HAMLYN POCKET GERMAN DICTIONARY

HAMLYN POCKET GERMAN DICTIONARY

GERMAN – ENGLISH
ENGLISH – GERMAN

HAMLYN

First published 1976
Published 1983 by Newnes Books,
a division of The Hamlyn Publishing Group Limited

This revised edition first published 1988 by
The Hamlyn Publishing Group Limited
a division of The Octopus Publishing Group plc
Michelin House, 81 Fulham Road
London SW3 6RB
and distributed for them by
Octopus Distribution Services
Rushden, Northamptonshire NN10 9RZ, England

ISBN 0 600 55905 X

Compiled by
Market House Books Limited,
Aylesbury, Bucks.

Printed in Great Britain

Foreword

This dictionary aims to give concise and accurate definitions of 24,000 of the most important words in use in the English and German languages today.

A pronunciation system based on the International Phonetic Alphabet is used (see *Key to symbols used in pronunciation*). Pronunciation is given for all headwords in both sections of the dictionary, and also for selected subentries in the German-English section.

Modern technical, commercial, and informal usage is given particular attention, in preference to outmoded terms or other expressions not in common contemporary use. Definitions are numbered in order to distinguish senses, and abbreviations are used to indicate use in specific technical, scientific, or commercial fields (see *Abbreviations used in the Dictionary*). An additional feature is the inclusion of idiomatic expressions and phrases, so necessary for the understanding and use of the foreign language.

This dictionary, with its emphasis on modernity, together with its compact form and clear typeface, should prove indispensable in the home, at school, in the office, and abroad.

Abbreviations used in the Dictionary

adj	adjective	*min*	minerals
adv	adverb	*mod*	modal
anat	anatomy	*mot*	motoring
arch	architecture	*mus*	music
aux	auxiliary	*n*	noun
aviat	aviation	*naut*	nautical
bot	botany	*neg*	negative
cap	capital	*neu*	neuter
comm	commerce	*pers*	person
comp	computer	*phot*	photography
conj	conjunction	*pol*	politics
cul	culinary	*poss*	possessive
def art	definite article	*pref*	prefix
derog	derogatory	*prep*	preposition
educ	education	*pron*	pronoun
f	feminine	*rel*	religion
fam	familiar	*s*	singular
fml	formal	*sci*	science
game	cards, chess, etc.	*sl*	slang
gram	grammar	*suff*	suffix
geog	geography	*tab*	taboo
indef art	indefinite article	*Tdmk*	trademark
inf	informal	*tech*	technical
infin	infinitive	*Th*	theatre
interj	interjection	*US*	United States
invar	invariable	*v*	verb
lit	literature	*vi*	intransitive verb
m	masculine	*v imp*	impersonal verb
math	mathematics	*vr*	reflexive verb
med	medical	*vt*	transitive verb
mil	military	*zool*	zoology

Key to symbols used in pronunciation

English

Vowels

i:	meet	u	p*u*t	ai	fl*y*
i	b*i*t	u:	sh*oo*t	au	h*ow*
e	g*e*t	ʌ	c*u*t	ɔi	b*oy*
æ	h*a*t	ə	*a*go	iə	h*ere*
ɑ:	h*ear*t	ə:	s*ir*	ɛə	*air*
ɔ	h*o*t	ei	l*a*te	uə	p*oor*
ɔ:	*ough*t	ou	g*o*		

Consonants

θ	*th*in	ʃ	*sh*ip
ð	*th*en	ʒ	mea*s*ure
ŋ	si*ng*	tʃ	*ch*in
j	*y*es	dʒ	*g*in

ˈ indicates that the following syllable is stressed as in *ago* (əˈgou).
ˌ placed under an *n* or *l* indicates that the *n* or *l* is pronounced as a syllable, as in *button* (ˈbʌtn̩) and *flannel* (ˈflænl̩).

German

Vowels

i	*i*st	u	r*u*nd
i:	w*ie*der	u:	K*u*gel
e	G*e*neral	y	H*ü*tte
e:	g*e*gen	y:	f*üh*len
ɛ	s*e*tzen	œ	H*ö*lle
ɛ:	F*äh*re	œ:	l*ö*sen
a	h*a*t	ə	bess*er*
a:	W*a*gen	ai	fr*ei*
ɔ	H*o*lz	au	H*au*s
o	F*o*relle	ɔy	tr*eu*
o:	*oh*ne		

Consonants

ç	i*ch*
ŋ	la*ng*
ʃ	Ti*sch*
j	*j*a
x	la*ch*en

ˈ indicates that the following syllable is stressed, as in *gegen̩* (ˈge:gən). In pronunciations of certain words borrowed from French, nasalization is indicated by a tilde (~) over the appropriate vowel, as in *Pension* (pãˈsjo:n).

Notes on the use of the Dictionary

An oblique stroke in a headword in the German-English section indicates that the part of the word before the oblique may be combined with other words or word endings shown in the text of the entry in heavy type after a dash, thus:-

einwillig/en . . . *vi* agree, consent. **—ung** *nf* . . . agreement, consent.

In headwords with no oblique, the ending combines with the whole word. Since all German nouns are spelt with a capital initial letter, the subentry above should be spelt *Einwilligung*. Verbs, adjectives, or adverbs entered under a noun headword with an initial capital should be written with a lower-case letter. Where a reflexive verb is the headword, subentries do not take the pronoun *sich*.

A swung dash (~) before a change of part of speech indicates that the part of speech refers to the headword, not the preceding subentry in heavy type.

Irregular verbs in the headword lists of both sections are marked with an asterisk. The principal parts of these verbs are shown in the verb tables. For compounds with either separable or inseparable prefixes, see the base form shown in the table, e.g. for *verstehen*, see *stehen*.

Plurals of German nouns are shown after a hyphen immediately after the part of speech, as follows:-

Feind . . . *nm* **-e** (plural is *die Feinde*)
Empfang . . . *nm* ¨**–e** (plural is *die Empfänge*)

However, a dash is used to indicate that a plural does not vary, or only takes an umlaut, as in the following examples:-

Kanzler . . . *nm* — (plural is *die Kanzler*)
Apfel . . . nm ¨— (plural is *die Äpfel*)

Exceptions are nouns that cannot form a plural, such as *Kost* or *Unterrichtung*. To form the plural of compounds, the user should refer to the headword of the principal (final) component, which is always the part that takes the plural, e.g. for *Armbanduhr*, see *Uhr*.

Parentheses are used to show optional forms, particularly in the English-German section, thus:

deliver . . . *vt* . . . (ab-, aus-) liefern . . . (indicates that *liefern* may be used alone or with the prefixes shown, as *abliefern* or *ausliefern*)
inoculation . . . *n* (Ein) Impfung *f* . . . (indicates that *Impfung* or *Einimpfung* may be used)
wash . . . (*vi*), *vt* . . . (sich) waschen . . . (indicates that *waschen* is transitive, but that the intransitive sense of *to wash* may be translated by *sich waschen*)

Adverbs: German adjectives can function as adverbs without modification. Therefore, in the German-English section, no translation of such adverbs is given where the adverbial form of the English adjective shown in the definition would be appropriate. In the English-German section, regular adverbial forms of English adjectives (i.e. those ending in *-ly*) are not shown where the given German translation could be used as an adverb, or where the English adverb has no special meaning requiring a separate translation.

English attributive adjectives can often be translated in German by using nouns to form compounds. This is shown by a dash as follows:-

manual . . . *adj* Hand—.

Thus, *manual worker* may be translated as *Handarbeiter*.

Feminine forms: Only the most common feminine forms of nouns have been selected for inclusion. However the feminine of agent nouns or nationalities ending in *-er* is formed by adding the suffix *-in* to the masculine; for example, *Arbeiterin* – a female worker; *Dichterin* – poetess; *Italienerin* – Italian woman, etc. Weak nouns drop the final *-e* and add *-in*; thus *Chinese* becomes *Chinesin*. Adjectival nouns, shown with a final *r* in parentheses, behave as a masculine or feminine adjective. Thus the feminine nominative singular of *Abgeordnete(r)* is *die Abgeordnete*.

English irregular verbs

Infinitive	*Past Tense*	*Past Participle*
abide	abode *or* abided	abode *or* abided
arise	arose	arisen
awake	awoke *or* awaked	awoke *or* awaked
be	was	been
bear[1]	bore	borne *or* born
beat	beat	beaten
become	became	become
begin	began	begun
bend	bent	bent
bet	bet	bet
beware[2]		
bid	bid	bidden *or* bid
bind	bound	bound
bite	bit	bitten *or* bit
bleed	bled	bled
blow	blew	blown
break	broke	broken
breed	bred	bred
bring	brought	brought
build	built	built
burn	burnt *or* burned	burnt *or* burned
burst	burst	burst
buy	bought	bought
can	could	
cast	cast	cast
catch	caught	caught
choose	chose	chosen
cling	clung	clung
come	came	come
cost	cost	cost
creep	crept	crept
crow	crowed *or* crew	crowed
cut	cut	cut
deal	dealt	dealt
dig	dug *or* digged	dug *or* digged
do	did	done

English irregular verbs

Infinitive	*Past Tense*	*Past Participle*
draw	drew	drawn
dream	dreamed *or* dreamt	dreamed *or* dreamt
drink	drank	drunk
drive	drove	driven
dwell	dwelt	dwelt
eat	ate	eaten
fall	fell	fallen
feed	fed	fed
feel	felt	felt
fight	fought	fought
find	found	found
flee	fled	fled
fling	flung	flung
fly	flew	flown
forbid	forbade *or* forbad	forbidden *or* forbid
forget	forgot	forgotten *or* forgot
forgive	forgave	forgiven
forsake	forsook	forsaken
freeze	froze	frozen
get	got	got
give	gave	given
go	went	gone
grind	ground	ground
grow	grew	grown
hang[3]	hung *or* hanged	hung *or* hanged
have	had	had
hear	heard	heard
hide	hid	hidden *or* hid
hit	hit	hit
hold	held	held
hurt	hurt	hurt
keep	kept	kept
kneel	knelt	knelt
knit	knitted *or* knit	knitted *or* knit
know	knew	known
lay	laid	laid
lead	led	led
lean	leant *or* leaned	leant *or* leaned
leap	leapt *or* leaped	leapt *or* leaped

Infinitive	*Past Tense*	*Past Participle*
learn	learnt *or* learned	learnt *or* learned
leave	left	left
lend	lent	lent
let	let	let
lie	lay	lain
light	lit *or* lighted	lit *or* lighted
lose	lost	lost
make	made	made
may	might	
mean	meant	meant
meet	met	met
mow	mowed	mown
must		
ought		
panic	panicked	panicked
pay	paid	paid
picnic	picnicked	picnicked
put	put	put
quit	quitted *or* quit	quitted *or* quit
read	read	read
rid	rid *or* ridded	rid *or* ridded
ride	rode	ridden
ring	rang	rung
rise	rose	risen
run	ran	run
saw	sawed	sawn *or* sawed
say	said	said
see	saw	seen
seek	sought	sought
sell	sold	sold
send	sent	sent
set	set	set
sew	sewed	sewn *or* sewed
shake	shook	shaken
shall	should	
shear	sheared	sheared *or* shorn
shed	shed	shed
shine	shone	shone
shoe	shod	shod

English irregular verbs

Infinitive	*Past Tense*	*Past Participle*
shoot	shot	shot
show	showed	shown
shrink	shrank *or* shrunk	shrunk *or* shrunken
shut	shut	shut
sing	sang	sung
sink	sank	sunk
sit	sat	sat
sleep	slept	slept
slide	slid	slid
sling	slung	slung
slink	slunk	slunk
slit	slit	slit
smell	smelt *or* smelled	smelt *or* smelled
sow	sowed	sown *or* sowed
speak	spoke	spoken
speed	sped *or* speeded	sped *or* speeded
spell	spelt *or* spelled	spelt *or* spelled
spend	spent	spent
spill	spilt *or* spilled	spilt *or* spilled
spin	spun	spun
spit	spat *or* spit	spat *or* spit
split	split	split
spread	spread	spread
spring	sprang	sprung
stand	stood	stood
steal	stole	stolen
stick	stuck	stuck
sting	stung	stung
stink	stank *or* stunk	stunk
stride	strode	stridden
strike	struck	struck
string	strung	strung
strive	strove	striven
swear	swore	sworn
sweep	swept	swept
swell	swelled	swollen *or* swelled
swim	swam	swum
swing	swung	swung
take	took	taken

Infinitive	*Past Tense*	*Past Participle*
teach	taught	taught
tear	tore	torn
tell	told	told
think	thought	thought
throw	threw	thrown
thrust	thrust	thrust
traffic	trafficked	trafficked
tread	trod	trodden *or* trod
wake	woke	woken
wear	wore	worn
weave	wove	woven *or* wove
weep	wept	wept
will	would	
win	won	won
wind	wound	wound
wring	wrung	wrung
write	wrote	written

[1] when *bear* means *give birth to* the past participle is always *born*.

[2] used only in the infinitive or as an imperative.

[3] the preferred form of the past tense and past participle when referring to death by hanging is *hanged*.

German irregular verbs

Infinitive	*Present Indicative*	*Imperfect Indicative*	*Past Participle*
backen	bäckt	backte	gebacken
befehlen	befiehlt	befahl	befohlen
beginnen	beginnt	begann	begonnen
beißen	beißt	biß	gebissen
bergen	birgt	barg	geborgen
bewegen[1]	bewegt	bewog	bewogen
biegen	biegt	bog	gebogen
bieten	bietet	bot	geboten
binden	bindet	band	gebunden
bitten	bittet	bat	gebeten
blasen	bläst	blies	geblasen
bleiben	bleibt	blieb	geblieben
bleichen[2]	bleicht	blich	geblichen
braten	brät	briet	gebraten
brechen	bricht	brach	gebrochen
brennen	brennt	brannte	gebrannt
bringen	bringt	brachte	gebracht
dreschen	drischt	drosch	gedroschen
dringen	dringt	drang	gedrungen
dürfen	darf	durfte	gedurft[2]
empfehlen	empfiehlt	empfahl	empfohlen
erschrecken[2]	erschrickt	erschrak	ershrocken
essen	ißt	aß	gegessen
fahren	fährt	fuhr	gefahren
fallen	fällt	fiel	gefallen
fangen	fängt	fing	gefangen
fechten	ficht	focht	gefochten
finden	findet	fand	gefunden
flechten	flicht	flocht	geflochten
fliegen	fliegt	flog	geflogen
fliehen	flieht	floh	geflohen
fließen	fließt	floß	geflossen
fressen	frißt	fraß	gefressen
frieren	friert	fror	gefroren
gären[4]	gärt	gor	gegoren
gebären	gebiert	gebar	geboren
geben	gibt	gab	gegeben
gedeihen	gedeiht	gedieh	gediehen

Infinitive	Present Indicative	Imperfect Indicative	Past Participle
gehen	geht	ging	gegangen
gelingen	gelingt	gelang	gelungen
gelten	gilt	galt	gegolten
genesen	genest	genas	genesen
genießen	genießt	genoß	genossen
gerinnen	gerinnt	gerann	geronnen
geschehen	geschieht	geschah	geschehen
gewinnen	gewinnt	gewann	gewonnen
gießen	gießt	goß	gegossen
gleichen	gleicht	glich	geglichen
gleiten	gleitet	glitt	geglitten
graben	gräbt	grub	gegraben
greifen	greift	griff	gegriffen
haben	hat	hatte	gehabt
halten	hält	hielt	gehalten
hangen	hängt	hing	gehangen
hauen	haut	haute *or* hieb	gehauen
heben	hebt	hob	gehoben
heißen	heißt	hieß	geheißen
helfen	hilft	half	geholfen
kennen	kennt	kannte	gekannt
klingen	klingt	klang	geklungen
kneifen	kneift	kniff	gekniffen
kommen	kommt	kam	gekommen
können	kann	konnte	gekonnt[3]
kriechen	kriecht	kroch	gekrochen
laden	lädt	lud	geladen
lassen	läßt	ließ	gelassen
laufen	läuft	lief	gelaufen
leiden	leidet	litt	gelitten
leihen	leiht	lieh	geliehen
liegen	liegt	lag	gelegen
lügen	lügt	log	gelogen
mahlen	mahlt	mahlte	gemahlen
meiden	meidet	mied	gemieden
melken	melkt	melkte *or* molk	gemelkt *or* gemolken
messen	mißt	maß	gemessen
mißlingen	mißlingt	mißlang	mißlungen

German irregular verbs

Infinitive	Present Indicative	Imperfect Indicative	Past Participle
mögen	mag	mochte	gemocht[3]
müssen	muß	mußte	gemußt[3]
nehmen	nimmt	nahm	genommen
nennen	nennt	nannte	genannt
pfeifen	pfeift	pfiff	gepfiffen
preisen	preist	pries	gepriesen
quellen[2]	quillt	quoll	gequollen
raten	rät	riet	geraten
reiben	reibt	rieb	gerieben
reißen	reißt	riß	gerissen
reiten	reitet	ritt	geritten
rennen	rennt	rannte	gerannt
riechen	riecht	roch	gerochen
ringen	ringt	rang	gerungen
rufen	ruft	rief	gerufen
saufen	säuft	soff	gesoffen
saugen	saugt	sog	gesogen
schaffen	schafft	schuf	geschaffen
scheiden	scheidet	schied	geschieden
scheinen	scheint	schien	geschienen
schieben	schiebt	schob	geschoben
schießen	schießt	schoß	geschossen
schinden	schindet	schund	geschunden
schlafen	schläft	schlief	geschlafen
schleichen	schleicht	schlich	geschlichen
schleifen[5]	schleift	schliff	geschliffen
schleißen	schleißt	schliß	geschlissen
schließen	schließt	schloß	geschlossen
schlingen	schlingt	schlang	geschlungen
schmeißen	schmeißt	schmiß	geschmissen
schmelzen	schmelzt	schmolz	geschmolzen
schneiden	schneidet	schnitt	geschnitten
schreiben	schreibt	schrieb	geschrieben
schreien	schreit	schrie	geschrie(e)n
schreiten	schreitet	schritt	geschritten
schweigen	schweigt	schwieg	geschwiegen
schwellen	schwillt	schwoll	geschwollen
schwimmen	schwimmt	schwamm	geschwommen
schwingen	schwingt	schwang	geschwungen

Infinitive	*Present Indicative*	*Imperfect Indicative*	*Past Participle*
schwören	schwört	schwur	geschworen
sehen	sieht	sah	gesehen
sein	ist	war	gewesen
senden	sendet	sandte	gesandt
singen	singt	sang	gesungen
sinken	sinkt	sank	gesunken
sinnen	sinnt	sann	gesonnen
sitzen	sitzt	saß	gesessen
sollen	soll	sollte	gesollt[3]
spinnen	spinnt	spann	gesponnen
sprechen	spricht	sprach	gesprochen
sprießen	sprießt	sproß	gesprossen
springen	springt	sprang	gesprungen
stechen	sticht	stoch	gestochen
stehen	steht	stand	gestanden
stehlen	stiehlt	stahl	gestohlen
steigen	steigt	stieg	gestiegen
sterben	stirbt	starb	gestorben
stinken	stinkt	stank	gestunken
stoßen	stößt	stieß	gestoßen
streichen	streicht	strich	gestrichen
streiten	streitet	stritt	gestritten
tragen	trägt	trug	getragen
treffen	trifft	traf	getroffen
trelben	treibt	trieb	getrieben
treten	tritt	trat	getreten
triefen	trieft	troff	getrieft
trinken	trinkt	trank	getrunken
trügen	trügt	trog	getrogen
tun	tut	tat	getan
verderben	verdirbt	verdarb	verdorben
verdrießen	verdrießt	verdroß	verdrossen
vergessen	vergißt	vergaß	vergessen
verlieren	verliert	verlor	verloren
verzeihen	verzeiht	verzieh	verziehen
wachsen	wächst	wuchs	gewachsen
weben	webt	wob	gewoben
weichen	weicht	wich	gewichen
weisen	weist	wies	gewiesen

German irregular verbs

Infinitive	Present Indicative	Imperfect Indicative	Past Participle
wenden	wendet	wandte *or* wendete	gewandt *or* gewendet
werben	wirbt	warb	geworben
werden	wird	wurde	geworden[3]
werfen	wirft	warf	geworfen
wiegen	wiegt	wog	gewogen
winden	windet	wand	gewunden
wissen	weiß	wußte	gewußt
wollen	will	wollte	gewollt[3]
ziehen	zieht	zog	gezogen
zwingen	zwingt	zwang	gezwungen

[1] strong conjugation in the meaning *induce*, *persuade*, but weak in the meaning *move*.
[2] strong conjugation when intransitive, but weak when transitive.
[3] when used as an auxiliary verb, the past participle has the same form as the infinitive.
[4] weak conjugation when figurative.
[5] strong conjugation in the meaning *polish*, *sharpen*, but weak in the meaning *drag*.

A

Aal (aːl) *nm* **-e** eel.

ab (ap) *adv* **1** off. **2** away. **3** down. **4** from. **ab und zu** sometimes, now and then. **weit ab** far off. *prep* from.

abänder/lich ('apɛndərliç) *adj* **1** alterable. **2** variable. **—n** *vt* **1** alter, change. **2** *pol* amend. **—ung** *nf* **-en** alteration.

abarbeiten ('aparbaitən) *vt* work off. **sich abarbeiten** *vr* overwork oneself.

Abbau ('apbau) *nm* reduction, dismantling, cutting down. **—en** *vt* **1** demolish. **2** reduce.

abberufen* ('apbəruːfən) *vt* recall.

abbestellen ('apbəʃtɛlən) *vt* cancel.

abbiegen* ('apbiːgən) *vi* turn off. *vt* turn aside.

Abbild ('apbilt) *n neu* **-er** **1** image, copy. **2** likeness. **—en** *vt* **1** copy. **2** illustrate. **3** model. **—ung** ('apbilduŋ) *nf* **-en** **1** copy(ing). **2** illustration. **3** picture.

abblenden ('apblɛndən) *vt* dim (one's headlights).

abbrechen* ('apbrɛçən) *vt,vi* **1** break off. **2** stop. *vt* tear down (houses).

abbremsen ('apbrɛmzən) *vi,vt* brake, slow down.

abbringen* ('apbriŋən) *vt* **1** divert. **2** dissuade.

Abbruch ('apbrux) *nm* **1** sudden end. **2** damage. **3** demolition.

abdank/en ('apdaŋkən) *vi* resign, abdicate. **—ung** *nf* **-en** abdication, resignation.

abdecken ('apdɛkən) *vt* **1** uncover. **2** *sport* protect or cover. **3** clear, strip.

abdichten ('apdiçtən) *vt* seal.

abdrehen ('apdreːən) *vt* turn off.

Abdruck ('apdruk) *nm* **1** *pl* **-e** copy, print. **2** *pl* cast, impression. **¨—en** ('apdrykən) *vt* squeeze. *vt,vi* shoot, fire (gun).

Abend ('aːbənt) *nm* **-e** evening, night. **gestern abend** last night. **heute abend** this evening. **abends** in the evening. **—brot** *n neu* supper. **—essen** *n neu* evening meal, supper. **—dämmerung** *nf* dusk. **—kleid** *n neu* evening dress or gown. **—land** *n neu* Occident, West. **—mahl** *n neu* (Holy) Communion.

Abenteuer ('aːbəntɔyər) *n neu* adventure. **—er** *nm* **— 1** adventurer. **2** crook. **—lich** *adj* **1** adventurous. **2** fantastic.

aber ('aːbər) *conj* **1** but. **2** however. *adv* **1** however. **2** again. **aber ja** yes indeed.

Aberglaub/e ('aːbərglaubə) *nm* superstition. **¨—isch** ('aːbərglɔybiʃ) *adj* superstitious.

Aberkennung ('apɛrkɛnuŋ) *nf* **-en** deprivation.

abermals ('aːbərmaːls) *adv* (once) again.

Abessin/ien (abɛ'siːniən) *n neu* Abyssinia. **—ier** *nm* **—** Abyssinian. **—isch** *adj* Abyssinian.

abfahr/en* ('apfaːrən) *vi* depart, start. *vt* drive off. **—t** *nf* **-en** departure.

Abfall ('apfal) *nm* **¨-e** **1** waste, rubbish. **2** slope. **3** decrease. **4** defection. **—eimer** *nm*

dustbin. **—en*** *vi* **1** fall down or off. **2** desert. **3** decrease.
abfällig ('apfɛliç) *adj* **1** disapproving, disparaging. **2** sloping.
abfassen ('apfasən) *vt* word, formulate.
abfertigen ('apfɛrtigən) *vt* **1** dispatch. **2** deal with.
Abfindung ('apfinduŋ) *nf* **-en** settlement, compensation.
abfliegen* ('apfli:gən) *vi* fly away, take off.
abfließen* ('apfli:sən) *vi* flow or drain away.
Abflug ('apfluk) *nm* **¨-e** take-off, departure.
Abfluß ('apflus) *nm* **-flüsse 1** drain(ing). **2** discharge.
Abfuhr ('apfu:r) *nf* **-en 1** removal. **2** *inf* rebuff. **¨—en** ('apfy:rən) *vt* lead off, take away. **¨—mittel** ('apfy:r mitəl) *n neu* laxative.
abfüllen ('apfylən) *vt* **1** fill. **2** bottle.
Abgabe ('apga:bə) *nf* **-n 1** delivery. **2** duty, tax, levy. **—nfrei** *adj* duty-free. **—npflichtig** *adj* taxable, liable to duty.
Abgang ('apgaŋ) *nm* **1** departure, exit. **2** loss.
Abgas ('apgas) *n neu* **-e** exhaust (gas).
abgeben* ('apge:bən) *vt* hand over, give up. **sich abgeben** *vr* associate with, occupy oneself with.
abgegriffen ('apgəgrifən) *adj* **1** worn. **2** (of a book) well-thumbed.
abgehen* ('apge:ən) *vi* **1** go away or off, leave. **2** come or fall off. **3** branch off. **es ist alles gut abgegangen** everything went well.
Abgeordnete(r) ('apgəɔrdnətə) *nm* **-n** deputy, representative, Member of Parliament. **Abgeordnetenhaus** *n neu* Chamber of Deputies.
abgestanden ('apgəʃtandən) *adj* stale, flat.
abgestorben ('apgəʃtɔrbən) *adj* dead, numb.
abgezehrt ('apgətsɛ:rt) *adj* emaciated.
Abgott ('apgɔt) *nm* **¨-er** idol.
abgrenz/en ('apgrɛntsən) *vt* mark off, delimit. **—ung** *nf* **-en** demarcation, delimitation.
Abgrund ('apgrunt) *nm* **¨-e 1** precipice. **2** abyss.
abhalten ('aphaltən) *vt* **1** keep or hold off. **2** prevent.
Abhandlung ('aphandluŋ) *nf* **-en** essay, treatise.
Abhang *nm* **¨-e** slope, incline. **¨—en** ('aphɛŋən) *vt* **1** take down or off. **2** unhook. **3** disconnect. *vi* **1** depend on. **2** slope. **¨—ig** ('aphɛŋiç) *adj* **1** dependent. **2** sloping. **3** subject (to). **¨—igkeit** *nf* dependence.
abhauen ('aphauən) *vt* cut down or off. *vi sl* leave, go away.
Abhilfe ('aphilfə) *nf* **-n** remedy, relief.
abholen ('apho:lən) *vt* fetch (away), call for.
abhören ('aphœ:rən) *vt* overhear, listen to.
Abitur (abi'tu:r) *n neu* **-e** school leaving examination or certificate.
abkanzeln ('apkantsəln) *vt* scold, rebuke.

abkehren ('apke:rən) *vi* turn away.

abklingen ('apkliŋən) *vi* (of sound) die out, fade away.

Abkommen ('apkɔmən) *n neu* — agreement, treaty. *vi* **1** deviate. **2** lose one's way.

abkühl/en ('apky:lən) *vt* chill, cool. **—ung** *nf* cooling.

abkürz/en ('apkyrtsən) *vt* shorten, abbreviate. **—ung** *nf* **-en** abbreviation.

abladen* ('apla:dən) *vt* unload, dump.

Ablauf ('aplauf) *nm* **¨-e 1** course of events. **2** end, expiry. **3** drain. **—en*** *vi* **1** run off or down. **2** expire. **gut ablaufen** pass off well, be a success.

Ablaut ('aplaut) *nm* **-e** gradation of vowels.

ablegen ('aple:gən) *vt* **1** take off (clothes). **2** lay down. **3** give up.

ablehn/en ('aple:nən) *vt* refuse, decline. **—ung** *nf* **-en** refusal, rejection.

ableit/en ('aplaitən) *vt* **1** divert. **2** derive. **3** draw off. **—ung** *nf* **-en 1** diversion. **2** derivation.

ablenk/en ('aplɛŋkən) *vt* turn aside, divert. **—ung** *nf* **-en** diversion, distraction.

abliefer/n ('apli:fərn) *vt* deliver. **—ung** *nf* **-en** delivery.

ablös/en ('aplœzən) *vt* **1** loosen, detach. **2** relieve (someone). **—ung** *nf* **-en 1** loosening, detachment. **2** relief.

abmach/en ('apmaxən) *vt* settle, arrange. **abgemacht!** agreed! **—ung** *nf* **-en** agreement, arrangement.

sich abmeld/en ('apmɛldən) *vr* announce one's departure. **—ung** *nf* **-en 1** notice of departure. **2** cancellation.

abmessen* ('apmɛsən) *vt* **1** measure off. **2** survey. **3** weigh (words).

Abnahme ('apna:me) *nf* **-n 1** removal, collection. **2** lessening, decrease. **3** acceptance.

abnehmen* ('apne:mən) *vt* take from or off. *vi* decrease.

Abneigung ('apnaiguŋ) *nf* **-en** dislike, aversion.

abnutzen ('apnutsən) *vt also* **abnützen** wear out.

Abonn/ement (abɔn'mã) *n neu* **-s** subscription. **—ent** (abɔ'nɛnt) *nm* **-en** subscriber. **—ieren** *vi* subscribe.

Abort (a'bɔrt) *nm* **-e** lavatory.

abräumen ('aprɔymən) *vt* clear away.

abrechn/en ('aprɛçnən) *vt* **1** deduct. **2** reckon up. **3** settle (with someone). **—ung** *nf* **-en** deduction, settlement.

Abrede ('apre:də) *nf* **-n** agreement. **in Abrede stellen** deny, dispute.

Abreise ('apraizə) *nf* **-n** departure. **—n** *vi* depart, set out.

abreißen* ('apraisən) *vt* **1** pull down. **2** tear off.

abrufen* ('apru:fən) *vt* **1** call back, recall. **2** cancel, call off.

Abrüstung ('aprystuŋ) *nf* **-en** disarmament.

Absage ('apza:gə) *nf* **-n 1** refusal. **2** cancellation. **—n** *vt* **1** refuse. **2** cancel. **3** renounce.

Absatz ('apzats) *nm* **¨-e 1** sale. **2** heel (of a shoe). **3** paragraph. **4** pause, intermission.

abschaff/en* ('apʃafən) *vt* abolish. **—ung** *nf* abolition.

abschalten ('apʃaltən) *vt* switch off.

abschätz/en ('apʃɛtsən) *vt* estimate, assess. **—ung** *nf* **-en** assessment, valuation.

Abscheu ('apʃɔy) *nm,f* horror, loathing. **—lich** (ap'ʃɔyliç) *adj* loathsome, repugnant.

abschicken ('apʃikən) *vt* send off, dispatch.

Abschied ('apʃi:t) *nm* **-e** parting, departure. **Abschied nehmen** take one's leave.

abschießen* ('apʃi:sən) *vt* **1** fire (a gun), shoot (off). **2** launch (a rocket).

Abschlag ('apʃla:k) *nm* **¨-e** reduction. **auf Abschlag** on account.

abschließen* ('apʃli:sən) *vt* **1** lock up, close (up). **2** settle, conclude.

Abschluß ('apʃlus) *nm* **-schlüsse** **1** conclusion, end. **2** settlement, deal.

abschnallen ('apʃnalən) *vt* unbuckle.

abschneiden* ('apʃnaidən) *vt* cut off or out. **gut/schlecht abschneiden** do well/badly.

Abschnitt ('apʃnit) *nm* **-e** section, portion.

abschrauben ('apʃraubən) *vt* unscrew.

abschrecken ('apʃrɛkən) *vt* frighten (off).

abschreiben* ('apʃraibən) *vt* **1** copy, write out. **2** write off.

Abschrift ('apʃrift) *nf* **-en** copy.

Abschuß ('apʃus) *nm* **-schüsse** **1** discharge, firing. **2** launching. **—rampe** *nf* launching pad.

abschwächen ('apʃvɛçən) *vt* weaken.

abseh/bar ('apze:ba:r) *adj* **1** within sight. **2** foreseeable. **—en*** *vt* **1** foresee. **2** perceive. **3** aim at. **4** copy. **abgesehen von** apart from.

absend/en ('apzɛndən) *vt* send, dispatch. **—er** *nm* — sender. **—ung** *nf* **-en** dispatch(ing).

absetzen ('apzɛtsən) *vt* **1** put down. **2** remove, dismiss (someone). **3** sell.

Absicht ('apziçt) *nf* **-en** intention, purpose. **—lich** *adj* intentional.

absolut (apzo'lu:t) *adj* absolute.

absonder/n ('apzɔndərn) *vt* separate, isolate. **—ung** *nf* **-en** separation.

Absorption (apzɔrptsi'o:n) *nf* **-en** absorption.

absperren ('apʃpɛrən) *vt* **1** cordon off, barricade. **2** shut off or away.

abspielen ('apʃpi:lən) *vt* perform (music). **sich abspielen** *vr* take place.

abspringen* ('apʃpriŋən) *vi* **1** jump off. **2** break off, shatter. **3** desert.

abspülen ('apʃpy:lən) *vt* **1** wash up. **2** rinse.

Abstammung ('apʃtamuŋ) *nf* **-en** descent, ancestry.

Abstand ('apʃtant) *nm* **¨-e** distance. **Abstand halten** keep one's distance.

abstatten ('apʃtatən) *vt* **1** give, render. **2** pay (a visit). **3** extend (thanks). **4** discharge (an obligation).

absteigen* ('apʃtaigən) *vi* **1** descend. **2** dismount, alight. **3** *sport* be relegated.

Abstieg ('apʃti:k) *nm* **-e 1** descent. **2** *sport* relegation.

Abstimmung ('apʃtimuŋ) *nf* **-en** vote, poll.

Abstinenz (apsti'nɛnts) *nf* **1** abstinence. **2** teetotalism. **—ler** *nm* — **1** abstainer. **2** teetotaller.

abstoßen* ('apʃto:sən) *vt* push away, repel.

abstrakt (ap'strakt) *adj* abstract.

Abstufung ('apʃtu:fuŋ) *nf* **-en** graduation.

Absturz ('apʃturts) *nm* **¨-e 1** fall. **2** *aviat* crash. **¨—en** ('apʃtyrtsən) *vi* **1** fall (down). **2** *aviat* crash.

absurd (ap'zurt) *adj* absurd.

Abszeß (aps'tsɛs) *nm* **-zesse** abcess.

Abt (apt) *nm* **¨-e** abbott. **Äbtissin** (ɛp'tisin) *nf* **-nen** abbess. **Abtei** (ap'tai) *nf* **-en** abbey.

Abteil (ap'tail) *n neu* **-e** compartment. **—en** ('aptailən) *vt* divide. **—ung** ('aptailuŋ) *nf* **-en** division, department, group, section.

abtreib/en ('aptraibən) *vt* **1** drive off. **2** abort. *vi* drift off. **—ung** *nf* **-en** abortion.

abtreten* ('aptre:tən) *vt* **1** cede. **2** wear out (shoes, etc). *vi* resign.

Abtritt ('aptrit) *nm* **-e 1** withdrawal. **2** lavatory.

abtrocknen ('aptrɔknən) *vt* dry (up).

abtrünnig ('aptryniç) *adj* disloyal, rebellious.

abtun* ('aptu:n) *vt* **1** abolish. **2** settle. **3** put aside. **4** take off (clothes).

abwägen* ('apvɛ:gən) *vt* consider, weigh.

abwand/eln ('apvandəln) *vt* **1** *gram* conjugate. **2** vary. **—lung** *nf* **-en 1** *gram* inflection. **2** variation.

abwarten ('apvartən) *vt* wait for.

abwärts ('apvɛrts) *adv* **1** downwards. **2** aside.

abwaschen* ('apvaʃən) *vt* **1** wash off or away. **2** wash up.

abwechsel/n ('apvɛksəln) *vi* alternate. *vt* change. **—nd** *adj* alternating. **—ung** *nf* **-en** change, alternation.

Abwehr ('apve:r) *nf* **-en** defence, guard. **—en** *vt* ward off. **—stoff** *nm* antibody.

abweichen* ('apvaiçən) *vi* deviate, differ from. **—d** *adj* irregular, different.

abweisen* ('apvaisən) *vt* **1** turn away, dismiss. **2** reject.

abwenden* ('apvɛndən) *vt* **1** turn away. **2** prevent. **sich abwenden von** turn away from.

abwerfen* ('apvɛrfən) *vt* **1** throw off or away. **2** knock down. **3** yield. **4** drop (bombs).

abwert/en ('apvɛrtən) *vt,vi* devalue, devaluate. **—ung** *nf* **-en** devaluation.

abwesen/d ('apve:zənt) *adj* **1** absent. **2** absent-minded. **—heit** *nf* **-en** absence.

abwischen ('apviʃən) *vt* wipe off.

abzahlen ('aptsa:lən) *vt* pay off.

abzäunen ('aptsɔynən) *vt* fence off or in.

Abzeichen ('aptsaiçən) *n neu* badge, mark.

abziehen* ('aptsi:ən) *vt* **1** draw off, remove. **2** subtract. **3** distract. *vi* go away.

Abzug ('aptsu:k) *nm* ¨**-e** **1** deduction. **2** copy. **3** departure. **4** trigger. **5** outlet, vent. **6** (printing) proof. ¨**—lich** ('aptsy:kliç) *adv* minus, less.

Abzweigung ('aptsvaiguŋ) *nf* **-en** branch.

ach (ax) *interj* oh!

Achse ('aksə) *nf* **-n** **1** axle. **2** axis.

Achsel ('aksəl) *nf* **-n** shoulder.

acht (axt) *adj,nf* eight. **—e** *adj* eighth. **heute in acht Tagen** today week.

Acht (axt) *nf* attention. **sich in Acht nehmen** look out, be on one's guard.

acht/en ('axtən) *vt* respect. **achten auf** pay attention to. **—sam** *adj* attentive. **—geben** *vi* pay attention. **—ung** *nf* respect. *interj* attention, look out! **—ungsvoll** *adj* respectful.

achtzehn ('axtse:n) *adj,nf* eighteen. **achtzehnte** *adj* eighteenth.

achtzig ('axtsiç) *adj,nf* eighty. **achtzigste** *adj* eightieth.

ächzen ('ɛçtsən) *vi* groan.

Acker ('akər) *nm* ¨**—** **1** field, arable land. **2** (German) acre. **—bau** *nm* agriculture.

addier/en (a'di:rən) *vt* add. **—maschine** *nf* adding machine.

ade, adieu (a'de:, a'djœ:) *interj* farewell.

Adel ('a:dəl) *nm* nobility, aristocracy. **adelig** *adj also* **adlig** noble. **Adlige(r)** ('a:dligə) *nm* **-n** nobleman, aristocrat. **Adelsstand** ('a:dəlsʃtant) *nm* **1** nobility. **2** peerage.

Ader ('a:dər) *nf* **-n** **1** vein. **2** artery.

Adjektiv ('atjɛkti:f) *n neu* **-e** adjective.

Adjutant (atju'tant) *nm* **-en** adjutant, aide.

Adler ('a:dlər) *nm* **—** eagle.

Admiral (atmi'ra:l) *nm* **-e** admiral.

adoptieren (adɔp'ti:rən) *vt* adopt. **Adoptivkind** (adɔp'ti:fkint) *n neu* adopted child.

Adrenalin (adre:na'li:n) *n neu* adrenaline.

Adress/e (a'drɛsə) *nf* **-n** address. **—ieren** (adrɛ'si:rən) *vt* address.

Adriatisches Meer (adri'a:tiʃəs) *n neu* Adriatic (Sea).

Advokat (atvo'ka:t) *nm* **-en** lawyer, advocate.

Affäre (a'fɛ:rə) *nf* **-n** **1** affair. **2** love affair.

Affe ('afə) *nm* **-n** **1** ape, monkey. **2** *inf* silly ass. ¨**—n** ('ɛfən) *vt* **1** deceive. **2** ape.

Afrika ('a:frika) *n neu* Africa. **—ner** *nm* **—** African. **—nisch** *adj* African.

Ägäisches Meer (a'gɛiʃəs) *n neu* Aegean (Sea).

Agent (a'gɛnt) *nm* **-en** agent. **—ur** (agɛn'tu:r) *nf* **-en** agency.

Agitation (agitatsi'o:n) *nf* **-en** agitation.

Agnost/iker (a'gnɔstikər) *nm* **—** agnostic. **—isch** *adj* agnostic. **—izismus** (agnɔsti'tsismus) *nm* agnosticism.

Ägypt/en (ɛ'gyptən) *n neu* Egypt. **—isch** *adj* Egyptian.

Ahn (aːn) *nm* **-en** ancestor.

ähneln ('ɛːnəln) *vi* resemble.

ahn/en ('aːnən) *vt* **1** suspect, guess. **2** foresee. **—ung** *nf* **-en 1** idea, suspicion. **2** presentiment.

ähnlich ('ɛːnliç) *adj* similar, like. **—keit** *nf* **-en** similarity, likeness.

Ahorn ('aːhɔrn) *nm* **-e** maple.

Akademie (akade'miː) *nf* **-n** academy, college. **Akademiker** (aka'deːmikər) *nm* — academic. **akademisch** (aka'deːmiʃ) *adj* academic.

Akkord (a'kɔrt) *nm* **-e 1** arrangement, settlement. **2** *mus* chord. **im Akkord arbeiten** do piecework. **—arbeit** *nf* piecework.

Akrobat (akro'baːt) *nm* **-en** acrobat.

Akt (akt) *nm* **-e 1** act, action. **2** nude study. **3** document.

Akte ('aktə) *nf* **-n 1** document. **2** report. **3** file. **—nmappe** *nf* **1** folder. **2** portfolio. **3** briefcase. **—nschrank** *nm* filing-cabinet. **—ntasche** *nf* briefcase.

Aktie ('aktsiə) *nf* **-n** *comm* share. **—ngesellschaft** *nf* limited company.

Aktionär (aktsio'nɛːr) *nm* **-e** shareholder.

aktiv (ak'tiːf) *adj* **1** active. **2** effective.

aktuell (aktu'ɛl) *adj* **1** topical. **2** present-day.

Akzent (ak'tsɛnt) *nm* **-e** accent, stress.

akzeptieren (aktsɛp'tiːrən) *vt* accept.

Alabaster (ala'bastər) *nm* alabaster.

Alarm (a'larm) *nm* **-e** alarm. **—ieren** *vt* alarm.

Alaun (a'laun) *nm* **-e** alum.

Alban/ien (al'baːniən) *n neu* Albania. **—ier** *nm* — Albanian. **—isch** *adj* Albanian.

Albatros ('albatrɔs) *nm* **-se** albatross.

albern ('albərn) *adj* silly, foolish.

Alge (algə) *nf* **-n** seaweed.

Alger/ien (al'geːriən) *n neu* Algeria. **—ier** *nm* — Algerian. **—isch** *adj* Algerian.

Alimente (ali'mɛntə) *n pl* alimony.

Alkohol ('alkohol) *nm* **-e** alcohol. **—frei** *adj* non-alcoholic. **—verbot** *n neu* prohibition. **—isch** (alko'hoːliʃ) *adj* alcoholic. **—iker** (alko'hoːlikər) *nm* alcoholic.

all (al) *pron* all everything. *adj* all, every. **alles in allem** on the whole. **—e** *adv inf* finished, all gone. **alledem** ('alədeːm) *pron* **bei** *or* **trotz alledem** in spite of all that.

All (al) *n neu* universe.

Allee (a'leː) *nf* **-n** avenue.

Allegorie (alego'riː) *nf* **-n** allegory.

allein (a'lain) *adv, adj* alone, single. *conj* but. **—ig** *adj* **1** sole. **2** exclusive.

allemal ('aləmaːl) *adv* always. **ein für allemal** once and for all.

allenfalls ('alənfals) *adv* if need be.

allerbest ('alərbɛst) *adj* best of all.
allerdings ('alərdiŋs) *adv* indeed, certainly.
allererst ('alərerːrst) *adj,adv* first of all.
allerhand ('alərhant) *adj* of all kinds, various.
allerhöchst ('alərhœçst) *adj* supreme.
allerlei ('alərlai) *adj* of all kinds, various.
allerliebst ('alərliːpst) *adj* **1** dearest (of all). **2** most lovely.
allerwenigst ('alərveːniçst) *adj* the very least.
allezeit ('alətsait) *adv* always.
allgemein ('algəmain) *adj* general, common.
Allierte(r) (a'liːrtə) *nm* **-n** ally.
alljährlich ('aljɛːrliç) *adj* annual, yearly.
Allmacht ('almaxt) *nf* omnipotence. **¨—ig** ('almɛçtiç) *adj* almighty.
allmählich ('almɛːliç) *adj* gradual.
allseitig ('alzaitiç) *adj* universal.
alltäglich ('altɛːkliç) *adj* daily, common(place).
allzu ('altsuː) *adv* much too, far too.
Almanach ('almanax) *nm* **-e** almanac.
Almosen ('almoːzən) *n neu* alms.
Alpen ('alpən) *n pl* Alps.
Alphabet (alfa'beːt) *n neu* **-e** alphabet.
Alptraum ('alptraum) *nm* **-e** *also* **Alpdrücken** *n neu* — nightmare.
als (als) *conj* **1** when. **2** as. **3** than. **als ob** *also* **als wenn** as if. *~prep* as. **nichts als** nothing but.
alsbald (als'balt) *adv* at once.
alsdann (als'dan) *adv* **1** then. **2** after.
also ('alzoː) *conj* therefore. *adv* so.
alt (alt) *adj* old, ancient. **—e(r)** ('altə) *nm* old one or man. **—klug** *adj* precocious. **—modisch** *adj* old-fashioned. **—papier** *n neu* wastepaper. **—stadt** *nf* old part of a town. **—warenhändler** *nm* second-hand dealer.
Alt (alt) *nm* **-e** *also* **Altstimme** *nf* alto (voice).
Alter ('altər) *n neu* — (old) age. **im Alter von** at the age of. **—sheim** *n neu* old people's home. **—sversicherung** *nf* life insurance.
Altertum ('altərtuːm) *n neu* antiquity.
Aluminium (alu'miːnium) *n neu* aluminium.
am (am) contraction of **an dem**
Amboß ('ambɔs) *nm* **-bosse** anvil.
Ameise ('aːmaizə) *nf* **-n** ant.
Amerika (a'meːrika) *n neu* America. **—ner** (ameri'kaːnər) *nm* — American. **amerikanisch** (ameri'kaːniʃ) *adj* American.
Ampel ('ampəl) *nf* **-n** **1** (hanging) lamp. **2** traffic light.
Amsel ('amzəl) *nf* **-n** blackbird.
Amt (amt) *n neu* **¨-er** **1** office, (official) position. **2** charge, responsibility. **von Amts wegen** officially, ex officio. **—lich** *adj* official. **—mann** *nm* **1** official. **2** bailiff. **—sgeheimnis** *n neu* official

secret. **—sgericht** *n neu* district court.

amüs/ant (amy'zant) *adj* amusing. **—ieren** (amy'ziːrən) *vt* amuse. **sich amusieren** *vr* enjoy oneself.

an (an) *prep* **1** at. **2** on. **3** to. **4** against. **5** in. **6** by. **an (und für) sich** in itself. **von jetzt an** from now on.

analog (ana'loːk) *adj* analogous. **—ie** (analo'giː) *nf* **-n** analogy.

Analphabet (analfa'beːt) *nm* **-en** illiterate.

Analys/e (ana'lyːzə) *nf* **-n** analysis. **—ieren** (analy'ziːrən) *vt* analyse.

Ananas ('ananas) *nf* **-se** pineapple.

Anarchie (anar'çiː) *nf* **-n** anarchy.

Anatomie (anato'miː) *nf* **-n** anatomy.

Anbau ('anbau) *nm* **1** *pl* **-e** cultivation. **2** *pl* **-ten** annexe, outbuilding. **—en** *vt* **1** cultivate. **2** build (an extension).

anbeißen* ('anbaisən) *vt* bite into. *vi* swallow the bait.

anbelangen ('anbəlaŋən) *vt* **was mich anbelangt** as for me.

anbet/en ('anbeːtən) *vt* worship, adore. **—ung** *nf* worship.

Anbetracht ('anbətraxt) *nf* **in Anbetracht** in view of.

anbetreffen* ('anbətrɛfən) *vt* concern.

anbieten* ('anbiːtən) *vt* offer.

Anblick ('anblik) *nm* **-e** view, sight. **—en** *vt* look at.

anbrechen* ('anbrɛçən) *vt* break into, open. *vi* dawn.

anbringen* ('anbriŋən) *vt* **1** attach. **2** place. **3** install. **4** bring (a complaint).

Anbruch ('anbrux) *nm* **¨-e** beginning, opening. **Anbruch des Tages** daybreak.

Andacht ('andaxt) *nf* **-en** devotion, prayers. **¨—ig** ('andɛçtiç) *adj* **1** devout. **2** attentive.

andauern ('andauərn) *vi* continue, last.

Anden ('andən) *n pl* Andes.

Andenken ('andɛŋkən) *n neu* **— 1** remembrance, memory. **2** souvenir, keepsake.

ander ('andər) *adj* other, different. **am anderen Tag** the next day. **einmal über das andere** again and again. **ein andermal** ('andərmaːl) *adv* another time. **andernfalls** ('andərnfals) *adv* otherwise. **anderntags** ('andərntaːks) *adv* the next day. **anderseits** ('andərzaits) *adv or* **andrerseits** on the other hand. **anders** ('andərs) *adv* differently, otherwise, else. **anderswo** ('andərsvo) *adv also* **anderwärts** elsewhere, in another place. **anderweit** ('andərvait) *adv* **1** in another place. **2** in another way.

änder/n ('ɛndərn) *vt* **sich ändern** *vr* change, alter. **—ung** *nf* **-en** change, alteration.

anderthalb ('andərthalp) *adj* one and a half.

andeut/en ('andɔytən) *vt* indicate, suggest. **—ung** *nf* **-en** indication, hint, suggestion.

Andrang ('andraŋ) *nm* press, rush, crowd.

andrehen ('andre:ən) *vt* turn or switch on.
aneignen ('anaignən) *vt* appropriate, acquire.
aneinander (anain'andər) *adv* **1** together. **2** to one another.
Anerbieten ('anɛrbi:tən) *n neu* — *also* **Anerbietung** *nf* **-en** offer, proposal.
anerkannt ('anɛrkant) *adj* recognized, acknowledged.
anerkenn/en* ('anɛrkɛnən) *vt* recognize, acknowledge. **—ung** *nf* **-en** recognition, acknowledgment.
anfahr/en* ('anfa:rən) *vt* **1** carry. **2** collide with. *vi* **1** approach. **2** (of a vehicle) begin to move. **—t** *nf* **-en 1** arrival. **2** drive(way).
Anfall ('anfal) *nm* **¨-e 1** attack. **2** fit.
Anfang ('anfaŋ) *nm* **¨-e 1** beginning, introduction. **2** basis. **am Anfang** at the beginning. **von Anfang an** from the outset. **—en*** *vt,vi* begin, start. **¨—er** ('anfɛŋər) *nm* **—** beginner, novice. **¨—lich** ('anfɛŋliç) *adj* initial. **—s** *adv* at first, at the beginning.
anfassen ('anfasən) *vt* **1** seize. **2** touch, handle.
anfecht/en ('anfɛçtən) *vt* **1** contest, oppose. **2** trouble, bother. **—ung** *nf* **-en 1** opposition. **2** temptation.
anfertig/en ('anfɛrtigən) *vt* manufacture, produce. **—ung** *nf* **-en** manufacture, fabrication.
Anforderung ('anfɔrdəruŋ) *nf* **-en 1** claim, demand. **2** requirement.
Anfrage ('anfra:gə) *nf* **-n** enquiry. **anfragen** ('anfra:gən) *vi,vt* enquire, ask.
anführ/en ('anfy:rən) *vt* **1** lead. **2** quote, state. **3** deceive. **—er** *nm* **— 1** commander, leader. **2** agitator. **—ung** *nf* **-en 1** lead(ership). **2** quotation. **—ungszeichen** *n pl* quotation marks, inverted commas.
anfüllen ('anfylən) *vt* fill up.
Angabe ('anga:bə) *nf* **-n 1** announcement, declaration. **2** information, details.
angeb/en* ('ange:bən) *vt* announce, state, give (reasons). *vi* **1** boast, pretend. **2** *game* deal first, serve. **—er** *nm* **— 1** informer. **2** show-off, poseur. **—lich** ('ange:pliç) *adj* supposed, alleged.
angeboren ('angəbo:rən) *adj* inborn.
Angebot ('angəbo:t) *n neu* **-e 1** bid, offer. **2** supply.
angehen* ('ange:ən) *vi* begin. **das geht nicht an** that won't do. *vt* **1** approach (a person). **2** concern (a person). **3** tackle, attack. **das geht dich nichts an** that's none of your business.
angehör/en ('angəhœ:rən) *vi* belong. **—ige(r)** *nm* **-n 1** member. **2** relative.
Angeklagte(r) ('angəkla:ktə) *nm* **-n** accused, defendant.
Angelegenheit ('angəle:gənhait) *nf* **-en** matter, affair, business.
angeln ('aŋəln) *vt,vi* angle, fish (for). *n neu* fishing, angling.
Angelsachs/e ('aŋəlzaksə) *nm* **-n** Anglo-Saxon. **¨—isch** ('aŋəlzɛksiʃ) *adj* Anglo-Saxon.

angemessen ('angəmɛsən) *adj* suitable.

angenehm ('angəneːm) *adj* pleasant, agreeable.

angenommen ('angənɔmən) *adj* **1** supposing, assuming. **2** approved.

angesehen ('angəzeːn) *adj* respected, distinguished.

Angesicht ('angəziçt) *n neu* **-er** face. **—s** *prep* in view of, considering.

angespannt ('angəʃpant) *adj* uptight.

Angestellte(r) ('angəʃtɛltə) *nm* **-n 1** employee. **2** office worker.

angetan ('angətaːn) *adj* **1** dressed up. **2** likely.

angewandt ('angəvant) *adj* applied.

angewöhnen ('angəvœːnən) *vt* accustom. **sich angewöhnen** *vr* grow accustomed to.

Angewohnheit ('angəvoːnhait) *nf* **-en** habit, custom.

Angler ('aŋlər) *nm* — angler.

anglikanisch (angli'kaːniʃ) *adj* Anglican.

angreif/en* ('angraifən) *vt* **1** attack, assault. **2** touch, grasp. **3** undertake. **—er** *nm* — aggressor, assailant.

angrenzen ('angrɛntsən) *vi* border on.

Angriff ('angrif) *nm* **-e 1** attack. **2** undertaking. **—slustig** *adj* aggressive.

Angst (aŋst) *nf* **¨-e** fear, fright, anxiety. **Angst haben** be afraid. **jemandem Angst machen** frighten someone. **¨—igen** ('ɛŋstigən) *vt* frighten. **sich ¨—igen** *vr* worry, be anxious. **¨—lich** ('ɛŋstliç) *adj* timid, anxious, cautious.

anhaben* ('anhaːbən) *vt* wear, have on.

Anhalt ('anhalt) *nm* **-e 1** support, hold. **2** clue, essential fact. **3** halt, stop. **—en*** *vt* check, stop. *vi* **1** stop. **2** continue, persist. **per Anhalter fahren** hitch-hike. **—spunkt** *nm* clue, lead.

Anhang ('anhaŋ) *nm* **¨-e 1** appendix. **2** following. **¨—en** ('anhɛŋən) *vt* hang on, attach. **¨—er** ('anhɛŋər) *nm* — **1** follower, disciple. **2** (baggage) tag, label. **3** *mot* trailer.

anheimfallen* ('anhaimfalən) *vi* fall or come to (someone).

Anhöhe ('anhœːə) *nf* **-n** hill, rise.

anhören ('anhœːrən) *vt* listen to.

Ankauf ('ankauf) *nm* **¨-e** purchase. **—en** *vt* purchase.

Anker ('aŋkər) *nm* — anchor. **—n** *vi* anchor.

Anklage ('anklaːgə) *nf* **-n 1** accusation. **2** prosecution. **—n** *vt* accuse, charge.

Anklang ('anklaŋ) *nm* **¨-e 1** approval. **2** reminiscence.

anknüpf/en ('anknypfən) *vt* **1** fasten. **2** begin.

ankommen* ('ankɔmən) *vi* arrive. **es kommt darauf an 1** it depends (on) . **2** it is important (to).

ankündigen ('ankyndigən) *vt* announce.

Ankunft ('ankunft) *nf* **¨-e** arrival.

Anlage ('anlaːgə) *nf* **-n 1** plan, lay-out. **2** park, gardens. **3** tendency. **4** talent, gift. **5** investment. **6** equipment, apparatus.

anlangen ('anlaŋən) *vi* arrive. *vt* concern (someone).

Anlaß ('anlas) *nm* **—lässe 1** cause. **2** occasion. **anlassen*** *vt* **1** leave on (a machine, etc.). **2** start, begin. **3** *mot* start (engine). **4** scold. **anläßlich** ('anlɛsliç) *prep* on the occasion of.

Anlauf ('anlauf) *nm* **¨-e** start, take-off, run-up.

anlegen ('anle:gən) *vt* **1** lay or put on or against. **2** found. **3** invest. *vi naut* **1** berth. **2** land. **Feuer anlegen** start a fire.

Anleihe ('anlaiə) *nf* **-n** loan.

Anleitung ('anlaituŋ) *nf* **-en** instruction.

anlieg/en* ('anli:gən) *vi* **1** lie near. **2** fit well. *n neu* — request. **—end** *adj* adjacent.

anlocken ('anlɔkən) *vt* entice, attract.

Anmarsch ('anmarʃ) *nm* **¨-e** *mil* approach, advance.

Anmaßung ('anmasuŋ) *nf* **-en** **1** presumption. **2** insolence.

anmeld/en ('anmɛldən) *vt* **1** report. **2** declare, announce. **—ung** *nf* **-en 1** registration (with the police). **2** application. **3** announcement.

Anmerk/en ('anmɛrkən) *vt* note, observe. **—ung** *nf* **-en** **1** remark, observation. **2** footnote.

Anmut ('anmu:t) *nf* grace, charm. **—ig** *adj* graceful, charming.

annähernd ('annɛ:ərnt) *adj* **1** approaching. **2** approximate.

Annahme ('anna:mə) *nf* **-n 1** supposition. **2** acceptance.

annehmen* ('anne:mən) *vt* **1** accept, receive. **2** assume, suppose.

anonym (ano'ny:m) *adj* anonymous.

anordn/en ('anɔrdnən) *vt* arrange, order. **—ung** *nf* **-en 1** regulation. **2** direction, order.

anpacken ('anpakən) *vt* grasp, seize.

anpass/en ('anpasən) *vt* **1** fit. **2** adapt, adjust. **sich anpassen** *vr* adapt, conform. **—schaltung** *nf* **-en** *comp* interface.

anrechn/en ('anrɛçnən) *vt* **1** think well of, value. **2** charge. **3** credit. **—ung** *nf* **-en** charge.

Anrede ('anre:də) *nf* **-n** address, speech. **—n** *vt* address, speak to.

anreg/en ('anre:gən) *vt* stimulate, excite, stir up. **—end** *adj* stimulating, exciting. **—ung** *nf* **-en 1** excitement. **2** inspiration. **3** suggestion.

anrichten ('anriçtən) *vt* **1** serve. **2** prepare. **3** cause.

Anruf ('anru:f) *nm* **-e 1** shout, call. **2** (telephone) call. **—en*** *vt* **1** ring up. **2** call, hail.

anrühren ('anry:rən) *vt* **1** touch. **2** mix.

ans (ans) contraction of **an das**.

Ansag/e ('anza:gə) *nf* **-n** announcement. **—er** *nm* — (radio) announcer.

ansammeln ('anzaməln) *vt* collect, amass. **sich ansammeln** *vr* gather, assemble.

ansässig ('anzɛsiç) *adj* **1** resident. **2** settled.

Ansatz ('anzats) *nm* **¨-e** start onset.

anschaffen* ('anʃafən) *vt* procure, buy.
anschalten ('anʃaltən) *vt* switch on, plug in.
anschau/en ('anʃauən) *vt* look at, view. **—lich** *adj* **1** vivid. **2** evident. **—ung** *nf* **-en 1** opinion, view. **2** conception, idea.
Anschein ('anʃain) *nm* **-e** appearance. **allem Anschein nach** to all appearances. **—end** *adj* apparent.
Anschlag ('anʃla:k) *nm* **¨-e 1** striking, stroke. **2** poster. **3** plan, plot. **4** estimate. **5** (bomb) attack. **—en*** ('anʃla:gən) *vt* **1** strike at. **2** affix. **3** value. *vi* **1** take effect. **2** attack, strike.
anschließen* ('anʃli:sən) *vt* connect, add, chain (up). **sich anschließen** *vr* join.
Anschluß ('anʃlus) *nm* **-schlüsse** connection, addition. **im Anschluß an** following.
anschnallen ('anʃnalən) *vt* fasten, buckle (on).
Anschovis (an'ʃo:vis) *nf* — anchovy.
Anschrift ('anʃrift) *nf* **-en** address.
anschuldigen ('anʃuldigən) *vt* accuse, charge.
anseh/en* ('anze:ən) *vt* **1** look at or upon. **2** consider. **ansehen für** take for. **—nlich** ('anze:nliç) *adj* **1** good-looking. **2** considerable, important.
ansetzen ('anzɛtsən) *vt* **1** set or put on. **2** fasten. **3** add. **4** apply. *vi* begin.
Ansicht ('anziçt) *nf* **-en 1** view, sight. **2** opinion. **meiner Ansicht nach** in my opinion. **zur Ansicht** on approval. **—s(post)karte** *nf* picture postcard.
ansiedeln ('anzi:dəln) *vt* settle, colonize.
anspiel/en ('anʃpi:lən) *vt* allude, insinuate. **—ung** *nf* **-en** reference, allusion.
Anspruch ('anʃprux) *nm* **¨-e 1** claim, demand. **2** right, entitlement. **—slos** *adj* unassuming. **—svoll** *adj* **1** demanding. **2** sophisticated. **3** fastidious.
Anstalt ('anʃtalt) *nf* **-en 1** institution. **2** *pl* arrangements.
Anstand ('anʃtant) *nm* **¨-e 1** decency, decorum. **2** hesitation. **¨—ig** ('anʃtɛndiç) *adj* decent, nice, respectable. **¨—igkeit** *nf* decency, respectability.
anstatt (an'ʃtat) *prep* instead of.
ansteck/en ('anʃtɛkən) *vt* **1** fasten or pin on. **2** set fire to, light. **3** infect. **—end** *adj* infectious, contagious.
anstell/en ('anʃtɛlən) *vt* **1** employ, appoint. **2** turn on, start. **3** place near. **4** carry out, implement. *vi* **1** queue up. **2** behave, act. **—ung** *nf* **-en** appointment, post.
anstiften ('anʃtiftən) *vt* **1** cause. **2** instigate, incite.
Anstoß ('anʃto:s) *nm* **-stösse 1** impulse, stimulus. **2** knock, collision. **3** offence. **4** kickoff. **Anstoß nehmen** take offence. **—en*** *vt* **1** push (on or against). **2** knock. *vi* offend.
anstreng/en ('anʃtrɛŋən) *vt* **1** exert. **2** strain. **3** tire. **—ung** *nf* **-en 1** exertion. **2** strain.
Antarktis (ant'arktis) *nf*

Antarctic. **antarktisch** (ant'arktiʃ) *adj* Antarctic.

antasten ('antastən) *vt* **1** touch. **2** damage.

Anteil ('antail) *nm* **-e 1** share. **2** interest. **3** sympathy.

Antenne (an'tɛnə) *nf* **-n** antenna, aerial.

Anthropologie (antropolo'giː) *nf* anthropology.

Antibiotikum (antibi'oːtikum) *n neu* **-ka** antibiotic.

antik (an'tiːk) *adj* **1** classical, ancient. **2** antique. **Antike** (an'tiːkə) *nf* antiquity.

Antiquar (anti'kvaːr) *nm* **-e 1** second-hand bookseller. **2** antique dealer. **Antiquariat** (antikvari'aːt) *n neu* **-e** second-hand bookshop. **Antiquität** (antikvi'tɛːt) *nf* **-en** antique.

antisemitisch (antize'miːtiʃ) *adj* anti-Semitic.

antiseptisch (anti'zɛptiʃ) *adj* antiseptic.

Antonym (anto'nyːm) *n neu* **-e** antonym.

Antrag ('antraːk) *nm* **¨-e 1** application. **2** proposal. **—steller** *nm* **— 1** applicant. **2** mover (of a proposal).

antreffen* ('antrɛfən) *vt* meet (with).

antreiben* ('antraibən) *vt* push or drive on. *vi* drift ashore.

antreten* ('antreːtən) *vt* **1** begin. **2** take up. **3** enter into. **4** approach.

Antrieb ('antriːp) *nm* **-e 1** impulse. **2** power. **3** motive force.

Antritt ('antrit) *nm* **-e 1** beginning. **2** taking up, assumption.

antun* ('antuːn) *vt* **1** put on. **2** do to.

Antwerpen (ant'vɛːrpən) *n neu* Antwerp.

Antwort ('antvɔrt) *nf* **-en** answer, reply. **in Antwort auf** in reply to. **—en** *vi* answer, reply.

anvertrauen ('anfɛrtrauən) *vt* entrust.

Anwalt ('anvalt) *nm* **¨-e** lawyer, advocate.

anwärmen ('anvɛrmən) *vt* warm (gently).

anweis/en* ('anvaizən) *vt* **1** assign. **2** instruct. **3** *comm* remit. **—ung** *nf* **-en 1** money order, remittance. **2** instruction.

anwend/bar ('anvɛntbaːr) *adj* **1** applicable. **2** practicable. **—en*** ('anvɛndən) *vt* use, apply. **—ung** ('anvɛnduŋ) *nf* **-en** application, use.

anwesen/d ('anveːzənt) *adj* present. **—heit** *nf* **-en** presence.

Anzahl ('antsaːl) *nf* **1** number. **2** quantity.

Anzeichen ('antsaiçən) *n neu* sign, sympton.

Anzeig/e ('antsaigə) *nf* **-n 1** advertisement, notice, announcement. **2** denunciation. **3** notification, indication. **—en** *vt* **1** announce, advertise. **2** denounce. **—er** *nm* **1** indicator. **2** informer. **3** advertiser. **4** newspaper.

anzieh/en* ('antsiːən) *vt* **1** put on (clothes). **2** attract. **3** pull or draw on. **4** tighten. **sich anziehen** *vr* dress. **—ungskraft** *nf* **1** attractive force, gravitation. **2** attractiveness.

Anzug ('antsuːk) *nm* **¨-e 1** suit. **2** clothing, dress. **3** approach.

ızünden ('antsyndən) *vt* ight, set fire to.

pennin (apɛ'niːn) *nm also* **Ap-ɔenninen** *n pl* Apennines.

pfel ('apfəl) *nm* ¨— apple.

Apfelsine ('apfəlziːnə) *nf* **-n** orange.

Apostel (a'pɔstəl) *nm* — apostle.

Apotheke (apo'teːkə) *nf* **-n** chemist's shop, pharmacy. **—r** *nm* — chemist, pharmacist.

Apparat (apa'raːt) *nm* **-e** **1** apparatus, equipment. **2** device. **3** telephone. **am Apparat bleiben** hold the line.

appellieren (apɛ'liːrən) *vi* appeal.

Appetit (ape'tiːt) *nm* **-e** appetite. **—lich** *adj* appetizing.

Aprikose (apri'koːzə) *nf* **-n** apricot.

April (a'pril) *nm* **-e** April.

Aquarell (akva'rel) *n neu* **-e** watercolour.

Aquarium (a'kvaːrium) *n neu* **-rien** aquarium.

Äquator (ɛ'kvaːtɔr) *nm* Equator.

Äquivalent (ɛkviva'lɛnt) *n neu* **-e** equivalent.

Arab/er ('arabər) *nm* — Arab. **—ien** (a'raːbiən) *n neu* Arabia. **—isch** (a'raːbiʃ) *adj* Arabian, Arabic. *n neu* Arabic (language).

Arbeit ('arbait) *nf* **-en** **1** work, labour. **2** job. **3** effort. **—en** *vi,vt* work, labour. **—er** *nm* — worker, workman, labourer. **—erklasse** *nf also* **—erschaft** *nf* **-en** working class(es). **—geber** *nm* — employer. **—nehmer** *nm* — employee. **—sgemeinschaft** *nf* **1** syndicate. **2** partnership (employers and employees). **3** working party, study group. **—skräfte** *nf pl* personnel, staff, workforce. **—slos** *adj* unemployed. **—slosigkeit** *nf* unemployment.

Archäologie (arçɛolo'giː) *nf* archaeology.

Architekt (arçi'tɛkt) *nm* **-en** architect. **—ur** (arçitɛk'tuːr) *nf* **-en** architecture.

Archiv (ar'çiːf) *n neu* **-e** archives, records.

arg (ark) *adj* **1** bad, evil. **2** serious. *n neu* evil, malice. **—los** *adj* unsuspecting, innocent. **—wohn** ('arkvoːn) *nm* suspicion, distrust.

Argentin/ien (argɛn'tiːniən) *n neu* Argentina. **—ier** *nm* — Argentine. **—isch** *adj* Argentinian.

Ärger ('ɛrgər) *nm* **1** anger. **2** irritation, annoyance. **—lich** *adj* **1** angry. **2** annoying, troublesome. **—n** *vt* annoy, irritate, bother. **—nis** *n neu* **-se** **1** nuisance. **2** offence.

Argument (argu'mɛnt) *n neu* **-e** argument, case.

Aristokrat (aristo'kraːt) *nm* **-en** aristocrat. **—ie** *nf* **-n** aristocracy. **—isch** *adj* aristocratic.

Arithmetik (arit'meːtik) *nf* arithmetic.

Arktis ('arktis) *nf* Arctic. **arktisch** ('arktiʃ) *adj* arctic.

arm (arm) *adj* poor. **—e(r)** *nm* **-n** poor man. ¨**—lich** ('ɛrmliç) *adj* poor, lowly (of clothes, a house, etc.). **—selig** *adj* miserable, wretched (of persons). **—ut** ('armu:t) *nf* poverty.

Arm (arm) *nm* **-e 1** arm. **2** (of rivers, etc.) branch. **—band** *n neu* bracelet. **—banduhr** *nf* wrist-watch. **—stuhl** *nm* armchair.

Armee (ar'me:) *nf* **-n** army. **—korps** *n neu* army corps.

Ärmel ('ɛrməl) *nm* **—** sleeve. **—kanal** *nm* (English) Channel.

Arrest (a'rɛst) *nm* **-e 1** arrest, seizure. **2** detention, imprisonment.

Art (a:rt) *nf* **-en 1** sort, type, kind. **2** way, manner. **3** nature. **4** species. **—en nach** *vi* take after. **—ig** *adj* **1** well-behaved, polite. **2** kind. **3** good. **—igkeit** *nf* **-en 1** politeness, good behaviour. **2** compliment.

—artig ('a:rtiç) *suff* -like.

Artikel (ar'ti:kəl) *nm* **—** article.

Artillerie (artilə'ri:) *nf* **-n** artillery.

Artischocke (a:ti'ʃɔkə) *nf* **-n** artichoke.

Arznei (arts'nai) *nf* **-en,** *also* **Arzneimittel** *n neu* medicine, drug.

Arzt (a:rtst) *nm* **¨-e** doctor, physician. **¨—in** ('ɛ:rtstin) *nf* **-nen** (woman) doctor. **¨—lich** ('ɛ:rtstliç) *adj* medical.

As (as) *n neu* **-se** ace.

Asbest (as'bɛst) *nm* **-e** asbestos.

Asche ('aʃə) *nf* **-n** ash, ashes, cinders. **—nbahn** *nf* cinder-track, dirt-track. **—nbecher** *nm* ashtray. **—rmittwoch** (aʃər'mitvɔx) *nm* Ash Wednesday.

aß (a:s) *v* see **essen.**

Assistent (asis'tɛnt) *nm* **-en** assistant.

Ast (ast) *nm* **¨-e 1** bough, branch. **2** knot (in wood).

ästhetisch (es'te:tiʃ) *adj* aesthetic.

Astronaut (astro'naut) *nm* **-en** astronaut.

Astronom (astro'no:m) *nm* **-en** astronomer. **—ie** (astrono'mi:) *nf* astronomy.

Asyl (a'zy:l) *n neu* **-e** asylum, sanctuary.

Atelier (atə'lje:) *n neu* **-s** studio.

Atem ('a:təm) *nm* breath. **außer Atem** breathless. **—raubend** *adj* **1** breath-taking, terrifying. **2** fascinating. **—los** *adj* breathless.

Athe/ismus (ate'ismus) *nm* atheism. **—ist** (ate'ist) *nm* **-en** atheist.

Athen (a'te:n) *n neu* Athens.

Äther ('ɛ:tər) *nm* ether. **—isch** (ɛ'te:riʃ) *adj* ethereal.

Äthiop/ien (ɛti'o:piən) *n neu* Ethiopia. **—ier** *nm* **—** Ethiopian. **—isch** *adj* Ethiopian.

Athletik (at'le:tik) *nf* athletics.

Atlantik (at'lantik) *nm* *also* **Atlantischer Ozean** (at'lantiʃər) Atlantic.

Atlas[1] ('atlas) *nm* **-lasse** satin.

Atlas[2] ('atlas) *nm* **-lanten** atlas.

atmen ('a:tmən) *vi,vt* breathe, respire.

Atmosphäre (atmos'fɛ:rə) *nf* **-n** atmosphere. **atmosphärisch** (atmos'fɛ:riʃ) *adj* atmospheric.

Atom (a'to:m) *n neu* **-e** atom. **—bombe** *nf* atom(ic) bomb **—energie** *nf* atomic energy.

—kern *nm* atomic nucleus. **—kraftanlage** *nf* nuclear power station. **—waffen** *nf pl* nuclear weapons.

Atten/tat (atɛn'taːt) *n neu* **-e** murderous attack, assault, (attempted) assassination. **—täter** (atɛn'tɛːtər) *nm* — assassin, assailant.

ätzen ('ɛtsən) *vt* corrode, etch.

Aubergine (obɛr'ʒiːnə) *nf* **-n** aubergine.

auch (aux) *adv, conj* **1** also, as well, too. **2** even. **3** indeed. **auch wenn** *also* **wenn auch** even if. **nicht nur...sondern auch** not only...but also. **wer auch** whoever.

Audienz (audi'ɛnts) *nf* **-en** audience, hearing.

auf (auf) *prep* **1** (up)on. **2** in. **3** to. **4** at. **5** up. **6** against. **auf einmal** all at once. *~adv* open, up(wards). *interj* (get) up!

Aufbau ('aufbau) *nm* **-e** or **-ten** **1** construction, erection. **2** composition, organization. **3** superstructure. **—en** *vt* construct, build up.

Aufbesserung ('aufbɛsəruŋ) *nf* **-en** **1** improvement. **2** increase (of salary etc.).

aufbewahren ('aufbəvaːrən) *vt* store, keep.

aufbleiben* ('aufblaibən) *vi* **1** stay up. **2** remain open.

aufblicken ('aufblikən) *vi* look up.

aufbrauchen ('aufbrauxən) *vt* use up, consume.

aufbrechen* ('aufbrɛçən) *vt* break open. *vi* **1** burst, open. **2** set off.

aufbringen* ('aufbriŋən) *vt* **1** bring up, raise. **2** irritate, anger.

aufdrehen ('aufdreːən) *vt* **1** unscrew. **2** turn on.

aufdring/en* ('aufdriŋən) *vt* force on (someone). **—lich** *adj* intrusive, importunate.

aufeinander (aufain'andər) *adv* **1** successively. **2** one on or against the other.

Aufenthalt ('aufɛnthalt) *nm* **-e** **1** stop, halt, delay. **2** stay, period (of residence).

auferlegen ('aufɛrleːgən) *vt* impose.

aufersteh/en* ('aufɛrʃteːən) *vi* rise from the dead. **—ung** *nf* **-en** resurrection.

auffahren* ('auffaːrən) *vi* **1** rise (up). **2** drive up. **3** start, jump. **4** become angry.

auffallen* ('auffalən) *vi* **1** fall upon. **2** be noticeable, evident. **es fiel mir auf, daß** it struck me that. **auffallend** ('auffalənt) *adj also* **auffällig** ('auffɛliç) striking, remarkable.

auffangen* ('auffaŋən) *vt* catch up, intercept.

auffass/en ('auffasən) *vt* **1** understand, interpret. **2** pick up. **—ung** *nf* **-en** **1** comprehension. **2** opinion. **3** conception.

auffinden* ('auffindən) *vt* find (out), discover.

auffliegen* ('auffliːgən) *vi* **1** fly up. **2** explode. **3** (of a door) fly open.

aufforder/n ('auffɔrdərn) *vt* **1** challenge, invite. **2** summon. **—ung** *nf* **-en** **1** challenge, invitation. **2** summons.

auffressen* ('auffrɛsən) *vt* devour.

aufführ/en ('auffyːrən) *vt* **1**

build. **2** perform. **3** specify. **4** list. **5** bring forward, introduce. **—ung** *nf* **-en** performance, presentation.

Aufgabe ('aufga:bə) *nf* **-n 1** task, duty. **2** problem. **3** giving up. **4** delivery.

Aufgang ('aufgaŋ) *nm* **¨-e 1** ascent, rise. **2** staircase.

aufgeben* ('aufge:bən) *vt* **1** give up or in. **2** deliver, surrender. **3** post (mail, etc.).

Aufgebot ('aufgəbo:t) *n neu* **-e** public notice.

aufgehen* ('aufge:ən) *vi* **1** rise. **2** open. **3** *math* divide exactly, work out correctly.

aufgeklärt ('aufgəklɛ:rt) *adj* enlightened.

aufgelegt ('aufgəle:kt) *adj* disposed, inclined. **gut/schlecht aufgelegt** in a good/bad mood.

aufhalten* ('aufhaltən) *vt* **1** hold open. **2** delay. **sich aufhalten** *vr* stay.

aufhängen* ('aufhɛŋən) *vt* hang (up).

aufheb/en* ('aufhe:bən) *vt* **1** pick up, raise. **2** keep, store. **3** annul, cancel. **4** suspend. **5** reverse. *n neu* **— 1** lifting up. **2** fuss, ado. **—ung** *nf* **-en 1** abolition, repeal. **2** suspension.

aufhören ('aufhœ:rən) *vi* cease, stop, discontinue.

aufklappen ('aufklapən) *vt* open.

aufklär/en ('aufklɛ:rən) *vt,vi* **1** clear up. **2** enlighten. **3** correct. **—ung** *nf* **-en 1** clearing up. **2** enlightenment. **3** explanation.

aufkleben ('aufkle:bən) *vt* paste on, affix.

aufknüpfen ('aufknypfən) *vt* **1** tie or hang up. **2** untie.

aufkommen* ('aufkɔmən) *vi* **1** rise. **2** recover. **3** make good. *n neu* **— 1** yield (of taxes). **2** recovery, rise.

aufladen* ('aufla:dən) *vt* load.

Auflage ('aufla:gə) *nf* **-n 1** edition, impression. **2** circulation. **3** tax, duty.

auflassen* ('auflasən) *vt* leave open.

Auflauf ('auflauf) *nm* **¨-e 1** riot. **2** soufflé.

auflös/en ('auflœ:zən) *vt* **1** untie, loosen. **2** dissolve. **3** break up. **—ung** *nf* **-en 1** dissolution. **2** decomposition.

aufmachen ('aufmaxən) *vt* **1** open, undo. **2** put up (an umbrella). **sich aufmachen** *vr* set out.

Aufmarsch ('aufmarʃ) *nm* **¨-e** *mil* **1** approach, marching up (of troops). **2** deployment. **3** parade.

aufmerk/sam ('aufmɛrkza:m) *adj* attentive. **—samkeit** *nf* attentiveness.

aufmuntern ('aufmuntərn) *vt* **1** rouse, encourage. **2** cheer up.

Aufnahme ('aufna:mə) *nf* **-n 1** acceptance, reception, admission. **2** recording. **3** photograph.

aufnehmen* ('aufne:mən) *vt* **1** take or pick up. **2** receive, admit. **3** record. **4** photograph.

aufopfer/n ('aufɔpfərn) *vt* sacrifice. **—ung** *nf* **-en 1** sacrifice. **2** devotion.

aufpassen ('aufpasən) *vi* **1** watch. **2** pay attention.

Aufputz ('aufputs) *nm* finery, ornament.

aufräumen ('aufrɔymən) *vt* **1** tidy up. **2** clear away or out.

aufrecht ('aufrɛçt) *adj* **1** upright, erect. **2** honourable. **—erhalten*** *vt* maintain, support. **—erhaltung** *nf* maintenance.

aufreg/en ('aufre:gən) *vt* **1** excite. **2** irritate. **3** alarm. **sich aufregen** *vr* get excited. **—ung** *nf* **-en** excitement, agitation.

aufreiben* ('aufraibən) *vt* **1** chafe. **2** exhaust. **3** harass. **4** destroy, wipe out (an enemy).

aufricht/en ('aufriçtən) *vt* **1** erect, set up. **2** establish. **sich aufrichten** *vr* get or sit up. **—ig** *adj* honest, sincere. **—igkeit** *nf* sincerity.

Aufriß ('aufris) *nm* **1** sketch. **2** section. **3** plan.

aufrücken ('aufrykən) *vi* move up(wards).

Aufruf ('aufru:f) *nm* **-e** **1** call. **2** summons. **3** appeal.

Aufruhr ('aufru:r) *nm* **-e** **1** riot, uproar. **2** revolt. **¨—erisch** ('aufry:rəriʃ) *adj* mutinous.

aufrüsten ('aufrystən) *vt* (re)arm.

aufs (aufs) contraction of **auf das.**

aufsagen ('aufzagən) *vt* recite.

Aufsatz ('aufzats) *nm* **¨-e** **1** essay, article. **2** top piece. **3** centrepiece.

aufschieben* ('aufʃi:bən) *vt* **1** push open. **2** delay, postpone.

Aufschlag ('aufʃla:k) *nm* **¨-e** **1** hit, impact. **2** rise (of prices). **3** cuff, lapel, facing (of clothes). **4** *sport* service. **—en*** ('aufʃla:gən) *vt* **1** break open, open. **2** put up, erect. **3** look or glance up.

aufschließen* ('aufʃli:sən) *vt* **1** unlock. **2** open up.

Aufschluß ('aufʃlus) *nm* **1** information. **2** explanation. **—reich** *adj* informative.

aufschneiden* ('aufʃnaidən) *vt* cut open or up. *vi* brag, exaggerate.

Aufschnitt ('aufʃnit) *nm* **-e** slices of cold meats.

Aufschrei ('aufʃrai) *nm* **-e** **1** scream. **2** outcry.

aufschreiben* ('aufʃraibən) *vt* write down.

Aufschrift ('aufʃrift) *nf* **-en** **1** inscription. **2** address.

Aufschub ('aufʃup) *nm* **¨-e** delay, postponement.

Aufschwung ('aufʃvuŋ) *nm* **¨-e** **1** rise, upward impetus. **2** *comm* boom. **3** enthusiasm. **einen neuen Aufschwung nehmen** revive.

aufseh/en* ('aufze:ən) *vi* look up. *n neu* — sensation, stir. **—er** *nm* — inspector, overseer, superintendant.

aufsetzen ('aufzɛtsən) *vt* **1** set up. **2** put on. **sich aufsetzen** *vr* sit up.

Aufsicht ('aufziçt) *nf* **-en** **1** supervision. **2** charge, care. **—sbehörde** *nf* controlling authority. **—srat** *nm* board of directors.

aufspringen* ('aufʃpriŋən) *vi* **1** jump up. **2** fly open. **3** crack.

Aufstand ('aufʃtant) *nm* **¨-e** revolt, riot. **¨—isch** ('aufʃtɛndiʃ) *adj* rebellious.

aufstapeln ('aufʃta:pəln) *vt* **1** heap up. **2** store.

aufstehen* ('aufʃteːən) *vi* **1** get or stand up. **2** rebel. **3** stand open.
aufsteigen* ('aufʃtaigən) *vi* **1** climb (up), mount. **2** rise.
aufstell/en ('aufʃtɛlən) *vt* **1** put or set up. **2** draw up. **3** nominate. **4** display. **5** state. **—ung** *nf* **-en** **1** erection. **2** position. **3** arrangement. **4** list, table. **5** nomination.
Aufstieg ('aufʃtiːk) *nm* **-e** **1** ascent. **2** rise.
aufstützen ('aufʃtytsən) *vt* prop up.
aufsuchen ('aufzuːxən) *vt* seek (out). **jemanden aufsuchen** look up or visit someone.
auftanken ('auftaŋkən) *vt* fuel, fill up (with fuel).
auftauchen ('auftauxən) *vi* **1** emerge. **2** surface. **3** appear, crop up.
aufteilen ('auftailən) *vt* distribute, divide up.
Auftrag ('auftraːk) *nm* **¨-e** **1** instructions, order. **2** task. **3** contract. **4** mandate. **im Auftrag von** by order of. **—geber** *nm* — *comm* customer.
auftreiben* ('auftraibən) *vt* **1** procure, obtain. **2** startle, rouse. **3** swell.
auftreten* ('auftreːtən) *vi* **1** come forward. **2** occur, appear. *vt* kick open. *n neu* — **1** appearance. **2** behaviour, manner.
Auftritt ('auftrit) *nm* **-e** **1** appearance. **2** *Th* scene.
auftun* ('auftuːn) *vt* **1** open. **2** start (up).
aufwachen* ('aufvaxən) *vi* wake up.
aufwachsen* ('aufvaksən) *vi* grow up.
Aufwand ('aufvant) *nm* **¨-e** **1** expenditure. **2** extravagance.
aufwärmen ('aufvɛrmən) *vt* **1** warm up. **2** rake up, revive (a dispute, story, etc.).
aufwärts ('aufvɛrts) *adv* upward(s).
aufwecken ('aufvɛkən) *vt* wake, rouse.
aufweisen* ('aufvaizən) *vt* present, show.
aufwend/en* (aufvendən) *vt* spend, expend. **—ung** *nf* **-en** expenditure.
aufwerfen* ('aufvɛrfən) *vt* **1** cast up. **2** throw open. **3** raise (a question).
aufwert/en ('aufvɛrtən) *vt* revalue (upwards). **—ung** *nf* **-en** revaluation.
aufwischen ('aufviʃən) *vt* wipe up.
aufwühlen ('aufvyːlən) *vt* **1** dig up, turn up. **2** stir up.
aufzählen ('auftsɛːlən) *vt* count (up), enumerate.
aufzeichn/en ('auftsaiçnən) *vt* **1** draw, sketch. **2** note, record. **—ung** *nf* **-en** note, record.
aufziehen* ('auftsiːən) *vt* **1** pull or draw up, raise. **2** open. **3** bring up, rear.
Aufzug ('auftsuːk) *nm* **¨-e** **1** lift, elevator, hoist. **2** parade. **3** act (of a play). **4** attire.
Augapfel ('aukapfəl) *nm* eyeball.
Auge ('augə) *n neu* **-n** **1** eye. **2** bud. **blaues Auge** black eye. **ein Auge zudrücken** **1** wink at. **2** shut one's eyes to. **unter vier Augen** face to face (in private). **—nblick** *nm* instant,

moment. **—nfällig** *adj* conspicuous, obvious.
August (au'gust) *nm* August.
Aula ('aula) *nf* **-len** (great) hall.
au pair (o'pɛːr) *adj* au pair.
aus (aus) *prep* **1** out (of). **2** from. **3** of. **4** by. *adv* **1** out. **2** over, finished.
ausarbeiten ('ausarbaitən) *vt* **1** work out. **2** prepare.
Ausbau ('ausbau) *nm* **-e 1** completion. **2** extension (of a building).
ausbessern ('ausbɛsərn) *vt* **1** repair, refit. **2** rectify.
Ausbeut/e ('ausbɔytə) *nf* **-n 1** profit, gain. **2** output. **—en** *vt* exploit, profit from. **—ung** *nf* **-en** exploitation.
ausbild/en ('ausbildən) *vt* **1** educate, train. **2** form, develop. **—ung** *nf* **1** education, training. **2** development.
ausbleiben* ('ausblaibən) *vi* stay away or out, be absent. *n neu* **—** absence, default.
Ausblick ('ausblik) *nm* **-e** view, outlook.
ausbrechen* ('ausbrɛçən) *vi* break out. *vt* vomit.
ausbreit/en ('ausbraitən) *vt* **1** spread (out). **2** stretch, extend. **3** spread. **—ung** *nf* **-en** spread, increase.
ausbringen* ('ausbriŋən) *vt* bring out. **eine Gesundheit ausbringen** propose a toast.
Ausbruch ('ausbrux) *nm* **¨-e 1** burst. **2** outbreak. **3** eruption. **4** escape.
ausbrüten ('ausbrytən) *vt* **1** hatch. **2** plot.
Ausdauer ('ausdauər) *nf* **1** endurance. **2** perseverance.
ausdehn/en ('ausdeːnən) *vt* extend, stretch, expand. **—** *nf* **1** expansion. **2** range, extent.
ausdenken* ('ausdɛŋkən) *vt* think out, work out. **sich ausdenken** *vr* think up, invent.
ausdrehen ('ausdreːən) *vt* turn or switch off.
Ausdruck ('ausdruk) *nm* **¨-e 1** expression, look. **2** expression, term. **3** printout. **¨—en** ('ausdrykən) *vt* **1** express. **2** press or squeeze out. **¨—lich** ('ausdrykliç) *adj* explicit.
auseinander (ausain'andər) *adv* separately, apart (from one another). **—gehen* 1** disperse. **2** separate. **3** differ. **—setzen** *vt* explain, expound. **—setzung** *nf* **-en 1** discussion. **2** conflict. **3** arrangement. **—treiben*** *vt* disperse.
ausersehen* ('ausɛrzeːən) *vt* **1** select, choose. **2** destine. *adj* (pre)destined.
auserwählen ('ausɛrveːlən) *vt* choose, select.
ausfahr/en* ('ausfaːrən) *vi* go for a drive. *vt* take (someone) for a drive. **—t** *nf* **1** drive, excursion. **2** way out, gateway. **3** departure.
Ausfall ('ausfal) *nm* **¨-e 1** loss. **2** falling out. **3** result. **4** attack, sortie.
ausfertigen ('ausfɛrtigən) *vt* **1** complete. **2** draw up. **3** issue. **4** execute.
ausfind/en* ('ausfindən) *vt* find out. **ausfindig machen 1** trace. **2** find out.
Ausflug ('ausfluːk) *nm* **¨-e** excursion.
Ausfluß ('ausflus) *nm* **1** out-

2 outlet. 3 re-

('ausfra:gən) vt in-

...e, question.

...uhr ('ausfu:r) nf **-en** export(ing). **—handel** *nm* export trade.

ausführ/bar ('ausfy:rba:r) *adj* **1** practicable. **2** exportable. **—en** *vt* **1** lead out. **2** carry out, perform. **3** export. **—lich** *adj* detailed, full.

ausfüllen ('ausfylən) *vt* fill up or in.

Ausgabe ('ausga:bə) *nf* **-n 1** delivery. **2** issue. **3** edition. **4** expense, expenditure.

Ausgang ('ausgaŋ) *nm* **¨-e 1** door, exit. **2** result, end. **3** going out.

ausgeben* ('ausge:bən) *vt* **1** give out. **2** spend. **sich ausgeben für** pose as.

ausgeglichen ('ausgəgliçən) *adj* balanced.

ausgeh/en* ('ausge:ən) *vi* **1** go out, depart. **2** proceed. **3** end, run out. **4** fade. **—verbot** *n neu* curfew.

ausgelassen ('ausgəlasən) *adj* boisterous, unrestrained.

ausgemacht ('ausgəmaxt) *adj* settled, agreed.

ausgenommen ('ausgənɔmən) *prep* except.

ausgeprägt ('ausgəprɛ:kt) *adj* distinct, marked.

ausgerechnet ('ausgərɛçnət) *adv* just, precisely. **ausgerechnet ich** I of all people.

ausgeschlossen ('ausgəʃlɔsən) *adj* impossible, out of the question.

ausgesprochen ('ausgəʃprɔçən) *adj* marked, pronounced.

ausgezeichnet ('ausgətsaiçnət) *adj* excellent.

ausgießen ('ausgi:sən) *vt* pour out.

Ausgleich ('ausglaiç) *nm* **-e 1** balance. **2** agreement, settlement. **3** compromise. **4** compensation. **5** adjustment. **—en*** *vt* **1** equalize, balance. **2** settle. **3** adjust.

Ausguß ('ausgus) *nm* **-güsse 1** pouring out. **2** spout. **3** gutter. **4** sink.

aushalten* ('aushaltən) *vi* **1** hold out. **2** persevere. *vt* endure, bear.

Aushang ('aushaŋ) *nm* **¨-e** poster, notice. **¨—en*** ('aushɛŋən) *vt,vi* hang out.

ausharren ('ausharən) *vi* persevere.

ausheben* ('aushe:bən) *vt* **1** lift out. **2** enlist, recruit. **3** raid.

aushelfen* ('aushɛlfən) *vi* help out.

Aushilfe ('aushilfə) *nf* **-n** assistance, help, (temporary) aid.

sich auskennen* ('auskɛnən) *vr* know thoroughly.

auskleiden ('ausklaidən) *vt* **1** undress. **2** *tech* coat, line. **sich auskleiden** *vr* undress.

auskommen* ('auskɔmən) *vi* **1** come out. **2** escape. **3** manage, make do. **mit jemandem gut auskommen** get on well with someone. *n neu* **—** livelihood.

Auskunft ('auskunft) *nf* **-künfte** information, data. **—sbüro** *n neu* information bureau. **—smittel** *n neu* **1** escape. **2** expedient.

auslachen ('auslaxən) *vt* laugh at.

ausladen* ('auslaːdən) *vt* unload.

Auslage ('auslaːgə) *nf* **-n 1** outlay. **2** expense. **3** display.

Ausland ('auslant) *n neu* foreign countries. **im/ins Ausland** abroad, overseas. **¨—er** ('auslɛndər) *nm* — foreigner, alien. **¨—isch** ('auslɛndiʃ) *adj* foreign.

auslass/en* ('auslasən) *vt* **1** let out. **2** leave out, omit. **sich auslassen** *vr* express one's opinion. **—ung** *nf* **-en 1** omission. **2** remark. **—ungszeichen** *n neu* apostrophe.

Auslauf ('auslauf) *nm* **¨-e 1** flowing out. **2** outlet. **3** departure (of a ship). **4** *aviat* landing run. **5** (gradual) finish, runout. **—en*** *vi* **1** run out. **2** leak. **3** come to an end.

ausleg/en ('ausleːgən) *vt* **1** lay out. **2** spend. **3** explain, interpret. **—ung** *nf* **-en** interpretation, explanation.

Auslese ('ausleːzə) *nf* **-n 1** selection. **2** choice wine.

ausliefer/n ('ausliːfərn) *vt* hand over, deliver (up). **—ung** *nf* **1** delivery. **2** extradition.

auslöschen ('auslœʃən) *vt* **1** extinguish. **2** erase. **3** switch off.

auslös/en ('auslœːzən) *vt* **1** release. **2** loosen. **3** ransom, redeem. **4** cause. **5** arouse. **—er** *nm* — **1** trigger. **2** release.

ausmachen ('ausmaxən) *vt* **1** put out (fire, lights). **2** constitute, make up. **3** make out, discern. **4** arrange. **5** agree.

es macht nichts au[...] doesn't matter.

Ausnahm/e ('ausnaːmə) *nf* [...] exception. **—efall** *nm* excep[...]tional case. **—ezustand** *nm* state of emergency. **—slos** *adj* without exception. **—sweise** *adv* exceptionally, for once.

ausnehmen* ('ausneːmən) *vt* **1** take out. **2** except, exempt.

ausnutzen ('ausnytsən) *vt also* **ausnützen** exploit, utilize.

auspacken ('auspakən) *vt* unpack.

auspräg/en ('ausprɛːgən) *vt* **1** stamp, mark. **2** coin. **—ung** *nf* **1** coinage. **2** stamp(ing).

ausprobieren ('ausprobiːrən) *vt* try, sample.

Auspuff ('auspuf) *nm* **-e** exhaust. **—rohr** *n neu* exhaust pipe. **—topf** *nm* silencer.

ausradieren ('ausradiːrən) *vt* erase.

ausräumen ('ausrɔymən) *vt* **1** clear (out). **2** empty.

ausrechnen ('ausrɛçnən) *vt* calculate.

Ausrede ('ausreːdə) *nf* **-n** (false) excuse.

ausreichen ('ausraiçən) *vi* suffice. **—d** *adj* sufficient.

Ausreise ('ausraizə) *nf* **-n** departure.

ausrichten ('ausriçtən) *vt* **1** carry out, accomplish. **2** deliver. **3** adjust. **4** straighten.

ausrotten ('ausrɔtən) *vt* **1** root out. **2** destroy (utterly), eradicate.

Ausruf ('ausruːf) *nm* **-e 1** cry. **2** proclamation. **—en*** *vt, vi* cry out, exclaim. **—ewort** *n neu* interjection. **—ung** *nf* **-en 1**

... proclamation. ...**en** *n neu* exclam-...

...n ('ausruːən) *vi* rest.

...**st/en** ('ausrystən) *vt* **1** ...ovide with, equip. **2** arm. **—ung** *nf* **-en 1** equipment. **2** armament.

aussäen ('auszɛːən) *vt* sow.

Aussag/e ('auszaːgə) *nf* **-n 1** declaration, deposition. **2** evidence. **—en** *vt* **1** declare, state. **2** give evidence.

Aussatz ('auszats) *nm* leprosy. **¨—ig** ('auszɛtsiç) *adj* leprous.

ausschalten ('ausʃaltən) *vt* **1** switch off, disconnect, break. **2** eliminate, exclude.

ausscheid/en* ('ausʃaidən) *vt* **1** eliminate. **2** separate. *vi* withdraw, retire.

ausschicken ('ausʃikən) *vt* send out, dispatch.

ausschießen* ('ausʃiːsən) *vt* shoot or cast out.

ausschiffen ('ausʃifən) *vt* **1** disembark. **2** set sail.

ausschimpfen ('ausʃimpfən) *vt* scold.

ausschlafen* ('ausʃlaːfən) *vi* sleep late, lie in.

Ausschlag ('ausʃlaːk) *nm* **¨-e 1** deflection. **2** rash, eruption. **den Ausschlag geben** tip the scales. **—en*** ('ausʃlaːgən) *vt* **1** beat or knock out. **2** refuse, reject. **3** line or trim with. *vi* **1** lash out. **2** sprout, break into leaf. **3** turn out, develop. **—gebend** *adj* decisive.

ausschließ/en* ('ausʃliːsən) *vt* shut out, exclude, bar. **—lich** *adj* exclusive. *prep* excluding, exclusive of. **Ausschluß** ('ausʃlus) *nm* exclusion.

ausschneiden* ('ausʃnaidən) *vt* cut out.

ausschöpfen ('ausʃœpfən) *vt* **1** scoop out. **2** drain (off). **3** exhaust.

ausschreiben* ('ausʃraibən) *vt* **1** write out, copy. **2** announce, advertise.

Ausschreitung ('ausʃraituŋ) *nf* **-en 1** excess. **2** transgression.

Ausschuß ('ausʃus) *nm* **1** committee, commission. **2** scrap. **3** rejects.

ausschweif/en ('ausʃvaifən) *vi* lead an immoral or dissolute life. **—ung** *nf* debauchery.

aussehen* ('auszeːən) *vi* appear, look. **gut aussehend** good looking. *n neu* **— 1** appearance. **2** exterior.

außen ('ausən) *adv* **1** out(side), out of doors. **2** outwards. **—bordmotor** *nm* outboard motor. **—handel** *nm* foreign trade. **—minister** *nm* foreign minister. **—politik** *nf* foreign policy, foreign affairs. **—seite** *nf* outside. **—stände** *nm pl* arrears, outstanding debts or accounts. **—welt** *nf* **1** external world. **2** visible world.

aussenden* ('auszɛndən) *vt* **1** send out. **2** emit, transmit.

außer ('ausər) *prep* **1** outside. **2** out of. **3** besides. **4** except for. **außer Betrieb** out of order. **außer Dienst** off duty. **außer Fassung** disconcerted. **außer Kraft setzen** annul, cancel. *~conj* except, but. **außer daß** except that. **—dem** *adv, conj* besides, moreover. **—gewöhnlich** *adj* extraordinary. **—halb** *prep* outside, beyond. **—ordentlich** (ausər'ɔrdəntliç) *adj* extraordinary, uncommon.

äußer/e ('ɔysərə) *adj* external. *n neu* **-n** exterior, appearance. **—st** ('ɔysərst) *adj* **1** outermost. **2** utmost. **3** extreme.

äußerlich ('ɔysərliç) *adj* **1** external. **2** superficial.

äußer/n ('ɔysərn) *vt* utter, express. **—ung** *nf* **-en** remark.

aussetzen ('auszɛtsən) *vt* **1** set or put out. **2** suspend. **3** expose. **4** offer (money). **5** lower (a boat). *vi* stop, stall.

Aussicht ('ausziçt) *nf* **-en** outlook, prospect. **—slos** *adj* hopeless. **—spunkt** *nm* viewpoint.

aussondern ('auszɔndərn) *vt* single out, separate.

ausspannen ('ausʃpanən) *vt* stretch, extend. *vi* rest, relax.

ausspeien ('ausʃpaijən) *vt* spit out.

Aussprache ('ausʃpraːxə) *nf* **-n 1** pronunciation. **2** discussion.

aussprechen* ('ausʃprɛçən) *vt* **1** pronounce. **2** express, say.

Ausspruch ('ausʃprux) *nm* saying, utterance.

ausspülen ('ausʃpyːlən) *vt* **1** wash or rinse out. **2** clean.

Ausstand ('ausʃtant) *nm* strike.

ausstatt/en ('ausʃtatən) *vt* **1** equip. **2** furnish. **—ung** *nf* **-en 1** equipment. **2** fittings.

ausstehen* ('ausʃteːən) *vt* endure, bear.

ausstell/en ('ausʃtɛlən) *vt* **1** exhibit. **2** issue. **—ung** *nf* exhibition.

aussterben* ('ausʃtɛı die out.

Aussteuer ('ausʃtɔyər) *nf* dowry. **2** trousseau.

ausstoßen* ('ausʃtoːsən) *vt* push or drive out, expel. **2** u ter.

ausstrahlen ('ausʃtraːlən) *vt,vi* radiate.

ausstrecken ('ausʃtrɛkən) *vt* extend.

ausstreichen* ('ausʃtraiçən) *vt* cross out.

ausströmen ('ausʃtrœːmən) *vi* **1** stream out. **2** escape.

aussuchen ('auszuːxən) *vt* select, pick.

Austausch ('austauʃ) *nm* **-e** exchange, barter. **—en** *vt* exchange.

austeilen ('austailən) *vt* distribute, hand out.

Auster ('austər) *nf* **-n** oyster.

austragen* ('austraːgən) *vt* **1** distribute. **2** deliver. **3** decide (a contest).

Austral/ien (au'straːliən) *n neu* Australia. **—ier** *nm* Australian. **—isch** *adj* Australian.

austreiben* ('austraibən) *vt* **1** drive out, expel. **2** exorcize.

austreten* ('austreːtən) *vi* **1** go or step out. **2** withdraw. **3** resign from. *vt* tread out, stamp out. **Austritt** ('austrit) *nm* **-e 1** departure, exit. **2** resignation. **3** withdrawal.

ausüb/en ('ausyːbən) *vt* **1** practise. **2** carry out. **—ung** *nf* practice, execution.

Ausverkauf ('ausfɛrkauf) *nm* (clearance) sale.

Auswahl ('ausvaːl) *nf* **-en 1** selection. **2** variety. **¨—en** ('ausvɛːlən) *vt* choose, select.

…usvandərər) … —**n** *vi* emi-… **g** *nf* **-en** emigra-…

…**g** ('ausvɛrtiç) *adj* for-… **das auswärtige Amt** …reign office.

auswärts ('ausvɛrts) *adv* **1** outward(s). **2** abroad. **3** outside.

Ausweg ('ausveːk) *nm* way out, expedient.

ausweich/en* ('ausvaiçən) *vi* **1** make way for. **2** avoid.

ausweiden ('ausvaidən) *vt* gut, disembowel.

Ausweis ('ausvais) *nm* **-e** **1** ticket. **2** identity card. **3** passport. **4** statement. **—en*** ('ausvaizən) *vt* turn out, expel, banish. **sich —en** *vr* prove one's identity. **—karte** *nf* identity card. **—papiere** *n neu pl* identification papers. **—ung** ('ausvaizuŋ) *nf* expulsion, deportation.

auswendig ('ausvɛndiç) *adj* external. **auswendig lernen** learn by heart, memorize.

auswerfen* ('ausvɛrfən) *vt* throw out, cast out.

auswerten ('ausvɛrtən) *vt* evaluate, analyse.

auswirken ('ausvirkən) *vt* **1** work out. **2** effect, bring about.

auswischen ('ausviʃən) *vt* wipe out, obliterate.

Auswuchs ('ausvuks) *nm* growth, deformity.

auszahlen ('austsaːlən) *vt* pay out or off.

auszeichn/en ('austsaiçnən) *vt* **1** mark out. **2** honour. **3** label. **—ung** *nf* **1** distinction, honour. **2** mark.

ausziehen* ('austsiːən) *vt* **1** draw or pull out. **2** make out (a bill). **3** take off (clothes). *vi* **1** move (out). **2** set forth. **sich ausziehen** *vr* undress.

Auszug ('austsuːk) *nm* **1** departure. **2** extract, abstract. **3** move, removal. **4** statement of account.

Auto ('auto) *n neu* **-s** (motor) car, automobile. **—bahn** *nf* motorway. **—bus** *nm* **-se** bus. **—fahrer** *nm* motorist, driver. **—heber** *nm* jack. **—rennen** *n neu* motor racing. **—stop** *nm* hitchhiking. **per Autostop fahren** hitchhike. **—unfall** *nm* motoring accident.

Autogramm (autoː'gram) *n neu* **-e** autograph.

Auto/mat (auto'maːt) *nm* **-en** automat, vending machine. **—matisch** *adj* automatic. **—nom** (auto'noːm) *adj* autonomous.

Autor ('autɔr) *nm* **-en** writer, author.

Autorität (autori'tɛːt) *nf* **-en** authority.

Axt (akst) *nf* **¨-e** axe.

Azoren (a'tsoːrən) *n pl* Azores.

B

Baby ('beːbi) *n neu* **-s** baby.

Bach (bax) *nm* **¨-e** stream, brook.

Backbord ('bakbɔrt) *n neu naut* port (side).

Backe ('bakə) *nf* **-n** *also* **Backen** ('bakən) *nm* — cheek.

back/en* ('bakən) *vt* **1** bake. **2** fry. **¨—er** ('bɛkər) *nm* — baker. **¨—erei** (bɛkə'rai) *nf*

-en bakery. **—pulver** *n neu* baking powder.

Bad (baːt) *n neu* ¨**-er** **1** bath. **2** spa. **—ehose** ('baːdəhoːzə) *nf* bathing trunks. **—ekappe** ('baːdəkapə) *nf* bathing cap. **—en** ('baːdən) *vi,vt* bathe. **—etuch** ('baːdətuːx) *n neu* bath towel. **—ewanne** ('baːdəvanə) *nf* bath tub. **—ezimmer** ('baːdətsimər) *n neu* bathroom.

Bagger ('bagə) *nm* — excavator.

Bahn (baːn) *nf* **-en** **1** way, path, track. **2** railway. **—hof** *nm* (railway) station. **—steig** *nm* **-e** platform. **—übergang** *nm* level crossing.

Bahre ('baːrə) *nf* **-n** stretcher, bier.

Bai (bai) *nf* **-en** bay.

Bajonett (bajo'nɛt) *n neu* **-e** bayonet.

Bakterium (bak'teːrium) *n neu* **-rien** *also* **Bakterie** (bak'teːriə) *nf* **-n** bacterium.

balancieren (balã'siːrən) *vt* balance.

bald (balt) *adv* **1** soon, shortly. **2** almost. **bald...bald** now...now. **—ig** ('baldiç) *adj* **1** early. **2** quick, speedy. **—möglichst** *adv* as soon as possible.

Balken ('balkən) *nm* — beam, rafter, girder.

Balkon (bal'kõː) *nm* **-s** balcony.

Ball[1] (bal) *nm* ¨**-e** **1** ball. **2** globe.

Ball[2] (bal) *nm* ¨**-e** dance, ball.

Ballade (ba'laːdə) *nf* **-n** ballad.

Ballast ('balast) *nm* **-e** ballast.

Ballen ('balən) *nm* — **1** bale. **2** package.

Ballet (ba'lɛt) *n neu* **-e** ...

Ballon (ba'lõː) *nm* **-e** ball...

Balsam ('balzaːm) *nm* **-e** ... sam, balm.

baltisch ('baltiʃ) *adj* bal...

baltisches Meer *n neu* Balti... (sea).

Bambus ('bambus) *nm* **-se** bamboo.

Banane (ba'naːnə) *nf* **-n** banana.

Band[1] (bant) *n neu* **1** *pl* **-ër** band, tape, ribbon. **2** *pl* **-ër** ligament. **3** *pl* **-e** bond, tie. **—aufnahme** *nf* tape-recording.

Band[2] (bant) *nm* ¨**-e** volume, tome.

Bandage (ban'daːʒə) *nf* **-n** bandage.

Bande ('bandə) *nf* **-n** band, gang.

bändigen ('bɛndigən) *vt* tame, subdue.

Bandit (ban'diːt) *nm* **-en** bandit.

bang(e) (baŋ) *adj* afraid, anxious.

Bank[1] (baŋk) *nf* ¨**-e** bench, seat.

Bank[2] (baŋk) *nf* **-en** *comm* bank. **—ier** (baŋk'jeː) *nm* **-s** banker. **—konto** *n neu* bank account. **—note** *nf* bank note. **—wesen** *n neu* banking.

Bankett (baŋ'kɛt) *n neu* **-e** banquet.

bankrott (baŋ'krɔt) *adj* bankrupt. *nm* **-e** bankruptcy.

Bann (ban) *nm* **-e** **1** ban, proscription. **2** excommunication. **3** spell. **—en** *vt* **1** banish. **2** excommunicate. **3** enchant.

bar (baːr) *adj* (of money) ready,

...*adj* barefoot.
...sh, ready mon-
... *nf* **-s** tavern, bar.
...r) *nm* **-en** bear.
...**ar** (bar'ba:r) *nm* **-en** bar-
...arian. **—ei** (barba'rai) *nf* **-en** barbarism. **—isch** *adj* barbarous.

Barbiturat (bar'biturat) *n neu* barbiturate.

Bariton ('bariton) *nm* **-e** baritone.

Barmädchen ('barmɛ:dçən) *n neu* — barmaid.

barmherzig (barm'hɛrtsiç) *adj* merciful.

Barock (ba'rɔk) *nm,neu* baroque.

Barometer (ba'romɛtər) *n neu* — barometer.

Baron (ba'ro:n) *nm* **-e** baron. **—in** *nf* **-nen** baroness.

Barre ('barə) *nf* **-n** bar.

Barriere (bari'ɛ:rə) *nf* **-n** barrier, gate.

barsch (barʃ) *adj* **1** harsh, rough. **2** rude.

Bart (ba:rt) *nm* **¨-e** beard.

Base[1] ('ba:zə) *nf* **-n** female relative (especially a cousin).

Base[2] (be:s) *nf* **-n** base.

Basel ('ba:zəl) *n neu* Basle.

bas/ieren (ba'zi:rən) *vi* be based. **—is** ('ba:zis) *nf* **-sen** base, basis.

Baß (bas) *nm* **Bässe** bass. **—geige** *nf* double bass.

Bassist (ba'sist) *nm* **-en** bass singer, bass player.

Bastard ('bastart) *nm* **-e** **1** bastard. **2** hybrid.

bas/teln ('bastəln) *vt* tinker with, potter around with. **—tler** ('bastlər) *nm* — **1** dabbler. **2** handyman.

bat (ba:t) *v see* **bitten.**

Bataillon (batai'ljo:n) *n neu* **-e** battalion.

Batterie (batə'ri:) *nf* **-n** battery.

Bau (bau) *nm* **-e, -ten** **1** construction, building. **2** burrow. **3** mine. **4** cultivation. **—en** *vt* **1** build. **2** grow. **—fällig** *adj* in disrepair, dilapidated. **—herr** *nm* **1** builder. **2** person for whom a building is being constructed. **—kunst** *nf* architecture. **—meister** *nm* **1** builder. **2** architect. **—platz** *nm also* **—stelle** *nf* building site. **—sparkasse** *nf* building society. **—stein** *nm* building stone. **—werk** *n neu* building, structure.

Bauch (baux) *nm* **¨-e** belly, stomach. **—schmerzen** *nm pl* stomach-ache. **—tanz** *nm* belly dance.

Bauer ('bauər) *nm* **-n** **1** farmer. **2** peasant, rustic. **Bäuerin** ('bɔyərin) *nf* **-nen** farmer's wife, peasant woman. **Bauernhaus** ('bauərnhaus) *n neu* farmhouse. **Bauernhof** ('bauərnho:f) *nm* farm(yard).

Baum (baum) *nm* **¨-e** **1** tree. **2** *naut* boom, mast. **—garten** *nm* orchard. **—wolle** *nf* cotton.

Bay/er ('baiər) *nm* **-n** Bavarian. **—ern** ('baiərn) *n neu* Bavaria. **—risch** ('bairiʃ) *adj* Bavarian.

Bazillus (ba'tsilus) *nm* **-illen** bacillus.

beabsichtigen (bə'apziçtigən) *vt* intend.

beacht/en (bə'axtən) *vt* pay attention to. **—enswert** *adj* noteworthy, notable. **—ung** *nf* consideration, attention.

Beamte(r) (bə'amtə) *nm* **-n,** **Beamtin** (bə'amtin) *nf* **-nen 1** official. **2** civil servant.

beängstigen (bə'ɛŋstigən) *vt* frighten.

beanspruchen (bə'anʃpruxən) *vt* claim, require.

beanstand/en (bə'anʃtandən) *vt* object to. **—ung** *nf* **-en** objection.

beantragen (bə'antraːgən) *vt* **1** apply for. **2** propose.

beantwort/en (bə'antvɔrtən) *vt* answer. **—ung** *nf* **-en** reply, answer.

bearbeit/en (bə'arbaitən) *vt* **1** work. **2** revise, adapt. **3** cultivate. **—ung** *nf* **-en 1** working. **2** treatment. **3** revision, adaptation.

beaufsichtig/en (bə'aufziçtigən) *vt* **1** supervise. **2** inspect. **—ung** *nf* **-en** supervision, control.

beauftragen (bə'auftraːgən) *vt* commission.

bebauen (bə'bauən) *vt* **1** build on. **2** cultivate.

beben ('beːbən) *vi* shake, tremble, shiver.

Becher ('bɛçər) *nm* **— 1** cup. **2** beaker.

Becken ('bɛkən) *n neu* **— 1** basin. **2** cymbal. **3** pelvis.

bedacht (bə'daxt) *adj* thoughtful. **bedacht auf** intent on. ~*nm* **1** caution. **2** consideration. **mit Bedacht** deliberately. **¨—ig** (bə'dɛçtiç) *adj* **1** deliberate. **2** cautious.

Bedarf (bə'darf) *nm* **1** need, want. **2** demand.

bedauer/lich (bə'dauərliç) *adj* unfortunate, regrettable. **—n** *vt* **1** regret. **2** deplore. **3** pity. *n neu* **— 1** regret. **2** pity.

bedeck/en (bə'dɛkən) *vt* **1** cover. **2** protect. **—t** *adj* **1** covered. **2** (of the sky) overcast. **—ung** *nf* **1** covering. **2** protection. **3** escort.

bedenk/en* (bə'dɛŋkən) *vt* consider, think about. **sich bedenken** *vr* deliberate. ~*n neu* **— 1** doubt, reservation. **2** consideration. **—lich** *adj* **1** doubtful. **2** risky.

bedeut/en (bə'dɔytən) *vt* **1** mean. **2** signify. **—end** *adj also* **—sam** (bə'dɔytzaːm) significant, important. **—ung** *nf* **-en 1** meaning. **2** importance. **—ungslos** *adj* **1** meaningless. **2** insignificant. **—ungsvoll** *adj* significant.

bedien/en (bə'diːnən) *vt* **1** wait on, serve. **2** operate (a machine). **sich bedien/en** *vr* make use of. **bedienen Sie sich!** help yourself! **—te(r)** (bə'diːntə) *nm* **-n** servant. **—ung** *nf* **-en** service, attendance.

beding/t (bə'diŋkt) *adj* **1** conditional. **2** determined (by something). **—ung** *nf* **-en** condition, term. **—ungslos** *adj* unconditional.

Bedrängnis (bə'drɛŋnis) *nf* **-se 1** distress. **2** oppression.

bedrohen (bə'droːən) *vt* threaten.

bedürf/en* (bə'dyrfən) *vi* need, require. **—nis** *n neu* **-se** need, want, requirement.

sich beeilen (bə'ailən) *vr* hurry, hasten.

beeinflussen (bə'ainflusən) *vt* influence.

beeinträchtigen (bə'aintrɛçtigən) *vt* **1** injure. **2** wrong. **3** interfere with. **4** impair.

beenden (bə'ɛndən) *vt* conclude, end, finish.

Beerdigung (bə'eːrdiguŋ) *nf* **-en** burial.

Beere ('beːrə) *nf* **-n** berry.

Beet (beːt) *n neu* **-e** flower bed.

befähig/en (bə'fɛːigən) *vt* enable. **—ung** *nf* **-en 1** ability. **2** qualification.

befahl (bə'faːl) *v* see **befehlen.**

befahr/bar (bə'faːrbaːr) *adj* **1** passable, navigable. **2** practicable. **—en*** *vt* **1** drive over. **2** navigate.

befallen* (bə'falən) *vt* **1** befall. **2** strike.

befangen (bə'faŋən) *adj* **1** embarrassed. **2** confused. **3** biased.

befassen (bə'fasən) *vt* touch. **sich befassen mit** be occupied with.

Befehl (bə'feːl) *nm* **-e** command, order. **—en*** *vt* command, order. **—shaber** (bə'feːlshaːbər) *nm* — commander, commanding officer.

befestig/en (bə'fɛstigən) *vt* **1** fasten. fortify, strengthen. **—ung** *nf* **-en 1** fortification. **2** strengthening. **3** fastening.

Befind/en (bə'findən) *n neu* — **1** health. **2** opinion. **sich befinden*** *vr* **1** be, be present. **2** feel. **—lich** (bə'fintliç) *adj* situated, present, existing.

beflecken (bə'flɛkən) *vt* stain, soil, dishonour.

beflissen (bə'flisən) *adj* **1** studious. **2** assiduous.

befohlen (bə'foːlən) *v* see **befehlen.**

befolgen (bə'fɔlgən) *vt* **1** follow. **2** obey.

beförder/n (bə'fœrdərn) *vt* **1** transport, convey. **2** promote. **3** support. **—ung** *nf* **-en 1** forwarding. **2** transport. **3** advancement, promotion.

befragen (bə'fraːgən) *vt* question.

befrei/en (bə'fraiən) *vt* free, liberate. **—ung** *nf* **-en 1** liberation. **2** exemption.

sich befreunden (bə'frɔyndən) *vr* **sich mit jemandem befreunden** befriend someone.

befriedig/en (bə'friːdigən) *vt* **1** satisfy. **2** pacify. **—end** *adj* satisfactory. **—ung** *nf* **1** satisfaction. **2** pacification.

befruchten (bə'fruxtən) *vt* **1** fertilize. **2** impregnate. **3** stimulate.

befug/en (bə'fuːgən) *vt* empower, authorize. **—nis** (bə'fuːknis) *nf* **-se** authority, right.

befürcht/en (bə'fyrçtən) *vt* fear. **—ung** *nf* **-en** anxiety, fear.

befürworten (bə'fyːrvɔrtən) *vt* advocate.

begab/t (bə'gaːpt) *adj* talented, gifted. **—ung** (bə'gaːbuŋ) *nf* **-en** talent, ability.

begann (bə'gan) *v* see **beginnen.**

begeben* (bə'geːbən) *vt comm* **1** endorse. **2** negotiate. **sich begeben** *vr* **1** go, proceed. **2**

surrender, give up. **—heit** *nf* **-en** occurrence, event.

begegn/en (bə'ge:gnən) *vi* meet, encounter. **—ung** *nf* **-en** meeting, encounter.

begehen* (bə'ge:ən) *vt* **1** walk (on), go (along). **2** commit (a crime, error, etc.).

begehr/en (bə'ge:rən) *vt* desire, long for. *n neu* — desire, longing. **—enswert** *adj* desirable.

begeister/n (bə'gaistərn) *vt* inspire. **—t** *adj* enthusiastic. **—ung** *nf* enthusiasm.

Begier (bə'gi:r) *nf* — *also* **Begierde** (bə'gi:rdə) *nf* **-n 1** desire, longing. **2** lust. **—ig** *adj* **1** covetous. **2** eager.

Beginn (bə'gin) *nm* **-e** beginning. **—en*** *vt,vi* begin, start.

beglaubigen (bə'glaubigən) *vt* certify, authenticate.

begleit/en* (bə'glaitən) *vt* accompany. **—er** *nm* **1** companion, attendant. **2** accompanist. **—ung** *nf* **-en 1** escort, retinue. **2** accompaniment.

beglück/en (bə'glykən) *vt* make happy. **—wünschen** *vt* congratulate.

begnadig/en (bə'gna:digən) *vt* pardon, reprieve. **—ung** *nf* **-en** pardon, reprieve, amnesty.

sich begnügen (bə'gny:gən) *vr* be satisfied.

begonnen (bə'gɔnən) *v* see **beginnen.**

begrab/en* (bə'gra:bən) *vt* bury, inter. **¨—nis** (bə'grɛ:pnis) *n neu* **-se 1** burial, funeral. **2** tomb.

begreif/en* (bə'graifən) *vt* understand, grasp. **—lich** *adj* understandable.

begrenzt (bə'grɛntst) *adj* limited, restricted.

Begriff (bə'grif) *nm* **-e 1** idea, concept. **2** understanding. **—en** *adj* engaged or occupied (in).

begründ/en (bə'gryndən) *vt* **1** found, establish. **2** base. **3** substantiate. **—er** *nm* — founder. **—et** (bə'gryndət) *adj* established. **—ung** *nf* **-en 1** foundation. **2** reason, substantiation.

begrüßen (bə'gry:sən) *vt* greet, welcome.

begünstig/en (bə'gynstigən) *vt* **1** favour. **2** further, promote. **—ung** *nf* **-en 1** favour. **2** encouragement.

begütert (bə'gy:tərt) *adj* wealthy, well-off.

behäbig (bə'hɛ:biç) *adj* **1** comfortable. **2** stout.

behaftet (bə'haftət) *adj* **1** burdened. **2** afflicted.

behag/en (bə'ha:gən) *vi* please, suit. *n neu* — **1** pleasure. **2** comfort. **—lich** (bə'ha:kliç) *adj* comfortable, snug.

behalt/en* (bə'haltən) *vt* **1** keep. **2** remember. **3** retain. **¨—er** (bə'hɛltər) *nm* — *also* **¨—nis** (bə'hɛltnis) *n neu* **-se 1** container, holder. **2** case. **3** tank.

behand/eln (bə'handəln) *vt* treat, handle, manage. **—lung** *nf* treatment, handling, management.

beharr/en (bə'harən) *vi* **1** insist, remain firm. **2** endure. **—lich** *adj* persistent, stubborn. **—lichkeit** *nf* perseverance, determination.

behaupt/en (bə'hauptən) *vt*

maintain, affirm, assert. **sich behaupten** *vr* be firm, hold one's own. **—ung** *nf* **-en** statement, assertion.

behend/(e) (bə'hɛnt) *adj* **1** agile. **2** dexterous. **—igkeit** (bə 'hɛndiçkait) *nf* **1** agility. **2** dexterity.

beherbergen (bə'hɛrbɛrgən) *vt* lodge, put up, house, shelter.

beherrschen (bə'hɛrʃən) *vt* **1** rule, govern, reign over. **2** master (a language). **3** control.

beherzigen (bə'hɛrtsigən) *vt* take to heart.

behilflich (bə'hilfliç) *adj* helpful.

behinder/n (bə'hindərn) *vt* hinder, obstruct. **—un** *nf* **-en** hindrance, obstruction.

Behörd/e (bə'hœːrdə) *nf* **-n 1** authority. **2** administrative or governing body. **3** *comm* board. **—lich** *adj* official.

behüten (bə'hyːtən) *vt* **1** preserve. guard. **behutsam** (bə 'huːtzaːm) *adj* careful, cautious.

bei (bai) *prep* **1** by. **2** at. **3** near. **4** beside. **5** with. **bei mir 1** at my house or home. **2** with or on me.

beibehalt/en* ('baibəhaltən) *vt* retain, maintain. **—ung** *nf* **-en** retention.

beibringen* ('baibriŋən) *vt* **1** bring forward, produce. **2** teach, impart.

Beicht/e ('baiçtə) *nf* **-n** confession. **—en** *vi,vt* confess. **—stuhl** *nm* confessional.

beide ('baidə) *adj,pron* both. **—rseitig** ('baidərzaitiç) *adj* joint, mutual, on both sides. **—rseits** ('baidərzaits) *adv* on both sides, mutually.

Beifahrer ('baifaːrər) *nm* **1** passenger. **2** co-driver.

Beifall ('baifal) *nm* **1** applause. **2** approval.

beifügen ('baifyːgən) *vt* **1** add. **2** enclose.

beigeben* ('baigeːbən) *vt* add. **klein beigeben** give in, knuckle under.

Beigeschmack ('baigəʃmak) *nm* **1** flavour, (after)taste. **2** tang, savour. **3** tinge, hint.

Beiheft ('baihɛft) *n neu* supplement.

Beihilfe ('baihilfə) *nf* **1** aid, subsidy. **2** assistance, abetting.

Beil (bail) *n neu* **-e** hatchet, axe.

Beilage ('bailaːgə) *nf* **1** supplement, insert, enclosure. **2** garnish.

beiläufig ('bailɔyfiç) *adj* **1** incidental. **2** casual. *adv* by the way.

Beileid ('bailait) *n neu* condolence.

beiliegend ('bailiːgənt) *adj* enclosed.

beim (baim) contraction of **bei dem.**

Bein (bain) *n neu* **-e 1** leg. **2** bone. **—bruch** *nm* fractured leg.

beinah(e) ('bainaː) *adv* almost, nearly.

Beiname ('bainaːmə) *nm* **1** nickname. **2** surname.

beirren (bə'irən) *vt* **1** mislead. **2** dissuade.

beisammen (bai'zamən) *adv* together.

beiseite (bai'zaitə) *adv* aside, apart.

beisetz/en ('baizɛtsən) *vt* **1**

add. **2** put on or beside. **3** bury. **—ung** *nf* **-en** burial.

Beispiel ('baiʃpi:l) *n neu* example. **zum/als Beispiel** for example. **—haft** *adj* exemplary, model. **—los** *adj* unprecedented. **—sweise** *adv* for example, for instance.

beiß/en* ('baisən) *vt,vi* **1** bite. **2** burn. **3** itch.

Beistand ('baiʃtant) *nm* help, assistance.

beistehen* ('baiʃte:ən) *vi* aid, assist.

beistimmen ('baiʃtimən) *vi* agree (with).

Beitrag ('baitra:k) *nm* **¨-e 1** contribution. **2** fee. **—en*** ('baitra:gən) *vt* contribute. *vi* help.

beitreten* ('baitre:tən) *vi* **1** join. **2** assent (to).

Beiwagen ('baiva:gən) *nm* **1** side-car. **2** extra carriage.

beiwohnen ('baivo:nən) *vi* be present, attend.

beizeiten (bai'tsaitən) *adv* early, on time.

beizen ('baitsən) *vt* **1** corrode. **2** cauterize. **3** tan. **4** marinate. **5** stain (wood).

bejahen (bə'ja:ən) *vt* **1** affirm. **2** accept.

bekämpf/en (bə'kɛmpfən) *vt* **1** fight, combat. **2** oppose. **—ung** *nf* **-en 1** fight, struggle. **2** opposition.

bekannt (bə'kant) *adj* (well)-known. **—e(r)** *nm* acquaintance, friend. **—lich** *adv* as is well known. **—machen** *vt* announce, make known. **—machung** *nf* **-en 1** publication. **2** announcement. **—schaft** *nf* **-en** acquaintance.

bekehr/en (bə'ke:rən) *vt* convert (to a religion, etc.). **—ung** *nf* **-en** (religious) conversion.

bekenn/en* (bə'kɛnən) *vt* confess, acknowledge. **Farbe bekennen 1** be frank. **2** *game* follow suit. **—tnis** (bə'kɛntnis) *n neu* **-se 1** confession. **2** denomination.

beklag/en (bə'kla:gən) *vt* **1** mourn. **2** deplore. **sich beklag/en** *vr* complain. **—te(r)** (bə'kla:ktə) *nm* **-n** accused, defendant.

bekleid/en (bə'klaidən) *vt* **1** clothe, dress. **2** cover. **3** occupy (a position, office). **—ung** *nf* clothing.

beklemmen (bə'klɛmən) *vt* stifle, oppress.

bekommen* (bə'kɔmən) *vt* **1** get, obtain. **2** receive. *vi* agree with (one's health).

bekräftigen (bə'krɛftigən) *vt* **1** confirm. **2** strengthen.

bekreuz(ig)en (bə'krɔytsigən) *vt* make the sign of the cross over.

bekümmern (bə'kymərn) *vt* trouble, distress. **sich bekümmern um 1** care for. **2** worry about.

bekunden (bə'kundən) *vt* **1** state. **2** show.

beladen* (bə'la:dən) *vt* load, burden.

Belag (bə'la:k) *nm* **-e** coat(ing), cover(ing).

belager/n (bə'la:gərn) *vt* besiege. **—ung** *nf* **-en** siege.

Belang (bə'laŋ) *nm* **-e 1** importance. **2** interest. **—los** *adj* unimportant, insignificant.

belast/en (bə'lastən) *vt* **1** load.

2 weigh down (on), burden. **3** accuse. **—ung** *nf* **-en 1** burden, load. **2** charge.

belästig/en (bə'lɛstigən) *vt* molest, bother. **—ung** *nf* **-en 1** molestation. **2** inconvenience.

sich belaufen* (bə'laufən) *vr* **sich belaufen auf** total, amount to.

belauschen (bə'lauʃən) *vt* eavesdrop on.

beleb/en (bə'leːbən) *vt* **1** enliven, animate. **2** revive. **—t** *adj* **1** lively. **2** alive. **3** (of streets) crowded.

Beleg (bə'leːk) *n* **-e 1** proof. **2** record. **3** evidence. **4** document. **—en** (bə'leːgən) *vt* **1** cover, lay (on). **2** reserve. **—schaft** *nf* **-en 1** personnel, staff. **2** shift.

belehr/en (bə'leːrən) *vt* teach, instruct. **—ung** *nf* **-en** instruction.

beleidig/en (bə'laidigən) *vt* **1** insult. **2** offend. **—ung** *nf* **-en 1** insult. **2** offence.

beleucht/en (bə'lɔyçtən) *vt* **1** light (up), illuminate. **2** elucidate. **—ung** *nf* **-en 1** lighting. **2** elucidation.

Belg/ien ('bɛlgiən) *n neu* Belgium. **—ier** *nm* — Belgian. **—isch** *adj* Belgian.

Belgrad ('bɛlgraːt) *n neu* Belgrade.

belicht/en (bə'liçtən) *vt phot* expose. **—ung** *nf* **-en** exposure. **—ungsmesser** *nm* exposure or light meter.

belieb/en (bə'liːbən) *vt* like. *vi* please. *n neu* **— 1** liking. **2** pleasure. **3** wish. **nach Belieben** according to one's liking or taste. **—ig** *adj* any, whatever. **—t** (bə'liːpt) *adj* **1** beloved. **2** favourite. **—theit** (bə'liːpthait) *nf* **-en** popularity.

bellen ('bɛlən) *vi* bark, bay.

belohn/en (bə'loːnən) *vt* reward, remunerate. **—ung** *nf* **-en** reward, remuneration.

sich bemächtigen (bə'mɛçtigən) *vr* seize, take possession of.

bemerk/bar (bə'mɛrkbaːr) *adj* noticeable, perceptible. **—en** *vt* perceive, notice, observe. **—enswert** *adj* remarkable, notable. **—ung** *nf* **-en** remark.

bemessen* (bə'mɛsən) *vt* **1** measure, judge. **2** adjust. **3** regulate.

bemitleiden (bə'mitlaidən) *vt* pity, sympathize with.

sich bemüh/en (bə'myːən) *vr* **1** strive, endeavour. **2** take pains. **—ung** *nf* **-en** effort, trouble, pains.

benachbart (bə'naxbaːrt) *adj* neighbouring.

benachrichtig/en (bə'naxriçtigən) *vt* **1** inform. **2** report. **—ung** *nf* **-en 1** notification. **2** information.

Benehmen (bə'neːmən) *n neu* — behaviour. **sich benehmen** *vr* act, behave.

beneiden (bə'naidən) *vt* envy. **—swert** *adj* enviable.

Benennung (bə'nɛnuŋ) *nf* **-en** name, term.

Bengel ('bɛŋəl) *nm* **— 1** club, cudgel. **2** brat, urchin. **3** rascal. **4** lout.

benutz/en (bə'nutsən) *vt* use, make use of. **—ung** *nf* utilization.

Benzin (bɛn'tsiːn) *n neu* **-e** *mot* petrol. **—motor** *nm* petrol engine.

beobacht/en (bə'oːbaxtən) *vt* **1** observe, watch. **2** keep (silence, etc.). **—er** *nm* — observer. **—ung** *nf* **-en** observation.

bepflanzen (bə'pflantsən) *vt* plant.

bequem (bə'kveːm) *adj* **1** comfortable. **2** convenient. **—lichkeit** *nf* **-en 1** comfort. **2** convenience.

berat/en* (bə'raːtən) *vt* advise, counsel. **—er** *nm* — adviser. **—ung** *nf* **-en 1** consultation. **2** deliberation. **—ungsstelle** *nf* advisory board or office.

berauben (bə'raubən) *vt* **1** rob. **2** deprive.

berauschen (bə'rauʃən) *vt* intoxicate. **sich berauschen** *vr* become enchanted (with).

berechn/en (bə'rɛçnən) *vt* calculate, reckon. **—ung** *nf* calculation, estimate.

berechtig/en (bə'rɛçtigən) *vt* empower, authorize. **—ung** *nf* **-en** authorization, right, title.

bered/en (bə'reːdən) *vt* **1** talk over. **2** persuade. **—sam** (bə'reːtzaːm) *adj also* **—t** (bə'reːt) eloquent. **—samkeit** *nf* eloquence.

Bereich (bə'raiç) *nm* **-e 1** region, area, district. **2** range, scope.

bereichern (bə'raiçərn) *vt* enrich.

bereit (bə'rait) *adj* ready, prepared. **—en** *vt* prepare, make (ready). **—halten*** *vt* keep or hold in readiness. **—s** *adv* already. **—schaft** *nf* **-en 1** readiness. **2** (police) squad. **—stehen*** *vi* be prepared, stand by. **—ung** *nf* **-en** preparation. **—willig** *adj* willing, ready.

bereuen (bə'rɔyən) *vt* regret, repent of.

Berg (bɛrk) *nm* **-e** mountain, hill. **über Berg und Tal** over hill and dale. **—ab** (bɛrk'ap) *adv* downhill. **—auf** (bɛrk 'auf) *adv also* **—an** uphill, upwards. **—arbeiter** *nm* miner. **—bau** *nm* mining. **—kette** *nf* mountain range. **—mann** *nm* **-leute** miner. **—rutsch** *nm also* **—sturz** landslide. **—steiger** *nm* mountaineer, climber. **—werk** *n neu* mine.

bergen* ('bɛrgən) *vt* **1** save. **2** protect. **3** rescue. **4** conceal.

Bericht (bə'riçt) *nm* **-e** report, account. **—en** *vt,vi* report. **—erstatter** *nm* — reporter, informant.

berichtig/en (bə'riçtigən) *vt* correct, rectify. **—ung** *nf* **-en** correction, adjustment.

beritten (bə'ritən) *adj* mounted.

Bernstein ('bɛrnʃtain) *nm* amber.

berüchtigt (bə'ryçtiçt) *adj* notorious.

berücksichtig/en (bə'rykziçtigən) *vt* **1** consider. **2** take into account. **—ung** *nf* **-en** regard, consideration.

Beruf (bə'ruːf) *nm* **-e 1** occupation, profession, trade. **2** vocation. **—en*** *vt* **1** call. **2** summon. **3** appoint. *adj* competent. **sich —en** *vr* **1** appeal.

2 refer to. **—lich** *adj* professional. **—sberatung** *nf* career guidance. **—smäßig** *adj* professional. **—sschule** *n* **1** vocational school. **2** training college. **—ung** *nf* **-en 1** call(ing). **2** nomination. **3** appointment. **4** (law) appeal.

beruhen (bə'ruːən) *vi* rest on, be based on.

beruhig/en (bə'ruːigən) *vt* quieten, calm, pacify. **—ung** *nf* calming (down).

berühmt (bə'ryːmt) *adj* famous. **—heit** *nf* **-en 1** fame. **2** famous person, celebrity.

berühr/en (bə'ryːrən) *vt* **1** touch, affect. **2** mention. **—ung** *nf* **-en** contact, touch(ing).

besäen (bə'zɛːən) *vt* sow. **besät** (bə'zɛːt) *adj* strewn, covered.

besänftig/en (bə'zɛnftigən) *vt* calm, soothe.

Besatz/ung (bə'zatsuŋ) *nf* **-en 1** *mil* occupation. **2** garrison. **3** crew. **—ungsbehörde** *nf* military adminstration (in occupied territory).

beschädig/en (bə'ʃɛːdigən) *vt* damage, injure. **—ung** *nf* **-en** damage, injury.

beschaffen (bə'ʃafən) *vt* **1** obtain, procure. **2** provide. *adj* constituted. **gut beschaffen sein** be in good condition. **—heit** *nf* **-en** condition, character, nature.

beschäftig/en (bə'ʃɛftigən) *vt* employ. **sich beschäftig/en** *vr* busy oneself (with). **-ung** *nf* **-en** occupation, employment.

beschämen (bə'ʃɛːmən) *vt* shame.

beschatten (bə'ʃatən) *vt* **1** shade, overshadow. **2** shadow, tail.

Beschau/er (bə'ʃauər) *nm* **— 1** observer. **2** inspector (of food, goods, etc.). **—lich** *adj* contemplative.

Bescheid (bə'ʃait) *nm* **-e 1** answer. **2** information. **3** (law) decision. **Bescheid wissen** be well-informed, know. **—en** (bə'ʃaidən) *adj* modest, moderate, unassuming. **—enheit** *nf* modesty, moderation, discretion.

bescheinig/en (bə'ʃainigən) *vt* certify, attest. **—ung** *nf* **-en** certificate, acknowledgment.

beschenken (bə'ʃɛnkən) *vt* give a present to.

Bescherung (bə'ʃeːruŋ) *nf* **-en** presentation.

beschieß/en* (bə'ʃiːsən) *vt* shoot at, bombard.

beschimpf/en (bə'ʃimpfən) *vt* insult. **—ung** *nf* **-en** abuse, insult.

Beschlag (bə'ʃlaːk) *nm* **¨-e 1** metal-work, fittings. **2** moisture. **in Beschlag nehmen** seize. **—nahme** *nf* **-n** confiscation.

beschleunig/en (bə'ʃlɔynigən) *vt* accelerate, hasten. **—er** *nm* — accelerator. **—ung** *nf* acceleration.

beschließen* (bə'ʃliːsən) *vt* **1** enclose. **2** decide, resolve, conclude.

Beschluß (bə'ʃlus) *nm* **-schlüsse 1** resolution, decision. **2** conclusion. **—fassung** *nf* decision, resolution.

beschmutzen (bə'ʃmutsən) *vt* soil, blemish.
beschneid/en* (bə'ʃnaidən) *vt* **1** cut, clip, trim. **2** circumcise.
beschränk/en (bə'ʃrɛnkən) *vt* limit, restrict. **—t** *adj* **1** limited. **2** narrow(-minded). **—ung** *nf* **-en** restriction, limitation.
beschreib/en* (bə'ʃraibən) *vt* **1** describe. **2** write, draw on. **—ung** *nf* **-en** description.
beschuldig/en (bə'ʃuldigən) *vt* accuse, charge. **—ung** *nf* **-en** accusation.
beschützen (bə'ʃytsən) *vt* protect.
Beschwer/de (bə'ʃve:rdə) *nf* **-n** **1** complaint. **2** trouble, difficulty. **—en** *vt* burden, weigh down. **sich —en** *vr* complain. **—lich** *adj* **1** troublesome. **2** tiresome.
beschwichtigen (bə'ʃviçtigən) *vt* calm, pacify.
beschwipst (bə'ʃvipst) *adj* *inf* tipsy, merry.
beschwören (bə'ʃvœ:rən) *vt* **1** swear, take an oath (on). **2** implore, beg of. **3** summon, invoke or exorcize (spirits).
beseelen (bə'ze:lən) *vt* **1** inspire. **2** enliven.
besehen* (bə'ze:ən) *vt* look at, inspect.
beseitig/en (bə'zaitigən) *vt* **1** remove, do away with. **2** overcome. **—ung** *nf* **-en** removal.
Besen ('be:zən) *nm* — broom.
besessen (bə'zɛsən) *adj* **1** possessed (of the devil, etc.). **2** obsessed.
besetz/en (bə'zɛtsən) *vt* **1** occupy. **2** man. **3** fill. **4** trim, decorate. **—t** *adj* **1** occupied. **2** full, crowded. **3** (telephone) engaged. **—ung** *nf* **-en** **1** *mil* occupation. **2** *Th* cast(ing).
besichtig/en (bə'ziçtigən) *vt* **1** inspect, look at. **2** go sight-seeing (in). **—ung** *nf* **-en** **1** inspection. **2** sight-seeing.
besieg/en (bə'zi:gən) *vt* conquer, defeat. **—er** *nm* conqueror.
sich besinn/en* (bə'zinən) *vr* **1** consider, reflect. **2** remember, recall. **—ung** *nf* **1** consciousness. **2** contemplation.
Besitz (bə'zits) *nm* **-e** possession, property. **—en*** *vt* possess. **—er** *nm* — owner, proprietor. **—tum** *n neu* ¨**-er** property, possession. **—ung** *nf* **-en** **1** possession. **2** estate.
besoffen (bə'zɔfən) *adj* *inf* drunk.
Besoldung (bə'zɔlduŋ) *nf* **-en** pay, salary.
besonder/e (bə'zɔndərə) *adj* special, particular, peculiar. **—s** *adv* **1** especially. **2** separately.
besonnen (bə'zɔnən) *adj* **1** prudent, cautious. **2** thoughtful. **—heit** *nf* **1** prudence. **2** thoughtfulness.
besorg/en (bə'zɔrgən) *vt* **1** take care of, attend to. **2** provide, procure. **3** fear. **—nis** (bə'zɔrknis) *nf* **-se** fear, worry, anxiety. **—t** (bə'zɔrkt) *adj* anxious, apprehensive. **—ung** *nf* **-en** **1** care. **2** matter (to attend to).
bespannen (bə'ʃpanən) *vt* **1** harness. **2** stretch over (covering). **3** (re)string (a guitar, etc.).
besprech/en* (bə'ʃprɛçən) *vt*

1 discuss, debate, talk over. **2** review (a book, etc.). **—ung** *nf* **-en 1** discussion. **2** conference. **3** review.

bespritzen (bə'ʃpritsən) *vt* splash, sprinkle.

besser ('bɛsər) *adj* better. **desto besser** so much the better. **um so besser** all the better. **—n** *vt* improve, better. **—ung** *nf* **-en 1** improvement. **2** recovery. **—wisser** ('bɛsərvisər) *nm* — know-all.

Bestand (bə'ʃtant) *nm* **¨-e 1** continuance, duration. **2** *comm* stock, supply. **3** *comm* reserves, funds, (cash-)balance. **¨—ig** (bə'ʃtɛndiç) *adj* continuous, constant. **—teil** *nm* constituent, part.

bestärken (bə'ʃtɛrkən) *vt* **1** strengthen. **2** confirm.

bestätig/en (bə'ʃtɛːtigən) *vt* **1** confirm, verify. **2** acknowledge. **—ung** *nf* **-en** confirmation, verification.

bestatten (bə'ʃtatən) *vt* **1** bury. **2** cremate.

beste ('bɛstə) *adj* best. **aufs beste** in the best way possible. *~n neu* **-n** best.

bestech/en* (bə'ʃtɛçən) *vt* **1** bribe. **2** corrupt. **—lich** *adj* corrupt(ible). **—ung** *nf* **-en 1** bribery. **2** corruption.

Besteck (bə'ʃtɛk) *n neu* **-e 1** set of cutlery, place-setting. **2** set of instruments.

bestehen* (bə'ʃteːən) *vi* **1** be, exist. **2** last, endure. *vt* pass (a test, etc.). **bestehen auf** insist on. **bestehen aus/in** consist of/in.

besteigen* (bə'ʃtaigən) *vt* **1** ascend. **2** mount (a horse). **3** board (a ship).

bestell/en (bə'ʃtɛlən) *vt* **1** order. **2** appoint. **3** till (fields). **4** deliver (a message). **—ung** *nf* **1** order. **2** message. **3** cultivation. **4** arrangement.

bestenfalls ('bɛstənfals) *adv* at best. **bestens** ('bɛstəns) *adv* **1** at best. **2** in the best way.

besteuer/n (bə'ʃtɔyərn) *vt* tax. **—ung** *nf* **-en** taxation.

Bestie ('bɛstiə) *nf* **-n** beast, brute.

bestimm/en (bə'ʃtimən) *vt* **1** determine, fix. **2** assign, intend. **—t** *adj* **1** certain, definite. **2** assigned. **3** intended. **—theit** *nf* **-en** certainty. **—ung** *nf* **-en 1** determination. **2** destination. **3** regulation. **4** destiny.

bestrafen (bə'ʃtraːfən) *vt* punish.

Bestrahlung (bə'ʃtraːluŋ) *nf* **1** irradiation. **2** radiotherapy.

sich bestreben (bə'ʃtreːbən) *vr* strive. **Bestrebung** *nf* **-en** attempt, effort.

bestreiten* (bə'ʃtraitən) *vt* **1** contest. **2** deny. **3** meet, defray (expenses).

bestürmen (bə'ʃtyrmən) *vt* **1** attack, storm. **2** implore.

bestürz/t (bə'ʃtyrtst) *adj* **1** upset. **2** dismayed. **—ung** *nf* dismay.

Besuch (bə'zuːx) *nm* **-e 1** visit. **2** visitors, company. **—en** *vt* **1** visit. **2** attend (a school). **—er** *nm* — visitor, guest.

betagt (bə'taːkt) *adj* aged, elderly.

betätigen (bə'tɛːtigən) *vt* operate, set in action. **sich betä-**

tigen *vr* busy oneself, participate (in).
betäub/en (bə'tɔybən) *vt* **1** stun. **2** deafen. **3** deaden. **4** anaesthetize. **—ungsmittel** *n neu* **1** anaesthetic. **2** narcotic.
beteilig/en (bə'tailigən) *vt* give a share to. **sich beteiligen** *vr* take part (in). **—ung** *nf* **1** participation. **2** share.
Bete ('beːtə) *nf* **-n** beetroot.
bet/en ('beːtən) *vi,vt* pray.
beteuern (bə'tɔyərn) *vt* **1** protest. **2** declare, aver.
Beton (be'tõː) *nm* **-e** concrete.
betonen (bə'tonən) *vt* emphasize, stress.
Betracht (bə'traxt) *nm* **in Betracht kommen** come into question. **außer Betracht stehen** be out of the question. **—en** *vt* look at, view, regard. **¨—lich** (bə'trɛçtliç) *adj* considerable. **—ung** *nf* **-en** **1** view, consideration. **2** reflection. **3** meditation.
Betrag (bə'traːk) *nm* **¨-e** sum, amount. **—en*** (bə'traːgən) *vt* amount to. *n neu* behaviour. **sich —en** *vr* behave.
betrauen (bə'trauən) *vt* entrust (someone).
Betreff (bə'trɛf) *nm* **in Betreff** *also* **betreffs** with regard to, concerning. **—en*** (bə'trɛfən) *vt* **1** affect, concern. **2** catch (in the act). **—end** *adj* concerned, in question. *prep* concerning.
betreiben* (bə'traibən) *vt* operate, carry on (a business, etc.).
betreten* (bə'treːtən) *vt* **1** step on. **2** enter, set foot in. *adj* **1** embarrassed. **2** disconcerted.
Betrieb (bə'triːp) *nm* **-e** **1** works, factory. **2** business. **3** working, operation, running. **4** bustle. **5** traffic. **außer Betrieb** out of order. **in Betrieb** in operation, working. **—sfähig** *adj* in working order. **—skapital** *n neu* working capital. **—skosten** *nf pl* working costs or expenses. **—sleiter** *nm* (works) manager. **—sordnung** *nf* company rules. **—sstoff** *nm mot* fuel. **—sunfall** *nm* industrial accident, accident at work.
betroffen (bə'trɔfən) *adj* **1** affected. **2** perplexed.
betrüb/en (bə'tryːbən) *vt* grieve, sadden. **—nis** *nf* **-se** sorrow, grief.
Betrug (bə'truːk) *nm* deceit, fraud. **¨—en** (bə'tryːgən) *vt* defraud, deceive, cheat. **¨—er** (bə'tryːgər) *nm* **—** swindler, cheat, deceiver.
betrunken (bə'truŋkən) *adj* drunk. **—heit** *nf* drunkenness.
Bett (bɛt) *n neu* **-en** bed. **—decke** *nf* **1** bedspread. **2** blanket. **—en** *vt* put to bed. **—tuch** *n neu* sheet. **—wäsche** *nf also* **—zeug** *n neu* bedding.
betteln ('bɛtəln) *vi* beg. **Bettler** ('bɛtlər) *nm* **—** beggar.
beugen ('bɔygən) *vt* **1** bend. **2** *gram* inflect. **sich beugen** *vr* **1** bend down or over. **2** bow. **3** humble oneself.
Beule ('bɔylə) *nf* **-n** **1** swelling, boil. **2** dent.
beunruhigen (bə'unruːigən) *vt* disturb, upset.
beurkunden (bə'uːrkundən) *vt*

prove, authenticate (by means of documents).

beurlauben (bə'u:rlaubən) *vt* give leave (of absence) to.

beurteil/en (bə'u:rtailən) *vt* judge, pass judgment on. **—ung** *nf* **-en** judgment.

Beute ('bɔyte) *nf* booty, spoil(s).

Beutel ('bɔytəl) *nm* **— 1** bag. **2** purse.

bevölker/n (bə'fœlkərn) *vt* populate. **—ung** *nf* **-en** population. **—ungsdichte** *nf* population density.

bevollmächtig/en (bə'fɔlmɛçtigən) *vt* empower, authorize, allow. **—te(r)** (bə 'fɔlmɛçtiçtə) *nm* **1** (authorized) representative. **2** proxy. **3** deputy.

bevor (bə'fo:r) *conj* before. **bevor...nicht** until

bevorstehen* (bə'fo:rʃte:ən) *vi* be near, be imminent.

bevorzugen (bə'fo:rtsu:gən) *vt* prefer.

bewachen (bə'vaxən) *vt* guard.

bewaffnen (bə'vafnən) *vt* arm.

bewahr/en (bə'va:rən) *vt* preserve, keep. **sich —en** *vr* prove oneself (efficient, successful, etc.). **—ung** *nf* **-en** test, trial. **—ungsfrist** *nf* probation.

bewältigen (bə'vɛltigən) *vt* **1** overcome. **2** finish.

bewandert (bə'vandərt) *adj* knowledgeable, expert.

Bewandtnis (bə'vantnis) *nf* **-se** condition, circumstance.

bewässer/n (bə'vɛsərn) *vt* water, irrigate. **—ung** *nf* watering, irrigation.

beweg/en* (bə've:gən) *vt* **1** move. **2** induce, persuade. **sich —en** *vr* move. **—grund** *nm* motive. **—lich** (bə 've:kliç) *adj* **1** movable, mobile, moving. **2** versatile. **—lichkeit** *nf* mobility. **—ung** *nf* **-en** motion, movement.

Beweis (bə'vais) *nm* **-e** proof. **—aufnahme** *nf* hearing of evidence. **—en*** (bə'vaizən) *vt* prove, demonstrate, show. **—grund** *nm* argument. **—kraft** *nf* conclusiveness. **—mittel** *n neu* evidence. **—stück** *n neu* **1** exhibit. **2** evidence.

bewenden (bə'vɛndən) *vi* **es dabei bewenden lassen** let the matter rest (at that).

sich bewerb/en* (bə'vɛrbən) *vr* **sich bewerben um 1** apply for. **2** seek. **—er** *nm* **— 1** applicant. **2** competitor. **3** suitor.

bewerkstelligen (bə'vɛrkʃtɛligən) *vt* manage, accomplish.

bewillig/en (bə'viligən) *vt* **1** allow, grant. **2** approve. **—ung** *nf* **-en 1** consent, approval. **2** grant, allowance.

bewirken (bə'virkən) *vt* cause, effect.

bewirten (bə'virtən) *vt* **1** entertain. **2** receive.

bewohn/en (bə'vo:nən) *vt* inhabit. **—er** *nm* — inhabitant.

bewölkt (bə'vœlkt) *adj* cloudy, overcast.

Bewunder/er (bə'vundərər) *nm* — admirer. **—n** *vt* admire. **—nswert** *adj* admirable. **—ung** *nf* admiration.

bewußt (bə'vust) *adj* **1** conscious, aware. **2** deliberate.

adv knowingly. **die bewußten Personen** the people in question. **—heit** *nf* awareness, consciousness. **—los** *adj* unconscious. **—sein** *n neu* consciousness.

bezahl/en (bə'tsaːlən) *vt* pay (for). **—ung** *nf* **-en** payment.

bezaubern (bə'tsaubərn) *vt* bewitch, enchant, charm.

bezeichn/en (bə'tsaiçnən) *vt* **1** mark. **2** designate, indicate. **—end** *adj* characteristic. **—ung** *nf* **-en** **1** mark, sign. **2** marking. **3** designation.

bezeugen (bə'tsɔygən) *vt* bear witness to, certify.

bezieh/en* (bə'tsiːən) *vt* **1** cover. **2** move into. **3** receive. **4** obtain. **sich beziehen auf** *vr* relate to, refer to. **—ung** *nf* **-en** **1** reference. **2** relation(ship), connection. **—ungsweise** *adv* **1** or. **2** that is to say.

Bezirk (bə'tsirk) *nm* **-e** district, area.

Bezug (bə'tsuːk) *nm* **1** cover(ing). **2** *comm* supply, purchase. **3** *pl* income. **bezüglich (auf)** *also* **in Bezug auf** with regard to, concerning.

bezwecken (bə'tsvɛkən) *vt* aim at.

bezweifeln (bə'tsvaifəln) *vt* doubt, question.

bezwingen* (bə'tsviŋən) *vt* **1** overcome. **2** master.

Bibel ('biːbəl) *nf* **-n** Bible.

Biber ('biːbər) *nm* — beaver.

Bibliographie (bibliogra'fiː) *nf* **-n** bibliography.

Bibliothek (biblio'teːk) *nf* **-en** library. **—ar** (bibliote'kaːr) *nm* **-e** librarian.

biblisch ('biːbliʃ) *adj* biblical.

bieder ('biːdər) *adj* **1** upright, honest. **2** simpleminded. **—mann** *nm* honest fellow.

biegen* ('biːgən) *vt* bend.

Biene ('biːnə) *nf* **-n** bee. **—nkorb** *nm* beehive.

Bier (biːr) *n neu* **-e** beer. **—garten** *nm* beer garden, (open air) cafe. **—krug** *nm* beermug.

bieten* ('biːtən) *vt* offer.

Bifokal ('biːfokaːl) *nf* — bifocals.

Bigamie (biga'miː) *nf* **-n** bigamy.

bigott (bi'gɔt) *adj* bigoted.

Bikini (bi'kiːniː) *nm* **-s** bikini.

Bilanz (bi'lants) *nf* **-en** balance (sheet).

Bild (bilt) *n neu* **-er** picture, image. **—erbuch** ('bildərbuːx) *n neu* picture book. **—fläche** *nf* **1** field of vision. **2** television or cinema screen. **—hauer** *nm* — sculptor. **—nis** *n neu* **-se** likeness, portrait. **—säule** *nf* statue. **—schirm** *nm* **-e** monitor. **—schön** *adj* lovely, (most) beautiful.

bild/en ('bildən) *vt* **1** form. **2** educate. **—ung** *nf* **-en** **1** education. **2** culture. **3** formation, creation.

Billard ('biljart) *n neu* **-s** billiards.

Billett (bil'jɛt) *n neu* **-e** **1** note. **2** ticket.

billig ('biliç) *adj* **1** cheap. **2** reasonable, just. **—en** ('biligən) *vt* approve (of), sanction. **—keit** *nf* **-en** **1** cheapness. **2** fairness. **—ung** ('biliguŋ) *nf* approval.

Bimsstein ('bimsʃtain) *nm* pumice-stone.

bin (bin) *v* see **sein**[2].

Bind/e ('bində) *nf* **-n 1** band. **2** bandage, sling. **3** sanitary towel. **—eglied** *n neu* connecting link. **—estrich** *nm* hyphen. **—ewort** *n neu* conjunction. **—faden** ('bintfa:dən) *nm* string, twine. **—ung** *nf* **-en 1** bond. **2** binding.

binden* ('bindən) *vt* bind, tie.

binnen ('binən) *prep* within. **—handel** *nm* domestic trade. **—land** *n neu* interior, inland.

Biographie (biogra'fi:) *nf* **-n** biography.

Biolog/e (bio'lo:gə) *nm* **-n** biologist. **—ie** (biolo'gi:) *nf* biology. **—isch** (bio'lo:giʃ) *adj* biological. **—isch abbaubar** *adj* biodegradable.

Birne ('birnə) *nf* **-n 1** pear. **2** (light) bulb.

bis (bis) *prep* **1** to. **2** up to. **3** until. *conj* **1** until. **2** by. **er wird bis morgen ankommen** he will arrive by tomorrow.

Bisam ('bi:zam) *nm* **-e** musk.

Bischof ('biʃɔf) *nm* **¨-e** bishop.

bisexuell (bizɛksu'ɛl) *adj* hermaphroditic, bisexual.

bisher (bis'he:r) *adv* until now, so far. **—ig** *adj* previous, until now.

biß (bis) *v* see **beißen.**

Biß (bis) *nm* **Bisse** bite. **—chen** ('bisçən) *n neu,adj* a little, a bit. **Bissen** ('bisən) *nm* — morsel, bite. **bissig** ('bisiç) *adj* **1** (of dogs) snappish. **2** cutting, biting.

bist (bist) *v* see **sein**[2].

Bistum ('bistu:m) *n neu* **¨-er** bishopric.

bisweilen (bis'vailən) *adv* sometimes.

bitt/e ('bitə) *interj* please! *nf* **-n** request. **—en*** ('bitən) *vt* ask, beg, request. **—schreiben** *n neu also* **—schrift** *nf* petition.

bitter ('bitər) *adj* **1** bitter. **2** severe. **—keit** *nf* bitterness.

Biwak ('bi:vak) *n neu* **-s** bivouac.

Bizeps ('bi:tsɛps) *nm* **-e** biceps.

Blam/age (bla'ma:ʒə) *nf* **-n** disgrace, scandal. **—ieren** (bla'mi:rən) *vt* disgrace, compromise (someone). **sich —ieren** *vr* make a fool of oneself.

blank (blaŋk) *adj* **1** shiny, bright. **2** bare, naked.

blanko ('blaŋko) *adj* blank. **—scheck** *nm* blank cheque. **—vollmacht** *nf* full power of attorney.

Blas/e ('bla:zə) *nf* **-n 1** blister. **2** bubble. **3** bladder. **—en*** *vi,vt* blow. **—instrument** *n neu* wind instrument. **—kapelle** *nf* brass band.

blaß (blas) *adj* pale. **Blässe** ('blɛsə) *nf* pallor, paleness.

Blatt (blat) *n neu* **¨-er 1** leaf, blade. **2** page, sheet (of paper). **3** newspaper. **¨—ern** ('blɛtərn) *vi* **1** turn over the pages. **2** skim through a book. **¨—erteig** ('blɛtərtaik) *nm* puff-pastry.

blau (blau) *adj* **1** blue. **2** *inf* tipsy. *n neu* blue. **—beere** *nf* bilberry. **¨—e** ('blɔyə) *nf* blueness, azure. **—papier** *n neu* carbon paper.

Blech (blɛç) *n neu* **-e 1** sheet metal. **2** tin.

Blei (blai) *n neu* **-e** lead.

bleiben* ('blaibən) *vi* remain, stay.

bleich (blaiç) *adj* pale, pallid.

—e *nf* **-n** paleness, pallor. **—en*** *vt* bleach, *vi* turn white or pale. **—sucht** *nf* anaemia.

Bleistift ('blaiʃtift) *nm* **-e** pencil. **—spitzer** *nm* — pencil-sharpener.

Blend/e ('blɛndə) *nf* **-n 1** blind, shutter. **2** *phot* diaphragm. **—en** *vt* **1** blind, dazzle. **2** deceive.

Blick (blik) *nm* **-e 1** look, glance. **2** gaze. **—en** *vi* look, glance.

blieb (bliːp) *v* see **bleiben.**

blind (blint) *adj* **1** blind. **2** false. **3** hidden. **4** tarnished. **blinder Passagier** *nm* stowaway. **—darm** *nm anat* appendix. **—darmentzündung** *nf* appendicitis. **—heit** *nf* blindness.

blinzeln ('blinstəln) *vi* **1** twinkle. **2** blink. **3** wink.

Blitz (blits) *nm* **-e** lightning. **—ableiter** *nm* — lightning-conductor. **—en** *vi* flash, lighten. **—krieg** *nm* lightning war, blitzkrieg. **—licht** *n neu* (photographic) flash. **—schnell** *adj* as quick as lightning.

Block/ade (blɔ'kaːdə) *nf* **-n** blockade. **—flöte** ('blɔkflœːtə) *nf mus* recorder. **—ieren** (blɔ 'kiːrən) *vt* **1** obstruct, block. **2** blockade. **3** jam.

blöd ('blœːt) *adj* **1** silly, stupid. **2** imbecile. **3** shy, timid. **—heit** ('blœːthait) *nf* **-en** stupidity. **—sinn** ('blœːtsin) *nm* **1** nonsense. **2** idiocy. **—sinnig** ('blœːtsiniç) *adj* idiotic, silly.

blond (blɔnt) *adj* blond, light-coloured, fair.

bloß (blɔs) *adj* **1** bare. **2** mere. *adv* only, simply. **—stellen** *vt* expose.

blühen ('blyːən) *vi* **1** bloom, blossom. **2** flourish.

Blume ('bluːmə) *nf* **-n 1** flower. **2** aroma. **3** (of wine) bouquet. **—nkohl** *nm* cauliflower. **—nstrauß** *nm* bouquet. **—nzwiebel** *n* bulb.

Bluse ('bluːzə) *nf* **-n** blouse.

Blut (bluːt) *n neu* blood. **—arm** *adj* **1** anaemic. **2** extremely poor. **—egel** *nm* — leech. **—en** *vi* bleed. **—ig** *adj* **1** bloody. **2** complete, total. **—rünstig** *adj* bloody, bloodthirsty. **—schande** *nf* incest. **—spender** *nm med* blood-donor. **—sturz** *nm* bleeding, haemorrhage. **—übertragung** *nf* blood transfusion. **—wurst** *nf* black pudding.

Blüte ('blyːtə) *nf* **-n 1** blossom, flower. **2** prime. **—zeit** *nf* **1** blossom-time. **2** prosperity, heyday.

Bö (bœː) *nf* **-en** squall, gust.

Bock (bɔk) *nm* **¨-e 1** ram, he-goat. **2** buck. **3** *sport* buck (for vaulting). **4** trestle. **5** strut. **—bier** *n neu* strong dark beer. **—wurst** *nf* (thick) frankfurter sausage.

Boden ('boːdən) *nm* **¨— 1** ground, soil. **2** bottom, bed. **—reform** *nf* land reform. **—schätze** *nm pl* mineral resources. **—tür** *nf* trap-door.

Bodensee ('boːdənzeː) *nm* Lake Constance.

Bogen ('boːgən) *nm* **— 1** curve, arch. **2** *mus, sport* bow. **3** sheet (of paper). **—gang** *nm* arcade, colonnade. **—linie** *nf* curve. **—schütze** *nm* archer.

Böhm/e ('bœ:mə) *nm* **-n** Bohemian. **—en** *n neu* Bohemia. **—isch** *adj* Bohemian.
Bohne ('bo:nə) *nf* **-n** bean.
Bohnenkaffee ('bo:nənkafe:) *nm* pure coffee.
bohr/en ('bo:rən) *vt,vi* bore, drill. **—er** *nm* — borer, drill, gimlet.
Boje ('bo:jə) *nf* **-n** buoy.
Bollwerk ('bɔlvɛrk) *n neu* bulwark.
Bolzen ('bɔltsən) *nm* — **1** bolt, peg. **2** bolt, arrow.
Bombe ('bɔmbə) *nf* **-n** bomb. **—nerfolg** *nm* huge success. **—r** *nm* — bomber.
Bonbon (bõ'b˜ɔ) *nm,neu* **-s** sweet.
Bonze ('bɔntsə) *nm* **-n** *sl* boss, bigwig.
Boot (bo:t) *n neu* **-e** boat.
Bord (bɔrt) *nm* **-e** border, rim. **an Bord** on board.
Bordell (bɔr'dɛl) *n neu* **-e** brothel.
borgen ('bɔrgən) *vt* borrow.
Borke ('bɔrkə) *nf* **-n** bark, rind.
Börse ('bœ:rstə) *nf* **-n** bristle.
bös/artig ('bœ:zartiç) *adj* **1** evil, malicious. **2** (illness) malignant. **—e** ('bœ:zə) *adj* **1** evil, bad. **2** angry. **3** (of disease) malignant. **—ewicht** ('bœ:zəviçt) *nm* **-e** villain, evil person.
bos/haft ('bo:shaft) *adj* spiteful, malicious. **—heit** ('bo:shait) *nf* **-en** **1** spite, malice. **2** wickedness.
Boß (bɔs) *nm* **-e** *inf* boss, manager.
bot (bo:t) *v* see **bieten.**
Botan/ik (bo'ta:nik) *nf* botany. **—iker** *nm* — botanist. **—isch** *adj* botanic(al).
Bot/e ('bo:tə) *nm* **-n** messenger. **—schaft** *nf* **-en** **1** embassy. **2** message. **—schafter** *nm* — ambassador.
Bottich ('bɔtiç) *nm* **-e** vat, tub.
Bowle ('bo:lə) *nf* **-n** **1** bowl. **2** fruit cup, punch.
box/en ('bɔksən) *vi* box. **—er** *nm* — boxer.
brach[1] (brax) *v* see **brechen.**
brach[2] (brax) *adj* fallow, uncultivated.
brachte ('braxtə) *v* see **bringen.**
Branche ('brãʃə) *nf* **-n** **1** trade, line (of business). **2** department, branch.
Brand (brant) *nm* **¨-e** **1** fire, burning. **2** gangrene. **3** mildew. **in Brand setzen** or **stecken** set on fire. **—bombe** *nf* incendiary bomb. **—sohle** *nf* inner sole, welt. **—stifter** *nm* incendiary, fire-raiser. **—stiftung** *nf* arson.
Brandung ('branduŋ) *nf* **-en** surf, breakers.
Branntwein ('brantvain) *nm* **-e** brandy.
Brasil/ianer (brazili'a:nər) *nm* — Brazilian. **—ianisch** *adj* Brazilian. **—ien** (bra'zi:liən) *n neu* Brazil.
brat/en* ('bra:tən) *vt,vi* **1** roast. **2** fry. **3** grill, broil. *n neu* — roast, joint. **—kartoffel** *nf* fried or roast potato. **—pfanne** *nf* frying pan. **—wurst** *nf* fried sausage.
Brauch (braux) *nm* **¨-e** **1** custom. **2** usage. **—bar** *adj* **1** useful. **2** serviceable. **—en** *vt* **1** need, want. **2** use.

Braue ('brauə) *nf* **-n** brow.
brau/en ('brauən) *vt* brew. **—er** *nm* — brewer. **—erei** (brauə'rai) *nf* **-en** brewery.
braun (braun) *adj* brown. **¨—en** ('brɔynən) *vi,vt* brown, tan.
Braunschweig ('braunʃvaik) *n neu* Brunswick.
Brause ('brauzə) *nf* **-n 1** shower. **2** nozzle, spray. **3** mineral water. **4** lemonade. **—n** *vi* **1** effervesce. **2** spray, shower. **3** roar, rage.
Braut (braut) *nf* **¨-e 1** bride. **2** fiancée. **¨—igam** ('brɔytigam) *nm* **-e 1** bridegroom. **2** fiancé. **—jungfer** *nf* bridesmaid. **—kleid** *n neu* wedding dress. **—paar** *n neu* **1** bridal pair. **2** engaged couple.
brav (braːf) *adj* **1** good. **2** honest. **3** brave.
brech/en* ('brɛçən) *vt* **1** break, crush. **2** refract. **—bohne** *nf* French bean.
Brei (brai) *nm* **-e 1** pap, pulp **2** porridge.
breit (brait) *adj* broad, wide. **—e** *nf* **-n 1** breadth, width. **2** latitude. **3** verbosity. **—en** *vt* spread (out), broaden. **—engrad** *nm* degree of latitude.
Brems/e[1] ('brɛmzə) *nf* **-n** brake. **—en** *vt,vi* brake, apply the brakes. **—schuh** *nm* brake shoe.
Bremse[2] ('brɛmzə) *nf* **-n** gadfly, horse-fly.
brenn/bar ('brɛnbaːr) *adj* inflammable. **—en*** *vi* burn, sting. *vt* **1** burn. **2** roast. **3** distil. **—er** *nm* — **1** (gas) burner. **2** distiller. **3** fire-raiser. **—erei** (brɛnə'rai) *nf* **-en** distillery, still. **—essel** ('brɛnnɛsəl) *nf* **-n** stinging-nettle. **—holz** *n neu* firewood. **—material** *n neu* fuel. **—punkt** *nm* focus, focal point. **—stoff** *nm* fuel.
Brett (brɛt) *n neu* **-er 1** board, plank. **2** shelf.
Brezel ('breːtsəl) *nf* **-n** pretzel.
bricht (briçt) *v* see **brechen.**
Brief (briːf) *nm* **-e** letter. **—fach** *n neu* **1** pigeon-hole. **2** post-office box. **—kasten** *nm* letter box. **-lich** *adj* by letter. **—marke** *nf* (postage) stamp. **—tasche** *nf* wallet, pocket-book. **—träger** *nm* postman. **—umschlag** *nm* envelope. **—wechsel** *nm* correspondence.
Brigade (bri'gaːdə) *nf* **-n** brigade.
Brikett (bri'kɛt) *n neu* **-s** briquette.
brillant (bril'jant) *adj* brilliant.
Brille ('brilə) *nf* **-n 1** spectacles. **2** goggles.
bringen* ('briŋən) *vt* **1** bring. **2** take. **3** fetch. **4** lead. **5** carry. **jemanden um etwas bringen** deprive someone of something. **jemanden dazu bringen** induce someone to.
Brit/annien (bri'taniən) *n neu* Britain. **—e** ('britə) *nm* **—n** Briton. **—isch** ('britiʃ) *adj* British.
bröckel/ig ('brœkəliç) *adj* crumbly. **—n** *vt,vi* crumble.
Brokkoli ('brɔkoli) *n pl* broccoli.
Brom (broːm) *n neu* bromine.
Brombeere ('brɔmbeːrə) *nf* **-n** blackberry.
Bronze ('br˜ɔsə) *nf* **-n** bronze.

Brosche ('brɔʃə) *nf* **-n** brooch.
Broschüre (brɔ'ʃy:rə) *nf* **-n** pamphlet, booklet, brochure.
Brot (bro:t) *n neu* **-e 1** bread. **2** loaf. **¨—chen** ('broe:tçən) *n neu* — roll, bun.
Bruch (brux) *nm* **¨-e 1** break(ing), breach. **2** fracture. **3** rupture. **4** fraction. **5** crease, fold. **¨—ig** ('bryçiç) *adj* **1** fragile, brittle. **2** cracked. **—stück** *n neu* fragment. **—teil** *nm* fraction.
Brücke ('brykə) *nf* **-n** bridge.
Bruder ('bru:dər) *nm* **¨—** brother. **¨—lich** ('bry:dərliç) *adj* fraternal. **—schaft** *nf* **-en** fraternity, brotherhood. **¨—schaft** ('bry:dərʃaft) *nf* **-en** friendship.
Brühe ('bry:ə) *nf* **-n** broth, stock, soup.
brüllen ('brylən) *vi* **1** bellow. **2** roar.
Brumm/bär ('brumbɛ:r) *nm,inf* grumbler. **—en** *vi* **1** hum, buzz. **2** growl, grumble.
brünett (bry'nɛt) *adj* brunette.
Brunnen ('brunən) *nm* — **1** well. **2** fountain. **3** spring. **—kresse** *nf* watercress.
Brunst (brunst) *nf* **¨-e 1** *zool* rut, heat. **2** (sexual) lust. **¨—ig** ('brynstiç) *adj* **1** in heat. **2** lustful.
Brüssel ('brysəl) *n neu* Brussels.
Brust (brust) *nf* **¨-e** breast, chest. **—bild** *n neu* half-length portrait. **—kasten** *nm* chest, thorax.
brutal (bru'ta:l) *adj* brutal.
brüten ('brytən) *vi,vt* **1** brood. **2** incubate.
brutto ('bruto) *adj* gross.
Bub(e) ('bu:bə) *nm* **-(e)n 1** boy. **2** rogue. **3** *game* knave.
Buch (bu:x) *n neu* **¨-er** book. **¨—erei** (by:çə'rai) *nf* **-en** library. **¨—erschrank** ('by:çərʃraŋk) *nm* bookcase. **—fink** *nm* chaffinch. **—halter** *nm comm* bookkeeper. **—handel** *nm* **1** book trade. **2** bookselling. **—händler** *nm* bookseller. **—handlung** *nf* bookshop. **¨—lein** ('by:çlain) *n neu* — booklet.
Buche ('bu:xə) *nf* **-n** beech.
Büchse ('byksə) *nf* **-n 1** box. **2** tin, can.
Buchstab/e ('bu:xʃta:bə) *nm* **-n** letter, character. **großer Buchstabe** capital letter. **—ieren** (bu:xʃta'bi:rən) *vt* spell. **—ierung** (bu:xʃta'bi:ruŋ) *nf* **-en** spelling. **¨—lich** ('bu:xʃtɛ:pliç) *adj* literal.
Bucht (buxt) *nf* **-en 1** bay, inlet. **2** bight.
Buck/el ('bukəl) *nm* — **1** bulge, hump. **2** humpback. **3** stud, boss.
sich bücken ('bykən) *vr* **1** bow. **2** stoop.
Bude ('bu:də) *nf* **-n 1** stall, booth. **2** *inf* digs, rooms.
Büfett (by'fɛt) *n neu* **-s** buffet.
Büffel ('byfəl) *nm* — buffalo, bison.
Bug (bu:k) *nm* **-e 1** *naut* bow. **2** *aviat* nose. **3** (of animals) shoulder.
Bügel ('by:gəl) *nm* — **1** hanger. **2** grip. **3** stirrup. **—eisen** *n neu* (clothes) iron. **—n** *vt* iron, press.
Bühne ('by:nə) *nf* **-n 1** stage. **2** theatre.

bulgar/ien (bul'gaːriən) *n neu* Bulgaria. **—ier** *nm* — Bulgarian. **—isch** *adj* Bulgarian.

Bulle ('bulə) *nm* **—n 1** bull. **2** *sl* policeman, copper.

Bumm/el ('buməl) *nm* — stroll. **—eln** *vi* **1** stroll. **2** loiter. **—ler** *nm* — idler, loafer.

bumsen ('bumzən) *vi* bump. *vi,vt tab* copulate, have sexual intercourse.

Bund (bunt) *nm* **¨-e 1** band. **2** league, (con)federation. *n neu* **-e** bundle, bunch. **—esgenosse** *nm* ally, confederate. **—eskanzler** *nm* Federal Chancellor. **—espräsident** *nm* president (of a federal state). **—esrat** *nm* **1** Upper House of Parliament (in Austria and West Germany). **2** Executive Federal Council (in Switzerland). **—esrepublik** *nf* Federal Republic. **Bundesrepublik Deutschland, B.R.D.** *nf* Federal Republic of Germany, F.R.G. **—esstaat** *nm* **1** federal state. **2** member state of a federation. **—estag** *nm* (Lower House of) West German Parliament. **—eswehr** *nf* West German armed forces. **¨—nis** ('byntnis) *n neu* **-se** alliance.

Bündel ('byndəl) *n neu* — bundle, bunch.

bunt (bunt) *adj* colourful, bright.

Bürde ('byrdə) *nf* **-n** burden.

Burg (burk) *nf* **-en 1** castle. **2** fortress.

Bürg/e ('byrgə) *nm* **-n** surety, guarantor, bail. **—en** *vi* **1** vouch (for). **2** stand bail (for). **—schaft** ('byrkʃaft) *nf* surety, bond.

Bürger ('byrgər) *nm* **—, Bürger/in** *nf* **-nen 1** citizen. **2** townsman or townswoman. **3** bourgeois. **—krieg** *nm* civil war. **—lich** *adj* **1** middle-class. **2** civil(ian). **3** unpretentious, simple. **—meister** *nm* mayor. **—recht** *n neu* **1** civic rights. **2** citizenship. **—schaft** *nf* **-en** citizens. **—stand** *nm* middle class(es). **—steig** *nm* pavement.

Büro (by'roː) *n neu* **-s** office. **—krat** (byro'kraːt) *nm* **-en** bureaucrat. **—kratie** (byrokra'tiː) *nf* bureaucracy.

Bursche ('burʃə) *nm* **-n 1** youth, lad. **2** student. **3** orderly. **4** servant. **5** apprentice.

Bürst/e ('byrstə) *nf* **-n** brush. **—en** *vt* brush.

Busch (buʃ) *nm* **¨-e 1** bush(land). **2** shrub(s). **3** thicket. **4** tuft. **—ig** *adj* bushy.

Busen ('buːzən) *nm* — **1** breast, bosom. **2** gulf, bay.

Buß/e ('buːsə) *nf* **-n 1** penance. **2** fine. **¨—en** ('byːsən) *vt,vi* atone for, pay (for), do penance (for). **¨—er** ('byːsər) *nm* penitent.

Büste ('bystə) *nf* **-n** bust. **—nhalter** *nm* bra, brassiere.

Butter ('butər) *nf* butter. **—brot** *n neu* (slice of) bread and butter.

C

Café (ka'feː) *n neu* **-s** cafe, coffee-house.

Camping ('kɛmpiŋ) *n neu* camping.

Cape (keːp) *n neu* **-s** cape.
CD-Platte (tseː'deː platə) *nf* **-n** compact disc.
Cell/ist (tʃɛ'list) *nm* **-en** cellist. **—o** ('tʃɛlo) *n neu* **-s** cello.
Champagner (ʃam'panjər) *nm* — champagne.
Champignon ('ʃampinj˜ɔ) *nm* **-s** mushroom.
Chance ('ʃãːsə) *nf* **-n** chance.
Chao/s ('kaːɔs) *n neu* chaos. **—tisch** (ka'oːtiʃ) *adj* chaotic.
Charakter ('karaktər) *nm* **-e** **1** character, nature. **2** letter, character. **—isieren** (karaktəri'ziːrən) *vt* characterize. **—istik** (karaktə'ristik) *nf* **-en** characterization. **—istisch** (karaktə'ristiʃ) *adj* characteristic.
charmant (ʃar'mant) *adj* charming.
Chauffeur (ʃɔ'fœːr) *nm* **-e** driver, chauffeur.
Chaussee (ʃo'seː) *nf* **-n** main or high road.
Chef (ʃɛf) *nm* **-s** head, boss.
Chemi/e (çe'miː) *nf* chemistry. **—kalien** (çemi'kaːliən) *nf pl* chemicals. **—ker** ('çeːmikər) *nm* — chemist (in science or industry). **—sch** ('çeːmiʃ) *adj* chemical. **chemische Reinigung** dry cleaning.
Chil/e ('tʃiːlə) *n neu* Chile. **—ene** (tʃi'leːnə) *nm* **-n** Chilean. **—enisch** (tʃi'leːniʃ) *adj* Chilean.
Chin/a ('çiːna) *n neu* China. **—ese** (çi'neːzə) *nm* **-n** Chinaman, Chinese. **—esisch** (çi'neːziʃ) *adj* Chinese.
Chirurg (çi'rurk) *nm* **-en** surgeon. **—ie** (çirur'giː) *nf* surgery.
Chlor (kloːr) *n neu* chlorine.
Chloroform (kloro'fɔrm) *n neu* **-e** chloroform.
Chor (koːr) *nm* **¨-e** choir, chorus.
Christ (krist) *nm* **-en** Christian. **—baum** *nm* Christmas tree. **—enheit** *nf* Christendom. **—entum** *n neu* Christianity. **—kind** *n neu* Christ-child. **—lich** *adj* Christian. **—us** *nm* Christ.
Chrom (kroːm) *n neu* chromium, chrome.
Chronik ('kroːnik) *nf* **-en** chronicle.
Computer (kɔm'pjuːtər) *nm* — computer. **—isieren** (kɔm'pjuːtəri'ziːrən) *vt* computerize.
Creme (kreːm) *nf* **-s** **1** cream. **2** cream pudding.

D

da (da) *adv* **1** there. **2** here. **3** then. *conj* **1** as. **2** when. **3** since.
dabei (da'bai) *adv* **1** by it. **2** nearby. **3** present. **4** at the same time. **5** thereby.
Dach (dax) *n neu* **¨-er** roof. **—boden** *nm* attic. **—fenster** *n neu also* **—luke** *nf* **-n** skylight. **—rinne** *also* **—traufe** *nf* **-n** **1** eaves. **2** gutter.
Dachs (daks) *nm* **-e** badger.
Dachshund ('dakshunt) *nm* dachshund.
dachte ('daxtə) *v* see **denken.**
dadurch (da'durç) *adv* **1** through there. **2** thus, in that way.
dafür (da'fyːr) *adv* for that, in return.
dagegen (da'geːgən) *adv* **1**

against it. **2** in comparison. *conj* on the other hand, but.

daher (da'heːr) *adv* **1** from there. **2** therefore.

dahin (da'hin) *adv* there, to that place. **bis dahin** until then. **dahin sein** be lost or gone.

dahinten (da'hintən) *adv* behind (there).

dahinter (da'hintər) *adv* behind it or that. **—kommen*** *vi* find out (about it).

damals ('daːmaːls) *adv* then, at that time.

Dame ('daːmə) *nf* **-n 1** lady. **2** *game* queen. **—spiel** *n neu* draughts.

damit (da'mit) *adv* **1** with or by it. **2** thereby. *conj* in order to, so (that).

Damm (dam) *nm* **¨-e 1** dam, dyke, embankment. **2** roadway. **¨—en** ('dɛmən) *vt* dam, restrain.

Dämmerung ('dɛməruŋ) *nf* **-en 1** dawn. **2** dusk, twilight.

Dampf (dampf) *nm* **¨-e** steam, vapour. **—en** *vi* **1** steam. **2** *inf* smoke. **—maschine** *nf* steam engine. **—schiff** *n neu* steamship.

dämpf/en ('dɛmpfən) *vt* **1** quieten, muffle. **2** steam. **—er** *nm* **— 1** damper, silencer. **2** extinguisher.

danach (da'naːx) *adv* **1** after(wards). **2** accordingly.

Dän/e ('dɛːnə) *nm* **-n** Dane. **—emark** ('dɛːnəmark) *n neu* Denmark. **—isch** ('dɛːniʃ) *adj* Danish. *n neu* Danish (language).

daneben (da'neːbən) *adv* **1** near it. **2** nearby. **3** beside. *conj*. moreover, as well.

Dank (daŋk) *nm* thanks. **vielen** or **schönen Dank!** many thanks! **—bar** *adj* thankful, grateful. **—barkeit** *nf* gratitude. **—e** *interj* thanks! thank you! **—en** *vi* thank.

dann (dan) *adv* then.

daran (da'ran) *adv also* **dran** at, on or by it or that. **daran gehen** set to work.

darauf (da'rauf) *adv also* **drauf 1** on it or that, thereupon. **2** later.

daraus (da'raus) *adv also* **draus 1** from or out of it or that. **2** from there.

darbieten* ('daːrbiːtən) *vt* offer, tender.

darein (da'rain) *adv also* **drein** into it or that, therein.

darf (daːrf) *v* see **dürfen.**

darin (da'rin) *adv also* **drin** in it, that or there, within.

Darlegung ('daːrleːguŋ) *nf* **-en** statement, exposition.

Darlehen ('daːrleːən) *n neu* **—** loan.

Darm (darm) *nm* **¨-e** intestine, bowel, gut.

darstell/en ('daːrʃtɛlən) *vt* **1** present, show. **2** represent, depict. **—ung** *nf* **-en 1** presentation. **2** description, statement.

darüber (da'ryːbər) *adv* **1** about it or that. **2** over, above or beyond it or that. **darüber hinaus 1** moreover. **2** over and above that, beyond that.

darum (da'rum) *adv* **1** about or around it or that. **2** therefore.

darunter (da'runtər) *adv* **1**

under it or that, underneath. **2** among them.

das (das) *def art* the. *pron* that, which.

dasein* ('da:zain) *vi* exist, be present. *n neu* existence, being, presence.

daß (das) *conj* that. **daß nicht** lest. **so daß** so that.

datieren (da'ti:rən) *vt* date.

Datum ('da:tum) *n neu* **-ten** date.

Dauer ('dauər) *nf* duration, period. **auf die Dauer** in the long run. **—haft** *adj* durable, lasting. **—lauf** *nm* endurance run. **—n** *vi* last, continue, take (time). **lange dauern** take a long time. **—nd** *adj* lasting, constant, permanent.

Daumen ('daumən) *nm* — thumb.

Daunendecke ('daunəndɛkə) *nf* (continental) quilt, duvet, eiderdown.

davon (da'fɔn) *adv* of, from or about it or that. **—kommen*** *vi* get away. **—tragen*** *vt* carry off.

davor (da'fo:r) *adv* **1** before or in front of it or that. **2** of or from it or that.

dawider (da'vi:dər) *adv* against it or that.

dazu (da'tsu:) *adv* **1** to or for it or that. **2** for that purpose. **3** in addition. **—kommen*** *vi* arrive, happen. **—tun*** *vt* add.

dazwischen (da'tsviʃən) *adv* **1** between or among (them). **2** meanwhile. **—kommen*** *vi* **1** intervene, prevent. **2** come between. **—treten*** *vi* intervene.

Debatt/e (de'batə) *nf* **-n** debate, discussion.

Debet ('de:bɛt) *n neu* **-s** debit.

Deck (dɛk) *n neu* **-e** *naut* deck.

Deck/e ('dɛkə) *nf* **-n 1** cover, blanket. **2** ceiling. **—el** *nm* — lid, cover. **—en** *vt* cover. **den Tisch decken** set or lay the table. **—mantel** *nm* **1** pretext. **2** cloak. **3** cover. **—name** *nm* assumed name. **—ung** *nf* **-en 1** cover(ing), protection. **2** *mil* cover. **3** *comm* security.

defensiv (defɛn'zi:f) *adj* defensive. **—e** (defɛn'zi:və) *nf* **-n 1** defensive. **2** defence.

defin/ieren (defi'ni:rən) *vt* define. **—ition** (definitsi'o:n) *nf* **-en** definition.

Defizit ('de:fitsit) *n neu* **-e** deficit.

Degen ('de:gən) *nm* — sword.

degenerieren (degene'ri:rən) *vi* degenerate.

dehnen ('de:nən) *vt* stretch, lengthen, expand.

Deich (daiç) *nm* **-e** dyke, embankment.

dein (dain) *poss adj,pron 2nd pers s fam* your, yours. **—er** *poss pron 2nd pers s fam also* **der —e** *or* **der —ige** yours. **—erseits** ('dainərzaits) *adv* on your part. **—esgleichen** *pron* people like you. **—ethalben** *adv* also **—etwegen** *or* **—etwillen** for your sake, on your account.

dekaden/t (deka'dɛnt) *adj* decadent. **—z** (deka'dɛnts) *nf* decadence.

Dekan (de'ka:n) *nm* **-e** dean.

Deklination (deklinatsi'o:n) *nf* **-en** *gram* declension.

Dekret (de'kreːt) *n neu* **-e** decree.
delikat (deli'kaːt) *adj* **1** delicate. **2** delicious.
Delikt (de'likt) *n neu* **-e** offence, crime.
Delphin (dɛl'fiːn) *nm* **-e** dolphin.
dem (deːm) *def art* to the. *pron* to it, that or whom.
dementieren (demɛn'tiːrən) *vt* deny.
demgemäß ('deːmgəmɛːs) *adv* accordingly.
Demission (demisi'oːn) *nf* **-en** resignation.
demnach ('deːmnaːx) *adv* accordingly.
demnächst ('deːmnɛːçst) *adv* soon.
Demokrat (demo'kraːt) *nm* **-en** democrat. **—isch** *adj* democratic. **—ie** (demokra'tiː) *nf* **-n** democracy.
Demonstr/ation (demɔnstratsi'oːn) *nf* **-en** demonstration. **—ieren** (demɔn'striːrən) *vt,vi* demonstrate.
Demut ('deːmuːt) *nf* humility. **¨—ig** ('deːmyːtiç) *adj* humble. **¨—igen** ('deːmyːtigən) *vt* humble, humiliate.
demzufolge ('deːmtsufɔlgə) *adv* accordingly.
den (deːn) *def art* **1** the. **2** *pl* (to) the. *pron* **1** that, which, whom. **2** *pl* to these or those. **denen** *pron* to these or those.
denk/en* ('dɛŋkən) *vt,vi* think. **denken an** or **über** think of or about. **—bar** *adj* conceivable. **—er** *nm* — thinker. **-mal** *n neu* **¨-er** monument, memorial. **—schrift** *nf* **-en** **1** inscription, memorial. **2** report. **3** memorandum. **—(ungs)art** *nf* **-en** way of thinking, mentality. **—würdig** *adj* notable, memorable.
denn (dɛn) *conj* for. *adv* then. **es sei denn, (daß)** unless.
dennoch ('dɛnɔx) *adv* yet, however.
Departement (depart'mãː) *n neu* **-s** department.
Depesche (de'pɛʃə) *nf* **-n** **1** dispatch. **2** telegram.
deponieren (depo'niːrən) *vt* deposit.
Depression (depresi'oːn) *nf* **-en** depression.
deprimieren (depri'miːrən) *vt* depress.
der (deːr) *def art* **1** the. **2** of the. *pron* that, which, who.
derart ('deːraːrt) *adv* in such a way. **—ig** *adj* such, of that kind.
derb (dɛrp) *adj* **1** sturdy, sound. **2** rough, coarse, crude.
deren ('deːrən) *pron* whose, of which.
dergestalt ('deːrgəʃtalt) *adv* in such a way.
dergleichen (deːr'glaiçən) *pron* such (a thing), the like, of the kind.
derjenige, diejenige, dasjenige ('deːrjeːnigə, 'diːjeːnigə, 'dasjeːnigə) *pron m,f,neu* he or she who, that which, the one which.
dermaßen ('deːrmaːsən) *adv* to such a degree.
derselbe, dieselbe, dasselbe (deːr'zɛlbə, diː'zɛlbə, das 'zɛlbə) *pron m,f,neu* the same.
derzeitig ('deːrtsaitiç) *adj* **1** present. **2** of or at that time.

des (dɛs) *def art* of the.
desgleichen (dɛs'glaiçən) *pron* such (a thing). *adv* likewise.
deshalb ('dɛshalp) *adv* therefore.
Desin/fektionsmittel (dezinfɛktsi'oːnzmitəl) *n neu* — disinfectant. **—fizieren** (dezinfi-'tsiːrən) *vt* disinfect.
dessen ('dɛsən) *pron* whose, of which. **—ungeachtet** (dɛsənunge'axtət) *adv* nevertheless.
desto ('dɛsto) *adv* so much, the. **je...desto** the...the. **je mehr, desto besser** the more the better.
deswegen ('dɛsveːgən) *adv* therefore.
Detail (de'tai) *n neu* **-s** detail, item. **—handel** *nf* retail trade. **en detail** *adv* retail.
deut/en ('dɔytən) *vi* point (to). *vt* **1** explain. **2** show. **—lich** *adj* clear, distinct. **—lichkeit** *nf* distinctness. **—ung** *nf* **-en** explanation, interpretation.
deutsch (dɔytʃ) *adj* German. *n neu* German (language). **auf Deutsch** in German. **—e(r)** *nm* German. **—e Demokratische Republik, D.D.R.** *nf* German Democratic Republic, G.D.R. **—kunde** *nf* German studies. **—land** *n neu* Germany. **—sprachig** *adj* German-speaking. **—tum** *n neu* German nature or culture.
Devise (de'viːzə) *nf* **-n** **1** *pl* foreign exchange. **2** motto, slogan.
Dezember (de'tsɛmbər) *nm* December.
Dialekt (dia'lɛkt) *nm* **-e** dialect.
Diamant (dia'mant) *nm* **-en** diamond.
Diapositiv (diːapɔzi'tiːf) *n neu* slide, transparency.
Diät (di'ɛːt) *nf* — diet.
Diäten (di'ɛːtən) *nf pl* allowance(s).
dich (diç) *pron 2nd pers s fam* you, yourself.
dicht (diçt) *adj* **1** dense, thick. **2** tight. **3** close (to). **—igkeit** *nf* **-en** *also* **—heit** **1** density, thickness. **2** imperviousness.
dicht/en ('diçtən) *vt* compose (poetry). **—er** *nm* — poet. **—ung** *nf* **-en** **1** poetry, poem. **2** fiction.
dick (dik) *adj* thick, fat, large. **—e** *nf* **-n** **1** thickness, fatness. **2** size. **—kopf** *nm* thickhead. **—icht** *n neu* **-e** thicket.
die *def art* the. *pron* that, which, who, whom.
Dieb (diːp) *nm* **-e** thief, robber. **—isch** ('diːbiʃ) *adj* thieving, dishonest. **—stahl** *nm* ¨**-e** theft.
Diele ('diːlə) *nf* **-n** **1** board, plank. **2** hall(way).
dien/en ('diːnən) *vi* serve. **—er** *nm* — man-servant. **—erin** *nf* **-nen** maid-servant. **—erschaft** *nf* **-en** servants. **—st** (diːnst) *nm* **-e** **1** service. **2** duty. **außer Dienst** off duty. **—stbereit** *adj* ready for service. **—ststelle** *nf* place of work or service.
Dienstag ('diːnstaːk) *nm* Tuesday.
dieser, diese, dieses ('diːzər, 'diːzə, 'diːzəs) *pron,adj m,f,neu* this.
diesmal ('diːsmaːl) *adv* this time.

diesseits ('di:szaits) *adv* on this side.

Dietrich ('di:triç) *nm* **-e** skeleton key.

Diktat (dik'ta:t) *n neu* **-e** **1** dictation. **2** command, decree. **—or** (dik'ta:tɔr) *nm* **-en** dictator. **—ur** (dikta'tu:r) *nf* **-en** dictatorship.

diktieren (dik'ti:rən) *vt* dictate.

Diner (di'ne:) *n neu* **-s** dinner.

Ding (diŋ) *n neu* **-e** thing, object.

Diplom (di'plo:m) *n neu* **-e** diploma, certificate.

dir (di:r) *pron 2nd pers s fam* (to) you, yourself.

Dirig/ent (diri'gɛnt) *nm* **-en** *mus* conductor. **—ieren** (diri 'gi:rən) *vt* **1** direct. **2** *mus* conduct.

Dirne ('dirnə) *nf* **-n** **1** prostitute. **2** girl.

diskont/ieren (diskɔn'ti:rən) *vt comm* discount. **—satz** *nm* bank rate.

Diskothek (disko:'te:k) *nf* **-en** discotheque.

Disku/ssion (diskusi'o:n) *nf* **-en** discussion. **—tieren** (disku'ti:rən) *vt,vi* discuss, debate.

disponieren (dispo'ni:rən) *vt,vi* arrange, dispose.

Distel ('distəl) *nf* **-n** thistle.

Disziplin (distsi'pli:n) *nf* **-en** discipline.

doch (dɔx) *adv* **1** nevertheless. **2** indeed, really. *conj* but, however, yet.

Docht (dɔxt) *nm* **-e** wick.

Dock (dɔk) *n neu* **-s** dock(yard). **—arbeiter** *nm* docker.

Dogge ('dɔgə) *nf* **-n** bulldog.

Dogma ('dɔgma) *n neu* **-s** dogma. **—tisch** (dɔg'ma:tiʃ) *adj* dogmatic.

Doktor ('dɔktɔr) *nm* **-en** doctor.

Dolch (dɔlç) *nm* **-e** dagger.

dolmetsch/en ('dɔlmɛtʃən) *vt,vi* interpret. **—er** *nm* — interpreter.

Dom (do:m) *nm* **-e** cathedral. **—herr** *nm rel* canon.

dominieren (domi'ni:rən) *vi,vt* dominate, domineer.

Donau ('do:nau) *nf* Danube.

Donner ('dɔnər) *nm* thunder. **—n** *vi* thunder, roar.

Donnerstag ('dɔnərsta:k) *nm* Thursday.

Doppel ('dɔpəl) *n neu* — **1** duplicate. **2** double. **—bett** *n neu* double bed. **—deckerbus** *nm* double-decker bus. **—ehe** *nf* bigamy. **—n** *vt* double. **—punkt** *nm* colon. **—sinn** *nm* ambiguity. **—t** *adj* double.

Dorf (dɔrf) *n neu* **¨-er** village, hamlet. **—bewohner** also **¨—ler** ('dɔrfbəvo:nər, 'doerflər) *nm* — villager.

Dorn (dɔrn) *nm* **-en** thorn. **—ig** *adj* thorny.

Dorsch (dɔrʃ) *nm* **-e** cod.

dort (dɔrt) *adv* there. **—her** *adv* from there. **—hin** *adv* to there or that place. **—ig** *adj* of that place or there.

Dose ('do:zə) *nf* **-n** **1** box. **2** tin, can.

dösen ('dœzən) *vi inf* doze.

Dosis ('do:zis) *nf* **-sen** dose (of medicine etc.). **zu starke Dosis** overdose.

Dotter ('dɔtə) *nm* — yolk.

Dozent (do'tsɛnt) *nm* **-en** university or college lecturer.

Drache ('draxə) *nm* **-n** dragon.

Draht (dra:t) *nm* **¨-e** wire, cable. **—los** *adj* wireless. **—seilbahn** *nf* funicular, cable railway.

Drama ('dra:ma) *n neu* **-men** drama. **—tiker** (dra'ma:tikər) *nm* — playwright. **—tisch** (dra'ma:tiʃ) *adj* dramatic.

dran (dran) *adv* see **daran.**

Drang (draŋ) *nm* **¨-e 1** drive, urge, stress. **2** pressure. **¨—en** ('drɛŋən) *vi,vt* **1** press, hurry, urge. **2** crowd.

drapieren (dra'pi:rən) *vt* drape.

drauf (drauf) *adv* see **darauf.**

draußen ('drausən) *adv* outside, out of doors.

Dreck (drɛk) *nm* **1** filth, dirt. **2** excrement. **—ig** *adj* filthy, dirty, muddy.

dreh/en ('dre:ən) *vt,vi* **1** turn, twist, wind. **2** shoot (a film). **—bank** *nf* **¨-e** lathe. **—buch** *n neu* (film) script. **—punkt** *nm* pivot. **—scheibe** *nf* turntable. **—ung** *nf* **-en** turn, rotation, revolution.

drei (drai) *adj,nf* three. **—bein** *n neu* tripod. **—eck** *n neu* triangle. **—eckig** *adj* triangular. **—einigkeit** *nf also* **—faltigkeit** Trinity. **—erlei** ('draiərlai) *adj* of three kinds. **—fach** *adj* triple, threefold. **—mal** *adv* three times. **—rad** *n neu* tricycle.

dreißig ('draisiç) *adj,nf* thirty. **dreißigste** *adj* thirtieth.

dreist (draist) *adj* **1** impudent. **2** bold.

dreizehn ('draitse:n) *adj,nf* thirteen. **dreizehnte** *adj* thirteenth.

dresch/en* ('drɛʃən) *vt* thresh. **—flegel** *nm* flail.

dressieren (dre'si:rən) *vt* train (an animal).

drin (drin) *adv* see **darin. —nen** *adv* inside, indoors.

dring/en* ('driŋən) *vi* **1** urge, force, press. **2** penetrate. **—end** *adj also* **—lich** urgent.

dritt(e) (drit) *adj* third. **—el** *n neu* — one third, third part. **—ens** *adv* thirdly.

Drog/e ('dro:gə) *nf* **-n** drug. **—erie** (drogə'ri:) *nf* **-n** chemist's shop.

droh/en ('dro:ən) *vi* threaten. **—ung** *nf* **-en** threat.

Drohne ('dro:nə) *nf* **-n** drone.

drollig ('drɔliç) *adj* droll, funny.

Drossel ('drɔsəl) *nf* **-n 1** thrush. **2** *tech* throttle.

drüben ('dry:bən) *adv* on the other side, over there.

drüber ('dry:bər) *adv* see **darüber.**

Druck (druk) *nm* **1 -e** print, printing. **2 -e** pressure. **—en** *vt* print. **—er** *nm* — printer. **—erei** (drukə'rai) *nf* **-en** printing works. **—fehler** *nm* misprint. **—knopf** *nm* **1** snap fastener. **2** push-button.

drück/en ('drykən) *vt,vi* **1** press (on), squeeze. **2** oppress. **sich drücken** *vr* dodge work, shirk.

drunten ('druntən) *adv* (there) below, down there.

drunter ('druntər) *adv* see **darunter.**

Drüse ('dry:zə) *nf* **-n** gland.

Dschungel ('dʒuŋəl) *nm,f,neu* **-n** jungle.

du (duː) *pron 2nd pers s fam* you.
ducken ('dukən) *vt* duck.
Dudelsack ('duːdəlzak) *nm* **¨-e** bagpipes.
Duell (du'ɛl) *n neu* **-e** duel. **sich —ieren** (duɛ'liːrən) *vr* duel.
Duett (du'ɛt) *n neu* **-e** duet.
Duft (duft) *nm* **¨-e** aroma, scent. **—en** *vi* smell (sweet), be fragrant.
dulden ('duldən) *vt* suffer, bear, tolerate.
dumm (dum) *adj* stupid, silly. **—heit** *nf* **-en** **1** stupidity. **2** foolish action. **—kopf** *nm* blockhead, fool.
dumpf (dumpf) *adj* **1** musty, close (atmosphere). **2** dull, hollow (sound).
Düne ('dyːnə) *nf* **-n** dune.
Dünger ('dyŋər) *nm* dung, manure.
dunkel ('dyŋkəl) *adj* **1** dark, dim, gloomy. **2** obscure. **—kammer** *nf* darkroom.
dünn (dyn) *adj* **1** thin. **2** sparse.
Dunst (dunst) *nm* **¨-e** vapour, haze, mist, smoke. **¨—en** ('dynstən) *vt cul* **1** steam. **2** stew.
Dur (duːr) *n neu mus* major.
durch (durç) *prep* through, during, by. *adv* completely, thoroughly.
durchaus (durç'aus) *adv* absolutely, completely.
durchblicken ('durçblikən) *vt,vi* look through, see through. **durchblicken lassen** give to understand.
durchbohren ('durçboːrən) *vt* bore through, pierce.
durchbrechen* ('durçbrɛçən) *vt,vi* break through or out. (durç'brɛçən) *vt* break through.
durchdringen* (*vi* 'durçdriŋən; *vt* durç'driŋən) *vi* press or get through. *vt* **1** permeate. **2** penetrate.
durcheinander (durçain'andər) *adv* **1** in confusion. **2** upset. *n neu* — disorder.
Durchfahrt ('durçfaːrt) *nf* **-en** **1** passage or journey through. **2** passageway. **3** gateway.
Durchfall ('durçfal) *nm* **¨-e** **1** failure. **2** diarrhoea.
durchforschen (durç'fɔrʃən) *vt* investigate.
durchführen ('durçfyːrən) *vt* **1** lead through. **2** carry out.
Durchgang ('durçgaŋ) *nm* **¨-e** passage. **durchgehen*** ('durçgeːən) *vi* **1** go or walk through. **2** run away. *vt* **1** examine. **2** wear out.
durch/lassen* ('durçlasən) *vt* let through, pass. **—lässig** ('durçlɛsiç) *adj* permeable.
durchlaufen* ('durçlaufən) *vi* run through. *vt* wear out. (durç'laufən) *vt* run through.
durchleuchten (*vi* 'durçlɔyçtən; *vt* durç'lɔyçtən) *vi* shine through. *vt* **1** X-ray. **2** investigate. **3** search.
durchlöchern (durç'lœçərn) *vt* perforate, pierce.
durchmachen ('durçmaxən) *vt* go through, experience, endure.
Durchmesser ('durçmɛsər) *nm* — diameter.
durchqueren (durç'kveːrən) *vt* cross, traverse.
Durchreise ('durçraizə) *nf* **-n**

passage, transit, journey through.

durchs (durçs) contraction of **durch das.**

durchschauen (*vi* 'durçʃauən; *vt* durç'ʃauən) *vi* look through. *vt* **1** see through. **2** penetrate.

Durchschlag ('durçʃlaːk) *nm* ¨**-e** **1** carbon (copy). **2** strainer. **3** *tech* punch. **—papier** *n neu* carbon paper.

Durchschnitt ('durçʃnit) *nm* **-e** **1** average. **2** cutting through. **3** (cross-)section. **—lich** *adj* average. **—smensch** *nm* man in the street.

durchsehen* ('durçzeːən) *vt* **1** look through. **2** examine.

durchsichtig ('durçziçtiç) *adj* transparent.

durchsuchen ('durçzuːxən) *vt* examine (closely).

durchtrieben (durç'triːbən) *adj* cunning.

durchweg ('durçvɛk) *adv* throughout.

durchwinden* ('durçvindən) *vr* struggle through, overcome.

durchziehen* ('durçtsiːən) *vi* march through. *vt* interlace. (durç'tsiːən) *vt* draw or pass through.

dürfen* ('dyrfən) *v mod aux* be allowed, may.

dürftig ('dyrftiç) *adj* needy, poor.

dürr (dyr) *adj* **1** dry, arid. **2** thin. **3** barren.

Durst (durst) *nm* thirst. **—ig** *adj* thirsty.

Dusche ('duʃə) *nf* **-n** shower. **—n** *vt* shower.

Düse ('dyːzə) *nf* **-n** jet, nozzle. **—nflugzeug** *n neu* jet (plane).

düster ('dyːstər) *adj* dark, dusky, gloomy.

Dutzend ('dutsənt) *n neu* **-e** dozen.

duzen ('duːtsən) *vt* address (someone) familiarly with **du.**

Dynam/ik (dy'naːmik) *nf* dynamics. **—isch** *adj* dynamic.

Dynamit (dyna'miːt) *n neu* **-e** dynamite.

Dynast/ie (dynas'tiː) *nf* **-n** dynasty.

D-Zug ('deːtsuːk) *nm* ¨**-e** express train.

E

Ebbe ('ɛbə) *nf* **-n** ebb, low-tide. **—n** *vi* ebb.

eben ('eːbən) *adj* **1** level, even. **2** smooth. *adv* just, precisely. **—bild** *n neu* image. **—bürtig** ('eːbənbyrtiç) *adj* equal, of equal rank. **—e** *nf* **-n** **1** plain. **2** *math* plane. **—falls** *adv* likewise. **—heit** *nf* **-en** evenness, smoothness. **—holz** *n neu* ebony. **—so** *adv* just as. **der eine ist ebenso gut wie der andere** the one is just as good as the other. **—soviel** *adv* just as much.

Eber ('eːbər) *nm* — boar.

ebnen ('eːbnən) *vt* level, make smooth.

Echo ('ɛço) *n neu* **-s** echo.

echt (ɛçt) *adj* **1** genuine, real, authentic. **2** pure.

Eck (ɛk) *n neu* **-e** also **Eck/e** ('ɛkə) *nf* **-n** **1** corner. **2** angle. **—ig** *adj* angular. **—stein** *nm* **1** corner stone. **2** *game* diamonds.

edel ('eːdəl) *adj* noble, aristocratic. **—frau** *nf* noblewoman. **—mann** *nm, pl* **-leute** nobleman, aristocrat. **—mütig** ('eːdəlmyːtiç) *adj* magnanimous, generous. **—stein** *nm* precious stone, gem.

Edikt (e'dikt) *n neu* **-e** edict.

Edinburg ('eːdinburk) *n neu* Edinburgh.

Efeu ('eːfɔy) *nm* **-s** ivy.

Effekt/en (ɛ'fɛktən) *n pl* **1** *comm* securities, bonds. **2** personal effects, belongings. **—iv** (ɛfɛk'tiːv) *adj* **1** actual. **2** effective.

egal (e'gaːl) *adv* **1** even. **2** equal, the same.

Egoismus (ego'ismus) *nm* egoism.

ehe (eː) *conj* before. **—dem** (eːə'deːm) *adv also* **—mals** formerly, previously. **—malig** ('eːəmaːliç) *adj* former. **—r** *adv* **1** sooner, before. **2** rather.

Ehe ('eːə) *nf* **-n** marriage. **—brecher** *nm* — adulterer. **—brecherin** *nf* **-nen** adulteress. **—bruch** *nm* adultery. **—frau** *nf* wife. **—lich** *adj* **1** matrimonial. **2** (of a child) legitimate. **—mann** *nm* husband. **—paar** *n neu* married couple. **—stand** *nm* matrimony, married state. **—scheidung** *nf* divorce.

Ehr/e ('eːrə) *nf* **-n** honour. **—en** *vt* honour. **—enwort** *n neu* word of honour. **—erbietig** *adj* respectful, deferential. **—furcht** *nf* reverence, awe, respect. **—geiz** *nm* ambition. **—geizig** *adj* ambitious. **—lich** *adj* **1** honest. **2** sincere. **3** fair. **—lichkeit** *nf* honesty. **—würdig** *adj* venerable.

Ei (ai) *n neu* **-er** egg.

Eich/e ('aiçə) *nf* **-n** oak. **—el** *nf* **-n** **1** acorn. **2** *game* clubs. **—hörnchen** ('aiçhœrnçən) *n neu* — squirrel.

Eid (ait) *nm* **-e** oath. **einen Eid abnehmen** administer an oath. **unter Eid** on oath. **—bruch** *nm* perjury. **—genosse** *nm* — **1** confederate. **2** Swiss. **—genossenschaft** *nf* **-en** **1** confederation. **2** Swiss Confederation, Switzerland. **—genössisch** ('aitgənœsiʃ) *adj* **1** federal. **2** Swiss.

Eidechse ('aidɛksə) *nf* **-n** lizard.

Eier/becher ('aiərbɛçər) *nm* eggcup. **—kuchen** *nm* **1** (sweet) omelette. **2** pancake. **—schale** *nf* eggshell.

Eif/er ('aifər) *nm* zeal, fervour. **—ersucht** *nf* jealousy. **—ersüchtig** *adj* jealous. **—rig** *adj* zealous, eager.

Eigelb ('aigɛlp) *n neu* **-e** (egg) yolk.

eigen ('aigən) *adj* **1** own, proper. **2** characteristic. **3** strange. **4** particular, exact.

Eigenart ('aigənaːrt) *nf* **-en** **1** peculiarity. **2** character. **—ig** *adj* peculiar.

eigenhändig ('aigənhɛndiç) *adj* in or by one's own hand, by oneself.

eigenmächtig ('aigənmɛçtiç) *adj* arbitrary.

Eigenname ('aigənnaːmə) *nm* proper name.

Eigennutz ('aigənnuts) *nm* self-interest, selfishness. **¨—ig** *adj* selfish.

Eigenschaft ('aigənʃaft) *nf* **-en**

characteristic, trait, quality. **—swort** *n neu* adjective.

Eigensinn ('aigənzin) *nm* obstinacy. **—ig** *adj* obstinate, inflexible.

eigentlich ('aigəntliç) *adj* **1** real. **2** proper. **3** true. *adv* **1** actually. **2** just. **3** indeed.

Eigentum ('aigəntu:m) *n neu* **-er** property. **¨—er** *nm* **—** owner. **¨—lich** *adj* **1** peculiar, characteristic. **2** peculiar, strange.

sich eignen ('aignən) *vr* suit, be qualified.

Eil/bote ('ailbo:tə) *nm* express messenger. **—brief** *nm* express letter. **—e** *nf* haste, hurry, speed. **—en** *vi* also **sich —en** *vr* hurry, hasten. **—ig** *adj* hurried, hasty. **—zug** *nm* fast train.

Eimer ('aimər) *nm* **—** bucket, pail.

ein, eine, ein (ain, 'ainə) *indef art m,f,neu* a, an. *adj* one. **einer, eine, eins** ('ainər, 'ainə, ains) *pron* one.

einander (ai'nandər) *pron* each other, one another.

einatmen ('aina:tmən) *vt,vi* inhale, breathe in.

Einbahnstraße ('ainba:nʃtra:sə) *nf* one-way street.

einbalsamieren (ainbalza'mi:rən) *vt* embalm.

Einband ('ainbant) *nm* **¨-e** binding, cover (of a book).

einbegreifen* ('ainbəgraifən) *vt* comprise, include.

einbiegen* ('ainbi:gən) *vt* bend in(wards). *vi* turn in(to).

sich einbild/en ('ainbildən) *vr* imagine. **—ung** *nf* imagination. **—ungskraft** *nf* (power of) imagination.

Einblick ('einblik) *nm* **1** insight. **2** glimpse.

einbrech/en* ('ainbrɛçən) *vt,vi* **1** break open, down or into. **2** burgle. **—er** *nm* **—** burglar.

einbürgern ('ainbyrgərn) *vt* naturalize. **sich einbürgern** *vr* **1** settle. **2** (of a word, etc.) come into use.

einbüßen ('ainby:sən) *vt* **1** lose. **2** forfeit.

eindeutig ('aindɔytiç) *adj* unequivocal, clear.

eindring/en* ('aindriŋən) *vi* **1** enter by force, invade. **2** penetrate.

Eindruck ('aindruk) *nm* **¨-e** impression. **—svoll** *adj* impressive.

einerlei ('ainərlai) *adj* of one sort or kind.

einerseits ('ainərzaits) *adv* on the one hand.

einfach ('ainfax) *adj* **1** simple, plain. **2** single.

einfahr/en* ('ainfa:rən) *vi* drive in. *vt* **1** bring in. **2** break in (horses). **—t** *nf* **-en** entrance, drive.

Einfall ('ainfal) *nm* **¨-e** **1** collapse, fall. **2** invasion. **3** brainwave, sudden idea. **—en*** *vi* collapse, fall. *v imp* occur (to someone). **es fiel mir ein** it (suddenly) occurred to me.

einfältig ('ainfɛltiç) *adj* simple, stupid.

Einfassung ('ainfassuŋ) *nf* **-en** **1** border (of a dress). **2** enclosure.

sich einfinden* ('ainfindən) *vr* turn up, appear.

einflechten* ('ainflεçtən) *vt* **1** plait, interlace. **2** put in (a word, etc.).

Einfluß ('ainflus) *nm* **-flüsse** **1** influx. **2** influence. **—reich** *adj* influential.

einförmig ('ainfœrmiç) *adj* **1** uniform. **2** monotonous.

einfügen ('ainfy:gən) *vt* **1** insert. **2** join. **sich einfügen** *vr* adapt, fit in.

Einfuhr ('ainfu:r) *nf* **-en** import, importation. **¨—en** ('ainfy:rən) *vt* **1** bring in, introduce. **2** import. **3** install. **¨—er** ('ainfy:rər) *nm* **—** importer. **¨—ung** ('ainfy:ruŋ) *nf* **-en** introduction. **—zoll** *nm* import duty.

Eingang ('aingaŋ) *nm* **¨-e** **1** entrance. **2** arrival, receipt (of a letter, etc.). **3** introduction, beginning.

eingebildet ('aingəbildət) *adj* **1** imaginary. **2** conceited.

eingeboren ('aingəbo:rən) *adj* **1** native. **2** innate. **—e(r)** *nm* native.

Eingebung ('ainge:buŋ) *nf* **-en** inspiration.

eingehen* ('ainge:ən) *vi* **1** go or walk in(to), enter. **2** cease. **3** shrink, wither. **4** die. *vt* conclude (agreement, etc.). **ein Risiko eingehen** run a risk.

eingenommen ('aingənɔmən) *adj* biased, prejudiced.

Eingeweide ('aingəvaidə) *n neu pl* intestines, bowels.

eingießen* ('aingi:sən) *vt* pour in or out.

eingreifen* ('aingraifən) *vi* **1** intervene, interfere. **2** catch.

einhalten* ('ainhaltən) *vt* **1** observe, respect (conditions). **2** restrain. *vi* stop.

einhändigen ('ainhεndigən) *vt* deliver, hand over.

einheimisch ('ainhaimiʃ) *adj* native.

Einheit ('ainhait) *nf* **-en** **1** unit. **2** unity. **—lich** *adj* uniform.

einholen ('ainho:lən) *vt* **1** gather (in). **2** shop. **3** catch up.

einig ('ainiç) *adj* united, agreed. **—e** ('ainigə) *pron,adj* a few, some. **—en** *vt* unite. **sich —en** *vr* agree. **—ermaßen** (ainigər'ma:sən) *adv* to a certain extent, somewhat. **—keit** ('ainiçkait) *nf* unity, concord. **—ung** ('ainiguŋ) *nf* **-en** **1** unification. **2** agreement.

einkassieren ('ainkasi:rən) *vt* cash.

Einkauf ('ainkauf) *nm* **¨-e** purchase. **—en** *vt* buy. **einkaufen gehen** go shopping. **¨—er** ('ainkɔyfər) *nm* **—** purchaser. **—spreis** *nm* wholesale or trade price.

einkehren ('ainke:rən) *vi* stop or stay overnight.

Einklang ('ainklaŋ) *nm* unison, harmony.

einkommen* ('ainkɔmən) *vi* **1** come in. **2** apply. *n neu* **—** income, revenue. **—steuer** *nf* income tax.

einkreisen ('ainkraizən) *vt* encircle.

Einkünfte ('ainkynftə) *nf pl* revenue, income.

einlad/en* ('ainla:dən) *vt* **1** invite. **2** load. **—ung** *nf* **-en** **1** invitation. **2** loading.

Einlage ('ainla:gə) *nf* **-n** **1** insert, enclosure. **2** deposit, investment. **3** *med* arch-support. **4** *cul* meat or vegetables, etc., added to soup. **—rn** *vt* store up.

Ein/laß ('ainlas) *nm* **-lässe** entrance, admission. **—lassen*** *vt* admit, put or let in. **sich —lassen*** *vr* engage in.

einlaufen* ('ainlaufən) *vi* **1** enter, arrive. **2** shrink.

einleg/en ('ainle:gən) *vt* **1** lay or put in, inlay. **2** insert, enclose. **3** deposit. **4** preserve, pickle. **—er** *nm* — depositor.

einleit/en ('ainlaitən) *vt* **1** introduce. **2** begin. **—ung** *nf* **-en** introduction.

einlösen ('ainlœzən) *vt comm* redeem.

einmachen ('ainmaxən) *vt* preserve, pickle (food).

einmal ('ainma:l) *adv* **1** once, one time. **2** formerly, sometime. **noch einmal** once again. **—eins** *n neu* multiplication table. **—ig** *adj* unique.

Einmarsch ('ainmarʃ) *nm* **¨-e** marching in, entry. **—ieren** (ainmar'ʃi:rən) *vi* march in.

sich einmischen ('ainmiʃən) *vr* interfere.

einmünden ('ainmyndən) *vi* **1** flow into. **2** join, run into.

Ein/nahme ('ainna:mə) *nf* **-n 1** income, revenue. **2** takings. **—nehmen*** ('ainne:mən) *vt* **1** take in (food etc.). **2** receive. **3** influence.

Einöde ('ainœ:də) *nf* **-n 1** desert. **2** isolated place.

einordnen ('ainɔrdnən) *vt* **1** arrange, order. **2** file. **3** *mot* get in lane.

einpacken ('ainpakən) *vt* pack or wrap up. *vi* pack or give up.

einprägen ('ainprɛ:gən) *vt* impress, imprint.

einrahmen ('ainra:mən) *vt* frame.

einräumen ('ainrɔymən) *vt* **1** give up, vacate. **2** clear away. **3** concede, admit.

einreden ('ainre:dən) *vt* persuade. *vi* interrupt.

einreichen ('ainraiçən) *vt* hand in, submit.

einreihen ('ainraiən) *vt* **1** arrange, order. **2** insert. **3** enrol.

Einreise ('ainraizə) *nf* **-n** entry (into a country). **—n** *vi* enter (a country).

einricht/en ('ainriçtən) *vt* **1** arrange. **2** establish, set up. **3** fit out, furnish. **—ung** *nf* **-en 1** arrangement. **2** institution. **3** furnishing, fittings.

einrücken ('ainrykən) *vi* enter. *vt* insert.

eins (ains) *nf* **-en 1** one. **2** ace. *pron* see **ein.**

einsam ('ainza:m) *adj* lonely. **—keit** *nf* loneliness, solitude.

Einsatz ('ainzats) *nm* **1** insertion, putting in. **2** stake, deposit. **3** employment, engagement.

einschalten ('ainʃaltən) *vt* **1** insert. **2** switch on. **3** tune in.

einschiffen ('ainʃifən) *vt* load onto a ship.

einschlafen* ('ainʃla:fən) *vi* fall asleep.

Einschlag ('ainʃla:k) *nm* **1** impact. **2** jacket (of a book). **3** touch, hint. **4** woof, weft. **—en*** ('ainʃla:gən) *vt* **1** drive in. **2** strike. **3** wrap. *vi* shake hands (on a deal).

einschließ/en* ('ainʃli:sən) *vt*

1 lock up or in, confine. **2** include. **—lich** *adj* inclusive of.
einschränk/en ('ainʃrɛŋkən) *vt* **1** restrict, confine. **2** curb. **—ung** *nf* **-en** **1** restriction. **2** reduction.
Einschreib/ebrief ('ainʃraibəbri:f) *nm* registered letter. **—en*** *vt* **1** write in. **2** take down. **3** register. **—ung** *nf* **-en** registration.
einschüchtern ('ainʃyçtərn) *vt* intimidate.
einsehen* ('ainze:ən) *vt* **1** understand. **2** look into.
einseitig ('ainzaitiç) *adj* one-sided. **—keit** *nf* bias, one-sidedness.
einsetz/en ('ainzɛtsən) *vt* **1** set or put in. **2** insert. **3** institute. **4** employ. *vi* begin. **—ung** *nf* **-en** **1** putting in. **2** institution. **3** appointment.
Einsicht ('ainziçt) *nf* **-en** **1** insight, understanding. **2** judgment. **3** inspection.
Einsiedler ('ainzi:dlər) *nm* — hermit, recluse.
einspannen ('ainʃpanən) *vt* **1** harness. **2** stretch. **3** clamp.
einsperren ('ainʃpɛrən) *vt* lock up, imprison.
einspritzen ('ainʃpritsən) *vt* inject.
Einspruch ('ainʃprux) *nm* objection, protest. **—srecht** *n neu* veto.
einst (ainst) *adv* **1** once. **2** some day.
einsteigen* ('ainʃtaigən) *vi* get or climb in.
einstell/en ('ainʃtɛlən) *vt* **1** put in. **2** stop, cease, shut down. **3** employ. **4** strike. **5** adjust, tune in. **—ung** *nf* **-en** **1** attitude. **2** adjustment. **3** stoppage, suspension. **4** appointment, taking on.
einstig ('ainstiç) *adj* former.
einstimm/en ('ainʃtimən) *vi* **1** agree. **2** join in. **—ig** *adj* unanimous, in unison. **—igkeit** *nf* unanimity, unison.
einstmalig ('ainstma:liç) *adj* former.
einstoßen* ('ainʃto:sən) *vt* **1** push in. **2** knock down.
einströmen ('ainʃtrœ:mən) *vi* stream or flock in, pour in.
einstufen ('ainʃtu:fən) *vt* grade, classify.
einstürmen ('ainʃtyrmən) *vi* **1** rush in. **2** assault.
Einsturz ('ainʃturts) *nm* **1** collapse. **2** fall. **¨—en** ('ainʃtyrtsən) *vi* fall in. *vt* demolish.
einstweil/en ('ainstvailən) *adv* **1** meanwhile. **2** for now. **—ig** *adj* temporary.
eintägig ('aintɛ:giç) *adj* one-day.
Eintausch ('aintauʃ) *nm* **-e** exchange. **—en** *vt* barter, exchange.
Einteilung ('aintailuŋ) *nf* **-en** **1** division. **2** classification.
eintönig ('aintœ:niç) *adj* monotonous. **—keit** *nf* monotony.
Eintopf ('aintɔpf) *nm* stew, casserole.
Eintracht ('aintraxt) *nf* harmony, unity.
Eintrag ('aintra:k) *nm* **¨-e** **1** *comm* registration, entry. **2** damage, detriment. **—en*** ('aintra:gən) *vt* **1** bring in, yield. **2** register, enter.
eintreten* ('aintre:tən) *vi* **1**

step or come in. **2** happen. **3** intercede. *vt* kick in.
Eintritt ('aintrit) *nm* **1** entry. **2** beginning. **—skarte** *nf* admission ticket.
einüben ('ainyːbən) *vt* **1** practise. **2** train.
einverleiben ('ainfɛrlaibən) *vt* **1** incorporate. **2** annex.
einverstanden ('ainfɛrʃtandən) *adj* **1** agreed. **2** agreeable.
Einwand ('ainvant) *nm* **¨-e** **1** objection. **2** pretext. **—frei** *adj* faultless.
Einwander/er ('ainvandərər) *nm* **—** immigrant. **—n** *vi* immigrate. **—ung** *nf* **-en** immigration.
einwärts ('ainvɛrts) *adv* inward(s).
einwechseln ('ainvɛksəln) *vt* (ex)change.
einweichen* ('ainvaiçən) *vt* soak, steep.
einweih/en ('ainvaiən) *vt* **1** inaugurate. **2** consecrate. **3** initiate. **—ung** *nf* **-en** **1** inauguration. **2** consecration. **3** initiation.
Einwendung ('ainvɛnduŋ) *nf* **-en** objection.
einwickel/n ('ainvikəln) *vt* **1** wrap (up). **2** entangle, implicate (someone). **—papier** *n neu* wrapping paper.
einwillig/en ('ainviligən) *vi* agree, consent. **—ung** *nf* **-en** consent.
Einwirkung ('ainvirkuŋ) *nf* **-en** **1** influence. **2** effect.
Einwohner ('ainvoːnər) *nm* **—** inhabitant.
Einzahl ('aintsaːl) *nf gram* singular. **—en** *vt* pay in. **—ung** *nf* **-en** **1** payment. **2** deposit.
Einzel/fall ('aintsəlfal) *nm* individual case. **—gänger** *nm* **—** outsider, loner. **—heit** *nf* **-en** detail, item. **—person** *nf* individual.
einziehen* ('aintsiːən) *vt* **1** draw in. **2** collect. **3** call up. **4** seize. *vi* **1** move in. **2** enter.
einzig ('aintsiç) *adj* single, sole, unique. **—artig** *adj* unique, singular.
Einzug ('aintsuːk) *nm* entry.
Eis (ais) *n neu* **-e** **1** ice. **2** ice cream. **—bahn** *nf* skating rink. **—bär** *nm* polar bear. **—bein** *n neu* knuckle of pork. **—berg** *nm* iceberg. **—ig** *adj* icy. **—kalt** *adj* ice-cold. **—schrank** *nm* refrigerator. **—zapfen** *nm* icicle. **—zeit** *nf* ice age.
Eisen ('aizən) *n neu* iron. **—bahn** *nf* **1** railway. **2** train. **—bahnwagen** *nm* railway carriage. **—beton** *nm* reinforced concrete. **—warenhändler** *nm* ironmonger.
eisern ('aizərn) *adj* **1** iron. **2** hard, inflexible. **Eiserner Vorhang** *nm* Iron Curtain.
eitel ('aitəl) *adj* **1** vain, conceited. **2** frivolous. **3** idle. **—keit** *nf* vanity.
Eiter ('aitər) *nm* pus. **—n** *vi* suppurate.
Eiweiß ('aivais) *n neu* **-e** egg white, albumen.
Ekel ('eːkəl) *nm* aversion, disgust. **—haft** *adj* loathsome, repulsive. **sich —n** *vr* feel disgust or loathing.
elastisch (e'laːstiʃ) *adj* elastic.

Elefant (ele'fant) *nm* **-en** elephant.

elegant (ele'gant) *adj* elegant.

elektr/ifizieren (elɛktrifi'tsiːrən) *vt* electrify (railway). **—iker** (e'lɛktrikər) *nm* — electrician. **—isch** (e'lɛktriʃ) *adj* electric(al). **—isieren** (elɛktri'ziːrən) *vt* electrify. **—izität** (elɛktritsi'tɛːt) *nf* electricity.

Elektrode (elɛk'troːdə) *nf* **-n** electrode.

Elektromagnet (e'lɛktromagneːt) *nm* — electromagnet. **—isch** (elɛktromag'neːtiʃ) *adj* electromagnetic.

Elektron (e'lɛktrɔn) *n neu* **-en** electron. **—isch** *adj* electronic.

Element (ele'mɛnt) *n neu* **-e 1** element. **2** battery, cell. **—ar** (elemɛn'taːr) *adj* elementary, elemental.

elend ('eːlɛnt) *adj* miserable. *n neu* **1** misery. **2** poverty. **—sviertel** *n neu* slum(s).

elf (ɛlf) *adj,nf* eleven. **—te** *adj* eleventh.

Elf (ɛlf) *nm* **-en** *also* **Elfe** *nf* **-n** elf, fairy.

Elfenbein ('ɛlfənbain) *n neu* ivory.

Elite (e'liːtə) *nf* **-n** elite.

Ellbogen ('ɛlboːgən) *nm* — elbow.

Ellipse (ɛ'lipsə) *nf* **-n** ellipse.

El/saß ('ɛlzas) *n neu* Alsace. **—sässich** *adj* Alsatian. **—sässer** *nm* — Alsatian.

Elster ('ɛlstər) *nf* **-n** magpie.

elter/lich ('ɛltərliç) *adj* parental. **—n** *n pl* parents.

Email (e'maːj) *n neu* **-s** enamel.

Emigr/ant (emi'grant) *nm* **-en 1** emigrant. **2** refugee. **—ieren** (emi'griːrən) *vi* emigrate.

empfahl (ɛm'pfaːl) *v* see **empfehlen.**

Empfang (ɛm'pfaŋ) *nm* **¨-e** reception, welcome. **in Empfang nehmen** receive. **—en*** *vt* receive. *vi* conceive. **¨—er** ('ɛm'pfɛŋər) *nm* — receiver. **¨—lich** (ɛm'pfɛŋliç) *adj* susceptible, impressionable.

empfehl/en* (ɛm'pfɛːlən) *vt* recommend, advise. **sich empfehlen** *vr* take one's leave. **—ung** *nf* **-en** recommendation.

empfind/en* (ɛm'pfindən) *vt* feel, sense. **—lich** (ɛm'pfinliç) *adj* **1** sensitive. **2** grievous, severe. **—lichkeit** *nf* sensitivity, touchiness. **—ung** *nf* **-en 1** perception. **2** feeling. **3** sentiment.

empfohlen (ɛm'pfoːlən) *v* see **empfehlen.** *adj* recommended.

empor (ɛm'poːr) *adv* up(wards). **¨—en** (ɛm'pœːrən) *vt* **1** rouse. **2** shock. **sich ¨—en** *vr* revolt. **¨—end** (ɛm'pœːrənt) *adj* revolting. **—kommen*** *vi* rise. **—kömmling** (ɛm'poːrkœmliŋ) *nm* **-e** upstart. **¨—ung** (ɛm'pœːruŋ) *nf* **-en 1** indignation. **2** rebellion.

emsig ('ɛmziç) *adj* busy, industrious.

End/e ('ɛndə) *n neu* **-n** end. **am Ende** in the end. **zu dem Ende** to that purpose. **zu Ende** over. **—en** *vi,vt also* **—igen** end, stop, finish. **—gültig** ('ɛntgyːltiç) *adj* final, definitive. **—lich** ('ɛntliç) *adj* **1** final. **2** finite. *adv* at last. **—los** ('ɛntlo:s) *adj* endless. **—punkt** ('ɛntpuŋkt) *nm* end point, extremity. **—spiel** ('ɛntʃpi:l) *n neu sport* final. **—station** ('ɛntstatsio:n) *nf* **-en** terminus. **—ung** *nf* **-en** ending.

Energi/e (enɛr'gi:) *nf* **-n** energy. **—sch** (e'nɛrgiʃ) *adj* energetic.

eng (ɛŋ) *adj* **1** narrow. **2** tight. **3** close. **—e** *nf* **-n** **1** narrowness. **2** defile, straits. **—herzig** *adj* petty. **—paß** *nm* **1** narrow pass. **2** bottleneck. **—stirnig** *adj* narrow-minded.

Engel ('ɛŋəl) *nm* — angel. **—gleich** *adj also* **—haft** angelic.

Eng/land ('ɛŋlant) *n neu* England. **—länder** ('ɛŋlɛndər) *nm* — Englishman. **—länderin** *nf* **-nen** Englishwoman. **—lisch** *adj, n neu* English (language).

en gros (ã'gro:) *adv* wholesale.

Enkel ('ɛŋkəl) *nm* — grandson, grandchild. **—in** *nf* **-nen** granddaughter. **—kind** *n neu* grandchild.

enorm (e'nɔrm) *adj* enormous.

entart/en (ɛnt'artən) *vi* degenerate. **—ung** *nf* degeneration, degeneracy.

entbehrlich (ɛnt'be:rliç) *adj* superfluous.

entbinden* (ɛnt'bindən) *vt* **1** untie, release. **2** *med* deliver.

entblößen (ɛnt'blœ:sən) *vt* **1** uncover, bare. **2** denude, deprive.

entdeck/en (ɛnt'dɛkən) *vt* discover, disclose, invent. **—er** *nm* — discoverer, explorer. **—ung** *nf* **-en** **1** discovery. **2** disclosure. **3** invention.

Ente ('ɛntə) *nf* **-n** **1** duck. **2** hoax.

entehren (ɛnt'e:rən) *vt* dishonour.

enteign/en (ɛnt'aignən) *vt* expropriate. **—ung** *nf* **-en** expropriation.

enterben (ɛnt'ɛrbən) *vt* disinherit.

entfallen* (ɛnt'falən) *vi* **1** escape the memory of. **2** fall out of. **entfällt** not applicable.

entfalt/en (ɛnt'faltən) *vt* **1** unfold. **2** exhibit, display. **—ung** *nf* **-en** **1** unfolding. **2** display.

entfern/en (ɛnt'fɛrnən) *vt* remove. **sich entfernen** *vr* go away, withdraw. **—t** *adj* distant. **—ung** *nf* **-en** **1** distance. **2** removal, departure.

entfliehen* (ɛnt'fli:ən) *vi* escape, flee.

entfremd/en (ɛnt'frɛmdən) *vt* alienate, antagonize. **—ung** *nf* alienation.

entführ/en (ɛnt'fy:rən) *vt* carry off, abduct, kidnap. **—ung** *nf* **-en** abduction, kidnapping.

entgegen (ɛnt'ge:gən) *prep,adv* **1** contrary (to), against. **2** towards. **—gehen*** *vi* go to meet. **—gesetzt** *adj* opposite, opposed. **—halten*** *vt* **1** hold out (towards). **2** point out. **3** contrast. **—kommen*** *vi* (come to) meet. *n neu* **1** cooperation. **2** kindness. **—laufen*** *vi* **1** run to meet. **2** oppose. **—setzen** *vt* oppose.

—stellen *vt* set against, contrast.

entgeg/nen (ɛnt'geːgnən) *vi* answer. **—nung** *nf* **-en** answer.

entgehen* (ɛnt'geːən) *vi* **1** escape. **2** avoid.

Entgelt (ɛnt'gɛlt) *n neu* **1** compensation. **2** remuneration. **—en*** *vt* **1** pay for. **2** compensate.

entgleisen (ɛnt'glaizən) *vi* run off the rails.

entgräten (ɛnt'grɛːtən) *vt* bone (fish).

enthaaren (ɛnt'haːrən) *vt* remove hair from, depilate.

enthalt/en* (ɛnt'haltən) *vt* contain, include. **sich enthalten** *vr* abstain. **—sam** *adj* abstemious. **—samkeit** *nf* moderation, abstemiousness.

enthaupten (ɛnt'hauptən) *vt* behead.

enthüllen (ɛnt'hylən) *vt* reveal, disclose, unveil.

Enthusiasmus (ɛntuzi'asmus) *nm* enthusiasm.

entkernen (ɛnt'kɛrnən) *vt* stone (fruit, etc.).

entkommen* (ɛnt'kɔmən) *vi* escape.

entkuppeln (ɛnt'kupəln) *vt* **1** disconnect. **2** declutch.

entladen* (ɛnt'laːdən) *vt* **1** unload. **2** (of guns) fire. **sich entladen** *vr* get rid (of).

entlang (ɛnt'laŋ) *adv,prep* along.

entlarven (ɛnt'larfən) *vt* unmask.

entlass/en* (ɛnt'lasən) *vt* dismiss. **—ung** *nf* **-en** dismissal.

entlast/en (ɛnt'lastən) *vt* **1** unload. **2** relieve. **3** clear, exonerate. **—ung** *nf* **1** relief. **2** exoneration. **—sstraße** *nf* bypass.

sich entledigen (ɛnt'leːdigən) *vr* rid oneself of.

entlegen (ɛnt'leːgən) *adj* remote, distant.

entmilitarisieren (ɛntmilitari'ziːrən) *vt* demilitarize.

entmutig/en (ɛnt'muːtigən) *vt* discourage. **—ung** *nf* discouragement.

entnehmen* (ɛnt'neːmən) *vt* **1** take out or away, remove. **2** infer. **3** learn.

entrahmen (ɛn'traːmən) *vt* skim.

entrüst/en (ɛnt'rystən) *vt* anger, provoke. **sich entrüsten** *vr* grow angry. **—et** *adj* indignant, angry. **—ung** *nf* indignation, anger.

entsagen (ɛnt'zaːgən) *vi* give up, renounce.

entschädig/en (ɛnt'ʃɛːdigən) *vt* **1** compensate. **2** indemnify. **—ung** *nf* **-en** **1** compensation. **2** indemnity.

Entscheid (ɛnt'ʃait) *nm* **-en** *also* **Entscheid/ung** (ɛnt'ʃaiduŋ) *nf* **-en** decision, verdict. **—en*** *vt,vi* decide, resolve. **sich —en** *vr* make up one's mind, decide (on). **—end** *adj* decisive.

entschieden (ɛnt'ʃiːdən) *adj* **1** decided. **2** determined. **—heit** *nf* determination.

sich entschließ/en* (ɛnt'ʃliːsən) *vr* decide. **—ung** *nf* **-en** resolution.

entschlossen (ɛnt'ʃlɔsən) *adj* determined. **—heit** *nf* resoluteness, determination.

Entschluß (ɛnt'ʃlus) *nm* **-schlüsse** decision.
entschlüsseln (ɛnt'ʃlysəln) *vt* decode, decipher.
entschuldig/en (ɛnt'ʃuldigən) *vt* **1** pardon. **2** justify. **sich entschuldigen** *vr* apologize. **—ung** *nf* **-en** excuse, apology. **Entschuldigung!** sorry! excuse me!
entsetz/en (ɛnt'zɛtsən) *vt* **1** frighten. **2** relieve. *n neu* terror. **—lich** *adj* terrible, dreadful.
entspann/en (ɛnt'ʃpanən) *vt* **1** release. **2** relax. **sich entspannen** *vr* relax, rest. **—ung** *nf* **1** relaxation. **2** recreation. **3** détente.
entsprechen* (ɛnt'ʃprɛçən) *vi* correspond (to), answer (to).
entspringen* (ɛnt'ʃpriŋən) *vi* **1** rise or spring from. **2** escape.
entstammen (ɛnt'ʃtamən) *vi* descend (from), spring (from).
entsteh/en* (ent'ʃteːən) *vi* arise. **—ung** *nf* **-en** origin.
enttäusch/en (ɛnt'tɔyʃən) *vt* disappoint, disillusion. **—ung** *nf* **-en** disappointment.
entvölkern (ɛnt'fœlkərn) *vt* depopulate.
entwaffnen (ɛnt'vafnən) *vt* disarm.
entwässer/n (ɛnt'vɛsərn) *vt* **1** drain. **2** dehydrate. **—ung** *nf* **1** drainage. **2** dehydration.
entweder (ɛnt'veːdər) *conj* **entweder...oder** either...or.
entweichen* (ɛnt'vaiçən) *vi* **1** flee. **2** escape.
entweihen (ɛnt'vaiən) *vt* desecrate.
entwerf/en* (ɛnt'vɛrfən) *vt* **1** design, plan. **2** sketch, draw up. **—er** *nm* **—** designer, planner.
entwert/en (ent'vɛrtən) *vt* **1** devalue. **2** cancel (postage stamps, etc.). **—ung** *nf* **-en 1** devaluation. **2** cancellation.
entwick/eln (ɛnt'vikəln) *vt* **1** develop. **2** explain. **3** unfold. **—ler** *nm* **—** developer. **—lung** *nf* **-en 1** development. **2** exposition. **—lungsländer** *n neu pl* developing countries.
entwirren (ɛnt'virən) *vt* unravel.
entwischen (ɛnt'viʃən) *vi* escape, slip away.
entwürdigen (ɛnt'wyrdigən) *vt* degrade.
Entwurf (ɛnt'vurf) *nm* **¨-e** plan, draft, outline.
entwurzeln (ɛnt'vurtsəln) *vt* uproot.
entziehen* (ɛnt'tsiːən) *vt* withdraw, take away. **sich entziehen** *vr* evade, shun.
entziffern (ɛnt'tsifərn) *vt* decipher.
entzück/en (ɛnt'tsykən) *vt* charm, delight. *n neu* **—** delight. **—end** *adj* charming, delightful.
entzünd/bar (ɛnt'tsyntbaːr) *adj* inflammable. **—en** (ɛnt 'tsyndən) *vt* **1** inflame. **2** ignite. **—ung** (ɛnt'tsynduŋ) *nf* **-en 1** inflammation. **2** ignition.
entzwei (ɛnt'tsvai) *adj* in two, broken.
Enzyklopäd/ie (ɛntsyklopɛ'diː) *nf* **-n** encyclopedia. **-isch** (ɛntsyklo'pɛːdiʃ) *adj* encyclopedic.

Enzym (ɛn'tsym) *n neu* **-e** enzyme.
Epidem/ie (epide'miː) *nf* **-n** epidemic. **—isch** (epi'deːmiʃ) *adj* epidemic.
Epik ('eːpik) *nf* epic poetry.
Epilepsie (epilɛp'siː) *nf* epilepsy.
Episode (epi'zoːdə) *nf* **-n** episode.
Epos ('eːpɔs) *n neu* **Epen** epic.
er (eːr, er) *pron 3rd pers s* he.
erachten (ɛr'axtən) *vt* think, deem. *n neu* — opinion. **meines Erachtens** in my opinion.
Erbarm/en (ɛr'barmən) *n neu* pity, mercy. **sich erbarmen** *vr* have pity. ¨**—lich** (ɛr 'bɛrmliç) *adj* pitiful. **—ungslos** *adj* merciless.
erbauen (ɛr'bauən) *vt* construct, build.
Erb/e ('ɛrbə) *n neu* **-n** inheritance. *nm* **-n** heir. **—en** ('ɛrbən) *vt* inherit. **—feind** ('ɛrpfaint) *nm* traditional enemy, sworn enemy. **—folge** ('ɛrpfɔlgə) *nf* hereditary succession. **—in** ('ɛrbin) *nf* **-nen** heiress. **—sünde** *nf* original sin. **—lich** ('ɛrpliç) *adj* hereditary. **—schaft** ('ɛrpʃaft) *nf* **-en** inheritance. **—stück** ('ɛrpʃtyk) *n neu* heirloom.
erbittern (ɛr'bitərn) *vt* embitter.
erblassen (ɛr'blasən) *vi also* **erbleichen*** **1** grow pale. **2** die.
erblinden (ɛr'blindən) *vi* grow or go blind.
Erbse ('ɛrpsə) *nf* **-n** pea.
Erd/beben ('eːrtbeːbən) *n neu* — earthquake. **—beere** *nf* strawberry. **—boden** *nm* soil, ground. **—e** ('eːrdə) *nf* **-n 1** earth, world. **2** ground. **3** soil. **auf der Erde** on earth. **zu ebener Erde** at ground level. **—en** ('eːrdən) *vt sci, tech* earth. **—geschoß** *n neu* ground floor. **—kreis** *nm* globe. **—kunde** *nf* geography. **—nuß** *nf* peanut. **—öl** *n neu* petroleum. **—teil** *nm* continent.
erdenk/en* (ɛr'dɛŋkən) *vt* **1** invent, think up. **2** imagine. **—lich** *adj* conceivable.
Erdichtung (ɛr'diçtuŋ) *nf* **-en** figment, fiction.
erdrosseln (ɛr'drɔsəln) *vt* strangle, throttle.
sich ereign/en (ɛr'aignən) *vr* happen. **—is** *n neu* **-se** event.
erfahr/en* (ɛr'faːrən) *vt* **1** experience. **2** learn. *adj* experienced. **—ung** *nf* **-en** experience.
erfassen (ɛr'fasən) *vt* **1** grasp. **2** include. **3** understand.
erfind/en* (ɛr'findən) *vt* **1** invent. **2** find out. **—er** *nm* — inventor. **—erisch** *adj* inventive. **—ung** *nf* **-en** invention, discovery.
Erfolg (ɛr'fɔlk) *nm* **-e 1** success. **2** result. **—en** (ɛr 'fɔlgən) *vi* follow, ensue. **—los** *adj* unsuccessful. **—reich** *adj* successful.
erforder/lich (ɛr'fɔrdərliç) *adj* necessary, required. **—n** *vt* call for, necessitate, require. **—nis** *n neu* **-se** requisite, requirement.
erforsch/en (ɛr'fɔrʃən) *vt* **1** investigate. **2** explore. **—er** *nm* — **1** investigator. **2** explorer.

—ung *nf* **-en** **1** investigation. **2** exploration.
erfreu/en (ɛr'frɔyən) *vt* delight. **sich erfreuen** *vr* **1** enjoy. **2** be pleased. **—lich** *adj* delightful, pleasing.
erfrieren (ɛr'friːrən) *vi* freeze to death.
erfrisch/en (ɛr'friʃən) *vt* refresh. **—ung** *nf* **-en** refreshment. **—ungsraum** *nm* snack bar.
erfüllen (ɛr'fylən) *vt* **1** fill (up). **2** fulfil.
ergänz/en (ɛr'gɛntsən) *vt* **1** complete. **2** supplement. **3** replenish. **—ung** *nf* **-en** completion.
ergeb/en* (ɛr'geːbən) *vt* **1** yield, produce. **2** show, prove. **sich ergeben** *vr* surrender, yield. **sich ergeben aus** follow from. *adj* **1** devoted. **2** addicted. **—enheit** *nf* **-en** **1** devotion. **2** submission. **3** resignation. **—nis** (ɛr'geːpnis) *n neu* **-se** result. **—nislos** *adj* without result, vain. **—ung** *nf* **-en** **1** surrender. **2** resignation.
ergehen* (ɛr'geːən) *vi* be published or issued. **sich ergehen** *vr* **1** (take a) walk. **2** indulge.
ergiebig (ɛr'giːbiç) *adj* productive, fertile.
ergreifen* (ɛr'graifən) *vt* **1** seize. **2** take up.
erhaben (ɛr'haːbən) *adj* **1** raised. **2** sublime. **3** noble.
erhalt/en* (ɛr'haltən) *vt* **1** receive. **2** maintain, support. **—ung** *nf* **1** maintenance. **2** preservation.
erheb/en* (ɛr'heːbən) *vt* **1** raise (up). **2** demand. **3** levy. **4** praise. **sich erheben** *vr* **1** rise up. **2** rebel. **—lich** (ɛr'heːpliç) *adj* considerable.
erheitern (ɛr'haitərn) *vt* cheer (up).
erhöh/en (ɛr'hœːən) *vt* raise, increase. **—ung** *nf* **-en** **1** rise, increase. **2** elevation.
sich erhol/en (ɛr'hoːlən) *vr* **1** recover. **2** recuperate. **—ung** *nf* **-en** **1** recovery. **2** recreation.
erinner/n (ɛr'inərn) *vt* remind. **sich erinnern** *vr* remember. **—ung** *nf* **-en** **1** memory. **2** reminder.
erkält/en (ɛr'kɛltən) *vt* cool, chill. **sich erkälten** *vr* catch cold. **—ung** *nf* **-en** cold.
erkämpfen (ɛr'kɛmpfən) *vt* win or gain by fighting.
erkenn/bar (ɛr'kɛnbaːr) *adj* recognizable. **—en*** *vt* **1** recognize. **2** perceive. **3** realize. **—ung** *nf* **-en** recognition. **—ungswort** *n neu* password.
Erkenntnis[1] (ɛr'kɛntnis) *n neu* **-se** judgment.
Erkenntnis[2] (ɛr'kɛntnis) *nf* **-se** recognition, realization.
erklär/en (ɛr'klɛːrən) *vt* **1** explain. **2** declare. **—ung** *nf* **-en** **1** explanation. **2** declaration.
erkrank/en (ɛr'kraŋkən) *vi* fall ill. **—ung** *nf* **-en** illness.
sich erkund/igen (ɛr'kundigən) *vr* inquire. **—igung** *nf* **-en** enquiry.
erlahmen (ɛr'laːmən) *vi* become tired or lame.
erlangen (ɛr'laŋən) *vt* attain, obtain.
Erlaß (ɛr'las) *nm* **-lasse** **1** de-

cree, ordinance. **2** remission.
erlassen* (ɛr'lasən) *vt* **1** proclaim. **2** issue. **3** remit, pardon.
erlaub/en (ɛr'laubən) *vt* permit, allow. **—nis** (ɛr'laupnis) *nf* **-se** permission.
erläutern (ɛr'lɔytərn) *vt* explain, illustrate.
erleb/en (ɛr'leːbən) *vt* experience, live to see. **—nis** (ɛr 'leːpnis) *n neu* **-se** **1** experience. **2** adventure.
erledig/en (ɛr'leːdigən) *vt* **1** settle. **2** finish (off). **3** deal with. **—ung** *nf* **-en** **1** completion. **2** execution.
erlegen (ɛr'leːgən) *vt* kill, shoot.
erleichter/n (ɛr'laiçtərn) *vt* lighten, relieve, ease. **—ung** *nf* relief.
erlernen (ɛr'lɛrnən) *vt* learn.
erleucht/en (ɛr'lɔyçtən) *vt* **1** illuminate. **2** enlighten. **—ung** *nf* **-en** **1** illumination. **2** enlightenment.
erliegen* (ɛr'liːgən) *vi* be defeated, succumb.
Erlös (ɛr'lœːs) *nm* **-e** proceeds. **-en** (ɛr'lœːzən) *vt* **1** release. **2** save. **—er** (ɛr'lœːzər) *nm* **—** **1** liberator, deliverer. **2** saviour. **—ung** (ɛr'lœːzuŋ) *nf* **1** deliverance. **2** salvation.
ermächtig/en (ɛr'mɛçtigən) *vt* empower. **—ung** *nf* **-en** authorization.
ermäßig/en (ɛr'mɛːsigən) *vt* reduce, moderate. **—ung** *nf* **-en** reduction, moderation.
ermitteln (ɛr'mitəln) *vt* find out, ascertain.
ermöglichen (ɛr'mœːgliçən) *vt* render possible, enable.
ermorden (ɛr'mɔrdən) *vt* murder, assassinate.
ermüden (ɛr'myːdən) *vi,vt* tire.
ermuntern (ɛr'muntərn) *vt* rouse, cheer (up).
ermutig/en (ɛr'muːtigən) *vt* encourage, hearten. **—ung** *nf* **-en** encouragement.
ernähr/en (ɛr'nɛːrən) *vt* **1** feed. **2** maintain, support. **—er** *nm* **—** breadwinner. **—ung** *nf* **1** nourishment. **2** nutrition. **3** maintenance.
ernenn/en* (ɛr'nɛnən) *vt* **1** appoint. **2** nominate. **—ung** *nf* **-en** **1** appointment. **2** nomination.
erneuer/n (ɛr'nɔyərn) *vt* **1** renew. **2** restore. **—ung** *nf* **-en** **1** renewal. **2** restoration.
erniedrigen (ɛr'niːdrigən) *vt* **1** lower. **2** degrade, humiliate.
ernst (ɛrnst) *adj* serious, earnest. *nm* **1** seriousness. **2** severity. **—haft** *adj* earnest. **—lich** *adj* serious, earnest.
Ernte ('ɛrntə) *nf* **-n** harvest, crop. **—dankfest** *n neu* harvest festival. **—n** *vt,vi* harvest, gather in.
ernüchtern (ɛr'nyçtərn) *vt* **1** sober (up). **2** disillusion.
Erober/er (ɛr'oːbərər) *nm* **—** conqueror. **—n** *vt* conquer. **—ung** *nf* **-en** conquest.
eröffn/en (ɛr'œfnən) *vt* **1** open. **2** inaugurate, begin. **—ung** *nf* **-en** **1** opening. **2** inauguration, beginning.
erörter/n (ɛr'œrtərn) *vt* discuss. **—ung** *nf* **-en** discussion.
Eroti/k (e'roːtik) *nf* eroticism. **—sch** *adj* erotic.
erpress/en (ɛr'prɛsən) *vt*

blackmail. **—er** *nm* — blackmailer. **—ung** *nf* **-en** blackmail.
erproben (ɛr'pro:bən) *vt* try, test.
erraten* (ɛr'ra:tən) *vt* **1** guess. **2** solve.
erreg/bar (ɛr're:kba:r) *adj* excitable. **—en** (ɛr're:gən) *vt* **1** excite. **2** irritate. **—ung** (ɛr 're:guŋ) *nf* **-en** excitement.
erreich/bar (ɛr'raiçba:r) *adj* attainable. **—en** *vt* reach, obtain.
erricht/en (ɛr'riçtən) *vt* **1** erect. **2** establish. **—ung** *nf* **-en** **1** erection. **2** establishment.
erröten (ɛr'rœ:tən) *vi* blush.
Errungenschaft (ɛr'ruŋənʃaft) *nf* **-en** **1** acquisition. **2** achievement.
Ersatz (ɛr'zats) *nm* **1** substitute, replacement. **2** reserve. **3** compensation. **—reifen** *nm* spare tyre. **—teil** *n neu* spare (part).
erschaff/en* (ɛr'ʃafən) *vt* create.
erschein/en* (ɛr'ʃainən) *vi* appear. **—ung** *nf* **-en** **1** appearance. **2** vision. **3** phenomenon.
erschlagen* (ɛr'ʃla:gən) *vt* kill.
erschließen* (ɛr'ʃli:sən) *vt* **1** open (up). **2** infer.
erschöpf/en (ɛr'ʃœpfən) *vt* exhaust. **—ung** *nf* exhaustion.
erschrak (ɛr'ʃra:k) *v* see **erschrecken.**
erschrecken* (ɛr'ʃrɛkən) *vt* frighten. *vi* be frightened.
erschrocken (ɛr'ʃrɔkən) *v* see **erschrecken.** *adj* frightened.
erschüttern (ɛr'ʃytərn) *vt* shake, upset.
ersehen* (ɛr'ze:ən) *vt* **1** see, perceive. **2** observe.
ersetzen (ɛr'zɛtsən) *vt* replace, make good.
ersichtlich (ɛr'ziçtliç) *adj* evident.
erspar/en (ɛr'ʃpa:rən) *vt* spare, save. **—nis** *nf* **-se** **1** saving. **2** savings.
erst (ɛrst) *adj* first. *adv* **1** at first. **2** only, not till. **der erste beste** the first that comes, anyone or anything. **erste Hilfe** first aid.
erstarren (ɛr'ʃtarən) *vi* grow stiff or rigid.
erstatten (ɛr'ʃtatən) *vt* **1** compensate, repay. **2** return. **3** give.
Erstaufführung ('ɛrstauffy:ruŋ) *nf* **-en** premiere, first night.
erstaun/en (ɛr'ʃtauən) *vt* astonish. *vi* be astonished. *n neu* amazement. **-lich** *adj* astonishing.
erstens ('ɛ:rstəns) *adv* first(ly).
ersticken (ɛr'ʃtikən) *vt,vi* suffocate, choke.
erstklassig ('e:rstklasiç) *adj* first-class, prime.
ersuchen (ɛr'zu:xən) *vt* request.
ertappen (ɛr'tapən) *vt* **1** surprise. **2** catch. **auf frischer Tat ertappt** caught red-handed.
Ertrag (ɛr'tra:k) *nm* **¨-e** yield, return, profit. **—en*** (ɛr 'tra:gən) *vt* bear, endure. **¨—lich** (ɛr'trɛ:kliç) *adj* bearable, tolerable.
ertränken (ɛr'trɛŋkən) *vt* drown.

ertrinken* (ɛr'triŋkən) *vi* drown.

erwachen (ɛr'vaxən) *vi* awake.

erwachsen* (ɛr'vaksən) *vi* **1** grow up. **2** arise (from). *adj* adult. **—e(r)** *nm* adult.

erwäg/en* (ɛr'vɛːgən) *vt* **1** consider. **2** weigh. **—ung** *nf* **—en** consideration.

erwähnen (ɛr'vɛːnən) *vt* mention.

erwärmen (ɛr'vɛrmən) *vt* warm.

erwart/en (ɛr'vartən) *vt* **1** await. **2** expect. **—ung** *nf* **-en** expectation.

erwecken (ɛr'vɛkən) *vt* awaken, (a)rouse.

erweisen* (ɛr'vaizən) *vt* **1** render. **2** prove.

erweiter/n (ɛr'vaitərn) *vt* enlarge. **—ung** *nf* **-en** extension.

Erwerb (ɛr'vɛrp) *nm* **-e 1** acquisition. **2** gain, profit. **3** livelihood. **—en*** (ɛr'vɛrbən) *vt* **1** acquire. **2** earn. **—stätig** *adj* (gainfully) employed.

erwider/n (ɛr'viːdərn) *vt* respond (to), reply (to). **—ung** *nf* **-en** reply, response.

erwischen (ɛr'viʃən) *vt* **1** catch. **2** surprise.

erwünscht (ɛr'vynʃt) *adj* desired.

erwürgen (ɛr'vyrgən) *vt* strangle.

Erz (eːrts) *n neu* **-e** ore.

erzähl/en (ɛr'tsɛːlən) *vt* tell, report, relate. **—er** *nm* **— 1** narrator, story-teller. **2** reporter. **—ung** *nf* **-en 1** narrative, story. **2** report.

Erz/bischof ('ɛrtsbiʃɔf) *nm* archbishop. **—engel** *nm* archangel. **—feind** *nm* archenemy.

erzeug/en (ɛr'tsɔygən) *vt* **1** beget, breed. **2** produce, manufacture. **—nis** (ɛr'tsɔyknis) *n neu* **-se 1** product. **2** produce. **—ung** *nf* **1** procreation. **2** production.

erzieh/en* (ɛr'tsiːən) *vt* **1** bring up. **2** educate. **—ung** *nf* education.

erzwingen* (ɛr'tsviŋən) *vt* obtain by force.

es (ɛs) *pron neu s* it.

Esche ('ɛʃə) *nf* **-n** ash (tree).

Esel ('eːzəl) *nm* **—** ass, donkey.

esoterisch (ezo'teːriʃ) *adj* esoteric.

essen* ('ɛsən) *vt,vi* eat. *n neu* **— 1** food. **2** meal.

eß/bar ('ɛsbar) *adj* edible. **—löffel** *nm* tablespoon. **—tisch** *nm* dining table. **—zimmer** *n neu* dining room.

Essenz (ɛ'sɛnts) *nf* **-en** essence.

Essig ('ɛsiç) *nm* **-e** vinegar.

etablieren (eta'bliːrən) *vt* establish.

Etage (e'taːʒə) *nf* **-n** floor, storey.

Etat (e'taː) *nm* **-s 1** budget. **2** balance-sheet.

Eth/ik ('eːtik) *nf* ethics. **—isch** *adj* ethical.

ethnisch ('eːtniʃ) *adj* ethnic.

Etikett (eti'kɛt) *n neu* **-e** (price) label, tag.

Etikette (eti'kɛtə) *nf* **-en** etiquette.

etliche ('ɛtliçə) *pron,adj pl* some, a few.

Etui (ɛt'viː) *n neu* **-s** small case or box.

etwa ('ɛtva) *adv* **1** about, nearly **2** perhaps. **—ig** *adj* possible.

etwas ('ɛtvas) *pron invar* some(thing), anything. *adj* some. *adv* somewhat. *n neu* a something.

Etymologie (etymolo'giː) *nf* **-n** etymology.

euch (ɔyç) *pron 2nd pers pl fam* you, to you.

euer ('ɔyər) *poss adj 2nd pers pl fam* your. *poss pron 2nd pers pl also* **eure, der —e,** *or* **der —ige** yours. **—ethalben** *adv also* **—etwegen** *or* **—etwillen** for your sake, on your account.

Eukalyptus (ɔyka'lyptus) *nm* **-ten** eucalyptus.

Eule ('ɔylə) *nf* **-n** owl.

Eunuch (ɔy'nuːx) *nm* **-en** eunuch.

Europa (ɔy'roːpa) *n neu* Europe. **¨—er** (ɔyro'pɛːər) *nm* — European. **¨—isch** (ɔyro'pɛːiʃ) *adj* European.

evakuieren (evaku'iːrən) *vt* **1** empty. **2** evacuate.

evangel/isch (evan'geːliʃ) *adj* **1** Protestant. **2** evangelical. **—ist** (evange'list) *nm* **-en** evangelist. **—ium** (evan'geːlium) *n neu* **-ien** gospel.

eventuell (evɛntu'ɛl) *adj* possible.

ewig ('eːviç) *adj* eternal. **—keit** *nf* eternity.

exakt (ɛ'ksakt) *adj* exact, accurate.

Examen (ɛ'ksaːmən) *n neu* — examination.

Exekutionskommando (ɛksekutsi'oːnskɔmando) *n neu* **—s** firing squad.

Exempel (ɛ'ksɛmpəl) *n neu* — example.

Exemplar (ɛksɛm'plaːr) *n neu* **-e** **1** specimen. **2** copy. **—isch** *adj* model, exemplary.

Exil (e'ksiːl) *n neu* **-e** exile.

Exist/enz (ɛksis'tɛnts) *nf* **-en** **1** existence. **2** livelihood. **—ieren** (ɛksis'tiːrən) *vi* exist.

exklusiv (ɛksklu'ziːf) *adj* exclusive.

exotisch (ɛ'ksoːtiʃ) *adj* exotic.

Expedition (ɛkspeditsi'oːn) *nf* **-en** **1** expedition. **2** dispatching.

Experiment (ɛksperi'mɛnt) *n neu* **-e** experiment. **—ell** (ɛksperimɛn'tɛl) *adj* experimental. **—ieren** (ɛksperimɛn'tiːrən) *vi* experiment.

explodieren (ɛksplo'diːrən) *vi* explode.

explosiv (ɛksplo'ziːf) *adj* explosive.

Export (ɛks'pɔrt) *nm* **-e** export. **—ieren** (ɛkspɔr'tiːrən) *vt* export.

extrem (ɛks'treːm) *adj* extreme.

exzentrisch (ɛks'tsɛntriʃ) *adj* eccentric.

F

Fabel ('faːbəl) *nf* **-n** **1** fable. **2** plot, story. **—haft** *adj* fabulous.

Fabrik (fa'briːk) *nf* **-en** factory. **—at** (fabri'kaːt) *n neu* **-e** manufacture, product.

fabrizieren (fabri'tsiːrən) *vt* manufacture.

Fach (fax) *n neu* **¨-er** **1** compartment, pigeon-hole. **2** drawer. **3** subject, field. **4** department. **5** speciality. **—arbeiter** *nm* skilled worker.

—arzt *nm med* specialist. **—berater** *nm* technical consultant. **—bildung** *nf* technical education. **—lehrer** *nm* specialist teacher. **—lich** *adj* **1** professional. **2** technical. **—mann** *nm* ¨ **-er** *or* **-leute** specialist, expert. **—schule** *nf* technical school. **—werk** *n neu* **1** half-timbered work. **2** framework.

fächeln ('fɛçəln) *vt* fan.

Fackel ('fakəl) *nf* **-n** torch.

fade ('faːdə) *adj* **1** dull. **2** insipid. **3** stale.

Faden ('faːdən) *nm* ¨— thread, string.

Fagott (fa'gɔt) *n neu* **-e** bassoon.

fähig ('fɛːiç) *adj* **1** able, capable. **2** competent. **—keit** *nf* **—en** ability, capacity, capability.

fahl (faːl) *adj* pale, faded.

fahnd/en ('faːndən) *vi* **nach jemandem fahnden** search for someone. **—ung** *nf* **-en** search.

Fahne ('faːnə) *nf* **-n** flag, standard.

fahr/en* ('faːrən) *vt,vi* **1** go. **2** drive. **3** travel. **4** sail. **—bahn** *nf* roadway, carriageway. **—bar** *adj* **1** passable, negotiable, navigable. **2** mobile. **—er** *nm* — driver. **—gast** *nm* passenger. **—geld** *n neu* fare. **—karte** *nf* ticket. **—lässig** *adj* negligent. **—plan** *nm* timetable. **—rad** *n neu* bicycle. **—schein** *nm* ticket. **—schule** *nf* driving school. **—stuhl** *nm* lift, elevator. **—zeug** *n neu* **1** vehicle. **2** vessel.

Fähre ('fɛːrə) *nf* **-n** ferry.

Fahrt (faːrt) *nf* **-en** **1** drive. **2** ride. **3** journey. **4** voyage. **—enschreiber** *nm* tachograph.

Fährte ('fɛːrtə) *nf* **-n** **1** track, trail. **2** scent.

Faktur (fak'tuːr) *nf* **-en** invoice. **—ieren** (faktu'riːrən) *vt* invoice.

Fakultät (fakul'tɛːt) *nf* **-en** (university) faculty.

Falke ('falkə) *nm* **-n** falcon.

Fall (fal) *nm* ¨**-e** **1** fall, downfall. **2** case. **auf jeden Fall** in any case. **für diesen Fall, in diesem Fall** in this case. **—s** *conj* in case, if.

Fall/e ('falə) *nf* **-n** **1** trap, snare. **2** catch, latch. **—en*** *vi* fall. **es fällt mir leicht/schwer** I find it easy/hard. **fallen lassen** lower, drop, let fall. **—schirm** *nm* **-e** parachute. **—schirmjäger** *nm* paratrooper. **—schirmspringer** *nm* parachutist. **—sucht** *nf* epilepsy.

fäll/en ('fɛlən) *vt* **1** fell (a tree, etc.). **2** pass (judgment).

fällig ('fɛliç) *adj* payable, due.

falsch (falʃ) *adj* **1** false. **2** wrong. ¨**—en** ('fɛlʃən) *vt* **1** falsify, forge. **2** adulterate. ¨**—er** ('fɛlʃər) *nm* — falsifier, forger. **—heit** *nf* **-en** **1** falsehood. **2** deceitfulness.

Falt/e ('faltə) *nf* **-n** fold, crease, wrinkle. **—en** *vt* fold, crease, wrinkle.

familiär (famil'jɛːr) *adj* familiar.

Familie (fa'miːliə) *nf* **-n** family. **—nname** *nm* surname.

Fanati/ker (fa'naːtikər) *nm* — fanatic. **—sch** *adj* fanatic(al).

Fanfare (fan'faːrə) *nf* **-n** fanfare.

fand (fant) *v* see **finden.**

Fang (faŋ) *nm* **¨-e** **1** catching, capture. **2** catch, prey. **3** *pl* fangs. **4** *pl* claws. **—en*** *vt* catch, capture. **sich —en** *vr* become entangled or ensnared.

Farb/e ('farbə) *nf* **-n** **1** colour. **2** paint, dye. **3** *game* suit. **Farbe bekennen** show one's true colours. **¨—en** ('fɛrbən) *vt* dye, colour. **—enblind** ('farbənblint) *adj* colour-blind. **¨—er** ('fɛrbər) *nm* — dyer. **—film** *nm* colour film. **—ig** ('farbiç) *adj* coloured. **—ige(r)** ('farbigə) *nm* **-n** coloured man. **—los** *adj* colourless. **—stoff** *nm* pigment, dye.

Fasan (fa'zaːn) *nm* **-e** pheasant.

Fasching ('faʃiŋ) *nm* **-e** (Shrovetide) carnival.

Faschis/mus (fa'ʃismus) *nm* fascism. **—t** *nm* **-en** fascist.

Faser ('faːzər) *nf* **-n** fibre, strand.

Faß (fas) *n neu* **Fässer** barrel, cask, drum.

fass/en ('fasən) *vt* **1** take hold of, seize, catch. **2** contain, hold. **3** comprehend, grasp. **sich fassen** *vr* **1** pull oneself together. **2** control oneself. **sich kurz fassen** express oneself briefly, be brief. **—ung** *nf* **-en** **1** composure, self control. **2** setting (of gems). **3** wording, version.

fast (fast) *adv* almost, nearly.

fast/en ('fastən) *vi* fast. **—nacht** *nf* **1** the night of Shrove Tuesday. **2** carnival.

fatal (fa'taːl) *adj* **1** unfortunate. **2** disastrous. **—ist** (fata'list) *nm* **-en** fatalist.

faul (faul) *adj* **1** lazy. **2** rotten. **—enzen** *vi* idle, loaf about. **—heit** *nf* laziness. **¨—nis** ('fɔylnis) *nf* decay, rottenness.

Faust (faust) *nf* **¨-e** fist.

Februar ('feːbruaːr) *nm* February.

fechten* ('fɛçtən) *vi* fence, fight.

Feder ('feːdər) *nf* **-n** **1** feather. **2** pen(-nib). **3** spring. **—ball** *nm* shuttlecock. **—n** *vi* **1** moult. **2** spring, be elastic. **—ung** *nf* **1** (spring) suspension. **2** elasticity.

Fee (feː) *nf* **-n** fairy.

fegen ('feːgən) *vt,vi* sweep.

fehl/bar ('feːlbaːr) *adj* fallible. **—betrag** *nm* loss, deficit. **—druck** *nm* misprint. **—en** *vi* **1** be absent. **2** be wanting. **3** fail. **4** err. **—er** *nm* — **1** fault, failing. **2** mistake. **—geburt** *nf* miscarriage. **—schlag** *nm* **1** failure, error. **2** miss. **—schlagen*** *vi* **1** fail. **2** miss. **—schuß** *nm* bad shot, miss. **—zünden** *vi* misfire.

Feier ('faiər) *nf* **-n** celebration, festival. **—abend** *nm* **1** evening leisure. **2** (at work) finishing-time, knocking-off time. **—lich** *adj* **1** ceremonial. **2** festive. **3** solemn, dignified. **—lichkeit** *nf* **1** ceremony, pomp. **2** solemnity. **—n** *vt,vi* celebrate. *vi* rest (from work). **—tag** *nm* holiday.

feig/e ('faigə) *adj* cowardly.

—heit ('faikhait) *nf* cowardice. **—ling** ('faikliŋ) *nm* **-e** coward.
Feige ('faigə) *nf* **-n** fig.
feil (fail) *adj* **1** for sale. **2** venal.
Feil/e ('failə) *nf* **-n** file. **—en** *vt,vi* **1** file. **2** polish.
feilschen ('failʃən) *vi* barter, haggle.
fein (fain) *adj* **1** fine. **2** delicate. **3** elegant. **4** distinguished. **5** acute. **6** sensitive. **—fühlig** *adj* sensitive, delicate. **—schmecker** *nm* — gourmet. **—sinnig** *adj* subtle, sensitive.
Feind (faint) *nm* **-e** enemy. **—schaft** *nf* enmity. **—selig** *adj* hostile.
Feld (fɛlt) *n neu* **-er** field. **—bett** *n neu* camp bed. **—herr** *nm* commander, general. **—messer** *nm* surveyor. **—stecher** *nm* — field-glasses. **—wache** *nf mil* picket. **—webel** *nm* — sergeant. **—zug** *nm* **1** campaign. **2** expedition.
Fell (fɛl) *n neu* **-e** **1** hide, skin. **2** fur.
Fels (fɛls) *nm* **-en** *also* **Felsen** ('fɛlzən) *nm* — **1** cliff. **2** rock.
Fenster ('fɛnstər) *n neu* — window. **—brett** *n neu* window-sill. **—laden** *nm* shutter. **—scheibe** *nf* window-pane.
Ferien ('feːrjən) *n pl* holidays.
Ferkel ('fɛrkəl) *n neu* — piglet.
fern (fɛrn) *adj* distant, far. **Ferne(r) Osten** *nm* Far East. **—e** *nf* **-n** distance, remoteness. **—er** *adj* farther. *adv* moreover. **—erhin** *adv* **1** in the future. **2** moreover. **—gespräch** *n neu* trunk call, long-distance call. **—meldung** *nf* **1** telecommunication. **2** remote signalling. **—rohr** *n neu* telescope. **—sehapparat** *nm* television set. **—sehen*** *vi* watch television. *n neu* television. **—sprecher** *nm* telephone. **—sprechzelle** *nf* call-box.
Ferse ('fɛrzə) *nf* **-n** heel.
fertig ('fɛrtiç) *adj* **1** ready. **2** finished. **—en** ('fɛrtigən) *vt* manufacture, produce. **—keit** *nf* dexterity, proficiency. **—machen** *vt* finish.
Fessel ('fɛsəl) *nf* **-n** fetter, bond. **—n** *vt* **1** fetter. **2** captivate.
fest (fɛst) *adj* **1** solid, hard. **2** stable, fixed. **—halten*** *vt* **1** seize. **2** hold tight. **3** record. **4** portray. *vi* hold fast, stick to (something). **—igen** *vt* make firm or stable. **—land** *n neu* mainland. **—machen** *vt* make fast, fasten. **—stehen*** *vi* stand firm. **—stellen** *vt* establish, ascertain. **—ung** *nf* **-en** fortress.
Fest (fɛst) *n neu* **-e** festival, feast. **—lich** *adj* festive. **—lichkeit** *nf* **-en** festivity.
fett (fɛt) *adj* **1** fat. **2** fertile. **3** greasy. *n neu* **-e** fat, grease. **—arm** *adj* low in fat. **—en** *vt* oil. **—ig** *adj* **1** fatty. **2** oily.
Fetzen ('fɛtsən) *nm* — **1** scrap, piece. **2** rag.
feucht (fɔyçt) *adj* damp, moist. **—igkeit** *nf* damp, moisture, humidity.
Feuer ('fɔyər) *n neu* — fire. **—fest** *adj* fireproof. **—löscher** *nm* fire-extinguisher. **—melder** *nm* fire-alarm. **—n** *vi* **1** fire (on). **2** make a fire. **—wehr** *nf* fire brigade.

—werk *n neu* fireworks. **—zeug** *n neu* cigarette-lighter.
Feuilleton ('fœjətõ) *n neu* **-s** cultural section of a newspaper.
feurig ('fɔyriç) *adj* fiery.
Fibel ('fiːbəl) *nf* **-n 1** primer, spelling-book. **2** brooch.
Fichte ('fiçtə) *nf* **-n** pine, spruce.
ficken ('fikən) *vi* move to and fro. *vt* rub. *vi,vt tab* copulate.
Fieber ('fiːbər) *n neu* — fever. **—haft** *adj* feverish.
Fied/el ('fiːdəl) *nf* **-n** fiddle, violin. **—eln** *vt* fiddle. **—ler** *nm* — fiddler.
fiel (fiːl) *v* see **fallen.**
Figur (fi'guːr) *nf* **-en 1** figure. **2** chessman.
Filiale (fili'aːlə) *nf* **-n** *comm* branch.
Film (film) *nm* **-e** film. **—star** *nm* **-s** film star.
Filt/er ('filtər) *nm,neu* — filter. **—ern** *vt also* **—rieren** (fil'triːrən) filter, strain.
Filz (filts) *nm* **-e 1** felt. **2** miser, skin-flint. **—en** *vt* **1** line with felt. **2** *sl* search, frisk. **—ig** *adj* **1** felt. **2** miserly.
Finanz (fi'nants) *nf* **-en** finance. **—iell** (finan'tsjɛl) *adj* financial. **—ieren** (finan'tsiːrən) *vt* finance. **—mann** *nm* financier.
find/en* ('findən) *vt* **1** find. **2** think, consider. **—igkeit** *nf* ingenuity.
fing (fiŋ) *v* see **fangen.**
Finger ('fiŋər) *nm* — finger. **—abdruck** *nm* fingerprint. **—hut** *nm* thimble. **—nagel** *nm* fingernail. **—spitze** *nf* fingertip.
Fink (fiŋk) *nm* **-en** finch.
Finn/e ('finə) *nm* **-n** *also* **Finn/länder** *nm* — Finn. **—isch** *adj* Finnish. *n neu* Finnish (language). **—land** *n neu* Finland.
finster ('finstər) *adj* **1** dark, gloomy. **2** ominous, sinister. **—nis** *nf* **-se 1** darkness, gloom. **2** *sci* eclipse.
Firma ('firmə) *nf* **Firmen** firm.
Firnis ('firnis) *nm* **-e** varnish. **—sen** *vt* varnish.
Fisch (fiʃ) *nm* **-e 1** fish. **2** *pl* Pisces. **—en** *vt* fish (for), catch. **—er** *nm* — fisherman. **—erei** (fiʃə'rai) *nf* **-en** fishery, fishing. **—heber** *nm* fish-slice.
fix (fiks) *adj* **1** fixed. **2** quick, agile. **—ieren** (fi'ksiːrən) *vt* **1** fix. **2** stare at.
flach (flax) *adj* **1** flat. **2** shallow. **¨—e** ('flɛçə) *nf* **-n 1** surface. **2** plain. **3** expanse. **4** (surface) area. **¨—enmaß** ('flɛçənmas) *n neu* square measure. **—land** *n neu* plain, lowland.
Flachs (flaks) *nm* flax.
flackern ('flakərn) *vi* (of light, flame) flicker.
Flagge ('flagə) *nf* **-n** flag, standard.
Flamme ('flamə) *nf* **-n** flame. **—n** *vi* flame, blaze.
Flanell (fla'nɛl) *n neu* **-e** flannel.
Flank/e ('flaŋkə) *nf* **-n** flank. **—ieren** (flaŋ'kiːrən) *vt* (out)flank.
Flasche ('flaʃə) *nf* **-n** bottle, flask. **—nöffner** *nm* bottle opener.
flattern ('flatərn) *vi* flutter.

flau (flau) *adj* **1** weak. **2** slack. **3** dull. **4** stale.

Flaute ('flautə) *nf* **-n** lull, calm.

Flechte ('flɛçtə) *nf* **-n** **1** plait, braid. **2** lichen. **—n*** *vt* braid, plait.

Fleck (flɛk) *nm* **-e** **1** spot. **2** blemish. **3** patch. **—en** *vt,vi* spot, stain. *nm* **—** **1** spot. **2** blemish. **3** market town. **—ig** *adj* spotted, stained.

Fledermaus ('fleːdərmaus) *nf* **¨-e** bat.

flehen ('fleːən) *vi* implore.

Fleisch (flaiʃ) *n neu* **-e** meat, flesh. **—er** *nm* **—** *also* **—hauer** butcher. **—erei** (flaiʃə'rai) *nf* **-en** butcher's shop. **—fressend** *adj* carnivorous. **—ig** *adj* fleshy, meaty. **—lich** *adj* **1** carnal, of the flesh. **2** sensual.

Fleiß (flais) *nm* industry, diligence. **—ig** *adj* industrious, diligent, hard-working.

flicken ('flikən) *vt* mend, patch. *nm* **—** patch.

Fliege ('fliːgə) *nf* **-n** fly. **—nklappe** *nf* fly-swatter.

flieg/en* ('fliːgən) *vi* fly. **—er** *nm* **—** flier, aviator.

fliehen* ('fliːən) *vi,vt* flee (from).

Fließ/band ('fliːsbant) *n neu* **1** conveyor belt. **2** production line. **—en*** *vi* flow. **—end** *adj* **1** flowing. **2** fluent.

flimmern ('flimərn) *vi* glimmer, twinkle.

flink (fliŋk) *adj* nimble, quick. **—heit** *nf* nimbleness, quickness.

Flinte ('flintə) *nf* **-n** **1** rifle. **2** shotgun.

Flitterwochen ('flitərvɔxən) *nf pl* honeymoon.

Flocke ('flɔkə) *nf* **-n** **1** flake. **2** flock, tuft.

flog (floːk) *v* see **fliegen.**

Floh (floː) *nm* **¨-e** flea.

Florenz (flo'rɛnts) *n neu* Florence.

floß (flɔs) *v* see **fließen.**

Floß (floːs) *n neu* **¨-e** **1** raft. **2** (fishing) float.

Flosse ('flɔsə) *nf* **-n** fin, flipper.

Flöt/e ('flœːtə) *nf* **-n** flute. **—ist** *nm* **-en** flautist.

flott (flɔt) *adj* **1** afloat. **2** brisk. **3** stylish, gay. **—e** ('flɔtə) *nf* **-n** fleet, navy.

Fluch (fluːx) *nm* **¨-e** curse, swear word. **—en** *vi* curse, swear.

Flucht (fluxt) *nf* **-en** **1** flight, escape. **2** row, line. **¨—ig** ('flyçtiç) *adj* **1** fleeing. **2** fugitive. **3** brief, fleeting. **4** superficial. **¨—ling** ('flyçtliŋ) *nm* **-e** **1** refugee. **2** fugitive.

Flug (fluːk) *nm* **¨-e** **1** flight, flying. **2** flock, flight. **—abwehr** *nf* anti-aircraft defence. **—blatt** *n neu* leaflet, pamphlet. **—deck** *n neu* flight deck. **—hafen** *nm* airport. **—post** *nf* airmail. **—zeug** *n neu* aeroplane, aircraft.

Flügel ('flyːgəl) *nm* **—** wing.

Fluor ('fluːɔr) *n neu* fluorine.

Flur (fluːr) *nm* **-e** (entrance) hall. *nf* **-en** field, meadowland.

Fluß (flus) *nm* **Flüsse** **1** river, stream. **2** flow.

flüssig ('flysiç) *adj* liquid, flu-

id. **—keit** *nf* **-en 1** liquid, fluid. **2** liquidity.
flüstern ('flystərn) *vi,vt* whisper.
Flut (fluːt) *nf* **-en 1** flood. **2** (high) tide.
Fohlen ('foːlən) *n neu* — foal.
Föhn (fœːn) *nm* **-e** warm south wind.
Folg/e ('fɔlgə) *nf* **-n 1** succession, series. **2** consequence, result. **—en** *vi* **1** follow. **2** ensue. **3** obey. **—endermaßen** *adv* in the following manner. **—ern** *vt* infer, conclude. **—erung** *nf* **-en** inference, conclusion. **—lich** ('fɔlkliç) *conj* consequently.
Folter ('fɔltər) *nf* **-n** torture. **—n** *vt* torture.
Fön (fœːn) *nm Tdmk* **-e** hair-dryer.
Fonds (fɔ̃) *nm comm* fund(s), stock.
forcieren (fɔr'siːrən) *vt* **1** force, take by force. **2** overdo.
forder/n ('fɔrdərn) *vt* **1** demand, claim. **2** challenge, summon. **—ung** *nf* **-en 1** demand. **2** challenge.
förder/n ('fœːrdərn) *vt* **1** further, promote. **2** transport, convey. **—lich** *adj* **1** conducive. **2** advantageous. **—ung** *nf* **-en** advancement.
Forelle (fo'rɛlə) *nf* **-n** trout.
Form (fɔrm) *nf* **-en 1** form, shape. **2** mould. **—el** *nf* **-n** formula. **—ell** (for'mɛl) *adj also* **¨—lich** ('fœrmliç) formal. **—en** *vt* form, mould. **—ieren** (fɔr'miːrən) *vt* **1** form. **2** arrange. **sich —ieren** *vr mil* fall in. **—ular** (fɔrmu'laːr) *n neu* **-e 1** form. **2** schedule. **—ulieren** (fɔrmu'liːrən) *vt* formulate.
forsch/en ('fɔrʃən) *vi* **1** search. **2** investigate. **3** research. **—er** *nm* — **1** researcher. **2** investigator. **3** explorer. **—ung** *nf* **-en 1** research. **2** investigation.
Forst (fɔrst) *nm* **-e** forest, wood. **¨—er** ('fœrstər) *nm* — forester.
fort (fɔrt) *adv* **1** away. **2** off. **3** on. **4** forward.
fortan (fɔrt'an) *adv* henceforth.
fortbestehen* ('fɔrtbəʃteːən) *vi* **1** continue (to exist). **2** persist.
Fortbildung ('fɔrtbilduŋ) *nf* further education or training.
fortdauern ('fɔrtdauərn) *vi* continue, last.
fortfahren* ('fɔrtfaːrən) *vi* **1** keep or go on. **2** depart. *vt* **1** remove. **2** drive away.
fortgehen* ('fɔrtgeːən) *vi* go away or on.
fortkommen* ('fɔrtkɔmən) *vi* **1** get away. **2** make progress.
fortlaufend ('fɔrtlaufənt) *adj* continuous.
fortpflanzen ('fɔrtpflantsən) *vt* propagate. **sich fortpflanzen** *vr* multiply, propagate.
fortschreiten* ('fɔrtʃraitən) *vi* **1** proceed. **2** progress. **—d** *adj* **1** advancing. **2** progressive.
Fortschritt ('fɔrtʃrit) *nm* **-e** progress. **—lich** *adj* progressive.
fortsetz/en ('fɔrtzɛtsən) *vt* continue. **—ung** *nf* **-en** continuation.
fortwährend ('fɔrtvɛːrənt) *adj* perpetual, continual.
Fossil (fɔ'siːl) *n neu* **-ien** fossil.

Fötus ('fœtus) *nm* **-usse** foetus.
Fracht (fraxt) *nf* **-en** freight, cargo. **—en** *vt* ship, freight. **—er** *nm* **—** freighter. **—gut** *n neu* freight, goods.
Frack (frak) *nm* **¨-e** dress coat, tails.
Frag/e ('fraːgə) *nf* **-n** question. **—ebogen** *nm* questionnaire. **—en** *vt* ask, question, inquire. **—ezeichen** *n neu* question mark. **—lich** ('fraːkliç) *adj* questionable, doubtful. **—los** ('fraːkloːs) *adv* unquestionably. **—würdig** ('fraːkvyrdiç) *adj* doubtful.
Fragment (frag'mɛnt) *n neu* **-e** fragment.
Fraktion (fraktsi'oːn) *nf* **-en** **1** fraction. **2** parliamentary party.
Fraktur (frak'tuːr) *nf* **-en** **1** fracture. **2** Gothic type or script.
Franken ('fraŋkən) *nm* **—** (Swiss) franc.
frankieren (fraŋ'kiːrən) *vt* frank, stamp.
Frankreich ('fraŋkraiç) *n neu* France.
Franse ('franzə) *nf* **-n** fringe.
Franz/ose (fran'tsoːzə) *nm* **-n** Frenchman. **—ösin** (fran'tsœːzin) *nf* **-nen** Frenchwoman. **—ösisch** (fran'tsœːziʃ) *adj* French. *n neu* French (language).
Fratze ('fratsə) *nf* **-n** grimace. **Fratzen schneiden** pull faces.
Frau (frau) *nf* **-en** woman, wife. **—enarzt** *nm* gynaecologist. **—enzimmer** *n neu* **1** woman, female. **2** slut.
Fräulein ('frɔylain) *n neu* **— 1** young or unmarried woman. **2** Miss.
frech (frɛç) *adj* impudent, cheeky. **—heit** *nf* impudence, cheek.
frei (frai) *adj* **1** free, at liberty, unconstrained. **2** free (of charge). **3** vacant. **freier Grundbesitz** *nm* freehold.
Freibad ('fraibat) *n neu* open-air swimming pool.
Freibrief ('fraibriːf) *nm* charter.
Freie ('fraiə) *n neu* open air. **im Freien** out of doors.
freigebig ('fraigeːbiç) *adj* generous.
Freiheit ('fraihait) *nf* freedom. **—sstrafe** *nf* imprisonment.
Frei/herr ('fraihɛr) *nm* baron. **—herrin** *nf* baroness.
freilassen* ('frailasən) *vt* release.
Freilauf ('frailauf) *nm* freewheel. **im Freilauf fahren** *vi* freewheel.
freilich ('frailiç) *adv* certainly, of course.
freimütig ('fraimyːtiç) *adj* frank, candid.
freisprechen* ('fraiʃprɛçən) *vt* acquit.
Freitag ('fraitaːk) *nm* Friday.
frei/willig ('fraiviliç) *adj* willing, voluntary. **—willige(r)** ('fraiviligə) *nm* volunteer.
Freizeit ('fraitsait) *nf* leisure, spare time.
fremd (frɛmt) *adj* **1** foreign. **2** strange. **—artig** *adj* strange, odd. **—e** ('frɛmdə) *nf* **-n** foreign country. **—e(r)** ('frɛmdə) *nm* **1** foreigner. **2** stranger, alien. **—enführer** ('frɛmdənfyːrər) *nm* guide. **—enverkehr** ('frɛmdən-

fɛrkeːr) *nm* tourism, travel. **—enzimmer** ('frɛmdəntsimər) *n neu* **1** guest-room. **2** room to let. **—sprache** *nf* foreign language. **—wort** *n neu* foreign word.

Frequenz (fre'kvɛnts) *nf* **-en** frequency.

fressen* ('frɛsən) *vt* (of animals) eat.

Freud/e ('frɔydə) *nf* **-n** joy, pleasure. **—ig** *adj* joyful. **—igkeit** *nf* joyfulness.

freuen ('frɔyən) *vt* please. **sich freuen** *vr* be glad. **sich freuen auf** look forward to.

Freund (frɔynt) *nm* **-e** friend, boyfriend. **—in** ('frɔyndin) *nf* **-nen** friend, girlfriend. **—lich** *adj* **1** friendly. **2** kind, pleasant. **—schaft** *nf* **-en** friendship.

Frevel ('freːfəl) *nm* — crime, outrage.

Fried/e(n) ('friːdə) *nm* peace. **—ensstifter** *nm* peace-maker. **—ensvertrag** *nm* peace treaty. **—fertig** ('friːtfɛrtiç) *adj* peaceable. **—hof** ('friːthoːf) *nm* cemetery. **—lich** ('friːtliç) *adj* peaceful, peaceable.

frieren* ('friːrən) *vi,vt* freeze.

Fries (friːs) *nm* **-e** frieze.

frigid (fri'giːt) *adj* frigid. **—ität** (frigidi'tɛːt) *nf* frigidity.

frisch (friʃ) *adj* **1** fresh. **2** cool. **3** new. **—e** *nf* freshness.

Fris/eur (fri'zœːr) *nm* **-e** hairdresser, barber. **—iersalon** (fri'ziːrzal˜ɔ) *nm* hairdresser's salon. **—ur** (fri'zuːr) *nf* **-en** hair style, hairdo.

Frist (frist) *nf* **-en** (period of) time, time-limit. **—los** *adj* without notice.

froh (froː) *adj* happy, glad, merry. **¨—lich** ('frœːliç) *adj* happy, merry. **¨—lichkeit** *nf* joyfulness, mirth. **—sinn** *nm* cheerfulness.

fromm (frɔm) *adj* **1** devout, pious. **2** docile. **¨—eln** ('frœməln) *vi* feign piety. **¨—igkeit** ('frœmiçkait) *nf* piety. **¨—ler** ('frœmlər) *nm* — bigot.

Fronleichnam (froːn'laiçnaːm) *nm rel* Corpus Christi Day.

Front (frɔnt) *nf* **-en** front, facade.

fror (froːr) *v* see **frieren.**

Frosch (frɔʃ) *nm* **¨-e** frog.

Frost (frɔst) *nm* **¨-e** frost, chill. **—ig** *adj* frosty, chilly.

Frucht (fruxt) *nf* **¨-e** fruit. **—bar** *adj* fruitful, fertile. **—barkeit** *nf* fertility. **—los** *adj* fruitless.

früh (fryː) *adj* early. *adv* **1** early. **2** in the morning. **—e** *nf* early hour, morning. **—er** *adj* earlier, former, sooner. **—jahr** *n neu also* **—ling** *nm* **-e** spring. **—reif** *adj* precocious, premature, forward. **—stück** *n neu* breakfast. **—stücken** *vi* breakfast. **—zeitig** *adj* early, premature.

Fuchs (fuks) *nm* **¨-e** fox.

Fug/e ('fuːgə) *nf* **-n** **1** joint. **2** fugue. **¨—en** ('fyːgən) *vt* **1** add. **2** join. **sich ¨—en** *vr* submit, acquiesce.

fühl/en ('fyːlən) *vt* **1** feel, touch. **2** sense. **sich fühlen** *vr* feel. **sich traurig fühlen** feel sad. **—er** *nm* — feeler.

führ/en ('fyːrən) *vt* **1** lead. **2** direct. **3** manage, control, carry on. **4** keep (books). **—er** *nm*

— **1** leader. **2** manager. **3** guide(book). **4** driver. **5** pilot. **—erschein** *nm* driving. licence. **—ung** *nf* **1** direction, control. **2** leadership. **3** administration.

Füll/e ('fylə) *nf* **1** fullness. **2** abundance. **—en** *vt* fill. **—feder** *nf also* **—er** *nm* — fountain pen.

Fundament (funda'mɛnt) *n neu* **-e** foundation.

fünf (fynf) *adj,nf* five. **—te** *adj* fifth. **—zehn** *adj,nf* fifteen. **—zehnte** *adj* fifteenth. **—zig** *adj,nf* fifty. **—zigste** *adj* fiftieth.

fungieren (fuŋ'giːrən) *vi* **fungieren als** act as.

Funk (fuŋk) *nm* radio, wireless. **—eln** *vi* sparkle, twinkle. **—en** *nm* — spark. *vi* spark. *vt* **1** radio. **2** broadcast. **—er** *nm* — radio operator. **—gerät** *n neu* radio (set).

Funktion (fuŋktsi'oːn) *nf* **-en** function. **—är** (fuŋktsio'nɛːr) *nm* **-e** functionary, official. **—ieren** (fuŋktsio'niːrən) *vi* function.

für (fyːr) *prep* **1** for. **2** in place of. **3** in favour of. **4** on behalf of. **für sich 1** for oneself. **2** exceptional. **was für** what sort of. **—sorge** *nf* **1** care. **2** welfare. **—sorger** *nm* — social or welfare worker. **—wahr** *adv* truly, indeed. **—wort** *n neu* pronoun.

Furch/e ('furçə) *nf* **-n 1** furrow. **2** wrinkle. **—en** *vt* furrow.

Furcht (furçt) *nf* fear. **—bar** *adj* frightful, horrible. **¨—en** ('fyrçtən) *vt* fear. **sich ¨—en** *vr* be afraid. **—los** *adj* fearless.

Furnier (fur'niːr) *nm* **-e** veneer.

Fürst (fyrst) *nm* **-en** prince. **—entum** ('fyrstentuːm) *n neu* **¨-er** principality. **—in** *nf* **-nen** princess. **—lich** *adj* princely.

Fuß (fuːs) *nm* **¨-e** foot. **zu Fuß gehen** walk, go on foot. **—ball** *nm* football. **—boden** *nm* floor. **—bremse** *nf* footbrake. **—gänger** ('fuːsgɛŋər) *nm* — pedestrian. **—tritt** *nm* **1** kick. **2** footstep.

Futter ('futər) *n neu* **1** feed, fodder. **2** lining. **¨—n** ('fytərn) *vt* **1** feed. **2** line.

G

gab (gaːp) *v* see **geben.**

Gabe ('gaːbə) *nf* **-n** gift.

Gabel ('gaːbəl) *nf* **-n** fork.

gackern ('gakərn) *vi* cackle.

gähnen ('gɛːnən) *vi* yawn.

galant (ga'lant) *adj* gallant.

Galeere (ga'leːrə) *nf* **-n** galley.

Galerie (galə'riː) *nf* **-n** gallery.

Galgen ('galgən) *nm* — gallows.

Galione (gali'oːnə) *nf* **-n** galleon.

Galopp (ga'lɔp) *nm* **-e** gallop. **—ieren** (galɔ'piːrən) *vi* gallop.

galvanisieren (galvani'ziːrən) *vt* galvanize.

Gang (gaŋ) *nm* **¨-e 1** gait. **2** walking, progress. **3** functioning, operation. **4** corridor, aisle. **5** (of a meal) course. **6** *mot* gear. **im Gang 1** going on. **2** working. **—art** *nf* walk, gait.

Gans (gans) *nf* **¨-e** goose. **¨—ebraten** ('gɛnzəbratən) *nm*

roast goose. ¨**—efüßchen** ('gɛnzəfyːsçən) *n neu pl inf* quotation marks. ¨**—emarsch** ('gɛnzəmarʃ) *nm* single file. ¨**—erich** ('gɛnzəriç) *nm* **-e** gander.
ganz (gants) *adj* whole, all. *adv* **1** quite. **2** wholly, very. **im ganzen** on the whole. **—e(s)** *n neu* whole. ¨**—lich** ('gɛntsliç) *adj* whole, entire.
gar (gaːr) *adj* **1** ready, finished. **2** *cul* tender, done. *adv* **1** quite. **2** about. **3** very. **gar nicht** not at all.
Garantie (garan'tiː) *nf* **-n** guarantee. **—ren** *vt* guarantee.
Garde ('gardə) *nf* **-n** guard(s).
Garderobe (gardə'roːbə) *nf* **-n** **1** cloakroom. **2** wardrobe.
Gardine (gar'diːnə) *nf* **-n** curtain.
gär/en* ('gɛːrən) *vi* ferment. **—ung** *nf* fermentation.
garnieren (gar'niːrən) *vt* **1** garnish. **2** trim.
Garnison (garni'zoːn) *nf* **-en** garrison.
Gart/en ('gartən) *nm* ¨**—** garden. ¨**—ner** ('gɛrtnər) *nm* **—** gardener.
Gas (gaːs) *n neu* **-e** gas. **—herd** *nm* gas cooker or stove. **—ofen** *nm* gas stove or oven, gas fire.
Gasse ('gasə) *nf* **-n** alley, lane.
Gast (gast) *nm* ¨**-e** **1** guest, visitor. **2** stranger. **3** customer. **—arbeiter** *nm* immigrant manual worker. ¨**—ebuch** ('gɛstəbuːx) *n neu* visitors' book. **—freundlich** *adj* hospitable. **—freundschaft** *nf* hospitality. **—geber** *nm* **—** host. **—geberin** *nf* **-nen** hostess. **—haus** *n neu* **1** inn. **2** restaurant. **—hof** *nm* **1** hotel. **2** restaurant. **—stätte** *nf* restaurant, cafe.
Gatt/e ('gatə) *nm* **-n** husband, spouse. **—in** *nf* **-nen** wife, spouse.
Gattung ('gatuŋ) *nf* **-en** **1** kind, sort. **2** species.
gaukeln ('gaukəln) *vi* **1** juggle. **2** conjure.
Gaul (gaul) *nm* **-e** horse, nag.
Gaumen ('gaumən) *nm* **—** palate.
Gauner ('gaunər) *nm* **—** swindler, rogue.
Gaze ('gaːzə) *nf* **-n** gauze.
Gazelle (ga'tsɛlə) *nf* **-n** gazelle.
Gebäck (gə'bɛk) *n neu* **-e** cakes, pastries.
Gebärde (gə'bɛːrdə) *nf* **-n** gesture.
gebär/en* (gə'bɛːrən) *vt* give birth to, bear. **—mutter** *nf* womb, uterus.
Gebäude (gə'bɔydə) *n neu* **—** building.
geben* ('geːbən) *vt* give, present. **sich geben** *vr* **1** act, behave. **2** pass, abate. **es gibt** there is or are. **von sich geben** utter.
Gebet (gə'beːt) *n neu* **-e** prayer.
gebeten (gə'beːtən) *v* see **bitten.**
Gebiet (gə'biːt) *n neu* **-e** territory, district, area. **—en*** *vt,vi* command. **—er** *nm* **—** commander, master. **—erisch** *adj* masterful, imperious.
Gebilde (gə'bildə) *n neu* **—** **1** creation, work. **2** form.
gebildet (gə'bildət) *adj* educated.
Gebirg/e (gə'birgə) *n neu* **—**

mountains, mountain range. **—ig** *adj* mountainous.

Gebiß (gə'bis) *n neu* **-bisse 1** teeth. **2** denture. **3** bit.

gebissen (gə'bisən) *v* see **beißen.**

Gebläse (gə'blɛːzə) *n neu* **—** bellows.

geblieben (gə'bliːbən) *v* see **bleiben.**

Gebot (gə'boːt) *n neu* **-e** command(ment).

gebracht (gə'braxt) *v* see **bringen.**

Gebrauch (gə'braux) *nm* **¨-e 1** use. **2** custom. **—en** *vt* use. **¨—lich** (gə'brɔyçliç) *adj* customary, usual, normal. **—sanweisung** *nf* directions for use. **—t** *adj* used, second-hand.

gebrechlich (gə'brɛçliç) *adj* fragile, weak.

gebrochen (gə'brɔxən) *v* see **brechen.**

Gebrüder (gə'brydər) *nm pl comm* brothers, bros.

Gebühr (gə'byːr) *nf* **-en 1** fee, charge. **2** tax, duty. **—lich** *adj* proper, appropriate.

gebunden (gə'bundən) *adj* **1** bound. **2** connected.

Geburt (gə'burt) *nf* **-en** birth. **—enbeschränkung** *nf also* **—enkontrolle** birth control. **—sort** *nm* birthplace. **—sschein** *nm also* **—surkunde** *nf* birth certificate. **—stag** *nm* birthday.

Gebüsch (gə'byʃ) *n neu* **-e** undergrowth, (clump of) bushes.

gedacht (gə'daxt) *v* see **denken.**

Gedächtnis (gə'dɛçtnis) *n neu* **-se** memory, remembrance.

Gedanke (gə'daŋkə) *nm* **-n** thought, idea.

Gedärm (gə'dɛrm) *n neu* **-e** bowels, intestines.

Gedeck (gə'dɛk) *n neu* **-e 1** cover. **2** menu.

gedeih/en* (gə'daiən) *vi* prosper, flourish.

gedenk/en* (gə'dɛŋkən) *vi* **1** remember. **2** mention. **3** intend. **—stätte** *nf* memorial.

Gedicht (gə'diçt) *n neu* **-e** poem.

gediegen (gə'diːgən) *adj* **1** pure. **2** solid, reliable, good-quality.

Gedräng/e (gə'drɛŋə) *n neu* crowd, press.

Geduld (gə'dult) *nf* patience. **—ig** (gə'duldiç) *adj* patient.

geeignet (gə'aignət) *adj* suitable, appropriate.

Gefahr (gə'faːr) *nf* **-en** danger. **¨—den** (gə'fɛːrdən) *vt* endanger. **¨—lich** (gə'fɛːrliç) *adj* dangerous.

Gefährte (gə'fɛːrtə) *nm* **-n** companion.

gefall/en* (gə'falən) *vi* please. **dieses Bild gefällt mir** I like this picture, this picture pleases me. *~n neu* **—** pleasure. *nm* **—** favour. **¨—ig** (gə'fɛliç) *adj* pleasing, agreeable. **¨—igkeit** (gə'fɛliçkait) *nf* **-en 1** kindness. **2** favour. **¨—igst** (gə'fɛliçst) *adv* please.

gefangen (gə'faŋən) *adj* captive. **gefangen nehmen** take prisoner. **—e(r)** *nm* prisoner, captive. **—schaft** *nf* imprisonment, captivity.

Gefängnis (gə'fɛŋnis) *n neu* **-se 1** prison. **2** imprisonment. **—wärter** *nm* warder, jailer.

Gefäß (gə'fɛːs) *n neu* **-e** vessel, container.
Gefecht (gə'fɛçt) *n neu* **-e** **1** fight. **2** action.
geflogen (gə'floːgən) *v* see **fliegen.**
geflossen (gə'flɔsən) *v* see **fließen.**
Geflügel (gə'flyːgəl) *n neu* poultry.
Gefolge (gə'fɔlgə) *n neu* retinue, followers.
gefräßig (gə'frɛːsiç) *adj* gluttonous, greedy.
Gefreite(r) (gə'fraitə) *nm* **1** lance corporal. **2** able seaman.
Gefrierpunkt (gə'friːrpuŋkt) *nm* freezing point.
gefroren (gə'froːrən) *v* see **frieren.**
gefügig (gə'fyːgiç) *adj* pliant, compliant.
Gefühl (gə'fyːl) *n neu* **-e** **1** sense, touch. **2** feeling, emotion.
gefunden (gə'fundən) *v* see **finden.**
gegangen (gə'gaŋən) *v* see **gehen.**
gegebenenfalls (gə'geːbənənfals) *adv* should the occasion or need arise.
gegen ('geːgən) *prep* **1** against. **2** towards. **3** about. **—angriff** *nm* counter-attack. **—einander** (geːgənain'andər) *adv* against one another. **—gewicht** *n neu* counterweight. **—gift** *n neu* antidote. **—satz** *nm* **1** contrast. **2** opposition. **im Gegensatz zu** **1** contrary to. **2** as opposed to. **—seitig** *adj* **1** mutual. **2** reciprocal. **—stand** *nm* object. **—teil** *n neu* **1** contrary. **2** reverse. **im Gegenteil** on the contrary. **—über** (geːgən 'yːbər) *prep,adv* opposite. *n neu* **—** person or object opposite. **—verkehr** *nm* contraflow. **—wart** *nf* **-en** **1** the present (time). **2** presence. **—wärtig** *adj* present, current. **—wehr** *nf* defence.
Gegend ('geːgənt) *nf* **-en** district, area, neighbourhood.
gegessen (gə'gɛsən) *v* see **essen.**
Gegner ('geːgnər) *nm* **—** opponent, enemy.
gegossen (gə'gɔsən) *v* see **gießen.**
gegriffen (gə'grifən) *v* see **greifen.**
gehabt (gə'haːpt) *v* see **haben.**
Gehalt (gə'halt) *n neu* **¨-er** salary. *nm* **-e** content, contents, capacity.
gehässig (gə'hɛsiç) *adj* **1** hateful. **2** spiteful.
geheim (gə'haim) *adj* secret. **—dienst** *nm* secret service. **—nis** *n neu* **-se** secret. **—nisvoll** *adj* mysterious.
gehen* ('geːən) *vi* **1** go, walk. **2** function, work. **es geht** it's all right. **wie geht es Ihnen?** how are you?
Gehilfe (gə'hilfə) *nm* **-n** assistant.
Gehirn (gə'hirn) *n neu* **-e** brain. **—erschütterung** *nf* concussion.
geholfen (gə'hɔlfən) *v* see **helfen.**
Gehör (gə'hœːr) *n neu* hearing.
gehorchen (gə'hɔrçən) *vi* obey.
gehör/en (gə'hœːrən) belong. **es gehört sich** it is proper.

—ig *adj* **1** belonging. **2** suitable, proper.
gehorsam (gə'hoːrzaːm) *adj* obedient. *nm* obedience.
Gehrock ('geːrɔk) *nm* frock coat.
Gehsteig ('geːʃtaik) *nm* **-e** pavement.
Gehwerk ('geːvɛrk) *n neu* clockwork.
Geier ('gaiər) *nm* — vulture.
Geifer ('gaifər) *nm* **1** spittle. **2** foam.
Geige ('gaigə) *nf* **-n** violin, fiddle. **—nspieler** *nm* violinist, fiddler.
Geisel ('gaizəl) *nm* —, *nf* **-n** hostage.
Geist (gaist) *nm* **-er** **1** spirit. **2** mind, intellect. **3** ghost. **—esabwesend** *adj* absent-minded. **—esgestört** *adj also* **—eskrank** insane, mentally ill. **—eswissenschaften** *nf pl* humanities, the Arts. **—ig** *adj* **1** spiritual. **2** intellectual, mental. **3** alcoholic (beverage, etc.). **—lich** *adj* **1** spiritual. **2** clerical. **—liche(r)** *nm* **-n** cleric. **—reich** *adj also* **—voll** **1** witty. **2** ingenious.
Geiz (gaits) *nm* **1** avarice. **2** miserliness. **—hals** *nm* miser. **—ig** *adj* miserly.
gekannt (gə'kant) *v* see **kennen.**
gekünstelt (gə'kynstəlt) *adj* **1** artificial. **2** affected. **3** feigned.
Gelächter (gə'lɛçtər) *n neu* laughter.
geladen (gə'laːdən) *adj* loaded.
Gelage (gə'laːgə) *n neu* — feast, drinking-bout.
Gelände (gə'lɛndə) *n neu* — ground, land.
Geländer (gə'lɛndər) *n neu* — railing, banisters.
gelang *v* see **gelingen.**
gelangen (gə'laŋən) *vi* arrive at, reach.
gelassen (gə'lasən) *adj* calm. **—heit** *nf* calmness, composure.
Gelatine (ʒɛla'tiːnə) *nf* gelatine. **—dynamit** *n neu* gelignite.
geläufig (gə'lɔyfiç) *adj* **1** common. **2** current. **3** familiar. **4** fluent.
gelb (gɛlp) *adj,n neu* yellow. **—sucht** *nf* jaundice.
Geld (gɛlt) *n neu* **-er** money. **—anweisung** *nf* money order. **—mittel** *n neu pl* funds, means. **—schrank** *nm* safe, strong-box. **—strafe** *nf* fine.
Gelee (ʒe'leː) *n neu* **-s** jelly.
gelegen (gə'leːgən) *adj* **1** situated. **2** convenient. **—heit** *nf* **-en** **1** opportunity. **2** occasion. **—tlich** *adj* **1** occasional. **2** incidental.
gelehr/t (gə'leːrt) *adj* learned. **—te(r)** *nm* scholar.
Geleit (gə'lait) *n neu* **-e** retinue, escort. **—en** *vt* escort.
Gelenk (gə'lɛŋk) *n neu* **-e** joint.
gelernt (gə'lɛrnt) *adj* trained, skilled.
Geliebte(r) (gə'liːptə) *nm* sweetheart, lover.
gelinde (gə'lində) *adj* mild, soft.
gelingen* (gə'liŋən) *vi imp* succeed. **es gelingt mir, etwas zu tun** I am successful or I succeed in doing something.
gelitten (gə'litən) *v* see **leiden.**
geloben (gə'loːbən) *vt* vow.

Gelübde (gə'lyptə) *n neu* — vow.

gelogen (gə'lo:gən) *v* see **lügen.**

gelt/en* ('gɛltən) *vi* **1** be valid. **2** be worth. **3** pass for. **4** apply to. **—ung** *nf* **-en 1** value. **2** validity.

gelungen (gə'luŋən) *v* see **gelingen.**

Gemach (gə'max) *n neu* ¨**-er** room, apartment. ¨**—lich** (gə'mɛçliç) *adj* **1** comfortable. **2** leisurely.

Gemahl (gə'ma:l) *nm* **-e** husband, consort. **—in** *nf* **-nen** wife, consort.

Gemälde (gə'mɛ:ldə) *n neu* — picture, painting.

gemäß (gə'mɛ:s) *prep* according to. *adj* conformable, appropriate. **—igt** *adj* moderate.

gemein (gə'main) *adj* **1** common, general. **2** vulgar. **3** mean. **4** nasty. **—e(r)** *nm mil* private. **—gut** *n neu* public property. **—heit** *nf* **-en 1** vulgarity. **2** mean trick. **—hin** *adv* ordinarily, commonly. **—sam** *adj* common, joint. **—schaft** *nf* **-en 1** community. **2** association, union.

Gemeinde (gə'maində) *nf* **-n 1** community. **2** municipality. **3** parish. **4** congregation, communion. **—steuer** *nf* rates.

Gemenge (gə'mɛŋə) *n neu* — **1** mixture. **2** scuffle.

gemessen (gə'mɛsən) *adj* **1** measured, precise. **2** dignified, deliberate.

Gemisch (gə'miʃ) *n neu* **-e** mixture. **—trassig** *adj* multiracial.

gemocht (gə'mɔxt) *v* see **mögen.**

Gemse ('gɛmzə) *nf* **-n** chamois.

Gemurmel (gə'murməl) *n neu* murmuring.

Gemüse (gə'my:zə) *n neu* — vegetable(s). **—händler** *nm* greengrocer.

Gemüt (gə'my:t) *n neu* **-er 1** mind, soul. **2** temperament, disposition. **—lich** *adj* **1** good-natured, genial. **2** comfortable, cosy, agreeable. **—lichkeit** *nf* **1** geniality, kindliness. **2** comfort, cosiness.

Gen (gɛn) *n neu* **-e** gene.

genannt (gə'nant) *v* see **nennen.**

genau (gə'nau) *adj* exact, precise.

genehmig/en (gə'ne:migən) *vt* **1** approve. **2** ratify. **—ung** *nf* **-en 1** approval. **2** permit. **3** ratification.

geneigt (gə'naikt) *adj* inclined or prone (to).

General (gene'ra:l) *nm* **-e** general. **—bevollmächtigte(r)** *nm* **1** chief representative. **2** commissioner. **—direktor** *nm* **1** general manager. **2** managing director. **—probe** *nf* dress rehearsal.

Generation (generatsi'o:n) *nf* **-en** generation.

genesen* (gə'ne:zən) *vi* recover, convalesce.

Genetik (ge'ne:tik) *nf* genetics.

Genf (gɛnf) *n neu* Geneva.

genial (geni'a:l) *adj* brilliant, inspired. **—ität** (geniali'tɛ:t) *nf* genius, brilliance.

Genick (gə'nik) *n neu* **-e** nape of the neck.

Genie (ʒe'ni:) *n neu* **-s** genius.

genieren (ʒe'niːrən) *vt* **1** embarrass. **2** inconvenience. **sich genieren** *vr* feel embarrassed.

genieß/bar (gə'niːsbaːr) *adj* **1** enjoyable. **2** edible. **3** drinkable. **—en*** *vt* **1** enjoy. **2** eat. **3** drink.

Genitalien (geni'taliən) *n pl* genitals.

genommen (gə'nɔmən) *v* see **nehmen.**

genoß (gə'nɔs) *v* see **genießen.**

Genosse (gə'nɔsə) *nm* **-n** comrade, colleague. **—nschaft** *nf* **-en** **1** association. **2** company. **3** cooperative.

genossen (gə'nɔsən) *v* see **genießen.**

genug (gə'nuːk) *adj* enough, sufficient. **¨—e** (gə'nyːgə) *nf* sufficiency, abundance. **¨—en** (gə'nyːgən) *vi* suffice. **¨—end** (gə'nyːgənt) *adj* sufficient. **¨—sam** (gə'nyːkzaːm) *adj* **1** easily satisfied. **2** unassuming. **3** frugal. **—tuung** (gə'nuːktuːuŋ) *nf* **-en** satisfaction.

Genuß (gə'nus) *nm* **-nüsse** **1** enjoyment, pleasure. **2** use. **3** consumption (of food, etc.).

Geograph (geo'graːf) *nm* **-en** geographer. **—ie** (geogra'fiː) *nf* geography. **—isch** *adj* geographic(al).

Geolog/e (geo'loːgə) *nm* **-n** geologist. **—ie** (geolo'giː) *nf* geology. **—isch** *adj* geological.

Geometrie (geome'triː) *nf* **-n** geometry.

Gepäck (gə'pɛk) *n neu* luggage. **—aufbewahrung** *nf* left-luggage office. **—netz** *n neu* luggage rack. **—träger** *nm* porter.

gepfiffen (gə'pfifən) *v* see **pfeifen.**

Gepflogenheit (gə'pfloːgənhait) *nf* **-en** habit, custom.

Geplapper (gə'plapər) *n neu* babble, prattle.

Geplauder (gə'plaudər) *n neu* chatter, talk.

Gepräge (gə'prɛːgə) *n neu* **—** **1** impression, stamp. **2** character.

gerade (gə'raːdə) *adj* **1** straight. **2** even. **3** upright. **4** exact. *adv* **1** precisely. **2** just (now). **3** directly. **—aus** (gəradə'aus) *adv* straight ahead or on. **—zu** (gəraːdə'tsuː) *adv* directly, frankly.

Geradheit (gə'raːthait) *nf* **1** straightness, evenness. **2** honesty.

Geranie (gɛ'raːniə) *nf* **-n** *bot* geranium.

gerannt (gə'rant) *v* see **rennen.**

Gerät (gə'rɛːt) *n neu* **-e** tool, implement, appliance.

geraten* (gə'raːtən) *vi* **1** come or get into. **2** turn out. *adj* advisable.

geräumig (gə'rɔymiç) *adj* spacious, roomy.

Geräusch (gə'rɔyʃ) *n neu* **-e** noise.

gerben ('gɛrbən) *vt* tan (hides).

gerecht (gə'rɛçt) *adj* **1** straight. **2** just, fair. **3** suitable. **4** righteous. **—igkeit** *nf* **1** justice, fairness. **2** righteousness.

Gerede (gə'reːdə) *n neu* talk, gossip, rumour.

Gericht (gə'riçt) *n neu* **-e** **1**

(law) court. **2** judgment. **—lich** *adj* judicial, legal. **—sbarkeit** *nf* jurisdiction. **—sdiener** *nm* bailiff. **—shof** *nm* (law) court.

gerieben (gə'riːbən) *v* see **reiben.**

gering (gə'riŋ) *adj* **1** small, insignificant. **2** poor, inferior. **—fügig** *adj* insignificant, trivial. **—schätzung** *nf* disdain.

gerinnen* (gə'rinən) *vi* coagulate, congeal.

Gerippe (gə'ripə) *n neu* — skeleton.

gerissen (gə'risən) *v* see **reißen.** *adj* **1** torn. **2** clever, wily.

geritten (gə'ritən) *v* see **reiten.**

German/e (gɛr'maːnə) *nm* **-n** Teuton. **—isch** *adj* Germanic, Teutonic.

gern(e) (gɛrn) *adv* gladly, readily. **etwas gern haben** like something.

gerochen (gə'rɔxən) *v* see **riechen.**

Gerste ('gɛrstə) *nf* barley.

Geruch (gə'ruːx) *nm* ¨**-e** smell, odour. **—sinn** *nm* sense of smell.

Gerücht (gə'ryçt) *n neu* **-e** rumour.

Gerüst (gə'ryst) *n neu* **-e** scaffold(ing), frame.

gesamt (gə'zamt) *adj* total, whole, entire. **—ausgabe** *nf* complete edition. **—schule** *nf* comprehensive school.

gesandt (gə'zant) *v* see **senden.**

Gesand/te(r) (gə'zantə) *nm* envoy, diplomatic representative. **—schaft** *nf* **-en** legation, embassy.

Gesang (gə'zaŋ) *nm* ¨**-e** **1** singing. **2** song.

Gesäß (gə'zɛːs) *n neu* **-e** buttocks, seat.

Geschäft (gə'ʃɛft) *n neu* **-e** **1** business. **2** shop. **—lich** *adj* commercial. **—sführer** *nm* manager. **—smann** *nm* **-leute** businessman. **—sträger** *nm* **1** representative. **2** chargé d'affaires.

geschah (gə'ʃaː) *v* see **geschehen.**

gescheh/en* (gə'ʃeːən) *vi* happen, occur. *n neu* events, occurrences. **—nis** *n neu* **-se** event.

gescheit (gə'ʃait) *adj* intelligent, clever.

Geschenk (gə'ʃɛŋk) *n neu* **-e** present.

Geschicht/e (gə'ʃiçtə) *nf* **-n** **1** history. **2** story. **3** affair. **—lich** *adj* historical. **—sschreiber** *nm* historian.

geschichtet (gə'ʃiçtət) *adj* laminated.

Geschick (gə'ʃik) *n neu* **-e** **1** skill, aptitude. **2** fate. **—lichkeit** *nf* **-en** skill, dexterity. **—t** *adj* skilful, dexterous.

geschieden (gə'ʃiːdən) *v* see **scheiden.** *adj* divorced.

geschienen (gə'ʃiːnən) *v* see **scheinen.**

Geschirr (gə'ʃir) *n neu* **-e** **1** dishes, crockery. **2** harness. **—tuch** *n neu* tea-towel.

Geschlecht (gə'ʃlɛçt) *n neu* **-er** **1** sex. **2** race. **3** species, kind. **4** family, blood. **5** gender. **—lich** *adj* sexual, venereal. **—skrankheit** *nf* venereal disease. **—sreife** *nf* puberty, sexual maturity. **—steile** *nm* *pl* genitals. **—sverkehr** *nm* sexual intercourse.

geschlossen (gəˈʃlɔsən) *v* see **schließen.**

Geschmack (gəˈʃmak) *nm* ¨**-e** **1** taste. **2** flavour. **3** liking, fancy. **—los** *adj* tasteless. **—ssinn** *nm* sense of taste. **—voll** *adj* tasteful.

Geschnatter (gəˈʃnatər) *n neu* cackling.

geschnitten (gəˈʃnitən) *v* see **schneiden.**

geschoben (gəˈʃoːbən) *v* see **schieben.**

Geschöpf (gəˈʃœpf) *n neu* **-e** **1** creature. **2** creation.

Geschoß (gəˈʃɔs) *n neu* **-schosse** **1** missile. **2** bullet. **3** storey, floor.

geschossen (gəˈʃɔsən) *v* see **schießen.**

Geschrei (gəˈʃrai) *n neu* **1** shouting, clamour. **2** fuss.

geschrieben (gəˈʃriːbən) *v* see **schreiben.**

geschrie(e)n (gəˈʃriː(ə)n) *v* see **schreien.**

geschritten (gəˈʃritən) *v* see **schreiten.**

Geschütz (gəˈʃyts) *n neu* **-e** gun, cannon.

geschwätzig (gəˈʃvɛtsiç) *adj* talkative.

geschweige (gəˈʃvaigə) *adv,conj also* **geschweige denn** not to mention, let alone.

geschwiegen (gəˈʃviːgən) *v* see **schweigen.**

geschwind (gəˈʃvint) *adj* swift, quick. **—igkeit** (gəˈʃvindiçkait) *nf* **-en** speed. **—igkeitsmesser** *nm* speedometer. **—igkeitsbegrenzung** *nf* speed limit.

Geschwister (gəˈʃvistər) *n pl* brothers and sisters.

Geschworene(r) (gəˈʃvoːrənə) *nm* juror, juryman.

Geschwür (gəˈʃvyːr) *n neu* **-e** **1** ulcer. **2** abscess.

Gesell/e (gəˈzɛlə) *nm* **-n** **1** companion, fellow. **2** assistant. **3** journeyman. **—ig** *adj* sociable, companionable, gregarious. **—igkeit** *nf* sociability. **—schaft** *nf* **-en** **1** society. **2** company. **3** firm. **4** party, social gathering. **—schaftlich** *adj* **1** social. **2** sociable.

Gesetz (gəˈzɛts) *n neu* **-e** **1** law. **2** statute. **—gebend** *adj* legislative. **—geber** *nm* — legislator. **—gebung** *nf* **-en** legislation. **—lich** *adj* lawful, legal. **—los** *adj* lawless. **—mäßig** *adj* **1** legal. **2** legitimate. **3** regular. **—widrig** *adj* illegal.

gesetzt (gəˈzɛtst) *adj* **1** calm. **2** grave.

Gesicht (gəˈziçt) *n neu* **-er** face. **—skreis** *nm* horizon. **—spunkt** *nm* point of view.

Gesims (gəˈzims) *n neu* **-e** **1** moulding, cornice. **2** ledge.

gesinn/t (gəˈzint) *adj* minded, disposed. **—ung** *nf* **-en** **1** convictions, beliefs. **2** attitude.

Gespann (gəˈʃpan) *n neu* **-e** team (of horses, oxen, etc.). **—t** *adj* **1** tense, strained. **2** curious. **3** anxious, agog.

Gespenst (gəˈʃpɛnst) *n neu* **-er** ghost, spectre.

Gespräch (gəˈʃprɛːç) *n neu* **-e** conversation, talk.

gesprochen (gə'ʃprɔxən) *v* see **sprechen.**
gesprungen (gə'ʃpruŋən) *v* see **springen.**
Gestalt (gə'ʃtalt) *nf* **-en 1** form, shape. **2** aspect. **3** figure. **4** stature. **—en** *vt* form. **sich —en** *vr* take shape.
gestanden (gə'ʃtandən) *v* see **stehen.**
Geständnis (gə'ʃtɛntnis) *n neu* **-nisse** confession.
Gestank (gə'ʃtaŋk) *nm* stench.
gestatten (gə'ʃtatən) *vt* permit, allow. **sich gestatten** *vr* **1** venture. **2** presume.
Geste ('gɛstə) *nf* **-n** gesture.
gestehen* (gə'ʃteːən) *vt* confess.
Gestein (gə'ʃtain) *n neu* **-e 1** stone. **2** mineral.
Gestell (gə'ʃtɛl) *n neu* **-e 1** stand. **2** frame. **3** trestle.
gest/ern ('gɛstərn) *adv* yesterday. **—rig** ('gɛstriç) *adj* yesterday's.
gestiegen (gə'ʃtiːgən) *v* see **steigen.**
gestohlen (gə'ʃtoːlən) *v* see **stehlen.**
Gesträuch (gə'ʃtrɔyç) *n neu* **-e** bush(es), shrubbery.
Gesuch (gə'zuːx) *n neu* **-e** petition, request.
gesund (gə'zunt) *adj* healthy, wholesome. **—heit** *nf* health, fitness.
gesungen (gə'zuŋən) *v* see **singen.**
gesunken (gə'zuŋkən) *v* see **sinken.**
getan (gə'taːn) *v* see **tun.**
Getränk (gə'trɛŋk) *n neu* **-e** drink.
Getreide (gə'traidə) *n neu* cereals, grain, corn.
getreu (gə'trɔy) *adj* faithful, true, loyal.
getrieben (gə'triːbən) *v* see **treiben.**
getroffen (gə'trɔfən) *v* see **treffen.**
getrost (gə'troːst) *adj* confident.
getrunken (gə'truŋkən) *v* see **trinken.**
Getto ('getoː) *n neu* **-s** ghetto.
gewagt (gə'vaːkt) *adj* risky, bold.
gewählt (gə'vɛːlt) *adj* **1** selected. **2** refined.
Gewähr (gə'vɛːr) *nf* guarantee, surety. **—en** *vt* allow, grant. **—leisten** *vt* guarantee.
Gewalt (gə'valt) *nf* **-en 1** violence, force. **2** power, might. **—ig** *adj* powerful, mighty. **—sam** *adj* violent, forcible.
Gewand (gə'vant) *n neu* **¨-er** gown, robe.
gewandt (gə'vant) *v* see **wenden.** *adj* agile, skilful.
gewann (gə'van) *v* see **gewinnen.**
Gewässer (gə'vɛsər) *n neu* — waters, stretch of water.
Gewebe (gə'veːbə) *n neu* — **1** tissue. **2** textile, fabric.
geweckt (gə'vɛkt) *adj* alert, bright.
Gewehr (gə'veːr) *n neu* **-e** gun, rifle.
Gewerb/e (gə'vɛrbə) *n neu* — trade, business, industry. **—lich** (gə'vɛrpliç) *adj* commercial.
Gewerkschaft (gə'vɛrkʃaft) *nf* **-en** trade union. **—ler** *nm* — trade-unionist.

gewesen (gə'veːzən) *v* see **sein.**
Gewicht (gə'viçt) *n neu* **-e 1** weight. **2** importance. **—ig** *adj* important, weighty.
gewiesen (gə'viːzən) *v* see **weisen.**
Gewimmel (gə'viməl) *n neu* swarms, throngs.
Gewinn (gə'vin) *nm* **-e 1** winning. **2** profit, gain. **3** winnings. **—en*** *vt* **1** win. **2** earn.
Gewirr (gə'vir) *n neu* **-e** confusion, tangle.
gewiß (gə'vis) *adj* sure, certain. **ein gewisser Herr** a certain gentleman. *~adv* indeed, certainly. **—ermaßen** *adv* to a certain extent. **—heit** *nf* **-en** certainty.
Gewissen (gə'visən) *n neu* conscience. **—los** *adj* unscrupulous.
Gewitter (gə'vitər) *n neu* — (thunder)storm. **—n** *vi* thunder.
gewogen (gə'voːgən) *v* see **wiegen.** *adj* **1** affectionate. **2** well-disposed.
gewöhnen (gə'vœːnən) *vt* accustom. **sich gewöhnen** *vr* become accustomed or used (to).
Gewohnheit (gə'voːnhait) *nf* **-en** habit. **—srecht** *n neu* common law.
gewöhnlich (gə'vœːnliç) *adj* usual, ordinary.
gewohnt (gə'voːnt) *adj* accustomed.
Gewölbe (gə'vœlbə) *n neu* — arch, vault.
gewonnen (gə'vɔnən) *v* see **gewinnen.**
geworden (gə'vɔːrdən) *v* see **werden.**
geworfen (gə'vɔːrfən) *v* see **werfen.**
Gewürz (gə'vyrts) *n neu* **-e** seasoning, spice. **—ig** *adj* spicy.
gewußt (gə'vust) *v* see **wissen.**
gezogen (gə'tsoːgən) *v* see **ziehen.**
gezwungen (gə'tsvuŋən) *v* see **zwingen.** *adj* **1** forced. **2** unnatural.
gibt (giːbt) *v* see **geben.**
Gicht (giçt) *nf* **-en** gout.
Giebel ('giːbəl) *nm* — gable.
Gier (giːr) *nf* greed(iness). **—ig** *adj* greedy.
gießen* ('giːsən) *vt* **1** pour. **2** water. **3** mould, found.
Gift (gift) *n neu* **-e** poison. **—ig** *adj* poisonous.
Gigue (ʒiːg) *nf* **-n** jig.
ging (giŋ) *v* see **gehen.**
Gipfel ('gipfəl) *nm* — peak, summit. **—höhe** *nf aviat* ceiling. **—n** *vi* culminate.
Gips (gips) *nm* **-e** plaster (of Paris), gypsum.
Giraffe (gi'rafə) *nf* **-n** giraffe.
Giro ('dʒiːroː) *n neu* **-s 1** giro transfer. **2** endorsement.
Gischt (giʃt) *nm* **-e** spray, foam.
Gitarre (gi'tarə) *nf* **-n** guitar.
Gitter ('gitər) *n neu* — **1** grating, lattice. **2** railings, fence.
Glanz (glants) *nm* **1** brilliance, shine, lustre. **2** splendour. **¨—en** ('glɛntsən) *vi* shine, gleam.
Glas (glaːs) *n neu* **¨-er 1** glass. **2** drinking-glass. **¨—ern** ('glɛːzərn) *adj* glass(y). **—ur**

(gla'zu:r) *nf* **-en 1** glaze. **2** enamel. **3** *cul* icing.
glatt (glat) *adj* **1** smooth, even. **2** slippery. **3** plain, downright. *adv* smoothly, easily. **¨—en** ('glɛtən) *vt* smooth, plane, polish.
Glaub/e ('glaubə) *nm* belief, faith. **—en** *vi* believe (in), trust. *vt* think, judge. **¨—ig** ('glɔybiç) *adj* believing, faithful. **¨—ige(r)** ('glɔybigə) *nm* believer. **¨—iger** ('glɔybigər) *nm* — creditor. **—würdig** ('glaupvyrdiç) *adj* credible, trustworthy.
gleich (glaiç) *adj* **1** same, like. **2** equal. **3** level, even. *adv* **1** equally, alike. **2** just. **3** at once, immediately.
gleichbedeutend ('glaiçbədɔytənt) *adj* **1** synonymous. **2** equivalent.
gleichberechtigt ('glaiçbərɛçtikt) *adj* having equal rights.
gleichen* ('glaiçən) *vi* be like or equal.
gleichermaßen ('glaiçərmasən) *adv* in like manner, equally.
gleichfalls ('glaiçfals) *adv* likewise, equally.
Gleichgewicht ('glaiçgəviçt) *n neu* balance, equilibrium.
gleichgültig ('glaiçgyltiç) *adj* **1** indifferent. **2** unimportant.
Gleichheit (glaiçhait) *nf* **-en 1** equality. **2** uniformity.
gleichmäßig ('glaiçmɛsiç) *adj* **1** equal. **2** uniform. **3** symmetrical.
Gleichnis ('glaiçnis) *n neu* **-se 1** parable. **2** simile. **3** image.
gleichschalten ('glaiçʃaltən) *vt* coordinate, synchronize.
Gleichschritt ('glaiçʃrit) *nm* marching in step.
Gleichstrom ('glaiçʃtro:m) *nm* direct current.
Gleichung ('glaiçuŋ) *nf* **-en** equation.
gleichviel ('glaiçvi:l) *adv* **1** no matter. **2** just as much.
gleichwohl ('glaiçvo:l) *adv* nevertheless.
gleichzeitig ('glaiçtsaitiç) *adj* simultaneous.
Gleis (glais) *n neu* **-e 1** track. **2** rails.
gleiten* ('glaitən) *vi* **1** glide. **2** slide.
Gletscher ('glɛtʃər) *nm* — glacier.
Glied (gli:t) *n neu* **-er 1** member, limb. **2** row, rank. **—erung** ('gli:dəruŋ) *nf* **-en 1** arrangement. **2** structure. **3** division. **—maßen** *n pl anat* extremities.
glimpflich ('glimpfliç) *adj* **1** gentle. **2** lenient.
Glocke ('glɔkə) *nf* **-n** bell. **—nblume** *nf* **1** bluebell. **2** harebell. **—nstuhl** *nm* belfry.
glor/ifizieren (glorifi'tsi:rən) *vt* glorify. **—reich** ('glo:raiç) *adj* glorious.
glotzen ('glɔtsən) *vi* stare, gape.
Glück (glyk) *n neu* **1** (good) luck. **2** fortune. **3** happiness. **—en** *vi* succeed, prosper. **—lich** *adj* **1** lucky. **2** happy. **—licherweise** *adv* fortunately. **—wunsch** *nm* congratulation(s).
glüh/en ('gly:ən) *vi* glow, burn. **—birne** *nf* (light) bulb.
Glut (glu:t) *nf* **-en 1** blaze,

glow. **2** live coals, embers. **3** passion.

Gnad/e ('gna:də) *nf* **-n 1** grace. **2** mercy. **3** favour. **—enfrist** *nf* reprieve, respite. **¨—ig** ('gnɛ:diç) *adj* **1** gracious. **2** merciful. **gnädige Frau** Madam.

Gold (gɔlt) *n neu* gold. **—en** ('gɔldən) *adj* gold(en). **—ig** ('gɔldiç) *adj* sweet, lovely, cute.

Golf[1] (gɔlf) *nm* **-e** gulf. **—strom** *nm* Gulf Stream.

Golf[2] (gɔlf) *n neu* golf.

gönn/en ('gœnən) *vt* grant, allow. **—er** *nm* — patron, benefactor.

goß (gɔs) *v* see **gießen.**

Gosse ('gɔsə) *nf* **-n** gutter.

Gott (gɔt) *nm* **¨-er** god. **—esdienst** ('gɔtəsdi:nst) *nm* **1** church service. **2** worship, revere. **—eslästerung** ('gɔtəslɛstəruŋ) *nf* blasphemy. **¨—in** ('gœtin) *nf* **-nen** goddess. **¨—lich** ('gœtliç) *adj* divine.

Götze ('gœtsə) *nm* **-n** idol.

Grab (gra:p) *n neu* **¨-er** grave. **—en*** ('gra:bən) *vt* dig. **—mal** *n neu* **1** tomb. **2** tombstone. **—schrift** *nf* epitaph. **—stätte** *nf* tomb, grave. **—stein** *nm* tombstone.

Grad (gra:t) *nm* **-e 1** degree. **2** grade, rank.

Graf (gra:f) *nm* **-en** count, earl. **¨—in** ('grɛ:fin) *nf* **-nen** countess. **—schaft** *nf* **-en** county.

Gram (gra:m) *nm* grief, sorrow.

Gramm (gram) *n neu* **-e** gramme.

Grammat/ik (gra'matik) *nf* **-en** grammar. **—isch** *adj* grammatical.

Granatapfel (gra'na:tapfəl) *nm* pomegranate.

Granat/e (gra'na:tə) *nf* **-n** grenade, shell.

Granit (gra'ni:t) *nm* **-e** granite.

graphisch ('gra:fiʃ) *adj* graphic.

Gras (gra:s) *n neu* **¨-er** grass. **—en** ('gra:zən) *vi* graze.

gräßlich ('grɛsliç) *adj* terrible, horrible.

Grat (gra:t) *nm* **-e 1** edge. **2** ridge. **3** crest.

Gräte ('grɛ:tə) *nf* **-n** fishbone.

gratis ('gra:tis) *adj,adv* free (of charge).

gratulieren (gratu'li:rən) *vi* congratulate.

grau (grau) *adj* grey.

grauen[1] ('grauən) *vi* **1** become grey. **2** dawn.

grauen[2] ('grauən) *n neu* — horror, dread. **sich grauen** *vr* be afraid or horrified. **grauenhaft** *adj* horrible, dreadful.

grausam ('grauza:m) *adj* cruel, ferocious.

grausig ('grauzic) *adj* horrible, fearful.

gravieren (gra'vi:rən) *vt* engrave.

greifen* ('graifən) *vt* grasp, seize. *vi* **1** touch. **2** reach. **3** grope.

Greis (grais) *nm* **-e** old man. **—in** ('graisin) *nf* **-nen** old woman.

grell (grɛl) *adj* **1** harsh, sharp. **2** glaring.

Grenz/e ('grɛntsə) *nf* **-n 1** frontier. **2** boundary, limit. **—en** *vi* border (on). **—enlos** *adj*

limitless, boundless. **—schicht** *nf* **-en** interface.
Greuel ('grɔyəl) *nm* — horror, abomination.
Griech/e ('gri:çə) *nm* **-n** Greek. **—enland** *n neu* Greece. **—isch** *adj* Greek. *n neu* Greek (language).
Grieß (gri:s) *nm* **-e** **1** gravel, grit. **2** semolina.
griff (grif) *v* see **greifen.**
Griff (grif) *nm* **-e** **1** grip, hold. **2** handle.
Grille ('grilə) *nf* **-n** **1** *zool* cricket. **2** whim.
grinsen ('grinzən) *vi* grin.
Grippe ('gripə) *nf* **-n** influenza, flu.
grob (gro:p) *adj* **1** coarse, crude. **2** gross.
Groll (grɔl) *nm* **1** grudge. **2** resentment.
Grönland ('grœ:nlant) *n neu* Greenland.
Gros (grɔs) *n neu* **1** gross. **2** main body. **en gros** wholesale.
Groschen ('grɔʃən) *nm* — tenpfennig (piece).
groß (gro:s) *adj* **1** large, big. **2** tall. **3** great. **im großen** **1** in bulk. **2** wholesale. **im großen und ganzen** on the whole.
großartig ('gro:sa:rtiç) *adj* **1** grand, splendid. **2** lofty.
Großbritannien (gro:sbri'taniən) *n neu* Great Britain.
Größe ('grœ:sə) *nf* **1** size. **2** height. **3** greatness. **4** importance.
Großeltern ('gro:seltern) *n pl* grandparents.
großenteils ('gro:sentails) *adv* in large part, mostly.
Großhandel ('gro:shandəl) *nm* wholesale trade.
großherzig ('gro:she:rtsik) *adj* magnanimous.
Großindustrie ('gro:sindustri:) *nf* heavy industry.
Großmacht ('gro:smaxt) *nf* great power.
Großmaul ('gro:smaul) *n neu* braggart, boaster.
Großmutter ('gro:smutər) *nf* grandmother.
Großstadt ('gro:sʃtat) *nf* (big) city.
größtenteils ('grœ:stəntails) *adv* for the most part, largely.
Großteil ('gro:stail) *nm* bulk.
Großvater ('gro:sfatə) *nm* grandfather.
großzügig ('gro:stsy:giç) *adj* **1** on a large scale. **2** generous.
grotesk (gro'tɛsk) *adj* grotesque.
Grube ('gru:bə) *nf* **-n** **1** hole, pit. **2** mine, quarry.
grübeln ('gry:bəln) *vi* brood, ponder.
grün (gry:n) *adj,n neu* green. **—kohl** *nm* kale.
Grund (grunt) *nm* **¨-e** **1** ground. **2** (plot of) land. **3** soil. **4** bottom, depth. **5** reason. **6** basis.
Grundbau ('gruntbau) *nm* foundation.
Grundbesitz ('gruntbəzits) *nm* landed property.
gründ/en ('gryndən) *vt* **1** found. **2** ground. **¨—er** *nm* — founder.
Grundgesetz ('gruntgəzɛts) *n neu* **1** basic law. **2** constitution.
Grundlage ('gruntla:gə) *nf* foundation.

gründlich ('gryntliç) *adj* **1** thorough. **2** complete.
grundlos ('gruntlo:s) *adj* baseless, groundless.
Grundriß ('gruntris) *nm* **1** outline. **2** plan.
Grundsatz ('gruntzats) *nm* **1** basic or fundamental principle. **2** axiom. ¨**—lich** *adj* fundamental.
Grundstück ('grunt∫tyk) *n neu* piece of land.
Gründung ('grynduŋ) *nf* **-en** foundation, establishment.
grunzen ('gruntsən) *vi* grunt.
Grupp/e ('grupə) *nf* **-n** group. **—ieren** (gru'pi:rən) *vt* group, arrange.
gruselig ('gru:zəliç) *adj* uncanny, creepy.
Gruß (gru:s) *nm* ¨**-e** greeting. ¨**—en** ('gry:sən) *vt* greet. **grüß Gott!** good day!
gucken ('gukən) *vi* look, peep.
Gulasch ('gu:la∫) *nm,neu* **-e** goulash.
gültig ('gyltiç) *adj* **1** valid, good. **2** current. **—keit** *nf* **1** validity. **2** currency.
Gummi ('gumi) *nm,neu* **-s** **1** rubber. **2** gum. **3** eraser. **—band** *n neu* rubber band, elastic. **—schuh** *nm* overshoe, galosh.
Gunst (gunst) *nf* ¨**-e** goodwill, favour. ¨**—ig** ('gynstiç) *adj* favourable. ¨**—ling** ('gynstliŋ) *nm* **-e** favourite.
gurgel/n ('gurgəln) *vi* **1** gargle. **2** gurgle. **—wasser** *n neu* gargle.
Gurke ('gurkə) *nf* **-n** cucumber.
Gürtel ('gyrtəl) *nm* **—** **1** belt. **2** zone.
Guß (gus) *nm* **-üsse** **1** pouring out, gush. **2** downpour. **3** casting. **4** *cul* icing.
gut (gu:t) *adj* good. *adv* well. **—achten** *n neu* **—** (expert) opinion. ¨**—e** ('gy:tə) *nf* **1** goodness. **2** kindness. **3** excellence. **—heißen** *vt* approve (of). ¨**—ig** ('gy:tiç) *adj* **1** kind. **2** good. **3** good-natured. **—willig** *adj* voluntary, willing.
Gut (gu:t) *n neu* ¨**-er** **1** possession. **2** landed estate. **3** goods, wares. ¨**—erbahnhof** ('gy:tərba:nhɔf) *nm* goods yard. ¨**—erzug** ('gy:tərtsu:k) *nm* goods train. **—sherr** *nm* **1** lord of the manor. **2** landlord.
Gymnasium (gym'na:zium) *n neu* **-sien** grammar school.

H

Haag, Den (ha:k) *nm* The Hague.
Haar (ha:r) *n neu* **-e** hair. **—bürste** *nf* hairbrush. **—ig** *adj* hairy. **—schnitt** *nm* haircut. **—sträubend** *adj* hair-raising.
Hab/e ('ha:bə) *nf* **-n** property, possessions. **—en*** *vt* have, possess. *n neu* credit. **—enichts** *nm* **-e** pauper. **—gier** ('ha:pgi:r) *nf* avarice, greed. **—seligkeiten** ('ha:pze:liçkaitən) *nf pl* belongings, possessions.
Habicht ('ha:biçt) *nm* **-e** hawk.
hack/en ('hakən) *vt* **1** hash. **2** hack. **3** chop. **—fleisch** *n neu* minced meat, mince.
Hafen ('ha:fən) *nm* ¨**—** harbour, port. **—arbeiter** *nm* docker. **—damm** *nm* jetty. **—stadt** *nf* port.
Hafer ('ha:fər) *nm* **—** oat(s).

—brei *nm* porridge. **—flocken** *nf pl* oat-flakes, rolled oats.
Haft (haft) *nf* **1** arrest. **2** imprisonment. **—befehl** *nm* warrant of arrest. **—en** *vi* **1** adhere, cling (to). **2** guarantee, answer (for). **—pflichtversicherung** *nf* **-en** third-party insurance. **—ung** *nf* **-en** liability.
Hagedorn ('ha:gədɔrn) *nm* **-e** hawthorn.
Hagel ('ha:gəl) *nm* — hail. **—n** *vi* hail.
hager ('ha:gər) *adj* gaunt.
Hahn (ha:n) *nm* **¨-e** **1** cock. **2** tap. **¨—chen** ('hɛ:nçən) *n neu* — **1** cockerel. **2** *cul* chicken.
Hai (hai) *nm* **-e** *also* **Haifisch** shark.
häkeln ('hɛ:kəln) *vt* crochet.
haken ('ha:kən) *vi* hook (on). *nm* — **1** hook. **2** difficulty, snag. **—kreuz** *n neu* swastika.
halb (halp) *adj* half. **—e(r)** ('halbə) *nm* half litre (of beer, wine, etc.). **—insel** *nf* peninsula. **—jährlich** *adj* half-yearly. **—kreis** *nm* semicircle. **—kugel** *nf* hemisphere. **—laut** *adj* (of a voice) low. *adv* in a low voice. **—messer** *nm* radius. **—mond** *nm* half-moon, crescent. **—wegs** ('halpve:ks) *adv* **1** halfway. **2** to some or any extent.
half (half) *v* see **helfen.**
Hälfte ('hɛlftə) *nf* **-n** **1** half. **2** middle.
Halfter ('halftər) *nm,neu* —, *nf* **-n** halter.
Hall (hal) *nm* **-e** **1** clang. **2** peal. **—en** *vi* **1** resound. **2** clang.
Halle ('halə) *nf* **-n** **1** hall. **2** porch, lobby. **3** hangar. **—nbad** *n neu* indoor swimming pool.
Halm (halm) *nm* **-e** **1** blade (of grass). **2** stalk.
Hals (hals) *nm* **¨-e** **1** neck. **2** throat. **—starrig** ('halsʃtariç) *adj* obstinate, stubborn. **—tuch** *n neu* scarf. **—weh** *n neu* sore throat.
Halt (halt) *nm* **-e** **1** stop, halt. **2** support. **—bar** *adj* **1** tenable. **2** firm, lasting. **haltbar sein** (of foodstuffs) keep. **Haltbarkeitsdatum** *n neu* shelf-life. **—los** *adj* **1** untenable. **2** unsteady.
halt/en* ('haltən) *vt* **1** hold. **2** keep. *vi* **1** stop, halt. **2** hold out. **halten fur** consider, deem. **sich halten** *vr* maintain oneself. **—estelle** *nf* (bus) stop.
Hamburger ('hamburgər) *nm* — beefburger.
hämisch ('hɛ:miʃ) *adj* malicious.
Hammelfleisch ('haməlflaiʃ) *n neu* mutton.
Hammer ('hamər) *nm* **¨**— hammer. **¨—n** ('hɛmərn) *vi,vt* hammer.
Hamster ('hamstər) *nm* — hamster.
Hand (hant) *nf* **¨-e** hand. **an Hand von** with the aid of. **die Hand geben** shake hands. **in der Hand haben** have under one's control.
Handarbeit ('hanta:rbait) *nf* **1** manual work. **2** handwork, craft. **3** needlework.
Handbremse ('hantbrɛmzə) *nf* handbrake.

Handbuch ('hantbux) *n neu* handbook.
Händedruck ('hɛndədruk) *nm* handshake.
Handel ('handəl) *nm* **1** trade, commerce. **2** transaction, deal. **—n** *vi* **1** act, do. **2** deal with. **3** haggle. **4** trade. **es handelt sich um** it is a question of. **—skammer** *nf* chamber of commerce. **—smarke** *nf* trademark, brand name. **—ssperre** *nf* embargo.
handfest ('hantfɛst) *adj* sturdy, strong.
Handfläche ('hantflɛçə) *nf* palm.
Handgelenk ('hantgəlɛnk) *n neu* wrist.
Handgepäck ('hantgəpɛk) *n neu* hand luggage.
handhaben* ('hanthaːbən) *vt* **1** handle. **2** manage.
Handschelle ('hantʃɛlə) *nf* **-n** handcuff.
Handschrift ('hantʃrift) *nf* **1** handwriting. **2** manuscript.
Handschuh ('hantʃuː) *nm* glove.
Handstreich ('hantʃtraiç) *nm* **1** raid. **2** surprise.
Handtasche ('hanttaʃə) *nf* handbag.
Handtuch ('hanttux) *n neu* towel.
Handwerk ('hantvɛrk) *n neu* craft, trade. **—er** *nm* artisan, craftsman.
Händler ('hɛndlər) *nm* — merchant, trader.
Handlung ('handluŋ) *nf* **-en** **1** act, action. **2** trade. **3** business, shop.
Hang (haŋ) *nm* **¨-e** **1** slope. **2** tendency, leaning. **¨—ebrücke** ('hɛŋəbrykə) *nf* suspension bridge. **¨—ematte** ('hɛŋəmatə) *nf* hammock. **¨—en*** ('hɛŋən) *vi* **1** hang. **2** be attached. **3** depend (on). *vt* **1** hang. **2** attach.
Hannover (ha'noːfər) *n neu* Hanover.
Harfe ('harfə) *nf* **-n** harp.
harmlos ('harmloːs) *adj* harmless.
Harmon/ie (harmɔ'niː) *nf* **-n** harmony. **—ika** (har'moːnika) *nf* **-s** **1** concertina. **2** harmonica. **—isch** (har'moːniʃ) *adj* harmonious, harmonic.
Harnisch ('harniʃ) *nm* **-e** armour.
Harpune (har'puːnə) *nf* **-n** harpoon.
harren ('harən) *vi* **1** wait for. **2** await. **3** hope for.
hart (hart) *adj* **1** hard. **2** rough. **3** severe. **¨—e** ('hɛrtə) *nf* **1** hardness. **2** roughness. **3** severity. **¨—en** ('hɛrtən) *vt* harden, temper. **—näckig** ('hartnɛkiç) *adj* obstinate.
Harz (harts) *n neu* **-e** resin.
Haschisch ('haʃiʃ) *n neu* hashish.
Hase ('haːzə) *nm* **-n** hare.
Haselnuß ('həːzəlnus) *nf* hazelnut.
Haspe ('haspə) *nf* **-n** hasp, hinge.
Haß (has) *nm* hate, hatred. **¨—lich** ('hɛsliç) *adj* **1** ugly. **2** nasty, horrid.
hassen ('hasən) *vt* hate.
hast (hast) *v* see **haben.**
hasten ('hastən) *vi* hasten, hurry.
hat (hat) *v* see **haben.**

hätscheln ('hɛːtʃəln) *vt* **1** caress. **2** pamper, spoil.
hatte ('hate) *v* see **haben.**
hätte ('hetə) *v* see **haben.**
Haube ('haubə) *nf* **-n 1** cap, hood. **2** *mot* bonnet. **3** dome.
Hauch (haux) *nm* **-e** breath.
Haue ('hauə) *nf* **-n 1** hoe. **2** thrashing, beating. **—n*** *vt* **1** chop. **2** fell. **3** thrash, spank.
Haufen ('haufən) *nm* **— 1** heap, pile. **2** mass, large amount. **¨—en** ('hɔyfən) *vt* heap up, accumulate. **—enweise** ('haufənvaizə) *adv* in great quantities, in heaps.
häufig ('hɔyfiç) *adj* frequent. **—keit** *nf* **-en** frequency.
Haupt (haupt) *n neu* **¨-er 1** head. **2** leader. **—bahnhof** *nm* main or central railway station. **—buch** *n neu* ledger. **—fach** *n neu* main subject. **—mann** *nm* captain. **—quartier** *n neu* headquarters. **—sache** *nf* main point or thing. **—sächlich** *adj* main, principal. **—stadt** *nf* capital. **—wort** *n neu* noun.
Haus (haus) *n neu* **¨-er 1** house. **2** building. **3** home. **nach Hause gehen** go home. **zu Hause** at home. **—arbeit** *nf* **1** housework. **2** homework. **—en** ('hauzən) *vi* **1** live (economically). **2** play havoc. **—frau** *nf* housewife. **—halt** *nm* **1** housekeeping. **2** household. **3** budget. **—halten*** *vi* **1** keep house. **2** economize. **—herr** *nm* **1** head of the family. **2** landlord. **—ieren** (hau'ziːrən) *vi* peddle. **—meister** *nm* caretaker. **—tier** *n neu* domestic animal, pet.
Haut (haut) *nf* **¨-e 1** skin, hide. **2** membrane, film. **¨—en** ('hɔytən) *vt* skin.
Hebamme ('heːpamə) *nf* **-n** midwife.
Heb/el ('heːbəl) *nm* **—** lever. **—en*** ('heːbən) *vt* lift, raise. **sich —en** *vr* **1** rise. **2** cancel. **—er** ('heːbər) *nm* **—** syphon. **—estange** ('heːbəʃtaŋə) *nf* crowbar. **—ung** ('heːbuŋ) *nf* **-en 1** elevation. **2** removal.
Hecht (hɛçt) *nm* **-e** pike.
Heck (hɛk) *n neu* stern, rear.
Hecke ('hɛkə) *nf* **-n** hedge. **—nschütze** *nm* sniper.
Hecktürmodell ('hɛktyːrmoːdel) *n neu* **-e** hatchback.
Heer (heːr) *n neu* **-e** army.
Hefe ('heːfə) *nf* **-n 1** yeast. **2** dregs.
Heft (hɛft) *n neu* **-e 1** handle. **2** exercise book. **3** (journal) volume, number. **—en** *vt* **1** fasten. **2** fix. **3** sew. **—klammer** *nf* paper clip. **—zwecke** *nf* drawing-pin.
heftig ('hɛftiç) *adj* **1** violent. **2** strong. **3** vehement. **4** fierce.
hegen ('heːgən) *vt* cherish, harbour.
Hehl (heːl) *n neu* **1** secret. **2** secrecy. **—en** *vt* **1** conceal. **2** receive (stolen property).
hehr (heːr) *adj* lofty, sublime.
Heide[1] ('haidə) *nf* **-n** heath. **—kraut** *n neu* heather. **—lbeere** *nf* bilberry.
Heid/e[2] ('haidə) *nm* **-n** heathen, pagan. **—nisch** *adj* heathen, pagan.
heikel ('haikəl) *adj* **1** critical. **2** delicate. **3** awkward.
heil (hail) *adj* **1** well. **2** unhurt.

3 whole. 4 sound, undamaged. *n neu* 1 welfare. 2 salvation. **—butt** ('hailbut) *nm* halibut. **—en** *vt,vi* heal. **—kraft** *nf* healing power. **—mittel** *n neu* remedy, cure. **—sam** *adj* 1 wholesome. 2 beneficial. **—sarmee** ('hailsarme:) *nf* Salvation Army. **—ung** *nf* **-en** 1 cure. 2 healing.

Heiland ('hailant) *nm* **-e** Saviour.

heilig ('hailiç) *adj* holy, sacred. **Heiliger Abend** Christmas Eve. **—e(r)** ('hailigə) *nm* saint. **—en** ('hailigən) *vt* sanctify. **—enschein** *nm* halo. **—keit** *nf* holiness, saintliness.

heim (haim) *adv* home(ward). *n neu* **-e** home. **—isch** *adj* domestic. **—kehr** *nf* homecoming. **—lich** *adj* secret. **—suchen** *vt* 1 visit. 2 punish. 3 afflict. **—tückisch** *adj* malicious. **—wärts** ('haimvɛrts) *adv* homeward(s). **—weh** *n neu* homesickness.

Heimat ('haima:t) *nf* 1 home. 2 homeland, native place. **—land** *n neu* homeland. **—los** *adj* homeless.

Heirat ('haira:t) *nf* **-en** marriage. **—en** *vt* marry. *vi* get married.

heiser ('haizər) *adj* hoarse.

heiß (hais) *adj* hot.

heißen* ('haisən) *vi* 1 be called. 2 mean. *vt* 1 name. 2 command. **das heißt, d.h.** that is, i.e.

heiter ('haitər) *adj* 1 cheerful. 2 serene, calm. 3 (of weather) bright, clear. **—keit** *nf* 1 cheerfulness. 2 brightness. 3 serenity.

Heiz/apparat ('haitsapara:t) *nm* heater. **—en** *vt* heat. **—körper** *nm* radiator. **—stoff** *nm* fuel. **—ung** *nf* **-en** heating.

Held (hɛlt) *nm* **-en** hero. **—enhaft** ('hɛldənhaft) *adj* heroic. **—in** ('hɛldin) *nf* **-nen** heroine.

helf/en* ('hɛlfən) *vi* help, assist. **—er** *nm* — helper, assistant.

hell (hɛl) *adj* 1 bright. 2 light. 3 clear. **—e** *nf* 1 brightness. 2 daylight. 3 clearness.

Helm (hɛlm) *nm* **-e** helmet.

Hemd (hɛmt) *n neu* **-en** 1 shirt. 2 vest.

hemm/en ('hɛmən) *vt* 1 restrain, inhibit. 2 block. 3 hinder. 4 stop. **—ung** *nf* **-en** 1 restriction. 2 restraint. 3 check. 4 inhibition. **—unglos** *adj* unrestrained, uninhibited.

Hengst (hɛŋst) *nm* **-e** stallion.

Henker ('hɛŋkər) *nm* — hangman, executioner.

her (he:r) *adv* 1 here, hither. 2 ago. 3 from.

herab (hɛ'rap) *adv* down, downward. **—lassen*** *vt* lower. **sich —lassen** *vr* condescend. **—setzen** *vt* 1 lower. 2 reduce. 3 degrade. **—setzung** *nf* **-en** 1 reduction. 2 degradation.

heran (hɛ'ran) *adv* 1 on (here). 2 up to. 3 along. **—kommen*** *vi* draw near. **—treten*** *vi* step up (to), approach. **—ziehen*** *vt* 1 pull or draw up. **2** grow, raise. **3** make use of, call on. *vi* approach.

herauf (hɛ'rauf) *adv* **1** up (here). **2** upwards.

heraus (hɛ'raus) *adv* **1** out. **2** forth. **—finden*** *vt* find out. **—fordern** *vt* **1** challenge. **2** provoke. **—gabe** *nf* **1** publication, publishing. **2** delivering (up). **—geben*** *vt* **1** publish. **2** deliver up. **3** restore, give back. **—geber** *nm* publisher. **—stellen** *vt* put or bring out. **sich —stellen** *vr* turn out, prove to be.

herb (hɛrp) *adj* **1** (of taste, etc.) sharp, tart. **2** (of wine) dry.

herbei (hɛr'bai) *adv* **1** here, hither. **2** on. **—führen** *vt* **1** lead, bring (on). **2** cause, induce.

Herberge ('hɛrbɛrgə) *nf* **-n** **1** hostel. **2** shelter, lodging. **—n** *vt,vi* lodge, shelter.

Herbst (hɛrpst) *nm* **-e** autumn.

Herd (heːrt) *nm* **-e** **1** hearth, fireplace. **2** cooker, stove.

Herde ('heːrdə) *nf* **-n** herd, flock.

herein (hɛ'rain) *adv* in (here). *interj* come in! **—lassen*** *vt* admit, allow in.

hergeben* ('heːrgeːbən) *vt* hand over.

hergebracht ('heːrgəbraxt) *adj* **1** traditional, handed down. **2** established.

Hering ('heːriŋ) *nm* **-e** herring.

her/kommen* ('heːrkɔmən) *vi* **1** come from. **2** approach. *n neu* **— 1** custom. **2** descent. **—kömmlich** ('heːrkœmliç) *adj* traditional. **—kunft** ('heːrkunft) *nf* descent, origin.

hernach (hɛr'naːx) *adv* after(wards).

Heroin (hero'iːn) *n neu* heroin.

Herr (hɛr) *nm* **-en** **1** gentleman. **2** master, lord. **3** Mr. **—enhaus** *n neu* manor-house. **—gott** *nm* the Lord God. **—in** *nf* **-nen** mistress, lady. **—lich** *adj* **1** wonderful. **2** grand. **3** glorious. **—schaft** *nf* **-en** **1** rule, dominion. **2** power. **3** distinguished people. **4** manor. **5** estate. **—schen** ('hɛrʃən) *vi* **1** rule, govern. **2** dominate. **3** exist. **4** prevail. **—scher** ('hɛrʃər) *nm* **—** ruler. **—schsucht** ('hɛrʃzuːxt) *nf* **1** love of power. **2** ambition.

herstell/en ('heːrʃtɛlən) *vt* manufacture, produce. **—ung** *nf* **-en** manufacture, production.

herüber (hɛ'ryːbər) *adv* **1** over, across. **2** to this side or place.

herum (hɛ'rum) *adv* (a)round, about. **—führen** *vt* show or take (a)round. **—ziehen*** *vi* wander about.

herunter (hɛ'runtər) *adv* down, downwards. **—kommen*** *vi* **1** come down. **2** decay.

hervor (hɛr'foːr) *adv* **1** forth, out. **2** forward. **—bringen*** *vt* produce. **—gehen*** *vi* **1** arise. **2** result. **—heben*** *vt* **1** stress. **2** highlight. **—ragend** *adj* **1** eminent. **2** projecting. **3** outstanding, excellent. **—rufen*** *vt* **1** call forth. **2** cause. **—treten*** *vi* come forward or out.

Herz (hɛrts) *n neu* **-en** heart. **—anfall** *nm* heart attack. **—lich** *adj* hearty, cordial.

—los *adj* heartless. **—schlag** *nm med* stroke.

Herzog ('hɛrtso:k) *nm* **¨-e** duke. **—in** ('hɛrtso:gin) *nf* **-nen** duchess. **—tum** *n neu* **-tümer** duchy, dukedom.

herzu (hɛr'tsu:) *adv* **1** (to) here. **2** near. **3** up (to).

Hessen ('hɛsən) *n neu* Hesse.

Hetze ('hɛtsə) *nf* **-n** **1** hurry. **2** hunt. **3** agitation. **—n** *vt* **1** hunt. **2** set (dogs) on. **3** incite.

Heu (hɔy) *n neu* hay. **—gabel** *nf* pitchfork. **—schnupfen** *nm* hayfever. **—schrecke** *nf* **-n** **1** grasshopper. **2** locust.

Heuch/elei (hɔyçə'lai) *nf* **-en** hypocrisy. **—ler** ('hɔyçlər) *nm* **—** hypocrite.

heulen ('hɔylən) *vi* howl, cry, scream.

heut/e ('hɔytə) *adv* today. **—ig** *adj* **1** of today. **2** modern, present. **—zutage** ('hɔytt-suta:gə) *adv* these days, nowadays.

Hexe ('hɛksə) *nf* **-n** **1** witch. **2** hag. **—rei** (hɛksə'rai) *nf* witchcraft.

Hieb (hi:p) *nm* **-e** **1** blow, stroke. **2** cut.

hielt (hi:lt) *v* see **halten.**

hier (hi:r) *adv* here. **—auf** (hi:'rauf) *adv* hereupon. **—bei** (hi:r'bai) *adv* **1** at this. **2** enclosed. **—durch** (hi:r'durç) *adv* hereby. **—her** (hi:r'he:r) *adv* **1** this way. **2** here. **—in** (hi:'rin) *adv* in this. **—von** (hi:r'fɔn) *adv* of this. **—zu** (hi:r'tsu:) *adv* in addition, moreover, hereto. **—zulande** ('hi:rtsulandə) *adv* in this country, in these parts, around here.

hiesig ('hi:ziç) *adj* of this place, local.

Hilf/e ('hilfə) *nf* **-n** help, assistance. **erste Hilfe** first aid. **—eleistung** *nf* assistance. **—los** *adj* helpless. **—reich** *adj* helpful. **—sarbeiter** *nm* unskilled or temporary worker. **—smittel** *n neu* **1** remedy. **2** resource.

Himbeere ('himbe:rə) *nf* **-n** raspberry.

Himmel ('himəl) *nm* **—** **1** sky. **2** heaven. **—fahrt** *nf* Ascension. **—reich** *n neu* (kingdom of) heaven.

himmlisch ('himliʃ) *adj* heavenly.

hin (hin) *adv* **1** (to) there. **2** gone, lost. **3** ruined. **hin und her** to and fro.

hinab (hi'nap) *adv* down, downwards.

hinan (hi'nan) *adv* up (to), upward(s).

hinauf (hi'nauf) *adv* **1** up (to). **2** on high.

hinaus (hi'naus) *adv* out. **—gehen*** *vi* **1** go out. **2** result (in). **—gehen über** go beyond, exceed. **—wollen*** *vi* **1** want to go out. **2** aim at.

Hinblick ('hinblik) *nm* **im Hinblick auf** with regard to.

hinder/lich ('hindərliç) *adj* **1** in the way. **2** inconvenient. **—n** *vt* **1** prevent. **2** hinder. **—nis** *n neu* **-se** obstacle.

hindeuten ('hindɔytən) *vi* point (to or at).

hindurch (hin'durç) *adv* **1** through(out). **2** across.

hinein (hi'nain) *adv* in(to). **—gehen*** *vi* **1** go in(to). **2**

contain. **—ziehen*** *vt* draw or pull in.

Hinfahrt ('hinfa:rt) *nf* outward journey.

hinfall/en* ('hinfalən) *vi* fall (down). **¨—ig** ('hinfɛliç) *adj* **1** obsolete. **2** decaying. **3** weak.

Hin/gabe ('hinga:bə) *nf* **1** delivery. **2** devotion. **3** surrender. **—geben*** ('hinge:bən) *vt* give away or up.

hingegen ('hinge:gən) *adv* on the other hand.

hingehen* ('hinge:ən) *vi* **1** go there or to. **2** pass away or over.

hinken ('hiŋkən) *vi* limp.

hinlegen ('hinle:gən) *vt* lay down. **sich hinlegen** *vr* lie down.

hinnehmen* ('hinne:mən) *vt* **1** receive, accept. **2** put up with.

hinreichend ('hinraiçənt) *adj* sufficient.

Hinreise ('hinraizə) *nf* outward journey or voyage.

hinricht/en ('hinriçtən) *vt* execute, put to death. **—ung** *nf* **-en** execution.

Hinsicht ('hinziçt) *nf* **in dieser Hinsicht** in this respect. **—lich** *prep* with regard to, as for.

hinten ('hintən) *adv* behind, at the back.

hinter ('hintər) *prep* behind, after. *adj* posterior, back. **—backe** *nf* buttock. **—einander** (hintərain'andər) *adv* one after another. **—gehen*** *vt* deceive. **—grund** *nm* background. **—halt** *nm* ambush, trap. **—her** (hintər'he:r) *adv* after(wards), behind. **—lassen*** *vt* **1** leave (behind). **2** bequeath. **—list** *nf* **1** cunning. **2** fraud. **—teil** *n neu* **1** back part or side. **2** *inf* bottom, bum, backside. **—tür** *nf* backdoor.

hinüber (hi'ny:bər) *adv* **1** over (there). **2** across. **3** beyond.

hinunter (hi'nuntər) *adv* down (there).

hinweg (hin'vɛk) *adv* **1** away. **2** off. *nm* outward journey.

Hinweis ('hinvais) *nm* **-e** **1** indication. **2** direction. **—en*** ('hinvaizən) *vi* **1** point to. **2** allude to. *vt* **1** show. **2** direct (someone).

hinwerfen* ('hinvɛrfən) *vt* **1** throw down. **2** sketch. **3** note.

hinziehen* ('hintsi:ən) *vt* draw out or along. *vi* move (house). **sich hinziehen** *vr* drag or stretch out.

hinzu (hin'tsu:) *adv* **1** in addition. **2** near. **—fügen** *vt* **1** add. **2** enclose.

Hirn (hirn) *n neu* **-e** brain(s). **—schale** *nf* skull, cranium.

Hirsch (hirʃ) *nm* **-e** deer, stag.

Hirt (hirt) *nm* **-en** shepherd, herdsman. **—in** *nf* **-nen** shepherdess.

hissen ('hisən) *vt* hoist (up).

Histor/iker (hi'sto:rikər) *nm* — historian. **—isch** *adj* historic(al).

Hitz/e ('hitsə) *nf* heat. **—ig** *adj* hot, heated, fiery. **—kopf** *nm* hothead.

hoch (ho:x) *adj* high, tall. *adv* up. *n neu* **-s** **1** cheer. **2** high (pressure).

Hochachtung ('ho:xaxtuŋ) *nf* respect, esteem. **—svoll** *adj*

respectful. *adv* yours respectfully or sincerely.
Hochdruck ('hoːxdruk) *nm* high pressure.
Hochebene ('hoːxeːbənə) *nf* plateau.
hochfahrend ('hoːxfaːrənt) *adj* haughty.
Hochflut ('hoːxfluːt) *nf* high tide.
hochhalten* ('hoːxhaltən) *vt* **1** raise. **2** cherish.
Hochhaus ('hoːxhaus) *n neu* high-rise building.
Hochland ('hoːxlant) *n neu* highland, upland.
Hochmut ('hoːxmut) *nm* pride. **¨—tig** ('hoːxmyːtiç) *adj* proud.
hochnäsig ('hoːxnɛziç) *adj inf* stuck-up, pretentious.
Hochschätzung ('hoːxʃɛtsuŋ) *nf* esteem.
Hochschule ('hoːxʃulə) *nf* college, university.
höchst (hœːxst) *adj* **1** highest. **2** extreme. *adv* **1** most. **2** highly. **—ens** ('hœːxstəns) *adv* at most or best. **—geschwindigkeit** ('hœːxstgəʃvindiçkait) *nf* maximum speed.
Hochstapler ('hoːxʃtaːplər) *nm* — swindler, confidence trickster.
Hochverrat ('hoːxfɛraːt) *nm* high treason.
Hochwasser ('hoːxvasə) *n neu* high water or tide.
Hochzeit ('hɔxtsait) *nf* **-en** wedding.
hock/en ('hɔkən) *vi* squat, crouch. **—er** *nm* — stool.
Hoden ('hoːdən) *nm* — *also* **Hode** *nf* **-n** testicle.
Hof (hoːf) *nm* **¨-e** **1** court. **2** yard. **3** farm. **4** halo. **jemandem den Hof machen** court or woo someone. **—rat** *nm* privy councillor.
hoff/en ('hɔfən) *vt,vi* hope (for). **—entlich** *adv* **1** hopefully. **2** it is to be hoped that. **—nung** *nf* **-en** hope. **—nungslos** *adj* hopeless. **—nungsvoll** *adj* hopeful.
höflich ('hœfliç) *adj* polite, courteous. **—keit** *nf* **-en** courtesy, politeness.
Höhe ('hœːə) *nf* **-n** **1** height, altitude. **2** hill. **3** top. **—punkt** *nm* **1** summit. **2** climax. **—r** *adj* higher, upper.
Hoheit ('hoːhait) *nf* **—en** grandeur, majesty.
hohl (hoːl) *adj* **1** empty, hollow. **2** concave. **¨—e** ('hœːlə) *nf* **-n** **1** cave. **2** den. **—maß** *neu* **1** capacity. **2** volume. **¨—ung** ('hœːluŋ) *nf* **-en** **1** excavation. **2** cavity.
Hohn (hoːn) *nm* scorn. **¨—isch** ('hoeːniʃ) *adj* scornful.
hold (hɔlt) *adj* charming, lovely.
holen ('hoːlən) *vt* **1** fetch. **2** call for.
Hölle ('hœlə) *nf* **-n** hell.
Holunder (ho'lundər) *nm* — *bot* elder.
Holz (hɔlts) *n neu* **¨-er** wood. **¨—ern** ('hoeltsərn) *adj* wooden. **—kohle** *nf* charcoal. **—schnitt** *nm* woodcut.
Honig ('hoːniç) *nm* honey.
Honorar (hono'raːr) *n neu* **-e** **1** honorarium. **2** royalty (payment).
Hopfen ('hɔpfən) *nm* — *bot* hop(s).

hör/bar ('hœːrbaːr) *adj* audible. **—en** *vt,vi* hear, listen (to). *n neu* hearing. **—er** *nm* — **1** hearer, listener. **2** student. **3** receiver. **4** headset. **—gerät** *n neu* hearing aid. **—saal** *nm* **1** auditorium. **2** lecture room. **—spiel** *n neu* radio play. **—weite** *nf* earshot.
horchen ('hɔrçən) *vi* listen (secretly).
Horde ('hɔrdə) *nf* **-n 1** horde. **2** gang.
Horizont (hori'tsɔnt) *nm* **-e** horizon.
Hormon (hɔr'moːn) *n neu* **-e** hormone.
Horn (hɔrn) *n neu* **¨-er** horn.
Horoskop (horo'skoːp) *n neu* **-e** horoscope.
Hose ('hoːzə) *nf* **-n** trousers. **—nbandorden** *nm* Order of the Garter. **—nträger** *nm pl* braces.
Hotel (ho'tɛl) *n neu* **-s** hotel.
Hub (huːp) *nm* **¨-e 1** *tech* stroke. **2** lift(ing). **—schrauber** *nm* — helicopter.
hübsch (hypʃ) *adj* **1** pretty. **2** nice, fine.
Huf (huːf) *nm* **-e** hoof.
Hüfte ('hyftə) *nf* **-n** hip.
Hügel ('hyːgəl) *nm* — hill, knoll.
Huhn (huːn) *n neu* **¨-er 1** chicken. **2** hen. **¨—erauge** ('hyːnəraugə) *n neu med* corn.
Huldigung ('huldiguŋ) *nf* **-en** homage.
Hülle ('hylə) *nf* **-n 1** cover(ing), wrapping. **2** case. **—n** *vt* wrap, cover.
Hülse ('hylzə) *nf* **-n** husk, shell, case.
human (hu'maːn) *adj* humane. **—itär** (humani'tɛr) *adj* humanitarian.
Hummel ('huməl) *nf* **-n** bumblebee.
Hummer ('humər) *nm* — lobster.
Humor (hu'moːr) *nm* **-e** (sense of) humour.
humpeln ('humpəln) *vi* hobble.
Hund (hunt) *nm* **-e** dog. **¨—in** ('hyndin) *nf* **-nen** bitch.
hundert ('hundərt) *adj,n neu* **-s** hundred. **—jahrfeier** (hundərt'jaːrfaiər) *nf* centenary.
Hung/er ('huŋər) *nm* hunger. **—ersnot** *nf* famine. **—rig** *adj* hungry.
Hupe ('huːpə) *nf* **-n** *mot* horn, hooter. **—n** *vi* sound the horn.
hüpfen ('hypfən) *vi* hop, skip.
Hürde ('hyrdə) *nf* **-n 1** hurdle. **2** pen, fold.
Hure ('huːrə) *nf* **-n** whore, prostitute.
husten ('huːstən) *vi* cough. *nm* — cough.
Hut[1] (huːt) *nm* **¨-e** hat.
Hut[2] (huːt) *nf* care, charge, protection.
hüten ('hyːtən) *vt* guard, watch over. **sich hüten** *vr* take care, be on one's guard.
Hütte ('hytə) *nf* **-n 1** hut, cabin. **2** cottage. **3** forge.
Hyäne (hy'ɛːnə) *nf* **-n** hyena.
Hygien/e (hygi'eːnə) *nf* hygiene. **—isch** *adj* hygienic.
Hymne ('hymnə) *nf* **-n** hymn.
Hypno/se (hyp'noːzə) *nf* **-n** hypnosis. **—tisch** *adj* hypnotic.

Hypothek (hypo'teːk) *nf* **-en** mortgage.
Hypothe/se (hypo'teːzə) *nf* **-n** hypothesis. **—tisch** *adj* hypothetical.
Hysterie (hyste'riː) *nf* **-n** hysteria.

I

ich (iç) *pron 1st pers s* I. *n neu* self, ego.
ideal (ide'aːl) *adj* ideal. *n neu* **-e** ideal. **—ismus** (idea'lismus) *nm* idealism.
Idee (i'deː) *nf* **-n** idea.
identisch (i'dɛntiʃ) *adj* identical.
idiomatisch (idio'maːtiʃ) *adj* idiomatic. **idiomatischer Ausdruck** *nm* idiom.
Idiot (idi'oːt) *nm* **-en** idiot. **—isch** *adj* idiotic, stupid.
ignorieren (igno'riːrən) *vt* ignore, disregard.
ihm (iːm) *pron 3rd pers s* (to) him or it.
ihn (iːn) *pron 3rd pers s* him, it.
ihnen ('iːnən) *pron* **1** *3rd pers pl* (to) them. **2** *cap 2nd pers s,pl fml* (to) you.
ihr (iːr) *pron* **1** *3rd pers s* (to) her or it. **2** *2nd pers pl fam* you. *poss adj* **1** *3rd pers s* her. **2** *3rd pers pl* their. **3** *cap 3rd pers s,pl* your. **—er** *poss pron also* **der —e** or **der —ige 1** *3rd pers s* hers. **2** *cap 3rd pers s,pl fml* yours. **3** *3rd pers pl* theirs. **—erseits** ('iːrərzaits) *adv* **1** on her or their part. **2** *cap* on your part. **—ethalben** *adv also* **—etwegen** *or* **—etwillen 1** for her or their sake. **2** *cap* for your sake.
Illusion (iluzi'oːn) *nf* **-en** illusion.
illustrier/en (ilu'striːrən) *vt* illustrate. **—te** *nf* **-n** (illustrated or colour) magazine.
im (im) contraction of **in dem.**
Imbiß ('imbis) *nm* **-bisse** snack, light meal. **Imbiß-Stube** *nf* snack bar.
Immatrikulation (imatrikulatsi'oːn) *nf* **-en** matriculation.
immer ('imər) *adv* always, ever. **—grün** *adj* evergreen. *n neu* **-e** evergreen. **—hin** *adv* nevertheless, yet, still.
Immigrant (imi'grant) *nm* **-en** immigrant.
Immobilien (imo'biːliən) *nm pl* real estate.
Imperfekt ('impɛrfɛkt) *n neu* **-e** *gram* imperfect.
impf/en ('impfən) *vt* vaccinate, inoculate. **—stoff** *nm* vaccine, serum.
imponieren (impo'niːrən) *vt* impress.
Import (im'pɔrt) *nm* **-e** import(ation). **—ieren** (impɔr'tiːrən) *vt* import.
impotent ('impotɛnt) *adj* impotent.
improvisieren (imprɔvi'ziːrən) *vt,vi* improvise, ad-lib.
imstande (im'ʃtandə) *adv* **imstande sein** be able or capable, be in a position (to).
in (in) *prep* **1** in(to). **2** at. **3** to. **4** during.
Inbegriff ('inbəgrif) *nm* **1** embodiment. **2** contents.
Inbrunst ('inbrunst) *nf* ardour, fervour.
indem (in'deːm) *conj* **1** while. **2** as, because. *adv* meanwhile.

Inder ('indər) *nm* — (Asian) Indian.

indes (in'dɛs) *adv also* **indessen** (in'dɛsən) **1** meanwhile. **2** however. **3** nevertheless. *conj* yet.

Indian/er (indi'a:nər) *nm* — (American) Indian. **—isch** *adj* Indian.

Indi/en ('indiən) *n neu* India. **—sch** ('indiʃ) *adj* Indian.

Indikativ ('indikati:f) *nm* **-e** *gram* indicative.

indirekt ('indirɛkt) *adj* indirect.

individu/ell (individu'ɛl) *adj* individual. **—um** (indi'vi:duum) *n neu* **-uen** individual, person.

Indones/ien (indo'ne:ziən) *n neu* Indonesia. **—ier** *nm* — Indonesian. **—isch** *adj* Indonesian.

Industrie (indus'tri:) *nf* **-n** industry. **—ll** (industri'ɛl) *adj* industrial. **—lle(r)** (industri'ɛlə) *nm* industrialist.

ineinander (inain'andər) *adv* into one another.

Infanterie (infantə'ri:) *nf* **-n** infantry, foot.

infizieren (infi'tsi:rən) *vt* infect.

Inflation (inflatsi'o:n) *nf* **-en** *comm* inflation.

infolge (in'fɔlgə) *prep* in consequence of, due to. **—dessen** (infɔlgə'dɛsən) *adv* **1** accordingly, then. **2** as a result of this, due to which.

Inform/ation (infɔrmatsi'o:n) *nf* **-en** (item of) information. **—ationsbüro** *n neu* information bureau or centre. **—ieren** (infɔr'mi:rən) *vt* **1** inform. **2** instruct.

Infrastruktur ('infra:ʃtruktu:r) *nf* **-en** infrastructure.

Ingenieur (inʒe'njœ:r) *nm* **-e** engineer. **—wesen** *n neu* engineering.

Inhaber ('inha:bər) *nm* — possessor, holder.

Inhalt ('inhalt) *nm* **-e** **1** contents. **2** volume. **3** meaning. **—sverzeichnis** *n neu* **1** table of contents. **2** index.

Initiative (initsia'ti:və) *nf* initiative.

inklusive (inklu'zi:və) *adv* inclusive, including.

Inkrafttreten (in'krafttre:tən) *n neu* coming into force or effect.

Inland ('inlant) *n neu* **1** native country. **2** inland.

inmitten (in'mitən) *prep* amid(st).

inne ('inə) *adv* within. **—halten*** *vi* stop. *vt* keep to.

innen ('inən) *adv* within, inside.

inner ('inər) *adj* inner, interior. **—halb** *prep,adv* within, inside. **—lich** *adj* inward, inner. **—st** *adj* inmost.

innig ('iniç) *adj* heartfelt, sincere.

ins (ins) contraction of **in das. —besondere** (insbə'zɔndərə) *adv* in particular. **—geheim** (insgə'haim) *adv* secretly. **—gesamt** (insgə'zamt) *adv* altogether.

Insasse ('inzasə) *nm* **-n** inmate, occupant.

Inschrift ('inʃrift) *nf* **-en** inscription.

Insekt (in'zɛkt) *n neu* **-en** insect. **—engift** *n neu* insecticide.

Insel ('inzəl) *nf* **-n** island, isle.

Inserat (inze'ra:t) *n neu* **-e** advertisement, announcement.
insofern (inzo'fɛrn) *adv also* **insoweit** (inzo'vait) in this respect, to that extent. *conj* in so far as, inasmuch as.
instand halten* (in 'ʃtanthaltən) *vt* maintain (in good order).
Instanz (in'stants) *nf* **-en 1** *law* court. **2** authority.
Instinkt (in'stiŋkt) *nm* **-e** instinct.
Institut (insti'tu:t) *n neu* **-e** institute.
Instrument (instru'mɛnt) *n neu* **-e** instrument.
inszenieren (instse'ni:rən) *vt* stage, produce.
intelligen/t (intɛli'gɛnt) *adj* intelligent. **—z** (intɛli'gɛnts) *nf* **1** intelligence. **2** intelligentsia.
interess/ant (intərɛ'sant) *adj* interesting. **—e** (intə'rɛsə) *n neu* **-n** interest. **—ieren** (intərɛ'si:rən) *vt* interest. **sich —ieren** *vr* be interested.
international (internatsio'na:l) *adj* international. **—e** *nf pol* International.
intim (in'ti:m) *adj* intimate.
Intrige (in'tri:gə) *nf* **-n** intrigue, plot.
inwendig ('invɛndiç) *adj* interior, inside.
inwiefern (invi:'fɛrn) *adv also* **inwieweit** (invi:'vait) to what extent, how far.
inzwischen (in'tsviʃən) *adv* meanwhile.
Irak (i'ra:k) *nm* Iraq. **—er** *nm* Iraqi. **—isch** *adj* Iraqi.
irdisch ('irdiʃ) *adj* **1** worldly, earthly. **2** mortal.
irgend ('irgənt) *pron,adv* some, any. **irgend etwas** something (or other). **irgend jemand** anybody, somebody or other. **—ein** (irgənt'ain) *pron,adj* some(one), any(one). **—wann** (irgənt'van) *adv* at some time. **—was** (irgənt 'vas) *pron* something (or other). **—wie** (irgənt'vi:) *adv* somehow. **—wo** (irgənt'vo:) *adv* somewhere.
Iris ('i:ris) *nf* — *anat* iris.
Ir/land ('irlant) *n neu* Ireland. **—e** ('i:rə) *nm* **-n** *also* **—länder** — Irishman. **—in** *nf* **-nen** *also* **—länderin** Irishwoman. **—isch** *adj* Irish.
Iron/ie (iro'ni:) *nf* **-n** irony. **—isch** (i'ro:niʃ) *adj* ironical.
irr/e ('irə) *adj* **1** stray. **2** mad. **3** unsettled. **4** confused. **—e(r)** *nm* lunatic. **—eführen** *vt* **1** mislead. **2** deceive. **—en** *vi* wander, stray. **sich —en** *vr* **1** err. **2** be mistaken. **—ig** *adj also* **—tümlich** erroneous, false. **—tum** *nm* **¨-er** error, fault.
isolieren (izo'li:rən) *vt* **1** isolate. **2** insulate.
ißt (ist) *v* see **essen.**
ist (ist) *v see* **sein**[2].
Italien (i'ta:liən) *n neu* Italy. **—er** (itali'e:nər) *nm* — Italian. **—isch** (itali'e:niʃ) *adj* Italian. *n neu* Italian (language).

J

ja (ja) *adv* yes, indeed. *n neu* **-s** assent. **mit Ja antworten** reply in the affirmative.
Jacht (jaxt) *nf* **-en** yacht.
Jacke ('jakə) *nf* **-n** jacket.
Jagd (ja:kt) *nf* **-en** hunt, hunting.

jag/en ('ja:gən) *vt* **1** hunt. **2** shoot. **3** drive. *vi* **1** hunt. **2** rush. **¨—er** ('jɛ:gər) *nm* — **1** hunter. **2** rifleman. **3** fighter pilot. **4** fighter plane.
jäh (jɛ:) *adj* **1** sudden. **2** steep.
Jahr (ja:r) *n neu* **-e** year. **—elang** *adj* lasting for one or several years. *adv* for years. **—eswechsel** *nm* turn of the year, New Year. **—eszeit** *nf* season. **—hundert** (ja:r 'hundərt) *n neu* **-e** century. **¨—lich** ('jɛ:rliç) *adj* annual. **—tausend** (ja:r'tauzənt) *n neu* **-e** millennium. **—zehnt** (ja:r 'tse:nt) *n neu* **-e** decade.
Jammer ('jamər) *nm* **1** misery, sorrow. **2** lamentation. **¨—lich** ('jɛ:mərliç) *adj* pitiful. **—n** *vi* lament, bewail.
Januar ('janua:r) *nm* January.
Japan ('ja:pan) *n neu* Japan. **—er** (ja'pa:nər) *nm* — Japanese. **—isch** (ja'pa:niʃ) *adj* Japanese. *n neu* Japanese (language).
jauchzen ('jauxtsən) *vi* rejoice, shout with joy.
jawohl (ja'vo:l) *adv* yes indeed, certainly.
Jazz (dʒɛs) *nm* jazz.
je (je:) *adv* **1** ever. **2** each, apiece. **je...desto** the...the. **je nachdem** according as or to.
jedenfalls ('je:dənfals) *adv* in any case.
jeder, jede, jedes ('je:dər, 'je:də, 'je:dəs) *pron,adj m,f,neu* every, each.
jedermann ('je:dərman) *pron* everyone.
jederzeit ('je:dərtsait) *adv* at any time.
jedesmal ('je:dəsma:l) *adv* every time, each time.
jedoch (je'dɔx) *adv* however, yet.
jeglicher ('je:kliçər) *pron,adj* every, each.
jemals ('je:ma:ls) *adv* at any time, ever.
jemand ('je:mant) *pron* someone, anyone.
jener, jene, jenes ('je:nər, 'je:nə, 'je:nəs) *pron,adj m,f,neu* **1** that. **2** the former.
jenseits ('je:nzaits) *adv* on the other side. *prep* beyond. *n neu* the other world, the life to come.
jetz/ig ('jɛtsiç) *adj* present, actual, current. **—t** *adv* at present, now.
Joch (jɔx) *n neu* **-e** yoke.
Jockei ('dʒɔki) *nm* **-s** jockey.
Jod (jo:t) *n neu* iodine.
jodeln ('jo:dəln) *vi* yodel.
Joghurt ('jo:gurt) *n neu* **-s** yoghurt.
Johannisbeere (jo'hanisbe:rə) *nf* redcurrant. **schwarze Johannisbeere** blackcurrant.
Journalist (ʒurna'list) *nm* **-en** journalist.
Jubel ('ju:bəl) *nm* rejoicing. **—n** *vi* rejoice.
jucken ('jukən) *vt,vi* itch.
Jud/e ('ju:də) *nm* **-n** Jew. **—entum** *n neu* Judaism, Jewry. **¨—in** ('jy:din) *nf* **-nen** Jewess. **¨—isch** ('jy:diʃ) *adj* Jewish.
Judo ('ju:do) *n neu* judo.
Jugend ('ju:gənt) *nf* youth. **—lich** *adj* youthful, juvenile. **—herberge** *nf* youth hostel.
Jugoslaw/e (jugo'sla:və) *nm* **-n** Yugoslav. **—ien** *n neu* Yugo-

slavia. **—isch** *adj* Yugoslav(ian).
Juli ('juːli) *nm* July.
jung (juŋ) *adj* young. **—e** *nm* **-n** youth, boy, lad. **¨—er** ('jyŋər) *adj* **1** younger. **2** junior. *nm* — disciple. **—fer** *nf* **-n** maid, virgin. **alte Jungfer** old maid, spinster. **—frau** *nf* **1** virgin, maiden. **2** Virgo. **—geselle** *nm* bachelor. **¨—ling** ('jyŋliŋ) *nm* **-e** youth, young man. **¨—st** (jyŋst) *adj* **1** youngest. **2** latest. **das Jüngste Gericht** the Last Judgment.
Juni ('juːni) *nm* June.
Junker ('juŋkər) *nm* — (young) nobleman, squire.
Jur/a[1] ('juːra) *n pl* (study of) law. **—ist** (ju'rist) *nm* **-en** lawyer.
Jura[2] ('juːra) *nm* **-s** the Juras.
just (just) *adv* **1** exactly. **2** just (now). **3** only just.
Justiz (jus'tiːts) *nf* **1** legal administration. **2** justice.
Juwel (ju'veːl) *n neu* **-en** jewel. **—ier** (juvə'liːr) *nm* **-e** jeweller.
Jux (juks) *nm* **-e** joke, prank.

K

Kabarett (kaba'rɛt) *n neu* **-e** cabaret.
Kabel ('kaːbəl) *n neu* — cable.
Kabine (ka'biːnə) *nf* **-n** **1** cabin. **2** cubicle.
Kabinett (kabi'nɛt) *n neu* **-e** **1** *pol* cabinet. **2** closet.
Kadett (ka'dɛt) *nm* **-en** cadet.
Käfer ('kɛːfər) *nm* — beetle.
Kaffee ('kafe) *nm* **-s** coffee.
Käfig ('kɛːfiç) *nm* **-e** cage.
kahl (kaːl) *adj* **1** bald. **2** bare. **—kopf** *nm* bald head.
Kahn (kaːn) *nm* **¨-e** **1** boat, skiff. **2** barge.
Kai (kai) *nm* **-e** quay, wharf.
Kaiser ('kaizər) *nm* — emperor. **—in** *nf* **-nen** empress. **—lich** *adj* imperial. **—reich** *n neu* empire.
Kakao (ka'kaːo) *nm* cocoa.
Kaktus ('kaktus) *nm* **-teen** cactus.
Kalb (kalp) *n neu* **¨-er** calf. **—fleisch** *n neu* veal. **—sbraten** *nm* roast veal.
Kalender (ka'lɛndər) *nm* — calendar.
Kali ('kaːli) *n neu* potash.
Kalk (kalk) *nm* **-e** lime. **—stein** *nm* limestone.
kalt (kalt) *adj* **1** cold. **2** frigid. **—blütig** ('kaltblyːtiç) *adj* cold-blooded. **¨—e** ('kɛltə) *nf* cold, coldness.
kam (kaːm) *v* see **kommen.**
Kamel (ka'meːl) *n neu* **-e** camel.
Kamera ('kamera) *nf* **-s** camera.
Kamerad (kamə'raːt) *nm* **-en, —in** (kamə'raːdin) *nf* **-nen** comrade, companion.
Kamin (ka'miːn) *nm* **-e** **1** chimney. **2** fireplace.
Kamm (kam) *nm* **¨-e** **1** comb. **2** crest. **3** ridge. **¨—en** ('kɛmən) *vt* comb.
Kammer ('kamər) *nf* **-n** **1** small room, chamber. **2** *pol,comm* chamber. **—diener** *nm* valet. **—musik** *nf* chamber music.
Kampf (kampf) *nm* **¨-e** fight, struggle, battle, contest. **¨—en** ('kɛmpfən) *vi* fight, struggle. **¨—er** ('kɛmpfər) *nm* — fighter, combatant.
Kanad/a ('kanada) *n neu* Can-

ada. **—ier** (ka'naːdiːr) *nm* — Canadian. **—isch** (ka'naːdiʃ) *adj* Canadian.
Kanal (ka'naːl) *nm* ¨-e **1** channel. **2** canal. **3** drain. **4** pipe. **Ärmelkanal** English Channel.
Kanarienvogel (ka'naːriənfoːgəl) *nm* canary.
Kandid/at (kandi'daːt) *nm* **-en** candidate. **—ieren** (kandi 'diːrən) *vi* be a candidate, stand.
Känguruh ('kɛŋguruː) *n neu* **-s** kangaroo.
Kaninchen ('kaninçən) *n neu* — rabbit.
kann (kan) *v* see **können.**
Kannabis ('kanabis) *n neu* cannabis.
Kanne ('kanə) *nf* **-n** **1** can. **2** jug. **3** pot.
kannte ('kantə) *v* see **kennen.**
Kanon (ka'noːn) *nm* **-s** canon.
Kanone (ka'noːnə) *nf* **-n** **1** cannon. **2** gun. **3** *inf* wizard, ace.
Kante ('kantə) *nf* **-n** **1** edge. **2** brim, rim.
Kantine (kan'tiːnə) *nf* **-n** canteen.
Kanton (kan'toːn) *nm* **-e** canton.
Kanzel ('kantsəl) *nf* **-n** **1** pulpit. **2** *aviat* cockpit.
Kanzler ('kantslər) *nm* — chancellor.
Kap (kap) *n neu* **-s** cape, headland.
Kapazität (kapatsi'tɛːt) *nf* **-en** **1** capacity. **2** authority.
Kapelle (ka'pɛlə) *nf* **-n** **1** chapel. **2** band. **3** choir.
Kaper ('kaːpər) *nf* **-n** *bot* caper.
Kapital (kapi'taːl) *n neu* **-ien** capital. **—anlage** *nf* investment. **—ismus** (kapita'lismus) *nm* capitalism. **—ist** (kapita'list) *nm* **-en** capitalist.
Kapitän (kapi'tɛːn) *nm* **-e** captain, skipper.
Kapitel (ka'pitəl) *n neu* — chapter.
Kaplan (ka'plaːn) *nm* ¨-e chaplain.
Kappe ('kapə) *nf* **-n** **1** cap. **2** hood. **3** top. **4** dome.
kaputt (ka'put) *adj inf* **1** bust, broken. **2** exhausted.
Kapuze (ka'puːtsə) *nf* **-n** **1** hood. **2** cowl.
Karat (ka'raːt) *n neu* **-e** carat.
Karate (ka'raːtə) *n neu* karate.
Karawane (kara'vaːnə) *nf* **-n** caravan.
Kardinal (kardi'naːl) *nm* ¨-e cardinal.
Karfreitag (kaːr'fraitaːk) *nm* Good Friday.
karg (kark) *adj* **1** thrifty. **2** miserly. **3** poor. **4** meagre. **5** barren. ¨**—lich** ('kɛrkliç) *adj* **1** scanty. **2** poor.
kariert (ka'riːrt) *adj* **1** checked. **2** chequered.
Karies ('kaːriɛs) *nf med* caries.
Karikatur (karika'tuːr) *nf* **-en** caricature.
Karneval ('karneval) *nm* **-e** carnival.
Karo ('kaːro) *n neu* **-s** *game* diamonds.
Karosserie (karɔsə'riː) *nf* **-n** *mot* bodywork.
Karotte (ka'rɔtə) *nf* **-n** carrot.
Karpfen ('karpfən) *nm* — carp.
Karre ('karə) *nf* **-n** *also* **Karren** *nm* — cart, (wheel-)barrow.
Karriere (ka'rjɛːrə) *nf* **-n** **1** career. **2** gallop.
Karte ('kartə) *nf* **-n** **1** card. **2** map. **3** ticket. **4** menu.

Kartell (kar'tɛl) *n neu* **-e** cartel.
Kartoffel (kar'tɔfəl) *nf* **-n** potato. **—brei** *nm also* **—püree** *n neu* mashed or creamed potatoes.
Karton (kar'tɔn) *nm* **-e, -s** cardboard (box), carton.
Kartusche (kar'tuʃə) *nf* **-n** cartridge.
Karussell (karu'sɛl) *n neu* **-e** merry-go-round.
Kaschmir ('kaʃmir) *n neu* Cashmere.
Käse ('kɛːzə) *nm* — cheese.
Kaserne (ka'zɛrnə) *nf* **-n** barracks.
Kasino (ka'ziːno) *n neu* **-s 1** casino. **2** officers' mess.
Kasse ('kasə) *nf* **-n 1** till, cash register. **2** cash-desk. **3** booking office. **4** cash. **5** cash-box. **6** strongbox.
Kassette (ka'sɛtə) *nf* **-n 1** casket, box. **2** film spool. **3** cassette (tape). **—nrecorder** *nm* — cassette-recorder.
kassier/en (ka'siːrən) *vt* **1** cash. **2** cashier. **3** cancel. **4** annul. **—er** *nm* — **1** cashier. **2** treasurer.
Kastanie (ka'staːniə) *nf* **-n** chestnut.
Kasten ('kastən) *nm* **¨—** box, chest.
kastrieren (ka'striːrən) *vt* castrate.
Kasus ('kaːzus) *nm* — *gram* case.
Katalog (kata'loːk) *nm* **-e** catalogue.
Katarrh (ka'tar) *nm* **-e** catarrh.
katastroph/al (katastro'faːl) *adj* catastrophic. **—e** (kata'stroːfə) *nf* **-n** catastrophe.
Kategorie (katego'riː) *nf* **-n** category.
Kater ('kaːtər) *nm* — **1** tomcat. **2** *inf* hangover.
Kathedrale (kate'draːlə) *nf* **-n** cathedral.
Kathol/ik (kato'liːk) *nm* **-en, —ikin** *nf* **-nen** Catholic. **—isch** (ka'toːliʃ) *adj* Catholic.
Katze ('katsə) *nf* **-n** cat.
Kauderwelsch ('kaudərvɛlʃ) *n neu* double-dutch.
kauen ('kauən) *vt* chew.
kauern ('kauərn) *vi* cower.
Kauf (kauf) *nm* **¨-e 1** purchase, buy(ing). **2** bargain. **in Kauf nehmen 1** accept. **2** put up with. **—en** *vt* buy, purchase. **¨—er** ('kɔyfər) *nm* — buyer, purchaser. **—haus** *n neu* department store. **—kraft** *nf* purchasing power. **—laden** *nm* shop. **¨—lich** ('kɔyfliç) *adj* **1** purchasable, for sale. **2** venal, corrupt. **—mann** *nm* **-leute 1** shopkeeper. **2** merchant. **3** businessman.
Kaugummi ('kaugumi) *nm* chewing gum.
Kaukasus ('kaukazus) *nm* Caucasus.
kaum (kaum) *adv* hardly, scarcely, barely.
Kaution (kau'tsjoːn) *nf* **-en 1** security. **2** bail.
Kauz (kauts) *nm* **¨-e 1** owl. **2** odd fellow.
Kavallerie (kavalə'riː) *nf* **-n** cavalry.
Kaviar ('kaːviar) *nm* **-e** caviar.
keck (kɛk) *adj* **1** bold, daring. **2** cheeky.
Kegel ('keːgəl) *nm* — **1** skittle(s), ninepin(s). **2** cone. **—bahn** *nf* bowling alley.

Kehl/e ('ke:lə) *nf* **-n** throat. **—kopf** *nm* larynx. **—kopfentzündung** *nf* laryngitis.

kehren[1] ('ke:rən) *vt* turn.

kehr/en[2] ('ke:rən) *vt* sweep. **—icht** ('ke:riçt) *nm* **1** sweepings. **2** rubbish.

Keil (kail) *nm* **-e** wedge. **—en** *vt* **1** (fix or split with a) wedge. **2** thrash. **sich —en** *vr* fight. **—er** *nm* **—** boar.

Keim (kaim) *nm* **-e** **1** germ. **2** bud. **3** embryo. **—en** *vi* **1** germinate. **2** sprout.

kein, kein/e, kein (kain, 'kaine, kain) *adj* no, not any. **es war kein Mensch zu sehen** there was not a soul to be seen. **—er, —e, —es** ('kainər, 'kainə, 'kainəs) *pron* **1** none. **2** no one. **—erlei** ('kainərlai) *adj* of no sort, not any. **—esfalls** ('kainəsfals) *adv* on no account. **—eswegs** ('kainəsve:ks) *adv* not at all, by no means.

Keks (ke:ks) *nm,neu* **-e** biscuit.

Keller ('kɛlər) *nm* **—** cellar.

Kellner ('kɛlnər) *nm* **—** **1** waiter. **2** barman. **—in** *nf* **-nen** **1** waitress. **2** barmaid.

kenn/en* ('kɛnən) *vt* know, be acquainted with. **—er** *nm* **—** expert, connoisseur. **—enlernen** *vt* become acquainted with, get to know. **—tnis** *nf* **-se** knowledge. **—zeichen** *n neu* characteristic, (distinguishing) feature. **—zeichnen** *vt* **1** mark. **2** distinguish.

Kerbe ('kɛrbə) *nf* **-n** **1** notch. **2** slot.

Kerker ('kɛrkər) *nm* **—** prison, jail.

Kerl (kɛrl) *nm* **-e** **1** fellow, man. **2** *inf* bloke.

Kern (kɛrn) *nm* **-e** **1** core. **2** kernel, pip, stone. **3** nucleus. **—energie** *nf* nuclear energy. **—gesund** *adj* thoroughly healthy. **—physik** *nf* nuclear physics. **—waffen** *nf pl* nuclear weapons.

Kerze ('kɛrtsə) *nf* **-n** candle.

Kessel ('kɛsəl) *nm* **—** **1** kettle. **2** boiler. **3** basin. **4** hollow.

Kette ('kɛtə) *nf* **-n** chain. **—nbrücke** *nf* suspension bridge. **—reaktion** *nf* chain reaction.

Ketzer ('kɛtsər) *nm* **—** heretic. **—ei** (kɛtsə'rai) *nf* **-en** heresy.

keuchen ('kɔyçən) *vi* pant, gasp.

Keule ('kɔylə) *nf* **-n** **1** club, cudgel. **2** thigh (of an animal). **3** *cul* leg.

keusch (kɔyʃ) *adj* chaste.

kichern ('kiçərn) *vi* giggle.

Kiefer[1] ('ki:fər) *nm* **—** jaw.

Kiefer[2] ('ki:fər) *nf* **-n** pine, fir.

Kiel (ki:l) *nm* **-e** **1** keel. **2** quill.

Kieme ('ki:mə) *nf* **-n** *zool* gill.

Kies (ki:s) *nm* **-e** gravel.

Kieselstein ('ki:zəlʃtain) *nm* pebble.

Kilo ('ki:lo) *n neu* kilo. **—gramm** (ki:lo'gram) *n neu* kilogram.

Kind (kint) *n neu* **-er** child. **—erei** (kində'rai) *nf* **-en** childishness, nonsense. **—erspiel** ('kindərʃpi:l) *n neu* child's play, child's game. **—erstube** ('kindərʃtu:bə) *nf* nursery. **—erwagen** ('kindərva:gən) *nm* pram. **—heit** ('kinthait) *nf* childhood. **—isch** ('kindiʃ) *adj* childish. **—lich** ('kintliç) *adj* childlike.

Kinn (kin) *n neu* **-e** chin.

Kino ('kiːno) *n neu* **-s** cinema.

Kiosk (ki'ɔsk) *nm* **-e 1** kiosk. **2** newsstand.

Kirch/e ('kirçə) *nf* **-n** church. **—hof** *nm* **1** churchyard. **2** cemetery. **—lich** *adj* ecclesiastical, church. **-spiel** *n neu* parish. **—turm** *nm* steeple, church tower.

Kirsch (kirʃ) *nm also* **Kirschwasser** ('kirʃvasər) *n neu* kirsch.

Kirsche ('kirʃə) *nf* **-n** cherry.

Kissen ('kisən) *n neu* — cushion, pillow.

Kiste ('kistə) *nf* **-n** box, case, crate.

Kitsch (kitʃ) *nm* tasteless rubbish, trash.

kitzeln ('kitsəln) *vt* tickle.

klaffen ('klafən) *vi* gape, yawn.

Klag/e ('klaːgə) *nf* **-n 1** complaint. **2** *law* action. **3** lament. **—en** *vi* **1** complain. **2** *law* bring an action. **3** lament. **¨—er** ('klɛːgər) *nm* — plaintiff. **¨—lich** ('klɛːkliç) *adj* wretched, plaintive.

Klammer ('klamər) *nf* **-n 1** clip, clamp. **2** peg. **3** bracket. **—n** *vt* fasten.

Klang (klaŋ) *nm* **¨-e** (ringing) sound. **—farbe** *nf* timbre, tone.

Klapp/e ('klapə) *nf* **-n 1** flap. **2** lid. **3** stop. **4** valve. **5** *sl* mouth. **—en** *vt* clap. *vi* **1** flap. **2** collapse, fold. **es klappt** it works (well).

Klapper ('klapər) *nf* **-n** rattle. **—n** *vi* rattle.

klar (klaːr) *adj* **1** clear. **2** bright. **3** distinct. **4** evident. **5** pure. **¨—en** ('klɛːrən) *vt* **1** clarify. **2** purify. **—heit** *nf* clarity, clearness. **—legen** *vt also* **—machen** clear up, explain, point out.

Klarinette (klari'nɛtə) *nf* **-n** clarinet.

Klasse ('klasə) *nf* **-n 1** class. **2** category. **—nzimmer** *n neu* classroom.

Klass/iker ('klasikər) *nm* — classic (author). **—isch** *adj* classic(al).

Klatsch (klatʃ) *nm* **-e 1** clap. **2** gossip. **3** smack. **—en** *vi* **1** clap. **2** gossip. **3** slap, smack.

Klaue ('klauə) *nf* **-n 1** hoof. **2** claw. **3** *sl* scrawl, handwriting. **—n** *vt* **1** claw. **2** *sl* pinch, steal.

Klausel ('klauzəl) *nf* **-n** clause.

Klavier (kla'viːr) *n neu* **-e** piano.

kleb/en ('kleːbən) *vt* glue, stick. *vi* **1** stick. **2** cling. **—(e)rig** *adj* sticky. **—estreifen** *nm* adhesive tape. **—stoff** *nm* adhesive, glue.

kleck/ern ('klɛkərn) *vi* dribble, slobber. **—s** (klɛks) *nm* **-e 1** blot. **2** stain.

Klee (kleː) *nm* clover.

Kleid (klait) *n neu* **-er 1** dress. **2** garment. **3** *pl* clothes. **—en** ('klaidən) *vt* clothe, dress. **—erschrank** ('klaidərʃraŋk) *nm* wardrobe. **—ung** ('klaiduŋ) *nf* clothing.

klein (klain) *adj* **1** small, little. **2** short. **3** petty, mean. **—asien** (klain'aːziən) *n neu* Asia Minor. **—geld** *n neu* (small) change. **—handel** *nm* retail trade. **—heit** *nf* smallness. **—igkeit** *nf* **-en** trifle, petty detail. **—laut** *adj* subdued, quiet. **—lich** *adj* petty, mean. **—stadt** *nf* small city or town.

Kleinod ('klaino:t) *n neu* **-ien** gem.

Kleister ('klaistər) *nm* — paste.

Klemme ('klɛmə) *nf* **-n 1** clamp. **2** (electrical) terminal. **3** dilemma, difficulty.

Klempner ('klɛmpnər) *nm* — plumber.

Klerus ('kle:rus) *nm* clergy.

klettern ('klɛtərn) *vi* climb.

Klima ('kli:ma) *n neu* **-te** climate. **—anlage** *nf* **1** air-conditioner. **2** air-conditioning.

Klinge ('kliŋə) *nf* **-n** blade. **—n*** *vi* **1** sound. **2** ring, chink.

Klingel ('kliŋəl) *nf* **-n 1** bell. **2** door-bell. **—n** *vi* ring, tinkle.

Klinik ('kli:nik) *nf* **-en** clinic, hospital.

Klinke ('kliŋkə) *nf* **-n 1** latch. **2** handle.

Klippe ('klipə) *nf* **-n** reef, rocks.

klirren ('klirən) *vi* **1** clink. **2** clash, jangle.

Klo (klo:) *n neu* **-s** *inf* toilet, loo.

Kloben ('klo:bən) *nm* — **1** pulley, block. **2** vice. **3** pincers. **4** log.

klopfen ('klɔpfən) *vi,vt* beat, knock.

Klosett (klɔ'zɛt) *n neu* **-e** toilet, lavatory. **—papier** *n neu* toilet paper.

Kloster ('klo:stər) *n neu* **¨— 1** convent. **2** monastery.

Klotz (klɔts) *nm* **¨-e 1** log. **2** block.

Klub (klup) *nm* **-s** club, society.

Kluft (kluft) *nf* **¨-e 1** gap. **2** chasm. **3** cleft.

klug (klu:k) *adj* **1** clever, intelligent. **2** prudent. **—heit** *nf* **1** cleverness, intelligence. **2** prudence.

Klumpen ('klumpən) *nm* — **1** lump, clod. **2** heap.

knabbern ('knabərn) *vi,vt* gnaw, nibble.

Knabe ('kna:bə) *nm* **-n** boy, lad.

knacken ('knakən) *vt,vi* crack, snap.

Knall (knal) *nm* **¨-e 1** crack. **2** bang, report. **—en** *vi* **1** crack, snap. **2** bang.

knapp (knap) *adj* **1** tight, close-fitting. **2** scarce, meagre. **3** bare, barely sufficient.

knarren ('knarən) *vi* **1** creak. **2** rattle.

Knecht (knɛçt) *nm* **-e 1** servant. **2** farmhand. **—schaft** *nf* servitude.

kneif/en* ('knaifən) *vt* pinch. *vi* **1** flinch. **2** retreat. **—zange** *nf* pliers, pincers.

Kneipe ('knaipə) *nf* **-n** public house, tavern.

kneten ('knɛ:tən) *vt* knead, massage.

Knicks (kniks) *nm* **-e** curtsey.

Knie (kni:) *n neu* — knee. **—(e)n** ('kni:ən) *vi* kneel. **—hose** *nf* kneebreeches.

Kniff (knif) *nm* **-e 1** crease. **2** pinch. **3** trick, knack.

knipsen ('knipsən) *vt* **1** clip. **2** snap (a photograph). *vi* snap one's fingers.

knirschen ('knirʃən) *vi* **1** grate. **2** grind.

Knoblauch ('kno:plaux) *nm* garlic.

Knöchel ('knœçəl) *nm* — **1** ankle. **2** knuckle.
Knoch/en ('knɔxən) *nm* — bone. **—ig** *adj* bony.
Knödel ('knœːdəl) *nm* — dumpling.
Knopf (knɔpf) *nm* **¨-e** button. **¨—en** ('knœpfən) *vt* button.
Knorpel ('knɔrpəl) *nm* — cartilage.
Knospe ('knɔspə) *nf* **-n** bud. **—n** *vi* **1** bud. **2** sprout.
Knoten ('knoːtən) *nm* — **1** knot. **2** node. **3** difficulty. **—punkt** *nm* junction.
knüpfen ('knypfən) *vt* tie, bind.
knusprig ('knuspriç) *adj* crisp.
Koalition (koalitsi'oːn) *nf* **-en** coalition.
Kobra ('koːbra) *nf* **-s** cobra.
Koch (kɔx) *nm* **¨-e, Köchin** ('kœçin) *nf* **-nen** cook. **—buch** *n neu* cookery book. **—en** *vt,vi* **1** cook. **2** boil.
Kodex ('koːdeks) *nm* **-e** code.
Koexistenz (koɛksis'tɛnts) *nf* co-existence.
koffeinfrei (kɔfe'iːnfrai) *adj* decaffeinated.
Koffer ('kɔfər) *nm* — **1** suitcase. **2** trunk. **—radio** *n neu* portable radio. **—raum** *nm* *mot* boot.
Kohl (koːl) *nm* **-e** cabbage.
Kohle ('koːlə) *nf* **-n** **1** coal. **2** charcoal, coke. **3** carbon. **—nbergwerk** *n neu* coalmine. **—nsäure** *nf* **1** carbonic acid. **2** carbon dioxide. **—nstoff** *nm* carbon. **—papier** *n neu* carbon paper.
Koje ('koːjə) *nf* **-n** **1** cabin. **2** bunk.
kokettieren (kokɛ'tiːrən) *vi* flirt.
Kokosnuß ('koːkɔsnus) *nf* coconut.
Koks (koːks) *nm* **-e** coke.
Kolben ('kɔlbən) *nm* — **1** butt(-end). **2** club. **3** piston. **4** *sci* retort, flask.
Kollege (kɔ'leːgə) *nm* **-n, Kollegin** *nf* **-nen** colleague.
kollektiv (kɔlɛk'tiːf) *adj* collective.
Köln (kœln) *n neu* Cologne.
kolon/ial (koloni'aːl) *adj* colonial. **—ie** (kolo'niː) *nf* **-n** colony. **—ist** (kolo'nist) *nm* **-en** colonist, settler.
Kolonne (ko'lɔnə) *nf* **-n** column.
kolossal (kolɔ'saːl) *adj* huge, immense.
Kombination (kɔmbinatsi'oːn) *nf* **-en** **1** combination. **2** conjecture, deduction.
Komet (ko'meːt) *nm* **-en** comet.
Komfort (kɔm'foːr) *nm* **1** luxury. **2** comfort.
komisch ('koːmiʃ) *adj* **1** funny. **2** strange.
Komitee (komi'teː) *n neu* **-s** committee.
Komma ('kɔma) *n neu* **-s** comma.
Kommand/ant (kɔman'dant) *nm* **-e** commander. **—ieren** (kɔman'diːrən) *vi,vt* command.
kommen* ('kɔmən) *vi* **1** come, approach. **2** arrive. **3** happen. **auf etwas kommen** think of, hit upon something. **zu etwas kommen** come to, obtain something.
Kommiss/ar (kɔmi'saːr) *nm* **-e** **1** commissioner. **2** (police) in-

spector. **3** commissar. **—ion** (kɔmisi'oːn) *nf* **-en** commission.
Kommode (kɔ'moːdə) *nf* **-n** chest of drawers.
kommun (kɔ'muːn) *adj* common. **—al** (kɔmu'naːl) *adj* **1** communal. **2** municipal. **—e** (kɔ'muːnə) *nf* **-n** **1** commune. **2** community.
Kommunikation (kɔmuːnikatsi'oːn) *nf* **-en** communication.
Kommunismus (kɔmu'nismus) *nm* communism. **—ist** (kɔmu'nist) *nm* **-en** communist. **—istisch** (kɔmu'nistiʃ) *adj* communist.
Komödie (ko'mœːdiə) *nf* **-n** comedy, farce.
Kompaß ('kɔmpas) *nm* **-passe** compass.
kompetent (kɔmpe'tɛnt) *adj* competent.
Kompliment (kɔmpli'mɛnt) *n neu* **-e** compliment.
kompliziert (kɔmpli'tsiːrt) *adj* complicated.
kompo/nieren (kɔmpo'niːrən) *vt* compose. **—nist** (kɔmpo'nist) *nm* **-en** composer. **—sition** (kɔmpozitsi'oːn) *nf* **-en** composition.
Kompott (kɔm'pɔt) *n neu* **-e** stewed fruit.
Kompromiß (kɔmpro'mis) *nm* **-misse** compromise.
Konditorei (kɔndito'rai) *nf* **-en** coffee-shop, cake-shop.
Kondom (kɔn'doːm) *nm* **-e** condom.
Konferenz (kɔnfe'rɛnts) *nf* **-en** conference, meeting.
Konflikt (kɔn'flikt) *nm* **-e** **1** conflict. **2** dispute.
konfus (kɔn'fuːs) *adj* confused.
Kongreß (kɔn'grɛs) *nm* **-gresse** congress.
König ('kœːniç) *nm* **-e** king. **—in** ('kœːnigin) *nf* **-nen** queen. **—lich** *adj* royal, regal. **—reich** *n neu* kingdom.
Konjugation (kɔnjugatsi'oːn) *nf* **-en** conjugation.
Konjunktiv ('kɔnjunktiːf) *nm* **-e** subjunctive.
Konjunktur (kɔnjunk'tuːr) *nf* **-en** economic or commercial situation.
Konkurrenz (kɔnku'rɛnts) *nf* **-en** competition.
Konkurs (kɔn'kurs) *nm* **-e** bankruptcy.
können* ('kœnən) *v mod aux* **1** be able. **2** be allowed. *vi,vt* know (how to do something).
konsequen/t (kɔnze'kvɛnt) *adj* consistent. **—z** (kɔnze'kvɛnts) *nf* **-en** **1** consistency. **2** consequence. **Konsequenzen ziehen** draw conclusions.
konservativ (kɔnzɛrva'tiːf) *adj* conservative.
Konserve (kɔn'zɛrvə) *nf* **-n** tinned food, preserve.
Konsonant (kɔnzo'nant) *nm* **-en** consonant.
Konstruktion (kɔnstruktsi'oːn) *nf* **-en** **1** construction. **2** design.
Konsul ('kɔnzul) *nm* **-n** consul. **—at** (kɔnzu'laːt) *n neu* **-e** consulate.
Konsum (kɔn'zuːm) *nm* consumption. **—ent** (kɔnzu'mɛnt) *nm* **-en** consumer. **—verein** *nm* cooperative society.
Kontakt (kɔn'takt) *nm* **-e** contact.

Kontinent ('kɔntinɛnt) *nm* **-e** continent.

kontinuierlich (kɔntinu'iːrliç) *adj* continuous.

Konto ('kɔnto) *n neu* **-ten** account.

Kontrast (kɔn'trast) *nm* **-e** contrast.

Kontroll/e (kɔn'trɔlə) *nf* **-n 1** control. **2** supervision. **—ieren** (kɔntrɔ'liːrən) *vt* **1** control. **2** supervise. **3** check. **4** audit. **—punkt** *nm* checkpoint.

konventionell (kɔnvɛntsio'nɛl) *adj* conventional.

Konversation (kɔnvɛrzatsi'oːn) *nf* **-en** conversation. **—slexikon** *n neu* encyclopaedia.

Konzentr/ation (kɔntsɛntratsi'oːn) *nf* **-en** concentration. **—ieren** (kɔntsɛn'triːrən) *vt* concentrate.

Konzept (kɔn'tsɛpt) *n neu* **-e 1** (rough) draft, sketch. **2** design.

Konzert (kɔn'tsɛrt) *n neu* **-e 1** concert. **2** concerto.

Kopf (kɔpf) *nm* **¨-e** head. **—haut** *nf* scalp. **—hörer** *nm* headphone(s). **—kissen** *n neu* pillow. **—schmerz** *nm also* **—weh** *n neu* headache.

Kopie (ko'piː) *nf* **-n** copy.

Koralle (ko'ralə) *nf* **-n** coral.

Korb (kɔrp) *nm* **¨-e 1** basket. **2** refusal.

Korinthe (ko'rintə) *nf* **-n** currant.

Kork (kɔrk) *nm* **-e** cork. **—enzieher** *nm* corkscrew.

Korn (kɔrn) *n neu* **¨-er 1** grain, corn. **2** seed. **3** whisky. **4** schnaps.

Koronarthrombose (kɔrɔ'nartrɔmboːzə) *nf* **-n** coronary thrombosis.

Körper ('kœrpər) *nm* **— 1** body. **2** substance. **—haltung** *nf* bearing, deportment. **—lich** *adj* **1** physical, corporeal. **2** material. **—schaft** *nf* **-en** corporation, body. **—übung** *nf* physical exercise.

korrekt (kɔ'rɛkt) *adj* correct. **-ur** (kɔrɛk'tuːr) *nf* **-en 1** correction. **2** (printing) proof.

Korresponden/t (kɔrɛspɔn'dɛnt) *nm* **-en** correspondent. **—z** (kɔrɛspɔn'dɛnts) *nf* **-en** correspondence.

Korridor ('kɔridoːr) *nm* **-e** corridor.

korrigieren (kɔri'giːrən) *vt* correct.

Kosename ('koːzənaːmə) *nm* pet name.

Kosmetik (kɔs'meːtik) *nf* **-en** cosmetics.

Kost (kɔst) *nf* **1** food, fare. **2** diet.

kostbar ('kɔstbaːr) *adj* **1** expensive. **2** precious.

kosten[1] ('kɔstən) *vt* cost. *n pl* cost(s). **—los** *adj* free (of charge).

kosten[2] ('kɔstən) *vt* taste, sample.

köstlich ('kœstliç) *adj* **1** delightful. **2** delicious.

Kostüm (kɔs'tyːm) *n neu* **-e 1** costume, dress. **2** suit.

Kot (kɔt) *nm* **1** mud, dirt. **2** excrement.

Kotelett (kotə'lɛt) *n neu* **-e** cutlet, chop. **—en** *n pl* sideburns.

kotzen ('kɔtsən) *vi inf* spew up, vomit.

Krabbe ('krabə) *nf* **-n 1** crab. **2** shrimp.

Krach (krax) *nm* **-e 1** noise. **2** crash. **3** quarrel.

kraft (kraft) *prep* by virtue of. *nf* **¨-e 1** strength, force, power. **2** efficacy. **3** worker. **außer Kraft setzen** annul. **in Kraft sein** be in force. **in Kraft treten** come into force. **—fahrzeug** *n neu* motor vehicle. **¨—ig** ('krɛftiç) *adj* strong, powerful. **¨—igen** ('krɛftigən) *vt* strengthen. **—wagen** *nm* **1** motor vehicle. **2** car. **3** lorry. **—werk** *n neu* power station.

Kragen ('kra:gən) *nm* — collar.

Krähe ('krɛ:ə) *nf* **-n** crow.

Kralle ('kralə) *nf* **-n** claw, talon.

Kram (kra:m) *nm* **¨-e** *inf* **1** junk, rubbish. **2** things, stuff. **3** affair, business.

Krampf (krampf) *nm* **¨-e 1** cramp. **2** convulsion.

Kran (kra:n) *nm* **¨-e** crane, hoist.

Kranich ('kra:niç) *nm* **-e** *zool* crane.

krank (kraŋk) *adj* sick, ill. **—e(r)** *nm* patient. **¨—en** ('krɛŋkən) *vt* **1** hurt. **2** offend. **sich ¨—en** *vr* worry. **—enhaus** *n neu* hospital. **—enkasse** *nf* health insurance (company). **—enschwester** *nf* nurse. **—enversicherung** *nf* health insurance. **—enwagen** *nm* ambulance. **—haft** *adj* **1** morbid. **2** diseased. **—heit** *nf* **-en 1** illness. **2** disease.

Kranz (krants) *nm* **¨-e** wreath, garland.

Kratzbürste ('kratsbyrstə) *nf* **-n 1** wire brush. **2** shrew, bad-tempered woman.

kratzen ('kratsən) *vt,vi* scratch, scrape.

Kraul (kraul) *n neu* crawl (swimming stroke).

Kraut (kraut) *n neu* **¨-er 1** plant. **2** herb. **3** cabbage.

Krawall (kra'val) *nm* **-e 1** row. **2** riot. **3** noise.

Krawatte (kra'vatə) *nf* **-n** (neck)tie.

Krebs (kre:ps) *nm* **-e 1** crayfish. **2** crab. **3** *med* cancer. **4** Cancer.

Kredit (kre'di:t) *nm* **-e** credit.

Kreide ('kraidə) *nf* **-n** chalk.

Kreis (krais) *nm* **-e 1** circle. **2** district. **3** sphere, field. **—en** ('kraizən) *vi* **1** circle. **2** circulate. **—förmig** ('kraisfœrmiç) *adj* circular, round. **—lauf** *nm* **1** circulation. **2** cycle, circuit.

kreischen ('kraiʃən) *vi* shriek, screech.

Krematorium (krema'to:rjum) *n neu* **-rien** crematorium.

Kreml ('kre:məl) *nm* Kremlin.

Krempe ('krɛmpə) *nf* **-n** brim.

krepieren (kre'pi:rən) *vi* **1** (of an animal) die. **2** explode.

Kresse ('krɛsə) *nf* **-n** cress.

Kreuz (krɔyts) *n neu* **-e 1** cross. **2** *mus* sharp (symbol). **3** *game* club. **4** (small of the) back, rump. **kreuz und quer** criss-cross. **—en** *vt* cross. *vi* cruise. **—er** *nm* — cruiser. **—fahrt** *nf* **1** cruise. **2** crusade. **—gang** *nm* cloister(s). **—igen** ('krɔytsigən) *vt* crucify. **—igung** *nf* **-en** crucifixion. **—otter** *nf* **-n** adder.

—**ung** *nf* **-en** crossing. —**zug** *nm* crusade.
kriech/en* ('kriːçən) *vi* **1** creep. **2** crawl. **3** cringe. **4** grovel. —**tier** *n neu* reptile.
Krieg (kriːk) *nm* **-e** war. —**er** ('kriːgər) *nm* — warrior. —**sgefangene(r)** *nm* prisoner of war. —**sgericht** *n neu mil* court martial. —**srecht** *n neu* martial law. —**sverbrechen** *n neu* war crime.
Krimi ('kriːmi) *n neu* **-s** *inf* detective story.
kriminal (krimi'naːl) *adj* criminal. —**beamte(r)** *nm* detective. —**roman** *nm* detective novel.
Krippe ('kripə) *nf* **-n** **1** crib. **2** crèche.
Krise ('kriːzə) *nf* **-n** crisis.
Kristall (kri'stal) *nm* **-e** crystal.
Krit/ik (kri'tiːk) *nf* **-en** **1** criticism. **2** review. —**iker** ('kriːtikər) *nm* — critic. —**isch** ('kriːtiʃ) *adj* critical.
Krokodil (kroko'diːl) *n neu* **-e** crocodile.
Kron/e ('kroːnə) *nf* **-n** crown. —**leuchter** *nm* chandelier. ¨—**en** ('krœːnən) *vt* crown. ¨—**ung** ('krœːnuŋ) *nf* **-en** coronation.
Kröte ('krœːtə) *nf* **-n** toad.
Krücke ('krykə) *nf* **-n** crutch.
Krug (kruːk) *nm* ¨**-e** **1** jug. **2** mug.
krumm (krum) *adj* **1** crooked. **2** bent. **3** curved. ¨—**en** ('krymən) *vt* **1** bend. **2** curve.
Krüppel ('krypəl) *nm* — cripple.
Kruste ('krustə) *nf* **-n** crust.
Kruzifix (krutsi'fiks) *n neu* **-e** crucifix.
Küche ('kyçə) *nf* **-n** **1** kitchen. **2** cookery. —**nschabe** *nf* **-n** cockroach.
Kuchen ('kuːxən) *nm* — cake.
Kuckuck ('kukuk) *nm* **-e** cuckoo.
Kugel ('kuːgəl) *nf* **-n** **1** ball. **2** sphere, globe. **3** bullet. —**förmig** ('kuːgəlfœrmiç) *adj* spherical. —**schreiber** *nm* — ballpoint pen.
Kuh (kuː) *nf* ¨**-e** cow.
kühl (kyːl) *adj* cool, chilly. —**e** *nf* coolness, cool. —**en** *vt,vi* **1** cool. **2** refrigerate. —**schrank** *nm* refrigerator.
kühn (kyːn) *adj* bold, daring. —**heit** *nf* **-en** boldness, daring.
Kulissen (ku'lisən) *nf pl Th* **1** scenery. **2** wings. **hinter den Kulissen** backstage.
Kult (kult) *nm* **-e** **1** cult. **2** worship.
Kultur (kul'tuːr) *nf* **-en** **1** culture. **2** cultivation. —**ell** (kultu'rɛl) *adj* cultural.
Kummer ('kumər) *nm* **1** grief. **2** distress. **3** worry. ¨—**lich** ('kymərliç) *adj* miserable. ¨—**n** ('kymərn) *vt* worry, be anxious. **sich kümmern um** care about, concern oneself with.
kund (kunt) *adj* known.
Kund/e[1] ('kundə) *nf* information, knowledge. —**geben*** ('kuntgeːbən) *vt* make known, declare. ¨—**igen** ('kyndigən) *vt,vi* **1** give notice. **2** cancel.
Kund/e[2] ('kundə) *nm* **-n** customer, client. —**schaft** ('kuntʃəft) *nf* customers, clientele.
künftig ('kynftiç) *adj* future.
Kunst (kunst) *nf* ¨**-e** **1** art. **2**

skill. **—griff** *nm* trick, knack. **¨—ler** ('kynstlər) *nm* — artist. **¨—lerisch** ('kynstləriʃ) *adj* artistic. **¨—lich** ('kynstliç) *adj* artificial, synthetic. **—stück** *n neu* **1** trick. **2** feat. **3** stunt. **—werk** *n neu* work of art.

Kupfer ('kupfər) *n neu* copper. **—stich** *nm* etching.

Kupp/el ('kupəl) *nf* **-n** dome, cupola. **—eln** *vt* **1** couple, pair. **2** join. *vi* pimp, procure. **—ler** ('kuplər) *nm* — **1** matchmaker. **2** pimp. **—lung** *nf* **-en** **1** coupling. **2** clutch.

Kur (kur) *nf* **-en** cure, treatment. **—ort** *nm* spa, health resort.

Kurbel ('kurbəl) *nf* **-n** **1** crank. **2** winch.

Kürbis ('kyrbis) *nm* **-se** **1** pumpkin. **2** marrow.

Kurs (kurs) *nm* **-e** **1** course. **2** rate (of exchange). **—buch** *n neu* timetable.

Kurve ('kurvə) *nf* **-n** **1** curve. **2** bend. **3** turn.

kurz (kurts) *adj* **1** short, brief. **2** abrupt, brusque. **in kurzem** soon, shortly. **kurz gesagt, um es kurz zu sagen** in a word, to cut a long story short. **vor kurzem** a short time ago. **—arbeit** *nf* short-time work. **¨—e** ('kyrtsə) *nf* **-n** shortness. **¨—en** ('kyrtsən) *vt* **1** shorten. **2** reduce. **—erhand** *adv* **1** without hesitation. **2** briefly. **—fristig** *adj* short-term. **¨—lich** ('kyrtsliç) *adv* lately, recently. **—schrift** *nf* shorthand.

Kusine (ku'ziːnə) *nf* **-n** cousin.

Kuß (kus) *nm* **Küsse** kiss. **küssen** *vt* kiss.

Küste ('kystə) *nf* **-n** coast, shore.

L

Laboratorium (labora'toːrium) *n neu* **-rien** laboratory.

lächeln ('lɛçəln) *vi* smile. *n neu* — smile.

lach/en ('laxən) *vi* laugh. *n neu* — laugh, laughter. **¨—erlich** ('lɛçərliç) *adj* ridiculous.

Lachs (laks) *nm* **-e** salmon.

Lack (lak) *nm* **-e** varnish, lacquer.

lad/en* ('laːdən) *vt* load. **—eraum** *nm* hold. **—ung** *nf* **-en** load(ing), freight.

Laden ('laːdən) *nm* **¨—** **1** shop, store. **2** shutter. **—diebstahl** *nm* shoplifting.

lag (laːk) *v* see **liegen.**

Lage ('laːgə) *nf* **-n** **1** situation, position. **2** site, location. **3** layer. **4** *mus* pitch.

Lager ('laːgər) *n neu* — **1** camp. **2** warehouse, store. **3** couch, bed. **4** *tech* bearing. **5** (geological) layer. **—haus** *n neu* warehouse. **—n** *vt* store. *vi* lie down. **sich lagern** *vr* camp.

Lagune (la'guːnə) *nf* **-n** lagoon.

lahm (laːm) *adj* lame. **lahm legen** paralyse. **¨—en** ('lɛːmən) *vt* **1** paralyse. **2** lame.

Laib (laip) *nm* **-e** loaf.

Laie ('laiə) *nm* **-n** layman.

Lakritze (la'kritsə) *nf* **-n** liquorice.

Lamm (lam) *n neu* **¨-er** lamb.

Lampe ('lampə) *nf* **-n** lamp.

Land (lant) *n neu* **¨-er** **1** land. **2**

ground, earth. **3** country. **4** state, province. **auf dem Lande** in the country(side).

Landarbeiter ('lantaːrbaitə) *nm* farm worker.

landen ('landən) *vt,vi* land.

Landenge ('lanteŋə) *nf* isthmus.

Landgut ('lantgut) *n neu* estate.

Landhaus ('lanthaus) *n neu* country house.

Landkarte ('lantkaːrtə) *nf* map.

ländlich ('lɛntliç) *adj* rural, rustic.

Landmann ('lantman) *nm* **-leute 1** countryman. **2** farmer.

Landschaft ('lantʃaft) *nf* **-en 1** landscape, countryside, scenery. **2** district.

Landsmann ('lantsman) *nm* **-sleute** fellow countryman.

Landstraße ('lantʃtraːsə) *nf* highway, main road.

Landstreicher ('lantʃtraiçə) *nm* — tramp.

Landtag ('lanttaːg) *nm* **1** provincial assembly. **2** state parliament.

Landung ('landuŋ) *nf* **-en** landing (of ships, aeroplanes, etc.). **—sbrücke** *nf* jetty.

Landwirtschaft ('lantvirtʃaft) *nf* agriculture.

lang (laŋ) *adj,adv* long, tall. **ein Jahr lang** for a year. **lang und breit** at length.

lange ('laŋə) *adv* long, a long time.

Länge ('lɛŋə) *nf* **-n 1** length, tallness. **2** duration. **3** size. **4** longitude. **—ngrad** ('lɛŋəngraːt) *nm* degree of longitude.

Lang(e)weile ('laŋ(ə)vailə) *nf* boredom.

langjährig ('laŋjɛriç) *adj* of long standing.

längs (lɛŋs) *adv* lengthways. *prep* along(side).

langsam ('laŋzaːm) *adj* slow.

längst (lɛŋst) *adj* longest. *adv* for a long time, long ago. **längst nicht** not nearly.

längstens ('lɛŋstəns) *adv* at the latest or most.

langweil/en ('laŋvailən) *vt* **1** bore. **2** tire. **—ig** *adj* boring.

Lanze ('lantsə) *nf* **-n** lance.

Lappen ('lapən) *nm* **— 1** rag, cloth. **2** lobe.

Lärche ('lɛrçə) *nf* **-n** larch.

Lärm (lɛrm) *nm* noise, din.

las (laːz) *v* see **lesen.**

Laser-Strahlen ('laːzər-ʃtraːlən) *nm pl* laser beams.

lassen* ('lasən) *vt,vi* **1** allow, let, permit. **2** cause. **3** have (done). **4** leave.

lässig ('lɛsiç) *adj* **1** careless. **2** idle.

Last (last) *nf* **-en 1** burden, load. **2** cargo. **3** change. **—auto** *n neu* lorry, van. **—en** *vi* weigh (upon). **¨—ig** ('lɛstiç) *adj* **1** troublesome, annoying. **2** burdensome. **—kahn** *nm* barge. **—kraftwagen** *nm* lorry, truck, van.

Laster ('lastər) *n neu* — vice. **¨—lich** ('lɛstərliç) *adj* **1** scandalous. **2** slanderous. **¨—n** ('lɛstərn) *vt* slander. **¨—ung** ('lɛstəruŋ) *nf* **-en** defamation, slander.

Latein (la'tain) *n neu* Latin.

Laterne (la'tɛrnə) *nf* **-n 1** lantern. **2** (street) lamp.

Latte ('latə) *nf* **-n 1** slat. **2** board.

lau (lau) *adj* **1** lukewarm. **2** half-hearted.

Laub (laup) *n neu* foliage, leaves. **—baum** *nm* deciduous tree. **—säge** *nf* fretsaw.

Lauch (laux) *nm* **-e** leek.

lauern ('lauərn) *vi* lie in wait, lurk.

Lauf (lauf) *nm* **¨-e 1** run(ning). **2** course. **3** race. **4** path, passage. **5** (gun) barrel. **—bahn** *nf* **1** career. **2** course. **—en*** *vi* **1** run. **2** walk. **3** go, move. **4** flow. **—end** *adj* **1** running. **2** current. **3** regular, routine. **¨—er** ('lɔyfər) *nm* **— 1** runner. **2** *game* bishop.

Laun/e ('launə) *nf* **-n 1** mood. **2** whim. **—enhaft** *adj* moody, capricious. **—isch** *adj* **1** bad-tempered. **2** moody. **3** capricious.

Laus (laus) *nf* **¨-e** louse. **—bube** *nm* (young) rascal. **—ig** *adj sl* lousy.

lauschen ('lauʃən) *vi* listen, eavesdrop.

laut (laut) *adj* loud. *adv* loudly, aloud. *prep* according to. *nm* **-e** sound. **—en** *vi* **1** sound. **2** (of a text, letter, etc.) read, run. **—los** *adj* silent, mute. **—sprecher** *nm* (loud)speaker. **—stärke** *nf* loudness, volume.

läuten ('lɔytən) *vi* ring, sound.

lauter ('lautər) *adj invar* **1** only, nothing but. **2** pure. **3** genuine.

lauwarm ('lauvarm) *adj* lukewarm, tepid.

Lawine (la'viːnə) *nf* **-n** avalanche.

lax (laks) *adj* **1** lax. **2** licentious.

leb/en ('leːbən) *vi* live. *n neu* — life.

lebend ('leːbənt) *adj* living, alive.

lebendig (le'bɛndiç) *adj* **1** alive. **2** lively.

Lebensart ('leːbənzaːrt) *nf* way of life.

Lebensgefahr ('leːbənzgəfaːr) *nf* danger to (one's) life.

Lebenskraft ('leːbənskraft) *nf* vitality.

Lebenslänglich ('leːbənslɛŋliç) *adj* lifelong.

Lebenslauf (leːbənslauf) *nm* curriculum vitae.

Lebensmittel ('leːbənsmitəl) *n neu pl* food.

Lebensstandard ('leːbənsstandaːrt) *nm* standard of living.

Lebensunterhalt ('lebənsuntərhalt) *nm* livelihood.

Lebensversicherung ('leː-bənsvɛrsiçərun) *nf* life insurance.

Lebensweise ('leːbənzvaizə) *nf* way of life.

Leber ('leːbər) *nf* **-n** liver. **—wurst** *nf* liver sausage.

Lebewesen ('leːbəveːzən) *n neu* creature.

Lebewohl ('leːbəvoːl) *n neu,interj* farewell.

Lebhaft ('leːphaft) *adj* lively, vivid.

Lebkuchen ('leːpkuːxən) *nm* gingerbread.

leblos ('leːploːs) *adj* **1** lifeless. **2** dull.

leck (lɛk) *adj* leaky, leaking. *n neu* **-e** leak.

lecken ('lɛkən) *vt* lick.
lecker ('lɛkər) *adj* **1** delicious. **2** delicate. **—bissen** *nm* delicacy, titbit.
Leder ('le:dər) *n neu* — leather.
ledig ('le:diç) *adj* **1** unmarried, single. **2** unrestrained, free. **—lich** ('le:dikliç) *adv* merely, only.
Lee (le:) *nf* lee(side).
leer (le:r) *adj* **1** empty. **2** vacant. **—e** *nf* **-en** **1** vacuum. **2** emptiness. **—en** *vt* empty.
legal (le'ga:l) *adj* legal.
legen ('le:gən) *vt* lay, place, put. **sich legen** *vr* lie down.
Legende (le'gɛndə) *nf* **-n** legend.
legieren (le'gi:rən) *vt* **1** alloy (metals). **2** thicken (soup).
legitim (legi'ti:m) *adj* legitimate.
Lehm (le:m) *nm* **-e** loam, clay.
Lehn/e ('le:nə) *nf* **-n** **1** support. **2** back or arm (of a chair). **—en** *vt,vi,* lean. **—sessel** *nm also* **—stuhl** armchair.
lehr/en ('le:rən) *vt* teach, instruct. **—buch** *n neu* textbook. **—e** *nf* **-n** **1** teaching, lesson. **2** theory, doctrine. **3** apprenticeship. **4** gauge. **—er** *nm* **—**, **—erin** *nf* **-nen** teacher, instructor. **—gang** *nm* course, syllabus. **—ling** *nm* **-e** apprentice. **—reich** *adj* instructive. **—stuhl** *nm* professorial chair.
Leib (laip) *nm* **-er** body. **—chen** ('laipçən) *n neu* **—** bodice, vest. **—esübung** ('laibəsy:buŋ) *nf* physical exercise. **—wache** *nf* bodyguard.
Leich/e ('laiçə) *nf* **-n** corpse. **—enhemd** *n neu* shroud. **-enschau** *nf* **1** inquest. **2** autopsy. **—schauhaus** *n neu* morgue. **—enwagen** *nm* hearse. **—nam** ('laiçna:m) *nm* **-e** corpse.
leicht (laiçt) *adj* **1** light. **2** easy. **3** slight. **4** unimportant. **5** superficial. **—athletik** *nf* athletics. **—fertig** *adj* **1** frivolous. **2** thoughtless. **—hin** *adv* lightly, casually. **—igkeit** *nf* **1** lightness. **2** ease. **—sinn** *nm* **1** carelessness, thoughtlessness. **2** frivolity.
leid (lait) *adv* **es tut mir leid** I am sorry, I regret. *n neu* **1** sorrow. **2** harm, pain. **—en*** ('laidən) *vt* **1** suffer. **2** permit. **3** tolerate. *vi* suffer. *n neu* **— 1** suffering, pain, illness. **2** misfortune.
Leidenschaft ('laidənʃaft) *nf* **-en** passion. **—lich** *adj* passionate.
leider ('laidər) *adv* unfortunately.
leihen* ('laiən) *vt* lend, loan.
Leim (laim) *nm* **-e** glue, size.
Lein (lain) *nm* **-e** flax. **—en** *adj* linen. *n neu* **—** linen. **—wand** *nf* **1** (cinema) screen. **2** linen. **3** canvas.
Leine ('lainə) *nf* **-n** **1** rope, line. **2** lead.
leise ('laizə) *adj* quiet, low, soft.
leist/en ('laistən) *vt* **1** achieve, do. **2** perform. **3** give. **4** offer. **ich kann es mir nicht leisten** I can't afford it. **—ung** *nf* **-en** **1** achievement. **2** work. **3** performance. **4** *sci* power. **—ungsfähig** *adj* **1** capable (of work). **2** productive.
leit/en ('laitən) *vt* **1** lead, guide.

2 manage. **3** direct. **4** conduct (electricity). **—artikel** *nm* leader, editorial. **—faden** *nm* **1** clue. **2** manual. **—gedanke** *nm* main thought or idea. **—ung** *nf* **-en** **1** direction. **2** management. **3** lead. **4** circuit.

Leiter[1] ('laitər) *nm* — **1** leader. **2** head. **3** director. **4** conductor (of electricity, etc.).

Leiter[2] ('laitər) *nf* **-n** **1** ladder. **2** *mus* scale.

Lektüre (lɛk'tyːrə) *nf* **-n** reading (material).

Lende ('lɛndə) *nf* **-n** **1** loin. **2** haunch, hip.

lenk/en ('lɛŋkən) *vt* **1** steer. **2** direct. **3** lead. **—rad** *n neu* steering wheel. **—stange** *nf* handlebars. **—ung** *nf* **-en** **1** steering. **2** direction.

Leopard (leo'part) *nm* **-en** leopard.

Lepra ('leːpra) *nf* leprosy.

Lerche ('lɛrçə) *nf* **-n** lark.

lernen (lɛrnən) *vt* learn.

les/bar ('leːsbaːr) *adj* legible, readable. **—e** ('leːzə) *nf* **-n** **1** harvest. **2** vintage. **—en*** *vt* **1** read. **2** lecture on. **3** gather, pick. **4** select. *vi* read. **—er** *nm* — **1** reader. **2** picker.

letzt (lɛtst) *adj* **1** last. **2** latest, newest. **zum letzen Mal** for the last time. **—ens** *adv* lastly. **—ere** *adj* latter. **—hin** *adv* lately, recently.

Leucht/e ('lɔyçtə) *nf* **-n** light, lamp, lantern. **—en** *vi* give light, shine. **—er** *nm* — **1** candlestick. **2** chandelier. **—turm** *nm* lighthouse.

leugnen ('lɔygnən) *vt* **1** deny. **2** contradict.

Leukämie (lɔykɛ'miː) *nf* leukaemia.

Leukoplast (lɔyko'plast) *n neu* *Tdmk* (sticking) plaster.

Leumund ('lɔymunt) *nm* **-e** reputation.

Leute ('lɔytə) *n pl* people, persons.

Leutnant ('lɔytnant) *nm* **-e** lieutenant.

leutselig ('lɔytzeːliç) *adj* affable.

Lexikon ('lɛksikɔn) *n neu* **-ka** dictionary.

Liban/on ('liːbanɔn) *nm* Lebanon. **—ese** (liːba'neːzə) *nm* **-n** Lebanese. **—esisch** *adj* Lebanese.

Libelle (li'bɛlə) *nf* **-n** dragonfly.

liberal (libe'raːl) *adj* liberal.

licht (liçt) *adj* **1** bright. **2** light. *n neu* **-er** **1** light. **2** candle. **3** lamp. **—bild** *n neu* photograph. **—en** *vt* **1** clear. **2** thin (out). **3** weigh (anchor). **sich —en** *vr* **1** grow thinner. **2** grow brighter. **—ung** *nf* **-en** clearing, glade.

Lid (liːt) *n neu* **-er** eyelid.

lieb (liːp) *adj* **1** dear, beloved. **2** pleasant, nice. **3** kind. **4** sweet.

liebäugeln ('liːpɔygəln) *vi* **1** ogle. **2** flirt.

Liebchen ('liːpçən) *n neu* — sweetheart, love.

Liebe ('liːbə) *nf* **-n** love.

Liebelei (liːbə'lai) *nf* **-en** flirtation.

lieben ('liːbən) *vt* love, like.

liebenswert ('liːbənzveːrt) *adj* lovely.

liebenswürdig ('liːbənzvyrdiç) *adj* **1** amiable. **2** kindly.

lieber ('li:bər) *adj* dearer. *adv* rather.

Liebesaffäre ('li:bəsafε:rə) *nf* **-n** *also* **Liebschaft** *nf* **-en** affair.

liebhab/en* ('li:pha:bən) *vt* love (a person). **—er** *nm* **— 1** lover. **2** amateur. **3** connoisseur.

liebkosen ('li:pko:zən) *vt* cuddle, caress.

lieblich ('li:pliç) *adj* charming, lovely.

Liebling ('li:pliŋ) *nm* **-e** darling.

Liebreiz ('li:praits) *nm* charm, attraction.

Lied (li:t) *n neu* **-er 1** song. **2** hymn. **3** tune.

liederlich ('li:dərliç) *adj* **1** disorderly, slovenly. **2** dissolute.

lief (li:f) *v* see **laufen.**

Liefer/ant (li:fə'rant) *nm* **-en** supplier. **—n** *vt* **1** deliver. **2** supply. **3** produce. **4** submit. **—ung** *nf* **-en 1** delivery. **2** supply(ing).

Liege ('li:gə) *nf* **-n** couch. **—n*** *vi* **1** lie. **2** be (situated). **—stuhl** *nm* deckchair.

ließ (li:s) *v* see **lassen.**

Liga ('li:ga) *nf* **-gen** league.

Likör (li'kœ:r) *nm* **-e** liqueur.

lila ('li:la) *adj* **1** lilac. **2** violet.

Lilie ('li:liə) *nf* **-n** lily.

Limonade (limo'na:də) *nf* **-n** lemonade.

Linde ('lində) *nf* **-n** linden or lime tree.

Lineal (line'a:l) *n neu* **-e** rule(r).

Linie ('li:niə) *nf* **-n** line.

link (liŋk) *adj* left. **—e** *nf* **-n 1** left (side). **2** *pol* Left. **—isch** *adj* awkward, clumsy. **—s** *adv* on the left. **—shändig** *adj* left-handed.

Linse ('linzə) *nf* **-n 1** lentil. **2** lens.

Lippe ('lipə) *nf* **-n** lip. **—nstift** *nm* lipstick.

lispeln ('lispəln) *vi* **1** lisp. **2** whisper. **3** rustle.

List (list) *nf* **-en 1** trick, ruse. **2** cunning. **—ig** *adj* cunning, artful.

Liste ('listə) *nf* **-n 1** list. **2** register.

Litanei (lita'nai) *nf* **-en** litany.

Liter ('li:tər) *n neu* or *m* **—** litre.

litera/risch (lite'ra:riʃ) *adj* literary. **—tur** (litəra'tu:r) *nf* **-en** literature.

litt (lit) *v* see **leiden.**

Lizenz (li'tsεnts) *nf* **-en** licence.

Lob (lo:p) *n neu* **-e** praise. **—en** ('lo:bən) *vt* praise. **—enswert** *adj* praiseworthy. **—rede** *nf* eulogy.

Loch (lɔx) *n neu* **¨-er 1** hole. **2** *sl* prison. **—en** *vt* puncture, perforate.

Lock/e ('lɔkə) *nf* **-n** curl, lock (of hair). **—ig** *adj* curly.

lock/en ('lɔkən) *vt* lure, entice. **—mittel** *n neu* bait.

locker ('lɔkər) *adj* **1** loose, slack. **2** light. **3** spongy. **4** lax. **5** dissolute. **—n** *vt* loosen.

lodern ('lo:dərn) *vi* flame, blaze.

Löffel ('lœfəl) *nm* **—** spoon. **—n** *vt* **1** spoon, ladle. **2** eat with a spoon.

log (lo:g) *v* see **lügen.**

Loge ('lo:ʒə) *nf* **-n** *Th* box.

Log/ik ('lo:gik) *nf* logic. **—isch** *adj* logical.

Lohn (lo:n) *nm* **¨-e 1** wages, pay. **2** reward, desert. **—ar-**

beiter *nm* labourer, workman. **—en** *vt* pay, reward. **sich —en** *vr* be worthwhile. **—steuer** *nf* income tax. **—tag** *nm* pay day. **—tüte** *nf* pay-packet.

lokal (lo'ka:l) *adj* local. *n neu* **-e** **1** restaurant. **2** pub.

Lokomotive (lokomo'ti:və) *nf* **-n** locomotive.

Lorbeer ('lɔrbe:r) *nm* **-en** laurel, bay.

los (lo:s) *adj,adv* free, loose. *adv* off, away. **es ist heute nicht viel los** there is not much happening or going on today. **was ist los?** what is the matter? *~suff* without, free of. **arbeitslos** *adj* unemployed. **mühelos** *adj* effortless.

Los (lo:s) *n neu* **-e** **1** fate, destiny. **2** lot, share. **3** lottery ticket. **—en** ('lo:zən) *vi* draw lots. **—ung** ('lo:zuŋ) *nf* **-en** password.

lösbar ('lœ:sba:r) *adj* soluble.

losbinden* (lo:sbindən) *vt* untie.

lösch/en* ('lœʃən) *vt* **1** extinguish, quench. **2** turn off or out. **3** erase. **4** cancel. **—er** *nm* **— 1** (fire) extinguisher. **2** blotter. **—papier** *n neu* blotting paper.

lose ('lo:zə) *adj* free, loose.

Lösegeld ('lœ:zəgɛlt) *n neu* ransom.

lösen ('lœ:zən) *vt* **1** loosen, free. **2** solve. **3** dissolve.

losgeben* ('lo:sgɛbən) *vt* set free.

loslassen* ('lo:slasən) *vt* let go, release.

losmachen ('lo:smaxən) *vt* unfasten, free.

losreißen* ('lo:sraisən) *vt* tear off or away.

lossprechen* ('lo:sʃprɛxən) *vt* **1** acquit. **2** free.

Lösung ('lœ:zuŋ) *nf* **-en** **1** solution. **2** loosening.

losziehen* ('lo:stsi:ən) *vi* **1** set out. **2** insult, abuse. **3** denounce.

löten ('lœ:tən) *vt* solder.

Lothringen ('lo:triŋən) *n neu* Lorraine.

Lotse ('lo:tsə) *nm* **-n** pilot. **—n** *vt naut* pilot.

Lotterie (lɔtə'ri:) *nf* **-n** lottery.

Löw/e ('lœ:və) *nm* **-n** **1** lion. **2** Leo. **—in** *nf* **-nen** lioness.

Luchs (luks) *nm* **-e** lynx.

Lücke ('lykə) *nf* **-n** **1** gap, chink. **2** omission.

lud (lu:d) *v* see **laden.**

Luft (luft) *nf* **¨-e** **1** air. **2** draught, breeze. **in der freien Luft** in the open air. **—dicht** *adj* airtight. **—druck** *nm* air pressure. **¨—en** ('lyftən) *vt* **1** air, ventilate. **2** disclose. **3** lift, raise. **—fahrt** *nf* aviation. **—hafen** *nm* airport. **—ig** *adj* airy. **—post** *nf* airmail. **¨—ung** ('lyftuŋ) *nf* ventilation. **—verkehrslinie** *nf* **-n** *also* **—gesellschaft** **-en** airline. **—waffe** *nf* air force.

Lüg/e ('ly:gə) *nf* **-n** lie. **—en*** *vi* lie, tell a lie. **—ner** ('ly:gnər) *nm* **—** liar.

Luke ('lu:kə) *nf* **-n** **1** skylight. **2** trapdoor.

Lump (lump) *nm* **-en** rascal, lout.

Lumpen ('lumpən) *nm* — rag(s).

Lunge ('luŋə) *nf* **-n** lung. **—nentzündung** *nf* pneumonia.

Lupe ('lu:pə) *nf* **-n** magnifying glass.

Lust (lust) *nf* **¨-e** **1** pleasure. **2** joy. **3** desire. **keine Lust haben** have no desire. **Lust auf etwas haben** want or be in the mood for something. **¨—ern** ('lystərn) *adj* **1** longing. **2** lustful. **—ig** *adj* **1** funny, amusing. **2** merry, jolly.

Luxus ('luksus) *nm* luxury.

Luzern (lu'tsɛrn) *n neu* Lucerne.

M

Maat (ma:t) *nm* **-e** petty officer, mate.

machen ('maxən) *vt* **1** make. **2** do. **3** produce, manufacture. **4** cause to. **5** amount or come to. **das macht nichts** it doesn't matter.

Macht (maxt) *nf* **¨-e** power, force, might. **¨—ig** ('mɛçtiç) *adj* **1** powerful, mighty. **2** thick. **3** immense. **—los** *adj* powerless.

Mädchen ('mɛ:tçən) *n neu* — girl.

Made ('ma:də) *nf* **-n** maggot, grub.

mag (ma:k) *v* see mögen.

Magazin (maga'tsi:n) *n neu* **-e** **1** storehouse. **2** magazine.

Magen ('ma:gən) *nm* — stomach.

mager ('ma:gər) *adj* **1** thin, lean. **2** meagre. **3** poor. **4** scanty.

Magnet (mag'ne:t) *nm* **-en** magnet. **—isch** *adj* magnetic.

Mahagoni (maha'go:ni) *n neu* mahogany.

mäh/en ('mɛ:ən) *vt* mow, reap. **—maschine** *nf* reaping or mowing machine.

Mahl (ma:l) *n neu* **-e** meal. **—zeit** *nf* meal.

mahlen* ('ma:lən) *vt* mill, grind.

Mähne ('mɛ:nə) *nf* **-n** mane.

mahn/en ('ma:nən) *vt* **1** warn. **2** remind. **—ung** *nf* **-en** **1** warning. **2** reminder.

Mai (mai) *nm* **-e** May. **—glöckchen** *n neu* lily of the valley.

Mais (mais) *nm* maize, corn. **—kolben** *nm* corn cob.

Majestät (majɛs'tɛ:t) *nf* **-en** majesty.

Makel ('ma:kəl) *nm* — **1** blemish. **2** stain.

Makler ('ma:klər) *nm* — broker, middleman.

Makrele (ma'kre:lə) *nf* **-n** mackerel.

mal (ma:l) *adv* **1** just. **2** times, multiplied by.

Mal[1] (ma:l) *n neu* **-e** time. **zum ersten/letzten Mal** for the first/last time.

Mal[2] (ma:l) *n neu* **-e, ¨-er** **1** sign, mark. **2** spot. **3** boundary. **4** monument.

mal/en ('ma:lən) *vt* paint. **—er** *nm* — painter, artist. **—erei** (ma:lə'rai) *nf* **-en** painting.

Malz (malts) *n neu* malt.

Mama (ma'ma:, 'mama) *nf* **-s** mummy.

man (man) *pron 3rd pers s* **1**

one. **2** you. **3** they. **man sagt** it is said, people say.
Manager ('mɛnidʒər) *nm* — manager.
manch (manç) *adj,pron* **1** many a. **2** *pl* some, many, several. **—erlei** (mançər'lai) *adj* various, different (sorts of). **—mal** *adv* sometimes.
Mandat (man'da:t) *n neu* **-e** **1** mandate. **2** brief.
Mandel ('mandəl) *nf* **-n** **1** almond. **2** tonsil.
Mangel ('maŋəl) *nm* ¨— **1** lack, deficiency. **2** defect. **—haft** *adj* **1** incomplete. **2** faulty. **—n** *vi* be wanting, lacking.
Mani/e (ma'ni:) *nf* mania. **—sch** ('ma:niʃ) *adj* manic.
Manier (ma'ni:r) *nf* **-en** **1** style. **2** *pl* manners.
Manifest (mani'fɛst) *n neu* **-e** manifesto.
Mann (man) *nm* ¨**-er** **1** man. **2** husband. **—esalter** *n neu* manhood. **—eskraft** *nf* virility. ¨**—lich** ('mɛnliç) *adj* masculine, male. **—schaft** *nf* **-en** **1** team. **2** crew.
Mannequin (manə'kɛ̃) *n neu* **-s** (fashion) model.
mannigfaltig ('maniçfaltiç) *adj* manifold.
Manöver (ma'nœ:vər) *n neu* — manoeuvre.
Manschette (man'ʃɛtə) *nf* **-n** cuff.
Mantel ('mantəl) *nm* ¨— **1** (over)coat, cloak. **2** case. **3** cover(ing).
Manuskript (manu'skript) *n neu* **-e** manuscript.
Mappe ('mapə) *nf* **-n** **1** briefcase. **2** file, folder.
Märchen ('mɛ:rçən) *n neu* — fairytale.
Margarine (marga'ri:nə) *nf* **-n** margarine.
Marihuana (mariu'a:nə) *n neu* marijuana.
Marine (ma'ri:nə) *nf* **-n** navy.
marinieren (mari'ni:rən) *vt* marinate.
Marionette (mario'nɛtə) *nf* **-n** marionette, puppet.
Mark[1] (mark) *nf* — mark (coin or currency).
Mark[2] (mark) *n neu* **1** (bone) marrow. **2** pith.
Marke ('markə) *nf* **-n** **1** mark, sign. **2** trademark, brand. **3** postage stamp. **4** ticket.
Markt (markt) *nm* ¨**-e** market.
Marmelade (marmə'la:də) *nf* **-n** **1** jam. **2** marmalade.
Marmor ('marmɔr) *nm* **-e** marble.
Marokko (ma'rɔko) *n neu* Morocco.
Marsch[1] (marʃ) *nm* ¨**-e** march. **—ieren** (mar'ʃi:rən) *vi* march.
Marsch[2] (marʃ) *nf* **-en** marsh.
Marschall ('marʃal) *nm* ¨**-e** marshal.
Märtyrer ('mɛrtyrər) *nm* — martyr.
März (mɛrts) *nm* **-e** March.
Masche ('maʃə) *nf* **-n** **1** stitch. **2** mesh.
Maschine (ma'ʃi:nə) *nf* **-n** machine, engine. **—nbau** *nm* mechanical engineering. **—ngewehr** *n neu* machine gun. **—npistole** *nf* submachine gun.
Maske ('maskə) *nf* **-n** mask.
maß (ma:s) *v* see **messen.**
Maß (ma:s) *n neu* **-e** **1** measure. **2** size. **3** moderation.

—gebend *adj* **1** authoritative. **2** standard. **¨—ig** ('mɛːsiç) *adj* moderate, modest. **¨—igen** ('mɛːsigən) *vt* moderate. **¨—igung** ('mɛːsiguŋ) *nf* moderation. **—nahme** *nf* **-n** measure, step. **—stab** *nm* **1** measure. **2** standard.

Masse ('masə) *nf* **-n** **1** mass, bulk, substance. **2** quantity, mass. **3** crowd. **4** assets. **—nhaft** *adj* **1** enormous. **2** in great quantities, in a mass. **—nmedien** *n neu pl* mass media.

massiv (ma'siːf) *adj* **1** massive. **2** solid.

Mast (mast) *nm* **-e(n)** mast, pole.

mästen ('mɛstən) *vt* fatten.

Material (materi'aːl) *n neu* **-ien** **1** material, matter. **2** stores. **—ismus** (materia'lismus) *nm* materialism.

Materie (ma'teːriə) *nf* **-n** matter, substance. **—ll** (materi'ɛl) *adj* material.

Mathemat/ik (matema'tiːk) *nf* mathematics. **—iker** (mate'maːtikər) *nm* **—** mathematician. **—isch** (mate'maːtiʃ) *adj* mathematical.

Matratze (ma'tratsə) *nf* **-n** mattress.

Mätresse (mɛ'trɛsə) *nf* **-n** mistress, lover.

Matrize (ma'triːtsə) *nf* **-n** **1** stencil. **2** mould.

Matrose (ma'troːzə) *nm* **-n** sailor.

matschig ('matʃiç) *adj* slushy, muddy.

matt (mat) *adj* **1** tired. **2** faint. **3** matt, dull. **4** checkmate. *n neu* **-s** checkmate.

Matte ('matə) *nf* **-n** mat.

Mau/er ('mauər) *nf* **-n** wall. **—rer** ('maurər) *nm* **—** bricklayer, mason.

Maul (maul) *n neu* **¨-er** mouth (of an animal). **—esel** *nm* mule. **—held** *nm* boaster, loud-mouth. **—korb** *nm* muzzle. **—tier** *n neu* mule. **—wurf** *nm* **¨-e** mole.

Maus (maus) *nf* **¨-e** mouse. **—efalle** ('mauzəfallə) *nf* mousetrap. **—eloch** ('mauzəlɔx) *n neu* mousehole.

maximal (maksi'maːl) *adj* maximum.

Mechan/ik (me'çaːnik) *nf* **-en** **1** mechanics. **2** mechanism. **—iker** *nm* **—** mechanic. **—isch** *adj* mechanical. **—ismus** (meça'nismus) *nm* **-men** mechanism.

meckern ('mɛkərn) *vi* **1** grumble. **2** bleat.

Medaille (me'daijə) *nf* **-n** medal.

Medikament (medika'mɛnt) *n neu* **-e** medicine, drug.

Medizin (medi'tsiːn) *nf* **-en** medicine.

Meer (meːr) *n neu* **-e** sea. **—enge** *nf* **-n** straits. **—rettich** *nm* horseradish.

Mehl (meːl) *n neu* **-e** flour, meal.

mehr (meːr) *adv,adj* more. **immer mehr** more and more. **—deutig** *adj* ambiguous. **—ere** *adj pl* several. **—fach** *adj* **1** repeated. **2** multiple. **—fach ungesättigt** *adj* polyunsaturated. **—heit** *nf* **-en** majority. **—mals** *adv* several times, repeatedly. **—wert-**

steuer *nf* value added tax. **—zahl** *nf* **1** majority. **2** plural.

meiden* ('maidən) *vt* **1** avoid. **2** shun.

Meile ('mailə) *nf* **-n** mile.

mein (main) *poss adj 1st pers s* my. **—er** *poss pron 1st pers s also* **der —e** or **der —ige** mine. **—erseits** ('mainər-zaits) *adv* on or for my part. **—esgleichen** ('mainəsglaiçən) *pron* people like me. **—ethalben** ('mainəthalbən) *adv also* **—etwegen** or **—etwillen** for my sake, on my account.

Meineid ('mainait) *nm* **-e** perjury. **meineidig werden** commit perjury.

mein/en ('mainən) *vt,vi* **1** mean. **2** think. **—ung** *nf* **-en** **1** opinion. **2** meaning. **—ungsforschung** *nf* opinion poll.

Meißel ('maisəl) *nm* — chisel.

meist (maist) *adj* most. **am meisten** most (of all). **—ens** *adv* mostly.

Meister ('maistər) *nm* — **1** master. **2** champion. **—haft** *adj* masterly. **—n** *vt* master. **—schaft** *nf* **-en** **1** mastery. **2** championship. **—stück** *n neu* masterpiece.

meld/en ('mɛldən) *vt* **1** inform of, report. **2** mention. **3** announce. **sich melden** *vr* report, present oneself. **—eamt** *n neu* registration office. **—ung** *nf* **-en** **1** announcement. **2** report. **3** application. **4** message.

melken* ('mɛlkən) *vt* milk.

Melone (me'lo:nə) *nf* **-n** **1** melon. **2** bowler hat.

Membran (mem'bra:n) *nf* **-en** *also* **Membrane -n** membrane, diaphragm.

Menge ('mɛŋə) *nf* **-n** **1** crowd. **2** quantity.

Mensch (mɛnʃ) *nm* **-en** human being, person. **—enfreundlich** *adj* philanthropic, humanitarian. **—enliebe** *nf* philanthropy. **—enskind!** *interj* good gracious! **—heit** *nf* humanity, mankind. **—lich** *adj* **1** human. **2** humane. **—lichkeit** *nf* humaneness, humanity.

Menstruation (mɛnstruatsi'o:n) *nf* **-en** menstruation.

merk/bar ('mɛrkba:r) *adj* noticeable. **—en** *vt* **1** observe, notice. **2** note, mark. **sich —en** *vr* remember, make a note of. **—mal** *n neu* **-e** **1** characteristic. **2** mark. **—würdig** *adj* remarkable, strange.

Messe ('mɛsə) *nf* **-n** **1** *rel* mass. **2** fair, market. **3** *mil* mess.

messen* ('mɛsən) *vt* **1** measure. **2** survey (land). **sich messen** *vr* compete (with).

Messer ('mɛsər) *n neu* — knife.

Meßgewand ('mɛsgəvant) *n neu* ¨**-er** vestment.

Messing ('mɛsiŋ) *n neu* brass.

Metall (me'tal) *n neu* **-e** metal. **—isch** *adj* metallic, metal.

Metaphysik (metafy'zi:k) *nf* metaphysics.

Meteor (mete'o:r) *nm,neu* **-e** meteor.

Meter ('me:tər) *nm,neu* — metre.

Method/e (me'to:də) *nf* **-n**

method. **—isch** *adj* methodical.

metrisch ('meːtriʃ) *adj* metric(al).

Mettwurst ('mɛtvurst) *nf* type of lean pork sausage.

metz/eln ('mɛtsəln) *vt* **1** slaughter. **2** massacre. **—ger** ('mɛtsgər) *nm* — butcher.

Meuchelmord ('mɔyçəlmɔrt) *nm* assassination.

Meuter/ei (mɔytə'rai) *nf* **-en** mutiny. **—er** ('mɔytərər) *nm* — mutineer. **—n** ('mɔytərn) *vi* mutiny, rebel.

mich (miç) *pron 1st pers s* me, myself.

Mieder ('miːdər) *n neu* — bodice.

Miene ('miːnə) *nf* **-n 1** air. **2** expression.

mies (miːs) *adj* miserable, wretched.

Miet/auto ('miːtauto) *n neu* **-s 1** hire car. **2** taxi. **—e** *nf* **-n 1** rent. **2** lease. **—en** *vt* **1** rent. **2** hire. **3** lease. **—er** *nm* — tenant.

Mikrochip (mikro'tʃip) *nm* microchip.

Mikrophon (mikro'foːn) *n neu* **-e** microphone.

Mikroskop (mikro'skoːp) *n neu* **-e** microscope.

Milbe ('milbə) *nf* **-n** mite.

Milch (milç) *nf* milk. **—straße** *nf* Milky Way.

mild (milt) *adj* **1** mild, gentle. **2** charitable. **—e** ('mildə) *nf* mildness, gentleness. **—ern** ('mildərn) *vt* mitigate, soften.

Militär (mili'tɛːr) *n neu* army, military. *nm* **-s** soldier. **—isch** *adj* military.

Milliarde (mil'jardə) *nf* **-n 1** thousand million. **2** *US* billion.

Million (mil'joːn) *nf* **-en** million. **—är** (miljo'nɛːr) *nm* **-e** millionaire. **—ste** *adj* millionth.

Mimik ('miːmik) *nf* **-en 1** mimicry. **2** mime.

minder ('mindər) *adj* **1** less. **2** lower. **3** inferior. **—heit** *nf* **-en** minority. **—jährig** *adj* under age, minor. **—n** *vt* diminish, reduce. **—wertig** *adj* inferior.

mindest ('mindəst) *adj* least. **—ens** *adv* at least.

Mine ('miːnə) *nf* **-n** mine.

Mineral (mine'raːl) *n neu* **-ien** mineral. **—wasser** *n neu* mineral water.

Miniatur (minia'tuːr) *nf* **-en** miniature.

Minimum ('miːnimum) *n neu* **-ima** minimum.

Minister (mi'nistər) *nm* — *pol* minister. **—iell** (ministeri'ɛl) *adj* ministerial. **—ium** (mini'steːrium) *n neu* **-ien** ministry. **—präsident** *nm* prime minister.

minus ('miːnus) *adv* minus, less.

Minute (mi'nuːtə) *nf* **-n** minute.

mir (miːr) *pron 1st pers s* to or for me, myself.

misch/en ('miʃən) *vt* **1** mix, blend. **2** shuffle (cards). **—ehe** *nf* mixed marriage. **—masch** ('miʃmaʃ) *nm* **-e** medley, hotchpotch. **—ung** *nf* **-en** mixture, blend.

mißachten (mis'axtən) *vt* **1** despise. **2** disregard.

Mißbilligung ('misbiliguŋ) *nf* disapproval.

Mißbrauch ('misbraux) *nm* misuse, abuse. **—en** (mis'brauxən) *vt* misuse, abuse.

mißdeuten (mis'dɔytən) *vt* misinterpret.

Mißerfolg ('misɛrfɔlk) *nm* failure.

Missetat ('misəta:t) *nf* misdeed, crime.

mißfallen* (mis'falən) *vi* displease.

Mißgeschick ('misgəʃik) *n neu* misfortune.

mißglücken (mis'glykən) *vi* fail.

Mißgriff ('misgrif) *nm* mistake.

mißhandeln (mis'handəln) *vt* maltreat, abuse.

Mission (misi'o:n) *nf* **-en** mission. **—ar** (misio'na:r) *nm* **-e** missionary.

mißlich ('misliç) *adj* awkward, difficult.

mißlingen* (*v* mis'liŋən; *n* 'misliŋən) *vi* fail. *n neu* — failure.

mißtrau/en (mis'trauən) *vi* distrust. *n neu* distrust. **—ensvotum** *n neu* vote of no confidence. **—isch** ('mistrauiʃ) *adj* distrustful, suspicious.

Mißverständnis ('misfɛrʃtɛntnis) *n neu* misunderstanding.

Mist (mist) *nm* **-e** **1** manure, dung. **2** trash. **—haufen** *nm* dung heap.

mit (mit) *prep* **1** with. **2** by. **3** at. **4** upon. *adv* also, as well.

Mitarbeiter ('mita:rbaitər) *nm* fellow worker.

miteinander (mitain'andər) *adv* together, with one another, jointly.

Mitgefühl ('mitgəfy:l) *n neu* sympathy.

Mitglied ('mitgli:t) *n neu* member. **—schaft** *nf* membership.

mithin (mit'hin) *adv* consequently, therefore.

Mitlaut ('mitlaut) *nm* consonant.

Mitleid ('mitlait) *n neu* compassion, sympathy.

mitmachen ('mitmaxən) *vt,vi* join in, be involved in, be in on.

mitnehmen* ('mitne:mən) *vt* **1** take with one, take away. **2** wear out, tire.

mitnichten (mit'niçtən) *adv* by no means, on no account.

Mittag ('mita:k) *nm* **-e** midday, noon. **—essen** *n neu* lunch, dinner. **—s** *adv* (at) noon or midday.

Mitte ('mitə) *nf* **-n** **1** middle. **2** centre. **3** mean.

mitteil/en ('mittailən) *vt* inform of, communicate. **—ung** *nf* **-en** communication, information.

Mittel ('mitəl) *n neu* — **1** means. **2** average, mean. **3** remedy. **—alter** *n neu* Middle Ages. **—alterlich** *adj* medieval. **—bar** *adj* indirect. **—mäßig** *adj* mediocre. **—meer** *n neu* Mediterranean (Sea). **—punkt** *nm* centre, focus. **—s** *prep* by means of, with the help of. **—schule** *nf* middle school. **—stand** *nm* middle classes.

mitten ('mitən) *adv* in the middle. **—drin** (mitən'drin) *adv* in the middle (of it).

Mitternacht ('mitərnaxt) *nf* midnight.
mittler ('mitlər) *adj* **1** middle. **2** central. **im mittleren Alter** middle-aged. **Mittlere(r) Osten** *nm* Middle East. *~nm* — mediator.
Mittwoch ('mitvɔx) *nm* Wednesday. **—s** *adv* on Wednesdays.
mitwirken ('mitvirkən) *vi* **1** co-operate. **2** contribute.
Möbel ('mœːbəl) *n neu* — (piece of) furniture.
mobil (mo'biːl) *adj* movable, mobile. **—isieren** (mobili'ziːrən) *vt* mobilize. **—machung** *nf* mobilization.
möblieren (mœ'bliːrən) *vt* furnish.
mochte ('mɔxtə) *v* see **mögen.**
Mod/e ('moːdə) *nf* **-n** fashion, vogue. **—isch** ('moːdiʃ) *adj* fashionable, stylish.
Modell (mo'dɛl) *n neu* **-e** model, pattern.
Moder ('moːdər) *nm* mould, decay.
modern (mo'dɛrn) *adj* modern, up-to-date. **—isieren** (modɛrni'ziːrən) *vt* modernize.
modifizieren (modifi'tsiːrən) *vt* modify, alter.
mogeln ('moːgəln) *vi* cheat.
mögen* ('mœːgən) *vt,vi* like, wish. *v mod aux* may, might. **er mag kommen** he may or might come. **das mag sein** that may be, that's as may be. **ich möchte etwas** I would like or I desire something. **ich möchte etwas tun** I would like to do something.
möglich ('mœːgliç) *adj* possible, feasible. **—erweise** *adv* possibly. **—keit** *nf* **-en** possibility. **—st** *adv* **möglichst bald/schnell** as soon/quickly as possible.
Mohammedaner (mohame'daːnər) *nm* — Muslim.
Mohn (moːn) *nm* **-e** poppy.
Mohrrübe ('moːrryːbə) *nf* **-n** carrot.
Molekül (mole'kyːl) *n neu* **-e** molecule.
Molkerei (mɔlkə'rai) *nf* **-en** dairy.
Moll (mɔl) *n neu mus* minor.
Moment (mo'mɛnt) *nm* **-e** moment, instant. *n neu* **-e** **1** momentum. **2** motive. **3** impulse. **4** element. **—an** (momɛn'taːn) *adj* momentary, passing.
Monarch (mo'narç) *nm* **-en** monarch.
Monat ('moːnat) *nm* **-e** month. **—lich** *adj* monthly.
Mönch (mœnç) *nm* **-e** monk.
Mond (moːnt) *nm* **-e** moon. **—schein** *nm* moonlight.
Monetarismus (moːnetə'rismus) *nm* monetarism.
Monopol (mono'poːl) *n neu* **-e** monopoly. **—isieren** (monopoli'ziːrən) *vt* monopolize.
Montag ('moːntaːk) *nm* Monday. **—s** *adv* on Mondays.
Moor (moːr) *n neu* **-e** **1** moor. **2** fen. **3** swamp.
Moos (moːs) *n neu* **-e** **1** moss. **2** *sl* money.
Moral (mo'raːl) *nf* **-en** **1** moral. **2** morality, morals. **3** morale. **—isch** *adj* moral. **—isieren** (morali'ziːrən) *vi* moralize. **—ität** (morali'tɛːt) *nf* morality.
Mord (mɔrt) *nm* **-e** murder. **—anschlag** *nm* **1** murderous attack. **2** attempted murder.

¨—er ('mœrdər) *nm* — murderer.

morgen ('mɔrgən) *adv* **1** tomorrow. **2** in the morning. *nm* — morning. *n neu* — following day. **(guten) Morgen** *interj* (good) morning! **morgen früh** (early) tomorrow morning. **—dämmerung** *nf also* **—grauen** *n neu* daybreak, dawn. **—land** *n neu* East, Orient. **—ländisch** *adj* oriental. **—rot** *n neu* dawn, (red) morning sky. **—s** *adv* in the morning.

Morphium ('mɔrfium) *n neu* morphine.

morsch (mɔrʃ) *adj* decayed, rotten.

Mosaik (moza'iːk) *n neu* **-en** mosaic.

Moschee (mɔ'ʃeː) *nf* **-n** mosque.

Mosel ('moːzəl) *nf* Moselle.

Moskau ('mɔskau) *n neu* Moscow.

Most (mɔst) *nm* **-e** **1** fruit juice or wine. **2** must, new wine. **3** cider.

Motiv (mo'tiːf) *n neu* **-e** **1** motive. **2** theme.

Motor ('moːtɔr) *nm* **-en** motor, engine. **—boot** *n neu* motor boat. **—isieren** (motori'ziːrən) *vt* motorize. **—rad** *n neu* motorcycle.

Motte ('mɔtə) *nf* **-n** moth.

Möwe ('mœːvə) *nf* **-n** seagull.

Mücke ('mykə) *nf* **-n** gnat, mosquito.

müde ('myːdə) *adj* tired, exhausted, weary.

Muff (muf) *nm* **¨-e** **1** muff. **2** musty smell. **—ig** *adj* **1** surly. **2** musty.

Muff/el ('mufəl) *nm* — grumbler, surly person. **—elig** *adj* surly, grumpy.

Müh/e ('myːə) *nf* **-n** trouble, effort. **sich Mühe geben** **1** take pains. **2** make great efforts.

Mühle ('myːlə) *nf* **-n** **1** mill. **2** grinder.

Mulde ('muldə) *nf* **-n** **1** trough. **2** valley.

Mull (mul) *nm* muslin.

Müll (myl) *nm* rubbish, refuse. **—eimer** *nm* dustbin. **—wagen** *nm* dust cart.

Müller ('mylər) *nm* — miller.

multiplizieren (multipli'tsiːrən) *vt* multiply.

Mummenschanz ('mumənʃants) *nm* masquerade.

München ('mynçən) *n neu* Munich.

Mund (munt) *nm* **¨-er** mouth. **—art** *nf* **-en** dialect. **¨—en** ('myndən) *vi* flow (into). **—harmonika** *nf* **-s** mouth organ. **¨—lich** ('myntliç) *adj* oral, verbal. **¨—ung** ('myndʊŋ) *nf* **-en** **1** mouth. **2** estuary. **3** (gun) muzzle.

mündig ('myndiç) *adj* of age, major.

Munition (munitsi'oːn) *nf* **-en** ammunition.

munter ('muntər) *adj* **1** lively, cheerful, merry. **2** awake.

Münze ('myntsə) *nf* **-n** **1** coin. **2** mint.

mürbe ('myrbə) *adj* **1** (of wood, stone, etc.) brittle, fragile. **2** (of food) soft, tender. **3** unnerved. **4** worn out.

murmeln ('murməln) **1** murmur. **2** mutter.

mürrisch ('myriʃ) *adj* surly, morose.

Muschel ('muʃəl) *nf* **-n** **1** mussel. **2** shell. **3** earpiece (of a telephone).

Mu/seum (mu'ze:um) *n neu* **-seen** museum.

Musik (mu'zi:k) *nf* **1** music. **2** (military) band. **—alisch** (muzi'ka:liʃ) *adj* of music, musical. **—antenknochen** (muzi'kantənknɔxən) *nm* funny bone. **—er** ('mu:zikər) *nm* — musician.

Muskat (mus'ka:t) *nm* **-e** nutmeg.

Muskel ('muskəl) *nm* **-n** muscle.

Muß/e ('mu:sə) *nf* leisure (time), spare time. **¨—ig** ('my:siç) *adj* **1** idle, lazy. **2** useless, superfluous.

müssen* ('mysən) *v mod aux* have to, be obliged to, must.

Muster ('mustər) *n neu* **— 1** model, pattern. **2** paragon. **3** sample. **—n** *vt* **1** inspect, examine. **2** decorate with a pattern.

Mut (mu:t) *nm* courage. **—ig** *adj* brave, courageous. **—maßen** ('mu:tma:sən) *vt* guess, suppose.

Mutter ('mutər) *nf* ¨— mother. **—leib** *nm* womb. **¨—lich** ('mytərliç) *adj* maternal, motherly. **—schaf** *n neu* ewe. **—schaft** *nf* maternity, motherhood. **—sprache** *nf* mother tongue.

Mütze ('mytsə) *nf* **-n** cap.

mysteriös (mysteri'œ:s) *adj* mysterious.

mystifizieren (mystifi'tsi:rən) *vt* mystify.

Mystik ('mystik) *nf* mysticism. **—er** *nm* — mystic.

Mythos ('my:tos) *nm* **-then** *also* **Mythus** ('my:tus) myth.

N

Nabe ('na:bə) *nf* **-n** (wheel) hub.

Nabel ('na:bəl) *nm* — navel.

nach (na:x) *prep* **1** after, behind. **2** according to. **3** by. **4** to(wards). **nach London, nach Frankreich** to London, to France. ~*adv* after, behind. **nach und nach** gradually. **nach wie vor** as usual.

nachahmen ('na:xa:mən) *vt* imitate.

Nachbar ('na:xba:r) *nm* **-n** neighbour. **—schaft** *nf* **-en** neighbourhood.

nachdem (na:x'de:m) *conj* after. *adv* afterwards.

nachdenk/en* ('na:xdɛŋkən) *vi* reflect, consider, ponder. *n neu* — reflection, consideration. **—lich** *adj* thoughtful, pensive.

Nachdruck ('na:xdruk) *nm* **-e** **1** reproduction, reprint. **2** emphasis. **3** energy. **¨—lich** ('na:xdrykliç) *adj* **1** emphatic. **2** energetic. **—srecht** *n neu* copyright.

nacheifern ('na:xaifərn) *vi* emulate.

nacheinander (na:xain'andər) *adv* one after the other.

Nachfolge ('na:xfɔlgə) *nf* succession. **—n** *vi* succeed, follow. **—r** *nm* — successor.

Nachfrage ('na:xfra:gə) *nf* **1** demand. **2** enquiry. **Angebot und Nachfrage** supply and demand.

nachgeben* ('na:xge:bən) *vi* give in, yield, give way.

nachgehen* ('na:xge:ən) *vi* **1** follow. **2** investigate. **3** (of a clock) be slow.

Nachgeschmack ('na:xgəʃmak) *nm* aftertaste.

nachgiebig ('na:xgi:biç) *adj* indulgent.

nachher (na:x'he:r) *adv* afterwards. **bis nachher!** see you later!

Nachhilfe ('na:xhilfə) *nf* assistance.

nachholen ('na:xho:lən) *vi* catch up, make up.

Nachhut ('na:xhu:t) *nf* **-en** rearguard.

Nachklang ('na:xklaŋ) *nm* resonance, echo.

Nachkomm/e ('na:xkɔmə) *nm* **-n** descendant. **—en*** *vi* **1** follow. **2** comply (with), fulfil. **—enschaft** *nf* posterity, descendants.

Nachkriegszeit ('na:xkri:kstsait) *nf* post-war period.

Nachlaß ('na:xlas) *nm* **-lässe 1** inheritance. **2** estate. **3** reduction.

nachlassen* ('na:xlasən) *vt* **1** leave behind. **2** reduce. **3** temper. *vi* **1** slacken. **2** stop. **3** subside. **4** diminish.

nachmachen ('na:xmaxən) *vt* **1** imitate, copy. **2** counterfeit.

Nachmittag ('na:xmita:k) *nm* **-e** afternoon. **—s** *adv* in the afternoon.

Nachnahme ('na:xna:mə) *nf* **-n** cash on delivery, C.O.D.

nachprüfen ('na:xpry:fən) *vt* **1** check. **2** control. **3** verify.

Nachricht ('na:xriçt) *nf* **-en 1** report, information. **2** *pl* news.

Nachruf ('na:xru:f) *nm* **-e** obituary.

nachschlag/en* ('na:xʃla:gən) *vt* **1** look up, consult (books). **2** take after (a person). **—ewerk** *n neu* reference book.

Nachschrift ('na:xʃrift) *nf* **1** transcript. **2** notes. **3** postscript.

Nachschub ('na:xʃu:p) *nm* **1** reinforcement. **2** supplies.

nachsehen* ('na:xze:ən) *vt* **1** examine, inspect. **2** consult, look up. **3** excuse, overlook. *vi* watch, follow (with one's gaze).

nachsenden* ('na:xzɛndən) *vt* forward, send on.

Nachspeise ('na:xʃpaizə) *nf* **-n** dessert, sweet.

nachsprechen* ('na:xʃprɛçən) *vt* repeat.

nächst (nɛ:çst) *adj* nearest, next. *prep* next to. **—e(r)** *nm* fellow, man, neighbour. **—enliebe** *nf* love for one's fellow men or one's neighbour. **—ens** *adv* shortly.

nachstellen ('na:xʃtɛlən) *vt* **1** place behind. **2** adjust. *vi* **1** pursue. **2** persecute.

nachstreben ('na:xʃtre:bən) *vi* **1** strive (for). **2** emulate.

Nacht (naxt) *nf* **¨-e** night. **—essen** *n neu* supper. **—hemd** *n neu* nightdress, nightshirt. **¨—lich** ('nɛçtliç) *adj* nocturnal, nightly. **—s** *adv* at night. **—wächter** *nm* night watchman. **—wandeln** *vi* sleepwalk.

Nachteil ('na:xtail) *nm* **-e 1** disadvantage. **2** loss. **—ig** *adj* detrimental, disadvantageous.

Nachtigall ('naxtigal) *nf* **-en** nightingale.

Nachtisch ('naxtiʃ) *nm* **-e** dessert, sweet.

Nachtrag ('na:xtra:k) *nm* **¨-e** supplement, postscript. **¨—lich** ('na:xtrɛ:kliç) *adj* supplementary.

Nachwahl ('naxva:l) *nf* by-election.

Nachweis ('na:xvais) *nm* **-e 1** proof. **2** information. **—en*** ('na:xvaizən) *vt* **1** prove. **2** point out.

Nachwelt ('na:xvɛlt) *nf* posterity.

Nachwirkung ('na:xvirkuŋ) *nf* after-effect.

Nachwuchs ('na:xvuks) *nm* new or rising generation.

nachziehen* ('na:xtsi:ən) *vt* **1** draw along or after, drag. **2** trace. *vi* follow.

Nachzügler ('na:xtsy:klər) *nm* — straggler.

Nacken ('nakən) *nm* — (nape of the) neck.

nackt (nakt) *adj* naked. **—kultur** *nf* nudism.

Nadel ('na:dəl) *nf* **-n** needle, pin. **—baum** *nm, pl* **Nadelhölzer** conifer.

Nagel ('na:gəl) *nm* **¨— 1** nail, pin. **2** (finger)nail. **—feile** *nf* nail file. **—lack** *nm* nail polish or varnish. **—n** *vt* nail. **—neu** *adj* brand-new.

nag/en ('na:gən) *vi,vt* **1** gnaw. **2** erode. **—etier** *n neu* rodent.

nah/(e) ('na:ə) *adj* near, close. **Nahe(r) Osten** *nm* Middle or Near East. **¨—e** ('nɛ:ə) *nf* **1** proximity, vicinity. **2** neighbourhood. **in der Nähe** nearby, in the vicinity. **—elegen** *vt* suggest. **—eliegen*** *vi* **1** lie near. **2** be obvious. **¨—er** ('nɛ:ər) *adj* **1** nearer. **2** more detailed. **¨—eres** ('nɛ:ərəs) *n neu* details. **¨—ern** ('nɛ:ərn) *vt* bring near. **sich ¨—ern** *vr* approach. **—estehen*** *vi* **1** be connected (with). **2** be friendly or sympathize (with). **—ezu** (na:ə'tsu:) *adv* nearly, almost.

näh/en ('nɛ:ən) *vt,vi* sew. **—maschine** *nf* sewing machine.

nahm (na:m) *v* see **nehmen.**

nähren ('nɛ:rən) *vt* feed, nourish. *vi* be nourishing. **sich nähren** *vr* live (on).

nahr/haft ('na:rhaft) *adj* **1** nutritious. **2** productive. **—ung** *nf* nourishment, food, sustenance. **—ungsmittel** *n neu pl* food(stuffs).

Naht (na:t) *nf* **¨-e 1** seam. **2** *med* stitch(es).

naiv (na'i:f) *adj* naive, simple.

Nam/e ('na:mə) *nm* **-n** name. **—enlos** *adj* nameless. **—ens** *prep* **1** named. **2** in the name of. **—entlich** *adj* by name. *adv* especially. **¨—lich** ('nɛ:mliç) *adv* that is to say, namely. *adj* same.

nannte ('nantə) *v* see **nennen.**

Napf (napf) *nm* **¨-e** bowl, basin.

Narbe ('narbə) *nf* **-n** scar.

Narko/se (nar'ko:zə) *nf* **-n** anaesthesia. **—tisch** (nar'ko:tiʃ) *adj* narcotic.

Narr (nar) *nm* **-en** fool. **—enhaus** *n neu* madhouse. **—heit** *nf* **-en** folly, madness.

Nase ('na:zə) *nf* **-n** nose. **die Nase voll haben von** be fed up with. **—weis** *adj* cheeky.
naß (nas) *adj* wet, moist.
Nässe ('nɛsə) *nf* **-n 1** moisture. **2** humidity. **—n** *vt* wet, moisten.
Nation (natsi'o:n) *nf* **-en** nation. **—al** (natsio'na:l) *adj* national. **—alhymne** *nf* national anthem. **—alismus** (natsiona'lismus) *nm* nationalism. **—alität** (natsionali'tɛ:t) *nf* **-en** nationality. **—alsozialismus** *nm* national socialism, Nazism. **—alsozialist** *nm* Nazi.
Natter ('natər) *nf* **-n** adder.
Natur (na'tu:r) *nf* **-en 1** nature. **2** disposition, temper. **—alien** (natu'ra:liən) *n pl* natural produce. **—erscheinung** *nf* natural phenomenon. **—gemäß** *adj* natural. **—geschichte** *nf* natural history. **—gesetz** *n neu* law of nature, natural law. **¨—lich** (na'ty:rliç) *adj* natural. *adv* of course, naturally. **—wissenschaft** *nf* (natural) science.
Navigation (navigatsi'o:n) *nf* **-en** navigation.
Nazi ('na:tsi) *nm* **-s** Nazi.
Nebel ('ne:bəl) *nm* — fog, mist.
neben ('ne:bən) *prep* **1** beside, near, next to. **2** in addition to. **—an** (ne:bən'an) *adv* **1** close or near by. **2** next door. **—bei** (ne:bən'bai) *adv* **1** incidentally. **2** besides, moreover. **—einander** (ne:bənain'andər) *adv* side by side, next to one another. **—fach** *n neu* subsidiary subject. **—fluß** *nm* tributary. **—gebäude** *n neu* annexe. **—her** (ne:bən'he:r) *adv* **1** incidentally. **2** alongside. **—kosten** *n pl* incidental costs, extras. **—sächlich** *adj* incidental.
nebst (ne:pst) *prep* together with.
neck/en ('nɛkən) *vt* tease. **—isch** *adj* **1** teasing. **2** comical.
Neffe ('nɛfə) *nm* **-n** nephew.
negativ (nega'ti:f) *adj* negative. *n neu* **-e** negative.
Neger ('ne:gər) *nm* — Negro. **—in** *nf* **-nen** Negress.
nehmen* ('ne:mən) *vt* **1** take. **2** receive.
Neid (nait) *nm* envy. **—en** ('naidən) *vi* envy. **—isch** ('naidiʃ) *adj* envious.
Neig/e ('naigə) *nf* **-n 1** slope, decline. **2** remnant, dregs. **—en** *vt* **1** lean. **2** lower. *vi* incline (to), tend (to). **sich —en** *vr* **1** incline (to), tend (to). **2** dip. **3** bow. **—ung** *nf* **-en 1** inclination, tendency, preference. **2** slope, incline.
nein (nain) *adv* no. **mit Nein antworten** reply in the negative.
Nelke ('nɛlkə) *nf* **-n 1** carnation. **2** clove.
nenn/en* ('nɛnən) *vt* name, call. **—enswert** *adj* worth mentioning. **—ung** *nf* **-en 1** naming. **2** *sport* entry.
Neon ('ne:ɔn) *n neu* neon.
Nerv (nɛrf) *nm* **-en** nerve. **—enzusammenbruch** *nm* nervous breakdown. **—ös** (nɛr'vœ:s) *adj* nervous.
Nessel ('nɛsəl) *nf* **-n** nettle.
Nest (nɛst) *n neu* **-er** nest.

nett (nɛt) *adj* **1** nice. **2** neat. **3** pretty.
netto ('nɛto) *adv* net, clear.
Netz (nɛts) *n neu* **-e 1** net, netting. **2** mains. **3** network, grid. **—haut** *nf* retina.
neu (nɔy) *adj* **1** new. **2** modern, recent. **3** fresh.
Neubau ('nɔybau) *nm* **1** new building. **2** building under construction.
neuerdings ('nɔyərdiŋs) *adv* lately, recently.
Neuerung ('nɔyəruŋ) *nf* **-en** innovation.
neu(e)stens ('nɔystəns) *adv* lately, of late.
Neugier ('nɔygiːr) *nf also* **Neugier/de** ('nɔygiːrdə) curiosity. **—ig** *adj* curious.
Neuheit ('nɔyhait) *nf* **-en 1** novelty. **2** newness.
Neuigkeit ('nɔyiçkait) *nf* **-en** news.
Neujahr ('nɔyjaːr) *n neu* New Year.
neulich ('nɔyliç) *adj* recently.
Neuphilologie ('nɔyfilɔlɔgiː) *nf* (study of) modern languages.
Neureiche(r) ('nɔyraiçə) *nm* new rich, nouveau riche.
Neuzeit ('nɔytsait) *nf* modern age or times. **—lich** *adj* modern.
neun (nɔyn) *adj,nf* nine. **—te** *adj* ninth. **—zehn** *adj,nf* nineteen. **—zehnte** *adj* nineteenth. **—zig** ('nɔyntsiç) *adj,nf* ninety. **—zigste** *adj* ninetieth.
Neurose (nɔy'roːzə) *nf* **-n** neurosis.
Neuseeland (nɔy'zeːlant) *n neu* New Zealand.
neutr/al (nɔy'traːl) *adj* neutral, impartial. **—alität** (nɔytrali'tɛːt) *nf* neutrality. **—um** ('nɔytrum) *n neu* neuter.
nicht (niçt) *adv* not. *pref* non-. **nicht wahr?** is that not so? isn't it? **—raucher** *nm* non-smoker. **—wissen** *n neu* ignorance. **—zutreffend** *adj* not applicable.
Nichte ('niçtə) *nf* **-n** niece.
Nichtigkeit ('niçtiçkait) *nf* **-en 1** invalidity. **2** worthlessness.
nichts (niçts) *pron* nothing. *n neu* nothing, nothingness. **—destoweniger** (niçtsdɛsto'veːnigər) *adv* nevertheless. **—sagend** *adj* meaningless. **—tuer** ('niçtstuːər) *nm* — idler, slacker.
Nickel ('nikəl) *n neu* nickel.
nick/en ('nikən) *vi* **1** nod. **2** doze. **—erchen** ('nikərçən) *n neu* — doze, nap.
nie (niː) *adv* never.
nieder ('niːdər) *adv* down. *adj* **1** low. **2** inferior.
niederdrücken (niːdər'drykən) *vt* **1** press down, weigh down. **2** depress.
Niedergang ('niːdərgaŋ) *nm* **1** decline. **2** descent.
niedergehen* ('niːdərgeːən) *vi* **1** go down. **2** alight, land.
niedergeschlagen ('niːdərgəʃlaːgən) *adj* downcast, depressed.
Niederlage ('niːdərlaːgə) *nf* **1** defeat. **2** warehouse. **3** *comm* branch.
Niederland/e ('niːdərlandə) *n pl* Netherlands. **¨—er** *nm* — Dutchman. **¨—isch** *adj* Dutch.
Niederlassung ('niːdərlasuŋ) *nf* **-en** settlement.

niederlegen ('niːdərleːgən) *vt* **1** lay down. **2** demolish. **3** resign, stop. **sich niederlegen** *vr* lie down.
Niedersachsen ('niːdəzaksən) *n neu* Lower Saxony.
Niederschlag ('niːdərʃlaːk) *nm* **1** precipitation. **2** knock-out. **3** sediment. **—en*** *vt* **1** knock down. **2** defeat. **3** kill. **4** press or move down(wards). **5** calm down. **6** depress. **7** precipitate.
niederträchtig (niːdətrɛçtiç) *adj* base, mean.
niedlich ('niːdliç) *adj* nice, dainty, pretty.
niedrig ('niːdriç) *adj* **1** low. **2** humble.
niemals ('niːmaːls) *adv* never.
niemand ('niːmant) *pron* nobody, no one.
Niere ('niːrə) *nf* **-n** kidney.
nieseln ('niːzəln) *vi* drizzle.
niesen ('niːzən) *vi* sneeze.
Niet (niːt) *nm* **-e** rivet. **—en** *vt* rivet.
Nikotin (niko'tiːn) *n neu* nicotine.
Nil (niːl) *nm* Nile. **—pferd** *n neu* hippopotamus.
nimmer ('nimər) *adv* never. **—mehr** *adv* never again.
nimmt (nimt) *v* see **nehmen.**
nippen ('nipən) *vi* sip.
nirgends ('nirgənts) *adv also* **nirgendwo** ('nirgəntvoː) nowhere.
Nische ('niːʃə) *nf* **-n** niche.
nisten ('nistən) *vi* (build a) nest.
Niveau (niː'voː) *n neu* **-s** **1** standard. **2** level.
noch (nɔx) *adv* **1** still. **2** yet. **3** besides. **noch nicht** not yet. **weder...noch** neither...nor. **—mal** *adv also* **—mals** once more, again.
Nomade (no'maːdə) *nm* **-n** nomad.
Nominativ ('noːminatiːf) *nm* **-e** nominative.
nominell (nomi'nɛl) *adj* nominal.
Nonne ('nɔnə) *nf* **-n** nun.
Nord (nɔrt) *nm also* **Norden** ('nɔrdən) north.
Nordamerika ('nɔrdameːrika) *n neu* North America.
nordisch ('nɔrdiʃ) *adj* **1** Norse, Nordic. **2** northern.
nördlich ('nœrtliç) *adj* northern.
Nordost (nɔrd'ɔst) *nm also* **Nordosten** (nɔrd'ɔst'ən) north-east. **¨—lich** *adj* north-eastern.
Nordpol ('nɔrdpoːl) *nm* North Pole.
Nordrhein-Westfalen (nɔrtrainvɛst'faːlən) *n neu* North Rhine-Westphalia.
Nordsee ('nɔrdzeː) *nf* North Sea.
nordwärts ('nɔrtvɛrts) *adv* northward(s), north.
Nordwest (nɔrd'vest) *nm also* **Nordwesten** (nɔrd'vestən) north-west. **—lich** *adj* north-western.
normal (nɔr'maːl) *adj* normal.
Normann/e (nɔr'manə) *nm* **-n** Norman. **—isch** *adj* Norman.
Norweg/en ('nɔrveːgən) *n neu* Norway. **—er** *nm* — Norwegian. **—isch** *adj* Norwegian. *n neu* Norwegian (language).
Not (noːt) *nf* **¨-e** **1** need, necessity. **2** emergency. **3** danger. **4**

trouble. **5** poverty, misery, distress.

Notar (no'ta:r) *nm* **-e** notary.

Notbremse ('no:tbrɛmsə) *nf* emergency brake.

Notfall ('no:tfal) *nm* case of emergency or need. **—s** *adv* if necessary, in an emergency.

Nothilfe ('no:thilfə) *nf* emergency or relief service.

notieren (no'ti:rən) *vt* make a note of, take down.

nötig ('nœ:tiç) *adj* necessary. **—en** ('nœ:tigən) *vt* compel, urge.

Notiz (no'ti:ts) *nf* **-en 1** notice. **2** note. **—buch** *n neu* notebook.

Notlage ('no:tla:gə) *nf* **1** crisis, emergency. **2** distress.

Notruf ('no:tru:f) *nm* emergency (telephone) call.

Notstand ('no:tʃtand) *nm* (state of) emergency.

notwendig ('no:tvɛndiç) *adj* necessary, requisite. **—keit** *nf* **-en** necessity.

Notzucht ('no:ttsuxt) *nf* rape.

Novelle (no'vɛlə) *nf* **-n** short novel or story.

November (no'vɛmbər) *nm* November.

Novize (no'vi:tsə) *nm,f* **-n** novice.

nüchtern ('nyçtərn) *adj* **1** sober. **2** prosaic, dull.

Nudeln ('nu:dəln) *nf pl* noodles.

null (nul) *adj* **1** nil. **2** null. *nf* **-en** nought, zero.

numerieren (nume'ri:rən) *vt* number.

Nummer ('numər) *nf* **-n 1** number. **2** issue, edition (of a magazine, etc.). **3** number, piece, song. **—nschild** *n neu mot* number plate.

nun (nu:n) *adv* now. *interj* well, well now. **—mehr** *adv* **1** (by) now. **2** from now on.

nur (nu:r) *adv* **1** only, solely. **2** merely. *conj* but.

Nürnberg ('nyrnbɛrk) *n neu* Nuremberg.

Nuß (nus) *n* **Nüsse** nut. **—baum** *nm* walnut tree.

nutz/bar ('nutsba:r) *adj* useful. **—en** ('nutsən) *n neu* **1** use. **2** advantage. **3** gain. *vt also* **¨—en** ('nytsən) make use of. *vi* be useful, help. **¨—lich** ('nytsliç) *adj* useful. **—los** *adj* useless.

Nylon ('nailɔn) *n neu* nylon. **—strümpfe** *nm pl* nylon stockings, nylons.

Nymphe ('nymfə) *nf* **-n** nymph.

O

Oase (o'a:zə) *nf* **-n** oasis.

ob (ɔp) *conj* whether. *prep* **1** above. **2** beyond. **3** on account of. **als ob** *conj* as if, as though.

Obdach ('ɔpdax) *n neu* shelter. **—los** *adj* homeless.

oben ('o:bən) *adv* **1** above. **2** (high) up. **3** upstairs. **nach oben gehen** go upstairs. **—an** (o:bən'an) *adv* **1** at the top. **2** at the beginning. **3** at the head. **—drein** (o:bən'drain) *adv* in addition, into the bargain.

ober ('o:bər) *adj* **1** upper, higher. **2** superior. **3** senior. *nm* **—** (head) waiter.

Oberarm ('o:bərarm) *nm* upper arm.

Oberbefehlshaber (o:bərbə'fɛ:lshabər) *nm* commander-in-chief.

Oberfläch/e ('o:bərflɛçə) *nf* **1** surface. **2** area. **—lich** ('o:bərflɛçliç) *adj* superficial.

oberhalb ('o:bərhalp) *adv,prep* above.

Oberhand ('o:bərhant) *nf* upper hand.

Oberhaupt ('o:bərhaupt) *nm* leader, head.

Oberhemd ('o:bərhɛmt) *n neu* shirt.

Oberin ('o:bərin) *nf* **-nen** matron.

oberirdisch (o:bər'irdiʃ) *adj* **1** above ground. **2** overhead.

Oberkellner ('o:bərkɛlnər) *nm* head waiter.

Oberlicht ('o:bərliçt) *n neu* skylight.

Oberschicht ('o:bəʃiçt) *nf* **1** top layer. **2** upper classes, elite.

Oberschule ('o:bərʃu:lə) *nf* secondary school.

Oberst ('o:bərst) *nm* **-en** colonel. **—leutnant** *nm mil* lieutenant colonel.

obgleich (ɔp'glaiç) *conj* although.

Obhut ('ɔphu:t) *nf* protection, care.

obig ('o:biç) *adj* above(-mentioned).

Objekt (ɔp'jɛkt) *n neu* **-e** object. **—iv** (ɔpjɛk'ti:f) *adj* objective.

obliegen* ('ɔpli:gən) *vi* **einem obliegen** be one's duty.

obligat (obli'ga:t) *adj* **1** obligatory. **2** necessary. **—orisch** (obliga'to:riʃ) *adj* compulsory.

Obmann ('ɔpman) *nm* **1** leader. **2** chairman. **3** spokesman.

Obo/e (o'bo:ə) *nf* **-n** oboe. **—ist** (obo'ist) *nm* **-en** oboe player.

Obrigkeit ('o:briçkait) *nf* **-en** **1** authorities. **2** *pl* government.

obschon (ɔp'ʃo:n) *conj* although.

Obst (o:pst) *n neu* fruit. **—garten** *nm* orchard.

obszön (ɔps'tsœ:n) *adj* obscene, indecent. **—ität** (ɔpstsœ:ni'tɛ:t) *nf* **-en** obscenity.

obwohl (ɔp'vo:l) *conj* although.

Ochse ('ɔksə) *nm* **-n** ox.

Ode ('o:də) *nf* **-n** ode.

öde ('œ:də) *adj* **1** bleak, barren. **2** deserted. **3** dull. *nf* **-n** **1** desert. **2** dullness.

oder ('o:dər) *conj* or. **entweder...oder** either ...or.

Ofen ('o:fən) *nm* **¨—** **1** stove, oven. **2** heater. **3** furnace.

offen ('ɔfən) *adj* **1** open. **2** public. **3** frank, candid. **4** vacant. **—bar** (ɔfən'ba:r) *adj* obvious. **—baren** (ɔfən'ba:rən) *vt* disclose, reveal. **—barung** (ɔfən'ba:ruŋ) *nf* **-en** revelation, disclosure. **—heit** *nf* openness, frankness. **—sichtlich** *adj* obvious. **¨—tlichkeit** ('œfəntliçkait) *nf* **1** public. **2** publicity.

offensiv (ɔfɛn'zi:f) *adj* offensive. **—e** (ɔfɛn'zi:və) *nf* **-n** offensive.

offiziell (ɔfi'tsjɛl) *adj* official.

Offizier (ɔfi'tsi:r) *nm* **-e** officer.

öffn/en ('œfnən) *vt* **1** open. **2** unlock. **—er** *nm* — opener. **—ung** *nf* **-en** opening, hole.

oft (ɔft) *adv also* **öfters**

('œftərs) *or* **oftmals** ('ɔftma:ls) often, frequently. **¨—er** ('œftər) *adv* (more) often. **—malig** ('ɔftma:liç) *adj* frequent.
Oheim ('o:haim) *nm* **-e** uncle.
ohn/e ('o:nə) *prep* without. **—edies** (o:nə'di:s) *adv also* **—ehin** (o:nə'hin) **1** in any case. **2** besides. **—macht** *nf* **1** unconsciousness. **2** powerlessness, impotence. **—mächtig** *adj* **1** unconscious. **2** powerless.
Ohr (o:r) *n neu* **-en** ear. **—feige** *nf* box on the ear. **—ring** *nm* **-e** earring.
Öhr (œ:r) *n neu* **-e** eye (of a needle).
Ökonom (œko'no:m) *nm* **-en** **1** farmer. **2** steward. **3** economist. **—ie** (œkono'mi:) *nf* **-n** **1** economics. **2** economy. **3** agriculture. **—isch** (œko'no:miʃ) *adj* economical.
Oktave (ɔk'ta:və) *nf* **-n** octave.
Oktober (ɔk'to:bər) *nm* October.
Okzident ('ɔktsidɛnt) *nm* Occident.
Öl (œ:l) *n neu* **-e** oil. **—bild** *n neu* oil painting. **—en** *vt* **1** oil. **2** anoint. **—feld** *n neu* oil field. **—ig** *adj* oily. **—ung** *nf* **-en** **1** lubrication. **2** anointment.
Olive (o'li:və) *nf* **-n** olive.
Oma ('o:ma) *nf* **-s** *inf* grandma.
Omelett (ɔmə'lɛt) *n neu* **-s** *also* **Omelette** *nf* **-n** omelette.
Omnibus ('ɔmnibus) *nm* **-busse** bus, coach.
ondulieren (ɔndu'li:rən) *vt* wave (hair).
Onkel ('ɔŋkəl) *nm* — uncle.
Opa ('o:pa) *nm* **-s** *inf* grandpa.
Opal (o'pa:l) *nm* **-e** opal.
Oper ('o:pər) *nf* **-n** opera. **—ette** (opə'rɛtə) *nf* **-n** operetta. **—nhaus** *n neu* opera house.
Oper/ation (operatsi'o:n) *nf* **-en** operation. **—ationssaal** *nm* operating theatre. **—ieren** (ope'ri:rən) *vt,vi* operate (on).
Opfer ('ɔpfər) *n neu* — **1** victim. **2** sacrifice. **—n** *vt* sacrifice.
Opium ('o:pium) *n neu* opium.
opportun (ɔpɔr'tu:n) *adj* opportune.
Opposition (ɔpozitsi'o:n) *nf* **-en** opposition.
Opt/ik ('ɔptik) *nf* optics. **—iker** *nm* — optician. **—isch** ('ɔptiʃ) *adj* optical.
Optimist (ɔpti'mist) *nm* **-en** optimist. **—isch** *adj* optimistic.
Orange (o'rã:ʒə) *nf* **-n** orange. **—nmarmelade** *nf* marmelade.
Orchester (ɔr'kɛstər) *n neu* — **1** orchestra. **2** band.
Orchidee (ɔrçi'de:ə) *nf* **-n** orchid.
Orden ('ɔrdən) *nm* — **1** order. **2** decoration. **—sbruder** *nm* member of an order, monk. **—sschwester** *nf* sister, nun.
ordentlich ('ɔrdəntliç) *adj* **1** orderly, tidy. **2** decent, proper. **3** regular. **—keit** *nf* **1** orderliness. **2** respectability. **3** regularity.
Order ('ɔrdər) *nf* **-n** command, order.
ordinär (ɔrdi'nɛ:r) *adj* ordinary, vulgar.
Ordinarius (ɔrdi'na:rius) *nm* **-rien** **1** professor. **2** class teacher.

ordn/en ('ɔrdnən) *vt* **1** (put in) order. **2** sort. **3** regulate. **—er** *nm* — **1** organizer. **2** steward. **3** file, folder. **—ung** *nf* **-en 1** order. **2** regulation. **3** arrangement.
Organ (ɔr'ga:n) *n neu* **-e** organ. **—isation** (ɔrganizatsi'o:n) *nf* **-en** organization. **—isieren** (ɔrgani'zi:rən) *vt* organize. **—isch** (ɔr'ga:niʃ) *adj* organic. **—ismus** (ɔrga'nismus) *nm* **-ismen** organism.
Orgel ('ɔrgəl) *nf* **-n** *mus* organ.
Orgie ('ɔrgiə) *nf* **-n** orgy.
Orient ('o:riɛnt) *nm* Orient. **—alisch** (oriɛn'ta:liʃ) *adj* oriental.
orientieren (oriɛn'ti:rən) *vt* **1** orientate. **2** inform. **sich orientieren** *vr* take one's bearings.
origin/al (origi'na:l) *adj* original, first. *n neu* **-e** original. **—ell** (origi'nɛl) *adj* **1** original. **2** unusual. **3** clever.
Orkan (ɔr'ka:n) *nm* **-e** hurricane.
Ornat (ɔr'nat) *nm* **-e** (official) robes.
Ornithologie (ɔrnitolo'gi:) *nf* ornithology.
Ort (ɔrt) *nm* **-e 1** place, spot. **2** point. **3** town. **¨—lich** ('œrtliç) *adj* local. **—schaft** *nf* **-en 1** (small) town, village. **2** place.
Orthopädie (ɔrtopɛ'di:) *nf* orthopaedics.
Ost (ɔst) *nm also* **Ost/en** east. **—deutschland** *n neu* East Germany. **¨—lich** ('œstliç) *adj* eastern. **—see** *nf* Baltic Sea. **—wärts** ('ɔstvɛrts) *adv* eastward(s), east.
Oster/n ('o:stərn) *n neu pl* Easter. **—ei** *n neu* Easter egg.
Österreich ('œ:stərraiç) *n neu* Austria. **—er** *nm* — Austrian. **—isch** *adj* Austrian.
Otter[1] ('ɔtər) *nm* — otter.
Otter[2] ('ɔtər) *nf* **-n** adder.
Ouvertüre (uvɛr'ty:rə) *nf* **-n** overture.
oval (o'va:l) *adj* oval.
Oxyd (ɔ'ksy:t) *n neu* **-e** oxide.
Ozean ('o:tsea:n) *nm* **-e** ocean. **—isch** (o:tse'a:niʃ) *adj* oceanic.
Ozon (o'tso:n) *n neu* **-e** ozone.

P

Paar (pa:r) *n neu* **-e** pair, couple. **ein paar** a few. **—en** *vt* pair, couple. **sich —en** *vr* mate.
Pacht (paxt) *nf* **-en 1** lease, tenure. **2** rent. **—en** *vt* lease, rent. **¨—er** ('pɛçtər) *nm* — tenant, leaseholder. **—vertrag** *nm* lease.
Pack (pak) *nm* **¨-e 1** packet, parcel. **2** pack. *n neu* mob, rabble. **¨—chen** ('pɛkçən) *n neu* — small parcel, packet. **—en** *vt* **1** grasp, seize. **2** pack. **3** thrill. **—papier** *n neu* wrapping paper. **—ung** *nf* **-en** packing.
Pädagog/ik (pɛda'go:gik) *nf* (theory of) education. **—isch** *adj* educational, teaching. **pädagogische Hochschule** *nf* teacher training college.
Paddel ('padəl) *n neu* — paddle. **—boot** *n neu* canoe. **—n** *vi* paddle.
Page ('pa:ʒə) *nm* **-n** page (boy).
Paket (pa'ke:t) *n neu* **-e** packet, package.

Pakt (pakt) *nm* **-e** pact, agreement.

Palast (pa'last) *nm* **¨-e** palace.

Palästin/a (palɛ'stiːna) *n neu* Palestine. **—ense(r)** *nm* Palestinian. **—isch** *adj* Palestinian.

Palm/e ('palmə) *nf* **-n** palm. **—sonntag** *nm* Palm Sunday.

Pampelmuse ('pampəlmuːzə) *nf* **-n** grapefruit.

panieren (pa'niːrən) *vt* coat with breadcrumbs.

Panik ('paːnik) *nf* **-en** panic.

Panne ('panə) *nf* **-n** *mot* breakdown.

Panther ('pantər) *nm* — panther.

Pantoffel (pan'tɔfəl) *nm* **-n** slipper.

Pantomime (panto'miːmə) *nf* **-n** pantomime.

Panzer ('pantsər) *nm* armour. **—(kampf)wagen** *nm mil* tank. **—n** *vt* **1** armour. **2** arm.

Papa (pa'paː, 'papa) *nm* **-s** dad, daddy.

Papagei (papa'gai) *nm* **-en** parrot.

Papier (pa'piːr) *n neu* **-e** paper. **—en** *adj* paper. **—geld** *n neu* paper money. **—korb** *nm* wastepaper basket.

Papp/e ('papə) *nf* **-n** cardboard. **—schachtel** *nf* cardboard box, carton.

Pappel ('papəl) *nf* **-n** poplar.

Paprika ('paprika) *nm* paprika, capsicum.

Papst (paːpst) *nm* **¨-e** pope. **¨—lich** ('pɛːpstliç) *adj* papal.

Parabel (pa'raːbəl) *nf* **-n 1** parable. **2** parabola.

Parad/e (pa'raːdə) *nf* **-n 1** parade. **2** parry. **—ieren** (para'diːrən) *vi* parade.

Paradies (para'diːs) *n neu* **-e** paradise.

paradox (para'dɔks) *adj* paradoxical. **—on** (para'dɔkson) *n neu* **-oxa** paradox.

Paragraph (para'graːf) *nm* **-en** paragraph, article, section.

parallel (para'leːl) *adj* parallel. **—e** *nf* **-n** parallel.

Paralyse (para'lyːzə) *nf* **-n** paralysis.

Parasit (para'ziːt) *nm* **-en** parasite.

Parenthese (parɛn'teːzə) *nf* **-n** parenthesis.

Parfüm (par'fyːm) *n neu* **-e** or **-s** perfume.

parieren (pa'riːrən) *vt* **1** parry. **2** rein in (a horse). *vi* obey.

Parität (pari'tɛːt) *nf* **-en** parity.

Park (park) *nm* **-s** park. **—anlage** *nf* park, grounds. **—en** *vt* park. **—platz** *nm* car park. **—uhr** *nf* parking meter.

Parkett (par'kɛt) *n neu* **-s 1** parquet (floor). **2** *Th* stalls.

Parlament (parla'mɛnt) *n neu* **-e** parliament. **—arisch** (parlamɛn'taːriʃ) *adj* parliamentary.

Parodie (paro'diː) *nf* **-n** parody.

Parole (pa'roːlə) *nf* **-n 1** password. **2** *pol* slogan.

Partei (par'tai) *nf* **-en** *pol* party. **—gänger** (par'taigɛŋər) *nm* party man, partisan. **—isch** *adj also* **—lich** partial, partisan, biased. **—los** *adj* impartial, independent.

Parterre (par'tɛr) *n neu* **-s 1** ground floor. **2** *Th* pit.

Partie (par'tiː) *nf* **-n 1** part. **2**

party, excursion. **3** match. **4** *comm* lot.

Partikel (par'ti:kəl) *nf* **-n** particle.

Partisan (parti'za:n) *nm* **-e** partisan, guerrilla.

Partitur (parti'tu:r) *nf* **-en** *mus* score.

Partizip (parti'tsi:p) *n neu* **-ien** participle.

Party ('pa:rti) *nf* **-ties** party.

Parzell/e (par'tsɛlə) *nf* **-n** allotment. **—ieren** (partsɛ'li:rən) *vt* divide into lots.

Paß (pas) *nm* **Pässe 1** passport. **2** pass. **3** passage. **—kontrolle** *nf* passport control.

Passag/e (pa'sa:ʒə) *nf* **-n** passage. **—ier** (pasa'ʒi:r) *nm* **-e** passenger.

Passant (pa'sant) *nm* **-en** passer-by.

passen ('pasən) *vi* **1** fit, suit. **2** *sport,game* pass. **sich passen** *vr* be proper or fitting. **—d** *adj* suitable, fit(ting).

passier/en (pa'si:rən) *vt* **1** pass (through), cross. **2** sieve, strain. *vi* happen, occur. **—schein** *nm* pass, permit.

Passion (pasi'o:n) *nf* **-en** passion. **—sspiel** *n neu* Passion Play.

passiv ('pasi:f) *adj* passive. *n neu* **-e** *gram* passive. **—ität** (pasivi'tɛ:t) *nf* passivity.

Pastete (pa'ste:tə) *nf* **-n** (meat) pie, pasty.

pasteurisieren (pastœri'zi:rən) *vt* pasteurize.

Pastor ('pastɔr) *nm* **-en** pastor, vicar. **—al** (pastɔ'ra:l) *adj* pastoral.

Pate ('pa:tə) *nm* **-n** godfather. **—nkind** *n neu* godchild.

patent (pa'tɛnt) *adj* splendid. *n neu* **-e 1** patent. **2** commission. **—ieren** (patɛn'ti:rən) *vt* patent. **—inhaber** *nm* patent-holder.

pathetisch (pa'te:tiʃ) *adj* pathetic.

Pathologie (patolo'gi:) *nf* **-n** pathology.

Patient (patsi'ɛnt) *nm* **-en** patient.

Patin ('pa:tin) *nf* **-nen** godmother.

Patriot (patri'o:t) *nm* **-en** patriot. **—isch** *adj* patriotic. **—ismus** (patrio'tismus) *nm* patriotism.

Patrizier (pa'tri:tsiər) *nm* — patrician.

Patron (pa'tro:n) *nm* **-e** patron. **—in** *nf* **-nen** patroness.

Patrone (pa'tro:nə) *nf* **-n 1** cartridge. **2** pattern.

Patrouille (pa'truljə) *nf* **-n** patrol.

Patt (pat) *n neu* **-s** stalemate.

Pauke ('paukə) *nf* **-n** kettledrum. **—n** *vi* **1** play the kettledrum **2** *inf* study, swot.

pauschal (pau'ʃa:l) *adj* inclusive. **—e** *nf* **-n 1** lump sum. **2** all-in price. **—reise** *nf* package tour.

Pause ('pauzə) *nf* **-n** pause, interval.

Pavian ('pa:via:n) *nm* **-e** baboon.

Pazifik (pa'tsi:fik) *nm* Pacific (Ocean).

Pazifismus (patsi'fismus) *nm* pacifism.

Pech (pɛç) *n neu* **-e 1** pitch. **2** *inf* hard luck.

Pedal (pe'daːl) *n neu* **-e** pedal.
Pedant (pe'dant) *nm* **-en** pedant.
Pegel ('peːgəl) *nm* — water-gauge.
peilen ('pailən) *vt naut* **1** sound. **2** take the bearings of.
Pein (pain) *nf* pain, torture. **—lich** *adj* **1** embarrassing. **2** painful. **3** meticulous.
Peitsche ('paitʃə) *nf* **-n** whip. **—n** *vt* whip.
Pelikan ('peːlikaːn) *nm* **-e** pelican.
Pell/e ('pɛlə) *nf* **-n** **1** skin. **2** peel. **—en** *vt* **1** skin. **2** peel. **—kartoffeln** *nf pl* potatoes boiled in their skins.
Pelz (pɛlts) *nm* **-e** pelt, fur. **—ig** *adj* furry. **—mantel** *nm* fur coat.
Pend/el ('pɛndəl) *n neu* — pendulum. **—elverkehr** *nm* **1** commuter traffic. **2** shuttle service. **—ler** *nm* — commuter.
penibel (pe'niːbəl) *adj* meticulous.
Pension (pã'sjoːn) *nf* **-en** **1** guest house. **2** pension. **¨—ar** (pãsjo'nɛːr) *nm* **-e** **1** paying guest. **2** pensioner. **—ieren** (pãsjo'niːrən) *vt* pension (off).
per (pɛr) *prep* by, per.
perfekt (pɛr'fɛkt) *adj* perfect. *n neu* **-e** *gram* perfect.
Pergament (pɛrga'mɛnt) *n neu* **-e** parchment.
Period/e (peri'oːdə) *nf* **-n** period, cycle. **—isch** *adj* periodic(al).
Perl/e ('pɛrlə) *nf* **-n** pearl. **—mutter** *nf* mother-of-pearl.
Pers/ien ('pɛrziən) *n neu* Persia. **—er** *nm* Persian. **—isch** *adj* Persian. *n neu* Persian (language).
Person (pɛr'zoːn) *nf* **-en** **1** person. **2** *Th* character. **—al** (pɛrzo'naːl) *n neu* **-e** personnel, staff. *adj* personal. **—alien** (pɛrzo'naːliən) *n pl* personal particulars. **—ell** (pɛrzo'nɛl) *adj* personal. **¨—lich** (pɛr'zœːnliç) *adj* personal, private. **¨—lichkeit** *nf* **-en** personality.
Perspektive (pɛrspɛk'tiːvə) *nf* **-n** perspective.
Perücke (pe'rykə) *nf* **-n** wig.
pervers (pɛr'vɛrs) *adj* perverse.
Pessimis/mus (pɛsi'mismus) *nm* pessimism. **—t** (pɛsi'mist) *nm* **-en** pessimist. **—tisch** *adj* pessimistic.
Pest (pɛst) *nf* **-en** pestilence, plague.
Petersilie (petər'ziːliə) *nf* **-n** parsley.
Petroleum (pe'troːleum) *n neu* **1** petroleum. **2** paraffin.
Pfad (pfaːt) *nm* **-e** path. **—finder** *nm* Boy Scout. **—finderin** *nf* Girl Guide.
Pfahl (pfaːl) *nm* **¨-e** stake, post.
Pfalz (pfalts) *nf* **-en** the Palatinate.
Pfand (pfant) *n neu* **¨-er** **1** pledge, security. **2** deposit. **3** mortgage. **—brief** *nm* mortgage deed. **¨-en** ('pfɛndən) *vt law* seize, take possession of. **—haus** *n neu* pawnshop. **—leiher** *nm* pawnbroker.
Pfann/e ('pfanə) *nf* **-n** pan. **—kuchen** *nm* pancake.
Pfarr/er ('pfarər) *nm* — parson, rector, minister. **—haus** *n neu* parsonage, rectory. **—kirche** *nf* parish church.

Pfau (pfau) *nm* **-en** peacock.
Pfeffer ('pfɛfər) *nm* pepper. **—dose** *nf* pepper-pot. **—korn** *n neu* **¨-er** peppercorn. **—minze** *nf* **-n** peppermint. **—n** *vt* pepper.
Pfeife ('pfaifə) *nf* **-n 1** pipe. **2** whistle. **—n*** *vi* whistle.
Pfeil (pfail) *nm* **-e** arrow.
Pfeiler ('pfailər) *nm* **— 1** pillar. **2** pier.
Pfennig ('pfɛniç) *nm* **-e 1** a coin, one hundredth of a mark. **2** penny.
Pferch (pfɛrç) *nm* **-e** fold, pen.
Pferd (pfeːrt) *n neu* **-e** horse. **—ebremse** ('pfeːrdəbrɛmzə) *nf* horsefly. **—erennen** ('pfeːrdərɛnən) *n neu* **1** horse-race. **2** horse-racing. **—estall** ('pfeːrdəʃtal) *nm* stable. **—estärke** ('pfeːrdəʃtɛrkə) *nf* horse-power.
pfiff (pfif) *v* see **pfeifen.**
Pfiff (pfif) *nm* **-e** whistle. **—ig** *adj* cunning.
Pfifferling ('pfifərliŋ) *nm* **-e** type of mushroom.
Pfingst/en ('pfiŋstən) *n neu* or *nf pl* Whitsun(tide). **—rose** *nf* peony.
Pfirsich ('pfirziç) *nm* **-e** peach.
Pflanze ('pflantsə) *nf* **-n** plant. **—en** *vt* plant. **—ung** *nf* **-en** plantation.
Pflaster ('pflastər) *n neu* **— 1** pavement, road-surface. **2** (sticking-)plaster. **—n** *vt* pave. **—stein** *nm* paving stone.
Pflaume ('pflaumə) *nf* **-n** plum.
Pflege ('pfleːgə) *nf* **-n 1** care. **2** cultivation. **—eltern** *n pl* foster-parents. **—kind** *n neu* **1** foster-child. **2** nurseling. **—mutter** *nf* foster-mother **—vater** *nm* foster-father. **—n** *vt* **1** care for, tend, foster. **2** cultivate. *vi* be accustomed to, be in the habit of. **—er** *nm* **—, —erin** *nf* **-nen 1** nurse. **2** guardian.
Pflicht (pfliçt) *nf* **-en** duty, obligation. **—gefühl** *n neu* sense of duty. **—gemäß** *adv* according to duty, dutifully. **—treu** *adj* dutiful. **—vergessen** *adj* disloyal.
Pflock (pflɔk) *nm* **¨-e 1** peg. **2** plug.
pflücken ('pflykən) *vt* pluck, gather.
Pflug (pfluːk) *nm* **¨-e** plough. **¨—en** ('pflyːgən) *vt* plough.
Pfort/e ('pfɔrtə) *nf* **-n 1** door, gate. **2** porthole. **¨—ner** ('pfœrtnər) *nm* **—** porter, gate-keeper.
Pfosten ('pfɔstən) *nm* **— 1** post. **2** door-post.
Pfote ('pfoːtə) *nf* **-n** paw.
Pfropf (pfrɔpf) *nm* **-e** plug, wad. **—en** *vt* **1** stop, plug. **2** fill, cram. **3** *bot* graft. *nm* **—** stopper, cork.
pfui (pfui) *interj* **1** shame! **2** ugh! pooh!
Pfund (Pfunt) *n neu* **-e 1** pound, half-kilogram. **2** pound (sterling).
pfusch/en ('pfuʃən) *vi,vt* bungle, blunder. **—erei** (pfuʃə'rai) *nf* **-en 1** bungling. **2** mess.
Pfütze ('pfytsə) *nf* **-n** puddle.
Phänomen (fɛno'meːn) *n neu* **-e** phenomenon.
Phantas/ie (fanta'ziː) *nf* **-n 1** imagination, fancy. **2** fantasy. **—ieren** (fanta'ziːrən) *vi* **1** day-

dream. **2** *mus* improvise. **3** talk feverishly. **—tisch** (fan'tastiʃ) *adj* fantastic, fanciful.
Phantom (fan'toːm) *n neu* **-e** phantom, vision.
Phase ('faːzə) *nf* **-n** phase.
Philist/er (fi'listər) *nm* — Philistine. **—erhaft** *adj also* **—rös** philistine.
Philosoph (filo'zoːf) *nm* **-en** philosopher. **—ie** (filozo'fiː) *nf* philosophy. **—isch** *adj* philosophical.
Phonet/ik (fo'neːtik) *nf* phonetics. **—isch** *adj* phonetic.
Phosphor ('fɔsfɔr) *nm* phosphorus.
Photo ('foːto) *n neu* **-s** photo(graph). **—apparat** *nm* camera. **—graph** (foto'graːf) *nm* **-en** photographer. **—graphie** (fotogra'fiː) *nf* photography. **—graphieren** (fotogra'fiːrən) *vt* photograph. **—graphisch** (foto'graːfiʃ) *adj* photographic. **—kopie** (fotoko'piː) *nf* photocopy.
Phrase ('fraːzə) *nf* **-n** **1** phrase. **2** empty words, cliché. **3** *mus* phrase, theme.
Physik (fy'ziːk) *nf* physics. **—alisch** (fyzi'kaːliʃ) *adj* physical. **—er** ('fyːzikər) *nm* — physicist.
Physiologie (fyziolo'giː) *nf* physiology.
physisch ('fyːziʃ) *adj* physical, material, corporeal.
Pianist (pia'nist) *nm* **-en** pianist.
Picke ('pikə) *nf* **-n** pickaxe. **—l** *nm* — **1** pimple. **2** pickaxe. **3** ice-axe. **—n** *vi* pick, peck.
Piep (piːp) *nm* **-e** chirp. **—en** *vi* chirp.
Pietät (pie'tɛːt) *nf* piety.
pikant (pi'kant) *adj* spicy.
Pikkoloflöte ('pikoloflœːtə) *nf* **-n** piccolo.
Pilger ('pilgər) *nm* — pilgrim. **—n** *vi* go on a pilgrimage.
Pille ('pilə) *nf* **-n** pill.
Pilot (pi'loːt) *nm* **-en** pilot.
Pilz (pilts) *nm* **-e** **1** fungus. **2** mushroom.
Pinguin (piŋgu'iːn) *nm* **-e** penguin.
Pinne ('pinə) *nf* **-n** **1** pin, peg. **2** tiller.
Pinsel ('pinzəl) *nm* — **1** brush. **2** simpleton.
Pionier (pio'niːr) *nm* **-e** **1** pioneer. **2** *mil* engineer.
Pistole (pi'stoːlə) *nf* **-n** pistol.
Plackerei (plakə'rai) *nf* drudgery.
plädieren (plɛ'diːrən) *vt* plead (a case).
Plage ('plaːgə) *nf* **-n** **1** nuisance. **2** irony. **—n** *vt* plague, worry. **sich —n** *vr* toil.
Plakat (pla'kaːt) *n neu* **-e** poster.
Plan (plaːn) *nm* **¨-e** **1** plan. **2** design, draft. **3** project. **4** schedule. **—en** *vt,vi* **1** plan. **2** design, draft. **—gemäß** *adj also* **—mäßig** according to plan. **—ung** *nf* planning.
Plane ('plaːnə)) *nf* **-n** **1** awning. **2** tarpaulin.
Planet (pla'neːt) *nm* **-en** planet.
planieren (pla'niːrən) *vt* plane, level.
Planke ('plaŋkə) *nf* **-n** plank.
Plänkelei (plɛŋkə'lai) *nf* **-en** skirmish(ing).
Plantage (plan'taːʒə) *nf* **-n** plantation.

plappern ('plapərn) *vi,vt* babble, chatter.

Plasti/k ('plastik) *nf* **-en** sculpture, plastic art. **—sch** *adj* plastic.

Plastilin (plasti'li:n) *n neu* **-s** *Tdmk* Plasticine *Tdmk*.

Platin (pla'ti:n) *n neu* platinum.

platt (plat) *adj* **1** flat, even. **2** insipid. **3** silly. **—deutsch** *n neu* Low German.

Platte ('platə) *nf* **-n** **1** record, disc. **2** plate. **3** tray. **—nspieler** *nm* record-player.

Platz (plats) *nm* **¨-e** **1** place. **2** square. **3** seat. **4** space. **5** locality. **—karte** *nf* (seat) reservation ticket.

platz/en ('platsən) *vi* burst, explode. **—regen** *nm* **1** heavy shower. **2** downpour.

plaudern ('plaudərn) *vi* chat, talk.

plausibel (plau'zi:bəl) *adj* plausible.

plombieren (plɔm'bi:rən) *vt* fill (a tooth).

plötzlich ('plœtsliç) *adj* sudden.

plump (plump) *adj* **1** coarse, crude. **2** awkward, clumsy.

plündern ('plyndərn) *vt,vi* plunder, pillage.

Plural ('plu:ra:l) *nm* **-e** plural.

Plusquamperfekt ('pluskvampɛrfɛkt) *n neu* **-e** pluperfect.

pneumatisch (pnɔy'ma:tiʃ) *adj* pneumatic.

Pöbel ('pœ:bəl) *nm* rabble, mob.

pochen ('pɔxən) *vi* knock, beat.

Pocken ('pɔkən) *nf pl* smallpox.

Poesie (poe'zi:) *nf* **-en** poetry.

Pokal (po'ka:l) *nm* **-e** **1** goblet. **2** *sport* cup.

Pökel ('pœ:kəl) *nm* — brine. **—n** *vt* pickle, salt.

Pol (po:l) *nm* **-e** pole (of the earth or of a magnet). **—ar** (po'la:r) *adj* polar. **—arisieren** (polari'zi:rən) *vt* polarize. **—arkreis** (po'la:rkrais) *nm* Arctic Circle.

Polem/ik (po'le:mik) *nf* **-en** polemic. **—isch** *adj* polemic.

Pol/en ('po:lən) *n neu* Poland. **—e** *nm* Pole.

Police (po'li:s, po'li:sə) *nf* **-n** (insurance) policy.

polieren (po'li:rən) *vt* polish.

Polit/ik (poli'ti:k) *nf* **1** politics. **2** policy. **—iker** (po'li:tikər) *nm* — politician. **—isch** (po'li:tiʃ) *adj* political. **—isieren** (politi'zi:rən) *vt* politicize. *vi* talk politics.

Poliz/ei (poli'tsai) *nf* **-en** police. **—eibeamte(r)** *nm* police officer. **—eilich** *adj* (of, by or with the) police. **—eiwache** *nf* police station. **—ist** (poli'tsist) *nm* **-en** policeman.

polnisch ('pɔlniʃ) *adj* Polish. *n neu* Polish (language).

Polster ('pɔlstər) *n neu* **1** cushion. **2** stuffing. **—n** *vt* **1** stuff, pad. **2** upholster.

Poltergeist ('pɔltərgaist) *nm* **-er** poltergeist.

Polypen (po'ly:pən) *nm pl med* adenoids.

Polystyrol ('pɔli:sty:ro:l) *nm* polystyrene.

Polytechnikum (poly'tɛçnikum) *n neu* **—ken** technical college.

Pommern ('pɔmərn) *n neu* Pommerania.

Pommes frites (pɔm'frit) *n pl* chips, chipped potatoes.
populär (popu'lɛːr) *adj* popular.
Pore ('poːrə) *nf* **-n** pore.
Pornographie (pɔrnogra'fiː) *nf* pornography. **—isch** (pɔrno 'graːfiʃ) *adj* pornographic.
Portion (pɔrtsi'oːn) *nf* **-en** portion, helping.
Porto ('pɔrto) *n neu* **-s** postage, carriage. **—frei** *adj* postage paid, post-free.
Porträt (pɔr'trɛː, pɔr'trɛːt) *n neu* **-s** portrait, picture.
Porzellan (pɔrtsɛ'laːn) *n neu* **-e** porcelain, china.
Posaune (po'zaunə) *nf* **-n** trombone.
Pose ('poːzə) *nf* **-n** pose.
Position (pozitsi'oːn) *nf* **-en** position.
positiv ('poːzitiːf) *adj* positive.
Poss/e ('pɔsə) *nf* **-n 1** *Th* farce. **2** trick. **—ierlich** (pɔ'siːrliç) *adj* comic, funny.
possessiv ('pɔsɛsiːf) *adj* possessive.
Post (pɔst) *nf* **1** post, mail. **2** (the) Post Office.
Postamt ('pɔstamt) *n neu* post office.
Postanweisung ('pɔstanvaizuŋ) *nf* postal order.
Postbote ('pɔstboːtə) *nm* postman.
Posten ('pɔstən) *nm* — **1** post, station. **2** *comm* entry, item. **3** lot. **4** picket. **5** guard.
Postfach ('pɔstfax) *n neu also* **Postschließfach** post-office box, P.O. box.
Postkarte ('pɔstkartə) *nf* postcard.
postlagernd ('pɔstlaːgərnt) *adj* poste restante.
Postleitzahl ('pɔstlaitsaːl) *nf* postal code.
Poststempel ('pɔststɛmpəl) *nm* postmark.
Postulat (pɔstu'laːt) *n neu* **-e** postulate.
postwendend ('pɔstvɛndənt) *adv* by return of post.
Postwertzeichen ('pɔstvɛrtsaiçən) *n neu* postage stamp.
potent (po'tɛnt) *adj* potent, capable.
poten/tial (potɛntsi'aːl) *adj also* **poten/tiell** (potɛntsi'ɛl) potential. *n neu* **-e** potential. **—z** (po 'tɛnts) *nf* **-en 1** potency. **2** *math* power.
Pottasche ('pɔtaʃə) *nf* potash.
Pracht (praxt) *nf* **1** splendour, pomp. **2** luxury. **¨—ig** ('prɛçtiç) *adj* **1** splendid, magnificent. **2** pompous. **—voll** *adj* splendid, magnificent.
Prädikat (prɛdi'kaːt) *n neu* **-e 1** predicate. **2** title.
Präfix (prɛ'fiks) *n neu* **-e** prefix.
Prag (praːk) *n neu* Prague.
prägen ('prɛːgən) *vt* **1** stamp. **2** coin.
pragmatisch (prag'maːtiʃ) *adj* pragmatic.
prägnant (prɛg'nant) *adj* **1** precise. **2** meaningful.
prahl/en ('praːlən) *vi* boast. **—erei** (praːlə'rai) *nf* boasting. **—erisch** ('praːləriʃ) *adj* boastful.
Prakt/iker ('praktikər) *nm* — practical or experienced man. **—isch** *adj* **1** practical. **2** experienced. **3** handy.

Praline (pra'liːnə) *nf* **-n** chocolate cream.
prall (pral) *adj* **1** taut, tight. **2** stuffed, full. **3** plump. **4** (of the sun) blazing. *nm* **-e** collision, impact. **—en** *vi* **1** bump (into), crash. **2** (of the sun) glare.
Prämie ('prɛmiə) *nf* **-n 1** premium. **2** prize, bonus.
Präparat (prɛpa'raːt) *n neu* **-e** preparation (of medicine, etc.).
Präposition (prɛpozitsi'oːn) *nf* **-en** preposition.
Präsens ('prɛːzɛns) *n neu gram* present.
präsentieren (prɛzɛn'tiːrən) *vt* present.
Präsid/ent (prɛzi'dɛnt) *nm* **-en 1** president. **2** chairman. **—ieren** (prɛzi'diːrən) *vi* act as president. *vt* preside over. **—ium** (prɛ'ziːdium) *n neu* **-ien 1** presidium. **2** presidency. **3** chair.
prasseln ('prasəln) *vi* patter, drum, crackle.
Präteritum (prɛ'teːritum) *n neu* **-ita** past tense.
Praxis ('praksis) *nf* **-xen 1** practice. **2** (doctor's) surgery. **3** (lawyer's) office.
Präzedenzfall (prɛtse'dɛntsfal) *nm* precedent.
präzis (prɛ'tsiːs) *adj* **1** precise. **2** punctual.
predig/en ('preːdigən) *vi,vt* preach. **—er** *nm* — preacher. **—t** ('preːdiçt) *nf* **-en** sermon.
Preis (prais) *nm* **-e 1** price. **2** prize. **3** praise. **—beaufsichtigung** *nf* **—en** price control. **—en*** ('praizən) *vt* praise. **—geben*** *vt* **1** give up, sacrifice. **2** expose. **—richter** *nm* umpire, judge. **—stopp** *nm* **-s** price freeze. **—wert** *adj* cheap, good value.
Preiselbeere ('praizəlbeːrə) *nf* **-n** cranberry.
prellen ('prɛlən) *vt* **1** deceive. **2** bang.
Premiere (prem'jɛːrə) *nf* **-n** premiere, first night.
Premierminister (prem 'jeːrministər) *nm* prime minister.
Presse ('prɛsə) *nf* **-n 1** press, journalism. **2** *tech* press. **—ausweis** *nm* press card. **—freiheit** *nf* freedom of the press. **—n** *vt* **1** (com)press. **2** urge.
Preßkohle ('prɛskoːlə) *nf* briquette.
Preßluftbohrer ('prɛsluftboːrər) *nm* pneumatic drill.
Preuß/en ('prɔysən) *n neu* Prussia.**-e** *nm* **-n** Prussian. **—isch** *adj* Prussian.
prickeln ('prikəln) *vi* prickle, itch.
Priester ('priːstər) *nm* — priest. **—in** *nf* priestess.
prima ('priːma) *adj,interj* first class. *nf* **-men** sixth form.
primär (pri'mɛːr) *adj* primary.
Primel ('priːməl) *nf* **-n** primrose.
primitiv (primi'tiːf) *adj* primitive.
Prinz (prints) *nm* **-en** prince. **—essin** (prin'tsɛsin) *nf* **-nen** princess.
Prinzip (prin'tsiːp) *n neu* **-ien** principle. **—iell** (printsipi'ɛl) *adj* principle. *adv* on or in principle.

Prise ('priːzə) *nf* **-n 1** pinch (of salt, etc.). **2** *naut* prize, spoils.
Prisma ('prisma) *n neu* **-men** prism.
privat (pri'vaːt) *adj* private. **—eigentum** *n neu* private property. **—isieren** (privati 'siːrən) *vt* privatize. **—recht** *n neu* civil law.
Privileg (privi'leːk) *n neu* **-ien** privilege. **—iert** (privili'giːrt) *adj* privileged.
Prob/e ('proːbə) *nf* **-n 1** experiment. **2** test. **3** rehearsal. **4** sample. **—en** *vt,vi* **1** test. **2** rehearse. **—ezeit** *nf* probation, trial period. **—ieren** (pro'biːrən) *vt* **1** try (out), attempt. **2** sample.
Problem (pro'bleːm) *n neu* **-e** problem. **—atisch** (proble 'maːtiʃ) *adj* problematic.
Produkt (pro'dukt) *n neu* **-e 1** product. **2** result. **—ion** (produktsi'oːn) *nf* production. **—ionsmittel** *n neu pl* means of production. **—iv** (produk'tiːf) *adj* productive. **—ivität** (produktivi'tɛːt) *nf* productivity.
Produz/ent (produ'tsɛnt) *nm* **-en** producer. **—ieren** (produ 'tsiːrən) *vt* produce.
Profess/or (pro'fɛsɔr) *nm* **-en** professor. **—ur** (profɛ'suːr) *nf* **-en** professorship.
Profil (pro'fiːl) *n neu* **-e** profile.
Profit (pro'fiːt) *nm* **-e** profit. **—ieren** (profi'tiːrən) *vi* profit.
Prognose (pro'gnoːzə) *nf* **-n** forecast, prognosis.
Programm (pro'gram) *n neu* **-e** programme. **—ieren** *vt* program.
Projekt (pro'jɛkt) *n neu* **-e** project. **—ion** (projɛktsi'oːn) *nf* **-en** projection.
projizieren (proji'tsiːrən) *vt* project.
Prolet (pro'leːt) *nm* **-en** *also* **Prolet/arier** (prole'tariər) **—** proletarian. **—ariat** (proletari 'aːt) *n neu* proletariat.
Prolog (pro'loːk) *nm* **-e** prologue.
Promenade (promə'naːdə) *nf* **-n** promenade.
Promotion[1] (promotsi'oːn) *nf* *comm* promotion.
Promo/tion[2] (promotsi'oːn) *nf* **-en** award of a doctorate. **—vieren** (promo'viːrən) *vt,vi* award or be awarded a doctorate.
Pronomen (pro'noːmɛn) *n neu* **-mina** pronoun.
Propaganda (propa'ganda) *nf* propaganda.
Propeller (pro'pɛlər) *nm* **—** propeller.
Proph/et (pro'feːt) *nm* **-en** prophet. **—ezeien** (profe 'tsaiən) *vt,vi* prophesy.
Proportion (propɔrtsi'oːn) *nf* **-en** proportion.
Prosa ('proːza) *nf* **-sen** prose. **—isch** (pro'zaːiʃ) *adj* prosaic.
prosit ('proːzit) *interj* cheers! good health!
Prospekt (pro'spɛkt) *nm* **-e 1** prospect, view. **2** prospectus.
prostituier/en (prostitu'iːrən) *vt* prostitute. **—te** *nf* **-n** prostitute.
Protektorat (protɛkto'raːt) *n neu* **-e 1** protectorate. **2** patronage.
Protest (pro'tɛst) *nm* **-e** protest. **—ant** (protɛ'stant) *nm* **-en** Protestant. **—antisch**

(protɛ'stantiʃ) *adj* Protestant. **—ieren** (protɛ'stiːrən) *vi* protest.

Protokoll (proto'kɔl) *n neu* **-e 1** minutes, record. **2** protocol.

Proton ('proːtɔn) *neu* **-en** proton.

Protz (prɔts) *nm* **-en** snob. **—en** *vi* show off (one's wealth), be ostentatious. **—ig** *adj* **1** snobbish, ostentatious. **2** gaudy.

Proviant (provi'ant) *nm* **-e** provisions, food.

Provinz (pro'vints) *nf* **-en** province. **—ial** (provintsi'aːl) *adj* provincial. **—iell** (provintsi'ɛl) *adj* provincial, narrow-minded, petty.

provisorisch (provi'zoːriʃ) *adj* provisional.

provozieren (provo'tsiːrən) *vt* provoke.

Prozedur (protse'duːr) *nf* **-en 1** procedure. **2** *law* proceedings.

Prozent (pro'tsɛnt) *n neu* **-e** percent. **—satz** *nm* percentage.

Prozeß (pro'tsɛs) *nm* **-zesse 1** lawsuit, case, trial. **2** process.

prüde ('pryːdə) *adj* prudish.

prüf/en ('pryːfən) *vt* **1** examine. **2** test. **3** inspect. **—er** *nm* — examiner, auditor. **—stein** *nm* yardstick. **—ung** *nf* **-en 1** examination. **2** test, inspection.

Prügel ('pryːgəl) *nm* **1** stick. **2** beating. **—ei** (pryːgə'lai) *nf* **-en** brawl. **—n** *vt* beat.

Prunk (pruŋk) *nm* splendour, pomp. **—en** *vi* make a show. **—voll** *adj* showy, ornate.

Psalm (psalm) *nm* **-en** psalm.

Psych/iatrie (psyçia'triː) *nf* psychiatry. **—isch** ('psyːçiʃ) *adj* psychic. **—oanalyse** (psyçoana'lyːzə) *nf* psychoanalysis. **—ologie** (psyçolo'giː) *nf* psychology. **—osomatisch** (psyçoso'maːtiʃ) *adj* psychosomatic.

Pubertät (pubɛr'tɛːt) *nf* puberty.

Publikum ('puːblikum) *n neu* public.

publizieren (publi'tsiːrən) *vt* publish.

Pudding ('pudiŋ) *nm* **-e** pudding.

Pudel ('puːdəl) *nm* — poodle.

Puder ('puːdər) *nm* powder. **—n** *vt* powder.

Puff (puf) *nm* **¨-e 1** push. **2** thump. **3** bang, crash. **4** *inf* brothel. **—er** *nm* — buffer. **—spiel** *n neu* backgammon.

Puls (puls) *nm* **-e** pulse. **—ieren** (pul'ziːrən) *vi* pulsate, throb.

Pult (pult) *n neu* **-e** desk.

Pulver ('pulvər) *n neu* powder. **—isieren** (pulvəri'ziːrən) *vt* pulverize.

Pumpe ('pumpə) *nf* **-n** pump. **—n** *vt* **1** pump. **2** *inf* borrow or lend.

Punker ('pʌnkə) *nm* punk.

Punkt (puŋkt) *nm* **-e 1** point. **2** dot, spot. **3** full stop. **4** item. **—ieren** (puŋk'tiːrən) *vt* **1** punctuate. **2** *med* puncture. **¨—lich** ('pynktliç) *adj* **1** punctual. **2** exact. **¨—lichkeit** *nf* punctuality.

Pupille (pu'pilə) *nf* **-n** *anat* pupil.

Puppe ('pupə) *nf* **-n 1** doll, puppet. **2** chrysalis, pupa. **—nspiel** *n neu* puppet show.

pur (puːr) *adj* pure.
Purpur ('purpur) *nm* purple.
Purzel/baum ('purtsəlbaum) *nm* somersault. **—n** *vi* fall over, tumble down.
Pustel ('pustəl) *nf* **-n** pimple.
Pute ('puːtə) *nf* **-n** turkey-hen. **—r** *nm* — turkey-cock.
Putsch (putʃ) *nm* **-e** **1** putsch, coup. **2** uprising.
putz/en ('putsən) *vt* **1** clean(se). **2** polish. **3** wipe. **4** sweep. **5** adorn. **sich putzen** *vr* dress up. **—frau** *nf* charwoman, cleaner. **—lappen** *nm* cleaning rag, duster.
Pyjama (pi'dʒaːma) *nm,neu* **-s** pyjamas.
Pyramide (pyra'miːdə) *nf* **-n** pyramid.
Pyrenäen (pyre'nɛːən) *n pl* Pyrenees.

Q

quabbelig ('kvabəliç) *adj* flabby, wobbly.
Quadrat (kva'draːt) *n neu* **-e** square. **—meter** *nm,neu* square metre.
quadrieren (kva'driːrən) *vt* *math* square.
quäken ('kvɛːkən) *vi* (of a child, etc.) whine, squeal.
Qual (kvaːl) *nf* **-en** pain, torment. **¨—en** ('kvɛːlən) *vt* torment, torture. **¨—erei** (kvɛːlə'rai) *nf* torment, torture.
qualifizieren (kvalifi'tsiːrən) *vt* qualify.
Qualität (kvali'tɛːt) *nf* **-en** quality.
Qualle ('kvalə) *nf* **-n** jelly-fish.
Quantität (kvanti'tɛːt) *nf* **-en** quantity.
Quarantäne (kvaran'tɛːnə) *nf* **-n** quarantine.
Quark (kvark) *nm* **-e** **1** curds. **2** *sl* rubbish, trash. **—käse** *nm* **1** curd cheese. **2** cream cheese.
Quart (kvart) *n neu* **-e** **1** quarto. **2** quart. **—al** (kvar'taːl) *n neu* **-e** quarter (of a year).
Quartett (kvar'tɛt) *n neu* **-e** quartet.
Quarz (kvarts) *nm* **-e** quartz.
Quatsch (kvatʃ) *nm* nonsense. **—en** *vi* talk nonsense.
Quecksilber ('kvɛkzilbər) *n neu* mercury.
Quelle ('kvɛlə) *nf* **-n** **1** source. **2** spring, fountain. **—n*** *vi* **1** well, flow. **2** swell. *vt* soak.
quer (kveːr) *adj* cross, diagonal. *adv* crosswise, obliquely. **—en** *vt* traverse, cross. **—schiff** *n neu* transept. **—schnitt** *nm* cross-section **—straße** *nf* crossroad.
quetschen ('kvɛtʃən) *vt* **1** press, crush. **2** squeeze, pinch.
quietschen ('kviːtʃən) *vi* squeak.
Quintett (kvin'tɛt) *n neu* **—e** quintet.
Quirl (kvirl) *nm* **-e** whisk. **—en** *vt* whisk.
quitt (kvit) *adj* even, quits.
Quitte ('kvitə) *nf* **-n** quince.
Quittung ('kvituŋ) *nf* **-en** receipt.

R

Rabatt (ra'bat) *nm* **-e** discount.
Rabbiner (ra'biːnər) *nm* — rabbi.
Rabe ('raːbə) *nm* **-n** raven.
rabiat (rabi'aːt) *adj* rabid, raging, furious.
Rach/e ('raxə) *nf* revenge, ven-

geance. **—durstig** *adj* vengeful. **¨—en** ('rɛçən) *vt* avenge, revenge. **sich ¨—en** *vr* take revenge (on).
Rachen ('raxən) *nm* — **1** throat. **2** jaws.
Rad (raːt) *n neu* **¨-er 1** wheel. **2** (bi)cycle. **—fahren*** *vi* cycle. **—fahrer** *nm* cyclist.
Radar ('raːdaːr) *n neu* radar.
Rädelsführer ('rɛːdəlsfyːrər) *nm* ringleader.
radier/en (ra'diːrən) vt **1** erase. **2** etch. **—gummi** *nm* rubber, eraser. **—ung** *nf* **-en 1** etching. **2** erasure.
Radieschen (ra'diːsçən) *n neu* — radish.
radikal (radi'kaːl) *adj* radical.
Radio ('raːdio) *n neu* **-s** radio.
radioaktiv (radioak'tiːf) *adj* radioactive.
Radium ('raːdium) *n neu* radium.
raffen ('rafən) *vt* **1** snatch (up), grab. **2** gather up (cloth).
raffinier/en (rafi'niːrən) *vt* refine. **—t** *adj* cunning, clever, artful.
ragen ('raːgən) *vi* tower (up), project.
Rahm (raːm) *nm* cream. **—käse** *nm* cream cheese.
Rahmen ('raːmən) *nm* — **1** frame, framework. **2** setting. *vt* frame.
Rakete (ra'keːtə) *nf* **-n** rocket.
Rakett (ra'kɛt) *n neu* **-s** *sport* racket.
Ramme ('ramə) *nf* **-n** pile-driver. **—n** *vt* ram (in).
Rampe ('rampə) *nf* **-n** ramp.
'ran (ran) contraction of **heran.**
Rand (rant) *nm* **¨-er 1** edge. **2** brink. **3** border. **¨—ern** ('rɛndərn) *vt* **1** border. **2** mill (coins).
Rang (raŋ) *nm* **¨-e 1** rank, order. **2** row. **—erhöhung** *nf* promotion.
rangieren (rã'ʒiːrən) *vt* **1** arrange, classify. **2** shunt. *vi* **1** be classified. **2** rank.
Ranke ('raŋkə) *nf* **-n 1** shoot. **2** branch.
rannte ('rantə) *v* see **rennen.**
ranzig ('rantsiç) *adj* rancid.
Rapier (ra'piːr) *n neu* **-e** rapier.
rar (raːr) *adj* **1** rare. **2** exquisite. **sich rar machen** make oneself scarce.
rasch (raʃ) *adj* hasty, swift.
rascheln ('raʃəln) *vi* rustle.
rasen ('raːzən) *vi* **1** rage. **2** rush. **—d** *adj* mad, raving.
Rasen ('raːzən) *nm* — grass, lawn, turf.
rasier/en (ra'ziːrən) *vt,vi* shave. **—apparat** *nm* shaver, safety razor. **—klinge** *nf* razor blade. **—krem** *nm* shaving cream. **—messer** *n neu* razor **—wasser** *n neu* aftershave lotion.
Raspel ('raspəl) *nf* **-n 1** rasp, file. **2** grater. **—n** *vt* **1** file. **2** grate.
Rass/e ('rasə) *nf* **-n 1** race. **2** breed. **—enhaß** *nm* racialism. **—entrennung** *nf* racial segregation. **—ig** *adj* **1** thoroughbred. **2** fiery. **—ist** *adj* racist.
rasseln ('rasəln) *vi* rattle.
Rast (rast) *nf* **-en** rest(ing). **—en** *vi* rest. **—los** *adj* restless. **—platz** *nm* layby.
Rasur (ra'zuːr) *nf* **-en** shave.
Rat (raːt) *nm* **¨-e 1** advice, counsel. **2** council. **3** council-

lor. **mit Rat und Tat** by word and deed. **—en*** *vt* **1** advise. **2** guess. **—geber** *nm* adviser. **—haus** *n neu* town hall. **—los** *adj* at a loss. **—sam** *adj* advisable. **—schlag** *nm* (piece of) advice, recommendation.

Rate ('ra:tə) *nf* **-n 1** instalment. **2** rate.

Ratif/ikation (ratifikatsi'o:n) *nf* **-en 1** ratification. **2** confirmation. **—izieren** (ratifi'tsi:rən) *vt* ratify.

Ration (ratsi'o:n) *nf* **-en** ration. **—al** (ratsio'na:l) *adj* rational, sensible. **—alisieren** (rationali'zi:rən) *vt* rationalize. **—ell** (ratsio'nɛl) *adj* **1** rational, logical. **2** economical. **—ieren** (ratsio'ni:rən) *vt* ration.

Rätsel ('rɛ:tsəl) *n neu* **— 1** puzzle, riddle. **2** mystery. **3** enigma. **—haft** *adj* mysterious, puzzling.

Ratte ('ratə) *nf* **-n** rat.

raub/en ('raubən) *vt* rob. **¨—er** (rɔybər) *nm* **—** robber. **—tier** ('raupti:r) *n neu* beast of prey. **—überfall** ('raupy:bərfal) *nm* armed robbery, robbery with violence.

Rauch (raux) *nm* smoke. **—en** *vt,vi* smoke. *n neu* smoking. **—er** *nm* **—** smoker. **¨—ern** ('rɔyçərn) *vt* smoke, cure (meat, etc.). **—fang** *nm* **¨-e** chimney, flue. **—ig** *adj* smoky.

'rauf (rauf) contraction of **herauf.**

Raufbold ('raufbɔlt) *nm* **-e** bully, rowdy.

rauh (rau) *adj* **1** rough. **2** coarse. **3** hoarse. **—elt** ('rauhait) *nf* roughness, coarseness.

Raum (raum) *nm* **¨-e 1** space. **2** room. **3** area. **¨—en** ('rɔymən) *vt* **1** remove. **2** clear away. **3** clear, evacuate. **—fahrt** *nf* space travel. **¨—lich** ('rɔymliç) *adj* spatial. **—schiff** *n neu* space ship.

Raupe ('raupə) *nf* **-n 1** caterpillar. **2** caterpillar track.

Rausch (rauʃ) *nm* **¨-e** intoxication. **—en** *vi* **1** rustle. **2** rush. **—gift** *n neu* narcotic, drug. **—giftsüchtige(r)** *nm* (drug) addict. **—mittel** *n neu* drug, intoxicant.

Reagenzglas (re'a:gɛntsgla:s) *n neu* test tube.

reagieren (rea'gi:rən) *vi* react.

Reakt/ion (reaktsi'o:n) *nf* **-en** reaction. **—ionär** (reaktsio'nɛ:r) *nm* **-e** reactionary. **—or** (re'aktɔr) *nm* **-en** reactor.

real (re'a:l) *adj* real. **—isieren** (reali'zi:rən) *vt* **1** realize. **2** perform. **3** convert into money. **—ismus** (rea'lismus) *nm* realism. **—ität** (reali'tɛ:t) *nf* **-en** reality. **—schule** *nf* (technical) secondary school.

Reb/e ('re:bə) *nf* **-n** vine. **—stock** ('rɛpstɔk) *nm* vine.

Rebell (re'bɛl) *nm* **-en** rebel. **—ion** (rebɛli'o:n) *nf* **-en** rebellion.

Rebhuhn ('rɛphu:n) *n neu* **¨-er** partridge.

rechen ('rɛçən) *vt* rake. *nm* **—** rake.

Rechen/maschine ('rɛçənmaʃi:nə) *nf* calculating machine, calculator. **—schaft** *nf* account. **Rechen-**

schaft ablegen account for.
rechn/en ('rɛçnən) *vt,vi* calculate, reckon, count. **—er** *nm* — calculator. **—ung** *nf* **-en 1** bill. **2** calculation.
recht (rɛçt) *adj* **1** right, correct. **2** right, right-hand. **3** correct, suitable. **4** real. **5** just. **recht haben** be right or correct. ~ *adv* **1** correctly. **2** very. **3** really. **4** justly. *n neu* **-e 1** right, privilege. **2** law.
Rechteck ('rɛçtɛk) *n neu* **-e** rectangle.
rechtfertigen ('rɛçtfɛrtigən) *vt* justify, vindicate.
rechtgläubig ('rɛçtglɔybiç) *adj* orthodox.
rechthaberisch ('rɛçthaːbəriʃ) *adj* dogmatic, obstinate.
rechtmäßig ('rɛçtmɛsiç) *adj* legal, lawful.
rechts (rɛçts) *adv* on or to the right.
Rechtsanwalt ('rɛçtsanvalt) *nm* lawyer, solicitor, barrister.
rechtschaffen ('rɛçtʃafən) *adj* upright, just.
Rechtschreibung ('rɛçtʃraibuŋ) *nf* **-en** spelling.
Rechtsfall ('rɛçtsfal) *nm* lawsuit.
Rechtsprechung ('rɛçtʃprɛxuŋ) *nf* **-en 1** administration of justice. **2** jurisdiction.
Rechtsstaat ('rɛçtsʃtaːt) *nm* constitutional state.
rechtzeitig ('rɛçttsaitiç) *adj* timely.
recken ('rɛkən) *vt* stretch (one's arms, legs, etc.). **sich recken** *vr* stretch oneself.
Redakt/eur (redak'tœːr) *nm* **-e** editor. **—ion** (redaktsi'oːn) *nf* **-en 1** editorial staff. **2** editing.
Red/e ('reːdə) *nf* **-n 1** talk. **2** speech. **nicht der Rede wert** not worth mentioning. **—efreiheit** *nf* freedom of speech. **—egewandt** *adj* eloquent. **—en** *vi* speak, talk. **—ensart** *nf* **1** phrase, expression. **2** empty phrase, cliché. **—ewendung** *nf* **-en** idiom, expression.
redigieren (redi'giːrən) *vt* edit, revise.
redlich ('reːtliç) *adj* honest, fair.
Redner ('reːdnər) *nm* — speaker, orator.
redselig ('reːtzeːliç) *adj* talkative.
reduzieren (redu'tsiːrən) *vt* reduce, decrease.
Reeder ('reːdər) *nm* — shipowner.
reell (re'ɛl) *adj* **1** honest. **2** (of business, etc.) fair. **3** respectable.
Referat (refe'raːt) *n neu* **-e 1** report. **2** lecture.
Referent (refe'rɛnt) *nm* **-en 1** expert adviser. **2** lecturer, speaker.
reflektieren (reflɛk'tiːrən) *vt,vi* reflect.
reflexiv (reflɛk'siːf) *adj* reflexive.
Reform (re'fɔrm) *nf* **-en** reform. **—ieren** (refɔr'miːrən) *vt* reform.
Refrain (rə'frɛ̃ː) *nm* **-s** refrain.
Regal (re'gaːl) *n neu* **-e** shelf, book-shelf.
rege ('reːgə) *adj* lively, active. **—n** *vt* move, stir.
Regel ('reːgəl) *nf* **-n 1** rule. **2**

regulation. **3** menstruation, menses, period. **—n** *vt* regulate. **—mäßig** *adj* regular, periodic. **—recht** *adj* regular, proper. **—ung** *nf* **-en** regulation, rule.

Regen ('re:gən) *nm* rain. **—bogen** *nm* rainbow. **—mantel** *nm* raincoat. **—schirm** *nm* umbrella.

Regent (re'gɛnt) *nm* **-en** regent.

Regie (re'ʒi:) *nf* **-n** **1** *Th* production, direction. **2** administration. **3** state monopoly.

regier/en (re'gi:rən) *vt,vi* govern, reign (over). **—ung** *nf* **-en** government, administration.

Regiment (regi'mɛnt) *n neu* **-er** **1** regiment. **2** rule, authority.

Regisseur (reʒi'sœ:r) *nm* **-e** *Th* producer, director.

Regist/er (re'gistər) *n neu* **—** **1** register. **2** table of contents. **3** index. **—rieren** (regi'stri:rən) *vt* **1** register. **2** index.

regn/en ('re:gnən) *vi* rain. **—erisch** ('re:gnəriʃ) *adj* rainy.

regulär (regu'lɛ:r) *adj* regular.

regulieren (regu'li:rən) *vt* regulate, adjust.

Regung ('re:guŋ) *nf* **-en** **1** movement. **2** emotion. **3** impulse. **—slos** *adj* motionless.

Reh (re:) *n neu* **-e** roe (deer). **—bock** *nm* **-e** roebuck. **—kalb** *n neu* fawn.

reib/en* ('raibən) *vt* **1** rub. **2** grate. **—erei** (raibə'rai) *nf* **-en** **1** friction. **2** conflict. **—ung** *nf* **-en** **1** rubbing, friction. **2** clash, conflict. **—ungslos** *adj* frictionless, smooth.

reich (raiç) *adj* wealthy, rich. **—haltig** *adj* copious, ample. **—lich** *adj* plentiful, abundant. **—tum** *nm* **¨-er** wealth, abundance.

Reich (raiç) *n neu* **-e** empire, realm.

reich/en ('raiçən) *vt* hand, offer, pass. *vi* **1** suffice. **2** reach. **—weite** *nf* **1** reach. **2** range.

reif (raif) *adj* mature, ripe. **—e** *nf* maturity, ripeness. **—ezeugnis** *n neu* school-leaving certificate.

Reif [1] (raif) *nm* hoarfrost.

Reif [2] (raif) *nm* **-e** **1** band. **2** ring.

Reifen ('raifən) *nm* **—** **1** tyre. **2** hoop. **3** collar. **—panne** *nf mot* puncture.

Reihe ('raiə) *nf* **-n** **1** file, row, rank. **2** series. **3** queue. **—n** *vt* **1** place in a row. **2** arrange. **—nfolge** *nf* sequence, order. **—nhäuser** *n neu pl* terraced houses.

Reiher ('raiər) *nm* **—** heron.

Reim (raim) *nm* **-e** rhyme. **—en** *vt,vi* rhyme.

rein [1] (rain) *adj* **1** clean. **2** pure. **3** absolute. **—machefrau** *nf* cleaner, charwoman. **—heit** *nf* cleanliness, purity. **—igen** *vt* **1** clean(se). **2** purify, refine. **—igung** *nf* **-en** **1** cleaning. **2** cleansing, purification. **—lich** *adj* **1** clean. **2** neat.

'rein [2] (rain) contraction of **herein.**

Reis (rais) *nm* rice.

Reise ('raizə) *nf* **-n** journey, trip, tour. **—büro** *n neu* **1** tourist office. **2** travel agency. **—führer** *nm* guide(book). **—n** *vi* travel. **—nde(r)** *nm* **1**

traveller. **2** passenger. **—scheck** *nm* traveller's cheque.
reiß/en* ('raisən) *vt* **1** tear. **2** drag. *vi* tear, split. **sich reißen um** fight for or over, scramble for. *~n neu inf* rheumatism. **—er** *nm* **— 1** thriller. **2** (box-office) success. **—verschluß** *nm* zip(-fastener).
reit/en* ('raitən) *vt,vi* ride. **—er** *nm* — rider. **—erei** (raitə'rai) *nf* **-en** cavalry.
Reiz (raits) *nm* **-e 1** attraction, charm. **2** irritation, annoyance. **—bar** *adj* **1** sensitive. **2** irritable. **—en** *vt* **1** attract, charm. **2** irritate. **3** excite. *vi game* bid. **—end** *adj* charming, enchanting. **—mittel** *n neu* stimulant. **—ung** *nf* **-en 1** irritation. **2** provocation. **3** enticement, charm.
Reklame (re'kla:mə) *nf* **-n 1** advertising, publicity. **2** advertisement.
Rekord (re'kɔrt) *nm* **-e** record.
Rekrut (re'kru:t) *nm* **-en** recruit. **—ieren** (rekru'ti:rən) *vt* recruit. **sich —ieren** *vr* pick or take on recruits.
Rektor ('rɛktɔr) *nm* **-en** rector, vice-chancellor, principal.
relativ (rela'ti:f) *adj* relative.
Relief (reli'ɛf) *n neu* **-s** *Art,geog* relief.
Religi/on (religi'o:n) *nf* **-en** religion. **—ös** (religi'œ:s) *adj* religious, pious.
Ren (rɛn) *n neu* **-e** reindeer.
Renn/bahn ('rɛnba:n) *nf* **-en** racecourse or racetrack. **—en*** *vi* **1** run. **2** race. *vt* run. *n neu* **— 1** running. **2** race. **3** racing. **—pferd** *n neu* racehorse. **—wagen** *nm* racing car.
Renomm/ee (reno'me:) *n neu* **-s** reputation. **—iert** (reno'mi:rt) *adj* widely respected.
renovieren (reno'vi:rən) *vt* renovate.
rentabel (rɛn'ta:bəl) *adj* profitable.
Rent/e ('rɛntə) *nf* **-n 1** pension. **2** annuity, (unearned) income. **3** interest. **—ner** *nm* — pensioner.
Repar/ation (reparatsi'o:n) *nf* **-en** reparation. **—atur** (repara'tu:r) *nf* **-en** repair. **—ieren** (repa'ri:rən) *vt* repair.
Report/age (repɔr'ta:ʒə) *nf* **-n 1** news report. **2** commentary. **—er** (re'pɔrtər) *nm* — reporter.
Repressalien (reprɛ'sa:liən) *n pl* reprisals.
Reproduktion (reproduktsi'o:n) *nf* **-en** reproduction.
Reptil (rɛp'ti:l) *n neu* **-ien** reptile.
Republik (repu'bli:k) *nf* **-en** republic.
Reserv/e (re'zɛrvə) *nf* **-n** reserve. **—ereifen** *n neu mot* spare tyre. **—ieren** *vt* reserve.
Residenz (rezi'dɛnts) *nf* **-en 1** residence (of a government, court, prince, etc.). **2** capital.
Resonanz (rezo'nants) *nf* **-en** resonance, echo.
Respekt (re'spɛkt) *nm* respect. **—abel** (respɛk'ta:bəl) *adj* respectable. **—ieren** (respɛk'ti:rən) *vt* respect. **—ive** (respɛk'ti:və) *adv* respectively. **—voll** *adj* respectful.

Rest (rɛst) *nm* **-e** rest, remainder. **—lich** *adj* remaining.
Restaurant (rɛsto'rã:) *n neu* **-s** restaurant.
Restauration (restauratsi'o:n) *nf* **-en** **1** restoration. **2** restaurant.
Resultat (rezul'ta:t) *n neu* **-e** result, outcome.
Retorte (re'tɔrtə) *nf* **-n** *sci* retort.
rett/en ('rɛtən) *vt* save, rescue. **—ung** *nf* **-en** **1** rescue. **2** escape. **—ungsboot** *n neu* lifeboat.
Reue ('rɔyə) *nf* **1** remorse, regret. **2** repentance. **—n** *v imp* **es reut mich** I regret.
Revanche (re'vã:ʃə) *nf* **-n** revenge.
Revers[1] (re'vɛrs) *nm* **-e** bond.
Revers[2] (re'vɛrs) *nm* **-e** back, reverse (side).
Revers[3] (re'vɛ:r) *nm,neu* **—** lapel.
revidieren (revi'di:rən) *vt* **1** revise. **2** audit.
Revier (re'vi:r) *n neu* **-e** **1** district. **2** (policeman's) beat. **3** (delivery) round.
Revision (revizi'o:n) *nf* **-en** **1** revision. **2** audit, auditing. **3** *law* appeal.
Revolte (re'vɔltə) *nf* **-n** revolt.
Revolution (revolutsi'o:n) *nf* **-en** revolution. **—är** (revolutsio'nɛ:r) *nm* **-e** revolutionary. *adj* revolutionary.
Revolver (re'vɔlvər) *nm* **—** revolver.
rezens/ieren (retsɛn'zi:rən) *vt* *Th,lit* review. **—ion** (retsɛnzi'o:n) *nf* **-en** review.
Rezept (re'tsɛpt) *n neu* **-e** **1** prescription. **2** recipe.
Rhabarber (ra'barbər) *nm* **—** rhubarb.
Rhein (rain) *nm* Rhine. **—land** *n neu* Rhineland. **—land-Pfalz** *nf* Rhineland-Palatinate.
Rhetor/ik (re'to:rik) *nf* rhetoric. **—isch** *adj* rhetorical.
Rheumatismus (rɔyma'tismus) *nm* rheumatism.
Rhythmus ('rytmus) *nm* **-men** rhythm.
richt/en ('riçtən) *vt* **1** set. **2** direct, aim. **3** prepare. **4** arrange. **5** adjust. **6** judge. *vi* judge. **sich richten** *vr* **1** prepare. **2** comply. **—er** *nm* **—** **1** judge. **2** umpire. **—maß** *n neu* gauge. **—ung** *nf* **-en** direction.
richtig ('riçtiç) *adj* **1** correct, right. **2** real. **3** just. **—keit** *nf* **1** correctness. **2** accuracy.
rieb (ri:p) *v* see **reiben.**
riechen* ('ri:çən) *vt,vi* smell.
rief (ri:f) *v* see **rufen.**
Riegel ('ri:gəl) *nm* **—** bolt, bar. **—n** *vt* bolt, bar.
Riemen ('ri:mən) *nm* **—** **1** strap, band. **2** belt.
Ries/e ('ri:zə) *nm* **-n** giant. **—enhaft** *adj* gigantic, huge. **—ig** *adj* giant, enormous.
riet (ri:t) *v* see **raten.**
Riff (rif) *n neu* **-e** reef.
Rille ('rilə) *nf* **-n** groove, furrow.
Rind (rint) *n neu* **-er** **1** ox, cow. **2** *pl* cattle. **—fleisch** *n neu* beef. **—vieh** *n neu* cattle.
Rinde ('rində) *nf* **-n** **1** rind. **2** crust. **3** bark.
Ring (riŋ) *nm* **-e** **1** ring. **2** *comm* combine, trust, syndicate. **—förmig** ('riŋfœrmiç) *adj*

ring-shaped. **—straße** *nf* ring-road.

ring/en* ('riŋən) *vi* **1** wrestle, struggle. **2** fight (for), strive (after). *vt* wring (one's hands, etc.). **—kampf** *nm* wrestling match.

rings (riŋs) *adv* (a)round. **—um** (riŋs'um) *adv also* **—umher** or **—herum** all about or around.

Rinn/e ('rinə) *nf* **-n** **1** gutter, drain. **2** groove, channel. **—stein** *nm* gutter, drain.

Ripp/e ('ripə) *nf* **-n** **1** rib. **2** *cul* cutlet, chop. **—chen** *n neu* **—** cutlet.

Ris/iko ('ri:ziko) *n neu* **-s, -ken** risk. **—kant** (ris'kant) *adj* risky. **—kieren** (ris'ki:rən) *vt* risk.

riß (ris) *v* see **reißen.**

Riß (ris) *nm* **Risse** **1** tear. **2** crack, crevice. **3** *tech* drawing, design. **4** fracture.

ritt (rit) *v* see **reiten.**

Ritt (rit) *nm* **-e** ride.

Ritter ('ritər) *nm* **—** knight. **—gut** *n neu* manor, estate. **—lich** *adj* chivalrous.

rittlings ('ritliŋs) *adv* astride.

Ritus ('ri:tus) *nm* **-ten** rite.

Ritz (rits) *nm* **-e** *also* **Ritze** ('ritsə) *nf* **-n** **1** cleft, fissure. **2** scratch.

Rizinusöl ('ri:tsinusœ:l) *n neu* castor oil.

roch (rox) *v* see **riechen.**

Rock (rɔk) *nm* **¨-e** **1** skirt. **2** jacket, coat.

rod/en ('ro:dən) *vt* clear (woodland for cultivation). **—ung** *nf* **-en** cleared woodland.

Roggen ('rɔgən) *nm* rye. **—brot** *n neu* ryebread.

roh (ro:) *adj* **1** raw. **2** crude. **3** rough, brutal. **—eit** ('ro:hait) *nf* **-en** **1** rawness. **2** roughness, brutality. **—stoff** *nm* raw material.

Rohr (ro:r) *n neu* **-e** **1** tube, pipe. **2** reed, cane. **3** barrel (of a gun). **¨—e** ('rœ:rə) *nf* **-n** **1** tube, pipe. **2** (radio) valve. **3** oven. **—geflecht** *n neu* wickerwork. **—weite** *nf tech* bore.

Roll/aden ('rɔlladən) *nm* roller blind. **—bahn** *nf aviat* runway. **—en** ('rɔlən) *vt,vi* roll. **—er** *nm* **—** **1** (motor) scooter. **2** roller, breaker. **—holz** *n neu* rolling pin. **—schuh** *nm* roller skate. **—stuhl** *nm* wheelchair. **—treppe** *nf* escalator.

Rolle ('rɔlə) *nf* **-n** **1** roll. **2** *Th* role. **3** pulley. **4** castor. **5** mangle. **das spielt keine Rolle** that doesn't matter.

Rom (ro:m) *n neu* Rome.

Roman (ro'ma:n) *nm* **-e** novel.

Roman/tik (ro'mantik) *nf* romantic poetry, romanticism. **—tiker** *nm* **—** romanticist. **—tisch** *adj* romantic.

röntgen ('rœntgən) *vt* X-ray. **—aufnahme** *nf also* **—bild** *n neu* X-ray (photograph). **—strahlen** *nm pl* X-rays.

rosa ('ro:za) *adj* pink.

Ros/e ('ro:zə) *nf* **-n** rose. **—enkohl** *nm* Brussels sprout. **—enkranz** *nm* rosary.

Rosine (ro'zi:nə) *nf* **-n** raisin.

Rosmarin (rɔsma'ri:n) *nm* **-e** rosemary.

Roß (rɔs) *n neu* **Rosse** horse, steed.

Rost[1] (rɔst) *nm* **—e** **1** grating. **2** *cul* grill. **—braten** *nm* roast (meat). ¨—**n** ('rœːstən) *vt* **1** roast. **2** toast. **3** grill.

Rost[2] (rɔst) *nm* rust. **—en** *vi* rust.

rot (roːt) *adj,n neu* red. ¨**—e** ('rœːtə) *nf* red, redness.

Röteln ('rœtəln) *n pl* German measles.

Rotor ('roːtɔr) *nm* **-en** rotor, armature.

Rübe ('ryːbə) *nf* **gelbe Rübe** carrot. **weiße Rübe** turnip. **—nzucker** *nm* beet sugar.

Rubin (ru'biːn) *nm* **-e** ruby.

Rubrik (ru'briːk) *nf* **-en** **1** rubric. **2** heading.

ruch/bar ('ruːxbaːr) *adj* notorious. **—los** *adj* wicked, impious.

rückbezüglich ('rykbətsyːkliç) *adj* reflexive.

Rückblende ('rybklɛndə) *nf* flashback.

Rückblick ('rykblik) *nm* **1** retrospect. **2** backward glance.

rücken ('rykən) *vt,vi* move, shift.

Rücken ('rykən) *nm* — back.

Rückfahrkarte ('rykfaːrkartə) *nf* return ticket.

Rückfahrt ('rykfaːrt) *nf* return voyage or trip.

Rückfall ('rykfal) *nm* **1** relapse. **2** reversion.

Rückgang ('rykgaŋ) *nm* decline, decrease.

rückgängig ('rykgɛŋiç) *adj* retrograde. **rückgängig machen** cancel, revoke.

Rückgrat ('rykgrat) *n neu* **-e** backbone, spine.

Rückhalt ('rykhalt) *nm* support.

Rückkehr ('rykkɛːr) *nf* return.

Rucksack ('rukzak) *nm* **1** rucksack. **2** sack.

Rückschlag ('rykʃlak) *nm* **1** setback. **2** recoil.

Rücksicht ('rykziçt) *nf* respect, consideration. **—slos** *adj* inconsiderate.

Rückspiegel ('rykʃpiːgəl) *nm* rear-view mirror.

rückständig ('rykʃtɛndiç) *adj* **1** backward. **2** in arrears.

Rückstoß ('rykʃtɔs) *nm* recoil.

Rücktritt ('ryktrit) *nm* **1** resignation. **2** withdrawal.

rückwärts ('rykvɛrts) *adv* backwards.

Rückzug ('ryktsuːk) *nm* retreat.

Rudel ('ruːdəl) *n neu* — pack, herd, band.

Ruder ('ruːdər) *n neu* — **1** oar. **2** rudder. **—boot** *n neu* rowing boat. **—n** *vi,vt* row.

Ruf (ruːf) *nm* **-e** **1** cry, call. **2** reputation. **3** summons. **—en*** *vt* **1** cry, call. **2** summon. *vi* cry, call. **—nummer** *nf* telephone number.

Rüge ('ryːgə) *nf* **-n** reprimand, reproach. **—n** *vt* **1** reproach, admonish. **2** blame.

Ruh/e ('ruːə) *nf* **1** quiet. **2** stillness, calm. **3** rest, relaxation. **—elos** *adj* restless. **—en** *vi* **1** rest, sleep. **2** be still. **3** be based (on). **—estand** *nm* retirement. **—ig** ('ruːiç) *adj* **1** quiet, still. **2** calm, peaceful.

Ruhm (ruːm) *nm* fame, glory. ¨**—en** ('ryːmən) *vt* praise. **sich ¨en** *vr* boast. ¨**—lich** ('ryːmliç) *adj* glorious.

Ruhr (ruːr) *nf* dysentery.

rühr/en ('ryːrən) *vt,vi* **1** move. **2** stir. **3** touch. **—ei** *n neu*

scrambled eggs. **—selig** *adj* sentimental, touchy, emotional. **—ung** *nf* emotion.
Ruhrgebiet ('ru:rgəbi:t) *n neu* Ruhr region.
Ruin/e (ru'i:nə) *nf* **-n** ruin(s). **—ieren** (rui'ni:rən) *vt* ruin.
Rülps (rylps) *nm* **-e** belch. **—en** *vi* belch.
Rum (rum) *nm* **-s** rum.
Rumän/ien (ru'mɛ:niən) *n neu* Rumania. **—e** *nm* Rumanian. **—isch** *adj* Rumanian. *n neu* Rumanian (language).
Rummel ('ruməl) *nm* **1** uproar, din. **2** bustle. **—platz** *nm* fairground, fun-fair.
Rumpf (rumpf) *nm* **¨-e** **1** trunk, torso. **2** hull. **3** fuselage.
rümpfen ('rympfən) *vt* turn up (one's nose).
rund (runt) *adj* **1** round. **2** plump. *adv* about, approximately. **—e** ('rundə) *nf* **-n** **1** round. **2** lap. **3** circuit. **4** circle. **—fahrt** *nf* round trip. **—funk** *nm* **1** radio, wireless. **2** broadcasting. **—gang** *nm* **1** round. **2** circuit. **—heraus** (runthɛ'raus) *adv* in plain terms. **—herum** (runthɛ'rum) *adv* round about. **—schau** *nf* panorama, display, review. **—schreiben** *n neu* circular.
Runzel ('runtsəl) *nf* **-n** wrinkle. **—n** *vt* wrinkle, fold.
rupfen ('rupfən) *vt* **1** pluck. **2** *inf* fleece.
Ruß (ru:s) *nm* soot. **—ig** *adj* sooty.
Russ/e ('rusə) *nm* **-n** Russian. **—isch** *adj* Russian. *n neu* Russian (language). **—land** *n neu* Russia.
rüst/en ('rystən) *vt* **1** prepare. **2** equip. **3** arm. **—ig** *adj* vigorous. **—ung** *nf* **-en** **1** preparation(s). **2** equipment. **3** armament. **4** armour.
Rute ('ru:tə) *nf* **-n** rod.
Rutsch (rutʃ) *nm* **-e** slide, slip. **—bahn** *nf* **1** slide. **2** chute. **—en** *vi* slide, slip, skid. **—ig** *adj* slippery.
rütteln ('rytəln) *vt,vi* shake (up), jolt.

S

Saal (za:l) *nm* **Säle** large room, hall.
Saat (za:t) *nf* **-en** **1** seed(s). **2** sowing.
Sabbat ('zabat) *nm* **-e** sabbath.
sabbern ('zabərn) *vi inf* **1** slobber. **2** drivel.
Säbel ('zɛ:bəl) *nm* — sabre.
Saccharin (zaxa'ri:n) *n neu* saccharin.
Sach/e ('zaxə) *nf* **-n** **1** matter. **2** thing. **3** affair, business. **4** *law* case, issue. **—bearbeiter** *nm* official or expert (with responsibility for a particular case or field). **—lage** *nf* state of affairs, situation. **—lich** *adj* **1** to the point. **2** real. **3** factual. **4** objective, impartial. **¨—lich** ('zɛçliç) *adj* neuter.
Sachs/e ('zaksə) *nm* Saxon. **—en** *n neu* Saxony. **¨—isch** ('zɛksiʃ) *adj* Saxon.
sacht (zaxt) *adj* gentle, soft. *adv* **1** gradually. **2** cautiously.
Sack (zak) *nm* **¨-e** **1** sack, bag. **2** pocket, pouch. **—en** *vi* **1** sink. **2** sag. **—gasse** *nf* **1** blind alley, cul-de-sac. **2** deadlock.
Sadismus (za'dismus) *nm* sadism.

säen ('sɛːən) *vt* sow.
Saft (zaft) *nm* **¨-e 1** juice. **2** sap. **3** gravy. **—ig** *adj* juicy.
Sage ('zaːgə) *nf* **-n** legend, myth. **—nhaft** *adj* **1** legendary. **2** *inf* fabulous.
Säge ('zɛːgə) *nf* **-n** saw. **—n** *vt,vi* saw.
sagen ('zaːgən) *vt,vi* **1** say, tell. **2** express, declare. **3** mean.
sah (zaː) *v* see **sehen.**
Sahn/e ('zaːnə) *nf* cream. **—ig** *adj* creamy.
Saison (zɛ'zõː) *nf* **-s** (high) season.
Saite ('zaitə) *nf* **-n** string, chord. **—ninstrument** *n neu* stringed instrument.
Sakrament (zakra'mɛnt) *n neu* **-e** sacrament.
Salat (za'laːt) *nm* **-e 1** salad. **2** lettuce. **—soße** *nf* salad dressing.
Salbe ('zalbə) *nf* **-n** ointment, salve.
Salbei (zal'bai) *nm,f cul* sage.
Salut (za'luːt) *nm* **-e** salute. **—ieren** (zalu'tiːrən) *vt,vi* salute.
Salve ('zalvə) *nf* **-n** *mil* volley.
Salz (zalts) *n neu* **-e** salt. **—en** *vt* salt. **—faß** *n neu* saltcellar. **—ig** *adj* salty.
Sam/en ('zaːmən) *nm* **— 1** seed. **2** sperm, semen. **¨—ling** ('zɛmliŋ) *nm* **-e** seedling.
Sämischleder ('zɛmiʃleːdər) *n neu* chamois (leather).
samm/eln ('zaməln) *vt,vi* collect, gather. **sich sammeln** *vr* **1** assemble. **2** compose oneself. **—ler** *nm* **— 1** collector, gatherer. **2** *tech* accumulator.
—lung *nf* **-en 1** collection. **2** concentration.
Samstag ('zamstaːk) *nm* **-e** Saturday. **—s** *adv* on Saturdays.
samt (zamt) *prep* together with. **¨—lich** ('zɛmtliç) *adj* **1** all. **2** complete, entire.
Sand (zant) *nm* **-e** sand. **—uhr** *nf* hourglass.
Sandale (zan'daːlə) *nf* **-n** sandal.
sandte ('zantə) *v* see **senden.**
sanft (zanft) *adj* **1** gentle, mild. **2** smooth, soft. **—mut** *nf* gentleness, sweetness.
sang (zaŋ) *v* see **singen.**
Sang (zaŋ) *nm* **¨-e** song. **¨—er** ('zɛŋər) *nm* **—, ¨—erin** ('zɛŋərin) *nf* **-nen** singer.
sanier/en (za'niːrən) *vt* **1** *comm* restore, reorganize. **2** heal. **—ung** *nf* **-en 1** restoration, reconstruction. **2** sanitation.
sanit/är (zani'tɛːr) *adj* sanitary. **—äter** (zani'tɛːtər) *nm* **— 1** ambulance man. **2** *med* orderly.
sank (zaŋk) *v* see **sinken.**
Sankt (zaŋkt) *adj Saint, St.*
Sanktion (zaŋktsi'oːn) *nf* **-en** sanction.
Saphir ('zaːfir) *nm* **-e** sapphire.
Sardine (zar'diːnə) *nf* **-n** sardine.
Sarg (zark) *nm* **¨-e** coffin.
sarkastisch (zar'kastiʃ) *adj* **1** sarcastic. **2** ironic.
saß (zaːs) *v* see **sitzen.**
Satan ('zaːtan) *nm* Satan.
Satellit (zatɛ'liːt) *nm* **-en** satellite. **—enstaat** *nm* satellite state.
Satin (sa'tɛ̃ː) *nm* satin.
Satir/e (za'tiːrə) *nf* **-n** satire. **—isch** *adj* satirical.

satt (zat) *adj* **1** satisfied. **2** full. **3** tired (of), sick (of). **4** (of colour) rich, deep. **¨—igen** ('zɛtigən) *vt* **1** satisfy, satiate. **2** saturate.
Sattel ('zatəl) *nm* **¨—** saddle.
Satz (zats) *nm* **¨-e** **1** sentence, clause. **2** leap, bound. **3** theorem, thesis. **4** *mus* movement. **5** dregs. **—lehre** *nf* syntax.
Satzung ('zatsuŋ) *nf* **-en** statute, regulation.
Sau (zau) *nf* **¨-e** sow. **—arbeit** *nf sl* drudgery. **—erei** (zauə'rai) *nf* **-en** dirty business.
sauber ('zaubər) *adj* **1** clean. **2** neat, tidy. **3** *inf* pretty, fine. **¨—n** ('zɔybərn) *vt* **1** clean. **2** purge. **¨—ung** ('zɔybəruŋ) *nf* **-en** **1** cleaning, clearing. **2** purge.
Saudi-Arabien ('zaudiara:biən) *n neu* Saudi-Arabia.
sauer ('zauər) *adj* **1** sour, acid. **2** (of work, etc.) hard. **3** sulky. **—stoff** *nm* oxygen.
sauf/en* ('zaufən) *vt,vi* **1** *inf* booze, drink (excessively). **2** (of animals) drink. **¨—er** ('zɔyfər) *nm* **—** drunkard.
saug/en* ('zaugən) *vt,vi* suck. **—er** *nm* **—** **1** sucker. **2** teat (of a baby's bottle). **—etier** *n neu* mammal. **—heber** *nm* siphon.
säug/en ('zɔygən) *vt* suckle. **—etier** *n neu* mammal. **—ling** ('zɔykliŋ) *nm* **-e** baby, suckling.
Säule ('zɔylə) *nf* **-n** column, pillar.
Saum (zaum) *nm* **¨-e** **1** seam. **2** hem. **3** border.
säumen[1] ('zɔymən) *vt* **1** hem. **2** border.
säumen[2] ('zɔymən) *vi* **1** delay. **2** hesitate.
Saumtier ('zaumti:r) *n neu* **-e** beast of burden.
Sauna ('zauna) *nf* **-s** sauna (bath).
Säure ('zɔyrə) *nf* **-n** **1** acid. **2** sourness.
Saxophon (zakso'fo:n) *n neu* **-e** saxophone.
schab/en ('ʃa:bən) *vt* **1** scrape. **2** grate. **—er** *nm* **—** scraper.
schäbig ('ʃɛ:biç) *adj* **1** shabby. **2** mean.
Schablone (ʃa'blo:nə) *nf* **-n** stencil, pattern.
Schach (ʃax) *n neu* chess. **—matt** *adj* checkmate.
Schacher ('ʃaxər) *nm* bargaining, haggling. **—n** *vi* haggle, barter.
Schacht (ʃaxt) *nm* **¨-e** **1** pit, shaft. **2** tunnel. **3** mine.
Schachtel ('ʃaxtəl) *nf* **-n** box.
schad/e ('ʃa:də) *interj* what a pity or shame! *adj* **es/das ist schade** it's/that's a pity or shame. **—en** *vi* **1** harm. **2** damage. *nm* **¨—** **1** damage. **2** harm. **3** loss, damages. **—enersatz** *nm* compensation. **—enfreude** *nf* malicious pleasure (in the misfortunes of others). **¨—igen** ('ʃɛ:digən) *vt* **1** harm. **2** damage. **¨—lich** ('ʃɛ:tliç) *adj* harmful, injurious.
Schädel ('ʃɛ:dəl) *nm* **—** skull.
Schaf (ʃa:f) *n neu* **-e** sheep. **¨—er** ('ʃɛ:fər) *nm* **—** shepherd, herdsman. **¨—erhund** ('ʃɛ:fərhunt) *nm* sheep dog. **deutscher ¨—erhund** Alsatian.
schaffen[1] ('ʃafən) *vt* **1** re-

move, shift. **2** accomplish, manage. *vi* work.

schaffen*[2] ('ʃafən) *vt* create, make.

Schaffner ('ʃafnər) *nm* — **1** conductor. **2** ticket-collector. **3** guard. **4** steward.

Schaft (ʃaft) *nm* **¨-e** **1** shaft. **2** stalk. **3** gunstock. **4** handle.

Schale ('ʃaːlə) *nf* **-n** **1** peel. **2** shell. **3** skin. **4** bowl, dish. **¨—n** ('ʃɛːlən) *vt* **1** peel. **2** skin. **3** shell.

Schalk (ʃalk) *nm* **-e** rogue, joker.

Schall (ʃal) *nm* **-e** **1** sound. **2** noise. **3** ring. **—dämpfer** *nm* silencer. **—dicht** *adj* soundproof. **—en** *vi* (re)sound. **—(geschwindigkeits)grenze** *nf* sound barrier. **—platte** *nf* (gramophone) record.

Schalt/brett ('ʃaltbrɛt) *n neu* **-er** **1** switchboard. **2** dashboard. **—en** *vi* **1** switch. **2** *mot* change gear. **3** rule. *vt* switch. **—er** *nm* — **1** switch. **2** ticket office. **3** counter. **—hebel** *nm mot* gear lever. **—jahr** *n neu* leap year. **—ung** *nf* **-en** **1** *mot* gear change. **2** (electric) circuit.

Scham (ʃaːm) *nf* shame, embarrassment. **sich ¨—en** ('ʃɛːmən) *vr* be ashamed.

Schampun (ʃam'puːn) *n neu* shampoo.

Schand/e ('ʃandə) *nf* shame, disgrace. **¨—en** ('ʃɛndən) *vt* **1** dishonour, disgrace. **2** rape. **3** desecrate. **4** disfigure. **5** soil. **¨—lich** ('ʃɛntliç) *adj* shameful, base, dishonourable. **—tat** ('ʃanttaːt) *nf* shameful deed, crime. **¨—ung** ('ʃɛnduŋ) *nf* **-en** **1** shaming, dishonouring. **2** disfigurement. **3** violation, rape.

Schanze ('ʃantsə) *nf* **-n** **1** fortification, earthwork. **2** *naut* quarterdeck.

Schar (ʃaːr) *nf* **-en** troop, host. **sich scharen** *vr* assemble, crowd together.

scharf (ʃarf) *adj* **1** sharp. **2** caustic. **3** pungent. **4** severe. **5** shrewd. **6** strong. **7** (of explosives, etc.) live. **¨—e** ('ʃɛrfə) *nf* **-n** **1** sharpness. **2** shrewdness. **3** severity. **¨—en** ('ʃɛrfən) *vt* **1** sharpen. **2** intensify. **—richter** *nm* executioner. **—schütze** *nm* sniper.

Scharlachfieber ('ʃarlaxfiːbər) *n neu* scarlet fever.

scharmant (ʃar'mant) *adj* charming.

Scharmützel (ʃar'mytsəl) *n neu* — skirmish. **—n** *vi* skirmish.

Scharnier (ʃar'niːr) *n neu* **-e** hinge.

Schatten ('ʃatən) *nm* — shadow, shade. **—bild** *n neu* silhouette. **—haft** *adj* shadowy. **—seite** *nf* **1** dark side. **2** drawback, snag.

Schatz (ʃats) *nm* **¨-e** **1** treasure. **2** darling, sweetheart. **—amt** *n neu* treasury. **¨—en** ('ʃɛtsən) *vt* **1** estimate, assess. **2** esteem, regard (highly). **—meister** *nm* treasurer. **¨—ung** ('ʃɛtsuŋ) *nf* **-en** **1** estimate. **2** approximation. **3** esteem. **4** tax. **¨—ungsweise** ('ʃɛtsuŋsvaizə) *adv* approximately.

Schau (ʃau) *nf* **-en** **1** show. **2** exhibition. **3** view. **—bühne** *nf* stage, theatre. **—en** *vt,vi* **1**

see. **2** look (at). **—fenster** *n neu* shop window. **—spiel** *n neu* play, drama. **—spieler** *nm* actor. **—spielerin** *nf* actress.

schauder/haft ('ʃaudərhaft) *adj* horrible. **—n** *vi* shudder.

Schauer ('ʃauər) *nm* — **1** shower. **2** shiver, shudder. **3** terror, awe.

Schaufel ('ʃaufəl) *nf* **-n** **1** shovel. **2** paddle, blade.

Schaukel ('ʃaukəl) *nf* **-n** swing. **—n** *vt,vi* swing, rock.

Schaum (ʃaum) *nm* **¨-e** foam, froth. **¨—en** ('ʃɔymən) *vi* foam, effervesce.

Scheck (ʃɛk) *nm* **-s** cheque.

Scheibe ('ʃaibə) *nf* **-n** **1** slice. **2** disc. **3** pane. **4** target. **—nwischer** *nm* — windscreen-wiper.

Scheid/e ('ʃaidə) *nf* **-n** **1** border. **2** sheath. **3** vagina. **—en*** *vt* **1** separate, divide. **2** divorce. **sich scheiden lassen** get divorced. *vi* depart, retire. **—ung** *nf* **-en** **1** separation. **2** divorce.

Schein (ʃain) *nm* **-e** **1** appearance, semblance. **2** shine. **3** light. **4** banknote. **5** certificate. **6** licence. **7** receipt. **—bar** *adj* apparent. **—en*** *vi* **1** seem. **2** shine. **—heilig** *adj* hypocritical. **—werfer** *nm* **1** searchlight, spotlight. **2** *mot* headlight. **3** reflector.

Scheiße ('ʃaisə) *nf tab* excrement.

Scheitel ('ʃaitəl) *nm* — **1** crown (of the head). **2** apex. **3** parting (of the hair). **—punkt** *nm* zenith, highest point.

scheitern ('ʃaitərn) *vi* **1** fail. **2** be wrecked.

Schellfisch ('ʃɛlfiʃ) *nm* **-e** haddock.

Schelm (ʃɛlm) *nm* **-e** **1** rogue, rascal. **2** joker.

Schemel ('ʃeːməl) *nm* — (foot)stool.

schenk/en ('ʃɛŋkən) *vt* **1** give (as a present). **2** endow. **3** pour (out). **—ung** *nf* **-en** donation.

Scherbe ('ʃɛrbə) *nf* **-n** **1** fragment. **2** chip. **3** splinter (of glass, pottery, etc.).

Scher/e ('ʃeːrə) *nf* **-n** **1** scissors, shears. **2** *zool* pincer, claw.

Scherz (ʃɛrts) *nm* **-e** **1** joke, jest. **2** prank, lark. **—en** *vi* **1** joke. **2** lark about. **—haft** *adj* playful, joking.

scheu (ʃɔy) *adj* shy, bashful. *nf* shyness. **—en** *vt* avoid. **sich —en** *vr* **1** be afraid (to). **2** be shy (of).

Scheuche ('ʃɔyçə) *nf* **-n** scarecrow.

Scheune ('ʃɔynə) *nf* **-n** barn.

Scheusal ('ʃɔyzaːl) *n neu* **-e** monster.

scheußlich ('ʃɔysliç) *adj* hideous.

Schi (ʃiː) *nm* **-er** ski. **Schi laufen** ski.

Schicht (ʃiçt) *nf* **-en** **1** layer. **2** coat(ing). **3** (social) class. **4** shift. **—arbeit** *nf* shift work. **—en** *vt* pile, stack.

schick (ʃik) *adj* chic, elegant. *nm* elegance.

schicken ('ʃikən) *vt* send. **sich schicken** *vr* **1** happen. **2** be proper, fitting, or decent.

schicklich ('ʃikliç) *adj* decent, proper.

Schicksal ('ʃikzaːl) *n neu* **-e** fate, destiny.

schieb/en* ('ʃiːbən) *vt* push, shove. *vi* profiteer. **—er** *nm* **—** **1** slide. **2** bolt (of a door, etc.). **3** profiteer. **—ung** *nf* **-en** **1** pushing. **2** profiteering. **3** underhand dealings, corrupt practice.

schied (ʃiːt) *v* see **scheiden.**

Schieds/gericht ('ʃiːtsgəriçt) *n neu* **-e** arbitration court. **—richter** *nm* **1** *sport* referee. **2** arbitrator.

schief (ʃiːf) *adj* **1** slanting, oblique. **2** sloping, inclined. **3** wrong, false.

schielen ('ʃiːlən) *vi* squint.

schien (ʃiːn) *v* see **scheinen.**

Schien/e ('ʃiːnə) *nf* **-n** **1** rail (of a railway track). **2** *med* splint. **—bein** *n neu* **-e** shinbone.

schieß/en* ('ʃiːsən) *vt* shoot. *vi* **1** shoot. **2** rush. **—pulver** *n neu* gunpowder.

Schiff (ʃif) *n neu* **-e** **1** ship, vessel. **2** nave. **—ahrt** ('ʃiffaːrt) *nf* shipping, navigation. **—bruch** *nm* shipwreck.

Schikan/e (ʃi'kaːnə) *nf* **-n** **1** annoyance. **2** chicanery. **—ieren** (ʃika'niːrən) *vt* annoy.

Schild (ʃilt) *n neu* **-er** **1** name plate. **2** signboard. **3** badge. **4** label. *nm* **-e** **1** shield. **2** coat-of-arms. **3** shell (of a tortoise or crab). **—ern** ('ʃildərn) *vt* describe, portray. **—kröte** ('ʃiltkrœːtə) *nf* **1** turtle. **2** tortoise.

Schilf (ʃilf) *n neu* **-e** reed, rush.

Schilling ('ʃiliŋ) *nm* **-e** **1** Austrian unit of currency. **2** shilling.

Schimmel ('ʃiməl) *nm* **1** mould, mildew. **2** *pl* **—** white horse. **—ig** *adj* mouldy.

Schimmer ('ʃimər) *nm* gleam, glimmer. **—n** *vi* gleam, glimmer.

Schimpanse (ʃim'panzə) *nm* **-n** chimpanzee.

Schimpf (ʃimpf) *nm* **-e** **1** insult. **2** disgrace. **—en** *vt* abuse, insult. *vi* grumble, scold. **—wort** *n neu* **1** insult. **2** swear word.

schind/en* ('ʃindən) *vt* **1** torment. **2** exploit. **3** skin (an animal). **sich schinden** *vr* toil, slave. **—er** *nm* **—** **1** exploiter. **2** tormentor.

Schinken ('ʃiŋkən) *nm* ham.

Schirm (ʃirm) *nm* **-e** **1** umbrella. **2** shade. **3** screen. **4** protection, shelter. **—en** *vt* shelter, protect. **—herr** *nm* patron.

Schlacht (ʃlaxt) *nf* **-en** battle. **—en** *vt* slaughter, butcher. **¨—erei** (ʃlɛçtə'rai) *nf* **-en** **1** butcher's shop. **2** massacre. **—feld** *n neu* battlefield. **—haus** *n neu* slaughterhouse, abattoir. **—schiff** *n neu* battleship.

Schlaf (ʃlaːf) *nm* sleep. **—anzug** *nm* pyjamas. **—en*** *vi* sleep. **—tablette** *nf* sleeping pill. **¨—rig** ('ʃlɛːfriç) *adj* **1** sleepy. **2** dozy. **—sack** *nm* sleeping bag. **—wagen** *nm* sleeping car. **—zimmer** *n neu* bedroom.

schlaff (ʃlaf) *adj* **1** slack. **2** soft. **3** lax. **4** weak.

Schlag (ʃlaːk) *nm* **¨-e** **1** blow, stroke. **2** punch, slap. **3** (electric) shock. **4** peal, clap. **5** kind, sort. **—ader** *nf* artery. **—anfall** *nm med* stroke, fit. **—en*** ('ʃlaːgən) *vt* **1** strike, beat. **2** defeat. **3** fell. *vi* **1** beat, strike. **2** ring. **sich —en** *vr* **1** fight (with). **2** side (with). **—fertig** *adj* quick-witted, ready. **—sahne** *nf* whipped cream. **—wort** *n neu* slogan. **—zeile** *nf* headline.

Schlager ('ʃlaːgər) *nm* — **1** pop song, dance tune. **2** (smash) hit, great success.

Schläger ('ʃlɛːgər) *nm* — **1** thug. **2** *cul* beater. **3** rapier. **4** *sport* racket, club, stick.

Schlamm (ʃlam) *nm* **-e** mud, sludge.

Schlamp/e ('ʃlampə) *nf* **-n** slut. **—erei** (ʃlampə'rai) *nf* **-en** slovenliness. **—ig** *adj* slovenly, sluttish.

Schlange ('ʃlaŋə) *nf* **-n 1** snake, serpent. **2** queue.

schlank (ʃlaŋk) *adj* slender, slim.

schlapp (ʃlap) *adj* **1** slack. **2** flabby.

schlau (ʃlau) *adj* **1** sly, cunning. **2** shrewd.

Schlauch (ʃlaux) *nm* **¨-e 1** tube. **2** hose. **3** *mot* inner tube.

schlecht (ʃlɛçt) *adj* **1** bad, wicked. **2** inferior. **—hin** *adv* simply, perfectly.

Schlegel ('ʃleːgəl) *nm* — **1** mallet. **2** club. **3** drumstick.

schleichen* ('ʃlaiçən) *vi* sneak, creep.

Schleier ('ʃlaiər) *nm* — veil. **—n** *vt* veil.

Schleif/e ('ʃlaifə) *nf* **-n 1** bow, slipknot. **2** slide, chute. **3** curve, loop. **—en*** *vt,vi* drag. *vt* **1** polish. **2** sharpen.

Schleim (ʃlaim) *nm* **-e** mucus, phlegm.

schleißen* ('ʃlaisən) *vt* **1** wear out. **2** slit, split.

schlendern ('ʃlɛndərn) *vi* stroll, dawdle.

schlepp/en ('ʃlɛpən) *vt* **1** drag, haul. **2** carry. **—er** *nm* — *also* **—dampfer** tug(boat).

Schlesien ('ʃleːziən) *n neu* Silesia.

Schleuder ('ʃlɔydər) *nf* **-n 1** sling, catapult. **2** spin-drier. **—n** *vt* **1** hurl, sling. **2** spin-dry. *vi mot* skid.

schleunig ('ʃlɔyniç) *adj* quick, prompt. **—st** *adv* in all haste, as quickly as possible.

Schleuse ('ʃlɔyzə) *nf* **-n 1** sluice. **2** lock (of a canal).

schlicht (ʃliçt) *adj* **1** plain, simple. **2** smooth. **—en** *vt* **1** settle (a quarrel). **2** smooth.

schlief (ʃliːf) *v* see **schlafen.**

schließ/en* ('ʃliːsən) *vi,vt* close, shut. *vt* **1** lock. **2** end, finish. **3** infer, conclude. **—fach** *n neu* **1** locker. **2** safe-deposit box. **—lich** ('ʃliːsliç) *adj* final. *adv* **1** finally. **2** after all.

schlimm (ʃlim) *adj* **1** bad, serious. **2** sick, ill. **—stenfalls** ('ʃlimstənfals) *adv* at (the) worst.

Schlinge ('ʃliŋə) *nf* **-n 1** loop, noose. **2** *med* sling. **3** snare.

schlingen*[1] ('ʃliŋən) *vt* **1** wind, coil. **2** weave, plait. **3** tie, knot. **4** fling.

schlingen*[2] ('ʃliŋən) *vi* gulp, eat greedily.

Schlitt/en ('ʃlitən) *nm* —

sledge, sleigh. **—schuh** *nm* skate. **—schuhlaufen** *vi* skate.
Schlitz (ʃlits) *nm* **-e** slit, slot.
schloß (ʃlɔs) *v* see **schließen.**
Schloß (ʃlɔs) *n neu* **Schlösser** **1** castle, palace. **2** lock, clasp.
Schlosser ('ʃlɔsər) *nm* — **1** locksmith. **2** metal worker, fitter.
schlotterig ('ʃlɔtəriç) *adj* shaky, tottery.
Schluck (ʃluk) *nm* **-e** **1** gulp, swig. **2** sip. **—en** *vt* gulp (down), swallow. *nm* hiccup(s).
schlug (ʃlu:k) *v* see **schlagen.**
Schlund (ʃlunt) *nm* ¨**-e** **1** throat, gullet. **2** gulf, chasm.
schlüpf/en ('ʃlypfən) *vi* slip. **—er** *nm* (ladies') knickers, panties. **—rig** *adj* **1** slippery. **2** (of a joke, remark, etc.) obscene.
Schlupfloch ('ʃlupflɔx) *n neu* **1** loophole. **2** hiding place.
Schluß (ʃlus) *nm* **Schlüsse** **1** end, close. **2** conclusion, deduction. **—folgerung** *nf* conclusion. **—licht** *n neu* taillight. **—stein** *nm* keystone.
Schlüssel ('ʃlysəl) *nm* — **1** key. **2** spanner. **3** *mus* clef. **—bein** *n neu* collarbone.
schmächtig ('ʃmɛçtiç) *adj* slender, slim.
schmackhaft ('ʃmakhaft) *adj* appetizing, tasty.
schmal (ʃma:l) *adj* **1** narrow, thin. **2** meagre.
Schmalz (ʃmalts) *n neu* **1** dripping, fat. **2** (exaggerated) sentimentality.
schmarotz/en (ʃma'rɔtsən) *vi* scrounge, sponge. **—er** *nm* — sponger, parasite.
Schmarren ('ʃmarən) *nm* — **1** pancake. **2** trash.
schmatzen ('ʃmatsən) *vi* smack (one's lips).
schmecken ('ʃmɛkən) *vt* **1** taste. **2** sample. *vi* taste (good).
Schmeich/elei (ʃmaiçə'lai) *nf* **-en** flattery. **—eln** ('ʃmaiçəln) *vi* flatter. **—ler** ('ʃmaiçlər) *nm* — flatterer.
schmeißen* ('ʃmaisən) *vt inf* throw, chuck.
schmelzen* ('ʃmɛltsən) *vt,vi* melt.
Schmerz (ʃmɛrts) *nm* **-en** **1** pain. **2** grief. **—haft** *adj also* **—lich** painful.
Schmetterling ('ʃmɛtərliŋ) *nm* **-e** butterfly.
Schmied (ʃmi:t) *nm* **-e** blacksmith. **—e** ('ʃmi:də) *nf* **-n** (blacksmith's) forge. **—en** ('ʃmi:dən) *vt* **1** forge. **2** construct.
Schmier/e ('ʃmi:rə) *nf* **-n** **1** grease. **2** ointment. **—en** *vt* **1** grease, lubricate. **2** smear. **3** spread (butter, etc.). **—ig** *adj* **1** greasy. **2** dirty. **3** sordid.
Schmink/e ('ʃmiŋkə) *nf* **-n** make-up. **—en** *vt* make up.
Schmor/en ('ʃmo:rən) *vt* **1** stew. **2** braise. **—braten** *nm* — stewed or braised meat.
Schmuck (ʃmuk) *nm* **-e** **1** ornament(s), jewellery. **2** decoration. ¨**—en** ('ʃmykən) *vt* decorate, adorn.
schmugg/eln ('ʃmugəln) *vt,vi* smuggle. **—ler** ('ʃmuglər) *nm* — smuggler.
Schmutz (ʃmuts) *nm* dirt. **—ig** *adj* dirty.
Schnabel ('ʃna:bəl) *nm* ¨— **1** beak. **2** nozzle.

Schnall/e ('ʃnalə) *nf* **-n** buckle, fastener. **—en** *vt* buckle, fasten.
Schnaps (ʃnaps) *nm* ¨**-e** spirit, liquor.
schnarchen ('ʃnarçən) *vi* snore.
schnattern ('ʃnatərn) *vi* cackle.
schnaufen ('ʃnaufən) *vi* wheeze, gasp, pant.
Schnauz/e ('ʃnautsə) *nf* **-n** **1** muzzle. **2** snout. **—en** *vi* shout, bellow.
Schneck/e ('ʃnɛkə) *nf* **-n** snail. **—engang** *nm* snail's pace.
Schnee (ʃne:) *nm* snow. **—ball** *nm* snowball. **—flocke** *nf* snowflake. **—glöckchen** *n neu* snowdrop.
Schneid/e ('ʃnaidə) *nf* **-n** edge, blade. **—en*** *vt* **1** cut, carve. **2** reap, mow. **—er** *nm* — tailor.
schneien ('ʃnaiən) *vi* snow.
schnell (ʃnɛl) *adj* fast, quick, rapid. **—en** *vt* **1** jerk. **2** flick. *vi* spring. **—er Direkttransport** *nm* shuttle. **—igkeit** *nf* speed, rapidity. **—zug** *nm* express train.
schnippisch ('ʃnipiʃ) *adj* saucy, cheeky.
schnitt (ʃnit) *v* see **schneiden.**
Schnitt (ʃnit) *nm* **-e** **1** cut. **2** slice. **3** pattern. **4** cut, fashion. **5** woodcut. **6** crop. **—lauch** *nm* chive(s).
Schnitz/el ('ʃnitsəl) *nm* — **1** cutlet. **2** chip. **—eln** *vt,vi* chip, shred.
Schnitzer ('ʃnitzər) *nm* — **1** carver, cutter. **2** blunder, (bad) mistake.
Schnörkel ('ʃnœrkəl) *nm* — **1** flourish, scroll. **2** squiggle.
schnüffeln ('ʃnyfəln) *vi* **1** sniff. **2** snoop.
Schnupfen ('ʃnupfən) *nm* — cold, chill.
Schnur (ʃnu:r) *nf* ¨**-e** **1** string, cord. **2** flex, (electrical) lead. **—gerade** *adv* straight as a die.
Schnür/band ('ʃny:rbant) *n neu* ¨**-er** lace. **—en** *vt* lace or tie (up). **—senkel** *nm* shoelace.
Schnurrbart ('ʃnurba:rt) *nm* moustache.
schob (ʃo:p) *v* see **schieben.**
Schock (ʃɔk) *nm* **-s** shock. **—ieren** (ʃɔ'ki:rən) *vt* shock.
Schokolade (ʃoko'la:də) *nf* **-n** chocolate.
Scholle ('ʃɔlə) *nf* **-n** **1** clod, lump. **2** plaice.
schon (ʃo:n) *adv* **1** already. **2** yet.
schön (ʃœ:n) *adj* **1** beautiful, handsome. **2** nice, fine. **—heit** *nf* beauty. **—heitskönigin** *nf* beauty queen.
schon/en ('ʃo:nən) *vt* spare, preserve. **—ung** *nf* **-en** **1** clemency, mercy. **2** consideration, care.
Schopf (ʃɔpf) *nm* ¨**-e** **1** tuft, lock (of hair). **2** crest (of birds).
schöpf/en ('ʃœpfən) *vt* **1** scoop, ladle. **2** get, obtain. **—kelle** *nf* **-n** scoop, ladle.
Schöpf/er *nm* — creator. **—erisch** *adj* creative. **—ung** *nf* **-en** creation.
Schornstein ('ʃɔrnʃtain) *nm* **-e** chimney, funnel. **—feger** *nm* chimney-sweep.
schoß (ʃɔs) *v* see **schießen.**

Schoß[1] (ʃoːs) *nm* **¨-e** **1** lap. **2** womb.

Schoß[2] (ʃɔs) *nm* **Schosse** *bot* shoot, sprout.

Schote ('ʃoːtə) *nf* **-n** pod, shell.

Schott/e ('ʃɔtə) *nm* **-n** Scot, Scotsman. **—isch** *adj* Scottish. **—land** *n neu* Scotland.

schräg (ʃrɛːk) *adj* oblique, slanting.

Schrank (ʃraŋk) *nm* **¨-e** cupboard, wardrobe.

Schranke ('ʃraŋkə) *nf* **-n** **1** barrier. **2** enclosure, arena. **—nlos** *adj* boundless.

Schraub/e ('ʃraubə) *nf* **-n** screw. **—en** *vt* screw, twist. **—enschlüssel** *nm* spanner, wrench. **—enzieher** *nm* screwdriver.

Schrebergarten ('ʃreːbərgartən) *nm* allotment.

Schreck (ʃrɛk) *nm* **-e** *also* **Schrecken** **—** **1** fright. **2** terror, horror. **—en** *vt* frighten. **—lich** *adj* terrible, dreadful, horrible.

Schrei (ʃrai) *nm* **-e** cry, scream. **—en*** *vi* cry, scream.

schreib/en* ('ʃraibən) *vt,vi* **1** write. **2** spell. *n neu* **—** letter. **—maschine** ('ʃraipmaʃiːnə) *nf* typewriter. **—papier** ('ʃraippapiːr) *n neu* notepaper. **—tisch** ('ʃraiptiʃ) *nm* desk.

Schrein (ʃrain) *nm* **-e** chest, cabinet. **—er** *nm* **—** cabinet-maker, carpenter.

schreiten* ('ʃraitən) *vi* step, stride.

schrie (ʃriː) *v* see **schreien.**

schrieb (ʃriːp) *v* see **schreiben.**

Schrift (ʃrift) *nf* **-en** **1** writing, work. **2** handwriting. **3** type, script. **4** scripture(s). **—lich** *adj* written, in writing. **—sprache** *nf* written language. **—steller** *nm* **—** writer, author.

schritt (ʃrit) *v* see **schreiten.**

Schritt (ʃrit) *nm* **-e** **1** step. **2** pace. **—macher** *nm* pacemaker.

schroff (ʃrɔf) *adj* **1** brusque, abrupt. **2** steep, rugged.

Schrot (ʃroːt) *nm,neu* **-e** (lead) shot. **—flinte** *nf* shotgun.

Schrott (ʃrɔt) *nm* **-e** scrap metal. **—haufen** *nm* scrap heap.

schrubben ('ʃrubən) *vt* scrub.

schrumpfen ('ʃrumpfən) *vi* **1** shrink. **2** become wrinkled.

Schub (ʃuːp) *nm* **¨-e** **1** push, thrust. **2** batch. **—karren** *nm* wheelbarrow. **—fach** *n neu also* **—lade** *nf* drawer.

schüchtern ('ʃyçtərn) *adj* shy, bashful, timid. **—heit** *nf* shyness.

Schuft (ʃuft) *nm* **-e** scoundrel.

Schuh (ʃuː) *nm* **-e** shoe, boot. **—löffel** *nm* shoehorn. **—macher** *nm* shoemaker.

Schul/e ('ʃuːlə) *nf* **-n** school, college. **—arbeit** *nf* **1** homework. **2** lesson. **—en** *vt* school, train. **¨—er** ('ʃyːlər) *nm* **—** schoolboy. **¨—erin** ('ʃyːlərin) *nf* **-nen** schoolgirl. **—rat** *nm* school inspector. **—ung** *nf* schooling.

Schuld (ʃult) *nf* **-en** **1** debt. **2** guilt. **3** offence. **—en** ('ʃuldən) *vt* owe. **—ig** ('ʃuldiç) *adj* **1** guilty. **2** indebted. **—los** ('ʃultloːs) *adj* innocent.

Schulter ('ʃultər) *nf* **-n** shoulder.
Schund (ʃunt) *nm* trash, rubbish.
Schuppe ('ʃupə) *nf* **-en** **1** *zool* scale. **2** *pl* dandruff.
schüren ('ʃyːrən) *vt* stir up.
Schurke ('ʃurkə) *nm* **-n** villain, scoundrel.
Schürze ('ʃyrtsə) *nf* **-n** apron, pinafore.
Schuß (ʃus) *nm* **Schüsse** shot. **—waffe** *nf* firearm.
Schüssel ('ʃysəl) *nf* **-n** **1** bowl, dish. **2** dish, course.
Schuster ('ʃuːstər) *nm* — shoemaker, cobbler.
Schutt (ʃut) *nm* **1** rubbish. **2** rubble. **—haufen** *nm* rubbish or rubble heap.
schütteln ('ʃytəln) *vt* shake.
schütten ('ʃytən) *vt,vi* pour.
Schutz (ʃuts) *nm* **1** protection, defence. **2** shelter. **—brille** *nf* goggles. **¨—e** ('ʃytsə) *nm* **-n** **1** marksman, rifleman. **2** Sagittarius. **¨—en** ('ʃytsən) *vt* **1** protect, defend. **2** shelter. **¨—er** ('ʃytsər) *nm* — protector, patron. **—heilige(r)** *nm* patron saint. **¨—ling** ('ʃytsliŋ) *nm* **—e** protégé. **—mann** *nm* policeman. **—mittel** *n neu* preservative. **—polizei** *nf* police.
Schwabe ('ʃvaːbə) *nm* **-n** Swabian. **—n** *n neu* Swabia.
schwach (ʃvax) *adj* weak. **¨—e** ('ʃvɛçə) *nf* **-n** *also* **-heit** weakness. **¨—lich** ('ʃvɛçliç) *adj* sickly, feeble. **—sinn** *nm* imbecility.
Schwadron (ʃva'droːn) *nf* **-en** squadron.
Schwager ('ʃvaːgər) *nm* **¨—** brother-in-law. **¨—in** ('ʃvɛːgərin) *nf* **-nen** sister-in-law.
Schwalbe ('ʃvalbə) *nf* **-n** swallow.
Schwall (ʃval) *nm* **-e** swell, torrent.
Schwamm (ʃvam) *nm* **¨-e** **1** sponge. **2** fungus.
Schwan (ʃvaːn) *nm* **¨-e** swan. **—engesang** *nm* swan song.
schwanger ('ʃvaŋər) *adj* pregnant. **—schaft** *nf* **-en** pregnancy. **—sverhütung** *nf* contraception.
schwanken ('ʃvaŋkən) *vi* **1** rock, sway. **2** hesitate, waver.
Schwanz (ʃvants) *nm* **¨-e** **1** tail. **2** trail, train.
schwärm/en ('ʃvɛrmən) *vi* **1** swarm. **2** be enthusiastic, rave (about). **—erisch** *adj* wildly enthusiastic.
schwarz (ʃvarts) *adj,n neu* black. **—brot** *n neu* black bread. **—e(r)** *nm* Black, Negro. **¨—e** ('ʃvɛrtsə) *nf* black, blackness. **¨—en** ('ʃvɛrtsən) *vt* **1** blacken. **2** slander, defame. **3** *inf* smuggle. **—markt** *nm* black market. **—wald** *nm* Black Forest. **—weiß** *adj* black and white.
schwatzen ('ʃvatsən) *vi* prattle, chatter.
Schweb/ebahn ('ʃveːbəbaːn) *nf* **-en** cable railway. **—en** *vi* **1** hover, soar. **2** hang. **3** waver.
Schwed/en ('ʃveːdən) *n neu* Sweden. **—e** *nm* **-n** Swede. **—isch** *adj* Swedish. *n neu* Swedish (language).
Schwefel ('ʃveːfəl) *nm* sulphur.

schweig/en* ('ʃvaigən) *vi* fall or be silent. **—sam** ('ʃvaikzaːm) *adj* silent, taciturn.

Schwein (ʃvain) *n neu* **-e** pig, swine. **Schwein haben** *inf* be in luck. **—efleisch** *n neu* pork. **—ehund** *nm inf* swine. **—erei** (ʃvainə'rai) *nf* **-en** mean trick. **—estall** *nm* pigsty.

Schweiß (ʃvais) *nm* sweat. **—en** *vt* weld.

Schweiz (ʃvaits) *nf* Switzerland. **—er** *nm* — Swiss. **—erisch** *adj* Swiss.

Schwelle ('ʃvɛlə) *nf* **-n** **1** threshold. **2** sill. **3** beam. **4** (railway) sleeper.

schwellen* ('ʃvɛlən) *vi,vt* swell. *vi* expand, increase.

schwemmen ('ʃvɛmən) *vt* **1** water. **2** rinse. **3** float, drift.

Schwengel ('ʃvɛŋəl) *nm* — **1** clapper (of a bell). **2** handle (of a pump).

schwenk/en ('ʃvɛŋkən) *vi* **1** swivel, swing. **2** tilt. *vt* **1** swing. **2** shake, flourish. **3** *cul* toss. **4** rinse.

schwer (ʃveːr) *adj* **1** heavy. **2** difficult. **3** serious, grave. **4** clumsy. **5** (of food) stodgy. **—e** *nf* **-n** **1** weight. **2** *sci* gravity. **3** seriousness. **4** difficulty. **5** severity. **—beschädigt** *adj* **1** disabled, crippled. **2** badly damaged. **—fällig** *adj* clumsy, ponderous. **—hörig** *adj* hard of hearing. **—industrie** *nf* heavy industry. **—lich** *adv* with difficulty, scarcely. **—punkt** *nm* **1** centre of gravity. **2** main point. **—verletzt** *adj* **1** disabled. **2** badly wounded, seriously injured. **—wiegend** *adj* grave, weighty.

Schwert (ʃveːrt) *n neu* **-er** **1** sword. **2** *naut* centre-board, keel. **—lilie** *nf bot* iris.

Schwester ('ʃvɛstər) *nf* **-n** sister.

schwieg (ʃviːk) *v* see **schweigen.**

Schwieger/mutter ('ʃviːgərmutər) *nf* ¨— mother-in-law. **—sohn** *nm* son-in-law. **—tochter** *nf* daughter-in-law. **—vater** *nm* father-in-law.

schwierig ('ʃviːriç) *adj* difficult, hard. **—keit** *nf* **-en** difficulty, trouble.

Schwimm/bad ('ʃvimbaːt) *n neu also* **Schwimm/becken** swimming pool. **—en*** *vi* **1** swim. **2** float. **—er** *nm* — **1** swimmer. **2** float. **—weste** *nf* life jacket.

Schwind/el ('ʃvindəl) *nm* — **1** dizziness, vertigo. **2** swindle. **3** lie, fib. **—(e)lig** *adj* dizzy. **—eln** *vi* **1** swindle, cheat. **2** lie. **3** be dizzy. **mir schwindelt** I feel dizzy. **—ler** ('ʃvindlər) *nm* — swindler, fraud.

Schwindsucht ('ʃvintzuxt) *nf med* consumption, tuberculosis.

schwingen* ('ʃviŋən) *vt,vi* **1** swing. **2** vibrate.

schwitzen ('ʃvitsən) *vi* sweat, perspire.

schwören* ('ʃvœːrən) *vi,vt* swear, take (an oath).

schwul (ʃvuːl) *adj sl* queer, homosexual.

schwül (ʃvyːl) *adj* sultry, hu-

mid. **—e** *nf* sultriness, oppressive heat.
Schwulst (ʃvulst) *nm* ¨**-e** bombast.
Schwung (ʃvuŋ) *nm* ¨**-e** **1** swing. **2** impetus. **3** enthusiasm, verve. **4** flair.
Schwur (ʃvu:r) *nm* ¨**-e** oath. **—gericht** *n neu* assize court.
sechs (zɛks) *adj,nf* six. **—te** *adj* sixth.
sechzehn ('zɛçtse:n) *adj,nf* sixteen. **—te** *adj* sixteenth.
sechzig ('zɛçtsiç) *adj,nf* sixty. **—ste** *adj* sixtieth.
See (se:) *nm* **-n** lake. *nf* **-n** sea. **—bad** *n neu* seaside resort. **—fahrt** *nf* **1** voyage. **2** navigation. **—krank** *adj* seasick. **—mann** *nm* **-leute** sailor, marine. **—meile** *nf* nautical mile, knot. **—räuber** *nm* — pirate. **—zunge** *nf zool* sole.
Seel/e ('ze:lə) *nf* **-n** soul, mind. **—sorger** *nm* — clergyman.
Segel ('ze:gəl) *n neu* — sail. **—boot** *n neu* sailing boat. **—fliegen** *n neu* gliding. **—n** *vi* **1** sail. **2** soar, glide. **—tuch** *n neu* canvas.
Seg/en ('ze:gən) *nm* — **1** blessing. **2** prayer(s). **3** grace. **—nen** ('ze:gnən) *vt* bless. **—nung** ('ze:gnuŋ) *nf* **-en** blessing.
seh/en* ('ze:ən) *vt,vi* see, look. **—enswert** *adj* worth seeing. **—enswürdigkeit** *nf* **-en** object of interest, sight. **—er** *nm* — prophet.
Sehn/e ('ze:nə) *nf* **-n** **1** tendon, sinew. **2** *math* chord. **3** (bow) string. **sich —en** *vr* long (for). **—sucht** *nf* longing.
sehr (ze:r) *adv* very, much.
sei (zai) *v* see **sein**[2].
seicht (zaiçt) *adj* **1** shallow. **2** insipid. **3** superficial.
seid (zait) *v* see **sein**[2].
Seide ('zaidə) *nf* **-n** silk.
Seidel ('zaidəl) *n neu* — (beer) mug.
Seif/e ('zaifə) *nf* **-n** soap. **—en** *vt* soap.
Seil (zail) *n neu* **-e** rope, cable. **—bahn** *nf* cable railway.
sein[1] (zain) *poss adj 3rd pers s* his, its. **—er** *poss pron 3rd pers s also* **der —e** or **der —ige** his. **—erseits** ('zainərzaits) *adv* for his part. **—esgleichen** ('zainəsglaiçən) *pron* people like him. **—ethalben** ('zainəthalbən) *adv also* **—etwegen** ('zainətve:gən) or **—etwillen** ('zainətvilən) for his sake.
sein[2] (zain) *vi* be, exist. *n neu* being, existence.
seit (zait) *prep,conj* since. **—dem** (zait'de:m) *conj* since. *adv* since then. **—her** (zait 'he:r) *adv* **1** since then. **2** till now.
Seit/e ('zaitə) *nf* **-n** **1** side. **2** page. **—engasse** *nf* (small) side street. **—ens** *adv* on the part or side of. **—lich** *adj* lateral, side. **—wärts** ('zaitvɛrts) *adv* sideways.
Sekretär (zekre'tɛ:r) *nm* **-e, Sekretärin** *nf* **-nen** secretary.
Sekt (zɛkt) *nm* **-e** champagne.
Sekte ('zɛktə) *nf* **-n** sect.
Sekunde (ze'kundə) *nf* **-n** second.
selber ('zɛlbər) *pron* self.
selbst (zɛlpst) *pron* **1** self. **2** unaided, alone. **ich selbst** I myself. *~n neu* self. *adv* even.

Selbstachtung ('zɛlpstaxtuŋ) *nf* self-respect.
selbständig ('zɛlpstɛndiç) *adj* independent, autonomous. **—keit** *nf* independence.
Selbstbedienung ('zɛlpstbədi:nuŋ) *nf* self-service. **—srestaurant** *n neu* cafeteria.
Selbstbeherrschung ('zɛlpstbəhɛrʃuŋ) *nf* self-control.
selbstbewußt ('zɛlpstbəvust) *adj* self-confident.
Selbstgefühl ('zɛlpstgəfy:l) *n neu* self-respect, self-reliance, self-confidence.
selbstlos ('zɛlpstlo:s) *adj* selfless.
Selbstmord ('zɛlpstmɔrt) *nm* suicide. **¨—er** *nm* (person) suicide.
selbstsicher ('zɛlpstziçər) *adj* self-confident.
Selbstsucht ('zɛlpstzuxt) *nf* selfishness. **¨—ig** ('zɛlpstzyçtiç) *adj* selfish.
selbstversorgend ('zɛlpstfɛrzɔrgənd) *adj* self-catering.
selbstverständlich ('zɛlpstfɛrʃtɛntliç) *adj* obvious. *adv* naturally, of course, obviously.
Selbstvertrauen ('zɛlpstfɛrtrauən) *n neu* self-confidence.
selig ('ze:liç) *adj* **1** blessed. **2** happy. **3** deceased, late. **—keit** *nf* **-en** bliss.
Sellerie ('zɛləri:) *nm,f* celery.
selten ('zɛltən) *adj* rare. *adv* seldom, rarely. **—heit** ('zɛltənhait) *nf* **-en** **1** rarity. **2** scarcity.
seltsam ('zɛltza:m) *adj* strange, singular.
Semester (ze'mɛstər) *n neu* — semester.
Seminar (zemi'na:r) *n neu* **-e** **1** seminar. **2** teacher-training college. **3** (academic) department.
Semmel ('zɛməl) *nf* **-n** roll, bun.
Senat (ze'na:t) *nm* **-e** senate.
send/en* ('zɛndən) *vt* **1** send. **2** broadcast. **—er** *nm* — **1** sender. **2** transmitter. **—ung** *nf* **-en** **1** shipment. **2** transmission. **3** mission.
Senf (zɛnf) *nm* **-e** mustard.
Senkel ('zɛŋkəl) *nm* — (shoe)lace.
senk/en ('zɛŋkən) *vt* sink, lower. **sich senken** *vr* **1** sink. **2** slope. **—recht** *adj* vertical, perpendicular.
Sensation (zɛnzatsi'o:n) *nf* **-en** **1** sensation. **2** thrill. **—ell** (zɛnzatsio'nɛl) *adj* sensational.
Sense ('zɛnzə) *nf* **-n** scythe.
sensuell (zɛnzu'ɛl) *adj* sensual.
sentimental (zɛntimɛn'ta:l) *adj* sentimental.
September (zɛp'tɛmbər) *nm* September.
Serie ('ze:riə) *nf* **-n** series. **—nbau** *nm also* **—nherstellung** *nf* mass production.
seriös (zeri'œ:s) *adj* **1** serious. **2** reliable.
Serv/ice (zɛr'vi:s) *n neu* — **1** (dinner) service. **2** service. **—ieren** (zɛr'vi:rən) *vt,vi* serve (food).
Serviette (zɛrvi'ɛtə) *nf* **-n** napkin, serviette.
Sessel ('zɛsəl) *nm* — armchair. **—lift** *nm* chair-lift.

seßhaft ('zɛshaft) *adj* **1** resident. **2** settled.
setzen ('zɛtsən) *vt* **1** set, put, place, lay. **2** erect. **3** wager. **4** compose. *vi* leap. **sich setzen** *vr* **1** sit down. **2** subside.
Seuche ('zɔyçə) *nf* **-n** epidemic.
seufz/en ('zɔyftsən) *vi* **1** sigh. **2** groan. **—er** *nm* **— 1** sigh. **2** groan.
Sex (zɛks) *nm* **1** sex, sexual intercourse. **2** sexuality. **—uell** (zɛksu'ɛl) *adj* sexual.
sezieren (ze'tsiːrən) *vt* dissect.
Sibir/ien (zi'biːriən) *n neu* Siberia. **—ier** *nm* **—** Siberian. **—isch** *adj* Siberian.
sich (ziç) *pron* **1** himself, herself, itself. **2** oneself. **3** themselves. **4** one another, each other.
Sichel ('ziçəl) *nf* **-n 1** sickle. **2** crescent.
sicher ('ziçər) *adj* **1** safe, secure. **2** certain. **3** reliable. **—heit** *nf* **-en 1** certainty. **2** security. **3** safety. **—heitsdienst** *nm* security service. **—lich** *adv* certainly, surely. **—n** *vt* **1** protect. **2** secure. **3** fasten. **4** guarantee. **—stellen** *vt* safeguard, secure. **—ung** *nf* **-en 1** safety mechanism. **2** protection. **3** *comm* security, guarantee. **4** fuse.
Sicht (ziçt) *nf* **1** sight. **2** visibility. **auf lange** or **weite Sicht** on a long-term basis. **—bar** *adj* visible. **—lich** *adj* obvious.
sie (ziː) *pron 3rd pers* **1** *s* she, her, it. **2** *pl* they, them. **Sie** *pron 2nd pers fml s,pl* you.
Sieb (ziːp) *n neu* **-e** sieve.
sieben[1] ('ziːbən) *vt* **1** sieve, sift. **2** select.
sieb/en[2] ('ziːbən) *adj,nf* seven. **—ente** *adj also* **—te** ('ziːptə) seventh.
siebzehn ('ziːptseːn) *adj,nf* seventeen. **—te** *adj* seventeenth.
siebzig ('ziːptsiç) *adj,nf* seventy. **—ste** *adj* seventieth.
sied/eln ('ziːdəln) *vi* settle, colonize. **—ler** ('ziːdlər) *nm* **—** settler. **—ung** ('ziːdluŋ) *nf* **-en 1** settlement. **2** housing estate.
Siedepunkt ('ziːdəpuŋkt) *nm* boiling point.
Sieg (ziːk) *nm* **-e 1** victory. **2** conquest. **—en** ('ziːgən) *vi* be victorious, win. **—er** ('ziːgər) *nm* **—** victor. **—reich** *adj* victorious.
Siegel ('ziːgəl) *n neu* **—** seal. **—n** *vt* seal.
sieht (ziːt) *v* see **sehen.**
Signal (zig'naːl) *n neu* **-e** signal. **—wärter** *nm* signalman.
Signatur (zigna'tuːr) *nf* **-en 1** sign. **2** mark, stamp. **3** signature.
Silbe ('zilbə) *nf* **-n** syllable.
Silber ('zilbər) *n neu* silver.
Silikon (ziliː'koːn) *n neu* silicon. **—chip** (ziliːkoːn'tʃip) *nm* silicon chip.
Silvester (zil'vɛstər) *nm* New Year's Eve.
simpel ('zimpəl) *adj* **1** simple. **2** foolish.
Sims (zims) *nm,neu* **-e 1** ledge, sill. **2** shelf.
simulieren (zimu'liːrən) *vt* simulate, feign. *vi* **1** malinger. **2** feign.
sind (zint) *v* see **sein**[2].

Sinfonie (zinfo'niː) *nf* **-n** symphony.
singen* ('ziŋən) *vt,vi* sing.
sinken* ('ziŋkən) *vi* **1** sink. **2** drop, slump.
Sinn (zin) *nm* **-e** **1** sense. **2** faculty. **3** meaning. **4** mind, consciousness. **—bild** *n neu* symbol. **—en*** *vt,vi* **1** think, reflect. **2** plan, scheme. **—lich** *adj* sensual, sensuous. **—los** *adj* senseless. **—voll** *adj* meaningful.
Sintflut ('zintfluːt) *nf* **-en** deluge.
Sipp/e ('zipə) *nf* **-n** **1** clan, tribe. **2** kin.
Sirup ('ziːrup) *nm* **-e** syrup.
Sitt/e ('zitə) *nf* **-n** **1** custom. **2** *pl* manners. **3** *pl* morals. **—lich** *adj* **1** moral. **2** decent, respectable. **—lichkeit** *nf* morality, morals.
Situation (zituatsi'oːn) *nf* **-en** situation.
Sitz (zits) *nm* **-e** **1** seat. **2** residence. **3** fit. **—en*** ('zitsən) *vi* **1** sit. **2** fit. **—ung** *nf* **—en** **1** sitting, session. **2** meeting.
Sizil/ien (zi'tsiːliən) *n neu* Sicily. **—ianer** (zitsili'aːnər) *nm* — Sicilian. **—ianisch** (zitsili 'aːniʃ) *adj* Sicilian.
Skala ('skaːla) *nf* **Skalen** scale.
Skandal (skan'daːl) *nm* **-e** **1** scandal. **2** row, noise. **—ös** (skanda'lœːs) *adj* scandalous.
Skandinav/ien (skandi 'naːviən) *n neu* Scandinavia. **—ier** *nm* — Scandinavian. **—isch** *adj* Scandinavian.
Skelett (ske'lɛt) *n neu* **-e** skeleton.
skeptisch ('skɛptiʃ) *adj* sceptical.
Ski (ʃiː) *nm* see **Schi.**
Skizz/e ('skitsə) *nf* **-n** sketch. **—ieren** (ski'tsiːrən) *vt* sketch.
Sklav/e ('sklaːvə) *nm* **-n** slave. **—erei** (sklaːvə'rai) *nf* slavery. **—isch** ('sklaːviʃ) *adj* **1** slavish. **2** servile.
Skorpion ('skɔrpiɔn) *nm* **-e** **1** scorpion. **2** Scorpio.
Skrupel ('skruːpəl) *nm* — scruple. **—los** *adj* unscrupulous.
Smaragd (sma'rakt) *nm* **-e** emerald.
Smoking ('smoːkiŋ) *nm* **-s** dinner-jacket.
so (zoː) *adv* so, thus. **so daß** *conj* so that. **—bald** (zo'balt) *conj* as soon as.
Socke ('zɔkə) *nf* **-n** sock. **—nhalter** *nm* garter.
Sockel ('zɔkəl) *nm* — pedestal, base.
sodann (zo'dan) *conj* then.
Sodawasser ('zoːdavasər) *n neu* soda water.
Sodbrennen ('zoːtbrɛnən) *n neu* heartburn.
soeben (zo'eːbən) *adv* just (now).
Sofa ('zoːfa) *n neu* **-s** sofa, couch.
sofern (zo'fɛrn) *conj* **1** as far as, so far as. **2** provided that.
sofort (zo'fɔrt) *adv* immediately, at once.
Sog (zoːk) *nm* **-e** **1** suction. **2** wake.
sogar (zo'gaːr) *adv* even.
sogenannt ('zoːgənant) *adj* so-called.
Sohle ('zoːlə) *nf* **-n** sole (of a shoe). **—n** *vt* sole.
Sohn (zoːn) *nm* **¨-e** son.
solang (zo'laŋ) *conj* while, so long as.

solch (zɔlç) *adj,pron* such.
Soldat (zɔl'daːt) *nm* **-en** soldier.
Söldner ('zœldnər) *nm* — mercenary.
solid (zo'liːt) *adj* **1** solid. **2** reliable.
Solist (zo'list) *nm* **-en** soloist.
sollen* ('zɔlən) *v mod aux* **1** should, ought (to). **2** be said, be supposed (to).
Solo ('zoːlo) *n neu* **-s** solo.
Sommer ('zɔmər) *nm* — summer. **—sprosse** *nf* freckle.
Sonate (zo'naːtə) *nf* **-n** sonata.
Sonde ('zɔndə) *nf* **-n** probe.
Sonder/angebot ('zɔndərangəboːt) *n neu* **-e** special offer. **—ausgabe** *nf* special edition. **—bar** ('zɔndərbaːr) *adj* strange, singular.
sondern[1] ('zɔndərn) *vt* separate.
sondern[2] ('zɔndərn) *conj* but. **nicht nur ...sondern auch** not only...but also.
Sonett (zo'nɛt) *n neu* **-e** sonnet.
Sonnabend ('zɔnaːbənt) *nm* **-e** Saturday. **—s** *adv* on Saturdays.
Sonn/e ('zɔnə) *nf* **-n** sun. **—enaufgang** *nm* sunrise. **—enbrand** *nm* sunburn. **—enfinsternis** *nf* solar eclipse. **—enschein** *nm* sunshine. **—enstich** *nm* sunstroke. **—enuhr** *nf* sundial. **—enuntergang** *nm* sunset. **—ig** *adj* sunny.
Sonntag ('zɔntaːk) *nm* **-e** Sunday. **—s** *adv* on Sundays.
sonst (zɔnst) *adv* **1** otherwise. **2** else. **3** besides. **—ig** *adj* **1** other. **2** former. **—wo** ('zɔnstvo) *adv* elsewhere.
Sopran (zo'praːn) *nm* **-e** soprano, treble. **—istin** (zopra'nistin) *nf* **-nen** soprano (singer).
Sorg/e ('zɔrgə) *nf* **-n** **1** care. **2** trouble, worry. **3** grief. **—en** *vi* care, take care. **—en für** care or provide for, take care of, look after. **sich —en** *vr* worry. **—falt** ('zɔrkfalt) *nf* care, carefulness.
Sort/e ('zɔrtə) *nf* **-n** sort, type. **—ieren** (zɔr'tiːrən) *vt* sort, arrange.
soso (zo'zoː) *adv inf* passably, so-so.
Soße ('zoːsə) *nf* **-n** **1** sauce. **2** gravy.
soweit (zo'vait) *conj* so far as.
sowie (zo'viː) *conj* **1** as soon as. **2** just as.
sowieso (zoviː'zoː) *adv* anyhow, anyway.
Sowjet (zɔ'vjɛt) *nm* **-s** Soviet. **—isch** *adj* Soviet. **—union** *nf* Soviet Union.
sowohl (zo'voːl) *conj* **sowohl...als auch** both... and.
sozial (zotsi'aːl) *adj* social. **—demokrat** *nm* social democrat. **—ismus** (zotsia'lismus) *nm* socialism. **—ist** (zotsia'list) *nm* **-en** socialist. **—produkt** *n neu pol* national product.
Soziolog/e (zotsio'loːgə) *nm* **-n** sociologist. **—ie** (zotsiolo'giː) *nf* sociology. **—isch** (zotsio'loːgi *adj* sociological.
sozusagen (zotsu'zaːgən) *adv* so to speak.
Spachtel ('ʃpaxtəl) *nm,f* **-n** **1** scraper. **2** spatula.

spähen ('ʃpɛːən) *vi* look out, watch.

Spalt (ʃpalt) *nm* **-e** crack, split. **—e** *nf* **-n 1** crack, split. **2** column (of print, etc.). **3** rift. **—en** *vt* split, divide. **—pilz** *nm* bacteria.

Span (ʃpaːn) *nm* **¨-e** chip, splinter.

Span/ien ('ʃpaːniən) *nm* Spain. **—ier** ('ʃpaːniər) *nm* — Spaniard. **—isch** ('ʃpaːniʃ) *adj* Spanish. *n neu* Spanish (language).

Spann (ʃpan) *nm* **-e** instep.

Spann/e ('ʃpanə) *nf* **-n** span. **—en** *vt* **1** stretch. **2** tighten. **3** harness. **4** excite. **—ung** *nf* **-en 1** tension. **2** suspense. **3** voltage.

spar/en ('ʃpaːrən) *vt,vi* save. *vt* spare. **—kasse** *nf* savings bank. **¨—lich** ('ʃpɛːrliç) *adj* meagre, scanty. **—sam** *adj* thrifty.

Spargel ('ʃpargəl) *nm* asparagus.

Spaß (ʃpaːs) *nm* **¨-e 1** fun, amusement. **2** joke.

spät (ʃpɛːt) *adj* late. **—estens** *adv* at the latest.

Spaten ('ʃpaːtən) *nm* — spade.

Spatz (ʃpats) *nm* **-en** sparrow.

spazier/en (ʃpa'tsiːrən) *vi* (take a) walk, stroll. **—engehen*** *vi* go for a walk. **—gang** *nm* walk.

Speck (ʃpɛk) *nm* **1** bacon. **2** fat.

spedieren (ʃpe'diːrən) *vt* dispatch, forward.

Speer (ʃpeːr) *nm* **-e** spear, lance.

Speichel ('ʃpaiçəl) *nm* saliva, spittle.

Speicher ('ʃpaiçər) *nm* **-e 1** storeroom. **2** loft. **3** granary. **4** reservoir. **—n** *vt* store (up).

Speise ('ʃpaizə) *nf* **-n 1** food. **2** meal. **3** dish. **—eis** *n neu* ice cream. **—kammer** *nf* pantry, larder. **—karte** *nf* menu. **—n** *vi* eat, dine. **—saal** *nm* dining room or hall. **—wagen** *nm* dining car.

Spektakel (ʃpɛk'taːkəl) *nm* — uproar, row.

spekulieren (ʃpeku'liːrən) *vi* speculate.

Sperr/e ('ʃpɛrə) *nf* **-n 1** closing. **2** barrier. **3** block. **4** blockade, embargo. **—en** *vt* **1** close, block (off). **2** shut (out). **3** cut off, stop.

Spesen ('ʃpeːzən) *n pl* expenses, charges.

spez/ialisieren (ʃpetsiali'ziːrən) *vt* specialize. **sich spezialisieren auf** specialize in. **—ialität** (ʃpetsiali'tɛːt) *nf* **-en** speciality. **—iell** (ʃpetsi'ɛl) *adj* special.

spezifisch (ʃpe'tsiːfiʃ) *adj* specific.

Sphäre ('sfɛːrə) *nf* **-n** sphere.

Spiegel ('ʃpiːgəl) *nm* — mirror. **—ei** *n neu* fried egg. **—n** *vt* reflect. *vi* shine. **—ung** *nf* **-en** reflection.

Spiel (ʃpiːl) *n neu* **-e 1** game. **2** play. **3** pack (of cards). **—en** *vt,vi* **1** play. **2** perform. **3** gamble. **—karte** *nf* playing card. **—platz** *nm* playground. **—zeug** *n neu* toy.

Spieß (ʃpiːs) *nm* **-e 1** spear. **2** *cul* spit. **—bürger** *nm* Philistine, (petit) bourgeois. **—ig** *adj* narrow-minded, Philistine.

Spinat (ʃpi'naːt) *nm* **-e** spinach.

Spinne ('ʃpinə) *nf* **-n** spider. **—n*** ('ʃpinən) *vt* **1** spin. **2** plot, think. *vi inf* **1** spin yarns, fib. **2** be crazy. **—r** *nm* — *inf* idiot.

Spion (ʃpi'oːn) *nm* **-e** spy.

Spirale (ʃpi'raːlə) *nf* **-n** spiral.

Spital (ʃpi'taːl) *n neu* **¨-er** hospital.

spitz (ʃpits) *adj* pointed, sharp. **—bube** *nm* rogue, rascal. **—e** *nf* **-n** **1** point. **2** peak, top. **3** lace. **—en** *vt* point, sharpen. **—findig** *adj* subtle. **—ig** *adj* pointed, sharp. **—name** *nm* nickname.

Splitter ('ʃplitər) *nm* — splinter. **—nackt** *adj* stark naked.

spontan (ʃpɔn'taːn) *adj* spontaneous.

Sporn (ʃpɔrn) *nm* **Sporen** spur.

Sport (ʃpɔrt) *nm* **-e** sport, games. **—ler** ('spɔrtlər) *nm* — sportsman, athlete. **—platz** *nm* sports field. **—wagen** *nm* sports car.

Spott (ʃpɔt) *nm* mockery, ridicule. **—en** *vi* mock, ridicule.

sprach (ʃpraːx) *v* see **sprechen.**

Sprach/e ('ʃpraːxə) *nf* **-n** **1** speech. **2** language. **—lehre** *nf* grammar. **—lich** *adj* linguistic. **—los** *adj* speechless.

sprang (ʃpraŋ) *v* see **springen.**

sprech/en* ('ʃprɛçən) *vi,vt* speak, talk. **—stunde** *nf* consulting hours, surgery.

spreng/en ('ʃprɛŋən) *vt* **1** explode, blast. **2** sprinkle. *vi* gallop. **—körper** *nm* explosive (charge). **—stoff** *nm* explosive.

spricht (ʃpriçt) *v* see **sprechen.**

Sprichwort ('ʃpriçvɔrt) *n neu* **¨-er** proverb, saying.

sprießen* ('ʃpriːsən) *vi* sprout, bud.

spring/en* ('ʃpriŋən) *vi* **1** leap, jump. **2** dive.

Sprit (ʃprit) *nm* **-e** **1** spirit, alcohol. **2** *inf* petrol.

Spritze ('ʃpritsə) *nf* **-n** **1** syringe. **2** spray. **3** injection. **4** fire engine. **—n** *vt* **1** spray, squirt. **2** inject. *vi* spurt.

Sproß (ʃprɔs) *nm* **-e** *also* **Sprößling** ('ʃprœsliŋ) shoot, sprout.

Spruch (ʃprux) *nm* **¨-e** **1** saying. **2** judgment, sentence.

Sprudel ('ʃpruːdəl) *nm* **—e** **1** mineral water. **2** spring.

Sprung (ʃpruŋ) *nm* **¨-e** **1** leap, spring. **2** dive. **3** short distance, stone's throw. **4** crack. **—brett** *n neu* **1** diving board. **2** stepping stone. **—feder** *nf* spring.

spucken ('ʃpukən) *vi,vt* spit.

Spuk (ʃpuːk) *nm* **-e** ghost. **—en** *vi* haunt.

Spule ('ʃpuːlə) *nf* **-n** **1** spool, reel. **2** coil.

spül/en ('ʃpyːlən) *vt* **1** rinse, wash (up). **2** flush. **—maschine** *nf* dishwasher. **—mittel** *n neu* washing-up liquid.

Spur (ʃpuːr) *nf* **-en** **1** track, trail. **2** trace, vestige, mark. **3** footprint.

Staat (ʃtaːt) *nm* **-en** **1** state. **2** pomp. **—lich** *adj* state. **—sangehörigkeit** *nf* nationality. **—sanwalt** *nm* public prosecutor. **—smann** *nm* statesman. **—sstreich** *nm* coup d'état.

Stab (ʃtaːp) *nm* **¨-e** staff. **—springen*** *vi* pole-vault.

stabil (ʃta'biːl) *adj* stable.

Stachel ('ʃtaxəl) *nm* **-n** **1** prickle. **2** sting. **3** quill, spine. **4** spike. **—beere** *nf* gooseberry. **—draht** *nm* barbed wire. **—schwein** *nm* porcupine.

Stadt (ʃtat) *nf* **¨-e** city, town. **¨—isch** ('ʃtɛːtiʃ) *adj* municipal, town. **—viertel** *n neu* quarter, district.

Staffel ('ʃtafəl) *nf* **-n** **1** step, rung. **2** stage, degree. **3** *aviat* squadron. **4** *sport* relay. **—ei** (ʃtafə'lai) *nf* **-en** easel.

stahl (ʃtaːl) *v* see **stehlen.**

Stahl (ʃtaːl) *nm* **-e** steel. **¨—ern** ('ʃtɛːlərn) *adj* steel.

Stall (ʃtal) *nm* **¨-e** **1** stable. **2** cowshed. **3** pigsty. **4** (dog-) kennel.

Stamm (ʃtam) *nm* **¨-e** **1** trunk. **2** stem. **3** family. **4** race. **—baum** *nm* **1** family tree. **2** pedigree. **—en** *vi* originate, be descended. **—tisch** *nm* (table for) regular customers.

stampfen ('ʃtampfən) *vt,vi* **1** stamp. **2** pound.

stand (ʃtant) *v* see **stehen.**

Stand (ʃtant) *nm* **¨-e** **1** stand. **2** situation. **3** location. **4** class, rank. **5** position. **auf den neuesten Stand bringen** *vt* update. **—bild** *n neu* statue. **—esamt** ('ʃtandəsamt) *n neu* registry office. **—haft** *adj* steadfast, constant. **—halten*** *vi* stand firm. **—ort** *nm* **1** location. **2** garrison. **—punkt** *nm* point of view, standpoint.

ständig ('ʃtɛndiç) *adj* permanent, continuous. *adv* constantly, continually.

Stange ('ʃtaŋə) *nf* **-n** pole, stick. **—nbohne** *nf* runner bean.

Stänker ('ʃtɛŋkər) *nm* — *inf* trouble-maker. **—n** *vi* *inf* cause trouble, stir things up.

Stanniol (ʃtani'oːl) *n neu* **-e** tinfoil.

Stapel ('ʃtaːpəl) *nm* — **1** pile. **2** stocks. **—lauf** *nm* launch(ing). **—n** *vt* pile up.

stark (ʃtark) *adj* **1** strong. **2** stout. **3** large. *adv* **1** strongly. **2** very, greatly. **¨—e** ('ʃtɛrkə) *nf* **-n** **1** strength. **2** starch. **¨—en** ('ʃtɛrkən) *vt* **1** strengthen. **2** starch.

starr (ʃtar) *adj* stiff, rigid. **—köpfig** ('ʃtarkœpfiç) *adj* stubborn.

Start (ʃtart) *nm* **-e** **1** start. **2** *aviat* take-off. **—en** *vi* **1** start. **2** *aviat* take off. **—erklappe** *nf* *mot* choke.

Station (ʃtatsi'oːn) *nf* **-en** **1** station, stop. **2** (hospital) ward.

Statist/ik (ʃta'tistik) *nf* **-en** statistics. **—isch** *adj* statistical.

statt (ʃtat) *prep* instead of. *nf* place, stead. **—finden*** *vi* take place, occur. **—haft** *adj* **1** permissible. **2** legal.

Stätte ('ʃtɛtə) *nf* **-n** **1** place, spot. **2** abode. **3** scene (of an accident, etc.).

Statut (ʃta'tuːt) *n neu* **-en** statute.

Staub (ʃtaup) *nm* **1** dust. **2** pollen. **—ig** ('ʃtaubiç) *adj* dusty. **—sauger** *nm* — vacuum cleaner.

Stau/damm ('ʃtaudam) *nm* **¨-e** dam. **—en** *vt* dam up.

staunen ('ʃtaunən) *vi* be amazed, wonder. *n neu* — amazement.

Steak (steːk) *n neu* steak.

stechen* ('ʃtɛçən) *vt* **1** stab, pierce. **2** cut. **3** *game* trump. *vi* **1** sting. **2** burn. **—d** *adj* stinging.

steck/en ('ʃtɛkən) *vt* **1** put, stick. **2** insert. *vi* be (found). *nm* — stick. **—brief** *nm* (arrest) warrant. **—dose** *nf* (electric) socket. **—enpferd** ('ʃtɛkənpfert) *n neu* **-e** hobby-horse. **—er** *nm* — (electric) plug.

Steg (ʃteːk) *nm* **-e** **1** footpath. **2** footbridge. **3** *mus* bridge.

stehen* ('ʃteːən) *vi* **1** stand. **2** be. **—bleiben*** *vi* stand still, stop.

stehlen* ('ʃteːlən) *vt* steal.

steif (ʃtaif) *adj* stiff.

steig/en* ('ʃtaigən) *vi* **1** climb. **2** rise. **3** mount. **—bügel** *nm* stirrup.

steiger/n ('ʃtaigərn) *vt* **1** increase. **2** raise. **—ung** *nf* **-en** **1** rise. **2** increase. **3** intensification.

steil (ʃtail) *adj* steep.

Stein (ʃtain) *nm* **-e** stone, rock. **—alt** *adj* ancient, as old as the hills. **—bock** *nm* **1** ibex. **2** Capricorn. **—bruch** *nm* quarry. **—ern** ('ʃtainərn) *adj* stone. **—ig** *adj* stony. **—schlag** *nm* rockfall, avalanche.

Stell/e ('ʃtɛlə) *nf* **-n** **1** place, site, spot. **2** job, position. **3** office, authority. **—en** *vt* **1** place, put. **2** arrange. **3** adjust, set. **4** provide, supply. **sich —en** *vr* **1** present oneself. **2** sham, pretend to be. **—enlos** *adj* unemployed. **—envermittlung** *nf* employment agency. **—vertreter** *nm* deputy, representative.

Stellung ('ʃtɛluŋ) *nf* **-en** **1** situation. **2** post, job. **—nahme** *nf* **1** attitude. **2** opinion.

Stelze ('ʃtɛltsə) *nf* **-n** stilt.

Stempel ('ʃtɛmpəl) *nm* — stamp. **—n** *vt* stamp, frank.

Stengel ('ʃtɛŋəl) *nm* — stalk, stem.

Stenographie (ʃtenogra'fiː) *nf* **-n** shorthand.

Steppe ('ʃtɛpə) *nf* **-n** steppe.

sterb/en* ('ʃtɛrbən) *vi* die. **—lich** ('ʃtɛrpliç) *adj* mortal.

Stereoanlage ('ʃtereoanlaːgə) *nf* **-n** music centre.

steril (ʃte'riːl) *adj* sterile.

Stern (ʃtɛrn) *nm* **-e** star. **—bild** *n neu* constellation. **—chen** ('ʃtɛrnçən) *n neu* — asterisk. **—deuterei** *nf* astrology. **—kunde** *nf* astronomy. **—warte** *nf* **-n** observatory.

stet (ʃteːt) *adj also* **stet/ig** constant, steady. **—s** *adv* always, constantly.

Steuer[1] ('ʃtɔyər) *n neu* — helm, rudder. **—bord** *nm,neu* starboard. **—mann** *nm* helmsman. **—n** *vt,vi* steer.

Steuer[2] ('ʃtɔyər) *nf* **-n** tax.

Stich (ʃtiç) *nm* **-e** **1** prick, sting. **2** stitch. **3** *game* trick. **4** engraving. **5** taunt. **—wort** *n neu* **1** key-word. **2** cue.

sticken ('ʃtikən) *vt,vi* embroider.

Stickstoff ('ʃtikʃtɔf) *nm* nitrogen.

Stief/bruder ('ʃtiːfbruːdər) *nm* stepbrother. **—mutter** *nf*

stepmother. **—mütterchen** *n neu* — pansy. **—schwester** *nf* stepsister. **—sohn** *nm* stepson. **—tochter** *nf* stepdaughter. **—vater** *nm* stepfather.
Stiefel ('ʃtiːfəl) *nm* — boot.
stieg (ʃtiːk) *v* see **steigen.**
Stiel (ʃtiːl) *nm* **-e 1** handle. **2** stalk.
Stier (ʃtiːr) *nm* **-e 1** bull. **2** Taurus.
stieß (ʃtiːs) *v* see **stoßen.**
Stift[1] (ʃtift) *n neu* **-e** (charitable) institution.
Stift[2] (ʃtift) *nm* **-e 1** peg, pin. **2** pencil.
stift/en ('ʃtiftən) *vt* **1** give, donate. **2** found. **3** cause. **—ung** *nf* **-en 1** institution. **2** donation.
Stil (ʃtiːl) *nm* **-e** style.
still (ʃtil) *adj* **1** still, calm. **2** quiet. **3** silent. **Stiller Ozean** Pacific Ocean. **—e** *nf* **-n 1** peace, stillness. **2** quiet, silence. **—egen** ('ʃtilleːgən) *vt* shut down, stop. **—en** *vt* **1** still. **2** appease. **3** suckle (a child). **4** quench. **5** quieten. **—schweigend** ('ʃtilʃvaigənt) *adj* **1** silent, taciturn. **2** tacit. **—stand** *nm* standstill.
Stimm/e ('ʃtimə) *nf* **-n 1** voice. **2** vote. **—en** *vi* **1** be correct. **2** agree. **3** vote. *vt* tune. **—ung** *nf* **-en 1** mood, feeling. **2** tuning.
stinken* ('ʃtiŋkən) *vi* stink.
Stipendium (ʃti'pɛndium) *n neu* **-ien** scholarship, grant.
Stirn (ʃtirn) *nf* **-en** forehead, brow.
stöbern ('ʃtœːbərn) *vi* rummage (around).
Stock (ʃtɔk) *nm* **¨-e 1** stick, cane. **2** storey, floor. **—en** *vi* **1** stop, pause. **2** rot. **3** curdle. **4** thicken. **—werk** *n neu* storey, floor.
Stoff (ʃtɔf) *nm* **-e 1** matter, substance. **2** material, fabric, cloth. **3** topic.
stöhnen ('ʃtœːnən) *vi* groan.
Stoi/ker ('ʃtoːikər) *nm* — Stoic. **—sch** ('ʃtoːiʃ) *adj* stoical.
stolpern ('ʃtɔlpərn) *vi* stumble.
stolz (ʃtɔlts) *adj* **1** proud. **2** noble. **3** vain. *nm* pride.
stopfen ('ʃtɔpfən) *vt* **1** stuff, fill. **2** darn. **3** constipate.
Stoppel ('ʃtɔpəl) *nf* **-n** stubble.
stoppen ('ʃtɔpən) *vt,vi* stop, halt.
Stör (ʃtœːr) *nm* **-e** sturgeon.
Storch (ʃtɔrç) *nm* **¨-e** stork.
stör/en ('ʃtœːrən) *vt* bother, trouble, disturb. **—ung** *nf* **-en 1** disturbance. **2** inconvenience. **3** interference (on a radio, etc.).
Stoß (ʃtoːs) *nm* **¨-e 1** push, thrust. **2** punch, kick, blow. **3** impact. **4** pile (of books, etc.). **—dämpfer** *nm* shock-absorber. **—en*** *vt* **1** push. **2** hit. **3** stab. **4** thrust. *vi* **1** bump, hit. **2** run (into). **sich —en** *vr* **1** bump. **2** take offence. **—stange** *nf mot* bumper.
stottern ('ʃtɔtərn) *vi,vt* stammer, stutter.
Straf/anstalt ('ʃtraːfanʃtalt) *nf* **-en** prison, penal institution. **—bar** *adj* punishable. **—e** *nf* **-n 1** punishment, penalty. **2** fine. **—en** *vt* punish. **¨—ling** ('ʃtrɛːfliŋ) *nm* **-e** convict. **—recht** *n neu* criminal law.

Strahl (ʃtra:l) *nm* **-en 1** ray, beam. **2** jet. **3** flash. **—en** *vt,vi* **1** radiate. **2** beam. **—ung** *nf* **-en** radiation.
stramm (ʃtram) *adj* **1** taut. **2** robust.
Strand (ʃtrant) *nm* **¨-e** shore, coast, beach. **—gutjäger** *nm* beachcomber.
strapazieren (ʃtrapa'tsi:rən) *vt* **1** tire, exhaust. **2** wear out.
Straße ('ʃtra:sə) *nf* **-n 1** street, road. **2** straits. **—nbahn** *nf* tram.
sträuben ('ʃtrɔybən) *vt* ruffle (up). **sich sträuben** *vr* oppose, refuse.
Strauch (ʃtraux) *nm* **¨-er** bush, shrub.
Strauß[1] (ʃtraus) *nm* **¨-e** bouquet, bunch.
Strauß[2] (ʃtraus) *nm* **-e** ostrich.
streb/en ('ʃtre:bən) *vi* strive (for). **—epfeiler** *nm* buttress. **—er** *nm* — climber, pusher.
Strecke ('ʃtrɛkə) *nf* **-n 1** stretch, section. **2** distance.
Streich (ʃtraiç) *nm* **-e 1** stroke, blow. **2** trick. **—eln** *vt* stroke, caress. **—en*** *vt* **1** stroke. **2** strike (out). **3** spread. *vi* rush, run. **—holz** *n neu* match. **—instrument** *n neu* stringed instrument.
Streif (ʃtraif) *nm* **-e** *also* **Streifen** *nm* — stripe, streak.
Streife ('ʃtraifə) *nf* **-n 1** patrol. **2** raid.
streifen ('ʃtraifən) *vt* **1** streak, stripe. **2** graze. **3** touch on. **4** strip off. *vi* rove, ramble.
Streik (ʃtraik) *nm* **-e** (industrial) strike. **—brecher** *nm* strikebreaker, blackleg. **—en** *vi* strike. **—posten** *nm* picket.
Streit (ʃtrait) *nm* **-e 1** dispute, quarrel. **2** brawl, struggle. **—en*** *vi* **1** quarrel, argue. **2** fight. **—frage** *nf* matter in dispute. **—ig** *adj* in dispute. **—kräfte** *nf pl* armed forces.
streng (ʃtrɛŋ) *adj* **1** harsh. **2** rigorous. **—e** *nf* **1** harshness. **2** rigour. **—gläubig** *adj* orthodox.
streuen ('ʃtrɔyən) *vt* **1** scatter, sprinkle. **2** sow.
Strich (ʃtriç) *nm* **-e 1** stroke. **2** line. **3** district. **4** touch. **5** (compass) point. **6** (wood) grain. **—punkt** *nm* semicolon.
Strick (ʃtrik) *nm* **-e** cord, rope. **—en** *vt,vi* knit.
strittig ('ʃtritiç) *adj* in dispute.
Stroh (ʃtro:) *n neu* straw. **—halm** *nm* (blade of) straw.
Strolch (ʃtrɔlç) *nm* **-e** tramp.
Strom (ʃtro:m) *nm* **¨-e 1** (large) river. **2** current. **3** electricity, electric current. **4** flood, torrent. **—abwärts** (ʃtro:m 'apvɛrts) *adv* downstream. **—aufwärts** (ʃtro:m'aufvɛrts) *adv* upstream. **¨—en** ('ʃtroe:mən) *vi* **1** stream, flow. **2** flock. **¨—ung** ('ʃtroe:muŋ) *nf* **-en 1** current. **2** trend. **3** flow.
Struktur (ʃtruk'tu:r) *nf* **-en** structure.
Strumpf (ʃtrumpf) *nm* **¨-e** stocking. **—band** *n neu* garter. **—halter** *nm* — suspender. **—hose** *nf* tights.
Stube ('ʃtu:bə) *nf* **-n** room, chamber. **—nrein** *adj* house-trained.

Stück (ʃtyk) *n neu* **-e 1** piece. **2** head, item. **3** play. **—arbeit** *nf* piecework. **—chen** ('ʃtykçən) *n neu* — scrap, bit.

Student (ʃtu'dεnt) *nm* **-en, —in** *nf* **-nen** student.

Stud/ie ('ʃtu:diə) *nf* **-n 1** study. **2** sketch. **—ienrat** *nm* secondary-school teacher. **—ieren** (ʃtu'di:rən) *vt,vi* study. **—ium** ('ʃtu:dium) *n neu* **-ien 1** studies. **2** university education or course.

Stufe ('ʃtu:fə) *nf* **-n 1** step, stair. **2** rung. **3** stage. **4** *mus* interval. **—nweise** *adv* gradually, in stages.

Stuhl (ʃtu:l) *nm* **¨-e** chair, seat.

stumm (ʃtum) *adj* **1** dumb, mute. **2** silent.

stumpf (ʃtumpf) *adj* **1** blunt. **2** dull. *nm* **¨—e** stump. **—sinn** *nm* dullness, stupidity.

Stund/e ('ʃtundə) *nf* **-n 1** hour. **2** lesson. **—enplan** *nm* (school) timetable. **¨—lich** ('ʃtyntliç) *adj* hourly.

stur (ʃtu:r) *adj inf* obstinate.

Sturm (ʃturm) *nm* **¨-e 1** storm, gale. **2** attack. **¨—isch** ('ʃtyrmiʃ) *adj* stormy.

Sturz (ʃturts) *nm* **¨-e 1** fall. **2** downfall. **3** overthrow. **4** collapse. **¨—en** ('ʃtyrtsən) *vt* **1** overthrow. **2** throw down. *vi* **1** fall. **2** rush. **3** crash. **sich ¨—en** *vr* rush, plunge.

Stute ('ʃtu:tə) *nf* **-n** mare. **—nfüllen** *n neu* filly.

Stütze ('ʃtytsə) *nf* **-n 1** support, prop. **2** buttress. **3** help. **—n** *vt* prop (up), support.

Styropor (ʃty:ro'po:r) *nm* polystyrene.

Subjekt (zup'jεkt) *n neu* **-e** subject.

Substantiv (zupstan'ti:f) *n neu* **-e** noun, substantive.

subtil (zup'ti:l) *adj* subtle.

Such/e ('zu:xə) *nf* **-n** search. **—en** *vt,vi* seek, search (for).

süchtig ('zyçtiç) *adj* **1** addicted (to). **2** sickly.

Süd (zy:t) *nm also* **Süden** ('zy:dən) south.

Südafrika (zy:t'afrika) *n neu* South Africa.

Südamerika (zyda'mεrika) *n neu* South America.

südlich ('zy:tliç) *adj* south(ern).

Südost (zyd'ɔst) *nm also* **Sudost/en** (zyd'ɔstən) south-east. **—lich** *adj* south-eastern.

Südpol ('zy:tpo:l) *nm* South Pole.

südwärts ('zy:tvεrts) *adv* southward(s), south.

Südwest (zyd'vest) *nm also* **Südwest/en** (zyd'vestən) south-west. **—lich** *adj* south-western.

Sultanine (zulta'ninə) *nf* **-n** *cul* sultana.

Sülze ('zyltsə) *nf* **-n 1** jellied meat. **2** brine.

Summe ('zumə) *nf* **-n** sum, total.

summen ('zumən) *vt,vi* hum, buzz.

Sumpf (zumpf) *nm* **¨-e 1** swamp, marsh, bog. **2** *tech* sump. **—ig** *adj* swampy.

Sund (zunt) *nm* **-e** *naut* straits.

Sünd/e ('zyndə) *nf* **-n** sin. **—enbock** *nm* scapegoat. **—er** *nm* — sinner.

Suppe ('zupə) *nf* **-n** soup.

süß (zy:s) *adj* sweet. **—e** *nf*

sweetness. **—igkeit** *nf* **-en 1** sweetness. **2** *pl* sweets.
Sylvester (zyl'vɛstər) *nm* see **Silvester.**
Symbol (zym'boːl) *n neu* **-e** symbol. **—isch** *adj* symbolic.
Synagoge (zyna'goːgə) *nf* **-n** synagogue.
Synonym (zyno'nyːm) *n neu* **-e** synonym.
Syphilis ('zyːfilis) *nf* syphilis.
Syr/ien ('zyːriən) *n neu* Syria. **—ier** *nm* — Syrian. **—isch** *adj* Syrian.
System (zys'teːm) *n neu* **-e 1** system. **2** method. **3** doctrine. **—atisch** (zyste'maːtiʃ) *adj* systematic.
Szene ('stseːnə) *nf* **-n 1** scene. **2** stage, set. **3** row, argument.

T

Tabak ('taːbak) *nm* **-e** tobacco. **—händler** *nm* tobacconist.
Tabelle (ta'bɛlə) *nf* **-n 1** table. **2** index.
Tadel ('taːdəl) *nm* — **1** blame. **2** reprimand, reproach. **3** fault. **—los** *adj* blameless, flawless. **—n** *vt* **1** blame. **2** scold, reproach.
Tafel ('taːfəl) *nf* **-n 1** board, panel. **2** blackboard. **3** tablet, bar. **4** index. **5** table. **¨—n** ('tɛːfəln) *vt* panel.
Taffet ('tafət) *nm* **-e** *also* **Taft** (taft) taffeta.
Tag (taːk) *nm* **-e 1** day. **2** daylight. **3** open air. **—ebuch** ('taːgəbuːx) *n neu* diary. **—en** ('taːgən) *vi* **1** dawn. **2** meet. **—esordnung** ('taːgəsɔrdnuŋ) *nf* agenda. **—esanbruch** ('taːgəsanbrux) *nm* daybreak. **—esmutter** ('taːgəsmutər) *nf* childminder. **¨—lich** ('tɛːkliç) *adj* daily. **—undnachtgleiche** *nf* **-n** equinox. **—ung** ('taːguŋ) *nf* **-en 1** meeting. **2** conference.
Taille ('taljə) *nf* **-n** waist.
Takelwerk ('taːkəlvɛrk) *n neu* rigging.
Takt (takt) *nm* **-e 1** *mus* time, beat. **2** tact. **—gefühl** *n neu* tact. **—los** *adj* tactless. **—stock** *nm mus* baton. **—voll** *adj* tactful.
Taktik ('taktik) *nf* **-en** tactics.
Tal (taːl) *n neu* **¨-er** valley.
Talent (ta'lɛnt) *n neu* **-e** talent, gift.
Talg (talk) *nm* **-e 1** suet. **2** tallow.
Talk (talk) *nm* **-e** talc, talcum powder.
tändeln ('tɛndəln) *vi* **1** dawdle. **2** flirt.
Tang (taŋ) *nm* **-e** seaweed.
Tanger ('taŋər) *n neu* Tangier(s).
Tank (taŋk) *nm* **-s 1** (fuel) tank. **2** *mil* tank. **—en** *vi* fill up, refuel. **—stelle** *nf* petrol or filling station.
Tanne ('tanə) *nf* **-n** fir, pine. **—nbaum** *nm* fir, pine tree.
Tante ('tantə) *nf* **-n** aunt.
Tanz (tants) *nm* **¨-e** dance. **—en** *vt,vi* dance. **¨—er** ('tɛntsər) *nm* **—, ¨—erin** ('tɛntsərin) *nf* **—nen** dancer. **—gesellschaft** *nf* dance, ball.
Tap/ete (ta'petə) *nf* **-n** wallpaper. **—ezieren** (tape'tsiːrən) *vt* paper.
tapfer ('tapfər) *adj* brave, bold. **—keit** *nf* courage.
tappen ('tapən) *vi* grope, fumble.

Tarif (ta'riːf) *nm* **-e** **1** price list, tariff. **2** list of fares. **3** wage scale.

tarn/en ('tarnən) *vt* camouflage. **—ung** *nf* **-en** camouflage.

Tasch/e ('taʃə) *nf* **-n** **1** pocket. **2** wallet. **3** handbag. **—enbuch** *n neu* pocketbook. **—endieb** *nm* pickpocket. **—engeld** *n neu* pocket money. **—enmesser** *n neu* pocket knife. **—entuch** *n neu* handkerchief.

Tasse ('tasə) *nf* **-n** cup.

Tast/e ('tastə) *nf* **-n** key. **—atur** (tasta'tuːr) *nf* **-en** keyboard. **—en** ('tastən) *vi* feel, grope. *vt* touch. **sich —en** *vr* feel one's way.

tat (taːt) *v* see **tun.**

Tat (taːt) *nf* **-en** deed, action, act. **in der Tat** in fact. **—bestand** *nm* **1** facts. **2** state of affairs. **¨—er** ('tɛːtər) *nm* — perpetrator, doer. **¨—ig** ('tɛːtiç) *adj* **1** active. **2** working, at work. **¨—igen** ('tɛːtigən) *vt* **1** carry out. **2** *comm* conclude, execute. **—kraft** *nf* energy. **—sache** *nf* fact. **—sächlich** ('taːtzɛçliç) *adj* **1** real. **2** factual. **3** effective. *adv* really, indeed.

tätowieren (tɛto'viːrən) *vt* tattoo.

Tatze ('tatsə) *nf* **-n** **1** paw. **2** claw.

Tau[1] (tau) *n neu* **-e** cable, rope. **—en** ('tauən) *vt* tow.

Tau[2] (tau) *nm* dew. **—en** ('tauən) *vi* melt. **es taut** dew is falling.

taub (taup) *adj* **1** deaf. **2** empty. **3** numb.

Taube ('taubə) *nf* **-n** pigeon, dove.

tauch/en ('tauxən) *vi* dive, plunge. *vt* plunge, dip. **—eranzug** *nm* wet suit. **—sieder** *nm* — immersion heater.

Tauf/becken ('taufbɛkən) *n neu also* **Tauf/stein** *nm* (baptismal) font. **—e** *nf* **-n** baptism. **—en** *vt* baptize.

taug/en ('taugən) *vi* be worth, be of use. **—enichts** *nm* **-e** good-for-nothing. **—lich** ('taukliç) *adj* **1** useful. **2** suitable. **3** fit, capable.

Taumel ('tauməl) *nm* — **1** staggering. **2** dizziness. **3** frenzy. **—n** *vi* **1** stagger. **2** be giddy or dizzy.

Tausch (tauʃ) *nm* **-e** exchange, swap. **—en** *vt* exchange, swap. **—handel** *nm* barter.

täusch/en ('tɔyʃən) *vt* **1** deceive. **2** cheat. **—ung** *nf* **-en** **1** deception. **2** cheating.

tausend ('tauzənt) *adj,nf* thousand. **—ste** *adj* thousandth.

Tauwerk ('tauvɛrk) *n neu* rigging, ropes.

Tax/e ('taksə) *nf* **-n** **1** estimate. **2** rate, fee. **3** duty, tax. **—ieren** (ta'ksiːrən) *vt* evaluate, assess.

Taxi ('taksi) *n neu* **-s** taxi.

Techn/ik ('tɛçnik) *nf* **-en** **1** skill, technique. **2** technical sciences. **—iker** *nm* — technician, engineer. **—isch** *adj* technical. **—ologie** (tɛçnolo'giː) *nf* technology.

Tee (teː) *nm* **-s** tea. **—beutel** *nm* teabag. **—kanne** *nf* teapot. **—löffel** *nm* teaspoon.

Teer (teːr) *nm* **-e** tar.

Teich (taiç) *nm* **-e** pond, pool.

Teig (taik) *nm* **-e 1** dough, batter. **2** paste. **—waren** *nf pl* pasta.

Teil (tail) *nm,neu* **-e 1** part. **2** share, portion. **3** piece. **—bar** *adj* separable, divisible. **—chen** ('tailçən) *n neu* — particle. **—en** *vt* divide. **—haber** *nm* — partner, associate. **—nahme** *nf* **1** participation. **2** interest. **3** sympathy. **—nehmen*** *vi* take part (in). **—nehmer** *nm* — participant, member. **—s** *adv* also **—weise** partly, in part. **—ung** *nf* **-en 1** division. **2** scale.

Telekommunikation (teləkɔmuːnikatsi'oːn) *nf* telecommunications.

Tele/gramm (tele'gram) *n neu* **-e** telegram. **—fon** see **—phon. —graph** (tele'graːf) *nm* **-en** cable, telegraph. **—graphieren** (telegra'fiːrən) *vi,vt* wire, telegraph. **—phon** (tele'foːn) *n neu* **-e** telephone. **—phonanruf** *nm* telephone call. **—phonieren** (telefo 'niːrən) *vi,vt* telephone. **—phonisch** *adj* by telephone. **—phonzelle** *nf* callbox. **—skop** (tele'skoːp) *n neu* **-e** telescope.

Teller ('tɛlər) *nm* — plate.

Tempel ('tɛmpəl) *nm* — temple.

Temperament (tɛmpera'mɛnt) *n neu* **-e 1** temperament. **2** liveliness, vivacity. **—voll** *adj* temperamental.

Temperatur (tɛmpera'tuːr) *nf* **-en** temperature.

Tempo ('tɛmpo) *n neu* **-pi** tempo, pace.

Tendenz (tɛn'dɛnts) *nf* **-en** tendency.

Tender ('tɛndər) *nm* — (railway) tender.

Tennis ('tɛnis) *n neu* tennis. **—platz** *nm* tennis court.

Teppich ('tɛpiç) *nm* **-e** carpet, rug. **—kehrmaschine** *nf* carpet sweeper.

Termin (tɛr'miːn) *nm* **-e 1** deadline. **2** term. **3** (fixed) date.

Terminologie (tɛrminolo'giː) *nf* **-n** terminology.

Terpentin (tɛrpɛn'tiːn) *n neu* turpentine.

Terrasse (tɛ'rasə) *nf* **-n** terrace.

Terror ('tɛrɔr) *nm* terror. **—isieren** (tɛrori'ziːrən) *vt* terrorize. **—ismus** (tɛro'rismus) *nm* terrorism. **—ist** (tɛro'rist) *nm* **-en** terrorist.

Terz (tɛrts) *nf* **-en** *mus* third. **—ett** (tɛr'tsɛt) *n neu* **-e** trio.

Testament (tɛsta'mɛnt) *n neu* **-e 1** (last) will. **2** *rel* Testament.

testieren (tɛ'stiːrən) *vt* **1** bequeath. **2** testify.

teuer ('tɔyər) *adj* **1** expensive. **2** cherished, dear.

Teuf/el ('tɔyfəl) *nm* — devil. **—elei** (tɔyfə'lai) *nf* **-en** devilry. **—lisch** ('tɔyfliʃ) *adj* devilish, fiendish.

Text (tɛkst) *nm* **-e** text.

Textil/ien (tɛks'tiːliən) *n pl* textiles.

Theater (te'aːtər) *n neu* — theatre. **—stück** *n neu* play.

Thema ('teːma) *n neu* **-men** theme, topic.

Themse ('tɛmzə) *nf* Thames.

Theolog/e (teo'loːgə) *nm* **-n** theologian. **—ie** (teolo'giː) *nf*

theology. **—isch** (teo'loːgiʃ) *adj* theological.
Theor/etiker (teo'reːtikər) *nm* — theorist, theoretician. **—etisch** (teo'reːtiʃ) *adj* theoretical. **—etisieren** (teoreti 'ziːrən) *vi* theorize. **—ie** (teo 'riː) *nf* **-n** theory.
Therapie (tera'piː) *nf* **-n** therapy.
therm/isch ('tɛrmiʃ) *adj* thermal, thermic. **—odynamik** (tɛrmody'naːmik) *nf* thermodynamics. **—ometer** (tɛrmo 'meːtər) *n neu* thermometer. **—osflasche** ('tɛrmosflaʃə) *nf* *Tdmk* Thermos flask.
Thron (troːn) *nm* **-e** throne. **—erbe** *nm* heir to the throne. **—folge** *nf* succession to the throne.
Thunfisch ('tuːnfiʃ) *nm* tunny (fish).
Thüringen ('tyːriŋən) *n neu* Thuringia.
Thymian ('tyːmiaːn) *nm* **-e** thyme.
ticken ('tikən) *vi* tick, click.
tief (tiːf) *adj* **1** deep. **2** low. **3** profound. *n neu* **-s** (barometric) depression. **—druck** *nm* low pressure. **—e** *nf* **-n** depth. **—kühlen** *vt* deep-freeze. **—kühlkost** *nf* frozen food. **—kühltruhe** *nf* freezer.
Tiegel ('tiːgəl) *nm* **-e** **1** saucepan. **2** crucible.
Tier (tiːr) *n neu* **-e** animal, beast. **—arzt** *nm* veterinary surgeon, vet. **—isch** *adj* **1** animal. **2** brutish. **3** brutal. **—kreis** *nm* zodiac.
Tiger ('tiːgər) *nm* — tiger.
tilg/en ('tilgən) *vt* **1** erase. **2** eradicate. **3** cancel. **4** repay. **—ung** *nf* **-en** **1** eradiction. **2** cancellation. **3** repayment.
Tint/e ('tintə) *nf* **-n** ink. **in der Tinte sitzen** be in a nice mess. **—enfaß** *n neu* inkwell.
tippen ('tipən) *vt,vi* **1** type. **2** tap.
Tirol (ti'roːl) *n neu* Tyrol.
Tisch (tiʃ) *nm* **-e** **1** table. **2** board. **—decke** *nf also* **—tuch** *n neu* tablecloth. **—ler** ('tiʃlər) *nm* — **1** joiner, cabinetmaker. **2** carpenter. **—tennis** *n neu* table tennis.
Titel ('tiːtəl) *nm* — title.
titulieren (titu'liːrən) *vt* give a title to, entitle.
Toast (toːst) *nm* **-e** toast. **—brot** *n neu* toasting bread. **-er** *nm* — toaster.
tob/en ('toːbən) *vi* **1** rage. **2** roar.
Tochter ('tɔxtər) *nf* ¨— daughter.
Tod (toːt) *nm* **-e** death. **—esanzeige** ('toːdəsantsaigə) *nf* obituary. **—esfall** ('toːdəsfal) *nm* death, casualty. **—eskampf** ('toːdəskampf) *nm* death agony. **—esstrafe** ('toːdəsʃtraːfə) *nf* death penalty. **—feind** ('toːtfaint) *nm* mortal enemy. **¨—lich** ('tœːtliç) *adj* deadly, fatal. **—müde** ('toːtmyːdə) *adj* dead tired.
Toilette (toa'lɛtə) *nf* **-n** **1** toilet. **2** dressing table. **3** toilette. **—npapier** *n neu* toilet paper.
toleran/t (tole'rant) *adj* tolerant. **—z** (tole'rants) *nf* **1** toleration. **2** tolerance.
toll (tɔl) *adj* **1** mad. **2** raving. **3** wild. **4** *inf* terrific. **—heit** *nf* **-en** **1** madness. **2** mad trick.

—kühn *adj* foolhardy. **—wut** *nf* rabies.

Tölpel ('tœlpəl) *nm* — clumsy person, fool.

Tomate (to'maːtə) *nf* **-n** tomato.

Ton[1] (ton) *nm* **-e** clay.

Ton[2] (toːn) *nm* **¨-e 1** sound. **2** *mus* tone, note. **3** fashion. **4** stress, accent. **—art** *nf mus* key. **—band** *n neu* (magnetic) tape. **—bandgerät** *n neu* tape-recorder. **¨—en** ('tœːnən) *vi* resound. *vt* shade, tint. **—fall** *nm* intonation. **—leiter** *nf mus* scale.

Tonne ('tɔnə) *nf* **-n 1** ton. **2** barrel.

Topf (tɔpf) *nm* **¨-e** pot. **¨—er** ('tœpfər) *n* — potter. **¨—erwaren** ('tœpfərvaːrən) *nf pl* pottery, earthenware.

Tor[1] (toːr) *n neu* **-e 1** gate, door. **2** *sport* goal.

Tor[2] (toːr) *nm* **-en** fool. **—heit** *nf* **-en** folly. **¨—icht** ('tœːriçt) *adj* foolish.

Torf (tɔrf) *nm* peat.

torkeln ('tɔrkəln) *vi* stagger.

Torpedo (tɔr'peːdo) *nm* **-s** torpedo.

Torte ('tɔrtə) *nf* **-n** tart, flan.

tot (toːt) *adj* dead. **Totes Meer** *n neu* Dead Sea.

total (to'taːl) *adj* total, complete. **—itär** (totali'tɛːr) *adj* totalitarian.

Tote(r) ('toːtə) *nm* **1** dead man. **2** corpse.

töten ('tœːtən) *vt* kill.

Totenbett ('toːtənbɛt) *n neu* deathbed.

Totengräber ('toːtəngrɛːbər) *nm* — gravedigger.

Totenhemd ('toːtənhɛmt) *n neu* shroud.

totgeboren ('toːtgəbɔːrən) *adj* still-born.

sich totlachen ('toːtlaxən) *vr* roar with laughter, kill oneself laughing.

totschießen* ('toːtʃiːsən) *vt* shoot dead.

Totschlag ('toːtʃlak) *nm* manslaughter.

totschweigen* ('toːtʃvaigən) *vt* hush up.

totsicher ('toːtziçər) *adj* dead certain.

Tour (tuːr) *nf* **-en 1** tour, trip. **2** turn. **—ist** (tu'rist) *nm* **-en** tourist.

Trab (traːp) *nm* trot. **—en** ('traːbən) *vi* trot.

Tracht (traxt) *nf* **-en 1** (national) costume. **2** dress. **3** load.

Tradition (traditsi'oːn) *nf* **-en** tradition. **—ell** (traditsio'nɛl) *adj* traditional.

traf (traːf) *v* see **treffen.**

träg/e ('trɛːgə) *adj* lazy, sluggish. **—heit** ('trɛːkhait) *nf* laziness, sluggishness.

trag/en* ('traːgən) *vt* **1** carry. **2** wear. **3** bear, endure. **4** support. **—bahre** ('traːkbaːrə) *nf* **-n** stretcher. **¨—er** ('trɛːgər) *nm* — **1** porter. **2** carrier. **3** support. **4** pillar, beam. **—flächenboot** ('traːkflɛçənboːt) *n neu* **-e** hydrofoil. **—weite** ('traːkvaitə) *nf* **1** range. **2** importance.

trag/isch ('traːgiʃ) *adj* tragic. **—ödie** (tra'gœːdiə) *nf* **-n** tragedy.

Train/er ('trɛːnər) *nm* — *sport* trainer, coach. **—ing** *n neu* training.

Traktor ('traktɔr) *nm* **-en** tractor.
trampeln ('trampəln) *vi* trample, stamp.
Tran (traːn) *nm* **-e** blubber, whale oil.
tranchieren (trãː'ʃiːrən) *vt* carve (up).
Träne ('trɛːnə) *nf* **-n** tear. **—ngas** *n neu* tear-gas.
trank (traŋk) *v* see **trinken.**
transatlantisch (transat'lantiʃ) *adj* transatlantic.
transitiv ('tranzitiːf) *adj* transitive.
Transmission (transmisi'oːn) *nf* **-en** transmission.
Transport (trans'pɔrt) *nm* **-e** transport. **—ieren** (transpɔr'tiːrən) *vt* transport.
trat (trat) *v* see **treten.**
Traube ('traubə) *nf* **-n 1** grape. **2** bunch of grapes.
trau/en ('trauən) *vi* trust. *vt* (of a priest, etc.) marry (a man and a woman). **sich trauen** *vr* dare, venture. **—ring** *nm* wedding-ring. **—ung** *nf* **-en** wedding.
Trau/er ('trauər) *nf* **1** sorrow. **2** mourning. **—ern** *vi* mourn. **—erspiel** *n neu* tragedy. **—rig** ('trauriç) *adj* sad.
Trauf/e ('traufə) *nf* **-n 1** eaves. **2** gutter. **¨—eln** ('trɔyfəln) *vi* drip, sprinkle. **—rinne** *nf* **-n** gutter (of a house).
traulich ('trauliç) *adj* cosy, familiar.
Traum (traum) *nm* **¨-e** dream. **¨—en** ('trɔymən) *vt,vi* dream (of). **¨—er** ('trɔymər) *nm* — dreamer. **—haft** *adj* dreamlike.
treff/en* ('trɛfən) *vt,vi* **1** hit, strike. **2** befall. **3** meet, encounter. **sich treffen** *vr* **1** meet. **2** happen. **eine Entscheidung treffen** come to a decision. *~n neu* — meeting. **—er** *nm* — (direct or lucky) hit. **—lich** *adj* excellent. **—punkt** *nm* meeting place.
treib/en* ('traibən) *vt* **1** drive. **2** urge. **3** force. **4** carry on, do. **5** work (metal). *vi* drift. *n neu* activity. **—haus** ('traiphaus) *n neu* hothouse. **—stoff** ('traipʃtɔf) *nm* fuel.
trenn/bar ('trɛnbaːr) *adj* divisible. **—en** *vt* **1** divide, separate. **2** cut off (a telephone call). **—ung** *nf* **-en** separation.
Trepp/e ('trɛpə) *nf* **-n** stairs, staircase. **—enhaus** *n neu* stairwell.
tret/en* ('treːtən) *vi* **1** step, walk. **2** pedal. *vt* **1** kick. **2** tread on. **—mühle** *nf* treadmill.
treu (trɔy) *adj* **1** faithful, loyal. **2** accurate. **—bruch** *nm* breach of faith. **—e** *nf* loyalty. **—händer** ('trɔyhɛndər) *nm* — trustee. **—lich** *adv* faithfully. **—los** *adj* disloyal.
Tribut (tri'buːt) *nm* **-e** tribute.
Trichter ('triçtər) *nm* **-e 1** funnel. **2** crater.
Trick (trik) *nm* **-s** trick, dodge. **—film** *nm* animated cartoon.
trieb (triːp) *v* see **treiben.**
Trieb (triːp) *nm* **-e 1** drive, force. **2** impulse. **3** *bot* shoot, sprout. **4** instinct. **—feder** *nf* (main)spring. **—haft** *adj* **1** instinctive. **2** unbridled. **—kraft** *nf* momentum. **—sand** *nm* quicksand.

triefen* ('tri:fən) *vi* drip.
trifft (trift) *v* see **treffen.**
triftig ('triftiç) *adj* **1** conclusive. **2** valid.
Trigonometrie (trigonome'tri:) *nf* trigonometry.
Triller ('trilər) *nm* — *mus* trill.
trimmen ('trimən) *vt* trim.
trink/bar ('triŋkba:r) *adj* drinkable. **—en*** *vt,vi* drink. **—geld** *n neu* tip.
Tripper ('tripər) *nm* gonorrhoea.
tritt (trit) *v* see **treten.**
Tritt (trit) *nm* **-e** **1** step. **2** kick.
Triumph (tri'umf) *nm* **-e** triumph. **—ieren** (trium'fi:rən) *vi* triumph.
trock/en ('trɔkən) *adj* dry. **—nen** *vt,vi* dry.
Trog (tro:k) *nm* **¨-e** trough.
Tromm/el ('trɔməl) *nf* **-n** drum. **—eln** *vi* drum. **—ler** ('trɔmlər) *nm* — drummer.
Trompete (trɔm'pe:tə) *nf* **-n** trumpet.
Trop/en ('tro:pən) *n pl* tropics. **—enhelm** *nm* sun-helmet. **—isch** *adj* tropical.
Tropf (trɔpf) *nm* **¨-e** simpleton. **¨—eln** ('trœpfəln) *vt,vi* drip, trickle. **—en** ('trɔpfən) *nm* — drop. *vt,vi* drip, trickle.
Trost (tro:st) *nm* consolation. **¨—en** ('trœ:stən) *vt* console, comfort. **—los** *adj* **1** inconsolable. **2** bleak, desolate.
Trott (trɔt) *nm* **-e** trot.
Trottel ('trɔtəl) *nm* — idiot.
trotz (trɔts) *prep* in spite of, despite. *nm* **1** defiance. **2** obstinacy. **jemandem zum Trotz** in defiance of someone. **—dem** ('trɔtsde:m) *adv* nevertheless. *conj* notwithstanding. **—ig** *adj* defiant, obstinate.
trüb (try:p) *adj* **1** gloomy, dismal. **2** cloudy, muddy. **—en** ('try:bən) *vt* **1** make gloomy. **2** dull, tarnish. **—sal** *nf* **-e** distress, affliction. **—sinn** *nm* melancholy, depression.
Trug (tru:k) *nm* **1** deceit, deception. **2** fraud. **—bild** *n neu* phantom, mirage. **¨—en*** ('try:gən) *vt* deceive. *vi* be deceptive, mislead. **¨—erisch** ('try:gəriʃ) *adj* **1** deceptive. **2** deceitful.
Trümmer ('trymər) *n neu pl* **1** ruins. **2** rubble.
Trumpf (trumpf) *nm* **¨-e** trump. **—en** *vt,vi* trump.
Trunk (truŋk) *nm* **¨-e** drink. **—en** *adj* drunk, drunken. **—sucht** *nf* alcoholism.
Trupp (trup) *nm* **-s** band, party. **—e** *nf* **-n** **1** troop. **2** company, unit. **3** *pl* troops.
Truthahn ('tru:tha:n) *nm* turkey(-cock).
Tschech/e ('tʃɛçə) *nm* **-n** Czech. **—isch** *adj* Czech. *n neu* Czech (language). **—oslowakei** (tʃɛçoslova'kai) *nf* Czechoslovakia. **—oslowakisch** *adj* Czechoslovakian.
Tuberkulose (tubɛrku'lo:zə) *nf* tuberculosis.
Tuch (tu:x) *n neu* **-e** **1** cloth. **2** rag, duster. **3** scarf.
tüchtig ('tyçtiç) *adj* **1** able. **2** efficient.
Tück/e ('tykə) *nf* **-n** malice, spite. **—isch** *adj* **1** malicious. **2** insidious.
Tugend ('tu:gənt) *nf* **-en** virtue. **—haft** *adj* virtuous.
Tulpe ('tulpə) *nf* **-n** tulip.

tun* (tu:n) *vt,vi* **1** do. **2** make. **3** act. **4** put. **5** pretend. *n neu* doings. **—lich** *adj* practicable.

Tünche ('tynçə) *nf* **-n** whitewash, distemper. **—n** *vt* whitewash, distemper.

Tunke ('tuŋkə) *nf* **-n** sauce, gravy. **—n** *vt* **1** dip. **2** steep.

Tunnel ('tunəl) *nm* — tunnel.

Tür (ty:r) *nf* **-en** door, doorway.

Türk/e ('tyrkə) *nm* Turk. **—ei** (tyr'kai) *nf* Turkey. **—isch** *adj* Turkish. *n neu* Turkish (language).

Türkis (tyr'ki:s) *nm* **-e** turquoise.

Turm (turm) *nm* **¨-e** **1** tower, steeple. **2** *game* rook, castle. **¨—chen** ('tyrmçən) *n neu* — turret.

turn/en ('turnən) *vi* do gymnastics. *n neu* gymnastics. **—halle** *nf* gymnasium.

Turnier (tur'ni:r) *n neu* **-e** tournament.

Tusch/e ('tuʃə) *nf* **-n** Indian ink. **—farbe** *nf* water-colour.

tuscheln ('tuʃəln) *vi* whisper.

Tüte ('ty:tə) *nf* **-n** **1** paper bag. **2** carrier bag.

Twen (tvɛn) *nm* **-s** man or woman in his or her twenties.

Typ (ty:p) *nm* **-en** **1** type. **2** model. **—isch** *adj* typical.

Typhus ('ty:fus) *nm* typhoid (fever).

Tyrann (ty'ran) *nm* **-en** tyrant. **—ei** (tyra'nai) *nf* tyranny.

U

U-Bahn ('u:ba:n) *nf* underground (railway).

übel ('y:bəl) *adj* **1** evil, wrong. **2** bad, nasty. **3** sick. *n neu* — **1** evil. **2** nuisance. **3** disease. **—keit** *nf* **-en** nausea, sickness. **—nehmen*** *vt* take amiss, take badly.

üben ('y:bən) *vt,vi* practise, exercise.

über ('y:bər) *prep* **1** over. **2** above. **3** (up)on. **4** beyond, across. **5** about.

überall (y:bər'al) *adv* everywhere.

überanstrengen (y:bər'anʃtrɛŋən) *vt* overexert.

überaus ('y:bəraus) *adv* exceedingly.

überbelichten ('y:bərbəliçtən) *vt* overexpose (a photograph).

überbieten (y:bər'bi:tən) *vt* outbid.

Überbleibsel ('y:bərblaipsəl) *n neu* — remainder, remnant.

Überblick ('y:bərblik) *nm* **1** survey. **2** summary. **—en** (y:bər'blikən) *vt* survey.

überbringen* (y:bər'briŋən) *vt* deliver, hand over.

überdies (y:bər'di:s) *adv* besides, moreover.

Überdruß ('y:bərdrus) *nm* **1** disgust. **2** boredom, weariness.

übereilen (y:bər'ailən) *vt* rush, hurry.

überein/ander (y:bərain'andər) *adv* one on top of another. **—kommen*** (y:bər'ainkɔmən) *vi* come to an agreement. *n neu* — agreement, contract. **—kunft** (y:bər'ainkunft) *nf* **¨-e** agreement, compromise. **—stimmen** (y:bər'ainʃtimən) *vi* agree.

überfahr/en* ('y:bərfa:rən) *vt* **1** drive or pass over. **2** run over. **—t** *nf* passage, crossing.

Überfall ('y:bərfal) *nm* surprise

attack, raid. **—en*** (y:bər'falən) *vt* attack suddenly. **¨—ig** ('y:bərfɛliç) *adj* overdue.
Über/fluß ('y:bərflus) *nm* abundance, excess. **—flüssig** ('y:bərflysiç) *adj* superfluous, excess.
überfordern (y:bər'fɔrdərn) *vt* overcharge.
überführ/en ('y:bərfy:rən) *vt* **1** transport. **2** convict. **3** convince. **—ung** (y:bər'fy:ruŋ) *nf* **1** transportation. **2** fly-over.
Übergabe ('y:bərga:bə) *nf* **1** surrender. **2** delivery.
Übergang ('y:bərgaŋ) *nm* **1** passage, crossing. **2** transition.
übergeben* ('y:bərge:bən) *vt* hand over, deliver. **sich übergeben** *vr* vomit.
übergehen* (*vi* 'y:bərge:ən; *vt* y:bər'ge:ən) *vi* **1** pass or cross over. **2** change. *vt* **1** omit. **2** pass or run over. **3** revise.
Übergewicht ('y:bərgeviçt) *n neu* **-e 1** overweight. **2** preponderance.
überhandnehmen* (y:bər'hantne:mən) *vi* increase or spread rapidly.
überhäufen (y:bər'hɔyfən) *vt* overwhelm.
überhaupt (y:bər'haupt) *adv* **1** in general. **2** altogether. **3** at all.
überheblich (y:bər'he:pliç) *adj* presumptuous.
überholen ('y:bərho:lən) *vt* fetch or bring over. (y:bər'ho:lən) *vt* **1** overtake. **2** recondition.
überkochen ('y:bərkɔxən) *vi* boil over.
überkommen* (y:bər'kɔmən) *vt* **1** obtain, receive. **2** befall.
überlassen* (y:bər'lasən) *vt* **jemandem etwas überlassen** leave something to someone.
überlaufen* ('y:bərlaufən) *vi* run or go over.
überleben (y:bər'le:bən) *vt* survive, outlive.
überleg/en (y:bər'le:gən) *vt* consider. *adj* superior. **—ung** *nf* **-en** consideration.
überliefer/n (y:bər'li:fərn) *vt* **1** hand down. **2** deliver. **3** surrender. **—ung** *nf* **-en 1** tradition. **2** delivery. **3** surrender.
überlisten (y:bər'listən) *vt* outwit.
Übermacht ('y:bərmaxt) *nf* superiority, superior strength.
übermäßig ('y:bərmɛsiç) *adj* excessive.
Übermensch ('y:bərmɛnʃ) *nm* superman.
übermitteln (y:bər'mitəln) *vt* **1** transmit. convey.
übermorgen ('y:bərmɔrgən) *adv* the day after tomorrow.
Übermut ('y:bərmu:t) *nm* **1** high spirits. **2** insolence. **3** arrogance. **¨—ig** ('y:bərmy:tiç) *adj* **1** high-spirited. **2** insolent. **3** arrogant.
übernachten (y:bər'naxtən) *vi* spend the night.
übernehmen* (y:bər'ne:mən) *vt* **1** take over. **2** undertake.
überprüfen (y:bər'pry:fən) *vt* examine, check.
überqueren (y:bər'kve:rən) *vt* traverse, cross.
überragen (y:bər'ra:gən) *vt* surpass.
überrasch/en (y:bər'raʃən) *vt* surprise. **—ung** *nf* **-en** surprise.

überreden (yːbər'reːdən) *vt* persuade.
überreichen (yːbər'raiçən) *vt* **1** hand over, present. **2** submit.
Überrest ('yːbərrɛst) *nm* remains, remnant.
überrumpeln (yːbər'rumpəln) *vt* take unawares.
übers ('yːbərs) contraction of **über das.**
überschätzen (yːbər'ʃɛtsən) *vt* overrate, overestimate.
überschauen (yːbər'ʃauən) *vt* survey.
überschreiten* (yːbər'ʃraitən) *vt* **1** step over. **2** exceed, transgress.
Überschrift ('yːbərʃrift) *nf* title, heading.
Überschuh ('yːbərʃuː) *nm* overshoe.
Überschuß ('yːbərʃus) *nm* surplus.
überschwemm/en (yːbər 'ʃvɛmən) *vt* flood, swamp. **—ung** *nf* **-en** flood, inundation.
überschwenglich ('yːbərʃvɛŋliç) *adj* effusive, rapturous.
Übersee ('yːbərzeː) *nf* overseas.
übersehen* (yːbər'zeːən) *vt* **1** overlook. **2** survey.
übersenden (yːbər'zɛndən) *vt* send, forward.
übersetz/en ('yːbərzɛtsən) *vt* ferry over. *vi* pass. (yːbər 'zɛtsən) *vt* translate. **—ung** (yːbər'zɛtsuŋ) *nf* **-en** **1** translation. **2** *tech* gear.
Übersicht ('yːbərziçt) *nf* **-en** survey, summary. **—lich** *adj* easily understood, clear.
übersiedeln ('yːbərziːdəln) *vi* **1** (re)move. **2** emigrate.
übersinnlich ('yːbərzinliç) *adj* psychic, supernatural.
überspannen (yːbər'ʃpanən) *vt* **1** stretch over, cover. **2** overstrain. **3** exaggerate.
überspringen* (*vi* 'yːbərʃpriŋən; *vt* yːbər'ʃpriŋən) *vi* leap or jump, skip, over. *vt* **1** leap over, jump. **2** omit.
überstehen* (yːbər'ʃteːən) *vt* survive, overcome.
Überstunden ('yːbərʃtundən) *nf pl* overtime.
überstürzen (yːbər'ʃtyrtsən) *vt* hurry, rush.
übertrag/en* (yːbər'traːgən) *vt* **1** carry over. **2** transport. **3** transmit, broadcast. **4** translate. **—ung** *nf* **-en** **1** transfer. **2** transportation. **3** transmission.
übertreffen* (yːbər'trɛfən) *vt* surpass, excel, outdo.
übertreiben* (yːbər'traibən) *vt* **1** overdo. **2** exaggerate.
übertreten* (*vi* 'yːbərtreːtən; *vt* yːbər'treːtən) *vi* go or change over. *vt* violate, infringe.
übertrieben (yːbər'triːbən) *adj* overdone, exaggerated.
überwachen (yːbər'vaxən) *vt* supervise, control.
überwältigen (yːbər'vɛltigən) *vt* overpower.
überweis/en* (yːbər'vaizən) *vt* **1** transfer. **2** remit. **—ung** *nf* **-en** **1** remittance. **2** transfer.
überwiegen* (yːbər'viːgən) *vt* outweigh, prevail.
überwinden (yːbər'vindən) *vt* overcome.
überzeug/en (yːbər'tsɔygən) *vt*

convince. **—ung** *nf* **-en** conviction.

überzieh/en* ('y:bərtsi:ən) *vt* put on. (y:bər'tsi:ən) *vt* **1** cover. **2** overdraw (an account).

Überzug ('y:bərtsu:k) *nm* coating, cover.

üblich ('y:pliç) *adj* customary, usual.

U-Boot ('u:bo:t) *n neu* submarine.

übrig ('y:briç) *adj* left over, remaining. **—ens** ('y:brigəns) *adv* **1** by the way. **2** besides. **3** after all.

Übung ('y:buŋ) *nf* **-en** **1** exercise. **2** practice. **3** use.

Ufer ('u:fər) *n neu* **— 1** bank. **2** shore.

Uhr (u:r) *nf* **-en** **1** clock, watch. **2** time, hour. **wieviel Uhr ist es?** what time is it? **—feder** *nf* watch spring.

ulkig ('ulkiç) *adj* funny, comical.

Ulme ('ulmə) *nf* **-n** elm.

um (um) *prep* **1** (a)round, about. **2** at, by, for. **3** on account of. *adv* **1** around, about. **2** over, up, finished. **um...zu** *conj* in order to.

umändern ('umɛndərn) *vt* alter, modify.

umarm/en (um'armən) *vt* embrace, hug. **—ung** *nf* **-en** embrace, hug.

umbauen ('umbauən) *vt* rebuild, remodel.

umbilden ('umbildən) *vt* **1** transform. **2** reform. **3** reconstruct.

umbinden* ('umbindən) *vt* **1** put on. **2** tie round.

sich umblicken ('umblikən) *vr* look round or about.

umbringen* ('umbriŋən) *vt* kill.

umdrehen ('umdre:ən) *vt* turn or twist round. **sich umdrehen** *vr* turn round.

umeinander (umain'andər) *adv* (a)round each other.

umfahren* ('umfa:rən) *vt* knock down, run over. (um'fa:rən) *vt* drive round.

umfallen* ('umfalən) *vi* **1** fall down or over. **2** collapse.

Umfang ('umfaŋ) *nm* **1** circumference. **2** girth. **3** extent, range.

umfassen (um'fasən) *vt* **1** include. **2** enclose. **3** embrace.

Umfrage ('umfra:gə) *nf* inquiry, poll.

Umgang ('umgaŋ) *nm* **1** relations, (social) intercourse. **2** rotation, circuit. **—ssprache** *nf* colloquial or everyday speech.

umgeb/en* (um'ge:bən) *vt* surround. **—ung** *nf* **-en** surroundings, environment.

umgeh/en* (*vi* 'umge:ən; *vt* um'ge:ən) *vi* **1** go round. **2** associate (with). (um'ge:ən) *vt* go round. **2** avoid. **—ungsstraße** (um'ge:uŋsʃtra:sə) *nf* bypass.

umgekehrt ('umgəke:rt) *adj* **1** reversed. **2** contrary. *adv* vice versa.

umgraben* ('umgra:bən) *vt* dig up.

umher (um'he:r) *adv* about, around. **—gehen*** *vi* walk about. **—schweifen** *vi* wander, roam.

umhüllen (um'hylən) *vt* wrap (up), cover.

Umkehr ('umke:r) *nf* return. **—en** *vi,vt* turn round.
umkippen ('umkipən) *vt,vi* turn or tip over.
umklammern (um'klamərn) *vt* clasp, cling (to).
sich umkleiden ('umklaidən) *vr* change (one's clothes).
umkommen* ('umkɔmən) *vi* **1** die, perish. **2** (of food) spoil.
Umkreis ('umkrais) *nm* **1** circumference. **2** surroundings.
Umlauf ('umlauf) *nm* **1** circulation. **2** rotation. **—en*** (*vt* um 'laufən; *vi* 'umlaufən) *vt* move or run round. *vi* **1** circulate. **2** rotate.
Umlaut ('umlaut) *nm* **-e** vowel modification, umlaut.
umleit/en ('umlaitən) *vt* divert. **—ung** *nf* **-en** diversion.
umlernen ('umlɛrnən) *vt* relearn.
umrahmen (um'ra:mən) *vt* frame.
umrechn/en ('umrɛçnən) *vt* convert, exchange. **—ung** *nf* conversion, exchange.
umreißen (um'raisən) *vt* outline, sketch. ('umraisən) *vt* pull down.
umringen (um'riŋən) *vt* surround.
Umriß ('umris) *nm* outline, sketch.
umrühren ('umry:rən) *vt* stir up or around.
ums (ums) contraction of **um das.**
Umsatz ('umzats) *nm comm* **1** turnover. **2** sale.
umschalten ('umʃaltən) *vt* **1** switch over. **2** change over.
umschauen ('umʃauən) *vi* look round.
Umschlag ('umʃla:k) *nm* **1** envelope. **2** cover, wrapper. **3** hem, cuff, turn-up. **4** (sudden) change, transformation. **5** poultice. **6** *comm* turnover. **—en*** (um'ʃla:gən) *vi* **1** turn or tip over. **2** change. ('umʃla:gən) *vt* **1** knock down or over. **2** turn over.
umschließen* (um'ʃli:sən) *vt* enclose, embrace.
umschulen ('umʃu:lən) *vt* **1** retrain, re-educate. **2** change (a child's) school.
Umschwung ('umʃvuŋ) *nm* **1** change. **2** *tech* revolution.
sich umsehen* ('umze:ən) *vr* **1** look round or back. **2** look out (for).
umsetzen ('umzɛtsən) *vt* **1** transpose. **2** transform. **3** sell, turn over.
umsichtig ('umziçtiç) *adj* cautious, prudent.
umsiedeln ('umzi:dəln) *vt,vi* resettle.
umsonst (um'zɔnst) *adv* **1** in vain. **2** free, for nothing.
Umstand ('umʃtant) *nm* **1** circumstance, condition. **2** *pl* ceremonies, fuss. **in anderen Umständen** *inf* pregnant, expecting, with child. **¨—lich** ('umʃtɛntliç) *adj* **1** complicated, involved. **2** ceremonious.
umsteigen* ('umʃtaigən) *vi* change (trains or buses).
umstoßen* ('umʃto:sən) *vt* **1** overturn, overthrow. **2** invalidate. **3** reverse (a judgment).
Umsturz ('umʃturts) *nm* **1** overthrow, downfall. **2** revolution. **¨—en** ('umʃtyrtsən) *vt* overthrow. *vi* fall down.

umtauschen ('umtauʃən) *vt* exchange.
umwälzen ('umvɛltsən) *vt* **1** revolutionize. **2** roll round. **sich umwälzen** *vr* whirl round.
Umweg ('umveːk) *nm* roundabout way, detour.
Umwelt ('umvɛlt) *nf* environment.
umwenden* ('umvɛndən) *vt* turn over. **sich umwenden** *vr* turn back or round.
umwerben* (um'vɛrbən) *vt* seek the favour of, court.
umwerfen* ('umvɛrfən) *vt* **1** overturn. **2** put on.
umziehen* ('umtsiːən) *vt* change (one's clothing). *vi* remove, move (house).
umzingeln (um'tsiŋəln) *vt* encircle, surround.
Umzug ('umtsuːk) *nm* **1** removal. **2** procession.
unabänderlich (unap'ɛndərliç) *adj* **1** unchangeable. **2** irrevocable.
unabhängig ('unaphɛŋiç) *adj* independent. **—keit** *nf* independence.
unachtsam ('unaxtzaːm) *adj* inattentive.
unanfechtbar (unan'fɛçtbaːr) *adj* incontestable.
unangemessen ('unangəmɛsən) *adj* **1** inadequate, unfit. **2** improper. **3** unsuitable.
unangenehm ('unangəneːm) *adj* unpleasant.
Unannehmlichkeit ('unanneːmliçkait) *nf* **-en** inconvenience, unpleasantness.
unanständig ('unanʃtɛndiç) *adj* indecent.
unartig ('unaːrtiç) *adj* naughty, badly behaved.
unauffällig ('unauffɛliç) *adj* **1** inconspicuous. **2** unassuming.
unausstehlich (unaus'ʃteːliç) *adj* insufferable.
unbändig ('unbɛndiç) *adj* **1** unruly. **2** *inf* tremendous, excessive.
unbeachtet ('unbəaxtət) *adj* unnoticed.
unbedeutend ('unbədɔytənt) *adj* insignificant.
unbedingt ('unbədiŋt) *adj* **1** unconditional, absolute. **2** definite. *adv* definitely.
Unbehag/en ('unbəhaːgən) *n neu* **1** uneasiness. **2** discomfort. **—lich** (unbə'haːkliç) *adj* uneasy, uncomfortable.
unbeholfen ('unbəhɔlfən) *adj* clumsy, awkward.
unbekümmert (unbə'kymərt) *adj* **1** carefree, unconcerned. **2** careless.
unbemannt ('unbəmant) *adj* unmanned.
unbemittelt ('unbəmitəlt) *adj* without means.
unbequem ('unbəkveːm) *adj* **1** uncomfortable. **2** inconvenient. **—lichkeit** *nf* **1** discomfort. **2** incovenience.
unberufen (unbə'ruːfən) *adj* uncalled for. *interj* touch wood!
unbeschreiblich (unbə'ʃraipliç) *adj* indescribable.
unbesonnen ('unbəzɔnən) *adj* thoughtless, rash.
unbestimmt ('unbəʃtimt) *adj* indefinite.
unbestreitbar (unbə'ʃtraitbaːr) *adj* indisputable.
unbestritten ('unbəʃtritən) *adj* undisputed.

unbeweglich ('unbəve:kliç) *adj* **1** immovable. **2** motionless.

unbewußt ('unbəvust) *adj* **1** unconscious, unknowing. **2** instinctive, involuntary.

unbotmäßig ('unbo:tmɛ:siç) *adj* unruly.

unbrauchbar ('unbrauxba:r) *adj* useless, unserviceable.

und (unt) *conj* and. **na und?** so what?

undankbar ('undaŋkba:r) *adj* ungrateful.

undenkbar (un'dɛŋkba:r) *adj* unthinkable.

undeutlich ('undɔytliç) *adj* indistinct, blurred.

undurchdringlich ('undurçdriŋliç) *adj* impenetrable.

uneben ('une:bən) *adj* **1** uneven. **2** rough.

unecht ('unɛçt) *adj* artificial, counterfeit.

unehelich ('une:əliç) *adj* (of a child) illegitimate.

unehrlich ('une:rliç) *adj* dishonest.

unendlich (un'ɛntliç) *adj* endless, infinite.

unentbehrlich (unɛnt'be:rliç) *adj* indispensable.

unerbittlich (unɛr'bitliç) *adj* relentless, unrelenting, unyielding.

unerfahren ('unɛfa:rən) *adj* inexperienced.

unerhört (unɛr'hœ:rt) *adj* **1** unheard of. **2** outrageous.

unerläßlich (unɛr'lɛsliç) *adj* indispensable.

unerlaubt ('unɛrlaupt) *adj* **1** unauthorized. **2** illegal.

unermeßlich (unɛr'mɛsliç) *adj* immeasurable.

unermüdlich (unɛr'my:tliç) *adj* untiring.

unerreicht (unɛr'raiçt) *adj* unequalled.

unerschrocken ('unɛrʃrɔkən) *adj* undaunted.

unerwünscht ('unɛrvynʃt) *adj* undesirable, unwelcome.

unfähig ('unfɛ:iç) *adj* **1** incapable. **2** incompetent. **—keit** *nf* **1** incapacity. **2** incompetence.

Unfall ('unfal) *nm* **1** accident. **2** disaster.

unfaßbar ('unfasba:r) *adj* inconceivable.

unfehlbar (un'fe:lba:r) *adj* **1** unfailing. **2** infallible.

unfreundlich ('unfrɔyntliç) *adj* unfriendly.

Unfug ('unfu:k) *nm* **1** mischief. **2** offence. **3** disturbance. **4** (public) nuisance. **¨—sam** ('unfy:kza:m) *adj* unruly, unmanageable.

Ungar ('uŋgar) *nm* **-n** Hungarian. **—isch** *adj* Hungarian. *n neu* Hungarian (language). **—n** *n neu* Hungary.

ungeachtet ('ungəaxtət) *prep* regardless of.

ungebührlich ('ungəby:rliç) *adj* improper.

Ungeduld ('ungədult) *nf* impatience. **—ig** ('ungəduldiç) *adj* impatient.

ungefähr ('ungəfɛ:r) *adv* about, approximately.

ungeheuer ('ungəhɔyər) *adj* huge, monstrous. *n neu* **—** monster. **—lich** (ungə'hɔyərliç) *adj* monstrous.

ungekürzt ('ungəkyrtst) *adj* unabridged.

ungelegen ('ungəle:gən) *adj* incovenient.

Ungemach ('ungəma:x) *n neu* **-e 1** adveristy. **2** discomfort.
ungemein ('ungəmain) *adj* uncommon, extraordinary.
ungemütlich ('ungəmy:tliç) *adj* unpleasant, uncomfortable.
ungeniert ('unʒəni:rt) *adj* unceremonious.
ungeraten ('ungəra:tən) *adj* **1** (of children) spoilt. **2** degenerate.
ungerecht ('ungərɛçt) *adj* unjust.
ungereimt ('ungəraimt) *adj* absurd.
ungern ('ungɛrn) *adv* reluctantly, unwillingly.
ungestüm ('ungəʃty:m) *adj* **1** impetuous. **2** violent. *n neu* **1** impetuosity. **2** violence.
unge/wöhnlich ('ungəvœ:nliç) *adj* unusual, uncommon, strange. **—wohnt** ('ungəvo:nt) *adj* unaccustomed.
Ungeziefer ('ungətsi:fər) *n neu* — vermin.
ungezogen ('ungətso:gən) *adj* **1** ill-mannered, uncivil, rude. **2** naughty, disobedient.
ungezwungen ('ungətsvuŋən) *adj* natural, unconstrained, easy(-going).
ungläubig ('unglɔybiç) *adj* incredulous, unbelieving.
unglaublich ('unglaupliç) *adj* unbelievable, incredible.
ungleich ('unglaiç) *adj* unequal, unlike.
Unglimpf ('unglimpf) *nm* **1** insult. **2** harshness.
Unglück ('unglyk) *n neu* misfortune. **—lich** *adj* **1** unhappy. **2** unfortunate. **—licherwise** *adv* unfortunately. **—sfall** *nm* accident.
Ungnade ('ungna:də) *nf* **1** disgrace. **2** displeasure.
ungünstig ('ungynstiç) *adj* unfavourable.
unhaltbar ('unhaltba:r) *adj* untenable.
Unheil ('unhail) *n neu* **1** harm. **2** disaster, misfortune. **—bar** *adj* incurable.
unheimlich ('unhaimliç) *adj* **1** weird, sinister, uncanny. **2** *inf* tremendous, terrific.
universal (univɛr'za:l) *adj* universal.
Universität (univɛrzi'tɛ:t) *nf* **-en** university.
Universum (uni'vɛrzum) *n neu* universe.
unkennt/lich ('unkɛntliç) *adj* unrecognizable. **—nis** *nf* ignorance.
unklug ('unklu:k) *adj* unwise, imprudent.
Unkosten ('unkɔstən) *nf pl* expenses, costs.
Unkraut ('unkraut) *n neu* weed(s).
unlängst ('unlɛŋst) *adv* lately, recently.
unlauter ('unlautər) *adj* impure, unfair.
unlösbar ('unlœ:sba:r) *adj* insoluble.
unmäßig ('unmɛ:siç) *adj* immoderate.
Unmenge ('unmɛŋə) *nf* enormous number.
Unmensch ('unmɛnʃ) *nm* brute, barbarian. **—lich** *adj* brutal, inhuman, barbarous.
unmittelbar ('unmitəlba:r) *adj* direct.
unmöglich ('unmœ:kliç) *adj* impossible.

unmoralisch ('unmora:liʃ) *adj* immoral.

unnötig ('unnœ:tiç) *adj* unnecessary.

unnütz ('unnyts) *adj* useless, vain, idle.

unord/entlich ('unɔrdəntliç) *adj* untidy, disorderly. **—nung** ('unɔrdnuŋ) *nf* disorder, confusion.

unparteiisch ('unpartaiiʃ) *adj* impartial.

unpassend ('unpasənt) *adj* unsuitable.

Unrat ('unra:t) *nm* **1** dirt, filth. **2** rubbish.

unratsam ('unra:tza:m) *adj* inadvisable.

unrecht ('unrɛçt) *adj* **1** incorrect. **2** unjust. *n neu* injustice, wrong. **—mäßig** *adj* illegal.

unrein ('unrain) *adj* unclean, dirty.

Unruh/e ('unru:ə) *nf* **1** uneasiness, anxiety. **2** disturbance, riot. **3** unrest. **—ig** *adj* **1** restless, uneasy. **2** turbulent. **—stifter** *nm* agitator, troublemaker.

uns (uns) *pron 1st pers pl* **1** us. **2** ourselves.

unsagbar (un'za:kba:r) *adj* unspeakable.

unsauber ('unzaubər) *adj* dirty, untidy.

unscheinbar ('unʃainba:r) *adj* **1** insignificant. **2** unpretentious, plain.

unschlüssig ('unʃlysiç) *adj* irresolute, undecided.

Unschuld ('unʃult) *nf* innocence. **—ig** ('unʃuldiç) *adj* innocent.

unselig ('unze:liç) *adj* **1** unfortunate. **2** fatal.

unser ('unzər) *poss adj 1st pers pl* our. **—er** *poss pron 1st pers pl also* **der uns(e)re** or **der uns(e)rige** ours. **—(e)seits** ('unzər(ə)zaits) *adv* for our part, as for us. **—(e)sgleichen** ('unzər(ə)sglaiçən) *pron* people like us. **—thalben** ('unzərthalbən) *adv also* **—twegen** ('unzərtve:gən) or **—twillen** ('unzərtvilən) for our sake(s), on our account.

unsicher ('unziçər) *adj* **1** unsafe, insecure. **2** uncertain.

unsichtbar ('unziçtba:r) *adj* invisible.

Unsinn ('unzin) *nm* nonsense. **—ig** *adj* foolish, stupid.

Unsitt/e ('unzitə) *nf* bad habit. **—lich** *adj* immoral, indecent.

unsterblich ('unʃtɛrpliç) *adj* immortal. **—keit** *nf* immortality.

unstet ('unʃte:t) *adj* unsteady, inconstant.

Untat ('unta:t) *nf* crime, outrage.

untätig ('untɛ:tiç) *adj* inactive.

untauglich ('untaukliç) *adj* unfit, useless.

unten ('untən) *adv* **1** below. **2** downstairs.

unter ('untər) *prep* **1** below, under. **2** among. **3** between. **4** of. **5** during. *adj* lower, inferior.

Unterarm ('untərarm) *nm* forearm.

Unterbau ('untərbau) *nm* **-ten** substructure, foundation.

unterbewußt ('untərbəvust) *adj* subconscious. **—sein** *n neu* subconscious.

unterbleiben* (untər'blaibən) *vi* not take place, be cancelled.

unterbrechen* (untər'brɛçən) *vt* interrupt.
unterbringen* ('untərbriŋən) *vt* **1** lodge, shelter. **2** place.
unterdes (untər'dɛs) *adv also* **unterdessen** meanwhile.
unterdrücken (untər'drykən) *vt* **1** suppress, repress. **2** oppress.
untereinander (untərain 'andər) *adv* **1** among one another, mutually. **2** one beneath the other.
Unterführung (untər'fy:ruŋ) *nf* underpass.
Untergang ('untərgaŋ) *nm* **1** (of the sun) setting. **2** decline, (down)fall.
Untergebene(r) (untər'ge:bənə) *nm* subordinate.
untergehen* ('untərge:ən) *vi* **1** perish, die. **2** set, sink.
untergeordnet ('untərgəɔrdnət) *adj* minor, subordinate.
Untergestell ('untərgəʃtɛl) *n neu* **-e** undercarriage, base.
untergraben* ('untər'gra:bən) *vt* **1** undermine. **2** corrupt.
Untergrund ('untərgrunt) *nm* subsoil. **—bahn** *nf* underground (railway).
unterhalb ('untərhalp) *prep* below, under.
Unterhalt ('untərhalt) *nm* livelihood, subsistence. **—en*** (untər'haltən) *vt* **1** entertain. **2** maintain. **3** support. **sich —en** *vr* talk, converse. **—ung** *nf* **-en** **1** entertainment. **2** conversation.
unterhand/eln (untər'handəln) *vi* negotiate. **—lung** (untər 'handluŋ) *nf* negotiation.
Unterhemd ('untərhɛmt) *n neu* vest.
Unterhosen ('untərho:zən) *n pl* underpants.
unterirdisch ('untərirdiʃ) *adj* underground, subterranean.
unterkommen* ('untərkɔmən) *vi* **1** find work. **2** find accommodation or shelter. *n neu also* **Unterkunft** ('untərkunft) *nf* **¨-e** **1** lodging(s), accommodation. **2** *mil* quarters.
Unterlage ('untərla:gə) *nf* **1** basis, foundation. **2** (documentary) proof, documents.
unterlassen* (untər'lasən) *vt* **1** omit. **2** abstain from.
unterlegen (*v* 'untərle:gən; *adj* untər'le:gən) *vt* put under. *adj* inferior.
Unterleib ('untərlaip) *nm* abdomen.
unterliegen (untər'li:gən) *vi* be defeated.
unternehm/en* (untər'ne:mən) *vt* undertake, attempt. *n neu* **—** undertaking, enterprise. **—er** *nm* **—** **1** contractor. **2** entrepreneur. **3** employer.
Unteroffizier ('untərɔfitsi:r) *nm* non-commissioned or petty officer.
Unterredung (untər're:duŋ) *nf* **-en** **1** conversation. **2** conference. **3** talk, interview.
Unterricht ('untərriçt) *nm* instruction, lessons. **—en** (untər'riçtən) *vt* instruct, teach, inform.
Unterrock ('untərrɔk) *nm* petticoat.
unters ('untərs) contraction of **unter das.**
untersagen (untər'za:gən) *vt* forbid, prohibit.

Untersatz ('untərzats) *nm* **1** support. **2** saucer.

unterscheid/en* (untər'ʃaidən) *vt* distinguish, discriminate. **sich unterscheiden** *vr* differ. **—ung** *nf* **-en** distinction, difference.

unterschieben* (untər'ʃiːbən) *vt* attribute, impute.

Unterschied ('untərʃiːt) *nm* **-e** difference. **—lich** *adj* different.

unterschlagen* (untər'ʃlaːgən) *vt* **1** embezzle. **2** suppress.

Unterschlupf ('untərʃlupf) *nm* **¨-e** refuge.

unterschreiben* (untər'ʃraibən) *vt* **1** sign. **2** subscribe to.

Unterschrift ('untərʃrift) *nf* signature.

Untersee/boot ('untərzeːboːt) *n neu* submarine. **—isch** ('untərzeːiʃ) *adj* submarine.

untersetzt (untər'zɛtst) *adj* thick-set, stocky.

unterst ('untərst) *adj* lowest, last, bottom.

Unterstand ('untərʃtant) *nm* dugout, shelter.

unterstütz/en (untər'ʃtytsən) *vt* support, back. **—ung** *nf* **-en** support.

untersuch/en (untər'zuːxən) *vt* examine, inspect. **—ung** *nf* **-en** **1** examination. **2** inquiry.

Untertan ('untərtaːn) *nm* **-en** subject. **¨—ig** ('untərtɛːniç) *adj* **1** subject. **2** submissive.

Untertasse ('untərtasə) *nf* saucer.

Untertitel ('untərtitəl) *nm* subtitle, caption.

unterwärts ('untərvɛrts) *adv* downwards.

Unterwäsche ('untərvɛʃə) *nf* underwear.

unterwegs (untər'veːks) *adv* **1** on the way, en route. **2** bound (for).

unterweisen* (untər'vaizən) *vt* teach, instruct.

Unterwelt ('untərvelt) *nf* underworld.

unterwerfen* (untər'vɛrfən) *vt* subdue, subject. **sich unterwerfen** *vr* submit.

unterwürfig (untər'vyrfiç) *adj* submissive, servile.

unterzeichn/en (untər'tsaiçnən) *vt* sign. **—ung** *nf* signature.

unterziehen* (untər'tsiːən) *vt* subject to. **sich unterziehen** *vr* undergo.

untreu ('untrɔy) *adj* **1** unfaithful. **2** disloyal.

untrüglich (un'tryːkliç) *adj* infallible, unerring.

Untugend ('untuːgənt) *nf* vice, bad habit.

unumgänglich (unum'gɛŋliç) *adj* **1** indispensable. **2** unavoidable.

unumwunden ('unumvundən) *adj* **1** plain, blunt. **2** candid.

ununterbrochen ('ununtərbrɔxən) *adj* uninterrupted, continuous.

unverantwortlich (unfɛr'antvɔrtliç) *adj* **1** irresponsible. **2** inexcusable.

unverbesserlich (unfɛr'bɛsərliç) *adj* incorrigible.

unverbindlich ('unfɛrbintliç) *adj* **1** not binding, without obligation. **2** unkind.

unverdient ('unfɛrdiːnt) *adj* undeserved.

unverdorben ('unfɛrdɔrbən) *adj* unspoilt.
unverdrossen ('unfɛrdrɔsən) *adj* indefatigable.
unvereinbar (unfɛr'ainba:r) *adj* incompatible.
unvergeßlich (unfɛr'gɛsliç) *adj* unforgettable.
unvermeidlich (unfɛr'maitliç) *adj* unavoidable, inevitable.
unvermittelt ('unfɛrmitəlt) *adj* abrupt.
Unvermögen ('unfɛrmœ:gən) *n neu* impotence, inability.
unvermutet ('unfɛrmu:tət) *adj* unexpected.
unvernünftig ('unfɛrnynftiç) *adj* unreasonable.
unverschämt ('unfɛrʃɛ:mt) *adj* **1** insolent, cheeky. **2** shameless.
unversehens ('unfɛrze:əns) *adv* unawares.
unversehrt ('unfɛrze:rt) *adj* uninjured.
unverständlich ('unfɛrʃtɛntliç) *adj* obscure, unintelligible.
unverträglich ('unfɛrtrɛ:kliç) *adj* **1** quarrelsome. **2** incompatible.
unverzüglich (unfɛr'tsy:kliç) *adj* immediate.
unwahr ('unva:r) *adj* untrue, false, wrong. **—scheinlich** *adj* **1** improbable. **2** *inf* incredible.
unweigerlich (un'vaigərliç) *adj* definite, certain. *adv* without fail.
unweit ('unvait) *adv* not far (off). *prep* near.
Unwetter ('unvɛtər) *n neu* storm, stormy weather.
unwichtig ('unviçtiç) *adj* unimportant.
unwiderruflich (unvi:dər'ru:fliç) *adj* irrevocable.
unwiderstehlich (unvi:dər'ʃte:liç) *adj* irresistible.
unwillig ('unviliç) *adj* indignant.
unwillkürlich ('unvilky:rliç) *adj* involuntary, instinctive.
unwirksam ('unvi:rkza:m) *adj* ineffective.
unwissen/d ('unvisənt) *adj* ignorant. **—heit** *nf* ignorance.
unwürdig ('unvyrdiç) *adj* unworthy.
Unzahl ('untsa:l) *nf* great or countless number. **¨—bar** (un'tsɛ:lba:r) *adj also* **¨—ig** (un'tsɛ:liç) innumerable, countless.
Unze ('untsə) *nf* **-n** ounce.
unzeitgemäß ('untsaitgəmɛ:s) *adj* inopportune.
unzerbrechlich (untsɛr'brɛçliç) *adj* unbreakable.
unzertrennlich (untsɛr'trɛnliç) *adj* inseparable.
unziemlich ('untsi:mliç) *adj* unseemly.
Unzucht ('untsuxt) *nf* indecent act, sexual offence.
unzufrieden ('untsufri:dən) *adj* dissatisfied.
unzugänglich ('untsu:gɛŋliç) *adj* inaccessible.
unzulänglich ('untsu:lɛŋliç) *adj* inadequate.
unzulässig ('untsu:lɛsiç) *adj* inadmissible.
üppig ('ypiç) *adj* **1** abundant, plentiful. **2** well-developed. **3** voluptuous. **4** presumptuous, cocky. **—keit** *nf* **1** abundance. **2** voluptuousness. **3** presumption.
uralt ('u:ralt) *adj* **1** very old.

2 prehistoric. **3** primeval.
Uran (u'raːn) *n neu* uranium.
Uraufführung ('uːrauffyːruŋ) *nf* first night, premiere.
urbar ('uːrbaːr) *adj* arable.
Ureinwohner ('uːrainvoːnər) *nm pl* aborigines.
Ureltern ('uːrɛltərn) *n pl* ancestors.
Urgeschichte ('uːrgəʃiçtə) *nf* earliest history, earliest times.
Urheber ('uːrheːbər) *nm* — author, originator.
Urin (u'riːn) *nm* urine.
Urkund/e ('uːrkundə) *nf* **-n** document, deed. **—lich** ('uːrkuntliç) *adj* documentary.
Urlaub ('uːrlaup) *nm* **-e** holidays, leave.
Urmensch ('uːrmɛnʃ) *nm* primitive man.
Urne ('urnə) *nf* **-n** urn.
urplötzlich ('uːrplœtsliç) *adj* sudden, abrupt.
Ursache ('uːrzaxə) *nf* cause, reason.
Ursprung ('uːrʃpruŋ) *nm* origin, source, beginning. **¨—lich** ('uːrʃpryŋliç) *adj* original, primary.
Urteil ('urtail) *n neu* **1** judgment. **2** opinion. **—en** *vi* judge.
Urwald ('uːrvalt) *nm* primeval or virgin forest, jungle.
Urzeit ('uːrtsait) *nf* remotest antiquity, primitive times.
Utop/ie (uto'piː) *nf* **-n** Utopia. **—isch** (u'toːpiʃ) *adj* Utopian.

V

vag (vaːk) *adj also* **vage** ('vaːgə) vague.
Vagabund (vaga'bunt) *nm* **-en** vagabond, tramp.
vakant (va'kant) *adj* vacant.
Vakuum ('vaːkuum) *n neu* **-kua** vacuum.
Valuta (va'luːtə) *nf* **-ten** **1** rate of exchange. **2** currency. **3** value.
Vanille (va'niljə) *nf* vanilla.
Variation (variatsi'oːn) *nf* **-en** variation.
Vase ('vaːzə) *nf* **-n** vase.
Vater ('faːtər) *nm* **¨—** father. **—land** *n neu* native country. **—ländisch** ('faːtərlɛndiʃ) *adj* national, patriotic. **¨—lich** ('fɛːtərliç) *adj* fatherly. **—unser** (faːtər'unzər) *n neu* Lord's Prayer.
Vegetar/ier (vege'taːriər) *nm* — vegetarian. **—isch** *adj* vegetarian.
Veilchen ('failçən) *n neu* — violet.
Vene ('veːnə) *nf* **-n** vein.
Venedig (ve'neːdiç) *n neu* Venice.
Ventil (vɛn'tiːl) *n neu* **-e** valve.
verabred/en (fɛr'apreːdən) *vt* agree (upon), fix. **sich verabreden** *vr* make an appointment. **—ung** *nf* **-en** **1** agreement. **2** appointment.
verabschieden (fɛr'apʃiːdən) *vt* **1** dismiss. **2** pass (laws). **sich verabschieden** *vr* take one's leave.
veracht/en (fɛr'axtən) *vt* despise. **¨—lich** (fɛr'ɛçtliç) *adj* **1** contemptuous, scornful. **2** contemptible, despicable.
verallgemeiner/n (fɛralgə'mainərn) *vt* generalize. **—ung** *nf* **-en** generalization.

veralten (fɛr'altən) *vi* become obsolete or out-of-date.

veränder/lich (fɛr'ɛndərliç) *adj* changeable, variable. **—n** *vt* change, alter.

veranlag/t (fɛr'anlaːkt) *adj* talented. **—ung** (fɛr'anlaːguŋ) *nf* **-en 1** aptitude, talent. **2** assessment.

veranlassen (fɛr'anlasən) *vt* give rise to.

veranschaulichen (fɛr'anʃauliçən) *vt* **1** make clear. **2** illustrate.

veranstalt/en (fɛr'anʃtaltən) *vt* arrange, organize. **—ung** *nf* **-en 1** arrangement. **2** entertainment, show. **3** *sport* event.

verantwort/en (fɛr'antvɔrtən) *vt* answer for. **—lich** *adj* responsible. **—ung** *nf* **-en** responsibility.

verarbeiten (fɛr'arbaitən) *vt* work, process.

verargen (fɛr'argən) *vt* blame. **jemandem etwas verargen** blame someone for something.

verärgern (fɛr'ɛrgərn) *vt* annoy, vex.

veräußer/n (fɛr'ɔysərn) *vt* sell, dispose of. **—ung** *nf* **-en 1** sale. **2** transfer.

Verb (vɛrp) *n neu* **-en** verb.

Verband (fɛr'bant) *nm* **¨-e 1** bandage, dressing. **2** association, union.

verbannen (fɛr'banən) *vt* banish.

verbergen* (fɛr'bɛrgən) *vt* hide, conceal.

verbessern (fɛr'bɛsərn) *vt* **1** improve. **2** correct.

sich verbeugen (fɛr'bɔygən) *vr* bow.

verbieten* (fɛr'biːtən) *vt* forbid, prohibit.

verbilligen (fɛr'biligən) *vt* **1** cheapen. **2** reduce (the price of).

verbind/en* (fɛr'bindən) *vt* **1** bandage. **2** bind, join. **—lich** (fɛr'bintliç) *adj* **1** obligatory, binding. **2** obliging. **—ung** (fɛr'binduŋ) *nf* **-en 1** union. **2** bond. **3** connection. **4** relation.

verbissen (fɛr'bisən) *adj* grim, dogged.

verbittern (fɛr'bitərn) *vt* embitter.

verblassen (fɛr'blasən) *vi* grow pale, fade.

Verbleib (fɛr'blaip) *nm* whereabouts. **—en*** (fɛr'blaibən) *vi* **1** remain. **2** persist, stick (to).

verblenden (fɛr'blɛndən) *vt* **1** delude. **2** dazzle. **3** screen. **4** *arch* face.

verblüffen (fɛr'blyfən) *vt* **1** amaze, astonish. **2** confuse, bewilder.

verbluten (fɛr'bluːtən) *vi* bleed to death.

verbohrt (fɛr'boːrt) *adj* stubborn.

verborgen (fer'bɔrgən) *adj* hidden, secret.

Verbot (fɛr'boːt) *n neu* **-e** prohibition. **—en** *adj* forbidden.

Verbrauch (fɛr'braux) *nm* consumption, use. **—en** *vt* **1** consume. **2** wear out. **—er** *nm* — consumer, user.

verbrech/en* (fɛr'brɛçən) *vt* commit (a crime). *n neu* — crime. **—er** *nm* — criminal. **—erisch** *adj* criminal.

verbreiten (fɛr'braitən) *vt* spread.

verbrennen* (fɛr'brɛnən) *vt* **1**

burn (up). **2** cremate. *vi* burn to death.
verbringen* (fɛr'briŋən) *vt* spend (time).
sich verbrüdern (fɛr'bryːdərn) *vr* fraternize.
Verbum ('vɛrbum) *n neu* **-ben** verb.
verbünd/en (fɛr'byndən) *vt* ally. **sich verbünden** *vr* ally oneself. **—ete(r)** *nm* ally, confederate.
Verdacht (fɛr'daxt) *nm* **-e** suspicion, distrust. **¨—ig** (fɛr 'dɛçtiç) *adj* **1** suspicious. **2** suspect. **¨—igen** (fɛr'dɛçtigən) *vt* suspect.
verdamm/en (fɛr'damən) *vt* condemn, damn. **—nis** *nf* damnation.
verdampfen (fɛr'dampfən) *vi* evaporate.
verdanken (fɛr'daŋkən) *vt* be indebted for, owe.
verdauen (fɛr'dauən) *vt* digest.
Verdeck (fɛr'dɛk) *n neu* **-e** **1** *naut* deck. **2** *mot* hood, top. **3** covering. **—en** *vt* cover (up).
Verderb (fɛr'dɛrp) *nm* ruin, destruction. **—en*** (fɛr'dɛrbən) *vt* spoil, corrupt. *vi* spoil, decay. **—lich** (fɛr'dɛrpliç) *adj* **1** perishable. **2** contaminating. **—nis** (fɛr'dɛrpnis) *nf* corruption.
verdeutlichen (fɛr'dɔytliçən) *vt* make clear, explain.
verdichten (fɛr'diçtən) *vt* condense, compress.
verdicken (fɛr'dikən) *vt* thicken.
verdien/en (fɛr'diːnən) *vt* **1** deserve. **2** earn. **—st** *n neu* **-e** merit. *nm* **-e** earnings, gain.
verdingen (fɛr'diŋən) *vt* hire out.
verdoppeln (fɛr'dɔpəln) *vt* double.
verdorben (fɛr'dɔrbən) *adj* spoilt, damaged.
verdrängen (fɛr'drɛŋən) *vt* **1** thrust aside. **2** displace. **3** supplant. **4** suppress, repress.
verdrehen (fɛr'dreːən) *vt* **1** distort. **2** twist.
verdrieß/en* (fɛr'driːsən) *vt* annoy, vex. **—lich** *adj* **1** annoyed. **2** sulky. **3** annoying.
verdrossen (fɛr'drɔsən) *adj* **1** sulky. **2** annoyed.
verdummen (fɛr'dumən) *vt* make stupid, stupefy. *vi* become stupid.
verdunkeln (fɛr'duŋkəln) *vt* **1** darken, black out. **2** overshadow.
veredeln (fɛr'eːdəln) *vt* **1** ennoble. **2** improve. **3** *bot* graft.
verehr/en (fɛr'eːrən) *vt* honour, venerate, worship. **—ung** *nf* worship, veneration.
Verein (fɛr'ain) *nm* **-e** **1** association, union. **2** society, club. **—bar** *adj* consistent, compatible. **—baren** *vt* agree upon, arrange. **—barung** *nf* **-en** agreement. **—fachen** *vt* simplify. **—igen** *vt also* **—en** unite, join, combine. **die Vereinigten Staaten** the United States. **die Vereinten Nationen** the United Nations. **—igung** *nf* **-en** union, alliance.
vereiteln (fɛr'aitəln) *vt* frustrate, thwart.
vererben (fɛr'ɛrbən) *vt* **1** bequeath. **2** transmit. **sich vererben** *vr* be hereditary.

verewigen (fɛr'eːvigən) *vt* immortalize.

verfahren* (fɛr'faːrən) *vi* act, deal. *vt* muddle. **sich verfahren** *vr* lose one's way. *~adj* bungled. *n neu* — **1** method. **2** process. **3** *law* proceedings.

Verfall (fɛr'fal) *nm* **1** decay, decline. **2** *comm* maturity. **3** *law* forfeiture. **—en*** *vi* **1** decay, decline. **2** *comm* mature. **3** be forfeited.

verfälschen (fɛr'fɛlʃən) *vt* **1** falsify. **2** adulterate.

verfass/en (fɛr'fasən) *vt* compose, write. **—er** *nm* — author. **—ung** *nf* **-en 1** *pol* constitution. **2** disposition, frame of mind. **—ungsgemäß** *adj also* **—ungsmäßig** constitutional. **—ungswidrig** *adj* unconstitutional.

verfechten (fɛr'fɛçtən) *vt* **1** defend. **2** advocate.

verfehl/en (fɛr'feːlən) *vt* **1** miss. **2** fail (to do). **—t** *adj* unsuccessful.

verfeinern (fɛr'fainərn) *vt* **1** refine. **2** improve.

verfluchen (fɛr'fluːxən) *vt* curse.

verfolg/en (fɛr'fɔlgən) *vt* **1** pursue. **2** follow up. **3** persecute. **4** *law* prosecute. **—er** *nm* — **1** pursuer. **2** persecutor. **—ung** *nf* **-en 1** pursuit. **2** persecution. **3** *law* prosecution.

verfüg/en (fɛr'fyːgən) *vi* **1** have at one's disposal. **2** dispose (of). *vt* order. **—ung** *nf* **-en 1** disposal. **2** order, instruction.

verführ/en (fɛr'fyːrən) *vt* **1** lead astray. **2** seduce. **3** tempt, lure. **—er** *nf* — **1** seducer. **2** tempter. **—erisch** *adj* seductive, alluring. **—ung** *nf* **1** seduction. **2** temptation.

vergang/en (fɛr'gaŋən) *adj* past, gone. **—enheit** *nf* past. **¨—lich** (fɛr'gɛŋliç) *adj* transitory, transient.

Vergaser (fɛr'gaːzər) *nm* — carburettor.

vergaß (fɛr'gaːs) *v* see **vergessen.**

vergeb/en* (fɛr'geːbən) *vt* **1** forgive. **2** give away. **—ens** *adv* in vain. **—lich** (fɛr'geːpliç) *adj* **1** fruitless. **2** futile.

vergegenwärtigen (fɛrgeːgən'vɛrtigən) *vt* **1** bring to mind. **2** represent, imagine. **sich vergegenwärtigen** *vr* imagine, picture.

vergehen* (fɛr'geːən) *vi* **1** pass or fade (away). **2** cease. **3** perish. **sich vergehen** *vr* commit an offence. *n neu* — offence.

vergelten* (fɛr'gɛltən) *vt* repay, pay back.

vergessen* (fɛr'gɛsən) *vt* forget.

vergeuden (fɛr'gɔydən) *vt* squander.

vergewaltig/en (fɛrgə'valtigən) *vt* **1** rape. **2** violate. **—ung** *nf* **-en 1** rape. **2** violence.

sich vergewissern (fɛrgə'visərn) *vr* ascertain.

vergießen* (fɛr'giːsən) *vt* **1** shed (blood or tears). **2** spill.

vergiften (fɛr'giftən) *vt* poison.

Vergißmeinnicht (fɛr'gismainniçt) *n neu* **-e** forget-me-not.

vergißt (fɛr'gist) *v* see **vergessen.**

verglasen (fɛr'glaːzən) *vt* glaze.

Vergleich (fɛr'glaiç) *nm* **-e 1** comparison. **2** *law* arrangement, compromise. **—en*** *vt* **1** compare. **2** settle.

vergnüg/en (fɛr'gny:gən) *vt* entertain, amuse. **sich vergnügen** *vr* enjoy or amuse onself. *~n neu* — pleasure, enjoyment.

vergöttern (fɛr'gœtərn) *vt* **1** deify. **2** idolize.

vergraben* (fɛr'gra:bən) *vt* bury.

vergriffen (fɛr'grifən) *adj* **1** sold out. **2** out of print.

vergrößern (fɛr'grœ:sərn) *vt* enlarge, magnify.

Vergünstigung (fɛr'gynstiguŋ) *nf* **-en** concession, privilege.

vergüten (fɛr'gy:tən) *vt* compensate for, reimburse, make good.

verhaften (fɛr'haftən) *vt* arrest.

verhalt/en* (fɛr'haltən) *vt* keep back, check, suppress. **sich verhalten** *vr* behave. *~n neu* behaviour, conduct. **¨—nis** (fɛr 'hɛltnis) *n neu* **-se 1** relation(ship). **2** proportion, ratio. **¨—nismäßig** (fɛr 'hɛltnismɛ:siç) *adj* proportional. *adv* relatively.

verhand/eln (fɛr'handəln) *vi* **1** negotiate. **2** deal (with). *vt* **1** dispose of, sell. **2** discuss. **3** *law* plead. **—lung** (fɛr'handluŋ) *nf* **1** negotiation. **2** discussion.

verhäng/en (fɛr'hɛŋən) *vt* **1** impose, inflict. **2** drape. **3** cover. **—nis** *n neu* **-se** destiny, fate.

verhaßt (fɛr'hast) *adj* **1** hated, despised. **2** hateful, despicable.

Verhau (fɛr'hau) *nm,neu* **-e** entanglement. **—en** *vt inf* thrash.

verheimlichen (fɛr'haimliçən) *vt* conceal, keep secret.

verheiraten (fɛr'haira:tən) *vt* marry. **sich verheiraten** *vr* marry, get married.

verheißen* (fɛr'haisən) *vt* promise.

verhelfen* (fɛr'hɛlfən) *vi* **jemandem zu etwas verhelfen** help someone in (doing) something.

verherrlichen (fɛr'hɛrliçən) *vt* glorify.

verhindern (fɛr'hindərn) *vt* **1** prevent. **2** hamper.

Verhör (fɛr'hœ:r) *n neu* **-e 1** examination. **2** interrogation. **—en** *vt* **1** examine. **2** question.

verhungern (fɛr'huŋərn) *vi* die of hunger, starve.

verhüten (fɛr'hy:tən) *vt* avert, prevent.

sich verirren (fɛr'irən) *vr* lose one's way.

verjüngen (fɛr'jyŋən) *vt* rejuvenate.

Verkauf (fɛr'kauf) *nm* **¨-e** sale. **—en** *vt* sell. **¨—er** (fɛr 'kɔyfər) *nm* — **1** retailer. **2** salesman, shop assistant. **¨—erin** *nf* **-nen** saleswoman, shop assistant.

Verkehr (fɛr'ke:r) *nm* **1** traffic. **2** communication, intercourse. **—en** *vt* **1** reverse. **2** pervert. *vi* **1** associate (with). **2** (of a vehicle or transport service) run, operate. **—sampel** *nf* traffic light. **—t** *adj* **1** wrong. **2** inverted, reversed.

verkennen* (fɛr'kɛnən) *vt* **1** misjudge. **2** fail to recognize.

verklagen (fɛr'kla:gən) *vt* **1** accuse. **2** sue.
verklären (fɛr'klɛ:rən) *vt* transfigure.
verkleiden (fɛr'klaidən) *vt* **1** disguise. **2** coat, face.
verkleinern (fɛr'klainərn) *vt* **1** diminish, reduce. **2** belittle.
verknüpfen (fɛr'knypfən) *vt* connect.
verkommen* (fɛr'kɔmən) *vi* **1** decay. **2** decline. *adj* **1** decayed. **2** depraved.
verkörpern (fɛr'kœrpərn) *vt* **1** embody. **2** represent.
verkrüppeln (fɛr'krypəln) *vt* cripple.
verkündig/en (fɛr'kyndigən) *vt* proclaim, announce. **—ung** *nf* **-en** proclamation or announcement.
verkürz/en (fɛr'kyrtsən) *vt* shorten. **—ung** *nf* **-en 1** reduction. **2** abbreviation.
verladen* (fɛr'la:dən) *vt* load, ship.
Verlag (fɛr'la:k) *nm* **-e** publishing house.
verlangen (fɛr'laŋən) *vt* **1** demand. **2** require. **verlangen nach** long for. *~n neu* **— 1** desire. **2** demand.
verlängern (fɛr'lɛŋərn) *vt* **1** lengthen. **2** prolong.
verlangsamen (fɛr'laŋza:mən) *vt* slow down.
Verlaß (fɛr'las) *nm* **1** reliance. **2** dependability. **¨—lich** (fɛr 'lɛsliç) *adj* reliable.
verlassen* (fɛr'lasən) *vt* **1** desert. **2** relinquish. **sich verlassen** *vr* rely.
Verlauf (fɛr'lauf) *nm* **1** course. **2** development. **—en*** *vi* **1** elapse. **2** develop. *adj* lost. **sich —en** *vr* lose one's way.
verlautbaren (fɛr'lautba:rən) *vt* divulge.
verleg/en (fɛr'le:gən) *vt* **1** misplace. **2** publish. **3** shift. **4** bar. *adj* embarrassed, confused. **—enheit** *nf* **-en** embarrassment, confusion. **—er** *nm* **—** publisher.
verleihen* (fɛr'laiən) *vt* **1** lend. **2** bestow.
verleiten (fɛr'laitən) *vt* **1** mislead. **2** seduce. **3** induce.
verlernen (fɛr'lɛrnən) *vt* forget.
verletzen (fɛr'lɛtsən) *vt* **1** wound. **2** violate.
verleugnen (fɛr'lɔygnən) *vt* **1** deny. **2** disavow. **3** renounce.
verleumd/en (fɛr'lɔymdən) *vt* slander. **—ung** *nf* **-en** slander, libel.
sich verlieben (fɛr'li:bən) *vr* fall in love.
verlieren* (fɛr'li:rən) *vt,vi* lose. **sich verlieren** *vr* **1** lose oneself or one's way. **2** disappear.
Verlob/te (fɛr'lo:ptə) *nf* fiancée. **—te(r)** *nm* fiancé. **—ung** (fɛr'lo:buŋ) *nf* **-en** engagement.
verlocken (fɛr'lɔkən) *vt* entice, tempt.
verlogen (fɛr'lo:gən) *adj* untruthful.
verlor (fɛr'lɔ:r) *v* see **verlieren.**
verloren (fɛr'lo:rən) *v* see **verlieren.** *adj* lost.
Verlust (fɛr'lust) *nm* **-e 1** loss. **2** damage. **3** waste.
vermach/en (fɛr'maxən) *vt* bequeath. **¨—tnis** (fɛr'mɛçtnis) *n neu* **-se 1** legacy. **2** bequest.
vermähl/en (fɛr'mɛ:lən) *vt*

marry. **sich vermählen** *vr* get married. **—ung** *nf* **-en** marriage.

vermehren (fɛr'meːrən) *vt* increase, multiply.

vermeid/en* (fɛr'maidən) avoid, elude. **—lich** (fɛr 'maitliç) *adj* avoidable.

vermeintlich (fɛr'maintliç) *adj* supposed.

Vermerk (fɛr'mɛrk) *nm* **-e** note, notice. **—en** *vt* note (down).

vermess/en* (fɛr'mɛsən) *vt* **1** measure. **2** survey. **sich vermessen** *vr* dare. *~adj* bold, insolent. **—ung** *nf* **-en** **1** measuring. **2** survey.

vermiet/en (fɛr'miːtən) *vt* let, lease. **—er** *nm* — landlord.

vermindern (fɛr'mindərn) *vt* diminish, decrease.

vermischen (fɛr'miʃən) *vt* mix, blend.

vermissen (fɛr'misən) *vt* miss.

vermitt/eln (fɛr'mitəln) *vi,vt* **1** mediate. **2** negotiate. *vt* obtain. **—lung** (fɛr'mitluŋ) *nf* **-en** **1** mediation. **2** intervention.

vermög/e (fɛr'mœːgə) *prep* by virtue of. **—en*** *vt* be able. *n neu* **1** wealth, assets. **2** ability, power.

vermut/en (fɛr'muːtən) *vt* suppose, presume. **—lich** *adj* likely, presumable. **—ung** *nf* **-en** **1** conjecture. **2** suspicion.

vernachlässigen (fɛr'naːxlɛsigən) *vt* neglect.

vernehmen* (fɛr'neːmən) *vt* **1** perceive, hear. **2** learn. **3** interrogate.

verneinen (fɛr'nainən) *vt* deny.

vernicht/en (fɛr'niçtən) *vt* annihilate, destroy. **—ung** *nf* annihilation, destruction.

vernieten (fɛr'niːtən) *vt* rivet.

Vernunft (fɛr'nunft) *nf* reason, (common) sense. **jemandem zur Vernunft bringen** bring someone to his senses. **¨—ig** (fɛr'nynftiç) *adj* **1** sensible, reasonable. **2** rational.

veröden (fɛr'œːdən) *vt* lay waste. *vi* become desolate.

veröffentlichen (fɛr'œfəntliçən) *vt* publish.

verpachten (fɛr'paxtən) *vt* **1** farm (out). **2** lease.

verpacken (fɛr'pakən) *vt* **1** pack (up or away). **2** wrap up.

verpassen (fɛr'pasən) *vt* **1** miss (a train, etc.). **2** fit (clothes).

verpfänden (fɛr'pfɛndən) *vt* pawn, pledge.

verpfleg/en (fɛr'pfleːgən) *vt* cater for, feed. **—ung** *nf* **1** catering. **2** board.

verpflicht/en (fɛr'pfliçtən) *vt* **1** oblige. **2** engage. **—ung** *nf* **-en** commitment, obligation.

verplempern (fɛr'plɛmpərn) *vt inf* fritter away.

verpönt (fɛr'pœːnt) *adj* taboo.

verputzen (fɛr'putsən) *vt* **1** plaster. **2** *inf* squander.

verquicken (fɛr'kvikən) *vt* **1** amalgamate. **2** mix up.

Verrat (fɛr'raːt) *nm* **1** treason. **2** betrayal. **—en*** *vt* betray. **¨—er** (fɛr'rɛːtər) *nm* — traitor. **¨—erisch** (fɛr'rɛːtəriʃ) *adj* treacherous.

verrechnen (fɛr'rɛçnən) *vt* reckon up. **sich verrechnen** *vr* miscalculate.

verrenk/en (fɛr'rɛŋkən) *vt med*

1 sprain. **2** dislocate. **—ung** *nf* **-en 1** sprain. **2** dislocation.
verrichten (fɛr'riçtən) *vt* perform, execute.
verringern (fɛr'riŋərn) *vt* diminish, lessen.
verrück/en (fɛr'rykən) *vt* shift, move. **—t** *adj* mad, crazy.
Verruf (fɛr'ru:f) *nm* ill repute, disrepute.
Vers (fɛrs) *nm* **-e** verse, stanza.
versag/en (fɛr'za:gən) *vi* fail. *vt* refuse. **—er** *nm* — failure.
versamm/eln (fɛr'zaməln) *vt* assemble, collect. **—lung** (fɛr 'zamluŋ) *nf* assembly, meeting.
Versand (fɛr'zant) *nm* dispatch.
versäum/en (fɛr'zɔymən) *vt* **1** neglect, fail (to). **2** miss (a train, etc.). **—nis** *nf,neu* **-se 1** neglect, omission. **2** delay.
verschaffen (fɛr'ʃafən) *vt* procure, provide.
verschämt (fɛr'ʃɛ:mt) *adj* **1** bashful, shy. **2** ashamed.
verschanzen (fɛr'ʃantsən) *vt* entrench.
verschärfen (fɛr'ʃɛrfən) *vt* **1** sharpen. **2** intensify.
verschieb/en* (fɛr'ʃi:bən) *vt* **1** postpone. **2** displace. **3** sell illegally. **—ung** *nf* **-en 1** postponement. **2** displacement.
verschieden (fɛr'ʃi:dən) *adj* **1** different. **2** *pl* several, various. **—es** *n neu* miscellany, variety (of things). **—heit** *nf* **-en 1** difference. **2** variety.
verschiffen (fɛr'ʃifən) *vt* ship.
verschimmeln (fɛr'ʃiməln) *vi* grow mouldy.
verschlafen* (fɛr'ʃla:fən) *vt* sleep through. *vi* oversleep.
Verschlag (fɛr'ʃla:k) *nm* **1** partition. **2** crate, box. **3** compartment. **—en*** (fɛr'ʃla:gən) *vt* **1** partition. **2** board up. *adj* cunning.
verschlechtern (fɛr'ʃlɛçtərn) *vt* make worse. **sich verschlechtern** *vr* deteriorate.
verschleiern (fɛr'ʃlaiərn) *vt* veil.
Verschleiß (fɛr'ʃlais) *nm* wear (and tear).
verschleudern (fɛr'ʃlɔydərn) *vt* **1** squander. **2** sell extremely cheaply or at a loss.
verschließen* (fɛr'ʃli:sən) *vt* **1** shut, close. **2** lock. **3** seal (a letter).
verschlimmern (fɛr'ʃlimərn) *vt* make worse. *vi* get worse.
verschlingen* (fɛr'ʃliŋən) *vt* **1** devour. **2** twist.
verschlucken (fɛr'ʃlukən) *vt* swallow.
Verschluß (fɛr'ʃlus) *nm* **1** fastening. **2** seal. **3** stopper.
verschmähen (fɛr'ʃmɛ:ən) *vt* disdain, despise.
verschmitzt (fɛr'ʃmitst) *adj* crafty, sly.
verschollen (fɛr'ʃɔlən) *adj* (of a person) missing.
verschönern (fɛr'ʃœ:nərn) *vt* **1** adorn, embellish. **2** improve.
verschränken (fɛr'ʃrɛŋkən) *vt* cross, fold.
verschreiben* (fɛr'ʃraibən) *vt* **1** prescribe. **2** order.
verschulden (fɛr'ʃuldən) *vt* be guilty of. *n neu* — **1** wrong. **2** fault.
verschweigen* (fɛr'ʃvaigən) *vt* keep secret.
verschwend/en (fɛr'ʃvɛndən) *vt* squander, waste. **—erisch** *adj* wasteful, extravagant.

verschwiegen (fɛr'ʃviːgən) *adj* **1** discreet. **2** reserved, reticent. **—heit** *nf* **1** discretion. **2** reticence.
verschwinden* (fɛr'ʃvindən) *vi* disappear. *n neu* — disappearance.
verschwommen (fɛr'ʃvɔmən) *adj* vague, blurred.
verschwör/en (fɛr'ʃvœːrən) *vt* renounce, forswear. **sich verschwören** *vr* conspire, plot. **—er** *nm* — conspirator. **—ung** *nf* **-en** conspiracy, plot.
versehen* (fɛr'zeːən) *vt* **1** furnish, provide, equip. **2** overlook. **3** fulfil, perform. **sich versehen** *vr* err, make a mistake. *~n neu* — mistake, error. **—tlich** (fɛr'zeːəntliç) *adv* by mistake, mistakenly.
versenden* (fɛr'zɛndən) *vt* **1** send. **2** ship.
versengen (fɛr'zɛŋən) *vt* singe, scorch.
versenk/en (fɛr'zɛŋkən) *vt* **1** submerge, sink, immerse. **2** countersink. **—ung** *nf* **-en** sinking, submersion, immersion.
versessen (fɛr'zɛsən) *adj* **auf etwas versessen sein 1** be bent on something. **2** be crazy about something
versetzen (fɛr'zɛtsən) *vt* **1** (re)move, transfer. **2** displace. **3** pawn.
verseuchen (fɛr'zɔyçən) *vt* infect, contaminate.
versicher/n (fɛr'ziçərn) *vt* **1** insure. **2** affirm. **sich versichern** *vr* make sure of. **—ung** *nf* **-en 1** insurance. **2** assurance. **3** confirmation. **—ungsstatistiker** *nm* actuary.
versiegeln (fɛr'ziːgəln) *vt* seal (up).
versöhnen (fɛr'zœːnən) *vt* reconcile.
versorg/en (fɛr'zɔrgən) *vt* **1** provide, supply. **2** look after. **—ung** *nf* **-en 1** maintenance. **2** supply.
verspät/en (fɛr'ʃpɛːtən) *vt* delay. **sich verspäten** *vr* be late. **—ung** *nf* **-en** delay.
verspielen (fɛr'ʃpiːlən) *vt* gamble away.
verspotten (fɛr'ʃpɔtən) *vt* mock, deride.
versprech/en* (fɛr'ʃprɛçən) *vt* promise. *n neu* — promise. **—ung** *nf* **-en** promise.
versprengen (fɛr'ʃprɛŋən) *vt* disperse.
verstaatlichen (fɛr'ʃtaːtliçən) *vt* nationalize.
Verstand (fɛr'ʃtant) *nm* **1** reason. **2** understanding. **3** intellect. **¨—igen** (fɛr'ʃtɛndigən) *vt* inform. **sich ¨—igen** *vr* **1** come to an understanding. **2** make oneself understood. **¨—igung** (fɛr'ʃtɛndiguŋ) *nf* **-en 1** agreement. **2** information. **¨—lich** (fɛr'ʃtɛntliç) *adj* intelligible, clear. **¨—nis** (fɛr'ʃtɛntnis) *n neu* **1** comprehension. **2** appreciation.
verstärk/en (fɛr'ʃtɛrkən) *vt* strengthen. **—er** *nm* — amplifier. **—ung** *nf* **-en 1** reinforcement(s). **2** strengthening. **3** amplification.
verstauchen (fɛr'ʃtauxən) *vt* sprain.
Versteck (fɛr'ʃtɛk) *n neu* **-e** hiding-place. **—en** *vt* hide.

verstehen* (fɛr'ʃteːən) *vt* understand. **sich verstehen** *vr* **1** agree. **2** get on (with someone).
versteiger/n (fɛr'ʃtaigərn) *vt* auction, sell by auction. **—ung** *nf* **-en** auction.
versteinern (fɛr'ʃtainərn) *vt* petrify.
verstell/bar (fɛr'ʃtɛlbaːr) *adj* adjustable. **—en** *vt* **1** adjust. **2** shift. **3** disguise. **4** pretend, feign. **5** misplace. **—ung** *nf* **1** pretence. **2** disguise. **3** displacement. **4** adjustment.
verstimmt (fɛr'ʃtimt) *adj* **1** bad-tempered, annoyed. **2** out of tune.
verstockt (fɛr'ʃtɔkt) *adj* **1** stubborn. **2** callous.
verstohlen (fɛr'ʃtoːlən) *adj* furtive, stealthy.
Verstoß (fɛr'ʃtɔs) *nm* **1** offence. **2** error. **—en*** *vt* **1** repudiate. **2** reject. *vi* **1** offend. **2** violate.
verstricken (fɛr'ʃtrikən) *vt* entangle.
verstümmeln (fɛr'ʃtyməln) *vt* mutilate.
Versuch (fɛr'zuːx) *nm* **-e** **1** attempt, trial. **2** experiment. **—en** *vt* **1** try, test. **2** tempt. **—ung** *nf* **-en** temptation.
vertagen (fɛr'taːgən) *vt* adjourn, postpone.
vertauschen (fɛr'tauʃən) *vt* **1** exchange. **2** mistake for.
verteidig/en (fɛr'taidigən) *vt* defend. **—er** *nm* — defender, advocate. **—ung** *nf* **-en** defence.
verteil/en (fɛr'tailən) *vt* **1** distribute. **2** divide. **—ung** *nf* distribution, allocation.
vertiefen (fɛr'tiːfən) *vt* deepen. **sich vertiefen** *vr* be absorbed (in).
vertikal (vɛrti'kaːl) *adj* vertical.
vertilgen (fɛr'tilgən) *vt* exterminate, destroy.
Vertrag (fɛr'traːk) *nm* **¨-e** **1** treaty. **2** agreement, contract. **—lich** *adj* stipulated, agreed.
vertrag/en* (fɛr'traːgən) *vt* **1** endure, stand, bear. **2** carry away. **sich vertragen** *vr* **1** get on (with someone). **2** agree. **¨—lich** (fɛr'trɛːkliç) *adj* **1** compatible. **2** sociable, good-natured.
vertrau/en (fɛr'trauən) *vi* trust, have confidence in. *n neu* confidence, trust. **—ensvoll** *adj* trustful. **—ensvotum** *n neu* vote of confidence. **—enswürdig** *adj* trustworthy. **—lich** *adj* **1** confidential. **2** intimate. **—t** *adj* intimate, familiar.
vertreiben* (fɛr'traibən) *vt* **1** expel, banish. **2** sell.
vertret/en* (fɛr'treːtən) *vt* represent. **—er** *nm* — **1** representative. **2** advocate.
vertrösten (fɛr'trœːstən) *vt* **1** console. **2** put off.
vertun* (fɛr'tuːn) *vt* spend, squander.
vertuschen (fɛr'tuʃən) *vt* hush up.
verunglimpfen (fɛr'unglimpfən) *vt* disparage, slander.
verunglücken (fɛr'unglykən) *vi* **1** meet with or have an accident. **2** perish.
verursachen (fɛr'uːrzaxən) *vt* cause.

verurteilen (fɛr'uːrtailən) *vt* condemn, sentence.
vervielfältigen (fɛr'fiːlfɛltigən) *vt* **1** reproduce. **2** multiply.
vervollkommnen (fɛr'fɔlkɔmnən) *vt* perfect.
vervollständigen (fɛr'fɔlʃtɛndigən) *vt* complete.
verwachsen* (fɛr'vaksən) *vi* **1** grow out of (clothes). **2** grow deformed. **3** heal, close up. **4** become involved, be closely connected (with). *adj* **1** deformed, stunted. **2** healed. **3** overgrown.
verwahren (fɛr'vaːrən) *vt* keep (safe).
verwahrlost (fɛr'vaːrloːst) *adj* **1** depraved. **2** neglected, unkempt.
verwalt/en (fɛr'valtən) *vt* **1** administer, administrate. **2** supervise, control. **—er** *nm* — **1** administrator, controller. **2** steward. **—ung** *nf* **—en** administration. **—ungsbeamte(r)** *nm* Civil Servant.
verwandt (fɛr'vant) *adj* related. **—e(r)** *nm* relative, relation. **—schaft** *nf* **-en** **1** relations. **2** relationship.
verwaschen (fɛr'vaʃən) *adj* faded.
verwechseln (fɛr'vɛksəln) *vt* mistake (for), confuse.
verwegen (fɛr'veːgən) *adj* bold.
verweichlicht (fɛr'vaiçliçt) *adj* effeminate.
verweigern (fɛr'vaigərn) *vt* refuse, deny.
verweilen (fɛr'vailən) *vi* linger, stay.
Verweis (fɛr'vais) *nm* **-e** reprimand, reproach. **—en*** (fɛr'vaizən) *vt* **1** banish, expel. **2** reprimand.
verwenden (fɛr'vɛndən) *vt* use, apply.
verwerf/en* (fɛr'vɛrfən) *vt* refuse, reject. **—lich** *adj* objectionable.
verwesen (fɛr'veːsən) *vi* decay, rot. *vt* administer.
verwickeln (fɛr'vikəln) *vt* entangle, involve.
verwirken (fɛr'virkən) *vt* **1** forfeit. **2** incur.
verwirklichen (fɛr'virkliçən) *vt* realize. *vi* be realized, materialize.
verwirren (fɛr'virən) *vt* **1** confuse. **2** entangle.
verwischen (fɛr'viʃən) *vt* **1** wipe or blot out. **2** blur.
verwöhnen (fɛr'vœːnən) *vt* spoil, pamper.
verworfen (fɛr'vɔrfən) *adj* depraved.
verworren (fɛr'vɔrən) *adj* **1** confused. **2** tangled.
verwund/en[1] (fɛr'vundən) *vt* wound, hurt. **—ete(r)** *nm* injured person, casualty.
verwunden[2] (fɛr'vundən) *adj* twisted.
verwundern (fɛr'vundərn) *vt* astonish. **sich verwundern** *vr* wonder.
verwünschen (fɛr'vynʃən) *vt* curse.
verwüsten (fɛr'vyːstən) *vt* lay waste.
verzagt (fɛr'tsaːkt) *adj* despondent, depressed.
verzaubern (fɛr'tsaubərn) *vt* enchant, bewitch.
verzehren (fɛr'tseːrən) *vt* consume.
verzeichn/en (fɛr'tsaiçnən) *vt*

catalogue, enter. **—is** *n neu* **-se 1** list, register. **2** index.
verzeih/en* (fɛr'tsaiən) *vt* forgive, pardon. **—ung** *nf* pardon. *interj* excuse me! sorry!
verzerren (fɛr'tsɛrən) *vt* distort.
Verzicht (fɛr'tsiçt) *nm* **-e** renunciation. **—en** *vi* renounce.
verzögern (fɛr'tsœːgərn) *vt* delay.
verzollen (fɛr'tsɔlən) *vt* pay duty on.
verzuckern (fɛr'tsukərn) *vt* sweeten, sugar.
verzückt (fɛr'tsykt) *adj* enraptured.
verzweif/eln (fɛr'tsvaifəln) *vi* despair. **—lung** *nf* despair, desperation.
sich verzweigen (fɛr'tsvaigən) *vr* branch out or off.
verzwickt (fɛr'tsvikt) *adj* complicated, involved, awkward.
Veterinär (veteri'nɛːr) *nm* **-e** veterinary surgeon.
Vetter ('fɛtər) *nm* **-n** (male) cousin.
Vieh (fiː) *n neu* **1** cattle. **2** beast. **—isch** *adj* **1** bestial. **2** brutal.
viel (fiːl) *adj,adv* much. *adj pl* many. **—erlei** ('fiːlərlai) *adj* of many kinds. **—fach** ('fiːlfax) *adj also* **—fältig** ('fiːlfɛltiç) manifold, multiple. **—leicht** (fiː'laiçt) *adv* perhaps, maybe, possibly. **—mal(s)** *adv* many times, frequently, often. **—mehr** (fiːl'meːr) *adv* rather. **—seitig** ('fiːlzaitiç) *adj* many-sided.
vier (fiːr) *adj,nf* four. **—eck** ('fiːrɛk) *n neu* square. **—eckig** *adj* square. **—te** *adj* fourth. **—tel** *n neu* **—** quarter, fourth. **—teljährlich** ('fiːrtəljɛːrliç) *adj* quarterly. **—telstunde** (fiːrtəl'ʃtundə) *nf* quarter of an hour.
vierzehn ('fiːrtseːn) *adj,nf* fourteen. **—te** *adj* fourteenth.
vierzig ('fiːrtsiç) *adj,nf* forty. **—ste** *adj* fortieth.
Villa ('vila) *nf* **Villen** villa.
Vio/la (vi'oːla) *nf* **-len** viola. **—line** (vio'liːnə) *nf* **-n** violin.
Visum ('viːzum) *n neu* **-sa** visa.
Vlies (fliːs) *n neu* **-e** fleece.
Vogel ('foːgəl) *nm* **¨—** bird. **—scheuche** *nf* **-en** scarecrow.
Vogesen (vo'geːzən) *n pl* Vosges.
Vokabel (vo'kaːbəl) *nf* **-n** word.
Vokal (vo'kaːl) *nm* **-e** vowel.
Volk (fɔlk) *n neu* **¨-er 1** people, folk. **2** nation, race.
Völkerbund ('fœlkərbunt) *nm* League of Nations.
Völkerkunde ('fœlkərkundə) *nf* ethnology.
Völkerrecht ('fœlkərrɛçt) *n neu* international law.
volkreich ('fɔlkraiç) *adj* populous.
Volksabstimmung ('fɔlksapʃtimuŋ) *nf* plebiscite, referendum.
volkseigen ('fɔlksaigən) *adj* nationalized.
Volkskunde ('fɔlkskundə) *nf* folklore.
Volkslied ('fɔlksliːt) *n neu* folksong.
Volksschule ('fɔlksʃuːlə) *nf* primary school.
volkstümlich ('fɔlkstyːmliç) *adj* **1** popular. **2** national.

Volkswirtschaft ('fɔlksvirtʃaft) *nf* economics.

voll (fɔl) *adj* **1** full. **2** complete. **—bringen*** (fɔl'briŋən) *vt* accomplish. **—enden** (fɔl 'ɛndən) *vt* **1** finish, end. **2** complete. **¨—ig** ('fœliç) *adv* fully, completely, totally. **—jährig** ('fɔljɛːriç) *adj* of age. **—kommen** (fɔl'kɔmən) *adj* perfect. **—macht** *nf* **1** power of attorney. **2** proxy. **—ständig** *adj* complete. **—strekken** *vt* carry out, execute, discharge. **—wertkost** ('fɔlvɛrtkɔst) *nf* health food. **—ziehen*** (fɔl'tsiːən) *vt* carry out, accomplish.

Volontär (volɔn'tɛːr) *nm* **-e** volunteer, trainee.

vom (fɔm) contraction of **von dem.**

von (fɔn) *prep* **1** of. **2** from. **3** by. **von...an** from, since. **—nöten** (fɔn'nœːtən) *adj* necessary.

vor (foːr) *prep* before, in front of. **—ab** (foːr'ap) *adv* **1** first (of all). **2** in advance.

Vorabend ('foːraːbənt) *nm* eve.

Vorahnung ('foːraːnuŋ) *nf* premonition.

voran (fo'ran) *adv* before, ahead. **—gehen*** *vi* go at the head, precede.

voraus (fo'raus) *adv* in advance, in front, ahead. **im voraus** in advance, beforehand. **—sage** *nf* prediction. **—sagen** *vt* predict, forecast. **—setzung** *nf* **-en** **1** (pre)condition, prerequisite. **2** assumption. **—sichtlich** *adj* probable.

Vorbau ('foːrbau) *nm* **-ten** **1** front structure. **2** porch.

Vorbedacht ('foːrbədaxt) *nm* forethought, premeditation.

Vorbedingung ('foːrbədiŋuŋ) *nf* condition, prerequisite.

Vorbehalt ('foːrbəhalt) *nm* **-e** **1** reservation. **2** proviso. **—en*** *vt* reserve.

vorbei (fɔr'bai) *adv* **1** by, along, past. **2** past, done, over. **—gehen*** *vi* go past, pass (by).

vorbereit/en ('foːrbəraitən) *vt* prepare. **—ung** *nf* **-en** preparation.

vorbeug/en ('foːrbɔygən) *vi* prevent. **—ung** *nf* prevention.

Vorbild ('foːrbilt) *n neu* **1** model. **2** original. **—lich** *adj* **1** model. **2** typical.

vorbringen* ('foːrbriŋən) *vt* **1** bring forward or up. **2** propose. **3** argue.

vordem (fɔr'deːm) *adv* formerly.

vorder ('fɔrdər) *adj* front, fore. **—asien** (fɔrdər'aːziən) *n neu* Near East. **—grund** *nm* foreground. **—hand** *adv* for the present.

vordring/en* ('foːrdriŋən) *vi* advance, press on or forward. **—lich** *adj* **1** urgent. **2** intrusive.

voreilig ('foːrailiç) *adj* hasty, premature.

voreingenommen ('foːraingənɔmən) *adj* biased, prejudiced.

vorenthalten* ('foːrɛnthaltən) *vt* withhold.

vorerst ('foːreːrst) *adv* **1** first of all. **2** for the present.

vorerwähnt ('foːrɛrvɛːnt) *adj* above-mentioned, aforesaid.
Vorfahr ('foːrfaːr) *nm* **-en** ancestor.
Vorfahrt ('foːrfaːrt) *nf also* **Vorfahrt(s)recht** *n neu mot* right-of-way, priority.
Vorfall ('foːrfal) *nm* incident, occurrence.
vorführen ('foːrfyːrən) *vt* **1** present, perform, display. **2** project (films).
Vorgang ('foːrgaŋ) *nm* **1** proceedings. **2** event. **3** precedent. **¨—er** ('foːrgɛŋər) *nm* — predecessor.
vorgeb/en* ('foːrgeːbən) *vt* pretend, feign. **—lich** ('foːrgepliç) *adj* alleged, pretended.
vorgefaßt ('foːrgəfast) *adj* preconceived.
vorgehen* ('foːrgeːən) *vi* **1** go forward, first, or before. **2** (of a clock) be fast. **3** occur. *n neu* — **1** procedure. **2** *law* action.
vorgenannt ('foːrgənant) *adj* aforementioned.
Vorgeschichte ('foːrgəʃiçtə) *nf* prehistory.
Vorgeschmack ('foːrgəʃmak) *nm* foretaste.
Vorgesetzte(r) ('foːrgəzɛtstə) *nm* superior, senior.
vorgestern ('foːrgɛstərn) *adv* the day before yesterday.
vorhaben* ('foːrhaːbən) *vt* intend. *n neu* — plan, purpose.
Vorhalle ('foːrhalə) *nf* entrance-hall, porch.
vorhanden (foːr'handən) *adj* **1** available. **2** existing.
Vorhang ('foːrhaŋ) *nm* curtain.
vorher ('foːrheːr) *adv* previously, before(hand). **—ig** (foːr'heːriç) *adj* previous.
vorhin (foːr'hin) *adv* a little while ago.
Vorhut ('foːrhuːt) *nf* **-en** vanguard.
vorig ('foːriç) *adj* former, preceding, previous.
vorjährig ('foːrjɛːriç) *adj* last year's.
Vorkehrung ('foːrkeːruŋ) *nf* **-en 1** precaution. **2** provision.
Vorkenntnis ('foːrkɛntnis) *nf* **-se** previous experience or knowledge.
vorkommen* ('foːrkɔmən) *vi* **1** happen, occur. **2** be found.
vorlad/en* ('foːrlaːdən) *vt law* summon. **—ung** *nf* **-en** summons.
vorläufig ('foːrlɔyfiç) *adj* provisional, preliminary, tentative.
vorlaut ('foːrlaut) *adj* presumptuous, impudent.
vorlegen ('foːrleːgən) *vt* **1** propose. **2** display. **3** submit.
vorles/en* ('foːrleːzən) *vt* read aloud. **—ung** *nf* **-en 1** lecture. **2** reading.
vorletzt ('foːrlɛtst) *adj* penultimate.
Vorliebe ('foːrliːbə) *nf* preference, fondness.
vorliegen* ('foːrliːgən) *vi* be present or at hand.
vormals ('foːrmaːls) *adv* formerly.
vormerken ('foːrmɛrkən) *vt* note (down).
Vormittag ('foːrmitaːk) *nm* morning. **—s** *adv* in the morning.
Vormund ('foːrmunt) *nm* **¨-er** guardian.
vorn (fɔrn) *adv* in front, before,

ahead. **von vornherein** from the first or start.
Vorname ('fo:rna:mə) *nm* first or Christian name.
vornehm ('fo:rne:m) *adj* **1** distinguished, noble. **2** elegant. **—en*** *vt* **1** put on (an apron). **2** undertake. **sich —en** *vr* resolve (to do something). **—lich** *adj* chiefly, especially.
Vorort ('fo:rɔrt) *nm* suburb.
Vorposten ('fo:rpɔstən) *nm* outpost.
Vorrang ('fo:rraŋ) *nm* precedence, priority.
Vorrat ('fo:rra:t) *nm* stock, store, supply.
Vorrede ('fo:rre:də) *nf* **1** preface. **2** introduction.
vorrücken ('fo:rrykən) *vt,vi* move forward.
Vorsatz ('fo:rzats) *nm* **1** purpose. **2** intention.
Vorschau ('fo:rʃau) *nf* **1** preview. **2** trailer (for a film).
Vorschein ('fo:rʃain) *nm* appearance.
vorschieben* ('fo:rʃi:bən) *vt* **1** push forward. **2** pretend. **3** plead.
Vorschlag ('fo:rʃla:k) *nm* suggestion, proposal. **—en*** ('fo:rʃla:gən) *vt* propose, suggest.
vorschreiben* ('fo:rʃraibən) *vt* prescribe, order.
Vorschrift ('fo:rʃrift) *nf* **1** decree. **2** regulation. **3** instructions. **4** prescription.
Vorschub ('fo:rʃu:p) *nm* aid, help, assistance.
Vorschuß ('fo:rʃus) *nm* advance (of money).
Vorsehung ('fo:rse:uŋ) *nf* **-en** providence.
vorsetzen ('fo:rzɛtsən) *vt* **1** set over. **2** put forward. **3** appoint. **4** prefix. **5** offer.
Vorsicht ('fo:rziçt) *nf* caution. **—ig** *adj* cautious.
Vorsilbe ('fo:rzilbə) *nf* prefix.
Vorsitz ('fo:rzits) *nm* chair(manship). **—ende(r)** *nm* chairman, president.
Vorsorg/e ('fo:rzɔrgə) *nf* **1** care. **2** provision. **—en** *vi* provide (for). **—lich** ('fo:rzɔrkliç) *adj* provident.
Vorspeise ('fo:rʃpaizə) *nf* hors d'oeuvre.
vorspiegeln ('fo:rʃpi:gəln) *vt* simulate, pretend.
Vorspiel ('fo:rʃpi:l) *n neu* prelude.
vorspringen* ('fo:rʃpriŋən) *vi* **1** project. **2** leap forward.
Vorsprung ('fo:rʃpruŋ) *nm* **1** projection. **2** advantage, start.
Vorstadt ('fo:rʃtat) *nf* suburb.
Vorstand ('fo:rʃtant) *nm* **1** board of directors. **2** executive, management.
vorsteh/en* ('fo:rʃte:ən) *vi* **1** protrude. **2** head, manage. **—er** *nm* — superintendent, chief.
vorstell/en ('fo:rʃtɛlən) *vt* **1** introduce, present, put forward. **2** represent. **sich vorstellen** *vr* imagine. **—ung** *nf* **1** (re)presentation. **2** idea. **3** introduction. **4** performance.
Vorstoß ('fo:rʃtɔs) *nm* advance, attack. **—en*** *vi,vt* advance (suddenly).
vorstrecken ('fo:rʃtrɛkən) *vt* **1** stretch forward or out. **2** advance (money).
Vorstufe ('fo:rʃtu:fə) *nf* first

step(s), preliminary or primary stage.

Vorteil ('fɔrtail) *nm* **1** advantage. **2** profit. **—haft** *adj* advantageous, profitable.

Vortrag ('foːrtraːk) *nm* **¨-e 1** lecture. **2** report. **3** delivery, performance. **4** *comm* balance carried forward. **—en*** ('foːrtraːgən) *vt* **1** lecture (on). **2** *comm* carry forward. **3** perform.

vortrefflich (foːr'trɛfliç) *adj* excellent, admirable.

Vortritt ('foːrtrit) *nm* precedence.

vorüber (fo'ryːbər) *adv* past, gone (by). **—gehen*** *vi* pass (by or over). **—gehend** *adj* passing, transitory.

Vorurteil ('foːrurtail) *n neu* prejudice.

Vorwand ('foːrvant) *nm* pretext.

vorwärts ('foːrvɛrts) *adv* forward, onward.

vorweg (for'vɛk) *adv* before, beforehand. **—nehmen*** *vt* anticipate.

vorwerfen* ('foːrvɛrfən) *vt* **1** reproach with. **2** throw forward.

vorwiegend ('foːrviːgənt) *adj* predominant.

Vorwissen ('foːrvisən) *n neu* previous knowledge.

Vorwort ('foːrvɔrt) *n neu* **-e 1** preface, foreword. **2** *gram* preposition.

Vorwurf ('foːrvurf) *nm* **1** reproach. **2** subject, theme. **—svoll** *adj* reproachful.

Vorzeichen ('foːrtsaiçən) *n neu* omen.

vorzeigen ('foːrtsaigən) *vt* exhibit, show.

vorzeitig ('foːrtsaitiç) *adj* premature.

vorziehen* ('foːrtsiːən) *vt* **1** prefer. **2** draw (forward).

Vorzug ('foːrtsuːk) *nm* **1** preference. **2** advantage. **3** priority. **4** good quality, merit. **¨—lich** (for'tsyːkliç) *adj* excellent, superior.

vulgär (vul'gɛːr) *adj* vulgar.

Vulkan (vul'kaːn) *nm* **-e** volcano.

W

Waag/e ('vaːgə) *nf* **-n 1** balance, scale. **2** Libra. **—recht** ('vaːkrɛçt) *adj* horizontal, level.

wabbelig ('vabəliç) *adj* flabby, wobbly.

Wabe ('vaːbə) *nf* **-n** honeycomb.

wach (vax) *adj* **1** awake. **2** alert, alive. **—e** *nf* **-n** guard, watch. **—en** *vi* **1** watch (over). **2** be awake. **—sam** *adj* watchful, alert.

Wachs (vaks) *n neu* **-e** wax.

wachs/en* ('vaksən) *vi* grow. **—tum** *n neu* growth.

Wacht (vaxt) *nf* **-en** guard. **¨—er** ('vɛçtər) *nm* **—** guard, keeper, warder. **—meister** *nm* **1** policeman. **2** cavalry sergeant.

Wachtel ('vaxtəl) *nf* **-n** quail.

wackel/ig ('vakəliç) *adj* shaky, wobbly. **—n** *vi* shake, totter.

wacker ('vakər) *adj* **1** valiant. **2** decent.

Wade ('vaːdə) *nf* **-n** *anat* calf.

Waff/e ('vafə) *nf* **-n** weapon.

—enstillstand *nm* armistice, truce, cease-fire.

Waffel ('vafəl) *nf* **-n** **1** waffle. **2** wafer.

wag/en ('va:gən) *vt* risk, dare. **—emut** ('va:gəmu:t) *nm* daring. **—halsig** ('va:khalsiç) *adj* reckless. **—nis** ('va:knis) *n neu* **-se** risk.

Wagen ('va:gən) *nm* — **1** car. **2** van, lorry. **3** carriage. **4** wagon, cart.

wägen* ('vɛ:gən) *vt* weigh. **erst wägen, dann wagen** look before you leap.

Wahl (va:l) *nf* **-en** **1** choice, selection. **2** election, vote. **¨—en** ('vɛ:lən) *vt* **1** choose, select. **2** elect, vote. **3** dial. **¨—er** ('vɛ:lər) *nm* — voter. **¨—erisch** ('vɛ:lərɪʃ) *adj* fastidious, fussy. **¨—erschaft** ('vɛ:lərʃaft) *nf* **-en** voters. **—recht** *n neu* franchise, vote. **¨—erscheibe** ('vɛlərʃaibə) *nf* dial. **—stimme** *nf* vote. **—zettel** *nm* ballot paper.

Wahn (va:n) *nm* **1** delusion, illusion. **2** madness, folly. **—bild** *n neu* **1** phantom. **2** hallucination. **—sinn** *nm* **1** madness, insanity. **2** frenzy. **—sinnig** *adj* mad, insane.

wahr (va:r) *adj* true, real. **—haft** *adj also* **—haftig** **1** truthful, true. **2** genuine. **—haftigkeit** *nf* truthfulness. **—heit** *nf* **-en** truth. **—nehmen*** *vt* **1** perceive, notice. **2** protect (interests). **—sagen** *vt* prophesy. **—scheinlich** (va:r'ʃainliç) *adj* probable, likely. **—scheinlichkeit** (va:r'ʃainliçkait) *nf* **-en** probability. **—zeichen** *n neu* **1** token. **2** emblem.

wahren ('va:rən) *vt* **1** defend. **2** maintain.

während ('vɛ:rənt) *prep* during. *conj* while. **—dem** (vɛ:rənt'de:m) *adv also* **—des** or **—dessen** meanwhile.

Währung ('vɛ:ruŋ) *nf* **-en** currency, standard.

Waise ('vaizə) *nf* **-n** *also* **Waisenkind** *n neu* orphan. **—nhaus** *n neu* orphanage.

Wal (va:l) *nm* **-e** *also* **Walfisch** ('va:lfiʃ) whale. **—fischspeck** *nm* blubber.

Wald (valt) *nm* **¨-er** wood, forest.

Wall (val) *nm* **¨-e** **1** rampart. **2** dam, dike.

wall/en[1] ('valən) *vi* see **wallfahren.**

wall/en[2] ('valən) *vi* **1** boil (up). **2** flutter. **—ung** *nf* **-en** **1** agitation. **2** boiling.

wallfahr/en* ('valfa:rən) *vi* go on a pilgrimage. **—er** *nm* pilgrim. **—t** *nf* pilgrimage.

Walnuß ('valnus) *nf* walnut.

Walroß ('valrɔs) *n neu* **-rosse** walrus.

Walz/e ('valtsə) *nf* **-n** *tech* roller, drum. **—en** *vi* waltz. *vt* roll, crush. **—er** ('valtsər) *nm* — waltz.

Wand (vant) *nf* **¨-e** wall. **—karte** *nf* wall map.

Wand/el ('vandəl) *nm* **1** change, transformation. **2** conduct. **—eln** *vt* change. *vi* wander. **—lung** *nf* **-en** change, transformation.

Wander/er ('vandərər) *nm* — wanderer, rambler. **—lust** *nf* love of rambling or travelling.

—n *vi* **1** walk, hike. **2** migrate. **—ung** *nf* **-en** **1** hike, excursion. **2** migration.
wandte ('vantə) *v* see **wenden.**
Wange ('vaŋə) *nf* **-n** cheek.
wanken ('vaŋkən) *vi* **1** sway, shake. **2** waver.
wann (van) *conj,adv* when.
Wanne ('vanə) *nf* **-n** tub, bath.
Wanze ('vantsə) *nf* **-n** bug, bedbug.
Wappen ('vapən) *n neu* **—** (coat of) arms.
war (vaːr) *v* see **sein**[2].
wäre ('vɛːrə) *v* see **sein**[2].
Ware ('vaːrə) *nf* **-n** **1** article, ware. **2** *pl* merchandise, goods. **—nhaus** *n neu* department store. **—nzeichen** *n neu* trademark.
warf (vaːrf) *v* see **werfen.**
warm (varm) *adj* warm, hot. **¨—e** ('vɛrmə) *nf* warmth. **¨—en** ('vɛrmən) *vt* warm. **¨—flasche** ('vɛrmflaʃə) *nf* hot-water bottle.
warn/en ('varnən) *vt* warn. **—ung** *nf* **-en** warning.
Warschau ('varʃau) *n neu* Warsaw.
wart/en ('vartən) *vi* wait. *vt* look after. **¨—er** ('vɛrtər) *nm* **—** attendant, keeper. **—esaal** *nm* waiting room.
warum (va'rum) *adv* why.
Warze ('vaːrtsə) *nf* **-n** wart.
was (vas) *pron* what, (that) which.
wasch/en* ('vaʃən) *vt,vi* wash. **—automat** ('vaʃautomaːt) *nm* automatic washing machine. **—becken** *n neu* hand-basin, wash-basin. **¨—e** ('vɛʃə) *nf* **1** wash(ing). **2** underwear. **—echt** *adj* **1** (of colour) fast. **2** genuine. **¨—erei** (vɛʃə'rai) *nf* **-en** washing, laundry. **¨—etrockner** ('vɛʃətrɔknər) *nm* tumble drier. **—lappen** *nm* face cloth. **—maschine** *nf* washing machine. **—mittel** *n neu* soap powder, detergent.
Wasser ('vasər) *n neu* **¨—** water. **—dicht** *adj* watertight, waterproof. **—fall** *nm* waterfall. **—hahn** *nm* tap. **¨—ig** ('vɛsəriç) *adj* watery. **—leitung** *nf* water supply. **—mann** *nm* Aquarius. **¨—n** ('vɛsərn) *vt* **1** water, irrigate. **2** soak. **—stoff** *nm* hydrogen.
Watte ('vatə) *nf* **-n** **1** wadding. **2** cotton wool.
weben* ('veːbən) *vt* weave. **—er** *nm* **—** weaver.
Wechsel ('vɛksəl) *nm* **—** **1** (ex)change. **2** bill of exchange. **—geld** *n neu* (small) change. **—n** *vt,vi* **1** change. **2** exchange. **3** vary.
weck/en ('vɛkən) *vt* wake, rouse. **—er** *nm* **—** alarm clock.
wedeln ('veːdəln) *vi* **1** fan. **2** wag.
weder ('veːdər) *conj* **weder... noch** neither...nor.
weg (vɛk) *adv* **1** away. **2** gone. **3** off.
Weg (veːk) *nm* **-e** **1** way, route. **2** path. **3** road. **—weiser** ('veːkvaizər) *nm* **—** **1** signpost. **2** guide.
wegbleiben* ('vɛkblaibən) *vi* **1** stay away. **2** be omitted.
wegblicken ('vɛkblikən) *vi* look away.
wegen ('veːgən) *prep* **1** because of. **2** for.

weggehen* ('vɛkgeːən) *vi* depart, leave.
weglassen* ('vɛklasən) *vt* **1** omit. **2** let go.
wegmüssen* ('vɛkmysən) *vi* have to go, be obliged to leave.
wegräumen ('vɛkrɔymən) *vt* clear away.
wegreißen* ('vɛkraisən) *vt* tear or snatch away.
wegschaffen* ('vɛkʃafən) *vt* get rid of.
wegtun* ('vɛktuːn) *vt* put away.
wegwerfen* ('vɛkvɛrfən) *vt* throw away or out.
weh (veː) *adj* **1** sore, painful. **2** sad. *interj* woe! **weh tun** hurt, be painful. ~*n neu* **-e 1** pain. **2** grief. **—en** *n pl* labour pains. **—mut** *nf* melancholy.
Weh/e ('veːə) *nf* **-n** (snow)drift. **—en** *vi* blow.
Wehr[1] (veːr) *nf* **-en 1** defence. **2** weapon. **3** bulwark. **—dienst** *nm* military service. **—en** *vt* **1** restrain. **2** forbid. **sich —en** *vr* resist. **—macht** *nf* armed forces. **—pflicht** *nf* compulsory service, conscription.
Wehr[2] (veːr) *n neu* **-e** weir.
Weib (vaip) *n neu* **-er** *inf* **1** woman, female. **2** wife. **—isch** ('vaibiʃ) *adj* effeminate, womanish. **—lich** *adj* feminine, female.
weich (vaiç) *adj* **1** soft. **2** smooth. **—lich** *adj* soft, effeminate. **—ling** *nm* **-e** weakling.
Weiche ('vaiçə) *nf* **-n 1** (railway) points. **2** *anat* flank.
weichen* ('vaiçən) *vi* **1** yield. **2** flinch.
Weichsel ('vaiksəl) *nf* Vistula.
Weide ('vaidə) *nf* **-n 1** pasture. **2** willow. **—n** *vi* graze. **sich —n** *vr* gloat.
sich weigern ('vaigərn) *vr* refuse.
Weih/e ('vaiə) *nf* **-n 1** consecration, dedication **2** initiation. **—en** *vt* **1** consecrate, dedicate. **2** initiate. **—rauch** *nm* incense.
Weihnacht/en ('vainaxtən) *n pl* Christmas. **—slied** *n neu* carol.
weil (vail) *conj* because, since.
Weile ('vailə) *nf* **-n 1** while. **2** time.
Wein (vain) *nm* **-e 1** wine. **2** *also* **Weinstock** ('vainʃtɔk) *nm* vine. **—bau** *nm* vine-growing. **—lese** *nf* vintage, gathering, grape-harvest.
weinen ('vainən) *vi* cry, weep.
weis/e ('vaizə) *adj* wise, prudent. *nm* **-n** wise man, sage. **—heit** ('vaishait) *nf* wisdom. **—lich** (vaisliç) *adv* wisely.
Weise ('vaizə) *nf* **-n 1** manner, way, method. **2** tune, melody.
weis/en* ('vaizən) *vt* indicate, show. **—ung** *nf* **-en** direction, instruction.
weiß[1] (vais) *adj,n neu* white. **—e(r)** *nm* white man. **—kohl** *nm* (white) cabbage.
weiß[2] (vais) *v* see **wissen.**
weit (vait) *adj* **1** distant. **2** wide. **—aus** (vait'aus) *adv* by far. **—e** *nf* **-n 1** distance. **2** width. **3** scope, size. **—läufig** ('vaitlɔyfiç) *adj* **1** distant. **2** extensive. **3** diffuse. **4** spacious. **—reichend** ('vaitraiçənt) *adj*

far-reaching. **—sichtig** *adj* **1** long-sighted. **2** far-sighted.
weiter ('vaitər) *adj* **1** further. **2** farther. **3** wider. *adv* **1** further on. **2** else.
Weizen ('vaitsən) *nm* wheat.
welch (vɛlç) *pron* who, which, what, that. *pron,adj* some, any.
welk (vɛlk) *adj* withered, limp.
Welle ('vɛlə) *nf* **-n 1** wave. **2** axle. **3** shaft. **—nlänge** *nf* wavelength.
Welt (vɛlt) *nf* **-en** world. **—all** *n neu* universe. **—anschauung** *nf* philosophy of life, ideology. **—klug** *adj* worldly-wise. **—lich** *adj* secular, worldly. **—macht** *nf* world power. **—männisch** ('vɛltmɛniʃ) *adj* sophisticated.
wem (veːm) *pron* to whom.
wen (veːn) *pron* whom.
Wend/e ('vɛndə) *nf* **-n** turn, turning point. **—en*** *vt* turn. **—epunkt** *nm* turning point, crisis. **—ung** *nf* **-en 1** turn(ing). **2** figure of speech.
wenig ('veːniç) *adj,pron* **1** little. **2** *pl* few. **—st** *adj* least. **—stens** *adv* at least.
wer (veːr) *pron* who, which.
werb/en* ('vɛrbən) *vi* **1** court. **2** advertise (for). *vt* recruit. **—ung** *nf* **-en 1** advertising. **2** recruiting. **3** courting.
Werdegang ('vɛrdəgaŋ) *nm* **1** career. **2** development.
werden* ('vɛrdən) *v mod aux* shall, will. *vi* **1** become. **2** happen. *n neu* **1** growth. **2** origin.
werfen* ('vɛrfən) *vt* throw. *vi* bring forth young.
Werft (vɛrft) *nf* **-en 1** shipyard. **2** wharf.
Werk (vɛrk) *n neu* **-e 1** work(s). **2** deed. **3** mechanism. **—statt** *nf* workshop. **—stoff** *nm* (raw) material. **—zeug** *n neu* tool.
Wermut ('veːrmuːt) *nm* vermouth.
wert (vɛrt) *adj* **1** worth. **2** worthy. *nm* **-e** worth, value. **—brief** *nm* registered money letter. **—en** *vt* value. **—sache** *nf* valuable. **—voll** *adj* valuable.
Wesen ('veːzən) *n neu* **— 1** being, creature. **2** essence, character. **3** way, manners. **4** fuss. **—tlich** *adj* **1** substantial. **2** essential.
weshalb (vɛs'halp) *adv,conj also* **weswegen** (vɛs'veːgən) why, wherefore.
Wespe ('vɛspə) *nf* **-n** wasp.
wessen ('vɛsən) *pron* **1** of whom, whose. **2** of which, of what.
West (vɛst) *nm also* **West/en** ('vɛstən) west. **—deutschland** *n neu* West Germany. **—lich** *adj* west(ern), westerly. **—wärts** ('vɛstvɛrts) *adv* westward(s), west.
Westfalen (vɛst'faːlən) *n neu* Westphalia.
Westindien (vɛst'indiən) *n neu* West Indies.
wett (vɛt) *adj* even, quits.
Wett/e ('vɛtə) *nf* **-n** bet, wager. **—büro** *n neu* betting shop or office. **—en** *vt,vi* bet, wager. **—kampf** *nm* competition, contest, match. **—laufen*** *vi* (run a) race.
Wetter ('vɛtər) *n neu* **— 1** weather. **2** storm. **—bericht** *nm* weather report or forecast.

wetzen ('vɛtsən) *vt* sharpen, whet.
wichtig ('viçtiç) *adj* important.
Widder ('vidər) *nm* — **1** ram. **2** Aries.
wider ('viːdər) *prep* against.
widerfahren* (viːdər'faːrən) *vi* happen (to).
Widerhaken ('viːdərhaːkən) *nm* barb, hook.
Widerhall ('viːdərhal) *nm* **-e** **1** echo. **2** response.
widerleg/en (viːdər'leːgən) *vt* refute. **—ung** *nf* **-en** refutation.
widerlich ('viːdərliç) *adj* repulsive.
widerrechtlich ('viːdərrɛçtliç) *adj* illegal.
Widerruf ('viːdərruːf) *nm* countermand, disavowal. **—en*** (viːdər'ruːfən) *vt* revoke.
widersetz/en (viːdər'zɛtsən) *vr* oppose. **—lich** *adj* insubordinate. **—lichkeit** *nf* insubordination.
widerspenstig ('viːdərʃpɛnstiç) *adj* obstinate.
widersprechen* (viːdər'ʃprɛçən) *vi* contradict.
Widerspruch ('viːdərsprux) *nm* **1** opposition. **2** contradiction.
Widerstand ('viːdərʃtant) *nm* **1** resistance. **2** opposition.
widerstehen* (viːdər'ʃteːən) *vi* withstand.
widerwärtig ('viːdərvɛrtiç) *adj* disagreeable, offensive.
widerwillig ('viːdərviliç) *adj* unwilling.
widmen ('vitmən) *vt* dedicate, devote.
widrig ('viːdriç) *adj* adverse, contrary, hostile. **—enfalls** ('viːdrigənfals) *adv* failing which.
wie (viː) *adv* how. *conj* **1** how. **2** as. **3** like.
wieder ('viːdər) *adv* **1** again. **2** back.
Wiederaufnahme (viːdər'aufnaːmə) *nf* **-n** resumption.
wiederaufbereiten (viːdər 'aufbəraitən) *vt* recycle.
wiederbringen* ('viːdərbriŋən) *vt* bring back, restore.
wiedererkennen* ('viːdərɛrkɛnən) *vt* recognize.
Wiedergabe ('viːdərgaːbə) *nf* **1** restitution. **2** reproduction.
wiedergeben* ('viːdərgeːbən) *vt* **1** return. **2** reproduce.
Wiedergeburt ('viːdərgəbuːrt) *nf* **1** rebirth, regeneration. **2** reincarnation.
wiedergutmachen (viːdər 'guːtmaxən) *vt* compensate for.
wiederhol/en (viːdər'hoːlən) *vt* repeat. **—ung** *nf* repetition.
wiederhören ('viːdərhœːrən) *vt* hear again. **auf Wiederhören** (in a telephone conversation) goodbye.
wiederkäuen ('viːdərkɔyən) *vt* ruminate.
wiederkehren ('viːdərkeːrən) *vi* return.
wiederkommen* ('viːdərkɔmən) *vi* come back.
wiedersehen* ('viːdərzeːən) *vt* see again. **auf Wiedersehen** goodbye.
wiederum ('viːdərum) *adv* again, anew.
Wieg/e ('viːgə) *nf* **-n** cradle. **—enlied** *n neu* lullaby.
wiegen* ('viːgən) *vt,vi* weigh.
Wien (viːn) *n neu* Vienna.

wies (viːs) *v* see **weisen.**
Wiese ('viːzə) *nf* **-n** meadow.
Wiesel ('viːzəl) *n neu* — weasel.
wieso (viː'zoː) *adv* why.
wieviel (viː'fiːl) *adv* how much.
wild (vilt) *adj* **1** wild, savage. **2** fierce. **3** angry. *n neu* game. **—dieb** *nm* poacher. **—ern** ('vildərn) *vi* poach. **—hüter** *nm* gamekeeper. **—nis** *nf* **-se** wilderness.
will (vil) *v see* **wollen.**
Will/e ('vilə) *nm* **-n** will. **—enlos** *adj* irresolute, half-hearted. **—enskraft** *nf* will-power. **—kommen** (vil'kɔmən) *adj,n neu,interj* welcome. **—kür** ('vilkyːr) *nf* discretion, choice. **—kürlich** ('vilkyːrliç) *adj* arbitrary.
wimmeln ('viməln) *vi* swarm (with).
Wimper ('vimpər) *nf* **-n** eyelash. **ohne mit der Wimper zu zucken** without batting an eyelid.
Wind (vint) *nm* **-e** wind. **—beutel** *nm* **1** eclair. **2** *sl* windbag. **—hund** *nm* greyhound. **—ig** ('vindiç) *adj* windy. **—schutzscheibe** *nf* windscreen. **—stille** *nf* calm, lull.
Winde ('vində) *nf* **-n** winch, reel.
Windel ('vindəl) *nf* **-n** nappy.
winden* ('vindən) *vt* wind.
Wink (viŋk) *nm* **-e** **1** sign. **2** nod. **3** wave. **—en** *vi* **1** make a sign. **2** wink. **3** wave. **4** nod.
Wink/el ('viŋkəl) *nm* — **1** angle. **2** corner. **3** nook. **—elmesser** *nm* protractor. **—lig** ('viŋkliç) *adj* angular.
winseln ('vinzəln) *vi* whimper, whine.
Winter ('vintər) *nm* — winter. **—lich** *adj* wintry.
Winzer ('vintsər) *nm* — vinegrower.
winzig ('vintsiç) *adj* tiny, minute.
Wipfel ('vipfəl) *nm* — treetop.
Wippe ('vipə) *nf* **-n** seesaw.
wir (viːr) *pron 1st pers pl* we.
Wirbel ('virbəl) *nm* — **1** whirl, eddy. **2** vertebra. **3** peg. **—n** *vi* whirl, swirl. **—säule** *nf* spine, vertebral column.
wird (virt) *v see* **werden.**
wirk/en ('virkən) *vi* work. *vt* **1** work. **2** effect. **3** weave. **—sam** *adj* effective. **—ung** *nf* **-en** **1** effect, result. **2** action.
wirklich ('virkliç) *adj* real, actual. **—keit** *nf* **-en** reality.
wirr (vir) *adj* confused, chaotic. **—warr** ('virvar) *nm* muddle, disorder.
wirst (virst) *v see* **werden.**
Wirt (virt) *nm* **-e** **1** host. **2** innkeeper, landlord. **—in** *nf* **-nen** **1** hostess. **2** landlady. **—schaft** *nf* **-en** **1** economy. **2** housekeeping, household. **3** inn, pub. **—schaften** *vi* **1** keep house. **2** manage (well). **—schaft(l)er** *nm* — manager. **—schaftlich** *adj* **1** economic. **2** economical. **—schaftsprüfer** *nm* — chartered accountant. **—shaus** *n neu* inn, pub.
wisch/en ('viʃən) *vt* wipe, rub. **—lappen** *nm* — duster.
wispern ('vispərn) *vi,vt* whisper.
Wißbegier ('visbəgiːr) *nf also*

Wißbegierde *nf* craving for knowledge, curiosity. **—ig** *adj* eager to learn, inquisitive.
wissen* ('visən) *vt,vi* know. *n neu* knowledge, learning.
Wissenschaft ('visənʃaft) *nf* **-en 1** science. **2** learning. **—ler** *nm* **— 1** scientist. **2** scholar. **—lich** *adj* **1** scientific. **2** learned, scholarly.
wittern ('vitərn) *vt* scent, smell.
Witwe ('vitvə) *nf* **-n** widow. **—r** ('vitvər) *nm* — widower.
Witz (vits) *nm* **-e 1** joke. **2** wit. **—eln** *vi* joke. **—ig** *adj* witty.
wo (vo:) *adv,conj* where.
woanders (vo:'andərs) *adv* elsewhere.
wobei (vo:'bai) *adv* whereby. *pron* **1** in or at which. **2** in doing which.
Woche ('vɔxə) *nf* **-n** week. **—nblatt** *n neu* weekly (newspaper). **—nende** *n neu* weekend. **¨—ntlich** ('vœçəntliç) *adj* weekly.
wodurch (vo:'durç) *adv* whereby. *pron* **1** by or through which. **2** in doing which.
wofür (vo:'fy:r) *adv,pron* for which.
wog (vo:k) *v* see **wiegen.**
wogegen (vo:'ge:gən) *adv* in return for which. *conj* whereas.
woher (vo:'he:r) *adv* whence, wherefrom.
wohin (vo:'hin) *adv* whither, (to) where.
wohl (vo:l) *adv* **1** well. **2** probably, presumably. *n neu* welfare, wellbeing.
wohlan (vo:l'an) *interj* come on! well!
wohlauf (vo:l'auf) *adv* well. *interj* well then!
Wohlbehagen ('vo:lbəha:gən) *n neu* comfort.
Wohlfahrt ('vo:lfa:rt) *nf* welfare. **—sstaat** *nm* welfare state. **—sgesellschaft** *nf* affluent society.
wohlfeil ('vo:lfail) *adj* cheap.
wohlhabend ('vo:lha:bənt) *adj* well-off, prosperous.
Wohlklang ('vo:lklaŋ) *nm* harmony.
Wohlstand ('vo:lʃtant) *nm* prosperity.
Wohltat ('vo:lta:t) *nf* benefit. **¨—er** ('vo:ltɛ:tər) *nm* benefactor.
wohltun* ('vo:ltu:n) *vi* do good, benefit.
Wohlwollen ('vo:lvɔlən) *n neu* goodwill, favour.
wohn/en ('vo:nən) *vi* live, dwell. **—haft** *adj* resident. **—ung** *nf* **-en 1** dwelling, residence. **2** flat, apartment. **—wagen** *nm* caravan. **—zimmer** *n neu* sitting room.
Wölbung ('vœlbuŋ) *nf* **-en 1** vault. **2** dome. **3** arch.
Wolf (vɔlf) *nm* **¨-e** wolf.
Wolk/e ('vɔlkə) *nf* **-n** cloud. **—enkratzer** *nm* — skyscraper. **—ig** *adj* cloudy, clouded.
Woll/e ('vɔlə) *nf* **-n** wool. **—en** *adj* woollen. **—ig** *adj* woolly, fleecy. **—jacke** *nf* cardigan.
wollen* ('vɔlən) *vi,vt* want, desire. *v mod aux* **1** want or desire (to). **2** intend (to). **3** be about (to).
Wollust ('vɔlust) *nf* **¨-e** sensual pleasure, lust.
womit (vo:'mit) *adv* with or by which.

womöglich (vo:'mœ:kliç) *adv* where or if possible.
wonach (vo:'na:x) *adv* **1** according to which. **2** after which.
Wonne ('vɔnə) *nf* **-n** delight, joy, bliss.
woran (vo:'ran) *adv,pron* at or about which or what.
worauf (vo:'rauf) *adv,pron* (up)on which or what.
woraus (vo:'raus) *adv,pron* of or from which or what.
worden ('vɔ:rdən) *v* see **werden.**
worin (vo:'rin) *adv* in(to) which or what.
Wort (vɔrt) *n neu* **¨-er** (written) word. *n neu* **-e 1** (spoken) word, expression. **2** word, pledge. **—bruch** *nm* breach of one's word. **¨—erbuch** ('vœrtərbu:x) *n neu* dictionary. **—führer** *nm* **1** spokesman. **2** speaker. **—karg** *adj* taciturn. **—laut** *nm* wording, text. **¨—lich** ('vœrtliç) *adj* **1** literal. **2** verbal. **3** word-for-word. **—reich** *adj* verbose. **—schatz** *nm* vocabulary.
wovon (vo:'fɔn) *adv,pron* of or from which or what.
wozu (vo:'tsu:) *adv,pron* **1** to or for what, why. **2** in addition to which.
Wrack (vrak) *n neu* **-s** *naut* wreck.
wringen* ('vriŋən) *vt* wring.
Wucher ('vu:xər) *nm* **1** usury. **2** profiteering. **—er** *nm* **— 1** usurer. **2** profiteer. **—isch** *adj* **1** usurious. **2** profiteering. **—n** *vi* **1** grow luxuriantly or abundantly. **2** profiteer.
Wuchs (vu:ks) *nm* **1** growth. **2** figure, size.
Wucht (vuxt) *nf* **-en** force, weight.
wühl/en ('vy:lən) *vt* stir up, agitate. *vi* burrow. **—er** *nm* — agitator.
Wulst (vulst) *nm* **¨-e 1** roll, pad. **2** swelling.
wund (vunt) *adj* **1** sore. **2** wounded. **—e** ('vundə) *nf* **-en** wound.
Wunder ('vundər) *n neu* **— 1** miracle. **2** wonder. **—bar** *adj* wonderful, great, marvellous. **—kind** *n neu* child prodigy. **—lich** *adj* strange, odd. **—n** *vt* astound, surprise. **sich —n** *vr* wonder (at). **—schön** *adj* beautiful, exquisite.
Wunsch (vunʃ) *nm* **¨-e** wish, desire. **¨—en** ('vynʃən) *vt* wish, desire. **¨—enswert** ('vynʃənsve:rt) *adj* desirable.
wurde ('vu:rdə) *v* see **werden.**
würde ('vyrdə) *v* see **werden.**
Würd/e ('vyrdə) *nf* **-n 1** dignity, honour. **2** rank. **—enträger** *nm* dignitary. **—ig** *adj* worthy.
Wurf (vurf) *nm* **¨-e 1** throw, cast. **2** litter, brood. **—scheibe** *nf* discus.
Würfel ('vyrfəl) *nm* **— 1** *game* die, dice. **2** cube. **—zucker** *nm* lump sugar.
würgen ('vyrgən) *vi,vt* choke.
Wurm (vurm) *nm* **¨-er** worm.
Wurst (vurst) *nf* **¨-e** sausage.
Württemberg ('vyrtəmbɛrk) *n neu* Wurtemberg.
Würz/e ('vyrtsə) *nf* **-n 1** seasoning, spice. **2** flavour. **—en** *vt* season, spice. **—ig** *adj* spicy, seasoned.

Wurzel ('vurtsəl) *nf* **-n** root. **—n** *vi* take root.
wußte ('vustə) *v* see **wissen.**
wüst (vy:st) *adj* **1** desert, waste. **2** disorderly. **3** depraved. **—e** *nf* **-n** desert, wilderness. **—ling** *nm* **-e** libertine, depraved person.
Wut (vu:t) *nf* rage, fury. **¨—end** ('vy:tənt) *adj* furious.

X

Xenophobie (ksɛnofo'bi:) *nf* xenophobia.
x-mal ('iksma:l) *adv inf* umpteen times.
Xylophon (ksylo'fo:n) *n neu* **-e** xylophone.

Z

Zack/e ('tsakə) *nf* **-n** *also* **Zack/en** *nm* **— 1** prong. **2** tooth. **3** peak. **—en** *vt* **1** notch. **2** indent. **—ig** *adj* **1** jagged. **2** spirited.
zaghaft ('tsa:khaft) *adj* timid.
zäh (tsɛ:) *adj* **1** tough. **2** resistant. **—igkeit** *nf* **1** toughness. **2** pertinacity.
Zahl (tsa:l) *nf* **-en** number, numeral. **—bar** *adj* payable. **—en** *vt,vi* pay. **—los** *adj* countless. **—reich** *adj* numerous. **—tag** *nm* payday. **—ung** *nf* **-en** payment. **—ungsfähig** *adj* solvent. **—wort** *n neu* numeral.
zähl/en ('tsɛ:lən) *vt,vi* count, number. **—ung** *nf* **-en** counting.
zahm (tsa:m) *adj* tame. **¨—en** ('tsɛ:mən) *vt* **1** tame. **2** break in (a horse).
Zahn (tsa:n) *nm* **¨-e** tooth. **—arzt** *nm* dentist. **—bürste** *nf* toothbrush. **—pasta** *nf* toothpaste. **—rad** *n neu* cog wheel. **—schmerz** *nm also* **—weh** *n neu* toothache. **—stocher** *nm* toothpick.
Zange ('tsaŋə) *nf* **-n 1** pincers, tweezers. **2** tongs.
Zank (tsaŋk) *nm* **¨-e** quarrel. **—en** *vi* quarrel. **¨—isch** ('tsɛŋkiʃ) *adj* quarrelsome.
zapfen ('tsapfən) *vt* tap. *nm* **— 1** bung, plug. **2** pin. **3** pivot.
zappeln ('tsapəln) *vi* **1** wriggle. **2** fidget.
Zar (tsa:r) *nm* **-en** tsar.
zart (tsa:rt) *adj* **1** tender. **2** delicate. **¨—lich** ('tsɛ:rtliç) *adj* tender, affectionate.
Zauber ('tsaubər) *nm* **— 1** magic. **2** spell, charm. **—ei** (tsaubə'rai) *nf* magic. **—er** *nm* **—** magician, sorcerer. **—haft** *adj* **1** magical. **2** enchanting. **—n** *vi,vt* conjure (up).
zaudern ('tsaudərn) *vi* hesitate, delay. *n neu* hesitation.
Zaum (tsaum) *nm* **¨-e** bridle, rein. **¨—en** ('tsɔymən) *vt* bridle.
Zaun (tsaun) *nm* **¨-e** fence.
Zeche ('tsɛçə) *nf* **-n 1** bill. **2** mine.
Zehe ('tse:ə) *nf* **-n** toe.
zehn (tse:n) *adj,nf* ten. **—te** *adj* tenth.
zehren ('tse:rən) *vi* **1** feed. **2** waste (away).
Zeichen ('tsaiçən) *n neu* **— 1** sign. **2** signal.
zeichn/en ('tsaiçnən) *vt* **1** draw. **2** mark. **3** design. **4** subscribe. **—er** *nm* **— 1** designer. **2** draughtsman. **3** subscriber. **—ung** *nf* **-en 1** drawing.

2 sketch. **3** design. **4** subscription.

Zeig/efinger ('tsaigəfiŋər) *nm* index finger. **—en** *vt* show. **sich —en** *vr* appear. **—er** *nm* — hand, pointer.

Zeile ('tsailə) *nf* **-n** line.

Zeit (tsait) *nf* **-en** time. **zur Zeit** at present.

Zeitalter ('tsaitaltər) *n neu* age, era.

Zeitfolge ('tsaitfɔlgə) *nf* chronological order.

Zeitgenoss/e ('tsaitgənɔsə) *nm* contemporary. **¨—isch** ('tsaitgənœsiʃ) *adj* contemporary.

zeitig ('tsaitiç) *adj* **1** early. **2** timely. **—en** *vt* **1** ripen, mature. **2** cause, produce.

Zeitkarte ('tsaitkartə) *nf* season ticket.

Zeitlang ('tsaitlaŋ) *nf* **eine Zeitlang** for some time.

zeitlich ('tsaitliç) *adj* temporal.

Zeitpunkt ('tsaitpuŋkt) *nm* **1** moment. **2** point.

Zeitraum ('tsaitraum) *nm* interval, period.

Zeitschrift ('tsaitʃrift) *nf* periodical, magazine.

Zeitung ('tsaituŋ) *nf* **-en** newspaper, journal. **—swesen** *n neu* journalism.

zeitweilig ('tsaitvailiç) *adj* **1** temporary. **2** intermittent.

zeitweise ('tsaitvaizə) *adv* **1** for a time. **2** at times.

Zeitwort ('tsaitvɔrt) *n neu* **¨—er** verb.

Zelle ('tsɛlə) *nf* **-n** **1** cell. **2** callbox.

Zelt (tsɛlt) *n neu* **-e** tent. **—en** *vi* camp. *n neu* camping.

Zement (tse'mɛnt) *nm* **-e** cement.

Zensur (tsɛn'zu:r) *nf* **-en** **1** censorship. **2** *educ* marks, report.

Zentimeter (tsɛnti'me:tər) *nm,neu* — centimetre.

Zentner ('tsɛntnər) *nm* — hundredweight, fifty kilograms.

zentral (tsɛn'tra:l) *adj* central. **—e** *nf* **-n** **1** head office, headquarters. **2** power station. **—heizung** *nf* central heating. **—isieren** (tsɛntrali'zi:rən) *vt* centralize.

zerbrech/en* (tsɛr'brɛçən) *vt,vi* break into pieces, shatter. **—lich** *adj* fragile.

zerdrücken (tsɛr'drykən) *vt* crush, grind.

Zeremonie (tseremo'ni:) *nf* **-n** ceremony.

Zerfall (tsɛr'fal) *nm* decay, ruin. **—en*** *vi* fall into ruin, decay.

zerfetzen (tsɛr'fɛtsən) *vt* shred.

zergliedern (tsɛr'gli:dərn) *vt* **1** dismember. **2** analyse. **3** *anat* dissect.

zerhauen (tsɛr'hauən) *vt* cut up, mince.

zerlegen (tsɛr'le:gən) *vt* **1** take apart, divide, dissect. **2** analyse. **3** carve. **4** dispense.

zerlumpt (tsɛr'lumpt) *adj* ragged, tattered.

zermürben (tsɛr'myrbən) *vt* wear down.

zerplatzen (tsɛr'platsən) *vi* burst.

zerquetschen (tsɛr'kvɛtʃən) *vt* squash, crush.

Zerr/bild ('tsɛrbilt) *n neu* caricature. **—en** *vt* **1** tug, pull. **2** strain.

zerreiben* (tsɛr'raibən) *vt* grind, pulverize.
zerreißen* (tsɛr'raisən) *vt,vi* tear or rip up.
zerrinnen* (tsɛr'rinən) *vi* melt away, vanish.
zerschellen (tsɛr'ʃɛlən) *vt,vi* shatter, smash.
zerschlagen* (tsɛr'ʃla:gən) *vt* break into pieces. *vi* come to nothing.
zerschneiden* (tsɛr'ʃnaidən) *vt* cut up.
zersetz/en (tsɛr'zɛtsən) *vt* **1** decompose, disintegrate. **2** undermine. **—ung** *nf* decomposition.
zersplittern (tsɛr'ʃplitərn) *vt* split up, splinter.
zersprengen (tsɛr'ʃprɛŋən) *vt* blow up, burst.
zerstäub/en (tsɛr'ʃtɔybən) *vt* **1** spray. **2** disperse, scatter. **—er** *nm* **—** spray.
zerstör/en (tsɛr'ʃtœ:rən) *vt* destroy. **—er** *nm* **—** destroyer. **—ung** *nf* destruction.
zerstreu/en (tsɛr'ʃtrɔyən) *vt* **1** disperse, scatter. **2** diffuse. **3** divert, entertain, amuse. **—t** *adj* **1** absent-minded. **2** dispersed. **—theit** *nf* absent-mindedness. **—ung** *nf* **-en 1** dispersion. **2** amusement.
zerteilen (tsɛr'tailən) *vt* cut up, divide.
zertreten* (tsɛr'tre:tən) *vt* trample underfoot, stamp out.
zertrümmern (tsɛr'trymərn) *vt* lay waste, demolish, destroy, ruin.
zetern ('tse:tərn) *vi* **1** cry out (for help). **2** scold, nag.
Zettel ('tsɛtəl) *nm* **— 1** sheet or slip of paper, note. **2** ticket. **3** label.
Zeug (tsɔyk) *n neu* **-e 1** thing. **2** stuff. **3** material, cloth. **—haus** *n neu* arsenal.
Zeug/e ('tsɔygə) *nm* **-n** witness. **—nis** ('tsɔyknis) *n neu* **-se 1** evidence, testimony. **2** certificate. **3** reference.
zeug/en[1] ('tsɔygən) *vt* produce, beget. **—ung** *nf* **-en** procreation.
zeugen[2] ('tsɔygən) *vi* give testimony, testify.
Zickzack ('tsiktsak) *nm* **-e** zigzag.
Ziege ('tsi:gə) *nf* **-n** (she-)goat.
Ziegel ('tsi:gəl) *nm* **— 1** brick. **2** tile. **—ofen** *nm* brickkiln.
zieh/en* ('tsi:ən) *vt* **1** pull, draw (out). **2** cultivate, raise. **3** dig. *vi* **1** draw, pull. **2** move, go. **es zieht** there is a draught, it is draughty. **sich ziehen** *vr* **1** extend. **2** move. **3** withdraw. **—harmonika** *nf* accordion.
Ziel (tsi:l) *n neu* **-e 1** aim, end. **2** goal. **3** target. **—en** *vi* aim (at).
ziem/en ('tsi:mən) *vi also* **sich ziemen** *vr* **1** suit. **2** become. **—lich** *adv* quite, rather, moderately, fairly. *adj* suitable, fitting.
Zier (tsi:r) *nf* **-en** *also* **Zierat** *nm* **-e** ornament. **—en** *vt* decorate, adorn. **—lich** *adj* graceful, pretty, elegant.
Ziffer ('tsifər) *nf* **-n** figure, cipher.
Zigarette (tsiga'rɛtə) *nf* **-n** cigarette.
Zigarre (tsi'garə) *nf* **-n** cigar.

Zigeuner (tsi'gɔynər) *nm* — gipsy.
Zimmer ('tsimər) *n neu* — room. **—mann** *nm* carpenter.
zimperlich ('tsimpərliç) *adj* **1** prim, prudish. **2** affected.
Zimt (tsimt) *nm* **-e** cinnamon.
Zink (tsiŋk) *n neu* zinc.
Zinke ('tsiŋkə) *nf* **-n 1** prong. **2** dovetail.
Zinn (tsin) *n neu* tin.
Zins (tsins) *nm* **-en 1** interest. **2** rent. **—eszins** ('tsinzəstsins) *nm* compound interest. **—fuß** *nm also* **—satz** interest rate.
Zipfel ('tsipfəl) *nm* — tip, corner, edge.
Zirkus ('tsirkus) *nm* **-se** circus.
zirpen ('tsirpən) *vi* chirp.
Zitrone (tsi'tro:nə) *nf* **-n** lemon.
zittern ('tsitərn) *vi* tremble, quiver.
Zitze ('tsitsə) *nf* **-n** teat, nipple.
zivil (tsi'vi:l) *adj* **1** civil. **2** civilian. **—ist** (tsivi'list) *nm* **-en** civilian.
Zivil/isation (tsivilizatsi'o:n) *nf* **-en** civilization, culture. **—isieren** (tsivili'zi:rən) *vt* civilize.
Zofe ('tso:fə) *nf* **-n** lady's maid.
zog (tso:k) *v see* **ziehen.**
zöger/n ('tsœ:gərn) *vi* hesitate, linger. **—ung** *nf* **-en** delay, hesitation.
Zögling ('tsœ:kliŋ) *nm* **-e** pupil.
Zoll[1] (tsɔl) *nm* — inch.
Zoll[2] (tsɔl) *nm* **¨-e** custom, duty, toll. **—amt** *n neu* customs office. **—beamte(r)** *nm also* **¨—ner** ('tsœlnər) *nm* — customs officer. **—en** *vt* pay. **—frei** *adj* duty-free. **—pflichtig** *adj* dutiable, liable to (customs) duty.
Zone ('tso:nə) *nf* **-n** zone.
Zoo (tso:) *nm* **-s** zoo. **—loge** (tso:o'lo:gə) *nm* **-n** zoologist. **—logie** (tso:olo'gi:) *nf* zoology. **—logisch** (tso:o'lo:giʃ) *adj* zoological.
Zopf (tsɔpf) *nm* **¨-e** plait, pigtail.
Zorn (tsɔrn) *nm* anger. **—ig** *adj* angry.
zu (tsu:) *prep* **1** in, into. **2** to. **3** at. **4** by, with. **5** along with, in addition to. *adv* **1** too. **2** to(wards). **3** closed, shut.
Zubehör ('tsu:bəhœ:r) *n neu* **-e 1** accessories. **2** fittings.
zubereiten ('tsu:bəraitən) *vt* prepare.
zubringen* ('tsu:briŋən) *vt* **1** bring to. **2** pass (the time).
Zucht (tsuxt) *nf* **1** discipline. **2** breed(ing). **3** decency. **4** culture. **5** training. **¨—en** ('tsuçtən) *vt* **1** breed, rear. **2** grow, cultivate. **¨—er** ('tsyçtər) *nm* — **1** breeder. **2** grower. **¨—ig** ('tsyçtiç) *adj* chaste, modest. **¨—igen** ('tsyçtigən) *vt* **1** punish, discipline. **2** flog, thrash.
zucken ('tsukən) *vi* **1** twitch. **2** flash. *vt* **1** shrug (one's shoulders). **2** bat (an eyelid).
Zucker ('tsukər) *nm* sugar. **—n** *vt* sugar. **—rohr** *n neu* sugar cane. **—rübe** *nf* sugar beet.
zudecken ('tsu:dɛkən) *vt* cover (up).
zudem (tsu'de:m) *adv* besides.
Zudrang ('tsu:draŋ) *nm* rush (towards).
zudrehen ('tsu:dre:ən) *vt* turn or switch off.
zudringlich ('tsu:driŋliç) *adj* importunate.

zueinander (tsuain'andər) *adv* to each other.

zuerst (tsu'eːrst) *adv* (at) first, above all.

Zufahrt ('tsuːfaːrt) *nf* **1** approach, drive. **2** access (by road).

Zufall ('tsuːfal) *nm* chance, accident. **—en*** *vi* **1** fall to or on. **2** close. **¨—ig** ('tsuːfɛliç) *adj* accidental.

zufließen* ('tsuːfliːsən) *vi* flow (in)to.

Zuflucht ('tsuːfluxt) *nf* refuge, shelter.

zufolge (tsu'fɔlgə) *prep* **1** according to. **2** owing to.

zufrieden (tsu'friːdən) *adj* satisfied, content(ed). **—heit** *nf* satisfaction, contentment. **—stellen** *vt* satisfy.

zufügen ('tsuːfyːgən) *vt* **1** add (to). **2** cause, do.

Zufuhr ('tsuːfuːr) *nf* **-en** supply. **¨—en** ('tsuːfyːrən) *vt* **1** lead or bring to. **2** supply.

Zug (tsuːk) *nm* **¨-e** **1** train. **2** pull(ing), drawing. **3** draught. **4** procession. **5** trait, feature. **6** platoon, section. **—brücke** *nf* drawbridge.

Zugabe ('tsuːgaːbə) *nf* **-n** **1** addition. **2** supplement.

Zugang ('tsuːgaŋ) *nm* **1** access, entry. **2** increase. **¨—lich** ('tsuːgɛŋliç) *adj* accessible.

zugeben* ('tsuːgeːbən) *vt* **1** admit, confess. **2** permit. **3** add.

zugegen (tsu'geːgən) *adj* present.

zugehen* ('tsuːgeːən) *vi* **1** go on or to. **2** shut, close. **3** happen.

zugehör/en ('tsuːgəhœːrən) *vi* belong to. **—ig** *adj* belonging to.

Zügel ('tsyːgəl) *nm* — **1** rein, bridle. **2** restraint. **—los** *adj* unbridled. **—n** *vt* rein in, curb.

Zugeständnis ('tsuːgəʃtɛntnis) *n neu* **-se** **1** concession. **2** admission.

zugestehen* ('tsuːgəʃteːən) *vt* **1** admit. **2** concede.

Zugführer ('tsuːkfyːrər) *nm* (railway) guard.

zugig ('tsuːgiç) *adj* draughty.

zugreifen* ('tsuːgraifən) *vi* **1** grasp. **2** help oneself (at table).

zugrunde (tsu'grundə) *adv* **zugrunde gehen** **1** perish, die. **2** be ruined.

zugunsten (tsu'gunstən) *adv* in favour of.

zugute (tsu'guːtə) *adv* for the benefit of. **jemandem etwas zugute halten** give someone credit for something. **jemandem zugute kommen** stand someone in good stead.

zuhalt/en* ('tsuːhaltən) *vt* keep shut. *vi* make for, go towards. **¨—er** ('tsuːhɛltər) *nm* — procurer, pimp.

zuhanden (tsu'handən) *adv* at or to hand.

zuhör/en ('tsuːhœːrən) *vi* listen, attend (to). **—er** *nm* **1** listener. **2** *pl* audience.

zukommen* ('tsuːkɔmən) *vi* **1** come to, fall to. **2** be due to.

Zukunft ('tsuːkunft) *nf* future. **¨—ig** ('tsuːkynftiç) *adj* future.

Zulage ('tsuːlaːgə) *nf* **1** increase. **2** extra pay or allowance.

zulänglich ('tsuːlɛŋliç) *adj* sufficient.

zulass/en* ('tsu:lasən) *vt* **1** leave shut. **2** admit (a person). **3** allow. **4** license (a car, etc.). **¨—ig** ('tsu:lɛsiç) *adj* admissible, allowable. **—ung** *nf* **-en 1** admission. **2** permission. **3** (car) licence, registration.
Zulauf ('tsu:lauf) *nm* **1** rush. **2** crowd. **3** supply.
zuleide (tsu'laidə) *adv* **jemandem etwas zuleide tun** hurt or harm someone.
zuleiten ('tsu:laitən) *vt* lead in or to.
zuletzt (tsu'lɛtst) *adv* (at) last, finally.
zuliebe (tsu'li:bə) *adv* **jemandem zuliebe 1** to please someone. **2** for someone's sake.
zum (tsum) contraction of **zu dem.**
zumachen ('tsu:maxən) *vt* shut, fasten.
zumal (tsu'ma:l) *adv* especially.
zumeist (tsu'maist) *adv* mostly.
zumindest (tsu'mindəst) *adv* at least.
zumute (tsu'mu:tə) *adv* **mir ist gut zumute** I feel well, I am in good spirits.
zumut/en ('tsu:mu:tən) *vt* expect or ask of (a person). **—ung** *nf* **-en** (unreasonable) demand, presumption.
zunächst (tsu'nɛ:çst) *adv* first (of all). *prep* next to.
Zunahme ('tsu:na:mə) *nf* **-n** increase, growth.
Zuname ('tsu:na:mə) *nm* surname.
zünd/en ('tsyndən) *vi,vt* ignite. **—er** *nm* **— 1** fuse. **2** detonator. **—kerze** ('tsyntkɛrtsə) *nf* sparking plug. **—stoff** ('tsyntʃtɔf) *nm* **1** combustible matter. **2** fuel. **—ung** *nf* **-en 1** *mot* ignition. **2** priming.
Zunder ('tsundər) *nm* **—** tinder.
zunehmen* ('tsu:ne:mən) *vi* grow, increase, put on (weight).
zuneig/en ('tsu:naigən) *vi* **1** lean. **2** incline. **—ung** *nf* **-en 1** inclination. **2** sympathy.
Zunft (tsunft) *nf* **¨-e 1** guild. **2** clique.
Zunge ('tsuŋə) *nf* **-n 1** tongue. **2** *zool* sole.
zunichte (tsu'niçtə) *adv* ruined. **zunichte machen** ruin. **zunichte werden** come to nothing.
zunicken ('tsu:nikən) *vi,vt* nod (to).
zuoberst (tsu'o:bərst) *adv* at the top.
zupfen ('tsupfən) *vt* **1** pull. **2** pick.
zur (tsu:r) contraction of **zu der.**
zurechn/en ('tsu:rɛçnən) *vt* **1** add. **2** include. **3** ascribe. **—ung** *nf* **1** attribution. **2** addition.
zurecht (tsu'rɛçt) *adv* in order. **—legen** *vt* put out, arrange. **—machen** *vt* organize, prepare. **—setzen** *vt* set right. **—weisen*** *vt* **1** direct. **2** reprimand.
zureden ('tsu:re:dən) *vi* **1** urge, advise. **2** persuade.
zureichen ('tsu:raiçən) *vt* hand (over or to). *vi* suffice.
Zürich ('tsy:riç) *n neu* Zurich.
zurichten ('tsu:riçtən) *vt* **1** prepare. **2** *tech* dress.
zürnen ('tsyrnən) *vi* be angry.

zurück (tsu'ryk) *adv* back(wards), behind.
zurückbezahlen (tsu'rykbətsa:lən) *vt* repay.
zurückbleiben* (tsu'rykblaibən) *vi* remain or fall behind, be left behind.
zurückbringen* (tsu'rykbrŋən) *vt* bring back.
zurückeilen (tsu'rykailən) *vi* hurry back.
zurückfahren* (tsu'rykfa:rən) *vi* **1** drive or go back. **2** recoil. *vt* drive back.
zurückfinden* (tsu'rykfindən) *vr* find one's way back.
zurückführen (tsu'rykfy:rən) *vt* lead or trace back.
zurückgehen* (tsu'rykge:ən) *vi* **1** go or fall back. **2** decrease.
zurückgezogen (tsu'rykgətso:gən) *adj* retired, secluded.
zurückhalt/en* (tsu'rykhaltən) *vt* **1** hold back or in. **2** restrain. **3** detain. **4** repress. *vi* keep back. **—end** *adj* reserved. **—ung** *nf* reserve.
zurückkehren (tsu'rykke:rən) *vi* return.
zurückkommen* (tsu'rykkɔmən) *vi* **1** return. **2** recur.
zurücklegen (tsu'rykle:gən) *vt* **1** lay aside. **2** put by. **3** complete. **4** cover (distance). **sich zurücklegen** *vr* lie back.
zurücknehmen* (tsu'rykne:mən) *vt* take back.
zurückrufen* (tsu'rykru:fən) *vt* **1** call back. **2** recall.
zurückschlagen* (tsu'rykʃla:gən) *vt* **1** repel. **2** throw off or open. **3** return. *vi* strike back.
zurücksetzen (tsu'rykzɛtsən) *vt* **1** put back. **2** neglect (a person).
zurücktreten* (tsu'ryktre:tən) *vi* **1** step back. **2** resign. **3** retire.
zurückweichen* (tsu'rykvaiçən) *vi* **1** fall back. **2** recede. **3** yield.
zurückweisen* (tsu'rykvaizən) *vt* **1** send away or back. **2** decline, reject.
zurückziehen* (tsu'ryktsi:ən) *vt* withdraw.
Zuruf ('tsu:ru:f) *nm* shout, call.
Zusage ('tsu:za:gə) *nf* **1** consent. **2** promise, word. **—n** *vt* promise. *vi* agree.
zusammen (tsu'zamən) *adv* together.
Zusammenarbeit (tsu'zamənarbait) *nf* cooperation, teamwork. **—en** *vi* cooperate, work together.
zusammenballen (tsu'zamənbalən) *vt* **1** roll into a ball. **2** clench (one's fists).
zusammenbrechen* (tsu 'zamənbrɛçən) *vi* break down, collapse.
Zusammenbruch (tsu'zamənbrux) *nm* breakdown, collapse.
zusammenfahren* (tsu 'zamenfa:rən) *vi* **1** collide. **2** wince, start.
zusammenfass/en (tsu'zamənfasən) *vt* **1** comprise. **2** condense. **3** sum up. **—ung** *nf* summary.
zusammenfügen (tsu'zamənfy:gən) *vt* combine.
zusammengesetzt (tsu'zam-

əngəzɛtst) *adj* composed, assembled.

Zusammenhang (tsu'zamənhaŋ) *nm* **1** connection. **2** context. **3** continuity.

Zusammenkunft (tsu'zamənkunft) *nf* assembly.

zusammenlegen (tsu'zamənle:gən) *vt* **1** put together, combine. **2** fold (up). **3** pool.

zusammennehmen* (tsu 'zamənne:mən) *vt* gather up. **sich zusammennehmen** *vr* pull oneself together.

zusammenpassen (tsu'zamənpasən) *vi* go well together. *vt* adjust.

zusammenrücken (tsu'zamənrykən) *vt,vi* move closer together.

zusammenschließen* (tsu 'zamənʃli:sən) *vr* unite.

Zusammenschluß (tsu'zamənʃlus) *nm* **1** union. **2** *comm* merger.

zusammensetz/en (tsu'zamənzɛtsən) *vt* put together. **sich zusammensetzen** *vr* sit down together. **—ung** *nf* **1** composition. **2** construction.

zusammenstellen (tsu'zamənʃtɛlən) *vt* **1** put together. **2** make up.

zusammenstimmen (tsu 'zamənʃtimən) *vi* agree, harmonize.

Zusammenstoß (tsu'zamənʃtɔs) *nm* **1** collision. **2** conflict. **—en*** *vt* knock together. *vi* collide.

zusammentreffen* (tsu'zaməntrɛfən) *vi* **1** meet. **2** coincide. *n neu* **1** meeting. **2** coincidence.

zusammentreten* (tsu'zaməntre:tən) *vi* come together.

zusammenzieh/en* (tsu'zaməntsi:ən) *vt* draw together. **—ung** *nf* contraction.

Zusatz ('tsu:zats) *nm* **1** addition. **2** appendix.

zuschau/en ('tsu:ʃauən) *vi* look on. **—er** *nm* — spectator.

zuschicken ('tsu:ʃikən) *vt* send on, forward.

zuschieben* ('tsu:ʃi:bən) *vt* **1** push on. **2** shut.

zuschießen* ('tsu:ʃi:sən) *vt,vi* **1** rush (at). **2** contribute (money). *vt* shoot (a glance, etc.) at.

Zuschlag ('tsu:ʃla:k) *nm* **1** surcharge. **2** increase. **—en*** ('tsu:ʃla:gən) *vt* slam. *vi* hit out. **—spflichtig** *adj* liable to surcharge.

zuschließen* ('tsu:ʃli:sən) *vt* lock.

zuschneiden* ('tsu:ʃnaidən) *vt* **1** cut out. **2** cut to size.

zuschreiben* ('tsu:ʃraibən) *vt* ascribe to.

Zuschuß ('tsu:ʃus) *nm* **1** extra allowance. **2** subsidy, grant.

zuschütten ('tsu:ʃytən) *vt* **1** fill up with. **2** pour in or on.

zusehen* ('tsu:ze:ən) *vi* **1** look on. **2** wait. **—ds** *adv* visibly.

zusenden* ('tsu:zɛndən) *vt* send on, forward.

zusetzen ('tsu:zɛtsən) *vt* **1** add. **2** lose (money). *vi* importune, pester.

Zuspruch ('tsu:ʃprux) *nm* **1** encouragement. **2** consolation. **3** custom(ers).

Zustand ('tsu:ʃtant) *nm* **1** condition. **2** situation. **¨—ig** ('tsu:ʃtɛndiç) *adj* **1** appropriate. **2** competent, responsible.

zustatten (tsu'ʃtatən) *adv* **jemandem gut zustatten kommen** stand a person in good stead.
zustellen ('tsuːʃtɛlən) *vt* deliver (letters, mail).
zustimm/en ('tsuːʃtimən) *vi* agree, consent. **—ung** *nf* consent.
zustoßen* ('tsuːʃtoːsən) *vt* slam (shut). *vi* befall.
zustreben ('tsuːʃtreːbən) *vi* strive (for).
zutage (tsu'taːgə) *adv* **zutage bringen** bring to light.
Zutat ('tsuːtaːt) *nf* **1** *cul* ingredient. **2** seasoning. **3** trimming.
zuteil (tsuː'tail) *adv* **einem zuteil werden** fall to one's share.
zuteilen ('tsuːtailən) *vt* assign, allocate.
zutiefst (tsuː'tiːfst) *adv* deeply, intensely.
zutrag/en* ('tsuːtraːgən) *vt* carry (to). **sich zutragen** *vr* happen. **¨—er** ('tsuːtrɛːgər) *nm* — informer, gossipmonger, tell-tale. **¨—lich** ('tsuːtrɛːkliç) *adj* **1** wholesome. **2** advantageous.
zutrau/en ('tsuːtrauən) *vt* credit. *n neu* confidence. **—lich** *adj* trusting.
zutreffen* ('tsuːtrɛfən) *vi* prove true.
Zutritt ('tsuːtrit) *nm* access, admission.
zuverlässig ('tsuːfɛrlɛsiç) *adj* **1** reliable. **2** certain.
Zuversicht ('tsuːfɛrziçt) *nf* confidence. **—lich** *adj* confident.
zuviel (tsu'fiːl) *adv* too much.
zuvörderst (tsu'fœrdərst) *adv* first of all.
zuvorkommen* (tsu'foːrkɔmən) *vi* anticipate.
zuvortun* (tsu'foːrtuːn) *vi* outdo.
Zuwachs ('tsuːvaks) *nm* increase, growth.
zuweilen (tsu'vailən) *adv* at times, sometimes.
zuweisen* ('tsuːvaizən) *vt* allot.
zuwenden* ('tsuːvɛndən) *vt* **1** turn towards. **2** give. **3** procure.
zuwider (tsu'viːdər) *prep* **1** contrary to. **2** distasteful to. **—handlung** *nf* violation, infringement. **—laufen*** *vi* run counter (to).
zuzeiten (tsu'tsaitən) *adv* at times.
zuziehen* ('tsuːtsiːən) *vt* **1** draw (together), tighten, shut. **2** invite. *vi* **1** move in. **2** immigrate. **sich eine Krankheit zuziehen** catch or contract a disease. **sich Schwierigkeiten zuziehen** get into difficulties.
zwang (tsvaŋ) *v* see **zwingen.**
Zwang (tsvaŋ) *nm* **¨—e 1** compulsion. **2** force. **—los** *adj* unconstrained. **—släufig** ('tsvaŋslɔyfiç) *adj* inevitable.
zwängen ('tsvɛŋən) *vt* press, squeeze.
zwanzig ('tsvantsiç) *adj,nf* twenty. **—ste** *adj* twentieth.
zwar (tsvaːr) *adv* indeed. **und zwar** that is, namely, in fact.
Zweck (tsvɛk) *nm* **-e 1** purpose. **2** design. **—los** *adj* useless, purposeless. **—mäßig** *adj* **1** suitable. **2** expedient. **3** practical.

Zwecke ('tsvɛkə) *nf* **-n 1** drawing-pin. **2** tack. **3** peg.
zwei (tsvai) *adj,nf* two.
zweideutig ('tsvaidɔytiç) *adj* ambiguous.
zweierlei (tsvaiər'lai) *adj* of two kinds.
Zweifel ('tsvaifəl) *nm* — doubt. **—haft** *adj* doubtful. **—los** *adj* doubtless. **—n** *vi* doubt.
Zweig (tsvaik) *nm* **-e** branch, twig. **—stelle** *nf* branch office.
zweijährlich ('tsvaijɛːrliç) *adj* every two years.
Zweikampf ('tsvaikampf) *nm* duel.
zweimal ('tsvaimal) *adv* twice.
zweisprachig ('tsvaiʃpraːxiç) *adj* bilingual.
zweistimmig ('tsvaiʃtimiç) *adj* *mus* for two voices.
zwei/te ('tsvaitə) *adj* second. **zu Zweit** in twos, two by two. **—tens** ('tsvaitəns) *adv* secondly. **—tklassig** *adj* second-rate.
Zwerchfell ('tsvɛrçfɛl) *n neu* diaphragm.
Zwerg (tsvɛrk) *nm* **-e** dwarf.
zwicken ('tsvikən) *vt* pinch, tweak.
Zwieback ('tsviːbak) *nm* **-e** biscuit, rusk.
Zwiebel ('tsviːbəl) *nf* **-n 1** onion. **2** *bot* bulb.
Zwiegespräch ('tsviːgəʃprɛːx) *n neu* dialogue.
Zwiespalt ('tsviːʃpalt) *nm* **-e** dissension.
Zwietracht ('tsviːtraxt) *nf* discord.
Zwilling ('tsviliŋ) *nm* **-e 1** twin. **2** *pl* Gemini.
Zwinge ('tsviŋə) *nf* **-n 1** clamp. **2** ferrule.
zwingen* ('tsviŋən) *vt* **1** force. **2** overcome.
zwischen ('tsviʃən) *prep* between, among. **—durch** *adv* **1** through. **2** in the midst. **3** between. —fall *nm* incident. **—raum** *nm* interval, gap, space. **—spiel** *n neu* interlude. **—wand** *nf* partition. **—zeit** *nf* interim, interval.
Zwist (tsvist) *nm* **-e 1** discord. **2** quarrel. **—ig** *adj* **1** at variance. **2** in dispute.
zwitschern ('tsitʃərn) *vi* chirp, twitter.
zwo (tsvoː) *adj,nf* see **zwei.**
zwölf (tsvœlf) *adj,nf* twelve. **—te** *adj* twelfth.
Zyklon (tsy'kloːn) *nm* **-e** cyclone.
Zyklus ('tsyːklus) *nm* **-len 1** cycle. **2** series.
Zylinder (tsi'lindər) *nm* — **1** cylinder. **2** top-hat.
Zyn/iker ('tsyːnikər) *nm* — cynic. **—isch** ('tsyːniʃ) *adj* cynical.
Zyp/ern ('tsyːpərn) *n neu* Cyprus. **—riot** (tsypriː'oːt) *nm* **-en** Cypriot. **—riotisch** (tsypri 'oːtiʃ) *adj* Cypriot.

A

a, an (ə, ən; *stressed* ei, æn) *indef art* **1** ein, eine, ein *m,f,neu.* **2** pro, je.

aback (ə'bæk) *adv* nach hinten, zurück. **taken aback** bestürzt, verblüfft.

abandon (ə'bændən) *n* Ungezwungenheit, Hingabe *f. vt* **1** aufgeben, verlassen. **2** verzichten auf. **3** im Stich lassen.

abashed (ə'bæʃt) *adj* verlegen, sich schämend.

abate (ə'beit) *vi* (of wind) abnehmen, sich legen.

abattoir ('æbətwɑː) *n* Schlachthaus *neu.*

abbess ('æbis) *n* Äbtissin *f.*

abbey ('æbi) *n* Abtei *f.*

abbot ('æbət) *n* Abt *m.*

abbreviate (ə'briːvieit) *vt* abkürzen. **abbreviation** *n* Abkürzung *f.*

abdicate ('æbdikeit) *vi* abdanken. *vt* niederlegen. **abdication** *n* Abdankung *f.*

abdomen ('æbdəmən) *n* Unterleib, Bauch *m.*

abduct (æb'dʌkt) *vt* entführen. **abduction** *n* Entführung *f.*

abet (ə'bet) *vt* **1** begünstigen. **2** anstiften. **aid and abet** *law* Vorschub leisten.

abhor (əb'hɔː) *vt* verabscheuen. **abhorrence** *n* Abscheu *m.* **abhorrent** *adj* zuwider, verhaßt.

abide* (ə'baid) *vi* bleiben, fortdauern. *vt* vertragen, ausstehen. **abide by** treu bleiben, sich halten an.

ability (ə'biliti) *n* **1** Fähigheit *f.* **2** geistige Anlagen *f pl.*

abject ('abdʒekt) *adj* gemein, verächtlich.

ablaze (ə'bleiz) *adj,adv* **1** in Flammen. **2** glänzend. **3** erregt.

able ('eibəl) *adj* **1** fähig. **2** geschickt, tüchtig, begabt. **be able to** können.

abnormal (æb'nɔːməl) *adj* **1** ungewöhnlich. **2** anormal, abnorm. **abnormality** *n* **1** Abnormität *f.* **2** Mißbildung *f.*

aboard (ə'bɔːd) *adv* an Bord.

abode (ə'boud) *n* Wohnort *m.* Stätte *f.*

abolish (ə'bɔliʃ) *vt* abschaffen, aufheben. **abolition** *n* Abschaffung, Aufhebung *f.*

abominable (ə'bɔminəbəl) *adj* abscheulich.

Aborigine (æbə'ridʒini) *n* **1** Ureinwohner *m.* **2** *pl* Urbevölkerung *f.* **aboriginal** *adj* eingeboren.

abort (ə'bɔːt) *vi* **1** fehlgebären. **2** fehlschlagen. **abortion** *n* **1** Abtreibung *f.* **2** Fehlgeburt *f.* **abortive** *adj* **1** vorzeitig. **2** fehlgeschlagen, mißlungen.

abound (ə'baund) *vi* reichlich vorhanden sein.

about (ə'baut) *prep* **1** wegen, über. **2** gegen. *adv* **1** herum, umher. **2** ungefähr, etwa. **be about to do something** eben etwas tun wollen.

above (ə'bʌv) *prep* über, oberhalb. *adv* oben, darüber. *adj* obig, oben erwähnt. **aboveboard** *adj* offen, ehrlich.

abrasion (ə'breiʒən) *n* Abschleifen, Abreiben *neu.* **abrasive** *adj* abreibend, abschleifend.

abreast (ə'brest) *adv* **1** nebeneinander. **2** auf dem laufenden. **keep abreast of** Schritt halten mit.

abridge (ə'bridʒ) *vt* (ab-, ver-) kürzen.

abroad (ə'brɔːd) *adv* **1** ins *or* im Ausland. **2** draußen. **3** auswärts.

abrupt (ə'brʌpt) *adj* **1** abrupt, plötzlich. **2** schroff.

abscess ('æbses) *n* Abszeß *m*. Geschwür *neu*.

abscond (əb'skɔnd) *vi* sich heimlich davonmachen, flüchten.

absent (*adj* 'æbsənt; *v* əb'sent) *adj* **1** abwesend. **2** zerstreut. *v* **absent oneself from** sich entfernen von. **absence** *n* **1** Abwesenheit *f*. **2** Mangel *m*. **in the absence of** in Ermangelung von. **absentee** *n* Abwesende(r) *m*. **absenteeism** *n* (unerlaubtes) Fernbleiben *neu*. **absent-minded** *adj* zerstreut, geistesabwesend.

absinthe ('æbsinθ) *n* Absinth *m*.

absolute ('æbsəluːt) *adj* **1** absolut. **2** vollkommen. **absolutely** *adv* völlig, durchaus.

absolve (əb'zɔlv) *vt* freisprechen. **absolution** *n rel* Absolution *f*.

absorb (əb'zɔːb) *vt* **1** absorbieren, aufsaugen. **2** aufnehmen. **be absorbed in** vertieft sein in. **absorbent** *adj* aufsaugend. **absorption** *n* Absorption, Aufsaugung *f*.

abstain (əb'stein) *vi* sich enthalten. **abstainer** *n* Abstinenzler *m*. **abstention** *n* Enthaltung *f*. **abstinence** *n* Enthaltsamkeit, Abstinenz *f*.

abstract (*adj,n* 'æbstrækt; *v* əb'strækt) *adj* abstrakt, theoretisch. *n* **1** Abstrakte *neu*. **2** Auszug *m*. *vt* ablenken, absondern. **abstraction** *n* **1** *sci* Absonderung *f*. **2** Abstraktion *f*. **3** Zerstreutheit *f*.

absurd (əb'səːd) *adj* absurd, sinnwidrig, albern. **absurdity** *n* Albernheit *f*. Unsinn *m*.

abundance (ə'bʌndəns) *n* Überfluß *m*. Fülle *f*. **abundant** *adj* reichlich.

abuse (*v* ə'bjuːz; *n* ə'bjuːs) *vt* **1** mißbrauchen. **2** beschimpfen. *n* **1** Mißbrauch *m*. **2** Beschimpfung *f*. **abusive** *adj* beleidigend.

abyss (ə'bis) *n* Abgrund *m*. **abysmal** *adj* abgrundtief.

Abyssinia (æbi'siniə) *n* Abessinien *neu*. **Abyssinian** *adj* abessinisch. *n* Abessinier *m*.

academy (ə'kædəmi) *n* (Kunst)Akademie *f*. **academic** *adj* **1** akademisch. **2** rein theoretisch. *n* Akademiker *m*.

accelerate (ək'seləreit) *vt* **1** beschleunigen. **2** *mot* Gas geben. **acceleration** *n* Beschleunigung *f*. **accelerator** *n* Gaspedal *neu*.

accent (*n* 'æksənt; *v* æk'sent) *n* **1** Akzent *m*. **2** Betonung *f*. *vt* betonen. **accentuate** *vt* **1** betonen. **2** hervorheben.

accept (ək'sept) *vt* **1** (an-, entgegen-)nehmen, akzeptieren. **2** anerkennen, gelten lassen. *vi* annehmen, zusagen. **acceptable** *adj* **1** annehmbar. **2** angenehm. **acceptance** *n* **1** Annahme *f*. **2** Aufnahme *f*.

access ('ækses) *n* **1** Zugang, Zutritt *m.* **2** Zufahrt *f.* **accessible** *adj* zugänglich. **accession** *n* **1** Antritt *m.* **2** Thronbesteigung *f.* **accessory** Zubehörteil *m.*

accident ('æksidnt) *n* **1** Zufall *m.* **2** Unfall *m.* Unglück neu. **accidental** *adj* zufällig.

acclaim (ə'kleim) *vt* **1** (mit Beifall) begrüßen, zujubeln. **2** anerkennen, begrüßen. **acclamation** *n* **1** Beifall *m.* **2** Zuruf *m.*

acclimatize (ə'klaimətaiz) *(vi),vt* (sich) akklimatisieren, (sich) eingewöhnen. **acclimatization** *n* Akklimatisierung, Eingewöhnung *f.*

accommodate (ə'kɔmədeit) *vt* **1** unterbringen. **2** anpassen. **3** aushelfen. **acommodating** *adj* **1** gefällig. **2** anpassungsfähig. **accommodation** *n* **1** Unterkunft *f.* **2** Anpassung *f.*

accompany (ə'kʌmpəni) *vt* begleiten. **accompaniment** *n* Begleitung *f.* **accompanist** *n mus* Begleiter *m.*

accomplice (ə'kʌmplis) *n* Mittäter *m.*

accomplish (ə'kʌmpliʃ) *vt* vollenden, zustande bringen. **accomplishment** *n* **1** Vollendung *f.* **2** Leistung *f.* **3** *pl* Talente *neu pl.*

accord (ə'kɔːd) *vt* gewähren. *vi* übereinstimmen. *n* Übereinstimmung *f.* **of one's own accord** aus eigenem Antrieb. **accordance** *n* Übereinstimmung *f.* **in accordance with** in Übereinstimmung mit, gemäß. **according to** *prep* **1** gemäß. **2** laut, zufolge.

accordion (ə'kɔːdiən) *n* Ziehharmonika *f.*

accost (ə'kɔst) *vt* ansprechen.

account (ə'kaunt) *vi* Rechenschaft ablegen. *vt* ansehen als. *n* **1** Rechnung *f.* **2** Bericht *m.* **3** *comm* Konto *neu.* **on no account** auf keinen Fall. **accountable** *adj* verantwortlich. **accountancy** *n* Rechnungswesen *neu.* **accountant** *n* **1** Rechnungsführer *m.* **2** Bücherrevisor *m.*

accumulate (ə'kjuːmjuleit) *(vi),vt* (sich) anhäufen. **accumulation** *n* Anhäufung *f.* **accumulative** *adj* (sich) anhäufend.

accurate ('ækjurət) *adj* **1** genau. **2** richtig. **accuracy** *n* Genauigkeit *f.*

accusative (ə'kjuːzətiv) *n* Akkusativ *m.*

accuse (ə'kjuːz) *vt* anklagen, beschuldigen. **accused** *n* Angeklagte(r) *m.* **accuser** *n* Kläger *m.*

accustom (ə'kʌstəm) *vt* gewöhnen. **become accustomed to** sich gewöhnen an.

ace (eis) *n* As *neu.*

ache (eik) *vi* schmerzen, weh tun. *n* Schmerz *m.* **aching** *adj* schmerzhaft.

achieve (ə'tʃiːv) *vt* **1** ausführen. **2** zustande bringen. **3** erreichen, erzielen. **achievement** *n* **1** Ausführung, Vollendung *f.* **2** Leistung *f.* Werk *neu.*

acid ('æsid) *adj* sauer. *n* Säure *f.*

acknowledge (ək'nɔlidʒ) *vt* **1** anerkennen, zugeben. **2** *comm* bestätigen. **acknowledg-**

ment *n* **1** Anerkennung *f*. **2** Dank *m*. **3** *comm* Empfangsbestätigung *f*.

acne ('ækni) *n* Akne *f*. Hautausschlag *m*.

acorn ('eikɔːn) *n* Eichel *f*.

acoustic (ə'kuːstik) *adj* akustisch. **acoustics** *n* Akustik *f*.

acquaint (ə'kweint) *vt* bekannt machen. **be acquainted with** kennen. **acquaintance** *n* **1** Bekanntschaft *f*. **2** Bekannte(r) *m*. **make someone's acquaintance** jemanden kennenlernen.

acquiesce (ækwi'es) *vi* einwilligen, sich fügen. **acquiescent** *adj* ergeben, fügsam.

acquire (ə'kwaiə) *vt* erwerben, erlangen. **acquisition** *n* Erwerbung *f*. **acquisitive** *adj* gewinnsüchtig.

acquit (ə'kwit) *vt* freisprechen. **acquittal** *n* Freispruch *m*.

acre ('eikə) *n* Morgen *m*.

acrimony ('ækriməni) *n* Schärfe, Bitterkeit *f*. **acrimonious** *adj* scharf, beißend.

acrobat ('ækrəbæt) *n* Akrobat *m*. **acrobatic** *adj* akrobatisch. **acrobatics** *n pl* Akrobatik *f*.

across (ə'krɔs) *adv* **1** hinüber, herüber, (quer)durch. **2** kreuzweise. *prep* **1** über. **2** jenseits. **come across** stoßen auf.

acrylic (ə'krilik) *n* Polyacryl *Tdmk neu*.

act (ækt) *vt* darstellen, spielen. **act a part** eine Rolle spielen. *vi* handeln. **act as** fungieren als. **act on** wirken auf. ~*n* **1** Handlung, Tat *f*. **2** *Th* Aufzug *m*. **3** Gesetz *neu*. **acting** *adj* **1** handelnd. **2** amtierend. *n Th* Spielen *neu*.

action ('ækʃən) *n* **1** Handlung *f*. **2** Tat *f*. **3** Wirkung *f*. **4** *law* Klage *f*. **5** *mil* Gefecht *neu*.

active ('æktiv) *adj* tätig, wirksam, aktiv. *n gram* Aktiv *neu*. **activate** *vt* **1** in Tätigkeit setzen. **2** wirksam machen. **activity** *n* **1** Tätigkeit *f*. **2** Treiben *neu*. **3** *pl* Unternehmungen *f pl*.

actor ('æktə) *n* Schauspieler *m*.

actress ('æktris) *n* Schauspielerin *f*.

actual ('æktʃuəl) *adj* wirklich, tatsächlich, eigentlich.

acupuncture ('ækjupʌŋktʃə) *n* Akupunktur *f*.

acute (ə'kjuːt) *adj* **1** akut, heftig. **2** scharf. **acute angle** spitzer Winkel *m*.

adamant ('ædəmənt) *adj* unerbittlich.

adapt (ə'dæpt) *vt* **1** anpassen, zurechtmachen. **2** bearbeiten. **adaptable** *adj* anpassungsfähig. **adaptation** *n* **1** Anpassung *f*. **2** Bearbeitung *f*. **adaptor** *n* Zwischenstecker *m*.

add (æd) *vt* **1** addieren. **2** hinzufügen. *vi* hinzukommen. **add up** zusammenzählen, addieren. **adding machine** *n* Addiermaschine *f*. **addition** *n* **1** Hinzufügung *f*. **2** Zusatz *m*. Zutat *f*. **3** Addition *f*. **in addition** außerdem, noch dazu. **in addition to which** wozu (kommt noch). **additional** *adj* zusätzlich. **additive** *n* Zusatz *m*.

addendum (ə'dendəm) *n, pl* **addenda 1** Zusatz *m*. **2** Nachtrag *m*.

adder ('ædə) *n* Natter *f*.

addict ('ædikt) *n* Süchtige(r) *m*. **addicted** *adj* süchtig. **addiction** *n* Neigung, Sucht *f*.

addled ('ædld) *adj* **1** faul. **2** verwirrt.

address (ə'dres) *vt* **1** anreden, sprechen zu. **2** (a letter) adressieren. *n* **1** Adresse, Anschrift *f*. **2** Ansprache, Anrede *f*. **address book** *n* Adreßbuch *neu*.

adenoids ('ædinɔidz) *n pl* Polypen *m pl*.

adept ('ædept) *adj* geschickt.

adequate ('ædikwət) *adj* **1** ausreichend. **2** angemessen. **adequacy** *n* Angemessenheit *f*.

adhere (əd'hiə) *vi* **1** kleben, haften. **2** festhalten. **adherence** *n* Festhalten *neu*. **adherent** *n* Anhänger *m*. *adj* anhaftend. **adhesion** *n* **1** Anhaften *neu*. **2** Anhänglichkeit *f*. **adhesive** *adj* klebrig, gummiert. *n* Klebstoff *m*. **adhesive tape** *n* Klebestreifen *m*.

ad hoc (æd 'hɔk) *adj,adv* für diesen Fall bestimmt.

adjacent (ə'dʒeisənt) *adj* angrenzend.

adjective ('ædʒiktiv) *n* Adjektiv, Eigenschaftswort *neu*.

adjoin (ə'dʒɔin) *vt* angrenzen.

adjourn (ə'dʒə:n) *vt* aufschieben, vertagen. *vi* sich vertagen. **adjournment** *n* Vertagung *f*. Verschiebung *f*.

adjudicate (ə'dʒu:dikeit) *vt* gerichtlich entscheiden. *vi* als Schiedsrichter handeln. **adjudication** **1** richterliche Entscheidung *f*. **2** Zusprechung *f*. **adjudicator** *n* Schiedsrichter *m*.

adjust (ə'dʒʌst) *vt* **1** anpassen. **2** einstellen. *vi* sich anpassen. **adjustable** *adj* verstellbar. **adjustment** *n* **1** Anpassung *f*. **2** Einstellung *f*.

ad-lib (æd'lib) *vt,vi inf* improvisieren.

administer (əd'ministə) *vt* verwalten. *vi* als Verwalter fungieren. **administrate** *vt* verwalten. **administration** *n* **1** Verwaltung *f*. Verwaltungswesen *neu*. **2** Regierung *f*. **administration of justice** Rechtsprechung *f*. **administrative** *adj* Verwaltungs—, verwaltend. **administrator** *n* Verwalter *m*.

admiral ('ædmərəl) *n* Admiral *m*. **admiralty** *n* Admiralität *f*.

admire (əd'maiə) *vt* **1** bewundern. **2** hochschätzen. **admirable** *adj* bewundernswert, großartig. **admiration** *n* Bewunderung *f*. **admirer** *n* **1** Bewunderer *m*. **2** Verehrer *m*.

admit (əd'mit) *vt* **1** einlassen. **2** zugeben. **3** gelten lassen. **admission** *n* **1** Zulassung *f*. **2** Eintritt *m*. **3** Zugeständnis *neu*. **admittance** *n* Einlaß *m*. Zutritt *m*. **no admittance** Zutritt verboten.

ado (ə'du:) *n* Getue, Aufheben *neu*. **without further ado** ohne weitere Umstände.

adolescence (ædə'lesəns) *n* Jünglingsalter *neu*. **adolescent** *n* Jugendliche(r) *m*. *adj* jugendlich.

adopt (ə'dɔpt) *vt* **1** adoptieren. **2** annehmen, sich aneignen. **adoption** *n* Adoption, An-

nahme *f.* **adoptive** *adj* angenommen, Adoptiv—.
adore (ə'dɔː) *vt* **1** anbeten, verehren. **2** lieben, sehr gern haben. **adorable** *adj* **1** verehrungswürdig. **2** entzückend. **adoration** *n* Anbetung, Verehrung *f.*
adorn (ə'dɔːn) *vt* schmücken. **adornment** *n* Schmuck *m.*
adrenaline (ə'drenəlin) *n* Adrenalin *neu.*
Adriatic (eidri'ætik) *adj* adriatisch. **Adriatic (Sea)** *n* Adriatisches Meer *neu.*
adrift (ə'drift) *adj,adv* **1** (umher)treibend. **2** hilflos.
adroit (ə'drɔit) *adj* gewandt.
adulation (ædju'leiʃən) *n* Schmeichelei *f.*
adult ('ædʌlt) *adj* erwachsen. *n* Erwachsene(r) *m.*
adulterate (ə'dʌltəreit) *vt* **1** verfälschen. **2** verderben. **adulteration** *n* Verfälschung *f.*
adultery (ə'dʌltəri) *n* Ehebruch *m.* **adulterer** *n* Ehebrecher *m.* **adulteress** *n* Ehebrecherin *f.* **adulterous** *adj* ehebrecherisch.
advance (əd'vɑːns) *vt* **1** vorrücken, vorwärtsbringen. **2** (money) vorschießen. **3** befördern. *vi* **1** vorrücken, vordringen. **2** Fortschritte machen. *n* **1** Vorrücken *neu.* **2** (money) Vorschuß *m.* **3** *mil* Vormarsch *m.* **in advance** im voraus. **advanced** *adj* fortgeschritten. **advancement** *n* **1** Beförderung *f.* **2** Fortschritt *m.*
advantage (əd'vɑːntidʒ) *n* Vorteil *m.* **take advantage of** ausnutzen. **advantageous** *adj* vorteilhaft, günstig.
advent ('ædvent) *n* **1** Kommen *neu.* Ankunft *f.* **2** *cap rel* Advent *m.*
adventure (əd'ventʃə) *n* Abenteuer *neu.* **adventurer** *n* Abenteurer *m.* **adventurous** *adj* **1** abenteuerlich. **2** abenteuerlustig.
adverb ('ædvəːb) *n* Adverb, Umstandswort *neu.* **adverbial** *adj* adverbial.
adverse ('ædvəːs) *adj* **1** widrig. **2** feindlich. **3** ungünstig. **adversary** *n* Gegner *m.* **adversity** *n* Unglück *neu.* Not *f.*
advertise ('ædvətaiz) *vt* anzeigen. *vi* Reklame machen. **advertisement** *n* **1** Anzeige *f.* **2** Reklame *f.* **advertising** *n* Reklame, Werbung *f.*
advise (əd'vaiz) *vt* **1** raten, empfehlen. **2** beraten. **3** benachrichtigen, mitteilen. **advice** *n* **1** Rat *m.* **2** Ratschlag *m.* **3** *comm* Avis *m.* **advisable** *adj* ratsam. **adviser** *n* **1** Ratgeber *m.* **2** Berater *m.* **advisory** *adj* beratend, Beratungs—.
advocate (*v* 'ædvəkeit; *n* 'ædvəkət) *vt* **1** verteidigen. **2** befürworten. *n* **1** Advokat *m.* **2** Fürsprecher *m.* **advocacy** *n* Verteidigung *f.* Befürwortung *f.*
Aegean (i'dʒiːən) *adj* ägäisch. **Aegean (Sea)** *n* Ägäisches Meer *neu.*
aerial ('ɛəriəl) *adj* **1** Luft—. **2** leicht, gasförmig. *n tech* Antenne *f.*
aerodynamics (ɛəroudai'næmiks) *n pl* Aerodynamik *f.* **aerodynamic** *adj* aerodynamisch.

aeronautics (ɛərə'nɔːtiks) *n pl* Aeronautik *f.* Flugwesen *neu.* **aeronautical** *adj* aeronautisch.

aeroplane ('ɛərəplein) *n* Flugzeug *neu.*

aerosol ('ɛərəsɔl) *n* **1** Sprühdose *f.* Spray *neu.* **2** Aerosol *neu.*

aesthetic (is'θetik) *adj* ästhetisch, geschmackvoll.

afar (ə'fɑː) *adv* fern. **from afar** aus weiter Ferne.

affable ('æfəbəl) *adj* leutselig.

affair (ə'fɛə) *n* **1** Angelegenheit, Sache, Affäre *f.* **2** (Liebes)Affäre, Liebschaft *f.*

affect[1] (ə'fekt) *vt* **1** berühren, angehen. **2** beeinflussen, einwirken auf. **3** beeinträchtigen.

affect[2] (ə'fekt) *vt* vortäuschen, vorgeben.

affection (ə'fekʃən) *n* Zuneigung, Liebe *f.* **affectionate** *adj* liebevoll, zärtlich.

affiliate (ə'filieit) *vt* **1** (als Mitglied) aufnehmen. **2** angliedern. **affiliated company** *n* Tochtergesellschaft *f.*

affinity (ə'finiti) *n* enge Beziehungen *f pl.*

affirm (ə'fəːm) *vt* behaupten, versichern. *vi* bestätigen, zustimmen. **affirmation** *n* Behauptung *f.* **affirmative** *adj* bejahend, bestimmt. **answer in the affirmative** bejahen, mit Ja antworten.

affix (ə'fiks) *vt* **1** aufkleben. **2** aufdrücken.

afflict (ə'flikt) *vt* **1** betrüben. **2** quälen. **afflicted** *adj* leidend. **affliction** *n* **1** Kummer *m.* **2** Leiden *neu.*

affluent ('æfluənt) *adj* **1** reich. **2** wohlhabend. **affluent society** *n* Wohlstandsgesellschaft *f.*

afford (ə'fɔːd) *vt* **1** sich leisten (können). **2** gewähren.

affront (ə'frʌnt) *vt* beleidigen. *n* Beleidigung *f.*

Afghanistan (æf'gænistɑːn, -'stæn) *n* Afghanistan *neu.* **Afghanistani** *adj* afghanistanisch. *n* Afghanistaner *m.*

afield (ə'fiːld) *adv* **far afield** weit weg.

afloat (ə'flout) *adv* **1** schwimmend. **2** auf dem Meere. **keep afloat** sich über Wasser halten.

afoot (ə'fut) *adv* **1** im Gang(e). **2** zu Fuß.

aforesaid (ə'fɔːsed) *adj* vorerwähnt.

afraid (ə'freid) *adj* ängstlich, bange, erschrocken. **be afraid 1** Angst haben. **2** bedauern. **be afraid of** sich fürchten vor, Angst haben vor. **be afraid to do something** sich scheuen, etwas zu tun.

afresh (ə'freʃ) *adv* von neuem.

Africa ('æfrikə) Afrika *neu.* **African** *adj* afrikanisch. *n* Afrikaner *m.*

aft (ɑːft) *adv naut* achtern, hinten.

after ('ɑːftə) *prep* nach. *conj* nachdem. *adv* nachher. **shortly after** kurz darauf. **after-care** *n* Nachbehandlung *f.* **after-effect** *n* Nachwirkung *f.* **afterlife** *n* Leben nach dem Tode *neu.* **aftermath** *n* Nachwirkungen *f pl.* **afternoon** *n* Nachmittag *m.* **afterthought** nachträglicher Einfall *m*. **afterwards** *adv* später, nachher.

again (ə'gen) *adv* **1** wieder, nochmals. **2** ferner, außerdem. **once again** noch einmal.

against (ə'genst) *prep* **1** gegen, wider. **2** gegenüber.

age (eidʒ) *n* **1** Alter *neu*. **2** Zeitalter *neu*. **age-group** *n* Altersklasse *f*. **be of age** mündig sein. **old age** Alter *neu*. *vi* alt werden, altern. *vt* alt machen. **aged** *adj* **1** alt. **2** bejahrt, betagt.

agency ('eidʒənsi) *n* Agentur *f*.

agenda (ə'dʒendə) *n* Tagesordnung *f*.

agent ('eidʒənt) *n* **1** Agent, Vertreter *m*. **2** wirkende Kraft *f*. Mittel *neu*.

aggravate ('ægrəveit) *vt* **1** erschweren, verschlimmern. **2** *inf* ärgern. **aggravating** *adj* **1** erschwerend. **2** *inf* ärgerlich. **aggravation** *n* **1** Erschwerung *f*. **2** *inf* Verärgerung *f*.

aggregate (*adj,n* 'ægrigit; *v* 'ægrigeit) *adj* angehäuft, gesamt. *n* Anhäufung *f*. *vt* anhäufen.

aggression (ə'greʃən) *n* **1** Angriff *m*. **2** Aggression *f*. **aggressive** *adj* **1** angreifend. **2** streitsüchtig, aggressiv.

aggrieved (ə'griːvd) *adj* betrübt, gekränkt.

aghast (ə'gɑːst) *adj* entsetzt.

agile ('ædʒail) *adj* beweglich, behende, agil. **agility** *n* Beweglichkeit, Behendigkeit *f*.

agitate ('ædʒiteit) *vt* **1** bewegen, aufrühren. **2** erregen. *vi* agitieren. **agitation** *n* **1** Bewegung *f*. **2** Unruhe *f*. Aufruhr *m*. **agitator** *n* Agitator, Aufwiegler *m*.

aglow (ə'glou) *adj* glühend.

agnostic (æg'nɔstik) *n* Agnostiker *m*. *adj* agnostisch. **agnosticism** *n* Agnostizismus *m*.

ago (ə'gou) *adv* vor, her. **long ago** vor langer Zeit.

agog (ə'gɔg) *adv* gespannt.

agony ('ægəni) *n* Qual, Agonie *f*. **agonize** *vt* quälen. **agonizing** *adj* quälend.

agrarian (ə'grɛəriən) *adj* agrarisch.

agree (ə'griː) *vi* übereinstimmen, einwilligen, einverstanden sein. **agree (on)** einig werden (über). **agreeable** *adj* **1** angenehm. **2** einverstanden. **agreed** *adj* **1** einig. **2** vereinbart. *interj* einverstanden! **agreement** *n* **1** Übereinstimmung *f*. **2** Abkommen *neu*. Vertrag *m*. **make an agreement** ein Abkommen treffen.

agriculture ('ægrikʌltʃə) *n* Landwirtschaft *f*. **agricultural** *adj* landwirtschaftlich.

aground (ə'graund) *adv* **run aground** stranden.

ahead (ə'hed) *adv* vorwärts, voran. **go ahead** fangen Sie an! **straight ahead** gerade aus.

aid (eid) *vt* helfen. *n* Hilfe *f*.

aide (eid) *n mil* Adjutant *m*.

ailment ('eilmənt) *n* Leiden *neu*. **ailing** *adj* kränklich, leidend.

aim (eim) *vt* (a gun, etc.) richten. *vi* **1** zielen. **2** streben. *n* **1** Ziel *neu*. **2** Absicht *f*. Zweck *m*. **take aim** zielen. **aimless** *adj* ziellos.

air (ɛə) *n* **1** Luft *f.* **2** Miene *f.* Anschein *m.* **3** Melodie *f.* Lied *neu.* **go by air** fliegen. **put on the air** senden. *~vt* **1** (aus)lüften, trocknen. **2** bekanntmachen.
airborne ('ɛəbɔːn) *adj* im Flugzeug befördert. **be airborne** fliegen.
air-conditioning *n* Klimaanlage *f.*
aircraft ('ɛəkraːft) *n* Flugzeug *neu.*
airfield ('ɛəfiːld) *n* Flugplatz *m.*
airforce ('ɛəfɔːs) *n* Luftwaffe *f.*
air-hostess ('ɛəhoustis) *n* Stewardeß *f.*
air lift *n* Luftbrücke *f.*
airline ('ɛəlain) *n* Luftverkehrslinie, Luftgesellschaft *f.* **airline passenger** *n* Fluggast *m.*
airmail ('ɛəmeil) *n* Luftpost *f.*
airman ('ɛəmən) *n* Flieger *m.*
airport ('ɛəpɔːt) *n* Flughafen *m.*
air-raid *n* Luftangriff *m.*
airtight ('ɛətait) *adj* luftdicht.
airy ('ɛəri) *adj* **1** luftig. **2** unbekümmert.
aisle (ail) *n* Seitenschiff *neu.*
ajar (ə'dʒɑː) *adv* halb offen, angelehnt.
akin (ə'kin) *adj* **1** verwandt. **2** (sehr) ähnlich.
alabaster ('æləbɑːstə) *n* Alabaster *m.*
alarm (ə'lɑːm) *vt* **1** alarmieren. **2** beunruhigen. *n* **1** Alarm *m.* **2** Angst *f.* **alarm clock** *n* Wecker *m.* **alarming** *adj* beunruhigend.
alas (ə'læs) *interj* ach! o weh! leider!
Albania (æl'beiniə) *n* Albanien *neu.* **Albanian** *adj* albanisch. *n* Albanier *m.*
albatross ('ælbətros) *n* Albatros *m.*
albeit (ɔːl'biːit) *conj* obgleich, wenn auch.
album ('ælbəm) *n* Album *neu.*
alchemy ('ælkəmi) *n* Alchimie *f.* **alchemist** *n* Alchimist *m.*
alcohol ('ælkəhɔl) *n* Alkohol *m.* **alcoholic** *adj* alkoholisch. *n* Alkoholiker *m.* **alcoholism** *n* Alkoholismus *m.*
alderman ('ɔːldəmən) *n* Ratsherr, Stadtrat *m.*
ale (eil) *n* Bier *neu.*
alert (ə'ləːt) *adj* **1** wachsam. **2** flink, munter. *vt* warnen. *n* Warnung *f.* **be on the alert** auf der Hut sein.
algebra ('ældʒibrə) *n* Algebra *f.*
Algeria (æl'dʒiəriə) *n* Algerien *neu.* **Algerian** *adj* algerisch. *n* Algerier *m.*
alias ('eiliəs) *adv* alias, sonst...genannt.
alibi ('ælibai) *n* **1** *law* Alibi *neu.* **2** *inf* Ausrede *f.*
alien ('eiliən) *n* Fremde(r) *m.* Ausländer *m.* *adj* fremd, ausländisch. **alienate** *vt* entfremden. **alienation** *n* Entfremdung *f.*
alight[1] (ə'lait) *vi* **1** absteigen. **2** landen.
alight[2] (ə'lait) *adj* **1** brennend, in Flammen. **2** erleuchtet.
align (ə'lain) *(vi),vt* **1** (sich) in gerader Linie aufstellen. **2** (sich) ausrichten. **align oneself** sich anschließen.
alike (ə'laik) *adj* gleich, ähnlich. *adv* gleich, in gleicher Weise.

alimentary (æli'mentəri) *adj* Nahrungs—, nahrhaft. **alimentary canal** *n* Verdauungskanal *m*.
alimony ('æliməni) *n* Alimente *neu pl*.
alive (ə'laiv) *adj* **1** lebend, am Leben. **2** lebhaft. **alive to** empfänglich für.
alkali ('ælkəlai) *n* Alkali *neu*. **alkaline** *adj* alkalisch.
all (ɔːl) *adj* **1** all, ganz. **2** jeder, jede, jedes *m,f,neu*. **3** *pl* alle, sämtliche. *n* Ganze *neu*. *adv* ganz. *pron* alles. **above all** vor allem. **at all** überhaupt. **not at all** durchaus nicht.
allay (ə'lei) *vt* **1** beruhigen. **2** stillen.
allege (ə'ledʒ) *vt* **1** behaupten. **2** angeben. **allegation** *n* Behauptung *f*. Aussage *f*.
allegiance (ə'liːdʒəns) *n* **1** Untertanenpflicht *f*. **2** Treue *f*.
allegory ('æligəri) *n* Allegorie *f*.
allergy ('ælədʒi) *n* Allergie. **allergic** *adj* allergisch.
alleviate (ə'liːvieit) *vt* erleichtern, mildern. **alleviation** *n* Erleichterung, Milderung *f*.
alley ('æli) *n* **1** Allee *f*. **2** Gasse *f*. **3** Durchgang *m*. **bowling alley** *n* Kegelbahn *f*.
alliance (ə'laiəns) *n* **1** Verbindung *f*. **2** Bund *m*. Bündnis *neu*. **3** Verwandtschaft *f*.
allied (ə'laid, 'ælaid) *adj* verbündet, alliiert.
alligator ('æligeitə) *n* Alligator *m*.
allocate ('æləkeit) *vt* zuteilen, zuweisen. **allocation** *n* Zuteilung, Zuweisung *f*.
allot (ə'lɔt) *vt* **1** verteilen. **2** bestimmen (für). **allotment** *n* **1** Verteilung *f*. **2** Parzelle *f*. **3** Schrebergarten *m*.
allow (ə'lau) *vt* **1** erlauben, zulassen. **2** bewilligen. **3** zugeben. **allow for** berücksichtigen. **be allowed to** dürfen. **allowable** *adj* zulässig. **allowance** *n* **1** Erlaubnis *f*. **2** Zuschuß *m*. **3** Nachsicht *f*. **4** *comm* Nachlaß *m*. **make allowances for** berücksichtigen.
alloy ('ælɔi) *n* Legierung *f*. *vt* legieren.
allude (ə'luːd) *vi* **allude to** anspielen auf, andeuten. **allusion** *n* Andeutung, Anspielung *f*.
allure (ə'luə) *vt* (an-, ver-)locken.
ally (*v* ə'lai; *n* 'ælai) *(vi),vt* (sich) verbünden. *n* Verbündete(r) *m*.
almanac ('ɔːlmənæk) *n* Almanach *m*.
almighty (ɔːl'maiti) *adj* allmächtig. *n* Allmächtige(r) *m*.
almond ('ɑːmənd) *n* Mandel *f*.
almost ('ɔːlmoust) *adv* fast, beinahe.
alms (ɑːmz) *n pl* Almosen *neu*.
aloft (ə'lɔft) *adv* **1** (hoch) oben. **2** nach oben.
alone (ə'loun) *adj* allein. *adv* allein, nur. **leave alone** in Ruhe lassen.
along (ə'lɔŋ) *prep* entlang. *adv* **1** entlang. **2** vorwärts, weiter. **get along with someone** mit jemandem auskommen, sich mit jemandem verstehen.
alongside *prep* neben. *adv* *naut* längsseits.
aloof (ə'luːf) *adv* fern, abseits.

keep aloof sich fernhalten. **aloofness** *n* Zurückhaltung *f.*
aloud (ə'laud) *adv* laut, mit lauter Stimme.
alphabet ('ælfəbet) *n* Alphabet *neu.* **alphabetical** *adj* alphabetisch.
alpine ('ælpain) *adj* Alpen—. **alpinist** *n* Alpinist *m.*
Alps (ælps) *n pl* Alpen *f pl.*
already (ɔːl'redi) *adv* schon, bereits.
Alsace ('ælsas) *n* Elsaß *neu.* **Alsatian** *adj* elsässich. *n* Elsässer *m.* **Alsatian (dog)** deutscher Schäferhund *m.*
also ('ɔːlsou) *adv* auch, ferner.
altar ('ɔːltə) *n* Altar *m.* **altarpiece** *n* Altarblatt *neu.* **altarrail** *n* Altarschranke *f.*
alter ('ɔːltə) *vt* (um-, ver-)ändern. *vi* sich ändern. **alterable** *adj* veränderlich. **alteration** *n* Veränderung, (Um)Änderung.
alternate (*v* 'ɔːltəneit; *adj* ɔl'təːnit) *vi (vt)* abwechseln (lassen). *adj* abwechselnd. **alternating** *adj* abwechselnd. **alternating current** *n* Wechselstrom *m.* **alternation** *n* **1** Abwechslung *f.* **2** Wechsel *m.* **alternative** *adj* **1** alternativ. **2** ander. *n* Alternative, Wahl *f.*
although ('ɔːlðou) *conj* obgleich, obwohl.
altitude ('æltitjuːd) *n* Höhe *f.*
alto ('æltou) *n* Alt *m.* Altstimme *f.*
altogether (ɔːltə'geðə) *adv* **1** gänzlich, ganz und gar. **2** im ganzen (genommen).
aluminium (ælju'miniəm) *n* Aluminium *neu.*
always ('ɔːlweiz) *adv* immer, stets.
am (əm; *stressed* æm) *v* see **be.**
amalgamate (ə'mælgəmeit) *(vi),vt* **1** (sich) amalgamieren. **2** (sich) vereinigen. **3** *comm* fusionieren.
amass (ə'mæs) *vt* anhäufen.
amateur ('æmətə) *n* Amateur, Liebhaber *m.*
amaze (ə'meiz) *vt* erstaunen, verblüffen. **amazement** *n* (Er)Staunen *neu.* **amazing** *adj* **1** erstaunlich. **2** verblüffend.
ambassador (æm'bæsədə) *n* Botschafter, Gesandte(r) *m.*
amber ('æmbə) *adj* **1** Bernstein—. **2** bernsteinfarben. *n* **1** Bernstein *m.* **2** *mot* Gelb, gelbes Licht *neu.*
ambidextrous (æmbi'dekstrəs) *adj* **1** beidhändig. **2** ungewöhnlich geschickt.
ambiguous (æm'bigjuəs) *adj* **1** zweideutig. **2** unklar. **ambiguity** *n* Zweideutigkeit *f.* Doppelsinn *m.*
ambition (æm'biʃən) *n* **1** Ehrgeiz *m.* **2** Ziel *neu.* **ambitious** *adj* ehrgeizig.
ambivalent (æm'bivələnt) *adj* **1** ambivalent. **2** zwiespältig.
amble ('æmbəl) *vi* schlendern.
ambulance ('æmbjuləns) *n* Krankenwagen *m.*
ambush ('æmbuʃ) *n* Hinterhalt *m.* *vt* aus dem Hinterhalt überfallen.
amenable (ə'miːnəbəl) *adj* **1** zugänglich. **2** gefügig.
amend (ə'mend) *vt* **1** verbessern. **2** abändern. **3** berichtigen. **amendment** *n* **1** Verbesserung *f.* **2** Abänderung

f. **make amends for** wiedergutmachen.
amenity (ə'mi:niti) *n* **1** Annehmlichkeit *f.* **2** *pl* Vorzüge *m pl.*
America (ə'merikə) *n* Amerika *neu.* **American** *adj* amerikanisch. *n* Amerikaner *m.*
amethyst ('æmiθist) *n* Amethyst *m.*
amiable ('eimiəbəl) *adj* freundlich.
amicable ('æmikəbəl) *adj* freundschaftlich.
amid (ə'mid) *prep* mitten in *or* unter.
amiss (ə'mis) *adj,adv* verkehrt, falsch. **take amiss** übel nehmen.
ammonia (ə'mouniə) *n* Ammoniak *neu.*
ammunition (æmju'niʃən) *n* Munition *f.*
amnesty ('æmnəsti) *n* Amnestie *f.* Straferlaß *m.*
amoeba (ə'mi:bə) *n* Amöbe *f.*
among (ə'mʌŋ) *prep also* **amongst 1** unter. **2** inmitten, zwischen. **3** bei.
amoral (ei'mɔrəl) *adj* amoralisch.
amorous ('æmərəs) *adj* **1** verliebt. **2** Liebes—.
amorphous (ə'mɔ:fəs) *adj* **1** amorph. **2** formlos.
amount (ə'maunt) *n* **1** Betrag *m.* Summe *f.* **2** Menge *f.* *vi* sich belaufen, betragen.
ampere ('æmpɛə) *n* Ampere *neu.*
amphetamine (æm'fetəmi:n) *n* Benzedrin *neu.*
amphibian (æm'fibiən) *n* Amphibie *f.* *adj* amphibisch. **amphibious** *adj* **1** *zool* amphibisch. **2** *tech* Amphibien—.
amphitheatre ('æmfiθiətə) *n* Amphitheater *neu.*
ample ('æmpəl) *adj* **1** reichlich. **2** weit, groß.
amplify ('æmplifai) *vt* **1** *tech* verstärken. **2** erweitern, ausdehnen. **amplifier** *n* Verstärker *m.*
amputate ('æmpjuteit) *vt* amputieren, abnehmen. **amputation** *n* Amputation *f.*
amuse (ə'mju:z) *vt* amüsieren, unterhalten. **be amused** sich amüsieren *or* freuen. **amusement** *n* **1** Unterhaltung *f.* **2** Vergnügen *neu.* **amusing** *adj* amüsant, unterhaltend.
an (ən; *stressed* æn) *indef art see* **a.**
anachronism (ə'nækrənizəm) *n* Anachronismus *m.*
anaemia (ə'ni:miə) *n* Anämie, Blutarmut *f.* **anaemic** *adj* anämisch, bleichsüchtig.
anaesthetic (ænis'θetik) *n* Betäubungsmittel *neu.* *adj* betäubend, narkotisch. **anaesthetist** *n* Narkotiseur *m.* **anaesthetize** *vt* betäuben, narkotisieren.
anal ('einl̩) *adj* anal, After—.
analogy (ə'nælədʒi) *n* Analogie, Ähnlichkeit *f.* **analogous** *adj* analog, ähnlich.
analysis (ə'nælisis) *n, pl* **analyses 1** Analyse *f.* **2** Zergliederung *f.* **3** Untersuchung *f.* **analyse** *vt* **1** analysieren. **2** zergliedern, auswerten. **3** genau untersuchen. **analyst** *n* Analytiker *m.* **analytical** *adj* analytisch.
anarchy ('ænəki) *n* Anarchie,

Gesetzlosigkeit *f*. **anarchist** *n* Anarchist *m*.
anatomy (ə'nætəmi) *n* Anatomie *f*. **anatomical** *adj* anatomisch.
ancestor ('ænsəstə) *n* Vorfahr, Ahn *m*.
anchor ('æŋkə) *n* Anker *m*. *vt* verankern. *vi* ankern.
anchovy ('æntʃəvi) *n* Anschovis *f*.
ancient ('einʃənt) *adj* alt, aus alter Zeit.
ancillary (æn'siləri) *adj* **1** Hilfs—, Neben—. **2** untergeordnet.
and (ən, ənd; *stressed* ænd) *conj* und.
anecdote ('ænikdout) *n* Anekdote *f*.
anemone (ə'neməni) *n* Anemone *f*.
anew (ə'nju:) *adv* von neuem.
angel ('eindʒəl) *n* Engel *m*. **angelic** *adj* engelhaft.
anger ('æŋgə) *n* Zorn, Ärger *m*. *vt* ärgern.
angle[1] ('æŋgəl) *n* **1** *math* Winkel *m*. **2** Ecke *f*. **3** Standpunkt *m*. **4** Seite *f*.
angle[2] ('æŋgəl) *vi* angeln. **angler** *n* Angler *m*. **angling** *n* Angeln *neu*.
Anglican ('æŋglikən) *adj* anglikanisch. *n* Anglikaner *m*.
angry ('æŋgri) *adj* zornig, ärgerlich, böse.
anguish ('æŋgwiʃ) *n* Qual, Angst *f*. Schmerz *m*.
angular ('æŋgjulə) *adj* winklig, eckig.
animal ('æniməl) *n* Tier *neu*. *adj* tierisch.
animate ('ænimeit) *vt* **1** beleben. **2** aufmuntern. **animated** *adj* lebhaft, munter. **animation** *n* Lebhaftigkeit, Munterkeit *f*.
animosity (æni'mɔsiti) *n* Feindseligkeit *f*.
aniseed ('ænisi:d) *n* Anis *m*.
ankle ('æŋkəl) *n* (Fuß)Knöchel *m*.
annals ('ænlz) *n pl* Annalen *f pl*.
annex (ə'neks) *vt* **1** annektieren. **2** anhängen. **3** beifügen. **annexation** *n* Annexion *f*.
annexe *n* **1** Anbau *m*. **2** Nebengebäude *neu*.
annihilate (ə'naiəleit) *vt* vernichten. **annihilation** *n* Vernichtung *f*.
anniversary (æni'və:səri) *n* Jahrestag *m*. Jahresfeier *f*.
annotate ('ænəteit) *vt* mit Anmerkungen versehen.
announce (ə'nauns) *vt* **1** ankündigen, bekanntmachen. **2** anzeigen. **announcement** *n* **1** Ankündigung *f*. **2** Anzeige *f*. **announcer** *n* Ansager *m*.
annoy (ə'nɔi) *vt* ärgern, belästigen. **be annoyed** sich ärgern. **annoyance** *n* Belästigung *f*. Ärgernis *neu*. **annoying** *adj* ärgerlich.
annual ('ænjuəl) *adj* **1** jährlich, Jahres—. **2** *bot* einjährig. *n* **1** Jahrbuch *neu*. **2** einjährige Pflanze *f*.
annul (ə'nʌl) *vt* für ungültig erklären.
anode ('ænoud) *n* Anode *f*.
anoint (ə'nɔint) *vt* salben.
anomaly (ə'nɔməli) *n* Anomalie, Unregelmäßigkeit *f*.
anonymous (ə'nɔniməs) *adj* anonym, namenlos. **anonymity** *n* Anonymität *f*.

another (ə'nʌðə) *adj,pron* **1** ein anderer. **2** ein zweiter *or* weiterer. **3** noch einer.
answer ('ɑːnsə) *n* Antwort *f.* *vt* **1** (a question) beantworten. **2** (a person) antworten. **answer for** verantwortlich sein für. **answerable** *adj* verantwortlich.
ant (ænt) *n* Ameise *f.*
antagonize (æn'tægənaiz) *vt* zum Gegner *or* Feind machen. **antagonism** *n* **1** Feindseligkeit *f.* **2** Widerstand *m.* **antagonist** *n* Gegner *m.* **antagonistic** *adj* feindlich, gegnerisch.
Antarctic (æn'tɑːktik) *n* Antarktis *f.* *adj* antarktisch, Südpol—. **Antarctic Ocean** *n* südliches Polarmeer *neu.*
antelope ('æntiloup) *n* Antelope *f.*
antenatal (ænti'neitḷ) *adj* vor der Geburt. **antenatal care** *n* Schwangerschaftsfürsorge *f.*
antenna (æn'tenə) *n* **1** *pl* **antennae** *zool* Fühler *m.* **2** *pl* **antennas** *tech* Antenne *f.*
anthem ('ænθəm) *n* **1** Hymne *f.* **2** Choral *m.* **national anthem** Nationalhymne *f.*
anthology (æn'θɔlədʒi) *n* Anthologie *f.*
anthropology (ænθrə'pɔlədʒi) *n* Anthropologie *f.* **anthropological** *adj* anthropologisch. **anthropologist** *n* Anthropologe *m.*
antibiotic (æntibai'ɔtik) *n* Antibiotikum *neu.* *adj* antibiotisch.
antibody ('æntibɔdi) *n* Antikörper *m.*
anticipate (æn'tisipeit) *vt* **1** voraussehen, vorgreifen. **2** vorwegnehmen. **3** erwarten, erhoffen. **anticipation** *n* **1** Vorahnung *f.* **2** Vorwegnahme *f.* **3** Hoffnung, Erwartung *f.*
anticlimax (ænti'klaimæks) *n* Abfallen *neu.* Antiklimax *m.*
anticlockwise (ænti'klɔkwaiz) *adv* gegen den Uhrzeigersinn.
antics ('æntiks) *n pl* Posse, Fratze *f.*
anticyclone (ænti'saikloun) *n* Hochdruckgebiet *neu.*
antidote ('æntidout) *n* Gegengift *neu.*
antifreeze ('æntifriːz) *n* Frostschutzmittel *neu.*
antique (æn'tiːk) *n* Antike *f.* alter Kunstgegenstand *m.* *adj* **1** antik. **2** alt. **antique dealer** *n* Antiquitätenhändler *m.* **antique shop** *n* Antiquitätengeschäft *neu.* **antiquated** *adj* **1** altmodisch. **2** veraltet, überholt. **antiquity** *n* **1** Altertum *neu.* **2** *pl* Antiquitäten *f pl.*
anti-Semitic *adj* antisemitisch. **anti-Semitism** *n* Antisemitismus *m.*
antiseptic (ænti'septik) *adj* antiseptisch. *n* Antiseptikum *neu.*
antisocial (ænti'souʃəl) *adj* gesellschaftsfeindlich.
antithesis (æn'tiθəsis) *n, pl* **-ses** Antithese *f.* Gegensatz *m.*
antler ('æntlə) *n* **1** Geweihsprosse *f.* **2** *pl* Geweih *neu.*
antonym ('æntənim) *n* Antonym *neu.*
anus ('einəs) *n* After *m.*
anvil ('ænvil) *n* Amboß *m.*
anxious (æŋkʃəs) *adj* **1** ängstlich, besorgt. **2** begierig. **anxiety** *n* Angst, Sorge *f.*
any ('eni) *adj* **1** (irgend)einer,

(irgend)welcher. **2** jeder. **in any case** auf jeden Fall. **not any** kein. *~pron* irgendeiner, irgendwelcher. *adv* **1** etwas. **2** irgendwie. **anybody** *pron* (irgend) jemand, irgendeiner. **anyhow** *adv* **1** irgendwie. **2** jedenfalls. **anyone** *pron* (irgend) jemand, irgendeiner. **anything** *pron* **1** (irgend) etwas. **2** alles. **anything but** alles andere als. **if anything** wenn überhaupt. **anyway** *adv* **1** irgendwie. **2** jedenfalls, sowieso. **anywhere** *adv* **1** irgendwo(hin). **2** überall.

apart (ə'pɑːt) *adv* **1** beiseite. **2** getrennt, abgesondert. **apart from** abgesehen von.

apartheid (ə'pɑːtait) *n* Rassentrennung *f.*

apartment (ə'pɑːtmənt) *n* **1** Zimmer *neu.* **2** *US* Wohnung *f.* **3** *pl* Wohnung *f.*

apathy ('æpəθi) *n* Apathie, Gleichgültigkeit *f.* **apathetic** *adj* apathisch.

ape (eip) *n* Affe *m.* *vt* (nach)äffen.

aperitive (ə'peritiv) *n* Aperitif *m.*

aperture ('æpətʃə) *n* **1** Öffnung *f.* **2** *tech* Blende *f.*

apex ('eipeks) *n, pl* **apexes** *or* **apices** Höhepunkt, Gipfel *m.* Spitze *f.*

apiece (ə'piːs) *adv* **1** je, für jedes Stück. **2** pro Person.

apology (ə'pɔlədʒi) *n* **1** Entschuldigung *f.* **2** Rechtfertigung *f.* **apologetic** *adj* entschuldigend. **apologize** *vi* sich entschuldigen.

apostle (ə'pɔsəl) *n* Apostel *m.*

apostrophe (ə'pɔstrəfi) *n* Apostroph *m.*

appal (ə'pɔːl) *vt* erschrecken, entsetzen. **appalling** *adj* entsetzlich, schrecklich.

apparatus (æpə'reitəs) *n, pl* **-tus** *or* **-tuses** Apparat *m.* Gerät *neu.*

apparent (ə'pærənt) *adj* **1** augenscheinlich, offenbar. **2** sichtbar. **3** scheinbar. **apparently** *adv* anscheinend.

appeal (ə'piːl) *vi* **1** appellieren, sich wenden. **2** bitten. **3** gefallen, zusagen. **4** sich berufen auf. *n* **1** (dringende) Bitte *f.* **2** Appell *m.* **3** Anziehungskraft *f.*

appear (ə'piə) *vi* **1** erscheinen, sich zeigen. **2** scheinen, aussehen. **3** auftauchen. **appearance** *n* **1** Erscheinen *neu.* **2** Äußere *neu.* Erscheinung *f.* **3** Anschein *m.* **to all appearances** allem Anschein nach.

appease (ə'piːz) *vt* **1** beruhigen. **2** befriedigen.

appendix (ə'pendiks) *n, pl* **-dixes** *or* **-dices** **1** Anhang *m.* **2** *anat* Blinddarm *m.* **appendicitis** *n* Blinddarmentzündung *f.*

appetite ('æpətait) *n* **1** Appetit *m.* **2** Verlangen *neu.*

applaud (ə'plɔːd) *vt* **1** beklatschen, Beifall spenden. **2** billigen. *vi* applaudieren. **applause** *n* Beifall *m.*

apple ('æpəl) *n* Apfel *m.*

apply (ə'plai) *vt* **1** anwenden, verwenden. **2** auflegen. *vi* **1** sich bewerben. **2** sich wenden an. **3** sich anwenden lassen. **apply oneself** sich widmen. **appliance** *n* Gerät *neu.* Apparat *m.* **applicable** *adj* **1**

anwendbar. **2** geeignet. **not applicable** nicht zutreffend. **applicant** *n* Bewerber, Antragsteller *m*. **application** *n* **1** Anwendung *f*. **2** Antrag *m*. Bewerbung *f*. **3** Eifer *m*. **4** Auflegen *neu*.

appoint (ə'pɔint) *vt* **1** ernennen, anstellen. **2** verabreden. **3** ausstatten. **appointment** *n* **1** Ernennung, Anstellung *f*. **2** Verabredung *f*.

appraise (ə'preiz) *vt* abschätzen, bewerten. **appraisal** *n* Abschätzung *f*.

appreciate (ə'pri:ʃieit) *vt* **1** (richtig) schätzen. **2** Gefallen finden. **3** dankbar sein (für). **4** wahrnehmen, erkennen. *vi* im Wert steigen. **appreciable** *adj* merklich, nennenswert. **appreciation** *n* **1** Schätzung *f*. **2** Verständnis *neu*. **appreciative** *adj* **1** anerkennend. **2** verständnisvoll.

apprehend (æpri'hend) *vt* **1** verhaften. **2** begreifen. **3** befürchten. **apprehension** *n* **1** Besorgnis, Befürchtung *f*. **2** Verstand *m*. **3** Verhaftung *f*. **apprehensive** *adj* besorgt, bedenklich, ängstlich.

apprentice (ə'prentis) *n* Lehrling *m*. **apprenticeship** *n* Lehrzeit *f*.

approach (ə'proutʃ) *vt,vi* **1** sich nähern. **2** nahekommen. *vt* **1** sich wenden an. **2** herantreten an. *n* **1** (Heran)Nahen *neu*. Annäherung *f*. **2** Zugang *m*. Auffahrt, Zufahrt *f*. **3** Behandlung *f*. **approachable** *adj* zugänglich.

appropriate (*adj* ə'proupriət; *v* ə'proprieit) *adj* **1** angemessen, geeignet. **2** entsprechend. *vt* sich aneignen.

approve (ə'pru:v) *vt,vi* billigen, empfehlen, anerkennen, genehmigen. *vt* annehmen, akzeptieren. **approval** *n* Billigung, Genehmigung, Anerkennung *f*. **on approval** zur Ansicht.

approximate (*adj* ə'prɔksimət; *v* ə'prɔksimeit) *adj* ungefähr. *vt* nahekommen. *vi* sich nähern.

apricot ('eiprikɔt) *n* Aprikose *f*.

April ('eiprəl) *n* April *m*.

apron ('eiprən) *n* Schürze *f*.

apt (æpt) *adj* **1** geeignet. **2** geschickt.

aptitude ('æptitju:d) *n* Begabung *f*. Geschick *neu*.

aquarium (ə'kwɛəriəm) *n, pl* **-riums** *or* **-ria** Aquarium *neu*.

Aquarius (ə'kwɛəriəs) *n* Wassermann *m*.

aquatic (ə'kwætik) *adj* Wasser—.

aqueduct ('ækwədʌkt) *n* Aquädukt *m*.

Arabia (ə'reibiə) *n* Arabien *neu*. **Arab** *adj* arabisch. *n* Araber *m*. **Arabian** *adj* arabisch. *n* Araber *m*. **Arabic** *adj* arabisch. *n* (language) Arabisch *neu*.

arable ('ærəbəl) *adj* Acker—.

arbitrary ('ɑ:bitrəri) *adj* willkürlich, eigenmächtig.

arbitrate ('ɑ:bitreit) *vt* entscheiden, schlichten. *vi* Schiedsrichter sein. **arbitration** *n* Schiedsspruch *m*. **arbitrator** *n* Schiedsrichter *m*.

arc (ɑ:k) *n* Bogen *m*.

arcade (ɑ:'keid) *n* **1** Arkade *f*. **2** Durchgang *m*.

arch (ɑːtʃ) *n* **1** *arch* Bogen *m*. **2** Wölbung *f*. *vi* sich wölben.
archaeology (ɑːki'ɔlədʒi) *n* Archäologie *f*. **archaeological** *adj* archäologisch. **archaeologist** *n* Archäologe *m*.
archaic (ɑː'keiik) *adj* **1** veraltet. **2** altertümlich. **archaism** *n* veralteter Ausdruck *m*.
archbishop (ɑːtʃ'biʃəp) *n* Erzbischof *m*.
archduke (ɑːtʃ'djuːk) *n* Erzherzog *m*.
archery ('ɑːtʃəri) *n* Bogenschießen *m*. **archer** *n* Bogenschütze *m*.
archetype ('ɑːkitaip) *n* Archetyp *m*.
archipelago (ɑːki'peləgou) *n* Archipel *m*.
architect ('ɑːkitekt) *n* **1** Architekt *m*. **2** Schöpfer, Urheber *m*. **architecture** *n* **1** Architektur *f*. **2** Konstruktion *f*.
archives ('ɑːkaivz) *n pl* Archiv *neu*.
archway ('ɑːtʃwei) *n* Bogengang *m*.
Arctic ('ɑːktik) *n* Arktis *f*. Nordpolargebiet *neu*. *adj* arktisch. **Arctic Ocean** *n* Nördliches Polarmeer *neu*.
ardent ('ɑːdnt) *adj* **1** heiß, glühend. **2** eifrig, begeistert.
ardour ('ɑːdə) *n* **1** Hitze *f*. **2** Eifer *m*. Begeisterung *f*.
arduous ('ɑːdjuəs) *adj* schwierig, anstrengend.
are (ə; *stressed* ɑː) *v* see **be.**
area ('ɛəriə) *n* **1** Fläche *f*. Flächeninhalt *m*. **2** Gebiet *neu*. Gegend *f*. **3** Bereich *m*. Zone *f*.
arena (ə'riːnə) *n* Arena *f*.
Argentina (ɑːdʒən'tiːnə) *n* Argentinien *neu*. **Argentine** *adj also* **Argentinian** argentinisch. *n* Argentinier *m*.
argue ('ɑːgjuː) *vt* **1** erörtern, diskutieren. **2** behaupten. *vi* **1** streiten, argumentieren. **2** Einwände machen. **argument** *n* **1** Beweis *m*. Beweisführung *f*. **2** Streit *m*. **3** Argument *neu*. **argumentative** *adj* streitlustig.
arid ('ærid) *adj* trocken, dürr.
Aries ('ɛəriːz) *n* Widder *m*.
arise* (ə'raiz) *vi* **1** entstehen. **2** aufstehen.
aristocracy (æri'stɔkrəsi) *n* Aristokratie *f*. Adel *m*. **aristocrat** *n* Aristokrat, Adlige(r) *m*. **aristocratic** *adj* aristokratisch.
arithmetic (ə'riθmətik) *n* Arithmetik *f*. Rechnen *neu*. **arithmetical** *adj* arithmetisch.
arm[1] (ɑːm) *n* **1** Arm *m*. **2** (of a chair) Armlehne *f*. **with open arms** mit offenen Armen. **armchair** *n* Lehnstuhl, Sessel *m*. **armful** *n* Armvoll *m*. **armhole** *n* Ärmelloch *neu*. **armpit** *n* Achselhöhle *f*.
arm[2] (ɑːm) *n* Waffe *f*. **arms race** Wettrüsten *neu*. **coat of arms** Wappen *neu*. **up in arms** in Aufruhr. *~(vi),vt* (sich) bewaffnen, (sich) ausrüsten. **armed forces** *n* Streitkräfte *f pl*. **armament** *n* **1** Bewaffnung *f*. **2** (Kriegsaus)-Rüstung *f*.
armour ('ɑːmə) *n* Panzer *m*. **armour-plated** *adj also* **armoured** gepanzert, Panzer—.
army ('ɑːmi) *n* **1** Armee *f*. Heer *neu*. **2** Menge *f*.

aroma (ə'roumə) *n* Aroma *neu.* Duft *m.* **aromatic** (ærə'mætik) *adj* aromatisch, würzig.
arose (ə'rouz) *v* see **arise.**
around (ə'raund) *prep* **1** um, um...herum. **2** ungefähr. *adv* **1** rundherum. **2** in der Nähe.
arouse (ə'rauz) *vt* **1** aufwecken. **2** erregen.
arrange (ə'reindʒ) *vt* **1** anordnen. **2** einrichten. **3** erledigen. **4** vereinbaren. **5** *mus* bearbeiten. *vi* **1** sich verständigen. **2** Vorkehrungen treffen. **3** sich einigen. **arrangement** *n* **1** Anordnung *f.* **2** Einrichtung *f.* **3** Vereinbarung *f.* Abkommen *neu.* **4** *mus* Bearbeitung *f.*
array (ə'rei) *vt* **1** ordnen. **2** kleiden, putzen. *n* **1** Ordnung *f.* **2** Kleidung, Aufmachung *f.*
arrears (ə'riəz) *n pl* Rückstände *m pl.* Schulden *f pl.* **in arrears** im Rückstand *m.*
arrest (ə'rest) *vt* **1** verhaften. **2** aufhalten, hindern. *n* Haft, Verhaftung *f.* **under arrest** verhaftet. **arresting** *adj* interessant, fesselnd.
arrive (ə'raiv) *vi* **1** ankommen. **2** erreichen, gelangen. **3** erscheinen. **arrival** *n* **1** Ankunft *f.* **2** Erscheinen *neu.*
arrogant ('ærəgənt) *adj* arrogant, anmaßend, überheblich. **arrogance** *n* Arroganz, Anmaßung *f.*
arrow ('ærou) *n* **1** Pfeil *m.* **2** Pfeilzeichen *neu.*
arsenic ('ɑːsnik) *n* Arsenik *neu.*
arson ('ɑːsən) *n* Brandstiftung *f.*
art (ɑːt) *n* **1** Kunst *f.* **2** Geschick *neu.* **3** List *f.* **4** *pl educ* Geisteswissenschaften *f pl.* **work of art** Kunstwerk *n.* ~ *adj* Kunst—. **art gallery** *n* Kunstgalerie, Bildergalerie *f.* **art school** *n* Kunstschule *f.* **artful** *adj* **1** listig, schlau. **2** geschickt.
artery ('ɑːtəri) *n* Arterie, Pulsader *f.* **arterial** *adj* arteriell.
arthritis (ɑː'θraitis) *n* Arthritis *f.*
artichoke ('ɑːtitʃouk) *n* Artischocke *f.*
article ('ɑːtikəl) *n* **1** Artikel *m.* **2** Ware *f.* Gegenstand *m.*
articulate (*v* ɑː'tikjuleit: *adj* ɑː'tikjulət) *vt* **1** aussprechen, artikulieren. **2** gliedern. *vi* deutlich sprechen. *adj* **1** deutlich. **2** sich gut ausdrückend.
artificial (ɑːti'fiʃəl) *adj* **1** künstlich, Kunst—. **2** gekünstelt.
artillery (ɑː'tiləri) *n* Artillerie *f.*
artist ('ɑːtist) *n* **1** Künstler *m.* **2** Könner *m.* **artiste** *n* Artist *m.* **artistic** *adj* künstlerisch, Kunst—.
as (əz; *stressed* æz) *conj* **1** da, weil. **2** wie, sowie. **3** als, während. *adv* **1** so, wie, ebenso wie. **2** als. **as...as** (eben)so...wie. **as far as** soviel, sofern, soweit. **as if** als ob, als wenn. **as long as** solange. **as well** ebenfalls, auch.
asbestos (æs'bestəs) *n* Asbest *m.*
ascend (ə'send) *vi* (auf-, hinauf-)steigen. *vt* besteigen. **ascendant** *adj* **1** aufsteigend. **2** vorherrschend. **in the ascendant** im Aufsteigen. **As-**

cension *n rel* Himmelfahrt *f.*
ascent *n* Aufstieg *m.*
ascertain (æsə'tein) *vt* feststellen.
ash[1] (æʃ) *n* Asche *f.* **ashtray** *n* Aschenbecher *m.*
ash[2] (æʃ) *n bot* Esche *f.*
ashamed (ə'ʃeimd) *adj* beschämt. **be ashamed** sich schämen.
ashore (ə'ʃɔː) *adv* am *or* ans Ufer. **go ashore** an Land gehen.
Ash Wednesday *n* Aschenmittwoch *m.*
Asia ('eiʃə) *n* Asien *neu.* **Asia Minor** Kleinasien *neu.* **Asian** *adj* asiatisch. *n* Asiat *m.* **Asiatic** *adj* asiatisch.
aside (ə'said) *adv* beiseite.
ask (ɑːsk) *vt* **1** fragen. **2** fragen nach. **3** bitten. **4** fordern, verlangen. **ask about** *or* **after** sich erkundigen nach *or* wegen.
askew (ə'skjuː) *adv* schief, schräg.
asleep (ə'sliːp) *adv* schlafend. **be asleep** schlafen. **fall asleep** einschlafen.
asparagus (ə'spærəgəs) *n* Spargel *m.*
aspect ('æspekt) *n* **1** Aussehen *neu.* **2** Aspekt *m.* Hinsicht *f.* **3** Aussicht *f.*
asphalt ('æsfælt) *n* Asphalt *m.*
aspire (ə'spaiə) *vi* **1** streben. **2** sich erheben. **aspiring** *adj* hochstrebend.
aspirin ('æsprin) *n* Aspirin *neu.*
ass (æs) *n* Esel *m.*
assassinate (ə'sæsineit) *vt* ermorden. **assassin** *n* (politischer) Mörder *m.* **assassination** *n* Ermordung *f.*
assault (ə'sɔːlt) *vt* angreifen, überfallen. *n* Angriff, Überfall *m.*
assemble (ə'sembəl) *vt* **1** versammeln. **2** zusammensetzen, montieren. *vi* sich versammeln. **assembly** *n* **1** Versammlung *f.* **2** Montage *f.* **assembly hall** *n educ* Aula *f.* **assembly line** *n* Fließband *neu.*
assent (ə'sent) *vi* **1** zustimmen. **2** genehmigen. *n* **1** Zustimmung *f.* **2** Genehmigung *f.*
assert (ə'səːt) *vt* **1** behaupten, erklären. **2** bestehen auf. **assert oneself** sich durchsetzen.
assertion *n* Behauptung *f.*
assertive *adj* anmaßend.
assess (ə'ses) *vt* **1** zur Steuer einschätzen. **2** einschätzen. **assessment** *n* Einschätzung *f.*
asset ('æset) *n* **1** Vorteil *m.* **2** *pl comm* Vermögen *neu.*
assign (ə'sain) *vt* **1** anweisen. **2** bestimmen. **assignment** *n* **1** Anweisung *f.* **2** Aufgabe *f.*
assimilate (ə'simileit) *vt* **1** absorbieren, aufnehmen. **2** anpassen. **assimilation** *n* Aufnahme *f.*
assist (ə'sist) *vt* **1** helfen. **2** unterstützen. **3** fördern. *vi* **1** mithelfen. **2** teilnehmen. **3** beiwohnen. **assistance** *n* **1** Hilfe *f.* **2** Unterstützung *f.*
assistant *n* **1** Assistent *m.* **2** Verkäufer *m.*
assizes (ə'saiziz) *n pl* Gerichtssitzungen *f pl.*
associate (*v* ə'souʃieit; *adj,n* ə'souʃiit) *vt* **1** vereinigen, anschließen. **2** verbinden, verknüpfen. *vi* verkehren. *adj*

verbündet. *n* Kollege, Mitarbeiter *m.* **association** *n* **1** Vereinigung *f.* **2** Verein, Verband *m.* **3** Verkehr *m.* **4** Verbindung *f.*

assort (ə'sɔːt) *vt* assortieren. **assorted** *adj* gemischt. **assortment** *n* Sortiment *neu.*

assume (ə'sjuːm) *vt* **1** annehmen. **2** übernehmen. **3** sich aneignen. **assuming** *adj* anmaßend. **assumption** *n* **1** Annahme *f.* **2** Aneignung *f.*

assure (ə'ʃuə) *vt* **1** sichern, sicherstellen. **2** versichern. **assurance** *n* **1** Versicherung *f.* **2** Selbstsicherheit *f.*

asthma ('æsmə) *n* Asthma *neu.*

astonish (ə'stɔniʃ) *vt* erstaunen, überraschen. **be astonished** erstaunt sein. **astonishing** *adj* erstaunlich. **astonishment** *n* Erstaunen *neu.*

astound (ə'staund) *vt* verblüffen.

astray (ə'strei) *adv* **go astray** sich verlaufen. **lead astray** irreführen.

astride (ə'straid) *prep,adj,adv* rittlings.

astrology (ə'strɔlədʒi) *n* Astrologie, Sterndeuterei *f.* **astrologer** *n* Astrologe *m.* **astrological** *adj* astrologisch.

astronaut ('æstrənɔːt) *n* Astronaut *m.*

astronomy (ə'strɔnəmi) *n* Astronomie, Sternkunde *f.* **astronomer** *n* Astronom *m.* **astronomical** *adj* **1** astronomisch, Stern—. **2** riesengroß.

astute (ə'stjuːt) *adj* scharfsinnig.

asunder (ə'sʌndə) *adv* auseinander.

asylum (ə'sailəm) *n* **1** *pol* Asyl *neu.* Freistätte *f.* **2** Heim *neu.* **lunatic asylum** Irrenanstalt *f.*

at (ət; *stressed* æt) *prep* **1** an, auf. **2** in, zu. **3** bei. **4** für. **5** um. **6** über. **at two o'clock** um zwei Uhr.

ate (eit, et) *v* see **eat.**

atheism ('eiθiizəm) *n* Atheismus *m.* **atheist** *n* Atheist *m.*

Athens ('æθinz) *n* Athen *neu.*

athlete ('æθliːt) *n* (Leicht)-Athlet, Sportler *m.* **athletic** *adj* athletisch, Sport—. **athletics** *n pl* Athletik *f.*

Atlantic (ət'læntik) *adj* atlantisch. **Atlantic (Ocean)** *n* Atlantik, Atlantischer Ozean *m.*

atlas ('ætləs) *n* Atlas *m.*

atmosphere ('ætməsfiə) *n* **1** Atmosphäre *f.* **2** Luft *f.* **3** Stimmung *f.*

atom ('ætəm) *n* Atom *neu.* **atom bomb** *n* Atombombe *f.* **atomic** *adj* atomisch, Atom—.

atone (ə'toun) *vi* **1** büßen. **2** wiedergutmachen. **atonement** *n* Buße *f.*

atrocious (ə'trouʃəs) *adj* scheußlich, gräßlich. **atrocity** *n* Scheußlichkeit, Greueltat *f.*

attach (ə'tætʃ) *vt* **1** befestigen. **2** anheften. **3** verbinden. **attachment** *n* **1** Befestigung *f.* **2** Zusatzgerät *neu.* **3** Anhänglichkeit *f.*

attaché (ə'tæʃei) *n* Attaché *m.* **attaché case** *n* Aktentasche *f.*

attack (ə'tæk) *vt* **1** angreifen, überfallen. **2** in Angriff nehmen. **3** kritisieren. *n* **1** Angriff, Überfall *m*. **2** Kritik *f*. **3** *med* Anfall *m*. **attacker** *n* Angreifer *m*.

attain (ə'tein) *vt* erreichen, erlangen. **attain to** gelangen zu. **attainable** *adj* erreichbar. **attainment** *n* Erreichung *f*.

attempt (ə'tempt) *vt* **1** versuchen. **2** sich wagen (an). *n* **1** Versuch *m*. **2** Attentat *neu*.

attend (ə'tend) *vt* **1** beiwohnen. **2** (a school) besuchen. **3** pflegen. *vi* **1** achten. **2** sich besorgen. **3** erledigen. **4** erscheinen. **5** bedienen. **attendance** *n* **1** Anwesenheit *f*. **2** Beteiligung *f*. **3** Pflege, Bedienung *f*. **4** Besuch *m*. **attendant** *n* **1** Diener *m*. **2** Begleiter *m*. **3** Bedienungsmann, Wärter *m*. **attention** *n* **1** Aufmerksamkeit, Beachtung *f*. **2** Erledigung *f*. **3** *pl* Aufmerksamkeiten *f pl*. **4** Bedienung *f*. **pay attention** achtgeben. *interj* Achtung! **attentive** *adj* aufmerksam.

attic ('ætik) *n* Dachstube *f*.

attire (ə'taiə) *vt* ankleiden, schmücken. *n* Kleidung *f*. Schmuck *m*.

attitude ('ætitjuːd) *n* **1** Stellung, Haltung *f*. **2** Einstellung, Stellungnahme *f*.

attract (ə'trækt) *vt* **1** anziehen. **2** reizen, fesseln. **attract attention** Aufmerksamkeit erregen. **attraction** *n* **1** Anziehung, Attraktion *f*. **2** Anziehungskraft *f*. **attractive** *adj* **1** anziehend, reizvoll. **2** hübsch. **attractiveness** *n* Reiz *m*.

attribute (*v* ə'tribjuːt; *n* 'ætribjuːt) *vt* **1** zuschreiben. **2** zurückführen. *n* Eigenschaft *f*.

aubergine ('oubəʒiːn) *n* Aubergine *f*.

auburn ('ɔːbən) *adj* kastanienbraun.

auction ('ɔːkʃən) *n* Auktion, Versteigerung *f*. *v* **auction off** versteigern.

audacious (ɔː'deiʃəs) *adj* **1** kühn. **2** frech. **audacity** *n* **1** Kühnheit *f*. **2** Frechheit *f*.

audible ('ɔːdibəl) *adj* hörbar.

audience ('ɔːdiəns) *n* **1** Publikum *neu*. Zuhörer *m pl*. **2** Audienz *f*.

audit ('ɔːdit) *vt* prüfen, revidieren. *n* Bücherrevision *f*. **auditing** *n* Bücherrevision *f*. **auditor** *n* Bücherrevisor *m*.

audition (ɔː'diʃən) *n* Hörprobe *f*. *vt* einer Hörprobe unterziehen.

August ('ɔːgəst) *n* August *m*.

aunt (ɑːnt) *n* Tante *f*.

au pair (ou 'pɛə) *n also* **au pair girl** Au-pair-Mädchen *neu*.

aura ('ɔːrə) *n*, *pl* **auras** *or* **aurae 1** Aura, Atmosphäre *f*. **2** Hauch, Duft *m*.

austere (ɔː'stiə) *adj* **1** streng. **2** enthaltsam.

Australia (ɔ'streiliə) *n* Australien *neu*. **Australian** *adj* australisch. *n* Australier *m*.

Austria ('ɔːstriə) *n* Österreich *neu*. **Austrian** *adj* österreichisch. *n* Österreicher *m*.

authentic (ɔː'θentik) *adj* authentisch, echt.

author ('ɔːθə) *n* **1** Verfasser *m*. **2** Autor, Schriftsteller *m*. **3** Urheber *m*.

authority (ɔː'θɔriti) *n* **1** Autorität *f*. **2** Gewalt *f*. **3**

Vollmacht *f.* **4** Quelle *f.* **5** Fachmann *m.* **6** *pl* Behörde *f.*
authoritarian *adj* autoritär.
authoritative *adj* **1** maßgebend. **2** herrisch.
authorize ('ɔːθəraiz) *vt* **1** ermächtigen. **2** billigen, genehmigen. **authorization** *n* Genehmigung *f.*
autobiography (ɔːtəbai'ɔgrəfi) *n* Autobiographie *f.* **autobiographical** *adj* autobiographisch.
autograph ('ɔːtəgrɑːf) *n* eigenhändige Unterschrift *f.* Autogramm *neu.* *vt* (eigenhändig) unterschreiben.
automatic (ɔːtə'mætik) *adj* **1** automatisch, selbsttätig. **2** unwillkürlich. **automation** *n* Automation *f.*
autonomous (ɔː'tɔnəməs) *adj* autonom. **autonomy** *n* Autonomie, Selbständigkeit *f.*
autumn ('ɔːtəm) *n* Herbst *m.*
auxiliary (ɔːg'ziliəri) *adj* helfend, Hilfs—. *n* **1** Helfer *m.* **2** *pl* Hilfspersonal *neu.*
available (ə'veiləbəl) *adj* verfügbar, vorhanden. **availability** *n* Verfügbarkeit *f.* Vorhandensein *neu.*
avalanche ('ævəlɑːnʃ) *n* Lawine *f.*
avenge (ə'vendʒ) *vt* rächen.
avenue ('ævənjuː) *n* **1** Allee *f.* **2** Weg *m.*
average ('ævridʒ) *adj* durchschnittlich. *n* Durchschnitt *m.* **on average** im Durchschnitt.
aversion (ə'vəːʃən) *n* Abneigung *f.*
aviary ('eiviəri) *n* Vogelhaus *neu.*
aviation (eivi'eiʃən) *n* Flugwesen *neu.*
avid ('ævid) *adj* gierig.
avocado (ævə'kɑːdou) *n* Avocadobirne *f.*
avoid (ə'vɔid) *vt* **1** vermeiden. **2** ausweichen. **3** aus dem Wege gehen.
await (ə'weit) *vt* erwarten, warten auf.
awake* (ə'weik) *vt* **1** wecken. **2** erwecken. *vi* **1** aufwachen, erwachen. **2** bewußt werden. *adj* wach. **wide awake** munter. **awaken** *vt* **1** wecken. **2** erwecken. *vi* aufwachen, erwachen. **awakening** *n* Erwachen *neu.*
award (ə'wɔːd) *vt* **1** zusprechen, verleihen. **2** gewähren. *n* Belohnung *f.* Preis *m.*
aware (ə'wɛə) *adj* bewußt. **awareness** *n* Bewußtsein *neu.* Kenntnis *f.*
away (ə'wei) *adv* **1** weg, fort, hinweg. **2** entfernt. **3** fort, verreist.
awe (ɔː) *n* Ehrfurcht *f.* **awe-inspiring** *adj* furchtbar, ehrfurchtgebietend. **awestruck** *adj* von Ehrfurcht ergriffen. **awful** *adj* **1** schrecklich, furchtbar. **2** *inf* furchtbar, scheußlich. **awfully** *adv inf* furchtbar, sehr.
awkward ('ɔːkwəd) *adj* **1** ungeschickt, linkisch. **2** peinlich, unangenehm. **3** lästig, schwierig.
awoke (ə'wouk) *v* see **awake.**
axe (æks) *n* Axt *f.* Beil *neu.*
axis ('æksis) *n,pl* **axes** Achse, Mittellinie *f.*
axle ('æksəl) *n* (Rad)Achse *f.*

B

babble ('bæbəl) *vt* **1** schwatzen, plappern. **2** plätschern, murmeln. *n* Geschwätz *neu.*
baboon (bə'buːn) *n* Pavian *m.*
baby ('beibi) *n* Baby *neu.* Säugling *m.* Kleinkind *neu.* **baby-sit** *vi* Kinder beaufsichtigen, babysitten. **babyish** *adj* babyhaft.
bachelor ('bætʃələ) *n* Junggeselle *m.*
back (bæk) *n* **1** Rücken *m.* Kreuz *neu.* **2** Rückseite *f.* Hinterseite *f.* *adj* Nach—, Hinter—. *adv* **1** zurück. **2** rückwärts. *vt* **1** wetten auf. **2** unterstützen. **3** rückwärts fahren.
backache ('bækeik) *n* Rückenschmerz *m.*
backbone ('bækboun) *n* Wirbelsäule *f.* Rückgrat *neu.*
backdate ('bækdeit) *vt* zurückdatieren.
backfire ('bækfaiə) *vi* **1** fehlzünden, frühzünden. **2** fehlschlagen. *n* Fehlzündung *f.*
backgammon ('bækgæmən) *n* Puffspiel *neu.*
background ('bækgraund) *n* Hintergrund *m.*
backhand ('bækhænd) *n* Rückhand *f.* **backhander** *n* **1** Rückhandschlag *m.* **2** geheime Belohnung *f.*
backlash ('bæklæʃ) *n* **1** *tech* Spielraum *m.* **2** (politische) Reaktion *f.* **3** Rückschlag *m.*
backlog ('bæklɔg) *n* Rückstand *m.* Rücklage *f.*
backside (bæk'said) *n* *inf* Hinterteil *neu.*
backstage (bæk'steidʒ) *adj,adv* hinter den Kulissen.
backstroke ('bækstrouk) *n* Gegenschlag *m.* Rückenschwimmen *neu.*
backward ('bækwəd) *adj* **1** (geistig) zurückgeblieben. **2** rückständig. **3** widerwillig.
backwards ('bækwədʒ) *adv* zurück, rückwärts.
backwater ('bækwɔtə) *n* Stauwasser *neu.*
bacon ('beikən) *n* Speck *m.*
bacteria (bæk'tiəriə) *n pl* Bakterie *f.*
bad (bæd) *adj* **1** schlecht, schlimm. **2** böse. **bad-tempered** *adj* mißgelaunt.
bade (beid) *v* see **bid.**
badge (bædʒ) *n* Abzeichen *neu.* Medaille *f.*
badger ('bædʒə) *n* Dachs *m.* *vt* belästigen.
badminton ('bædmintən) *n* Federballspiel *neu.*
baffle ('bæfəl) *vt* verwirren, täuschen.
bag (bæg) *n* **1** Beutel *m.* Tüte *f.* **2** Tasche *f.* **3** Sack *m.* *vt* **1** abschießen. **2** erlegen. **baggage** *n* Gepäck *neu.* **baggy** *adj* bauschig, sackartig, schlotterig. **bagpipes** *n* Dudelsack *m.*
bail (beil) *n* *law* Bürgschaft, Kaution *f.*
bailiff ('beilif) *n* **1** Gerichtsdiener *m.* **2** Gutsverwalter *m.*
bait (beit) *n* **1** Köder *m.* Lockspeise *f.* **2** Lockung *f.* Reiz *m.* *vt* **1** ködern. **2** hetzen, quälen.
bake (beik) *vt* backen. **baker** *n* Bäcker *m.* **bakery** *n* Bäckerei *f.*
balance ('bæləns) *vt* **1**

balancieren. **2** erwägen. **3** saldieren. *n* **1** Waage *f.* **2** Gleichgewicht *neu.* **3** Saldo *m.* Guthaben *neu.* **balance sheet** *n* Bilanz *f.* Bilanzbogen *m.*

balcony ('bælkəni) *n* Balkon *m.*

bald (bɔːld) *adj* **1** kahl, haarlos. **2** nackt.

bale[1] (beil) *n* Ballen *m.*

bale[2] (beil) *vt,vi* ausschöpfen. **bale out** mit dem Fallschirm abspringen.

ball[1] (bɔːl) *n* **1** Ball *m.* **2** Kugel *f.* **ballpoint pen** *n* Kugelschreiber *m.*

ball[2] (bɔːl) *n* Ball *m.* Tanzgesellschaft *f.* **ballroom** *n* Tanzsaal, Ballsaal *m.*

ballad ('bæləd) *n* Ballade *f.* Lied *neu.*

ballast ('bæləst) *n* Ballast *m.*

ballet ('bælei) *n* Ballett *neu.* **ballet dancer** *n* Ballettänzer *m.* Ballettänzerin *f.*

ballistic (bə'listik) *adj* ballistisch.

balloon (bə'luːn) *n* Ballon *m.* Luftballon *m.*

ballot ('bælət) *n* Wahl *f.* Abstimmung *f.* **ballot paper** *n* Stimmzettel *m.*

Baltic ('bɔːltik) *adj* baltisch. **Baltic (Sea)** *n* Ostsee *f.*

bamboo (bæm'buː) *n* Bambus *m.*

ban (bæn) *vt* verbannen, ächten. *n* Bann *m.* Verbannung, Ächtung *f.*

banal (bə'nɑːl) *adj* banal, alltäglich.

banana (bə'nɑːnə) *n* Banane *f.*

band[1] (bænd) *n* **1** *mus* Kapelle *f.* Orchester *neu.* **2** Gruppe, Bande *f.*

band[2] (bænd) *n* **1** Band *neu.* Binde, Schnur *f.* **2** Riemen *m.*

bandage *n* Bandage, Binde *f.* Verband *m. vt* verbinden.

bandit ('bændit) *n* Bandit *m.*

bandy ('bændi) *adj* krummbeinig. *v* **bandy words** hin und herstreiten.

bang (bæŋ) *n* **1** Knall, schallender Schlag *m. vi,(vt)* knallen (lassen). **banger** *n inf* **1** Feuerwerkskörper *m.* **2** Wurst *f.*

bangle ('bæŋgəl) *n* Spange *f.* Armband *neu.*

banish ('bæniʃ) *vt* verbannen, vertreiben.

banister ('bænistə) *n* Treppengeländer *neu.*

banjo ('bændʒou) *n* Banjo *neu.*

bank[1] (bæŋk) *n* **1** Ufer *neu.* **2** Damm *m.*

bank[2] (bæŋk) *n* Bank, Sparkasse *f.* **bank account** *n* Bankkonto *neu.* **bankbook** *n* Bankbuch, Sparbuch *neu.* **bank holiday** *n* (amtlicher) Feiertag *m.* **banknote** *n* Banknote *f.* **banker** *n* Bankier *m.* **banker's card** *n* Scheckkarte, Bankkarte *f.*

bankrupt ('bæŋkrʌpt) *adj* bankrott, zahlungsunfähig. *n* Bankerotteur *m.*

banner ('bænə) *n* Banner *m.* Fahne *f.*

banquet ('bæŋkwit) *n* Bankett, Festessen *neu.*

baptize (bæp'taiz) *vt* taufen. **baptism** *n* Taufe *f.*

bar (bɑː) *n* **1** Stange *f.* Riegel, Stab *m.* **2** Bar, Schank *f. vt* **1** verriegeln, vergittern. **2** ausschließen, verbieten. **barmaid** *n* Kellnerin, Barmädchen *f.* **barman** *n* Kellner *m.*

barbarian (bɑː'bɛəriən) *n* Barbar *m.* **barbaric** *adj* barbarisch, roh, grausam. **barbarism** *n* Barbarismus *m.* **barbarity** *n* Barbarei, Roheit, Grausamkeit *f.*
barbecue ('bɑːbikjuː) *n* Bratrost *m.* Barbecue *neu.*
barbed wire (bɑːbd) *n* Stacheldraht *m.*
barber ('bɑːbə) *n* Barbier, (Herren)Friseur *m.*
barbiturate (bɑː'bitjurət) *n* Barbiturat *neu.*
bare (bɛə) *adj* **1** nackt, unbekleidet. **2** bloß, unbedeckt, kahl. **3** leer. *vt* **1** entblößen, enthüllen. **2** (one's teeth) blecken. **barefoot** *adj,adv* barfuß. **barely** *adv* kaum.
bargain ('bɑːgin) *n* (vorteilhaftes) Geschäft *neu.* Gelegenheitskauf *m.* **into the bargain** obendrein. *~vt,vi* feilschen, handeln. **bargain for** erwarten.
barge (bɑːdʒ) *n* Lastkahn *m.* *v* **barge into** *inf* stürzen in.
baritone ('bæritoun) *n* Bariton *m.*
bark[1] (bɑːk) *vi* bellen. *n* Gebell *neu.*
bark[2] (bɑːk) *n* (Baum)rinde, Borke *f.*
barley ('bɑːli) *n* Gerste *f.*
barn (bɑːn) *n* Scheune *f.*
barometer (bə'rɔmitə) *n* Barometer *neu.*
baron ('bærən) *n* Baron, Freiherr *m.* **baroness** *n* Baronin *f.*
baronet ('bærənit) *n* Baronet *m.*
barracks ('bærəks) *n pl* Kaserne *f.*
barrel ('bærəl) *n* **1** Faß *neu.* Tonne *f.* **2** (of a gun) Lauf *m.*
barren ('bærən) *adj* unfruchtbar, öde.
barricade ('bærikeid) *n* Barrikade, Sperre *f.* *vt* versperren.
barrier ('bæriə) *n* Barriere, Schranke *f.*
barrister ('bæristə) *n* Rechtsanwalt *m.*
barrow ('bærou) *n* Karren *m.*
barter ('bɑːtə) *vt* (ein)tauschen. *vi* Tauschhandel treiben. *n* Tauschhandel *m.*
base[1] (beis) *n* **1** Grundfläche, Basis *f.* **2** Fuß, Stützpunkt *m.* *vi* **1** basieren. **2** stützen. **be based on** sich beruhen auf. **baseball** *n* Baseballspiel *neu.* **basement** *n* Kellergeschoß *neu.*
base[2] (beis) *adj* niedrig, gemein, verächtlich.
bash (bæʃ) *vt* heftig schlagen. **have a bash** versuchen.
bashful ('bæʃfəl) *adj* scheu, schüchtern.
basic ('beisik) *adj* **1** einfach. **2** grundliegend. **basically** *adv* im Grunde, grundsätzlich.
basil ('bæzəl) *n* Basilienkraut *neu.*
basin ('beisən) *n* Becken *neu.* Schüssel *f.*
basis ('beisis) *n pl* **-ses** Basis, Grundlage *f.*
bask (bɑːsk) *vi* sich sonnen.
basket ('bɑːskit) *n* Korb *m.* **basketball** *n* Basketballspiel *neu.*
Basle (bɑːl) *n* Basel *neu.*
bass (beis) *mus adj* Baß—. *n* Baß *m.*
bassoon (bə'suːn) *n* Fagott *neu.*

bastard ('bɑːstəd) *n* Bastard *m*.
baste ('beist) *vt cul* (mit Fett) begießen.
bat[1] (bæt) *n* Schläger *m*. Schlagholz *neu*. *vt* **1** schlagen. **2** (eyelids, etc.) zucken, zwinkern. **batsman** *n* Schläger *m*.
bat[2] (bæt) *n zool* Fledermaus *f*.
batch (bætʃ) *n* Schub, Stoß *m*.
bath (bɑːθ) *n* **1** Bad *neu*. **2** Badewanne *f*. **bathroom** *n* Badezimmer *neu*. **bathtub** *n* Badewanne *f*.
bathe (beið) *(vi),vt* (sich) baden. **bathing costume** *n* Badeanzug *m*. **bathing trunks** *n* Badehose *f*.
baton ('bætɔn) *mus* Taktstock *m*.
battalion (bə'tæliən) *n* Bataillon *neu*.
batter[1] ('bætə) *vt* schlagen, prügeln.
batter[2] ('bætə) *n cul* Eierteig *m*.
battery ('bætəri) *n* Batterie *f*.
battle ('bætl̩) *n* Schlacht *f*. Gefecht *neu*. *vi* kämpfen. **battlefield** *n* Schlachtfeld *neu*. **battleship** *n* Schlachtschiff *neu*.
Bavaria (bə'vɛəriə) *n* Bayern *neu*. **Bavarian** *adj* bayrisch. *n* Bayer *m*.
bawl (bɔːl) *vi* schreien, brüllen.
bay[1] (bei) *n* **1** *geog* Bai, Bucht *f*. **2** Lücke, Nische *f*.
bay[2] (bei) *n* **1** Fach. *neu*. Abteilung *f*. **2** Fensternische *f*.
bay[3] (bei) *vi* (dumpf) bellen, kläffen. **keep at bay** in Schach halten.
bay[4] (bei) *n bot* Lorbeer *m*.
bayonet ('beiənit) *n* Bajonett *neu*.
be* (biː) *vi* **1** sein. **2** existieren. **3** sich befinden. *v aux* sein, werden. **there is, there are** es gibt.
beach (biːtʃ) *n* Strand *m*. *vt* stranden. **beachcomber** *n* Strandgutjäger *m*.
beacon ('biːkən) *n* **1** Signalfeuer *neu*. **2** Blinklicht *neu*.
bead (biːd) *n* Perle, Glasperle *f*.
beak (biːk) *n* Schnabel *m*.
beaker ('biːkə) *n* **1** Becher *m*. **2** *sci* Becherglas *neu*.
beam (biːm) *n* **1** Balken *m*. **2** Strahl *m*. *vt,vi* strahlen. *vi* strahlend lächeln.
bean (biːn) *n* Bohne *f*. **full of beans** lebhaft.
bear*[1] (bɛə) *vt* **1** tragen, stützen. **2** erleiden, aushalten. **3** gebären. **bearing** *n* **1** Haltung *f*. **2** Verhalten, Betragen *neu*. **3** Beziehung *f*. **4** Richtung **5** *tech* Lager *neu*.
bear[2] (bɛə) *n* Bär *m*.
beard (biəd) *n* Bart *m*.
beast (biːst) *n* **1** Tier, Vieh *neu*. **2** Bestie *f*.
beat* (biːt) *vt* **1** schlagen, prügeln, klopfen. **2** besiegen, schlagen. *n* **1** *mus* Rhythmus, Takt *m*. **2** Schlag *m*. **3** (of a policeman) Revier *neu*.
beauty ('bjuːti) *n* Schönheit *f*. **beauty queen** *n* Schönheitskönigin *f*. **beautiful** *adj* schön, hübsch.
beaver ('biːvə) *n* Biber *m*.
became (bi'keim) *v* see **become**.
because (bi'kɔːz) *conj* weil. **because of** wegen.
beckon ('bekən) *vt,vi* heranwinken.
become* (bi'kʌm) *vi* werden.

vt passen, geziemen. **becoming** *adj* passend, geziemend.
bed (bed) *n* Bett *neu*. **bed bug** *n* Wanze *f*. **bedclothes** *n pl* Bettwäsche *f*. **bedding** *n* **1** Bettzeug *neu*. **2** Streu *f*. **bedridden** *adj* bettlägerig. **bedroom** *n* Schlafzimmer, Schlafgemach *neu*. **bed-sitter** *n* Wohnschlafzimmer *neu*. **bedspread** *n* Bettdecke *f*.
bedraggled (bi'drægəld) *adj* beschmutzt, naß.
bee (biː) *n* Biene *f*. **beehive** *n* Bienenstock *m*.
beech (biːtʃ) *n* Buche *f*.
beef (biːf) *n* Rindfleisch *neu*. **beefburger** ('biːfbəːgə) *n* Hamburger *m*.
beer (biə) *n* Bier *neu*.
beet (biːt) *n* Bete, Rübe *f*. **beetroot** *n* rote Rübe *f*.
beetle ('biːtl̩) *n* Käfer *m*. Schabe *f*.
befall* (bi'fɔːl) *vi* sich ereignen. *vt* (jemandem) zustoßen.
before (bi'fɔː) *conj* bevor, ehe, bis. *adv* **1** voraus, vorn, voran. **2** vorher, früher, ehe. *prep* vor. **beforehand** *adv* zuvor, davor.
befriend (bi'frend) *vt* befreunden.
beg (beg) *vt,vi* **1** betteln. **2** bitten. *vi* erbitten. **beggar** *n* Bettler *m*.
begin* (bi'gin) *vt,vi* anfangen, beginnen. **beginner** *n* Anfänger *nm*. **beginning** *n* Anfang, Beginn *m*.
begrudge (bi'grʌdʒ) *vt* mißgönnen.
behalf (bi'hɑːf) *n* **on behalf of** **1** im Namen *or* im Auftrag von. **2** zugunsten. **on my behalf** um meinetwillen.
behave (bi'heiv) *vi* sich verhalten, sich betragen, sich benehmen. **behave oneself** sich gut betragen. **behaviour** *n* Betragen, Verhalten, Benehmen *neu*.
behind (bi'haind) *adv* **1** hinten. **2** zurück *prep* hinter. *n* Hinterteil *neu*. **behindhand** *adv* verspätet, im Rückstand.
behold* (bi'hould) *vt* erblicken, sehen.
beige (beiʒ) *adj* beige. *n* Beige *neu*.
being ('biːiŋ) *n* **1** (Da)Sein *neu*. Existenz *f*. **2** Geschöpf, Wesen *neu*.
belch (beltʃ) *vi* rülpsen. *n* Rülpsen *neu*.
belfry ('belfri) *n* Glockenturm *m*.
Belgium ('beldʒəm) *n* Belgien *neu*. **Belgian** *adj* belgisch. *n* Belgier *m*.
believe (bi'liːv) *vt* glauben. **belief** *n* **1** Glaube *m*. **2** Überzeugung *f*. **believer** *n* Gläubige(r) *m*.
bell (bel) *n* **1** Glocke *f*. **2** Klingel *f*. **bellringer** *n* Glöckner *m*.
belligerent (bə'lidʒərənt) *adj* kriegführend.
bellow ('belou) *vi* brüllen, schreien. *n* Gebrüll, Geschrei *neu*.
bellows ('belouz) *n pl* Gebläse *neu*.
belly ('beli) *n* Bauch *m*.
belong (bi'lɔŋ) *vi* **1** gehören. **2** (to a club, etc.) angehören. **belongings** *n pl* Eigentum *neu*.

below (bi'lou) *adv* unter. *prep* unter(halb).
belt (belt) *n* **1** Gürtel, Riemen *m*. Binde *f*. **2** Bereich *m*. Gebiet *neu*.
bench (bentʃ) *n* **1** Bank *f*. **2** Arbeitstisch *m*.
bend* (bend) *n* Kurve, Krümmung *f*. *vt* biegen, krümmen. *vi* (sich) beugen.
beneath (bi'ni:θ) *prep* unter(halb).
benefactor ('benifæktə) *n* Wohltäter, Gönner *m*.
benefit ('benifit) *n* **1** Nutzen, Vorteil *m*. **2** Wohltat *f*. *vi* nützen, Nutzen ziehen (aus). **beneficial** *adj* **1** wohltuend. **2** vorteilhaft, nützlich.
benevolent (bi'nevələnt) *adj* wohlwollend, gütig. **benevolence** *n* Wohlwollen *neu*. Güte *f*.
bent (bent) *v* see **bend.**
bereave* (bi'ri:v) *vt* berauben. **bereavement** *n* Beraubung *f*. Verlust *m*.
berry ('beri) *n* Beere *f*.
berth (bə:θ) *n* **1** Ankerplatz *m*. **2** Liegeplatz *m*. Koje *f*.
beside (bi'said) *prep* neben, dicht bei. **besides** *adv* außerdem, ferner. *prep* außer.
besiege (bi'si:dʒ) *vt* belagern.
best (best) *adj* best. *adv* am besten. **at best** im besten Fall(e). *n* Beste(r) *m*. **best man** *n* die rechte Hand des Bräutigams bei der Hochzeit. **best-seller** *n* Verkaufsschlager, Bestseller *m*.
bestow (bi'stou) *vt* geben, schenken.
bet* (bet) *n* Wette *f*. *vt,vi* wetten. **betting shop** *n* Wettbüro *neu*.
betray (bi'trei) *vt* verraten. **betrayal** *n* Verrat *m*.
better ('betə) *adj,adv* besser. *vt* **1** (ver)bessern. **2** übertreffen. **better oneself** sich bessern.
between (bi'twi:n) *prep* zwischen. *adv* dazwischen.
beverage ('bevridʒ) *n* Getränk *neu*.
beware* (bi'wɛə) *vi* sich vorsehen, sich hüten.
bewilder (bi'wildə) *vt* verwirren, bestürzen.
beyond (bi'jɔnd) *prep* jenseits, außer. *adv* darüber hinaus, jenseits.
bias ('baiəs) *n* **1** Neigung *f*. **2** Vorurteil *neu*. **biased** *adj* voreingenommen.
bib (bib) *n* Lätzchen *neu*.
Bible ('baibəl) *n* Bibel *f*. **biblical** *adj* biblisch.
bibliography (bibli'ɔgrəfi) *n* Bibliographie *f*.
biceps ('baiseps) *n* Bizeps *m*.
bicker ('bikə) *vi* zanken, streiten.
bicycle ('baisikəl) *n* Fahrrad *neu*.
bid* (bid) *n* **2** Angebot *neu*. **2** Versuch *m*. *vi* **1** bieten. **2** *game* reizen.
biennial (bai'eniəl) *adj* zweijährig.
bifocals (bai'foukəlz) *n pl* Bifokal *f pl*.
big (big) *adj* **1** groß. **2** dick.
bigamy ('bigəmi) *n* Bigamie, Doppelehe *f*.
bigot ('bigət) *n* Fanatiker, Frömmler *m*. **bigoted** *adj* bigott, blind ergeben.
bikini (bi'ki:ni) *n* Bikini *m*.

bilingual (bai'liŋgwəl) *adj* zweisprachig.
bilious ('biliəs) *adj* gallig.
bill[1] (bil) *n* **1** Rechnung *f.* **2** Gesetzesvorlage *f.*
bill[2] (bil) *n* (Vogel)Schnabel *m.*
billiards ('biliədz) *n* Billard(spiel) *neu.*
billion ('biljən) *n* **1** Billion *f.* **2** *US* Milliarde *f.*
bin (bin) *n* Behälter, Kasten *m.*
binary ('bainəri) *adj* binär.
bind* (baind) *vt* **1** binden, befestigen, festmachen. **2** verbinden, verpflichten. **binding** *adj* verbindlich. *n* **1** Bindung *f.* **2** Einband *m.*
binoculars (bi'nɔkjuləz) *n pl* Feldstecher *m.*
biodegradable (baioudi'greid-əbəl) *adj* biologisch abbaubar.
biography (bai'ɔgrəfi) *n* Biographie *f.*
biology (bai'ɔlədʒi) *n* Biologie *f.*
birch (bəːtʃ) *n* Birke *f.* *vt* züchtigen.
bird (bəːd) *n* Vogel *m.*
birth (bəːθ) *n* **1** Geburt *f.* **2** Entstehung *f.* **birth certificate** *n* Geburtsschein *m.* Geburtsurkunde *f.* **birth control** *n* Geburtenkontrolle, Geburtenbeschränkung *f.* **birthday** *n* Geburtstag *m.* **birthmark** *n* Muttermal *neu.* **birth rate** *n* Geburtenziffer *f.*
biscuit ('biskit) *n* Keks, Zwieback *m.*
bishop ('biʃəp) *n* Bischof *m.*
bit[1] (bit) *n* **1** Stück, Stückchen, Bißchen *neu.* **2** Gebiß *neu.*
bit[2] (bit) *v* see **bite.**
bitch (bitʃ) *n* **1** Hündin *f.* **2** *sl* gemeine Frau, Dirne *f.*
bite* (bait) *vt* beißen. *n* Biß, Bissen *m.*
bitter ('bitə) *adj* **1** bitter. **2** verbittert.
bizarre (bi'zɑː) *adj* bizarr, grotesk.
black (blæk) *adj* schwarz. *n* **1** Schwarz *neu.* **2** Schwarze(r), Farbige(r) *m.* **blacken** *vt* **1** schwärzen. **2** anschwärzen, verleumden. *vi* schwarz *or* dunkel werden. **blackness** *n* Schwärze *f.*
blackberry ('blækbəri) *n* Brombeere *f.*
blackbird ('blækbəːd) *n* Amsel *f.*
blackboard ('blækbɔːd) *n* (Wand)Tafel *f.*
blackcurrant (blæk'kʌrənt) *n* schwarze Johannisbeere *f.*
blackleg ('blækleg) *n* Streikbrecher *m.*
blackmail ('blækmeil) *n* Erpressung *f.* *vt* erpressen.
black market *n* Schwarzmarkt *m.*
blackout ('blækaut) *n* **1** Verdunkelung *f.* **2** Gedächtnisstörung *f.*
black pudding *n* Blutwurst *f.*
blacksmith ('blæksmiθ) *n* Schmied *m.*
bladder ('blædə) *n* Blase *f.*
blade (bleid) *n* **1** Klinge, Schneide *f.* **2** (of grass, etc.) Halm *m.*
blame (bleim) *n* Schuld, Verantwortung *f.* *vt* **1** tadeln. **2** beschuldigen.
blank (blæŋk) *adj* weiß, blank(o), leer, unausgefüllt.
blanket ('blæŋkit) *n* Wolldecke *f.* *vt* zudecken.

blare (blɛə) *vi* schmettern. *n* Geschmetter *neu*.

blaspheme (blæs'fiːm) *vi* lästern, fluchen. **blasphemy** *n* Gotteslästerung *f*.

blast (blɑːst) *n* **1** Windstoß, Sturm *m*. **2** (of trumpets) Schall *m*. **1** Sprengschuß *m*. Explosion *f*. *vt* sprengen.

blatant ('bleitn̩t) *adj* **1** lärmend. **2** offenkundig.

blaze (bleiz) *vi* brennen, lodern. *n* Feuer *neu*. Flammen *f*. **blazer** *n* Sportjacke *f*. Blazer *m*.

bleach (bliːtʃ) *n* Bleichmittel *neu*. *vt* bleichen.

bleak (bliːk) *adj* **1** kahl, öde. **2** trüb, freudlos.

bleat (bliːt) *vi* blöken, meckern. *n* Blöken *neu*.

bleed* (bliːd) *vi* bluten. *vt* **1** bluten lassen. **2** *inf* schröpfen. **bleeding** *n* Blutung *f*.

blemish ('blemiʃ) *n* **1** Flecken *m*. **2** Fehler *m*. *vt* verunstalten.

blend (blend) *vt* mischen, vermengen. *vi* sich vermischen. *n* Mischung *f*. Gemisch *neu*.

bless (bles) *vt* **1** segnen. **2** preisen, loben. **blessed** *adj* gesegnet. **blessing** *n* Segen *m*. Segnung *f*.

blew (bluː) *v* see **blow**².

blind (blaind) *adj* blind. *adv* blindlings. *vt* (ver)blenden. *n* (of a window) Vorhang *m*. Jalousie *f*. **blind alley** *n* Sackgasse *f*. **blindfold** *adj* blindlings. *vt* die Augen verbinden.

blink (bliŋk) *vi* blinzeln. *n* Blinzeln *neu*.

bliss (blis) *n* Wonne, Seligkeit *f*.

blister ('blistə) *n* (Haut)Blase *f*. *vt* Blasen ziehen. *vi* Blasen bekommen.

blizzard ('blizəd) *n* (dichter) Schneesturm *m*.

blob (blɔb) *n* Tropfen *m*.

bloc (blɔk) *n pol* Block *m*. **en bloc** *adv* im ganzen, en bloc.

block (blɔk) *n* Block, Klotz *m*. *vt* blockieren, sperren, aufhalten, verhindern. **blockade** *n* Blockade, Sperre *f*. *vt* blockieren, sperren.

blond (blɔnd) *adj* blond, hell(farbig). **blonde** *n* Blondine *f*.

blood (blʌd) *n* Blut *neu*. **bloodcurdling** *adj* schrecklich, furchtbar, Mark und Bein durchdringend. **blood donor** *n* Blutspender *m*. **blood pressure** *n* Blutdruck *m*. **bloodstream** *n* Blutkreislauf *m*. **bloodthirsty** *adj* blutdürstig, blutrünstig. **blood transfusion** *n* Blutübertragung *f*. **bloody** *adj* **1** blutig. **2** *sl* verdammt.

bloom (bluːm) *n* Blüte, Blume *f*. *vi* blühen.

blossom ('blɔsəm) *n* Blüte *f*. *vi* blühen, Blüten treiben.

blot (blɔt) *n* **1** Fleck, Klecks *m*. **2** Makel *m*. *vt* beflecken, beklecksen. **blotting paper** *n* Löschpapier *neu*.

blotch (blɔtʃ) *n* Klecks *m*.

blouse (blauz) *n* Bluse *f*.

blow¹ (blou) *n* **1** Schlag, Stoß *m*. **2** Unglück *neu*. Nachteil *m*.

blow*² (blou) *vi* **1** blasen. **2** (of wind) wehen. **3** keuchen, schnaufen.

blubber ('blʌbə) *n* Walfischspeck, Tran *m*. *vi inf* heulen, plärren.

blue (bluː) *adj* **1** blau. **2** *inf* traurig, deprimiert. *n* Blau *neu*. **bluebell** *n* Glockenblume *f*. **blueprint** **1** Blaudruck *m*. **2** Plan *m*.

bluff (blʌf) *vi* bluffen, täuschen. *n* Bluff *m*. Irreführung *f*. *adj* grob, derb.

blunder ('blʌndə) *n* Fehler, Schnitzer *m*. *vi* **1** stolpern. **2** irren, unbesonnen handeln.

blunt (blʌnt) *adj* **1** stumpf. **2** grob, offen. *vt* stumpfmachen.

blur (bləː) *vt* beflecken, verwischen. *n* Fleck *m*. Verschwommenheit *f*.

blush (blʌʃ) *vi* erröten. *n* Erröten *neu*.

boar (bɔː) *n* Eber, Keiler *m*.

board (bɔːd) *n* **1** Brett *neu*. **2** Tafel *f*. **3** Vorstand, Aufsichtsrat *m*. **4** Verpflegung *f*. **boarding house** *n* Pension *f*. **boarding school** *n* Internat *neu*.

boast (boust) *vi* prahlen, angeben. *n* Prahlerei *f*. **boaster** *n* Prahler, Angeber *m*.

boat (bout) *n* **1** Boot *neu*. **2** Dampfer *m*. Schiff *neu*.

bob (bɔb) *vi* sich auf und ab bewegen, baumeln.

bodice ('bɔdis) *n* Mieder *neu*.

body ('bɔdi) *n* **1** Körper *m*. **2** Leiche *f*. Leichnam *m*. **3** Gruppe *f*. **4** *mot* Karosserie *f*. **bodyguard** *n* Leibwächter *m*.

bog (bɔg) *n* Sumpf *m*. Moor *neu*.

bohemian (bə'hiːmiən) *adj* leichtlebig, ungebunden, zigeunerhaft.

boil[1] (bɔil) *vt* kochen, sieden. **boiler** *n* **1** Kocher, Kessel *m*. **2** Dampfkessel *m*. **boiling point** *n* Siedepunkt *m*.

boil[2] (bɔil) *n* Geschwür *neu*.

boisterous ('bɔistərəs) *adj* ungestüm, heftig, laut.

bold (bould) *adj* **1** kühn, mutig. **2** frech, unverschämt. **boldness** *n* Kühnheit *f*. Mut *m*.

Bolivia (bə'liviə) *n* Bolivien *neu*. **Bolivian** *adj* bolivianisch. *n* Bolivianer *m*.

bolster ('boulstə) *n* Kissen, Polster *neu*. *v* **bolster up** unterstützen.

bolt (boult) *n* **1** Bolzen *m*. **2** Riegel *m*. **3** Bund *m*. Rolle *f*. *vt* **1** verriegeln. **2** (food) hinunterschlingen. *vi* hastig fliehen.

bomb (bɔm) *n* Bombe *f*. *vt* bombardieren. **bombard** *vt* bombardieren, beschießen. **bombardment** *n* Beschuß *m*.

bond (bɔnd) *n* **1** Verbindung *f*. **2** Fesseln *f pl*. **3** Bürgschaft *f*. *vt* verbinden, aufschlichten, verkleben.

bone (boun) *n* **1** Knochen *m*. Bein *neu*. **2** (of fish) Gräte *f*. **bony** *adj* **1** knochig. **2** grätig.

bonfire ('bɔnfaiə) *n* (Garten)Feuer *neu*.

bonnet ('bɔnit) *n* **1** Haube, Damenmütze *f*. **2** Motorhaube *f*.

bonus ('bounəs) *n* Zulage, Extrazahlung *f*.

booby trap ('buːbi) *n* (Spreng)Falle *f*.

book (buk) *n* **1** Buch *neu*. **2**

Heft *neu.* *vt* aufschreiben, eintragen. **bookcase** *n* Bücherschrank *m.* Bücherregal *neu.* **booking office** *n* Fahrkartenschalter *m.* **bookkeeper** *n* Buchhalter *m.* **bookkeeping** *n* Buchhaltung, Buchführung *f.* **booklet** *n* Büchlein *neu.* Broschüre *f.* **bookmaker** *n* Buchmacher *m.* **bookshop** *n* Buchladen *m.* Buchhandlung *f.* **bookstall** *n* Bücherstand *m.*

boom (buːm) *n* **1** *comm* Hochkonjunktur, Hausse, *f.* Aufschwung *m.* **2** *naut* Baum *m.* **3** Dröhnen *neu.* *vi* dröhnen, brummen.

boost (buːst) *vt* **1** heben, unterstützen. **2** verstärken, aufladen. *n* Aufschwung *m.*

boot (buːt) *n* **1** Stiefel *m.* **2** *mot* Kofferraum *m.* *v* **boot out** *sl* hinauswerfen.

booth (buːð) *n* **1** Bude *f.* **2** Zelle *f.*

booze (buːz) *n inf* alkoholisches Getränk *neu.* *vi inf* saufen, trinken.

border ('bɔːdə) *n* **1** Rand, Saum *m.* **2** Grenze *f.* *vt* grenzen, begrenzen. **borderline** *adj* unsicher, zweifelhaft. *n* Grenze *f.*

bore[1] (bɔː) *vi,vt* bohren, durchdringen. *n* **1** Bohnrung, Höhlung *f.* **2** Kaliber *neu.*

bore[2] (bɔː) *vt* langweilen. *n* langweiliger *or* lästiger Mensch *m.* **boredom** *n* Langeweile *f.* **boring** *adj* langweilig.

bore[3] (bɔː) *v* see **bear**[1].

born (bɔːn) *adj* geboren.

borne (bɔːn) *v* see **bear**[1].

borough ('bʌrə) *n* Verwaltungsbezirk *m.*

borrow ('bɔrou) *vt* borgen, entleihen.

bosom ('buzəm) *n* Busen *m.* Brust *f.*

boss (bɔs) *n* **1** Chef, Boß *m.* **2** Arbeitgeber *m.* **bossy** *adj* herrisch, rechthaberisch.

botany ('bɔtəni) *n* Botanik, Pflanzenkunde *f.* **Botanist** *n* Botaniker, Pflanzenkenner *m.*

both (bouθ) *pron,adj* beide(s). **both...and** sowohl...als(auch).

bother ('bɔðə) *n* Belästigung, Störung *f.* *vt* belästigen, stören.

bottle ('bɔtl) *n* Flasche *f.* *vt* in Flaschen füllen. **bottleneck** Engpaß *m.*

bottom ('bɔtəm) *n* **1** Boden, Unterteil *m.* **2** Grund *m.* **3** *inf* Hintern *m.* *adj* **1** Grund—. **2** letzt.

bough (bau) *n* Ast, Hauptzweig *m.*

bought (bɔːt) *v* see **buy.**

boulder ('bouldə) *n* Felsbrocken *m.*

bounce (bauns) *vi* springen, aufprallen. *n* Sprung, Aufprall *m.*

bound[1] (baund) *v* see **bind.** *adj* **1** verpflichtet. **2** bestimmt.

bound[2] (baund) *n* Sprung, Satz *m.* *vi* springen, hüpfen.

bound[3] (baund) *n* Grenze, Schranke *f.* **boundary** *n* Grenze *f.* **boundless** grenzenlos.

bound[4] (baund) *adv* bestimmt, unterwegs nach.

bouquet (bu'kei) *n* **1** Bukett *neu.* Blumenstrauß *m.* **2** (of wine) Blume *f.*

bourgeois ('buəʒwaː) *n* Bürger, Bourgeois *m.* *adj* bürgerlich, bourgeois. **bourgeoisie** *n* Bürgertum *neu*. Bourgeoisie *f*.

bout (baut) *n* **1** Reihe, Tour *f*. **2** Kampf *m*. **3** *med* Anfall *m*.

bow[1] (bau) *n* Verbeugung, Verneigung *f*. *vi* sich verbeugen, sich verneigen.

bow[2] (bou) *n* **1** *mil* (Schieß)Bogen *m*. **2** *mus* Bogen *m*. **3** Schleife *f*. **4** Kurve *f*.

bow[3] (bau) *n naut* Bug *m*.

bowels ('bauəlz) *n pl* **1** Darm *m*. Eingeweide *neu pl*. **2** Innere *neu*.

bowl[1] (boul) *n* **1** Schüssel, Schale *f*. **2** Becken *neu*. **3** Pfeifenkopf *m*.

bowl[2] (boul) *n* Kugel *f*. *vt* werfen, kugeln, schieben, rollen.

box[1] (bɔks) *n* **1** Kasten *m*. Büchse, Schachtel *f*. **2** *Th* Loge *f*. *vt* einpacken, in Schachteln packen. **box number** *n* Postfachnummer *f*. **box office** *n* Theaterkasse *f*.

box[2] (bɔks) *(vi),vt* (sich) boxen. *n* **box on the ear** Ohrfeige *f*. **boxer** Boxer *m*. **boxing match** *n* Boxkampf *m*.

Boxing Day *n* zweite Weihnachtsfeiertag *m*.

boy (bɔi) *n* Junge, Knabe, Bube *m*. **boyfriend** Freund *m*. **boyhood** *n* Jugend *f*. Knabenalter *neu*.

boycott ('bɔikɔt) *vt* boykottieren. *n* Boykott *m*.

brace (breis) *n* **1** Stütze *f*. **2** Bohrwinde *f*. **3** Paar *neu*. **4** *pl* Hosenträger *m pl*. *vt* spannen, stützen, festziehen. **brace oneself** sich zusammennehmen.

bracelet ('breislət) Armband *neu*.

bracket ('brækit) *n* **1** Träger *m*. **2** Klammer *f*. **3** Klasse, Kategorie *f*.

brag (bræg) *vi* angeben, prahlen.

braille (breil) *n* Blindenschrift *f*.

brain (brein) *n* **1** (Ge)Hirn *neu*. **2** *pl* Verstand *m*. Intelligenz *f*. **brainwash** *vt* gehirnwaschen. **brainwashing** *n* Gehirnwäsche *f*. **brainwave** *n* Idee, Eingebung *f*. Einfall *m*.

braise (breiz) *vt* schmoren.

brake (breik) *n* Bremse *f*. *vt,vi* bremsen. *vt* aufhalten.

branch (brɑːntʃ) *n* **1** Ast, Zweig *m*. **2** *comm* Zweigstelle, Filiale *f*. *vi* (ab)zweigen.

brand (brænd) *n* **1** *comm* Marke *f*. Fabrikat *neu*. **2** (Feuer)Brand *m*. *vt* einbrennen, brandmarken. **brand-new** *adj* nagelneu.

brandy ('brændi) *n* Branntwein, Weinbrand *m*.

brass (brɑːs) *n* **1** Messing *neu*. **2** Blasinstrumente *neu pl*. **3** *sl* Geld *neu*. **brass band** *n* Blasorchester *neu*. Blaskapelle *f*.

brassiere ('bræziə) *n* Büstenhalter *m*.

brave (breiv) *adj* mutig, tapfer.

brawl (brɔːl) *n* Streit *m*. Schlägerei *f*. *vi* streiten, zanken, raufen.

bray (brei) *vi* schreien. *n* Eselsgeschrei *neu*.

brazen ('breizən) *adj* **1** ehern. **2** unverschämt.

Brazil (brə'zil) *n* Brasilien *neu*.

Brazilian *adj* brasilianisch. *n* Brasilianer *m*.

breach (briːtʃ) *n* **1** Bruch *m*. Lücke *f*. **2** Vergehen *neu*. Verstoß *m*. *vt* **1** durchbrechen. **2** verstoßen gegen.

bread (bred) *n* **1** Brot *neu*. **2** Nahrung *f*. **breadcrumb** *n* Brotkrume *f*. **coated with breadcrumbs** paniert. **breadwinner** *n* Brotverdiener, Ernährer *m*.

breadth (bredθ) *n* Breite *f*.

break* (breik) *vt* brechen, zerbrechen, kaputtmachen. *n* **1** Riß, Bruch *m*. **2** Pause *f*. **breakdown** *n* **1** *med* Zusammenbruch *m*. **2** *mot* (Auto)Panne *f*. **breakthrough** *n* Durchbruch *m*.

breakfast ('brekfəst) *n* Frühstück *neu*. *vi* frühstücken.

breast (brest) *n* Brust *f*. Busen *m*. **breaststroke** *n* Brustschwimmen *neu*.

breath (breθ) *n* **1** Atem, Hauch *m*. **2** Atemzug *m*. **breathtaking** *adj* atemraubend.

breathe (briːð) *vi,vt* atmen.

breed* (briːd) *vt* **1** erzeugen, hervorbringen. **2** aufziehen, züchten. *vi* sich fortpflanzen. *n* Rasse, Zucht *f*.

breeze (briːz) *n* Brise *f*. Wind *m*.

brew (bruː) *n* Gebräu, Getränk *neu*. *vt* brauen. *vi* (of a storm) sich zusammenziehen. **brewery** *n* Brauerei *f*.

bribe (braib) *n* Bestechung *f*. *vt* bestechen.

brick (brik) *n* Ziegelstein, Mauerstein *m*.

bride (braid) *n* Braut *f*. **bridegroom** *n* Bräutigam *m*.

bridesmaid *n* Brautjungfer *f*.

bridge[1] (bridʒ) *n* **1** Brücke *f*. **2** *mus* Steg *m*. *vt* überbrücken.

bridge[2] (bridʒ) *n* Bridgespiel *neu*.

bridle ('braidḷ) *n* Zaum, Zügel *m*. *vt* zügeln, bändigen. **bridlepath** *n* Reitweg *m*.

brief (briːf) *adj* kurz, flüchtig. **in brief** *adv* kurz gesagt, kurz gefaßt. ~*n law* Schriftsatz *m*.

briefcase *n* Aktentasche, Mappe *f*. **briefing** *n* Anweisung, Instruktion *f*.

briefs *n pl* (Herren) Unterhose *f*.

brigade (bri'geid) *n* Brigade *f*. **brigadier** *n* Brigadekommandeur *m*.

bright (brait) *adj* **1** hell, glänzend, leuchtend. **2** intelligent, klug. **brighten** *vt,vi* erhellen, aufleuchten, aufmuntern.

brilliant ('briliənt) *adj* **1** brillant, strahlend, glänzend. **2** hochbegabt.

brim (brim) *n* **1** Rand *m*. **2** (of a hat) Krempe *f*.

bring* (briŋ) *vt* (her-, mit-)bringen. **bring about** zustande bringen. **bring up 1** (a child) erziehen, aufziehen. **2** (a question, etc.) aufwerfen.

brink (briŋk) *n* **1** Rand *m*. **2** Ufer *neu*.

brisk (brisk) *adj* frisch, lebhaft, munter.

bristle ('brisəl) *n* Borste *f*.

Britain ('britṇ) *n* Großbritannien. **British** *adj* britisch. **Briton** *n* Brite *m*.

brittle ('britḷ) *adj* brüchig, zerbrechlich.

broad (brɔːd) *adj* breit, ausgedehnt. **broad bean** *n* Saubohne *f.* **broadcast** *n* Radiosendung *f.* *vt* **1** senden, funken. **2** verbreiten. *adj* weit verstreut. **broadcasting** *n* Rundfunk *m.* **broaden** *vt* verbreitern, ausdehnen. **broadminded** *adj* tolerant.

broccoli ('brɔkəli) *n* Brokkoli *pl.* Spargelkohl *m.*

brochure ('brouʃə) *n* Broschüre *f.*

broke (brouk) *v* see **break.** *adj inf* pleite.

broken ('broukən) *v* see **break.** *adj* kaputt.

broker ('broukə) *n* Vermittler, Makler *m.*

bronchitis (brɔŋ'kaitis) *n* Bronchitis *f.*

bronze (brɔnz) *n* **1** Bronze *f.* **2** Bronzefigur *f.*

brooch (broutʃ) *n* Spange, Brosche *f.*

brood (bruːd) *vi* brüten. *n* Brut *f.*

brook (bruk) *n* Bach *m.*

broom (bruːm) *n* Besen *m.*

brothel ('brɔθəl) *n* Bordell *neu.*

brother ('brʌðə) *n* Bruder *m.* **brotherhood** *n* Bruderschaft *f.* **brother-in-law** *n* Schwager *m.* **brotherly** *adj* brüderlich.

brought (brɔːt) *v* see **bring.**

brow (brau) *n* **1** Augenbraue *f.* **2** Stirn *f.* **3** (of a hill) Rand *m.*

brown (braun) *adj* braun. *n* Braun *neu.* *vt* bräunen.

browse (brauz) *vi* **1** grasen, (ab)weiden. **2** flüchtig lesen, durchblättern, schmökern.

bruise (bruːz) *n* Quetschung *f.* *vt* quetschen.

brunette (bruː'net) *n* Brünette *f.* *adj* brünett.

brush (brʌʃ) *n* **1** Bürste *f.* **2** Pinsel *m.* **3** Unterholz *m.* *vt* **1** bürsten, fegen. **2** berühren, streifen.

brusque (bruːsk) *adj* schroff, angebunden.

Brussels ('brʌsəlz) *n* Brüssel *neu.* **Brussels sprout** *n* Rosenkohl *m.*

brute (bruːt) *n* Unmensch *m.* *adj* roh. **brutal** *adj* brutal.

bubble ('bʌbəl) *n* Blase *f.* *vi* brodeln, aufwallen, sprudeln.

buck[1] (bʌk) *n* **1** (Reh)Bock *m.* **2** (of a rabbit) Männchen *neu.*

buck[2] (bʌk) *vi* bocken. **buck up** sich zusammenreißen, sich beeilen.

bucket ('bʌkit) *n* Eimer *m.*

buckle ('bʌkəl) *n* Schnalle, Spange *f.* *vt* anschnallen, (zu)schnallen.

bud (bʌd) *n* **1** Knospe *f.* **2** Keim *m.* **nip in the bud** im Keime ersticken. ~*vi* knospen, keimen.

Buddhism ('budizəm) *n* Buddhismus *m.*

budget ('bʌdʒit) *n* Budget *neu.* Staatshaushalt, Etat *m.* *vi* sparen, Geld einteilen.

buffalo ('bʌfəlou) *n* Büffel *m.*

buffer ('bʌfə) *n* Puffer, Prellbock *m.*

buffet[1] ('bʌfit) *n* Stoß, Schlag *m.* *vt* schlagen, Stoßen.

buffet[2] ('bufei) *n* Büfett *neu.*

bug (bʌg) *n* **1** Wanze *f.* **2** *inf* Bazillus *m.* **3** *inf* (microphone) Wanze *f.* *vt sl* stören.

bugger ('bʌgə) *n* **1** Sodomit *m.* **2** *sl* Kerl, Schuft *m.*

bugle ('bju:gəl) *n* (Jagd)Horn *neu.*

build* (bild) *vt* **1** bauen, errichten. **2** zusammenstellen. **building** *n* Gebäude *neu.* **building society** *n* Bausparkasse *f.*

bulb (bʌlb) *n* **1** Glühbirne *f.* **2** *bot* Knolle, Zwiebel *f.*

Bulgaria (bʌl'gɛəriə) *n* Bulgarien *neu.* **Bulgarian** *adj* bulgarisch. *n* Bulgare *m.*

bulge (bʌldʒ) *n* (Aus)-Bauchung, Ausbuchtung *f.* *vi* sich (aus)bauchen, vorstehen.

bulk (bʌlk) *n* **1** Maße, Größe *f.* **2** Großteil *m.*

bull (bul) *n* Bulle, Stier *m.* **bulldog** *n* Bulldogge *f.* **bulldozer** Bulldozer *m.* **bullfight** *n* Stierkampf *m.*

bullet ('bulit) *n* Kugel *f.* Geschoß *neu.* **bulletproof** *adj* kugelsicher, gepanzert.

bulletin ('bulətin) *n* Bulletin *neu.*

bully ('buli) *n* Raufbold, Tyrann *m.* *vt* einschüchtern, tyrannisieren.

bum (bʌm) *n inf* Hintern *m.* Hinterteil *neu.*

bump (bʌmp) *n* **1** Stoß, Schlag *m.* **2** Beule *f.* *vt* stoßen, schlagen. **bumper** *n mot* Stoßstange *f.* *adj* ungewohnlich gut *or* groß.

bun (bʌn) *n* **1** Semmel *f.* Brötchen *neu.* **2** (of hair) Kauz *m.*

bunch (bʌntʃ) *n* **1** Bund *neu.* **2** Strauß *m.* **2** Traube *f.* **4** Büschel *m.* **5** Gruppe *f.* *vt,vi* zusammenfügen, bündeln.

bundle ('bʌndḷ) *n* Bündel *neu.* *vt* einbündeln, (schnell) zusammenpacken.

bungalow ('bʌŋgəlou) *n* Bungalow, Landhaus *neu.*

bungle ('bʌŋgəl) *vt* pfuschen. *vi* verpfuschen.

bunk (bʌŋk) *n* Schlafkoje *f.*

bunker ('bʌŋkə) *n* **1** Bunker *m.* **2** Sandloch *neu.*

buoy (bɔi) *n* Boje *f.* **buoyant** *adj* **1** schwimmfähig. **2** tragfähig.

burden ('bə:dn̩) *n* Last, Bürde *f.* *vt* beladen, belasten.

bureau ('bjuərou) *n* **1** Schreibtisch *m.* **2** Büro *neu.*

bureaucracy (bju'rɔkrəsi) *n* Bürokratie *f.* **bureaucrat** *n* Bürokrat, Beamte(r) *m.*

burgle ('bə:gəl) *vt* einbrechen. **burglar** *n* Einbrecher *m.* **burglary** *n* Einbruch *m.*

burn* (bə:n) *vt* (ver)brennen, in Brand stecken. *vi* brennen. *n* Brandwunde *f.*

burrow ('bʌrou) *n* Höhle *f.* Bau *m.* *vi* sich eingraben, wühlen. *vt* aufwühlen, graben.

burst* (bə:st) *vi* platzen, zerspringen. *vt* sprengen. **burst into tears/out laughing** in Tränen/Lachen ausbrechen. ~ *n* Bruch *m.*

bury* ('beri) *vt* begraben. **burial** *n* Beerdigung *f.* Begräbnis *neu.* **burial ground** *n* Begräbnisplatz *m.*

bus (bʌs) *n* (Auto)Bus *m.* **bus-stop** *n* Bushaltestelle *f.*

bush (buʃ) *n* Busch, Strauch *m.* Gebüsch *neu.*

bushy ('buʃi:) *adj* buschig, dicht.

business ('biznis) *n* **1** Geschäft *neu.* **2** Gewerbe *neu.* **3**

Angelegenheit *f.* **4** Beruf *m.* **businessman** *n* Geschäftsmann *m.*
bust[1] (bʌst) *n* **1** Büste *f.* **2** (Frauen)Brust *f.* Busen *m.*
bust[2] (bʌst) *vt* brechen, zerbrechen. *adj sl* **1** kaputt. **2** bankrott, pleite.
bustle ('bʌsəl) *n* Gewühl, Gedränge *neu.* *vi* herumrennen.
busy ('bizi) *adj* (viel)beschäftigt, fleißig.
but (bət; *stressed* bʌt) *conj* **1** aber, jedoch, sondern. **2** außer, als. *adv* nur, bloß. **all but** fast, beinahe. **not only...but also** nicht nur...sondern auch.
butcher ('butʃə) *n* Fleischer *m.* *vt* schlachten. **butcher's shop** *n* Fleischerei *f.*
butler ('bʌtlə) *n* Butler, Diener *m.*
butt[1] (bʌt) *n* **1** dickes Ende *neu.* **2** Stummel *m.* **3** Gegenstand *m.*
butt[2] (bʌt) *vt* stoßen, schlagen. **butt in** sich einmischen. ~*n* Stoß *m.*
butt[3] (bʌt) *n* Faß *neu.* Tonne *f.*
butter ('bʌtə) *n* Butter *f.* **buttercup** *n* Butterblume *f.* **butterfly** *n* Schmetterling *m.*
buttocks ('bʌtəks) *n pl* Gesäß *neu.*
button ('bʌtn̩) *n* Knopf *m.* **buttonhole** *n* Knopfloch *neu.* *vt* anhalten.
buttress ('bʌtrəs) *n* Strebepfeiler *m.* Stütze *f.*
buy* (bai) *vt* kaufen, erwerben, einkaufen. *n* Kauf *m.*
buzz (bʌz) *n* Summen *neu.* *vi* summen.
by (bai) *prep* bei, neben, an, nahe bei, von, durch. *adv* vorbei, dabei. **by (the time that)** bis. **by the way** übrigens. **by and by** bald. **by bus** per Bus, mit dem Bus. **by-election** *n* Nachwahl *f.* **bylaw** *n* Ortsstatut *neu.* **bypass** *n* Umgehungsstraße *f.* *vt* umgehen, meiden.

C

cab (kæb) *n* **1** Droschke *f.* Taxi *neu.* **2** Fahrerhaus *neu.*
cabaret ('kæbərei) *n* Kabarett *neu.*
cabbage ('kæbidʒ) *n* **1** Kohl *m.* **2** Kohlkopf *m.*
cabin ('kæbin) *n* **1** Hütte *f.* Häuschen *neu.* **2** Kabine *f.* **cabin cruiser** *n* Kabinenboot *neu.*
cabinet ('kæbinət) *n* **1** Schrank *m.* **2** *pol* Kabinett *neu.* **cabinet maker** *n* Tischler *m.*
cable ('keibəl) *n* Kabel *neu.* Draht *m.* *vt,vi* telegraphieren, kabeln.
cackle ('kækəl) *vi* gackern, schnattern. *n* Geschnatter *neu.*
cactus ('kæktəs) *n* Kaktus *m.*
cadence ('keidn̩s) *n* *mus* Tonfall *m.*
cadet (kə'det) *n* Kadett *m.*
cafe ('kæfei) *n* Café, Kaffeehaus *neu.*
cafeteria (kæfi'tiəriə) *n* Selbstbedienungsrestaurant *neu.*
caffeine ('kæfiːn) *n* Koffein *neu.*
cage (keidʒ) *n* **1** Käfig *m.* **2** Fahrkorb *m.* *vt* einsperren.
cake (keik) *n* **1** Kuchen *m.* **2**

(of soap, etc.) Stück *neu.* *vt* überziehen, bedecken.
calamity (kə'læməti) *n* **1** Unheil *neu.* **2** Katastrophe *f.*
calcium ('kælsiəm) *n* Kalzium *neu.*
calculate ('kælkjuleit) *vt* kalkulieren, ausrechnen, berechnen. **calculator** *n* Rechenmaschine *f.*
calendar ('kælində) *n* Kalender *m.*
calf[1] (kɑːf) *n, pl* **calves** Kalb *neu.*
calf[2] (kɑːf) *n, pl* **calves** *anat* Wade *f.*
calibre ('kælibə) *n* **1** Kaliber *neu.* **2** Wert *m.*
call (kɔːl) *n* **1** Ruf *m.* **2** Anruf *m.* **3** Besuch *m.* **4** *comm* Einforderung, Nachfrage *f.* *vt* **1** rufen. **2** anrufen. **3** benennen. *vi* **1** rufen. **2** besuchen. **be called** heißen. **call for** fordern. **callbox** *n* Telefonzelle *f.*
callous ('kæləs) *adj* gefühllos, hart.
calm (kɑːm) *adj* ruhig, gelassen. *n* Ruhe, Stille *f.*
calorie ('kæləri) *n* Kalorie *f.*
Cambodia (kæm'boudiə) *n* Kambodscha *neu.* **Cambodian** *n* Kambodschaner *m.* *adj* kambodschanisch.
came (keim) *v* see **come.**
camel ('kæməl) *n* Kamel *neu.* **camelhair** *n* Kamelhaar *neu.*
camera ('kæmrə) *n* Kamera *f.* Photoapparat *m.* **cameraman** *n* Kameramann *m.*
camouflage ('kæməflɑːʒ) *n* Tarnung *f.* *vt* tarnen.
camp[1] (kæmp) *n* Lager *neu.* Lagerplatz *m.* *vi* lagern, zelten. **camp bed** *n* Feldbett *neu.* **camp fire** *n* Lagerfeuer *neu.* **camping** *n* Zelten, Camping *neu.* **camping site** *n* Zeltlager *neu.* Campingplatz *m.*
camp[2] (kæmp) *adj* **1** weibisch. **2** homosexuell.
campaign (kæm'pein) *n* **1** Feldzug *m.* **2** Kampagne *f.* *vi* kämpfen, Wahlpropaganda machen.
campus ('kæmpəs) *n* Universitätsgelände *neu.*
can*[1] (kæn) *v mod aux* **1** können. **2** dürfen. **3** fähig sein.
can[2] (kæn) *n* Dose, Kanne, Büchse *f.*
Canada ('kænədə) *n* Kanada *neu.* **Canadian** *adj* kanadisch. *n* Kanadier *m.*
canal (kə'næl) *n* Kanal *m.*
canary (kə'nɛəri) *n* Kanarienvogel *m.*
cancel ('kænsəl) *vt* **1** stornieren, abbestellen. **2** streichen, entwerten. **3** absagen.
cancer ('kænsə) *n* **1** *med* Krebs *m.* **2** *cap* Krebs *m.*
candid ('kændid) *adj* offen, ehrlich.
candidate ('kændidət) *n* Kandidat, Bewerber *m.*
candle ('kændl̩) *n* Kerze *f.* **candlelight** *n* Kerzenlicht *neu.* **candlestick** *n* Kerzenhalter *m.*
candour ('kændə) *n* Offenheit *f.*
cane ('kein) *n* **1** Zuckerrohr *neu.* **2** Spazierstock *m.* Rute *f.* *vt* mit der Rute schlagen.
canine ('keinain) *adj* Hunds—. **canine teeth** *n* Reißzähne *m pl.*

cannabis ('kænəbis) *n* Kannabis *neu.*

cannibal ('kænəbəl) *n* Kannibale *m.*

cannon ('kænən) *n* Kanone *f.* Geschütz *neu. vi* stoßen gegen. **cannonball** *n* Kanonenkugel *f.*

cannot ('kænət) contraction of **can not.**

canoe (kə'nu:) *n* Kanu *neu. vi* paddeln.

canon[1] ('kænən) *n* Kanon *m.* **canonize** *vt* kanonisieren, heiligsprechen.

canon[2] ('kænən) *n* Domherr *m.*

canopy ('kænəpi) *n* Dach *neu.* Traghimmel *m.*

cant (kænt) *n* **1** Jargon *m.* **2** Heuchelei *f.*

canteen (kæn'ti:n) *n* Kantine *f.*

canter ('kæntə) *n* leichter Galopp *m.*

canton ('kæntɔn) *n* **1** Kanton *m.* **2** Bezirk *m.*

canvas ('kænvəs) *n* **1** Segeltuch *neu.* **2** Zeltleinwand *f.*

canvass ('kænvəs) *vi* **1** untersuchen, prüfen. **2** um Stimmen werben.

canyon ('kænjən) *n* Schlucht *f.*

cap (kæp) *n* **1** Mütze *f.* **2** Kappe *f. vt* **1** bedecken. **2** übertreffen.

capable ('keipəbəl) *adj* fähig. **capability** *n* Fähigkeit *f.*

capacity (kə'pæsiti) *n* **1** Fassungsvermögen *neu.* **2** Leistungsfähigkeit *f.*

cape[1] (keip) *n* Cape *neu.* Umhang *m.*

cape[2] (keip) *n* Kap, Vorgebirge *neu.*

caper ('keipə) *n* Kapriole *f. vi* hüpfen.

capital ('kæpitl) *n* **1** Hauptstadt *f.* **2** Kapital *neu. adj* **1** hauptsächlich. **2** todeswürdig, Todes—. **3** großartig. **capitalism** *n* Kapitalismus *m.* **capitalist** *n* Kapitalist *m.* **capitalize** *vt* kapitalisieren.

capricious (kə'priʃəs) *adj* launisch.

Capricorn ('kæprikɔ:n) *n* Steinbock *m.*

capsicum ('kæpsikəm) *n* spanischer Pfeffer *m.*

capsize ('kæpsaiz) *vi* kentern, umschlagen.

capsule ('kæpsju:l) *n* Kapsel, Hülle *f.*

captain ('kæptin) *n* **1** Kapitän *m.* **2** Hauptmann *m.* **3** Führer *m. vt* anführen, leiten.

caption ('kæpʃən) *n* Überschrift *f.* Titel *m.*

captive ('kæptiv) *n* Gefangene(r) *m. adj* gefangen, eingesperrt. **captivate** *vt* fesseln, bezaubern. **captivity** *n* Gefangenschaft *f.*

capture ('kæptʃə) *n* **1** Gefangennahme *f.* **2** Fang *m.* **3** Eroberung *f. vt* **1** fangen, gefangennehmen. **2** erobern. **3** gewinnen.

car (ka:) *n* Wagen *m.* Auto(mobil) *neu.* **car park** *n* Parkplatz *m.*

caramel ('kærəməl) *n* Karamel *m.*

carat ('kærət) *n* Karat *neu.*

caravan ('kærəvæn) *n* **1** Karawane *f.* **2** Wohnwagen *m.*

caraway ('kærəwei) *n* Kümmel *m.*

carbohydrate (kaːbou'haidreit) *n* Kohlenhydrat *neu*.
carbon ('kaːbən) *n* Kohlenstoff *m*. **carbon dioxide** *n* Kohlensäure *f*. **carbon paper** *n* Kohlepapier *neu*.
carburettor (kaːbju'retə) *n* Vergaser *m*.
carcass ('kaːkəs) *n* Kadaver *m*.
card (kaːd) *n* **1** Karte *f*. **2** Spielkarte *f*. **3** Postkarte *f*. **cardboard** *n* Pappe *f*. **cardboard box** *n* Pappschachtel *f*.
cardigan ('kaːdigən) *n* Wolljacke *f*.
cardinal ('kaːdinl̩) *n* Kardinal *m*. *adj* hauptsächlich.
care (kɛə) *n* **1** Sorge *f*. **2** Pflege *f*. **3** Sorgfalt, Vorsicht *f*. **4** Kummer *m*. **take care of 1** aufpassen auf. **2** erledigen. *~vi* sich sorgen. **care for 1** sorgen für. **2** sich kummern um. **3** gern haben. **carefree** *adj* sorgenlos. **careful** *adj* **1** sorgfältig. **2** vorsichtig. **careless** *adj* **1** sorglos. **2** unordentlich, nachlässig. **3** unüberlegt. **caretaker** *n* Hausmeister, Hauswart *m*.
career (kə'riə) *n* Karriere, Laufbahn *f*. *vi* rasen, jagen.
caress (kə'res) *n* Liebkosung *f*. *vt* liebkosen, streicheln.
cargo ('kaːgou) *n* Fracht *f*. Frachtgut *neu*.
Caribbean (kæri'biən) *adj* karibisch. **Caribbean (Sea)** *n* Karibisches Meer *neu*.
caricature ('kærikətjuə) *n* Karikatur *f*.
carnal ('kaːnl̩) *adj* fleischlich, geschlectlich.
carnation (kaː'neiʃən) *n* Nelke *f*.
carnival ('kaːnivəl) *n* Karneval, Fasching *m*.
carnivorous (kaː'nivərəs) *adj* fleischfressend.
carol ('kærəl) *n* Weihnachtslied *neu*.
carpenter ('kaːpintə) *n* Zimmermann, Tischler *m*.
carpet ('kaːpit) *n* Teppich *m*. **carpet-sweeper** *n* Teppichkehrmaschine *f*.
carriage ('kæridʒ) *n* **1** Wagen *m*. Kutsche *f*. **2** (Körper)-Haltung *f*. **carriageway** *n* Fahrbahn *f*.
carrier ('kæriə) *n* **1** Träger *m*. **2** Spediteur *m*. **carrier bag** *n* Tragtasche *f*.
carrot ('kærət) *n* Karotte, Mohrrübe *f*.
carry ('kæri) *vt* **1** tragen. **2** befördern. **carrycot** *n* tragbares Babybett *neu*.
cart (kaːt) *n* Wagen, Karren *m*. Fuhrwerk *neu*. *vt* tragen, schleppen. **carthorse** *n* Zugpferd *neu*.
cartilage ('kaːtlidʒ) *n* Knorpel *m*.
carton ('kaːtn̩) *n* Pappschachtel *f*. Karton *m*.
cartoon (kaː'tuːn) *n* **1** Karikatur *f*. **2** Zeichentrickfilm *m*. **3** Musterzeichnung *f*.
cartridge ('kaːtridʒ) *n* Patrone *f*.
carve (kaːv) *vt* **1** schnitzen. **2** zerlegen, tranchieren. **carving-knife** *n* Vorlegemesser *neu*.
cascade (kæ'skeid) *n* Kaskade *f*. Wasserfall *m*. *vi* herabregnen.
case[1] (keis) *n* **1** Fall *m*. **2** *law* (Rechts)Fall *m*. **3** Sache *f*. **in**

case falls. **in case of** im Falle von.

case[2] (keis) *n* **1** Gehäuse *neu.* **2** Tasche, Mappe *f.* **3** Etui *neu.*

cash (kæʃ) *n* Bargeld *neu.* **cash desk** *n* Kasse *f.* **cash register** *n* Registrierkasse *f.* ~ *vt* einlösen.

cashier[1] (kæ'ʃiə) *n* Kassierer *m.*

cashier[2] (kæ'ʃiə) *vt* kassieren, entlassen.

cashmere (kæʃ'miə) *n* Kaschmir *m.*

casino (kə'siːnou) *n* Spiellokal, Kasino *neu.*

casket ('kɑːskit) *n* Kästchen *neu.*

casserole ('kæsəroul) *n* Schmorpfanne *f.*

cassette (kə'set) *n* Kassette *f.*

cassock ('kæsək) *n* Soutane *f.*

cast* (kɑːst) *n* **1** Wurf *m.* **2** *tech* Guß *m.* Gußform *f.* **3** *Th* Besetzung *f.* **4** Typ *m.* Art *f.* *vt* **1** werfen. **2** *tech* gießen. **3** *Th* Rollen verteilen.

castanets (kæstə'nets) *n* Kastagnetten *f pl.*

caste (kɑːst) *n* Kaste, Gesellschaftsklasse *f.*

castle ('kɑːsəl) *n* **1** Schloß *neu.* Burg, Festung *f.* **2** *game* Turm *m.*

castrate (kæ'streit) *vt* kastrieren.

casual ('kæʒuəl) *adj* **1** zufällig, beiläufig. **2** gleichgültig, nachlässig. **3** salopp. **4** lässig. **casualty** *n* **1** Verunglückte(r) *m.* **2** *pl* Verluste *m pl.*

cat (kæt) *n* Katze *f.* **cat's eye** *n mot* Katzenauge *neu.* **tom cat** Kater *m.*

catalogue ('kætələg) *n* Katalog *m.*

catamaran (kætəmə'ræn) *n* Katamaran, Auslegerboot *neu.*

catapult ('kætəpʌlt) *n* Katapult *m.* Wurfmaschine *f.* *vt* katapultieren, schleudern.

cataract ('kætərækt) *n* **1** Katarakt, Wasserfall *m.* **2** *med* Star *m.*

catarrh (kə'tɑː) *n* Katarrh, Schnupfen *m.*

catastrophe (kə'tæstrəfi) *n* Katastrophe *f.*

catch* (kætʃ) *n* Fang *m.* *vt* **1** fangen. **2** fassen. **3** (rechtzeitig) erreichen.

category ('kætigəri) *n* Kategorie, Klasse, Ordnung *f.* **categorical** *adj* kategorisch, unbedingt. **categorize** *vt* kategorisieren.

cater ('keitə) *vi* Lebensmittel anschaffen *or* liefern. **cater for** sorgen für. **catering** (Lebensmittel)Versorgung *f.* Verpflegungswesen *neu.*

caterpillar ('kætəpilə) *n* Raupe *f.* **caterpillar track** *n* Raupe, Gleiskette *f.*

cathedral (kə'θiːdrəl) *n* Dom *m.* Kathedrale *f.*

cathode ('kæθoud) *n* Kathode *f.*

catholic ('kæθlik) *adj* **1** allgemein, allumfassend. **2** katholisch.

catkin ('kætkin) *n* Kätzchen *neu.*

cattle ('kætl̩) *n* Vieh, Rindvieh *neu.*

caught (kɔːt) *v* see **catch.**

cauliflower ('kɔliflauə) *n* Blumenkohl *m.*

cause (kɔːz) *n* **1** Ursache *f.*

Anlaß, Grund *m*. **2** Sache *f*. *vt* verursachen, bewirken, veranlassen.
causeway ('kɔːzwei) *n* Damm, Fußweg *m*.
caustic ('kɔːstik) *adj* **1** ätzend, brennend. **2** scharf, beißend, sarkastisch.
caution ('kɔːʃən) *n* **1** Vorsicht *f*. **2** (Ver)Warnung *f*. *vt* verwarnen.
cavalry ('kævəlri) *n* Kavallerie, Reiterei *f*.
cave (keiv) *n* Höhle *f*.
caviar ('kæviɑː) *n* Kaviar *m*.
cavity ('kæviti) *n* Höhle *n*. Höhlung *f*.
cayenne (kei'en) *n* Cayennepfeffer *m*.
cease (siːs) *vi* aufhören, unterlassen, einstellen. **ceasefire** *n* Waffenstillstand *m*. Feuereinstellung *f*.
cedar ('siːdə) *n* Zeder *f*.
ceiling ('siːliŋ) *n* Decke *f*.
celebrate ('seləbreit) *vt* feiern. **celebration** *n* Feier *f*. Fest *neu*. **celebrity** *n* Berühmtheit, prominente Person *f*.
celery ('seləri) *n* Sellerie *m*.
celestial (si'lestiəl) *adj* himmlisch.
celibate ('selibət) *adj* unverheiratet.
cell (sel) *n* Zelle *f*.
cellar ('selə) *n* Keller(raum) *m*.
cello ('tʃelou) *n* Cello *neu*.
Cellophane ('seləfein) *n* *Tdmk* Cellophan *neu*.
cement (si'ment) *n* Zement *m*. *vt* zementieren.
cemetery ('semətri) *n* Friedhof *m*.
censor ('sensə) *n* Zensor *m*. *vt* zensieren. **censorship** *n* Zensur *f*.
censure ('senʃə) *vt* tadeln, verurteilen. *n* Tadel *m*. Rüge *f*. **vote of censure** Mißtrauensvotum *neu*.
census ('sensəs) *n* Zensus *m*. Volkszählung *f*.
cent (sent) *n* Cent *m*.
centenary (sen'tiːnəri) *adj* hundertjährig. *n* Hundertjahrfeier *f*.
centigrade ('sentigreid) *adj* Celsius.
centimetre ('sentimiːtə) *n* Zentimeter *m*.
centre ('sentə) *n* **1** Mittelpunkt *m*. Zentrum *neu*. Mitte *f*. **2** Zentrale, Zentralstelle *f*. *vi* sich konzentrieren auf. **central** *adj* zentral. **central heating** *n* Zentralheizung *f*. **centralize** *vt* zentralisieren. **centre-forward** *n* Mittelstürmer *m*. **centre-half** *n* Mittelläufer *m*.
centrifugal (sen'trifjugəl) *adj* zentrifugal.
century ('sentʃəri) *n* Jahrhundert *neu*.
ceramic (si'ræmik) *adj* keramisch. **ceramics** *n pl* Keramik *f*.
cereal ('siəriəl) *n* Getreidepflanze *f*. *adj* Getreide—.
ceremony ('serəməni) *n* **1** Zeremonie, Feier *f*. **2** Feierlichkeit *f*. **ceremonial** *adj* zeremoniell, feierlich. **ceremonious** *adj* steif, förmlich.
certain ('səːtn̩) *adj* **1** sicher, überzeugt. **2** gewiß, bestimmt, sicher. **3** gewiß.
certificate (sə'tifikət) *n* Schein *m*. Urkunde, Bescheinigung *f*.

certify *vi,vt* bescheinigen, bestätigen.
chaffinch ('tʃæfintʃ) *n* Buchfink *m*.
chain (tʃein) *n* **1** Kette *f*. **2** Reihe *f*. *vt* (an)ketten. **chain-smoke** *vi* kettenrauchen. **chain-store** *n* Filialgeschäft *neu*.
chair (tʃɛə) *n* **1** Stuhl *m*. **2** Lehrstuhl *m*. Professur *f*. *vt* den Vorsitz führen. **chair-lift** *n* Sessellift *m*. **chairman** *n* Vorsitzende(r) *m*.
chalet ('ʃælei) *n* Chalet, Landhaus *neu*.
chalk (tʃɔːk) *n* **1** Kreide *f*. **2** Kreidestift *m*. *vt* ankreiden.
challenge ('tʃæləndʒ) *n* **1** Herausforderung *f*. **2** Aufforderung *f*. **3** Anfechtung *f*. *vt* **1** herausfordern. **2** auffordern. **3** anzweifeln.
chamber ('tʃeimbə) *n* Kammer *f*. Zimmer *neu*. **chambermaid** *n* Zimmermädchen *neu*. **chamber music** *n* Kammermusik *f*.
chameleon (kə'miːliən) *n* Chamäleon *neu*.
chamois *n* **1** ('ʃæmwɑː) Gemse *f*. **2** ('ʃæmi) Sämischleder *neu*.
champagne (ʃæm'pein) *n* Champagner, Sekt *m*.
champion ('tʃæmpiən) *n* **1** Sieger, Meister *m*. **2** Verfechter *m*. *vt* unterstützen, verfechten, eintreten für. **championship** *n* Meisterschaft *f*.
chance (tʃɑːns) *n* **1** Zufall *m*. **2** Schicksal, Geschick *neu*. **3** Risiko *neu*. **4** Chance, Aussicht *f*. **5** Gelegenheit, Chance *f*. **by chance** zufällig. **take a chance** sein Glück versuchen. ~*vt* riskieren.
chancellor ('tʃɑːnsələ) *n* Kanzler *m*.
chandelier (ʃændə'liə) *n* Kronleuchter *m*.
change (tʃeindʒ) *vi,vt* **1** (ab-, ver-)ändern. **2** (ver)wandeln. **3** (ab)wechseln. *vt* **1** (um-, aus-)tauschen. **change one's clothes** sich umziehen. **change trains** umsteigen. ~*n* **1** (Ab-, Ver-)Änderung *f*. **2** Wechsel *m*. Abwechselung *f*. **3** Wendung *f*. **4** Wandlung *f*. **5** (Aus)Tausch *m*. **6** Kleingeld, Wechselgeld *neu*.
channel ('tʃænl) *n* **1** Kanal *m*. **2** Fahrrinne *f*. **3** (radio, etc.) Station *f*. Sender *m*. *vt* leiten, lenken.
Channel Islands *n pl* Kanalinseln *f pl*.
chant (tʃɑːnt) *n* (Kirchen)Gesang *m*. *vt* intonieren, singen.
chaos ('keiɔs) *n* Chaos, Durcheinander *neu*.
chap[1] (tʃæp) *vt* spalten, aufreißen. **chapped skin** aufgesprungene Haut.
chap[2] (tʃæp) *n* Junge, Kerl, Bursche *m*.
chapel ('tʃæpəl) *n* Kapelle *f*.
chaperon ('ʃæpəroun) *n* Anstandsdame *f*. *vt* (als Anstanddame) begleiten.
chaplain ('tʃæplin) *n* **1** Kaplan, Geistliche(r) *m*. **2** *mil* Feldgeistliche(r) *m*.
chapter ('tʃæptə) *n* Kapitel *neu*.
char[1] (tʃɑː) *vt* verkohlen, versengen.
char[2] (tʃɑː) *vi* scheuern,

putzen. *n* **1** Putzfrau *f*. **2** *inf* Tee *m*. **charwoman** *n* Scheuerfrau, Putzfrau *f*.

character ('kæriktə) *n* **1** Charakter *m*. Persönlichkeit *f*. Natur *f*. **2** (Schrift)Zeichen *neu*. **3** Figur, Gestalt *f*. **characteristic** *adj* **1** charakteristisch, bezeichnend. **2** typisch. **characterization** *n* Charakterisierung, Kennzeichnung *f*. **characterize** *vt* charakterisieren, kennzeichnen.

charcoal ('tʃɑːkoul) *n* (Holz)Kohle *f*.

charge (tʃɑːdʒ) *vt* **1** anstürmen, angreifen. **2** (be)laden, belasten. **3** beauftragen. **4** berechnen. **5** *law* anklagen. **6** befehlen. *n* **1** Ladung *f*. **2** Preis *m*. **3** Sorge, Verantwortung *f*. **4** Anklage *f*. **5** *comm* Belastung *f*. **6** Befehl *m*. **charge hand** *n* Vorarbeiter *m*.

chariot ('tʃæriət) *n* Streitwagen *m*.

charisma (kə'rizmə) *n* Charisma *f*.

charity ('tʃæriti) *n* **1** Wohltätigkeit, Nächstenliebe, Güte *f*. **2** Stiftung *f*. Wohltätigkeitsverein *m*. **charitable** *adj* mild, wohltätig.

charm (tʃɑːm) *n* **1** Zauber *m*. **2** Reiz, Charme *m*. **3** Amulett *neu*. *vt* entzücken, bezaubern.

chart (tʃɑːt) *n* **1** Seekarte *f*. **2** Übersichtstafel, Tabelle *f*. *vt* entwerfen, verzeichnen.

charter ('tʃɑːtə) *n* (Verfassungs)Urkunde *f*. Gnadenbrief *m*. *vt* chartern, mieten. **charter flight** *n* Charterflug *m*.

chase (tʃeis) *vt* jagen, verfolgen. *n* Jagd, Verfolgung *f*.

chasm ('kæzəm) *n* Spalte Kluft *f*.

chassis ('ʃæsi) *n* Fahrgestel *neu*.

chaste (tʃeist) *adj* rein, anständig, keusch.

chastise (tʃæ'staiz) *vt* strafen züchtigen.

chastity ('tʃæstiti) *n* Keuschheit, Reinheit *f*.

chat (tʃæt) *vi* schwatzen plaudern. *n* Plauderei, Unterhaltung *f*.

chatter ('tʃætə) *vi* **1** plaudern, schwatzen, plappern. **2** (of teeth) klappern.

chauffeur ('ʃoufə) *n* Chauffeur, Fahrer *m*.

chauvinism ('ʃouvinizəm) *n* Chauvinismus *m*.

cheap (tʃiːp) *adj* **1** billig. **2** gemein, minderwertig.

cheat (tʃiːt) *n* Betrüger, Schwindler *m*. *vi,vt* betrügen, schwindeln.

check (tʃek) *n* **1** Prüfung, Untersuchung, Kontrolle *f*. **2** *game* Schach *neu*. **3** *US* Scheck *m*. *vt* **1** prüfen, untersuchen, kontrollieren. **2** hindern, aufhalten. **checkmate** *n* Schachmatt *neu*. *vt* in Schachmatt stellen *neu*. **checkpoint** *n* Grenzübergang *m*. **checkup** *n* Untersuchung *f*.

cheek (tʃiːk) *n* **1** Wange, Backe *f*. **2** Frechheit *f*. *vt* frech sein gegen. **cheekbone** *n* Backenknochen *m*. **cheeky** *adj* frech, dreist, keck.

cheer (tʃiə) *n* **1** Laune, Stimmung *f*. **2** Hoch, Hurra *neu*. *vt* aufheitern, erfreuen. *vi* hurra rufen. **cheer up** *vt* aufmuntern, aufheitern. **cheerful** *adj* fröhlich, heiter.

cheese (tʃiːz) *n* Käse *m.*

cheetah ('tʃiːtə) *n* Gepard *m.*

chef (ʃef) *n* Küchenchef *m.*

chemistry ('kemistri) *n* Chemie *f.* **chemical** *n* **1** chemisches Präparat *neu.* **2** *pl* Chemikalien *f pl. adj* chemisch. **chemist** *n* **1** *sci* Chemiker *m.* **2** *med* Apotheker *m.* **chemist's shop** *n* Apotheke *f.*

cheque (tʃek) *n* Scheck *m.* **chequebook** *n* Scheckbuch *neu.* **cheque card** *n* Scheckkarte *f.*

cherish ('tʃeriʃ) *vt* **1** (wert)schätzen. **2** (feelings) hegen. **3** (an idea) festhalten an.

cherry ('tʃeri) *n* Kirsche *f.*

cherub ('tʃerəb) *n* Cherub *m.*

chess (tʃes) *n* Schachspiel *neu.* **chessboard** *n* Schachbrett *neu.* **chessman** *n* Schachfigur *f.* **chess set** *n* Schachspiel *neu.*

chest (tʃest) *n* **1** Brust *f.* **2** Truhe, Kiste *f.* **chest of drawers** *n* Kommode *f.*

chestnut ('tʃesnʌt) *n* Kastanie *f.*

chew (tʃuː) *vt* kauen. **chewing gum** *n* Kaugummi *m.*

chicken ('tʃikən) *n* Huhnchen, Hähnchen *neu. adj sl* feig. **chick** *n* Küchlein, Kuken *neu.* **chickenpox** *n* Windpocken *f pl.*

chicory ('tʃikəri) *n* Zichorie *f.*

chief (tʃiːf) *n* Häuptling, Anführer *m.* Chef *m. adj* haupt, Haupt—, hauptsächlich.

chilblain ('tʃilblein) *n* Frostbeule *f.*

child (tʃaild) *n, pl* **children** Kind *neu.* **childbirth** *n* Geburt, Entbindung *f.* **childhood** *n* Kindheit *f.* **childish** *adj* kindisch. **childlike** *adj* kindlich. **childminder** *n* Tagesmutter *f.*

Chile ('tʃili) *n* Chile *neu.* **Chilean** *adj* chilenisch. *n* Chilene *m.*

chill (tʃil) *n* **1** Kälte *f.* **2** Erkältung *f.* **3** Schauer *m. adj* kalt. *vt* kühlen. **chilly** *adj* kalt, kühl, frostig.

chilli ('tʃili) *n* spanischer Pfeffer *m.*

chime (tʃaim) *n* **1** Geläut *neu.* **2** Glockensatz *m. vi* klingen, tönen. **chime in** einstimmen.

chimney ('tʃimnı) *n* Schornstein, Rauchfang, Schlot *m.* **chimneypot** *n* Schornsteinaufsatz *m.* **chimneysweep** *n* Schornsteinfeger *m.*

chimpanzee (tʃimpæn'ziː) *n* Schimpanse *m.*

chin (tʃin) *n* Kinn *neu.*

china ('tʃainə) *n* Porzellan *neu.*

China ('tʃainə) *n* China *neu.* **Chinese** *adj* chinesisch. *n* Chinese *m.*

chink[1] (tʃiŋk) *n* Spalt *m.* Lücke *f.*

chink[2] (tʃiŋk) *n* Geklimper, Klingen *neu. vi* klingen, klimpern.

chip (tʃip) *n* **1** Span, Splitter *m.* Holzstückchen *neu.* **2** *pl cul* Pommes frites *pl. vt* behauen, beschneiden.

chiropody (ki'rɔpədi) *n*

Fußpflege *f.* **chiropodist** *n* Fußpfleger *m.*
chirp (tʃəːp) *vi* zwitschern, zirpen.
chisel ('tʃizəl) *n* Meißel *m.* Stemmeisen *neu.*
chivalry ('ʃivəlri) *n* Ritterlichkeit *f.*
chives (tʃaivz) *n* Schnittlauch *m.*
chlorine ('klɔːriːn) *n* Chlor *neu.*
chlorophyll ('klɔrəfil) *n* Blattgrün, Chlorophyll *neu.*
chocolate ('tʃɔklit) *n* Schokolade *f.*
choice (tʃɔis) *n* **1** Wahl *f.* **2** Auswahl *f. adj* auserlesen.
choir (kwaiə) *n* Chor *m.* **choirboy** *n* Chorknabe *m.* **choirmaster** *n* Chormeister *m.*
choke (tʃouk) *vt* würgen. *vt,vi* ersticken. *n mot* Starterklappe *f.*
cholera ('kɔlərə) *n* Cholera *f.*
choose* (tʃuːz) *vt* wählen, aussuchen, auslesen.
chop (tʃɔp) *vt* hacken, zerhacken. *n* Kotelett *neu.* **chopper** *n* Beil *neu.*
chopstick ('tʃɔpstik) *n* Eßstäbchen *neu.*
chord (kɔːd) *n* Akkord *m.*
chore (tʃɔː) *n* Hausarbeit *f.*
choreography (kɔri'ɔgrəfi) *n* Choreographie *f.*
chorus ('kɔːrəs) *n* **1** (Sänger)Chor *m.* **2** Refrain *m.* **choral** *n* Choral *m. adj* Chor —.
chose (tʃouz) *v* see **choose.**
chosen ('tʃouzən) *v* see **choose.** *adj* auserwählt.
Christ (kraist) *n* Christus *m.*
christen ('krisən) *vt* taufen. **christening** *n* Taufe *f.*
Christian ('kristʃən) *n* Christ *m.* **Christian name** *n* Vorname *m.* **Christianity** *n* Christentum *neu.*
Christmas ('krisməs) *n* Weihnachten *f pl.* **Christmas card** *n* Weihnachtskarte *f.* **Christmas tree** *n* Weihnachtsbaum *m.*
chromatic (krə'mætik) *adj* chromatisch.
chrome (kroum) *adj* **1** chromgelb. **2** aus Chrom.
chromium ('kroumiəm) *n* Chrom *neu.*
chronic ('krɔnik) *adj* **1** chronisch, (an)dauernd. **2** *inf* schlecht.
chronicle ('krɔnikəl) *n* Chronik, Zeitgeschichte *f.*
chronological (krɔnə'lɔdʒikəl) *adj* chronologisch.
chrysalis ('krisəlis) *n* Puppe *f.*
chrysanthemum (kri'zænθiməm) *n* Goldblume, Chrysantheme *f.*
chubby ('tʃʌbi) *adj* plump, pausbäckig.
chuck (tʃʌk) *vt inf* **1** werfen, schleudern. **2** aufgeben.
chuckle ('tʃʌkəl) *n* Kichern, Gekicher *neu. vi* kichern, vergnügt lachen.
chunk (tʃʌŋk) *n* Stück *neu.* Klotz *m.*
church (tʃəːtʃ) *n* Kirche *f.* **churchgoer** *n* Kirchengänger *m.* **churchyard** *n* Kirchhof *m.*
churn (tʃəːn) *n* Butterfaß *neu. vt* aufwühlen.
chute (ʃuːt) *n* Gleitbahn, Rinne *f.*

chutney ('tʃʌtni) *n* Chutney *neu*.
cider ('saidə) *n* Apfelwein *m*.
cigar (si'gɑː) *n* Zigarre *f*. **cigarette** *n* Zigarette *f*. **cigarette lighter** *n* Feuerzeug *neu*.
cinder ('sində) *n* **1** ausgeglühte Kohle *f*. **2** *pl* Asche *pl*.
cinecamera ('sinikæmrə) *n* Filmkamera *f*.
cinema ('sinəmə) *n* Kino *neu*.
cinnamon ('sinəmən) *n* Zimt *m*.
circle ('səːkəl) *n* **1** Kreis *m*. Ring *m*. **2** *Th* Rang *m*. *vt* umkreisen, umringen. **circular** *adj* kreisförmig, rund. **circulate** *vi* kreisen. *vt* in Umlauf setzen. **circulation** *n* **1** Kreislauf *m*. **2** Umlauf *m*. Verkehr *m*. **3** Auflage *f*.
circuit ('səːkit) *n* **1** Kreisbewegung *f*. **2** Runde *f*. **3** Stromkreis *m*.
circumcise ('səːkəmsaiz) *vt* beschneiden.
circumference (sə'kʌmfərəns) *n* Kreisumfang, Umkreis *m*.
circumscribe ('səːkəmskraib) *vt* umschreiben.
circumstance ('səːkəmstæns) *n* **1** Umstand *m*. **2** Tatsache *f*. **3** Formalität *f*. **circumstantial** *adj* zufällig, indirekt, nebensächlich.
circus ('səːkəs) *n* Zirkus *m*.
cistern ('sistən) *n* Zisterne *f*.
cite (sait) *vt* **1** zitieren, anführen. **2** vorladen. **citation** *n* **1** Zitat neu. **2** Vorladung *f*.
citizen ('sitizən) *n* (Staats)Bürger *m*.
citrus ('sitrəs) *n* Zitrusfrucht *f*.
city ('siti) *n* Stadt, Großstadt *f*.
civic ('sivik) *adj* bürgerlich, städtisch.
civil ('sivəl) *adj* **1** bürgerlich, städtisch. **2** höflich. **3** Staats—. **civil engineering** *n* Ingenieurbau *m*. **civil servant** *n* Staatsbeamte(r) *m*. **civil service** *n* Staatsverwaltung *f*. **civil war** *n* Bürgerkrieg *m*.
civilian (si'viliən) *n* Zivilist *m*. *adj* Zivil—.
civilization (sivilai'zeiʃən) *n* Zivilisation *f*. **civilize** *vt* zivilisieren.
clad (klæd) *adj* bekleidet, bedeckt.
claim (kleim) *n* **1** Anspruch *m*. (An)Recht *neu*. **2** Forderung *f*. **3** Behauptung *f*. *vt* beanspruchen, fordern.
clam (klæm) *n* Venusmuschel *f*.
clamber ('klæmbə) *vi* klettern.
clammy ('klæmi) *adj* feuchtkalt, klebrig.
clamour ('klæmə) *n* Lärm *m*. Geschrei *neu*. *vi* schreien, lärmen.
clamp (klæmp) *n* Klammer, Schelle *f*. *vt* festklemmen, befestigen.
clan (klæn) *n* Stamm *m*. Sippe *f*.
clandestine (klæn'destin) *adj* heimlich.
clang (klæŋ) *vi,(vt)* klingen *or* schallen (lassen). *n* Klang, Schall *m*.
clank (klæŋk) *vi,(vt)* rasseln *or* klirren (mit). *n* Gerassel *neu*.
clap (klæp) *vi,(vt)* klatschen (mit). *n* **1** Donnerschlag *m*. **2** Knall *m*. **clapper** *n* Klöppel *m*.
claret ('klærət) *n* Klarett *m*.

clarify ('klærifai) *vt* klarmachen, erläutern, klären. **clarification** *n* (Er)Klärung *f*. **clarity** *n* Klarheit, Reinheit *f*.

clarinet (klæri'net) *n* Klarinette *f*.

clash (klæʃ) *n* **1** Geklirr *neu*. **2** Zusammenstoß *m*. **3** Konflikt *m*. *vi* **1** klirren, rasseln. **2** zusammenstoßen.

clasp (klɑːsp) *n* Schnalle, Spange *f*. *vt* **1** schnallen. **2** festhalten, umklammern.

class (klɑːs) *n* **1** Klasse, Kategorie *f*. **2** (Schul)Klasse *f*. *vt* einstufen, einreihen. **classify** *vt* klassifizieren, einordnen, einteilen. **classification** *n* Klassifizierung, Einteilung *f*. **classroom** *n* Klassenzimmer *neu*.

classic ('klæsik) *adj* klassisch. *n* Klassiker *m*. **classical** *adj* klassisch.

clatter ('klætə) *vi* rasseln, klappern. *n* Geklapper *neu*.

clause (klɔːz) *n* **1** Satz *m*. **2** Klausel *f*.

claustrophobia (klɔstrə'foubiə) *n* Klaustrophobie *f*. **claustrophobic** *adj* eng, überfüllt.

claw (klɔː) *n* Klaue *f*. Kralle *f*.

clay (klei) *n* Ton *m*.

clean (kliːn) *adj* sauber, rein, gewaschen. *vt* **1** reinigen, säubern. *vi,vt* putzen.

cleanse (klenz) *vt* säubern, heilen.

clear (kliə) *adj* **1** klar, durchsichtig. **2** verständlich. **3** rein. **4** offen, frei. *vt* **1** leeren, räumen. **2** freisprechen. **3** (a cheque) einlösen. **4** verzollen. **5** springen über. *vi* sich (auf)klären. **clear away, out,** *or* **up** *vi,vt* ausräumen, aufräumen. **clear off** *vi inf* abhauen. **clearance** *n* **1** Aufräumen *f*. **2** Verzollung *f*. **3** *tech* Spielraum *m*. **4** Räumungsausverkauf *m*. **clear-headed** *adj* besonnen, klardenkend. **clearing** *n* Lichtung *f*.

clef (klef) *n* Notenschlüssel *m*.

clench (klentʃ) *vt* zusammenpressen, ballen.

clergy ('kləːdʒi) *n* Klerus *m*. **clergyman** *n* Geistliche(r) *m*.

clerical ('klerikəl) *adj* **1** geistlich. **2** Büro—. **clerical work** *n* Büroarbeit *f*.

clerk (klɑːk) *n* Büroangestellte(r) *m*.

clever ('klevə) *adj* geschickt, klug, intelligent.

cliché ('kliʃei) *n* Klischee *neu*.

click (klik) *vi,vt* knipsen, knacken, (zu)schnappen. *n* Schnappen *neu*. Schlag *m*.

client ('klaiənt) *n* Kunde *m*. **clientèle** *n* Kundschaft *f*.

cliff (klif) *n* Klippe *f*. Felsen *m*.

climate ('klaimit) *n* Klima *neu*.

climax ('klaimæks) *n* Höhepunkt *m*.

climb (klaim) *n* Aufstieg *m*. *vt,vi* klettern, steigen. **climber** *n* Kletterer, Bergsteiger *m*.

cling* (kliŋ) *vi* sich klammern, sich halten, haften.

clinic ('klinik) *n* Klinik *f*.

clip[1] (klip) *vt* schneiden, stutzen, knipsen. *n* Schlag *m*. **clipping** *n* (Zeitungs)Ausschnitt *m*.

clip[2] (klip) *n* Klammer *f*. *vt* befestigen, zusammenheften.

cloak (klouk) *n* Gewand *neu*.

Mantel *m.* *vt* ummanteln, umhüllen. **cloakroom** *n* Garderobe *f.*

clock (klɔk) *n* Uhr *f.* **three o'clock** drei Uhr. **clock-tower** *n* Uhrturm *m.* **clock-wise** *adj,adv* im Uhrzeigersinn. **clockwork** *n* Uhrwerk *neu.*

clog (klɔg) *n* Holzschuh *m.* *(vi),vt* (sich) verstopfen.

cloister ('klɔistə) *n* Kloster *neu.*

close *vt,vi* (klouz) zumachen, schließen. *adj* (klous) **1** dicht, nahe. **2** intim, vertraut. **3** knapp. *n* **1** (klous) Sackgasse *f.* **2** (klouz) Schluß *m.*

closet ('klɔzit) *n* Schrank *m.*

clot (klɔt) *n* Klumpen *m.* *vi* gerinnen.

cloth (klɔθ) *n* **1** Stoff *m.* Gewebe, Tuch *neu.* **2** Lappen *m.*

clothe (klouð) *vt* bekleiden. **clothes** *n pl* Kleider *neu pl.* Kleidung *f.* **clothes brush** *n* Kleiderbürste *f.* **clothes line** *n* Wäscheleine *f.* **clothes peg** *n* Wäscheklammer *f.* **clothing** *n* Kleidung *f.*

cloud (klaud) *n* Wolke *f.* *vi, vt* bewölken, umnebeln. **cloudburst** *n* Wolkenbruch *m.* **cloudy** *adj* **1** wolkig, bewölkt. **2** trübe.

clove[1] (klouv) *n* Gewürznelke *f.*

clove[2] (klouv) *n* (Knoblauch)Zehe *f.*

clover ('klouvə) *n* Klee *m.*

clown (klaun) *n* Clown *m.*

club (klʌb) *n* **1** Klub *m.* Verein *m.* **2** *sport* Schläger *m.* **3** Keule *f.*

clue (kluː) *n* Hinweis, Anhaltspunkt *m.*

clump (klʌmp) *n* **1** Haufen *m.* **2** Gruppe *f.*

clumsy ('klʌmzi) *adj* ungeschickt, schwerfällig.

clung (klʌŋ) *v* see **cling.**

cluster ('klʌstə) *n* **1** Gruppe *f.* **2** *bot* Traube *f.* *vi* sich (ver)sammeln, sich gruppieren.

clutch (klʌtʃ) *n* **1** Kupplung *f.* **2** *pl* Klauen *f pl.* *vt* packen, greifen, fassen.

clutter ('klʌtə) *n* Unordnung *f.* Durcheinander *neu.* *vt* vollstopfen.

coach (koutʃ) *n* **1** Kutsche *f.* **2** Bus *m.* **3** *sport* Trainer *m.* *vt* **1** *sport* trainieren. **2** *educ* Nachhilfeunterricht geben.

coal (koul) *n* (Stein)Kohle *f.* **coalmine** *n* Kohlenbergwerk *neu.*

coalition (kouə'liʃən) *n* Koalition *f.*

coarse (kɔːs) *adj* **1** grob. **2** rauh, unhöflich.

coast (koust) *n* Küste *f.* **coastguard** *n* Küstenwacht *f.* **coastline** *n* Küstenlinie *f.*

coat (kout) *n* **1** Mantel *m.* **2** Pelz *m.* Fell *neu.* **3** Belag *m.* **4** (of paint) Anstrich *m.* *vt* bedecken, beschichten. **coat-hanger** *n* Kleiderbügel *m.* **coating** *n* Schicht *f.* Belag *m.*

coax (kouks) *vt* (geduldig) überreden.

cobbler ('kɔblə) *n* Schuster *m.*

cobra ('koubrə) *n* Kobra *f.*

cobweb ('kɔbweb) *n* Spinngewebe *neu.*

cock[1] (kɔk) *n* **1** Hahn *m.* **2** (Vogel)Männchen *neu.* **3** *tab*

Penis *m.* **cockpit** *n* Kanzel, Kabine *f.* **cockroach** *n* Küchenschabe *f.* **cocktail** *n* Cocktail *neu.* **cocky** *adj inf* eingebildet, frech.
cock² (kɔk) *vt* **1** (one's ears) spitzen. **2** (a hat, etc.) schiefmachen, schief aufsetzen.
cockle ('kɔkəl) *n* Herzmuschel *f.*
cocoa ('koukou) *n* Kakao *m.*
coconut ('koukənʌt) *n* Kokosnuß *f.*
cocoon (kə'kuːn) *n* Puppe *f.*
cod (kɔd) *n* Dorsch *m.*
code (koud) *n* **1** Kodex *m.* **2** Schlüssel *m.* Geheimschrift *f.* *vt* verschlüsseln.
codeine ('koudiːn) *n* Kodein *neu.*
coeducation (kouedju'keiʃən) *n* Gemeinschaftserziehung *f.*
coerce (kou'əːs) *vt* zwingen.
coexist (kouig'zist) *vi* koexistieren, zusammenleben. **coexistence** *n* Koexistenz *f.*
coffee ('kɔfi) *n* Kaffee *m.* **coffee bar** *n* Kaffeehaus, Café *neu.* **coffee bean** *n* Kaffeebohne *f.*
coffin ('kɔfin) *n* Sarg *m.*
cog (kɔg) *n* Radzahn *m.*
cognac ('kɔnjæk) *n* Kognak *m.*
cohabit (kou'hæbit) *vi* zusammenleben.
cohere (kou'hiə) *vi* zusammenhängen, zusammenkleben. **coherence** *n* Zusammenhang *m.* **coherent** *adj* zusammenhängend, verständlich.
coil (kɔil) *n* Windung, Spule *f.* *vt* aufrollen, aufwinden. *vi* sich zusammenrollen.
coin (kɔin) *n* Münze *f.* *vt* prägen.
coincide (kouin'said) *vi* **1** zusammentreffen. **2** übereinstimmen. **coincidence** *n* Zufall *m.* Zusammentreffen *neu.*
colander ('kʌləndə) *n* Sieb *neu.*
cold (kould) *adj* kalt. *n* **1** Kälte *f.* **2** Erkältung *f.* Schnupfen *m.* **catch a cold** sich erkälten. **cold-blooded** *adj* kaltblütig.
collaborate (kə'læbəreit) *vi* **1** zusammenarbeiten, mitarbeiten. **2** mit dem Feind arbeiten, kollaborieren. **collaboration** *n* **1** Zusammenarbeit *f.* **2** Kollaboration *f.*
collapse (kə'læps) *n* Zusammenbruch, Einsturz *m.* *vi* zusammenbrechen, einstürzen.
collar ('kɔlə) *n* Kragen *m.*
collarbone *n* Schlüsselbein *neu.*
colleague ('kɔliːg) *n* Kollege, Mitarbeiter *m.*
collect (kə'lekt) *vt* sammeln, auflesen. **collection** *n* **1** Sammlung *f.* **2** Ansammlung *f.* Anhäufung *f.* **3** (of mail) Abholung *f.* **collective** *adj* vereint, zusammengefaßt, gesamt, kollektiv—. *n* Kollektiv *neu.*
college ('kɔlidʒ) *n* Kollegium *neu.* Hochschule *f.*
collide (kə'laid) *vi* zusammenstoßen. **collision** *n* Zusammenstoß *m.*
colloquial (kə'loukwiəl) *adj* familiär, umgangssprachlich.
Cologne (kə'loun) *n* Köln *neu.*
colon ('koulən) *n* **1** Doppelpunkt *m.* Kolon *neu.* **2** *anat* Dickdarm *m.*
colonel ('kəːnl̩) *n* Oberst *m.*

colony ('kɔləni) *n* Kolonie, Siedlung *f.* **colonial** *adj* kolonial.
colossal (kə'lɔsəl) *adj* kolossal, riesig.
colour ('kʌlə) *n* Farbe *f.* **colour-bar** *n* Farbschranke *f.* **colour-blind** *adj* farbenblind. **coloured** *adj* farbig, bunt. **coloured (man)** Farbige(r) *m.*
colt (koult) *n* Füllen, Fohlen *neu.*
column ('kɔləm) *n* **1** Säule *f.* Pfeiler *m.* **2** Kolonne *f.* **3** Rubrik *f.* **4** (Zeitungs)Spalte *f.* **columnist** *n* Kolumnist *m.*
coma ('koumə) *n* Koma, anhaltende Bewußtlosigkeit *f.*
comb (koum) *n* Kamm *m.* *vt* **1** kämmen. **2** durchsuchen.
combat ('kɔmbæt) *n* Kampf *m.* *vt* bekämpfen.
combine (*v* kəm'bain; *n* 'kɔmbain) *vt* vereinigen, verbinden. *n* **1** Verband *m.* **2** Kartell *neu.* **combine harvester** *n* Mähdrescher *m.*
combustion (kəm'bʌstʃən) *n* Verbrennung *f.*
come* (kʌm) *vi* kommen. **come about** geschehen. **come across** stoßen auf. **comeback** *n* Rückkehr *f.* Comeback *neu.*
comedy ('kɔmədi) *n* Lustspiel *neu.* Komödie *f.* **comedian** *n* Komiker *m.* **comic** *n* **1** Komiker *m.* **2** Witzblatt *neu.* *adj* witzig, komisch. **comical** *adj* witzig, spaßig.
comet ('kɔmit) *n* Komet *m.*
comfort ('kʌmfət) *n* **1** Trost *m.* **2** Komfort *m.* **3** Gemütlichkeit *f.* *vt* trösten. **comfortable** *adj* bequem, behaglich.
comma ('kɔmə) *n* Komma *neu.* Beistrich *m.*
command (kə'ma:nd) *n* **1** Befehl *m.* **2** Führung. *vt* **1** befehlen. **2** kommandieren. **commander** *n* Kommandant, Befehlshaber, Führer *m.* **commandment** *n* Gebot *neu.*
commemorate (kə'meməreit) *vt* feiern, gedenken.
commence (kə'mens) *vt,vi* anfangen, beginnen. **commencement** *n* Anfang, Beginn *m.*
commend (kə'mend) *vt* empfehlen, loben.
comment ('kɔment) *n* **1** Bemerkung *f.* **2** Stellungnahme *f.* *vi* bemerken, kommentieren. **commentary** *n* Kommentar *m.* **commentator** *n* Kommentator, Berichterstatter *m.*
commerce ('kɔmə:s) *n* Handel(sverkehr) *m.* **commercial** *adj* kommerziell, kaufmännisch, geschäftlich. *n* Fernsehreklame *f.* **commercialize** *vt* marktfähig machen. **commercial vehicle** *n* Nutzfahrzeug *neu.*
commission (kə'miʃən) *n* **1** Auftrag *m.* **2** *mil* Offizierspatent *neu.* **3** Kommission *f.* Ausschuß *m.* *vt* **1** bestellen, beauftragen. **2** eine Bestellung geben. **commissioner** *n* Kommissionär *m.*
commit (kə'mit) *vt* **1** begehen. **2** übergeben. **commit oneself** sich verpflichten.
committee (kə'miti) *n* Ausschuß *m.* Komitee *neu.*
commodity (kə'mɔditi) *n* Handelsgut *neu.* Ware *f.*
common ('kɔmən) *adj* **1**

allgemein, gemeinsam. **2** gewöhnlich, häufig. **3** alltäglich. *n* Allmende *f*. **Common Market** *n* Gemeinsamer Markt *m*. Europäische Wirtschaftsgemeinschaft *f*. **commonplace** *n* Gewöhnliche(s), Alltägliche(s) *neu*. Gemeinplatz *m*. *adj* gewöhnlich, alltäglich. **common sense** *n* gesunder Menschenverstand *m*. schlichte Vernunft *f*. **commonwealth** *n* **1** Staat *m*. Gemeinwesen *neu*. **2** Commonwealth *neu*.

commotion (kə'mouʃən) *n* Aufruhr *m*. Getue *neu*.

commune[1] (kə'mju:n) *vi* **1** sich unterhalten. **2** *rel* Kommunion empfangen. **communion** *n* Kommunion *f*.

commune[2] ('kɔmju:n) *n* Kommune, Gemeinde *f*. **communal** *adj* Kommunal—, Gemeinschafts—.

communicant (kəmju:nikənt) *n* Kommunikant *m*.

communicate (kə'mju:nikeit) *vt* **1** mitteilen. **2** übertragen. *vi* **1** in Verbindung stehen. **2** *rel* Kommunizieren. **communication** *n* **1** Mitteilung *f*. **2** Verbindung, Kommunikation *f*. Verkehr *m*.

communism ('kɔmjunizəm) *n* Kommunismus *m*. **communist** *n* Kommunist *m*. *adj* kommunistisch.

community (kə'mju:niti) *n* **1** Gemeinschaft, Gemeinde *f*. **2** Gemeinsamkeit *f*.

commute (kə'mju:t) *vt* umwandeln, austauschen. *vi* zur Arbeit reisen, pendeln. **commuter** *n* Pendler *m*.

compact[1] (kəm'pækt) *adj* dicht, fest, kompakt. *vt* verdichten, verbinden. **compact disc** ('kɔmpækt) *n* CD-Platte *f*.

compact[2] ('kɔmpækt) *n* Vertrag, Pakt *m*. Übereinkommen *neu*.

companion (kəm'pæniən) *n* Begleiter, Kamerad *m*. **companionship** *n* Gesellschaft, Kameradschaft *f*.

company ('kʌmpəni) *n* **1** *comm* Firma, Gesellschaft *f*. **2** Gesellschaft *f*.

compare (kəm'pɛə) *(vi),vt* (sich) vergleichen. **comparable** *adj* vergleichbar. **comparative** *adj* **1** vergleichend. **2** verhältnismäßig. **comparison** *n* Vergleich *m*.

compartment (kəm'pa:tmənt) *n* **1** Abteilung *f*. **2** Fach *neu*. **3** Abteil *neu*.

compass ('kʌmpəs) *n* Kompaß *m*.

compassion (kəm'pæʃən) *n* Mitleid, Erbarmen *neu*. **compassionate** *adj* mitleidsvoll.

compatible (kəm'pætibəl) *adj* vereinbar.

compel (kəm'pel) *vt* zwingen, nötigen.

compensate ('kɔmpənseit) *vi* **1** ausgleichen, ersetzen. **2** wiedergutmachen, entschädigen. **compensation** *n* Entschädigung *f*. Schadenersatz *m*.

compete (kəm'pi:t) *vi* **1** teilnehmen. **2** konkurrieren. **competition** *n* **1** Wettbewerb *m*. **2** Konkurrenz *f*. **competitive** *adj* **1** konkurrenzfähig. **2** wetteifernd, konkurrierend. **competitor** *n* Konkurrent *m*.

competent ('kɔmpitənt) *adj* kompetent, fähig. **competence** *n* Kompetenz, Befähigung *f.*
compile (kəm'pail) *vt* aufstellen, zusammenstellen.
complacent (kəm'pleisənt) *adj* gleichgültig. **complacency** *n* Selbstgefälligkeit *f.*
complain (kəm'plein) *vi* sich beklagen *or* beschweren. **complaint** *n* Klage, Beschwerde *f.*
complement ('kɔmplimənt) *n* **1** Ergänzung. **2** *math* Komplement *neu.* *vt* ergänzen.
complete (kəm'pliːt) *vt* vervollständigen, beenden, fertigstellen. *adj* ganz, vollständig.
complex ('kɔmpleks) *adj* komplex, kompliziert. *n* Komplex *m.* **complexity** *n* Kompliziertheit, Schwierigkeit *f.*
complexion (kəm'plekʃən) *n* Gesichtsfarbe *f.* Teint *m.*
complicate ('kɔmplikeit) *vt* komplizieren, erschweren. **complicated** *adj* kompliziert.
compliment ('kɔmplimənt) *n* Kompliment *neu.* *vt* loben, ein Kompliment machen. **complimentary** *adj* **1** höflich, schmeichelhaft. **2** Gratis—, Frei—.
comply (kəm'plai) *vi* einwilligen, nachgeben, sich fügen. **comply with** erfüllen, befolgen.
component (kəm'pounənt) *n* (Bestand)Teil *m.* *adj* teilbildend.
compose (kəm'pouz) *vt* **1** zusammensetzen. **2** dichten, verfassen. **3** *mus* komponieren. **compose oneself** sich beruhigen, sich fassen. **composed** *adj* ruhig, gelassen. **composition** *n* **1** Zusammensetzung *f.* **2** Aufsatz *m.* **3** *mus* Komposition *f.*
composure (kəm'pouʒə) *n* Gelassenheit *f.*
compound[1] (*v* kəm'paund; *n* 'kɔmpaund) *vt* **1** zusammensetzen, mischen. **2** verbinden. *n* **1** *sci* Verbindung *f.* **2** Gemisch *neu.* Mischung *f.*
compound[2] ('kɔmpaund) *n* eingezäuntes Gelände *neu.*
comprehend (kɔmpri'hend) *vt* **1** verstehen, begreifen. **2** umfassen, einschließen. **comprehensive** *adj* umfassend, allgemein. **comprehensive school** *n* Gesamtschule *f.*
compress (*v* kəm'pres; *n* 'kɔmpres) *vt* komprimieren, zusammendrücken. *n* Kompressionsbinde *f.* **compression** *n tech* Verdichtung *f.*
comprise (kəm'praiz) *vt* einschließen, umfassen.
compromise ('kɔmprəmaiz) *n* Kompromiß *m.* *vi* übereinkommen, einen Kompromiß schließen. *vt* kompromittieren, gefährden.
compulsion (kəm'pʌlʃən) *n* Zwang *m.* **compulsive** *adj* zwingend, Zwangs—. **compulsory** *adj* zwangsläufig, obligatorisch.
compunction (kəm'pʌnkʃən) *n* Gewissensbisse *m pl.*
computer (kəm'pjuːtə) *n* Rechenautomat *neu.* Computer, Datenverarbeiter *m.* **computerize** *vt* computerisieren.

comrade ('kɔmrəd, -reid) *n* **1** Kamerad, Gefährte *m*. **2** *pol* Genosse *m*.
concave ('kɔŋkeiv) *adj* konkav, hohl.
conceal (kən'siːl) *vt* **1** verstecken, verbergen. **2** verschweigen.
concede (kən'siːd) *vt* zugestehen, zugeben.
conceit (kən'siːt) *n* Eingebildetheit, Eitelkeit *f*.
conceive (kən'siːv) *vt* **1** (a child) empfangen. **2** begreifen, sich vorstellen, ersinnen.
concentrate ('kɔnsəntreit) *(vi),vt* (sich) konzentrieren. *vt* richten. **concentration** *n* Konzentration *f*.
concentric (kɔn'sentrik) *adj* konzentrisch.
concept ('kɔnsept) *n* Konzept *neu*. Begriff *m*. **conception** *n* **1** Empfängnis *f*. **2** Auffassungsvermögen *neu*. **3** Vorstellung *f*.
concern (kən'səːn) *n* **1** Teilnahme *f*. Belang *m*. **2** Interesse *neu*. **3** Sorge *f*. **4** *comm* Unternehmen *neu*. *vt* angehen. **concern oneself** sich beschäftigen.
concert ('kɔnsət) *n* Konzert *neu*.
concertina (kɔnsə'tiːnə) *n* Ziehharmonika *f*.
concerto (kən'tʃɛətou) *n* (Solo)Konzert *neu*.
concession (kən'seʃən) *n* **1** Konzession *f*. **2** Zugeständnis *neu*.
conciliate (kən'silieit) *vt* aussöhnen.
concise (kən'sais) *adj* knapp, kurz.
conclude (kən'kluːd) *vt,vi* beenden, schließen. **conclusion** *n* Schluß *m*. **draw conclusions (from)** Schlüsse ziehen (aus).
concoct (kən'kɔkt) *vt* zusammenbrauen.
concrete ('kɔŋkriːt) *n* Beton *m*. *adj* **1** fest, dicht. **2** konkret, greifbar.
concussion (kən'kʌʃən) *n* Gehirnerschütterung *f*.
condemn (kən'dem) *vt* verurteilen. **condemnation** *n* Verurteilung *f*.
condense (kən'dens) *vt* **1** kondensieren. **2** abkürzen, zusammenfassen. **condensation** *n* **1** Kondensation *f*. **2** Abkürzung *f*.
condescend (kɔndi'send) *vi* sich herablassen.
condition (kən'diʃən) *n* **1** Zustand *m*. **2** Bedingung, Voraussetzung *f*. **conditional** *adj* bedingt, abhängig.
condolence (kən'douləns) *n* Beileid *neu*.
condom ('kɔndəm) *n* Kondom *neu*.
condone (kən'doun) *vt* billigen.
conduct (*n* 'kɔndʌkt; *v* kən 'dʌkt) *n* **1** Betragen, Verhalten *neu*. **2** Führung *f*. *vt* **1** durchführen. **2** leiten, dirigieren. **conduct oneself** sich verhalten.
conductor (kən'dʌktə) *n* **1** Schaffner *m*. **2** *mus* Dirigent *m*.
cone (koun) *n* Kegel *m*.
confectioner (kən'fekʃənə) *n* Konditor *m*. **confectionery** *n* Konditorwaren *f pl*.
confederate (*n,adj* kən

'fedərət; *v* kən'fedəreit) *n* **1** Verbündete(r) *m*. **2** Mitschuldige(r) *m*. *adj* verbündet, Bundes—. *(vi),vt* (sich) verbünden.

confer (kən'fəː) *vt* verleihen, erteilen. **conference** *n* Konferenz, Tagung *f*.

confess (kən'fes) *vt,vi* **1** zugeben, bekennen, gestehen. **2** *rel* beichten. **confession** *n* **1** Zugeständnis *neu*. **2** *rel* Beichte *f*. **3** *law* Geständnis *neu*.

confide (kən'faid) *vi* vertrauen. *vt* anvertrauen. **confidence** *n* Vertrauen *neu*. Zuversicht *f*. **confidence trick** *n* Schwindel *m*. **confident** *adj* **1** zuversichtlich. **2** selbstsicher. **confidential** *adj* geheim, vertraulich.

confine (kən'fain) *vt* begrenzen, einschränken.

confirm (kən'fəːm) *vt* bestätigen, bekräftigen. **confirmation** *n* **1** Bestätigung *f*. **2** *rel* Konfirmation *f*.

confiscate ('kɔnfiskeit) *vt* konfiszieren, einziehen.

conflict (*v* kən'flikt; *n* 'kɔnflikt) *vi* **1** streiten. **2** widersprechen. *n* Konflikt, Kampf *m*.

conform (kən'fɔːm) *(vi),vt* (sich) anpassen.

confound (kən'faund) *vt* verwirren, verblüffen.

confront (kən'frʌnt) *vt* **1** gegenüberstehen, konfrontieren. **2** entgegenhalten. **confrontation** *n* Konfrontation *f*.

confuse (kən'fjuːz) *vt* **1** verwirren, durcheinanderbringen. **2** verwechseln. **confusion** *n* Verwirrung *f*. Durcheinander *neu*.

congeal (kən'dʒiːl) *vi* gerinnen, erstarren.

congenial (kən'dʒiːniəl) *adj* kongenial, gleichartig, übereinstimmend.

congested (kən'dʒestid) *adj* verstopft, überfüllt.

congratulate (kən'grætjuleit) *vt* beglückwünschen, gratulieren. **congratulation** *n* Glückwunsch *m*.

congregate ('kɔŋgrigeit) *vi* sich versammeln. **congregation** *n* **1** Versammlung *f*. **2** Kirchengemeinde *f*.

congress ('kɔŋgres) *n* Kongreß *m*.

conical ('kɔnikəl) *adj* kegelförmig.

conifer ('kɔnifə) *n* **1** Nadelbaum *m*. **2** *pl* Nadelhölzer *neu pl*.

conjugal ('kɔndʒugəl) *adj* ehelich.

conjugate ('kɔndʒugeit) *vt gram* konjugieren.

conjunction (kən'dʒʌŋkʃən) *n* **1** *gramm* Konjunktion *f*. **2** Verbindung *f*.

conjure ('kʌndʒə) *vi* zaubern. **conjure up** *vt* **1** heraufbeschwören. **2** hervorrufen. **conjurer** *n* Zauberer *m*.

connect (kə'nekt) *vt* verbinden, koppeln, verknüpfen, anschließen. **connection** *n* **1** Verbindung, Verknüpfung *f*. **2** Anschluß *m*. **3** Zusammenhang *m*.

connoisseur (kɔnə'səː) *n* Kenner *m*.

connotation (kɔnə'teiʃən) *n* Nebenbedeutung *f*.

conquer ('kɔŋkə) *vt* besiegen, erobern. **conqueror** *n* Sieger, Eroberer *m*. **conquest** *n* Eroberung *f*.

conscience ('kɔnʃəns) *n* Gewissen *neu*.

conscientious (kɔnʃi'enʃəs) *adj* gewissenhaft.

conscious ('kɔnʃəs) *adj* **1** bei Bewußtsein. **2** bewußt. **3** wissentlich. **consciousness** *n* Bewußtsein *neu*.

conscript (*n* 'kɔnskript; *v* kən 'skript) *n* Wehrdienstpflichtige(r) *m*. *vt* (zwangsweise) einziehen. **conscription** *n* Wehrpflicht *f*.

consecrate ('kɔnsikreit) *vt* weihen. **consecration** *n* Weihung *f*.

consecutive (kən'sekjutiv) *adj* aufeinanderfolgend.

consent (kən'sent) *vi* zustimmen, einwilligen. *n* Zustimmung *f*.

consequence ('kɔnsikwəns) *n* Folge *f*. Ergebnis *neu*. **consequent** *adj* folgend. **consequently** *adv* folglich, deshalb.

conserve (kən'səːv) *vt* **1** erhalten, bewahren. **2** einmachen. **conservation** *n* **1** Erhaltung *f*. **2** Schutz *m*. **conservative** *adj* konservativ. *n* Konservative(r) *m*. **conservatory** *n* Treibhaus *neu*.

consider (kən'sidə) *vt* betrachten (als). **2** bedenken, überlegen. **3** berücksichtigen. **considerable** *adj* beträchtlich, erheblich. **considerate** *adj* überlegt, rücksichtsvoll. **consideration** *n* **1** Betracht(ung), Überlegung, Berücksichtigung *f*. **2** Rücksicht *f*.

consign (kən'sain) *vt* übergeben, überliefern. **consignment** *n* Lieferung *f*.

consist (kən'sist) *vi* bestehen. **consistency** *n* **1** Dichtigkeit *f*. **2** Übereinstimmung *f*. **3** Konsequenz, Folgerichtigkeit *f*. **consistent** *adj* **1** konsequent, folgerichtig. **2** übereinstimmend.

console (kən'soul) *vt* trösten. **consolation** *n* Trost *m*.

consolidate (kən'sɔlideit) *vt* stärken, festigen, konsolidieren.

consonant ('kɔnsənənt) *n* Konsonant, Mitlaut *m*.

conspicuous (kən'spikjuəs) *adj* auffallend.

conspire (kən'spaiə) *vi* sich verschwören.

constable ('kɔnstəbəl) *n* Polizist *m*.

Constance, Lake ('kɔnstəns) *n* Bodensee *m*.

constant ('kɔnstənt) *adj* **1** dauernd, beständig. **2** treu. **3** unveränderlich. **constantly** *adv* stets, ständig.

constellation (kɔnstə'leiʃən) *n* Konstellation *f*.

constipation (kɔnsti'peiʃən) *n* (Darm)Verstopfung *f*.

constitute ('kɔnstitjuːt) *vt* **1** ausmachen, bilden. **2** gründen. **constituency** *n* Wahlkreis, Wahlbezirk *m*. **constituent** *adj* teilbildend. *n* **1** Bestandteil *m*. **2** Wähler *m*. **constitution** *n* **1** *pol* (Staats)Verfassung *f*. **2** Struktur, Konstitution *f*. **constitutional** *adj* verfassungsmäßig.

constraint (kən'streint) *n* **1** Zwang *m*. **2** Zurückhaltung *f*.
constrict (kən'strikt) *vt* **1** zusammenziehen. **2** hemmen, einengen.
construct (kən'strʌkt) *vt* bauen, errichten, konstruieren. **construction** *n* **1** Bau *m*. Errichtung *f*. **2** Bau *m*. Gebäude *neu*. **3** Konstruktion *f*. **constructive** *adj* konstruktiv.
consul ('kɔnsəl) *n* Konsul *m*. **consulate** *n* Konsulat *neu*.
consult (kən'sʌlt) *vi,vt* konsultieren, um Rat fragen. **consult a book** in einem Buch nachschlagen. **consultant** *n* **1** Berater *m*. **2** *med* Konsilarius *m*. **consultation** *n* **1** Beratung *f*. **2** Konsultation *f*.
consume (kən'sjuːm) *vt* **1** konsumieren, essen. **2** verbrauchen. **3** vernichten. **consumer** *n* Verbraucher *m*. **consumption** *n* **1** Verbrauch *m*. **2** Genuß *m*.
contact ('kɔntækt) *n* **1** Kontakt *m*. Berührung *f*. **2** Anschluß *m*. *vt* sich in Verbindung setzen mit. **contact lenses** *n* Kontaktlinsen *f pl*.
contagious (kən'teidʒəs) *adj* ansteckend.
contain (kən'tein) *vt* **1** enthalten. **2** zurückhalten. **container** *n* Behälter *m*.
contaminate (kən'tæmineit) *vt* verseuchen, vergiften. **contamination** *n* Verseuchung *f*.
contemplate ('kɔntəmpleit) *vt* **1** betrachten, nachdenken, erwägen. **2** vorhaben. **contemplation** *n* **1** Betrachtung *f*. Nachdenken *neu*. **2** Meditation *f*.
contemporary (kən'tempərəri) *adj* zeitgenössisch. *n* Zeitgenosse *m*.
contempt (kən'tempt) *n* **1** Verachtung *f*. **2** *law* Mißachtung (des Gerichts) *f*. **contemptible** *adj* verächtlich. **contemptuous** *adj* verachtungsvoll.
content[1] ('kɔntent) *n* **1** Inhalt *m*. **2** Gehalt *m*.
content[2] (kən'tent) *adj* zufrieden, genügsam. *vt* zufriedenstellen. **contentment** *n* Zufriedenheit *f*.
contest (*n* 'kɔntest; *v* kən'test) *n* **1** Streit *m*. **2** Wettkampf *m*. *vt* bestreiten, anfechten. **contestant** *n* Teilnehmer, Bewerber *m*.
context ('kɔntekst) *n* Zusammenhang *m*.
continent ('kɔntinənt) *n* Kontinent *m*. *adj* mäßig, keusch. **continental** *adj* kontinental.
contingency (kən'tindʒənsi) *n* **1** Möglichkeit *f*. **2** Zufälligkeit *f*. **contingent** *adj* zufällig, nicht notwendig.
continue (kən'tinjuː) *vt* fortsetzen, weitermachen. **continual** *adj* fortgesetzt. **continually** *adv* immer wieder, dauernd. **continuation** *n* Fortsetzung, Weiterführung *f*. **continuity** *n* Kontinuität, Stetigkeit *f*. **continuous** *adj* ununterbrochen, (fort)dauernd.
contour ('kɔntuə) *n* **1** Umriß *m*. Kontur *f*. **2** *geog* Höhenlinie *f*.
contraband ('kɔntrəbænd) *n* Schmuggelware *f*.
contraception (kɔntrə'sepʃən)

n Empfängnisverhütung *f*. **contraceptive** *n* Empfängnisverhütungsmittel *neu*.

contract (*n* 'kɔntrækt; *v* kən'trækt) *n* Vertrag, Kontrakt *m*. *vt* **1** verkürzen, zusammenziehen. **2** (an illness) sich zuziehen. *vi* sich zusammenziehen, kleiner werden.

contradict (kɔntrə'dikt) *vt* widersprechen. **contradiction** *n* Widerspruch *m*.

contraflow ('kɔntrəflou) *n* Gegenverkehr *m*.

contralto (kən'træltou) *n* Alt *m*. Altstimme *f*.

contraption (kən'træpʃən) *n inf* (neuartiges) Gerät *neu*. Kniff *m*.

contrary ('kɔntrəri) *adj* **1** entgegengesetzt, widrig. **2** widerspenstig.

contrast (*v* kən'trɑːst; *n* 'kɔntrɑːst) *vt* kontrastieren, entgegensetzen, gegenüberstellen. *vi* sich unterscheiden. *n* Kontrast, Gegensatz *m*.

contravene (kɔntrə'viːn) *vt* **1** übertreten. **2** zuwiderhandeln.

contribute (kən'tribjuːt) *vt,vi* beitragen, beisteuern. **contribution** *n* Beitrag *m*.

contrive (kən'traiv) *vt* **1** erdenken, erfinden. **2** zustande bringen.

control (kən'troul) *vt* **1** lenken, steuern. **2** beaufsichtigen. **3** beherrschen. **4** kontrollieren. *n* **1** Macht, Gewalt *f*. **2** Aufsicht, Kontrolle *f*. **controller** *n* **1** Aufseher. **2** (Strom)Regler *m*.

controversy ('kɔntrəvəːsi, kən'trɔvəsi) *n* Kontroverse *f*. Streit *m*. **controversial** *adj* umstritten.

convalesce (kɔnvə'les) *vi* genesen, gesund werden.

convenience (kən'viːniəns) *n* **1** Bequemlichkeit, Annehmlichkeit *f*. **2** Gelegenheit *f*. **convenient** *adj* passend, geeignet, gelegen.

convent ('kɔnvənt) *n* Kloster *neu*.

convention (kən'venʃən) *n* **1** Tagung, Versammlung *f*. **2** Brauch *m*. Sitte, Regel *f*. **conventional** *adj* konventionell.

converge (kən'vəːdʒ) *vi* zusammenlaufen, sich nähern.

converse (*v* kən'vəːs; *n* 'kɔnvəːs) *vi* sich unterhalten, sprechen. *n* Umkehrung *f*. Gegenteil *neu*. **conversation** *n* Unterhaltung *f*. Gespräch *neu*. **conversational** *adj* Unterhaltungs—.

convert (*v* kən'vəːt; *n* 'kɔnvəːt) *vt* **1** umwandeln, verwandeln. **2** umwechseln. **3** *rel* bekehren. *n* Bekehrte(r) *m*.

convex ('kɔnveks) *adj* konvex, gewölbt.

convey (kən'vei) *vt* **1** befördern, transportieren. **2** mitteilen, vermitteln. **conveyor belt** *n* Fließband *neu*.

convict (*v* kən'vikt; *n* 'kɔnvikt) *vt law* überführen. *n* Sträfling *m*.

conviction (kən'vikʃən) *n* **1** *law* Überführung, Verurteilung *f*. **2** Überzeugung *f*.

convince (kən'vins) *vt* überzeugen, überreden.

convoy ('kɔnvɔi) *n* **1** Geleitzug *m*. **2** *mil* Kolonne *f*.

cook (kuk) *n* Koch *m*. Köchin

f. *vt* kochen. **cookery** *n* Kochen *neu.*

cool (ku:l) *adj* kühl. *vt* kühlen. *vi* sich abkühlen.

coop (ku:p) *n* Brutkorb *m.* *vt* einsperren.

cooperate (kou'ɔpəreit) *vi* zusammenarbeiten, kooperieren. **cooperation** *n* **1** Zusammenarbeit *f.* **2** Hilfe *f.* **cooperative** *adj* **1** zusammenarbeitend. **2** hilfsbereit. **3** *pol* genossenschaftlich. *n* Arbeitsgenossenschaft *f.* **cooperative society** *n* Konsumverein *m.*

coordinate (*adj, n* kou'ɔ:dnət; *v* kou'ɔ:dineit) *adj* koordiniert. *n* Koordinate *f.* *vt* koordinieren, gleichstellen. **coordination** *n* Koordinierung, Gleichstellung *f.*

cope (koup) *vi* sich messen mit, meistern.

Copenhagen (koupən'heigən) *n* Kopenhagen *neu.*

copious ('koupiəs) *adj* reichlich.

copper[1] ('kɔpə) *n* Kupfer *neu.* *adj* Kupfer—.

copper[2] ('kɔpə) *n* *inf* Polyp, Polizist *m.*

copulate ('kɔpjuleit) *vi* sich paaren.

copy ('kɔpi) *vt* kopieren, nachmachen. *n* **1** Kopie, Abschrift *f.* **2** Exemplar *neu.* **copyright** *n* Verlagsrecht, Copyright *neu.*

coral ('kɔrəl) *n* Koralle *f.*

cord (kɔ:d) *n* Schnur *f.* Strick *m.*

cordial ('kɔ:diəl) *adj* freundlich, herzlich.

cordon ('kɔ:dn̩) *n* Kette *f.* Gürtel *m.* **cordon off** absperren.

corduroy ('kɔ:dərɔi) *n* Kord(samt) *m.*

core (kɔ:) *n* Kern *m.*

cork (kɔ:k) *n* Korken, Pfropfen *m.* **corkscrew** *n* Korkenzieher *m.*

corn[1] (kɔ:n) *n* Getreide, Korn *neu.* **cornflour** *n* Maismehl *neu.* **cornflower** *n* Kornblume *f.*

corn[2] (kɔ:n) *n* *med* Hühnerauge *neu.*

corner ('kɔ:nə) *n* Ecke *f.*

cornet ('kɔ:nit) *n* **1** *mus* (Ventil)kornett *neu.* **2** Eiswaffeltüte *f.*

coronary ('kɔrənəri) *adj* koronar. **coronary thrombosis** *n* Koronarthrombose *f.*

coronation (kɔrə'neiʃən) *n* Krönung *f.*

corporal[1] ('kɔ:prəl) *adj* körperlich, physisch.

corporal[2] ('kɔ:prəl) *n* Korporal, Gefreite(r) *m.*

corporation (kɔ:pə'reiʃən) *n* Körperschaft, Korporation *f.*

corps (kɔ:) *n* Armeekorps *neu.*

corpse (kɔ:ps) *n* Leiche *f.* Leichnam *m.*

correct (kə'rekt) *adj* **1** richtig. **2** korrekt. *vt* **1** berichtigen, richtigstellen. **2** korrigieren. **correction** *n* **1** Berichtigung, Verbesserung *f.* **2** Korrektur *f.*

correlate ('kɔrəleit) *vi* entsprechen. *vt* aufeinander beziehen.

correspond (kɔri'spɔnd) *vi* **1** übereinstimmen, entsprechen. **2** einen Briefwechsel führen, korrespondieren. **correspondence** *n* **1** Übereinstimmung

f. **2** Briefwechsel *m*. **3** Briefe *m pl*. **correspondent** *n* Korrespondent *m*.
corridor ('kɔridɔː) *n* Korridor, Gang *m*.
corrode (kə'roud) *vt* zerfressen. *vi* rosten.
corrupt (kə'rʌpt) *vt* **1** verderben. **2** verführen. *adj* **1** verdorben, verfault. **2** korrupt.
corset ('kɔːsit) *n* Korsett *neu*.
cosmetic (kɔz'metik) *adj* kosmetisch. *n* Schönheitsmittel *neu*.
cosmopolitan (kɔzmə'pɔlitən) *adj* weltbürgerlich.
cost* (kɔst) *n* **1** Preis *m*. Kosten *pl*. **2** Schaden *m*. *vi* kosten. *vt* die Kosten berechnen von. **costly** *adj* teuer.
costume ('kɔstjuːm) *n* Kostüm *neu*. Tracht *f*.
cosy ('kouzi) *adj* bequem, gemütlich.
cot (kɔt) *n* Kinderbett *neu*.
cottage ('kɔtidʒ) *n* Hütte *f*. Häuschen.
cotton ('kɔtn̩) *n* Baumwolle *f*. **cotton-wool** *n* Watte *f*.
couch (kautʃ) *n* Couch *f*. Liegesofa *neu*.
cough (kɔf) *n* Husten *m*. *vi* husten.
could (kud; *unstressed* kəd) *v* see **can.**
council ('kaunsəl) *n* Rat *m*. **councillor** Ratsherr *m*.
counsel ('kaunsəl) *n* Rat(schlag) *m*. *vt* beraten.
count[1] (kaunt) *vt* **1** zählen. **2** halten für. *vi* **1** zählen. **2** gelten. *n* Zählen *neu*. **countdown** Startzählung *f*.
count[2] (kaunt) *n* Graf *m*.
counter[1] ('kauntə) *n* **1** Ladentisch *m*. **2** Spielmarke *f*. **3** Zähler *m*.
counter[2] ('kauntə) *pref* gegen, entgegen.
counterattack ('kauntərətæk) *n* Gegenangriff *m*.
counterfeit ('kauntəfit) *adj* falsch, unecht, verfälscht. *vt* fälschen.
counterfoil ('kauntəfɔil) *n* Quittung *f*. Kontrollabschnitt *m*.
counterpart ('kauntəpɑːt) *n* Gegenstück *neu*.
countess ('kauntis) *n* Gräfin *f*.
country ('kʌntri) *n* **1** Land *neu*. **2** Staat *m*. **country house** *n* Landhaus *neu*. **countryside** *n* Landschaft *f*.
county ('kaunti) *n* Grafschaft *f*.
coup (kuː) *n* Coup, Putsch *m*. **coup d'état** *n* Staatsstreich *m*.
couple ('kʌpəl) *n* Paar *neu*. **a couple of** ein Paar. *vt* **1** paaren, verbinden. **2** koppeln.
coupon ('kuːpɔn) *n* Gutschein, Kupon *m*.
courage ('kʌridʒ) *n* Mut *m*. Tapferkeit *f*.
courgette (kuə'ʒet) *n* Courgette *f*.
courier ('kuriə) *n* **1** Kurier, Eilbote *m*. **2** Reiseleiter *m*.
course (kɔːs) *n* **1** Lauf, Gang *m*. **2** Kurs *m*. Richtung *f*. **3** Rennbahn *f*. **4** *educ* Kursus, Lehrgang *m*. **of course** natürlich, selbstverständlich.
court (kɔːt) *n* **1** Hof *m*. **2** Spielplatz *m*. *vt* werben um. **court martial** *n* Militärgericht, Kriegsgericht *neu*. **courtship** *n* Werbezeit, Werbung *f*.
courtyard *n* Hof *m*.
courteous ('kəːtiəs) *adj* höf-

lich, verbindlich. **courtesy** *n* Höflichkeit *f.*

cousin ('kʌzən) *n* Vetter, Cousin *m.* Kusine *f.*

cove (kouv) *n* Bucht *f.*

cover ('kʌvə) *n* **1** Decke *f.* **2** (Be)Deckung *f.* **3** Hülle *f.* *vt* decken, bedecken.

cow (kau) *n* Kuh *f.* **cowboy** *n* Cowboy *m.*

coward ('kauəd) *n* Feigling *m.*

cower ('kauə) *vi* sich ducken, kauern.

coy (kɔi) *adj* scheu, bescheiden.

crab (kræb) *n* Krebs *m.*

crack (kræk) *vi,vt* **1** knallen. **2** spalten, zerbrechen. *n* **1** Spalt, Riß *m.* **2** Knall *m.*

cracker ('krækə) *n* Keks *m.*

crackle ('krækəl) *vi* knistern. *n* Geknister *neu.*

cradle ('kreidl̩) *n* Wiege *f.* *vt* wiegen.

craft (krɑːft) *n* **1** Kunst, Fertigkeit *f.* **2** List, Schlauheit *f.* **craftsman** *n* Künstler, Handwerker *m.* **craftsmanship** *n* Kunstfertigkeit *f.* **crafty** *adj* listig, gerissen.

cram (kræm) *vt* vollstopfen, überladen.

cramp[1] (kræmp) *n* Krampf *m.* **cramped** *adj* beengt, zusammengepfercht.

cramp[2] (kræmp) *n* Klammer, Krampe *f.* *vt* mit Klammern befestigen.

crane (krein) *n* **1** *zool* Kranich *m.* **2** Kran *m.*

crash (kræʃ) *n* **1** Zusammenstoß, Aufprall *m.* **2** Absturz *m.* **3** Krachen *neu.* *vi* **1** zusammenstoßen. **2** abstürzen. **crash-helmet** *n* Sturzhelm *m.*

crate (kreit) *n* Kiste *f.* *vt* verpacken.

crater ('kreitə) *n* Krater, Trichter *m.*

crave (kreiv) *vt* sich sehnen nach, flehen um.

crawl (krɔːl) *vi* kriechen, sich schleppen. *n* **1** Kriechen *neu.* **2** *sport* Kraulschwimmen *neu.*

crayfish ('kreifiʃ) *n* (Fluß)-Krebs *m.*

crayon ('kreiən) *n* Buntstift *m.*

craze (kreiz) *n* Fimmel *m.* Manie, Mode *f.* **crazy** *adj* verrückt, toll.

creak (kriːk) *vi* knarren. *n* Knarren *neu.*

cream (kriːm) *n* **1** Sahne *f.* Rahm *m.* **2** Creme *f.*

crease (kriːs) *n* **1** Falte *f.* **2** Bügelfalte *f.* *vt* **1** falten. **2** bügeln. **crease-resistant** *adj* knitterfrei.

create (kri'eit) *vt* **1** (er)schaffen, kreieren. **2** verursachen. **3** erheben (zu). **creation** *n* Erschaffung, Schöpfung *f.* **creative** *adj* kreativ, schöpferisch. **creator** *n* Schöpfer *m.* **creature** *n* Geschöpf, Wesen *neu.*

credentials (kri'denʃəlz) *n pl* **1** Ausweispapiere *neu pl.* **2** Beglaubigungsschreiben *neu.*

credible ('kredibəl) *adj* glaubwürdig.

credit ('kredit) *n* **1** Kredit *m.* Guthaben *neu.* **2** Anerkennung *f.* **3** Glaube *m.* *vt* **1** kreditieren, gutschreiben. **2** zutrauen. **credit card** *n* Kreditkarte *f.*

credulous ('kredjuləs) *adj* leichtgläubig.

creep* (kriːp) *vi* **1** kriechen, schleichen. **2** sich heimlich nähern. *n sl* Kriecher *m.*

cremate (kri'meit) *vt* einäschern, verbrennen. **crematorium** *n* Krematorium *neu*.
crept (krept) *v* see **creep**.
crescent ('kresənt) *n* Halbmond *m*.
cress (kres) *n* Kresse *f*.
crest (krest) *n* **1** Familienwappen *neu*. **2** Kamm *m*. **3** Gipfel *m*.
crevice ('krevis) *n* Spalte *f*. Riß *m*.
crew[1] (kruː) *n* Mannschaft, Besatzung *f*.
crew[2] (kruː) *v* see **crow**[2].
crib (krib) *n* Krippe *f*. *vi inf* abschreiben.
cricket[1] ('krikit) *n* Grille *f*.
cricket[2] ('krikit) *n* Kricketspiel *neu*.
crime (kraim) *n* Verbrechen *neu*. **criminal** *n* Verbrecher *m*. *adj* kriminell, verbrecherisch.
crimson ('krimzən) *adj* karmesinrot.
cringe (krindʒ) *vi* sich krümmen, kauern.
crinkle ('kriŋkəl) *vi* sich kräuseln. **crinkly** *adj* kraus.
cripple ('kripəl) *n* Krüppel *m*. *vt* lahmlegen, schwer schädigen.
crisis ('kraisis) *n*, *pl* **crises** Krise *f*.
crisp (krisp) *adj* **1** knusprig. **2** frisch. **crisps** *n pl* Kartoffelscheiben *f pl*.
criterion (krai'tiəriən) *n* Kriterium *neu*.
criticize ('kritisaiz) *vt* kritisieren, tadeln. **critic** *n* Kritiker *m*. **critical** *adj* **1** kritisch. **2** entscheidend. **criticism** *n* Kritik *f*.
croak (krouk) *n* Quaken *neu*. *vi* quaken, krächzen.
crochet ('krouʃei) *vt* häkeln. *n* Häkelarbeit *f*.
crockery ('krɔkəri) Geschirr *neu*.
crocodile ('krɔkədail) *n* Krokodil *neu*.
crocus ('kroukəs) *n* Krokus *m*.
crook (kruk) *n* **1** Haken *m*. **2** Krummstab *m*. **3** Schwindler, Gauner *m*. *vt* krümmen.
crooked ('krukid) *adj* schief, gebogen, krumm.
crop (krɔp) *n* **1** Feldfrucht *f*. Getreide *neu*. **2** Ernte *f*. **3** Reitpeitsche *f*. *vi* **1** abgrasen, abweiden. **2** stutzen. **crop up** auftauchen.
croquet ('kroukei) *n* Krocketspiel *neu*.
cross (krɔs) *vt* **1** überqueren, hinübergehen. **2** kreuzen. *vi* sich kreuzen. *n* **1** Kreuz *neu*. **2** Querstrich *m*. *adj* **1** böse, verärgert. **2** Quer—, Kreuz—. **cross-examination** *n* Kreuzverhör *m*. **cross-eyed** *adj* schielend. **cross-fire** *n* Kreuzfeuer *neu*. **crossing** *n* **1** Übergang *m*. **2** Kreuzung *f*. **cross-reference** *vt* kreuzverweisen. *n* Kreuzverweis *m*. **crossroads** *n* **1** (Straßen)Kreuzung *f*. **2** Scheideweg *m*. **crossword** *n* Kreuzworträtsel *neu*.
crotchet ('krɔtʃit) *n mus* Viertelnote *f*.
crouch (krautʃ) *vi* sich bücken, hocken.
crow[1] (krou) *n* Krähe *f*.
crow*[2] (krou) *vi* krähen.
crowd (kraud) *n* **1** (Men-

schen)Menge *f*. **2** *inf* Clique *f*. *vi* sich drängen. *vt* überfüllen.
crown (kraun) *n* Krone *f*. *vt* krönen. **crowning** *adj* krönend, höchst. **crown prince** *n* Kronprinz *m*.
crucial ('kruːʃəl) *adj* kritisch, entscheidend.
crucify ('kruːsifai) *vt* kreuzigen. **crucifix** *n* Kruzifix *neu*.
crude (kruːd) *adj* **1** roh, unreif. **2** grob, ungehobelt. **crude oil** *n* Rohöl *neu*.
cruel ('kruəl) *adj* grausam, unbarmherzig. **cruelty** *n* **1** Grausamkeit *f*. **2** Quälerei *f*.
cruise (kruːz) *n* Kreuzfahrt *f*. *vi* kreuzen.
crumb (krʌm) *n* Krume *f*. Brösel *m*.
crumble ('krʌmbəl) *vt* zerkrümeln, zerbröckeln. *vi* zerfallen.
crumple ('krʌmpəl) *vt* zerknittern, zusammenbrechen. *vi* faltig werden.
crunch (krʌntʃ) *vt* zerknirschen. *vi* knirschen. **crunchy** *adj* knusprig.
crusade (kruː'seid) *n* Kreuzzug *m*. **crusader** *n* Kreuzfahrer *m*.
crush (krʌʃ) *vt* zerdrücken, zerquetschen.
crust (krʌst) *n* Kruste, Rinde *f*.
crustacean (krʌs'teiʃən) *n* Krustentier *neu*.
crutch (krʌtʃ) *n* Krücke *f*.
cry (krai) *vi* **1** schreien, rufen. **2** weinen. *n* Schrei, Ruf *m*.
crypt (kript) *n* Gruft *f*. **cryptic** *adj* geheim.
crystal ('kristl̩) *n* Kristall *m*. **crystallize** *vt,vi* kristallisieren.
cub (kʌb) *n* Welpe *m*.
cube (kjuːb) *n* Würfel, Kubus *m*. **cubic** *adj* **1** würfelförmig. **2** Kubik—. **cubicle** *n* Kabine *f*.
cuckoo ('kukuː) *n* Kuckuck *m*.
cucumber ('kjuːkʌmbə) *n* (Salat)Gurke *f*.
cuddle ('kʌdl̩) *vt* umarmen, hätscheln. *vi* sich (zusammen)kuscheln. *n* Umarmung *f*.
cue[1] (kjuː) *n* **1** *Th* Stichwort *neu*. **2** Wink *m*.
cue[2] (kjuː) *n* Billardstock *m*.
cuff[1] (kʌf) *n* Manschette *f*. Ärmelaufschlag *m*. **cufflink** *n* Manschettenknopf *m*.
cuff[2] (kʌf) *vt* schlagen, knuffen. *n* Ohrfeige *f*.
culinary ('kʌlinri) *adj* kulinarisch, Koch—.
culminate ('kʌlmineit) *vi* kulminieren, gipfeln.
culprit ('kʌlprit) *n* Schuldige(r), Täter *m*.
cult (kʌlt) *n* Kult *m*.
cultivate (kʌltiveit) *vt* **1** bebauen, kultivieren. **2** pflegen, hegen. **cultivation** *n* **1** Ackerbau *m*. **2** Bebauung, Kultivierung *f*.
culture ('kʌltʃə) *n* **1** Kultur *f*. **2** Zucht *f*. **cultural** *adj* kulturell.
cumbersome ('kʌmbəsəm) *adj* schwerfällig.
cunning ('kʌniŋ) *adj* listig, schlau.
cup (kʌp) *n* **1** Tasse *f*. **2** *sport* Pokal *m*. **cupful** *n* Tasse(voll) *f*.
cupboard ('kʌbəd) *n* Schrank *m*.
curate ('kjuəreit) *n* Unterpfarrer *m*.

curator (kju'reitə) *n* **1** Verwalter *m.* **2** Museumsdirektor *m.*
curb (kəːb) *vt* bändigen, zügeln. *n* **1** Kinnkette *f.* **2** Zügel *m.*
curdle ('kəːdl̩) *vi,(vt)* gerinnen (lassen).
cure (kjuə) *vt* **1** heilen. **2** *cul* räuchern. *n* **1** Heilung *f.* **2** Heilmittel *neu.* **3** Kur *f.*
curfew ('kəːfjuː) *n* Ausgehvebot *m.*
curious ('kjuəriəs) *adj* **1** neugierig. **2** merkwürdig, seltsam. **curiosity** *n* Neugier *f.*
curl (kəːl) *(vi),vt* **1** (sich) locken, (sich) kräuseln. **2** (sich) zusammenrollen. *n* **1** Locke *f.* **2** Windung *f.*
currant ('kʌrənt) *n* Korinthe *f.*
current ('kʌrənt) *n* Strom *m.* *adj* **1** laufend. **2** gegenwärtig. **current account** *n* Kontokorrent *neu.* **currency** *n* **1** *comm* Währung *f.* **2** Umlauf *m.*
curry ('kʌri) *n* *cul* Curry m.
curse (kəːs) *vi* fluchen, schimpfen. *vt* (ver)fluchen. *n* Fluch *m.*
curt (kəːt) *adj* knapp, barsch.
curtail (kəː'teil) *vt* **1** verkürzen. **2** beschneiden. **3** vermindern.
curtain ('kəːtn̩) *n* Gardine *f.* Vorhang *m.*
curtsy ('kəːtsi) *vi* einen Knicks machen. *n* Knicks *m.*
curve (kəːv) *(vi),vt* (sich) biegen, (sich) krümmen. *n* Kurve, Krümmung *f.*
cushion ('kuʃən) *n* Kissen, Polster *neu.* *vt* dämpfen.
custard ('kʌstəd) *n* Eierkrem *f.*
custody ('kʌstədi) *n* **1** Bewachung *f.* Schutz *m.* **2** *law* Haft *f.*
custom ('kʌstəm) *n* Brauch *m.* Gewohnheit, Sitte *f.* **customary** *adj* gebräuchlich, Gewohnheits—. **customer** *n* Kunde, Klient *m.*
cut* (kʌt) *vt* **1** schneiden. **2** vermindern, verkürzen. *n* Schnitt *m.* **2** Schlag *m.* **3** Anteil *m.* **4** Abzug *m.* **5** Kürzung *f.* **cut down 1** fällen. **2** verringern. **cut off** abschneiden. **cut up** zerschneiden. **cut-price** *adj* herabgesetzt. **cutting** *n* Ausschnitt *m.* *adj* beißend, scharf.
cute (kjuːt) *adj* süß, niedlich.
cuticle ('kjuːtikəl) *n* Oberhaut *f.*
cutlery ('kʌtləri) *n* Besteck *neu.*
cutlet ('kʌtlit) *n* Kotelett *neu.*
cycle ('saikəl) *n* **1** Fahrrad *neu.* **2** Zyklus *m.* Kreislauf *m.* *vi* radfahren.
cyclone ('saikloun) *n* Wirbelsturm *m.*
cygnet ('signit) *n* junger Schwan *m.*
cylinder ('silində) *n* Zylinder *m.*
cymbal ('simbəl) *n* Zimbel *f.* Becken *neu.*
cynic ('sinik) *n* Zyniker *m.* **cynical** *adj* zynisch.
cypress ('saiprəs) *n* Zypresse *f.*
Cyprus ('saiprəs) *n* Zypern *neu.* **Cypriot** *n* Zypriot *m.* *adj* zypriotisch.
Czech (tʃek) *n* Tscheche *m.* *adj* tschechisch.
Czechoslovakia (tʃekəslə'vækiə) *n* Tschechoslowakei *f.* **Czechoslovakian** *adj* tschech-

oslowakisch. *n* Tschechoslowake *m*.

D

dab (dæb) *vt* (be)tupfen.
dabble ('dæbəl) *vi* **1** benetzen. **2** hineinpfuschen. **dabbler** *n* Dilettant *m*.
dad (dæd) *n inf also* **daddy** Vati *m*.
daffodil ('dæfədil) *n* Narzisse *f*.
daft (dɑːft) *adj* blöd, dumm.
dagger ('dægə) *n* Dolch *m*.
daily ('deili) *adj* täglich.
dainty ('deinti) *adj* zierlich.
dairy ('dɛəri) *n* Molkerei *f*. **dairy farm** *n* Meierei *f*.
daisy ('deizi) *n* Gänseblümchen *neu*.
dam (dæm) *n* Damm, Deich *m*. *vt* eindämmen.
damage ('dæmidʒ) *n* Schaden *m*. Beschädigung *f*. *vt* beschädigen.
damn (dæm) *vt* **1** verdammen. **2** verfluchen. **3** verurteilen. *interj* verflucht! **damnable** *adj* verdammt, verflucht. **damnation** *n* Verdammung *f*.
damp (dæmp) *adj* feucht. **dampen** *vt* **1** anfeuchten. **2** *inf* niederschlagen.
damson ('dæmzən) *n* Zwetschge *f*.
dance (dɑːns) *n* Tanz *m*. *vi* tanzen. **dancer** *n* Tänzer *m*. Tänzerin *f*.
dandelion ('dændilaiən) *n* Löwenzahn *m*.
dandruff ('dændrʌf) *n* Schuppen *f pl*.
Dane (dein) *n* Däne *m*. **Danish** *adj* dänisch. *n* (language) Dänisch *neu*.
danger ('deindʒə) *n* Gefahr *f*. **dangerous** *adj* gefährlich.
dangle ('dæŋgəl) *vi,(vt)* baumeln, schwenken (lassen).
Danube ('dænjuːb) *n* Donau *f*.
dare (dɛə) *vi* wagen, sich getrauen. **daring** *adj* mutig, waghalsig.
dark (dɑːk) *adj* dunkel, finster. **darken** *vt* verdunkeln. *vi* sich verdunkeln, trüben. **darkness** *n* Dunkelheit, Finsternis *f*.
darling ('dɑːliŋ) *n* Liebling *m*.
darn (dɑːn) *vt* stopfen.
dart (dɑːt) *n* Wurfpfeil *m*. *vi* hervorschießen.
dash (dæʃ) *vt* **1** zerschlagen. **2** zerstören. *vi* eilen, stürzen. *n* Zusatz, Schuß *m*. **dashboard** *n* Armaturenbrett *neu*.
data ('deitə) *n pl* Daten *neu pl*. **data processing** *n* Datenverarbeitung *f*.
date[1] (deit) *n* **1** Datum *neu*. **2** Termin *m*. **3** Periode *f*. *vt* **1** datieren. **2** *inf* sich verabreden mit. **date line** *n* Datumsgrenze *f*.
date[2] (deit) *n* Dattel *f*.
dative ('deitiv) *adj* dativ. *n* Dativ *m*.
daughter ('dɔːtə) *n* Tochter *f*. **daughter-in-law** *n* Schwiegertochter *f*.
dawdle ('dɔːdḷ) *vi* bummeln, trödeln.
dawn (dɔːn) *n* Morgendämmerung *f*. Tagesanbruch *m*.
day (dei) *n* Tag *m*. **daybreak** *n* Tagesanbruch *m*. **daydream** *n* Träumerei *f*. **daylight** *n* Tageslicht *neu*.
daze (deiz) *n* Verwirrung *f*. *vt* verwirren, betäuben.

dazzle ('dæzəl) *vt* blenden.
dead (ded) *adj* tot, leblos. **deaden** *vt* abtöten, dämpfen. **deadline** *n* Frist *f*. Termin *m*. **deadlock** *n* Stillstand *m*.
deaf (def) *adj* taub, schwerhörig. **deaf-aid** *n* Hörgerät *neu*. **deafen** *vt* taub machen. **deaf-mute** *n* Taubstumme(r) *m*. *adj* taubstumm.
deal* (di:l) *vi* **1** handeln. **2** sich beschäftigen. *vt game* austeilen. *n* **1** Geschäft *neu*. **2** Abkommen *neu*. **3** Menge *f*. **a great** *or* **good deal** sehr viel, eine ganze Menge. **dealer** *n* **1** Händler. **2** Verteiler *m*.
dean (di:n) *n* Dekan *m*.
dear (diə) *adj* **1** lieb, geschätzt. **2** teuer. **3** (in letters) Liebe(r), Sehr geehrte(r). *n* Liebling *neu*. **oh dear!** ach je! **dearly** *adv* **1** herzlich. **2** teuer.
death (deθ) *n* Tod *m*. **death certificate** *n* Sterbeurkunde *f*.
debase (di'beis) *vt* verderben, in Wert mindern.
debate (di'beit) *vt* debattieren, besprechen.
debit ('debit) *vt* belasten. *n* Belastung *f*. Soll *neu*.
debris ('deibri) *n* Trümmer *pl*. Schutt *m*.
debt (det) *n* Schuld, Verpflichtung *f*. **debtor** *n* Schuldner *m*.
decade ('dekeid) *n* Jahrzehnt *neu*.
decadent ('dekədənt) *adj* dekadent. **decadence** *n* Dekadenz *f*.
decaffeinated (di:'kæfineitid) *adj* koffeinfrei.
decant (di'kænt) *vt* umfüllen. **decanter** *n* Karaffe *f*.
decay (di'kei) *n* Verfall *m*. *vi* verfallen, verfaulen.
decease (di'si:s) *vi* sterben. **deceased** *n* Verstorbene(r) *m*.
deceit (di'si:t) *n* Täuschung *f*. Betrug *m*.
deceive (di'si:v) *vt* irreführen, betrügen, täuschen.
December (di'sembə) *n* Dezember *m*.
decent ('di:sənt) *adj* dezent, anständig.
deceptive (di'septiv) *adj* täuschend, trügerisch.
decide (di'said) *vi* sich entscheiden, sich entschließen. *vt* bestimmen, entscheiden.
deciduous (di'sidjuəs) *adj* Laub—.
decimal ('desiməl) *adj* dezimal.
decipher (di'saifə) *vt* entziffern.
decision (di'siʒən) *n* Entscheidung *f*. Entschluß *m*. **decisive** *adj* entscheidend.
deck (dek) *n* **1** Deck *neu*. **2** *game* Spielkarten *f pl*. Pack *neu*. **deckchair** *n* Liegestuhl *m*.
declare (di'klɛə) *vt* erklären, bekanntgeben. *vi* erklären. **declaration** *n* Erklärung, Anmeldung *f*.
decline (di'klain) *vi* **1** verfallen, sich neigen. **2** ablehnen. **3** abnehmen. *vt* **1** ablehnen. **2** *gram* deklinieren. *n* Verfall *m*. **declension** *n* Deklination *f*.
decompose (di:kəm'pouz) *vt* **1** spalten. **2** scheiden. *vi* sich auflösen. **2** verfaulen.
decorate ('dekəreit) *vt* **1** schmücken, dekorieren. **2** tapezieren, streichen. **3** auszeichnen. **decoration** *n* **1**

Schmuck *m.* Verzierung *f.* **2** Ausstattung *f.* **3** Auszeichnung *f.* Order *m.*
decoy (*n* 'di:kɔi; *v* di'kɔi) *n* Lockvogel, Köder *m.* *vt* locken, verleiten.
decrease (di'kri:s) *n* Abnahme *f.* Verminderung *f.* *vt* verringern, vermindern. *vi* abnehmen, sich vermindern.
decree (di'kri:) *n* Erlaß, Bescheid *m.*
decrepit (di:krepit) *adj* **1** hinfällig. **2** verfallen.
dedicate ('dedikeit) *vt* **1** (ein)weihen. **2** widmen. **dedicated** *adj* pflichtgetreu. **dedication** *n* Widmung, Hingabe *f.*
deduce (di'dju:s) *vt* folgern, schließen, ableiten.
deduct (di'dʌkt) *vt* abziehen, abrechnen. **deduction** *n* **1** Abzug *m.* **2** Schlußfolgerung *f.*
deed (di:d) *n* **1** Tat, Handlung *f.* **2** Urkunde *f.*
deep (di:p) *adj* tief. *n* Tiefe *f.*
deep-freeze *n* Tiefkühltruhe *f.* *vt* tiefkühlen.
deer (diə) *n invar* Reh *neu.*
deface (di'feis) *vt* entstellen, verunstalten.
default (di'fɔ:lt) *n* Nichterfüllung, Unterlassung *f.* Versäumnis *neu.* *vi* in Verzug geraten.
defeat (di'fi:t) *n* Niederlage *f.* *vt* schlagen, überwinden, besiegen.
defect (*n* 'di:fekt; *v* di'fekt) *n* Mangel, Fehler *m.* *vi* übertreten. **defection** *n* Treubruch *m.* **defective** *adj* fehlerhaft, mangelhaft.
defend (di'fənd) *vt* verteidigen.
defence *n* Verteidigung *f.*
defender *n* Verteidiger *m.*
defer (di'fə:) *vt* verschieben. *vi* nachgieben, sich beugen.
deference *n* **1** Nachgiebigkeit *f.* **2** (Hoch)Achtung *f.* **deferential** *adj* rücksichtsvoll.
defiant (di'faiənt) *adj* trotzig, herausfordernd. **defiance** *n* Trotz, Widerstand *m.* Widerspenstigkeit *f.*
deficient (di'fiʃənt) *adj* mangelhaft, unzulänglich. **deficiency** *n* Mangel *m.* Unzulänglichkeit *f.*
deficit ('defisit) *n* Fehlbetrag, Ausfall *m.*
define (di'fain) *vt* **1** definieren, festlegen, bestimmen. **2** abgrenzen. **definition** *n* **1** Definition *f.* **2** Deutlichkeit *f.*
definite ('defənit) *adj* bestimmt, unbedingt.
deflate (di'fleit) *vt* entleeren, Luft ablassen aus.
deform (di'fɔ:m) *vt* deformieren, verunstalten.
defraud (di'frɔ:d) *vt* betrügen.
defrost (di'frɔst) *vt* entfrosten.
deft (deft) *adj* gewandt, geschickt.
defunct (di'fʌŋkt) *adj* **1** verstorben. **2** nicht mehr bestehend.
defy (di'fai) *vt* **1** trotzen. **2** herausfordern.
degenerate (di'dʒenəreit) *vi* entarten, degenerieren. **degeneration** *n* Entartung, Degeneration *f.*
degrade (di'greid) *vt* degradieren, erniedrigen.
degree (di'gri:) *n* **1** Grad *m.* **2** Stufe *f.* **3** *educ* Grad *m.*
dehydrate (di'haidreit) *vt*

trocknen, das Wasser entziehen.
deity ('deiiti) *n* Gott *m*. Gottheit *f*.
dejected (di'dʒektid) *adj* niedergeschlagen, traurig.
delay (di'lei) *n* Verzögerung, Verspätung *f*. *vt* verzögern, verschieben. *vi* zögern.
delegate (*n* 'deligət; *v* 'deligeit) *n* Delegierte(r), Abgeordnete(r) *m*. *vt* **1** bevollmächtigen, delegieren. **2** übertragen.
delete (di'liːt) *vt* (aus)streichen.
deliberate (*adj* di'libərət; *v* di'libəreit) *adj* absichtlich. *vi* nachdenken, überlegen. **deliberation** *n* Überlegung.
delicate ('delikət) *adj* **1** zart, fein. **2** empfindlich. **delicacy** *n* **1** Delikatesse *f*. **2** Feinheit *f*. **delicatessen** *n* Feinkostgeschäft *neu*.
delicious (di'liʃəs) *adj* köstlich, herrlich.
delight (di'lait) *n* Freude, Wonne *f*. *vt* erfreuen, entzücken. *vi* Freude haben, entzückt sein.
delinquency (di'liŋkwənsi) *n* Kriminalität *f*. **delinquent** *adj* kriminell. *n* Verbrecher *m*.
deliver (di'livə) *vt* **1** (ab-, aus-) liefern, austragen. **2** *med* entbinden. **3** befreien. **deliverance** *n* Befreiung *f*. **delivery** *n* **1** (Aus)Lieferung *f*. **2** *med* Entbindung *f*. **3** *sport* Wurf *m*.
delta ('deltə) *n* Delta *neu*.
delude (di'luːd) *vt* täuschen, irreführen. **delusion** *n* Wahn *m*. Täuschung *f*.
delve (delv) *vi* sich vertiefen.
demand (di'mɑːnd) *n* Forderung *f*. Verlangen *neu*. *vt* fordern, verlangen.
democracy (di'mɔkrəsi) *n* Demokratie *f*. **democratic** *adj* demokratisch.
demolish (di'mɔliʃ) *vt* abreißen, zerstören. **demolition** *n* Abreißen *neu*.
demon ('diːmən) *n* Dämon *m*.
demonstrate ('demənstreit) *vi,vt* demonstrieren, zeigen. **demonstration** *n* Demonstration *f*.
demoralize (di'mɔrəlaiz) *vt* entmutigen.
demure (di'mjuə) *adj* zurückhaltend, zimperlich.
den (den) *n* Höhle *f*. Loch *neu*.
denial (di'naiəl) *n* **1** Verweigerung *f*. **2** (Ab)-Leugnung *f*.
denim ('denim) *n* Drillich *m*.
Denmark ('denmɑːk) *n* Dänemark *neu*.
denomination (dinɔmi'neiʃən) *n* **1** *rel* Konfession *f*. **2** Einheit *f*. **3** Bezeichnung *f*.
denote (di'nout) *vt* kennzeichnen, bedeuten.
denounce (di'nauns) *vt* anzeigen, denunzieren.
dense (dens) *adj* **1** dicht. **2** beschränkt. **density** *n* Dichte *f*.
dent (dent) *vt* einbeulen. *n* Beule *f*.
dental ('dentḷ) *adj* zahnärztlich, Zahn—. **dentist** *n* Zahnarzt *m*. **denture** *n* Zahnprothese *f*.
denunciation (di'nʌnsieiʃən) *n* Verurteilung, Denunziation *f*.
deny (di'nai) *vt* **1** leugnen, verneinen. **2** verweigern.

deodorant (di'oudərənt) *n* Desodorans *neu.*

depart (di'pɑːt) *vi* **1** weggehen, abfahren. **2** abweichen. **departure** *n* Abfahrt *f.* Abflug *m.*

department (di'pɑːtmənt) *n* Abteilung *f.* **department store** *n* Warenhaus, Kaufhaus *neu.*

depend (di'pend) *vi* **1** abhängen. **2** ankommen. **dependant** *n* Abhängige(r), Angehörige(r) *m.* **dependence** *n* Abhängigkeit *f.* **dependent** *adj* abhängig.

depict (di'pikt) *vt* **1** zeichnen. **2** schildern.

deplete (di'pliːt) *vt* **1** (ent)leeren. **2** erschöpfen.

deplore (di'plɔː) *vt* bedauern, mißbilligen.

deport (di'pɔːt) *vt* deportieren, ausweisen. **deportation** *n* Deportation, Ausweisung *f.*

depose (di'pouz) *vt* absetzen.

deposit (di'pɔzit) *n* **1** Anzahlung *f.* **2** Niederschlag *m.* *vt* **1** niederlegen. **2** hinterlegen, anzahlen.

depot ('depou) *n* Depot, Lagerhaus *neu.*

deprave (di'preiv) *vt* (moralisch) verderben. **depraved** *adj* verdorben. **depravity** *n* Verdorbenheit *f.*

depreciate (di'priːʃieit) *vt* entwerten. *vi* im Wert sinken.

depress (di'pres) *vt* **1** bedrücken. **2** niederschlagen, deprimieren. **depression** *n* **1** Depression *f.* **2** Vertiefung *f.* **3** Tiefdruckgebiet *neu.*

deprive (di'praiv) *vt* berauben, vorenthalten. **deprivation** *n* Beraubung, Verlust *f.*

depth (depθ) *n* Tiefe *f.* **in depth** ausführlich, gründlich.

deputy ('depjuti) *n* Stellvertreter *m.*

derail (di'reil) *vt* entgleisen.

derelict ('derəlikt) *adj* verlassen, aufgegeben, verfallen.

deride (di'raid) *vt* verlachen, verhöhnen.

derive (di'raiv) *vt* ableiten, herleiten. *vi* abstammen. **derivation** *n* Ableitung, Abstammung *f.*

derogatory (di'rɔgətri) *adj* herabsetzend, abfällig.

descend (di'send) *vi* **1** herunterkommen. **2** absteigen. **3** aussteigen. **4** sinken. **5** herkommen. **descendant** *n* Nachkomme *m.* **descent** (di'sent) *n* **1** Abstieg *m.* **2** Niedergang *m.* **3** Herkunft *f.*

describe (di'skraib) *vt* beschreiben. **description** *n* Beschreibung *f.*

desert[1] ('dezət) *n* Wüste, Einöde *f.*

desert[2] (di'zəːt) *vt* verlassen. *vi* desertieren. **deserter** *n* *mil* Deserteur *m.*

desert[3] (di'zəːt) *n* Verdienst *m.*

deserve (di'zəːv) *vt* verdienen.

design (di'zain) *n* **1** Entwurf *m.* Zeichnung *f.* **2** Konstruktion *f.* **3** Muster *neu.* **4** Absicht *f.* Plan *m.* *vt* entwerfen, planen.

designate ('dezigneit) *vt* bezeichnen, vorsehen.

desire (di'zaiə) *vt* **1** wünschen. **2** begehren. *n* **1** Wunsch, Wille *m.* **2** Begierde *f.* Verlangen *neu.*

desk (desk) *n* Pult *neu*. Schreibtisch *m*.
desolate ('desələt) *adj* **1** wüst, öde. **2** traurig.
despair (di'spɛə) *vi* verzweifeln. *n* Verzweiflung *f*.
desperate ('desprət) *adj* verzweifelt, hoffnungslos.
despise (di'spaiz) *vt* verachten. **despicable** *adj* verächtlich.
despite (di'spait) *prep* trotz, ungeachtet.
despondent (di'spɔndənt) *adj* mutlos, verzweifelt.
dessert (di'zəːt) *n* Nachtisch *m*. **dessertspoon** *n* Dessertlöffel *m*.
destine ('destin) *vt* bestimmen, ausersehen. **destination** *n* Ziel *neu*. Bestimmungsort *m*. **destiny** *n* Schicksal *neu*.
destitute ('destitjuːt) *adj* mittellos, verarmt.
destroy (di'strɔi) *vt* zerstören. **destroyer** *n* Zerstörer *m*. **destruction** *n* **1** Zerstörung *f*. **2** Verwüstung *f*.
detach (di'tætʃ) *vt* loslösen, abtrennen. **detached** *adj* **1** abgetrennt. **2** objektiv. **detachment** *n* **1** Abtrennung. **2** Objektivität *f*.
detail ('diːteil) *n* Detail *neu*. Einzelheit *f*. **in detail** ausführlich. *vt* detaillieren. **detailed** *adj* ausführlich.
detain (di'tein) *vt* zurückhalten, festhalten.
detect (di'tekt) *vt* **1** entdecken, (heraus)finden. **2** spuren, empfinden. **detective** *n* Detektiv *m*.
détente (dei'taːnt) *n pol* Entspannung *f*.
detention (di'tenʃən) *n* Haft *f*.
deter (di'təː) *vt* abschrecken. **deterrent** *n* Abschreckmittel *neu*. Abschreckung *f*. *adj* abschreckend.
detergent (di'təːdʒənt) *n* Waschmittel *neu*.
deteriorate (di'tiəriəreit) *vi* sich verschlechtern. **deterioration** *n* Verschlechterung *f*.
determine (di'təːmin) *vt* **1** entschließen, entscheiden. **2** bestimmen, feststellen. **determination** *n* Entschlossenheit *f*.
detest (di'test) *vt* hassen.
detonate ('detəneit) *vi,(vt)* explodieren (lassen).
detour ('diːtuə) *n* Umweg *m*.
detract (di'trækt) *vi* herabsetzen. *vt* entziehen.
devalue (di'væljuː) *vt* entwerten. **devaluation** *n* Entwertung *f*.
devastate ('devəsteit) *vt* verwüsten, verheeren. **devastation** *n* Verwüstung *f*.
develop (di'veləp) *vt* entwickeln. **development** *n* Entwicklung *f*.
deviate ('diːvieit) *vi* abweichen. **deviation** *n* Abweichung *f*.
devious *adj* unaufrichtig.
device (di'vais) *n* **1** Plan *m*. **2** Apparat *m*. Gerät *neu*.
devil ('devəl) *n* Teufel *m*.
devise (di'vaiz) *vt,vi* ausdenken, erfinden.
devoid (di'vɔid) *adj* ohne, frei von.
devote (di'vout) *vt* widmen. **devote oneself** sich hingeben. **devotee** *n* **1** Verehrer *m*. **2** Anhänger *m*. **devotion** *n* Hingabe *f*.
devour (di'vauə) *vt* **1** fressen,

verschlingen. **2** verzehren. **3** vernichten.
devout (di'vaut) *adj* fromm, andächtig.
dew (djuː) *n* Tau *m*.
dexterous ('dekstrəs) *adj* gewandt. **dexterity** *n* Gewandtheit *f*.
diabetes (daiə'biːtiz) *n* Zuckerkrankheit *f*. **diabetic** *adj* zuckerkrank. *n* Zuckerkranke(r) *m*.
diagonal (dai'agənl̩) *adj* diagonal.
diagram ('daiəgræm) *n* Diagramm, Schema *neu*.
dial (dail) *n* **1** (telephone) Wählscheibe *f*. **2** Ziffernscheibe *f*. *vt,vi* wählen.
dialect ('daiəlekt) *n* Mundart *f*. Dialekt *m*.
dialogue ('daiəlɔg) *n* Dialog *m*. Zwiegespräch *neu*.
diameter (dai'æmitə) *n* Durchmesser *m*.
diamond ('daiəmənd) *n* Diamant *m*.
diaphragm ('daiəfræm) *n* **1** Membran *f*. **2** *anat* Zwerchfell *neu*. **3** *phot* Blende *f*.
diarrhoea (daiə'riə) *n* Durchfall *m*.
diary ('daiəri) *n* Tagebuch *neu*. Kalender *m*.
dice (dais) *n pl or s* Würfel *m*. *vi* würfeln. *vt cul* in Würfel schneiden.
dictate (*v* dik'teit; *n* 'dikteit) *vt* diktieren. *n* Gebot *neu*. **dictation** *n* **1** Vorschrift *f*. Diktieren *neu*. **2** Diktat *neu*. **dictator** *n* **1** Diktator *m*. **dictatorship** *n* Diktatur *f*.
dictionary ('dikʃənri) *n* Wörterbuch *neu*.
did (did) *v* see **do.**
die (dai) *vi* **1** sterben. **2** (of animals) eingehen.
diesel ('diːzəl) *n tech* Diesel *m*. **diesel engine** Dieselmotor *m*.
diet ('daiət) *n* **1** Ernährung, Kost *f*. **2** Diät *f*.
differ ('difə) *vi* **1** (sich) unterscheiden. **2** abweichen. **difference** *n* Unterschied *m*. Verschiedenheit *f*. **different** *adj* verschieden, ander(s).
difficult ('difikəlt) *adj* schwierig, schwer, mühsam. **difficulty** *n* Schwierigkeit, Mühe *f*.
dig* (dig) *vt,vi* graben.
digest (*v* dai'dʒest; *n* 'daidʒest) *vt* verdauen. *n* Auslese *f*. **digestion** *n* Verdauung *f*.
digit ('didʒit) *n* **1** Finger *m*. **2** *math* Stelle *f*.
dignified ('dignifaid) *adj* würdevoll.
dignity ('digniti) *n* Würde, Ehre *f*.
dilapidated (di'læpideitid) *adj* verfallen, schäbig.
dilemma (di'lemə) *n* Dilemma *neu*. Verlegenheit *f*.
diligent ('dilidʒənt) *adj* **1** sorgfältig. **2** fleißig.
dilute (dai'luːt) *vt* verdünnen, wässern.
dim (dim) *adj* **1** düster, trübe. **2** schwach. *vt* verdunkeln.
dimension (di'menʃən) *n* Dimension *f*. Ausmaß *neu*.
diminish (di'miniʃ) *vt* vermindern, verringern. *vi* sich vermindern, abnehmen.
diminutive (di'minjutiv) *adj* klein, winzig.
dimple ('dimpəl) *n* Grübchen *neu*.
din (din) *n* Lärm *m*. Getöse *neu*.

dine (dain) *vi* speisen, essen. **dining car** *n* Speisewagen *m*. **dining room** *n* Speisezimmer, Eßzimmer *neu*.
dinghy ('diŋgi) *n* Beiboot *neu*.
dingy ('dindʒi) *adj* schmutzig, schäbig.
dinner ('dinə) *n* (Haupt)-Mahlzeit *f*. Abendessen, Mittagessen *neu*.
diocese ('daiəsis) *n* Diözese *f*.
dip (dip) *vt* **1** eintauchen. **2** (one's headlights) abblenden. *vi* untertauchen. *n* **1** Vertiefung *f*. **2** Eintauchen *neu*.
diphthong ('difθɔŋ) *n* Doppellaut *m*.
diploma (di'ploumə) *n* Diplom *neu*.
diplomacy (di'ploumәsi) *n* Diplomatie *f*. **diplomat** *n* Diplomat *m*. **diplomatic** *adj* diplomatisch.
direct (di'rekt) *adj* **1** direkt. **2** gerade, unmittelbar. *vt* **1** führen, leiten. **2** richten. **3** anweisen. **direction** *n* **1** Richtung *f*. **2** *pl* Vorschrift, Anweisung *f*. **direct object** *n* direktes Objekt *neu*. **director** *n* Direktor *m*. Leiter *m*. **directory** *n* Telephonbuch *neu*.
dirt (dəːt) *n* Dreck, Schmutz *m*. **dirty** *adj* schmutzig.
disability (disə'biliti) *n* Unfähigkeit, Behinderung *f*. **disabled** *adj* (körper)behindert.
disadvantage ('disəd'vɑːntidʒ) *n* Nachteil *m*. **disadvantageous** *adj* nachteilig.
disagree (disə'griː) *vi* **1** nicht übereinstimmen, nicht einig sein. **2** sich widersprechen. **3** (sich) streiten. **disagreement** *n* **1** Uneinigkeit, Unstimmigkeit *f*. **2** (Meinungs)Verschiedenheit *f*. Streit *m*.
disappear (disə'piə) *vi* verschwinden. **disappearance** *n* Verschwinden *neu*.
disappoint ('disə'pɔint) *vt* enttäuschen. **disappointment** *n* Enttäuschung *f*.
disapprove (disə'pruːv) *vt* mißbilligen. **disapproval** *n* Mißbilligung *f*.
disarm (dis'ɑːm) *vt,vi* entwaffnen, abrüsten. **disarmament** *n* Abrüstung *f*.
disaster (di'zɑːstə) *n* Unglück *neu*. Katastrophe *f*. **disastrous** *adj* unglücklich, schrecklich.
disc (disk) *n* **1** Scheibe *f*. **2** Schallplatte *f*. **disc jockey** *n* Schallplattenansager *m*.
discard (di'skɑːd) *vt* ablegen, aufgeben.
discern (di'səːn) *vt* **1** unterscheiden. **2** wahrnehmen.
discharge (dis'tʃɑːdʒ) *vt* erfüllen. *n* **1** Entlassung *f*. **2** Erfüllung *f*. **3** *med* Absonderung *f*.
disciple (di'saipəl) *n* Schüler, Jünger *m*.
discipline ('disəplin) *n* **1** Disziplin *f*. **2** Wissenszweig *m*. *vt* bestrafen, zurechtweisen.
disclaim (dis'kleim) *vt* **1** verzichten auf. **2** nicht anerkennen, abstreiten.
disclose (dis'klouz) *vt* offenbaren, enthüllen.
discomfort (dis'kʌmfət) *n* Unbehagen *neu*.
disconnect (diskə'nekt) *vt* trennen, unterbrechen.
disconsolate (dis'kɔnsələt) *adj* trostlos.

discontinue (diskən'tinjuː) *vt* unterbrechen. *vi* aufhören.
discord ('diskɔːd) *n* Uneinigkeit *f.* Mißklang *m.*
discotheque ('diskətek) *n* Diskothek *f.*
discount ('diskaunt) *n* Rabatt *m.*
discourage (dis'kʌridʒ) *vt* **1** abraten. **2** entmutigen.
discover (dis'kʌvə) *vt* **1** entdecken. **2** herausfinden, erkennen. **discovery** *n* Entdeckung *f.*
discredit (dis'kredit) *vt* **1** in Verruf bringen. **2** anzweifeln. *n* **1** schlechter Ruf *m.* **2** Zweifel *m.*
discreet (dis'kriːt) *adj* besonnen, diskret. **discretion** *n* **1** Belieben *neu.* **2** Takt *m.*
discrepancy (dis'krepənsi) *n* Widerspruch *m.* Unstimmigkeit *f.*
discriminate (dis'krimineit) *vi* unterschiedlich behandeln. *vt* unterscheiden, absondern. **discrimination** *n* Diskriminierung, Unterscheidung *f.*
discus ('diskəs) *n sport* Diskus *m.*
discuss (dis'kʌs) *vt* besprechen, diskutieren, erörtern. **discussion** *n* Erörterung, Diskussion *f.*
disease (di'ziːz) *n* Krankheit *f.*
disembark (disim'bɑːk) *vi* ausschiffen.
disengage (disin'geidʒ) *vt* **1** (los)lösen, freimachen. **2** loskuppeln. *vi* sich freimachen.
disfigure (dis'figə) *vt* verunstalten.
disgrace (dis'greis) *n* **1** Schande *f.* **2** Ungnade *f.* *vt* schänden, entehren. **disgraceful** *adj* schändlich.
disgruntled (dis'grʌntəld) *adj* mürrisch.
disguise (dis'gaiz) *vt* **1** verkleiden. **2** verhüllen. *n* Verkleidung *f.* **in disguise** verkleidet.
disgust (dis'gʌst) *n* Ekel *m.* *vt* anekeln. **disgusting** *adj* ekelhaft, widerlich.
dish (diʃ) *n* **1** *cul* Gericht *neu.* **2** Schüssel *f.* **dishcloth** *n* Abwaschtuch *neu.* **dishwasher** *n* Spülmaschine *f.*
dishearten (dis'hɑːtn̩) *vt* entmutigen.
dishevelled (di'ʃevəld) *adj* zerzaust.
dishonest (dis'ɔnist) *adj* unehrlich. **dishonesty** *n* Unehrlichkeit *f.*
dishonour (dis'ɔnə) *vt* entehren. *n* Schande, Unehre *f.*
disillusion (disi'luːʒən) *n* Enttäuschung, Ernüchterung *f.* *vt* ernüchtern, enttäuschen. **disillusioned** *adj* enttäuscht, verbittert, ernüchtert.
disinfect (disin'fekt) *vt* desinfizieren. **disinfectant** *n* Desinfektionsmittel *neu.*
disinherit (disin'herit) *vt* enterben.
disintegrate (dis'intigreit) *(vi),vt* (sich) auflösen, (sich) zersetzen. *vi* verfallen. **disintegration** *n* Auflösung, Zersetzung *f.*
disinterested (dis'intrəstid) *adj* unbeteiligt.
dislike (dis'laik) *vt* nicht mögen. *n* Abneigung *f.*
dislocate ('disləkeit) *vt med*

verrenken. **dislocation** *n* Verrenkung *f*.
dislodge (dis'lɔdʒ) *vt* **1** entfernen. **2** vertreiben.
disloyal (dis'lɔiəl) *adj* untreu.
dismal ('dizməl) *adj* traurig, trübe.
dismantle (dis'mæntl̩) *vt* demontieren, auseinandernehmen.
dismay (dismei) *n* Bestürzung *f*. *vt* bestürzen.
dismiss (dis'mis) *vt* **1** entlassen. **2** gehen lassen. **3** abweisen. **dismissal** *n* Entlassung *f*.
dismount (dis'maunt) *vi* absteigen.
disobey (disə'bei) *vt* ungehorsam sein gegen, nicht gehorchen. **disobedience** *n* Ungehorsam *m*. **disobedient** *adj* ungehorsam.
disorder (dis'ɔːdə) *n* **1** Unordnung *f*. **2** Unruhe *f*. **3** *med* Störung *f*.
disorganized (dis'ɔːgənaizd) *adj* in Unordnung, aufgelöst.
disown (dis'oun) *vt* nicht anerkennen, verleugnen.
disparage (dis'pæridʒ) *vt* verunglimpfen, herabsetzen.
dispassionate (dis'pæʃənət) *adj* **1** leidenschaftslos. **2** sachlich.
dispatch (dis'pætʃ) *n* Absendung, Abfertigung *f*. *vt* (eilig) wegschicken, absenden.
dispel (dis'pel) *vt* zerstreuen, vertreiben.
dispense (dis'pens) *vt* verteilen, ausgeben. **dispense with** entbehren, verzichten auf. **dispensary** *n* Arzneiausgabe, Apotheke *f*.
disperse (dis'pəːs) *(vi),vt* (sich) zerstreuen, (sich) verteilen. **dispersal** *n* Zerstreuung, Vertreibung *f*.
displace (dis'pleis) *vt* **1** verschieben. **2** *naut* verdrängen. **displacement** *n* Verrückung, Verdrängung *f*.
display (dis'plei) *n* **1** Auslage *f*. **2** *mil* Vorführung *f*. *vt* **1** zur Schau stellen. **2** zeigen.
displease (dis'pliːz) *vt* mißfallen. **displeasure** *n* Mißfallen *neu*.
dispose (dis'pouz) *vt* anordnen. **dispose of** beseitigen, abschaffen. **disposal** *n* **1** Verfügung *f*. **2** Erledigung *f*.
disposition *n* **1** Neigung *f*. **2** Veranlagung *f*.
disproportion (disprə'pɔːʃən) *n* Mißverhältnis *neu*. **disproportionate** *adj* **1** unverhältnismäßig. **2** übertrieben.
disprove (dis'pruːv) *vt* widerlegen.
dispute (dis'pjuːt) *n* Streit *m*. Debatte *f*. *vi* (sich) streiten. *vt* bestreiten.
disqualify (dis'kwɔlifai) *vt* **1** ausschließen, disqualifizieren. **2** unfähig erklären.
disregard (disri'gɑːd) *vt* **1** mißachten. **2** außer Acht lassen.
disreputable (dis'repjutəbəl) *adj* verrufen.
disrespect (disri'spekt) *n* Respektlosigkeit *f*.
disrupt (dis'rʌpt) *vt* **1** spalten, zerbrechen. **2** unterbrechen, stören.
dissatisfy (di'sætisfai) *vt* nicht zufriedenstellen, mißfallen.

dissect (di'sekt) *vt* sezieren, zergliedern.
dissent (di'sent) *n* abweichende Meinung *f.* *vi* anderer Meinung sein.
dissimilar (di'similə) *adj* verschieden, unähnlich.
dissociate (di'souʃieit) *vt* trennen. **dissociate oneself** sich lossagen, abrücken.
dissolve (di'zɔlv) *vt* auflösen. *vi* sich auflösen, schmelzen.
dissuade (di'sweid) *vt* abraten.
distance ('distəns) *n* Entfernung *f.* Abstand *m.* **distant** *adj* weit, entfernt.
distaste (dis'teist) *n* Abneigung *f.* **distasteful** *adj* widerlich, unangenehm.
distil (dis'til) *vt* destillieren.
distinct (dis'tiŋkt) *adj* **1** verschieden. **2** deutlich. **3** ausgeprägt. **distinction** *n* **1** Unterschied *m.* **2** Auszeichnung *f.* **3** Würde *f.* **distinctive** *adj* deutlich, kennzeichnend.
distinguish (dis'tiŋgwiʃ) *vt,vi* unterscheiden. **distinguish oneself** sich auszeichnen.
distort (dis'tɔːt) *vt* verzerren.
distract (dis'trækt) *vt* **1** ablenken. **2** beunruhigen.
distraught (dis'trɔːt) *adj* **1** erregt, verwirrt. **2** wahnsinnig.
distress (dis'tres) *n* **1** Not *f.* Elend *neu.* **2** Leid *neu.* Schmerz *m.* *vt* beunruhigen, quälen.
distribute (dis'tribjuːt) *vt* verteilen, ausgeben. **distribution** *n* Verteilung, Verbreitung *f.*
district ('distrikt) *n* Bezirk *m.* Gegend *f.*
distrust (dis'trʌst) *n* Mißtrauen. *vt* mißtrauen.
disturb (dis'təːb) *vt* **1** stören. **2** beunruhigen. **disturbance** *n* **1** Störung *f.* **2** Unruhe *f.*
ditch (ditʃ) *n* Graben *m.* *vt inf* wegwerfen.
ditto ('ditou) *adv* dito, desgleichen.
divan (di'væn) *n* Diwan *m.*
dive (daiv) *n* **1** Kopfsprung *m.* **2** *aviat* Sturzflug *m.* *vi* **1** tauchen. **2** sich stürzen. **3** einen Kopfsprung machen. **4** einen Sturzflug machen. **diving board** *n* Sprungbrett *neu.*
diverge (dai'vəːdʒ) *vi* **1** auseinanderlaufen, sich trennen. **2** abweichen.
diverse (dai'vəːs) *adj* verschieden, vielfältig.
divert (dai'vəːt) *vt* **1** ablenken. **2** umleiten. **3** unterhalten. **diversion** *n* **1** Umleitung *f.* **2** Zerstreuung *f.*
divide (di'vaid) *vt* **1** teilen. **2** verteilen. **3** zerteilen, spalten. **divisible** *adj* teilbar. **division** *n* **1** Teilung *f.* **2** Trennung *f.* **3** *mil,sport* Division *f.*
dividend ('dividend) *n* Dividende *f.* (Gewinn)Anteil *m.*
divine (di'vain) *adj* göttlich, Gottes—. **divinity** *n* **1** Gottheit *f.* **2** Theologie *f.*
divorce (di'vɔːs) *n* Scheidung *f.* *vi* scheiden, sich scheiden lassen.
divulge (di'vʌldʒ) *vt* enthüllen, bekanntmachen.
dizzy ('dizi) *adj* **1** schwindelig. **2** unbesonnen.
do* (duː) *vt* **1** tun, machen. **2** ausführen. *vi* tun, handeln.

do away with abschaffen, beseitigen.
docile ('dousail) *adj* gelehrig, fügsam.
dock[1] (dɔk) *n* **1** Dock *neu*. **2** Hafenanlage *f*. **dockyard** *n* Werft *f*.
dock[2] (dɔk) *vt* **1** stutzen. **2** vermindern.
dock[3] (dɔk) *n law* Anklagebank *f*.
doctor ('dɔktə) *n* **1** *med* Doktor, Arzt *m*. **2** *educ* Doktor *m*.
doctrine ('dɔktrin) *n* Lehre, Doktrin *f*.
document ('dɔkjumənt) *n* Urkunde *f*. Dokument, Schriftstück *neu*. *vt* dokumentieren, beurkunden. **documentary** *n* Dokumentarfilm *m*. *adj* dokumentarisch, schriftlich.
dodge (dɔdʒ) *vi* ausweichen. *vt* vermeiden. *n* **1** Seitensprung *m*. **2** Trick, Kniff *m*.
does (dʌz) *v* see **do.**
dog (dɔg) *n* Hund *m*. *vt* nachspüren. **dogged** *adj* verbissen.
dogma ('dɔgmə) *n* Glaubenssatz *m*. Dogma *neu*. **dogmatic** *adj* dogmatisch.
dole (doul) *n* Arbeitslosenunterstützung *f*. *v* **dole out** austeilen, ausgeben.
doll (dɔl) *n* Puppe *f*.
dollar ('dɔlə) *n* Dollar *m*.
Dolomites ('dɔləmaits) *n* Dolomiten *pl*.
dolphin ('dɔlfin) *n* Delphin *m*.
domain (də'mein) *n* Bereich *m*.
dome (doum) *n* Kuppel *f*.
domestic (də'mestik) *adj* **1** häuslich. **2** inländisch. **domestic animal** *n* Haustier *neu*. **domesticate** *vt* **1** zähmen. **2** häuslich machen.
dominate ('dɔmineit) *vt* beherrschen, herrschen über, dominieren. **dominance** *n* (Vor)Herrschaft *f*. **dominant** *adj* (vor)herrschend. **domination** *n* Herrschaft *f*. **domineer** *vi* den Herrn spielen.
dominion (də'minjən) *n* Herrschaft *f*.
donate (dou'neit) *vt* schenken. *vi* eine Schenkung machen.
done (dʌn) *v* see **do.** *adj* fertig. *interj* abgemacht!
donkey ('dɔŋki) *n* Esel *m*.
donor ('dounə) *n* Spender *m*.
doom (du:m) *n* **1** Schicksal, Verhängnis *neu*. **2** Verderben *neu*. *vt* verdammen. **doomed** *adj* verloren, verdammt.
door (dɔ:) *n* Tür *f*. **door to door** von Haus zu Haus. **out of doors** draußen, im Freien. **doorbell** *n* Türklingel *f*. **doorhandle** *n* Türgriff *m*. Türklinke *f*. **doorstep** *n* Türschwelle *f*. **doorway** *n* Türeingang *m*.
dope (doup) *n sl* Rauschgift *neu*.
dormant ('dɔ:mənt) *adj* schlafend, untätig.
dormitory ('dɔ:mitri) *n* Schlafsaal *m*.
dormouse ('dɔ:maus) *n*, *pl* **dormice** *n* Haselmaus *f*.
dose (dous) *n* Dosis *f*. *vt* dosieren. **dosage** *n* Dosierung *f*.
dot (dɔt) *n* Punkt *m*. *vt* **1** punktieren. **2** verstreuen.
dote (dout) *vi* **dote on 1**

schwärmen für. **2** (zärtlich) lieben.
double ('dʌbəl) *adj* doppelt, Doppel—. *adv* doppelt, zu zweien. *n* **1** Doppelte *neu.* **2** Doppelgänger *m.* *(vi),vt* (sich) verdoppeln. **double bass** *n* Kontrabaß *m.* **doublecross** *vt inf* hintergehen, betrügen.
doubt (daut) *n* Zweifel *m.* *vi* zweifeln. *vt* bezweifeln. **no doubt** zweifellos, ohne Zweifel, gewiß. **doubtful** *adj* zweifelhaft, ungewiß.
dough (dou) *n* Teig *m.* **doughnut** *n* Berliner Pfannkuchen *m.*
dove (dʌv) *n* Taube *f.*
dowdy ('daudi) *adj* nachlässig, schlampig.
down[1] (daun) *adv* hinunter, herab, abwärts, nieder.
down[2] (daun) *n* Daunen *f pl.*
downcast ('daunkɑːst) *adj* niedergeschlagen.
downfall ('daunfɔːl) *n* **1** Fall *m.* **2** Niedergang *m.*
downhearted (daun'hɑːtid) *adj* mutlos, niedergeschlagen.
downhill ('daunhil) *adv* bergab. *adj* Abwärts—.
downpour ('daunpɔː) *n* Regenguß *m.*
downright ('daunrait) *adj* offen, völlig.
downstairs (daun'stɛəz) *adv* **1** nach unten, die Treppe hinunter. **2** unten. *adj* unter, im Erdgeschoß (liegend).
downstream (daun'striːm) *adv* flußabwärts.
downtrodden ('dauntrɔdn̩) *adj* getreten, unterdrückt.
downward ('daunwəd) *adj* Abwärts—.
downwards ('daunwədz) *adv* abwärts.
dowry ('dauəri) *n* Mitgift *f.*
doze (douz) *n* Nickerchen *neu.* kurzer Schlaf *m.* *vi* dösen. **dozy** *adj* schläfrig.
dozen ('dʌzən) *n* Dutzend *neu.*
drab (dræb) *adj* **1** gelbgrau. **2** eintönig, farblos.
draft (drɑːft) *n* **1** Skizze *f.* Entwurf *m.* **2** *comm* Abhebung *f.* **3** *mil* Aushebung *f.* *vt* **1** entwerfen. **2** (zur Armee) einziehen.
drag (dræg) *(vi),vt* (sich) schleppen, (sich) ziehen. *n sl* langweilige Sache.
dragon ('drægən) *n* Drachen *m.* **dragonfly** *n* Libelle *f.*
drain (drein) *n* **1** Abfluß *m.* **2** Abflußrohr *m.* Gosse *f.* *vt* **1** entwässern. **2** ableiten. *vi* abfliessen. **drainage** *n* Abfluß *m.* Entwässerung *f.* **draining-board** *n* Abtropfbrett *neu.* **drainpipe** *n* Abflußrohr *neu.*
drake (dreik) *n* Enterich *m.*
dram (dræm) *n* Schluck *m.* Gläschen *neu.*
drama ('drɑːmə) *n* Drama *neu.* **dramatic** *adj* **1** dramatisch. **2** spannend. **dramatist** *n* Dramatiker *m.* **dramatize** *vt* dramatisieren.
drank (dræŋk) *v* see **drink.**
drape (dreip) *vt* behängen, drapieren. *vi* schön fallen.
draper ('dreipə) *n* Tuchhändler *m.* **drapery** *n* **1** Tuchwaren *f pl.* **2** Tuchhandel *m.*
drastic ('dræstik) *adj* drastisch, gründlich.
draught (drɑːft) *n* **1** Zug *m.* **2** Entwurf *m.* **3** *pl* Damespiel *neu.* **draught beer** Faßbier

neu. **draughtsman** *n* Zeichner *m.* **draughty** *adj* zugig.
draw* (drɔː) *vt* **1** ziehen. **2** zeichnen. **3** anziehen. **4** dehnen. **5** (money) abheben. *vi* **1** ziehen. **2** zeichnen. **3** *sport* unentschieden spielen. **draw near** sich nähern. *~n* **1** Ziehen *neu.* Zug *m.* **2** Verlosung *f.* **3** *sport* Unentschieden *neu.* **drawback** *n* Nachteil *m.* **drawbridge** *n* Zugbrücke *f.* **drawer** *n* **1** Zeichner *m.* **2** Schublade *f.* **drawing** *n* Zeichnung *f.* **drawing-board** *n* Zeichenbrett *neu.* **drawing-pin** *n* Heftzwecke *f.* **drawing room** *n* Salon *m.*
drawl (drɔːl) *n* gedehnte Sprechweise *f.* *vi* gedehnt sprechen.
dread (dred) *n* Furcht *f.* Schrecken *m.* *vt* fürchten, sich fürchten vor. **dreadful** *adj* furchtbar, schrecklich.
dream* (driːm) *vi,vt* träumen. *n* Traum *m.* **dreamer** *n* Träumer *m.* **dreamlike** *adj* traumhaft.
dreary ('driəri) *adj* öde, eintönig.
dredge (dredʒ) *vt* **1** mit dem Schleppnetz fangen. **2** ausbaggern. **dredger** *n* Bagger *m.*
dregs (dregz) *n pl* Bodensatz *m.*
drench (drentʃ) *vt* durchnässen.
dress (dres) *n* **1** Kleidung *f.* Anzug *m.* **2** (Damen)Kleid *neu.* **3** Gewand *neu.* *vi* sich anziehen. *vt* **1** ankleiden. **2** schmücken. **3** bearbeiten. **dress circle** *n Th* erster Rang *m.* **dressing** *n* **1** Ankleiden *neu.* **2** *med* Verband *m.* **3** *cul* Zutat, Soße *f.* **dressing-gown** *n* Morgenrock *m.* **dressing-room** *n* Ankleidezimmer *neu.* **dressing-table** *n* Toilettentisch *m.* **dressmaker** *n* Damenschneiderin *f.*
dresser[1] ('dresə) *n* Anrichter, Dekorateur *m.*
dresser[2] ('dresə) *n* Küchenschrank *m.*
drew (druː) *v* see **draw.**
dribble ('dribəl) *vi* **1** tröpfeln. **2** geifern.
drier ('draiə) *n* Trockner *m.*
drift (drift) *n* **1** Treiben *neu.* **2** (Schnee)Wehe *f.* **3** Treibenlassen *neu.* **4** Tendenz *f.* *vi* **1** (dahin)treiben. **2** getrieben werden.
drill (dril) *n* **1** Bohrer *m.* **2** *mil* Exerzieren *neu.* *vt,vi* **1** bohren. **2** *mil* exerzieren.
drink* (driŋk) *vi,vt* trinken. *n* **1** Getränk *neu.* **2** Drink *m.* **3** Alkohol *m.* **drinking water** *n* Trinkwasser *neu.*
drip (drip) *vi* tröpfeln, triefen, tropfen. *n* Tröpfeln *neu.* **drip-dry** *adj* bügelfrei.
drive* (draiv) *n* **1** Fahrt *f.* **2** Auffahrt *f.* **3** Trieb, Drang *m.* **4** *tech* Antrieb *m.* *vt,vi* **1** fahren. **2** treiben. **driver** *n* **1** Fahrer, Chauffeur *m.* **2** Führer *m.* **3** Treiber *m.* **driving licence** *n* Führerschein *m.* **driving school** *n* Fahrschule *f.* **driving test** *n* Fahrprüfung *f.*
drivel ('drivəl) *vi* sabbern, geifern. *n inf* Unsinn *m.*
drizzle ('drizəl) *vi* nieseln,

sprühen. *n* Sprühregen, Nieselregen *m*.
drone[1] (droun) *n* **1** *zool* Drohne *f*. **2** Faulenzer *m*.
drone[2] (droun) *n* Summen *neu*. *vi* summen.
droop (druːp) *vi* **1** schlaff werden, herabhängen. **2** verwelken.
drop (drɔp) *n* **1** Tropfen *m*. **2** Fall, Sturz *m*. **3** Bonbon *m*. *vi* **1** tropfen. **2** fallen. *vt* fallen lassen, niederlassen. **drop someone a line** jemandem ein paar Zeilen schreiben. **drop out** *vi* ausscheiden, aufgeben. **dropout** *n* *inf* Aussteiger, Drop-out *m*.
drought (draut) *n* Trockenheit, Dürre *f*.
drove (drouv) *v* see **drive.**
drown (draun) *vi* ertrinken. *vt* ertränken, überschwemmen.
drowsy (drauzi) *adj* schläfrig.
drudge (drʌdʒ) *n* Kuli, Sklave *m*. *vi* schuften. **drudgery** *n* mühsame Arbeit, Plackerei *f*.
drug (drʌg) *n* **1** Droge *f*. **2** Rauschgift *neu*. **drug-addict** *n* Rauschgiftsüchtige(r) *m*.
drum (drʌm) *n* **1** Trommel *f*. **2** Faß *neu*. *vt,(vi)* trommeln (auf).
drunk (drʌŋk) *v* see **drink.** *adj* betrunken. **get drunk** sich betrinken. ~*n* Betrunkene(r) *m*. **drunken** *adj* betrunken.
dry (drai) *adj* **1** trocken. **2** (of wine) herb. *vt* (ab-, aus)-trocknen. *vi* trocknen. **dry-clean** *vt* chemisch reinigen. **dry-cleaning** *n* chemische Reinigung *f*.
dual ('djuəl) *adj* doppelt, zweifach. **dual carriageway** *n* Doppelfahrbahn *f*.
dubious ('djuːbiəs) *adj* zweifelhaft.
duchess ('dʌtʃis) *n* Herzogin *f*.
duck[1] (dʌk) *n* Ente *f*. **duckling** *n* Entchen *neu*.
duck[2] (dʌk) *vi* **1** untertauchen. **2** sich ducken. *vt* untertauchen.
duct (dʌkt) *n* Röhre *f*. Kanal *m*.
dud (dʌd) *n* *mil* Blindgänger *m*. *adj* falsch, verfälscht, wertlos.
due (djuː) *adj* **1** fällig. **2** erwartet. **3** angemessen, gebührend. **due to** infolge, wegen, zuzuschreiben. *adv* genau, gerade. *n* **1** Recht *neu*. Anteil *m*. **2** *pl* Gebühren *f pl*.
duel ('djuəl) *n* Duell *neu*.
duet (dju'et) *n* *mus* Duett *neu*.
dug (dʌg) *v* see **dig.**
duke (djuːk) *n* Herzog *m*.
dull (dʌl) *adj* **1** stumpfsinnig. **2** matt. **3** (of light) schwach. **4** langweilig. **5** stumpf. *vi,vt* abstumpfen.
dumb (dʌm) *adj* **1** stumm. **2** *inf* dumm. **dumbfound** *vt* sprachlos machen, verblüffen.
dummy ('dʌmi) *n* **1** Attrappe *f*. **2** Puppe *f*. **3** (for a baby) Schnuller *m*.
dump (dʌmp) *n* Müllabladeplatz *m*. *vt* abladen, auskippen.
dumpling ('dʌmpliŋ) *n* Kloß, Knödel *m*.
dunce (dʌns) *n* Dummkopf *m*.
dune (djuːn) *n* Düne *f*.
dung (dʌŋ) *n* Dung, Mist *m*.
dungeon ('dʌndʒən) *n* Kerker *m*.

duplicate (*adj,n* 'dju:plikət; *v* 'dju:plikeit) *adj* **1** doppelt. **2** Duplikat—. *n* Duplikat *neu.* Kopie *f.* *vt* **1** duplizieren. **2** verdoppeln.
durable ('djuərəbəl) *adj* dauerhaft.
duration (djuə'reiʃən) *n* Dauer *f.*
during ('djuəriŋ) *prep* während.
dusk (dʌsk) *n* (Abend)Dämmerung *f.* **dusky** *adj* **1** dämmerig. **2** dunkel.
dust (dʌst) *n* Staub *m.* *vt* abstauben. **dustbin** *n* Mülleimer *m.* **duster** *n* Staubtuch *neu.* **dustman** *n* Müllmann *m.* **dustpan** *n* Kehrichtschaufel *f.*
Dutch (dʌtʃ) *adj* holländisch. *n* (language) Holländisch *neu.* **Dutchman** *n* Holländer *m.*
dutiful ('dju:tifəl) *adj* pflichtgetreu.
duty ('dju:ti) *n* **1** Pflicht *f.* **2** Aufgabe *f.* **3** Zoll *m.* Abgabe *f.* **dutiful** *adj* pflichtbewußt. **duty-free** *adj* zollfrei, abgabenfrei.
duvet ('dju:vei) *n* Federbett *neu.* Daunendecke *f.*
dwarf (dwɔ:f) *n* Zwerg *m.* *vt* in den Schatten stellen.
dwell* (dwel) *vi* **1** wohnen. **2** verweilen. **dwelling** *n* Wohnung *f.* Wohnsitz *m.*
dwindle ('dwindḷ) *vi* schwinden, abnehmen.
dye (dai) *n* Färbemittel *neu.* Farbe *f.* *vt* färben.
dyke (daik) *n* Deich, Damm *m.*
dynamic (dai'næmik) *adj* dynamisch.
dynamite ('dainəmait) *n* Dynamit *neu.*
dynasty ('dinəsti) *n* Dynastie *f.*
dysentery ('disəntri) *n* *med* Ruhr *f.*
dyslexia (dis'leksiə) *n* Dyslexie, Wortblindheit *f.*

E

each (i:tʃ) *pron, adj* jeder, jede, jedes. *adv* je.
eager ('i:gə) *adj* begierig, eifrig.
eagle ('i:gəl) *n* Adler *m.*
ear[1] (iə) *n* **1** Ohr *neu.* **2** Gehör *neu.* **earache** *n* Ohrenschmerzen *m pl.* **eardrum** *n* Trommelfell *neu.* **earmark** *vt* **1** kennzeichnen. **2** bestimmen. **earring** *n* Ohrring *m.*
ear[2] (iə) *n* (of corn) Ähre *f.*
earl (ə:l) *n* Graf *m.*
early ('ə:li) *adj,adv* **1** früh. **2** vorzeitig.
earn (ə:n) *vt* verdienen, erwerben.
earnest ('ə:nist) *adj* **1** ernst(haft). **2** aufrichtig. *n* Ernst *m.*
earth (ə:θ) *n* **1** Erde *f.* **2** (Erd)Boden *m.* **earthenware** *n* Steingut *neu.* **earthquake** *n* Erdbeben *neu.*
ease (i:z) *n* **1** Leichtigkeit *f.* **2** Behagen *neu.* Ungezwungenheit *f.* *vt* erleichtern. **easy** *adj* **1** leicht, mühelos. **2** bequem. **3** ungezwungen. **easygoing** *adj* lässig, leichtlebig.
easel ('i:zəl) *n* Staffelei *f.*
east (i:st) *n* **1** Osten *m.* **2** Orient *m.* Morgenland *neu.* *adj* östlich, Ost—. *adv* nach Osten, ostwärts. **easterly** *adj* östlich. **eastern** *adj* **1** östlich.

2 oriental, morgenländisch. **eastward** *adj* ostwärts. **eastwards** *adv* ostwärts.
Easter ('iːstə) *n* Ostern *neu.*
eat* (iːt) *vt* **1** essen. **2** (of animals) fressen.
eavesdrop ('iːvzdrɔp) *vi* lauschen, heimlich zuhören.
ebb (eb) *n* **1** Ebbe *f.* **2** Abnahme *f.* *vi* **1** verebben. **2** abnehmen.
ebony ('ebəni) *n* Ebenholz *neu.*
eccentric (ik'sentrik) *adj* exzentrisch. *n* Exzentriker, Sonderling *m.*
ecclesiastical (ikliːzi'æstikəl) *adj* kirchlich.
echo ('ekou) *n, pl* **echoes** Echo *neu.* *vi* widerhallen.
eclair (ei'klɛə) *n* Cremekuchen *m.*
eclipse (i'klips) *n* Verfinsterung, Finsternis *f.* *vt* **1** verfinstern. **2** in den Schatten stellen.
ecology (iː'kɔlədʒi) *n* Ökologie *f.*
economy (i'kɔnəmi) *n* **1** Wirtschaft *f.* **2** Sparsamkeit *f.* **3** Sparmaßnahme *f.* **economic** *adj* wirtschaftlich, Wirtschafts—. **economical** *adj* wirtschaftlich, sparsam. **economics** *n pl* Ökonomie, (Volks)Wirtschaft *f.* **economize** *vt* (ein)sparen.
ecstasy ('ekstəsi) *n* Ekstase, Verzückung *f.* **ecstatic** *adj* ekstatisch, verzückt.
edge (edʒ) *n* **1** Rand *m.* **2** Schneide *f.* *vt* **1** schärfen. **2** umsäumen.
edible ('edibəl) *adj* eßbar.
Edinburgh ('edinbərə) *n* Edinburg *neu.*
edit ('edit) *vt* redigieren, druckfertig machen. **editor** *n* Redakteur *m.* **editorial** *n* Leitartikel *m.* *adj* Redaktions—.
edition (i'diʃən) *n* **1** Auflage *f.* **2** Ausgabe *f.*
educate ('edjukeit) *vt* erziehen, (aus)bilden. **education** *n* Erziehung, Bildung *f.* **educational** *adj* Erziehungs—, pädagogisch.
eel (iːl) *n* Aal *m.*
eerie ('iəri) *adj* unheimlich.
effect (i'fekt) *n* **1** Wirkung *f.* **2** Einfluß *m.* **3** Eindruck *m.* **4** Gültigkeit *f.* *vt* **1** bewirken. **2** einwirken auf. **3** ausführen. **effective** *adj* **1** wirksam. **2** eindrucksvoll.
effeminate (i'feminət) *adj* weibisch.
effervesce (efə'ves) *vi* aufbrausen, sprudeln.
efficient (i'fiʃənt) *adj* **1** leistungsfähig. **2** tüchtig. **3** wirksam. **efficiency** *n* **1** Leistungsfähigkeit *f.* **2** Tüchtigkeit *f.* **3** Wirksamkeit *f.*
effigy ('efidʒi) *n* Bildnis *neu.*
effort ('efət) *n* Anstrengung, Bemühung, Mühe *f.* **effortless** *adj* mühelos.
egg[1] (eg) *n* Ei *neu.* **eggcup** *n* Eierbecher *m.* **eggshell** *n* Eierschale *f.* **eggwhisk** *n* Schneebesen *m.*
egg[2] (eg) *vt* **egg on** aufreizen.
ego ('iːgou) *n* Ich *neu.* **egocentric** *adj* egozentrisch. **egoism** *n* Selbstsucht *f.* **egotism** *n* Selbstgefälligkeit *f.*
Egypt ('iːdʒipt) *n* Ägypten *neu.* **Egyptian** *adj* ägyptisch. *n* Ägypter *m.*

eiderdown ('aidədaun) *n* Daunendecke *f*.

eight (eit) *adj* acht. *n* Acht *f*. **eighth** *adj* achte.

eighteen (ei'ti:n) *adj* achtzehn. *n* Achtzehn *f*. **eighteenth** *adj* achtzehnte.

eighty ('eiti) *adj* achtzig. *n* Achtzig *f*. **eightieth** *adj* achtzigste.

either ('aiðə) *pron, adj* **1** einer (von zweien). **2** beide, jeder (von zweien). **either...or** entweder...oder.

ejaculate (i'dʒækjuleit) *vt* ausstoßen.

eject (i'dʒekt) *vt* ausstoßen, vertreiben.

eke (i:k) *vt* **eke out** ergänzen, verlängern.

elaborate (*adj* i'læbrət; *v* i'læbəreit) *adj* ausgearbeitet, kompliziert. *vt* ausarbeiten.

elapse (i'læps) *vi* vergehen, verstreichen.

elastic (i'læstik) *adj* dehnbar, elastisch. **elasticity** *n* Elastizität *f*.

elated (i'leitid) *adj* erfreut, erregt.

elbow ('elbou) *n* Ell(en)bogen *m*.

elder[1] ('eldə) *adj* älter. *n* **1** (Kirchen)Älteste(r) *m*. **2** Respektsperson *f*.

elder[2] ('eldə) *n bot* Holunder *m*. **elderberry** *n* Holunderbeere *f*.

eldest ('eldist) *adj* ältest.

elect (i'lekt) *vt* wählen, auserwählen. *vi* sich entschließen. **election** *n* Wahl *f*.

electorate (i'lɛktərət) *n* Wählerschaft *f*.

electricity (ilek'trisiti) *n* Elektrizität *f*. **electric** *adj also* **electrical** elektrisch. **electrician** *n* Elektriker *m*. **electrify** *vt* **1** elektrisieren. **2** elektrifizieren. **electrocute** *vt* durch elektrischen Strom töten.

electrode (i'lektroud) *n* Elektrode *f*.

electromagnet (ilektrou'mægnit) *n* Elektromagnet *m*. **electromagnetic** *adj* elektromagnetisch.

electron (i'lektrɔn) *n* Elektron *neu*. **electronic** *adj* elektronisch. **electronics** *npl* Elektronik *f*.

elegant ('eligənt) *adj* elegant, geschmackvoll.

element ('eləmənt) *n* **1** Element *neu*. **2** Grundbestandteil *neu*. **elemental** *adj* wesentlich. **elementary** *adj* elementar, einfach.

elephant ('eləfənt) *n* Elefant *m*.

elevate ('eləveit) *vt* aufrichten, erheben, erhöhen. **elevation** *n* **1** Erhebung *f*. **2** *math* Aufriß *m*. **elevator** *n* Aufzug, Fahrstuhl *m*.

eleven (i'levən) *adj* elf. *n* Elf *f*. **eleventh** *adj* elfte.

elf (elf) *n, pl* **elves** Elf *m*. Elfe *f*.

eligible ('elidʒəbəl) *adj* **1** annehmbar, wünschenswert. **2** berechtigt. **3** heiratsfähig.

eliminate (i'limineit) *vt* eliminieren, ausstoßen. **elimination** *n* Eliminierung, Ausstoßung *f*.

elite (ei'li:t) *n* Elite *f*.

ellipse (i'lips) *n* Ellipse *f*.

elm (elm) *n* Ulme *f*.

elocution (elə'kju:ʃən) *n* Vortragskunst *f*.

elope (i'loup) *vi* (mit ihrem *or* seiner Geliebten) entlaufen.

eloquent ('eləkwənt) *adj* redegewandt.

else (els) *adv* sonst. **anyone else 1** sonst noch jemand? **2** irgend ein anderer. **something else** etwas anderes. **elsewhere** *adv* anderswo, anderswohin.

elucidate (i'lu:sideit) *vt* erläutern, aufklären.

elude (i'lu:d) *vt* umgehen, ausweichen.

emaciated (i'meiʃieitəd) *adj* abgemagert.

emanate ('eməneit) *vi* ausströmen, ausfließen.

emancipate (i'mænsipeit) *vt* emanzipieren, befreien. **emancipation** *n* Befreiung *f*.

embalm (im'ba:m) *vt* einbalsamieren.

embankment (im'bæŋkmənt) *n* **1** Deich, Damm *m*. **2** Uferstraße.

embargo (im'ba:gou) *n* Handelssperre *f*. *vt* sperren.

embark (im'ba:k) *(vi),vt* (sich) einschiffen.

embarrass (im'bærəs) *vt* in Verlegenheit bringen. **embarrassed** *adj* verlegen.

embassy ('embəsi) *n* Botschaft *f*.

embellish (im'beliʃ) *vt* schmücken, verschönern.

ember ('embə) *n* glühende Asche *f*.

embezzle (im'bezəl) *vt* veruntreuen.

embitter (im'bitə) *vt* verbittern.

emblem ('embləm) *n* Abzeichen, Sinnbild *neu*.

embody (im'bɔdi) *vt* verkörpern.

emboss (im'bɔs) *vt* prägen, in Relief ausarbeiten.

embrace (im'breis) *vt* **1** umarmen. **2** umfassen. *n* Umarmung *f*.

embroider (im'brɔidə) *vt* besticken. **embroidery** *n* Stickerei *f*.

embryo ('embriou) *n* Embryo *m*.

emerald ('emrəld) *n* Smaragd *m*. *adj* smaragdgrün.

emerge (i'mə:dʒ) *vi* **1** auftauchen. **2** hervorkommen. **emergence** *n* Auftauchen, Hervorkommen *neu*.

emergency (i'mə:dʒənsi) *n* Notfall *m*.

emigrate ('emigreit) *vi* auswandern.

eminent ('eminənt) *adj* hervorragend, berühmt. **eminently** *adv* ganz besonders.

emit (i'mit) *vt* **1** ausstrahlen, aussenden. **2** von sich geben.

emotion (i'mouʃən) *n* Gemütsbewegung *f*. Gefühl *neu*. **emotional** *adj* **1** emotionell, gefühlvoll. **2** rührend.

empathy ('empəθi) *n* Einfühlung *f*.

emperor ('empərə) *n* Kaiser *m*.

emphasis ('emfəsis) *n* Betonung *f*. **emphasize** *vt* betonen, unterstreichen. **emphatic** *adj* nachdrücklich, betont.

empire ('empaiə) *n* Reich *neu*.

empirical (im'pirikəl) *adj* empirisch.

employ (im'plɔi) *vt* **1**

verwenden. **2** beschäftigen. **employee** *n* Arbeitnehmer *m.* **employer** *n* Arbeitgeber *m.* **employment** *n* **1** Beschäftigung, Arbeit *f.* **2** Verwendung *f.*

empower (im'pauə) *vt* bevollmächtigen, befähigen.

empress ('emprəs) *n* Kaiserin *f.*

empty ('empti) *adj* **1** leer. **2** unbeladen. **3** eitel. *vt* entleeren. **empty-handed** *adj* mit leeren Händen. **empty-headed** *adj* ohne Verstand.

emu ('iːmjuː) *n* Emu *m.*

emulate ('emjuleit) *vt* nacheifern.

emulsion (i'mʌlʃən) *n* Emulsion *f.*

enable (i'neibəl) *vt* befähigen, ermöglichen.

enact (i'nækt) *vt* **1** *law* erlassen. **2** *Th* aufführen, darstellen.

enamel (i'næməl) *n* Emaille *f.* *vt* glasieren, emaillieren.

encapsulate (in'kæpsjuleit) *vt* einkapseln.

enchant (in'tʃɑːnt) *vt* entzücken.

encircle (in'səːkəl) *vt* einkreisen, umkreisen.

enclose (in'klouz) *vt* **1** einschließen. **2** beifügen. **enclosure** *n* **1** Umzäunung *f.* **2** Anlage *f.*

encore ('ɔŋkɔː) *interj* noch einmal! *n* Zugabe *f.*

encounter (in'kauntə) *n* Begegnung *f.* *vt* begegnen, stoßen auf.

encourage (in'kʌridʒ) *vt* **1** ermutigen. **2** unterstützen, fördern. **encouragement** *n* Unterstützung, Ermutigung *f.*

encroach (in'kroutʃ) *vi* unbefugt eingreifen.

encumber (in'kʌmbə) *vt* belasten, beschweren.

encyclopedia (insaiklə'piːdiə) *n* Enzyklopädie *f.*

end (end) *n* **1** Ende *neu.* **2** Zweck *m.* Ziel *neu.* **3** Tod *m.* **be at an end** am Ende sein. ~*vi* enden, zu Ende kommen. *vt* beendigen, zu Ende führen. **endless** *vt* endlos, unendlich.

endanger (in'deindʒə) *vt* gefährden.

endeavour (in'devə) *n* Bestreben *neu.* *vi* streben, sich bemühen.

endemic (en'demik) *adj* endemisch.

endive ('endaiv) *n* *bot* Endivie *f.*

endorse (in'dɔːs) *vt* **1** vermerken. **2** bestätigen. **endorsement** *n* **1** Vermerk *m.* **2** Bestätigung *f.*

endow (in'dau) *vt* **1** schenken. **2** vermachen.

endure (in'djuə) *vi* (fort)dauern. *vt* ertragen.

enemy ('enəmi) *n* Feind, Gegner *m.* *adj* feindlich, Feind—.

energy ('enədʒi) *n* **1** Energie *f.* **2** Tatkraft *f.*

enfold (in'fould) *vt* einhüllen, einschlagen.

enforce (in'fɔːs) *vt* durchsetzen.

engage (in'geidʒ) *vt* **1** verpflichten. **2** anstellen. **3** *tech* einschalten. *vi* **1** sich verpflichten. **2** sich beschäftigen. **get engaged** sich verloben. **en-**

gagement *n* **1** Verlobung *f.* **2** Beschäftigung *f.* **3** Verabredung *f.*

engine ('endʒin) *n* **1** Motor *m.* **2** Lokomotive *f.* **3** Maschine *f.*

engineer (endʒi'niə) *n* Ingenieur, Techniker *m.* *vt* konstruieren, bauen. **engineering** *n* **1** Ingenieurwesen *neu.* **2** Maschinenbaukunst *f.*

England ('iŋglənd) *n* England *neu.* **English** *adj* englisch. *n* (language) Englisch *neu.* **Englishman** *n* Engländer *m.*

English Channel *n* (Ärmel)Kanal *m.*

engrave (in'greiv) *vt* gravieren.

engrossed (in'groust) *adj* vertieft, versunken.

engulf (in'gʌlf) *vt* **1** versenken. **2** verschlingen.

enhance (in'hɑːns) *vt* erhöhen.

enigma (i'nigmə) *n* Rätsel *neu.*

enjoy (in'dʒɔi) *vt* genießen, Freude haben an. **enjoy oneself** sich (gut) unterhalten. **enjoyment** *n* Genuß *m.* Freude *f.*

enlarge (in'lɑːdʒ) *(vi),vt* (sich) vergrößern, (sich) erweitern.

enlighten (in'laitn̩) *vt* erleuchten, aufklären. **enlightenment** *n* Aufklärung *f.*

enlist (in'list) *mil vt* anwerben. *vi* sich anwerben lassen.

enormous (i'nɔːməs) *adj* enorm, ungeheuer.

enough (i'nʌf) *adj,adv* genug.

enquire (in'kwaiə) *vi* sich erkundigen. **enquiry** *n* **1** Erkundigung *f.* **2** Untersuchung *f.*

enrage (in'reidʒ) *vt* wütend machen.

enrich (in'ritʃ) *vt* bereichern, verzieren.

enrol (in'roul) *vt* **1** einschreiben. **2** anwerben. *vi* sich einschreiben lassen.

ensign ('ensain) *n* Fahne *f.* Abzeichen *neu.*

enslave (in'sleiv) *vt* versklaven.

ensure (in'ʃuə) *vt* **1** sicherstellen, sichern. **2** dafür sorgen.

entail (in'teil) *vt* mit sich bringen.

entangle (in'tæŋgəl) *vt* verwickeln, verwirren.

enter ('entə) *vt* **1** eintreten (in), betreten. **2** eintragen.

enterprise ('entəpraiz) *n* **1** Unternehmen *neu.* **2** Unternehmungslust *f.* **enterprising** *adj* unternehmungslustig.

entertain (entə'tein) *vt* **1** unterhalten. **2** bewirten. **3** eingehen auf. *vi* Gäste haben *or* einladen. **entertainment** *n* Unterhaltung *f.*

enthral (in'θrɔːl) *vt* fesseln, bezaubern.

enthusiasm (in'θjuːziæzəm) *n* Begeisterung *f.* Enthusiasmus *m.* **enthusiastic** *adj* begeistert, enthusiastisch.

entice (in'tais) *vt* verlocken.

entire (in'taiə) *adj* vollständig, ganz.

entitle (in'taitl̩) *vt* berechtigen.

entity ('entiti) *n* Wesen, Dasein *neu.*

entrails ('entreilz) *n pl* Eingeweide *neu pl.*

entrance¹ ('entrəns) *n* **1** Eingang, Eintritt *m.* **2** Eintreten *neu.*

entrance² (in'trɑːns) *vt* entzücken, bezaubern.

entreat (in'tri:t) *vt* bitten, ersuchen.
entrench (in'trentʃ) *vt mil* verschanzen.
entrepreneur (ɔntrəprə'nə:) *n* Unternehmer *m*.
entrust (in'trʌst) *vt* anvertrauen.
entry ('entri) *n* **1** Eintritt *m*. **2** Einreise, Einfahrt *f*. **3** Eintragung *f*.
entwine (in'twain) *vi* verflechten.
enunciate (i'nʌnsieit) *vt* ausdrücken.
envelop (in'velɔp) *vt* einwickeln, umhüllen.
envelope ('envəloup) *n* (Brief)Umschlag *m*.
environment (in'vairənmənt) *n* **1** Umwelt *f*. **2** Umgebung. **environmental** *adj* Umwelt—.
envisage (in'vizidʒ) *vt* ins Auge fassen, sich vorstellen.
envoy ('envɔi) *n* Gesandte(r) *m*.
envy ('envi) *n* Neid *m*. *vt* beneiden. **envious** *adj* neidisch.
enzyme ('enzaim) *n* Enzym *neu*.
epaulet ('epəlet) *n* Epaulette *f*.
ephemeral (i'femərəl) *adj* vergänglich, flüchtig.
epic ('epik) *adj* episch.
epicure ('epikjuə) *n* Genießer, Feinschmecker *m*.
epidemic (epi'demik) *adj* epidemisch. *n* Epidemie, Seuche *f*.
epilepsy ('epilepsi) *n* Epilepsie, Fallsucht *f*.
epilogue ('epilɔg) *n* Nachwort *neu*, Epilog *m*.
Epiphany (i'pifəni) *n* Dreikönigsfest *neu*.
episcopal (i'piskəpəl) *adj* bischöflich.
episode ('episoud) *n* Episode *f*.
epitaph ('epitɑ:f) *n* Grabschrift *f*.
epitome (i'pitəmi) *n* Auszug, Abriß *m*.
epoch ('i:pɔk) *n* Epoche *f*.
equable ('ekwəbəl) *adj* ausgeglichen.
equal ('i:kwəl) *adj* **1** gleich. **2** entsprechend. **3** fähig, gewachsen. *n* **1** Gleiche(r) *m*. **2** Gleichgestellte(r) *m*. *vt* gleichen. **equality** *n* Gleichberechtigung *f*. **equalize** *vt* gleichstellen, ausgleichen. *vi sport* ausgleichen.
equate (i'kweit) *vt* gleichsetzen. **equation** *n* Gleichung *f*. **equator** *n* Äquator *m*.
equestrian (i'kwestriən) *n* Reiter *m*. *adj* Reiter—.
equilateral (i:kwi'lætərəl) *adj* gleichseitig.
equilibrium (i:kwi'libriəm) *n* Gleichgewicht *neu*.
equinox ('i:kwinɔks) *n* Tagundnachtgleiche *f*.
equip (i'kwip) *vt* ausstatten, ausrüsten. **equipment** *n* Ausrüstung, Ausstattung *f*.
equity ('ekwiti) *n* **1** Gerechtigkeit *f*. **2** *pl* Wertpapiere *neu pl*.
equivalent (i'kwivələnt) *adj* **1** gleichwertig. **2** entsprechend.
era ('iərə) *n* Ära *f*.
eradicate (i'rædikeit) *vt* ausrotten, vernichten.
erase (i'reiz) *vt* **1** ausradieren. **2** auslöschen.
erect (i'rekt) *adj* aufrecht. *vt* **1**

aufrichten. **2** bauen, errichten. **erection** *n* **1** Errichtung *f.* **2** Bau *m.*

ermine ('ə:min) *n zool* Hermelin *neu.*

erode (i'roud) *vt* **1** zerfressen. **2** erodieren. **erosion** *n* **1** Zerfressung *f.* **2** Erosion *f.*

erotic (i'rɔtik) *adj* erotisch.

err (ə:) *vi* **1** sich irren. **2** abweichen.

errand ('erənd) *n* Botengang, Auftrag *m.*

erratic (i'rætik) *adj* **1** unregelmäßig. **2** unberechenbar, nicht konstant.

error ('erə) *n* Irrtum, Fehler *m.*

erupt (i'rʌpt) *vi* ausbrechen. **eruption** *n* Ausbruch *m.*

escalate ('eskəleit) *(vi),vt* eskalieren, (sich) steigern. **escalator** *n* Rolltreppe *f.*

escalope (i'skæləp) *n cul* Schnitzel *neu.*

escape (i'skeip) *n* **1** Flucht *f.* Entkommen *neu.* **2** Befreiung *f.* *vi* **1** flüchten, entkommen. **2** ausfließen. *vt* **1** entgehen.

escort ('eskɔ:t) *n* **1** Begleitung *f.* **2** Begleiter *m.* **3** *mil* Eskorte *f.* *vt* **1** geleiten. **2** begleiten.

Eskimo ('eskimou) *n* Eskimo *m.*

esoteric (esə'terik) *adj* esoterisch.

especial (i'speʃəl) *adj* besonder, speziell. **especially** *adv* besonders, hauptsächlich.

espionage ('espiənɑ:ʒ) *n* Spionage *f.*

essay ('esei) *n* Aufsatz *m.* Abhandlung *f.*

essence ('esəns) *n* Essenz *f.* Kern *m.* **essential** *adj* **1** wesentlich. **2** unentbehrlich.

establish (i'stæbliʃ) *vt* **1** festlegen, aufstellen. **2** begründen, errichten. **establishment** *n* **1** Gründung, Errichtung *f.* **2** Firma *f.* **3** Anstalt *m.*

estate (i'steit) *n* **1** Besitz *m.* **2** Nachlaß *m.* **estate agent** *n* Häusermakler *m.* **estate car** *n mot* Kombiwagen *m.*

esteem (i'sti:m) *n* Achtung *f.* *vt* hochschätzen.

estimate (*n* 'estimət; *v* 'estimeit) *n* Schätzung *f.* *vt* schätzen. **estimation** *n* **1** Schätzung *f.* **2** Urteil *neu.*

estuary ('estʃuəri) *n* Flußmündung *f.*

eternal (i'tə:nl) *adj* ewig. **eternity** *n* Ewigkeit *f.*

ethereal (i'θiəriəl) *adj* ätherisch.

ethical ('eθikəl) *adj* ethisch, sittlich. **ethics** *n pl* **1** Sitten *f pl.* Moral *f.* **2** Sittenlehre *f.*

Ethiopia (i:θi'oupiə) *n* Äthiopien *neu.* **Ethiopian** *adj* äthiopisch. *n* Äthiopier *m.*

ethnic ('eθnik) *adj* ethnisch, Volks—.

etiquette ('etikit) *n* Etikette *f.*

etymology (eti'mɔlədʒi) *n* Etymologie *f.*

Eucharist ('ju:kərist) *n* heiliges Abendmahl *neu.*

eunuch ('ju:nək) *n* Eunuch *m.*

euphemism ('ju:fəmizəm) *n* Euphemismus *m.*

euphoria (ju:'fɔ:riə) *n* **1** Euphorie *f.* **2** (heftige) Begeisterung *f.*

Europe ('juərəp) *n* Europe *neu.*

European *adj* europäisch. *n* Europäer *m*.
European Economic Community *n* Europäische Wirtschaftsgemeinschaft, EWG *f*.
euthanasia (juːθəˈneiziə) *n* Sterbehilfe, Euthanasie *f*. Gnadentod *m*.
evacuate (iˈvækjueit) *vt* **1** entleeren. **2** evakuieren. **3** räumen.
evade (iˈveid) *vt,vi* ausweichen, umgehen, vermeiden. **evasive** *adj* ausweichend.
evaluate (iˈvæljueit) *vt* abschätzen, berechnen.
evangelical (iːvænˈdʒelikəl) *adj* evangelisch. **evangelist** *n* Evangelist *m*.
evaporate (iˈvæpəreit) *vi,(vt)* verdampfen (lassen).
eve (iːv) *n* Vorabend *m*.
even (ˈiːvən) *adj* **1** glatt, eben. **2** gleich. **3** *math* gerade. **4** quitt. *adv* gerade, sogar. **even better** noch besser. **not even** nicht einmal. **even-tempered** *adj* gleichmütig, gelassen.
evening (ˈiːvəniŋ) *n* Abend *m*. **evening dress** *n* **1** Abendkleid *neu*. **2** Smoking *m*.
event (iˈvent) *n* **1** Ereignis *neu*. Vorfall *m*. **2** Veranstaltung *f*. **eventual** *adj* schließlich. **eventually** *adv* schließlich, endlich.
ever (ˈevə) *adv* **1** immer, stets. **2** je, jemals. **3** überhaupt. **ever so** *inf* besonders, sehr. **for ever** für immer, auf ewig, stets. **evergreen** *n* Immergrün *neu*. *adj* immergrün. **everlasting** *adj* **1** ewig. **2** dauerhaft. **evermore** *adj* immerfort.
every (ˈevri) *pron* jeder, jede, jedes *m,f,neu*. all. **everybody** *pron also* **everyone** jeder, jedermann. **everyday** *adj* Alltags— alltäglich. **everything** *pron* alles. **everywhere** *adv* überall, überallhin.
evict (iˈvikt) *vt law* ausweisen.
evidence (ˈevidəns) *n* **1** Zeugnis *neu*. **2** Nachweis, Beweis *m*. **evident** *adj* offenbar, klar.
evil (ˈiːvəl) *adj* böse, übel. *n* Böse, Übel *neu*.
evoke (iˈvouk) *vt* hervorrufen.
evolve (iˈvɔlv) *vi* sich entwickeln, enstehen. *vt* entwickeln. **evolution** *n* Entwicklung, Evolution *f*.
ewe (juː) *n* Mutterschaf *neu*.
exact (igˈzækt) *adj* **1** genau, exakt. **2** streng. *vt* verlangen, fordern.
exaggerate (igˈzædʒəreit) *vt,vi* übertreiben.
exalt (igˈzɔːlt) *vt* verherrlichen. **exaltation** *n* Verherrlichung *f*.
examine (igˈzæmin) *vt* **1** prüfen. **2** untersuchen. **3** verhören. **examination** *n* **1** Prüfung *f*. **2** Untersuchung *f*. **3** Verhör *neu*.
example (igˈzaːmpəl) *n* **1** Beispiel *neu*. **2** Vorbild *neu*. **for example** zum Beispiel.
exasperate (igˈzaːspəreit) *vt* ärgern, reizen.
excavate (ˈekskəveit) *vt* ausgraben, aushöhlen.
exceed (ikˈsiːd) *vt* **1** überschreiten. **2** hinausgehen über. **exceedingly** *adv* äußerst, höchst.

excel (ik'sel) *vt* übertreffen. **excel oneself** sich auszeichnen. **excellence** *n* Vorzüglichkeit *f*. **excellent** *adj* vorzüglich, ausgezeichnet.

Excellency ('eksələnsi) *n* Exzellenz *f*.

except (ik'sept) *prep* ausgenommen, außer. **except for** abgesehen von. **except that** nur daß, außer daß. *vt* ausnehmen, ausschließen. **exception** *n* Ausnahme *f*.

excerpt ('eksə:pt) *n* Auszug *m*. Szene *f*.

excess (ik'ses) *n* **1** Übermaß *neu*. Überfluß *m*. **2** *pl* Unmäßigkeiten *f pl*. **in excess of** mehr als. **excessive** *adj* übermäßig.

exchange (iks'tʃeindʒ) *vt* (aus-, um-)tauschen, wechseln. *n* **1** (Aus)Tausch *m*. **2** Wechsel *m*. **3** *comm* Börse *f*. **4** (Telephon)Zentrale *f*. **exchange rate** *n* Wechselkurs *m*.

exchequer (iks'tʃekə) *n* Staatskasse *f*. Finanzministerium *neu*. **chancellor of the exchequer** *n* Finanzminister *m*.

excise ('eksaiz) *n* (indirekte) Steuer *f*.

excite (ik'sait) *vt* erregen, anregen, aufregen. **excitement** *n* Aufregung *f*.

exclaim (ik'skleim) *vt,vi* ausrufen.

exclamation (eksklə'meiʃən) *n* Ausruf *m*. **exclamation mark** *n* Ausrufungszeichen *neu*.

exclude (ik'sklu:d) *vt* ausschließen. **exclusive** *adj* **1** exklusiv. **2** ausschließlich.

excommunicate (ekskə'mju:nikeit) *vt* exkommunizieren.

excrete (ik'skri:t) *vi* ausscheiden, absondern. **excreta** *n pl* Auswurf, Kot *m*.

excruciating (ik'skru:ʃieitiŋ) *adj* qualvoll.

excursion (ik'skə:ʒən) *n* Ausflug *m*.

excuse (*n* ik'skju:s; *v* ik'skju:z) *n* Entschuldigung, Ausrede *f*. *vt* entschuldigen. **excuse me** entschuldigen Sie!

execute ('eksikju:t) *vt* **1** ausführen, vollziehen. **2** (a person) hinrichten. **executive** *n* **1** Verwaltung *f*. **2** (hoher) Angestellte(r), *adj* vollziehend.

exempt (ig'zempt) *adj* befreit, ausgenommen. *vt* ausnehmen, befreien.

exercise ('eksəsaiz) *n* **1** Übung *f*. **2** Ausübung *f*. **3** Schulaufgabe *f*. *vt* **1** üben, anwenden. **2** ausüben. **exercise book** *n* Schulheft *neu*.

exert (ig'zə:t) *vt* ausüben. **exert oneself** sich anstrengen. **exertion** *n* Anstrengung *f*.

exhale (eks'heil) *vt,vi* ausatmen.

exhaust (ig'zɔ:st) *n* **1** Abgas *neu*. **2** *mot* Auspuff *m*. *vt* **1** erschöpfen. **2** ermüden. **exhausted** *adj* erschöpft. **exhaust pipe** *n* Auspuffrohr *neu*.

exhibit (ig'zibit) *vt* **1** ausstellen. **2** zeigen, vorführen. *n* Ausstellungsstück *neu*. **exhibition** *n* **1** Ausstellung *f*. **2** Vorführung *f*. **exhibitionism** *n* Exhibitionismus, Öffentlichkeitsdrang *m*.

exhilarate (ig'ziləreit) *vt* erheitern.
exile ('egzail) *n* **1** Verbannung *f*. Exil *neu*. **2** Verbannte(r) *m*. *vt* verbannen, vertreiben.
exist (ig'zist) *vi* **1** existieren, sein. **2** leben. **existence** *n* Dasein *neu*. Existenz *f*.
exit ('eksit) *n* **1** Ausgang *m*. **2** Abgang *m*. *vi Th* (geht) ab.
exonerate (eg'zɔnəreit) *vt* freisprechen.
exorbitant (ig'zɔːbitənt) *adj* maßlos, ubermäßig.
exorcize ('eksɔːsaiz) *vt* beschwören, austreiben.
exotic (ig'zɔtik) *adj* exotisch.
expand (ik'spænd) *(vi),vt* **1** (sich) ausdehnen, (sich) ausbreiten. **2** (sich) erweitern. **expansion** *n* **1** Ausdehnung, Ausbreitung *f*. **2** *pol* Expansion *f*.
expanse (ik'spæns) *n* Weite, weite Fläche *f*.
expatriate (eks'pætriit) *vt* ausbürgern. *adj* im Ausland lebend. *n* Ausgebürgerte(r) *m*.
expect (ik'spekt) *vt* **1** erwarten. **2** annehmen. **expectancy** *n* Erwartung *f*.
expedient (ik'spiːdiənt) *adj* ratsam, zweckmäßig. *n* Ausweg *m*. Hilfsmittel *neu*.
expedition ('ekspi'diʃən) *n* Expedition *f*.
expel (ik'spel) *vt* (hin)ausstoßen, vertreiben.
expenditure (ik'spenditʃə) *n* **1** (Geld)Ausgabe *f*. **2** Verbrauch *m*.
expense (ik'spens) *n* **1** Kosten *f pl*. Ausgabe *f*. **2** *pl* Unkosten *f pl*. **at the expense of** auf Kosten. **expensive** *adj* teuer.
experience (ik'spiəriəns) *n* **1** Erfahrung *f*. **2** Erlebnis *neu*. *vt* erleben, erfahren. **experienced** *adj* erfahren.
experiment (ik'sperimənt) *n* Versuch *m*. Experiment *neu*. *vi* experimentieren. **experimental** *adj* Experimental—.
expert ('ekspəːt) *n* Fachmann, Experte *m*. *adj* erfahren, fachmännisch. **expertise** (ekspə'tiːz) *n* Spezialwissen *neu*. Erfahrung *f*.
expire (ik'spaiə) *vi* **1** ablaufen. **2** sterben. **3** ausatmen. **expiry** *n* Ablauf *m*.
explain (ik'splein) *vt* erklären, erläutern. **explain oneself** sich rechtfertigen. **explanation** *n* Erklärung, Erläuterung *f*.
expletive (ik'spliːtiv) *adj* ausfüllend. *n* **1** Füllwort *neu*. **2** Fluchwort *neu*.
explicit (ik'splisit) *adj* verständlich, ausdrücklich, deutlich.
explode (ik'sploud) *vi* explodieren. *vt* sprengen. **explosion** *n* Explosion *f*. **explosive** *adj* explosiv. *n* Sprengstoff *m*.
exploit[1] ('eksplɔit) *n* Heldentat *f*. Abenteuer *neu*.
exploit[2] (ik'splɔit) *vt* **1** ausbeuten, ausnutzen. **2** auswerten. **exploitation** *n* **1** Ausbeutung *f*. **2** Ausnutzung *f*.
explore (ik'splɔː) *vt* **1** erforschen. **2** untersuchen.
exponent (ik'spounənt) *n* Exponent, Vertreter *m*.
export (*v* ik'spɔːt; *n* 'ekspɔːt) *vt* exportieren, ausführen. *n* Ausfuhr *f*. Export(handel) *m*.
expose (ik'spouz) *vt* **1** aus-

setzen. **2** enthüllen. **3** bloßstellen. **4** *phot* belichten.
exposure *n* **1** Enthüllung *f*. **2** Aussetzung *f*. **3** *med* Entkräftung *f*. **4** *phot* Belichtung *f*.
express (ik'spres) *vt* ausdrücken, äußern. *adj* **1** ausdrücklich. **2** Expreß—. **expression** *n* Ausdruck *m*. **express letter** Eilbrief *m*. **express (train)** *n* Schnellzug *m*.
exquisite (ek'skwizit) *adj* vorzüglich, vornehm, auserlesen.
extend (ik'stend) *vt* **1** ausdehnen, erweitern. **2** ausbauen. **3** verlängern. **4** gewähren, erweisen. *vi* sich ausdehnen, erstrecken. **extension** *n* **1** Erweiterung, Ausdehnung *f*. **2** Verlängerung *f*. **3** Anbau *m*. **4** (Telephon)-Nebenanschluß *m*. **extensive** *adj* umfassend, ausgedehnt.
extent (ik'stent) *n* **1** Ausdehnung *f*. **2** Größe *f*. **3** (Aus)Maß *neu*. **to some extent** gewissermaßen. **to that/what extent** insofern/inwiefern.
exterior (ek'stiəriə) *adj* außer, Außen—. *n* **1** Äußere *neu*. **2** Außenseite *f*.
exterminate (ik'stə:mineit) *vt* ausrotten, vertilgen.
external (ek'stə:nl̩) *adj* äußer(lich), Außen—.
extinct (ik'stiŋkt) *adj* **1** ausgestorben. **2** erloschen.
extinguish (ik'stiŋgwiʃ) *vt* auslöschen.
extra ('ekstrə) *adj* zusätzlich, Extra—, Sonder—.
extract (ik'strækt) *vt* (heraus)ziehen. *n* **1** Auszug *m*. **2** Extrakt *m*.
extramural (ekstrə'mjuərəl) *adj* *educ* außerhalb der Mauern (einer Universität).
extraordinary (ik'strɔ:dənri) *adj* außerordentlich, außergewöhnlich.
extravagant (ik'strævəgənt) *adj* verschwenderisch. **extravagance** *n* Verschwendung *f*.
extreme (ik'stri:m) *adj* **1** äußerst. **2** extrem, radikal. **3** höchst, außerordentlich. *n* Äußerste *neu*. **extremist** *n* Radikale(r), Fanatiker *m*. **extremity** *n* **1** Äußerste *neu*. **2** Spitze *f*. **3** *pl* Gliedmaßen *pl*.
extricate ('ekstrikeit) *vt* herausziehen, freimachen.
extrovert ('ekstrəvə:t) *n* Extravertierte(r), Extravert *m*.
exuberant (ig'zju:bərənt) *adj* **1** üppig. **2** überschwenglich.
eye (ai) *n* **1** Auge *neu*. **2** Blick *m*. **3** Ansicht *f*. *vt* ansehen.
eyeball ('aibɔ:l) *n* Augapfel *m*.
eyebrow ('aibrau) *n* Augenbraue *f*.
eye-catching *adj* auffällig.
eyelash ('ailæʃ) *n* Wimper *f*.
eyelid ('ailid) *n* Augenlid *neu*.
eye-opener *n* aufschlußreiche *or* überraschende Entdeckung *f*.
eye shadow *n* Lidschatten, Augenschatten *m*.
eyesight ('aisait) *n* Sehkraft *f*.
eyesore ('aisɔ:) *n* Dorn im Auge *m*.
eyestrain ('aistrein) *n* Überanstrengung des Auges *f*.
eyewitness (ai'witnis) *n* Augenzeuge *m*.

F

fable ('feibəl) *n* Fabel *f*. Märchen *neu*.
fabric ('fæbrik) *n* **1** Stoff *m*. Gewebe *neu*. **2** Struktur *f*. **fabricate** *vt* erfinden, fabrizieren.
fabulous ('fæbjuləs) *adj* **1** fabelhaft. **2** *inf* toll, fantastisch.
facade (fə'sɑːd) *n* Fassade *f*.
face (feis) *n* **1** Gesicht *neu*. **2** Oberfläche *f*. **3** Vorderseite *f*. **in the face of** angesichts. **pull faces** Fratzen schneiden. ~*vt* **1** gegenüberstehen. **2** ansehen. **face up to 1** entgegentreten. **2** hinnehmen. **3** gewachsen sein. **face value** *n* Nennwert *m*. **take at face value** für bare Münze nehmen.
facet ('fæsit) *n* Seite *f*. Aspekt *m*.
facetious (fə'siːʃəs) *adj* witzig, spaßig.
facile ('fæsail) *adj* **1** leicht. **2** gefällig, nachgiebig. **facilitate** *vt* erleichtern, fördern. **facility** *n* **1** Möglichkeit *f*. **2** Leichtigkeit *f*. **3** *pl* Einrichtungen *f pl*.
facing ('feisiŋ) *prep* gegenüber.
facsimile (fæk'siməli) *n* Faksimile *neu*.
fact (fækt) *n* **1** Tatsache, Wahrheit *f*. **2** *pl* Tatbestand *m*. **in fact** tatsächlich, in der Tat. **factual** *adj* tatsächlich.
faction ('fækʃən) *n* **1** Partei, Splittergruppe *f*. **2** Zwietracht *f*.
factor ('fæktə) *n* Faktor, Umstand *m*.
factory ('fæktri) *n* Fabrik *f*. Betrieb *m*.
faculty ('fækəlti) *n* **1** Vermögen *neu*. Kraft *f*. **2** *educ* Fakultät *f*.
fad (fæd) *n* *inf* Liebhaberei, Mode *f*.
fade (feid) *vi* **1** verblassen. **2** verklingen. **3** verschwinden.
fag (fæg) *n* **1** *sl* Zigarette *f*. **2** Plackerei *f*.
fail (feil) *vi* **1** scheitern, versagen. **2** nachlassen. **3** versäumen. **4** *educ* durchfallen. *vt* **1** *educ* durchfallen lassen. **2** im Stich lassen. **without fail** unbedingt. **failing** *prep* in Ermangelung. *n* Schwäche *f*. **failure** *n* **1** Scheitern, Versagen *neu*. **2** Verfall *m*. **3** Versäumnis *neu*. **4** Mißerfolg *m*. **5** *educ* Durchfallen *neu*.
faint (feint) *adj* **1** schwach, matt. **2** leise. **3** ohnmächtig. *vi* ohnmächtig werden. **faint-hearted** *adj* zaghaft, verzagt.
fair[1] (fɛə) *adj* **1** hübsch, schön. **2** blond, hell. *adj,adv* gerecht, fair. **fairly** *adv* ziemlich, ganz schön. **fair-minded** *adj* gerecht, ehrlich. **fairness** *n* Gerechtigkeit *f*.
fair[2] (fɛə) *n* **1** Ausstellung, Messe *f*. **2** Jahrmarkt *m*. **fairground** *n* Rummelplatz *m*.
fairy ('fɛəri) *n* Fee *f*. Elf *m*. **fairytale** *n* Märchen *neu*.
faith (feiθ) *n* **1** Vertrauen *neu*. Glaube *m*. **2** Treue *f*. **3** Religion *f*. **faithful** *adj* **1** treu. **2** zuverlässig, genau. **3** gläubig. **yours faithfully** hochachtungsvoll.
fake (feik) *n* Fälschung *f*. *adj* verfälscht. *vt* fälschen, nachmachen.
falcon ('fɔːlkən) *n* Falke *m*.
fall* (fɔːl) *n* **1** Fall, Sturz *m*. **2**

Niedergang, Verfall *m.* **3** Sinken, Abnehmen *neu.* **3** *US* Herbst *m. vi* **1** fallen, stürzen. **2** sinken, abnehmen. **fall behind** zurückbleiben. **fall down** niederfallen. **fall through** durchfallen, scheitern.

fallacy ('fæləsi) *n* Täuschung *f.* Irrtum *m.*

fallible ('fæləbəl) *adj* fehlbar.

fallow ('fælou) *adj* **lie fallow** brachliegen.

false (fɔːls) *adj* **1** falsch. **2** trügerisch. **3** künstlich. **false alarm** *n* blinder Alarm *m.* **falsehood** *n* Falschheit, Unwahrheit *f.* **false pretences** *pl* Vorspiegelung falscher Tatsachen *f.* Betrug *m.* **false teeth** *n pl* künstliche Zähne *m pl.* **falsify** *vt* verfälschen, unrichtig darstellen.

falter ('fɔːltə) *vi* **1** stolpern. **2** zögern.

fame (feim) *n* Ruhm, Ruf *m.*

familiar (fə'miliə) *adj* **1** vertraut, bekannt. **2** gewohnt. **familiarity** *n* Vertrautheit *f.* **familiarize** *vt* vertraut machen.

family ('fæmili) *n* **1** Familie *f.* **2** Gruppe *f.*

famine ('fæmin) *n* Hungersnot *f.*

famous ('feiməs) *adj* berühmt.

fan[1] (fæn) *n* **1** Fächer *m.* **2** *tech* Ventilator *m.* **fanbelt** *n mot* Keilriemen *m.*

fan[2] (fæn) *n* Anhänger, Liebhaber *m.*

fanatic (fə'nætik) *n* Fanatiker *m. adj also* **fanatical** fanatisch.

fancy ('fænsi) *n* **1** Neigung, Vorliebe *f.* **2** Einbildung, Phantasie *f. adj* verziert, geschmückt. *vt* mögen, Lust haben auf. **fancy oneself** *inf* sich einbilden. **fancy someone** *inf* auf jemanden ein Auge haben. **fancy dress** *n* Maskenkostüm *neu.* **fanciful** *adj* phantasievoll.

fanfare ('fænfɛə) *n* Fanfare *f.*

fang (fæŋ) *n* Reißzahn *m.*

fantastic (fæn'tæstik) *adj* **1** phantastisch. **2** eingebildet. **3** *inf* wunderbar, toll.

fantasy ('fæntəsi) *n* Phantasie *f.*

far (fɑː) *adj* weit, entfernt. *adv* weit, fern. **by far** weitaus, bei weitem. **far and wide** weit und breit. **in so far as** insofern als. **faraway** *adj* **1** weit entfernt. **2** verträumt. **far-fetched** *adj* weit hergeholt, phantastisch. **far-off** *adj* entfernt, weit. **far-reaching** *adj* weitreichend.

farce (fɑːs) *n Th* Posse, Farce *f.*

fare (fɛə) *n* **1** Fahrgeld *neu.* **2** Kost *f. vi* (er)gehen.

Far East *n* Ferne(r) Osten *m.*

farewell (fɛə'wel) *n* Lebewohl *neu.* Abschied *m. interj* lebe wohl!

farinaceous (færi'neiʃəs) *adj* mehlig, Mehl—. **farinaceous food** *n* Teigwaren *f pl.*

farm (fɑːm) *n* **1** Bauernhof *m.* **2** Farm *f. vt* bewirtschaften. **farmer** *n* Bauer *m.* **farmhouse** *n* Bauernhaus *neu.* **farming** *n* Landwirtschaft *f.* **farmland** *n* Ackerland *neu.* **farmyard** *n* Hofplatz *m.*

farther ('fɑːðə) *adv* weiter, ferner. *adj* entfernter.

farthest ('fɑːðist) *adj* weitest, fernst. *adv* am weitesten.

farthing ('fɑːðiŋ) *n* **1** Farthing *m*. **2** Kleinigkeit *f*.
fascinate ('fæsineit) *vt* faszinieren.
fascism ('fæʃizəm) *n* Faschismus *m*. **fascist** *adj* faschistisch. *n* Faschist *m*.
fashion ('fæʃən) *n* **1** Mode *f*. **2** Art, Weise *f*. *vt* bilden, gestalten.
fast[1] (fɑːst) *adj,adv* **1** schnell. **2** fest, befestigt. **3** waschecht.
fast[2] (fɑːst) *n* Fasten *neu*. *vi* fasten.
fasten ('fɑːsən) *vt* **1** befestigen. **2** anschnallen. *vi* sich klammern an.
fastidious (fə'stidiəs) *adj* anspruchsvall, penibel, wählerisch.
fat (fæt) *adj* fett, dick. *n* Fett *neu*. *vt* **1** fett machen. **2** (animals) mästen. *vi* fett werden.
fatal ('feitḷ) *adj* **1** tödlich. **2** verhängnisvoll, fatal. **fatality** *n* Todesfall *m*.
fate (feit) *n* Schicksal *neu*.
father ('fɑːðə) *n* Vater *m*. *vt* zeugen. **father-in-law** *n* Schwiegervater *m*. **fatherland** *n* Vaterland *neu*. Heimat *f*.
fathom ('fæðəm) *n* Faden *m*. *vt* **1** ergründen, begreifen. **2** sondieren.
fatigue (fə'tiːg) *n* Ermüdung *f*. *vi* ermüden.
fatuous ('fætjuəs) *adj* albern, blödsinnig.
fault (fɔːlt) *n* **1** Fehler *m*. **2** Schuld *f*. **3** *tech* Störung *f*. Defekt *m*. **be at fault** sich irren. **find fault** tadeln.
fauna ('fɔːnə) *n* Fauna, Tierwelt *f*.
favour ('feivə) *n* **1** Gefallen *m*. **2** Begünstigung *f*. *vt* **1** begünstigen. **2** vorziehen. **favourable** *adj* günstig, vorteilhaft, gelegen. **favourite** *adj* Lieblings—. *n* Liebling *m*. Favorit *m*.
fawn[1] (fɔːn) *n* Rehkalb *neu*. *adj* rehbraun.
fawn[2] (fɔːn) *vi* **1** kriechen. **2** schmeicheln.
fear (fiə) *n* Furcht, Angst *f*. *vt* (be)fürchten, sich fürchten vor. **fearless** *adj* furchtlos.
feasible ('fiːzibəl) *adj* möglich, ausführbar.
feast (fiːst) *n* Fest, Festmahl *neu*. *vi* sich ergötzen. **feast-day** *n* Festtag *m*.
feat (fiːt) *n* **1** Kunststück *neu*. **2** Heldentat *f*.
feather ('feðə) *n* Feder *f*. **featherbed** *n* Federbett *neu*. **featherweight** *n* Federgewicht *neu*.
feature ('fiːtʃə) *n* **1** (Gesichts)Zug *m*. **2** Grundzug *m*. **3** Merkmal *neu*. **4** (in a newspaper) Feature *neu*. spezieller Artikel *m*. *vt* **1** charakterisieren. **2** in der Hauptrolle zeigen.
February ('februəri) *n* Februar *m*.
feckless ('fekləs) *adj* **1** hilflos. **2** wirkungslos.
fed (fed) *v* see **feed.**
federal ('fedərəl) *adj* **1** Bundes—, bundesstaatlich. **2** (in Switzerland) eidgenössisch. **federate** *adj* verbündet. **federation** *n* **1** Vereinigung *f*. **2** *pol* Bundesstaat *m*.
fee (fiː) *n* Gebühr, Bezahlung *f*. Honorar *neu*

feeble ('fiːbəl) *adj* schwach, lahm, kraftlos. **feeble-minded** *adj* geistesschwach. **feeble-mindedness** *n* Schwachsinn *m*.

feed* (fiːd) *vt* **1** ernähren. **2** füttern. *vi* **1** sich (er)nähren. **2** weiden. *n* **1** Nahrung *f*. **2** Futter *neu*. **be fed up with** satt haben. **feedback** *n* Feedback *m*.

feel* (fiːl) *vt* **1** betasten, (be)fühlen. **2** spüren, wahrnehmen. **3** empfinden. *vi* **1** sich fühlen, sich vorkommen. **2** glauben. **feel like doing something** Lust haben, etwas zu tun. **feeler** *n* Fühler *m*. **feeling** *n* **1** Gefühl *neu*. **2** Empfindung *f*. **3** Ahnung *f*. **with feeling** *adv* gefühlvoll.

feign (fein) *vi,vt* vorgeben, simulieren. *vt* heucheln. **feigned** *adj* vorgeblich, heuchlerisch.

feint[1] (feint) *n* **1** Finte *f*. **2** Verstellung *f*.

feint[2] (feint) *adj,adv* schwach.

feline ('fiːlain) *adj* Katzen—, katzenartig.

fell[1] (fel) *v* see **fall.**

fell[2] (fel) *vt* **1** niederschlagen. **2** fällen.

fellow ('felou) *n* **1** Gefährte *m*. **2** Mitglied *neu*. **3** Kerl, Bursche *m*. **fellow passenger** Mitreisende(r) *m*. **fellowship** *n* Gemeinschaft *f*. Gesellschaft *f*.

felon ('felən) *n* Verbrecher *m*. **felonious** *adj* verbrecherisch. **felony** *n* schwere Verbrechen *neu*.

felt[1] (felt) *v* see **feel.**

felt[2] (felt) *n* Filz *m*.

female ('fiːmeil) *n* **1** Weib *neu*. **2** (of animals) Weibchen *neu*. *adj* weiblich.

feminine ('feminin) *adj* weiblich. **femininity** *n* Weiblichkeit *f*. weibliches Wesen *neu*.

feminism ('feminizəm) *n* Frauenrechtlertum *neu*. **feminist** *n* Frauenrechtler *m*.

fence (fens) *n* **1** Einzäunung *f*. Zaun *m*. *vi* fechten. **fence in** einzäunen. **fencing** *n* **1** Fechtkunst *f*. **2** Einzäunung *f*.

fend (fend) *vt* **fend off** abwehren. *vi* **fend for** sorgen für.

fennel ('fenl̩) *n bot* Fenchel *m*.

ferment (*n* 'fəːment; *v* fə'ment) *n* Gärungsmittel *neu*. *vi* gären, fermentieren. *vt* gären lassen. **fermentation** *n* Gärung *f*.

fern (fəːn) *n* Farn *m*. Farnkraut *neu*.

ferocious (fə'rouʃəs) *adj* **1** wild. **2** grausam. **ferocity** *n* **1** Wildheit *f*. **2** Grausamkeit *f*.

ferret ('ferit) *n* Frettchen *neu*. *v* **ferret out** **1** herausjagen. **2** ausforschen.

ferry ('feri) *n* Fähre *f*. *vt* übersetzen.

fertile ('fəːtail) *adj* **1** fruchtbar. **2** ergiebig. **fertility** *n* Fruchtbarkeit *f*. **fertilize** *vt* **1** fruchtbar machen. **2** *bot* befruchten. **3** düngen. **fertilization** *n* **1** Befruchtung *f*. **2** Düngung *f*. **fertilizer** *n* Düngemittel *neu*.

fervent ('fəːvənt) *adj* glühend, leidenschaftlich. **fervour** *n* Leidenschaft *f*. Eifer *m*.

fester ('festə) *vi* **1** eitern. **2** verfaulen.

festival ('festivəl) *n* Fest *neu.* Feier *f.* **festive** *adj* festlich. **festivity** *n* Festlichkeit *f.*
festoon (fes'tu:n) *n* Girlande *f. vt* schmücken.
fetch (fetʃ) *vt* **1** holen. **2** (in a sale) bringen. **fetching** *adj inf* reizend, anziehend.
fete (feit) *n* Fest *neu. vt* feiern.
fetid ('fetid) *adj* stinkend.
fetish ('fetiʃ) *n* Fetisch *m.*
fetter ('fetə) *n* Fessel *f. vt* fesseln.
feud (fju:d) *n* **1** Fehde *f.* **2** Lehen *neu.* **feudal** *adj* feudal. **feudalism** *n* Feudalismus *m.*
fever ('fi:və) *n* **1** *med* Fieber *neu.* **2** fieberhafte Aufregung *f.* **feverish** *adj* **1** fiebrig. **2** aufgeregt, fieberhaft.
few (fju:) *adj,pron* wenige. **a few** ein paar.
fiance (fi'ɔnsei) *n* Verlobte(r) *m.* **fiancee** *n* Verlobte, Braut *f.*
fiasco (fi'æskou) *n* Fiasko *neu.*
fib (fib) *n* Schwindelei, (kleine) Lüge *f.*
fibre ('faibə) *n* Faser, Fiber *f.* **fibreglass** *n* Fiberglas *neu.* **fibrous** *adj* faserig.
fickle ('fikəl) *adj* wankelmutig, unbeständig. **fickleness** *n* Wankelmut *m.* Unbeständigkeit *f.*
fiction ('fikʃən) *n* **1** Romanliteratur *f.* **2** Erdichtung *f.* **fictional** *adj* erdichtet, erfunden. **fictitious** *adj* unwirklich, erfunden.
fiddle ('fidl̩) *n* **1** Geige, Fiedel *f.* **2** *inf* Schwindelei *f. vi* **1** fiedeln. **2** tändeln. **3** beschwindeln.
fidelity (fi'deliti) *n* Treue *f.*
fidget ('fidʒit) *vi* (herum)-zappeln. **fidgety** *adj* zappelig.
field (fi:ld) *n* **1** Feld *neu.* **2** Gebiet, Fach *neu.* Bereich *m.* **3** *sport* Platz *m.* **fieldwork** *n* praktische (wissenschaftliche) Arbeit *f.*
fiend (fi:nd) *n* **1** Teufel *m.* **2** Unhold *m.* **fiendish** *adj* teuflisch, unmenschlich.
fierce (fiəs) *adj* **1** wild, grimmig. **2** heftig. **3** (of light) grell. **fierceness** *n* **1** Wildheit *f.* **2** Heftigkeit *f.*
fiery ('faiəri) *adj* feurig, leidenschaftlich.
fifteen (fif'ti:n) *adj* fünfzehn. *n* Fünfzehn *f.* **fifteenth** *adj* fünfzehnte.
fifth (fifθ) *adj* fünfte. **fifthly** *adv* fünftens.
fifty ('fifti) *adj* fünfzig. *n* Fünfzig *f.* **fifty-fifty** *adv* halb und halb, **fiftieth** *adj* fünfzigste.
fig (fig) *n* Feige *f.*
fight* (fait) *n* **1** Kampf *m.* **2** Konflikt *m.* **3** Schlägerei *f. vt* bekämpfen. *vi* kämpfen, sich schlagen. **fighter** *n* Kämpfer *m.*
figment ('figmənt) *n* (reine) Einbildung *f.*
figure ('figə) *n* **1** Ziffer *f.* **2** Gestalt, Figur *f.* **3** Persönlichkeit *f.* **4** Statue *f. vi* **1** erscheinen, auftreten. **2** meinen, denken. *vt* bildlich darstellen. **figure out** ausrechnen. **figurative** *adj* bildlich, symbolisch. **figurehead** *n* Repräsentationsfigur *f.* Strohmann *m.*
filament ('filəmənt) *n* **1** Faden

m. Faser *f.* **2** (in an electric appliance) Glühfaden *m.*

file[1] (fail) *n* **1** Akte *f.* **2** Mappe *f.* Ordner *m.* **3** Reihe *f.* **in single file** hintereinander. *vt* (ein)ordnen, ablegen. **filing cabinet** *n* Aktenschrank *m.*

file[2] (fail) *n* Feile *f.* *vt* (zu)feilen, glätten.

filial ('filiəl) *adj* kindlich, Kindes—.

fill (fil) *vt* **1** (ab-, er-)füllen. **2** sättigen. **3** besetzen. **4** (a tooth) plombieren. *vi* sich füllen. **fill up (with petrol)** (auf)tanken. **filling** *n* **1** Einlage *f.* **2** Füllung *f.* **3** *med* Zahnplombe *f.* *adj* sättigend. **filling station** *n* Tankstelle *f.*

fillet ('filit) *n cul* Filet *neu.*

filly ('fili) *n* weibliches Füllen *or* Fohlen *neu.*

film (film) *n* **1** Film *m.* **2** Haut, Membrane *f.* **3** *med* Schleier. *vt* (ver)filmen, drehen. *vi* drehen. **film star** *n* Filmstar, Filmschauspieler *m.*

filter ('filtə) *n* Filter *m.* *vt* filtern, filtrieren.

filth (filθ) *n* Dreck, Schmutz *m.* **filthiness** *n* Schmutzigkeit *f.* **filthy** *adj* schmutzig, drekkig.

fin (fin) *n* Flosse, Finne *f.*

final ('fainl̩) *adj* **1** letzt. **2** End—, Schluß—. **3** endgültig. *n sport* Endspiel *neu.* **finale** *n* Finale *neu.* **finalize** *vt* **1** vollenden, abschließen. **2** endgültige Form geben. **finally** *adv* **1** endlich, schließlich. **2** zum Schluß.

finance ('fainæns) *n* Finanz *f.* Finanzwesen *neu.* *vt* finanzieren. **financial** *adj* finanziell, Finanz—. **financier** *n* Financier *m.*

finch (fintʃ) *n* Fink *m.*

find* (faind) *vt* **1** finden, entdecken. **2** halten für, denken. **find out** herausfinden. ~*n* Fund *m.*

fine[1] (fain) *adj* **1** fein. **2** schön. **3** scharf. **finery** *n* **1** Putz *m.* **2** Eleganz *f.*

fine[2] (fain) *n* **1** Geldstrafe *f.* *vt* zu einer Geldstrafe verurteilen.

finesse (fi'nes) *n* **1** Finesse *f.* **2** Schlauheit *f.*

finger ('fiŋgə) *n* Finger *m.* *vt* fingern, betasten. **fingermark** *n* Fingerabdruck *m.* **fingernail** *n* Fingernagel *m.* **fingerprint** *n* Fingerabdruck *m.* **fingertip** *n* Fingerspitze *f.*

finish ('finiʃ) *vt* **1** beenden. **2** vollenden. *vi* enden, aufhören. *n* **1** *sport* Ziel *neu.* **2** Ende *neu.*

finite ('fainait) *adj* begrenzt, endlich. **finite verb** *n gram* Verbum finitum *neu.*

Finland ('finlənd) *n* Finnland *neu.*

Finn *n* Finne *m.* **Finnish** *adj* finnisch. *n* (language) Finnisch *neu.*

fir (fəː) *n* Tanne *f.* **fircone** *n* Tannenzapfen *m.*

fire (faiə) *n* **1** Feuer *neu.* **2** Brand *m.* **on fire** in Flammen. ~*vt* **1** anzünden. **2** anfeuern. *vi* feuern. **fire away!** schieß los!

fire alarm *n* Feuermelder, Feueralarm *m.*

fire brigade *n* Feuerwehr *f.*

fire drill *n* Feueralarmübung *f.*

fire-engine *n* Motorspritze *f.* Feuerwehrauto *neu.*

fire-escape *n* Nottreppe *f.*

fire-extinguisher *n* Feuerlöscher *m*.
fireman ('faiəmən) *n* Feuerwehrmann *m*.
fireplace ('faiəpleis) *n* (offener) Kamin *m*.
fireproof ('faiəpru:f) *adj* feuerfest.
fireside ('faiəsaid) *n* Kamin *m*. *adj* häuslich.
fire station *n* Feuerwache *f*.
firework ('faiəwə:k) *n* Feuerwerk *neu*.
firing squad *n* Exekutionskommando *neu*.
firm[1] (fə:m) *adj* **1** fest. **2** standhaft. **3** entschlossen. **firmness** *n* **1** Festigkeit *f*. **2** Entschlossenheit *f*.
firm[2] (fəim) *n* Firma *f*.
first (fə:st) *adj* **1** erste. **2** beste. *adv* **1** erstens. **2** zuerst. **at first** anfangs, zuerst. **first of all** zuallererst. ~*n* Erste(r) *m*. **first aid** *n* Nothilfe *f*. *adj* Unfalls—. **first class** *n* erste Klasse *f*. **first-class** *adj* prima, erstklassig, ausgezeichnet. **first-hand** *adv* aus erster Hand, direkt. **first name** *n* Vorname *m*. **first person** *n gram* erste Person *f*. **first-rate** *adj* ausgezeichnet.
fiscal ('fiskəl) *adj* fiskalisch, Finanz—.
fish (fiʃ) *n, pl* **fishes** or **fish** Fisch *m*. **queer fish** *n* komischer Kauz *m*. **a pretty kettle of fish** eine schöne Bescherung *f*. *vi* fischen, angeln. **fisherman** *n* Fischer *m*. **fish finger** *n* Fischstäbchen *neu*. **fishing** *n* Fischen, Angeln *neu*. **fishing rod** *n* Angelrute *f*. **fishmonger** *n* Fischhändler *m*. **fish-slice** *n* Fischheber *m*. **fishy** *adj* **1** fischig. **2** verdächtig.
fission ('fiʃən) *n* Spaltung *f*.
fist (fist) *n* Faust *f*.
fit[1] (fit) *adj* **1** passend. **2** *sport* in Form, fit. **3** fähig. **fit as a fiddle** kerngesund. ~*vt* **1** passen. **2** passend machen, anpassen. *vi* **1** sich eignen. **2** (of clothes) sitzen. *n* (of clothes) Sitz *m*. **fitting** *adj* passend, schicklich.
fit[2] (fit) *n* **1** *med* Anfall *m*. **2** Ausbruch *m*. **fitful** *adj* **1** unbeständig. **2** launenhaft.
five (faiv) *adj* fünf. *n* Fünf *f*.
fix (fiks) *vt* **1** befestigen, anheften. **2** (one's eyes) richten, heften. **3** bestimmen, festsetzen. *vi* fest werden. **fix up** arrangieren. **fixation** *n* Fixierung *f*. **fixed** *adj* starr. **2** bestimmt. **fixture** *n* Zubehör(teil) *m*.
fizz (fiz) *vi* zischen, sprudeln. *n* Zischen *neu*. **fizzle** *vi* zischen. **fizzle out** verpuffen.
fjord (fjɔ:d) *n* Fjord *m*.
flabbergast ('flæbəgɑ:st) *vt* verblüffen.
flabby ('flæbi) *adj* schlaff, schlapp.
flag[1] (flæg) *n* Fahne, Flagge *f*. *vt* beflaggen. **flagpole** *n* Fahnenstange *f*.
flag[2] (flæg) *vi* **1** ermatten. **2** mutlos werden.
flagon ('flægən) *n* (bauchige) Flasche *f*.
flagrant ('fleigrənt) *adj* **1** schamlos. **2** offenkundig.
flair ('flɛə) *n* Spürsinn, Flair *m*.
flake (fleik) *n* **1** Flocke *f*. **2** Schuppe *f*. Blatt *neu*. *vi* (sich)

flocken. *vi,vt* abblättern. **flaky** *adj* flockig, schuppig.

flamboyant (flæm'bɔiənt) *adj* **1** auffallend. **2** überladen. **3** flammend.

flame (fleim) *n* **1** Flamme *f.* **2** Leidenschaft *f.* *vi* flammen, lodern.

flamingo (flə'miŋgou) *n* Flamingo *m.*

flan (flæn) *n* Torte *f.*

flank (flæŋk) *n* **1** *mil* Flanke *f.* **2** *zool* Weiche *f.* *vt* flankieren.

flannel ('flænl̩) *n* **1** Flanell *m.* **2** Waschlappen *m.*

flap (flæp) *n* **1** *anat* Lappen *m.* **2** Klappe *f.* **3** (Flügel)Schlag *m.* *vi* **1** flattern. **2** lose herabhängen.

flare (flɛə) *vi* **1** flackern. **2** sich bauschen. *n* **1** flackerndes Licht *neu.* **2** Lichtsignal *neu.* *v* **flare up 1** aufflackern. **2** aufbrausen.

flash (flæʃ) *n* **1** Blitz *m.* **2** Aufblitzen *neu.* *vi* (auf)blitzen. *vt* werfen. **flashback** *n* Rückblende *f.* **flashbulb** *n* Blitzlichtlampe *f.* **flashlight** *n* **1** Blitzlicht *neu.* Taschenlampe *f.*

flask (flɑːsk) *n* **1** (Taschen-, Reise-) Flasche *f.* **2** *sci* Kolben *m.*

flat[1] (flæt) *adj* **1** flach, platt. **2** eben. *n* **1** Fläche *f.* **2** Flachland *neu.* **flatfish** *n* Plattfisch *m.* **flat-footed** *adj* plattfüßig. **flatten** *vt* platt machen, (ein)ebnen. *vi* flach werden.

flat[2] (flæt) *n* Wohnung *f.*

flatter ('flætə) *vt* schmeicheln. **flatterer** *n* Schmeichler *m.* **flattering** *adj* schmeichelhaft. **flattery** *n* Schmeichelei *f.*

flaunt (flɔːnt) *vt* **1** prunken. **2** offen zeigen.

flautist ('flɔːtist) *n* Flötist *m.*

flavour ('fleivə) *n* Geschmack *m.* Aroma *neu.* **flavouring** *n* Würze *f.* Geschmackstoff *m.*

flaw (flɔː) *n* **1** Sprung *m.* **2** Makel *m.* **flawless** *adj* **1** makellos. **2** tadellos.

flax (flæks) *n* Flachs *m.*

flea (fliː) *n* Floh *m.*

fleck (flek) *n* Fleck *m.* *vt* sprenkeln.

fled (fled) *v* see **flee.**

flee* (fliː) *vi* fliehen. *vt* meiden.

fleece (fliːs) *n* Fell, Vlies *neu.* *vt* schröpfen. **fleecy** *adj* wollig.

fleet (fliːt) *n* Flotte *f.*

fleeting ('fliːtiŋ) *adj* flüchtig, vergänglich.

Flemish ('flemiʃ) *adj* flämisch. *n* (language) Flämisch *neu.*

flesh (fleʃ) *n* Fleisch *neu.* **fleshy** *adj* **1** fleischig. **2** fett.

flew (fluː) *v* see **fly**[1].

flex (fleks) *n* Kabel *neu.* *vt* biegen, beugen. **flexible** *adj* **1** biegsam. **2** flexibel. **flexibility** *n* Biegsamkeit *f.*

flick (flik) *vt* schnellen. *n* (leichter) Hieb *m.*

flicker ('flikə) *n* Flackern *neu.* *vi* flackern.

flight[1] (flait) *n* **1** Flug *m.* **2** Schwarm *m.* **flight deck** *n* Flugdeck *neu.* **flight of stairs** *n* Treppe *f.*

flight[2] (flait) *n* Flucht *f.* **flighty** *adj* flüchtig.

flimsy ('flimzi) *adj* **1** dünn. **2** schwach.

flinch (flintʃ) *vi* zurückschrecken, zucken.

fling* (fliŋ) *vt* werfen, schleudern. *n* Hieb *m*.

flint (flint) *n* **1** Kiesel *m*. **2** Flint *m*.

flip (flip) *n* Klaps *m*. *vt* klapsen, schnellen. **flipper** *n* **1** *zool* Flosse *f*. **2** Schwimmflosse *f*.

flippant ('flipənt) *adj* leichtfertig. **flippancy** *n* Leichtfertigkeit, Frechheit *f*.

flirt (flə:t) *vi* flirten. **flirtation** *n* Liebelei *f*. Flirt *m*. **flirtatious** *adj* kokett.

flit (flit) *vi* **1** flitzen. **2** wegziehen, sich entfernen.

float (flout) *vi* **1** (obenauf) schwimmen. **2** schweben. *vt* **1** bewässern. **2** flottmachen. **3** flößen. *n* **1** *tech* Schwimmer *m*. **2** Floß *neu*.

flock[1] (flɔk) *n* **1** Herde *f*. **2** Schar *f*. *vi* **1** sich scharen. **2** zusammenströmen.

flock[2] (flɔk) *n* (Woll)Flocke *f*.

flog (flɔg) *vt* **1** (aus)peitschen. **2** prügeln, züchtigen. **3** *sl* verkaufen. **flogging** *n* **1** Prügelstrafe *f*. **2** (Aus)Peitschen *neu*.

flood (flʌd) *n* **1** Flut *f*. **2** Überschwemmung *f*. *vt,vi* **1** überfluten. **2** überschwemmen. **floodlight** *n* Scheinwerfer *m*. Flutlicht *neu*.

floor (flɔ:) *n* **1** Fußboden *m*. **2** Stock *m*. Stockwerk, Geschoß *neu*. Etage *f*. *vt* **1** einen Fußboden legen. **2** *inf* verblüffen. **floorboard** *n* Diele *f*. Fußbodenbrett *neu*.

flop (flɔp) *vi* **1** (hin)plumpsen. **2** flattern, schlottern. **3** *Th* durchfallen. *n* **1** Plumps *m*. **2** Versager, Durchfall *m*. **floppy** *adj* schlapp.

flora ('flɔ:rə) *n* Flora, Pflanzenwelt *f*. **floral** *adj* Blumen—, Blüte—. **florist** *n* Blumenhändler *m*.

flounce[1] (flauns) *vi* stürzen.

flounce[2] (flauns) *n* Volant *m*.

flounder[1] ('flaundə) *vi* taumeln, stolpern.

flounder[2] ('flaundə) *n* Flunder *f*.

flour ('flauə) *n* Mehl *neu*. *vt* mit Mehl bestreuen.

flourish ('flʌriʃ) *n* **1** Schnörkel *m*. **2** Schwingen *neu*. **3** *mus* Verzierung *f*. *vi* **1** blühen, gedeihen. **2** Schnörkel machen. *vt* schwingen.

flout (flaut) *vt* verspotten, verhöhnen.

flow (flou) *vi* **1** fließen. **2** wallen. *n* Fluß *m*.

flower ('flauə) *n* **1** Blume *f*. **2** Blüte *f*. *vi* blühen. **flowerbed** *n* Blumenbeet *neu*. **flowerpot** *n* Blumentopf *m*. **flowery** *adj* blumig.

flown *v* see **fly**[1].

fluctuate ('flʌktʃueit) *vi* schwanken, fluktuieren. **fluctuation** *n* **1** Schwanken *neu*. Schwankung *f*. **2** *comm* Fluktuieren *neu*.

flue (flu:) *n* Kaminrohr, Abzugsrohr *neu*.

fluent ('flu:ənt) *adj* fließend. **fluency** *n* Fluß *m*. Geläufigkeit *f*.

fluff (flʌf) *n* **1** Flaum *m*. **2** Staubflocke *f*. **fluffy** *adj* **1** flaumig. **2** flockig.

fluid ('flu:id) *n* Flüssigkeit *f*. *adj* **1** flüssig. **2** fließend. **3** veränderlich.

flung (flʌŋ) *v* see **fling**.

fluorescent (fluə'resənt) *adj*

fluoreszierend. **fluorescence** *n* Fluoreszenz *f.*
fluoride ('fluəraid) *n* Fluor *neu.*
flush[1] (flʌʃ) *vi* erröten. *vt* (aus)spülen. *n* **1** Erröten *neu.* **2** Spülung *f.*
flush[2] (flʌʃ) *adj* eben, glatt. **be flush** *inf* gut bei Kasse sein.
fluster ('flʌstə) *n* Verwirrung *f.* *vt* verwirren.
flute (fluːt) *n mus* Flöte *f.*
flutter ('flʌtə) *vi,(vt)* flattern (lassen).
flux (flʌks) *n* **1** Fluß *m.* **2** beständiger Wechsel *m.*
fly*[1] (flai) *vi* **1** fliegen. **2** fliehen. *vt* fliegen (lassen). **flyover** *n* (Straßen)Überführung *f.*
fly[2] (flai) *n* Fliege *f.*
foal (foul) *n* Fohlen *neu.* *vi* fohlen.
foam (foum) *n* Schaum *m.* *vi* schäumen. **foamy** *adj* schaumig.
focal ('foukəl) *adj* im Brennpunkt stehend, fokal. **focus** *n* Fokus, Brennpunkt *m.* *vt* fokussieren, einstellen.
fodder ('fɔdə) *n* Futter *neu.* *vt* füttern.
foe (fou) *n* Feind *m.*
foetus ('fiːtəs) *n* Fötus *m.* Leibesfrucht *f.*
fog (fɔg) *n* **1** (dicker) Nebel *m.* **2** Schleier, Dunst *m.* *vt,vi* verschleiern. **foggy** *adj* **1** nebelig. **2** verschleiert, unklar. **foghorn** *n* Nebelhorn *neu.*
foible ('fɔibəl) *n* Schwäche *f.*
foil[1] (fɔil) *vt* vereiteln.
foil[2] (fɔil) *n* Folie *f.* Blattmetall *neu.*
foil[3] (fɔil) *n sport* Florett *neu.*
foist (fɔist) *vt* **1** aufhalsen. **2** unterschieben.
fold[1] (fould) *vt* **1** falten. **2** (one's arms) kreuzen. *vi* **1** sich falten. **2** sich zusammenklappen (lassen). *n* Falte *f.*
fold[2] (fould) *n* **1** (Schaf)Hürde *f.* **2** Herde *f.*
foliage ('fouliidʒ) *n* Laub *neu.*
folk (fouk) *n pl* Leute *pl.* *adj* Volks—. **folkdance** *n* Volkstanz *m.* **folklore** *n* Volkssagen *f pl.* **folksong** *n* Volkslied *neu.*
follicle ('fɔlikəl) *n* **1** Follikel *m.* **2** Haarbalg *m.*
follow ('fɔlou) *vt,vi* folgen, nachgehen. **follower** *n* **1** Nachfolger *m.* **2** Anhänger *m.* **following** *n* Anhängerschaft *f.*
folly ('fɔli) *n* Torheit, Narrheit *f.*
fond (fɔnd) *adj* **1** liebevoll. **2** (of a hope, etc.) töricht. **be fond of** gern haben.
fondle ('fɔndḷ) *vt* liebkosen, streicheln.
font (fɔnt) *n* Taufstein *m.*
food (fuːd) *n* **1** Nahrung, Kost *f.* Essen *neu.* Lebensmittel *neu pl.* **2** Futter *neu.*
fool (fuːl) *n* Narr, Dumme(r) *m.* *vt* zum Narren haben. *vi* Spaß machen. **foolish** *adj* **1** närrisch, albern, dumm. **2** unklug. **foolishness** *n* Dummheit *f.*
foolscap ('fuːlzkæp) *n* **1** Kanzleipapier *neu.* **2** Aktenformat *neu.*
foot (fut) *n, pl* **feet** **1** Fuß *m.* **2** Fußende *neu.* **on foot** zu Fuß. ~*vt* (bill) bezahlen. **foot it** *inf* zu Fuß gehen. **football** *n* **1** Fußball *m.* **2** Fußballspiel *neu.*

footbridge *n* Steg *m.* Fußgängerbrücke *f.* **foothold** *n* **1** fester Stand *m.* **2** Halt *m.* **footing** *n* **1** Halt *m.* **2** Grundlage *f.* **3** Verhältnis *neu.* **footlights** *n pl Th* **1** Rampenlichter *neu pl.* **2** Bühne *f.* **footnote** *n* Anmerkung, Fußnote *f.* **footprint** *n* Fußspur *f.* **footstep** *n* **1** Spur *f.* **2** Tritt *m.* **footwear** *n* Schuhwerk *neu.*

for (fə; *stressed* fɔː) *prep* **1** für. **2** zu, nach. **3** aus, vor. **4** lang. *conj* denn.

forage ('fɔridʒ) *n* Futter neu. *vi* **1** Futter holen. **2** durchstöbern, herumsuchen.

forbear* (fə'bɛə) *vi* **1** sich enthalten. **2** gedulden. *vt* sich enthalten, unterlassen. **forbearance** *n* **1** Geduld *f.* **2** Unterlassung *f.*

forbid* (fə'bid) *vt* verbieten, untersagen. **forbidding** *adj* **1** abstoßend. **2** gefährlich.

force (fɔːs) *n* **1** Kraft, Stärke *f.* **2** Zwang *m.* **3** Gewalt *f.* **4** *pl* Streitkräfte *f pl.* *vt* **1** zwingen. **2** (a door) aufbrechen. **force-feed** *vt* zwangsweise ernähren. **forceful** *adj* **1** kräftig. **2** eindringlich. **forcible** *adj* gewaltsam.

forceps ('fɔːseps) *n s or pl* Zange *f.*

ford (fɔːd) *n* Furt *f.* *vt* durchwaten.

fore (fɔː) *adv* vorn *n.* Vorderteil *neu.* *adj* vorder, Vorder—.

forearm[1] ('fɔːraːm) *n* Vorderarm *m.*

forearm[2] (fɔː'raːm) *vt* im voraus bewaffnen.

forebear (fə'bɛə) *n* Vorfahr *m.*

forecast ('fɔːkaːst) *n* Vorhersage, Voraussage *f.* **weather forecast** *n* Wetterbericht *m.* ~*vt* vorhersagen, voraussagen.

forefather ('fɔːfaːðə) *n* Vorfahr *m.*

forefinger ('fɔːfiŋgə) *n* Zeigefinger *m.*

forefront ('fɔːfrʌnt) *n* **1** Vorderseite *f.* **2** vorderste Reihe *f.*

foreground ('fɔːgraund) *n* Vordergrund *m.*

forehand ('fɔːhænd) *n* Vorhand *f.* *adj* mit Vorhand gespielt.

forehead ('fɔrid) *n* Stirn *f.*

foreign ('fɔrin) *adj* **1** fremd. **2** ausländisch. **foreigner** *n* **1** Ausländer *m.* **2** Fremde(r) *m.* **foreign exchange** *n* Devisen *f pl.*

foreleg ('fɔːleg) *n* Vorderbein *neu.*

forelock ('fɔːlɔk) *n* Stirnlocke *f.*

foreman ('fɔːmən) *n* Aufseher, Vorarbeiter *m.*

foremost ('fɔːmoust) *adj* vorderst, erst. *adv* zuerst.

forensic (fə'rensik) *adj* gerichtlich, Gerichts—.

forerunner ('fɔːrʌnə) *n* Vorläufer *m.*

foresee* (fɔː'siː) *vt* voraussehen. **forseeable** *adj* absehbar.

foresight ('fɔːsait) *n* Voraussicht *f.*

forest ('fɔrist) *n* Wald, Forst *m.* *adj* Wald—, Forst—. *vt* beforsten. **forester** *n* Förster *m.* **forestry** *n* Forstwirtschaft *f.*

forestall (fɔː'stɔːl) *vt* vereiteln.

foretaste ('fɔːteist) *n* Vorgeschmack *m.*

foretell* (fɔː'tel) *vt* **1** voraussagen. **2** vorbedeuten.
forethought ('fɔːθɔːt) *n* Vorbedacht *m*.
forfeit ('fɔːfit) *n* **1** Verwirkung *f*. **2** Buße *f*. **3** Pfand *neu*. *vt* **1** verwirken. **2** einbüßen. **3** verlieren. *adj* verwirkt.
forge[1] (fɔːdʒ) *n* Schmiede *f*. *vt* **1** schmieden. **2** fälschen.
forge[2] *vi* (fɔːdʒ) **forge ahead** sich vorwärtsdrängen, an die Spitze kommen.
forgery ('fɔːdʒəri) *n* Fälschung *f*.
forget* (fə'get) *vt* **1** vergessen. **2** vernachlässigen. **forgetful** *adj* vergeßlich.
forgive* (fə'giv) *vt* verzeihen, vergeben. **forgiveness** *n* Verzeihung, Vergebung *f*. **forgiving** *adj* versöhnlich.
forgo* (fɔː'gou) *vt* verzichten auf.
fork (fɔːk) *n* **1** Gabel *f*. **2** (in a road, etc.) Gabelung *f*. *vi* sich gabeln. **fork out** Geld herausrücken. **forked** *adj* gabelförmig.
forlorn (fə'lɔːn) *adj* **1** verloren. **2** hoffnungslos. **3** hilflos.
form (fɔːm) *n* **1** Form, Figur, Gestalt *f*. **2** Art, Weise, Methode *f*. **3** Förmlichkeit *f*. **4** Formular *neu*. **5** (Schul)Klasse *f*. **6** (Schul)Bank *f*. *vt* **1** formen, bilden, gestalten. **2** erdenken. **3** schließen. *vi* sich formen. **formal** *adj* **1** formal, förmlich. **2** formell, feierlich. **formality** *n* Formalität, Förmlichkeit *f*. **formation** *n* **1** Bildung, Gestaltung *f*. **2** Formation *f*. **formative** *adj* bildend, gestaltend. **formative years** *n pl* Entwicklungsjahre *neu pl*.
former ('fɔːmə) *adj* **1** vorig. **2** ehemalig. **3** jene. **formerly** *adv* ehemals.
formidable ('fɔːmidəbəl) *adj* **1** furchtbar, erschreckend. **2** ungeheuer, gewaltig.
formula ('fɔːmjulə) *n* Formel *f*. **formulate** *vt* formulieren.
forsake* (fə'seik) *vt* **1** aufgeben. **2** verlassen.
fort (fɔːt) *n* Fort *neu*. Festung *f*.
forte ('fɔːtei) *n* Stärke *f*. *adv mus* forte.
forth (fɔːθ) *adv* hervor. **from this day forth** von heute an. **forthcoming** *adj* bevorstehend.
fortify ('fɔːtifai) *vt* **1** befestigen. **2** stärken. **fortification** *n* **1** Befestigung *f*. **2** Stärkung *f*.
fortnight ('fɔːtnait) *n* vierzehn Tage *m pl*.
fortress ('fɔːtrəs) *n* Festung *f*.
fortune ('fɔːtʃən) *n* **1** Glück *neu*. **2** Schicksal *neu*. **3** Vermögen *neu*. **fortunate** *adj* glücklich. **fortunately** *adv* glücklicherweise.
forty ('fɔːti) *adj* vierzig. *n* Vierzig *f*. **fortieth** *adj* vierzigste.
forum ('fɔːrəm) *n* **1** Forum *neu*. **2** Tribunal *neu*.
forward ('fɔːwəd) *adj* **1** vorder, vornliegend. **2** fortschrittlich. **3** vorlaut. *adv* **1** vorwärts. **2** nach vorn. *vt* **1** befördern. **2** nachsenden. **forwards** *adv* vorwärts.
fossil ('fɔsəl) *n* Fossil *neu*. *adj* versteinert.
foster ('fɔstə) *vt* pflegen, aufziehen. *adj* Pflege—. **fos-**

terchild *n* Pflegekind *neu.* **fostermother** *n* Pflegemutter *f.*

fought (fɔːt) *v* see **fight.**

foul (faul) *adj* schmutzig, ekelhaft, übel, widrig. *vi* schmutzig werden. *vt* verschmutzen. *n sport* Regelverstoß *m.* Foul *neu.*

found[1] (faund) *v* see **find.**

found[2] (faund) *vt* (be)gründen, stiften. **foundation** *n* Gründung, Stiftung *f. adj* Grund—.

founder ('faundə) *vi* **1** *naut* sinken, untergehen. **2** scheitern. *vt* zum Scheitern bringen.

foundry ('faundri) *n* Gießerei, Hütte *f.*

fountain ('fauntin) *n* **1** Springbrunnen *m.* **2** Quelle *f.* **fountain pen** *n* Füllfeder *f.*

four (fɔː) *adj* vier. *n* Vier *f.* **four-poster** *n* Himmelbett *neu.* **foursome** *n* **1** *sport* Viererspiel *neu.* **2** Quartett *neu.* **fourth** *adj* vierte. **fourthly** *adv* viertens.

fourteen (fɔː'tiːn) *adj* vierzehn. *n* Vierzehn *f.* **fourteenth** *adj* vierzehnte.

fowl (faul) *n* **1** Geflügel *neu.* **2** Huhn *neu.*

fox (fɔks) *n* Fuchs *m. vt* täuschen, betrügen, verwirren. **foxglove** *n bot* Fingerhut *m.* **foxhunting** *n* Fuchsjagd *f.*

foyer ('fɔiei) *n* Foyer *neu.*

fraction ('frækʃən) *n* **1** *math* Bruch *m.* **2** Bruchteil *m.*

fracture ('fræktʃə) *n med* Knochenbruch *m. vt* brechen.

fragile ('frædʒail) *adj* zerbrechlich, zart.

fragment ('frægmənt) *n* Bruchstück *neu.* Splitter *m.* Scherbe *f.* **fragmentary** *adj* bruchstückhaft, unvollständig, fragmentarisch.

fragrant ('freigrənt) *adj* duftend.

frail (freil) *adj* **1** zerbrechlich. **2** schwach. **frailty** *n* Schwachheit *f.*

frame (freim) *n* **1** Rahmen *m.* **2** Gestell *neu. vt* **1** (ein)rahmen. **2** bilden, bauen. **framework** *n* **1** Gerippe *neu.* **2** Bau *m.* **3** Rahmen *m.*

franc (fræŋk) *n* **1** (französischer) Franc *m.* **2** (schweizerischer) Franken *m.*

France (frɑːns) *n* Frankreich *neu.*

franchise ('fræntʃaiz) *n* **1** Wahlrecht *neu.* **2** Bürgerrecht *neu.* **3** *US* Konzession *f.*

frank (fræŋk) *adj* offen, freimütig. *vt* (maschinell) frankieren.

frankfurter ('fræŋkfəːtə) *n* Frankfurter *f.*

frantic ('fræntik) *adj* **1** wahnsinnig. **2** verzweifelt, außer sich.

fraternal (frə'təːnḷ) *adj* brüderlich. **fraternity** *n* **1** Brüderlichkeit *f.* **2** Bruderschaft *f.* **fraternize** *vi* sich verbrüdern. **fraternization** *n* Verbrüderung *f.*

fraud (frɔːd) *n* **1** Betrug *m.* **2** Schwindel *m.* **3** Betrüger, Schwindler *m.* **fraudulence** *n* Betrügerei *f.* **fraudulent** *adj* betrügerisch.

fraught (frɔːt) *adj* beladen, voll (von).

fray[1] (frei) *n* Streit *m.* Schlägerei *f.*

fray[2] (frei) *(vt),vi* (sich) ausfransen.

freak (fri:k) *n* **1** Laune *f.* Einfall *m.* **2** Abnormität, Mißbildung *f. adj* **1** launenhaft. **2** abnorm, grotesk.

freckle ('frekəl) *n* Sommersprosse *f.*

free (fri:) *adj* **1** frei. **2** ungebunden, unabhängig. **3** kostenlos, umsonst, gratis. **4** freigebig, großzügig. *vt* befreien. **freedom** *n* Freiheit *f.* **freehand** *adj* freihändig. **freehold** *n* eigener Grundbesitz *m.* **freelance** *adj* freischaffend, selbständig. **freely** *adv* **1** freiwillig. **2** reichlich. **Freemason** *n* Freimaurer *m.* **freewheel** *n* Freilauf *m. vi* im Freilauf fahren. **free will** *n* freier Wille *m.*

freeze* (fri:z) *vi* **1** (ge)frieren. **2** erstarren. *vt* **1** frieren, tiefkühlen. **2** (credit) sperren. **3** (wages, prices) stoppen. *n* **1** (Ge)frieren *neu.* **2** Lohnstopp *m.* **3** Preisstopp *m.* **freezing** *adj* eisig. **freezing point** *n* Gefrierpunkt *m.*

freight (freit) *n* **1** Fracht *f.* **2** Frachtgeld *neu. vt* **1** beladen. **2** befrachten. **freight train** *n* Güterzug *m.*

French (frentʃ) *adj* französisch. *n* (language) Französisch *neu.* **French bean** *n* grüne Bohne *f.* **French horn** *n* Waldhorn *neu.* **Frenchman** *n* Franzose *m.* **French window** *n* Flügeltür *f.* **Frenchwoman** *n* Französin *f.*

frenzy ('frenzi) *n* Wahnsinn *m.* Raserei *f.* **frenzied** *adj* wahnsinnig, rasend.

frequency ('fri:kwənsi) *n* **1** Häufigkeit *f.* **2** *sci* Frequenz *f.* **frequent** *adj* häufig, öfters. *vt* häufig *or* öfters besuchen, frequentieren.

fresco ('freskou) *n* Fresko(gemälde) *neu.*

fresh (freʃ) *adj* **1** frisch. **2** unerfahren. **3** neu. **4** *sl* frech. **freshen up** *vt,vi* auffrischen. **freshwater** *n* Süßwasser *neu. adj* Süßwasser—.

fret[1] (fret) *vt* zerfressen. *vi* sich ärgern. **fretful** *adj* ärgerlich, mürrisch.

fret[2] (fret) *n* Flechtband *neu.* **fretsaw** *n* Laubsäge *f.*

friar ('fraiə) *n* Mönch *m.* **friary** *n* Mönchskloster *neu.*

friction ('frikʃən) *n* Reibung *f.*

Friday ('fraidi) *n* Freitag *m.*

fridge (fridʒ) *n inf* Kühlschrank *m.*

fried (fraid) *v* see **fry.** *adj* gebraten, Brat—. **fried egg** *n* Spiegelei *neu.*

friend (frend) *n* **1** Freund *m.* **2** Bekannte(r) *m.* **make friends with** sich anfreunden mit. **friendliness** *n* Freundlichkeit *f.* **friendly** *adj* **1** freundlich. **2** befreundet. **3** wohlwollend. **friendship** *n.* Freundschaft *f.*

frieze (fri:z) *n* Fries *m.*

fright (frait) *n* Schreck, Schrecken *m.* **frighten** *vt* erschrecken. **be frightened of** Angst haben vor. **frightful** *adj* schrecklich.

frigid ('fridʒid) *adj* **1** kalt. **2** frigid. **frigidity** *n* **1** Kälte *f.* **2** Frigidität *f.*

frill (fril) *n* Krause *f.* *vt* kräuseln.
fringe ('frindʒ) *n* **1** Franse *f.* **2** Rand *m.* *vt* **1** mit Fransen besetzen. **2** säumen.
frisk (frisk) *vi* hüpfen. *vt sl* durchsuchen, filzen. **frisky** *adj* **1** hüpfend. **2** munter.
fritter[1] ('fritə) *vt* **fritter away** verzetteln, verschwenden, vergeuden.
fritter[2] ('fritə) *n* in Eierteig gebackene Obstscheiben *f pl.*
frivolity (fri'vɔliti) *n* Leichtfertigkeit *f.* **frivolous** *adj* leichtfertig.
frizz (friz) *(vi),vt* (sich) kräuseln. **frizzy** *adj* kraus, gekräuselt.
frizzle[1] ('frizḷ) *(vi),vt* (sich) kräuseln.
frizzle[2] ('frizəl) *vi* zischen.
fro (fro) *adv* **to and fro** hin und her, auf und ab.
frock (frɔk) *n* **1** Damenkleid, Kinderkleid *neu.* **2** *rel* Kutte *f.* **frockcoat** *n* Gehrock *m.*
frog (frɔg) *n* Frosch *m.* **frogman** *n* Froschmann *m.*
frolic ('frɔlik) *n* **1** lustiger Streich, Spaß *m.* **2** Lustbarkeit *f.* *vi* scherzen. **frolicsome** *adj* lustig, vergnügt.
from (frəm; *stressed* frɔm) *prep* **1** von, aus, von...her. **2** seit. **3** nach.
front (frʌnt) *n* **1** Vorderseite *f.* Vorderteil *m.* **2** Front *f.* *adj* Vorder—. **in front** *adv* vorne. **in front of** *prep* vor.
frontier ('frʌntiə) *n* Grenze *f.* *adj* Grenz—.
frost (frɔst) *n* Frost *m.* **frostbite** *n* Erfrierung *f.* **frosty** *adj* frostig.
froth (frɔθ) *n* Schaum *m.* *vi* schäumen. *vt* zu Schaum schlagen. **frothy** *adj* schaumig.
frown (fraun) *n* **1** Stirnrunzeln *neu.* **2** finsterer Blick *m.* *vi* **1** die Stirn runzeln. **2** finster blicken.
froze (frouz) *v* see **freeze.**
frozen ('frouzṇ) *v* see **freeze.** *adj* **1** gefroren. **2** *cul* Gefrier—. **frozen food** *n* tiefgekühlte Lebensmittel *f pl.*
frugal ('fru:gəl) *adj* **1** frugal, mäßig. **2** sparsam. **frugality** *n* **1** Mäßigkeit. **2** Sparsamkeit *f.*
fruit (fru:t) *n* **1** Frucht *f.* **2** Früchte *f pl.* Obst *neu.* **fruitful** *adj* **1** fruchtbar. **2** ergiebig. **fruition** *n* **1** Genuß *m.* **2** Erfüllung *f.* **fruitless** *adj* **1** unfruchtbar. **2** vergeblich, fruchtlos. **fruit machine** *n* Spielautomat *m.* **fruit salad** *n* Obstsalat *m.* **fruity** *adj* fruchtig, saftig.
frustrate (frʌs'treit) *vt* vereiteln, verhindern. **frustration** *n* Vereitelung, Enttäuschung *f.*
fry (frai) *vt* braten, (in der Pfanne) backen. **frying pan** *n* Bratpfanne *f.* **out of the frying pan into the fire** aus dem Regen in die Traufe.
fuchsia ('fju:ʃə) *n* Fuschsie *f.*
fuck (fʌk) *vi,(vt)* *tab* sich paaren (mit).
fudge (fʌdʒ) *n* Weichkaramelle *f.* *vt inf* (zurecht)pfuschen.
fuel ('fju:əl) *n* **1** Brennstoff *m.* **2** Treibstoff *m.* *vt* **1** mit Brennstoff versehen. **2** tanken.

fugitive ('fjuːdʒitiv) *n* Flüchtling *m*. *adj* flüchtig.

fulcrum ('fʌlkrəm) *n* Drehpunkt *m*.

fulfil (ful'fil) *vt* erfüllen. **fulfilment** *n* Erfüllung *f*.

full (ful) *adj* **1** voll. **2** besetzt. **3** satt. *adv* direkt, gerade, völlig. **to the full** *adv* vollständig. **full-length** *adj* in Lebensgröße *f*. **full moon** *n* Vollmond *m*. **fullness** *n* Fülle *f*. **full stop** *n* Punkt *m*. **full-time** *adj* ganztägig, Vollzeit—. **fully** *adv* voll, ausführlich.

fumble ('fʌmbəl) *vi* umhertappen, fummeln. **fumbling** *adj* **1** tappend. **2** linkisch.

fume (fjuːm) *n* **1** Dunst, Dampf, Rauch *m*. **2** *pl* Abgase *neu*. *vi* **1** dunsten, rauchen. **2** wütend sein, aufgebracht sein.

fun (fʌn) *n* Spaß, Scherz *m*. **make fun of** *vi* sich lustig machen über. **funfair** *n* Rummelplatz, Jahrmarkt *m*.

function ('fʌŋkʃən) *n* **1** Funktion, Aufgabe *f*. **2** Veranstaltung *f*. *vi* funktionieren. **functional** *adj* funktionell. **functionary** *n* Beamte(r) *m*.

fund (fʌnd) *n* **1** Kapital *neu*. Fonds *m*. **2** Vorrat, Schatz *m*. **3** *pl* Geldmittel *neu pl*.

fundamental (fʌndə'mentḷ) *adj* Grund—, wesentlich, grundsätzlich, fundamental.

funeral ('fjuːnərəl) *n* Beerdigung. *adj* Trauer—.

fungus ('fʌŋgəs) *n*, *pl* **fungi** Schwamm, Pilz *m*.

funnel ('fʌnḷ) *n* **1** Trichter *m*. **2** Schornstein *m*.

funny ('fʌni) *adj* **1** komisch. **2** sonderbar. **funny bone** *n inf* Musikantenknochen *m*.

fur (fəː) *n* **1** Pelz *m*. **2** *med* Belag *m*. **3** *pl* Pelzwaren *f pl*. *adj* Pelz—.

furious ('fjuəriəs) *adj* wütend, rasend.

furnace ('fəːnis) *n* Schmelzofen *m*.

furnish ('fəːniʃ) *vt* **1** versehen. **2** möblieren. **furnished** *adj* möbliert. **furnishing** *n* Einrichtung *f*.

furniture ('fəːnitʃə) *n* Möbel *neu pl*.

furrow ('fʌrou) *n* Furche, Rinne *f*. *vt* (durch)furchen.

further ('fəːðə) *adj* weiter, ferner. *vt* fördern. **furthermore** *adv* überdies, weiter.

furthest ('fəːðist) *adj* weitest. *adv* am weitesten.

furtive ('fəːtiv) *adj* verstohlen, heimlich.

fury ('fjuəri) *n* Wut *f*. Zorn *m*.

fuse[1] (fjuːz) *n* **1** (Schmelz)-Sicherung *f*. **2** Zünder *m*. *vi* durchbrennen.

fuse[2] (fjuːz) *vt* schmelzen. *vi* verschmelzen.

fuselage ('fjuːzəlɑːʒ) *n* (Flugzeug)Rumpf *m*.

fusion ('fjuːʒən) *n* **1** Schmelzen *neu*. **2** Verschmelzung *f*. **3** *comm* Fusion *f*.

fuss (fʌs) *n* Getue *neu*. Aufregung *f*. *vi* sich aufregen über. **fussy** *adj* penibel.

futile ('fjuːtail) *adj* unnütz, nutzlos, vergeblich. **futility** *n* Nutzlosigkeit, Sinnlosigkeit *f*.

future ('fjuːtʃə) *n* **1** Zukunft *f*. **2** *gram* Futur *neu*. *adj* (zu)künftig.

fuzz (fʌz) *n* **1** Fussel *f*. Flaum

m. **2** *sl* Polizei *f.* **fuzzy** *adj* **1** fusselig. **2** verschwommen. **3** kraus.

G

gabble ('gæbəl) *n* Geschnatter, Geplapper *neu.* *vi,vt* schnattern, plappern.
gable ('geibəl) *n* Giebel *m.*
gadget ('gædʒit) *n* Apparat *m.* Dings *neu.*
gag[1] (gæg) *n* Knebel *m.* *vt* knebeln.
gag[2] (gæg) *n* Gag *m.* Pointe *f.*
gaiety ('geiəti) *n* Heiterkeit, Fröhlichkeit *f.*
gaily ('geili) *adv* heiter, fröhlich.
gain (gein) *n* **1** Gewinn *m.* **2** Profit *m.* *vt* **1** gewinnen. **2** erlangen, erreichen. *vi* (of a clock) vorgehen.
gait (geit) *n* **1** Gangart *f.* **2** Haltung *f.*
gala ('gɑːlə) *n* Fest *neu.* Festlichkeit *f.*
galaxy ('gæləksi) *n* Milchstraße *f.*
gale (geil) *n* Sturm *m.*
gallant ('gælənt) *adj* **1** tapfer, ritterlich. **2** galant, höflich.
galleon ('gæliən) *n* Galeone *f.*
gallery ('gæləri) *n* Galerie *f.*
galley ('gæli) *n* **1** Galeere *f.* **2** Schiffsküche *f.*
gallon ('gælən) *n* Gallone *f.*
gallop ('gæləp) *n* Galopp *m.* *vi* galoppieren.
gallows ('gælouz) *n pl* Galgen *m.*
galore (gə'lɔː) *adv* in Hülle und Fülle.
galvanize ('gælvənaiz) *vt* **1** galvanisieren. **2** beleben, anspornen.
gamble ('gæmbəl) *vi* (um Geld) spielen. **gamble away** verspielen. *~n* Risiko *neu.* **gambling** *n* Glücksspiel *neu.*
game (geim) *n* **1** Spiel *neu.* **2** Partie *f.* **3** (animals) Wild *neu.* *adj inf* bereit, aufgelegt (zu). **gamekeeper** *n* Wildhüter *m.*
gammon ('gæmən) *n* (geräucherter) Schinken *m.*
gander ('gændə) *n* Gänserich *m.*
gang (gæŋ) *n* **1** Arbeitskolonne *f.* **2** Gruppe, Bande *f.* *v* **gang up** sich zusammenrotten. **gangster** *n* Gangster, Verbrecher *m.*
gangrene (gæŋ'griːn) *n* Gangrän *f.*
gangway ('gæŋwei) *n* **1** Durchgang *m.* **2** *naut* Fallreep *neu.*
gap (gæp) *n* Lücke *f.*
gape (geip) *vi* **1** klaffen. **2** starren, glotzen. **gape at** angaffen.
garage ('gærɑːʒ) *n* **1** Garage *f.* **2** Reparaturwerkstatt *f.* *vt* einstellen, garagieren.
garble ('gɑːbəl) *vt* verstümmeln, entstellen.
garden ('gɑːdn̩) *n* Garten *m.* *vi* im Garten arbeiten. **gardner** *n* Gärtner *m.*
gargle ('gɑːgəl) *vi* gurgeln. *n* Gurgelwasser *neu.*
garland ('gɑːlənd) *n* Girlande *f.* Kranz *m.* *vt* bekränzen.
garlic ('gɑːlik) *n* Knoblauch *m.*
garment ('gɑːmənt) *n* Kleidungsstück, Gewand *neu.*
garnish ('gɑːniʃ) *vt* **1** *cul* garnieren. **2** verzieren, schmücken. *n* **1** Garnierung *f.* **2** Schmuck *m.* Verzierung *f.*

garrison ('gærisən) *n* Garnison *f.*
garter ('gɑːtə) *n* Strumpfband *neu.*
gas (gæs) *n* Gas *neu. vt* vergasen. **gas cooker** *n* Gasherd, Gasofen *m.* **gas fire** *n* Gasfeuer *neu.*
gash (gæʃ) *n* **1** (klaffende) Wunde *f.* **2** Riß *m. vt* tief schneiden in.
gasket ('gæskit) *n tech* Dichtung *f.*
gasp (gɑːsp) *vi* keuchen. *n* Keuchen *neu.*
gastric ('gæstrik) *adj* gastrisch, Magen—. **gastronomic** *adj* gastronomisch. **gastronomy** *n* Gastronomie, Kochkunst *f.*
gate (geit) *n* **1** Tor *neu.* **2** Pforte *f.* **gatecrasher** *n inf* uneingeladener Gast, Eindringling *m.*
gateau ('gætou) *n* Torte *f.*
gather ('gæðə) *vt* **1** (ein-, ver-) sammeln. **2** ernten, lesen. **3** pflücken. **4** (cloth) raffen. *vi* sich versammeln. **gathering** *n* Versammlung *f.*
gauche (gouʃ) *adj* linkish, taktlos.
gaudy ('gɔːdi) *adj* bunt, grell, protzig.
gauge (geidʒ) *n* **1** Normalmaß *neu.* **2** Maßstab *m.* **3** Meßgerät *neu. vt* **1** eichen. **2** (aus)messen. **3** abschätzen, beurteilen.
gaunt (gɔːnt) *adj* hager, mager.
gauze (gɔːz) *n* Gaze *f.*
gave (geiv) *v* see **give.**
gay (gei) *adj* **1** heiter. **2** bunt. **3** ausschweifend. **4** *sl* homosexuell.
gaze (geiz) *vi* starren. **gaze at** anstarren. *~n* (starrer) Blick *m.*
gazelle (gə'zel) *n* Gazelle *f.*
gear (giə) *n* **1** Zeug *neu.* **2** Ausrüstung *f.* **3** Getriebe *neu.* **4** *mot* Gang *m.* **5** (Be)Kleidung *f.* **gearbox** *n* Getriebe *neu.* **gear lever** *n* Schalthebel *m.*
gelatine ('dʒelətiːn) *n* Gelatine *f.*
gelignite ('dʒelignait) *n* Gelatinedynamit *neu.*
gem (dʒem) *n* **1** Edelstein *m.* **2** Gemme *f.*
Gemini ('dʒɛminai) *n pl* Zwillinge *m pl.*
gender ('dʒendə) *n* Geschlecht *neu.*
genealogy (dʒini'ælədʒi) *n* Genealogie *f.*
general ('dʒenərəl) *adj* **1** allgemein. **2** gewöhnlich. **3** Allgemein—. **in general** im allgemeinen. *~n* General *m.* **general election** *n* allgemeine Wahlen *f pl.* **general practitioner** *n* praktischer Arzt *m.* **generalize** *vi* verallgemeinern. **generalization** *n* Verallgemeinerung *f.*
generate ('dʒenəreit) *vt* **1** *tech* erzeugen, hervorbringen. **2** verursachen. **3** zeugen. **generation** *n* **1** Erzeugung *f.* **2** Menschenalter *neu.* Generation *f.* **generator** *n* **1** Erzeuger *m.* **2** *tech* Generator *m.*
generic (dʒi'nerik) *adj* **1** allgemein, generell. **2** generisch, Gattungs—.
generous ('dʒenərəs) *adj* **1** großzügig. **2** großmütig. **3** reichlich. **generosity** *n* **1** Großzügigkeit *f.* **2** Großmut *f.*
genetic (dʒi'netik) *adj* Ent-

stehungs—, genetisch. **genetics** *n pl* Genetik, Vererbungslehre *f*.
Geneva (dʒi'niːvə) *n* Genf *neu*.
genial ('dʒiːniəl) *adj* **1** freundlich, herzlich. **2** mild. **3** heiter, jovial. **geniality** *n* **1** Freundlichkeit *f*. **2** Herzlichkeit *f*.
genital ('dʒenitl̩) *adj* **1** Zeugungs—. **2** Geschlechts—. **genitals** *n pl*. Genitalien *neu pl*. Geschlechtsteile *m pl*.
genitive ('dʒenitiv) *n gram* Genitiv *m*.
genius ('dʒiːniəs) *n* Genie *neu*. Genius *m*.
genteel (dʒen'tiːl) *adj* **1** vornehm. **2** fein.
gentile ('dʒentail) *n* Heide *m*. *adj* heidnisch.
gentle ('dʒentl̩) *adj* **1** mild, sanft. **2** vornehm. **gentleman** *n* **1** Herr *m*. **2** Gentleman *m*.
genuflect ('dʒenjuflekt) *vi* die Knie beugen. **genuflection** *n* Kniebeugung *f*.
genuine ('dʒenjuin) *adj* **1** echt. **2** wirklich.
genus ('dʒiːnəs) *n* Gattung *f*.
geography (dʒi'ɔgrəfi) *n* Erdkunde, Geographie *f*.
geology (dʒi'ɔlədʒi) *n* Geologie *f*.
geometry (dʒi'ɔmətri) *n* Geometrie *f*.
geranium (dʒə'reiniəm) *n* Geranie *f*.
germ (dʒəːm) *n* Keim, Bazillus *m*. Bakterie *f*. **germinate** *vi* keimen.
Germany ('dʒəːməni) *n* Deutschland *neu*. **German** *adj* deutsch. *n* **1** Deutsche(r) *m*. **2** (language) Deutsch *neu*. **German measles** *n pl* Röteln *pl*. **Germanic** *adj* germanisch.
gerund ('dʒerənd) *n* Gerundium *neu*.
gesticulate (dʒis'tikuleit) *vi* gestikulieren, sich lebhaft gebärden.
gesture ('dʒestʃə) *n* Gebärde, Geste *f*.
get* (get) *vt* **1** bekommen, erhalten. **2** *inf* kriegen. **3** gewinnen. **4** veranlassen. **5** besorgen. *vi* **1** gelangen, kommen. **2** werden. **get in** einsteigen. **get off** aussteigen. **get over** hinwegkommen über. **get ready** fertig machen. **get up** aufstehen.
geyser ('giːzə) *n* **1** Geiser, Geysir *m*. **2** Durchlauferhitzer *m*.
ghastly ('gɑːstli) *adj* gräßlich, schrecklich.
gherkin ('gəːkin) *n* Essiggurke *f*.
ghetto ('getou) *n* Getto *neu*.
ghost (goust) *n* Gespenst *neu*. Geist *m*.
giant ('dʒaiənt) *n* Riese *m*. *adj* riesig.
giddy ('gidi) *adj* **1** schwindlig. **2** leichtsinnig.
gift (gift) *n* **1** Geschenk *neu*. **2** Begabung *f*.
gigantic (dʒai'gæntik) *adj* riesenhaft, gigantisch.
giggle ('gigəl) *vi* kichern. *n* Gekicher *neu*.
gild (gild) *vt* vergolden.
gill (gil) *n zool* Kieme *f*.
gilt (gilt) *adj* vergoldet. *n* Vergoldung *f*.
gimmick ('gimik) *n inf* Trick, Kniff *m*.

gin (dʒin) *n* Gin, Wacholderschnaps *m*.
ginger ('dʒindʒə) *n* Ingwer *m*. **ginger beer** *n* Ingwerbier *neu*. **gingerbread** *n* Pfefferkuchen *m*.
gipsy ('dʒipsi) *n* Zigeuner *m*.
giraffe (dʒi'rɑːf) *n* Giraffe *f*.
girder ('gəːdə) *n* Tragbalken, Träger *m*.
girdle ('gəːdl̩) *n* (Hüft)Gürtel *m*.
girl (gəːl) *n* Mädchen *neu*. **girlfriend** *n* Freundin *f*.
Giro ('dʒairou) *n* Giro *neu*.
girth (gəːθ) *n* **1** (Sattel)Gurt *m*. **2** Umfang *m*.
give* (giv) *vt* **1** geben, schenken. **2** erteilen. **give away** verschenken. **give back** zurückgeben. **give in** nachgeben. **give out 1** verteilen, ausgeben. **2** zu Ende gehen. **give up** aufgeben.
glacier ('glæsiə) *n* Gletscher *m*.
glad (glæd) *adj* **1** froh, erfreut. **2** fröhlich.
glamour ('glæmə) *n* Glanz, Zauber *m*. **glamorize** *vt* verherrlichen. **glamorous** *adj* bezaubernd, schön.
glance (glɑːns) *n* (flüchtiger) Blick, Schimmer *m*. *vi* flüchtig blicken.
gland (glænd) *n* Drüse *f*.
glare (glɛə) *vi* **1** (wütend) anblicken, starren. **2** hell glänzen. *n* **1** blendender Glanz *m*. **2** (wütender) Blick *m*.
glass (glɑːs) *n* **1** Glas *neu*. **2** *pl* Brille *f*.
glaze (gleiz) *n* Glasur *f*. *vt* **1** verglasen. **2** glasieren.
gleam (gliːm) *n* Schimmer, Lichtstrahl *m*. *vi* strahlen, schimmern.
glean (gliːn) *vt* (auf-, nach-) lesen.
glee (gliː) *n* Fröhlichkeit *f*.
glib (glib) *adj* zungenfertig, glatt.
glide (glaid) *vi* **1** (vorüber)gleiten, fließen. **2** im Gleitflug fliegen. **glider** *n* Segelflugzeug *neu*.
glimmer ('glimə) *n* Schimmer *m*.
glimpse (glimps) *n* flüchtiger Blick *m*.
glisten ('glisən) *vi* glänzen, schimmern.
glitter ('glitə) *vi* glitzern. *n* Glanz *m*.
gloat (glout) *vi* sich weiden, sich hämisch freuen.
globe (gloub) *n* (Erd)Kugel *f*. Globus *m*.
gloom[1] (gluːm) *n* Dunkelheit, Düsternis *f*.
gloom[2] (gluːm) *n* Schwermut *f*. Trübsinn *m*.
glory ('glɔːri) *n* Ruhm, Glanz *m*. **glorify** *vt* verherrlichen. **glorious** *adj* glorreich, herrlich, prachtvoll.
gloss[1] (glɔs) *n* Glanz, Schein *m*. *v* **gloss over** vertuschen.
gloss[2] (glɔs) *n* Randbemerkung, Glosse *f*.
glossary ('glɔsəri) *n* (Spezial)Wörterverzeichnis *neu*.
glove (glʌv) *n* Handschuh *m*.
glow (glou) *vi* glühen. *n* Glühen *neu*. Glut *f*.
glucose ('gluːkous) *n* Traubenzucker *m*.
glue (gluː) *n* Klebstoff *m*. *vt* kleben.

glum (glʌm) *adj* mürrisch, verdrießlich.

glut (glʌt) *n* **1** Sättigung, Stillung *f*. **2** *comm* Überangebot *neu*.

glutton ('glʌtn̩) *n* **1** Vielfraß *m*. **2** unersättliche(r) Mensch *m*.

gnarled (nɑːld) *adj* knorrig.

gnash (næʃ) *vt* knirschen.

gnat (næt) *n* Mücke *f*.

gnaw (nɔː) *vt,vi* nagen.

gnome (noum) *n* Zwerg, Erdgeist *m*. Gnom *m*.

go* (gou) *vi* **1** gehen, fahren, laufen. **2** funktionieren. **3** reichen. **go abroad** ins Ausland gehen. **go ahead 1** losgehen. **2** vorausgehen. **go away 1** weggehen. **2** verreisen. **go back** zurückkehren. **go down** hinuntergehen, untergehen. **go into** eintreten. **go off 1** weggehen. **2** (of food) schlecht werden. **go on** weitergehen. **go out** (hin)ausgehen. **go through 1** durchgehen. **2** durchmachen. **go up** (hinauf)steigen.

goad (goud) *vt* anspornen, anstacheln.

goal (goul) *n* **1** Ziel *m*. **2** *sport* Tor *neu*. **goalkeeper** *n* Torwart *m*. **goalpost** *n* Torpfosten *m*.

goat (gout) *n* Ziege *f*.

gobble ('gɔbəl) *vt* (hinunter-, ver-)schlingen.

goblin ('gɔblin) *n* Kobold *m*.

god (gɔd) *n* Gott *m*. **godchild** *n* Patenkind *neu*. **goddaughter** *n* Patentochter *f*. **godfather** *n* Pate *m*. **godmother** *n* Patin *f*. **godson** *n* Patensohn *m*.

goddess ('gɔdis) *n* Göttin *f*.

goggles ('gɔgəlz) *n pl* Schutzbrille *f*.

going ('gouiŋ) *adj* laufend, im Gang. *n* Gehen *neu*. Abreise *f*.

gold (gould) *n* Gold *neu*. *adj* golden. **golden** *adj* golden. **goldfish** *n* Goldfisch *m*.

golf (gɔlf) *n* Golf(spiel) *neu*. **golfball** *n* Golfball *m*. **golfclub** *n* Golfschläger *m*. **golfcourse** *n* Golfplatz *m*.

gondola ('gɔndələ) *n* Gondel *f*. **gondolier** *n* Gondoliere *m*.

gone (gɔn) *v* see **go.** *adj* **1** vergangen. **2** fort. **3** tot.

gong (gɔŋ) *n* Gong *m*.

good (gud) *adj* **1** gut. **2** ordentlich. **3** artig, brav. **4** *law* gültig. *n* **1** Gut(e) *neu*. **2** Wohl *neu*. **3** *pl* Waren, Güter *pl*. **for good** auf immer. **good afternoon** *interj* guten Tag. **goodbye** *interj* auf Wiedersehen. *n* Lebewohl *neu*. **good evening** *interj* guten Abend. **good-looking** *adj* gut aussehend, schön, hübsch. **good morning** *interj* guten Morgen. **good night** *interj* gute Nacht. **goods train** *n* Güterzug *m*. **goodwill** *n* **1** Wohlwollen *neu*. guter Wille *m*. **2** Kundschaft *f*.

Good Friday *n* Karfreitag *m*.

goose (guːs) *n*, *pl* **geese** Gans *f*. **gooseberry** *n* Stachelbeere *f*.

gore[1] (gɔː) *n* (geronnenes) Blut *neu*.

gore[2] (gɔː) *vt* durchbohren, aufspießen.

gorge (gɔːdʒ) *n* Schlucht *f*. *vt,vi* gierig essen. **gorge oneself** sich vollstopfen.

gorgeous ('gɔːdʒəs) *adj* **1** prächtig, großartig. **2** *inf* phantastisch. **3** *inf* sehr schmackhaft.

gorilla (gə'rilə) *n* Gorilla *m*.

gorse (gɔːs) *n* Stechginster *m*.

gory ('gɔːri) *adj* blutig.

gosh (gɔʃ) *interj* Donnerwetter!

gosling ('gɔzliŋ) *n* Gänschen *neu*.

gospel ('gɔspəl) *n* Evangelium *neu*.

gossip ('gɔsip) *n* **1** Geschwätz *neu*. **2** Klatschbase *f*. *vi* schwatzen.

got (gɔt) *v* see **get**.

Gothic ('gɔθik) *adj* gotisch.

goulash ('guːlæʃ) *n* Gulasch *neu*.

gourd (guəd) *n* Kürbis *m*.

gourmet (guə'mei) *n* Gourmet, Feinschmecker *m*.

govern ('gʌvən) *vt* **1** regieren, beherrschen. **2** bestimmen. *vi* regieren, herrschen. **government** *n* Regierung *f*. **governor** *n* **1** Gouverneur, Statthalter *m*. **2** Direktor *m*.

gown (gaun) *n* **1** (Damen)Kleid *neu*. **2** Robe *f*.

grab (græb) *vt* schnappen, ergreifen. *vi* gierig greifen.

grace (greis) *n* **1** Gnade *f*. **2** Reiz *m*. **3** Tischgebet *neu*. **4** Gunst *f*. **5** Anmut *f*. **His/Her/Your Grace** Sein/Ihr/Euer Gnaden. ~*vt* **1** schmücken. **2** ehren. **graceful** *adj* **1** anmutig. **2** taktvoll. **gracious** *adj* gütig, gnädig, anmutig.

grade (greid) *n* **1** Rang, Grad *m*. **2** Qualität *f*. *vt* ordnen, sortieren, einteilen. **gradient** *n* **1** Neigung *f*. **2** Hang *m*. **3** Steigerung *f*. **4** Gefälle *neu*. **gradual** *adj* allmählich, stufenweise, schrittweise.

graduate *n* Graduierte(r) *m*. *vi* ein Diplom erwerben. *vt* einteilen.

graffiti (grə'fiːti) *n pl* Graffiti *neu*.

graft[1] (grɑːft) *vt* **1** *bot* (auf-, ein-)pfropfen. **2** *med* verpflanzen. *n* **1** Propfreis *neu*. **2** Verpflanzung *f*.

graft[2] *inf n* **1** Schiebung, Bestechung *f*. **2** Gaunerei *f*. *vt* **1** schieben. **2** (er)gaunern.

grain (grein) *n* **1** Getreide *neu*. **2** Samenkorn *neu*. **3** (Holz)Faser *f*.

gram (græm) *n* Gramm *neu*.

grammar ('græmə) *n* Grammatik *f*. **grammar school** *n* Gymnasium *neu*. **grammatical** *adj* grammatisch, grammatikalisch.

gramophone ('græməfoun) *n* Plattenspieler *m*. Gramophon *neu*.

granary ('grænəri) *n* Kornspeicher *m*.

grand (grænd) *adj* groß, erhaben, stattlich. **grand piano** *n* Flügel *m*. **grandeur** *n* Erhabenheit, Größe *f*. **grandiose** *adj* großartig, grandios.

grandad ('grændæd) *n inf also* **grandpa** Opa *m*.

grandchild ('græntʃaild) *n* Enkelkind *neu*.

grand-daughter ('grændɔːtə) *n* Enkelin *f*.

grandfather ('grænfɑːðə) *n* Großvater *m*.

grandma ('grænmɑː) *n inf also* **granny** Oma *f*.

grandmother ('grænmʌðə) *n* Großmutter *f*.

grandparents ('grænpɛərənts) *n pl* Großeltern *pl*.

grandson ('grænsʌn) *n* Enkel *m.*
grandstand ('grændstænd) *n* Zuschauertribüne *f.*
granite ('grænit) *n* Granit *m.*
grant (grɑːnt) *n* **1** Bewilligung *f.* **2** Verleihung *f.* **3** Zuschuß *m.* **4** *educ* Stipendium. *vt* **1** bewilligen. **2** verleihen. **3** zugestehen.
grape (greip) *n* Weintraube *f.*
grapefruit *n* Grapefruit, Pampelmuse *f.*
graph (græf) *n* Diagramm *neu.* Kurve *f.* **graphic** *adj* **1** graphisch. **2** anschaulich.
grapple ('græpəl) *vi* ringen. *vt* **1** packen. **2** befestigen (an). **grapple with** in Angriff nehmen, sich auseinandersetzen mit.
grasp (grɑːsp) *vt* **1** greifen, fassen. **2** begreifen, verstehen. *n* Griff m.
grass (grɑːs) *n* **1** Gras *neu.* **2** Rasen *m.* **grassroots** *n pl* Wurzel *f. adj* volksnah, volkstümlich.
grate[1] (greit) *n* (Feuer)Rost *m.* Gitter *neu.*
grate[2] (greit) *vt* **1** *cul* reiben. **2** krächzen. **3** knirschen mit. *vi* kratzen, knirschen, knarren.
grateful ('greitfəl) *adj* dankbar.
gratify *vt* erfreuen, befriedigen, zufriedenstellen.
gratitude ('grætitjuːd) *n* Dankbarkeit *f.*
grave[1] (greiv) *n* Grab *neu.* **gravestone** *n* Grabstein *m.* **graveyard** *n* Friedhof *m.*
grave[2] (greiv) *adj* ernst(haft).
gravel ('grævəl) *n* Kies *m.*
gravity ('græviti) *n* **1** *sci* Gravität, Schwerkraft *f.* **2** Schwere *f.* Ernst *m.*
gravy ('greivi) *n* (Braten)Soße *f.*
graze[1] (greiz) *n* **1** flüchtige Berührung *f.* **2** Abschürfung *f. vt* **1** streifen. **2** abschürfen.
graze[2] (greiz) *vi* weiden, grasen.
grease (griːs) *n* **1** Fett *neu.* **2** Schmiere *f. vt* schmieren, einfetten. **greasepaint** *n* Bühnenschminke *f.* **greaseproof** *adj* fettdicht.
great (greit) *adj* **1** groß. **2** beträchtlich. **3** bedeutend. **4** berühmt. **5** *inf* toll, sagenhaft, prima.
Great Britain *n* Großbritannien *neu.*
Greece (griːs) *n* Griechenland *neu.* **Greek** *adj also* **Grecian** griechisch. *n* **1** Grieche *m.* **2** (language) Griechisch *neu.*
greed (griːd) *n* (Hab)Gier *f.* **greedy** *adj* gierig.
green (griːn) *adj* **1** grün. **2** *inf* unerfahren. *n* **1** Grün *neu.* **2** Grünfläche *f.* **3** *pl* Grüngemüse *neu pl.* **greenery** *n* Laub(werk) *neu.* **greenfly** *n* grüne Blattlaus *f.* **greengage** *n* Reineclaude *f.* **greengrocer** *n* Obst- und Gemüsehändler *m.* **greenhouse** *n* Treibhaus *neu.*
Greenland ('griːnlənd) *n* Grönland *neu.* **Greenlander** *n* Grönlander *m.*
greet (griːt) *vt* (be)grüßen. **greeting** *n* Gruß *m.*
gregarious (gri'gɛəriəs) *adj* gesellig.
grenade (gri'neid) *n* Granate *f.*
grew (gruː) *v* see **grow.**

grey (grei) *adj* grau. *n* Grau *neu.* **greyhound** *n* Windhund *m.*
grid (grid) *n* **1** Gitter *neu.* **2** Netz *neu.*
grief (gri:f) *n* Kummer, Schmerz *m.*
grieve (gri:v) *vi* trauern, sich kränken über. **grievance** *n* Beschwerde *f.* Groll *m.*
grill (gril) *n* Bratrost *m. vt* grillen, rosten.
grille (gril) *n* Gitter *neu.*
grim (grim) *adj* **1** grimmig, finster. **2** hart.
grimace (gri'meis) *n* Grimasse *f. vi* Grimassen schneiden.
grime (graim) *n* (fettiger) Schmutz *m.*
grin (grin) *vi* grinsen. *n* Grinsen *neu.*
grind* (graind) *vt* (zer)reiben, (zer)mahlen. *n inf* Plackerei *f.*
grip (grip) *vt* packen, (er)greifen. *n* Griff *m.*
gristle ('grisəl) *n* Knorpel *m.*
grit (grit) *n* grober Sand, Kies *m.*
groan (groun) *vi* stöhnen, seufzen. *n* Stöhnen *neu.*
grocer ('grousə) *n* Lebensmittelhändler *m.*
groin (grɔin) *n* Leiste *f.*
groom (gru:m) *n* **1** Stallknecht, Reitknecht *m.* **2** Bräutigam *m. vt* versorgen, pflegen.
groove (gru:v) *n* Rinne, Furche, Rille *f.*
grope (group) *vi* herumtasten, herumtappen.
gross (grous) *adj* **1** *comm* brutto. **2** dick. **3** grob, roh. *n* Gros *neu.*
grotesque (grou'tesk) *adj* grotesk.
grotto ('grɔtou) *n* Grotte *f.*
ground[1] (graund) *n* **1** Grund, Boden *m.* **2** *pl* Gelände *f.* Anlagen *f pl.* **3** (Beweg)Grund *m. vt* **1** begründen. **2** hinlegen. **ground floor** *n* Erdgeschoß *neu.* **groundsheet** *n* Zeltbahn *f.* **groundsman** *n* (Sportplatz)Wärter *m.*
ground[2] (graund) *v* see **grind.**
group (gru:p) *n* Gruppe *f. vt* gruppieren.
grouse[1] (graus) *n* Rebhuhn *neu.*
grouse[2] (graus) *vi inf* murren, meckern.
grove (grouv) *n* Gehölz *neu.* Waldung *f.*
grovel ('grɔvəl) *vi* (auf dem Bauch) kriechen.
grow* (grou) *vi* **1** wachsen. **2** werden. **3** zunehmen. *vt* (an)bauen, züchten, wachsen lassen. **growth** *n* **1** Wachstum *neu.* Entwicklung *f.* **2** Zunahme, Vergrößerung *f.*
growl (graul) *vi,vt* grollen, knurren, brummen. *n* Brummen, Knurren, Grollen *neu.*
grub (grʌb) *n* **1** Made *f.* **2** *sl* Futter *neu.* Fraß *m. vi* graben.
grubby ('grʌbi) *adj* schmutzig, dreckig.
grudge (grʌdʒ) *n* Groll *m. vt* beneiden, mißgönnen.
gruelling ('gru:əliŋ) *adj* erschöpfend.
gruesome ('gru:səm) *adj* grausig.
gruff (grʌf) *adj* **1** schroff, barsch. **2** mürrisch.
grumble ('grʌmbəl) *vi* murren, schimpfen.
grumpy ('grʌmpi) *adj* verdrießlich, mürrisch.

grunt (grʌnt) *vi* grunzen. *n* Grunzen *neu*.
guarantee (gærən'tiː) *n* Garantie, Bürgschaft *f*. *vt* garantieren, gewährleisten. **guarantor** *n* Bürge, Garant *m*.
guard (gɑːd) *vt* bewachen, (be)schützen. *vi* sich hüten. *n* **1** Wache *f*. **2** (railway) Schaffner *m*. **guardian** *n* **1** *law* Vormund *m*. **2** Wächter *m*. **guard's van** *n* Gepäckwagen *neu*.
guerrilla (gə'rilə) *n* Guerillakämpfer *m*.
guess (ges) *vt* erraten, vermuten. *n* Vermutung, Mutmaßung *f*. **guesswork** *n* Vermutungen *f pl*.
guest (gest) *n* Gast *m*. **guesthouse** *n* Pension *f*.
guide (gaid) *n* **1** Führer *m*. **2** Leitfaden *m*. **3** Ratgeber *m*. *vt* führen. **Girl Guide** *n* Pfadfinderin *f*. **guidebook** *n* Reiseführer *m*. **guide-dog** *n* Blindenhund *m*. **guidance** *n* Führung, Anleitung *f*.
guild (gild) *n* Zunft *f*.
guillotine (gilə'tiːn) *n* Guillotine *f*.
guilt (gilt) *n* Schuld *f*. **guilty** *adj* schuldig, schuldhaft.
guinea ('gini) *n* Guinee *f*. **guinea pig** *n* **1** *zool* Meerschweinchen *neu*. **2** Versuchskaninchen *neu*.
guitar (gi'tɑː) *n* Gitarre *f*.
gulf (gʌlf) *n* **1** Golf *m*. **2** Abgrund *m*. **3** Kluft *f*.
gull (gʌl) *n* Möwe *f*.
gullet ('gʌlit) *n* Speiseröhre *f*. Schlund *m*.
gulp (gʌlp) *n* Schluck *m*. *vt* hinunterschlingen. *vi* schlucken.
gum[1] (gʌm) *n* Gummi *neu*. *vt* (an)kleben.
gum[2] (gʌm) *n anat* Zahnfleisch *neu*.
gun (gʌn) *n* **1** Gewehr, Geschütz *neu*. **2** Flinte *f*. **3** Revolver *m*. **gunboat** *n* Kanonenboot *neu*. **gunman** *n* bewaffneter Verbrecher *m*. **gunpowder** *n* Schießpulver *neu*. **gunrunning** *n* Waffenschmuggel *m*. **gunshot** *n* **1** Schuß *m*. **2** Schußweite *f*.
gurgle ('gəːgəl) *vi* glucksen, gurgeln.
gush (gʌʃ) *vi* **1** sich ergießen. **2** strömen. *n* **1** Erguß *m*. **2** Flut *f*.
gust (gʌst) *n* Windstoß *m*.
gut (gʌt) *n* **1** Darm *m*. **2** *pl* Eingeweide *pl*. **3** *pl sl* Mut *f*. *vt* ausweiden.
gutter ('gʌtə) *n* **1** Rinnstein *m*. **2** Dachrinne *f*. **3** Gosse *f*.
guy[1] (gai) *n sl* Kerl, Bursche *m*.
guy[2] (gai) *n* Spannschnur *f*.
gymnasium (dʒim'neiziəm) *n* Turnhalle *f*. **gymnast** *n* Leichtathlet, Turner *m*. **gymnastic** *adj* gymnastisch, Turn—. **gymnastics** *n pl* Turnen *neu*. Gymnastik *f*.
gynaecology (gaini'kɔlədʒi) *n* Gynäkologie *f*. **gynaecologist** *n* Frauenarzt, Gynäkologe *m*.
gypsum ('dʒipsəm) *n* Gips *m*.
gyrate (dʒai'reit) *vi* wirbeln, kreisen.

H

haberdasher ('hæbədæʃə) *n* Kurzwarenhändler *m*. **haber-**

dashery *n* Kurzwarenhandlung *f*.

habit ('hæbit) *n* Gewohnheit *f*. **get into the habit of** sich angewöhnen. **habitual** *adj* gewohnt, üblich.

habitable ('hæbitəbəl) *adj* bewohnbar.

hack[1] (hæk) *vt* (zer)hacken. **hacksaw** *n* Metallsäge *f*.

hack[2] (hæk) *n* **1** Mietpferd *neu*. **2** Gaul *m*. **3** Lohnschreiber *m*.

hackneyed ('hæknid) *adj* abgedroschen.

had (hæd) *v* see **have.**

haddock ('hædək) *n* Schellfisch *m*.

haemorrhage ('heməridʒ) *n* Blutung *f*.

hag (hæg) *n* häßliches altes Weib *neu*.

haggard ('hægəd) *adj* **1** verstört. **2** hager.

haggle ('hægḷ) *vi* streiten, feilschen.

Hague, The (heig) *n* Den Haag *m*.

hail[1] (heil) *n* Hagel *m*. *vi* hageln. **hailstone** *n* Hagelkorn *neu*. **hailstorm** *n* Hagelschauer *m*.

hail[2] (heil) *vt* (be)grüßen, zurufen.

hair (hεə) *n* Haar *neu*. **hairbrush** *n* Haarbürste *f*. **haircut** *n* Haarschnitt *m*. **hairdresser** *n* Friseur *m*. Friseuse *f*. **hairpin** *n* Haarnadel *f*. **hair-raising** *adj* haarsträubend. **hairstyle** *n* Haartracht *f*.

half (hɑːf) *n*, *pl* **halves** Hälfte *f*. *adj,adv* halb.

half-dozen *n* halbes Dutzend *neu*.

half-and-half *adj,adv* halb und halb.

half-back *n sport* Läufer *m*.

half-breed *n also* **half-caste** Mischling *m*.

half-brother *n* Halbbruder *m*.

half-hearted *adj* lau, zaghaft.

half-hour *n* halbe Stunde *f*.

half-mast *n* Halbmast *m*. **at half-mast** halbmast.

half-sister *n* Halbschwester *f*.

half-term *n* Semesterhalbzeit *f*.

half-time *n* Halbzeit *f*.

halfway (hɑːf'wei) *adj,adv* auf halbem Wege, halbwegs.

halfwit ('hɑːfwit) *n* Schwachkopf, Idiot *m*.

halibut ('hælibət) *n* Heilbutt *m*.

hall (hɔːl) *n* **1** Halle *f*. **2** Saal *m*. **3** Diele *f*. Flur *m*.

hallelujah (hæli'luːjə) *interj* halleluja!

hallmark ('hɔːlmɑːk) *n* **1** Feingehaltsstempel *m*. **2** Kennzeichen *neu*.

hallo (hə'lou) *interj* **1** guten Tag! grüß Gott! **2** hallo!

hallowed ('hæloud) *adj* geheiligt.

Hallowe'en (hælou'iːn) *n* Abend vor Allerheiligen *m*.

hallucination (həluːsi'neiʃən) *n* Halluzination, Sinnestäuschung *f*.

halo ('heilou) *n pl* **-os** *or* **-oes** **1** Heiligenschein *m*. **2** *sci* Hof *m*.

halt (hɔːlt) *n* Halt *m*. Pause *f*. *vt,vi* (an)halten.

halter ('hɔːltə) *n* Halfter *neu*.

halve (hɑːv) *vt* halbieren.

ham (hæm) *n* Schinken *m*.

hamburger ('hæmbəːgə) *n* Frikadelle *f*.

hammer ('hæmə) *n* Hammer *m*. *vt,vi* hämmern.
hammock ('hæmək) *n* Hängematte *f*.
hamper[1] ('hæmpə) *vt* (be)hindern, hemmen.
hamper[2] ('hæmpə) *n* Packkorb *m*.
hamster ('hæmstə) *n* Hamster *m*.
hand (hænd) *n* Hand *f*. **give** *or* **lend a hand** behilflich sein. **on the one hand...on the other** einerseits...andererseits. ~*vt* überreichen. **hand in** einreichen. **hand on** weitergeben. **hand out** verteilen. **hand over** übergeben.
handbag ('hændbæg) *n* Handtasche *f*.
handbook ('hændbuk) *n* Handbuch *neu*.
handbrake ('hændbreik) *n* Handbremse *f*.
handcart ('hændkaːt) *n* Handwagen *m*.
handcuff ('hændkʌf) *vt* Handschellen anlegen. **handcuffs** *n pl* Handschellen *f pl*.
handful ('hændful) *n* Handvoll *f*.
handicap ('hændikæp) *n* **1** Nachteil *m*. **2** *sport* Vorgabe *f*. *vt* benachteiligen.
handicraft ('hændikraːft) *n* Handwerk *neu*.
handiwork ('hændiwəːk) *n* **1** Handarbeit *f*. **2** Werk *neu*.
handkerchief ('hæŋkətʃif) *n* Taschentuch *neu*.
handle ('hændl̩) *n* Griff *m*. *vt* **1** anfassen. **2** handhaben. **3** behandeln. **handlebars** *n pl* Lenkstange *f*.
handmade (hænd'meid) *adj* handgearbeitet, Hand—.
hand-out *n* **1** Almosen *neu*. **2** Werbezettel *m*.
hand-pick *vt* auslesen, auswählen.
handrail ('hændreil) *n* Geländer *neu*.
handshake ('hændʃeik) *n* Händedruck *m*.
handsome ('hænsəm) *adj* **1** hübsch, schön, gut aussehend. **2** beträchtlich.
handstand ('hændstænd) *n* *sport* Handstand *m*.
handwriting ('hændraitiŋ) *n* Handschrift *f*.
handy ('hændi) *adj* **1** handlich, zur Hand. **2** geschickt.
hang* (hæŋ) *vt* (auf-, ein-) hängen. *vi* hängen. **hanger** *n* Kleiderbügel *m*. **hangman** *n* Henker *m*. **hangover** *n inf* Kater *m*.
hanker ('hæŋkə) *vi* sich sehnen.
Hanover ('hænəvə) *n* Hannover *neu*.
haphazard (hæp'hæzəd) *adj* zufällig.
happen ('hæpən) *vi* geschehen, sich ereignen, vorkommen, passieren. **happen to do something** etwas zufällig tun.
happy ('hæpi) *adj* **1** glücklich, zufrieden. **2** erfreulich. **happily** *adv* glücklicherweise. **happiness** *n* Glück *neu*.
harass ('hærəs) *vt* belästigen, quälen.
harbour ('haːbə) *n* Hafen *m*. *vt* beherbergen.
hard (haːd) *adj* **1** hart. **2** schwer. **3** streng. **4** schlecht. *adv* **1** heftig. **2** mühsam. **3** flei-

ßig. **hardback** *n* Buch mit steifem Einband *or* Leineneinband *neu.* **hardboard** *n* Hartfaserplatte *f.* **hard-boiled** *adj* hartgekocht. **harden** *vt* (ab)härten, hart machen. *vi* hart werden. **hard-headed** *adj* nüchtern, eigensinnig. **hard-hearted** *adj* hartherzig. **hardship** *n* Strapaze, Bedrängnis *f.* **hardware** *n* Eisenwaren *f pl.*

hardly ('hɑːdli) *adv* **1** kaum, schwerlich. **2** mit Mühe.

hardy ('hɑːdi) *adj* abgehärtet, zäh.

hare ('hɛə) *n* Hase *m.*

haricot ('hærikou) *n* weiße Bohne *f.*

hark (hɑːk) *vi* horchen.

harm (hɑːm) *n* Schaden *m. vt* Leid *or* Schaden zufügen, schaden. **harmful** *adj* schädlich.

harmonic (hɑː'mɔnik) *adj* harmonisch. **harmonica** *n* Mundharmonika *f.* **harmonize** *vt* **1** *mus* harmonisieren. **2** in Einklang bringen. *vi* in Einklang sein. **harmony** *n* **1** *mus* Harmonie *f.* **2** Einklang *m.*

harness ('hɑːnis) *n* Geschirr *neu. vt* anschirren, anspannen.

harp (hɑːp) *n* Harfe *f.*

harpoon (hɑː'puːn) *n* Harpune *f.*

harpsichord ('hɑːpsikɔːd) *n* Spinett *neu.*

harsh (hɑːʃ) *adj* **1** rauh, hart. **2** streng.

harvest ('hɑːvist) *n* **1** Ernte *f.* **2** (Wein)Lese *f. vt* ernten, einbringen.

has (hæz) *v* see **have.**

haste (heist) *n* Eile, Hast *f.*

hasten *vi* eilen, sich beeilen. *vt* beschleunigen.

hat (hæt) *n* Hut *m.*

hatch[1] (hætʃ) *vt* ausbrüten. *vi* brüten. *n* Brut *f.*

hatch[2] (hætʃ) *n* Luke, Klapptür *f.*

hatchback ('hætʃbæk) *n* Hecktürmodell *neu.*

hatchet ('hætʃit) *n* Beil *neu.*

hate (heit) *vt* hassen. *n* Haß *m.*

hateful *adj* verhaßt.

haughty ('hɔːti) *adj* hochmütig.

haul (hɔːl) *vt* schleppen, zerren, transportieren. *n* Fang *m.*

haunch (hɔːntʃ) *n* Hüfte, Keule *f.*

haunt (hɔːnt) *vt* **1** häufig besuchen. **2** heimsuchen. **3** spuken. *n* Aufenthalt *m.*

have* (hæv) *vt* haben. *v aux* haben, sein. **have something done** etwas tun lassen. **have to do something** etwas tun müssen.

haven ('heivən) *n* Hafen, Zufluchtsort *m.*

haversack ('hævəsæk) *n* Rucksack *m.*

havoc ('hævək) *n* **1** Verwüstung *f.* **2** Zerstörung *f.* **cause havoc** große Zerstörungen verursachen.

hawk (hɔːk) *n* Habicht, Falke *m.*

hawthorn ('hɔːθɔːn) *n* Hagedorn *m.*

hay (hei) *n* Heu *neu.* **hayfever** *n* Heuschnupfen *m.* **haystack** *n* Heuschober *m.* **go haywire** kaputt gehen.

hazard ('hæzəd) *n* **1** Risiko *neu.* Gefahr *f.* **2** Zufall *m. vt* wagen, riskieren.

haze (heiz) *n* **1** Dunst *m*. **2** Unklarheit *f*.
hazel ('heizəl) *n* Hasel *f*. Haselstrauch *m*. **hazelnut** *n* Haselnuß *f*.
he (hiː) *pron 3rd pers s* er.
head (hed) *n* **1** Kopf *m*. Haupt *neu*. **2** Leiter, Chef *m*. **3** Spitze *f*. vorderes Ende *neu*. **4** Stück *neu*. **5** Höhepunkt *m*. *vt* führen, vorstehen.
headache ('hedeik) *n* Kopfweh *neu*. Kopfschmerzen *m pl*.
heading ('hediŋ) *n* Überschrift *f*.
headlight ('hedlait) *n* Scheinwerfer *m*.
headline ('hedlain) *n* Schlagzeile *f*.
headlong ('hedlɔŋ) *adv* kopfüber. *adj* ungestüm, unbesonnen.
headmaster (hed'mɑːstə) *n* (Schul)Direktor *m*.
headphones ('hedfouns) *n pl* Kopfhörer *m*.
headquarters ('hedkwɔːtəz) *n pl* **1** Hauptquartier *neu*. **2** Hauptgeschäftsstelle *f*.
headscarf ('hedskɑːf) *n* Kopftuch *neu*.
headstrong ('hedstrɔŋ) *adj* starrköpfig, halsstarrig.
headway ('hedwei) *n* Fortschritte *m pl*.
heal (hiːl) *vt,vi* heilen.
health (helθ) *n* Gesundheit *f*. **health food** *n* Vollwertkost *f*. **your health** *interj* prosit! auf Ihr Wohl! **healthy** *adj* **1** gesund. **2** kräftig.
heap (hiːp) *n* **1** Haufen *m*. **2** *inf* Menge *f*. *v* **heap up** anhäufen.
hear* (hiə) *vi,vt* hören. **hearing** *n* **1** Hören *neu*. **2** Verhör *neu*. **hearing aid** *n* Hörgerät *neu*.
hearse (həːs) *n* Leichenwagen *m*.
heart (hɑːt) *n* **1** Herz *neu*. **2** Kern *m*. **3** Mut *m*. **heart attack** *n* Herzanfall *m*. **heartbeat** *n* Herzchlag, Puls *m*. **heartbroken** *adj* untröstlich. **heartless** *adj* herzlos. **hearty** *adj* herzhaft, herzlich.
hearth (hɑːθ) *n* Herd *m*.
heat (hiːt) *n* **1** Hitze *f*. **2** Eifer *m*. **3** *sport* Runde *f*. *vt* heizen. **heater** *n* Heizapparat *m*. **heating** *n* Heizung *f*. **heatwave** *n* Hitzewelle *f*.
heath (hiːθ) *n* Heide *f*.
heathen ('hiːðən) *n* Heide *m*. *adj* heidnisch.
heather ('heðə) *n* Heidekraut *neu*. Erika *f*.
heave (hiːv) *vt* (hoch)heben. *vi* sich heben und senken.
heaven ('hevən) *n* Himmel *m*. **heavenly** *adj* himmlisch.
heavy ('hevi) *adj* **1** schwer, gewichtig. **2** schwerfällig. **heavyweight** *n* Schwergewicht *neu*.
Hebrew ('hiːbruː) *adj* hebräisch. *n* **1** Hebräer *m*. **2** (language) Hebräisch *neu*.
heckle ('hekəl) *vt* (jemandem) Fangfragen stellen. **heckler** *n* Zwischenrufer *m*.
hectare ('hektεə) *n* Hektar *neu*.
hectic ('hektik) *adj* hektisch, fieberhaft.
hedge (hedʒ) *n* Hecke *f*. **hedgehog** *n* Igel *m*.
heed (hiːd) *vt* achten auf.
heel (hiːl) *n* **1** Ferse *f*. **2** Absatz *m*.
hefty ('hefti) *adj* kräftig.

height (hait) *n* **1** Höhe *f.* **2** Höhepunkt *m.* **heighten** *vt* **1** erhöhen. **2** verstärken.
heir (ɛə) *n* Erbe *m.* **heirloom** *n* Erbstück *neu.*
held (held) *v* see **hold.**
helicopter ('helikɔptə) *n* Hubschrauber *m.*
hell (hel) *n* Hölle *f.* *interj* verdammt!
hello (hə'lou) *interj* **1** guten Tag! grüß Gott! **2** hallo!
helm (helm) *n* Ruder *neu.*
helmet ('helmit) *n* Helm *m.*
help (help) *vt* helfen, unterstützen. *vi* helfen. **help oneself** sich bedienen. ~*n* Hilfe *f.* **helpless** *adj* hilflos.
hem (hem) *n* Saum *m.* *vt* säumen.
hemisphere ('hemisfiə) *n* Halbkugel, Hemisphäre *f.*
hemp (hemp) *n* Hanf *m.*
hen (hen) *n* **1** Huhn *neu.* **2** Weibchen *neu.*
hence (hens) *adv* **1** hieraus, daher, daraus. **2** von hier.
henna ('henə) *n* Henna *f.*
her (həː) *pron 3rd pers s* **1** sie. **2** ihr. *poss adj 3rd pers s* ihr.
herald ('herəld) *n* Herold *m.* *vt* ankündigen.
herb (həːb) *n* Kraut *neu.*
herd (həːd) *n* Herde *f.* *vt* weiden, hüten. **herdsman** *n* Hirt *m.*
here (hiə) *adv* **1** hier. **2** hierher.
hereditary (hi'reditri) *adj* erblich.
heredity (hi'rediti) *n* Vererbung *f.*
heresy ('herəsi) *n* Ketzerei *f.*
heritage ('heritidʒ) *n* **1** Erbschaft *f.* **2** Erbrecht *neu.*
hermit ('həːmit) *n* Einsiedler *m.*
hero ('hiərou) *n, pl* **heroes** Held *m.* **heroine** *n* Heldin *f.*
heroin ('herouin) *n* Heroin *neu.*
heron ('herən) *n* Reiher *m.*
herring ('heriŋ) *n* Hering *m.*
hers (həːz) *poss pron 3rd pers s* ihrer, der ihre *or* ihrige. **herself** *pron 3rd pers s* **1** sich. **2** sich selbst. **3** sie selbst. **by herself** allein, von selbst.
hesitate ('heziteit) *vi* zögern. **hesitation** *n* Zögern, Schwanken *neu.*
hexagon ('heksəgən) *n* Sechseck *neu.*
hibernate ('haibəneit) *vi* überwintern.
hiccup ('hikʌp) *n* Schluckauf *m.* *vi* den Schluckauf haben.
hide*[1] (haid) *vt* **1** verstecken, verbergen. **2** verheimlichen. *vi* sich verbergen.
hide[2] (haid) *n* Fell *neu.* Haut *f.*
hideous ('hidiəs) *adj* **1** scheußlich, gräßlich. **2** häßlich.
hiding[1] ('haidiŋ) *n* Versteck *neu.* **hiding-place** *n* Schlupfwinkel *m.*
hiding[2] ('haidiŋ) *n* Prügel *f.*
hierarchy ('haiərɑːki) *n* Hierarchie *f.*
high (hai) *adj* **1** hoch. **2** groß. **3** bedeutend. **4** vornehm. **highly** *adv* **1** in hohem Maße, äußerst, hoch. **2** lobend.
highbrow ('haibrau) *adj inf* intellektuell.
high-fidelity *adj* Hi-Fi.
high frequency *n* Hochfrequenz *f.*
high jump *n* Hochsprung *m.*
highland ('hailənd) *n* Hochland *neu.*

highlight ('hailait) *n* **1** Glanzlicht *neu.* **2** Höhepunkt *m.* *vt* hervorheben.

highness ('hainis) *n* **His/Her/Your Highness** Seine/Ihre/Eure Hoheit *f.*

highpitched ('haipitʃd) *adj* schrill, hoch.

high-rise *adj* vielstöckig. **high-rise building** *n* Hochhaus *neu.*

high-spirited *adj* übermütig, wagemütig.

highway ('haiwei) *n* Landstraße *f.*

hijack ('haidʒæk) *vt* **1** (be)rauben. **2** (an aeroplane) entführen.

hike (haik) *vi* wandern. *n* Wanderung *f.*

hilarious (hi'lɛəriəs) *adj* lustig, fröhlich.

hill (hil) *n* Hügel, Berg *m.* **hillside** *n* Abhang *m.* **hilltop** *n* Bergspitze *f.*

him (him) *pron 3rd pers s* **1** ihn. **2** ihm. **himself** *pron 3rd pers s* **1** sich. **2** sich selbst. **3** er selbst. **by himself** allein, von selbst.

hind (haind) *adj* hinter. **hindleg** *n* Hinterbein *neu.* **hindsight** *n* späte Einsicht, Nachsicht *f.*

hinder ('hində) *vt* (ver)hindern, hemmen.

Hindu ('hindu:) *n* Hindu *m.* **Hinduism** *n* Hinduismus *m.*

hinge (hindʒ) *n* Scharnier *f.* Gelenk *neu.* *vi* abhängen, ankommen.

hint (hint) *n* Hinweis, Wink *m.* *vt* andeuten.

hip (hip) *n* Hüfte *f.*

hippopotamus (hipə'pɔtəməs) *n* Nilpferd *neu.*

hire (haiə) *vt* mieten. *n* Miete *f.* **hire car** Mietauto *neu.*

his (hiz) *poss adj 3rd pers s* sein. *poss pron 3rd pers s* seiner, der seine *or* seinige.

hiss (his) *vi* zischen. *n* Zischen *neu.*

history ('histri) *n* Geschichte *f.* **historian** *n* Historiker *m.* **historical** *adj* geschichtlich, historisch.

hit* (hit) *vt,vi* **1** schlagen. **2** treffen. *n* **1** Treffer *m.* **2** Schlag *m.* **3** *mus* Schlager *m.*

hitch (hitʃ) *vt* **1** festmachen. **2** rücken. **hitch-hike** *vi* per Anhalter fahren, trampen.

hive (haiv) *n* Bienenstock *m.*

hoard (hɔ:d) *n* Vorrat, Schatz *m.* *vi,vt* hamstern, horten.

hoarding ('hɔ:diŋ) *n* **1** Bauzaun *m.* **2** Reklamewand *f.*

hoarse (hɔ:s) *adj* heiser.

hoax (houks) *n* Täuschung, Fopperei *f.* *vt* zum besten haben, anführen.

hobble ('hɔbəl) *vi* humpeln.

hobby ('hɔbi) *n* Hobby, Steckenpferd *neu.*

hock[1] (hɔk) *n* Sprunggelenk *neu.*

hock[2] (hɔk) *n* Rheinwein *m.*

hockey ('hɔki) *n* Hockey *neu.*

hoe (hou) *n* Haue, Hacke *f.* *vt,vi* hacken.

hog (hɔg) *n* Schwein *neu.* *vt sl* an sich reißen.

hoist (hɔist) *vt* hochziehen. *n* Aufzug, Kran *m.* Winde *f.*

hold*[1] (hould) *vt* **1** (fest)halten. **2** zurückhalten. **3** besitzen. **4** abhalten. **5** fassen, enthalten. **6** vertreten. *vi* **1** gelten. **2** sich

halten. *n* Griff, Halt *m*. **hold-all** *n* Reisetasche *f*. **holder** *n* **1** Behälter *m*. **2** Inhaber *m*.
hold[2] (hould) *n* Laderaum, Schiffsraum *m*.
hole (houl) *n* Loch *neu*. Höhle *f*.
holiday ('hɔlidi) *n* **1** Feiertag *m*. **2** *pl* Ferien *pl*. Urlaub *m*. **holiday camp** *n* Ferienlager *neu*. **holiday-maker** *n* Urlauber *m*.
Holland ('hɔlənd) *n* Holland *neu*.
hollow ('hɔlou) *adj* hohl. *n* Höhle, Aushöhlung *f*.
holly ('holi) *n* Stechpalme *f*.
holster ('houlstə) *n* Pistolenhalfter *f*.
holy ('houli) *adj* heilig.
homage ('hɔmidʒ) *n* Huldigung *f*.
home (houm) *n* **1** Heim *neu*. **2** Heimat *f*. *adv* heim, nach Hause. **at home** zu Hause. ~*adj* **1** einheimisch. **2** häuslich. **homecoming** *n* Heimkehr *f*. **homeland** *n* Heimatland *neu*. Heimat *f*. **homesick** *adj* **be homesick** Heimweh haben. **homework** *n* Schularbeit *f*. Schulaufgaben *f pl*.
homosexual (houmə'sekʃuəl) *adj* homosexuell. *n* Homosexuelle(r) *m*.
honest ('ɔnist) *adj* ehrlich.
honey ('hʌni) *n* Honig *m*. **honeymoon** *n* Flitterwochen *f pl*.
honour ('ɔnə) *n* **1** Ehre, Würde *f*. **2** Ruf *m*. **3** Auszeichnung *f*. **His/Her/Your Honour** Sein/Ihr/Euer Ehrwürden *or* Gnaden. ~*vt* (be)ehren, verehren. **honorary** *adj* Ehren—.
hood (hud) *n* **1** Kapuze *f*. **2** *mot* Verdeck *neu*.
hoof (huːf) *n* Huf *m*.
hook (huk) *n* Haken *m*. *vt* (an-, zu-)haken, fangen.
hooligan ('huːligən) *n* Rowdy *m*.
hoop (huːp) *n* Reifen, Ring *m*.
hoot (huːt) *vi* **1** *mot* hupen. **2** schreien.
Hoover ('huːvə) *n* *Tdmk* Staubsauger *m*. *vt* (ab)saugen.
hop[1] (hɔp) *vi* hüpfen, springen. *n* Hüpfer, Sprung *m*.
hop[2] (hɔp) *n* *bot* Hopfen *m*.
hope (houp) *vt,vi* (er)hoffen. *n* Hoffnung *f*.
horde (hɔːd) *n* Horde *f*.
horizon (hə'raizən) *n* Horizont *m*. **horizontal** *adj* waagerecht, horizontal.
horn (hɔːn) *n* **1** Horn *neu*. **2** *mot* Hupe *f*.
horoscope ('hɔrəskoup) *n* Horoskop *neu*.
horrible ('hɔrəbl̩) *adj* **1** schrecklich, entsetzlich. **2** gräßlich.
horrid ('hɔrid) *adj* gräßlich, scheußlich.
horrify ('hɔrifai) *vt* entsetzen, erschrecken.
horror ('hɔrə) *n* **1** Entsetzen *neu*. **2** Grausen *neu*. **3** Greuel *m*.
hors d'oeuvres (ɔː 'dəːv) *n pl* Vorspeise *f*.
horse (hɔːs) *n* **1** Pferd *neu*. **2** *mil* Reiterei *f*. **on horseback** *adv* zu Pferde. **horse chestnut** *n* Roßkastanie *f*. **horseman** *n* Reiter *m*. **horsepower** *n* Pferdestärke *f*. **horse-**

racing *n* Pferderennen *neu.*
horseshoe *n* Hufeisen *neu.*
horticulture ('hɔːtikʌltʃə) *n* Gartenbau *m.*
hose (houz) *n* **1** Schlauch *m.* **2** (lange) Strümpfe *f pl.*
hosiery ('houziəri) *n* Strumpfwaren *f pl.*
hospitable ('hɔspitəbəl) *adj* gastfreundlich.
hospital ('hɔspitl̩) *n* Krankenhaus, Spital *neu.*
hospitality (hɔspi'tæliti) *n* Gastfreundschaft *f.*
host[1] (houst) *n* **1** Gastgeber *m.* **2** Wirt *m.*
host[2] (houst) *n* Menge *f.*
hostage ('hɔstidʒ) *n* Geisel *m,f.*
hostel ('hɔstl̩) *n* **1** Herberge *f.* **2** Wohnheim *neu.*
hostess ('houstis) *n* Gastgeberin *f.*
hostile ('hɔstail) *adj* feindlich.
hot (hɔt) *adj* **1** heiß. **2** scharf, pikant. **hotplate** *n* Kochplatte *f.* **hot-tempered** *adj* heißblütig, feurig. **hot-water bottle** *n* Wärmflasche *f.*
hotel (hou'tel) *n* Hotel *neu.*
hound (haund) *n* Jagdhund *m.*
hour (auə) *n* Stunde *f.*
house (*n* haus; *v* hauz) *n* Haus *neu.* *vt* unterbringen.
houseboat ('hausbout) *n* Hausboot *neu.*
housebound ('hausbaund) *adj* gezwungen, zu Hause zu bleiben.
household ('haushould) *n* Haushalt *m.*
housekeeper ('hauskiːpə) *n* Haushälterin *f.*
housemaid ('hausmeid) *n* Hausmädchen *neu.*
House of Commons *n* Abgeordnetenhaus, Unterhaus *neu.*
House of Lords *n* Herrenhaus, Oberhaus *neu.*
houseproud ('hauspraud) *adj* penibel.
housewife ('hauswaif) *n* Hausfrau *f.*
housework ('hauswəːk) *n* Hausarbeit *f.*
housing ('hauziŋ) *n* Unterkunft, Unterbringung *f.*
hover ('hɔvə) *vi* schweben.
hovercraft *n* Luftkissenfahrzeug *neu.*
how (hau) *adv* wie. **how do you do?** wie geht es (Ihnen)? **how much** wieviel. **however** *adv* wie auch (immer). *conj* dennoch, doch, jedoch, aber.
hub (hʌb) *n* **1** Nabe *f.* **2** Angelpunkt *m.*
huddle ('hʌdl̩) *vi* sich (zusammen)drängen.
huff (hʌf) *n* üble Laune *f.*
hug (hʌg) *vt* umarmen. *n* Umarmung *f.*
huge (hjuːdʒ) *adj* ungeheuer, riesig.
hulk (hʌlk) *n* **1** Schiffsgerippe *f.* **2** unförmige Masse *f.*
hull (hʌl) *n* Schiffsrumpf *m.*
hullo (hə'lou) *interj* **1** guten Tag! grüß Gott! **2** hallo!
hum (hʌm) *vi,vt* summen.
human ('hjuːmən) *adj* menschlich. *n* Mensch *m.* **humane** *adj* menschlich, human. **humanism** *n* Humanismus *m.* **human nature** *n* menschliche Natur *f.*
humanity (hjuː'mæniti) *n* **1** Menschheit *f.* **2** Menschlichkeit *f.* **humanitarian** *adj*

menschenfreundlich. *n* Menschenfreund *m*.
humble ('hʌmbəl) *adj* bescheiden, demütig.
humdrum ('hʌmdrʌm) *adj* eintönig, fad, langweilig. *n* Eintönigkeit *f*.
humid ('hjuːmid) *adj* feucht.
humiliate (hjuː'milieit) *vt* demütigen.
humility (hjuː'militi) *n* Demut, Bescheidenheit *f*.
humour ('hjuːmə) *n* **1** Humor *m*. **2** Laune *f*. *vt* willfahren, aufheitern. **humorist** *n* Humorist *m*. **humorous** *adj* komisch, lustig.
hump (hʌmp) *n* Buckel *m*.
hunch (hʌntʃ) *vi* nach vorn rücken. *vt* krümmen. *n inf* Ahnung *f*. Verdacht *m*. **hunchback** *n* Bucklige(r) *m*.
hundred ('hʌndrəd) *adj* hundert. *n* Hundert *neu*. **hundredth** *adj* hundertste. **hundredweight** *n* Zentner *m*.
hung (hʌŋ) *v* see **hang**.
Hungary ('hʌŋgəri) *n* Ungarn *neu*. **Hungarian** *adj* ungarisch. *n* **1** Ungar *m*. **2** (language) Ungarisch *neu*.
hunger ('hʌŋgə) *n* Hunger *m*. *vi* hungern (nach). **hunger-strike** *n* Hungerstreik *m*. **hungry** *adj* hungrig. **be hungry** Hunger haben.
hunt (hʌnt) *vt,vi* jagen. *n* Jagd *f*. **hunting** *n* Jagen *neu*. **huntsman** *n* Jäger, Weidmann *m*.
hurdle ('həːdḷ) *n* Hürde *f*.
hurl (həːl) *vt* schleudern.
hurrah (hu'rɑː) *interj* hurra!
hurricane ('hʌrikein) *n* Orkan *m*.
hurry ('hʌri) *vi* eilen, sich beeilen. *vt* beschleunigen, antreiben. *n* Eile, Hast *f*. **be in a hurry** Eile *or* es eilig haben.
hurt* (həːt) *vt* **1** verletzen. **2** weh tun. *vi* weh tun. *n* **1** Schmerz *m*. **2** Verletzung *f*.
husband ('hʌzbənd) *n* Ehemann, Mann, Gatte *m*.
hush (hʌʃ) *interj* still! *n* Stille *f*. *v* **hush up** verschweigen.
husk (hʌsk) *n* Hülse, Schale *f*. *vt* schälen.
husky ('hʌski) *adj* heiser.
hussar (hu'zɑː) *n* Husar *m*.
hustle ('hʌsəl) *vi* eilen. *vt* drängen. *n* Drängen *neu*.
hut (hʌt) *n* Hütte *f*.
hutch (hʌtʃ) *n* **1** Kasten *m*. **2** Verschlag *m*.
hyacinth ('haiəsinθ) *n* Hyazinthe *f*.
hybrid ('haibrid) *n* Mischling *m*. Hybride *f*.
hydraulic (hai'drɔːlik) *adj* hydraulisch.
hydro-electric *adj* hydroelektrisch.
hydrofoil ('haidroufɔil) *n* Tragflächenboot *neu*.
hydrogen ('haidrədʒən) *n* Wasserstoff *m*.
hyena (hai'iːnə) *n* Hyäne *f*.
hygiene ('haidʒiːn) *n* Hygiene *f*. **hygienic** *adj* hygienisch.
hymn (him) *n* Hymne *f*. Kirchenlied *neu*. **hymnbook** *n* Gesangbuch *neu*.
hyphen ('haifən) *n* Bindestrich *m*.
hypnosis (hip'nousis) *n* Hypnose *f*. **hypnotism** *n* Hypnotismus *m*.
hypochondria (haipə'kɔndriə)

n Hypochondrie *f*. **hypochondriac** *n* Hypochonder *m*.
hypocrisy (hi'pɔkrəsi) *n* Heuchelei *f*. **hypocrite** *n* Heuchler, Scheinheilige(r) *m*.
hypodermic (haipə'də:mik) *adj* **hypodermic syringe** Spritze *f*.
hypothesis (hai'pɔθəsis) *n pl* **-ses** Hypothese *f*.
hysterectomy (histə'rektəmi) *n* Hysterektomie *f*.
hysteria (his'tiəriə) *n* Hysterie *f*. **hysterical** *adj* hysterisch.

I

I (ai) *pron 1st pers sing* ich.
ice (ais) *n* Eis *neu*. **iceberg** *n* Eisberg *m*. **ice-cream** *n* Eiskrem *f*. (Speise)Eis *neu*. **ice-rink** *n* Eisbahn *f*. **ice skate** *n* Schlittschuh *m*. **icing** *n* Zuckerguß *m*. **icy** *adj* eisig.
Iceland ('aislənd) *n* Island *neu*. **Icelander** *n* Isländer *m*. **Icelandic** (ais'lændik) *adj* isländisch. *n* (language) Isländisch *neu*.
idea (ai'diə) *n* Idee *f*. Begriff, Gedanke *m*.
ideal (ai'diəl) *n* Ideal *neu*. *adj* ideal, vorbildlich. **idealistic** *adj* idealistisch. **idealize** *vt* idealisieren.
identify (ai'dentifai) *vt* identifizieren. **identification** *n* Identifizierung *f*.
identity (ai'dentiti) *n* **1** Identität, Gleichheit *f*. **2** Persönlichkeit *f*. **identical** *adj* **1** identisch. **2** derselbe. **identical twins** *n pl* eineiige Zwillinge *m pl*. **identity card** *n* (Personal)Ausweis *m*.
ideology (aidi'ɔlədʒi) *n* Ideologie *f*.
idiom ('idiəm) *n* **1** Idiom *neu*. **2** Mundart *f*.
idiosyncrasy (idiə'siŋkrəsi) *n* Eigenart *f*.
idiot ('idiət) *n* Idiot, Schwachsinnige(r) *m*.
idle ('aidḷ) *adj* **1** müßig. **2** faul. **3** unbenutzt.
idol ('aidḷ) *n* Idol *neu*. Abgott *m*. **idolatry** *n* Abgötterei *f*.
idyllic (i'dilik) *adj* idyllisch.
if (if) *conj* **1** wenn, falls. **2** ob. **as if** als ob.
igloo ('iglu:) *n* Iglu *m*.
ignite (ig'nait) *(vi),vt* (sich) entzünden. **ignition** *n* **1** Entzündung *f*. Anzünden *neu*. **2** *mot* Zündung *f*.
ignorant ('ignərənt) *adj* **1** unwissend, ungebildet. **2** nicht wissend.
ignore (ig'nɔ:) *vt* ignorieren, nicht beachten *or* berücksichtigen.
ill (il) *adj* krank. *adj,adv* übel, schlecht. **ill-bred** *adj* ungezogen, unhöflich, schlecht erzogen. **illness** *n* Krankheit *f*. **ill-treat** *vt* mißhandeln, mißbrauchen. **ill will** *n* Mißgunst *f*.
illegal (i'li:gəl) *adj* ungesetzlich, illegal.
illegible (i'ledʒəbəl) *adj* unlesbar.
illegitimate (ili'dʒitimət) *adj* unehelich.
illicit (i'lisit) *adj* gesetzwidrig.
illiterate (i'litərət) *adj* analphabetisch. *n* Analphabet *m*.
illogical (i'lɔdʒikəl) *adj* unlogisch.

illuminate (i'lu:mineit) *vt* beleuchten.

illusion (i'lu:ʒən) *n* Illusion, Täuschung *f*.

illustrate ('iləstreit) *vt* **1** illustrieren. **2** erläutern. **illustration** *n* **1** Illustration *f*. Bild *neu*. **2** Erläuterung *f*. **3** Beispiel *neu*.

illustrious (i'lʌstriəs) *adj* berühmt.

image ('imidʒ) *n* **1** Bild, Abbild *neu*. **2** Sinnbild *neu*. **imagery** *n* Bildersprache *f*.

imagine (i'mædʒin) *vt* sich vorstellen. **imaginary** *adj* imaginär, eingebildet. **imagination** *n* Einbildung(skraft), Phantasie, Vorstellungskraft *f*. **imaginative** *adj* phantasievoll, einfallsreich.

imbalance (im'bæləns) *n* Unausgewogenheit *f*.

imbecile ('imbəsi:l) *n* Schwachsinnige(r) *m*.

imitate ('imiteit) *vt* nachahmen. **imitation** *n* **1** Nachahmung *f*. **2** Nachbildung *f*. *adj* Kunst—.

immaculate (i'mækjulət) *adj* fleckenlos.

immature (imə'tjuə) *adj* unreif.

immediate (i'mi:diət) *adj* unmittelbar, sofortig. **immediately** *adv* sofort, gleich.

immense (i'mens) *adj* gewaltig, ungeheuer.

immerse (i'mə:s) *vt* eintauchen, vertiefen. **immersion** *n* Eintauchen, Vertieftsein *neu*. **immersion heater** *n* Tauchsieder *m*.

immigrate ('imigreit) *vi* einwandern. **immigrant** *n* Einwanderer *m*.

imminent ('iminənt) *adj* bevorstehend.

immobile (i'moubail) *adj* unbeweglich, bewegungslos. **immobilize** *vt* unbeweglich machen.

immoral (i'mɔrəl) *adj* unmoralisch, unsittlich.

immortal (i'mɔ:tl̩) *adj* unsterblich.

immovable (i'mu:vəbəl) *adj* **1** unbeweglich. **2** unerschütterlich.

immune (i'mju:n) *adj* **1** immun. **2** geschützt. **immunize** *vt med* immunisieren, impfen.

imp (imp) *n* **1** Kobold *m*. **2** Spitzbube *m*.

impact ('impækt) *n* **1** Zusammenstoß, Aufprall *m*. **2** Einfluß *m*. Wirkung *f*.

impair (im'pɛə) *vt* beeinträchtigen.

impart (im'pɑ:t) *vt* **1** mitteilen. **2** geben.

impartial (im'pɑ:ʃəl) *adj* unparteiisch.

impassable (im'pɑ:səbəl) *adj* unbefahrbar.

impatient (im'peiʃənt) *adj* ungeduldig. **impatience** *n* Ungeduld *f*.

impeach (im'pi:tʃ) *vt* **1** anklagen. **2** zur Rechenschaft ziehen.

impeccable (im'pekəbəl) *adj* **1** sündlos. **2** einwandfrei.

impediment (im'pedimənt) *n* **1** Hindernis *neu*. **2** (of speech) Sprachfehler *m*.

imperative (im'perətiv) *adj* **1** erforderlich. **2** befehlend. *n* Befehlsform *f*. Imperativ *m*.

imperfect (im'pə:fikt) *adj* **1**

unvollkommen. **2** mangelhaft. *n* Imperfekt *neu*.
imperial (im'piəriəl) *adj* kaiserlich, Reichs—.
impersonal (im'pəːsənl) *adj* unpersönlich.
impersonate (im'pəːsəneit) *vt* **1** verkörpern. **2** sich ausgeben als.
impertinent (im'pəːtinənt) *adj* unverschämt, frech.
impetuous (im'petʃuəs) *adj* ungestüm.
impetus ('impitəs) *n* Antrieb, Anstoß *m*.
impinge (im'pindʒ) *vi* **1** stoßen. **2** einwirken.
implement ('impləmənt) *n* Werkzeug, Gerät *neu*. *vt* durchführen.
implicate ('impləkeit) *vt* **1** hineinziehen, verwickeln. **2** implizieren.
implicit (im'plisit) *adj* implizit, inbegriffen.
implore (im'plɔː) *vt* anflehen.
imply (im'plai) *vt* **1** implizieren, in sich schließen. **2** andeuten, zu verstehen geben. **implication** *n* **1** Bedeutung *f*. **2** Folge *f*.
import (*v* im'pɔːt; *n* 'impɔrt) *vt* einführen, importieren. *n* **1** Einfuhr *f*. Import *m*. **2** *pl* Einfuhrwaren *f pl*. **3** Bedeutung *f*. **importation** *n* Einfuhr *f*. Import *m*.
importance (im'pɔːtn̩s) *n* **1** Wichtigkeit *f*. **2** Bedeutung *f*. **important** *adj* **1** wichtig. **2** bedeutend. **3** einflußreich.
impose (im'pouz) *vt* auferlegen, aufbürden. **impose upon** zu sehr beanspruchen. **imposing** *adj* imponierend, eindrucksvoll.
impossible (im'posəbəl) *adj* unmöglich.
impostor (im'pɔstə) *n* Betrüger, Hochstapler *m*.
impotent ('impətənt) *adj* **1** unfähig. **2** *med* impotent.
impound (im'paund) *vt* beschlagnehmen.
impoverish (im'pɔvəriʃ) *vt* arm machen.
impress (im'pres) *vt* **1** beeindrucken, Eindruck machen auf. **2** (ein)drücken, einprägen. **impression** *n* **1** Eindruck *m*. **2** Abdruck *m*. **3** (of a book) Auflage *f*.
imprint (*n* 'imprint; *v* im'print) *n* **1** Aufdruck *m*. **2** Eindruck *m*. *vt* aufdrücken, einprägen.
imprison (im'prizən) *vt* einsperren, ins Gefängnis werfen. **imprisonment** *n* **1** Gefangenschaft *f*. **2** Gefängnisstrafe *f*.
improbable (im'prɔbəbəl) *adj* **1** unwahrscheinlich. **2** unglaubhaft.
improper (im'prɔpə) *adj* **1** unanständig. **2** ungeeignet.
improve (im'pruːv) *vt* (ver)bessern. *vi* sich (ver)bessern, besser werden.
improvise ('imprəvaiz) *vt* improvisieren.
impudent ('impjudənt) *adj* unverschämt, frech.
impulse ('impʌls) *n* **1** (An)Trieb, Stoß *m*. **2** Impuls, Drang *m*.
impure (im'pjuə) *adj* unrein, unsauber.
in (in) *prep* **1** in. **2** an. **3** auf. **4** nach. *adv* **1** hinein, herein. **2** innen.

inability (inə'biliti) *n* Unfähigkeit *f*.
inaccurate (in'ækjurət) *adj* **1** ungenau, unrichtig. **2** fehlerhaft.
inadequate (in'ædikwit) *adj* unangemessen, unzulänglich, ungenügend.
inadvertent (inəd'vəːtnt) *adj* **1** unachtsam. **2** unabsichtlich. **3** nachlässig.
inane (i'nein) *adj* sinnlos, nichtig, geistlos.
inarticulate (inaː'tikjulət) *adj* **1** unartikuliert, undeutlich. **2** sich schlecht ausdrückend.
inasmuch (inəz'mʌtʃ) *conj* **inasmuch as** (in)sofern (als), da, weil.
inaugurate (i'nɔːgjureit) *vt* einweihen.
incapable (in'keipəbəl) *adj* unfähig.
incendiary (in'sendiəri) *n* **1** Brandstifter *m*. **2** Brandbombe *f*.
incense[1] ('insens) *n* Weihrauch *m*.
incense[2] (in'sens) *vt* in Wut bringen, erzürnen.
incessant (in'sesənt) *adj* unaufhörlich.
incest ('insest) *n* Blutschande *f*. Inzest *m*.
inch (intʃ) *n* Zoll *m*.
incident ('insidənt) *n* **1** Zwischenfall *m*. **2** Zufall *m*. **incidental** *adj* **1** beiläufig. **2** gelegentlich. **3** zufällig. **4** Neben—.
incite (in'sait) *vt* aufregen, anstacheln.
incline (in'klain) *vi* sich neigen, geneigt sein zu. *n* Hang, Abhang *m*.
include (in'kluːd) *vt* einschließen, enthalten.
incoherent (inkou'hiərənt) *adj* unzusammenhängend.
income ('inkʌm) *n* Einkommen *neu*. Einkünfte *f pl*.
incompatible (inkəm'pætibəl) *adj* unvereinbar, nicht zusammenpassend.
incompetent (in'kɔmpətənt) *adj* unfähig.
incomplete (inkəm'pliːt) *adj* unvollständig.
incomprehensible (inkɔmpri'hensibəl) *adj* **1** unverständlich. **2** unbegreiflich.
inconceivable (inkən'siːvəbəl) *adj* unbegreiflich.
incongruous (in'kɔŋgruəs) *adj* unvereinbar.
inconsiderate (inkən'sidərət) *adj* rücksichtslos.
inconsistent (inkən'sistənt) *adj* **1** widersprechend. **2** inkonsequent. **3** unbeständig.
inconvenient (inkən'viːniənt) *adj* ungelegen, unbequem, lästig.
incorporate (in'kɔːpəreit) *vt* einverleiben, aufnehmen, vereinigen.
incorrect (inkə'rekt) *adj* unrichtig, falsch.
increase (*v* in'kriːs; *n* 'inkriːs) *vt* **1** erhöhen, steigern. **2** vermehren. *vi* **1** sich vermehren. **2** sich vergrößern, zunehmen. *n* **1** Vergrößerung *f*. **2** Zunahme *f*. Wachstum *neu*.
incredible (in'kredəbəl) *adj* unglaublich.
incubate ('inkjubeit) *vt* ausbrüten.
incur (in'kəː) *vt* **1** sich

zuziehen. **2** herbeiführen. **3** eingehen. **4** (debts) machen.
incurable (in'kjuərəbəl) *adj* unheilbar.
indecent (in'di:sənt) *adj* unanständig. **indecency** *n* Unanständigkeit *f*.
indeed (in'di:d) *adv* **1** in der Tat, tatsächlich. **2** zwar. **3** gewiß. *interj* **1** wirklich? **2** so!
indefinite (in'defənit) *adj* unbestimmt.
indemnity (in'demniti) *n* Entschädigung *f*.
indent (in'dent) *vt* **1** auszacken, einschneiden. **2** bestellen. *n* **1** Einschnitt *m*. **2** Bestellung *f*.
independent (indi'pendənt) *adj* unabhängig, selbständig. **independence** *n* Unabhängigkeit, Selbständigkeit *f*.
index ('indeks) *n* **1** Zeiger *m*. **2** Inhaltsverzeichnis *neu*. **index finger** *n* Zeigefinger *m*.
India ('indiə) *n* Indien *neu*. **Indian** *adj* **1** indisch. **2** (of America) indianisch. *n* **1** Inder *m*. **2** (of America) Indianer *m*.
indicate ('indikeit) *vt* (an)zeigen, hinweisen. **indicator** *n* **1** Zeiger *m*. **2** *mot* Winker *m*.
indifferent (in'difrənt) *adj* **1** gleichgültig. **2** mittelmäßig.
indigenous (in'didʒənəs) *adj* eingeboren, einheimisch.
indigestion (indi'dʒestʃən) *n* Verdauungsstörung *f*.
indignant (in'dignənt) *adj* entrüstet, empört.
indirect (indi'rekt) *adj* indirekt.
indiscreet (indi'skri:t) *adj* indiskret.
indispensable (indi'spensəbəl) *adj* unentbehrlich.
individual (indi'vidʒuəl) *adj* **1** einzeln. **2** persönlich. **3** individuell. *n* Individuum *neu*.
indoctrinate (in'dɔktrineit) *vt* schulen, belehren. **indoctrination** *n* Schulung, Belehrung *f*.
indolent ('indələnt) *adj* lässig, träge.
Indonesia (ində'ni:ziə) *n* Indonesien *neu*. **Indonesian** *adj* indonesisch. *n* Indonesier *m*.
indoor ('indɔ:) *adj* **1** Innen—, Haus—, häuslich. **2** *sport* Hallen—. **indoors** *adv* innen, im Hause, drinnen.
induce (in'dju:s) *vt* **1** dazu bringen, bewegen. **2** herbeiführen.
indulge (in'dʌldʒ) *vt* **1** sich hingeben, nachgeben. **2** schwelgen. **3** verwöhnen. *vi* sich hingeben.
industry ('indəstri) *n* **1** Industrie *f*. **2** Fleiß *m*. **industrial** *adj* industriell, gewerblich. **industrialisation** *n* Industrialisierung *f*. **industrious** *adj* fleißig, arbeitsam.
inefficient (ini'fiʃənt) *adj* **1** unwirksam. **2** unwirtschaftlich. **3** untüchtig.
inept (i'nept) *adj* **1** unpassend. **2** ungeschickt.
inequality (ini'kwɔliti) *n* Ungleichheit *f*.
inert (i'nə:t) *adj* **1** träge. **2** *sci* wirkungslos. **inertia** *n* Trägheit, Untätigkeit *f*.
inevitable (in'evitəbəl) *adj* unvermeidlich.
inexpensive (inik'spensiv) *adj* preiswert, billig.

inexperienced (inik'spiəriənst) *adj* unerfahren.

infallible (in'fæləbəl) *adj* unfehlbar.

infamous ('infəməs) *adj* berüchtigt, ehrlos.

infancy ('infənsi) *n* (frühe) Kindheit *f*.

infant ('infənt) *n* (Klein)Kind *neu*.

infantry ('infəntri) *n* Infanterie *f*.

infatuate (in'fætʃueit) *vt* verblenden, betören. **be infatuated with** verliebt *or* vernarrt sein in. **infatuation** *n* Verblendung *f*.

infect (in'fekt) *vt* infizieren, anstecken. **infection** *n* Ansteckung, Infektion *f*. **infectious** *adj* ansteckend.

infer (in'fəː) *vt* folgern, schließen.

inferior (in'fiəriə) *adj* **1** minderwertig. **2** niedriger. **3** untergeordnet. **inferiority** *n* Minderwertigkeit *nf*. **inferiority complex** *n* Minderwertigkeitskomplex *m*.

infernal (in'fəːnl̩) *adj* teuflisch, höllisch.

infest (in'fest) *vt* **1** (in Schwärmen) überlaufen, überschwemmen. **2** heimsuchen, plagen.

infidelity (infi'deliti) *n* Untreue *f*.

infiltrate ('infiltreit) *vt* durchsickern lassen, infiltrieren. *vi* eindringen.

infinite ('infinit) *adj* unendlich. **infinity** *n* Unendlichkeit *f*.

infinitive (in'finitiv) *n* Infinitiv *m*.

infirm (in'fəːm) *adj* schwach, gebrechlich.

inflame (in'fleim) *vt* **1** *med* entzünden. **2** entflammen, erregen.

inflammable (in'flæməbəl) *adj* **1** (leicht) entzündlich. **2** feuergefährlich.

inflate (in'fleit) *vt* aufblasen, aufpumpen. **inflation** *n* Inflation *f*.

inflection (in'flekʃən) *n* **1** *gram* Flexion, Abwandlung *f*. **2** Modulation *f*.

inflict (in'flikt) *vt* **1** zufügen. **2** auferlegen.

influence ('influəns) *n* **1** Einfluß *m*. **2** Wirkung *f*.

influenza (influ'enzə) *n* Grippe *f*.

influx ('inflʌks) *n* **1** Zustrom *m*. **2** Einfließen *neu*.

inform (in'fɔːm) *vt* informieren, mitteilen.

informal (in'fɔːməl) *adj* **1** zwangslos, nicht formell. **2** ungezwungen. **informality** *n* Ungezwungenheit, Zwanglosigkeit *f*.

information (infə'meiʃən) *n* **1** Auskunft *f*. **2** Information, Nachricht *f*.

infrastructure ('infrəstrʌktʃə) *n* Infrastruktur *f*.

infringe (in'frindʒ) *vt,vi* verletzen, übertreten.

infuriate (in'fjuərieit) *vt* rasend machen, aufbringen.

ingenious (in'dʒiːniəs) *adj* geistreich, erfinderisch, originell.

ingredient (in'griːdiənt) *n* Bestandteil *m*. Zutat *f*.

inhabit (in'hæbit) *vt* bewohnen.

inhabitant *n* **1** Einwohner *m*. **2** Bewohner *m*.
inhale (in'heil) *vt* einatmen.
inherent (in'hiərənt) *adj* **1** innewohnend. **2** angeboren.
inherit (in'herit) *vt* erben. **inheritance** *n* Erbschaft *f*.
inhibit (in'hibit) *vt* **1** hemmen. **2** hindern. **inhibition** *n* **1** Hemmung *f*. **2** (Be)Hinderung *f*.
inhospitable (in'hɔspitəbəl) *adj* **1** nicht gastfreundlich. **2** ungastlich.
inhuman (in'hjuːmən) *adj* unmenschlich.
iniquity (i'nikwiti) *n* **1** Ungerechtigkeit *f*. **2** Schlechtigkeit *f*. **3** Schandtat *f*.
initial (i'niʃəl) *adj* ursprünglich, anfänglich. *n* Anfangsbuchstabe *m*.
initiate (i'niʃieit) *vt* einweihen. *vt,vi* anfangen, beginnen. *vi* die Initiative ergreifen.
initiative (i'niʃətiv) *n* Initiative *f*.
inject (in'dʒekt) *vt* **1** einspritzen. **2** ausspritzen. **injection** *n* **1** Einspritzung *f*. **2** *med* Injektion, Spritze *f*.
injure ('indʒə) *vt* **1** beschädigen. **2** verletzen. **3** schaden. **4** beleidigen. **injury** *n* **1** Verletzung *f*. **2** Unrecht *neu*. **3** Beleidigung *f*.
injustice (in'dʒʌstis) *n* Ungerechtigkeit *f*.
ink (iŋk) *n* **1** Tinte *f*. **2** Druckerschwärze *f*.
inkling ('iŋkliŋ) *n* Andeutung, Ahnung *f*.
inland ('inlənd) *adj* inländisch, Binnen—. *n* Binnenland *neu*. *adv* **1** landeinwärts. **2** im Inland. **Inland Revenue** *n* **1** Steuereinnahmen *f pl*. **2** (Einkommens)Steuerbehörde *f*.
inmate ('inmeit) *n* **1** Insasse *m*. **2** Mitbewohner *m*.
inn (in) *n* Wirtshaus, Gasthaus *neu*.
innate (i'neit) *adj* angeboren.
inner ('inə) *adj* inner, Innen—, innerlich.
innocent ('inəsənt) *adj* **1** unschuldig. **2** harmlos. **3** einfältig. **innocence** *n* **1** Unschuld *f*. **2** Harmlosigkeit *f*. **3** Einfalt *f*.
innocuous (i'nɔkjuəs) *adj* harmlos, unschädlich.
innovation (inə'veiʃən) *n* Neuerung *f*.
innuendo (inju'endou) *n* Anspielung *f*.
innumerable (i'njuːmərəbəl) *adj* unzählbar, zahllos.
inoculate (i'nɔkjuleit) *vt* (ein)impfen. **inoculation** *n* (Ein)Impfung *f*.
inquest ('inkwest) *n* gerichtliche Untersuchung *f*.
inquire (in'kwaiə) *vi* (nach)fragen, sich erkundigen. **inquiry** *n* **1** Nachfrage, Erkundigung *f*. **2** Untersuchung *f*. **3** *pl* Auskünfte *f pl*.
inquisition (inkwi'ziʃən) *n* **1** Untersuchung *f*. **2** Inquisition *f*.
inquisitive (in'kwizitiv) *adj* **1** neugierig. **2** wißbegierig. **inquisitiveness** *n* **1** Neugier *f*. **2** Wißbegierde *f*.
insane (in'sein) *adj* **1** wahnsinnig. **2** verrückt. **insanity** *n* **1** Wahnsinn *m*. **2** Verrücktheit *f*.
insatiable (in'seiʃəbəl) *adj* unersättlich.

inscribe (in'skraib) *vt* **1** einschreiben. **2** beschriften. **3** eintragen. **inscription** *n* **1** Inschrift *f.* **2** Eintragung *f.*
insect ('insekt) *n* Insekt *neu.* **insecticide** *n* Insektengift *neu.*
insecure (insi'kjuə) *adj* unsicher. **insecurity** *n* Unsicherheit *f.*
inseminate (in'semineit) *vt* **1** befruchten. **2** einpflanzen. **insemination** *n* Befruchtung *f.*
insensitive (in'sensitiv) *adj* unempfindlich.
inseparable (in'sepərəbəl) *adj* untrennbar.
insert (in'sə:t) *vt* **1** einsetzen. **2** (a coin, etc.) einwerfen. **3** (an advertisement, etc.) aufgeben. **insertion** *n* **1** Einsetzung *f.* **2** Einwurf *m.* **3** Inserat *neu.*
inside (in'said) *n* Innere *neu.* Innenseite *f.* *adj* inner, Innen—. *adv* **1** drinnen. **2** hinein, herein. *prep* innerhalb.
insidious (in'sidiəs) *adj* heimtückisch.
insight ('insait) *n* Einsicht *f.*
insignificant (insig'nifikənt) *adj* **1** unbedeutend. **2** bedeutunglos.
insincere (insin'siə) *adj* unaufrichtig. **insincerity** *n* Unaufrichtigkeit *f.*
insinuate (in'sinjueit) *vt* **1** anspielen auf. **2** unbemerkt hineinbringen. **3** zu verstehen geben. **4** sich einschmeicheln. **insinuation** *n* **1** Andeutung *f.* **2** Einschmeichelung *f.*
insist (in'sist) *vi* bestehen. **insistence** *n* Bestehen *neu.*
insolent ('insələnt) *adj* unverschämt, frech. **insolence** *n* Unverschämtheit, Frechheit *f.*
insomnia (in'sɔmniə) *n* Schlaflosigkeit *f.*
inspect (in'spekt) *vt* **1** untersuchen. **2** inspizieren, besichtigen. **inspection** *n* **1** Untersuchung *f.* **2** Inspektion, Besichtigung *f.*
inspire (in'spaiə) *vt,vi* **1** inspirieren, eingeben, begeistern. **2** einatmen. **inspiration** *n* **1** Eingebung, Begeisterung *f.* **2** Einatmung *f.* **inspiring** *adj* begeisternd, belebend.
instability (instə'biliti) *n* Unbeständigkeit *f.*
install (in'stɔ:l) *vt* **1** einsetzen. **2** installieren, einrichten. **installation** *n* **1** Einsetzung *f.* **2** Installierung, Einrichtung *f.* Montage *f.*
instalment (in'stɔ:lmənt) *n* **1** Rate *f.* **2** (Teil)Lieferung *f.* **by instalments** *adv* ratenweise.
instance ('instəns) *n* **1** Beispiel *neu.* **2** (besonderer) Fall *m.* **3** Bitte *f.* **4** *law* Instanz *f.* **for instance** zum Beispiel. **instant** *adj* **1** sofortig, augenblicklich. **2** dringend. *n* Augenblick *m.* **instantaneous** *adj* sofortig, augenblicklich. **instantly** *adv* sogleich, sofort.
instead (in'sted) *adv* statt dessen. **instead of** (an)statt.
instep ('instep) *n* Rist, Spann *m.*
instigate ('instigeit) *vt* anstiften. **instigation** *n* Anstiftung *f.* **instigator** *n* Anstifter *m.*
instil (in'stil) *vt* **1** einträufeln. **2** einflößen. **instillation** *n* **1**

Einträufeln *neu.* **2** Einflößung *f.*

instinct ('instiŋkt) *n* (Natur)-Trieb, Instinkt *m.* **instinctive** *adj* unwillkürlich, instinktiv.

institute ('institju:t) *vt* einsetzen, einführen, gründen. *n* Institut *neu.* **institution** *n* **1** Institut *neu.* Anstalt *f.* **2** Stiftung *f.* **3** Einführung. **4** Institution, Einrichtung *f.*

instruct (in'strʌkt) *vt* **1** unterrichten. **2** unterweisen. **3** anweisen. **instruction** *n* **1** Unterricht *m.* **2** Unterweisung *f.* **3** Vorschrift, Anordnung. **4** Anweisung *f.* **instructive** *adj* instruktiv, lehrreich.

instrument ('instrumənt) *n* **1** Instrument *neu.* **2** Werkzeug *neu.* **3** Mittel *neu.* **instrumental** *adj* **1** behilflich, förderlich. **2** Instrumental—.

insubordinate (insə'bɔ:dinət) *adj* aufsässig, widersetzlich, ungehorsam. **insubordination** *n* Widersetzlichkeit *f.* Ungehorsam *m.*

insular ('insjulə) *adj* **1** insular, Insel—. **2** beschränkt.

insulate ('insjuleit) *vt* isolieren. **insulation** *n* Isolierung *f.*

insulin ('insjulin) *n* Insulin *neu.*

insult (*v* in'sʌlt; *n* 'insʌlt) *vt* beleidigen, beschimpfen. *n* Beleidigung, Beschimpfung *f.*

insure (in'ʃuə) *vt* versichern. **insurance** *n* Versicherung *f.* *adj* Versicherungs—.

intact (in'tækt) *adj* unberührt, intakt.

intake ('inteik) *n* **1** *tech* Einlaß *m.* **2** (Neu)Aufnahme *f.*

integral ('intigrəl) *adj* **1** integral, ganz, vollständig. **2** *math* Integral—.

integrate ('intigreit) *vt* **1** ergänzen. **2** integrieren. **integration** *n pol* Integration *f.*

integrity (in'tegriti) *n* **1** Vollständigkeit *f.* **2** Redlichkeit, Integrität *f.*

intellect ('intəlekt) *n* Intellekt, Verstand *m.* **intellectual** *adj* **1** Verstandes—, geistig. **2** intellektuell. *n* Intellektuelle(r) *m.*

intelligent (in'telidʒənt) *adj* **1** intelligent. **2** klug. **intelligence** *n* **1** Intelligenz *f.* **2** Verstand *m.* **3** *pol* (geheimer) Nachrichtendienst *m.* **intelligentsia** *n* Intelligenz, Intelligentsia *f.* **intelligible** *adj* verständlich.

intend (in'tend) *vt* **1** vorhaben, die Absicht haben zu. **2** meinen. **3** bestimmen. **intended** *adj* absichtlich.

intense (in'tens) *adj* **1** intensiv. **2** angespannt. **3** heftig. **intensify** *(vi),vt* (sich) verstärken. **intensity** *n* **1** Intensität *f.* **2** Anspannung *f.* **3** Heftigkeit *f.* **intensive** *adj* **1** intensiv, heftig. **2** verstärkend.

intent[1] (in'tent) *n* **1** Absicht *f.* **2** Plan *m.*

intent[2] (in'tent) *adj* **1** versessen. **2** gespannt.

intention (in'tenʃən) *n* **1** Absicht *f.* **2** Zweck *m.* **intentional** *adj* absichtlich.

inter (in'tə:) *vt* beerdigen.

interact (intə'rækt) *vt* sich gegenseitig beeinflussen. **interaction** *n* Wechselwirkung *f.*

intercept (intə'sept) *vt* **1** abfangen. **2** unterbrechen. **in-**

terception *n* **1** Abfangen *neu.* **2** Unterbrechung *f.*
interchange (intə'tʃeindʒ) *vt* austauschen. *vi* abwechseln. *n* **1** Austausch *m.* **2** Abwechslung *f.* **interchangeable** *adj* austauschbar.
intercourse ('intəkɔːs) *n* Verkehr, Ungang *m.*
interest ('intrəst) *n* **1** Interesse *neu.* Anteilnahme *m.* **2** Beteiligung *f.* **3** Nutzen *m.* **4** *comm* Zins *m.* *vt* **1** interessieren. **2** angehen. **take an interest in** sich interessieren für. **interesting** *adj* interessant.
interface ('intəfeis) *n* **1** Grenzschicht *f.* **2** *comp* Anpaßschaltung *f.*
interfere (intə'fiə) *vi* **1** sich einmischen. **2** stören. **interference** *n* **1** Einmischung *f.* **2** Störung *f.* **3** Dazwischentreten *neu.*
interim ('intərim) *n* Interim *neu.* Zwischenzeit *f.* *adj* vorläufig, Interims—.
interior (in'tiəriə) *adj* inner, Innen—, innerlich. *n* **1** Innere *neu.* **2** Binnenland *neu.*
interjection (intə'dʒekʃn̩) *n* Ausruf, Einwurf *m.* Interjektion *f.*
interlude ('intəluːd) *n* Zwischenspiel *neu.*
intermediate (intə'miːdiət) *adj* **1** dazwischenliegend. **2** Mittel—, Zwischen—. **intermediary** *adj* **1** dazwischen befindlich. **2** vermittelnd. *n* Vermittler *m.*
interminable (in'təːminəbəl) *adj* endlos, unendlich.
intermission (intə'miʃən) *n* **1** Aussetzen *neu.* **2** Unterbrechung *f.* **3** Pause *f.*
intermittent (intə'mitn̩t) *adj* aussetzend, mit Unterbrechungen.
intern (in'təːn) *vt* internieren. **internment** *n* Internierung *f.*
internal (in'təːnl̩) *adj* **1** inner(lich). **2** inländisch. **internal-combustion engine** *n* Verbrennungsmotor *m.*
international (intə'næʃənəl) *adj* international. *n sport* internationaler Spieler *m.*
interpose (intə'pouz) *vt* **1** einlegen. **2** einwerfen. *vi* **1** dazwischenstellen. **2** vermitteln.
interpret (in'təːprit) *vt* **1** interpretieren, auslegen, erklären. **2** dolmetschen. **3** darstellen. **interpretation** *n* **1** Interpretation, Auslegung, Erklärung *f.* **2** Darstellung *f.* **interpreter** *n* Dolmetscher *m.*
interrogate (in'terəgeit) *vt* **1** befragen. **2** verhören. **interrogation** *n* **1** Befragen *neu.* **2** Verhör *neu.*
interrogative (intə'rɔgətiv) *adj* fragend, Frage—.
interrupt (intə'rʌpt) *vt* unterbrechen. **interruption** *n* Unterbrechung *f.*
intersect (intə'sekt) *vt* durchschneiden. *vi* (sich) schneiden. **intersection** *n* **1** Durchschnitt *m.* **2** Schnittpunkt *m.* **3** *mot* Kreuzung *f.*
interval ('intəvəl) *n* **1** Zwischenraum *m.* **2** Pause *f.* **3** *mus* Intervall *neu.*
intervene (intə'viːn) *vi* **1** dazwischenkommen. **2** dazwischenliegen. **3** intervenieren.

intervention *n* **1** Dazwischenkommen *neu.* **2** Intervention *f.*

interview ('intəvju:) *n* **1** Unterredung *f.* **2** Interview *neu.* *vt* interviewen. **interviewer** *n* Interviewer *m.*

intestine (in'testin) *n* **1** Darm *m.* **2** *pl* Eingeweide *neu pl.*

intimate[1] ('intimeit) *adj* **1** vertraut, intim. **2** innig. **intimacy** *n* Vertraulichkeit, Intimität *f.*

intimate[2] ('intimit) *vt* **1** andeuten. **2** zu verstehen geben.

intimidate (in'timideit) *vt* einschüchtern. **intimidation** *n* Einschüchterung *f.*

into ('intə; *stressed* 'intu:) *prep* in, in...hinein.

intolerable (in'tɔlərəbəl) *adj* unerträglich. **intolerant** *adj* intolerant, unduldsam. **intolerance** *n* Intoleranz, Unduldsamkeit *f.*

intonation (intə'neiʃən) *n* **1** Anstimmung *f.* **2** Tonfall *m.* **3** *mus* Tongebung *f.*

intoxicate (in'tɔksikeit) *vt* berauschen. **intoxication** *n* **1** Berauschung *f.* **2** Rausch *m.*

intransitive (in'trænsitiv) *adj* *gram* intransitiv.

intricate ('intrikət) *adj* **1** kompliziert. **2** schwierig. **intricacy** *n* **1** Kompliziertheit *f.* **2** Schwierigkeit *f.*

intrigue (in'tri:g) *n* **1** Intrige *f.* **2** (Liebes)Verhältnis *neu.* *vi* intrigieren. *vt* neugierig machen. **intriguing** *adj* interessant, faszinierend.

intrinsic (in'trinsik) *adj* **1** innerlich. **2** wahr, eigentlich, wesentlich.

introduce (intrə'dju:s) *vt* **1** einführen, einleiten. **2** (a person) vorstellen. **introduction** *n* **1** Einführung, Einleitung *f.* **2** Vorstellung *f.* **introductory** *adj* einführend, einleitend.

introspective (intrə'spektiv) *adj* beschaulich, nach innen gekehrt, introspektiv.

introvert ('intrəvə:t) *vt* einwärts kehren. *n* introvertierter Mensch *m.*

intrude (in'tru:d) *vt* einzwängen. *vi* **1** sich eindrängen. **2** stören. **intruder** *n* Eindringling *m.* **intrusion** *n* Eindringen *neu.*

intuition (intju'iʃən) *n* Intuition *f.* **intuitive** *adj* intuitiv.

inundate ('inʌndeit) *vt* überschwemmen. **inundation** *n* Überschwemmung *f.*

invade (in'veid) *vt* **1** einfallen in, eindringen in. **2** befallen. **invasion** *n* Einfall *m.* Invasion *f.*

invalid[1] ('invəli:d) *n* **1** Kranke(r) *m.* **2** Invalide *m.*

invalid[2] (in'vælid) *adj* ungültig. **invalidate** *vt* ungültig machen.

invaluable (in'væljubəl) *adj* unschätzbar.

invariable (in'vɛəriəbəl) *adj* unveränderlich. **invariably** *adv* immer, stets.

invent (in'vent) *vt* **1** erfinden. **2** erdichten. **invention** *n* **1** Erfindung *f.* **2** Erdichtung *f.* **inventive** *adj* erfinderisch. **inventor** *n* Erfinder *m.*

inventory ('invəntəri) *n* **1** Inventar *neu.* **2** *comm* Inventur *f.*

invert (in'vəːt) *vt* umkehren. **inverted commas** Anführungszeichen *neu pl.*
invertebrate (in'vəːtəbreit) *adj* **1** wirbellos. **2** rückgratlos. *n* wirbelloses Tier *neu.*
invest (in'vest) *vt* **1** *comm* anlegen, investieren. **2** bekleiden. **invest in** *inf* kaufen. **investor** *n* Geldanleger *m.* **investment** *n* Kapitalanlage *f.*
investigate (in'vestigeit) *vt* erforschen, untersuchen. **investigation** *n* Untersuchung *f.*
invincible (in'vinsəbəl) *adj* unüberwindlich.
invisible (in'vizəbəl) *adj* unsichtbar.
invite (in'vait) *vt* **1** einladen. **2** anlocken. **invitation** *n* Einladung *f.*
invoice ('invɔis) *n* Faktura, Rechnung *f.*
invoke (in'vouk) *vt* **1** anrufen. **2** (a spirit) beschwören. **invocation** *n* Anrufung, Beschwörung *f.*
involve (in'vɔlv) *vt* verwickeln, hineinziehen. **involvement** *n* **1** Verwicklung *f.* **2** Schwierigkeit *f.*
inward ('inwəd) *adj* **1** innerlich. **2** nach innen gehend. **inwards** *adv* einwärts, nach innen.
iodine ('aiədiːn) *n* Jod *neu.*
Iran (i'rɑːn) *n* Iran *m.* **Iranian** *adj* iranisch. *n* Iranier *m.*
Iraq (i'rɑːk) *n* Irak *m.* **Iraqi** *adj* irakisch. *n* Iraker *m.*
Ireland ('aiələnd) *n* Irland *neu.* **Irish** *adj* irisch. **Irishman** *n* Ire, Irländer *m.* **Irishwoman** *n* Irin, Irländerin *f.*
iris ('airis) *n* **1** *anat* Iris *f.* **2** *bot* Schwertlilie *f.*
iron ('aiən) *n* **1** Eisen *neu.* **2** *dom* Bügeleisen *neu. adj* eisern, Eisen—. *vt* bügeln. **ironing board** *n* Bügelbrett *neu.*
ironmonger *n* Eisenwarenhändler *m.*
Iron Curtain *n* Eiserner Vorhang *m.*
irony ('airəni) *n* Ironie *f.* **ironic** *adj* ironisch, spöttisch.
irrational (i'ræʃənl) *adj* irrational, unvernünftig. **irrationality** *n* Unvernunft *f.*
irregular (i'regjulə) *adj* unregelmäßig. **irregularity** *n* Unregelmäßigkeit *f.*
irrelevant (i'reləvənt) *adj* **1** irrelevant, nicht zur Sache gehörig. **2** belanglos. **irrelevance** *n* Belanglosigkeit *f.*
irresistible (iri'zistəbəl) *adj* unwiderstehlich.
irrespective (iri'spektiv) *adj* **irrespective of** ohne Rücksicht auf, unabhängig von.
irresponsible (iri'spɔnsəbəl) *adj* verantwortungslos. **Irresponsibility** *n* Verantwortungslosigkeit *f.*
irrevocable (i'revəkəbəl) *adj* unwiderruflich.
irrigate ('irigeit) *vt* bewässern. **irrigation** *n* Bewässerung *f.*
irritate ('iriteit) *vt* reizen. **irritable** *adj* reizbar. **irritating** *adj* aufreizend, ärgerlich.
is (iz) *v* see **be.**
Islam ('izlɑːm) *n* Islam *m.* **Islamic** *adj* islamisch.
island ('ailənd) *n* Insel *f.* **islander** *n* Inselbewohner *m.*
isle (ail) *n* Insel *f.*
isolate ('aisəleit) *vt* **1** abson-

dern. **2** isolieren. **isolated** *adj* **1** abgesondert. **2** abgeschieden, isoliert. **isolation** *n* **1** Absonderung *f*. **2** Isolierung *f*.

Israel ('izreiəl) *n* Israel *neu*. **Israeli** *adj* israelisch. *n* Israeli *m*.

issue ('iʃuː) *n* **1** Herauskommen, Herausgeben *neu*. **2** Ausgabe *f*. **3** Nummer *f*. **4** Ergebnis *neu*. **5** Streitfrage *f*. *vi* herauskommen. *vt* **1** aussenden. **2** emittieren. **3** herausgeben.

isthmus ('isməs) *n* Landenge *f*. Isthmus *m*.

it (it) *pron 3rd pers s* **1** er *m*. sie *f*. es *neu*. **2** ihn *m*. sie *f*. es *neu*. **3** ihm *m,neu*. ihr *f*.

italic (i'tælik) *adj* kursiv. **italics** *n pl* Kursivdruck *m*.

Italy ('itəli) *n* Italien *neu*. **Italian** *adj* italienisch. *n* **1** Italiener *m*. **2** (language) Italienisch *neu*.

itch (itʃ) *n* Jucken *neu*. Krätze *f*. *vi* jucken. **itchy** *adj* juckend, krätzig.

item ('aitəm) *n* **1** Einzelheit *f*. **2** (Zeitungs)Notiz *f*. **3** (Rechnungs)Posten *m*.

itinerary (ai'tinərəri) *n* **1** Reiseroute *f*. **2** Reisebericht *m*. **itinerant** *adj* **1** (herum)reisend. **2** Wander—, Reise—.

its (its) *poss adj 3rd pers s* sein *m*. *neu*. ihr *f*. **itself** *pron 3rd pers s* **1** selbst. **2** sich. **3** sich selbst. **by itself** allein, von selbst.

ivory ('aivəri) *n* Elfenbein *neu*. *adj* Elfenbein—.

ivy ('aivi) *n* Efeu *m*.

J

jab (dʒæb) *n* **1** Stich *m*. **2** *inf med* Spritze *f*. *vt* stechen.

jack (dʒæk) *n* **1** *mot* Wagenheber *m*. **2** *game* Bube *m*. **3** *naut* Bugflagge *f*. *vt* heben.

jackdaw ('dʒækdɔː) *n* Dohle *f*.

jacket ('dʒækit) *n* **1** Jacke *f*. **2** (Schutz)Umschlag *m*.

jackpot ('dʒækpɔt) *n game* Jackpot *m*.

jade (dʒeid) *n* Jade, Nephrit *m*.

jaded ('dʒeidid) *adj* abgehetzt, ermüdet.

jagged ('dʒægid) *adj* zackig.

jaguar ('dʒægjuə) *n* Jaguar *m*.

jail (dʒeil) *n* Gefängnis *neu*. *vt* ins Gefängnis bringen, einsperren. **jailer** *n* Gefängniswärter *m*.

jam[1] (dʒæm) *vt* **1** (fest)klemmen. **2** versperren. *vi* sich (ver-, ein-)klemmen. *n* Gedränge *neu*.

jam[2] (dʒæm) *n* Marmelade *f*. **jam-jar** *n* Marmeladenglas *neu*.

Jamaica (dʒə'meikə) *n* Jamaika *neu*. **Jamaican** *adj* jamaikisch. *n* Jamaiker *m*.

January ('dʒænjuəri) *n* Januar *m*.

Japan (dʒə'pæn) *n* Japan *neu*. **Japanese** (dʒæpə'niːz) *adj* japanisch. *n*. **1** Japaner *m*. **2** (language) Japanisch *neu*.

jar[1] (dʒɑː) *n* **1** Glas *neu*. **2** Krug *m*.

jar[2] (dʒɑː) *n* Knarren *neu*. *vi* knarren.

jargon ('dʒɑːgən) *n* Jargon *m*. Fachsprache *f*.

jasmine ('dʒæzmin) *n* Jasmin *m*.

jaundice ('dʒɔːndis) *n med*

Gelbsucht *f.* **jaundiced** *adj* **1** gelbsüchtig. **2** neidisch.
jaunt (dʒɔːnt) *n* Ausflug *m.* **jaunty** *adj* flott, munter.
javelin ('dʒævlin) *n* **1** Wurfspieß *m.* **2** *sport* Speer *m.*
jaw (dʒɔː) *n* **1** Kiefer *m.* **2** *pl* Rachen *m. vi sl* schwatzen. **jawbone** *n* Kieferknochen *m.*
jazz (dʒæz) *n* Jazz *m. v* **jazz up** *sl* Leben bringen in, aufmöbeln. **jazzy** *adj inf* grell, schreiend.
jealous ('dʒeləs) *adj* eifersüchtig, neidisch. **jealousy** *n* Eifersucht *f.* Neid *m.*
jeans (dʒiːnz) *n pl* Jeans *pl.*
jeep (dʒiːp) *n* Jeep *m.*
jeer (dʒiə) *vi* höhnen, spotten. *vt* verhöhnen. *n* Spott *m.* **jeering** *adj* spöttisch, höhnisch.
jelly ('dʒeli) *n* Gelee *neu.* **jellyfish** *n* Qualle *f.*
jeopardize ('dʒepədaiz) *vt* gefährden. **jeopardy** *n* Gefahr *f.*
jerk (dʒəːk) *vt* rucken. *vi* ziehen, schleudern. *n* **1** Ruck, plötzlicher Stoß *m.* **jerky** *adj* **1** ruckartig. **2** holperig.
jersey ('dʒəːzi) *n* (Woll)Pullover *m.*
Jersey ('dʒəːzi) *n* (Insel) Jersey *neu.*
jest (dʒest) *n* Scherz, Spaß, Witz *m. vi* scherzen. **jester** *n* (Hof)Narr *m.*
Jesus ('dʒiːzəs) *n* Jesus *m.*
jet (dʒet) *n* **1** (Wasser-, Gas-) Strahl *m.* **2** Düse *f.* **jet-plane** *n* Düsenflugzeug *neu.*
jetty ('dʒeti) *n* **1** Hafendamm *m.* **2** Landungsbrücke *f.*
Jew (dʒuː) *n* Jude *m.* **jewish** *adj* jüdisch. **Jewry** *n* Judentum *neu.*
jewel ('dʒuːəl) *n* Juwel *neu,m.* **jeweller** *n* Juwelier *m.* **jewellery** *n* Schmuck *m.*
jig (dʒig) *n* Gigue *f. vi* Gigue tanzen, (herum) hüpfen.
jiggle ('dʒigəl) *(vi),vt* (umher)wackeln.
jigsaw ('dʒigsɔː) *n* Zusammensetzspiel *neu.*
jilt (dʒilt) *vt* sitzen lassen.
jingle ('dʒiŋgəl) *n* **1** Geklingel *neu.* **2** Wortgeklingel *neu. vi,vt* klingeln, klimpern.
job (dʒɔb) *n* **1** Arbeit *f.* **2** Stelle *f.* Job *m.* **3** Sache, Aufgabe *f.*
jockey ('dʒɔki) *n* Jockei *m.*
jodhpurs ('dʒɔdpəz) *n pl* Reithose *f.*
jog (dʒɔg) *vt* (an)stoßen, rütteln. *vi* (dahin)trotten. *n* **1** Stoß *m.* **2** Rütteln *neu.* **3** Trott *m.*
join (dʒɔin) *vt* **1** verbinden. **2** fügen. **3** zusammenbringen, vereinigen. **4** eintreten in, Mitglied werden. *vi* **1** sich verbinden. **2** angrenzen. **join in** mitmachen, teilnehmen. ~*n* **1** Verbindung(sstelle) *f.* **2** Fuge *f.* **3** Naht *f.* **joiner** *n* Tischler *m.* **joinery** *n* Tischlerarbeit *f.* **joint** *n* **1** Verbindung(sstelle) *f.* **2** *anat* Gelenk *neu.* **3** *cul* Braten *m.* **4** *sl* Lokal *neu.* Bude *f.* **5** *sl* Marihuana-Zigarette *f.* Joint *m. adj* **1** verbunden. **2** gemeinsam. *vt* **1** zusammenfügen. **2** verbinden. **3** mit Gelenken versehen.
joist (dʒɔist) *n* Querbalken *m.*
joke (dʒouk) *n* Scherz, Witz, Spaß *m. vi* scherzen. **joker** *n*

1 Spaßvogel *m.* **2** *game* Joker *m.* **practical joke** *n* Streich *m.*
jolly ('dʒɔli) *adj* lustig. *adv inf* ganz schön.
jolt (dʒoult) *vt,vi* rütteln. *vi* holpern. *n* Rütteln *neu.*
Jordan ('dʒɔːdn̩) *n* Jordanien *neu.* **Jordanian** *adj* jordanisch. *n* Jordanier *m.*
jostle ('dʒɔsəl) *vt* anstoßen. *vi* sich drängen. *n* (Zusammen)Stoß *m.* Gedränge *neu.*
journal ('dʒəːnl̩) *n* **1** Journal *neu.* **2** Tagebuch *neu.* **3** Zeitschrift *f.* **journalism** *n* Zeitungswesen *neu.* Journalismus *m.* **journalist** *n* Journalist *m.*
journey ('dʒəːni) *n* **1** Reise *f.* **2** Fahrt *f.* *vi* reisen, wandern.
jovial ('dʒouviəl) *adj* heiter, jovial. **joviality** *n* Heiterkeit, Jovialität *f.*
joy (dʒɔi) *n* Freude *f.* **joyful** *adj* **1** freudig. **2** froh. **joyfulness** *n* Fröhlichkeit *f.*
jubilee ('dʒuːbiliː) *n* Jubiläum *neu.*
Judaism ('dʒuːdeiizəm) *n* Judaismus *m.*
judge (dʒʌdʒ) *n* **1** *law* Richter *m.* **2** Schiedsrichter *m.* **3** Beurteiler *m.* *vi* **1** urteilen. *vt* **1** beurteilen. **2** ein Urteil fällen über. **judgment** *n* **1** Urteil neu. **2** Meinung *f.* **3** Urteilvermögen *neu.*
judicial (dʒuː'diʃəl) *adj* **1** Gerichts—, gerichtlich. **2** richterlich. **3** kritisch.
judicious (dʒuː'diʃəs) *adj* einsichtsvoll.
judo ('dʒuːdou) *n* Judo *neu.*
jug (dʒʌg) *n* Krug *m.* Kanne *f.*
juggernaut ('dʒʌgənɔːt) *n inf* Fernlaster *m.*
juggle ('dʒʌgəl) *vi,vt* jonglieren, Kunststücke machen. **juggler** *n* Jongleur *m.*
juice (dʒuːs) *n* **1** Saft *m.* **2** *mot sl* Sprit *m.* **juicy** *adj* **1** saftig. **2** *inf* pikant.
jukebox ('dʒuːkbɔks) *n* Musikautomat *m.*
July (dʒu'lai) *n* Juli *m.*
jumble ('dʒʌmbəl) *n* Mischmasch *m.* Durcheinander *neu.* *vt* durcheinanderwerfen. *vi* durcheinandergeraten. **jumble sale** *n* Wohltätigkeitsbasar *m.*
jump (dʒʌmp) *vi* **1** springen, hüpfen. **2** auffahren. *vt* hinwegspringen über. **jump the queue** sich vordrängen. ~ *n* Sprung, Satz *m.*
jumper ('dʒʌmpə) *n* Pullover *m.*
junction ('dʒʌŋkʃən) *n* **1** Verbindung *f.* **2** Kreuzung *f.* **3** Knotenpunkt *m.*
June (dʒuːn) *n* Juni *m.*
jungle ('dʒʌŋgəl) *n* Dschungel *m.*
junior ('dʒuːniə) *adj* **1** jünger. **2** Unter—. *n* **1** Jüngere(r) *m.* **2** Junior *m.*
juniper ('dʒuːnipə) *n* Wachholder *m.*
junk[1] (dʒʌŋk) *n* Altwaren *f pl.* alter Kram *m.*
junk[2] (dʒʌŋk) *n* Dschunke *f.*
junta ('dʒʌntə) *n* Junta *f.*
Jupiter ('dʒuːpitə) *n* Jupiter *m.*
jurisdiction (dʒuəris'dikʃən) *n* **1** Rechtsprechung *f.* **2** Gerichtsbarkeit, Zuständigkeit *f.*
jury ('dʒuəri) *n* **1** die

Geschworenen *pl.* **2** Jury *f.* **juror** *n* Geschworene(r) *m.*
just (dʒʌst) *adj* **1** gerecht. **2** richtig. **3** gehörig. *adv* **1** gerade, eben. **2** genau.
justice ('dʒʌstis) *n* **1** Gerechtigkeit *f.* **2** Recht *neu.* **3** Richter *m.*
justify ('dʒʌstifai) *vt* rechtfertigen.
jut (dʒʌt) *vi* hervorragen, vorspringen. *n* Vorsprung *m.*
jute (dʒu:t) *n bot* Jute *f.*
juvenile ('dʒu:vənail) *adj* jung, jugendlich, Jugend—. **juvenile delinquency** *n* Jugendkriminilität *f.* **juvenility** *n* **1** Jugendlichkeit *f.* **2** Kinderei *f.*
juxtapose (dʒʌkstə'pouz) *vt* nebeneinanderstellen.

K

kaftan ('kæftæn) *n* Kaftan *m.*
kaleidoscope (kə'laidəskoup) *n* Kaleidoskop *neu.*
kangaroo (kæŋgə'ru:) *n* Känguruh *neu.*
karate (kə'ra:ti) *n* Karate *neu.*
kebab (kə'bæb) *n* Kebab *m.*
keel (ki:l) *n* Kiel *m.* **on an even keel** *n* gleichmäßig, ausgeglichen.
keen (ki:n) *adj* **1** scharf. **2** eifrig. **3** heftig. **keen on** *inf* erpicht auf, scharf auf.
keep* (ki:p) *vt* **1** halten. **2** unterhalten. **3** (auf)bewahren. **4** (accounts, etc.) führen. *vi* sich halten. *n* **1** Unterhalt *m.* **2** Bergfried *m.* **keeper** *n* Wärter *m.* **keepsake** *n* Andenken *neu.*
keg (keg) *n* Fäßchen *neu.*
kennel ('kenl̩) *n* **1** Hundehütte *f.* **2** *pl* Hundezwinger *m.*
Kenya ('kenjə) *n* Kenya *f.* **Kenyan** *adj* Kenianisch. *n* Kenianer *m.*
kept (kept) *v* see **keep.**
kerb (kə:b) *n* Strassenkante *f.*
kernel ('kə:nl̩) *n* **1** Kern *m.* **2** Korn *neu.*
kettle ('ketl̩) *n* Kessel *m.* **kettledrum** *n* (Kessel)Pauke *f.*
key (ki:) *n* **1** Schlüssel *m.* **2** Taste *f.* **3** *mus* Tonart *f.* **keyboard** *n* Tastatur *f.*
khaki ('ka:ki) *n* Khaki *neu. adj* khakifarben.
kibbutz (ki'buts) *n* Kibbuz *m.*
kick (kik) *vt* mit dem Fuß stoßen *or* treten. *vi* **1** ausschlagen. **2** (zurück)stoßen. **kick off** anstoßen. **kick-off** *n* Anstoß *m.* **kick one's heels** *inf* wartend herumstehen. **kick the bucket** ins Gras beißen. ~*n* **1** Fußtritt *m.* **2** Rückstoß *m.* **3** *inf* Schwung *m.* Energie *f.* **get a kick out of** Spaß daran haben.
kid[1] (kid) *n* **1** *zool* Zicklein *neu.* **2** Ziegenleder *neu.* **3** *inf* Kind *neu.*
kid[2] (kid) *vt* foppen, aufziehen. *vi* scherzen.
kidnap ('kidnæp) *vt* entführen. **kidnapper** *n* Entführer, Kidnapper *m.*
kidney ('kidni) *n* Niere *f.* **kidney bean** *n* weiße Bohne *f.*
kill (kil) *vt* **1** töten. **2** umbringen, morden. **3** abschlachten. **kill time** die Zeit totschlagen.
kiln (kiln) *n* Ziegelofen, Brennofen *m.*
kilo ('ki:lou) *n* Kilo *neu.*
kilogram ('kiləgræm) *n* Kilogramm *neu.*

kilometre (ki'lɔmitə) *n* Kilometer *m*.
kilt (kilt) *n* Schottenrock, Kilt *m*.
kimono (ki'mounou) *n* Kimono *m*.
kin (kin) *n* **1** Geschlecht *neu*. Sippe *f*. **2** (Bluts)-Verwandtschaft *f*. **the next of kin** die nächsten Verwandten.
kind[1] (kaind) *adj* freundlich, gütig, gut.
kind[2] (kaind) *n* **1** Art, Sorte *f*. **2** Geschlecht *neu*. **all kinds of** allerlei. **what kind of?** was für?
kindergarten ('kindəgɑːtn̩) *n* Kindergarten *m*.
kindle ('kindl̩) *vt* anzünden. *vi* (sich) entzünden, aufflammen.
kinetic (ki'netik) *adj* kinetisch, bewegend. **kinetics** *n pl* Kinetik *f*.
king (kiŋ) *n* König *m*. **kingdom** *n* Königreich *neu*. **kingfisher** *n* Eisvogel *m*.
kink (kiŋk) *n* **1** Schleife *f*. Knick *m*. **2** Fimmel *m*. *vt* knicken. *vi* (sich) verfilzen.
kiosk ('kiɔsk) *n* Kiosk *m*.
kipper ('kipə) *n* Räucherhering *m*.
kiss (kis) *vi,vt* küssen. *n* Kuß *m*.
kit (kit) *n* **1** Ausrüstung *f*. **2** Werkzeug *neu*. **3** Bausatz *m*.
kitchen ('kitʃin) *n* Küche *f*.
kite (kait) *n* (Papier)Drachen *m*.
kitten ('kitn̩) *n* Kätzchen *neu*. junge Katze *f*.
kitty ('kiti) *n* (gemeinsame) Kasse *f*.
kiwi ('kiːwi) *n* Kiwi *m*.
kleptomania (ˌkleptə'meiniə) *n* Kleptomanie *f*. **kleptomaniac** *n* Kleptomane *m*.
knack (næk) *n* **1** Kniff, Trick *m*. **2** Geschicklichkeit *f*.
knapsack ('næpsæk) *n* Rucksack *m*.
knead (niːd) *vt* kneten.
knee (niː) *n* Knie *neu*. **kneecap** *n anat* Kniescheibe *f*.
kneel* (niːl) *vi* knien.
knew (nuː) *v* see **know.**
knickers ('nikəz) *n pl* (Damen)Schlüpfer *m*. **knickerbockers** *n pl* Kniehosen *f pl*.
knife (naif) *n, pl* **knives** Messer *neu*. *vt* (er)stechen.
knight (nait) *n* **1** Ritter *m*. **2** *game* Springer *m*. *vt* zum Ritter schlagen. **knighthood** *n* Ritterwürde *f*.
knit* (nit) *vt* **1** stricken. **2** (ver)knüpfen. **knit one's brows** die Stirn runzeln. **knitting** *n* **1** Stricken *neu*. **2** Strickzeug *neu*. **knitting needle** *n* Stricknadel *f*. **knitwear** *n* Strickwaren *f pl*.
knob (nɔb) *n* Knopf *m*.
knobbly ('nɔbli) *adj* knorrig.
knock (nɔk) *vi,vt* klopfen, schlagen, pochen. **knock down 1** niederschlagen. **2** überfahren. **knock off 1** abschlagen, abziehen. **2** *inf* Feierabend machen. **3** *sl* stehlen. **knock out** k.o. schlagen. **knockout** *n* knockout *m*. ~*n* **1** Klopfen *neu* **2** Stoß, Schlag *m*.
knot (nɔt) *n* **1** Knoten *m*. **2** Ast *m*. **3** Schwierigkeit *f*. *vi,vt* (ver)knoten, (ver)knüpfen.
know* (nou) *vt* **1** wissen. **2** kennen. **get to know** ken-

nenlernen. **know the ropes** sich auskennen. **knowing** *adj* **1** erfahren. **2** verständnisvoll.
knowledge ('nɔlidʒ) *n* **1** Wissen *neu.* **2** Kenntnis *f.* **to my knowledge** meines Wissens. **knowledgeable** *adj* **1** kenntnisreich. **2** gut informiert.
knuckle ('nʌkəl) *n* Knöchel *m.* *v* **knuckle under** nachgeben.
Korea (kə'riə) *n* Korea *neu.* **Korean** *adj* koreanisch. *n* Koreaner *m.*
kosher ('kouʃə) *adj* koscher.
Kuwait (ku'weit) *n* Kuwait *neu.*

L

label ('leibəl) *n* **1** Zettel *neu.* **2** Bezeichnung *f.* *vt* beschriften, mit einem Zettel versehen.
laboratory (lə'bɔrətri) *n* Laboratorium, Labor *neu.* **laboratory assistant** *n* Laborant *m.*
labour ('leibə) *vi* **1** arbeiten. **2** sich anstrengen. **3** sich schwer bewegen. *vt* **1** ausarbeiten. **2** ausführlich eingehen. *n* **1** Arbeit *f.* **2** Mühe, Anstrengung *f.* **3** (Geburts)Wehen *f pl.* **4** Arbeitskräfte *f pl.* **hard labour** *n* Zwangsarbeit *f.* **labour force** *n* Arbeiterschaft *f.* **Labour Party** *n* Labour Party, Arbeiterpartei *f.* **labour-saving** *adj* arbeitssparend. **laborious** *adj* mühsam, anstrengend. **labourer** *n* Arbeiter *m.*
laburnum (lə'bəːnəm) *n* Goldregen *m.*
labyrinth ('læbərinθ) *n* Labyrinth *neu.*
lace (leis) *n* **1** Spitze *f.* **2** Schnur *f.* *vt* **1** mit Spitze besetzen. **2** (zu)schnüren.
lack (læk) *n* Mangel *m.* Fehlen *neu.* *vt* ermangeln. *vi* fehlen, mangeln.
lacquer ('lækə) *n* Lack *m.* *vt* lackieren. **lacquered** *adj* Lack—.
lad (læd) *n* Bursche, Junge *m.*
ladder ('lædə) *n* **1** Leiter *f.* **2** (in stockings) Laufmasche *f.* *vi* eine Laufmasche bekommen.
laden ('leidn̩) *adj* beladen.
ladle ('leidl̩) *n* Schöpflöffel *m.* Kelle *f.* *v* **ladle out** **1** schöpfen. **2** austeilen.
lady ('leidi) *n* **1** Dame *f.* **2** Herrin *f.* **Ladies and Gentleman!** Meine Damen und Herren! **ladybird** *n* Marienkäfer *m.*
lag[1] (læg) *vi* sich verzögern, zurückbleiben. *n* **1** Rückstand *m.* **2** Zeitabstand *m.*
lag[2] (læg) *vt* verschalen, verkleiden.
lager ('lɑːgə) *n* Lagerbier *neu.*
laid (leid) *v* see **lay**[1]. **laid up** *adj inf* bettlägerig.
lain (lein) *v* see **lie**[1].
laity ('leiəti) *n* Laien *m pl.*
lake (leik) *n* See *m.*
lamb (læm) *n* **1** Lamm *m.* **2** Lammfleisch *neu.*
lame (leim) *adj* lahm. *vt* lähmen. **lameness** *n* Lahmheit *f.*
lament (lə'ment) *n* **1** (Weh)-Klage *f.* **2** Klagelied *neu.* *vt* beklagen. *vi* trauern.
laminated ('læmineitid) *adj* geschichtet.
lamp (læmp) *n* Lampe *f.* **lamppost** *n* Laternenpfahl *m.*

lampshade *n* Lampenschirm *m.*
lance (lɑːns) *n* Lanze *f.*
land (lænd) *n* **1** (festes) Land *neu.* **2** Boden, Grund *m.* **3** Grundbesitz *m.* *vi,vt* landen. **landing** *n* **1** Landung *f.* **2** Treppenabsatz *m.* **landlady** *n* (Haus)Wirtin *f.* **landlord** *n* (Haus)Wirt *m.* **landmark** *n* **1** Grenzstein *m.* **2** Wendepunkt *m.* **landscape** *n* Landschaft *f.*
lane (lein) *n* **1** Feldweg *m.* **2** Gasse *f.* **3** (on motorways, etc.) Fahrbahn *f.*
language ('læŋgwidʒ) *n* **1** Sprache *f.* **2** *pl* Fremdsprachen *pl.* **bad language** Schimpfworte *m pl.* **language laboratory** *n* Sprachlabor *neu.*
lanky ('læŋki) *adj* schlaksig, schlank.
lantern ('læntən) *n* Laterne *f.*
lap[1] (læp) *n* Schoß *m.*
lap[2] (læp) *vt* **1** übereinanderlegen, umschlagen. **2** *sport* überrunden. *vi* (ein)hüllen. *n sport* Runde *f.*
lap[3] (læp) *vt* (auf)lecken. *vi* plätschern.
lapel (lə'pel) *n* Aufschlag *m.*
Lapland ('læplænd) *n* Lappland *neu.* **Lapp** *adj* lappisch. *n* **1** Lappländer, Lappe *m.* **2** (language) Lappisch *neu.*
lapse (læps) *n* **1** Verlauf *m.* **2** Verfallen *neu.* **3** Versehen *neu.* *vi* **1** verlaufen. **2** (ver)fallen.
larceny ('lɑːsəni) *n* Diebstahl *m.*
larch (lɑːtʃ) *n* Lärche *f.*
lard (lɑːd) *n* Schmalz, Schweinefett *neu.*
larder ('lɑːdə) *n* Speiseschrank *m.*
large (lɑːdʒ) *adj* **1** groß. **2** reichlich. **3** weitherzig. **largely** *adv* zum großen Teil.
lark[1] (lɑːk) *n zool* Lerche *f.*
lark[2] (lɑːk) *n* Streich *m.*
larva ('lɑːvə) *n* Larve, Puppe *f.*
larynx ('læriŋks) *n* Kehlkopf *m.* **laryngitis** *n med* Kehlkopfentzündung *f.*
laser ('leizə) *n* Laser *m.* **laser beams** *n* Laserstrahlen *m pl.*
lash (læʃ) *n* **1** Peitschenschnur *f.* **2** (Peitschen)Hieb *m.* **3** *anat* Wimper *f.* *vt* peitschen, geißeln. **lash out** ausschlagen.
lass (læs) *n inf* Mädchen *neu.*
lasso (læ'suː) *n* Lasso *m,neu.* *vt* mit dem Lasso fangen.
last[1] (lɑːst) *adj* **1** letzt. **2** vorig. *n* **1** Letzte(r) *m.* **2** Ende *neu.* **at last 1** schließlich. **2** zuletzt. **last but not least** nicht zuletzt.
last[2] (lɑːst) *vi* **1** dauern. **2** halten. **3** ausreichen.
latch (lætʃ) *n* **1** Klinke *f.* **2** Sicherheitsschloß *neu.* **on the latch** (nur) eingeklinkt. ~*vt* einklinken.
late (leit) *adj* **1** spät. **2** verspätet. **3** (jüngst) verstorben, selig. **4** ehemalig. **be late 1** zu spät kommen. **2** Verspätung haben. **lately** *adv* vor kurzem, neulich, in letzter Zeit.
latent ('leitn̩t) *adj* **1** verborgen. **2** latent.
lateral ('lætərəl) *adj* seitlich, Seiten—. Quer—.
latest ('leitist) *adj* spätest,

neuest, letzt. **at the latest** *adv* spätestens.
lathe (leið) *n* Drehbank *f.*
lather ('lɑːðə) *n* (Seifen)-Schaum *m. vt* einseifen. *vi* schäumen.
Latin ('lætin) *adj* lateinisch. *n* **1** Latiner *m.* **2** (language) Latein *neu.* **Latin America** *n* Lateinamerika *neu.*
latitude ('lætitjuːd) *n* **1** *geog* Breite *f.* **2** Spielraum *m.* **latitudinal** *adj* Breiten—.
latter ('lætə) *adj* **1** letzter. **2** neuer.
lattice ('lætis) *n* Gitter *neu.*
laugh (lɑːf) *vi* lachen. **laugh at** auslachen. ~*n* Lachen *neu.* **laughable** *adj* lächerlich. **laughter** *n* Gelächter *neu.*
launch[1] (lɔːntʃ) *vt* **1** *naut* vom Stapel lassen. **2** loslassen. **3** (a rocket) abschießen. **launch into** sich stürzen in. **launching pad** *n* Raketenabschußrampe *f.*
launch[2] (lɔːntʃ) *n* **1** Barkasse *f.* **2** Ausflugsdampfer *m.*
launder ('lɔːndə) *(vi),vt* (sich) waschen. **launderette** *n* Schnellwäscherei *f.* **laundry** *n* **1** Wäscherei *f.* **2** Wäsche *f.*
laurel ('lɔrəl) *n* Lorbeer *m.*
lava ('lɑːvə) *n* Lava *f.*
lavatory ('lævətri) *n* Toilette *f.*
lavender ('lævində) *n* Lavendel *m.*
lavish ('læviʃ) *adj* **1** verschwenderisch, freigebig. **2** reichlich. *vt* verschwenden. **lavishness** *n* (verschwenderische) Freigebigkeit *f.*
law (lɔː) *n* **1** Gesetz, Recht *neu.* **2** Jura *neu pl.* **law-abiding** *adj* gesetzestreu, friedlich.
lawsuit *n* **1** Verfahren *neu.* **2** Klage *f.* **lawyer** *n* **1** Rechtsanwalt *m.* **2** Jurist *m.*
lawn (lɔːn) *n* Rasen *m.* **lawnmower** *n* Rasenmäher *m.*
lax (læks) *adj* lax, locker, nachlässig.
laxative ('læksətiv) *n* Abführmittel *neu.*
lay*[1] (lei) *vt* **1** legen. **2** (the table) decken. **3** setzen, (hin)stellen. **layer** *n* Schicht, Lage *f. vt* überlagern. *vi* sich lagern.
lay[2] (lei) *v* see **lie.**
lay[3] (lei) *adj* **1** Laien—. **2** laienhaft. **layman** *n* Laie *m.*
laze (leiz) *vi* faulenzen. **laze away** vertrödeln. **laziness** *n* Faulheit, Trägheit *f.* **lazy** *adj* faul, träge. **lazy bones** *n inf* Faulenzer *m.*
lead*[1] (liːd) *vt,vi* **1** führen, leiten. **2** vorangehen. *n* **1** Führung *f.* **2** *tech* (Zu)Leitung *f.* **3** (Hunde)Leine *f.* **4** *Th* Hauptrolle *f.* **5** Hinweis *m.* Beispiel *neu.* **leading** *adj* Haupt—, herrschend, führend, Leit—. **leader** *n* **1** Führer *m.* **2** Leiter *m.* **3** (in a newspaper) Leitartikel *m.* **leadership** *n* Führerschaft *f.*
lead[2] (led) *n* **1** Blei *neu.* **2** Bleistiftmine *f. adj* bleiern.
leaf (liːf) *n* **1** Blatt *neu.* **2** Flügel *m.* **3** Klappe *f. v* **leaf through** durchblättern. **leaflet** *n* **1** Blättchen *neu.* **2** Prospekt *m.*
league (liːg) *n* **1** Bund *m.* **2** *sport* Liga *f.*
leak (liːk) *n* **1** Leck *neu.* **2** *pol* Durchsickern *neu. vi* **1** lecken. **2** durchsickern. **leakage** *n* **1**

Durchsickern *neu*. **2** Schwund *m*.

lean* [1] (liːn) *vi* sich lehnen, sich neigen. *vt* lehnen, stützen. **lean on** sich stützen auf.

lean [2] (liːn) *adj* mager.

leap* (liːp) *vi* springen, hüpfen. *vt* überspringen. *n* Sprung, Satz *m*. **look before you leap** erst wägen, dann wagen. **leapfrog** *n* Bockspringen *neu*. **leap year** *n* Schaltjahr *neu*.

learn* (ləːn) *vt* **1** lernen. **2** erfahren, erlernen. **learned** *adj* **1** gelehrt. **2** erfahren. **learner** *n* **1** Anfänger *m*. **2** *mot* Fahrschüler *m*.

lease (liːs) *n* **1** Pachtvertrag *m*. **2** Pacht *f*. *vt* (ver)pachten. **leasehold** *n* **1** Pacht *f*. **2** Pachtbesitz *m*. *adj* Pacht—. **leaseholder** *n* Pächter *m*.

leash (liːʃ) *n* (Koppel)Leine *f*.

least (liːst) *adj* wenigst, mindest. *adv* am wenigsten. *n* Wenigste, Mindeste *neu*. **at least** wenigstens, mindestens, zumindest.

leather ('leðə) *n* Leder *neu*. *adj* ledern, Leder—. **leathery** *adj* zäh.

leave [1] (liːv) *vt* **1** verlassen. **2** lassen. *vi* abfahren, (fort-, weg-)gehen.

leave [2] (liːv) *n* **1** Erlaubnis *f*. **2** Urlaub *m*. **take one's leave** Abschied nehmen.

Lebanon ('lebənən) *n* Libanon *m*. **Lebanese** *adj* libanesisch. *n* Libanese(r) *m*.

lecherous ('letʃərəs) *adj* wollüstig.

lectern ('lektən) *n* Lesepult *neu*.

lecture ('lektʃə) *n* **1** Vorlesung *f*. Vortrag *m*. **2** Strafpredigt *f*. *vi* eine Vorlesung halten. *vt* abkanzeln. **lecturer** *n* Dozent *m*.

led (led) *v* see **lead** [1].

ledge (ledʒ) *n* **1** Sims *m*. **2** Felsbank *f*.

ledger ('ledʒə) *n* *comm* Hauptbuch *neu*.

lee (liː) *n* **1** Schutz *m*. **2** *naut* Leeseite *f*.

leech (liːtʃ) *n* Blutegel *m*.

leek (liːk) *n* Lauch *m*.

leer (liə) *vi* schielen. *n* lüsterner Seitenblick *m*.

left [1] (left) *adj* link. *n* linke Seite, Linke *f*. *adv* (nach) links. **left-hand** *adj* link, linksseitig. **left-handed** *adj* linkshändig. **left-wing** *adj pol* Links—, linksradikal.

left [2] (left) *v* see **leave** [1]. *adj* übrig. **left-luggage office** *n* Gepäckaufbewahrung *f*.

leg (leg) *n* **1** Bein *neu*. **2** *cul* Keule *f*. **pull someone's leg** jemanden auf den Arm nehmen.

legacy ('legəsi) *n* Vermächtnis *neu*.

legal ('liːgəl) *adj* **1** gesetzlich. **2** juristisch. **3** Rechts—. **legality** *n* Gesetzlichkeit *f*. **legalize** *vt* rechtskräftig machen, legalisieren.

legend ('ledʒənd) *n* Legende *f*. Sage *f*.

legible ('ledʒiblzibəl) *adj* leserlich, lesbar.

legion ('liːdʒən) *n* Legion *f*. **legionary** *adj* Legions—. *n* Legionär *m*.

legislate ('ledʒisleit) *vi* Gesetze geben. **legislation** *n* Gesetzgebung *f*.

legitimate (li'dʒitimət) *adj* **1** legitim, rechtmäßig. **2** (of a child) ehelich. **legitimize** *vt* legitimieren, für rechtmäßig erklären.
leisure ('leʒə) *n* Muße, freie Zeit *f*. **at your leisure** wenn es Ihnen paßt. **be at leisure** Muße haben. ~*adj* müßig, Muße—. **leisurely** *adj,adv* gemächlich, ohne Hast.
lemon ('lemən) *n* Zitrone *f*. **lemonade** *n* (Zitronen) Limonade *f*.
lend* (lend) *vt* (ver-, aus-) leihen. **2** leisten, gewähren. **lend a hand** helfen.
length (leŋθ) *n* **1** Länge *f*. **2** Strecke *f*. **3** Dauer *f*. **at length** *adv* **1** ausführlich. **2** endlich. **lengthen** *(vi),vt* (sich) verlängern. **lengthy** *adj* **1** sehr lang. **2** weitschweifig.
lenient ('li:niənt) *adj* mild, nachsichtig.
lens (lenz) *n* Linse *f*.
lent (lent) *v* see **lend.**
Lent (lent) *n* Fastenzeit *f*. Fasten *f pl*.
lentil ('lentl) *n* Linse *f*.
Leo ('li:ou) *n* Löwe *m*.
leopard ('lepəd) *n* Leopard *m*.
leper ('lepə) *n* Aussätzige(r) *m*. **leprosy** *n* Aussatz *m*. Lepra *f*. **leprous** *adj* aussätzig.
lesbian ('lezbiən) *n* Lesbierin *f*. *adj* lesbisch.
less (les) *adv* weniger. *adj* kleiner, geringer. **lessen** *(vi),vt* (sich) vermindern.
lesson ('lesən) *n* **1** Lektion *f*. **2** *educ* Stunde *f*. **3** *rel* Lesung *f*. **4** *pl* Unterricht *m*. **teach someone a lesson** jemandem eine Lektion erteilen.
lest (lest) *conj* damit *or* daß nicht.
let* (let) *vt* **1** lassen. **2** vermieten. **let on** *inf* es verraten. **let someone down** jemanden im Stich lassen. ~*n sport* Netzball *m*.
lethal ('li:θəl) *adj* tödlich.
lethargy ('leθədʒi) *n* Lethargie *f*. **lethargic** *adj* lethargisch.
letter ('letə) *n* **1** Brief *m*. **2** Buchstabe *m*. **3** Type *f*. **man of letters** Literat *m*. **to the letter** buchstäblich. **letterbox** *n* Briefkasten *m*.
lettuce ('letis) *n* Kopfsalat *m*.
leukaemia (lu:'ki:miə) *n* Leukämie *f*.
level ('levəl) *adj* **1** eben. **2** ausgeglichen. **level crossing** *n* Bahnübergang *m*. **level-headed** *adj* vernünftig. ~*n* **1** ebene Fläche, Ebene *f*. **2** Niveau *neu*. Höhe *f*. *vt* **1** gleichmachen. **2** nivellieren. **3** ebnen, planieren.
lever ('li:və) *n* **1** Hebel *m*. **2** Hebestange *f*. *vt* mit einem Hebel bewegen. **leverage** *n* Hebelkraft *f*.
levy ('levi) *n* **1** Erhebung *f*. Beitrag *m*. **2** *mil* Aushebung *f*. *vt* **1** erheben. **2** ausheben.
lewd (lu:d) *adj* unzüchtig. **lewdness** *n* Unzucht *f*.
liable ('laiəbəl) *adj* **1** verantwortlich. **2** haftpflichtig. **3** ausgesetzt. **be liable to** neigen zu. **liability** *n* **1** Verantwortlichkeit *f*. **2** Haftpflicht *f*. **3** Neigung *f*. **4** *pl* Verbindlichkeiten *f pl*.

liaison *n* **1** Verbindung *f.* **2** Liebschaft *f.*

liar ('laiə) *n* Lügner *m.*

libel ('laibəl) *n* **1** Schmähschrift *f.* **2** Verleumdung *f. vt* **1** schmähen. **2** (schriftlich) verleumden.

liberal ('libərəl) *adj* **1** liberal. **2** großzügig, freigebig. **2** reichlich. **3** freisinnig. *n* Liberale(r) *m.*

liberate ('libəreit) *vt* befreien. **liberation** *n* Befreiung *f.*

liberty ('libəti) *n* Freiheit *f.*

Libra ('liːbrə) *n* Waage *f.*

library ('laibrəri) *n* Bücherei, Bibliothek *f.* **lending library** Leihbücherei *f.* **librarian** *n* Bibliothekar *m.*

libretto (li'bretou) *n* Libretto *neu.*

Libya ('libiə) *n* Libyen *neu.* **Libyan** *adj* libysch. *n* Libyer *m.*

licence ('laisəns) *n* **1** Lizenz *f.* **2** Erlaubnis *f.* **3** Konzession *f.* **4** Zügellosigkeit *f.* **5** Freiheit *f.* **driving licence** Führerschein *m.* **license** *vt* lizenzieren, genehmigen, zulassen. **licensing hours** *n pl* Ausschankstunden *f pl.* **licensee** *n* Lizenzinhaber *m.*

lick (lik) *vt* **1** lecken. **2** *inf* besiegen, übertreffen. *vi* (of flames) züngeln. *n* Lecken *neu.*

lid (lid) *n* **1** Deckel *m.* **2** *anat* Augenlid *neu.*

lie*[1] (lai) *vi* liegen. **lie down** sich (hin-, nieder-) legen. ~*n* Lage *f.*

lie[2] (lai) *n* Lüge *f.* **white lie** Notlüge *f. vi* lügen.

lieutenant (lef'tenənt) *n* Leutnant *m.* **lieutenant colonel** *n* Oberstleutnant *m.*

life (laif) *n, pl* **lives** **1** Leben *neu.* **2** Menschenleben *neu.* **3** Lebendigkeit *f.* **lifebelt** *n* Rettungsgürtel *m.* **lifeboat** *n* Rettungsboot *neu.* **lifebuoy** *n* Rettungsboje *f.* **lifeguard** *n* Bademeister *m.* **lifeline** *n* Rettungsleine *f.* **lifetime** *n* Lebenszeit *f.*

lift (lift) *vt* **1** (auf-, hoch-)heben. **2** erheben. *vi* sich heben. *n* **1** Aufzug, Fahrstuhl *m.* **2** (Auf)Heben *neu.* **3** Erhebung *f.* **give someone a lift** jemanden im Auto mitnehmen.

light*[1] (lait) *n* **1** Licht. **2** Beleuchtung *f.* **3** Lampe *f.* **4** (for tobacco) Feuer *neu.* **5** Leuchte *f.* **lighthouse** *n* Leuchtturm *m.* ~*vt* **1** anzünden. **2** beleuchten. *adj* hell. **lighter** *n* **1** Anzünder *m.* **2** Feuerzeug *neu.* **lighting** *n* Beleuchtung *f.*

light[2] (lait) *adj* leicht. **light-headed** *adj* leichtsinnig. **light-hearted** *adj* leichtherzig, fröhlich. **lightweight** *adj* leicht. *n* Leichtgewichtler *m.*

light[3] (lait) *vi* **light upon** stoßen auf.

lighten[1] ('laitn̩) *vi* **1** erleuchten. **2** sich erhellen. **3** blitzen.

lighten[2] ('laitn̩) *(vi),vt* (sich) erleichtern.

lightning ('laitniŋ) *n* Blitz *m.*

like[1] (laik) *adj,adv* gleich, ähnlich. *prep* wie. **like-minded** *adj* gleichgesinnt. **likeness** *n* **1** Ähnlichkeit *f.* **2** Abbild *neu.* **likewise** *adv* gleichfalls, auch, ebenso.

like[2] (laik) *vt* mögen, gern haben, lieben, gefallen. **like doing something** etwas gern tun. **I like this picture** dieses Bild gefällt mir.

likely ('laikli) *adj,adv* wahrscheinlich.

lilac ('lailək) *adj* lila. *n* **1** *bot* (spanischer) Flieder *m.* **2** Lila *neu.*

lily ('lili) *n* Lilie *f.* **lily-of-the-valley** *n* Maiglöckchen *neu.*

limb (lim) *n* **1** Glied *neu.* **2** Ast *m.* **artificial limb** *n* Prothese *f.*

limbo ('limbou) *n* **1** Vorhölle *f.* **2** Vergessenheit *f.* **3** Gefängnis, Kittchen *neu.*

lime[1] (laim) *n* Kalk *m. vt* mit Kalk düngen. **limelight** *n* **1** Kalklicht *neu.* **2** Scheinwerferlicht *neu.* **3** Rampenlicht *neu.* **limestone** *n* Kalkstein *m.*

lime[2] (laim) *n* **1** Limone *f.* **2** Linde *f.*

limerick ('limərik) *n* Limerick *m.*

limit ('limit) *n* Grenze *f.* Äußerste *neu.* **that is the limit!** das ist (doch wirklich) die Höhe! ~*vt* begrenzen, beschränken. **limitation** *n* **1** Begrenzung, Beschränkung *f.* **2** Grenze *f.*

limp[1] (limp) *vi* hinken. *n* Hinken *neu.*

limp[2] (limp) *adj* **1** schlaff. **2** kraftlos.

limpet ('limpit) *n* Napfschnecke *f.*

linden ('lindən) *n* Linde *f.* Lindenbaum *m.*

line[1] (lain) *n* **1** Linie *f.* **2** Reihe *f.* **3** Zeile *f.* **4** Fach *neu. vt* **1** linieren. **2** aufstellen. **3** (um)säumen. **lineage** *n* Abstammung *f.* **linear** *adj* linear, Linien—.

line[2] (lain) *vt* (a coat, etc.) füttern.

linen ('linin) *n* **1** Leinen *neu.* Leinwand *f.* **2** Wäsche *f.* **linen basket** *n* Wäschekorb *m.* ~*adj* leinen, Leinen—.

liner ('lainə) *n* Passagierdampfer *m.*

linger ('liŋgə) *vi* **1** zögern. **2** verweilen. **3** sich hinziehen. **4** schlendern.

lingerie ('lɔnʒəri:) *n* Damenunterwäsche *f.*

linguist ('liŋgwist) *n* Linguist, Sprachwissenschaftler *m.* **linguistic** *adj* linguistisch, sprachlich, Sprach—. **linguistics** *n pl* Linguistik, Sprachwissenschaft *f.*

lining ('lainiŋ) *n* **1** Futter *neu.* **2** Verkleidung *f.*

link (liŋk) *n* **1** Glied *neu.* **2** Verbindung *f.* *(vi),vt* (sich) verketten, (sich) verbinden.

linoleum (li'nouliəm) *n also* **lino** Linoleum *neu.*

linseed ('linsi:d) *n* Leinsamen *m.* **linseed oil** *n* Leinöl *neu.*

lion ('laiən) *n* Löwe *m.*

lip (lip) *n* **1** Lippe *f.* **2** Rand *m.* **3** *inf* Unverschämtheit *f.* **lip-read** von den Lippen ablesen. **lipstick** *n* Lippenstift *m.*

liqueur (li'kjuə) *n* Likör *m.*

liquid ('likwid) *adj* flüssig. *n* Flüssigkeit *f.* **liquidation** *n* **1** *comm* Liquidation *f.* **2** Beseitigung *f.* **go into liquidation** sich auflösen. **liquidize** *(vi),vt* (sich) verflüssigen.

liquor ('likə) *n* **1** Flüssigkeit *f.* **2** Alkohol *m.*

liquorice ('likəris) *n* Lakritze *f*.
lira ('liərə) *n, pl* **lire** *or* **liras** Lira *f*.
lisp (lisp) *vi* lispeln. *n* Lispeln *neu*.
list[1] (list) *n* Liste *f*. Verzeichnis *neu*. *vt* (in eine Liste) eintragen, verzeichnen.
list[2] (list) *vi naut* Schlagseite haben. *n* Schlagseite *f*.
listen ('lisən) *vi* **1** (an-, zu-)hören. **2** lauschen. **listener** *n* (Zu)Hörer *m*.
listless ('listləs) *adj* lustlos, träg. **listlessness** *n* Lustlosigkeit, Trägheit *f*.
lit (lit) *v* see **light**[1].
litany ('litəni) *n* Litanei *f*.
literal ('litərəl) *adj* **1** buchstäblich, wörtlich. **2** genau.
literary ('litərəri) *adj* **1** literarisch. **2** literarisch gebildet.
literate ('litərət) *adj* gebildet.
literature ('litərətʃə) *n* Literatur *f*.
litre ('liːtə) *n* Liter *m,neu*.
litter ('litə) *n* **1** Tragbahre *f*. **2** (of animals) Wurf *m*. **3** Abfall *m*. **litter-bin** *n* Abfallkorb *m*. ~*vt* **1** verstreuen. **2** verunreinigen.
little ('litl̩) *adj* **1** klein. **2** kurz. **3** wenig. *adv* wenig. *n* Wenige *neu*. **a little** ein wenig, ein bißchen.
liturgy ('litədʒi) *n* Liturgie *f*.
live[1] (liv) *vi* **1** leben. **2** wohnen. *vt* (a life) führen.
live[2] (laiv) *adj* **1** lebend, lebendig. **2** Direkt—. **3** stromführend. **livestock** *n* Vieh *neu*.
livelihood ('laivlihud) *n* Lebensunterhalt *m*.
lively ('laivli) *adj* lebhaft.
liver ('livə) *n* Leber *f*.
livid ('livid) *adj* **1** bläulich. **2** *inf* wütend.
living ('liviŋ) *adj* lebend(ig), Lebens—. *n* Lebensunterhalt *m*. **living room** *n* Wohnzimmer *neu*.
lizard ('lizəd) *n* Eidechse *f*.
llama ('lɑːmə) *n* Lama *neu*.
load (loud) *n* **1** Last *f*. **2** Belastung *f*. **3** Ladung *f*. **loads of** *inf* sehr viel, eine ganze Menge. ~*vt* **1** (be-, auf-)laden. **2** überhäufen, überladen.
loaf[1] (louf) *n* Brotlaib *m*.
loaf[2] (louf) *vi* bummeln, gammeln. **loafer** *n* Bummler, Gammler *m*.
loan (loun) *n* **1** Anleihe *f*. **2** Leihgabe *f*. **on loan** leihweise.
loathe (louð) *vt* sich ekeln vor, verabscheuen. **loathsome** *adj* ekelhaft, widerlich.
lob (lɔb) *n sport* Hochschlag *m*. *vt* hochschlagen.
lobby ('lɔbi) *n* **1** Vorhalle *f*. **2** Interessengruppe *f*. **3** Lobby *neu*. *vt* beeinflussen.
lobe (loub) *n* **1** Lappen *m*. **2** (of the ear) (Ohr)Läppchen *neu*.
lobster ('lɔbstə) *n* Hummer *m*.
local ('loukəl) *adj* örtlich, Orts—. Lokal—. *n* Ortsbewohner *m*. **local authority** *n* Ortsbehörden *f pl*. **locality** *n* **1** Örtlichkeit *f*. Ort *m*. **2** Lage *f*. **localize** *vt* lokalisieren. **locate** *vt* **1** ausfindig machen. **2** unterbringen, errichten. **location** *n* **1** Standort *m*. **2** Lage *f*.
loch (lɔx) *n* See *m*. Bucht *f*.
lock[1] (lɔk) *n* **1** Schloß *neu*. **2** (on a canal, etc.) Schleuse *f*. *vt*

(ver)schließen. *vi* sich schließen. **locksmith** *n* Schlosser *m*.

lock[2] (lɔk) *n* (of hair, etc.) Locke *f*.

locker ('lɔkə) *n* Kasten *m*.

locket ('lɔkit) *n* Medaillon *neu*.

locomotive (loukə'moutiv) *n* Lokomotive *f*.

locust ('loukəst) *n* Heuschrecke *f*.

lodge (lɔdʒ) *n* **1** (Jagd)Hütte *f*. **2** Forsthaus, Parkhaus *neu*. *vt* **1** aufnehmen. **2** unterbringen. **3** hinterlegen. **4** (a complaint) einreichen. *vi* **1** wohnen, logieren. **2** steckenbleiben. **lodger** *n* (Unter)Mieter *m*. **lodgings** *n pl* (Miets)-Wohnung *f*.

loft (lɔft) *n* Dachboden *m*. **lofty** *adj* **1** (sehr) hoch. **2** hochmütig. **3** erhaben.

log (lɔg) *n* (Holz)Klotz *m*. **log-book** *n* **1** Logbuch *neu*. **2** *mot* Zulassungsbuch *neu*.

logarithm ('lɔgəriðəm) *n* Logarithmus *m*.

logic ('lɔdʒik) *n* Logik *f*. **logical** *adj* logisch.

loins (lɔinz) *n pl* Lenden *f pl*.

loiter ('lɔitə) *vi* bummeln, herumlungern.

lollipop ('lɔlipɔp) *n* Lutscher *m*.

London ('lʌndən) *n* London *neu*.

lonely ('lounli) *adj* einsam. **loneliness** *n* Einsamkeit *f*.

long[1] (lɔŋ) *vi* sich sehnen.

long[2] (lɔŋ) *adj* lang. **in the long run** auf die Dauer. **long-distance** *adj* Fern—, Weit—. **long jump** *n* Weitsprung *m*. **long-playing record** *n* Langspielplatte *f*. **long-range** *adj* weittragend, auf weite Sicht. **long-sighted** *adj* weitsichtig. **longstanding** *adj* seit langer Zeit bestehend, alt. **long-term** *adj* langfristig. **long wave** *n* Langwelle *f*. **longwinded** *adj* langatmig.

longevity (lɔn'dʒeviti) *n* Langlebigkeit *f*.

longitude ('lɔndʒitjuːd) *n* Länge *f*.

loo (luː) *n inf* Klo *neu*.

look (luk) *n* **1** Blick *m*. **2** Aussehen *neu*. *vi* **1** (an)blicken, sehen, schauen **2** zusehen. **3** nachsehen. **4** aussehen. **look for** suchen. **look up** (for reference) nachschlagen.

loom[1] (luːm) *n* Webstuhl *m*.

loom[2] (luːm) *vi* (drohend) aufragen.

loop (luːp) *n* Schleife *f*. *vt* in Schleifen legen. *vi* eine Schleife machen.

loophole ('luːphoul) *n* Schlupfloch *neu*.

loose (luːs) *adj* **1** locker. **2** schlaff. **3** (of clothes) weit. **4** frei. **5** lose, nicht verpackt. **at a loose end** beschäftigungslos. **loosen** *(vi),vt* (sich) lösen, (sich) lockern.

loot (luːt) *n* Beute *f*. *vi,vt* plündern.

lop (lɔp) *vt* beschneiden, stutzen.

lopsided (lɔp'saidid) *adj* **1** schief. **2** einseitig.

lord (lɔːd) *n* **1** Herr *m*. **2** Edelmann *m*. **3** Lord *m*. **lordly** *adj* **1** edel. **2** herrisch. **lordship** *n* Herrlichkeit *f*.

lorry ('lɔri) *n* Lastkraftwagen, Lastwagen *m*.

lose* (luːz) *vt* verlieren. *vi* **1** sich verlieren. **2** (of a clock) nachgehen. **lose weight** abnehmen.

loss (lɔs) *n* **1** Verlust *m.* **2** Schaden *m.* **at a loss** in Verlegenheit.

lost (lɔst) *adj* verloren.

lot (lɔt) *n* **1** Los *neu.* **2** Schicksal *neu.* **3** Menge *f.* **draw lots** losen.

lotion ('louʃən) *n* Schönheitswasser *neu.*

lottery ('lɔtəri) *n* Lotterie *f.*

lotus ('loutəs) *n* Lotos *m.*

loud (laud) *adj* **1** laut. **2** grell. **loud-mouth** *n inf* Maulheld *m.* **loudness** *n* Lautheit, Lautstärke *f.* **loudspeaker** *n* Lautsprecher *m.*

lounge (laundʒ) *n* **1** Wohnzimmer *neu.* **2** Salon *m.* *vi* faulenzen, herumlungern. **lounge suit** *n* Straßenanzug *m.*

louse (laus) *n* Laus *f.* **lousy** *adj* lausig.

love (lʌv) *n* **1** Liebe *f.* **2** Liebling *m.* **3** liebe Grüße *m pl.* **4** *sport* Null *f.* **be in love with** verliebt sein in. **fall in love with** sich verlieben in. ~ *adj* Liebes—. *vt* **1** lieben. **2** gern haben. **love affair** *n* Liebschaft *f.* **lovesick** *adj* liebeskrank. **lovely** *adj* **1** lieblich, reizend. **2** *inf* wunderschön. **lover** *n* Liebhaber, Geliebte(r) *m.* **loving** *adj* liebevoll, liebend.

low[1] (lou) *adj* **1** niedrig. **2** tief. **3** niedergeschlagen. **4** gemein. **lowbrow** *adj* nicht intellektuel, geistig anspruchslos. **low frequency** *n* Niederfrequenz *f.* **low-grade** *n* Unterstufe *f.* **lowland** *n* Tiefland *neu.* **low-necked** *adj* tief ausgeschnitten. **low-pitched** *adj* tief.

low[2] (lou) *vi* muhen. *n* Muhen *neu.*

lower ('louə) *adj* **1** niedriger. **2** niedere, untere, Unter—. **lower class** *n* untere Klassen *f pl.* ~*vt* **1** niederlassen, herunterlassen. **2** senken. **3** (one's eyes) niederschlagen.

Lower Saxony ('sæksəni) *n* Niedersachsen *neu.*

loyal ('lɔiəl) *adj* treu. **loyalty** *n* Treue *f.*

lozenge ('lɔzindʒ) *n* Pastille *f.*

lubricate ('luːbrikeit) *vt* schmieren. **lubricant** *n* Schmiermittel *neu.* **lubrication** *n* Schmierung *f.* Ölen *neu.*

Lucerne (luː'səːn) *n* Luzerne *f.*

lucid ('luːsid) *adj* **1** hell. **2** klar, deutlich.

luck (lʌk) *n* **1** Glück *neu.* **2** Geschick *neu.* **bad luck** *n* Unglück, Pech *neu.* **lucky** *adj* glücklich. **be lucky** Glück haben. **luckily** *adv* glücklicherweise.

lucrative ('luːkrətiv) *adj* lukrativ.

ludicrous ('luːdikrəs) *adj* lächerlich.

lug (lʌg) *vt* schleppen, zerren.

luggage ('lʌgidʒ) *n* Gepäck *neu.*

lukewarm (luːk'wɔːm) *adj* lauwarm.

lull (lʌl) *vt* **1** einlullen. **2** beruhigen. *vi* sich legen. *n* Stille *f.* **lullaby** *n* Wiegenlied *neu.*

lumbago (ləm'beigou) *n* Hexenschuß *m*.

lumber[1] ('lʌmbə) *n* **1** Gerümpel *neu*. **2** Bauholz *neu*. **lumberjack** *n* Holzfäller *m*. ~ *vt* mit Gerümpel vollpacken.

lumber[2] ('lʌmbə) *vi* sich schwerfällig schleppen.

luminous ('luːminəs) *adj* **1** leuchtend, Leuchter—. **2** hellerleuchtet. **3** klar, einleuchtend.

lump (lʌmp) *n* **1** Klumpen *m*. **2** Beule *f*. **lump sum** Pauschalsumme *f*. ~*vt* zusammenwerfen.

lunacy ('luːnəsi) *n* Irrsinn, Wahnsinn *m*.

lunar ('luːnə) *adj* Mond—.

lunatic ('luːnətik) *adj* wahnsinnig. *n* Irre(r) *m*.

lunch (lʌntʃ) *n* Mittagessen *neu*. **lunch-hour** *n* Mittagspause *f*. ~*vi* zu Mittag essen.

lung (lʌŋ) *n* Lunge *f*.

lunge (lʌndʒ) *n* Ausfall, Stoß *m*. *vi* **1** ausfallen. **2** (dahin)stürmen.

lurch[1] (ləːtʃ) *vi* taumeln. *n* Taumeln *neu*.

lurch[2] (ləːtʃ) *n* **leave someone in the lurch** jemanden im Stich lassen.

lure (luə) *n* **1** Köder *m*. **2** Lockung *f*. *vt* **1** ködern. **2** (an)locken.

lurid ('luərid) *adj* unheimlich, düster.

lurk (ləːk) *vi* lauern.

luscious ('lʌʃəs) *adj* köstlich.

lush (lʌʃ) *adj* saftig, üppig.

lust (lʌst) *n* **1** (Wol)Lust *f*. **2** Sucht, Gier *f*. *v* **lust for** begehren, gelüsten (nach).

lustre ('lʌstə) *n* **1** Glanz *m*. **2** Lüster *m*.

Luxembourg ('lʌksəmbəːg) *n* Luxemburg *neu*.

luxury ('lʌkʃəri) *n* **1** Luxus *m*. **2** Luxusartikel *m*. **luxurious** *adj* luxuriös.

lynx (liŋks) *n* Luchs *m*.

lyre ('laiə) *n* Leier, Lyra *f*.

lyrical ('lirikəl) *adj* lyrisch.

lyrics ('liriks) *n pl* Lyrik *f*.

M

mac (mæk) *n inf* Regenmantel *m*.

macabre (mə'kaːb) *adj* grausig, makaber.

mace[1] (meis) *n* **1** Keule *f*. **2** Amtsstab *m*.

mace[2] (meis) *n bot* Muskatblüte *f*.

machine (mə'ʃiːn) *n* Maschine *f*. *vt* maschinell bearbeiten, herstellen. **machine-gun** *n* Maschinengewehr *neu*. **machinery** *n* **1** Mechanismus *m*. **3** Maschinerie *f*.

mackerel ('mækrəl) *n* Makrele *f*.

mackintosh ('mækintɔʃ) *n* Regenmantel *m*.

mad (mæd) *adj* **1** wahnsinnig, verrückt. **2** toll, wild. **3** *inf* wütend. **madness** *n* Wahnsinn *m*.

madam ('mædəm) *n* gnädige Frau *f*.

made (meid) *v* see **make.**

Madonna (mə'dɔnə) *n* Madonna *f*.

magazine (mægə'ziːn) *n* **1** Magazin *neu*. **2** Illustrierte *f*.

maggot ('mægət) *n* Made *f*.

magic ('mædʒik) *n* **1** Magie *f*. **2** Zauber *m*. Zauberei *f*.

adj **1** magisch. **2** zauberhaft, Zauber—. **magician** *n* Zauberer, Magier *m*.
magistrate ('mædʒistreit) *n* Friedensrichter *m*.
magnanimous (mæg'næniməs) *adj* großmütig.
magnate ('mægneit) *n* Magnat *m*.
magnet ('mægnit) *n* Magnet *m*. **magnetic** *adj* **1** magnetisch. **2** anziehend. **magnetic tape** *n* (Ton)Band *m*. **magnetism** *n* **1** Magnetismus *m*. **2** Anziehungskraft *f*. **magnetize** *vt* **1** magnetisieren. **2** anziehen, fesseln.
magnificent (mæg'nifisənt) *adj* herrlich, prächtig, großartig. **magnificence** *n* Herrlichkeit, Pracht *f*.
magnify ('mægnifai) *vt* vergrößern. **magnifying glass** *n* Vergrößerungsglas *neu*. Lupe *f*.
magnitude ('mægnitju:d) *n* **1** Größe *f*. **2** Bedeutung *f*.
magnolia (mæg'nouliə) *n* Magnolie *f*.
magpie ('mægpai) *n* Elster *f*.
mahogany (mə'hɔgəni) *n* Mahagoni(holz) *neu*.
maid (meid) *n* **1** Mädchen *neu*. **2** Dienstmädchen *neu*. **old maid** *n* alte Jungfer *f*. **maiden** *n* Jungfrau *f*. **maiden name** *n* Mädchenname *m*.
mail (meil) *n* Post *f*. *vt* (mit der Post) schicken. **mailbag** *n* Postsack *m*. **mail order firm** *n* Postversandhaus *neu*.
maim (meim) *vt* verstümmeln, zum Krüppel machen.
main (mein) *adj* Haupt—, hauptsächlich. *n* **1** Hauptleitung *f*. **2** *pl* Stromnetz *neu*. **mainland** *n* Festland *neu*. **mainsail** *n* Großsegel *neu*. **mainspring** *n* **1** Hauptfeder *f*. **2** treibende Kraft *f*. **mainstream** *n* Hauptstrom *m*.
maintain (mein'tein) *vt* **1** erhalten. **2** unterhalten. **3** behaupten. **maintenance** *n* **1** Erhaltung *f*. **2** Unterhalt *m*.
maize (meiz) *n* Mais *m*.
majesty ('mædʒisti) *n* Majestät *f*. **majestic** *adj* majestätisch.
major ('meidʒə) *adj* **1** größer. **2** bedeutend, wichtig. **3** *law* volljährig, mündig. *n* **1** *law* Volljährige(r). **2** *mil* Major *m*. **3** *mus* Dur *neu*. **major general** *n* Generalmajor *m*. **majority** *n* **1** Mehrheit *f*. größter Teil *m*. **2** *law* Volljährigkeit *f*.
make* (meik) *vt* **1** machen. **2** bauen. **3** herstellen. **4** zwingen. **5** sich belaufen auf. **6** *inf* erreichen. **7** *inf* schaffen. **make for** sich ergeben nach. **make good** wiedergutmachen. **make off** sich davonmachen. **make out** **1** ausmachen. **2** ausstellen. **3** vorgeben. **make up** **1** erdichten. **2** sich schminken. **3** sich versöhnen. **4** wiedergutmachen. **5** bilden. **make-believe** *n* Verstellung *f*. Vorwand *m*. **makeshift** *adj* Behelfs—. *n* Notbehelf *m*.
make-up *n* **1** Schminke *f*. Make-up *neu*. **2** Veranlagung, Natur *f*.
maladjusted (mælə'dʒʌstid) *adj* **1** schlecht angepaßt. **2** milieu gestört.
malaria (mə'lɛəriə) *n* Malaria *f*. Sumpffieber *m*.

male (meil) *adj* männlich, Männer—. *n* **1** Mann. **2** *zool* Männchen.
malfunction (mælˈfʌŋkʃən) *vi* schlecht funktionieren. *n* Funktionsstörung *f*.
malice (ˈmalis) *n* **1** Böswilligkeit *f*. **2** *law* böse Absicht *f*. **malicious** *adj* **1** böswillig. **2** boshaft.
malignant (məˈlignənt) *adj* **1** *med* bösartig. **2** boshaft.
malinger (məˈliŋgə) *vi* simulieren, sich krank stellen. **malingerer** *n* Simulant *m*.
mallet (ˈmælət) *n* **1** Holzhammer *m*. **2** *sport* Schlagholz *neu*.
malnutrition (mælnjuːˈtriʃən) *n* Unterernährung *f*.
malt (mɔːlt) *n* Malz *neu*. *vt* mälzen.
Malta (ˈmɔːltə) *n* Malta *neu*. **Maltese** *adj* maltesisch. *n* Malteser *m*.
maltreat (mælˈtriːt) *vt* mißhandeln, schlecht behandeln. **maltreatment** *n* Mißhandlung, schlechte Behandlung *f*.
mammal (ˈmæməl) *n* Säugetier *neu*.
mammoth (ˈmæməθ) *n* Mammut *neu*. *adj* riesig.
man (mæn) *n* **1** Mann *m*. **2** Mensch *m*. **3** Menschheit *f*. *vt* bemannen. **manhandle** *vt* **1** durch Menschenkraft bewegen. **2** rauh behandeln, mißhandeln. **manhole** *n* Einsteigeöffnung, Luke *f*. **manly** *adj* männlich. **manmade** *adj* künstlich, Kunst—. **manpower** *n* **1** Arbeitskräfte *f pl*. **2** Menschenkraft *f*. **manslaughter** *n* Totschlag *m*.
Man, Isle of (mæn) *n* (Insel) Man *neu*.
manage (ˈmænidʒ) *vt* **1** handhaben. **2** leiten, führen. **3** beaufsichtigen. *vi* **1** es schaffen. **2** auskommen. **management** *n* **1** Handhabung *f*. **2** (Geschäfts)Leitung *f*. Management *neu*. **manager** *n* (Betriebs)Leiter, Manager *m*.
mandarin (ˈmændərin) *n* **1** Mandarin *m*. **2** *bot* Mandarine *f*.
mandate (ˈmændeit) *n* **1** Mandat *neu*. Auftrag *m*. **2** Befehl *m*. **mandatory** *adj* **1** verbindlich, obligatorisch. **2** Mandats—.
mane (mein) *n* Mähne *f*.
mange (meindʒ) *n* Räude *f*.
mangle[1] (ˈmæŋgəl) *vt* zerstückeln, zerfleischen.
mangle[2] (ˈmæŋgəl) *n* Wäscherolle, Wringmaschine *f*. *vt* mangeln, rollen, wringen.
mango (ˈmæŋgou) *n* Mangopflaume *f*.
mania (ˈmeiniə) *n* **1** Manie *f*. **2** Wahnsinn *m*. **3** *inf* Fimmel *m*. **maniac** *n* Wahnsinnige(r), Verrückte(r) *m*. **manic** *adj* manisch.
manicure (ˈmænikjuə) *n* Maniküre, Nagelpflege *f*. *vt* maniküren. **manicurist** *n* Maniküre *f*.
manifest (ˈmænifest) *adj* offenbar, manifest, klar. *vt* **1** offenbaren. **2** zeigen. **manifestation** *n* **1** Offenbarung, Kundgebung *f*. **2** Erscheinung *f*.
manifesto (mæniˈfestou) *n* Manifest *neu*.

manifold ('mænifould) *adj* mannigfaltig.
manipulate (mə'nipjuleit) *vt* **1** (geschickt) handhaben. **2** manipulieren. **manipulation** *n* **1** Handhabung *f*. **2** Manipulation *f*.
mankind ('mænkaind) *n* Menschheit *f*.
manner ('mænə) *n* **1** Art, Weise *f*. **2** Manier *f*. **3** Benehmen *neu*. **4** *pl* Manieren *pl*. Betragen *neu*. **mannerism** *n* **1** Manieriertheit *f*. **2** (of style) Manierismus *m*.
manoeuvre (mə'nu:və) *n* Manöver *neu*. *vi,(vt)* manövrieren (lassen).
manor ('mænə) *n* Gut *neu*. **lord of the manor** *n* Gutsherr *m*. **manor house** *n* Herrensitz *m*.
mansion ('mænʃən) *n* **1** herrschaftliches Wohnhaus *neu*. **2** *pl* Mietshaus *neu*.
mantle ('mæntl) *n* **1** (Deck)Mantel *m*. **2** Hülle *f*. *vt* verhüllen. **mantlepiece** *n* Kaminsims *m*.
manual ('mænjuəl) *adj* **1** Hand—. **2** handgefertigt. **3** manuell. *n* **1** Handbuch *neu*. **2** *mus* Manual *neu*.
manufacture (mænju'fæktʃə) *n* **1** Herstellung, Fabrikation, Erzeugung *f*. **2** Fabrikat *neu*. *vt* **1** herstellen, erzeugen, anfertigen. **2** erfinden, erdichten. **manufactured** *adj* Fabrik—, Fertig—.
manure (mə'njuə) *n* Dünger *m*. *vt* düngen.
manuscript ('mænjuskript) *n* **1** Manuskript *neu*. Handschrift *f*. **2** Druckvorlage *f*.
many ('meni) *adj* viele. **how many** wieviele. **many a** manch (ein). **many times** oft, häufig. **the many** die Masse *f*. die Vielen *pl*.
map (mæp) *n* **1** Landkarte, Seekarte *f*. **2** Stadtplan *m*. *vt* aufzeichnen, eintragen.
maple ('meipəl) *n bot* Ahorn *m*.
mar (mɑ:) *vt* **1** verderben. **2** verunstalten.
marathon ('mærəθən) *adj* Dauer—. **marathon race** *n* Langstreckenlauf, Marathonlauf *m*.
marble ('mɑ:bəl) *n* **1** Marmor *m*. **2** Marmorkunstwerk *neu*. **3** Murmel *f*. *adj* marmorn.
march (mɑ:tʃ) *n* Marsch *m*. **march past** *n* Vorbeimarsch *m*. *~vi,(vt)* marschieren (lassen). **marching** *adj* Marsch—.
March (mɑ:tʃ) *n* März *m*.
marchioness ('mɑ:ʃənis) *n* Marquise *f*.
mare (mɛə) *n* Stute *f*.
margarine (mɑ:dʒə'ri:n) *n* Margarine *f*.
margin ('mɑ:dʒin) *n* **1** Rand *m*. **2** Grenze *f*.
marguerite (mɑ:gə'ri:t) *n* Gänseblümchen *neu*.
marigold ('mærigould) *n* Dotterblume *f*.
marijuana (mæri'wɑ:nə) *n* Marihuana *neu*.
marinade (*n* mæri'neid; *v* 'mærineid) *n cul* Marinade *f*. *vt* marinieren.
marine (mə'ri:n) *adj* **1** See—, Marine—. **2** Schiffs—. *n* **1** Marine *f*. **2** Marineinfantrist *m*. **maritime** *adj* **1** See—. **2** Küsten—. **3** Schiffahrts—.

marital ('mæritḷ) *adj* ehelich.
marjoram ('ma:dʒərəm) *n* Marjoran *m*.
mark[1] (ma:k) *n* **1** Marke *f*. Zeichen *neu*. **2** Fleck *m*. **3** Kennzeichen *neu*. **4** *educ* Note *f*. **5** Ziel *neu*. *vt* **1** (aus)zeichnen. **2** *educ* zensieren, korrigieren. **3** beachten. **4** markieren. *vi* beflecken. **marked** *adj* auffällig, deutlich, gezeichnet. **marksman** *n* (guter) Schütze *m*.
mark[2] (ma:k) *n* Mark *f*.
market ('ma:kit) *n* Markt *m*. *vt* auf den Markt bringen. **market garden** *n* Handelsgärtnerei *f*. **market place** *n* Marktplatz *m*. **market research** *n* Marktforschung *f*.
marmalade ('ma:məleid) *n* Orangenmarmelade *f*.
maroon[1] (mə'ru:n) *adj* dunkelrot.
maroon[2] (mə'ru:n) *vt* **1** (auf einer öden Insel) aussetzen. **2** verlassen, im Stich lassen.
marquee (ma:'ki:) *n* großes Zelt *neu*.
marquess ('ma:kwis) *n* Marquis *m*.
marriage ('mæridʒ) *n* **1** Ehe *f*. **2** Ehestand *m*. **3** Hochzeit, Heirat *f*. **civil marriage** *n* standesamtliche Trauung *f*. **marriage certificate** *n* Trauschein *m*.
marrow ('mærou) *n* **1** (Knochen)Mark *neu*. **2** Kern *m*. **3** *bot* Kürbis *m*. **marrowbone** *n* Markknochen *m*.
marry ('mæri) *vt* **1** (ver)heiraten, trauen. **2** sich verheiraten mit. *vi* sich verheiraten, heiraten.
Mars (ma:z) *n* Mars *m*.
marsh (ma:ʃ) *n* Sumpfland *neu*.
marshal ('ma:ʃəl) *n* **1** (Feld)Marschall *m*. **2** Zeremonienmeister, Festordner *m*. *vt* **1** ordnen. **2** (feierlich) führen.
martial ('ma:ʃəl) *adj* **1** kriegerisch. **2** Kriegs—.
martin ('ma:tin) *n* *zool* Mauerschwalbe *f*.
martyr ('ma:tə) *n* Märtyrer *m*. *vt* zum Märtyrer machen. **martyrdom** *n* **1** Märtyrertum *neu*. **2** Martyrium *neu*.
marvel ('ma:vəl) *n* Wunder *m*. *vi* sich wundern.
marvellous ('ma:vələs) *adj* wunderbar, erstaunlich.
Marxism ('ma:ksizəm) *n* Marxismus *m*. **Marxist** *adj* marxistisch. *n* Marxist *m*.
marzipan ('ma:zipæn) *n* Marzipan *neu*.
mascara (mæ'ska:rə) *n* Wimperntusche *f*.
mascot ('mæskɔt) *n* Maskottchen *neu*.
masculine ('mæskjulin) *adj* männlich. *n* *gram* Maskulinum *neu*.
mash (mæʃ) *n* **1** Gemisch *neu*. **2** Brei *m*. **3** Mengfutter *neu*. *vt* **1** mischen. **2** zerquetschen, zerstampfen. **mashed potatoes** *n pl* Kartoffelpüree *m*.
mask (ma:sk) *n* Maske *f*. *vt* verbergen.
mason ('meisən) *n* Maurer *m*. **masonry** *n* Mauerwerk *neu*.
masquerade (mæskə'reid) **1**

Maskenball *m.* **2** Maskerade *f.* *vi* sich maskieren.

mass[1] (mæs) *n* **1** Masse *f.* **2** Menge *f.* *(vi),vt* (sich) anhäufen, (sich) ansammeln. **mass media** *n pl* Massenmedien *neu pl.* **mass-produce** *vt* serienmäßig herstellen. **mass production** *n* Serienbau *m.* Serienproduktion *f.*

mass[2] (mæs) *n rel* Messe *f.*

massacre ('mæsəkə) *n* Gemetzel, Massaker *neu.* *vt* niedermetzeln.

massage ('mæsɑːʒ) *n* Massage *f.* *vt* massieren.

massive ('mæsiv) *adj* **1** massiv. **2** schwer. **3** massig. **4** fest.

mast (mɑːst) *n* Mast *m.* **masthead** *n* Mastkorb *m.*

mastectomy (mæs'tektəmi) *n med* Brustamputation *f.*

master ('mɑstə) *n* **1** Meister *m.* **2** Herr *m.* **3** Lehrer *m.* *vt* beherrschen. **masterpiece** *n* Meisterstück *neu.* **masterful** *adj* **1** herrisch. **2** meisterhaft. **mastery** *n* **1** Herrschaft *f.* **2** Beherrschung *f.*

masturbate ('mæstəbeit) *vi* masturbieren.

mat (mæt) *n* Matte *f.*

match[1] (mætʃ) *n* Streichholz, Zündholz *neu.* **matchbox** *n* Streichholzschachtel *f.*

match[2] (mætʃ) *n* **1** Passende(r), Gleiche(r) *m.* **2** Wettspiel *neu.* (Wett)Kampf *m.* **3** Partie *f.* **4** Match *neu.* *vt* **1** anpassen. **2** passen zu. *vi* zusammenpassen, dazupassen.

mate (meit) *n* **1** Gefährte *m.* Gefährtin *f.* **2** Gatte *m.* Gattin *f.* **3** *zool* Männchen, Weibchen *neu.* **4** *naut* Maat *m.* *(vi),vt* (sich) paaren.

material (mə'tiəriəl) *n* Material *neu.* Stoff *m.* *adj* materiell, stofflich. **materialism** *n* Materialismus *m.* **materialist** *n* Materialist *m.* **materialize** *vi* sich verwirklichen.

maternal (mə'təːnl) *adj* **1** mütterlich. **2** mütterlicherseits. **maternity** *n* Mutterschaft *f.* *adj* Schwangerschafts—, Umstands—.

mathematics (mæθə'mætiks) *n* Mathematik *f.*

matins ('mætinz) *n pl* Frühmesse *f.*

matinee ('mætinei) *n* Nachmittagsvorstellung *f.*

matriarchal ('meitriɑːkəl) *adj* matriarchalisch.

matrimony ('mætriməni) *n* Ehe *f.* Ehestand *m.*

matrix ('meitriks) *n, pl* **-ices** **1** Matrix *f.* **2** *tech* Matrize *f.* **3** Nährboden *m.*

matron ('meitrən) *n* **1** Matrone *f.* **2** Vorsteherin *f.*

matter ('mætə) *n* **1** Materie *f.* Stoff *m.* Substanz *f.* **2** Sache, Angelegenheit *f.* *vi* etwas bedeuten, etwas ausmachen. **it doesn't matter** es macht nichts. **what's the matter?** was ist los?

mattress ('mætrəs) *n* Matratze *f.*

mature (mə'tjuə) *adj* reif, entwickelt. *vi* reifen. **maturity** *n* Reife *f.*

maudlin ('mɔːdlin) *adj* sentimental.

maul (mɔːl) *vt* verprügeln, zerreißen.

mausoleum (mɔːsə'liəm) *n* Mausoleum *neu*.
mauve (mouv) *adj* malvenfarbig. *n* Malvenfarbe *f*.
maxim ('mæksim) *n* Grundsatz *m*. Maxime *f*.
maximum ('mæksiməm) *n* Maximum, Höchstmaß *neu*. **maximize** *vt* vergrößern, verstärken.
may* (mei) *v mod aux* **1** mögen, können. **2** dürfen. **maybe** *adv* vielleicht.
May (mei) *n* Mai *m*. **May Day** *n* erster Mai *m*. **maypole** *n* Maibaum *m*.
mayonnaise (meiə'neiz) *n* Mayonnaise *f*.
mayor ('mɛə) *n* Bürgermeister *m*.
maze (meiz) *n* Irrgarten *m*.
me (miː) *pron 1st pers s* **1** mich. **2** mir.
meadow ('medou) *n* Wiese *f*.
meagre ('miːgə) *adj* mager, ärmlich.
meal[1] (miːl) *n* Mahlzeit *f*. Mahl, Essen *neu*.
meal[2] (miːl) *n* (grobes) Mehl *neu*.
mean*[1] (miːn) *vt* bedeuten, heißen, meinen. *vi,vt* beabsichtigen.
mean[2] (miːn) *adj* **1** gering, niedrig. **2** geizig.
meander (mi'ændə) *vi* sich winden. *n* Windung *f*. Krümmung *f*.
meaning ('miːniŋ) *n* Bedeutung *f*. Sinn *m*.
means (miːnz) *n pl* Mittel *neu pl*. **by means of** mittels, durch.
meanwhile ('miːnwail) *adv* inzwischen.
measles ('miːzəlz) *n* Masern *f pl*.
measure ('meʒə) *vt* (ab-, aus-) messen. *n* **1** Maß *neu*. **2** Maßnahme *f*. **measurement** *n* **1** Messung *f*. **2** Maß *neu*.
meat (miːt) *n* **1** Fleisch *neu*. **2** Kern *m*.
mechanic (mi'kænik) *n* Mechaniker, Autoschlosser *m*. **mechanical** *adj* mechanisch. **mechanical engineering** *n* Maschinenbau *m*. **mechanics** *n pl* **1** Mechanik *f*. Konstruktion *f*. **mechanism** *n* Mechanismus *m*. Arbeitsweise *f*. **mechanize** *vt* mechanisieren.
medal ('medḷ) *n* Orden *m*. Medaille *f*. **medallion** *n* Medaille *f*.
meddle ('medḷ) *vi* sich einmischen.
media ('miːdiə) *n* Nachrichtenmittel, Medien *neu pl*.
medial ('miːdiəl) *adj* durchschnittlich, Mittel—.
median ('miːdiən) *adj* in der Mitte liegend, mittler. *n* Mittelwert *m*.
mediate ('miːdieit) *vi* vermitteln.
medical ('medikəl) *adj* medizinisch, ärztlich. **medication** *n* medizinische Behandlung, Verordnung *f*. **medicine** *n* **1** Medizin *f*. **2** Arzneimittel *neu*.
medieval (medi'iːvəl) *adj* mittelalterlich.
mediocre (miːdi'oukə) *adj* mittelmäßig. **mediocrity** *n* Mittelmäßigkeit *f*.
meditate ('mediteit) *vi* **1** medi-

tieren. **2** überlegen. **3** nachdenken.

Mediterranean (meditə'reiniən) *adj* Mittelmeer—. **Mediterranean (Sea)** *n* Mittelmeer *neu*.

medium ('mi:diəm) *n, pl* **media 1** Mitte *f*. **2** Mittel *neu*. **3** Medium *neu*. *adj* mittler.

meek (mi:k) *adj* sanft, demütig, mild.

meet* (mi:t) *vt* **1** begegnen. **2** treffen. **3** erfüllen. **meeting** *n* **1** Begegnung *f*. **2** Zusammenkunft *f*. **3** Versammlung, Sitzung *f*.

megaphone ('megəfoun) *n* Megaphon *neu*.

melancholy ('melənkəli) *n* Schwermut, Melancholie *f*. *adj* schwermütig, melancholisch.

mellow ('melou) *adj* **1** ausgereift. **2** mild.

melodrama ('melədrɑ:mə) *n* Melodrama *neu*.

melody ('melədi) *n* Melodie *f*. **melodic** *adj* melodisch.

melon ('melən) *n* Melone *f*.

melt* (melt) *vt,vi* schmelzen. **melting point** *n* Schmelzpunkt *m*.

member ('membə) *n* **1** Mitglied *neu*. **2** *anat* Glied *neu*. **membership** *n* Mitgliedschaft *f*.

membrane ('membrein) *n* Membrane *f*.

memento (mə'mentou) *n* Memento *neu*.

memo ('memou) *n inf* Notiz, Mitteilung *f*.

memoirs ('memwɑ:z) *n pl* Memoiren, Lebenserinnerungen *f pl*.

memorandum (memə'rændəm) *n, pl* **-da** Notiz, Mitteilung *f*.

memory ('meməri) *n* **1** Gedächtnis *neu*. **2** Erinnerung *f*. **memorable** *adj* denkwürdig. **memorial** *n* Denkmal *neu*. *adj* Gedächtnis—. **memorize** *vt* auswendig lernen, im Gedächtnis behalten.

menace ('menəs) *vt* (be)drohen. *n* **1** Drohung *f*. **2** *inf* lästiger Mensch *m*. lästiges Kind *neu*.

menagerie (mə'nædʒəri) *n* Menagerie *f*.

mend (mend) *vt* reparieren, ausbessern.

menial ('mi:niəl) *adj* niedrig, gemein.

menopause ('menəpɔ:z) *n* Menopause *f*. Wechseljahre *neu pl*.

menstrual ('menstruəl) *adj* **1** monatlich, Monats—. **2** Menstruations—. **menstruate** *vi* menstruieren, die Regel haben. **menstruation** *n* Monatsblutung, Menstruation, Regel *f*.

mental ('mentl̩) *adj* **1** geistig, intellektuell, Geistes—. **2** *sl* verrückt. **mental hospital** *n* Nervenklinik *f*. **mental illness** *n* Geisteskrankheit *f*.

mentality *n* Mentalität, Denkweise *f*.

menthol ('menθɔl) *n* Menthol *neu*.

mention ('menʃən) *vt* erwähnen. *n* Erwähnung *f*. **don't mention it!** bitte! gern geschehen! **not to mention** ganz zu schweigen von.

menu ('menju:) *n* Speisekarte *f*.

mercantile ('mə:kəntail) *adj* kaufmännisch.

mercenary ('mə:sənəri) *adj* **1** käuflich. **2** Gewinn—, Geld—. *n* Söldner *m*.

merchant ('mə:tʃənt) *n* **1** (Groß)Händler *m*. **2** (Groß)Kaufmann *m*. **merchant bank** *n* Handelsbank *f*. **merchant navy** *n* Handelsflotte *f*. **merchandise** *n* Güter *neu pl*. Waren *f pl*.

mercury ('mə:kjuri) *n* **1** *sci* Quecksilber *neu*. **2** *cap* Merkur *m*.

mercy ('mə:si) *n* Gnade, Barmherzigkeit *f*.

mere (miə) *adj* bloß.

merge (mə:dʒ) *vi* aufgehen, sich verschmelzen. *vt* verschmelzen, aufgehen lassen. *vt,vi comm* fusionieren. **merger** *n comm* Fusionierung *f*.

meridian (mə'ridiən) *n* Meridian *m*.

meringue (mə'ræŋ) *n* Meringe *f*. Baiser *neu*.

merit ('merit) *n* **1** Verdienst *neu*. **2** Wert *m*. *vt* verdienen.

mermaid ('mə:meid) *n* Meerjungfer, Seenixe *f*.

merry ('meri) *adj* **1** lustig, fröhlich. **2** *inf* beschwipst, leicht betrunken. **merry-go-round** *n* Karussell *neu*.

mesh (meʃ) *n* Masche *f*. Netz *neu*. *vt* verfangen. *vi tech* ineinandergreifen.

mesmerize ('mezməraiz) *vt* mesmerisieren.

mess (mes) *n* **1** Unordnung *f*. **2** Verwirrung *f*. Durcheinander *neu*. **3** Schmutz *m*. **4** *mil* Messe *f*.

message ('mesidʒ) *n* **1** Botschaft *f*. **2** Mitteilung *f*. **messenger** *n* Bote *m*.

met (met) *v* see **meet**.

metabolism (mi'tæbəlizəm) *n* Stoffwechsel *m*.

metal ('metl̩) *n* Metall *neu*. **metallurgy** *n* Metallurgie, Hüttenkünde *f*.

metamorphosis (metə'mɔ:fəsis) *n* Metamorphose, Verwandlung *f*.

metaphor ('metəfə) *n* Metapher *f*.

metaphysics (metə'fiziks) *n* Metaphysik *f*.

meteor ('mi:tiə) *n* Meteor *neu*. **meteorology** *n* Meteorologie, Wetterkunde *f*.

meter ('mi:tə) *n* Messer, Zähler *m*.

methane ('mi:θein) *n* Methan, Sumpfgas *neu*.

method ('meθəd) *n* **1** Methode *f*. **2** Weise *f*. **3** *tech* Verfahren *neu*. **methodical** *adj* methodisch. **methodology** *n* Methodologie *f*.

Methodist ('meθədist) *n* Methodist *m*.

meticulous (mi'tikjuləs) *adj* peinlich genau, penibel, übergenau.

metre ('mi:tə) *n* **1** Meter *m,neu*. **2** *lit* Versmaß *neu*. **metric** *adj* metrisch.

metropolis (mə'trɔpəlis) *n* Hauptstadt, Metropole *f*. **metropolitan** *adj* großstädtisch.

Mexico ('meksikou) *n* Mexiko *neu*. **Mexican** *adj* mexikanisch. *n* Mexikaner *m*.

miaow (mi'au) *n* Miauen *neu*. *vi* miauen.

microbe ('maikroub) *n* Mikrobe *f.*
microchip ('maikroutʃip) *n* Mikrochip *m.*
microphone ('maikrəfoun) *n* Mikrophon *neu.*
microscope ('maikrəskoup) *n* Mikroskop *neu.*
mid (mid) *adj* in der Mitte, mittler. **midday** *n* Mittag *m.* **midland** *n* Mittelland *neu.* **midnight** *n* Mitternacht *f.* **midstream** *n* Strommitte *f.* **midsummer** *n* Hochsommer *m.* **midway** *adj,adv* auf halbem Wege. **midweek** *n* Mitte der Woche *f.*
middle ('midḷ) *n* Mitte *f.* Zentrum *neu.* **middle-aged** *adj* im mittleren Alter. **middle class** *n* Mittelstand *m.* Bürgertum *neu.* **middle-class** *adj* Mittelstands—. **Middle Ages** *n* Mittelalter *neu.* **Middle East** *n* Nahe(r) Osten *m.*
midget ('midʒit) *n* Zwerg *m.*
midst (midst) *n* Mitte *f.* **in the midst of** mitten unter, inmitten.
midwife ('midwaif) *n* Hebamme *f.*
might[1] (mait) *v* see **may.**
might[2] (mait) *n* **1** Macht *f.* **2** Gewalt *f.* **mighty** *adj* mächtig.
migraine ('mi:grein) *n* Migräne *f.*
migrate (mai'greit) *vi* (aus)wandern.
mike (maik) *n sl* Mikrophon *neu.*
Milan (mi'læn) *n* Mailand *neu.*
mild (maild) *adj* **1** mild. **2** sanft.
mildew ('mildju:) *n* **1** Meltau *m.* **2** Moder *m.*
mile (mail) *n* Meile *f.* **mileage** *n* Meilenzahl *f.* **mileometer** *n* Meilenzähler, Kilometerzähler *m.* **milestone** *n* **1** Meilenstein *m.* **2** Markstein *m.*
militant ('militənt) *adj* militant, kämpferisch. *n* Kämpfer *m.*
military *adj* militärisch. *n* Militär *neu.*
milk (milk) *n* Milch *f.* **milkman** *n* Milchmann *m.* **Milky Way** *n* Milchstraße *f.*
mill (mil) *n* **1** Mühle *f.* **2** Fabrik *f.* *vt* mahlen. *vi* herumirren. **millstone** *n* Mühlstein *m.*
millennium (mi'leniəm) *n* Jahrtausend *neu.*
milligram ('miligræm) *n* Milligramm *neu.*
millilitre ('milili:tə) *n* Milliliter *m.*
millimetre ('milimi:tə) *n* Millimeter *m,neu.*
million ('miliən) *n* Million *f.* **millionth** *adj* millionste. **millionaire** *n* Millionär *m.*
mime (maim) *n* Mime *m.* *vt,vi* mimen. **mimic** *vt* nachahmen. *n* Mimiker, Nachahmer *m.*
minaret (minə'ret) *n* Minarett *neu.*
mince (mins) *vt* zerhacken, zerstückeln. *n* Hackfleisch *neu.*
mind (maind) *n* **1** Geist, Verstand *m.* **2** Sinn *m.* **3** Meinung *f.* **4** Gedächtnis *neu.* *vt* **1** achten *or* aufpassen auf. **2** sorgen für, sehen nach. **3** sich kümmern um. **4** sich hüten vor. *vt,vi* etwas dagegen haben. **never mind!** macht nichts!

mine[1] (main) *poss pron 1st pers s* meiner, der meine *or* meinige.
mine[2] (main) *n* **1** *min* Mine *f*. Bergwerk *neu*. **2** *mil* Mine *f*. *vi* graben. *vt* **1** *mil* verminen. **2** abbauen.
mineral ('minərəl) *n* Mineral *neu*. Bodenschatz *m*. *adj* mineralisch. **mineral water** *n* Mineralwasser *neu*.
mingle ('miŋgəl) *(vi),vt* (sich) vermischen.
miniature ('miniətʃə) *n* Miniatur *f*. *adj* Klein—. Miniatur—.
minim ('minim) *n* Halbnote *f*.
minimum ('miniməm) *n, pl* **-ma** Minimum *neu*. **minimal** *adj* Mindest—, minimal.
mining ('mainiŋ) *n* Bergbau *m*.
minister ('ministə) *n* Minister *m*. **ministry** *n* Ministerium *neu*.
mink (miŋk) *n* Nerz *m*.
minor ('mainə) *adj* **1** kleiner, geringer. **2** geringfügig. *n* **1** Minderjährige(r). **2** Moll *neu*. **minority** *n* Minderheit, Minorität *f*.
minstrel ('minstrəl) *n* **1** Minnesänger *m*. **2** Sänger *m*.
mint[1] (mint) *n bot* Minze *f*.
mint[2] (mint) *n* Münzanstalt *f*.
minuet (minju'et) *n* Menuett *neu*.
minus ('mainəs) *prep* weniger, minus.
minute[1] ('minit) *n* Minute *f*.
minute[2] (mai'nju:t) *adj* winzig.
miracle ('mirəkəl) *n* **1** Wunder *neu*. **2** Wundertat *f*. **miraculous** *adj* wunderbar.
mirage ('mirɑ:ʒ) *n* Täuschung *f*.
mirror ('mirə) *n* Spiegel *m*. *vt* widerspiegeln.
mirth (mə:θ) *n* **1** Fröhlichkeit *f*. **2** Heiterkeit *f*.
misbehave (misbi'heiv) *vi* sich schlecht benehmen.
miscarriage (mis'kæridʒ) *n* Fehlgeburt *f*. **miscarriage of justice** *n* Rechtsbeugung *f*.
miscellaneous (misə'leiniəs) *adj* verschiedenartig. *n* (newspaper column) Verschiedenes *neu*. **miscellany** *n* Gemisch *neu*. Sammlung *f*.
mischance (mis'tʃɑ:ns) *n* Mißgeschick *neu*.
mischief ('mistʃif) *n* **1** Unheil *neu*. Schaden *m*. **2** Unfug *m*. **mischievous** *adj* **1** schelmisch. **2** verderblich.
misconceive (miskən'si:v) *vt* mißverstehen, falsch begreifen. **misconception** *n* Mißverständnis *neu*.
misconduct (mis'kɔndʌkt) *n* schlechtes *or* unangemessenes Verhalten *neu*.
misdeed (mis'di:d) *n* Missetat *f*.
miser ('maizə) *n* Geizhals *m*.
miserable ('mizərəbəl) *adj* **1** elend, erbärmlich. **2** unglücklich.
misery ('mizəri) *n* Elend *neu*.
misfire (mis'faiə) *vi* **1** *mot* fehlzünden. **2** *mil* versagen. **3** scheitern.
misfit ('misfit) *n* **1** schlechtpassendes Stück *neu*. **2** Mensch, der sich seiner Umwelt nicht anpassen kann *m*.
misfortune (mis'fɔ:tʃən) *n* Unglück, Mißgeschick *neu*.
misgiving (mis'giviŋ) *n* Befürchtung *f*. Zweifel *m*.

misguided (mis'gaidid) *adj* irregeführt.
mishap ('mishæp) *n* Unfall *m*. Unglück *neu*.
mislay* (mis'lei) *vt* verlegen.
mislead* (mis'liːd) *vt* irreführen.
misprint ('misprint) *n* Druckfehler *m*.
miss[1] (mis) *vt* **1** verfehlen. **2** vermissen. **3** versäumen, verpassen. *n* Fehlschuß *m*. **missing** *adj* fehlend, abwesend.
miss[2] (mis) *n* **1** Fräulein *neu*. **2** *cap* (title of address) Fräulein, Frl.
missile ('misail) *n* Geschoß *neu*.
mission ('miʃən) *n* **1** Mission *f*. **2** Auftrag *m*. **missionary** *n* Missionar *m*.
mist (mist) *n* Nebel, Dunst *m*.
mistake* (mis'teik) *n* Fehler, Irrtum *m*. *vt* verwechseln, falsch verstehen.
mister ('mistə) *n* Herr *m*.
mistletoe ('misəltou) *n* Mistel *f*.
mistress ('mistrəs) *n* **1** Lehrerin *f*. **2** Geliebte *f*. **3** Herrin *f*. **4** Frau des Hauses *f*.
mistrust (mis'trʌst) *vt* mißtrauen. *n* Mißtrauen *neu*.
misunderstand* (misʌndə'stænd) *vt* mißverstehen. **misunderstanding** *n* Mißverständnis *neu*.
misuse (*v* mis'juːz; *n* mis'juːs) *vt* mißbrauchen. *n* Mißbrauch *m*.
mitre ('maitə) *n* Bischofsmütze *f*.
mitten ('mitn̩) *n* Fausthandschuh *m*.
mix (miks) *vt* (ver)mischen. **mix up 1** verwechseln. **2** vermischen. ~*n* Mischung *f*. **mixture** *n* Mischung *f*.
moan (moun) *vi* **1** stöhnen. **2** jammern, meckern.
moat (mout) *n* Burggraben *m*.
mob (mɔb) *n* **1** Pöbel *m*. Gesindel *neu*. **2** Bande *f*.
mobile ('moubail) *adj* mobil, beweglich. **mobility** *n* Beweglichkeit *f*. **mobilize** *vt* mobilisieren.
mock (mɔk) *vt* verspotten, verhöhnen. *adj* nachgemacht, unecht, Pseudo—.
mode (moud) *n* **1** Weise, Methode *f*. **2** Form, Art *f*.
model ('mɔdl̩) *n* **1** Modell *neu*. **2** Vorbild *neu*. *adj* **1** Modell—. **2** vorbildlich.
moderate ('mɔdərət) *adj* mäßig. **moderation** *n* Maß *neu*. Mäßigung *f*.
modern ('mɔdən) *adj* modern. **modernize** *vt* modernisieren.
modest ('mɔdist) *adj* bescheiden. **modesty** *n* Bescheidenheit *f*.
modify ('mɔdifai) *vt* abändern, modifizieren. **modification** *n* Abänderung, Modifikation *f*.
modulate ('mɔdjuleit) *vt* **1** abstimmen, anpassen. **2** abstufen. **3** dämpfen. **4** modulieren.
module ('mɔdjuːl) *n* Modul, Model *m*.
mohair ('mouhɛə) *n* Mohär *m*.
moist (mɔist) *adj* feucht. **moisten** *vt* (be-, an-)feuchten, nässen. **moisture** *n* Feuchtigkeit *f*. **moisturizing cream** *n* Feuchtigkeitscreme *f*.

mole[1] (moul) *n* Muttermal *neu.* Leberfleck *m.*
mole[2] (moul) *n* Maulwurf *m.*
molecule ('mɔlikju:l) *n* Molekül *neu.*
molest (mə'lest) *vt* belästigen.
mollusc ('mɔləsk) *n* Weichtier *neu.* Molluske *f.*
molten ('moultən) *adj* **1** geschmolzen. **2** (of metal) flüssig.
moment ('moumənt) *n* Moment, Augenblick *m.* **momentary** *adj* momentan, augenblicklich. **momentous** *adj* bedeutend, gewichtig. **momentum** *n* Triebkraft, Schwungkraft *f.* Impuls *m.*
monarch ('mɔnək) *n* Monarch *m.*
monastery ('mɔnəstri) *n* (Mönchs)Kloster *neu.*
Monday ('mʌndi) *n* Montag *m.*
money ('mʌni) *n* Geld *neu.* **get one's money's worth** etwas für sein Geld bekommen. **moneybox** *n* Sparbüchse *f.* **money order** *n* Postanweisung *f.* **monetarism** *n* Monetarismus *m.* **monetary** *adj* **1** Geld—. **2** finanziell.
mongrel ('mʌngrəl) *n* Mischling *m.* Kreuzung *f.*
monitor ('mɔnitə) *n* Monitor, Bildschirm *m.* *vt* **1** abhören. **2** kontrollieren, überwachen.
monk (mʌŋk) *n* Mönch *m.*
monkey ('mʌŋki) *n* Affe *m.*
monogamy (mə'nɔgəmi) *n* Monogamie, Einehe *f.*
monologue ('mɔnəlɔg) *n* Monolog *m.*
monopolize (mə'nɔpəlaiz) *vt* monopolisieren. **monopoly** *n* Monopol *neu.*
monosyllable ('mɔnəsiləbəl) *n* einsilbiges Wort *neu.* **speak in monosyllables** einsilbige Antworten geben.
monotone ('mɔnətoun) *n* Eintönigkeit, Monotonie *f.* **monotonous** *adj* eintönig, monoton.
monsoon (mɔn'su:n) *n* Monsun *m.*
monster ('mɔnstə) *n* **1** Ungeheuer *neu.* **2** Scheusal *neu.* **monstrous** *adj* **1** ungeheuer, riesig. **2** ungeheuerlich. **3** scheußlich.
month (mʌnθ) *n* Monat *m.*
monument ('mɔnjumənt) *n* Denkmal, Monument *neu.*
moo (mu:) *vi* muhen.
mood[1] (mu:d) *n* Laune, Stimmung *f.* **be in a good/bad mood** guter/schlechter Laune sein. **moody** *adj* launisch.
mood[2] (mu:d) *n* Modus *m.*
moon (mu:n) *n* Mond *m.* **moonlight** *n* Mondlicht *neu.* Mondschein *m.*
moor[1] (muə) *n* Moor *neu.* **moorhen** *n* Teichhuhn *neu.* **moorland** *n* Moor(land) *neu.*
moor[2] (muə) *vt* festmachen, verankern.
Moor (muə) *n* Maure *m.* **Moorish** *adj* maurisch.
mop (mɔp) *n* Mop, Staubbesen *m.* *vt* (auf)wischen.
mope (moup) *vi* traurig sein.
moped ('mouped) *n* Moped *neu.*
moral ('mɔrəl) *n* **1** Moral, Lehre *f.* **2** *pl* Moral *f.* Sitten *f pl.* *adj* moralisch. **morale** *n* Moral *f.* **morality** *n* **1** Mor-

al(ität) *f.* **2** Sittlichkeit *f.* **moralize** *vi* moralisieren.
morbid ('mɔːbid) *adj* krankhaft, morbid.
more (mɔː) *adj* **1** mehr. **2** mehr, noch (etwas), weiter. *adv* **1** mehr. **2** noch. **more and more** immer mehr. **more or less** mehr oder weniger. **moreover** *adv* außerdem, weiter, ferner.
morgue (mɔːg) *n* Leichenschauhaus *neu.*
morning ('mɔːniŋ) *n* **1** Morgen *m.* **2** Vormittag *m.* **in the mornings** morgens. **this morning** heute früh, heute morgen..
Morocco (mə'rɔkou) *n* Marokko *neu.* **Moroccan** *adj* marokkanisch. *n* Marokkaner *m.*
moron ('mɔːrɔn) *n* Schwachsinnige(r) *m.*
morose (mə'rous) *adj* mürrisch, verdrießlich.
morphine ('mɔːfiːn) *n* Morphium *neu.*
morse code (mɔːs) *n* Morsealphabet *neu.*
mortal ('mɔːt) *adj* sterblich. **mortality** *n* Sterblichkeit *f.*
mortar[1] ('mɔːtə) *n* Mörser *m.*
mortar[2] ('mɔːtə) *n* (for building) Mörtel *m.*
mortgage ('mɔːgidʒ) *n* Hypothek *f.* *vt* **1** eine Hypothek nehmen auf. **2** verpfänden.
mortify ('mɔːtifai) *vt* **1** demütigen. **2** abtöten.
mortuary ('mɔːtjuəri) *n* Leichenhalle *f.*
mosaic (mou'zeiik) *n* Mosaik *neu.*
Moselle (mou'zel) *n* **1** Mosel *f.* **2** Moselwein *m.*
mosque (mɔsk) *n* Moschee *f.*
mosquito (mə'skiːtou) *n pl* **-oes** *or* **-os** Mücke *f.* Moskito *m.*
moss (mɔs) *n* Moos *neu.*
most (moust) *adj* **1** die meisten. **2** meist, höchst. *adv* am meisten, Meist—. *n* **1** das meiste, das Höchste *neu.* **2** der größte Teil *m.* **mostly** *adv* **1** hauptsächlich. **2** größtenteils.
motel (mou'tel) *n* Motel *neu.*
moth (mɔθ) *n* Motte *f.*
mother ('mʌðə) *n* Mutter *f.* *vt* bemuttern. **motherhood** *n* Mutterschaft *f.* **mother-in-law** *n* Schwiegermutter *f.* **mother superior** *n* Äbtissin *f.*
motion ('mouʃən) *n* **1** Bewegung *f.* **2** Gang *m.* **3** Antrieb *m.* *vt* zuwinken.
motive ('moutiv) *n* Beweggrund *m.*
motor ('moutə) *n* Motor *m.* **motor car** *n* Auto(mobil) *neu.* Personenkraftwagen *m.* **motorcycle** *n* Motorrad *neu.* **motorcyclist** *n* Motorradfahrer *m.* **motorist** *n* Autofahrer *m.* **motorway** *n* Autobahn *f.*
mottled ('mɔtl̩d) *adj* gefleckt.
motto ('mɔtou) *n* Motto *neu.* Sinnspruch *m.*
mould[1] (mould) *n* **1** *tech* (Guß)Form *f.* **2** Art *f.* *vt* **1** *tech* gießen. **2** formen, bilden.
mould[2] (mould) *n* Schimmel *m.* **mouldy** *adj* schimm(e)lig.
moult (moult) *vi* **1** (of birds) sich mausern. **2** (of animals) sich häuten.

mound (maund) *n* Hügel, Erdwall *m*.

mount[1] (maunt) *vt* **1** besteigen. **2** hinaufgehen. **3** einbauen. **4** aufkleben. **5** montieren.

mount[2] (maunt) *n* Berg *m*.

mountain ('mauntin) *n* Berg *m*. **mountaineer** *n* Alpinist, Bergsteiger *m*.

mourn (mɔːn) *vt* betrauern. *vi* trauern. **mourning** *n* Trauer *f*. **go into mourning** Trauer anlegen.

mouse (maus) *n, pl* **mice** Maus *f*. **mousetrap** *n* Mausefalle *f*. **mousy** *adj* **1** mauseartig. **2** grau.

mousse (muːs) *n* Kremeis *neu*.

moustache (mə'stɑːʃ) *n* Schnurrbart *m*.

mouth (mauθ) *n* **1** Mund *m*. **2** Öffnung *f*. **3** *geog* Mündung *f*. **mouthpiece** *n* Mundstück *neu*. **mouth-watering** *adj* schmackhaft.

move (muːv) *(vi),vt* **1** (sich) bewegen. **2** (sich) rühren. **3** umziehen. *n* **1** Bewegung *f*. **2** Umzug *m*. **3** Schritt *m*. **4** (taktischer) Zug *m*. **movable** *adj* beweglich. **movement** *n* **1** Bewegung *f*. **2** *mus* Satz *m*. **3** Lauf *m*. **moving** *adj* **1** (sich) bewegend. **2** rührend, packend.

mow* (mou) *vt* mähen.

Mr ('mistə) (title of address) Herr.

Mrs ('misiz) (title of address) Frau.

much (mʌtʃ) *adj* viel. *adv* **1** sehr. **2** viel. **3** bei weitem. **how much** wieviel.

muck (mʌk) *n* **1** Mist *m*. **2** Dreck, Schmutz *m*. **mucky** *adj* dreckig.

mud (mʌd) *n* Schlamm, Schmutz *m*. **muddy** *adj* schlammig. **mudguard** *n* Kotflügel *m*.

muddle ('mʌdl̩) *n* Durcheinander *neu*. Wirrwarr *m*. *vt* verwirren. **muddle up** verwechseln. **muddle through** sich durchwursteln.

muff (mʌf) *n* Muff *m*. *vt inf* verpfuschen.

muffle ('mʌfəl) *vt* dämpfen, unterdrücken.

mug (mʌg) *n* **1** Becher, Krug *m*. **2** *inf* Dumme(r) *m*.

mulberry ('mʌlbəri) *n* Maulbeere *f*.

mule[1] (mjuːl) *n* Maultier *neu*.

mule[2] (mjuːl) *n* Pantoffel *m*.

multiple ('mʌltipəl) *adj* mehrfach, vielfach.

multiply ('mʌltiplai) *vt math* multiplizieren. *(vi),vt* (sich) vermehren.

multiracial (mʌlti'reiʃəl) *adj* gemischtrassig.

multitude ('mʌltitjuːd) *n* Menge, große Zahl *f*.

mum (mʌm) *n inf* Mutti *f*.

mumble ('mʌmbəl) *vi,vt* murmeln.

mummy[1] ('mʌmi) *n* Mumie *f*.

mummy[2] ('mʌmi) *n inf* Mutti *f*.

mumps (mʌmps) *n* Mumps, Ziegenpeter *m*.

munch (mʌntʃ) *vt,vi* hörbar kauen, schmatzen.

mundane ('mʌndein) *adj* **1** alltäglich, banal. **2** weltlich, irdisch.

Munich ('mjuːnik) *n* München *neu*.

municipal (mju'nisipəl) *adj* städtisch, Stadt—. **municipality** *n* Stadt *f*. Stadtbezirk *m*.
mural ('mjuərəl) *n* Wandgemälde *neu*.
murder ('mə:də) *n* Mord *m*. *vt* ermorden. **murderer** *n* Mörder *m*.
murmur ('mə:mə) *n* Murmeln *neu*. *vt* murmeln.
muscle ('mʌsəl) *n* Muskel *m*.
muse (mju:z) *n* Muse *f*. *vi* (nach)sinnen, (nach)denken.
museum (mju:'ziəm) *n* Museum *neu*.
mushroom ('mʌʃrum) *n* Pilz, Champignon *m*.
music ('mu:zik) *n* Musik *f*. **music centre** *n* Stereoanlage *f*. **musical** *adj* musikalisch. **musician** *n* Musiker *m*.
musk (mʌsk) *n* **1** *zool* Moschus *m*. **2** *bot* Moschuspflanze *f*.
musket ('mʌskit) *n* Muskete, Flinte *f*.
Muslim ('muzlim) *n* Muselmann, Mohammedaner *m*. *adj* mohammedanisch.
muslin ('mʌzlin) *n* Musselin *m*.
mussel ('mʌsəl) *n* Muschel *f*.
must* [1] (mʌst) *v mod aux* müssen.
must [2] (mʌst) *n* Most *m*.
mustard ('mʌstəd) *n* Senf *m*. *adj* senfgelb.
mute (mju:t) *adj* **1** stumm. **2** still, schweigend. *n* Stumme(r) *m*.
mutilate ('mju:tileit) *vt* verstümmeln, entstellen. **mutilation** *n* Verstümmelung *f*.
mutiny ('mju:tini) *n* Meuterei *f*.
mutter ('mʌtə) *vt,vi* murren, murmeln.
mutton ('mʌtn̩) *n* Hammelfleisch *neu*.
mutual ('mju:tjuəl) *adj* **1** gegenseitig. **2** gemeinsam.
muzzle ('mʌzəl) *n* **1** Maul *neu*. Schnauze *f*. **2** (of a gun) Mündung *f*. *vt* knebeln.
my (mai) *poss adj 1st pers s* mein. **myself** *pron 1st pers s* **1** mich. **2** mich selbst. **3** ich selbst. **by myself** allein.
myrrh (mə:) *n* Myrrhe *f*.
mystery ('mistəri) *n* **1** Geheimnis *neu*. **2** Rätsel *neu*. **mysterious** *adj* geheimnisvoll, mysteriös, rätselhaft.
mystic ('mistik) *n* Mystiker *m*. *adj* mystisch. **mysticism** *n* Mystizismus *m*.
mystify ('mistifai) *vt* **1** verwirren, irremachen. **2** täuschen. **3** in Dunkel hüllen.
mystique (mi'sti:k) *n* **1** Atmosphäre des Mysteriösen *f*. **2** Geheimnis *neu*.
myth (miθ) *n* Mythos *m*. **mythology** *n* Mythologie *f*.

N

nag [1] (næg) *vt* nörgeln.
nag [2] (næg) *n* Gaul *m*.
nail (neil) *n* Nagel *m*. **hit the nail on the head** den Nagel auf den Kopf treffen. **nailbrush** *n* Nagelbürste *f*. **nailfile** *n* Nagelfeile *f*. **nail varnish** *n* Nagellack *m*. ~*vt* nageln.
naive (nai'i:v) *adj* naiv.
naked ('neikid) *adj* **1** nackt. **2** bloß.
name (neim) *n* Name *m*. **namesake** *n* Namensvetter *m*. *vt* nennen. **nameless** *adj* **1** namenlos. **2** unbekannt. **3**

unerwähnt. **namely** *adv* nämlich.

nanny ('næni) *n* Kinderpflegerin *f*.

nap (næp) *n inf* Schläfchen, Nickerchen *neu*.

napkin ('næpkin) *n* Serviette *f*.

Naples ('neipəlz) *n* Neapel *neu*.

nappy ('næpi) *n* Windel *f*.

narcotic (nɑː'kɔtik) *n* Betäubungsmittel, Narkotikum *neu*. *adj* betäubend, narkotisch.

narrate (nə'reit) *vt* erzählen. **narrative** *n* Erzählung *f*.

narrow ('nærou) *adj* eng, schmal. **narrow-minded** *adj* beschränkt, kleinlich, engstirnig.

nasal ('neizəl) *adj* nasal, Nasen—.

nasturtium (nə'stəːʃəm) *n* Kapuzinerkresse *f*.

nasty ('nɑːsti) *adj* **1** unangenehm, widerlich. **2** gemein. **3** schlimm, ernst.

nation ('neiʃən) *n* Nation *f*. Volk *neu*. **nationwide** *adj* allgemein, die Nation umfassend, weit verbreitet. **national** *adj* national. **national anthem** *n* Nationalhymne *f*. **national insurance** *n* Sozialversicherung *f*. **national service** *n* Militärdienst *m*. **nationalism** *n* Nationalismus *m*. **nationality** *n* Nationalität, Staatsangehörigkeit *f*. **nationalize** *vt* nationalisieren, verstaatlichen.

native ('neitiv) *n* **1** Eingeborene(r) *m*. **2** Einheimische(r) *m*. *adj* einheimisch.

nativity (nə'tiviti) *n* Geburt (Christi) *f*. **nativity play** Christfestspiel *neu*.

natural ('nætʃərəl) *adj* natürlich. **natural gas** *n* Erdgas *neu*. **natural history** *n* Naturgeschichte *f*. **natural science** *n* Naturwissenschaft *f*. **naturalize** *vt* naturalisieren, einbürgern.

nature ('neitʃə) *n* **1** Natur *f*. **2** Wesen *neu*. Art *f*. **3** Charakter *m*.

naughty ('nɔːti) *adj* unartig, schlimm.

nausea ('nɔːsiə, -ziə) *n* **1** Übelkeit *f*. **2** Ekel *m*. **nauseate** *vt* anekeln.

nautical ('nɔːtikəl) *adj* nautisch, See—.

naval ('neivəl) *adj* Marine—, See—, Flotten—.

nave (neiv) *n* Kirchenschiff *neu*.

navel ('neivəl) *n* Nabel *m*.

navigate ('nævigeit) *vt* steuern, befahren. *vi* navigieren. **navigation** *n* Nautik, Navigation *f*.

navy ('neivi) *n* Kriegsmarine, (Kriegs)Flotte *f*. **navy blue** *adj* marineblau. *n* Marineblau *neu*.

near (niə) *prep* nahe, in der Nähe von. *adj,adv* nahe. **nearby** *adj* nahe(gelegen). *adv* in der Nähe. **nearly** *adv* nahe, fast, beinahe. **nearside** *n* Fahrerseite *f*.

neat (niːt) *adj* sauber, nett, ordentlich.

nebulous ('nebjuləs) *adj* nebelhaft, unbestimmt, verschwommen.

necessary ('nesəsəri) *adj* notwendig, nötig, erforderlich. **necessarily** *adv* **1**

notwendigerweise. **2** unbedingt. **necessity** *n* **1** Notwendigkeit *f.* **2** Bedürfnis *neu.*

neck (nek) *n* Hals, Nacken *m.* **neckband** *n* Halsband *m.* **necklace** *n* Halskette *f.*

nectar ('nektə) *n* Nektar *m.*

need (ni:d) *n* **1** Notwendigkeit *f.* **2** Bedarf *m.* Bedürfnis *neu.* **3** Not, Armut *f.* *vt* **1** benötigen. **2** brauchen. **needless** *adj* unnötig. **needless to say** selbstverständlich.

needle ('ni:dl̩) *n* Nadel *f.* **needlework** *n* Näherei *f.* ~*vt sl* sticheln, reizen.

negate (ni'geit) *vt* verneinen, leugnen, negieren. **negation** *n* Verneinung, Negation *f.* **negative** *adj* negativ. *n* **1** (of a photograph) Negativ *neu.* **2** Negation *f.* **answer in the negative** mit Nein antworten, verneinen.

neglect (ni'glekt) *n* Nachlässigkeit *f.* *vt* **1** vernachlässigen. **2** unterlassen. **negligent** *adj* nachlässig. **negligible** *adj* unbedeutend, geringfügig.

negotiate (ni'gouʃieit) *vt* **1** verhandeln. **2** überwinden. *vi* verhandeln. **negotiation** *n* **1** Verhandlung *f.* **2** Überwindung *f.*

Negro ('ni:grou) *n, pl* **-oes** Neger *m.* **Negress** *n* Negerin *f.*

neigh (nei) *vi* wiehern. *n* Wiehern *neu.*

neighbour ('neibə) *n* Nachbar *m.* **neighbourhood** *n* Nachbarschaft *f.* **neighbouring** *adj* angrenzend, benachbart.

neither ('naiðə) *conj* auch nicht. **neither...nor** weder... noch. *adj,pron* keiner (von beiden).

neon ('ni:ən) *n* Neon *neu.*

nephew ('nevju:) *n* Neffe *m.*

nepotism ('nepətizəm) *n* Nepotismus *m.*

Neptune ('neptju:n) *n* Neptun *m.*

nerve (nə:v) *n* **1** Nerv *m.* **2** *inf* Frechheit *f.* Mut *m.* **3** *pl* Nervosität *f.* **nerve-racking** *adj* nervenaufreibend. **nervous** *adj* **1** nervös. **2** Nerven—. **nervous breakdown** *n* Nervenzusammenbruch *m.* **nervous system** *n* Nervensystem *neu.*

nest (nest) *n* Nest *neu.* *vi* nisten.

nestle ('nesəl) *vi* sich schmiegen an.

net[1] (net) *n* Netz *neu.* *vt* fangen. **netball** *n* Korbballspiel *neu.* **network** *n* Netz *neu.*

net[2] (net) *adj* netto.

Netherlands ('neðələndz) *n pl* Niederlande *f pl.* **Netherlander** *n* Niederländer *m.*

nettle ('netl̩) *n* Nessel *f.*

neurosis (njuə'rousis) *n* Neurose *f.* **neurotic** *adj* neurotisch.

neuter ('nju:tə) *n* Neutrum *neu.* *adj* **1** sächlich. **2** geschlechtslos. *vt* kastrieren.

neutral ('nju:trəl) *adj* **1** neutral. **2** unparteiisch. **neutrality** *n* Neutralität *f.* **neutralize** *vt* neutralisieren.

never ('nevə) *adv* nie, niemals. **on the never-never** *inf* auf Abzahlung. **nevertheless**

adv dennoch, nichtsdestoweniger.

new (njuː) *adj* neu. **newcomer** *n* Neuankömmling *m*. **newly** *adv* neulich, kürzlich. **news** *n* Nachrichten *f pl*. **a piece of news** Neuigkeit, Nachricht *f*. **newsagent** *n* Zeitungshändler *m*. **newspaper** *n* Zeitung *f*. **newsreel** *n* Wochenschau *f*.

newt (njuːt) *n* Wassermolch *m*.

New Testament *n* Neues Testament *neu*.

New Year *n* Neujahr *neu*. **New Year's Day** *n* Neujahrstag *m*. **New Year's Eve** *n* Silvester *m*.

New Zealand ('ziːlənd) *n* Neuseeland *neu*. *adj* neuseeländisch. **New Zealander** *n* Neuseeländer *m*.

next (nekst) *adj* **1** nächst. **2** folgend. **next door** nebenan. ~*adv* **1** nächstens. **2** das nächste Mal. *n* Nächste(r) *m*.

nib (nib) *n* (of a pen) Spitze *f*.

nibble ('nibəl) *vi,(vt)* knabbern *or* nagen (an).

nice (nais) *adj* **1** nett. **2** schön. **3** lieb, freundlich.

niche (nitʃ) *n* **1** Nische *f*. **2** passende Stelle *f*.

nick (nik) *vt* einkerben. *n* Kerbe *f*. **in the nick of time** gerade rechtzeitig.

nickel ('nikəl) *n* Nickel *neu*.

nickname ('nikneim) *n* Spitzname *m*.

nicotine ('nikətiːn) *n* Nikotin *neu*.

niece (niːs) *n* Nichte *f*.

Nigeria (nai'dʒiəriə) *n* Nigeria *neu*. **Nigerian** *adj* nigerianisch. *n* Nigerianer *m*.

nigger ('nigə) *n derog* Neger, Schwarze(r) *m*.

niggle ('nigəl) *vi* nörgeln, herumtüfteln.

night (nait) *n* **1** Nacht *f*. **2** Abend *m*. **last night** gestern Abend. **spend the night** übernachten. **nightclub** *n* Nachtklub *m*. **nightdress** *n also* **nightgown** Nachthemd *neu*. **nightmare** *n* Alptraum *m*.

nightingale ('naitiŋgeil) *n* Nachtigall *f*.

nil (nil) *n* Null *f*.

Nile (nail) *n* Nil *m*.

nimble ('nimbəl) *adj* flink, behend.

nine (nain) *adj* neun. *n* Neun *f*. **ninth** *adj* neunte.

nineteen (nain'tiːn) *adj* neunzehn. *n* Neunzehn *f*. **nineteenth** *adj* neunzehnte.

ninety ('nainti) *adj* neunzig. *n* Neunzig *f*. **ninetieth** *adj* neunzigste.

nip[1] (nip) *n* leichter Biß, Kniff *m*. *vt* beißen, kneifen. *vi* flitzen. **nippy** *adj inf* spritzig.

nip[2] (nip) *n* Schlückchen *neu*.

nipple ('nipəl) *n* Brustwarze *f*.

nitrogen ('naitrədʒən) *n* Stickstoff *m*. Nitrogen *neu*.

no[1] (nou) *adv* nein.

no[2] (nou) *adj* kein. **in no way** keineswegs.

noble ('noubəl) *adj* **1** vornehm, edel. **2** adlig. *n* Edelmann *m*. **nobleman** *n* Edelmann, Adlige(r) *m*. **nobility** *n* **1** Adel *m*. **2** Vornehmheit *f*.

nobody ('noubədi) *pron also* **no-one** niemand, keiner. *n inf* Null *f*. Niemand *m*.

nocturnal (nɔk'tə:nl̩) *adj* nächtlich.
nod (nɔd) *vt,vi* (mit dem Kopf) nicken. *n* Kopfnicken *neu*.
node (noud) *n* Knoten *m*.
noise (nɔiz) *n* **1** Geräusch *neu*. Lärm *m*. **2** Krach *m*. **noisy** *adj* lärmend.
nomad ('noumæd) *n* Nomade *m*. **nomadic** *adj* nomadisch.
nominal ('nɔminl̩) *adj* nominell.
nominate ('nɔmineit) *vt* (er)nennen, nominieren.
nominative ('nɔminətiv) *n* Nominativ *m*.
non- *pref* nicht—.
nonchalant ('nɔnʃələnt) *adj* **1** gleichgültig. **2** unbekümmert. **3** nonchalant.
nondescript ('nɔndiskript) *adj* schwer zu beschreiben.
none (nʌn) *pron* **1** kein. **2** niemand. *adv* keineswegs.
nonentity (nɔn'entiti) *n* **1** *inf* unbedeutender Mensch, Null *f*. **2** Nichts *neu*.
nonsense ('nɔnsəns) *n* Unsinn *m*.
noodles ('nu:dl̩z) *n pl* Nudeln *f pl*.
noon (nu:n) *n* Mittag *m*.
noose (nu:s) *n* Schlinge *f*.
nor (nɔ:) *conj* noch, auch nicht. **neither...nor** weder...noch.
norm (nɔ:m) *n* Norm, Regel, Richtschnur *f*. **normal** *adj* normal.
Norman ('nɔ:mən) *adj* normannisch. *n* Normanne *m*.
Normandy ('nɔ:məndi) *n* Normandie *f*.
Norse (nɔ:s) *adj* altnorwegisch. *n* (language) Altnorwegisch *neu*.
north (nɔ:θ) *n* Nord(en) *m*. *adj* nördlich, Nord—. *adv* nördlich. **northeast** *n* Nordost(en) *m*. *adj,adv* nordöstlich. **northeasterly** *adj,adv* nordöstlich. **northeastern** *adj* nordöstlich. **northerly** *adj* nördlich. **northern** *adj* nördlich. **northwards** *adv* nordwärts. **northwest** *n* Nordwest(en) *m*. *adj,adv* nordwestlich. **northwesterly** *adj,adv* nordwestlich. **northwestern** *adj* nordwestlich.
North America *n* Nordamerika *neu*.
Northern Ireland *n* Nordirland *neu*.
North Pole *n* Nordpol *m*.
North Rhine-Westphalia (west'feiliə) *n* Nordrhein-Westfalen *neu*.
Norway ('nɔ:wei) *n* Norwegen *neu*. **Norwegian** *adj* norwegisch. *n* **1** Norweger *m*. **2** (language) Norwegisch *neu*.
nose (nouz) *n* Nase *f*. **nosy** *adj inf* neugierig.
nostalgia (nɔ'stældʒiə) *n* **1** Nostalgie, Sehnsucht *f*. **2** Heimweh *neu*. **nostalgic** *adj* wehmütig, voll Heimweh.
nostril ('nɔstril) *n* Nasenloch *neu*.
not (nɔt) *adv* nicht. **not a** kein.
notch (nɔtʃ) *n* Kerbe *f*. *vt* einkerben.
note (nout) *n* **1** Zettel *m*. **2** Notiz *f*. **3** Vermerk *m*. **4** Ton *m*. **5** Bedeutung *f*. **notebook** *n* Notizbuch *neu*. **notepaper** *n* Briefpapier *neu*. **noteworthy** *adj* bemerkenswert. ~*vt* **1** merken. **2** vermerken, auf-

schreiben. **notable** *adj* bemerkenswert, beträchtlich, hervorragend. **notation** *n* **1** Aufzeichnung *f.* **2** Schreibweise *f.*

nothing ('nʌθiŋ) *pron* nichts. *n* Nichts *neu.* **nothing of the kind** nichts dergleichen.

notice ('noutis) *n* **1** Notiz *f.* **2** Meldung *f.* Hinweis *m.* **3** Kündigung(sfrist) *f.* **4** Anschlag *m.* Plakat *neu.* **notice board** *n* Anschlagtafel *f.* *vt* bemerken. **noticeable** *adj* **1** bemerkenswert. **2** merklich.

notify ('noutifai) *vt* benachrichtigen, bekanntgeben. **notification** *n* Benachrichtigung *f.*

notion ('nouʃən) *n* **1** Begriff, Gedanke *m.* **2** Idee *f.* **3** Vorstellung *f.*

notorious (nou'tɔːriəs) *adj* berüchtigt, notorisch, allbekannt.

notwithstanding (nɔtwiθ'stændiŋ) *prep* ungeachtet, trotz.

nought (nɔːt) *n* Null *f.* *pron* nichts.

noun (naun) *n* Hauptwort *neu.* Substantiv *m.*

nourish ('nʌriʃ) *vt* (er)nähren. **nourishing** *adj* nahrhaft.

novel[1] ('nɔvəl) *n* Roman *m.* **novelist** *n* Romanschriftsteller *m.*

novel[2] ('nɔvəl) *adj* neuartig. **novelty** *n* **1** Neuheit *f.* **2** Ungewöhnlichkeit *f.*

November (nou'vembə) *n* November *m.*

novice ('nɔvis) *n* **1** Anfänger *m.* **2** *rel* Novize *m.*

now (nau) *adv* **1** nun, jetzt. **2** sofort. **3** eben. *conj* nun. **nowadays** *adv* heutzutage.

nowhere ('nouwɛə) *adv* nirgends, nirgendwo.

noxious ('nɔkʃəs) *adj* schädlich.

nozzle ('nɔzəl) *n* **1** Schnauze. **2** Ausgußröhre *f.* **3** Düse *f.*

nuance ('njuːəns) *n* **1** Nuance *f.* **2** Abtönung *f.* **3** Schattierung *f.*

nucleus ('njuːkliəs) *n* **1** *sci* Kern *m.* **2** Mittelpunkt *m.* **nuclear** *adj* Kern—, Atom—, nuklear.

nude (njuːd) *adj* nackt. *n* **1** Nackte(r) *m.* **2** *Art* Akt *m.*

nudge (nʌdʒ) *vt* leicht anstoßen.

nugget ('nʌgit) *n* Goldklumpen, Nugget *m.*

nuisance ('njuːsəns) *n* **1** Ärgernis *neu.* Belästigung *f.* **2** lästiger Mensch *m.*

null (nʌl) *adj* nichtig, ungültig, null.

numb (nʌm) *adj* starr, empfindungslos. *vt* starr machen, betäuben.

number ('nʌmbə) *n* **1** Nummer *f.* **2** Zahl, Ziffer *f.* **3** (An)Zahl *f.* **numberplate** *n* *mot* Nummernschild *neu.* **numeral** *n* **1** Zahlzeichen *neu.* **2** Zahlwort *neu.* **numerate** *adj* rechenkundig. **numerical** *adj* zahlenmäßig, numerisch. **numerous** *adj* zahlreich.

nun (nʌn) *n* Nonne *f.*

Nuremberg ('njuərəmbəːg) *n* Nürnberg *neu.*

nurse (nəːs) *n* Krankenschwester *f.* *vt* **1** pflegen. **2** aufzeihen. **nursing home** *n* (Privat)Klinik *f.* Sanatorium

neu. **nursery** *n* **1** Kinderzimmer *neu.* **2** *bot* Pflanzschule *f.* **nursery rhyme** *n* Kinderreim *m.* Kinderlied *neu.* **nursery school** *n* Kindergarten *m.*
nurture ('nəːtʃə) *vt* **1** ernähren. **2** hegen.
nut (nʌt) *n* **1** Nuß *f.* **2** *tech* (Schrauben)Mutter *f.* **3** *inf* Kopf *m.* **in a nutshell** kurz gefaßt. **nutcrackers** *n* Nußknacker *m.* **nutmeg** *n* Muskatnuß *f.* **nutshell** *n* Nußschale *f.*
nutrition (njuː'triʃən) *n* Nahrung, Ernährung *f.*
nuzzle ('nʌzəl) *vi* **1** schnüffeln. **2** sich anschmiegen.
nylon ('nailɔn) *n* Nylon *neu.* **nylon stockings** *n pl also* **nylons** Nylonstrümpfe *m pl.*
nymph (nimf) *n* Nymphe *f.*

O

oak (ouk) *n* Eiche *f.*
oar (ɔː) *n* Ruder *neu.* **oarsman** *n* Ruderer *m.*
oasis (ou'eisis) *n* Oase *f.*
oath (ouθ) *n* Eid, Schwur *m.*
oats (outs) *n pl* **1** Hafer *m pl.* **2** Haferflocken *f pl.* **oatmeal** *n* Hafermehl *m.*
obedient (ə'biːdiənt) *adj* gehorsam. **obedience** *n* Gehorsam *m.*
obese (ou'biːs) *adj* fettleibig.
obey (ə'bei) *vt* **1** gehorchen. **2** befolgen.
obituary (ə'bitjuəri) *n* Todesanzeige *f.*
object (*n* 'ɔbdʒikt; *v* əb'dʒekt) *n* **1** Gegenstand *m.* Objekt *neu.* **2** Ziel *neu.* Zweck *m.* *vi* **1** einwenden. **2** protestieren. **objection** *n* **1** Einwand *m.* **2** Abneigung *f.* **objective** *n* Ziel *neu.* Absicht *f.* *adj* sachlich, objektiv.
oblige (ə'blaidʒ) *vt* **1** binden, verpflichten. **2** nötigen. **3** gefällig sein. **be obliged to do something** etwas tun müssen. **be obliged to someone** jemandem dankbar sein. **obligation** *n* Verpflichtung *f.* **obligatory** *adj* verbindlich, verpflichtend.
oblique (ə'bliːk) *adj* schräg, schief.
obliterate (ə'blitəreit) *vt* **1** auslöschen, ausradieren. **2** unkenntlich machen.
oblivion (ə'bliviən) *n* Vergessenheit *f.* **oblivious** *adj* **1** vergeßlich. **2** nicht bewußt.
oblong ('ɔblɔŋ) *n* Rechteck *neu.* *adj* rechteckig, länglich.
obnoxious (əb'nɔkʃəs) *adj* anstößig, verhaßt.
oboe ('oubou) *n* Oboe *f.*
obscene (əb'siːn) *adj* obszön, unzüchtig.
obscure (əb'skjuə) *adj* **1** dunkel, finster. **2** unbekannt. *vt* verdecken, verdunkeln.
observe (əb'zəːv) *vt* **1** beobachten. **2** bemerken. **observance** *n* **1** Beobachtung *f.* **2** Befolgung *f.* **observant** *adj* aufmerksam, wachsam. **observation** *n* **1** Beobachtung *f.* **2** Bemerkung *f.* **observatory** *n* Sternwarte *f.* Observatorium *neu.*
obsess (əb'ses) *vt* verfolgen, quälen. **obsession** *n* Besessenheit *f.*
obsolescent (ɔbsə'lesənt) *adj* veraltend.

obsolete ('ɔbsəliːt) *adj* veraltet, überholt.
obstacle ('ɔbstəkəl) *n* Hindernis *neu.*
obstinate ('ɔbstinət) *adj* hartnäckig, eigensinnig. **obstinacy** *n* Hartnäckigkeit *f.*
obstruct (əb'strʌkt) *vt* **1** verstopfen, blockieren. **2** (ver)hindern. **obstruction** *n* **1** Verstopfung *f.* **2** Hindernis *neu.*
obtain (əb'tein) *vt* erhalten, bekommen.
obtrusive (əb'truːsiv) *adj* aufdringlich.
obtuse (əb'tjuːs) *adj* stumpf, stumpfwinkelig.
obverse ('ɔbvəːs) *adj* Vorder—. *n* Kehrseite *f.*
obvious ('ɔbviəs) *adj* offensichtlich, klar.
occasion (ə'keiʒən) *n* **1** Gelegenheit *f.* **2** Anlaß *m.* **on the occasion of** anläßlich.
Occident ('ɔksidənt) *n* Westen *m.* Abendland *neu.* **occidental** *adj* westlich, abendländisch.
occult (ɔ'kʌlt) *adj* okkult. **occultism** *n* Okkultismus *m.*
occupy ('ɔkjupai) *vt* **1** besetzen. **2** bewohnen. **3** beschäftigen. **occupy oneself** sich beschäftigen. **occupation** *n* **1** Beruf *m.* Beschäftigung *f.* **2** *mil* Besetzung, Besatzung *f.*
occur (ə'kəː) *vi* **1** vorkommen, sich ereignen. **2** einfallen. **occurrence** *n* **1** Ereignis *neu.* **2** Vorfall *m.*
ocean ('ouʃən) *n* Meer *neu.* Ozean *m.*
ochre ('oukə) *n* Ocker *m. adj* ockergelb.
octagon ('ɔktəgən) *n* Achteck *neu.* **octagonal** *adj* achteckig.
octane ('ɔktein) *n* Oktan *neu.*
octave ('ɔktiv) *n* Oktave *f.*
October (ɔk'toubə) *n* Oktober *m.*
octopus ('ɔktəpəs) *n, pl* **-puses** *or* **-pi** Krake *m.* Polyp *m.*
oculist ('ɔkjulist) *n* Augenarzt *m.*
odd (ɔd) *adj* **1** ungleich. **2** seltsam, sonderbar. **3** (of numbers) ungerade. **oddity** *n* Seltsamkeit, seltsame Sache *f.* **oddment** Überbleibsel *neu.* Rest *m.* **odds** *n pl* Gewinnchancen *f pl.*
ode (oud) *n* Ode *f.*
odious ('oudiəs) *adj* verhaßt.
odour ('oudə) *n* Geruch *m.*
oesophagus (i'sɔfəgəs) *n, pl* **-gi** Speiseröhre *f.*
of (əv; *stressed* ɔv) *prep* **1** von. **2** aus.
off (ɔf) *adv* **1** davon, fort, weg. **2** nicht frisch. **well/badly off** gut/schlecht daran.
offal ('ɔfəl) *n* Fleischabfall *m.*
offend (ə'fend) *vt* beleidigen. **offence** *n* **1** Beleidigung *f.* Anstoß *m.* **2** Vergehen *neu.* **take offence** Anstoß nehmen. **offensive** *adj* anstößig, beleidigend. *n* Offensive *f.* Angriff *m.*
offer ('ɔfə) *vt* anbieten. *n* Angebot *neu.*
offhand (ɔf'hænd) *adj* **1** kurz (angebunden). **2** improvisiert, spontan, aus dem Stegreif. *adv* spontan.

office ('ɔfis) *n* **1** Büro *neu.* **2** Dienst *m.* Amt *neu.* **officer** *n* **1** *mil* Offizier *m.* **2** Beamte(r) *m.* **official** *adj* offiziell. *n* Beamte(r) *m.*
officious (ə'fiʃəs) *adj* offiziös, aufdringlich.
offing ('ɔfiŋ) *n* offene See *f.* **in the offing** in (Aus)Sicht, im Werden.
off-licence *n* Ausschank über die Straße *m.*
off-peak *adj* außerhalb der Hauptverkehrszeit.
off-putting *adj* abstoßend.
off-season *adj* außer Saison.
offset ('ɔfset) *vt* ausgleichen.
offshore (ɔf'ʃɔː) *adj* **1** von der Küste entfernt. **2** vom Land kommend, ablandig.
offside (ɔf'said) *adj,adv sport* abseits. *n* rechte Seite *f.*
offspring ('ɔfspriŋ) *n* **1** Nachkomme *m.* **2** Nachkommenschaft *f.*
offstage (ɔf'steidʒ) *adj* hinter der Bühne *f.*
often ('ɔfən) *adv* oft, häufig.
ogre ('ougə) *n* Unhold, Riese *m.*
oil (ɔil) *n* **1** Öl *neu.* **2** Erdöl *neu.* *vt* ölen, schmieren. **oilfield** *n* Ölfeld neu. **oil painting** *n* Ölgemälde *neu.* **oil rig** *n* **1** Ölplattform *f.* **2** Ölbohrturm *m.* **oilskin** *n* **1** Öltuch *neu.* **2** *pl* Ölkleidung *f.*
ointment ('ɔintmənt) *n* Salbe *f.*
old (ould) *adj* alt. **six years old** sechs Jahre alt. **old age** *n* Alter *neu.* **old-fashioned** *adj* altmodisch, veraltet.
Old Testament *n* Altes Testament *neu.*
olive ('ɔliv) *n* **1** Olive *f.* Ölbaum *m.* **2** Olive *f.* *adj* olivgrün. **olive oil** *n* Olivenöl *neu.*
omelette ('ɔmlət) *n* Omelett *neu.*
omen ('oumen) *n* Omen *neu.* Vorzeichen *neu.*
ominous ('ɔminəs) *adj* unheilvoll, drohend.
omit (ə'mit) *vt* auslassen, weglassen. **omission** *n* Auslassung *f.*
omnibus ('ɔmnibəs) *n* Omnibus, Bus *m.*
omnipotent (ɔm'nipətənt) *adj* allmächtig.
on (ɔn) *prep* **1** auf. **2** an. **3** über, zu. *adv* **1** auf. **2** an. **3** weiter, vorwärts. **be on 1** an(geschaltet) sein. **2** los sein. **from...on** von...an.
once (wʌns) *adv* **1** einmal. **2** einst. **at once 1** auf einmal. **2** sofort. **once and for all** ein für allemal.
one (wʌn) *adj* eins. *n* Eins *f.* *pron 3rd pers s* einer, man. **oneself** *pron 3rd pers s* sich (selbst). **by oneself** allein. **one-sided** *adj* einseitig. **one-way** *adj* Einweg—. **one-way street** Einbahnstraße *f.*
onion ('ʌniən) *n* Zwiebel *f.*
onlooker ('ɔnlukə) *n* Zuschauer *m.*
only ('ounli) *adj* einzig. *adv* **1** nur. **2** erst. **not only...but also** nicht nur...sondern auch. *~conj* nur daß, jedoch.
onset ('ɔnset) *n* **1** Anfang *m.* **2** Angriff *m.*
onslaught ('ɔnslɔːt) *n* (plötzlicher) Angriff *m.*
onus ('ounəs) *n* Last *f.*
onward ('ɔnwəd) *adv* vorwärts,

weiter. *adj* weitergehend. **onwards** *adv* vorwärts, weiter.

ooze (u:z) *vi* (durch)sickern, triefen.

opal ('oupəl) *n* Opal *m*.

opaque (ou'peik) *adj* undurchsichtig.

open ('oupən) *vt* **1** (er)öffnen. **2** aufmachen. **3** anfangen. *adj* offen, offenstehend, auf. **open-air** *adj* Freiluft—. **in the open air** im Freien. **open-air swimming pool** Freibad *neu*. **open-ended** *adj* offenendig. **open-handed** *adj* großzügig, freigebig. **open-hearted** *adj* offenherzig. **open-minded** *adj* aufgeschlossen, unvoreingenommen. **open-mouthed** *adj* **1** mit offenen Mund. **2** verblüfft, erstaunt. **open-plan** *adj* Großraum—. **opening 1** Öffnung, Lücke *f*. **2** Eröffnung *f*.

opera ('ɔprə) *n* Oper *f*. **opera house** *n* Opernhaus *neu*. **operetta** *n* Operette *f*.

operate ('ɔpəreit) *vi* **1** laufen, funktionieren. **2** handeln, Geschäft betreiben. **3** *med* operieren. *vt* betätigen. **operation** *n* **1** Arbeitslauf, Betrieb *m*. **2** Betätigung *f*. **3** *med* Operation. **4** *mil* Unternehmung, Operation *f*. **operative** *adj* tätig, wirksam. *n* Arbeiter, Handwerker *m*.

opinion (ə'piniən) *n* Meinung, Ansicht *f*. **opinion poll** *n* Meinungsumfrage *f*.

opium ('oupiəm) *n* Opium *neu*.

opponent (ə'pounənt) *n* Gegner *m*.

opportune (ɔpə'tju:n) *adj* **1** günstig. **2** rechtzeitig.

opportunity (ɔpə'tju:niti) *n* Gelegenheit, Möglichkeit *f*.

oppose (ɔ'pouz) *vt* **1** ablehnend gegenüberstehen, bekämpfen. **2** gegenüberstellen. *vi* Widerstand leisten, opponieren. **opposed** *adj* **1** entegegengesetzt. **2** feindlich. **as opposed to** im Vergleich zu.

opposite ('ɔpəzit) *adj* **1** gegenüberliegend. **2** gegensätzlich. *n* Gegensatz *m*. **opposition** *n* **1** Widerstand *m*. **2** *pol* Opposition *f*.

oppress (ə'pres) *vt* unterdrücken, tyrannisieren. **oppression** *n* Unterdrückung *f*.

opt (ɔpt) *vi* wählen. **opt for** sich entscheiden für.

optical ('ɔptikəl) *adj* optisch. **optician** *n* Optiker *m*.

optimism ('ɔptimizəm) *n* Optimismus *m*. **optimist** *n* Optimist *m*. **optimistic** *adj* optimistisch.

option ('ɔpʃən) *n* **1** Wahl, Alternative *f*. **2** Option *f*. Vorkaufsrecht *neu*.

opulent ('ɔpjulənt) *adj* reich, üppig.

or (ɔ:) *conj* oder.

oral ('ɔ:rəl) *adj* mündlich.

orange ('ɔrindʒ) *n* Apfelsine, Orange *f*. *adj* orangenfarbig.

orator ('ɔrətə) *n* Redner *m*.

orbit ('ɔ:bit) *n* Umlaufbahn *f*. *vt* umkreisen.

orchard ('ɔ:tʃəd) *n* Obstgarten *m*.

orchestra ('ɔ:kistrə) *n* Orchester *neu*. **orchestral** *adj* orchestral.

orchid ('ɔːkid) *n* Orchidee *f*.
ordain (ɔː'dein) *vt* **1** bestimmen. **2** *rel* weihen.
ordeal (ɔː'diːl) *n* Qual, Plage, Nervenprobe *f*.
order ('ɔːdə) *n* **1** Befehl *m*. **2** Ordnung *f*. **3** *comm* Bestellung *f*. Auftrag *m*. **4** Stand *m*. **in order that** damit. **in order to** um...zu. *vt* **1** befehlen. **2** bestellen. **3** ordnen. **orderly** *n* Ordner *m*. *adj* ordentlich.
ordinal ('ɔːdinl) *adj* Ordinal—. *n* Ordnungszahl *f*.
ordinary ('ɔːdənri) *adj* **1** gewöhnlich, normal. **2** mittelmäßig, Durchschnitts—.
ore (ɔː) *n* Erz *neu*.
oregano (ɔri'gɑːnou) *n* Origanum *neu*.
organ ('ɔːgən) *n* **1** Organ *neu*. **2** *mus* Orgel *f*.
organism ('ɔːgənizəm) *n* Organismus *m*. **organic** *adj* **1** organisch. **2** geordnet.
organize ('ɔːgənaiz) *vt* **1** organisieren. **2** einrichten. **organization** *n* **1** Organisation *f*. **2** systematischer Aufbau *m*. **3** Gesellschaft *f*.
orgasm ('ɔːgæzəm) *n* Orgasmus *m*.
orgy ('ɔːdʒi) *n* Orgie *f*.
Orient ('ɔːriənt) *n* Orient, Osten *m*. Morgenland *neu*. **oriental** *adj* orientalisch, morgenländisch. *n* Orientale *m*.
orientate ('ɔːrienteit) *vt* orientieren, richten. **orientation** *n* Orientierung *f*.
origin ('ɔridʒin) *n* **1** Ursprung *m*. **2** Herkunft *f*. **original** *adj* **1** original, ursprünglich. **2** originell, schöpferisch. **originate** *vi* entspringen, entstehen, ausgehen.
Orlon ('ɔːlɔn) *n* *Tdmk* Orlon *neu*.
ornament ('ɔːnəmənt) *n* Schmuck *m*. Ornament *neu*. Verzierung *f*. **ornamental** *adj* ornamental. **ornamentation** *n* Verzierung *f*.
ornate (ɔː'neit) *adj* geschmückt, veriert.
ornithology (ɔːni'θɔlədʒi) *n* Ornithologie, Vogelkunde *f*.
orphan ('ɔːfən) *n* Waise *m*.
orthodox ('ɔːθədɔks) *adj* **1** *rel* orthodox, rechtgläubig. **2** konventionell.
orthopaedic (ɔːθə'piːdik) *adj* orthopädisch.
oscillate ('ɔsəleit) *vi* **1** schwingen, oszillieren. **2** schwanken.
ostensible (ɔ'stensəbəl) *adj* **1** scheinbar. **2** angeblich.
ostentatious (ɔsten'teiʃəs) *adj* prahlerisch, prunkhaft.
osteopath ('ɔstiəpæθ) *n* Chiropraktiker *m*.
ostracize ('ɔstrəsaiz) *vt* verbannen, ausstoßen.
ostrich ('ɔːstritʃ) *n* Strauß *m*.
other ('ʌðə) *adj* **1** ander. **2** weiter. **3** zweite. *adv* anders. *pron* ander. **each other** einander. **otherwise** *adv* **1** sonst. **2** anders. **3** anderweitig.
otter ('ɔtə) *n* Otter *m*.
ought* (ɔːt) *v mod aux* sollen.
ounce (auns) *n* Unze *f*.
our (auə) *poss adj 1st pers pl* unser. **ours** *poss pron 1st pers pl* unser, der uns(e)re *or* uns(e)rige. **ourselves** *pron 1st pers pl* **1** uns. **2** uns selbst. **3** wir selbst.

oust (aust) *vt* vertreiben, verdrängen.
out (aut) *adv* **1** aus. **2** heraus, hinaus. **3** draußen. **4** fort. **out and out** durch und durch.
outboard ('autbɔːd) *adj* Außenbord—.
outbreak ('autbreik) *n* Ausbruch *m*.
outburst ('autbəːst) *n* Ausbruch *m*.
outcast ('autkɑːst) *n* Ausgestoßene(r) *m*.
outcome ('autkʌm) *n* Resultat, Ergebnis *neu*.
outcry ('autkrai) *n* Aufschrei *m*.
outdo* (aut'duː) *vt* übertreffen.
outdoor ('autdɔː) *adj* Außen—, im Freien. **outdoors** *adv* draußen, im Freien.
outer ('autə) *adj* äußere, Außen—.
outfit ('autfit) *n* **1** Ausstattung, Ausrüstung *f*. **2** Gruppe, Mannschaft *f*.
outgoing ('autgouiŋ) *adj* **1** weggehend, abgehend. **2** gesellig. **outgoings** *n pl* Ausgaben *f pl*.
outgrow* (aut'grou) *vt* herauswachsen aus.
outhouse ('authaus) *n* Nebengebäude *neu*.
outing ('autiŋ) *n* Ausflug *m*.
outlandish (aut'lændiʃ) *adj* fremdartig.
outlaw ('autlɔː) *n* **1** Geächtete(r) *m*. **2** Bandit *m*. *vt* ächten.
outlay ('autlei) *n* Auslage *f*.
outlet ('autlet) *n* **1** Abfluß, Auslauf *m*. **2** Absatzmarkt *m*.
outline ('autlain) *n* **1** Umriß *m*. **2** Überblick *m*. **3** Abriß *m*. *vt* umreißen.
outlive (aut'liv) *vt* überleben.
outlook ('autluk) *n* **1** Aussicht *f*. **2** Standpunkt *m*. Weltanschauung *f*.
outlying ('autlaiiŋ) *adj* abgelegen, abseits liegend.
outnumber (aut'nʌmbə) *vt* an Zahl übertreffen.
outpatient ('autpeiʃənt) *n* ambulanter Patient *m*.
outpost ('autpoust) *n* Vorposten *m*.
output ('autput) *n* Leistung, Produktion *f*.
outrage (aut'reidʒ) *n* Gewalttat, Schandtat *f*. Exzeß *m*. *vt* schockieren, Gewalt antun.
outrageous (aut'reidʒəs) *adj* unerhört, empörend, schändlich.
outright ('autrait) *adj,adv* völlig, total.
outside (aut'said) *n* Außenseite *f*. *adv* **1** außen, draußen. **2** hinaus. **outsider** *n* Außenseiter *m*.
outsize ('autsaiz) *adj* übergroß.
outskirts ('autskəːts) *n pl* Randgebiet *neu*. Vororte *m pl*.
outspoken (aut'spoukən) *adj* freimütig, offen.
outstanding (aut'stændiŋ) *adj* hervorragend.
outstrip (aut'strip) *vt* überholen, übertreffen.
outward ('autwəd) *adj* **1** äußere. **2** Auswärts—. *adv* auswärts, nach außen. **outwards** *adv* auswärts, nach außen.
outweigh (aut'wei) *vt* überwiegen.
outwit (aut'wit) *vt* überlisten.

oval ('ouvəl) *adj* oval. *n* Oval *neu*.
ovary ('ouvəri) *n* Eierstock *m*.
ovation (ou'veiʃən) *n* Huldigung, Ovation *f*.
oven ('ʌvən) *n* Ofen, Backofen *m*.
over ('ouvə) *prep* **1** über. **2** zu Ende, aus. **3** während. *adv* **1** (hin-, her-)über. **2** drüben. **3** übermäßig. **over again** nochmals.
overall ('ɔvərɔːl) *adj* gesamt, Gesamt—. *n* Arbeitsanzug, Schutzanzug *m*.
overbalance (ouvə'bæləns) *vt,vi* umkippen.
overboard ('ouvəbɔːd) *adv* über Bord.
overcast ('ouvəkɑːst) *adj* bewölkt.
overcharge (ouvə'tʃɑːdʒ) *vt* **1** zu viel verlangen von. **2** überladen.
overcoat ('ouvəkout) *n* Mantel *m*.
overcome* (ouvə'kʌm) *vt* überwinden, überwältigen. *adj* überwältigt.
overdo* (ouvə'duː) *vt* übertreiben.
overdose ('ouvədous) *n* Überdosis *f*.
overdraft ('ouvədrɑːft) *n* Überziehung *f*.
overdraw* (ouvə'drɔː) *vt,vi* überziehen.
overdue (ouvə'djuː) *adj* **1** überfällig. **2** verspätet.
overestimate (ouvər'estimeit) *vt* überschätzen.
overfill (ouvə'fil) *vt* überfüllen, überladen.
overflow (*v* ouvə'flou; *n* 'ouvəð flou) *vi* überlaufen, überfließen. *n* Überlauf *m*. Überfließen *neu*.
overgrow* (ouvə'grou) *vt* überwachsen.
overhang (*v* ouvə'hæŋ; *n* 'ouvəhæŋ) *vt* überhängen über. *n* Überhang *m*.
overhaul (ouvə'hɔːl) *vt* überholen. *n* Überholung *f*.
overhead (*adv* ouvə'hed; *adj,n* 'ouvəhed) *adv* oben, droben. *adj* obenliegend, Hoch—.
overheads *n pl* (allgemeine) Unkosten *f pl*.
overhear* (ouvə'hiə) *vt* (zufällig) hören.
overheat (ouvə'hiːt) *vi* heißlaufen.
overjoyed (ouvə'dʒɔid) *adj* entzückt, überglücklich.
overland (*adv* ouvə'lænd; *adj* 'ouvəlænd) *adv* über Land. *adj* Überland—.
overlap (*v* ouvə'læp; *n* 'ouvəlæp) *vi,(vt)* sich überschneiden (mit). *n* Überschneidung *f*. Übergreifen *neu*.
overlay* (ouvə'lei) *vt* bedecken, überziehen.
overleaf (ouvə'liːf) *adv* umseitig.
overload (*v* ouvə'loud; *n* 'ouvəloud) *vt* überladen, überbelasten. *n* Überladung *f*.
overlook (ouvə'luk) *vt* übersehen.
overnight (*adv* ouvə'nait; *adj* 'ouvənait) *adv* über Nacht *f*. *adj* **1** Nacht—. **2** plötzlich.
overpower (ouvə'pauə) *vt* überwältigen.
overrate (ouvə'reit) *vt* überbewerten.
overreach (ouvə'riːtʃ) *vt* (zu weit) hinausreichen über.

overreach oneself sich übernehmen.
overrule (ouvə'ru:l) *vt* zurückweisen.
overrun* (ouvə'rʌn) *vt* überrennen.
overseas (ouvə'si:z) *adv* in Übersee. *adj* Übersee—.
overshadow (ouvə'ʃædou) *vt* überschatten.
overshoot* (ouvə'ʃu:t) *vt* hinausschießen über, zu weit gehen.
oversight ('ouvəsait) *n* Versehen *neu*.
oversleep* (ouvə'sli:p) *vi* verschlafen.
overspill* ('ouvəspil) *n* Überschuß *m*.
overt ('ouvə:t) *adj* offen(bar), offensichtlich.
overtake* (ouvə'teik) *vt* überholen.
overthrow* (*v* ouvə'θrou; *n* 'ouvəθrou) *vt* umwerfen, umstürzen. *n* Umsturz *m*.
overtime ('ouvətaim) *n* Überstunden *f pl*. **work overtime** Überstunden machen.
overtone ('ouvətoun) *n* **1** Unterton, Beiklang *m*. **2** *pl* Nebenbedeutungen, Assoziationen *f pl*.
overture ('ouvətʃə) *n* **1** Vorspiel *neu*. Einleitung *f*. **2** *mus* Ouvertüre *f*.
overturn (ouvə'tə:n) *vt* umstürzen, umstoßen, umkippen. *vi* umkippen, umschlagen, umfallen. *n* Umsturz *m*.
overweight (*n* 'ouvəweit; *adj* ouvə'weit) *n* Übergewicht *neu*. **be overweight** Übergewicht haben.
overwhelm (ouvə'welm) *vt* **1** überschütten, überhäufen. **2** überwältigen.
overwork (*v* ouvə'wə:k; *n* 'ouvəwə:k) *vt* **1** überanstrengen, mit Arbeit überlasten. *vi* sich überarbeiten. *n* Überarbeitung *f*.
overwrought (ouvə'rɔ:t) *adj* überarbeitet, überreizt.
ovulate ('ɔvjuleit) *vi* ovulieren. **ovulation** *n* Eiausstoßung, Ovulation *f*.
owe (ou) *vt* **1** schulden, schuldig sein. **2** verdanken. *vi* Schulden haben. **owing to** *prep* infolge.
owl (aul) *n* Eule *f*.
own (oun) *adj* eigen. **get one's own back** sich revanchieren. ~*vt* besitzen. *vi* sich bekennen. **own up** *inf* gestehen. **ownership** *n* **1** Eigentumsrecht *neu*. **2** Besitz *m*.
ox (ɔks) *n, pl* **oxen** Ochse *m*. Rind *neu*.
oxygen ('ɔksidʒən) *n* Sauerstoff *m*.
oyster ('ɔistə) *n* Auster *f*.

P

pace (peis) *n* **1** Schritt *m*. **2** Tempo *neu*. **3** Gangart *f*. **pacemaker** *n* Schrittmacher *m*. *vt* **1** durchschreiten, überschreiten. **2** *sport* Schritt machen für. *vi* (einher)-schreiten.
Pacific (pə'sifik) *adj* pazifisch. **Pacific (Ocean)** *n* Pazifik, Stiller Ozean *m*.
pacify ('pæsifai) *vt* **1** befrieden, den Frieden bringen. **2** besänftigen. **pacifism** *n* Pazifismus

m. **pacifist** *n* Pazifist *m.* *adj* pazifistisch.

pack (pæk) *n* **1** Paket, Bündel *neu.* **2** Menge *f.* Haufen *m.* **3** Pack *neu.* Bande *f.* **4** Päckchen *neu.* Packung *f.* *vt* **1** (ver)packen. **2** vollstopfen. *vi* **1** packen. **2** sich zusammendrängen. **package** *n* **1** Packung *f.* Paket *neu.* **2** Ballen *m.* *vt* (in Pakete) (ver)packen. **packet** *n* Paket, Päckchen *neu.* **packing** *n* **1** Pakken *neu.* **2** Packmaterial *neu.*

pact (pækt) *n* Pakt, Vertrag *m.*

pad[1] (pæd) *n* **1** Polster, Kissen *neu.* Bausch *m.* **2** Stempelkissen *neu.* **3** (Brief)Block *m.* **padding** *n* Wattierung, Polsterung *f.*

pad[2] (pæd) *n* (leises) Tappen, Trotten *neu.*

paddle[1] ('pædl̩) *n* Paddel *neu.* *vi* paddeln.

paddle[2] ('pædl̩) *vi* (im Wasser) spielen, herumpaddeln.

paddock ('pædɔk) *n* Pferdekoppel *f.*

paddyfield ('pædifi:ld) *n* Reisfeld *neu.*

padlock ('pædlɔk) *n* Vorhängeschloß *neu.*

paediatric (pi:di'ætrik) *adj med* pädiatrisch. **paediatrician** *n* Kinderarzt *m.*

pagan ('peigən) *n* Heide *m.* *adj* heidnisch.

page[1] (peidʒ) *n* Seite *f.* Blatt *neu.*

page[2] (peidʒ) *n* Page, Boy *m.*

pageant ('pædʒənt) *n* **1** (großartiges) Schauspiel *neu.* **2** Festspiel *neu.* **pageantry** *n* Prunk *m.* Gepränge *neu.*

paid (peid) *v* see **pay.**

pain (pein) *n* **1** Schmerz *m.* Pein *f.* **2** Leid *m.* **3** Strafe *f.* **be in pain** Schmerzen haben. **take pains** sich Mühe geben. ~*vt* weh tun. **painful** *adj* **1** schmerzhaft. **2** schmerzlich. **3** peinlich. **painstaking** *adj* sorgfältig, gewissenhaft.

paint (peint) *vt* **1** malen. **2** anstreichen. *vi* malen. *n* **1** Farbe *f.* **2** Anstrich *m.* **3** Lack *m.* **wet paint!** frisch gestrichen! **paintbrush** *n* Pinsel *m.* **painter** *n* **1** Maler *m.* **2** Anstreicher *m.* **painting** *n* **1** Malen *neu.* Malerei *f.* **2** Gemälde, Bild *neu.*

pair (pɛə) *n* Paar *neu.* *vi* **1** sich paaren. **2** sich verbinden. *vt* paarweise anordnen, paaren.

Pakistan (pɑ:ki'stɑ:n) *n* Pakistan *neu.* **Pakistani** *adj* pakistanisch. *n* Pakistaner *m.*

pal (pæl) *n inf* Kumpel, Freund, Kamerad *m.*

palace ('pælis) *n* Palast *m.* Schloß *neu.*

palate ('pælət) *n* **1** Gaumen *m.* **2** Geschmack *m.* **palatable** *adj* **1** wohlschmeckend. **2** annehmbar, angenehm.

pale (peil) *adj* blaß, bleich. *vi* blaß werden, erblassen. *vt* bleich machen.

Palestine ('pælistain) *n* Palastina *neu.* **Palestinian** *adj* palästinisch. *n* Palästiner *m.*

palette ('pælit) *n* Palette *f.* Farbenteller *m.*

palm[1] (pɑ:m) *n* Handfläche *f.* Handteller *m.* *vt* **1** berühren. **2** (in der Hand) verbergen. **palm off** abschieben. **palmistry** *n* Handlesekunst *f.*

palm[2] (pɑːm) *n bot* Palme *f.* **palm tree** Palmenbaum *m.* **Palm Sunday** *n* Palmsonntag *m.*

pamper ('pæmpə) *vt* verwöhnen, hätscheln.

pamphlet ('pæmflət) *n* **1** Flugschrift *f.* **2** Broschüre *f.* **pamphleteer** *n* Pamphletist *m.*

pan (pæn) *n* Pfanne *f.* **frying pan** Bratpfanne *f.* **pancake** *n* Pfannkuchen *m.* **flat as a pancake** flach wie ein Brett.

Panama ('pænəmɑː) *n* Panama *neu.*

pancreas ('pæŋkriəs) *n* Pankreas *neu.*

panda ('pændə) *n* Panda, Katzenbär *m.*

pander ('pændə) *n* Kuppler *m.* *vt* verkuppeln. *vi* **1** kuppeln. **2** Vorschub leisten.

pane (pein) *n* **1** (Fenster)Scheibe *f.*

panel ('pænl) **1** (Tür)Füllung, Täfelung *f.* **2** *law* Geschworene *m pl.* **3** Diskussionsteilnehmer *m pl.* Ausschuß *m.* **instrument panel** Armaturenbrett *neu.* ~*vt* täfeln, paneelieren. **panelling** *n* Täfelung *f.* Tafelwerk *neu.*

pang (pæŋ) *n* stechender Schmerz, Stich *m.*

panic ('pænik) *adj* panisch. *n* Panik *f.* *vi* Angst bekommen, in eine Panik ausbrechen. **panic-stricken** von panischem Schrecken ergriffen.

pannier ('pæniə) *n* (großer) Korb *m.*

panorama (pænə'rɑːmə) *n* Panorama *neu.*

pansy ('pænzi) *n bot* Stiefmütterchen *neu.*

pant (pænt) *vi* keuchen, schnaufen. *n* Keuchen, Schnaufen *neu.*

panther ('pænθə) *n* Panther *m.*

pantomime ('pæntəmaim) *n* Pantomime *f.*

pantry ('pæntri) *n* Speisekammer *f.*

pants (pænts) *n pl* **1** Herrenunterhose *f.* **2** (lange) Hose *f.*

papal ('peipəl) *adj* päpstlich.

paper ('peipə) *n* **1** Papier *neu.* **2** *pl* (Ausweis)Papiere, Urkunden *f.* **3** Zeitung *f.* **4** *educ* schriftliche Prüfung *f.* *adj* Papier—. **paper money** Papiergeld *neu.* ~*vt* tapezieren. **paperback** *n* **1** Buch im Pappeinband *neu.* **2** Taschenbuch, Paperback *neu.* **paperclip** *n* Heftklammer, Büroklammer *f.* **paperwork** *n* Schreibarbeit, Büroarbeit *f.*

papier-mâché (pæpiei'mæʃei) *n* Papiermaché *neu.*

paprika ('pæprikə) *n* Paprika *m.*

par (pɑː) *n* **1** Gleichheit *f.* Pari *neu.* **2** Nennwert *m.* **3** Normalmaß *neu.* **on a par with** auf derselben Ebene wie.

parable ('pærəbəl) *n* Parabel *f.* Gleichnis *neu.*

parachute ('pærəʃuːt) *n* Fallschirm *m.* **parachutist** *n* Fallschirmabspringer *m.*

parade (pə'reid) *vt* **1** *mil* vorführen, paradieren. **2** zur Schau stellen. *vi* **1** promenieren. **2** paradieren. *n* Parade, Vorführung *f.*

paradise ('pærədais) *n* Paradies *neu.*

paradox ('pærədɔks) *n*

Paradoxon *neu.* widersprüchliche Aussage *f.* **paradoxical** *adj* paradox, widersinnig.

paraffin ('pærəfin) *n* Paraffin *neu.*

paragon ('pærəgən) *n* Muster, Vorbild *neu.*

paragraph ('pærəgrɑːf) *n* Absatz, Paragraph *m.*

parallel ('pærəlel) *adj* **1** gleichlaufend, parallel. **2** entsprechend, Parallel—. *n math* Parallele *f.* **2** Parallelfall *m.* **draw a parallel** einen Vergleich anstellen. *~vt* **1** gleich sein mit. **2** parallel laufen.

paralyse ('pærəlaiz) *vt* paralysieren, lähmen. **paralysis** *n* Lähmung, Paralyse *f.*

paramilitary (pærə'militəri) *adj* halbmilitärisch.

paramount ('pærəmaunt) *adj* höchst, oberst.

paranoia (pærə'nɔiə) *n* Paranoia *f.* **paranoiac** *adj* paranoisch.

parapet ('pærəpit) *n* **1** *mil* Brustwehr *f.* **2** Geländer *neu.* Brüstung *f.*

paraphernalia (pærəfə'neiliə) *n pl* **1** *law* Paraphernalgüter *neu.* **2** Ausstattung *f.* Zubehör *neu.* **3** Drum und Dran *neu.*

paraphrase ('pærəfreiz) *n* Paraphrase, Umschreibung *f.* *vt* umschreiben, paraphrasieren.

parasite ('pærəsait) *n* Schmarotzer, Parasit *m.* **parasitic** *adj* schmarotzend, parasitisch.

paratrooper ('pærətruːpə) *n* Fallschirmjäger *m.*

parcel ('pɑːsəl) *n* **1** Paket, Bündel *neu.* **2** Los *neu.* **3** Parzelle *f.* *v* **parcel out** austeilen, verteilen.

parch (pɑːtʃ) *vt* (aus)dörren, austrocknen. **be parched** vor Durst verschmachten.

parchment ('pɑːtʃmənt) *n* Pergament *neu.*

pardon ('pɑːdn̩) *n* Verzeihung, Vergebung *f.* **I beg your pardon** ich bitte um Entschuldigung. *~vt* verzeihen, entschuldigen. **pardon me** entschuldigen Sie! **pardonable** *adj* verzeihlich.

pare (pɛə) *vt* **1** (be)schneiden. **2** schälen.

parent ('pɛərənt) *n* **1** Vater *m.* Mutter *f.* **2** *pl* Eltern *pl.* **3** Elternteil *m.* **parental** *adj* **1** elterlich. **2** väterlich. **3** mütterlich. **parenthood** *n* Elternschaft *f.*

parenthesis (pə'renθəsis) *n, pl* **-ses** **1** Parenthese *f.* **2** *pl* Klammern *f pl.*

Paris ('pæris) *n* Paris *neu.*

parish ('pæriʃ) *n* Pfarrbezirk *m.* Kirchspiel *neu adj* Pfarr—, zum Kirchspiel gehörig.

parity ('pæriti) *n* Gleichheit, Parität *f.*

park (pɑːk) *n* Park *m.* Parkanlagen *f pl.* **car park** Parkplatz *m.* *~vt* parken, abstellen. *vi* parken. **parking meter** *n* Parkuhr *f.*

parliament ('pɑːləmənt) *n* Parlament *neu.* **parliamentary** *adj* parlamentarisch.

parlour ('pɑːlə) *n* Wohnzimmer *neu.* Salon *m.*

parochial (pə'roukiəl) *adj* **1** Pfarr—, Gemeinde—. **2** beschränkt, begrenzt.

parody ('pærədi) *n* Parodie *f*. *vt* parodieren.

parole (pə'roul) *n* **1** Ehrenwort *neu*. **2** *mil* Losungswort *neu*. Parole *f*. **3** bedingte Haftentlassung *f*. **on parole** auf Ehrenwort.

paroxysm ('pærɔksizm) *n* **1** (krankhafter) Anfall, Krampf *m*. **2** Steigerung (einer Krankheit) *f*.

parquet ('pa:kei) *n* Parkett *neu*.

parrot ('pærət) *n* Papagei *m*.

parsley ('pa:sli) *n* Petersilie *f*.

parsnip ('pa:snip) *n* Pastinak *m*. Pastinake *f*.

parson ('pa:sən) *n* Pastor, Pfarrer, Geistliche(r) *m*. **parsonage** *n* Pfarrhaus *neu*.

part (pa:t) *n* **1** Teil *m*. Stück *neu*. **2** Aufgabe, Pflicht *f*. **3** *Th* Rolle *f*. **play a part** eine Rolle spielen. ~*vi* **1** sich trennen, auseinandergehen. **2** Abschied nehmen. *vt* **1** teilen, trennen. **2** (the hair) scheiteln. *adv* teils, zum Teil. **parting** *n* **1** Scheiden *neu*. Abschied *m*. **2** (of the hair) Scheitel *m*. *adj* scheidend, Trennungs—. **part-time** *adj* teilzeitbeschäftigt. *adv* halbtags. **part-time job** Nebenbeschäftigung, Teilzeitbeschäftigung *f*.

partake* (pa:'teik) *vi* **1** teilnehmen, teilhaben. **2** etwas an sich haben. *vt* teilen.

partial ('pa:ʃəl) *adj* **1** einseitig, parteiisch. **2** Teil—, partiell. **be partial to** eine Vorliebe haben für.

participate (pa:'tisipeit) *vi* teilnehmen, sich beteiligen. **participation** *n* Teilnahme *f*.

participle ('pa:tisəpəl) *n* Partizip *neu*.

particle ('pa:tikəl) *n* **1** Teilchen, Stückchen *neu*. **2** Partikel *f*.

particular (pə'tikjulə) *adj* **1** individuell, einzeln. **2** ungewöhnlich. **3** ausführlich. **4** peinlich, genau. **nothing particular** nichts Besonderes. ~*n* Einzelheit *f*. **in particular** besonders, insbesondere.

partisan (pa:ti'zæn) *n* **1** Anhänger, Parteigänger *m*. **2** *mil* Partisan *m*.

partition (pa:'tiʃən) *n* **1** (Auf)Teilung, Trennung *f*. **2** Trennwand *f*. **3** Abteilung *f*. *vt* (ver-, auf-)teilen. **partition off** abteilen, abtrennen.

partly ('pa:tli) *adv* teilweise, zum Teil.

partner ('pa:tnə) *n* **1** Teilhaber, Partner *m*. **2** Gatte *m*. Gattin *f*. *vt* sich zusammentun mit, zusammenarbeiten mit. **partnership** *n* Teilhaberschaft, Partnerschaft *f*.

partridge ('pa:tridʒ) *n* Rebhuhn *neu*.

party ('pa:ti) *n* **1** Partei *f*. **2** Gesellschaft, Party *f*. **3** Gruppe *f*. **4** Beteiligte(r) *m*. *adj* Partei—. **party line** *n* festgelegte Parteipolitik, Parteilinie *f*. **follow the party line** linientreu sein.

pass (pa:s) *vt* **1** vorbeigehen. **2** übergehen, überschlagen. **3** bestehen. **4** passieren. **5** verbringen. **6** durchgehen lassen. *vi* **1** vorbeigehen. **2** gehen. **pass away** sterben. **pass off** ausgeben. **pass through** durchfahren. ~*n* **1** Engpaß, enger Weg *m*. **2** Paß *m*. **3** (in an exam) Bestehen *neu*. **password** *n* Losungswort *neu*. Parole *f*.

passage ('pæsidʒ) *n* **1** Durchgang *m*. Passage, Durchfahrt, Überfahrt *f*. **2** enger Gang, Weg *m*. Gasse *f*. **3** (in a book) Stelle *f*.

passenger ('pæsindʒə) *n* Fahrgast, Passagier *m*.

passion ('pæʃən) *n* **1** Leidenschaft *f*. **2** Zorn *m*. Wut *f*. **3** Liebhaberei *f*. **passionate** *adj* leidenschaftlich.

passive ('pæsiv) *adj* **1** passiv. **2** zurückhaltend, still, widerstandslos. *n* Passiv *neu*.

Passover ('pɑːsouvə) *n* Passahfest *neu*.

passport ('pɑːspɔːt) *n* (Reise)Paß, Ausweis *m*.

past (pɑːst) *adj* **1** vergangen. **2** ehemalig. **past participle** *n* Partizip der Vergangenheit *neu*. *n* Vergangeheit *f*. Vergangene *neu*. *adv* vorbei, vorüber. *prep* **1** nach. **2** an...vorbei. **3** über...hinaus.

pasta ('pæstə) *n* Teigwaren *f pl*.

paste (peist) *n* **1** Kleister, Klebstoff *m*. **2** Teig *m*. Paste *f*. *vt* (fest)kleben, kleistern.

pastel ('pæstəl) *n* Pastellfarbe *f*.

pasteurize ('pæstəraiz) *vt* pasteurisieren.

pastime ('pɑːstaim) *n* **1** Zeitvertreib *m*. **2** Erholung *f*. Belustigung *f*.

pastoral ('pæstərəl) *adj* Hirten—, Schäfer—.

pastry ('peistri) *n* **1** Gebäck, Backwerk *neu*. **2** Torten *f pl*. **3** Blätterteig *m*.

pasture ('pɑːstʃə) *n* Weide *f*. Weideland *neu*.

pasty[1] ('peisti) *adj* **1** teigig, teigartig. **2** bläßlich, kränklich.

pasty[2] ('pæsti) *n* (Fleisch)Pastete *f*.

pat[1] (pæt) *n* Klopfen *neu*. Klaps *m*. *vt,vi* klopfen, klapsen.

pat[2] (pæt) *adj* bereit, glatt. *adv* genau.

patch (pætʃ) *n* **1** Lappen, Flicken *m*. **2** Fleck *m*. **3** (of land) kleines Stück *neu*. *vt* flicken. **patchwork** *n* **1** Flickarbeit *f*. **2** Buntgemustertes *neu*.

pâté ('pætei) *n* Pastete, Leberwurst *f*.

patent ('peitnt) *adj* **1** offen, offenkundig. **2** patentiert. **3** Patent—. *n* **1** Patent *neu*. Patentbrief *m*. *vt* patentieren. **patent leather** *n* Lackleder *neu*.

paternal (pə'təːnl) *adj* väterlich, Vater—. **paternity** *n* **1** Vaterschaft *f*.

path (pɑːθ) *n* **1** Pfad, Weg *m*. **2** Bahn *f*.

pathetic (pə'θetik) *adj* **1** rührend, ergreifend, pathetisch. **2** *inf* jämmerlich, armselig.

pathology (pə'θɔlədʒi) *n med* Krankheitslehre, Pathologie *f*. **pathologist** *n* Pathologe *m*.

patience ('peiʃəns) *n* **1** Geduld *f*. **2** Ausdauer *f*. **patient** *n* Kranke(r), Patient *m*. *adj* geduldig.

patio ('pætiou) *n* Innenhof, Terasse, Veranda *f*.

patriarchal (peitri'ɑːkəl) *adj* patriarchalisch.

patrician (pə'triʃən) *n* Patrizier

m. adj **1** patrizisch. **2** aristokratisch.
patriot ('peitriət) *n* Patriot *m.* **patriotic** *adj* **1** patriotisch. **2** vaterländisch.
patrol (pə'troul) *n* **1** *mil* Patrouille *f.* **2** (Polizei)Streife *f.* *(vt),vi* (ab)patrouillieren.
patron ('peitrən) *n* **1** Patron, Schutzherr *m.* **2** Gönner *m.* **3** Kunde *m.* **patronage** *n* **1** Gönnerschaft, Protektion *f.* **2** *law* Patronatsrecht *neu.* **3** Schutz *m.* **4** Kundschaft *f.* **patronize** *vt* **1** gönnerhaft behandeln, **2** in Schutz nehmen, beschützen. **3** Kunde sein bei. **patronizing** *adj* gönnerhaft, herablassend.
patter[1] ('pætə) *vi* **1** klatschen, platschen. **2** trappeln. *n* **1** Platschen, Prasseln. *neu.* **2** Getrappel *neu.*
patter[2] ('pætə) *n* **1** Jargon *m.* **2** Geplapper *neu. vi* schwatzen, plappern.
pattern ('pætən) *n* **1** Muster *neu.* Schablone *f.* **2** Plan *m.* Anlage *f.*
paunch (pɔːntʃ) *n* **1** Bauch, Wanst *m.* **2** *zool* Pansen *m.*
pauper ('pɔːpə) *n* Arme(r) *m.*
pause (pɔːz) *n* Pause, Unterbrechung *f. vi* innehalten, pausieren, warten.
pave (peiv) *vt* pflastern. **pave the way** den Weg bahnen. **pavement** *n* **1** Gehsteig *m.* **2** Pflaster *neu.*
pavilion (pə'viliən) *n* Pavillion *m.*
paw (pɔː) *n* Pfote, Tatze *f. vt* mit den Pfoten kratzen, scharren, stampfen. *vi* scharren, kratzen.
pawn[1] (pɔːn) *vt* verpfänden, versetzen. *n* Pfand *neu.* **pawnbroker** *n* Pfandleiher *m.*
pawn[2] (pɔːn) *n game* Bauer *m.*
pay* (pei) *vi* **1** zahlen, Zahlung leisten. **2** sich lohnen, sich rentieren. *vt* **1** bezahlen. **2** schenken. **3** abstatten, machen. *n* **1** Bezahlung *f.* **2** Lohn *m.* **3** Belohnung *f.* **paypacket** *n* Lohntüte *f.* **payroll** *n* Lohnliste *f.*
pea (piː) *n* Erbse *f.*
peace (piːs) *n* **1** Frieden *m.* **2** Ruhe *f.* **peaceful** *adj* friedlich, ruhig. **peacemaker** *n* Friedensstifter *m.*
peach (piːtʃ) *n* Pfirsich *m.*
peacock ('piːkɔk) *n* Pfau *m.*
peak (piːk) *n* **1** Spitze, Bergspitze *f.* **2** Gipfel, Höhepunkt *m. adj* Hoch—, Spitzen—. **peak hours** *n pl* Hauptverkehrszeit *f.*
peal (piːl) *n* **1** Geläute *neu.* **2** Getöse *neu.* Krach *m. vi* **1** läuten. **2** erschallen.
peanut ('piːnʌt) *n* Erdnuß *f.*
pear (pɛə) *n* Birne *f.*
pearl (pəːl) *n* Perle *f.*
peasant ('pezənt) *n* Bauer, Landmann *m. adj* bäuerlich, ländlich.
peat (piːt) *n* Torf *m.*
pebble ('pebəl) *n* Kieselstein *m.*
peck (pek) *n* **1** Picken, Hacken *neu.* **2** Küßchen *neu. vt,vi* picken, hacken.
peckish ('pekiʃ) *adj inf* hungrig.
peculiar (pi'kjuːliə) *adj* **1** eigen(tümlich). **2** eigenartig. **peculiarity** *n* Eigentümlichkeit *f.*

pedal ('pedḷ) *n* Pedal *neu.* Fußhebel *m.* *vt* fahren, treten. *vi* **1** das Pedal treten. **2** radfahren.

peddle ('pedḷ) *vt,vi* hausieren.

pedestal ('pedistəl) *n* Postament *neu.* Ständer, Sockel *m.* **put on a pedestal** aufs Podest heben.

pedestrian (pi'destriən) *n* Fußgänger *m.* *adj* **1** Fuß—, zu Fuß (gehend). **2** prosaisch, alltäglich. **pedestrian crossing** *n* Fußgängerübergang *m.*

pedigree ('pedigriː) *n* Stammbaum *m.*

pedlar ('pedlə) *n* Hausierer *m.*

peel (piːl) *n* Schale, Rinde, Haut *f.* *vt* **1** schälen, entrinden. **2** abstreifen. *vi* sich abschälen, sich abblättern.

peep (piːp) *n* Gucken *neu.* neugieriger Blick *m.* *vi* neugierig gucken.

peer[1] (piə) *n* **1** Peer, Adlige(r) *m.* **2** Gleiche(r) *m.*

peer[2] (piə) *vi* **1** spähen, scharf blicken. **2** sich zeigen, erscheinen.

peevish ('piːviʃ) *adj* verdrießlich, mürrisch.

peg (peg) *n* **1** Pflock, Stift *m.* **2** (Wäsche)Klammer *f.* *vt* **1** mit Pflocken befestigen, anpflocken. **2** (an)nageln.

pejorative (pi'dʒɔrətiv) *adj* verschlechternd, herabsetzend, pejorativ.

pelican ('pelikən) *n* Pelikan *m.*

pellet ('pelit) *n* **1** Kügelchen *neu.* **2** Schrotkugel *f.* *vt* mit Kugeln bewerfen.

pelmet ('pelmit) *n* Vorhangsfalbel *f.*

pelt[1] (pelt) *vt* (be)werfen. *vi* **1** niederprasseln. **2** eilen. **pelting rain** *n* Platzregen *m.* ~*n* **1** Wurf, Schlag *m.* **2** Prasseln, Klatschen *neu.* **3** Eile, Geschwindigkeit *f.*

pelt[2] (pelt) *n* Pelz, Fell *m.*

pelvis ('pelvis) *n* Becken *neu.*

pen[1] (pen) *n* (Schreib)Feder *f.* *vt* **1** schreiben. **2** verfassen. **penfriend** *n* Brieffreund *m.* **penknife** *n* Taschenmesser *neu.*

pen[2] (pen) *n* Gehege *neu.* Pferch *m.* Koppel *f.* *vt* einpferchen, einschließen.

penal ('piːnḷ) *adj* **1** Straf—. **2** strafbar. **penalize** *vt* **1** bestrafen. **2** belasten. **penalty** *n* Strafe, Buße *f.* **penalty (kick)** *sport* Strafstoß, Elfmeter *m.*

penance ('penəns) *n* Buße *f.*

pencil ('pensəl) *n* **1** Bleistift *m.* **2** Stift *m.* **pencil-sharpener** *n* Bleistiftspitzer *m.*

pendant ('pendənt) *n* **1** Anhänger *m.* **2** Hängeleuchter *m.* *adj also* **pendent** **1** herabhängend. **2** schwebend.

pending ('pendiŋ) *adj* **1** hängend. **2** schwebend, unentschieden. **3** bevorstehend. *prep* **1** bis zu. **2** während.

pendulum ('pendjuləm) *n* Pendel *neu.*

penetrate ('penitreit) *vt* **1** eindringen, durchdringen. **2** erforschen, ergründen. *vi* eindringen. **penetration** *n* Eindringen *neu.* Eindringungsvermögen *neu.* **3** Ergründung *f.*

penguin ('peŋgwin) *n* Pinguin *m.*

penicillin (peni'silin) *n* Penicillin *neu.*

peninsula (pə'ninsjulə) *n* Halbinsel *f.*

penis ('pi:nis) *n* **1** Penis *m.* **2** *zool* Rute *f.*

penitent ('penitənt) *adj* reuig, bußfertig. *n* Büßer *m.*

pennant ('penənt) *n* Wimpel *m.* Fähnchen *neu.*

penny ('peni) *n* **1** *pl* **pence** British unit of currency. **2** *pl* **pennies** Pfennig, Penny *neu.* **penniless** *adj* ohne Geld, mittellos. **be penniless** keinen roten Heller haben.

pension ('penʃən) *n* Pension, Rente *f.* *v* **pension off** pensionieren, in den Ruhestand versetzen. **pensioner** *n* Rentner, Pensionist *m.*

pensive ('pensiv) *adj* gedankenvoll, nachdenklich.

pent (pent) *adj* **pent up** **1** eingepfercht. **2** (of feelings) verhalten.

pentagon ('pentəgən) *n* *math* Fünfeck *neu.*

Pentecost ('pentikɔst) *n* Pfingsten *neu.*

penthouse ('penthaus) *n* **1** Schutzdach *neu.* **2** Dachterassenwohnung *f.*

people ('pi:pəl) *n pl* **1** Leute *pl.* **2** Volk *neu.* **3** Bevölkerung *f.* *vt* bevölkern, besiedeln. **people say** man sagt.

pepper ('pepə) *n* Pfeffer *m.* *vt* **1** pfeffern. **2** bestreuen. **peppercorn** *n* Pfefferkorn *neu.* **peppermill** *n* Pfeffermühle *f.* **peppermint** *n* **1** Pfefferminze *f.* **2** Pfefferminzbonbon *m,neu.* **pepperpot** *n* Pfefferstreuer *m.*

per (pə:) *pre* **1** pro. **2** per, durch, mit. **as per** gemäß, laut.

perambulator (pə'ræmbjuleitə) *n* Kinderwagen *m.*

perceive (pə'si:v) *vt,vi* **1** wahrnehmen, empfinden. **2** erkennen, begreifen.

per cent (pə 'sent) *n* Prozent *neu.* *adj* —prozentig.

percentage (pə'sentidʒ) *n* **1** Prozentsatz *m.* **2** Gewinnanteil *m.* Provision *f.*

perception (pə'sepʃən) *n* **1** (geistige) Wahrnehmung *f.* **2** Empfindungsvermögen *neu.* **3** Vorstellung *f.* **perceptive** *adj* **1** wahrnehmend, empfindend. **2** auffassungsfähig.

perch (pə:tʃ) *n* (Sitz)Stange *f.* *vi* sich setzen.

percolate ('pə:kəleit) *vt* **1** filtern, perkolieren. **2** klären. *vi* durchsickern, durchlaufen.

percussion (pə'kʌʃən) *n* **1** Schlag, Stoß *m.* **2** *mus* Schlaginstrumente *neu pl.*

perennial (pə'reniəl) *n* perennierende Pflanze *f.* *adj* **1** fortdauernd, beständig. **2** perennierend.

perfect (*adj,n* 'pə:fi:kt; *v* pə 'fekt) *adj* **1** vollkommen. **2** gründlich. **3** geschickt. **4** gänzlich, vollständig. *n* Perfekt *neu.* *vt* **1** vollenden. **2** vervollkommnen.

perforate ('pə:fəreit) *vt* durchbohren, durchlochen, perforieren.

perform (pə'fɔ:m) *vi* **1** eine Vorstellung geben. **2** seine Aufgabe erfüllen. **3** arbeiten, leisten. *vt* **1** verrichten, ausführen. **2** vollenden. **3** aufführen, vortragen. **perfor-**

mance *n* **1** Ausführung, Vollziehung *f*. **2** Aufführung, Darstellung *f*. **3** Leistung *f*. **4** Benehmen *neu*. **5** *inf* Theater, Getue *neu*.

perfume ('pəːfjuːm) *n* **1** Parfüm *neu*. **2** Duft *m*. *vt* parfümieren.

perhaps (pə'hæps) *adv* vielleicht.

peril ('perəl) *n* Gefahr *f*. Risiko *neu*. **at one's peril** auf eigene Gefahr.

perimeter (pə'rimitə) *n* **1** *math* Umkreis *m*. **2** Peripherie *f*.

period ('piəriəd) *n* **1** Periode *f*. Zeitabschnitt *m*. **2** Pause *f*. Absatz *m*. **3** Weile *f*. **4** *med* Periode, Menstruation *f*. **5** *educ* (Unterrichts)Stunde *f*. **periodical** *n* Zeitschrift *f*. Magazin *neu*. *adj* regelmäßig wiederkehrend, periodisch.

peripheral (pə'rifərəl) *adj* peripherisch, Umfangs—.

periscope ('periskoup) *n* Periskop *neu*.

perish ('periʃ) *vi* **1** umkommen, sterben. **2** verfallen, vergehen. *vt* zerstören.

perjure ('pəːdʒə) *vt* **perjure oneself** eidbrüchig *or* meineidig werden. **perjurer** *n* Meineidige(r) *m*. **perjury** *n* Meineid *m*.

perk (pəːk) *vi* **1** sich brüsten, den Kopf hochtragen. **2** sich vorrecken. **perk up** munter werden *or* machen, in Stimmung kommen. **perky** *adj* keck, munter.

perm (pəːm) *n inf* Dauerwelle *f*.

permanent ('pəːmənənt) *adj* **1** beständig, (fort)dauernd, permanent. **2** dauerhaft. **permanence** *n* Beständigkeit, Permanenz *f*.

permeate ('pəːmieit) *vt* durchdringen. *vi* eindringen.

permit (*v* pə'mit; *n* 'pəːmit) *vt,vi* erlauben, gestatten. *n* **1** Erlaubnis, Genehmigung *f*. **2** Passierschein *m*. **permissible** *adj* zulässig. **permission** *n* Erlaubnis, Zulassung, Bewilligung *f*. **permissive** *adj* gestattend, zulassend.

permutation (pəːmju'teiʃən) *n* Permutation *f*.

pernicious (pəː'niʃəs) *adj* verderblich, schädlich.

perpendicular (pəːpən'dikjulə) *adj* senkrecht, lotrecht. *n* Senkrechte *f*.

perpetrate ('pəːpətreit) *vt* verüben, begehen. **perpetrator** *n* Täter *m*.

perpetual (pə'petʃuəl) *adj* **1** unaufhörlich, beständig. **2** lebenslänglich.

perpetuate (pə'petʃueit) *vt* verewigen, immerwährend fortsetzen.

perplex (pə'pleks) *vt* verwirren, verblüffen.

persecute ('pəːsikjuːt) *vt* **1** verfolgen. **2** plagen, belästigen.

persevere (pəːsi'viə) *vi* beharren, nicht nachgeben.

Persia ('pəːʃə) *n* Persien *neu*. **Persian** *adj* persich. *n* **1** Perser *m*. **2** (language) Persisch *neu*.

persist (pə'sist) *vi* beharren, hartnäckig bestehen.

person ('pəːsən) *n* **1** Person *f*. Individuum *neu*. **2** Persönlichkeit *f*. **personal** *adj* per-

sönlich. **personality** *n* **1** Persönlichkeit *f*. **2** Ausstrahlung *f*.
personify (pə'sɔnifai) *vt* verkörpern, personifizieren.
personnel (pəːsə'nel) *n* Personal *neu*. Angestellte(n) *pl*. **personnel manager** *n* Personalchef *m*.
perspective (pə'spektiv) *n* **1** Perspektive *f*. **2** Aussicht, Fernsicht *f*. *adj* perspektivisch. **in perspective** in richtiger Perspektive.
Perspex ('pəːspeks) *n Tdmk* Plexiglas *Tdmk neu*.
perspire (pə'spaiə) *vi* schwitzen, transpirieren. *vt* ausschwitzen. **perspiration** *n* Schweiß *m*.
persuade (pə'sweid) *vt* **1** überreden, verleiten. **2** überzeugen. **persuasion** *n* **1** Überredung *f*. **2** Überzeugung *f*. **3** Glaube *m*.
pert (pəːt) *adj* **1** keck, schnippisch. **2** munter, flink.
pertain (pə'tein) *vi* **1** (an)gehören. **2** sich ziemen. **pertinent** *adj* **1** angemessen, passend. **2** gehörig.
perturb (pə'təːb) *vt* beunruhigen, ängstigen.
Peru (pə'ruː) *n* Peru *neu*. **Peruvian** *adj* peruanisch. *n* Peruaner *m*.
pervade (pə'veid) *vt* durchdringen, erfüllen.
perverse (pə'vəːs) *adj* **1** schlecht, böse. **2** pervers, widernatürlich. **3** verstockt, störrisch. **4** verkehrt.
pervert (*v* pə'vəːt; *n* 'pəːvəːt) *vt* **1** verkehren, verdrehen. **2** verführen. *n* **1** perverser Mensch *m*. **2** Abtrünnige(r) *m*.
pessimism ('pesimizəm) *n* Pessimismus *m*. **pessimist** *n* Pessimist *m*. **pessimistic** *adj* pessimistisch.
pest (pest) *n* **1** Pest *f*. **2** Schädling *m*. **pesticide** *n* Schädlingsbekämpfungsmittel *neu*.
pester ('pestə) *vt* plagen, belästigen.
pet[1] (pet) *n* **1** (zahmes) Haustier *neu*. **2** Liebling *m*. *adj* Lieblings—. *vt* verhätscheln.
pet[2] (pet) *n* üble Laune *f*. *vi* übler Laune *or* mürrisch sein.
petal ('petl̩) *n* Blumenblatt *neu*.
peter ('piːtə) *vi* **peter out** allmählich aufhören, sich totlaufen.
petition (pi'tiʃən) *n* Bitte, Bittschrift, Petition *f*. *vt* bitten, petitionieren. *vi* ansuchen.
petrify ('petrifai) *vt* **1** versteinern. **2** bestürzen, erschrecken. *vi* sich versteinern, zu Stein werden.
petroleum (pi'trouliəm) *n* Petroleum, Erdöl *neu*. **petrol** *n* Benzin *neu*.
petticoat ('petikout) *n* (Frauen)Unterrock *m*.
petty ('peti) *adj* **1** klein, unbedeutend. **2** engstirnig, kleinlich, beschränkt. **petty cash** *n* kleine Summen *f pl*. geringe Beträge *m pl*. **petty officer** *n* Maat *m*.
petulant ('petjulənt) *adj* **1** reizbar, launisch. **2** mürrisch, eigensinnig.
pew (pjuː) *n* Kirchenstuhl *m*.
pewter ('pjuːtə) *n* (Hart)Zinn *neu*.
phallus ('fæləs) *n* Phallus *m*.

phantom ('fæntəm) *n* Phantom *neu.* Erscheinung *f.*

pharmacy ('fɑːməsi) *n* **1** Pharmazie *f.* **2** Apotheke *f.* **pharmacist** *n* Apotheker *m.*

pharynx ('færiŋks) *n* Schlund, Rachen *m.*

phase (feiz) *n* **1** Phase *f.* **2** Entwicklungsstadium *neu.* **3** Aspekt *m.* *v* **phase out** abwickeln.

pheasant ('fezənt) *n* Fasan *m.*

phenomenon (fi'nɔminən) *n* Phänomen *neu.* Erscheinung *f.* **phenomenal** *adj* phänomenal, außerordentlich.

philanthropy (fi'lænθrəpi) *n* Menschenliebe *f.* **philanthropist** *n* Menschenfreund, Philanthrop *m.*

philately (fi'lætəli) *n* Philatelie, Briefmarkenkunde *f.*

Philippines ('filipiːnz) *n pl* Philippinen *pl.*

Philistine ('filistain) *n* **1** Philister *m.* **2** Spießbürger *m.* *adj* spießbürgerlich, beschränkt.

philosophy (fi'lɔsəfi) *n* Philosophie *f.* **philosopher** *n* Philosoph *m.* **philosophical** *adj* **1** philosophisch. **2** gleichmütig.

phlegm (flem) *n* **1** *med* Phlegma *neu.* Schleim *m.* **2** Gleichgültigkeit *f.*

phlegmatic (fleg'mætik) *adj* **1** phlegmatisch, schleimhaltig. **2** phlegmatisch, gleichgültig, träge.

phobia ('foubiə) *n* Phobie, krankhafte Angst *f.*

phoenix ('fiːniks) *n* Phoenix *m.*

phone (foun) *inf n* **1** Telefon *neu.* Fernsprecher *m.* *vi,vt* anrufen, telefonieren.

phonetic (fə'netik) *adj* phonetisch.

phoney ('founi) *adj* unecht, falsch, Schein—.

phosphate ('fɔsfeit) *n* Phosphat *neu.*

phosphorescence (fɔsfə'resəns) *n* Phosphoreszenz *f.* Nachleuchten *neu.*

phosphorous ('fɔsfərəs) *n* Phosphor *m.*

photo ('foutou) *n* Photo *neu.*

photocopy ('foutoukɔpi) *n* Photokopie *f.* *vt* photokopieren.

photogenic (foutə'dʒenik) *adj* photogen.

photograph ('foutəgrɑːf) *n* Photographie *f.* Lichtbild *neu.* *vt* photographieren. **photographer** *n* Photograph *m.* **photography** *n* Photographie *f.*

phrase (freiz) *n* **1** Redensart, (Rede)Wendung *f.* **2** Phrase *f.* **3** Satz *m.* *vt* formulieren, ausdrücken. **phrasebook** *n* Konversations-Handbuch *neu.*

physical ('fizikəl) *adj* **1** physisch, körperlich. **2** physikalisch. **physical education** *n* Leibeserziehung *f.*

physician (fi'ziʃən) *n* Arzt *m.*

physics ('fiziks) *n* Physik *f.* **physicist** *n* Physiker *m.*

physiology (fizi'ɔlədʒi) *n* Physiologie *f.*

physiotherapy (fiziou'θerəpi) *n* Physiotherapie *f.*

physique (fi'ziːk) *n* Körperbau *m.*

piano (pi'ænou) *n* Klavier, Piano *neu*. **pianist** *n* Klavierspieler, Pianist *m*.

pick[1] (pik) *vt* **1** hacken, picken. **2** auswählen. **3** pflücken, lesen. *vi* hacken, picken. **pick out** auswählen. **pick up** **1** aufheben. **2** *sl* auflesen. **3** *mot* mitnehmen. **4** sich erholen. **5** (sound) abnehmen. *~n* Auswahl, Auslese *f*. **pickpocket** *n* Taschendieb *m*. **pick-up** *n* **1** *sl* zufällige Bekanntschaft *f*. **2** kleiner Lieferwagen *m*.

pick[2] (pik) *n* Spitzhacke, Picke *f*.

picket ('pikit) *n* **1** Pfahl, Pflock *m*. **2** Streikposten *m*. *vt* einzäunen. *vi* (als) Streikposten stehen.

pickle ('pikəl) *n* **1** Eingepökeltes *neu*. **2** eingelegtes Gemüse *neu*. *vt* einpökeln, einsalzen, marinieren.

picnic ('piknik) *n* Mahlzeit im Freien *f*. Picknick *neu*.

pictorial (pik'tɔːriəl) *adj* bildlich, illustriert, Bild—. *n* Illustrierte *f*.

picture ('piktʃə) *n* **1** Bild *neu*. **2** Gemälde *neu*. Zeichnung *f*. **3** *pl* Kino *neu*. *vt* sich vorstellen, darstellen.

picturesque (piktʃə'resk) *adj* pittoresk, malerisch, anschaulich.

pidgin ('pidʒən) *n* Verkehrssprache *f*. **pidgin English** Pidgin-Englisch *neu*.

pie (pai) *n* **1** Pastete *f*. **2** Torte *f*. **have a finger in the pie** die Hand im Spiel haben.

piece (piːs) *n* **1** Stück *neu*. **2** Teil *m*. **3** (Geld)Stück *neu*. **4** *game* Figur *f*. **piecemeal** *adv* stückweise, Stück für Stück. **piecework** *n* Akkordarbeit *f*. *~v* **piece together** **1** zusammensetzen. **2** zusammenreimen.

pied (paid) *adj* buntscheckig.

pier (piə) *n* **1** Pier *m*. **2** Landungssteg *m*. **3** Hafendamm *m*. **4** Pfeiler *m*.

pierce (piəs) *vt* **1** durchstechen, durchbohren. **2** durchdringen. *vi* eindringen.

piety ('paiəti) *n* Frömmigkeit, Pietät *f*.

pig (pig) *n* Schwein, Ferkel *neu*. **pig-headed** *adj* dickschädelig, stur. **pig-iron** *n* Masseleisen, Roheisen *neu*. **piglet** *n* Schweinchen, Ferkel *neu*. **pigskin** *n* Schweinsleder *neu*. **pigsty** *n* Schweinestall *m*. **pigtail** *n* Zopf *m*.

pigeon ('pidʒən) *n* Taube *f*. **pigeonhole** *n* (Brief)Fach *neu*. *vt* einordnen.

piggyback ('pigibæk) *adj,adv* huckepack.

pigment ('pigmənt) *n* **1** Pigment *neu*. **2** Farbe *f*. Farbstoff *m*. *vt* pigmentieren, färben.

pike (paik) *n* Hecht *m*.

pilchard ('piltʃəd) *n* Sardine *f*.

pile[1] (pail) *n* Haufen, Stapel, Stoß *m*. *vt* anhaüfen, stapeln. **pile up** sich ansammeln, anhäufen. **pile-up** *n* *mot* (Massen)Zusammenstoß *m*.

pile[2] (pail) *n* **1** zugespitzter Pfahl *m*. **2** Pfeiler *m*. **pile-driver** *n* Ramme *f*.

pile[3] (pail) *n* **1** Flaum *m*. **2** Flor *m*. **3** Haar, Fell *neu*.

piles (pails) *n* *med* Hämorrhoiden *f pl*.

pilfer ('pilfə) *vt,vi* **1** stehlen. **2** mausen, klauen.

pilgrim ('pilgrim) *n* Pilger, Wallfahrer *m*. *adj* pilgernd, Wallfahrts—. **pilgrimage** *n* Pilgerfahrt, Wallfahrt *f*. **go on a pilgrimage** pilgern, wallfahren.

pill (pil) *n* Pille *f*. **the pill** *inf* die Pille.

pillage ('pilidʒ) *vt* ausplündern, rauben.

pillar ('pilə) *n* **1** Pfeiler *m*. **2** Säule *f*. **pillar-box** Briefkasten *m*.

pillion ('piliən) *n* **1** Damensattel *m*. **2** Soziussitz *m*.

pillow ('pilou) *n* Kopfkissen *neu*. **pillowcase** *n* Kissenbezug *m*.

pilot ('pailət) *n* Pilot, Flugzeugführer *m*. *vt* **1** steuern, lotsen. **2** leiten, führen. **pilot-light** *n* **1** Zündflamme *f*. **2** Kontrollampe *f*.

pimento (pi'mentou) *n* Piment *m*.

pimp (pimp) *n* Zuhälter, Kuppler *m*.

pimple ('pimpəl) *n* Pickel, Pustel *f*.

pin (pin) *n* **1** Nadel *f*. **2** Stift, Bolzen *m*. *vt* **1** mit einer Nadel festmachen. **2** festnageln, festhalten. **pinball** *n* Kugelspiel *neu*. Flipper *m*. **pincushion** *n* Nadelkissen *neu*. **pin-money** *n* **1** Geldbetrag für kleine Sonderausgaben *m*. **2** Nadelgeld *neu*. **pinpoint** *vt* genau feststellen. **pinstripe** *n* Nadelstreifen *m*.

pinafore ('pinəfɔː) *n* (Kinder)Schürze *f*.

pincers ('pinsəz) *n pl* **1** (Kneif) Zange *f*. **2** *zool* Krebsschere *f*.

pinch (pintʃ) *vt* **1** kneifen, drücken. **2** *inf* klauen. **3** beschränken, einschränken. *vi* drücken, kneifen. *n* **1** Kneifen, Zwicken *neu*. **2** Druck *m*. **3** *cul* Prise *f*.

pine[1] (pain) *n* *bot* Kiefer, Föhre *f*.

pine[2] (pain) *vi* sich sehnen, schmachten.

pineapple ('painæpəl) *n* Ananas *f*.

ping-pong ('piŋpɔŋ) *n* Tischtennis, Pingpong *neu*.

pinion ('piniən) *n* **1** Flügelspitze *f*. **2** Flügel *m*. *vt* **1** beschneiden, stutzen. **2** binden, fesseln.

pink (piŋk) *adj* rosa. *n* *bot* Nelke *f*.

pinnacle ('pinəkəl) *n* **1** Spitzturm *m*. **2** Gipfel *m*. Spitze *f*.

pint (paint) *n* **1** Pinte *f*. **2** Schoppen *m*.

pioneer (paiə'niə) *n* **1** Pionier *m*. **2** Wegbereiter *m*. *vt* den Weg bahnen für, bahnbrechende Arbeit leisten.

pious ('paiəs) *adj* fromm.

pip[1] (pip) *n* Obstkern *m*.

pip[2] (pip) *n* Ton *m*. *vi* piepsen.

pipe (paip) *n* **1** Pfeife *f*. **2** Röhre *f*. Rohr *neu*. **3** Rohrleitung *f*. **4** *pl* *mus* Dudelsack *m*. *vt* durch ein Rohr leiten. **pipedream** *n* Luftschloß *neu*. **pipeline** *n* Pipeline, Rohrleitung *f*. **pipette** *n* Pipette *f*.

piquant ('piːkənt) *adj* pikant, würzig.

pique (piːk) *n* Groll, Ärger *m*. *vt* ärgern.

pirate ('pairət) *n* Pirat, Seeräuber *m. vi* plündern.

pirouette (piru'et) *n* Pirouette, Kreiseldrehung *f. vi* pirouettieren.

Pisces ('pisiːz) *n* Fische *m pl.*

piss (pis) *vi tab* urinieren, harnen. **piss off!** *interj* schleich dich! verzieh dich!

pistol ('pistəl) *n* Pistole *f.*

piston ('pistən) *n* **1** *tech* Kolben *m.* **2** *mus* Ventil *neu.*

pit (pit) *n* **1** Grube, Höhle *f.* **2** Zeche *f.* **3** Abgrund *m.* **4** (Pocken)Narbe *f. vt* **1** mit Narben bedecken. **2** zerfressen. **pitfall** *n* **1** Falle, Fallgrube *f.* **2** Gefahr *f.*

pitch[1] (pitʃ) *vt* **1** werfen, schleudern. **2** errichten, aufstellen. **3** *mus* stimmen. **4** festsetzen. **5** gabeln. *vi* hinstürzen. *n* **1** Wurf *m.* **2** *mus* Tonhöhe. **3** Stufe *f.* Grad *m.* **pitchfork** *n* Heugabel, Mistgabel *f.*

pitch[2] (pitʃ) *n* Pech *neu. vt* (ver)pechen.

pith (piθ) *n* **1** Mark *neu.* **2** Innere *neu.* Kern *m.* **3** Bedeutung *f.*

pittance ('pitṇs) *n* **1** Hungerlohn *m.* **2** kleiner Anteil *m.*

pituitary gland (pi'tjuətri) *n* Hypophyse *f.* Hirnanhang *m.*

pity ('piti) *n* **1** Mitleid, Erbarmen *neu.* **2** Jammer *m.* **what a pity!** wie schade! ~*vt* bemitleiden.

pivot ('pivət) *n* **1** Drehpunkt *m.* **2** (Tür)Angel *f. vi* sich drehen. *vt* **1** schwenken. **2** mit Angeln versehen.

pizza ('piːtsə) *n* Pizza *f.*

placard ('plækaːd) *n* Plakat *neu.*

placate (plə'keit) *vt* besänftigen, beruhigen.

place (pleis) *n* **1** Ort *m.* **2** Stelle *f.* **3** Platz *m.* **4** Stand, Rang *m.* **5** Stadt *f.* **6** *inf* Wohnung *f.* Haus *neu.* **all over the place** *inf* überall. ~*vt* **1** stellen, legen, setzen. **2** unterbringen. **3** identifizieren. **placename** *n* Ortsname *m.*

placenta (plə'sentə) *n* Plazenta *f.*

placid ('plæsid) *adj* ruhig, gelassen.

plagiarize ('pleidʒəraiz) *vt* abschreiben, plagieren, nachahmen. *vi* ein Plagiat begehen.

plague (pleig) *n* **1** Plage *f.* **2** Seuche, Pest *f.* **3** Quälgeist *m. vt* quälen, verfolgen, belästigen.

plaice (pleis) *n* Scholle *f.*

plaid (plæd) *n* Plaid *m,neu* Schottenmuster *neu. adj* buntkariert.

plain (plein) *adj* **1** klar. **2** offen. **3** einfach, schlicht. **4** schmucklos, ungemustert. **5** unschön. **plain sailing** *n* einfache Sache, reibungslose Affäre *f.* ~*adv* klar. *n* Ebene, Fläche *f.* **plain-clothes** *n* Zivilkleidung *f.*

plaintiff ('pleintif) *n law* Kläger *m.*

plaintive ('pleintiv) *adj* **1** klagend, kläglich. **2** traurig.

plait (plæt) *n* **1** Falte *f.* **2** Zopf *m. vt* **1** (zu einem Zopf) flechten. **2** falten.

plan (plæn) *n* **1** Plan *m.* **2** Skizze *f.* Entwurf *m.* **3** Absicht *f. vt* **1** entwerfen, skizzieren. **2** planen, beabsichtigen.

plane[1] (plein) *adj* flach, eben. *n* **1** Ebene *f.* **2** Höhe *f.* Niveau *neu.* **3** Flugzeug *neu. vi* gleiten.

plane[2] (plein) Hobel *m. vt* ebnen, glätten, hobeln.

planet ('plænit) *n* Planet *m.*

plank (plæŋk) *n* Planke, Bohle *f.*

plankton ('plæŋktən) *n* Plankton *neu.*

plant (plɑːnt) *n* **1** *bot* Pflanze *f.* **2** Fabrik *f.* Werk *neu. vt* **1** pflanzen. **2** bepflanzen. **plantation** *n* (An)Pflanzung *f.* Plantage *f.*

plaque (plɑːk) *n* **1** (Schmuck)Platte *f.* **2** Brosche *f.* **3** Gedenktafel *f.*

plasma ('plæzmə) *n* Plasma *neu.*

plaster ('plɑːstə) *n* **1** Pflaster *neu.* **2** Mörtel *m.* **3** Gips *m.* **plaster of Paris** *n* (gebrannter) Gips *m.* **sticking plaster** Heftpflaster *neu.* ~*vt* **1** (be)pflastern. **2** verputzen.

plastic ('plæstik) *n* Kunststoff *m. adj* **1** Plastik—, Kunststoff—. **2** bildend. **3** plastisch.

Plasticine ('plæstisiːn) *n Tdmk* Plastilin *Tdmk neu.*

plate (pleit) *n* **1** Tafel, Platte *f.* **2** Teller *m.* **3** Silbergeschirr *neu. vt* plattieren, überziehen. **platelayer** *n* Schienenleger, Streckenarbeiter *m.*

plateau ('plætou) *n* Plateau *neu.* Hochebene *f.*

platform ('plætfɔːm) *n* **1** Rednerbühne *f.* **2** Bahnsteig *m.* **3** Plattform *f.*

platinum ('plætnəm) *n* Platin *neu.*

platonic (plə'tɔnik) *adj* platonisch.

plausible ('plɔːzəbəl) *adj* **1** plausibel, einleuchtend. **2** überzeugend.

play (plei) *n* **1** Spiel *neu.* **2** Schauspiel, Theaterstück *neu.* **3** Verhalten *neu.* **4** Spielraum *m. vi* **1** spielen. **2** tändeln, flirten. **3** *mus* Musik machen. *vt* spielen. **playboy** *n* Playboy *m.* **playful** *adj* spielerisch, scherzhaft. **playground** *n* **1** Spielplatz *m.* **2** Schulhof *m.* **playgroup** *n* Spielgruppe *f.* **playhouse** *n* **1** Schauspielhaus *neu.* **2** Puppenhaus *neu.* **playing card** *n* Spielkarte *f.* **playing field** *n* Sportplatz *m.* **playmate** *n* Spielkamerad *m.* **playschool** *n* Kindergarten *m.* **playwright** *n* Dramatiker *m.*

plea (pliː) *n* **1** Gesuch *neu.* Bitte *f.* **2** Vorwand *m.* **3** *law* Einspruch *m.*

plead (pliːd) *vi law* plädieren, sich verteidigen. *vt* **1** vertreten. **2** verteidigen. **3** vorbringen, geltend machen. **plead guilty** sich schuldig bekennen.

please (pliːz) *vt* **1** gefallen, Freude machen. **2** befriedigen. *vi* gefallen, angenehm sein. *adv* bitte. **please yourself** tun Sie, was Sie wollen. **pleasant** *adj* **1** angenehm. **2** freundlich, liebenswürdig. **pleasure** *n* **1** Vergnügen *neu.* Freude *f.* **2** Genuß *m.*

pleat (pliːt) *n* Falte *f. vt* in Falten legen, plissieren.

plectrum ('plektrəm) *n* Plektron *neu.*
pledge (pledʒ) *n* **1** Pfand *neu.* Bürgschaft *f.* **2** Versprechen *neu.* Zusage *f.* **3** Trinkspruch, Toast *m. vt* **1** verpfänden, als Pfand geben. **2** versprechen. **3** verplichten.
plenty ('plenti) *n* Fülle *f.* Reichtum *m. adj* reichlich. **in plenty** reichlich, im Überfluß. **plenty of** viel, reichlich.
pliable ('plaiəbəl) *adj* **1** biegsam. **2** nachgiebig, fügsam.
pliers ('plaiəz) *n* (Kneif)Zange *f.*
plight (plait) *n* Notlage, Zwangslage *f.*
plimsoll ('plimsəl) *n* Turnschuh *m.*
plod (plɔd) *vi* **1** (mühsam) daherstampfen, sich hinschleppen. **2** sich abmühen, sich mühsam durcharbeiten.
plonk (plɔŋk) *vt* hinplumpsen.
plot[1] (plɔt) *n* **1** *lit* Handlung *f.* **2** Plan *m.* **3** Verschwörung *f. vi* sich verschwören. *vt* **1** (heimlich) planen. **2** entwerfen. **3** ersinnen. **4** graphisch darstellen, aufzeichnen.
plot[2] (plɔt) *n* Parzelle *f.* Grundstück *neu.*
plough (plau) *n* Pflug *m. vt* pflügen.
pluck (plʌk) *vt* **1** pflücken. **2** rupfen. **3** reißen, zerren. *vi* reißen, zerren. *n* **1** Ruck, Zug *m.* **2** Mut *m.* Beherztheit *f.*
plug (plʌg) *n* Stöpsel, Pfropf *m. vt* verstopfen.
plum (plʌm) *n bot* Pflaume *f.*
plumage ('plu:midʒ) *n* Gefieder *neu.*
plumb (plʌm) *n* Senkblei, Lot *neu. adj* senkrecht, lotrecht. *vt* **1** sondieren. **2** erforschen. *vi* klempnern. **plumber** *n* Klempner, Installateur *m.* **plumbing** *n* **1** Klempnerarbeit *f.* **2** Ausloten *neu.*
plume (plu:m) *n* **1** Feder *f.* **2** Federbusch *m. vt* mit Federn schmücken.
plump[1] (plʌmp) *adj* rundlich, dick.
plump[2] (plʌmp) *vi* plumpsen. **plump for** sich entscheiden für.
plunder ('plʌndə) *n* **1** Plünderung *f.* **2** Beute *f.*
plunge (plʌndʒ) *vt* **1** tauchen. **2** stürzen. *vi* **1** tauchen. **2** sich hineinstürzen. *n* **1** Tauchen *neu.* **2** Sturz *m.*
pluperfect (plu:'pə:fikt) *n* Plusquamperfekt *neu.*
plural ('pluərəl) *adj* mehrfach, Plural—. *n* Plural *m.* Mehrzahl *f.*
plus (plʌs) *prep* plus, und. *n* Plus, Mehr *neu. adj* **1** positiv, Plus—. **2** mehr, Extra—.
plush (plʌʃ) *n* Plüsch *m. adj* Plüsch—.
Pluto ('plu:tou) *n* Pluto *m.*
ply[1] (plai) *vt* **1** ausüben. **2** handhaben. *vi* regelmässig fahren, verkehren.
ply[2] (plai) *n* **1** Schicht *f.* **2** Strähne *f.* **3** Neigung *f.* **plywood** *n* Sperrholz *neu.*
pneumatic (nju:'mætik) *adj* pneumatisch, Luft—. **pneumatic drill** *n* Preßluftbohrer *m.*
pneumonia (nju:'mouniə) *n* Lungenentzündung, Pneumonie *f.*

poach¹ (poutʃ) *vi* **1** wildern, unerlaubt jagen. **2** widerrechtlich betreten.
poach² (poutʃ) *vt cul* pochieren. **poached egg** *n* pochiertes *or* verlorenes Ei.
pocket ('pɔkit) *n* Tasche *f*. *vt* in die Tasche stecken. **pocket-money** *n* Taschengeld *neu*.
pod (pɔd) *n* Schote, Schale *f*. *vt* ausschoten.
poem ('pouim) *n* Gedicht *neu*.
poet ('pouit) *n* Dichter *m*. **poetic** *adj* dichterisch, poetisch. **poetry** *n* **1** Dichtung, Poesie *f*. **2** Gedichte *neu pl*.
poignant ('pɔinjənt) *adj* **1** scharf. **2** pikant. **3** rührend, ergreifend.
point (pɔint) *n* **1** Punkt *m*. **2** Spitze *f*. **3** Frage, Sache *f*. **4** Zweck *m*. Absicht *f*. **5** Stufe *f*. Zeitpunkt *m*. **6** Stelle *f*. **be on the point of doing** eben tun wollen. **beside the point** nicht zur Sache gehörig. **point-blank** *adj, adv* **1** (schnur)gerade. **2** direkt, offen. **3** *mil* Kern—, Kernschuß—. ~*vt* **1** richten. **2** spitzen. **3** deuten auf. **point out** aufmerksam machen auf. **point to** hinweisen auf. **pointed** *adj* **1** spitz. **2** scharf, treffend.
poise (pɔiz) *n* **1** Gleichgewicht *neu*. **2** Haltung *f*. **3** Ruhe, Gelassenheit *f*. *vt* **1** balancieren. **2** im Gleichgewicht halten. *vi* schweben.
poison ('pɔizən) *n* Gift *neu*. *vt* vergiften. **poisonous** *adj* giftig.
poke (pouk) *n* Stoß, Puff *m*. *vi* stoßen, stochern, tasten. *vt* **1** stoßen, knuffen. **2** (a fire) schüren.
poker¹ ('poukə) *n* Feuerhaken *m*.
poker² ('poukə) *n* Poker(spiel) *neu*.
Poland ('poulənd) *n* Polen *neu*.
polar ('poulə) *adj* polar, Polar—. **polar bear** *n* Eisbär *m*. **polarize** *vt* polarisieren.
pole¹ (poul) *n* **1** Pfahl *m*. **2** Stange *f*. Pfosten *m*. Stock *m*. *vt* staken. **pole-vault** *n* Stabhochsprung *m*.
pole² (poul) *n* Pol *m*. **Pole Star** *n* Polarstern *m*.
Pole (poul) *n* Pole *m*.
polemic (pə'lemik) *adj* **1** polemisch. **2** streitsüchtig. *n* Polemik *f*.
police (pə'li:s) *n* Polizei *f*. *vt* **1** polizeilich bewachen. **2** schützen. **3** kontrollieren. **policeman** *n* Polizist, Schutzmann *m*. **police station** *n* Polizeiwache *f*.
policy¹ ('pɔlisi) *n* **1** Politik, politische Linie *f*. **2** Taktik, Methode *f*.
policy² ('pɔlisi) *n* (Versicherungs)Police *f*.
polish ('pɔliʃ) *vt* **1** polieren, glätten. **2** bohnern. **3** verfeinern. *vi* glatt werden, Glanz annehmen. *n* **1** Glanz *m*. Politur *f*. **2** Putzmittel *neu*.
Polish ('pouliʃ) *adj* polnisch *n* (language) Polnisch *neu*.
polite (pə'lait) *adj* **1** höflich, zuvorkommend. **2** fein, schön.
politics ('pɔlitiks) *n* Politik *f*. **political** *adj* politisch. **politician** *n* Politiker *m*.
polka ('pɔlkə) *n* Polka *f*.
poll (poul) *n* **1** Wahl, Abstim-

mung *f.* **2** Wählerliste *f.* **3** Umfrage. **4** Stimmabgabe *f.* **go to the polls** zur Wahl gehen. ~*vt* **1** (votes) erhalten. **2** stutzen, abschneiden. *vi* wählen, stimmen.

pollen ('pɔlən) *n* Blütenstaub, Pollen *m.*

pollute (pə'luːt) *vt* **1** verschmutzen, verunreinigen. **2** schänden, entweihen. **pollution** *n* (Umwelts)-Verschmutzung *f.*

polyester (pɔli'estə) *n* Polyester *m.*

polygamy (pə'ligəmi) *n* Polygamie *f.*

polygon ('pɔligən) *n* Vieleck *neu.*

polystyrene (pɔli'stairiːn) *n* Polystyrol, Styropor *m.*

polytechnic (pɔli'teknik) *adj* polytechnisch. *n* polytechnische Hochschule *f.*

polythene ('pɔliθiːn) *n* **1** *sci* Polyäthylen *neu.* **2** Plastik—.

polyunsaturated (pɔliːʌn'sætjəreitid) *adj* mehrfach ungesättigt.

pomegranate ('pɔmigrænət) *n* Granatapfel *m.*

pomp (pɔmp) *n* Pomp, Prunk *m.* Pracht *f.* **pompous** *adj* **1** pompös, prunkvoll. **2** hochtrabend, anmaßend.

pond (pɔnd) *n* Teich *m.*

ponder ('pɔndə) *vt* erwägen, nachdenken über. *vi* tief nachdenken, nachsinnen.

pony ('pouni) *n* Pony *neu.*

ponytail *n* Pferdeschwanz *m.*

poodle ('puːdl) *n* Pudel *m.*

pool[1] (puːl) *n* **1** Teich *m.* **2** Pfütze *f.*

pool[2] (puːl) *n* **1** Pool, Ring *m.* Interessengemeinschaft *f.* **2** gemeinsame Kasse *f.* *vt* zusammenlegen, vereinigen.

poor (puə, pɔː) *adj* **1** arm, bedürftig. **2** schlecht. **3** jämmerlich.

pop[1] (pɔp) *n* **1** Knall, Puff *m.* **2** *inf* Sprudel *m.* Limonade *f.* *vt* knallen lassen. *vi* puffen, knallen. **pop up** plötzlich auftauchen *or* erscheinen. *interj* paff! **popcorn** *n* Popcorn *neu.* Puffmais *m.*

pop[2] (pɔp) *adj inf* populär, beliebt. **pop music** *n* Popmusik *f.* **pop song** *n* Schlager *m.*

pope (poup) *n* Papst *m.*

poplar ('pɔplə) *n* Pappel *f.*

poppy ('pɔpi) *n* Mohn *m.* Mohnpflanze *f.*

popular ('pɔpjulə) *adj* **1** populär. **2** beliebt. **3** volkstümlich.

population (pɔpju'leiʃən) *n* Bevölkerung *f.*

porcelain ('pɔːslin) *adj* Porzellan—. *n* Porzellan *neu.*

porch (pɔːtʃ) *n* **1** Portal *neu.* **2** Vorhalle *f.* **3** Veranda *f.*

porcupine ('pɔːkjupain) *n* Stachelschwein *neu.*

pore[1] (pɔː) *n anat* Pore *f.*

pore[2] (pɔː) *vi* **pore over** eifrig studieren, aufmerksam untersuchen.

pork (pɔːk) *n* Schweinefleisch *neu.*

pornography (pɔː'nɔgrəfi) *n* Pornographie *f.* **pornographic** *adj* pornographisch.

porous ('pɔːrəs) *adj* porös, durchlässig.

porpoise ('pɔːpəs) *n* Tümmler *m.*

porridge ('pɔridʒ) *n* Hafer(flocken)brei *m*.
port[1] (pɔːt) *n* Hafen *m*.
port[2] (pɔːt) *adj* Backbord—. *n* Backbord *neu*.
port[3] (pɔːt) *n* Portwein *m*.
port[4] (pɔːt) *n* Tor *neu*. Pforte *f*.
portable ('pɔːtəbəl) *adj* tragbar, portabel.
portent ('pɔːtent) *n* **1** Vorbedeutung *f*. übles Vorzeichen *neu*. **2** Wunder *neu*.
porter[1] ('pɔːtə) *n* Gepäcktrager *m*.
porter[2] ('pɔːtə) *n* Pförtner, Portier *m*.
portfolio (pɔːt'fouliou) *n* **1** (Brief)Mappe *f*. **2** Geschäftsbereich (eines Ministers) *m*.
porthole ('pɔːthoul) *n* Pfortluke *f*.
portion ('pɔːʃən) *n* **1** Portion *f*. **2** Anteil *m*. *vt* einteilen, zuteilen.
portrait ('pɔːtrit) *n* Porträt, Bildnis *neu*.
portray (pɔː'trei) *vt* **1** porträtieren, abmalen. **2** beschreiben, schildern.
Portugal ('pɔːtjugəl) *n* Portugal *neu*. **Portuguese** *adj* portugiesisch. *n* **1** Portugiese *m*. **2** (language) Portugiesisch *neu*.
pose (pouz) *n* Stellung, Pose *f*. *vi* posieren. *vt* **1** (questions) stellen. **2** aufstellen. **pose as** auftreten als.
posh (pɔʃ) *adj inf* elegant, schick, prima.
position (pə'ziʃən) *n* **1** Position, Stellung *f*. **2** Rang *m*. **3** Standpunkt *m*. Einstellung *f*. **4** Lage *f*. *vt* (richtig hin)stellen.
positive ('pɔzitiv) *adj* **1** positiv. **2** genau, exakt. **3** konstruktiv. **4** definitiv, eindeutig. *n* **1** Positivum *neu*. **2** *phot* Positiv *neu*.
possess (pə'zes) *vt* **1** besitzen, haben. **2** in Besitz nehmen. **3** beherrschen. **possession** *n* **1** Besitz *m*. **2** *pl* Habe *f*. Reichtum *m*. **be in possession of** besitzen. **possessive** *adj* **1** besitzgierig. **2** anhänglich. **3** *gram* Possessiv.
possible ('pɔsəbəl) *adj* **1** möglich. **2** eventuell.
post[1] (poust) *n* Pfosten, Pfahl *m*. *vt* ankleben, anschlagen.
post[2] (poust) *n* **1** Stellung *f*. **2** Posten *m*. *vt* postieren, aufstellen.
post[3] (poust) *n* **1** Post *f*. **2** Postamt *neu*. *vt* (per Post) schicken. **postage** *n* Porto *neu*. Postgebühr *f*. **postal order** *n* Postanweisung *f*. **postbox** *n* Briefkasten *m*. **postcard** *n* Postkarte *f*. **postcode** *n* Postleitzahl *f*. **postman** *n* Briefträger *m*. **postmark** *n* Poststempel *f*. *vt* abstempeln. **post office** *n* Postamt *neu*.
poster ('poustə) *n* Plakat *neu*.
posterior (pɔs'tiəriə) *adj* **1** später. **2** folgend, hinter. *n* Hinterteil *neu*.
posterity (pɔs'teriti) *n* **1** Nachkommenschaft *f*. **2** Nachwelt *f*.
postgraduate (poust'grædjuət) *n* Doktorand *m*. *adj* **1** vorgeschritten. **2** Forschungs—.
posthumous ('pɔstjuməs) *adj* **1** posthum. **2** nachträglich.
post-mortem (poust'mɔːtəm) *adj* nach dem Tode. **post mortem (examination)** *n* Autopsie *f*.

postpone (pəs'poun) *vt* **1** verschieben. **2** unterordnen.
postscript ('pouskript) *n* Postskriptum *neu.* Nachschrift *f.* Nachtrag *m.*
postulate (*v* 'pɔstjuleit; *n* 'pɔstjulət) *vt* **1** postulieren. **2** fordern, verlangen. *n* **1** Postulat *neu.* **2** Forderung *f.*
posture ('pɔstʃə) *n* **1** Stellung, Haltung *f.* **2** Lage *f.*
pot (pɔt) *n* **1** Topf *m.* **2** Krug *m.* *vt* **1** in einen Topf tun. **2** einmachen.
potassium (pə'tæsiəm) *n* **1** Pottasche *f.* **2** Kalium *neu.*
potato (pə'teitou) *n* Kartoffel *f.*
potent ('poutn̩t) *adj* **1** stark, kräftig. **2** potent.
potential (pə'tenʃəl) *adj* möglich, potentiell. *n* Potential *neu.*
pothole ('pɔthoul) *n* Schlagloch *neu.*
potion ('pouʃən) *n* Trank *m.*
potter ('pɔtə) *n* Töpfer *m.*
pottery ('pɔtəri) *n* **1** Töpferwaren *f pl.* **2** Töpferei *f.*
pouch (pautʃ) *n* Tasche *f.* Beutel *m.* *(vi),vt* (sich) bauschen.
poultice ('poultis) *n* Umschlag *m.* Packung *f.*
poultry ('poultri) *n* Geflügel *neu.*
pounce (pauns) *vi* sich stürzen, herabstoßen. *n* Sprung, Satz *m.*
pound[1] (paund) *vt* **1** zerstoßen, zerstampfen. **2** schlagen, stoßen. *vi* schlagen, hämmern.
pound[2] (paund) *n* Pfund *neu.*
pour (pɔː) *vt* gießen, schütten. *vi* **1** fließen, strömen. **2** stark regnen. *n* **1** Guß *m.* **2** (Regen)Guß *m.*
pout (paut) *vi* **1** die Lippen spitzen. **2** schmollen. *n* Schmollen *neu.*
poverty ('pɔvəti) *n* **1** Armut *f.* **2** Elend *neu.* Not *f.* **poverty-stricken** *adj* verarmt, bedürftig.
powder ('paudə) *n* Pulver *neu.* Puder *m.* *vt* **1** (ein)pudern, bestreuen. **2** pulverisieren. *vi* zu Pulver werden. **powder room** *n* Damentoilette *f.*
power ('pauə) *n* **1** Kraft, Stärke *f.* **2** Macht, Autorität *f.* **3** Gewalt *f.* **4** *math* Potenz *f.* **5** Energie. *vt* antreiben. **powerful** *adj* mächtig, stark, kräftig.
practicable ('præktikəbəl) *adj* ausführbar, möglich.
practical ('præktikəl) *adj* praktisch.
practice ('præktis) *n* **1** Praxis *f.* **2** Brauch *m.* Gewohnheit *f.* **3** Übung *f.* **4** Verfahren *neu.*
practise ('præktis) *vt* **1** ausüben, betreiben. **2** üben. *vi* **1** üben. **2** praktisch tätig sein. **3** *sport* trainieren.
practitioner (præk'tiʃənə) *n* **1** *med* praktischer Arzt *m.* **2** *law* Rechtsanwalt *m.* **3** Praktiker *m.*
pragmatic (præg'mætik) *adj* pragmatisch.
Prague (prɑːg) *n* Prag *neu.*
prairie ('prɛəri) *n* Prärie, Steppe *f.*
praise (preiz) *vt* preisen, loben. *n* Lob *neu.* Preis *m.* Anerkennung *f.* **praiseworthy** *adj* lobenswert.
pram (præm) *n* Kinderwagen *m.*
prance (prɑːns) *vi* **1** sich

bäumen. **2** umherspringen. **3** einherstolzieren.

prank (præŋk) *n* Streich, Ulk *m.*

prattle ('prætl) *vi* schwazen, plappern. *n* Geschwätz, Geplapper *neu.*

prawn (prɔːn) *n* Garnele *f.*

pray (prei) *vi* beten. *vt* bitten, anflehen. **prayer** *n* Gebet *neu.* **prayerbook** *n* Gebetbuch *neu.*

preach (priːtʃ) *vi,vt* predigen.

precarious (pri'kɛəriəs) *adj* **1** prekär, unsicher, riskant. **2** *law* widerruflich.

precaution (pri'kɔːʃən) *n* Vorsichtsmaßnahme *f.* **take precautions** Vorsichtsmaßnahmen treffen.

precede (pri'siːd) *vi,vt* vorausgehen, vorangehen. **precedence** *n* Vorrang *m.* Priorität *f.* **precedent** *n* Präzedenzfall *m.*

precinct ('priːsiŋkt) *n* **1** Bezirk *m.* **2** *pl* Umgebung *f.*

precious ('preʃəs) *adj* kostbar, vertvoll. *adv inf* recht, sehr.

precipice ('presipis) *n* Abgrund *m.*

precipitate (prə'sipiteit) *vt* **1** hinabstürzen. **2** überstürzen, übereilen. *vi* **1** sich übereilen. **2** sich niederschlagen. *adj* voreilig, überstürzt. **precipitation** *n* **1** Niederschlag *m.* **2** Überstürzung *f.*

precis ('preisi) *n* Zusammenfassung *f.* *vt* zusammenfassen.

precise (pri'sais) *adj* **1** präzis, genau. **2** korrekt. **precision** *n* Präzision *f.*

preclude (pri'kluːd) *vt* **1** ausschließen. **2** (ver)hindern.

precocious (pri'kouʃəs) *adj* frühreif, altklug.

preconceive (priːkən'siːv) *vt* sich vorher vorstellen, vorher ausdenken. **preconception** *n* Vorurteil *m.* vorgefaßte Meinung *f.*

predatory ('predətəri) *adj* räuberisch, Raub—.

predecessor ('priːdisesə) *n* Vorgänger *m.*

predestine (priː'destin) *vt* vorherbestimmen, vorher festlegen. **predestination** *n* Prädestination, Vorherbestimmung *f.*

predicament (pri'dikəmənt) *n* heikle *or* mißliche Lage *f.*

predicate (*n* 'predikit; *v* 'predikeit) *n* Prädikat *neu.* *vt* **1** aussagen, feststellen. **2** begründen.

predict (pri'dikt) *vt* vorhersagen, prophezeien.

predominate (pri'dɔmineit) *vi* **1** vorherrschen. **2** überlegen sein.

pre-eminent *adj* hervorragend.

preen (priːn) *vt* (of a bird) putzen.

prefabricate (pri'fæbrikeit) *vt* vorfabrizieren.

preface ('prefis) *n* Vorrede, Einleitung *f.* *vt* einleiten.

prefect ('priːfekt) *n* **1** *pol* Präfekt *m.* **2** *educ* Aufsichtsschüler *m.*

prefer (pri'fəː) *vt* **1** vorziehen, lieber tun *or* haben. **2** einreichen. **3** begünstigen. **preference** *n* **1** Bevorzugung *f.* **2** Vorliebe *f.* **3** Vortritt, Vorrecht *neu.*

prefix ('priːfiks) *n* Präfix *neu.* Vorsilbe *f.*

pregnant ('pregnənt) *adj* **1** schwanger. **2** wichtig, gehaltvoll, bedeutsam. **pregnancy** *n* Schwangerschaft *f.*
prehistoric (pri:his'tɔrik) *adj* vorgeschichtlich, urgeschichtlich, prähistorisch.
prejudice ('predʒədis) *n* **1** Vorurteil *neu.* **2** Beeinträchtigung *f.* Schaden *m.* *vt* ungünstig beeinflussen, beeinträchtigen. **prejudiced** *adj* voreingenommen.
preliminary (pri'liminəri) *adj* vorbereitend, einleitend, vorläufig.
prelude ('prelju:d) *n* **1** Einleitung *f.* **2** *mus* Vorspiel *neu.*
premarital (pri:'mæritl) *adj* voreheIich.
premature ('premətʃə) *adj* **1** frühreif. **2** vorzeitig, frühzeitig.
premeditate (pri:'mediteit) *vt* vorher überlegen. **premeditation** *n* Vorbedacht *m.*
premier ('premiə) *n* Premierminister *m.* *adj* **1** erst. **2** frühest.
premiere ('premiεə) *n* Erstaufführung, Premiere *f.*
premise ('premis) *n* **1** Prämisse, Voraussetzung *f.* **2** *pl* Grundstück *neu.* **3** *pl* Haus *neu.*
premium ('pri:miəm) *n* Prämie *f.*
preoccupied (pri:'ɔkjupaid) *adj* vertieft, in Gedanken versunken.
prepare (pri'pεə) *vt* **1** vorbereiten. **2** zubereiten. **3** präparieren. *vi* **1** Vorbereitungen treffen, sich vorbereiten. **2** *mil* sich rüsten. **preparation** *n* **1** Vorbereitung *f.* **2** *pl* Vorkehrungsmaßnahmen *f pl.* **preparatory** *adj* vorbereitend, Vorbereitungs—.
preposition (prepə'ziʃən) *n* Präposition *f.* Verhältniswort *neu.*
preposterous (pri'pɔstərəs) *adj* unnatürlich, unsinnig, grotesk, lächerlich.
prerogative (pri'rɔgətiv) *n* Vorrecht, Privileg *neu.* Prärogative *f.* *adj* bevorrechtet.
prescribe (pri'skraib) *vt* **1** vorschreiben. **2** *med* verordnen. *vi* Vorschriften machen, Anweisungen geben. **prescription** *n* **1** Vorschrift, Verordnung *f.* **2** *med* Rezept *neu.*
presence ('prezəns) *n* **1** Gegenwart *f.* **2** Anwesenheit. **3** Aussehen, Äußere *neu.*
present[1] ('prezənt) *adj* **1** gegenwärtig. **2** anwesend. **3** vorhanden. **4** augenblicklich. **present participle** *n* Partizip des Präsens *neu.* ~*n* Gegenwart *f.* **at present** im Augenblick. **presently** *adv* **1** bald. **2** kurz darauf.
present[2] (*v* pri'zent; *n* 'prezənt) *vt* **1** vorstellen. **2** schenken, überreichen. **3** darbieten, vorführen. *n* Geschenk *neu.*
preserve (pri'zə:v) *vt* **1** bewahren, schützen. **2** *cul* einmachen, konservieren. **3** beibehalten, aufrechterhalten. *n* Konserve *f.*
preside (pri'zaid) *vi* präsidieren, den Vorsitz führen.
president ('prezidənt) *n* **1** Präsident *m.* **2** Vorsitzende(r) *m.*

press (pres) *vt* **1** drücken, pressen. **2** bügeln. *vi* **1** Druck ausüben, drücken. **2** dringend bitten. **3** drängen. *n* **1** Druck *m*. **2** Presse *f*. **3** Gedränge *neu*. **press conference** *n* Pressekonferenz *f*. **press-gang** *n* Anwerbetrupp *m*. **press-stud** *n* Druckknopf *m*. **press-up** *n sport* Liegestütz *m*.

pressure ('preʃə) *n* **1** Druck *m*. Druckkraft *f*. **2** Dringlichkeit *f*. **3** Druck, Zwang *m*. **pressure cooker** *n* Schnellkochtopf *m*. **pressurize** *vt* **1** unter Druck setzen. **2** Druck ausüben auf, zwingen.

prestige (pres'tiːʒ) *n* Prestige, Ansehen *neu*.

presume (pri'zjuːm) *vt* vermuten, annehmen. *vi* **1** vermuten. **2** wagen, sich erlauben. **3** mißbrauchen. **presumption** *n* **1** Vermutung *f*. **2** Anmaßung *f*. **presumptuous** *adj* anmaßend.

pretend (pri'tend) *vt* vorgeben, vorspiegeln. *vi* vorgeben. **pretend to** **1** tun, als ob. **2** Anspruch machen auf. **pretence** *n* Vorwand *m*. **pretension** *n* Anspruch *m*. **pretentious** *adj* anspruchsvoll, angeberisch.

pretext ('priːtekst) *n* Vorwand *m*. Ausrede *f*.

pretty ('priti) *adj* hübsch, schön. *adv inf* ziemlich.

prevail (pri'veil) *vi* **1** die Oberhand gewinnen, sich durchsetzen. **2** vorherrschen. **prevalent** *adj* **1** vorherrschend. **2** überlegen.

prevent (pri'vent) *vt* abhalten, zurückhalten, verhindern, verhüten. **prevention** *n* Verhinderung *f*.

preview ('priːvjuː) *n* (private) Vorschau, Vorbesichtigung *f*. *vt* vorher sehen.

previous ('priːviəs) *adj* vorhergehend, früher. **previously** *adv* vorher, früher.

prey (prei) *n* Raub *m*. Beute *f*. **bird of prey** Raubvogel *m*. *v* **prey on** Jagd machen auf.

price (prais) *n* **1** Preis *m*. **2** Wert *m*. *vt* **1** bewerten. **2** den Preis festsetzen von. **price-list** *n* Preisliste *f*.

prick (prik) *n* **1** Dorn *m*. **2** Stich *m*. *vt* stechen. *vi* stechen, prickeln. **prickle** *n* Stachel, Dorn *m*. *vt* stechen, prickeln.

pride (praid) *n* **1** Stolz *m*. **2** Hochmut *m*. *v* **pride oneself on** stolz sein auf.

priest (priːst) *n* Priester, Geistliche(r) *m*. **priesthood** *n* Priesteramt *neu*.

prim (prim) *adj* gekünstelt, (über)korrekt, steif.

primary ('praiməri) *adj* **1** erst, ursprünglich, Grund—. **2** hauptsächlich, Haupt—. **3** elementar. **primary school** *n* Grundschule, Volksschule, Elementarschule *f*.

primate *n* **1** ('praimit) Erzbischof *m*. **2** ('praimeit) *zool* Primat *m*.

prime (praim) *adj* **1** erst, Haupt—, Ober—. **2** höchst. *n* Vollkommenheit, Blüte *f*. *vt* vorbereiten, fertigmachen. **prime minister** *n* Ministerpräsident, Premierminister *m*.

primitive ('primitiv) *adj* **1** ursprünglich, Ur—. **2** primitiv.

primrose ('primrouz) *n* Primel, Schlüsselblume *f.* *adj* blaßgelb.

prince (prins) *n* Fürst, Prinz *m.* **princess** *n* Fürstin, Prinzessin *f.*

principal ('prinsəpəl) *adj* **1** hauptsächlich, Haupt—. **2** wichtigst. *n* Chef, Vorsitzende(r) *m.* **principality** *n* Fürstentum *neu.*

principle ('prinsəpəl) *n* Prinzip *neu.* Grundsatz *m.* **in/on principle** im/aus Prinzip.

print (print) *vt* **1** drucken. **2** stempeln. **3** herausgeben, veröffentlichen. *n* **1** Druck *m.* **2** Abzug *m.* **3** Spur *f.* **printout** ('printaut) *n* Ausdruck *m.*

prior ('praiə) *adj* eher, früher, vorausgehend. *n* Prior *m.* **priority** *n* Priorität *f.* Vorrang *m.*

prise (praiz) *vt* **prise open** aufbrechen.

prism ('prizəm) *n* Prisma *neu.*

prison ('prizən) *n* Gefängnis *neu.* **prisoner** *n* Gefangene(r) *m.*

private ('praivit) *adj* **1** privat. **2** persönlich. **3** nicht öffentlich, Privat—. **4** heimlich. *n* gemeiner Soldat *m.* **in private** im Vertrauen, unter vier Augen. **private eye** *n* Privatdedektiv *m.* **privacy** *n* **1** Geheimhaltung *f.* **2** Ruhe, Ungestörheit *f.* **3** Privatleben *neu.* **privatize** *vt* privatisieren.

privet ('privit) *n* Liguster *m.* Rainweide *f.*

privilege ('privilidʒ) *n* Privileg, Vorrecht *neu.* *vt* privilegieren, bevorrechten.

privy ('privi) *adj* **1** eingeweiht, mitwissend. **2** Privat—, Geheim—.

prize[1] (praiz) *n* Preis *m.*

prize[2] (praiz) *vt* hoch einschätzen.

probable ('prɔbəbəl) *adj* wahrscheinlich.

probation (prə'beiʃən) *n* **1** Prüfung *f.* **2** Probezeit *f.* **3** *law* Bewährungsfrist *f.* **on probation** **1** auf Probe. **2** *law* auf Bewährung. **probation officer** *n* Bewährungshelfer *m.*

probe (proub) *n* **1** *med* Sonde *f.* **2** Untersuchung *f.* *vt* **1** sondieren. **2** untersuchen.

problem ('prɔbləm) *n* **1** Problem *neu.* **2** Schwierigkeit *f.* **3** *math* Aufgabe *f.* *adj* Problem—, problematisch. **problematic** *adj* problematisch.

proceed (prə'siːd) *vi* **1** vorwärtsgehen. **2** weitermachen, fortfahren. **3** übergehen. **4** handeln, verfahren. **procedure** *n* **1** Verfahren, Vorgehen *neu.* **2** Prozedur *f.*

process ('prouses) *n* **1** Vorgang *m.* **2** Verfahren *neu.* Prozeß *m.* **in process** im Gang. ~*vt* **1** behandeln, verarbeiten. **2** *law* prozessieren, gerichtlich belangen.

procession (prə'seʃən) *n* Prozession *f.* Umzug, (Fest) Zug *m.*

proclaim (prə'kleim) *vt* proklamieren, verkünden.

procreate ('proukrieit) *vt* **1** erzeugen. **2** hervorbringen.

procure (prə'kjuə) *vt* **1** verschaffen, anschaffen, besorgen. **2** zustandebringen, bewirken. *vi* Kuppelei betreiben. **procurer** *n* Kuppler *m.*

prod (prɔd) *n* **1** Stich *m.* **2** Stoß *m. vt* **1** stechen. **2** stoßen.

prodigal ('prɔdigəl) *adj* verschwenderisch.

prodigy ('prɔdidʒi) *n* Wunder *neu.* **child prodigy** Wunderkind *neu.*

produce (*v* prə'djuːs; *n* 'prɔdjuːs) *vt* **1** herstellen, erzeugen, produzieren. **2** vorzeigen. **3** veranlassen, bewirken. *n* Ertrag *m.* Frucht *f.* Produkt *neu.* **product** *n* **1** Erzeugnis, Produkt *neu.* **2** Ergebnis *neu.* **3** *math* Resultat *neu.* **production** *n* Erzeugung, Produktion *f.*

profane (prə'fein) *vt* entweihen, profanieren. *adj* **1** weltlich, profan. **2** gottlos.

profess (prə'fes) *vt* **1** gestehen, bekennen. **2** erklären. *vi* ein Bekenntnis ablegen. **profession** *n* **1** Beruf *m.* **2** Bekenntnis *neu.*

professor (prə'fesə) *n* Professor *m.*

proficient (prə'fiʃənt) *adj* **1** geübt, erfahren. **2** tüchtig.

profile ('proufail) *n* Profil *neu.* Querschnitt *m.*

profit ('prɔfit) *n* Gewinn, Profit *m. vi* profitieren, Nutzen ziehen.

profound (prə'faund) *adj* **1** (tief)liegend. **2** tiefsinnig, gründlich, profund.

profuse (prə'fjuːs) *adj* **1** überreichlich. **2** verschwenderisch.

programme ('prougræm) *n* **1** Programm *neu.* **2** Sendung *f.* **program** (computers) *n* Programm *neu. vt* programmieren.

progress (*n* 'prougres; *v* prə'gres) *n* Fortgang, Fortschritt *m. vi* fortschreiten, Fortschritte machen. **progression** *n* **1** Fortschreiten *neu.* Fortschritt *m.* **2** Progression *f.* **progressive** *adj* **1** fortschreitend. **2** fortschrittlich.

prohibit (prə'hibit) *vt* verbieten, verhindern.

project (*n* 'prɔdʒekt; *v* prə'dʒekt) *n* Projekt *neu.* Plan *m. vt* **1** schleudern. **2** werfen. **3** projizieren. **4** entwerfen. **projectile** *n* Projektil, (Wurf)Geschoß *neu.* **projection** *n* **1** Wurf *m.* **2** Entwurf, Plan *m.* **3** Projektion *f.* **projector** *n* Projektionsapparat *m.*

proletariat (prouli'tɛəriət) *n* Proletariat *neu.*

proliferate (prə'lifəreit) *vi* **1** sprossen. **2** *med* wuchern.

prolific (prə'lifik) *adj* **1** fruchtbar. **2** reich.

prologue ('proulɔg) *n* Prolog *m.* Einleitung *f.*

prolong (prə'lɔŋ) *vt* verlängern.

promenade (prɔmə'nɑːd) *n* **1** Promenade *f.* **2** Spaziergang *m. vi* spazierengehen.

prominent ('prɔminənt) *adj* **1** hervorragend. **2** berühmt, prominent.

promiscuous (prə'miskjuəs) *adj* **1** unterschiedslos. **2** gemeinsam. **3** vermischt.

promise ('prɔmis) *n* Versprechen *neu.* Zusage *f. vt* versprechen, zusagen.

promote (prə'mout) *vt* **1** begünstigen, fördern. **2** erheben, befördern. **3** anpreisen. **promotion** *n* **1**

Förderung *f.* **2** Beförderung *f.* **3** Werbung *f.*
prompt (prɔmpt) *adj* schnell, rasch, prompt. *vt* anspornen, veranlassen.
prone (proun) *adj* **1** geneigt, neigend. **2** auf dem Gesicht liegend.
prong (prɔŋ) *n* Zinke, Spitze *f.*
pronoun ('prounaun) *n gram* Pronomen, Fürwort *neu.*
pronounce (prə'nauns) *vt* **1** aussprechen. **2** verkünden. *vi* sich aussprechen. **pronunciation** *n* Aussprache *f.*
proof (pruːf) *n* **1** Beweis, Nachweis *m.* **2** Abzug *m.* **3** Probe *f. adj* fest, sicher, undurchdringlich. *vt* imprägnieren. **proofread** *vt* korrigieren.
prop[1] (prɔp) *n* Stütze, Strebe *f. vt* stützen.
prop[2] (prɔp) *n Th* (Bühnen)Requisit *neu.*
propaganda (prɔpə'gændə) *n* Propaganda *f.*
propagate ('prɔpəgeit) *vt* **1** fortpflanzen, übertragen. **2** ausbreiten.
propel (prə'pel) *vt* vorwärtstreiben. **propeller** *n* Propeller *m.*
proper ('prɔpə) *adj* **1** passend, angebracht. **2** eigen(tlich). **3** richtig, korrekt. **4** ordnungsgemäß. **proper noun** *n* Eigenname *m.*
property ('prɔpəti) *n* **1** Eigentum *neu.* Besitz *m.* **2** Eigenschaft, Eigentümlichkeit *f.* **3** Grundbesitz *m.* Immobilien *pl.*
prophecy ('prɔfisi) *n* Prophezeiung, Weissagung *f.* **prophesy** *vt* prophezeien, weissagen.
prophet ('prɔfit) *n* Prophet *m.*
proportion (prə'pɔːʃən) *n* **1** Proportion *f.* Verhältnis *neu.* **2** Maß *neu.* **3** *pl* Ausmaß *neu.*
propose (prə'pouz) *vt* **1** vorschlagen. **2** (a toast) ausbringen. *vi* **1** beabsichtigen. **2** einen Heiratsantrag machen.
proposal *n* **1** Vorschlag *m.* **2** (Heirats)Antrag *m.* **proposition** *n* **1** Vorschlag, Antrag *m.* **2** Behauptung *f.*
proprietor (prə'praiətə) *n* Besitzer, Eigentümer *m.*
propriety (prə'praiəti) *n* Anstand *m.* Angemessenheit *f.*
propulsion (prə'pʌlʃən) *n* Antrieb *m.*
prose (prouz) *n* Prosa *f. adj* Prosa—, prosaisch. **prosaic** *adj* prosaisch, alltäglich.
prosecute ('prɔsikjuːt) *vt* **1** *law* strafrechtlich verfolgen. **2** verfolgen. **3** betreiben. *vi law* Klage erheben.
prospect ('prɔspekt) *n* **1** Aussicht *f.* **2** Erwartung, Voraussicht *f.* **prospective** *adj* voraussichtlich, künftig. **prospectus** *n* Prospekt *m.*
prosper ('prɔspə) *vi* gedeihen. *vt* begünstigen. **prosperity** *n* Wohlstand *m.* **prosperous** *adj* **1** erfolgreich, gedeihend. **2** wohlhabend.
prostitute ('prɔstitjuːt) *n* Prostituierte, Dirne *f. vt* **1** prostituieren. **2** entehren. **prostitution** *n* Prostitution *f.*
prostrate (*v* prɔs'treit; *adj* 'prɔstreit) *vt* **1** niederwerfen. **2** entkräften. **3** demütigen. *adj* **1** auf der Erde hingestreckt. **2** unterwürfig. **3** kraftlos.
protagonist (prə'tægənist) *n lit*

Held *m.* Hauptperson *f.* Verfechter *m.*
protect (prə'tekt) *vt* (be)schützen, bewahren. **protection** *n* Schutz *m.* Beschützung *f.*
protégé ('prɔtiʒei) *n* Schützling *m.*
protein ('prouti:n) *n* Protein, Eiweiß *neu.*
protest (*n* 'proutest; *v* prə'test) *n* Protest, Einspruch *m.* *vt* **1** beteuern. **2** protestieren gegen. *vi* protestieren, Einspruch erheben.
Protestant ('prɔtistənt) *adj* protestantisch. *n* Protestant *m.*
protocol ('proutəkɔl) *n* Protokoll *neu.*
prototype ('proutətaip) *n* Prototyp, Urtyp *m.*
protractor (prə'træktə) *n* Winkelmesser *m.*
protrude (prə'tru:d) *vi* (her)vorragen, (her)vorstehen. *vt* (her)vortreten lassen.
proud (praud) *adj* **1** stolz. **2** hochmütig. **3** stattlich, prächtig.
prove (pru:v) *vt* **1** beweisen, erweisen. **2** bestätigen. *vi* sich herausstellen. **proven** *adj* **1** bewiesen. **2** bewährt.
proverb ('prɔvə:b) *n* Sprichwort *neu.*
provide (prə'vaid) *vt* **1** beschaffen, versorgen. **2** bereitstellen. *vi* Vorkehrungen treffen. **provision** *n* **1** Vorsorge, Vorkehrung *f.* **2** Bestimmung *f.* **3** *pl* Proviant *m.* *vt* mit Proviant versorgen. **provisional** *adj* provisorisch.
province ('prɔvins) *n* **1** Provinz *f.* **2** (Arbeits)Gebiet *neu.* **provincial** *adj* **1** provinziell. **2** engstirnig, beschränkt. *n* Provinzbewohner *m.*
proviso (prə'vaizou) *n law* Klausel *f.* Vorbehalt *m.*
provoke (prə'vouk) *vt* **1** provozieren, reizen. **2** hervorrufen. **3** veranlassen. **provocation** *n* **1** Provokation *f.* **2** Aufreizung *f.* **3** Anlaß *m.* **provocative** *adj* provozierend.
prow (prau) *n naut* Bug *m.*
prowess ('prauis) *n* **1** Geschicklichkeit *f.* Können *neu.* **2** Tapferkeit *f.*
prowl (praul) *vt* durchstreifen. *vi* umherstreifen. *n* Umherstreifen *neu.* **be on the prowl** umherstreifen.
proximity (prɔk'simiti) *n* Nähe *f.*
proxy ('prɔksi) *n* **1** Vollmacht *f.* **2** Bevollmächtigte(r) *m.* **3** (Stell)Vertreter *m.*
prude (pru:d) *n* Spröde, Prüde *f.* **prudish** *adj* prüde, zimperlich.
prudent ('pru:dnt) *adj* **1** klug, weis. **2** vorsichtig. **3** sparsam.
prune[1] (pru:n) *n* (Dörr)-Pflaume *f.*
prune[2] (pru:n) *vt* beschneiden, (zu)stutzen.
Prussia ('prʌʃə) *n* Preußen *neu.* **Prussian** *adj* preußisch. *n* Preuße *m.*
pry (prai) *vi* neugierig schauen, spähen. **pry into** seine Nase stecken in.
psalm (sa:m) *n* Psalm *m.*
pseudonym ('sju:dənim) *n* Pseudonym *neu.*
psychedelic (saiki'delik) *adj* psychedelisch.

psychiatry (sai'kaiətri) *n* Psychiatrie *f*. **psychiatric** *adj* psychiatrisch. **psychiatrist** *n* Psychiater *m*.
psychic ('saikik) *adj* **1** psychisch, seelisch. **2** übersinnlich.
psychoanalysis (saikouə'nælisis) *n* Psychoanalyse *f*. **psychoanalyst** *n* Psychoanalytiker *m*.
psychology (sai'kɔlədʒi) *n* Psychologie *f*. **psychological** *adj* psychologisch. **psychologist** *n* Psychologe *m*.
psychopathic (saikə'pæθik) *adj med* psychopathisch.
psychosomatic (saikousə'mætik) *adj* psychosomatisch.
pub (pʌb) *n inf* Kneipe *f*. Lokal, Wirtshaus *neu*.
puberty ('pjuːbəti) *n* Pubertät *f*.
public ('pʌblik) *adj* **1** öffentlich, allgemein. **2** national, Volks—. **3** bekannt. *n* **1** Publikum *neu*. **2** Öffentlichkeit *f*. **in public** öffentlich. **public house** *n* Wirtshaus *neu*. Gaststätte *f*. **public relations** *n* öffentliche Meinungspflege *f*. Public Relations *pl*. **public school** *n* Internat *neu*. Privatschule *f*.
publication (pʌbli'keiʃən) *n* **1** Veröffentlichung *f*. **2** Publikation, Druckschrift *f*.
publicity (pʌb'lisiti) *n* **1** Öffentlichkeit, Publizität *f*. **2** Reklame *f*.
publicize ('pʌblisaiz) *vt* bekanntmachen, publizieren.
publish ('pʌbliʃ) *vt* **1** herausgeben, verlegen, veröffentlichen. **2** bekanntmachen.
pucker ('pʌkə) *(vi),vt* (sich) falten, (sich) runzeln. *n* Falte, Runzel *f*.
pudding ('pudiŋ) *n* Pudding *m*. Süßspeise *f*. **black pudding** Blutwurst *f*.
puddle ('pʌdl̩) *n* Pfütze, Lache *f*.
puff (pʌf) *n* **1** Windstoß *m*. **2** Hauch *m*. **3** Zug *m*. Paffen *neu*. *vi* **1** puffen, blasen. **2** schnaufen, keuchen. **puff up** *or* **out** aufblasen, schwellen. **puff pastry** *n* Blätterteig *m*.
pull (pul) *vt* **1** ziehen. **2** zerren. **3** schleppen. *vi* ziehen, zerren. **pull down** niederreißen, abreißen. **pull oneself together** sich zusammenreißen. **pull through** *inf* durchkommen. ~*n* **1** Zug, Ruck *m*. **2** Anziehungskraft *f*. **pullover** *n* Pullover *m*.
pulley ('puli) *n* (Riemen) Scheibe, Rolle *f*.
pulp (pʌlp) *n* **1** Brei *m*. **2** Fruchtfleisch *neu*. **3** Pulpe *f*. Papierbrei *m*. *vt* in Brei verwandeln.
pulpit ('pʌlpit) *n* Kanzel *f*. Katheder *neu*.
pulsate (pʌl'seit) *vi* pulsieren, pochen.
pulse (pʌls) *n* Puls(schlag) *m*.
pulverize ('pʌlvəraiz) *vt* pulverisieren, zermahlen. *vi* zu Staub zerfallen.
pump (pʌmp) *n* Pumpe *f*. *vt* **1** pumpen. **2** ausfragen. *vi* pumpen.
pumpkin ('pʌmpkin) *n* Kürbis *m*.
pun (pʌn) *n* Wortspiel *neu*. *vi* ein Wortspiel machen, witzeln.
punch[1] (pʌntʃ) *vt* (mit der

Faust) schlagen. *n* Faustschlag, Knuff *m*.
punch[2] (pʌntʃ) *vt* **1** lochen. **2** stempeln. *n* **1** Locheisen *neu*. **2** Locher *m*. **3** Stempel *m*.
punch[3] (pʌntʃ) *n* Punsch *m*. Bowle *f*.
punctual ('pʌŋktʃuəl) *adj* pünktlich. **punctuality** *n* Pünktlichkeit *f*.
punctuate ('pʌŋktʃueit) *vt* **1** interpunktieren. **2** unterbrechen. **punctuation** *n* Interpunktion *f*.
puncture ('pʌŋktʃə) *n* **1** Loch *neu*. Stich *m*. **2** *mot* Reifenpanne *f*. **3** *med* Punktur *f*. *vt* **1** durchstoßen, perforieren. **2** *med* punktieren. *vi* (of a tyre) ein Loch bekommen.
pungent ('pʌndʒənt) *adj* scharf, beißend.
punish ('pʌniʃ) *vt* (be)strafen, züchtigen.
punk (pʌŋk) *n* Punker *m*.
punt[1] (pʌnt) *n* **1** Punt, Flachboot *neu*. **2** *sport* Fallstoß *m*. *vt* **1** staken. **2** stoßen.
punt[2] (pʌnt) *vi* wetten.
pupil[1] ('pju:pəl) *n* Schüler *m*. Schülerin *f*.
pupil[2] ('pju:pəl) *n* *anat* Pupille *f*.
puppet ('pʌpit) *n* Puppe, Marionette *f*.
puppy ('pʌpi) *n* junger Hund, Welpe *m*.
purchase ('pə:tʃis) *vt* kaufen. *n* Kauf *m*.
pure (pjuə) *adj* **1** rein, sauber. **2** unberührt. **purify** *vt* **1** reinigen. **2** klären.
purgatory ('pə:gətri) *n* Fegefeuer *neu*.
purge (pə:dʒ) *vt* **1** reinigen. **2** *pol* säubern. *n* **1** Reinigung *f*. **2** *pol* Säuberung *f*.
Puritan ('pjuəritən) *n* Puritaner *m*. *adj* *also* **puritanical** puritanisch.
purl (pə:l) *vt* linksstricken.
purple ('pə:pəl) *adj* purpurn. *n* Purpur *m*.
purpose ('pə:pəs) *n* Absicht *f*. Zweck *m*. **purposeful** *adj* **1** entschlossen. **2** zweckmäßig.
purr (pə:) *vi* schnurren.
purse (pə:s) *n* Geldbeutel *m*. Portemonnaie *neu*.
pursue (pə'sju:) *vt* **1** verfolgen. **2** fortsetzen. **3** betreiben. **pursuit** *n* Verfolgung *f*.
pus (pʌs) *n* Eiter *m*.
push (puʃ) *vt* **1** schieben, stoßen. **2** drängen. **3** treiben. **push off** **1** abstoßen. **2** *inf* abhauen. **push on** vordringen. **push through** durchsetzen. ~*n* **1** Stoß *m*. **2** Drang *m*. Energie *f*. **pushbike** *n* *inf* Fahrrad *neu*. **pushchair** *n* (leichter) Kinderwagen *m*.
pussy ('pusi) *n* *inf* Kätzchen *neu*. Mieze *f*.
put* (put) *vt* **1** setzen, stellen, legen. **2** ausdrücken. **3** richten, tun. **4** *sport* schleudern, werfen. **put away** **1** weglegen. **2** sparen. **put by** zurücklegen. **put down** **1** niedersetzen. **2** unterdrücken. **3** demütigen. **4** töten. **put forward** **1** vorschlagen. **2** vorbringen. **put off** **1** verschieben. **2** abhalten. **put on** **1** anziehen. **2** herausbringen. **3** zunehmen. **4** vorgeben. **put through** **1** durchführen. **2** verbinden.

put up 1 errichten, erhöhen. **2** unterbringen.
putrid ('pjuːtrid) *adj* verfault, verwest.
putt (pʌt) *vt sport* putten. *n* Putten *neu.*
putty ('pʌti) *n* (Fenster)Kitt *m.*
puzzle ('pʌzəl) *n* Rätsel *neu. vt* verwirren.
PVC *n* PVC *neu.*
Pygmy ('pigmi) *n* Pygmäe, Zwerg *m.*
pyjamas (pə'dʒɑːməz) *n pl* Schlafanzug, Pyjama *m.*
pylon ('pailən) *n* Leitungsmast *m.*
pyramid ('pirəmid) *n* Pyramide *f.*
Pyrenees (pirə'niːz) *n pl* Pyrenäen *pl.*
Pyrex ('paireks) *n Tdmk* Jenaer Glas *Tdmk neu.*
python ('paiθən) *n* Pythonschlange *f.*

Q

quack[1] (kwæk) *vi* (of a duck, etc.) quaken.
quack[2] (kwæk) *n* Quacksalber, Kurpfuscher *m.*
quadrangle ('kwɔdræŋgəl) *n* **1** Viereck *neu.* **2** Hof *m.*
quadrant ('kwɔdrənt) *n* Quadrant *m.*
quadrilateral (kwɔdri'lætərəl) *adj* vierseitig. *n* Viereck *neu.*
quadruped ('kwɔdruped) *n* Vierfüßer *m.*
quadruple ('kwɔdrupəl) *adj* vierfach. **quadruplet** *n* Vierling *m.*
quail (kweil) *n* Wachtel *f.*
quaint (kweint) *adj* malerisch, kurios.
quake (kweik) *vi* zittern, beben. *n* **1** Zittern *neu.* **2** Erdbeben *neu.*
Quaker ('kweikə) *n* Quäker *m.*
qualify ('kwɔlifai) *vt* **1** befähigen, qualifizieren. **2** einschränken. *vi* sich eignen. **qualification** *n* **1** Qualifikation, Befähigung *f.* **2** Voraussetzung *f.* **3** Einschränkung *f.*
quality ('kwɔliti) *n* **1** Eigenschaft *f.* **2** Qualität *f.*
qualm (kwɑːm) *n* **1** Skrupel, Zweifel *m.* **2** Übelkeit *f.*
quandary ('kwɔndəri) *n* Verlegenheit *f.*
quantify ('kwɔntifai) *vt* quantitativ bestimmen, messen.
quantity ('kwɔntiti) *n* Menge, Größe, Quantität *f.*
quarantine ('kwɔrəntiːn) *n* Quarantäne *f. vt* isolieren.
quarrel ('kwɔrəl) *n* Streit, Zank *m. vi* streiten, zanken.
quarry[1] ('kwɔri) *n* **1** Steinbruch *m.* **2** Quelle *f. vt* **1** brechen. **2** ausgraben.
quarry[2] ('kwɔri) *n* (verfolgtes) Wild *neu.* Beute *f.*
quart (kwɔːt) *n* Quart *neu.*
quarter ('kwɔːtə) *n* **1** Viertel *neu.* **2** *pl* Unterkunft *f.* Quartier *neu. vt* **1** vierteln. **2** einquartieren. **quarterdeck** *n* Achterdeck *neu.* **quartermaster** *n* **1** *mil* Quartiermeister *m.* **2** *naut* Steuerer *m.*
quartet (kwɔː'tet) *n* Quartett *neu.*
quartz (kwɔːts) *n* Quarz *m.*
quash[1] (kwɔʃ) *vt* unterdrücken, vernichten.
quash[2] (kwɔʃ) *vt law* annullieren, abweisen, niederschlagen.

quaver ('kweivə) *vi* **1** zittern. **2** trillern. *n mus* Achtelnote *f.*
quay (kiː) *n* Kai *m.*
queasy ('kwiːzi) *adj* unwohl.
queen (kwiːn) *n* Königin *f.*
queer (kwiə) *adj* **1** wunderlich, sonderbar. **2** komisch, kurios. **3** *sl* schwul, homosexuell.
quell (kwel) *vt* unterdrücken, bezwingen.
quench (kwentʃ) *vt* löschen.
query ('kwiəri) *n* Frage, Erkundigung *f.* *vt* (be)fragen, sich erkundigen.
quest (kwest) *n* Suche *f.*
question ('kwestʃən) *n* **1** Frage *f.* **2** Problem *neu.* *vt* **1** (be)fragen. **2** bezweifeln. **question mark** *n* Fragezeichen *neu.* **questionnaire** *n* Fragebogen *m.*
queue (kjuː) *n* Schlange, Reihe *f.* *vi* Schlange stehen.
quibble ('kwibəl) *n* Spitzfindigkeit *f.* *vi* spitzfindig sein, Haarspalterei betreiben.
quick (kwik) *adj* **1** schnell, rasch, geschwind. **2** flink. **3** scharf. **4** lebend. **quicken** *(vi),vt* **1** (sich) beschleunigen. **2** (sich) beleben. **quicksand** *n* Treibsand *m.* **quicksilver** *n* Quecksilber *neu.* **quickstep** *n* Quickstep *m.* **quick-tempered** *adj* jähzornig, reizbar. **quick-witted** *adj* schlagfertig.
quid (kwid) *n sl* Pfund (sterling) *neu.*
quiet[1] ('kwaiət) *n* Stille, Ruhe *f.* Frieden *m.* **quieten** *vt* beruhigen.
quiet[2] ('kwaiət) *adj* still, ruhig. **quietness** *n* Ruhe, Stille *f.*
quill (kwil) *adj* Feder *f.*
quilt (kwilt) *n* Steppdecke *f.* *vt* **1** steppen. **2** wattieren.
quinine (kwi'niːn) *n* Chinin *neu.*
quintessence (kwin'tesəns) *n* Quintessenz *f.*
quintet (kwin'tet) *n* Quintett *neu.*
quirk (kwəːk) *n* Eigenart, Verschrobenheit *f.*
quit* (kwit) *vi inf* seine Stelle aufgeben. *vt* **1** aufgeben. **2** verlassen.
quite (kwait) *adv* **1** ziemlich. **2** ganz, durchaus, völlig.
quiver[1] ('kwivə) *vi* zittern, beben *n.* Zittern, Beben *neu.*
quiver[2] ('kwivə) *n* Köcher *m.*
quiz (kwiz) *n, pl* **quizzes** *Quiz neu.*
quizzical ('kwizikəl) *adj* **1** seltsam, komisch. **2** spöttisch.
quota ('kwoutə) *n* Anteil *m.* Quote *f.*
quote (kwout) *vt* **1** anführen, zitieren. **2** angeben. *n* Zitat *neu.* **quotation** *n* **1** Zitat *neu.* **2** *comm* (Kurs)Notierung *f.* **quotation marks** *n pl* Anführungszeichen *neu pl.*

R

rabbi ('ræbai) *n* Rabbiner *m.*
rabbit ('ræbit) *n* Kaninchen *neu.*
rabble ('ræbəl) *n* Pöbel, Mob *m.*
rabies ('reibiːz) *n* Tollwut *f.* **rabid** *adj* **1** tollwütig. **2** wütend, rasend. **3** fanatisch.
race[1] (reis) *vi* rennen. *n* (Wett)Rennen *neu.* **racecourse** *n* Rennbahn *f.* **racehorse** *n* Rennpferd *neu.*
race[2] (reis) *n* Rasse *f.* **race**

relations *n pl* Rassenbeziehungen *f pl.* **racial** *adj* rassich, Rassen—. **racialism** *n* Rassenvorurteil *neu.* **racist** *adj* rassist.
rack (ræk) *n* **1** Gestell *neu.* **2** Ständer *m.* **3** Gepäcknetz *neu.* **4** Folterbank *f.*
racket[1] ('rækit) *n* **1** Lärm *m.* **2** Gaunerei *f.*
racket[2] ('rækit) *n* Schläger *m.* Rakett *neu.*
radar ('reidɑː) *n* Radar *neu.*
radial ('reidiəl) *adj* radial.
radiant ('reidiənt) *adj* strahlend, glänzend.
radiate ('reidieit) *vt,vi* ausstrahlen. **radiation** *n* (Aus) Strahlung *f.* Strahlen *m pl.* **radiator** *n* **1** Heizkörper *m.* **2** *mot* Kühler *m.*
radical ('rædikəl) *adj* **1** *pol* radikal. **2** gründlich.
radio ('reidiou) *n* Radio *neu.* Rundfunk *m.*
radioactive (reidiouæk'tiv) *adj* radioaktiv. **radioactivity** *n* Radioaktivität *f.*
radish ('rædiʃ) *n* Radieschen *neu.* Rettich *m.*
radium ('reidiəm) *n* Radium *neu.*
radius ('reidiəs) *n, pl* **radii** **1** Halbmesser, Radius *m.* **2** Bereich *m.*
raffia ('ræfiə) *n* Raffiabast *m.*
raffle ('ræfəl) *n* Verlosung *f.* *vt* verlosen.
raft (rɑːft) *n* Floß *neu.*
rafter ('rɑːftə) *n* Dachbalken *m.*
rag[1] (ræg) *n* **1** Fetzen, Lumpen, Lappen *m.* **2** Schundblatt *neu.* **ragged** *adj* zerlumpt.
rag[2] (ræg) *vt* **1** anschnauzen. **2** aufziehen. *n* Streich, Ulk, Unfug *m.*
rage (reidʒ) *n* Wut *f.* *vi* wüten.
raid (reid) *n* **1** Überfall, Angriff *m.* **2** (by the police) Razzia *f.*
rail (reil) *n* **1** Riegel *m.* **2** Geländer *neu.* **by rail** mit der Eisenbahn. **railway** *n* Eisenbahn *f.*
rain (rein) *n* Regen *m.* *vi* regnen. **rainbow** *n* Regenbogen *m.* **rainfall** *n* Niederschlagsmenge *f.*
raise (reiz) *vt* **1** (auf-, er-) heben. **2** errichten. **3** erhöhen, steigern. **4** aufbringen.
raisin ('reizən) *n* Rosine *f.*
rake (reik) *n* Rechen *m.* *vt* rechen.
rally ('ræli) *n* **1** Versammlung *f.* **2** *mot* Sternfahrt *f.* **3** *sport* Schlagwechsel *m.* *vt* **1** wieder sammeln. **2** aufmuntern. *vi* **1** sich wieder sammeln. **2** sich erholen. **rally round** sich scharen um.
ram (ræm) *n* **1** *zool* Widder *m.* **2** Ramme *f.* Rammbock *m.* *vt* rammen.
ramble ('ræmbəl) *vi* **1** wandern. **2** umherschweifen. *n* Wanderung *f.*
ramp (ræmp) *n* Rampe *f.*
rampage ('ræmpeidʒ) *vi* (herum)toben.
rampant ('ræmpənt) *adj* **1** zügellos. **2** wuchernd.
rampart ('ræmpɑːt) *n* (Schutz)Wall *m.*
ramshackle ('ræmʃækəl) *adj* baufällig.
ran (ræn) *v* see **run.**
ranch (rɑːntʃ) *n* Ranch, Viehfarm *f.*
rancid ('rænsid) *adj* ranzig.

rancour ('ræŋkə) *n* Groll *m.* Erbitterung *f.*
random ('rændəm) *adj* zufällig, planlos. **at random** aufs Geratewohl.
rang (ræŋ) *v* see **ring**[2].
range (reindʒ) *n* **1** Reihe *f.* **2** *geog* Kette *f.* **3** Reichweite *f.* **4** Kollektion *f.* **5** Herd *m.* *vt* **1** einreihen. **2** durchstreifen. *vi* **1** sich erstrekken. **2** reichen. **3** streifen.
rank[1] (ræŋk) *n* **1** Reihe *f.* **2** Rang *m.* **3** Stand *m.* Klasse *f.* *vt* **1** einordnen. **2** rangieren. *vi* gehören. **rank and file** *n* **1** Mannschaftstand *m.* **2** die Masse *f.*
rank[2] (ræŋk) *adj* **1** üppig, überwuchert. **2** stinkend. **3** unanständig. **4** rein, kraß.
rankle ('ræŋkəl) *vi* nagen, wühlen.
ransack ('rænsæk) *vt* durchwühlen, plündern.
ransom ('rænsəm) *n* Lösegeld *neu.* *vt* loskaufen.
rap (ræp) *vi* klopfen. *n* Klopfen *neu.*
rape (reip) *vt* vergewaltigen. *n* Vergewaltigung, Notzucht *f.*
rapid ('ræpid) *adj* schnell, eilig, rapid.
rapier ('reipiə) *n* Rapier *neu.* (Stoß)Degen *m.*
rapture ('ræptʃə) *n* Entzücken *neu.* Verzückung *f.*
rare[1] (rɛə) *adj* selten, rar.
rare[2] (rɛə) *adj* nicht durchgebraten.
rascal ('rɑːskəl) *n* **1** Schurke *m.* **2** Spitzbube *m.*
rash[1] (ræʃ) *adj* **1** übereilt. **2** tollkühn.
rash[2] (ræʃ) *n* Hautausschlag *m.*
rasher ('ræʃə) *n* Speckschnitte *f.*
raspberry ('rɑːzbri) *n* Himbeere *f.*
rat (ræt) *n* Ratte *f.*
rate (reit) *n* **1** Grad *m.* **2** Verhältnis *neu.* Maßstab *m.* **3** Geschwindigkeit *f.* **4** *comm* Kurs *m.* **5** Gebühr *f.* **6** *pl* Gemeindesteuer *f.* **at any rate** auf jeden Fall. *vt* einschätzen.
rather ('rɑːðə) *adv* **1** eher, lieber. **2** ziemlich.
ratio ('reiʃiou) *n* Verhältnis *neu.*
ration ('ræʃən) *n* Ration *f.* *vt* rationieren.
rational ('ræʃənəl) *adj* rational, vernünftig. **rationalize** *vt* **1** rational erklären. **2** rationalisieren.
rattle ('rætl̩) *vt,vi* rasseln, klappern. *n* **1** Gerassel *neu.* **2** Klapper *f.*
raucous ('rɔːkəs) *adj* heiser, rauh.
ravage ('rævidʒ) *vt* verwüsten, verheeren.
rave (reiv) *vi* rasen, toben, wüten. **rave about** schwärmen für.
raven ('reivən) *n* Rabe *m.*
ravenous *adj* gefräßig, heißhungrig.
ravine (rə'viːn) *n* (Berg)Schlucht *f.*
ravish ('ræviʃ) *vt* **1** entzücken, hinreißen. **2** vergewaltigen. **3** fortraffen.
raw (rɔː) *adj* **1** rauh. **2** roh. **3** unreif, unerfahren.
ray (rei) *n* Strahl *m.*
rayon ('reiɔn) *n* Kunstseide *f.* Rayon *neu.*
razor ('reizə) *n* Rasiermesser

neu. **electric razor** elektrischer Rasierapparat *m.* **safety razor** Rasierapparat *m.* **razor blade** Rasierklinge *f.*

reach (riːtʃ) *vt* (er)reichen. *vi* reichen. **1** Reichweite *f.* **2** Bereich *m.*

react (ri'ækt) *vi* reagieren. **reaction** *n* **1** Reaktion *f.* **2** Rückwirkung *f.* **reactionary** *adj* reaktionär. *n* Reaktionär *m.* **reactor** *n* Reaktor *m.*

read* (riːd) *vt,vi* lesen.

readjust (riːə'dʒʌst) *vt* wieder anpassen, einstellen. *vi* sich umorientieren, sich wieder anpassen.

ready ('redi) *adj* **1** bereit, fertig. **2** schnell. **readily** *adv* bereitwillig, ohne weiteres.

real (riəl) *adj* **1** wirklich, tatsächlich. **2** echt, wahr. **real estate** *n* Grundbesitz *m.* **really** *adv* wirklich, tatsächlich. **realism** *n* Realismus *m.* **realize** *vt* **1** verwirklichen. **2** sich vorstellen. **3** begreifen. **4** *comm* realisieren.

realm (relm) *n* **1** Reich *neu.* **2** Bereich *m.*

reap (riːp) *vt* **1** ernten. **2** mähen, schneiden.

reappear (riːə'piə) *vi* wieder erscheinen.

rear[1] (riə) *n* **1** Rückseite *f.* **2** Hintergrund *m.* *adj* hinterst. **rear admiral** *n* Konteradmiral *m.* **rearguard** *n* Nachhut *f.*

rear[2] (riə) *vt* **1** züchten, (er)ziehen. **2** erheben. *vi* **1** sich (auf)bäumen. **2** hochfahren.

rearrange (riːə'reindʒ) *vt* neuordnen.

reason ('riːzən) *n* **1** Vernunft *f.* **2** Grund, Anlaß *m.* *vi* vernünftig denken. **reasonable** *adj* **1** vernünftig. **2** angemessen, annehmbar.

reassure (riːə'ʃuə) *vt* **1** beruhigen. **2** wieder beteuern.

rebate ('riːbeit) *n* **1** Rabatt *m.* **2** Zurückzahlung *f.*

rebel (*n,adj* 'rebəl; *v* ri'bel) *n* Rebell *m.* *adj* aufrührerisch. *vi* sich empören, sich auflehnen.

rebound (*v* ri'baund; *n* 'riːbaund) *vi* zurückprallen. *n* **1** Rückprall *m.* **2** Rückschlag *m.*

rebuff (ri'bʌf) *n* Abweisung *f.* *vt* abweisen.

rebuild* (riː'bild) *vt* wiederaufbauen.

rebuke (ri'bjuːk) *vt* tadeln. *n* Tadel *m.*

recall (ri'kɔːl) *vt* **1** zurückrufen. **2** sich erinnern an. *n* Widerruf *m.*

recede (ri'siːd) *vi* zurückweichen, zurückgehen.

receipt (ri'siːt) *n* **1** Quittung *f.* **2** Empfang *m.*

receive (ri'siːv) *vt* **1** empfangen. **2** erhalten. **3** annehmen. **receiver** *n* **1** Empfänger *m.* **2** *comm* Konkursverwalter *m.* **3** (telephone) Hörer *m.*

recent ('riːsənt) *adj* letzt, neu, jung. **recently** *adv* kürzlich, in letzter Zeit, neulich.

receptacle (ri'septəkəl) *n* Behälter *m.*

reception (ri'sepʃən) *n* **1** Empfang *m.* **2** Aufnahme *f.* **receptive** *adj* empfänglich, aufnahmebereit.

recess (ri'ses) *n* **1** Pause *f.* Ferien *pl.* **2** Nische *f.* *vt* einsenken.

recession (ri'seʃən) *n* **1** Rezession *f*. Konjunkturrückgang *m*. **2** Zurücktreten *neu*.
recipe ('resipi) *n* Rezept *neu*.
recipient (ri'sipiənt) *n* Empfänger *m*. *adj* empfänglich.
reciprocate (ri'siprəkeit) *vi* einen Gegendienst leisten. *vt* **1** erwidern. **2** austauschen. **reciprocal** *adj* gegenseitig, wechselseitig.
recite (ri'sait) *vt* **1** vortragen. **2** Aufzählung *f*. **3** Bericht *m*.
reckless ('rekləs) *adj* **1** unbekümmert. **2** rücksichtslos. **3** fahrlässig.
reckon ('rekən) *vt* **1** zählen, rechnen. **2** *inf* meinen, glauben.
reclaim (ri'kleim) *vt* **1** zurückfordern. **2** urbar machen.
recline (ri'klain) *vi* sich zurücklehnen.
recluse (ri'klu:s) *n* Einsiedler *m*. *adj* **1** abgeschieden. **2** einsiedlerisch.
recognize ('rekəgnaiz) *vt* **1** wiedererkennen. **2** (an)erkennen. **3** zugeben. **recognition** **1** Erkenntnis *f*. **2** Anerkennung *f*.
recoil (ri'kɔil) *vi* **1** zurückschrecken, zurückfahren. **2** zurückweichen. *n* Rückstoß *m*.
recollect (rekə'lekt) *vt* sich erinnern an.
recommence (ri:kə'mens) *vt,vi* wieder beginnen *or* anfangen.
recommend (rekə'mend) *vt* empfehlen. **recommendation** *n* Empfehlung *f*. Vorschlag *m*.
recompense ('rekəmpəns) *vt* **1** entschädigen, belohnen. **2** wiedergutmachen. *n* **1** Entschädigung, Belohnung *f*. **2** Rückerstattung *f*.
reconcile ('rekənsail) *vt* versöhnen.
reconstruct (ri:kən'strʌkt) *vt* **1** wiederaufbauen. **2** rekonstruieren.
record (*v* ri'kɔ:d; *n,adj* 'rekɔ:d) *vt* **1** aufzeichnen. **2** *tech* aufnehmen. **3** eintragen. *n* **1** Niederschrift *f*. Bericht *m*. **2** Schallplatte *f*. **3** *sport* Rekord *m*. *adj* Rekord—. **recording** *n* Aufnahme *f*. **record-player** *n* Plattenspieler *m*.
recount (ri'kaunt) *vt* erzählen.
recover (ri'kʌvə) *vt* wiederfinden, zurückgewinnen. *vi* sich erholen. **recovery** *n* **1** Rettung *f*. **2** Erholung *f*.
recreation (rekri'eiʃən) *n* Erholung *f*. **recreation ground** Sportplatz, Spielplatz *m*.
recruit (ri'kru:t) *vt* rekrutieren, anwerben. *n* Rekrut *m*. **recruitment** *n* Rekrutierung *f*.
rectangle ('rektæŋgəl) *n* Rechteck *neu*. **rectangular** *adj* rechteckig.
rectify ('rektifai) *vt* berichtigen, korrigieren.
recuperate (ri'kju:pəreit) *vi* sich erholen. **recuperation** *n* Erholung *f*.
recur (ri'kə:) *vi* wiederkehren, zurückkehren.
recycle (ri'saikəl) *vt* wiederaufbereiten.
red (red) *adj* rot. *n* Rot *neu*. **caught red-handed** auf frischer Tat ertappt. **redcur-**

rant *n* Rote Johannisbeere *f.* **redden** *vi* **1** erröten. **2** rot werden.

redeem (ri'di:m) *vt* **1** zurückkaufen. **2** einlösen. **3** wiedergutmachen. **4** (er)retten. **5** *rel* erlösen. **redemption** *n* **1** Rückkauf *m.* **2** Einlösung *f.* **3** Wiedergutmachung *f.* **4** (Er)Rettung *f.* **5** *rel* Erlösung *f.*

redevelop (ri:di'veləp) *vt,vi* neu entwickeln.

Red Indian *n* Indianer *m.*

redress (ri'dres) *vt* **1** abhelfen, beseitigen. **2** wiederherstellen. *n* Abhilfe, Behebung *f.*

reduce (ri'dju:s) *vt* **1** vermindern. **2** erniedrigen. **3** verwandeln. **4** zwingen. *vi* abnehmen. **reduction** *n* **1** Verminderung *f.* **2** Abnahme *f.*

redundant (ri'dʌndənt) *adj* **1** überflüssig. **2** übermäßig. **make redundant** entlassen. **redundancy** *n* **1** Entlassung *f.* **2** Überfluß *m.*

reed (ri:d) *n* **1** Rohr *neu.* **2** *mus* (Rohr)Blatt *neu.*

reef (ri:f) *n* (Felsen)Riff *m.*

reek (ri:k) *vi* stinken. *n* Gestank *m.*

reel[1] (ri:l) *n* Spule, Rolle *f. vt* spulen.

reel[2] (ri:l) *vi* **1** taumeln. **2** schwanken.

re-establish (ri:i'stæbliʃ) *vt* wiederherstellen.

refectory (ri'fektəri) *n* **1** Speisesaal *m.* **2** Mensa *f.*

refer (ri'fə:) *vt* verweisen. *vi* **1** sich beziehen. **2** hinweisen. **referee** *n* Schiedsrichter *m.* **reference** *n* **1** Hinweis *m.* **2** Bezugnahme *f.* **3** Quellenangabe *f.* **4** Zeugnis *neu.* **referendum** *n, pl* **-da** Volksabstimmung *f.* Referendum *neu.*

refill (*v* ri:'fil; *n* 'ri:fil) *vt* nachfüllen, auffüllen. *n* Nachfüllung, Ersatzfüllung *f.*

refine (ri'fain) *vt* **1** läutern, raffinieren. **2** verfeinern. **refined** *adj* **1** raffiniert. **2** kultiviert. **refinement** *n* **1** Feinheit, Kultiviertheit *f.* **2** Raffinierung *f.* **refinery** *n* Raffinerie *f.*

reflation (ri'fleiʃən) *n* Wirtschaftsbelebung, Reflation *f.*

reflect (ri'flekt) *vt* wiederspiegeln. *vi* **1** zurückstrahlen, reflektieren. **2** nachdenken. **reflection** *n* **1** Rückstrahlung, Reflexion *f.* **2** Spiegelbild *neu.* **3** Überlegung *f.* **reflector** *n* **1** Reflektor *m.* **2** *mot* Rückstrahler *m.*

reflex (*adj,n* 'ri:fleks) *adj* **1** rückwirkend. **2** Reflex—. *n* Reflex *m.* **reflexive** *adj gram* rückbezüglich, reflexiv.

reform (ri'fɔ:m) *n* Reform, Verbesserung *f. vt* reformieren. *vi* sich bessern. **reformation** *n* **1** Umgestaltung *f.* **2** *cap rel* Reformation *f.*

refract (ri'frækt) *vt* brechen.

refrain[1] (ri'frein) *vi* sich enthalten, unterlassen.

refrain[2] (ri'frein) *n mus* Refrain, Kehrreim *m.*

refresh (ri'freʃ) *vt* **1** erfrischen. **2** erneuern. **refreshment** *n* Erfrischung *f.*

refrigerator (ri'fridʒəreitə) *n* Kühlschrank *m.*

refuel (ri:'fju:əl) *vt,vi* (auf)tanken.

refuge ('refju:dʒ) *n* Zuflucht *f.*

Zufluchtsort *m*. **refugee** *n* Flüchtling *m*.
refund (*v* ri'fʌnd; *n* 'riːfʌnd) *vt* zurückzahlen. *n* Rückzahlung *f*.
refuse[1] (ri'fjuːz) *vt* **1** ablehnen. **2** verweigern. *vi* sich weigern.
refuse[2] ('refjuːs) *n* Abfall, Müll *m*.
refute (ri'fjuːt) *vt* widerlegen.
regain (ri'gein) *vt* wiedergewinnen.
regal ('riːgəl) *adj* **1** königlich. **2** prunkvoll.
regard (ri'gɑːd) *vt* **1** ansehen, betrachten. **2** berücksichtigen. *n* **1** Rücksicht *f*. **2** Achtung *f*. **regardless** *adj, adv* ohne Rücksicht.
regatta (ri'gɑːtə) *n* Regatta *f*.
regent ('riːdʒənt) *n* Regent *m*.
regime (rei'ʒiːm) *n* Regime *neu*.
regiment ('redʒimənt) *n* Regiment *neu*. *vt* reglementieren. **regimental** *adj* Regiments—.
region ('riːdʒən) *n* Gegend *f*. Gebiet *neu*. Bereich *m*. **in the region of** ungefähr.
register ('redʒistə) *n* **1** Liste *f*. Verzeichnis *neu*. **2** *mus,lit* Register *neu*. *vt* **1** eintragen. **2** zeigen. *vi* sich eintragen, sich (an)melden. **registrar** *n* Standesbeamte(r) *m*.
regress (ri'gres) *vi* zurückgehen. *n* Rückschritt *m*.
regret (ri'gret) *vt* bedauern. *n* Bedauern *neu*. **regrettable** *adj* bedauerlich.
regular ('regjulə) *adj* **1** regelmäßig. **2** ordentlich. **3** gewöhnlich. **regularity** *n* Regelmäßigkeit *f*.
regulate ('regjuleit) *vt* regeln, ordnen, regulieren. **regulation** *n* **1** Vorschrift *f*. **2** Regelung *f*.
rehabilitate (riːə'biliteit) *vt* rehabilitieren.
rehearse (ri'həːs) *Th vt,vi* proben. **rehearsal** *n* Probe *f*.
reign (rein) *n* Regierung(szeit) *f*. *vi* regieren.
reimburse (riːim'bəːs) *vt* **1** entschädigen. **2** zurückzahlen.
rein (rein) *n* Zügel *m*. *vt* zügeln.
reincarnation (riːinkɑː'neiʃən) *n* **1** Wiedergeburt *f*. **2** (Wieder)Verkörperung *f*.
reindeer ('reindiə) *n* Renntier, Ren *neu*.
reinforce (riːin'fɔːs) *vt* **1** verstärken. **2** bewehren. **reinforced concrete** *n* Eisenbeton *m*.
reinstate (riːin'steit) *vt* wiedereinsetzen.
reinvest (riːin'vest) *vt* wieder anlegen.
reissue (riː'iʃuː) *vt* wieder ausgeben. *n* Neuausgabe *f*.
reject (*v* ri'dʒekt; *n* 'riːdʒekt) *vt* **1** zurückweisen, ablehnen. **2** abstoßen. *n* Ausschußartikel *m*. **rejection** *n* Zurückweisung, Ablehnung *f*.
rejoice (ri'dʒɔis) *vi* sich freuen.
rejoin (ri'dʒɔin) *vi* erwidern.
rejuvenate (ri'dʒuːvəneit) *vt* verjüngen.
relapse (ri'læps) *n* Rückfall *m*. *vi* wieder verfallen, rückfällig werden.
relate (ri'leit) *vt* **1** berichten, erzählen. **2** verbinden. *vi* sich beziehen.
relation (ri'leiʃən) *n* **1** Verwandte(r) *m*. **2** Verhältnis *neu*.

Beziehung *f*. **relationship** *n* **1** Verwandtschaft *f*. **2** Verbindung *f*. Verhältnis *neu*.
relative ('relətiv) *adj* **1** bezüglich, relativ. **2** verhältnismäßig. *n* Verwandte(r) *m*. **relatively** *adv* verhältnismäßig. **relativity** *n* Relativität *f*.
relax (ri'læks) *vi* **1** sich entspannen. **2** sich lockern. **3** nachlassen. *vt* **1** lockern. **2** entspannen. **3** abschwächen. **relaxation** *n* **1** Entspannung *f*. **2** Lockerung *f*. **3** Nachlassen *neu*.
relay (*n* 'ri:lei; *v* ri'lei) *n* **1** *sport* Staffel *f*. **2** *tech* Relais *neu*. *vt* **1** übertragen. **2** weitergeben. **relay race** Staffellauf *m*.
release (ri'li:s) *vt* **1** freilassen, loslassen. **2** aufgeben. **3** freigeben. *n* **1** Entlassung, Befreiung *f*. **2** Aufgabe *f*.
relent (ri'lent) *vi* sich erweichen lassen. **relentless** *adj* unbarmherzig.
relevant ('reləvənt) *adj* relevant, belangvoll. **relevance** *n* Relevanz, Bedeutung *f*.
reliable (ri'laiəbəl) *adj* zuverlässig, verläßlich. **reliability** *n* Zuverlässigkeit *f*.
relic ('relik) *n* **1** *rel* Reliquie *f*. **2** Überbleibsel *neu*.
relief (ri'li:f) *n* **1** Erleichterung *f*. **2** Ablösung *f*. **3** Entlastung *f*.
relieve (ri'li:v) *vt* **1** erleichtern. **2** entlasten. **3** entheben. **4** ablösen.
religion (ri'lidʒən) *n* Religion *f*. Glaube *m*. **religious** *adj* **1** religiös. **2** fromm.
relinquish (ri'liŋkwish) *vt* aufgeben, loslassen.
relish ('reliʃ) *vt* genießen. *n* **1** pikante Würze *f*. **2** Geschmack *m*.
relive (ri:'liv) *vt* wieder erleben.
reluctant (ri'lʌktənt) *adj* widerwillig, ungern. **reluctance** *n* Abneigung *f*. Widerwille *m*.
rely (ri'lai) *vi* **rely on** sich verlassen auf.
remain (ri'mein) *vi* **1** bleiben. **2** übrigbleiben. **remains** *n pl* Reste *m pl*. **remainder** *n* Rest *m*.
remand (ri'ma:nd) *vt* in die Untersuchungshaft zurückschicken. *n* Untersuchungshaft *f*.
remark (ri'ma:k) *vt* bemerken. *n* Bemerkung *f*. **remarkable** *adj* bemerkenswert.
remarry (ri:'mæri) *vi* (sich) wieder (ver)heiraten.
remedy ('remədi) *n* **1** Heilmittel *neu*. **2** Gegenmittel *neu*. *vt* **1** abhelfen. **2** in Ordnung bringen.
remember (ri'membə) *vt* **1** sich erinnern an. **2** sich merken. **3** grüßen. **remembrance** *n* **1** Erinnerung *f*. **2** Gedenken *neu*.
remind (ri'maind) *vt* erinnern, mahnen.
reminiscence (remi'nisəns) *n* Erinnerung *f*. **reminiscent** *adj* (sich) erinnernd.
remiss (ri'mis) *adj* nachlässig, säumig. **remission** *n* Erlaß *m*. Ermäßigung *f*.
remit (ri'mit) *vt* **1** überweisen. **2** erlassen. **remittance** *n*

(Geld)Sendung, Überweisung *f.*

remnant ('remnənt) *n* **1** Überrest *m.* **2** Spur *f.*

remorse (ri'mɔːs) *n* Reue *f.*

remote (ri'mout) *adj* entfernt, abgelegen.

remove (ri'muːv) *vt* **1** entfernen, beseitigen. **2** zurückziehen, wegnehmen. **3** ausziehen. *vi* umziehen. **removal** *n* **1** Entfernung *f.* **2** Abhebung *f.* **3** Umzug *m.*

remunerate (ri'mjuːnəreit) *vt* **1** belohnen. **2** vergüten. **remuneration** *n* **1** Lohn *m.* Honorar *neu.* **2** Belohnung *f.*

renaissance (ri'neisəns) *n* **1** Wiedergeburt *f.* **2** *cap* Renaissance *f.*

rename (riː'neim) *vt* umbenennen.

render ('rendə) *vt* **1** übergeben. **2** leisten, erweisen. **3** machen. **4** interpretieren, darstellen. **5** übertragen.

rendezvous ('rɔndivuː) *n* **1** Treffpunkt *m.* **2** Verabredung *f.* Rendezvous *neu.*

renew (ri'njuː) *vt* **1** erneuern. **2** wieder aufnehmen.

renounce (ri'nauns) *vt* verzichten auf, entsagen, ablehnen.

renovate ('renəveit) *vt* renovieren, erneuern.

renown (ri'naun) *n* Ruhm, Ruf *m.* Ansehen *neu.* **renowned** *adj* berühmt, renommiert.

rent (rent) *n* Miete *f.* *vt* **1** mieten. **2** vermieten. **rental** *n* Mietbetrag *m.*

reopen (riː'oupən) *vt,vi* wieder (er)öffnen.

reorganize (riː'ɔːgənaiz) *vt* reorganisieren.

repair (ri'pɛə) *vt* reparieren, ausbessern. *n* Reparatur, Ausbesserung *f.*

repartee (repə'tiː) *n* **1** Schlagfertigkeit *f.* **2** schlagfertige Antwort *f.*

repatriate (ri'pætrieit) *vt* repatriieren.

repay (ri'pei) *vt* **1** zurückzahlen. **2** erwidern.

repeal (ri'piːl) *vt* aufheben. *n* Aufhebung *f.*

repeat (ri'piːt) *vt* **1** wiederholen. **2** nachsagen. *n* Wiederholung *f.*

repel (ri'pel) *vt* **1** zurücktreiben, zurückschlagen. **2** abweisen, abstoßen, zuwider sein.

repent (ri'pent) *vt* bereuen. *vi* Reue empfinden. **repent of** bereuen.

repercussion (riːpə'kʌʃən) *n* Rückwirkung *f.*

repertoire ('repətwɑː) *n* Spielplan *m.* Repertoire *neu.*

repetition (repə'tiʃən) *n* Wiederholung *f.*

replace (ri'pleis) *vt* **1** ersetzen. **2** wieder hinstellen.

replay ('riːplei) *n* *sport* Wiederholungsspiel *neu.*

replenish (ri'pleniʃ) *vt* (wieder) auffüllen.

replica ('replikə) *n* **1** Kopie *f.* **2** Ebenbild *neu.*

reply (ri'plai) *vi* antworten, erwidern. *n* Antwort, Erwiderung *f.*

report (re'pɔːt) *n* **1** Bericht *m.* **2** Gerücht *neu.* **3** Knall *m.* *vt* **1** berichten. **2** melden. *vi* **1** berichten. **2** sich melden.

reporter *n* Reporter, Berichterstatter *m*.
repose (ri'pouz) *n* Ruhe *f*. *vi* ruhen.
represent (repri'zent) *vt* **1** vertreten, repräsentieren. **2** darstellen. **3** bedeuten. **representation** *n* **1** Vertretung, Repräsentation *f*. **2** Darstellung *f*. **3** Vorstellung, Aufführung *f*. **representative** *adj* **1** darstellend. **2** (stell)-vertretend. **3** typisch. *n* **1** Vertreter, Repräsentant *m*. **2** Beauftragte(r) *m*.
repress (ri'pres) *vt* **1** unterdrücken. **2** verdrängen. **repression** *n* **1** Unterdrückung *f*. **2** Verdrängung *f*.
reprieve (ri'pri:v) *vt* begnadigen. *n* Begnadigung, Gnadenfrist *f*.
reprimand ('reprimɑ:nd) *n* Verweis *m*. *vt* einen Verweis erteilen.
reprint (*v* ri:'print; *n* 'ri:print) *vt* neu auflegen *or* drucken. *n* Neudruck *m*.
reprisal (ri'praizəl) *n* Repressalie *f*.
reproach (ri'proutʃ) *vt* vorwerfen. *n* Vorwurf *m*. **reproachful** *adj* vorwurfsvoll.
reproduce (ri:prə'dju:s) *vt* **1** (wieder) hervorbringen. **2** wiedergeben. **3** erzeugen. **4** kopieren. *vi* sich fortpflanzen. **reproduction** *n* **1** Wiedergabe *f*. **2** Kopie, Nachbildung *f*. **3** Fortpflanzung, Vermehrung *f*.
reptile ('reptail) *n* Kriechtier, Reptil *neu*.
republic (ri'pʌblik) *n* Republik *f*.
repudiate (ri'pju:dieit) *vt* **1** nicht anerkennen. **2** ablehnen, abweisen.
repugnant (ri'pʌgnənt) *adj* zuwider, widerlich.
repulsion (ri'pʌlʃən) *n* **1** Widerwille *m*. Abscheu *f*. **2** Abstoßung *f*. **repulsive** *adj* **1** widerwärtig. **2** abstoßend.
repute (ri'pju:t) *n* Ruf *m*. *vt* halten für. **reputed** *adj* angeblich. **reputable** *adj* **1** angesehen. **2** geachtet. **reputation** *n* **1** Ruf *m*. **2** Ansehen *neu*.
request (ri'kwest) *n* Bitte *f*. Gesuch, Verlangen *neu*. *vt* **1** bitten. **2** beantragen.
requiem ('rekwiəm) *n* Requiem *neu*.
require (ri'kwaiə) *vt* **1** verlangen. **2** erfordern.
re-route (ri:'ru:t) *vt* umleiten.
resale ('ri:seil) *n* Weiterverkauf *m*.
rescue ('reskju:) *vt* **1** retten. **2** befreien. *n* **1** Rettung *f*. **2** Befreiung *f*.
research (ri'sə:tʃ) *n* **1** Forschung *f*. **2** Untersuchung *f*.
resell* (ri:'sel) *vt* weiterverkaufen.
resemble (ri'zembəl) *vt* ähnlich sein, gleichen. **resemblance** *n* Ähnlichkeit *f*.
resent (ri'zent) *vt* übelnehmen. **resentful** *adj* ärgerlich, aufgebracht. **resentment** *n* Ressentiment *neu*.
reserve (ri'zə:v) *vt* **1** aufbewahren. **2** reservieren. **3** sich vorbehalten. *n* **1** Reserve *f*. **2** Zurückhaltung *f*. **reservation** *n* **1** Vorbestellung, Reservierung *f*. **2** Vorbehalt *m*.

reserved *adj* **1** reserviert, zurückgelegt. **2** zurückhaltend.
reservoir ('rezəvwa:) *n* **1** Reservoir *neu.* **2** Staubecken *neu.*
reside (ri'zaid) *vi* wohnen, leben. **residence** *n* **1** Wohnsitz *m.* **2** Aufenthalt *m.* **resident** *adj* wohnhaft, ansässig. *n* Einwohner *m.*
residue ('rezidju:) *n* Rest *m.*
resign (ri'zain) *vi* zurücktreten. *vt* **1** aufgeben. **2** niederlegen. **resign oneself to** sich versöhnen mit. **resignation** *n* **1** Rücktritt *m.* **2** Resignation *f.*
resilient (ri'ziliənt) *adj* **1** federnd. **2** elastisch. **3** nicht unterzukriegen.
resin ('rezin) *n* Harz *neu.*
resist (ri'zist) *vt* **1** sich widersetzen. **2** widerstehen. *vi* sich widersetzen. **resistance** *n* Widerstand *m.*
resit (ri:'sit) *vt* (an exam) wiederholen.
resolve (ri'zɔlv) *vt* **1** auflösen. **2** lösen. **3** beschließen. *vi* **1** sich auflösen. **2** sich entschließen. **resolute** *adj* entschlossen. **resolution** *n* **1** Beschluß *m.* Resolution *f.* **2** Lösung *f.* **3** Entschlossenheit *f.*
resonant ('rezənənt) *adj* **1** widerhallend. **2** mitschwingend.
resort (ri'zɔ:t) *vi* **resort to 1** sich begeben nach. **2** zurückgreifen auf. ~*n* **1** Mittel *neu.* **2** Ferienort *m.* **last resort** letzter Ausweg *m.*
resound (ri'zaund) *vi* widerhallen.
resource (ri'zɔ:s) *n* **1** Hilfsquelle *f.* **2** Findigkeit *f.* **3** *pl* Rohstoffquellen. **4** *pl* Bodenschätze *m pl.* **resourceful** *adj* findig, einfallsreich.
respect (ri'spekt) *n* **1** Respekt *m.* Achtung *f.* **2** Rücksicht *f.* **3** Hinsicht *f.* **4** *pl* Grüße *m pl.* *vt* **1** achten. **2** respektieren. **respectable** anständig, respektabel. **respective** *adj* jeweilig. **respectively** *adv* beziehungsweise.
respite ('respit) *n* **1** Frist *f.* Aufschub *m.* **2** Ruhepause *f.*
respond (ri'spɔnd) *vi* **1** antworten. **2** entgegenkommen. **3** reagieren. **response** *n* **1** Antwort *f.* **2** Reaktion *f.*
responsibility *n* **1** Verantwortlichkeit *f.* **2** Verantwortung *f.* **3** *pl* Verpflichtungen *f pl.* **responsible** *adj* **1** verantwortlich. **2** verantwortungsbewußt. **responsive** *adj* **1** empfänglich. **2** zugänglich. **3** entgegenkommend.
rest[1] (rest) *n* **1** Ruhe *f.* **2** Rast *f.* **3** Pause *f.* **4** Stütze *f.* *vi* **1** ruhen. **2** sich verlassen. *vt* **1** stützen. **2** begründen. **restless** *adj* **1** unruhig. **2** ruhelos.
rest[2] (rest) *n* **1** Rest *m.* **2** das Übrige.
restaurant ('restərɔnt) *n* Restaurant *neu.*
restore (ri'stɔ:) *vt* **1** zurückgeben. **2** wiederherstellen. **3** restaurieren. **restoration** *n* **1** Wiederherstellung *f.* **2** Rückerstattung *f.* **3** *cap* Restauration *f.*
restrain (ri'strein) *vt* **1** zurückhalten. **2** hindern. **3** einschränken. **restraint** *n* **1** Zurückhaltung *f.* **2** Zwang *m.*
restrict (ri'strikt) *vt* einschränken, beschränken.

result (ri'zʌlt) *n* Ergebnis *neu.* Folge *f.* *vi* **1** sich ergeben. **2** zur Folge haben.
resume (ri'zjuːm) *vt* **1** wiederaufnehmen. **2** zurücknehmen.
résumé ('rezumei) *n* Zusammenfassung *f.* Resümee *neu.*
resurrect (rezə'rekt) *vt* **1** ausgraben. **2** wieder aufleben lassen. **resurrection** *n* Auferstehung *f.*
retail ('riːteil) *n* Kleinhandel *m.* *adj* Einzelhandels—. *vt* im kleinen verkaufen. *adv* en detail.
retain (ri'tein) *vt* **1** bewahren. **2** zurückhalten.
retaliate (ri'tælieit) *vi* sich rächen, Vergeltung üben. **retaliation** *n* Vergeltung *f.*
retard (ri'tɑːd) *vt* verzögern, verlangsamen. **retarded** *adj* *med* zurückgeblieben.
reticent ('retisənt) *adj* verschwiegen, zurückhaltend.
retina ('retinə) *n* Netzhaut, Retina *f.*
retire (ri'taiə) *vi* **1** in den Ruhestand treten. **2** sich zurückziehen. *vt* **1** in den Ruhestand versetzen.
retort[1] (ri'tɔːt) *vi* erwidern. *n* Erwiderung *f.*
retort[2] (ri'tɔːt) *n* *sci* Retorte *f.*
retrace (ri'treis) *vt* zurückverfolgen.
retract (ri'trækt) *vt* **1** zurücknehmen. **2** widerrufen. **3** einziehen.
retreat (ri'triːt) *n* **1** Rückzug *m.* **2** Zurückweichen *neu.* **3** Zuflucht *f.* *vi* **1** sich zurückziehen. **2** zurückweichen.
retrieve (ri'triːv) *vt* **1** wiederbekommen. **2** wiedergewinnen.
retrograde ('retrəgreid) *adj* **1** rückläufig. **2** rückschrittlich. **3** retrograd.
retrogress (retrə'gres) *vi* zurückgehen, sich verschlechtern.
retrospect ('retrəspekt) *n* Rückblick *m.* **in retrospect** rückblickend.
return (ri'təːn) *vi* zurückkehren. *vt* **1** zurückgeben. **2** erwidern. *n* **1** Rückkehr *f.* **2** Rückgabe *f.* **3** *comm* Umsatz *m.* **4** Bericht *m.*
reunite (riːjuː'nait) *vt* wiedervereinigen.
reveal (ri'viːl) *vi* **1** offenbaren, enthüllen. **2** zeigen. **revelation** *n* Offenbarung, Enthüllung *f.*
revel ('revəl) *vi* sich weiden an.
revenge (ri'vendʒ) *n* Rache *f.* *vt* (sich) rächen.
revenue ('revənjuː) *n* Einkommen *neu.* Einnahmen *f pl.*
reverberate (ri'vəːbəreit) *vi* widerhallen, reflektiert werden.
reverence ('revərəns) *n* **1** Ehrfurcht *f.* **2** Verehrung *f.*
reverse (ri'vəːs) *adj* umgekehrt. *n* **1** Gegenteil *neu.* **2** Rückseite *f.* **3** Rückschlag *m.* **4** *tech,mot* Rückwärtsgang *m.* *vt* **1** umkehren, umdrehen. **2** rückwärts fahren. *vi* rückwärts fahren.
revert (ri'vəːt) *vi* **1** zurückfallen. **2** sich zurückverwandeln.
review (ri'vjuː) *n* **1** Überblick *m.* **2** Nachprüfung *f.* **3** Rezension, Besprechung *f.* **4** Rund-

schau *f.* *vt* **1** nachprüfen. **2** überblicken. **3** rezensieren.
revise (ri'vaiz) *vt* **1** überprüfen. **2** verbessern, bearbeiten. *vi* studieren.
revive (ri'vaiv) *vt* wiederbeleben.
revoke (ri'vouk) *vt* widerrufen, aufheben.
revolt (ri'voult) *vi* sich erheben, rebellieren. *vt* abstoßen. *n* Revolte *f.* Aufstand *m.* **revolting** *adj* abstoßend.
revolution (revə'luːʃən) *n* **1** *pol* Revolution *f.* **2** Umdrehung *f.*
revolve (ri'vɔlv) *vi* sich drehen. *vt* kreisen. **revolver** *n* Revolver *m.*
revue (ri'vjuː) *n* Revue *f.*
revulsion (ri'vʌlʃən) *n* Abscheu *f.* Ekel *m.*
reward (ri'wɔːd) *n* Belohnung *f.* *vt* belohnen.
rhetoric ('retərik) *n* Rhetorik, Redekunst *f.* **rhetorical** *adj* rhetorisch.
rheumatism ('ruːmətizəm) *n* Rheumatismus *m.*
Rhine (rain) *n* Rhein *m.*
Rhineland-Palatinate *n* Rheinland-Pfalz *neu.*
rhinoceros (rai'nɔsərəs) *n* Nashorn *neu.*
Rhodesia (rou'diːʃə) *n* Rhodesien *neu.* **Rhodesian** *adj* rhodesisch. *n* Rhodesier *m.*
rhododendron (roudə'dendrən) *n* Rhododendron *m,neu.*
rhubarb ('ruːbɑːb) *n* Rhabarber *m.*
rhyme (raim) *n* Reim *m.* *vt,vi* reimen.
rhythm ('riðəm) *n* Rhythmus *m.*
rib (rib) *n* Rippe *f.*
ribbon ('ribən) *n* Band *neu.* Streifen *m.*
rice (rais) *n* Reis *m.*
rich (ritʃ) *adj* **1** reich. **2** fett. **3** voll. **4** kräftig.
rickety ('rikiti) *adj* wackelig, baufällig.
rid* (rid) *vt* befreien. *adj* los, frei. **get rid of** los werden.
riddance ('ridns) *n* Loswerden *neu.* Befreiung *f.* **good riddance** den wäre ich glücklich los.
riddle[1] ('ridl) *n* Rätsel *neu.*
riddle[2] ('ridl) *vt* **1** durchlöchern. **2** durchsieben.
ride (raid) *vt,vi* **1** reiten. **2** fahren. *n* **1** Ritt *m.* **2** Fahrt *f.*
ridge (ridʒ) *n* **1** *geog* Kamm *m.* **2** Rücken *m.*
ridicule ('ridikjuːl) *n* Spott *m.* Verspottung *f.* *vt* verspotten, lächerlich machen. **ridiculous** *adj* lächerlich.
rife (raif) *adj* **1** weit verbreitet. **2** zahlreich. **3** voll von.
rifle[1] ('raifəl) *n* *mil* Gewehr *neu.* Büchse *f.*
rifle[2] ('raifəl) *vt* plündern, berauben.
rift (rift) *n* **1** Spalt *m.* **2** Riß *m.*
rig (rig) *n* **1** *naut* Takelwerk *neu.* **2** Ausrüstung *f.* *vt* **1** einrichten. **2** (auf)takeln.
right (rait) *adj* **1** richtig. **2** recht. *n* **1** Recht *neu.* **2** Rechte *f.* *adv* **1** richtig. **2** rechts. **3** sehr, ganz. *vt* **1** aufrichten. **2** in Ordnung bringen. **right angle** *n* rechter Winkel *m.* **right-hand** *adj* recht. **right-handed** *adj* rechtshändig. **right of way** *n* **1** Vorfahrtsrecht *neu.* **2** Wegerecht *neu.*

right wing *n* rechter Flügel *m*. *adj* Rechts—, rechtradikal.

righteous ('raitʃəs) *adj* gerecht, rechtschaffen.

rigid ('ridʒid) *adj* **1** steif. **2** unbeugsam.

rigour ('rigə) *n* **1** Strenge *f*. **2** Härte *f*.

rim (rim) *n* Rand *m*. Kante *f*.

rind (raind) *n* Rinde, Schale *f*.

ring[1] (riŋ) *n* **1** Ring *m*. **2** Kreis *m*. **3** Bande *f*. *vt* einkreisen. **ringleader** *n* Rädelsführer *m*. **ringroad** *n* Ringstraße *f*.

ring*[2] (riŋ) *vt* **1** läuten. **2** erklingen. **3** anrufen. *vi* läuten, klingeln, ertönen. **ring up** anrufen. ~*n* **1** Klingeln, Geklingel *neu*. **2** Klang *m*. **3** *inf* Anruf *m*.

rink (riŋk) *n* Eisbahn *f*.

rinse (rins) *vt* (aus)spülen.

riot ('raiət) *n* Aufruhr, Tumult *m*. *vi* an einem Aufruhr teilnehmen. **run riot 1** sich austoben. **2** umherschwärmen.

rip (rip) *vt* (zer)reißen. *vi* reißen. *n* Riß *m*.

ripe (raip) *adj* reif. **ripen** *vi* reifen, reif werden. *vt* reifen lassen.

ripple ('ripəl) *n* kleine Welle *f*. *(vi),vt* (sich) kräuseln.

rise* (raiz) *vi* **1** aufstehen. **2** sich erheben. **3** sich empören. **4** aufgehen. **5** (an)steigen. *n* **1** Steigen *neu*. **2** Erhebung *f*. **3** Aufstieg *m*. **4** Erhöhung *f*.

risk (risk) *n* Risiko *neu*. *vt* riskieren, wagen.

rissole ('risoul) *n cul* Frikadelle *f*.

rite (rait) *n* Ritus *m*. Zeremonie *f*.

ritual ('ritjuəl) *adj* feierlich. *n* Ritual *neu*.

rival ('raivəl) *n* Rivale, Nebenbuhler *m*. *adj* rivalisierend, wetteifernd. *vt* wetteifern mit, rivalisieren mit. **rivalry** *n* Rivalität, Wetteifer *m*.

river ('rivə) *n* Fluß, Strom *m*. **riverbed** *n* Flußbett *neu*. **riverside** *n* Flußufer *neu*.

rivet ('rivit) *n* Niet *m*. Niete *f*. *vt* **1** (ver)nieten. **2** (attention) fesseln.

road (roud) *n* **1** (Land)Straße *f*. **2** Weg *m*. **roadblock** *n* Straßensperre *f*. **roadside** *n* Straßenrand *m*.

roam (roum) *vi* umherstreifen. *vt* durchstreifen.

roar (rɔː) *vi* brüllen. *n* Gebrüll *neu*.

roast (roust) *vt* braten, rösten. *n* Braten *m*. *adj* gebraten, geröstet.

rob (rɔb) *vt* (be)rauben. **robber** *n* Räuber *m*.

robe (roub) *n* **1** Gewand, Kleid *neu*. **2** *rel,law* Talar *m*.

robin ('rɔbin) *n* Rotkehlchen *neu*.

robot ('roubɔt) *n* Roboter *m*.

robust (rou'bʌst) *adj* stark, kräftig, robust.

rock[1] (rɔk) *n* **1** Gestein *neu*. **2** Fels(en) *m*. **rock-bottom** *adj* allerniedrigst. **rockery** *n* Steingarten *m*.

rock[2] (rɔk) *vt,vi* schaukeln. **rocker** *n* **1** Kufe *f*. **2** *tech* Wippe *f*. **rocking-chair** *n* Schaukelstuhl *m*. **rocking-horse** *n* Schaukelpferd *neu*.

rocket ('rɔkit) *n* Rakete *f*. *vi* hochschießen.

rod (rɔd) *n* **1** Rute *f.* **2** Stange *f.*
rode (roud) *v* see **ride.**
rodent ('roudn̩t) *n* Nagetier *neu.*
roe (rou) *n* Fischlaich, Rogen *m.*
rogue (roug) *n* Schurke, Schelm *m.*
role (roul) *n* Rolle *f.*
roll (roul) *vi* **1** rollen. **2** schwanken. **3** sich wälzen. *vt* **1** rollen, wälzen. **2** walzen. **3** zusammenrollen. *n* **1** Rolle *f.* **2** Verzeichnis *neu.* **3** Brötchen *neu.* **4** Rollen *neu.* **rollcall** *n* **1** Namensaufruf *m.* **2** *mil* Appell *m.* **roller** *n* Rolle, Walze *f.* **roller-skate** *n* Rollschuh *m.* *vi* Rollschuh laufen. **rolling pin** *n* Teigrolle *f.*
Roman Catholic *adj* (römisch-) katholisch. *n* Römisch-Katholische(r), Katholik *m.*
romance ('roumæns) *n* **1** *lit* Romanze *f.* **2** Liebschaft *f.* **3** Übertreibung *f.* **romantic** *adj* romantisch. *n* Romantiker *m.* **romanticize** *vt* romantisch darstellen, romantisieren.
Rome (roum) *n* Rom *neu.* **Roman** *adj* römisch. *n* Römer *m.*
romp (rɔmp) *vi* herumspielen, balgen. *n* Balgerei *f.* **rompers** *n pl* Spielanzug *m.*
roof (ru:f) *n* Dach *neu.* *vt* bedachen.
rook (ruk) *n* Saatkrähe *f.* *vt sl* betrügen.
room (ru:m) *n* **1** Zimmer *neu.* Stube *f.* **2** Raum, Platz *m.*
roost (ru:st) *vi* **1** auf der Stange sitzen. **2** schlafen. *n* **1** Hühnerstange *f.* **2** Ruheplatz *m.*
root[1] (ru:t) *n* **1** Wurzel *f.* **2** Quelle *f.* Kern *m.* *vi* einwurzeln. **take root** Wurzel schlagen.
root[2] (ru:t) *vi* wühlen. *vt* durchwühlen.
rope (roup) *n* Seil, Tau *neu.* *vt* anseilen.
rosary ('rouzəri) *n rel* Rosenkranz *m.*
rose[1] (rouz) *n* **1** Rose *f.* *adj* rosa. **rosette** *n* Rosette *f.* **rosy** *adj* rosig.
rose[2] (rouz) *v* see **rise.**
rosemary ('rouzməri) *n* Rosmarin *m.*
rot (rɔt) *vi* verfaulen. *n* **1** Fäulnis *f.* **2** *inf* Unsinn, Quatsch *m.* **rotten** *adj* **1** faul, verfault, zersetzt. **2** verdorben. **3** *sl* gemein.
rota ('routə) *n* Dienstturnus *m.* Dienstliste *f.* **rotary** *adj* (sich) drehend. **rotate** *vi* sich drehen. *vt* **1** drehen. **2** wechseln. **rotation** *n* **1** Umdrehung *f.* **2** Abwechselung *f.*
rotor ('routə) *n* Rotor *m.*
rouge (ru:ʒ) *n* (rote) Schminke *f.* Rouge *neu.*
rough (rʌf) *adj* **1** rauh. **2** roh, grob. **3** wild. **roughly** *adv* ungefähr.
roulette (ru:'let) *n* Roulett *neu.*
round (raund) *adj* rund, kreisförmig. *adv* herum, rundum. *n* **1** Runde *f.* **2** Serie *f.* *vt* runden. *prep* um. **roundabout** *adj* indirekt, umständlich, weitschweifig. *n* **1** Kreisverkehr *m.* **2** Karussell *neu.*
rouse (rauz) *vt* (auf)wecken, erregen.
route (ru:t) *n* Route *f.* Weg *m.* *vt* leiten, senden.

routine (ru:'ti:n) *n* Routine *f. adj* üblich, Routine—.
rove (rouv) *vi* umherschweifen.
row[1] (rou) *n* Reihe, Zeile *f.*
row[2] (rou) *vi,vt* rudern.
row[3] (rau) *n inf* Krach, Streit *m. vi* streiten.
rowdy ('raudi) *n* Raufbold, Rowdy *m. adj* rauflustig.
royal ('rɔiəl) *adj* königlich. **royalty** *n* **1** königlicher Rang *m.* **2** Mitglieder der königlichen Familie *pl.* **3** Verfasserhonorar *neu.*
rub (rʌb) *vt,vi* reiben.
rubber ('rʌbə) *n* **1** Gummi *neu.* **2** Radiergummi *neu.* **rubber band** *n* Gummiband *neu.*
rubbish ('rʌbiʃ) *n* **1** Müll, Abfall *m.* **2** *inf* Quatsch *m.*
rubble ('rʌbəl) *n* Bauschutt *m.*
ruby ('ru:bi) *n* Rubin *m.*
rucksack ('rʌksæk) *n* Rucksack *m.*
rudder ('rʌdə) *n* (Steuer)Ruder *neu.*
rude (ru:d) *adj* **1** unhöflich. **2** roh. **3** rauh.
rudiment ('ru:dimənt) *n* **1** Rudiment *neu.* **2** *pl* Rudimente *neu pl.* Grundlagen *f pl.*
rueful ('ru:fəl) *adj* kummervoll, reumütig.
ruff (rʌf) *n* Halskrause *f.*
ruffian ('rʌfiən) *n* Raufbold *m.*
ruffle ('rʌfəl) *vt* **1** kräuseln. **2** sträuben. **3** verärgern. *n* **1** Kräuselung *f.* **2** Kräuseln *neu.*
rug (rʌg) *n* **1** Decke *f.* **2** Vorleger *m.* kleiner Teppich *m.*
rugby ('rʌgbi) *n* Rugby *neu.*
rugged ('rʌgid) *adj* uneben, rauh, derb.
ruin ('ru:in) *n* **1** Ruine *f.* **2** Verfall *m.* **3** Trümmer *m pl. vt* **1** verderben. **2** zugrunde richten, ruinieren.
rule (ru:l) *n* **1** Regel *f.* **2** Gewohnheit *f.* **3** Herrschaft *f.* **4** Lineal *neu. vt* **1** regeln, bestimmen. **2** regieren, beherrschen. **3** ziehen. **ruler** *n* **1** Herrscher *m.* **2** Lineal *neu.*
rum (rʌm) *n* Rum *m.*
Rumania (ru:'meiniə) *n* Rumänien *neu.* **Rumanian** *adj* rumänisch. *n* **1** Rumäne *m.* **2** (language) Rumänisch *m.*
rumble ('rʌmbəl) *vi* rumpeln. *n* Rumpeln *neu.*
rummage ('rʌmidʒ) *vi* (herum)stöbern. **rummage through** durchstöbern.
rumour ('ru:mə) *n* Gerücht *neu.* **rumour has it** es geht das Gerücht.
rump (rʌmp) *n* Steiß *m.* **rump steak** *n* Rumpsteak *neu.*
run* (rʌn) *vi* **1** rennen, laufen. **2** fließen. **3** lauten. **4** im Gang sein. *vt* **1** betreiben. **2** rennen, laufen. **3** in Gang halten. **4** befördern. **run away** davonlaufen. **run out 1** hinauslaufen. **2** zu Ende gehen. **run over** überfahren. ~*n* **1** Lauf *m.* Rennen *neu.* **2** Zustrom *neu.* **3** *comm* Zulauf *m.* **runner** *n* **1** Läufer *m.* **2** Bote *m.* **runner bean** *n* Stangenbohne *f.* **runner-up** *n* Zweitbeste(r) *m.* **running** *n* **1** Laufen, Rennen *neu.* **2** Betrieb *m.* **runway** *n aviat* Startbahn, Landebahn *f.*
rung[1] (rʌŋg) *v* see **ring**[2].
rung[2] (rʌŋ) *n* **1** (of a ladder) Sprosse *f.* **2** Stufe *f.*
rupture ('rʌptʃə) *n* Bruch, Riß

m. *vt* sprengen, brechen, (zer)reißen. *vi* einen Bruch *or* Riß bekommen.
rural ('ruərəl) *adj* ländlich, Land—.
rush[1] (rʌʃ) *vi* (sich) stürzen, stürmen. *vt* **1** drängen, hetzen. **2** sich stürzen auf. *n* **1** Hast *f*. **2** Andrang *m*. **rush hour** Hauptverkehrszeit *f*.
rush[2] (rʌʃ) *n bot* Binse *f*.
Russia ('rʌʃə) *n* Rußland *neu*. **Russian** *adj* russisch. *n* **1** Russe *m*. **2** (language) Russisch *neu*.
rust (rʌst) *n* Rost *m*. *vi* (ver)rosten. **rusty** *adj* **1** verrostet. **2** außer Übung.
rustic ('rʌstik) *adj* **1** bäuerisch. **2** ländlich, rustikal.
rustle ('rʌsəl) *vi,(vt)* rascheln (mit). *n* Geraschel *neu*.
rut (rʌt) *n* **1** Furche *f*. **2** (Rad)Spur *f*. **be in a rut** stagnieren.
ruthless ('ru:θləs) *adj* **1** erbarmungslos. **2** rücksichtslos.
rye (rai) *n* Roggen *m*.

S

Sabbath ('sæbəθ) *n* Sabbat *m*.
sable ('seibəl) *n* Zobel *m*.
sabotage ('sæbətɑ:ʒ) *n* Sabotage *f*. *vt* sabotieren.
sabre ('seibə) *n* Säbel *m*.
saccharin ('sækərin) *n* Saccharin *neu*.
sachet ('sæʃei) *n* **1** Sachet *neu*. **2** Schampoobeutel *m*. **3** Duftkissen *neu*.
sack (sæk) *n* Sack *m*. **get the sack** *sl* entlassen werden. ~*vt sl* entlassen.
sacrament ('sækrəmənt) *n* Sakrament *neu*.
sacred ('seikrid) *adj* heilig, geweiht.
sacrifice ('sækrifais) *n* **1** Opfer *neu*. **2** Verlust *m*. *vt* opfern.
sacrilege ('sækrilidʒ) *n* Sakrileg *neu*. Entweihung, Kirchenschändung *f*.
sad (sæd) *adj* **1** traurig. **2** ernst, schlimm. **3** düster. **sadden** *vt* betrüben, traurig machen. *vi* traurig werden.
saddle ('sædl̩) *n* Sattel *m*. *vt* satteln.
sadism ('seidizəm) *n* Sadismus *m*. **sadist** *n* Sadist *m*. **sadistic** *adj* sadistisch.
safari (sə'fɑ:ri) *n* Safari *f*.
safe (seif) *adj* **1** sicher. **2** heil. **3** vorsichtig. **play safe** kein Risiko eingehen. ~*n* Geldschrank, Safe *m*. **safeguard** *n* Vorsichtsmaßnahme *f*. Schutz *m*. *vt* **1** schützen. **2** sichern. **safety** *n* Sicherheit *f*. **safety belt** *n* Sicherheitsgürtel *m*. **safety pin** *n* Sicherheitsnadel *f*.
saffron ('sæfrən) *n* Safran *m*. *adj* safrangelb.
sag (sæg) *vi* **1** sacken. **2** nachlassen.
saga ('sɑ:gə) *n* Saga *f*.
sage[1] (seidʒ) *n* Weise(r) *m*. *adj* weise.
sage[2] (seidʒ) *n* Salbei *m,f*.
Sagittarius (sædʒi'tɛəriəs) *n* Schütze *m*.
sago ('seigou) *n* Sago *m*.
said (sed) *v* see **say**.
sail (seil) *n* **1** Segel *neu*. **2** Seefahrt *f*. *vi,vt* segeln, fahren. **sailor** *n* Matrose, Seemann *m*.
saint (seint) *n* Heilige(r) *m*.

sake (seik) *n* **for the sake of** um...willen. **for my sake** um meinetwillen.
salad ('sæləd) *n* Salat *m*. **salad dressing** *n* Salatsoße *f*.
salami (sə'lɑːmi) *n* Salami *f*.
salary ('sæləri) *n* Gehalt *neu*. *vt* besolden.
sale (seil) *n* **1** Verkauf *m*. **2** Ausverkauf *m*. **3** Absatz *m*. **salesman** *n* Verkäufer *m*.
saliva (sə'laivə) *n* Speichel *m*. **salivate** *vi* Speichel absondern.
sallow ('sælou) *adj* bläßlich, gelblich.
salmon ('sæmən) *n* Lachs *m*.
salon ('sælɔn) *n* Salon *m*.
saloon (sə'luːn) *n* Salon, Saal *m*. **saloon car** Limousine *f*.
salt (sɔːlt) *n* Salz *neu*. *adj* salzig, Salz—. *vt* (ein)salzen. **salt-cellar** *n* Salzfäßchen *neu*. **salty** *adj* salzig.
salute (sə'luːt) *n* **1** Gruß *m*. **2** *mil* Ehrenbezeichnung *f*. *vi* grüßen. *vt* **1** (be)grüßen. **2** *mil* salutieren vor.
salvage ('sælvidʒ) *n* Bergung *f*. *vt* bergen.
salvation (sæl'veiʃən) *n* **1** *rel* Erlösung *f*. **2** (Er)Rettung *f*.
same (seim) *adj,pron* derselbe, der gleiche. *adv* ebenso. **all the same** trotzdem.
sample ('sɑːmpəl) *n* **1** Probe *f*. **2** Auswahl *f*. **3** Muster *neu*. *vt* (aus)probieren.
sanatorium (sænə'tɔːriəm) *n*, *pl* **-iums** *or* **-ia** Sanatorium *neu*. Heilanstalt *f*.
sanction ('sæŋkʃən) *n* **1** Sanktion, Billigung *f*. **2** Zwangsmaßnahme *f*. *vt* billigen, gutheißen.
sanctity ('sæŋktiti) *n* Heiligkeit *f*.
sanctuary ('sæŋktʃuəri) *n* **1** Asyl *neu*. **2** *rel* Heiligtum *neu*.
sand (sænd) *n* **1** Sand *m*. **2** *pl* Sandfläche *f*. Strand *m*.
sandal ('sændl̩) *n* Sandale *f*.
sandwich ('sænwidʒ) *n* Sandwich, belegtes Brot, Butterbrot *neu*.
sane (sein) *adj* **1** geistig gesund. **2** vernünftig.
sang (sæŋ) *v* see **sing.**
sanitary ('sænitri) *adj* gesundheitlich, hygienisch. **sanitary towel** *n* Damenbinde *f*.
sank (sæŋk) *v* see **sink.**
sap (sæp) *n bot* Saft *m*.
sapphire ('sæfaiə) *n* Saphir *m*.
sarcasm ('sɑːkæzəm) *n* Sarkasmus, bitterer Hohn *m*. **sarcastic** *adj* sarkastisch.
sardine (sɑː'diːn) *n* Sardine *f*.
Sardinia (sɑː'diniə) *n* Sardinien *neu*.
sardonic (sɑː'dɔnik) *adj* höhnisch, sardonisch.
sash[1] (sæʃ) *n* Schärpe *f*.
sash[2] (sæʃ) *n* Fensterrahmen *m*. **sash-window** *n* Schiebefenster *neu*.
sat (sæt) *v* see **sit.**
Satan ('seitn̩) *n* Satan *m*.
satchel ('sætʃəl) *n* Schultasche *f*.
satellite ('sætəlait) *n* Satellit *m*.
satin ('sætin) *n* Atlas, Satin *m*.
satire ('sætaiə) *n* **1** Satire *f*. **2** Spott *m*. **satirical** *adj* satirisch.
satisfy ('sætisfai) *vt* **1** zufriedenstellen, befriedigen. **2** genügen. **3** überzeugen. **sat-**

isfaction *n* **1** Zufriedenheit *f.* **2** Genugtuung *f.*
saturate ('sætʃəreit) *vt* sättigen.
Saturday ('sætədi) *n* Sonnabend, Samstag *m.*
Saturn ('sætən) *n* Saturn *m.*
sauce (sɔːs) *n* **1** Soße *f.* **2** *inf* Frechheit *f.* **saucepan** *n* Kochtopf *m.* **saucer** *n* Untertasse *f.* **saucy** *adj* frech.
Saudi Arabia ('saudi) *n* Saudi-Arabien *neu.*
sauna ('sɔːnə) *n* Sauna *f.*
saunter ('sɔːntə) *vi* schlendern. *n* Schlendern *neu.*
sausage ('sɔsidʒ) *n* Wurst *f.*
savage ('sævidʒ) *adj* wild. *n* Wilde(r) *m.*
save[1] (seiv) *vt* **1** (er)retten. **2** bewahren. **3** (money) sparen. **savings** *n pl* Ersparnisse *f pl.*
save[2] (seiv) *prep* außer, ausgenommen.
saviour ('seiviə) *n* **1** *rel* Erlöser, Heiland *m.* **2** Retter *m.*
savoury ('seivəri) *adj* **1** schmackhaft. **2** würzig. *n* pikantes Gericht *neu.*
saw*[1] (sɔː) *n* Säge *f.* *vi,vt* sägen. **sawdust** *n* Sägemehl *neu.*
saw[2] (sɔː) *v* see **see**[1].
Saxon ('sæksən) *adj* **1** sächsisch. **2** angelsächsisch. *n* **1** Sachse *m.* **2** Angelsachse *m.*
saxophone ('sæksəfoun) *n* Saxophon *neu.*
say* (sei) *vt,vi* **1** sagen. **2** sprechen. **3** äußern. **4** heißen, bedeuten. *n* Wort *neu.* Rede *f.* **saying** *n* **1** Sprichwort *neu.* **2** Redensart *f.*
scab (skæb) *n* Schorf *m.* Krätze *f.*
scaffold ('skæfəld) *n* **1** (Bau)Gerüst *neu.* **2** Schafott *neu.* **scaffolding** *n* Gerüst *neu.*
scald (skɔːld) *vt* (ver)brühen. *n* Verbrühung *f.* **scalding** *adj* **1** brühend. **2** brühheiß.
scale[1] (skeil) *n* **1** *zool* Schuppe *f.* **2** Kesselstein *m.* *vt* abschuppen.
scale[2] (skeil) *n* **1** Waagschale *f.* **2** *pl* Waage *f.*
scale[3] (skeil) *n* **1** Maßstab *m.* **2** Skala *f.* **3** Ausmaß *neu.* **4** *mus* Tonleiter *f.* *vt* ersteigen.
scallop ('skɔləp) *n* Kammuschel *f.*
scalp (skælp) *n* Kopfhaut *f.*
scalpel ('skælpəl) *n* Skalpell *neu.*
scampi ('skæmpi) *n* Kaiserhummer *m.*
scan (skæn) *vt* **1** untersuchen, prüfen. **2** abtasten. **3** *lit* skandieren.
scandal ('skændl̩) *n* **1** Skandal *m.* **2** Verleumdung *f.* **scandalous** *adj* skandalös.
Scandinavia (skændi'neiviə) *n* Skandinavien *neu.* **Scandinavian** *adj* skandinavisch. *n* Skandinavier *m.*
scapegoat ('skeipgout) *n* Sündenbock *m.*
scar (skɑː) *n* Narbe, Schramme *f.* *vt* **1** schrammen. **2** entstellen. *vi* vernarben.
scarce (skɛəs) *adj* **1** knapp. **2** spärlich. **scarcely** *adv* kaum.
scare (skɛə) *vt* erschrecken. *n* Schreck(en) *m.*
scarf (skɑːf) *n* Schal *m.* Halstuch *neu.*
scarlet ('skɑːlit) *adj*

scharlachrot. **scarlet fever** *n* Scharlachfieber *neu*.
scathing ('skeiðiŋ) *adj* scharf, beißend, ätzend.
scatter ('skætə) *vt* **1** (ver)streuen. **2** zerstreuen. *vi* sich zerstreuen.
scavenge ('skævindʒ) *vt* reinigen. *vi* Nährung suchen. **scavenger** *n* **1** Aasgeier *m*. **2** Straßenkehrer *m*.
scene (siːn) *n* **1** Szene *f*. **2** Schauplatz *m*. **3** Bild *neu*. **behind the scenes** hinter den Kulissen.
scenery ('siːnəri) *n* **1** Bühnenbild *neu*. **2** Landschaft *f*.
scent (sent) *n* **1** Geruch, Duft *m*. **2** Parfüm *neu*. **3** Spur *f*. *vt* **1** riechen. **2** parfümieren.
sceptic ('skeptik) *n* Skeptiker *m*. **sceptical** *adj* skeptisch. **scepticism** *n* Skeptizismus *m*.
sceptre ('septə) *n* Zepter *neu*.
schedule ('ʃedjuːl) *n* **1** Arbeitsplan *m*. **2** Fahrplan *m*. **3** Liste *f*. *vt* **1** aufzeichnen. **2** planen.
scheme (skiːm) *n* **1** Plan *m*. **2** Intrige *f*. **3** Schema *neu*. *vi* Ränke schmieden, intrigieren.
schizophrenia (skitsou'friːniə) *n* Schizophrenie *f*. **schizophrenic** *adj* schizophren. *n* Schizophrene(r) *m*.
scholar ('skɔlə) *n* **1** Gelehrete(r) *m*. **2** Studierende(r) *m*. *f*. **3** Stipendiat *m*. **scholarship** *n* **1** Stipendium *neu*. **2** Gelehrsamkeit *f*.
scholastic (skə'læstik) *adj* **1** akademisch. **2** Schul—, schulisch.
school[1] (skuːl) *n* Schule *f*. *vt* schulen. **schoolboy** *n* Schüler *m*. **schoolgirl** *n* Schülerin *f*. **schoolmaster** *n* Lehrer, Schulleiter *m*. **schoolmistress** *n* Lehrerin *f*.
school[2] (skuːl) *n zool* Schule *f*. Schwarm *m*.
schooner ('skuːnə) *n* **1** *naut* Schoner *m*. **2** (hohes) Bierglas *or* Weinglas *neu*.
science ('saiəns) *n* **1** Wissenschaft *f*. **2** Naturwissenschaft *f*. **science fiction** *n* Zukunftsroman *m*. **scientific** *adj* wissenschaftlich. **scientist** *n* (Natur)Wissenschaftler *m*.
scissors ('sizəz) *n pl* Schere *f*.
scoff[1] (skɔf) *vi* spotten. *n* Spott *m*.
scoff[2] (skɔf) *vt sl* fressen.
scold (skould) *vt* ausschimpfen. *vi* schimpfen.
scone (skoun) *n* (flaches) Teegebäck *neu*.
scoop (skuːp) *n* **1** Schaufel *f*. **2** Schöpfkelle *f*. **3** Schub *m*. **4** Erstmeldung *f*. *vt* schaufeln, schöpfen.
scooter ('skuːtə) *n* (Motor)Roller *m*.
scope (skoup) *n* **1** Spielraum *m*. **2** Gebiet *neu*. Bereich *m*.
scorch (skɔːtʃ) *vt* **1** versengen. **2** verbrennen. *vi* verbrennen.
score (skɔː) *n* **1** *sport* (Punkt)Zahl *f*. **2** Rechnung *f*. **4** *mus* Partitur *f*. **5** Kerbe *f*. *vt* **1** gewinnen. **2** einkerben. **3** (a goal) schießen. *vi* Punkte gewinnen. **scoreboard** *n* Anschreibetafel *f*.
scorn (skɔːn) *n* Hohn *m*. Verachtung *f*. *vt* verachten. **scornful** *adj* verächtlich.

Scorpio ('skɔːpiou) *n* Skorpion *m.*

scorpion ('skɔːpiən) *n* Skorpion *m.*

Scotland ('skɔtlənd) *n* Schottland *neu.* **Scot** *n* Schotte *m.* **Scotch** *adj* schottisch. *n* (schottischer) Whisky *m.* **Scots** *n* schottischer Dialekt. *adj* schottisch. **Scottish** *adj* schottisch.

scoundrel ('skaundrəl) *n* Schurke, Schuft *m.*

scour[1] ('skauə) *vt* **1** scheuern. **2** wegwischen.

scour[2] ('skauə) *vt* durchsuchen, durchstreifen.

scout (skaut) *n* **1** Späher, Kundschafter *m.* **2** Pfadfinder *m. vi,vt* kundschaften, spähen.

scowl (skaul) *vi* finster blicken. *n* finsterer Blick *m.*

scramble ('skræmbəl) *vi* **1** krabbeln. **2** sich balgen. *n* **1** Krabbelei *f.* **2** Balgerei *f.*

scrap (skræp) *n* **1** Stückchen *neu.* Brocken *m.* **2** Schrott *m. vt* **1** wegwerfen. **2** verzichten auf. **3** verschrotten. *adj* Schrott—. **scrapbook** *n* Einklebebuch *neu.*

scrape (skreip) *vt* **1** kratzen, schaben. *vi* kratzen. *n* **1** Kratzen *neu.* **2** Klemme *f.*

scratch (skrætʃ) *vt* kratzen. *n* **1** Kratzen *neu.* **2** Schramme *f.* Riß *m.*

scrawl (skrɔːl) *vt,vi* kritzeln. *n* Gekritzel *neu.*

scream (skriːm) *vi,vt* schreien. *n* Schrei *m.*

screech (skriːtʃ) *vi,vt* kreischen, schreien. *n* Kreischen *neu.*

screen (skriːn) *n* **1** Schirm *m.* **2** (Lein)Wand *f. vt* **1** (ab)schirmen. **2** überprüfen. **3** (a film) vorführen.

screw (skruː) *n* Schraube *f. vt* schrauben. **screwdriver** *n* Schraubenzieher *m.*

scribble ('skribəl) *vt,vi* kritzeln. *n* Gekritzel *neu.*

script (skript) *n* **1** *Th* Manuskript *neu.* **2** (of a film) Drehbuch *neu.* **3** Schrift *f.*

Scripture ('skriptʃə) *n* Heilige Schrift *f.*

scroll (skroul) *n* **1** Schriftrolle *f.* **2** Schnörkel *m.*

scrounge (skraundʒ) *vt,vi* schnorren, klauen.

scrub[1] (skrʌb) *vi,vt* schrubben, scheuern. *n* Schrubben *neu.* **scrubbing brush** *n* Scheuerbürste *f.*

scrub[2] (skrʌb) *n* Gestrüpp *neu.* Busch *m.*

scruffy ('skrʌfi) *adj inf* schäbig.

scruple ('skruːpəl) *n* Skrupel *m.* Bedenken *neu.* **have scruples** sich ein Gewissen machen. **scrupulous** *adj* gewissenhaft.

scrutiny ('skruːtini) *n* **1** Untersuchung *f.* **2** prüfender Blick *m.* **scrutinize** *vt* **1** (genau) prüfen, untersuchen. **2** genau ansehen.

scuffle ('skʌfəl) *n* Balgerei, Schlägerei *f. vi* sich balgen, raufen.

scullery ('skʌləri) *n* Spülküche *f.*

sculpt (skʌlpt) *vt* (heraus)meißeln, schnitzen. *vi* bildhauern. **sculptor** *n* Bildhauer *m.* **sculpture** *n* Bildhauerei, Skulptur *f.*

scum (skʌm) *n* **1** Schaum *m*. **2** Abschaum *m*.
scurf (skəːf) *n* **1** Schuppen *f pl*. **2** Schorf *m*.
scythe (saið) *n* Sense *f*. *vt* (ab)mähen.
sea (siː) *n* See *f*. Meer *neu*. **by the sea** an der See.
seabed ('siːbed) *n* Meeresgrund *m*.
seafront ('siːfrʌnt) *n* Strandpromenade *f*.
seagull ('siːgʌl) *n* Möwe *f*.
seal[1] (siːl) *n* **1** Siegel *neu*. **2** Stempel *m*. **3** Dichtung *f*. *vt* **1** (ver)siegeln. **2** bestätigen. **3** abdichten.
seal[2] (siːl) *n* Seehund *m*. Robbe *f*. **sealskin** *n* Seehundfell *neu*.
sea-level *n* Meersspiegel *m*. Meereshöhe *f*.
sea-lion *n* Seelöwe *m*.
seam (siːm) *n* **1** Saum *m*. Naht *f*. **2** Spalt *m*. **3** Schicht *f*. *vt* säumen.
seaman ('siːmən) *n* Seemann, Matrose *m*.
search (səːtʃ) *vt* durchsuchen. **2** erforschen. *vi* suchen, forschen. *n* Suche *f*. **searchlight** *n* Scheinwerfer *f*.
seashore ('siːʃɔː) *n* Seeküste *f*.
seasick ('siːsik) *adj* seekrank.
seaside ('siːsaid) *n* Seeküste *f*. **go to the seaside** an die See fahren. *~adj* See—. **seaside resort** *n* Seebad *neu*.
season ('siːzən) *n* **1** Jahreszeit *f*. **2** Saison *f*. **season ticket** *n* Dauerkarte *f*. *vt* **1** *cul* würzen. **2** ausreifen lassen. **seasoning** *n* Würze *f*.
seat (siːt) *n* **1** Sitz, Platz *m*. **2** Bank *f*. **3** Wohnsitz *m*. **3** Gesäß *neu*. *vt* **1** setzen. **2** Raum haben für. **seat-belt** *n* Sitzgurt *m*.
seaweed ('siːwiːd) *n* Alge *f*.
secluded (si'kluːdid) *adj* abgelegen, abgeschlossen.
second[1] ('sekənd) *adj* **1** zweite. **2** nächst. **second best** *adj* zweitbest. **second-class** *adj,adv* zweiter Klasse. *adj* zweitrangig. **second-hand** *adj* aus zweiter Hand, gebraucht. **secondly** *adv* zweitens. **second-rate** *adj* zweitrangig, minderwertig.
secondary *adj* **1** untergeordnet. **2** sekundär. **3** Neben—. **secondary school** *n* Oberschule *f*.
second[2] ('sekənd) *n* Sekunde *f*.
secret ('siːkrət) *n* Geheimnis *neu*. *adj* geheim, heimlich. **secrecy** *n* Geheimhaltung, Verschwiegenheit *f*. **secretive** *adj* geheimtuerisch.
secretary ('sekrətri) *n* **1** Sekretär *m*. Sekretärin *f*. **2** Schriftführer *m*. **3** Schreibtisch *m*.
secrete (si'kriːt) *vt* **1** verbergen, verheimlichen. **2** *anat* absondern.
sect (sekt) *n* Sekte *f*. **sectarian** *adj* sektiererisch.
section ('sekʃən) *n* **1** Abschnitt, Teil *m*. **2** Abteilung *f*. **3** Schnitt *m*. **4** Sektion *f*.
sector ('sektə) *n* **1** Abschnitt *m*. **2** *math* Sektor *m*.
secular ('sekjulə) *adj* weltlich, säkular.
secure (si'kjuə) *adj* **1** sicher. **2** fest. *vt* **1** sichern. **2** sicherstel-

len. **3** festbinden, festmachen. **security** *n* Sicherheit *f*.

sedate (si'deit) *adj* gesetzt, ernst, ruhig. **sedation** *n* Beruhigung *f*. **sedative** *adj* beruhigend, stillend. *n* Beruhigungsmittel *neu*.

sediment ('sedimənt) *n* **1** Satz *m*. **2** Sediment *neu*. **3** Ablagerung *f*.

seduce (si'dju:s) *vt* verführen. **seduction** *n* Verführung *f*.

see* [1] (si:) *vt,vi* **1** sehen. **2** verstehen. **3** besichtigen, ansehen. **4** besuchen. **see off** fortbegleiten. **see out** hinausbegleiten. **see through 1** durchschauen. **2** durchführen.

see [2] (si:) *n* Bischofssitz *m*.

seed (si:d) *n* **1** Same(n) *m*. Saat *f*. **2** Keim *m*. **seedling** *n* Sämling *neu*. **seedy** *adj* schäbig, mies.

seek* (si:k) *vt,vi* suchen.

seem (si:m) *vi* **1** (er)scheinen. **2** aussehen. **seeming** *adj* anscheinend.

seep (si:p) *vi* sickern.

seesaw ('si:sɔ:) *n* Wippe *f*. *vi* wippen.

seethe (si:ð) *vi* **1** sieden, kochen. **2** brodeln.

segment ('segmənt) *n* Abschnitt *m*.

segregate ('segrigeit) *vt* absondern, trennen. *vi* sich absondern.

seize (si:z) *vt* **1** ergreifen, packen. **2** an sich reißen. **3** begreifen.

seldom ('seldəm) *adv* selten.

select (si'lekt) *vt* aussuchen, auswählen. *adj* ausgewählt. **selection** *n* Auswahl *f*. **selective** *adj* auswählend, selektiv.

self (self) *n, pl* **selves** Selbst, Ich *neu*. *pron* selbst.

self-assured *adj* selbstsicher.

self-aware *adj* selbstbewußt.

self-catering *adj* selbstversorgend.

self-centred *adj* egozentrisch, ichbezogen.

self-confident *adj* selbstsicher.

self-conscious *adj* **1** befangen. **2** selbstbewußt.

self-contained *adj* **1** selbständig. **2** zurückhaltend. **3** (in sich) geschlossen.

self-defence *n* Notwehr, Selbstverteidigung *f*.

self-discipline *n* Selbstdisziplin *f*.

self-employed *adj* selbständig.

self-expression *n* Ausdruck der eigenen Persönlichkeit *m*.

self-indulgent *adj* schwächlich, genußsüchtig.

self-interest *n* Eigennutz *m*.

selfish ('selfiʃ) *adj* selbstsüchtig, eigennützig. **selfishness** *n* Selbstsucht *f*.

self-pity *n* Selbstbemitleidung *f*.

self-portrait *n* Selbstporträt *neu*.

self-respect *n* Selbstachtung *f*.

self-righteous *adj* selbstgerecht, pharisäisch.

self-sacrifice *n* Selbstaufopferung *f*.

selfsame ('selfseim) *adj* eben derselbe.

self-satisfied *adj* selbstzufrieden.

self-service *n* Selbstbedienung *f*.

self-sufficient *adj* unabhängig, selbständig.
self-will *n* Eigensinn *m*.
sell* (sel) *vt* verkaufen. *vi* handeln. **sell out** *or* **up** ausverkaufen.
Sellotape ('seləteip) *n Tdmk* Klebestreifen *m*.
semantic (si'mæntik) *adj* semantisch. **semantics** *n* Semantik *f*.
semaphore ('seməfɔː) *n* Semaphor *m*.
semibreve ('semibriːv) *n mus* ganze Note *f*.
semicircle ('semisəːkəl) *n* Halbkreis *m*.
semicolon (semi'koulən) *n* Strichpunkt *m*.
semidetached (semidi'tætʃt) *adj* halb freistehend.
semifinal (semi'fainl̩) *n* Vorschlußrunde *f*. Semifinale *neu*.
seminar ('seminɑː) *n* Seminar *neu*.
semiprecious (semi'preʃəs) *adj* Halbedel—.
semiquaver (semi'kweivə) *n mus* Sechzehntelnote *f*.
semivowel ('semivauəl) *n* Halbvokal *m*.
semolina (seməliːnə) *n* Grieß *m*.
senate ('senət) *n* Senat *m*. **Senator** *n* Senator *m*.
send* (send) *vt* schicken, (ab)senden. **send for** kommen lassen. **send word** mitteilen. **sender** *n* (Ab)Sender *m*.
senile ('siːnail) *adj* altersschwach.
senior ('siːniə) *adj* **1** älter. **2** Senior—. *n* **1** Ältere(r) *m*. **2** Senior *m*.
sensation (sen'seiʃən) *n* **1** Empfindung *f*. **2** Sensation *f*. **sensational** *adj* sensationell.
sense (sens) *n* **1** Sinn *m*. **2** Empfindung *f*. **3** Vernunft *f*. **4** Bedeutung *f*. **talk sense** vernünftig reden. *~vt* empfinden, spüreng fühlen. **senseless** *adj* **1** sinnlos. **2** bewußtlos.
sensible ('sensəbəl) *adj* **1** verständig, vernünftig. **2** fühlbar. **3** empfänglich. **sensibility** *n* **1** Empfindungsvermögen *neu*. **2** Empfindlichkeit *f*.
sensitive ('sensitiv) *adj* empfindlich, sensibel, feinfühlig. **sensitivity** *n* **1** Empfindlichkeit *f*. **2** Empfindungsvermögen *neu*. **3** Feingefühl *neu*.
sensual ('senʃuəl) *adj* sinnlich. **sensuality** *n* Sinnlichkeit *f*.
sensuous ('senʃuəs) *adj* sinnenfreudig, sinnlich.
sentence ('sentəns) *n* **1** Satz *m*. **2** Urteil *neu*. *vt* verurteilen.
sentiment ('sentimənt) *n* **1** Gefühl *neu*. Empfindung *f*. **2** *pl* Gesinnung *f*. **sentimental** *adj* sentimental. **sentimentality** *n* Sentimentalität *f*.
sentry ('sentri) *n* Wache *f*.
separate (*v* 'sepəreit; *adj* 'seprit) *(vi),vt* (sich) trennen, (sich) scheiden. *adj* getrennt, gesondert. **separation** *n* Trennung, Scheidung *f*.
September (sep'tembə) *n* September *m*.
septic ('septik) *adj* septisch, eitrig.

sequel ('siːkwəl) *n* **1** Folge *f*. **2** Fortsetzung *f*.

sequence ('siːkwəns) *n* **1** (Reihen)Folge *f*. **2** Szene *f*.

sequin ('siːkwin) *n* Zechine *f*.

serenade (serə'neid) *n* Ständchen *neu*. Serenade *f*. *vt* ein Ständchen bringen.

serene (si'riːn) *adj* **1** heiter. **2** ruhig. **serenity** *n* **1** Heiterkeit *f*. **2** Ruhe *f*.

serf (səːf) *n* **1** Leibeigene(r) *m*. **2** Sklave *m*.

sergeant ('sɑːdʒənt) *n* **1** *mil* Feldwebel *m*. **2** (Polizei)Sergeant *m*. **sergeant-major** *n* *mil* Hauptfeldwebel *m*.

serial ('siəriəl) *adj* **1** Fortsetzungs—. **2** serienmäßig. *n* Fortsetzungsroman *m*. **serialize** *vt* in Fortsetzungen veröffentlichen.

series ('siəriːz) *n* **1** Reihe *f*. **2** Serie *f*. **3** Folge *f*.

serious ('siəriəs) *adj* ernst, ernsthaft. **seriousness** *n* Ernst *m*. Ernsthaftigkeit *f*.

sermon ('səːmən) *n* Predigt *f*.

serpent ('səːpənt) *n* Schlange *f*.

servant ('səːvənt) *n* Diener *m*.

serve (səːv) *vt,vi* **1** (be)dienen. **2** erfüllen. **3** nützen. **4** *sport* aufschlagen. **it serves him right** das geschieht ihm recht. *n sport* Aufschlag *m*.

service ('səːvis) *n* **1** Dienst *m*. **2** Bedienung *f*. **3** *sport* Aufschlag *m*. **4** *rel* Gottesdienst *m*. **5** Kundendienst *m*. **6** *mot* Service *neu*. **serviceable** *adj* **1** dienlich. **2** betriebsfähig. **service station** *n* Tankstelle *f*.

serviette (səːvi'et) *n* Serviette *f*.

servile ('səvail) *adj* **1** unterwürfig, servil. **2** sklavisch.

session ('seʃən) *n* Sitzung *f*. **be in session** tagen.

set* (set) *vt* **1** setzen. **2** stellen. **3** legen. **4** (ein)richten. *vi* **1** (of the sun) untergehen. **2** *cul* gerinnen. **set an example** ein Beispiel geben. **set off** sich auf den Weg machen.~*adj* **1** fest. **2** bestimmt. **3** vorgeschrieben. *n* **1** Satz *m*. Sammlung *f*. **2** Serie *f*. **setback** *n* Rückschlag *m*. **setting** *n* **1** Setzen *neu*. **2** (of a gem) Fassung *f*. **3** Bühnenausstattung *f*.

settee (se'tiː) *n* Sofa *neu*.

settle ('setḷ) *vt* **1** (fest)setzen. **2** erledigen. **3** entscheiden. **4** beruhigen. *vi* **1** sich ansiedeln. **2** (of the weather) beständig werden. **settle down** sich niederlassen. **settle with** sich begnügen mit. **settlement** *n* **1** Regelung *f*. **2** (Be)Siedlung *f*. **settler** *n* Siedler m.

seven ('sevən) *adj* sieben. *n* Sieben *f*. **seventh** *adj* siebente, siebte.

seventeen (sevən'tiːn) *adj* siebzehn. *n* Siebzehn *f*. **seventeenth** *adj* siebzehnte.

seventy ('sevənti) *adj* siebzig. *n* Siebzig *f*. **seventieth** *adj* siebzigste.

several ('sevrəl) *adj* **1** mehrere. **2** einige. **3** besonder, eigen. **several times** mehrmals.

severe (si'viə) *adj* **1** streng, hart. **2** schwer. **3** heftig. **severity** *n* **1** Strenge, Härte *f*. **2** Schwere *f*.

sew* (sou) *vt,vi* nähen. **sew up** zunähen. **sewing** *n*

Nähen *neu*. **sewing machine** *n* Nähmaschine *f*.

sewage ('su:idʒ) *n* Abwasser *neu*.

sewer ('su:ə) *n* Abwasserkanal *m*. Kloake *f*.

sex (seks) *n* Geschlecht *neu*. *adj* Geschlechts—. **sexual** *adj* geschlechtlich, Geschlechts—, sexuell, Sexual—. **sexual intercourse** *n* Geschlechtsverkehr *neu*. **sexy** *adj* sexy.

sextet (seks'tet) *n* Sextett *neu*.

shabby ('ʃæbi) *adj* schäbig.

shack (ʃæk) *n* Hütte *f*.

shade (ʃeid) *n* **1** Schatten *m*. **2** Spur *f*. **3** (of a lamp, etc.) Schirm *m*. *vt* **1** beschatten. **2** abschirmen. **3** schattieren. **shady** *adj* **1** schattig. **2** anrüchig, fragwürdig.

shadow ('ʃædou) *n* **1** Schatten *m*. **2** Phantom *neu*. **3** Spur *f*. *vt* **1** beschatten. **2** verfolgen. **shadow cabinet** *n* Schattenkabinett *neu*.

shaft (ʃɑ:ft) *n* **1** Schaft *m*. **2** *tech* Welle *f*. **3** (of light) Strahl *m*.

shaggy ('ʃægi) *adj* zottig.

shake* (ʃeik) *vt* **1** schütteln. **2** erschüttern. *vi* zittern, wackeln. **shake hands with someone** jemandem die Hand geben. ~*n* **1** Schütteln *neu*. **2** Erschütterung *f*. **3** Beben *neu*. **shaky** *adj* **1** wacklig. **2** zitterig.

shall* (ʃəl; *stressed* ʃæl) *v mod aux* **1** werden. **2** wollen. **3** sollen.

shallot (ʃə'lɔt) *n* Schalotte *f*.

shallow ('ʃælou) *adj* seicht. *n* Untiefe *f*.

sham (ʃæm) *adj* **1** falsch. **2** Schein—. *vt* vortäuschen, vorgeben. *n* Täuschung *f*.

shame (ʃeim) *n* **1** Scham *f*. **2** Schamgefühl *neu*. **3** Schande *f*. **what a shame!** wie schade! ~ *vt* beschämen. **shamefaced** *adj* schamhaft, verschämt. **shameful** *adj* schändlich, schmächlich. **shameless** *adj* schamlos.

shampoo (ʃæm'pu:) *n* Shampoo, Haarwaschmittel *neu*. *vt* schampunieren.

shamrock ('ʃæmrɔk) *n* **1** Feldklee *m*. **2** (Irish emblem) Kleeblatt *neu*.

shanty[1] ('ʃænti) *n* Matrosenlied *neu*.

shanty[2] ('ʃænti) *n* Bude *f*. **shanty town** *n* Elendsviertel *neu*. schäbige Vorstadt *f*.

shape (ʃeip) *n* Gestalt, Form *f*. **in good shape** in gutem Zustand. ~*vt* gestalten, formen, bilden. *vi* sich entwickeln. **shapely** *adj* wohlgestaltet.

share (ʃεə) *n* **1** Anteil *m*. **2** Beitrag *m*. **3** *comm* Aktie *f*. **have a share in** teilhaben an. **shareholder** *n* Aktionär *m*. *vt* teilen. **share out** verteilen.

shark (ʃɑ:k) *n* **1** Hai(fisch) *m*. **2** Gauner *m*.

sharp (ʃɑ:p) *adj* **1** scharf. **2** spitz. **3** schrill. *n mus* Kreuz *neu*. **sharp-sighted** *adj* scharfsichtig. **sharpen** *vt* **1** (ver)schärfen. **2** (a pencil) spitzen. **sharpener** *n* **1** Schärfer *m*. **2** Spitzer *m*. **sharpness** *n* Schärfe *f*.

shatter ('ʃætə) *vt* zerschmettern, zerbrechen. **shattered** *adj* **1** erschüttert. **2** erschöpft.

shave (ʃeiv) *vt* **1** rasieren. **2**

(wood) (ab)schälen. *vi* sich rasieren. *n* Rasieren *neu.* **have a close shave** knapp davonkommen.

shawl (ʃɔːl) *n* Schal *m.*

she (ʃiː) *pron 3rd pers s* sie.

sheaf (ʃiːf) *n* **1** Garbe *f.* **2** Bündel *neu.*

shear* (ʃiə) *vt* scheren. **shears** *n pl* (große) Schere *f.*

sheath (ʃiːθ) *n* Scheide *f.* **sheathe** *vt* **1** in die Scheide stecken. **2** umhüllen.

shed[1] (ʃed) *n* Hütte *f.* Schuppen *m.*

shed*[2] (ʃed) *vt* **1** vergießen. **2** verbreiten. **3** abwerfen.

sheen (ʃiːn) *n* Glanz *m.*

sheep (ʃiːp) *n, pl* **sheep** Schaf *m.* **sheepdog** *n* Schäferhund *m.* **sheepskin** *n* **1** Schaffell *neu.* **2** Schafleder *neu.* **sheepish** *adj* blöd.

sheer[1] (ʃiə) *adj* **1** steil. **2** rein, bloß.

sheer[2] (ʃiə) *vi naut* abscheren.

sheet (ʃiːt) *n* **1** Bettuch *neu.* **2** Platte *f.* **3** Blatt *neu.* **4** (of water) Fläche *f.*

shelf (ʃelf) *n, pl* **shelves 1** Brett *neu.* **2** Regal *neu.* **3** *geog* Riff *m.* **shelf-life** *n* Haltbarkeitsdatum *neu.*

shell (ʃel) *n* **1** Muschel *f.* **2** Schale *f.* **3** (of a building) Gerippe *neu.* **4** Granate *f.* *vt* **1** schälen. **2** beschießen, bombardieren. **shellfish** *n* Schalentier *neu.*

shelter ('ʃeltə) *n* **1** Obdach *neu.* Schutz *m.* **2** Schirm *m.* *vt* **1** (be)schützen. **2** Zuflucht gewähren. *vi* Schutz suchen.

shelve (ʃelv) *vt* **1** auf ein Brett stellen. **2** beiseite legen. **3** aufschieben.

shepherd ('ʃepəd) *n* Hirt, Schäfer *m.* *vt* **1** hüten. **2** geleiten, (an)führen.

sheriff ('ʃerif) *n* Sheriff *m.*

sherry ('ʃeri) *n* Sherry *m.*

shield (ʃiːld) *n* **1** Schild *neu.* **2** Schutz, Schirm *m.* *vt* (be)schirmen.

shift (ʃift) *vt* **1** (ver-, weg-) schieben. **2** umlegen. **3** wechseln. **4** verändern. *vi* sich bewegen. *n* **1** Wechsel *m.* **2** Arbeitsschicht *f.* **shifty** *adj* schlau, raffiniert. **shiftwork** *n* Schichtarbeit *f.*

shilling ('ʃiliŋ) *n* Schilling *m.*

shimmer ('ʃimə) *vi* schimmern. *n* Schimmer *m.*

shin (ʃin) *n* Schienbein *neu.*

shine* (ʃain) *vi* **1** scheinen, leuchten. **2** glänzen. *vt* polieren. *n* **1** Schein *m.* **2** Glanz *m.*

ship (ʃip) *n* Schiff *neu.* *vt* **1** an Bord nehmen. **2** verschiffen. **shipment** *n* **1** Verschiffung *f.* **2** Ladung *f.* **shipshape** *adj* ordentlich. **shipwreck** *n* Schiffbruch *m.* *vi* scheitern, Schiffbruch leiden. **shipyard** *n* Schiffswerft *f.*

shirk (ʃəːk) *vt* sich drücken, vermeiden. **shirker** *n* Drückeberger *m.*

shirt (ʃəːt) *n* Hemd *neu.*

shit (ʃit) *n tab* Kot *m.* Exkremente *pl.*

shiver ('ʃivə) *n* Schauer *m.* *vi* **1** schauern. **2** frösteln.

shock[1] (ʃɔk) *n* **1** (An)Stoß *m.* **2** Erschütterung *f.* *vt* **1** (an)stoßen. **2** erschüttern, schockieren. **shock absorber** *n* Stoßdämpfer *m.*

shock[2] (ʃɔk) *n* (Haar)Schopf *m*.

shoddy ('ʃɔdi) *adj* minderwertig, schlecht.

shoe* (ʃuː) *n* **1** Schuh *m*. **2** (of a horse) Hufeisen *neu*. *vt* (a horse) beschlagen. **shoelace** *n* Schnürsenkel *m*.

shone (ʃɔn) *v* see **shine.**

shook (ʃuk) *v* see **shake.**

shoot* (ʃuːt) *n* **1** *bot* Sproß *m*. **2** Jagdgesellschaft *f*. *vt* **1** schießen. **2** erschießen. **3** (a film) drehen. *vi* schießen.

shop (ʃɔp) *n* **1** Laden *m*. Geschäft *neu*. **2** Fabrik, Werkstatt *f*. *vi* einkaufen gehen. **shop assistant** *n* Verkäufer *m*. **shop floor 1** Werkstatt *f*. **2** Arbeiter *m pl*. **shopkeeper** *n* Ladeninhaber *m*. **shoplifter** *n* Ladendieb *m*. **shop steward** *n* Betriebsrat *m*. **shopwindow** *n* Schaufenster *neu*. **shopping** *n* **1** Einkaufen *neu*. **2** Einkäufe *m pl*. *adj* Einkaufs—.

shore[1] (ʃɔː) *n* **1** Strand *m*. **2** Küste *f*.

shore[2] (ʃɔː) *n* Stütze *f*. *v* **shore up** stützen.

shorn (ʃɔːn) *v* see **shear.**

short (ʃɔːt) *adj* **1** kurz. **2** klein. **3** knapp. **short cut** *n* Abkürzung *f*. **shorts** *n pl* kurze Hose *f*. **shorten** *vt* (ab-, ver-)kürzen. *vi* kürzer werden.

shortage ('ʃɔːtidʒ) *n* Mangel *m*. Knappheit *f*.

shortbread ('ʃɔːtbred) *n* Mürbekuchen *m*.

shortcoming ('ʃɔːtkʌmiŋ) *n* Unzulänglichkeit *f*.

shorthand ('ʃɔːthænd) *n* Stenographie *f*. **shorthand typist** *n* Stenotypistin *f*.

shortlived ('ʃɔːtlivd) *adj* kurzlebig.

short-sighted *adj* kurzsichtig.

short-tempered *adj* reizbar, leicht aufgebracht.

short-term *adj* kurzfristig.

short-wave *adj* Kurzwellen—.

shot[1] (ʃɔt) *n* **1** Schuß *m*. **2** Kugel *f*. **3** Schütze *m*. **4** *sport* Stoß *m*. **5** *phot* Aufnahme *f*. **6** Schrotkugel *f*. **have a shot at** *inf* versuchen. **like a shot** wie der Blitz. **shotgun** *n* Schrotflinte *f*.

shot[2] (ʃɔt) *v* see **shoot.**

should (ʃəd; *stressed* ʃud) *v* see **shall.**

shoulder ('ʃouldə) *n* Schulter *f*. *vt* auf sich nehmen. **shoulder-blade** *n* Schulterblatt *neu*.

shout (ʃaut) *vi* **1** (laut) schreien. **2** jauchzen. *n* (lauter) Schrei *m*.

shove (ʃʌv) *n* Schub *m*. *vt* schieben.

shovel ('ʃʌvəl) *n* Schaufel *f*. *vt* schaufeln.

show* (ʃou) *vt* **1** zeigen. **2** ausstellen. **3** erweisen. *vi* erscheinen. **show off** angeben, sich aufspielen. ~*n* **1** Schau *f*. **2** Ausstellung *f*. **3** Anschein *m*. **4** *Th* Aufführung *f*. **show business** *n* Unterhaltungsindustrie *f*. **showcase** *n* Schaukasten *m*. **show-jumping** *n* Schauspringen *neu*. **showroom** *n* Ausstellungsraum *m*.

shower ('ʃauə) *n* **1** Guß, (Regen)Schauer *m*. **2** Dusche *f*. **3** Fülle *f*. *vt* **1** herabschütten. **2** übergießen. *vi* sich dus-

chen. **showerproof** *adj* wasserdicht.
shrank (ʃræŋk) *v* see **shrink.**
shred (ʃred) *n* **1** Schnitzel *m.* **2** Fetzen *m. vt* **1** (zer)schnitzeln. **2** zerfetzen. **3** reißen.
shrew (ʃruː) *n* **1** *zool* Spitzmaus *f.* **2** *inf* Kratzbürste *f.*
shrewd (ʃruːd) *adj* scharfsinnig.
shriek (ʃriːk) *vi* schreien, kreischen. *n* (greller) Schrei *m.*
shrill (ʃril) *adj* **1** schrill, gellend. **2** grell. *vi* schrillen, gellen.
shrimp (ʃrimp) *n* **1** Garnele *f.* **2** Knirps *m.*
shrine (ʃrain) *n* **1** Reliquienschrein *m.* **2** Altar *m.*
shrink* (ʃriŋk) *vi* **1** (ein-, zusammen-)schrumpfen. **2** sich zurückziehen. *vt* einschrumpfen lassen.
shrivel ('ʃrivəl) *vi,(vt)* schrumpfen (lassen).
shroud (ʃraud) *n* **1** Leichentuch *neu.* **2** Umhüllung *f. vt* **1** in ein Leichentuch einhüllen. **2** (ein)hüllen.
Shrove Tuesday (ʃrouv) *n* Fastnachtsdienstag *m.*
shrub (ʃrʌb) *n* Strauch, Busch *m.* **shrubbery** *n* Strauchpflanzung *f.* Strauchwerk *neu.*
shrug (ʃrʌg) *(vi),vt* (die Achseln) zucken. **shrug off** abtun. *n* (Achsel)Zucken *neu.*
shrunk (ʃrʌŋk) *v* see **shrink.** *adj* **1** eingeschrumpft. **2** eingefallen.
shudder ('ʃʌdə) *vi* **1** schaudern. **2** erbeben. *n* **1** Schauder *m.* **2** Erbeben *neu.*
shuffle ('ʃʌfəl) *vt* **1** *game* mischen. **2** hin und herschieben. *vi* schlurfen. *n* **1** Mischen *neu.* **2** Schlurfen *neu.* **3** Schiebung *f.*
shun (ʃʌn) *vt* (ver)meiden.
shunt (ʃʌnt) *vt* rangieren. *n* Rangieren *neu.*
shut* (ʃʌt) *vt* (ver)schließen, zumachen. *vi* (sich) schließen, zugehen. **shut out** ausschließen. **shut up!** *inf* halt den Mund! *~adj* zu, geschlossen.
shutter ('ʃʌtə) *n* **1** Rolladen *m.* **2** *phot* Verschluß *m.*
shuttle ('ʃʌtəl) *n* schneller Direkttransport *m.*
shuttlecock ('ʃʌtəlkɔk) *n* Federball *m.*
shy (ʃai) *adj* **1** scheu. **2** schüchtern. *vi* scheuen.
Sicily ('sisəli) *n* Sizilien *neu.* **Sicilian** *adj* sizilianisch *n* Sizilianer *m.*
sick (sik) *adj* **1** krank. **2** übel. **3** überdrüssig. **4** *inf* (of humour) schwarz. **be sick** sich erbrechen. **be sick of** satt haben. **sicken** *vi* krank werden. *vt* anekeln. **sickening** *adj* ekelhaft. **sickness** *n* **1** Krankheit *f.* **2** Übelkeit *f.*
sickle ('sikəl) *n* Sichel *f.*
side (said) *n* **1** Seite *f.* **2** Flanke *f.* **3** Partei *f. adj* Seiten—, Neben—. *v* **side with** Partei ergreifen für. **sideboard** *n* Büffett *neu.* Anrichte *f.* **side effect** *n* Nebenwirkung *f.* **sidelight** *n* Seitenlampe *f.* **sideline** *n* Nebenbeschäftigung, Seitenlinie *f.* **sideshow** *n* Nebenvorstellung *f.* **sidestep** *vi* beiseite treten. **sidetrack** *vt inf* **1** ablenken. **2** abschieben. **sideways** *adv*

seitwärts. **siding** *n* Nebengleis *neu.*

sidle ('saidl̩) *vi* **sidle up to** sich heranschleichen an.

siege (si:dʒ) *n* Belagerung *f.* **lay siege to** belagern.

sieve (siv) *n* Sieb *neu. vt* sieben.

sift (sift) *vt* **1** sieben. **2** prüfen.

sigh (sai) *vi* seufzen. *n* Seufzer *m.*

sight (sait) *n* **1** Sehkraft *f.* **2** Anblick *m.* **3** Sicht *f.* **4** *pl* Sehenswürdigkeiten *f pl.* **catch sight of** erblicken. **know by sight** vom Sehen kennen. ~*vt* sichten. **sight-read** *vt* vom Blatt singen *or* spielen. **sightseeing** *n* Besichtigung von Sehenswürdigkeiten *f.*

sign (sain) *n* **1** Zeichen *neu.* **2** Schild *neu.* **3** Wink *m. vi* winken. *vt* unterschreiben. **signpost** *n* Wegweiser *m.*

signal ('signl̩) *n* **1** Signal *neu.* **2** Zeichen *neu. vi,vt* signalisieren.

signature ('signətʃə) *n* Unterschrift *f.*

signify ('signifai) *vt* **1** bedeuten. **2** bezeichnen. **significant** *adj* **1** bedeutsam. **2** bezeichnend. **significance** *n* **1** Bedeutsamkeit *f.* **2** Bedeutung *f.*

silence ('sailəns) *n* **1** Schweigen *neu.* **2** Ruhe *f. vt* zum Schweigen bringen. **silencer** *n* **1** Schalldämpfer *m.* **2** *mot* Auspufftopf *m.*

silent ('sailənt) *adj* **1** still. **2** ruhig. **3** schweigsam. **4** stumm.

Silesia (sai'li:ziə) *n* Schlesien *neu.*

silhouette (silu:'et) *n* Silhouette *f.* **be silhouetted against** sich abheben gegen.

silicon ('silikən) *n* Silikon *neu.* **silicon chip** *n* Silikonchip *m.*

silk (silk) *n* Seide *f. adj* Seiden—. **silkworm** *n* Seidenraupe *f.*

sill (sil) *n* **1** Fensterbrett *neu.* **2** Schwelle *f.*

silly ('sili) *adj* albern, dumm.

silt (silt) *n* Schlamm *m.*

silver ('silvə) *n* Silber *neu. adj* silbern, Silber—. *vt* versilbern. *vi* silberweiß werden.

similar ('similə) *adj* ähnlich. **similarity** *n* Ähnlichkeit *f.*

simile ('simili) *n* Gleichnis, Simile *neu.*

simmer ('simə) *vi,(vt)* sieden (lassen).

simple ('simpəl) *adj* **1** einfach. **2** einfältig. **simply** *adv* einfach, nur. **simplify** *vt* vereinfachen.

simultaneous (siməl'teiniəs) *adj* gleichzeitig.

sin (sin) *n* Sünde *f. vi* sündigen.

since (sins) *prep* seit. *adv* seitdem, seither. *conj* **1** seitdem. **2** da, weil.

sincere (sin'siə) *adj* aufrichtig, ehrlich. **yours sincerely** Ihr ergebener. **sincerity** *n* Aufrichtigkeit *f.*

sinew ('sinju:) *n* Sehne *f.*

sing* (siŋ) *vt* **1** singen. **2** summen. **singer** *n* Sänger *m.* Sängerin *f.*

singe (sindʒ) *vt* (ver)sengen.

single ('siŋgəl) *adj* **1** einzig. **2** einzeln. **3** ledig. **4** einfach. *v*

single out auswählen. **single file** *n* Gänsemarsch *m*. **single-handed** *adj,adv* allein, eigenhändig. **single-minded** *adj* **1** zielbewußt. **2** aufrichtig.
singular ('siŋgjulə) *adj* **1** einzigartig. **2** sonderbar. *n gram* Singular *m*. Einzahl *f*.
sinister ('sinistə) *adj* unheilvoll, finster.
sink* (siŋk) *vi* **1** sinken. **2** sich senken. **3** eindringen. *vt* versenken. *n* Spülbecken *neu*.
sinner ('sinə) *n* Sünder *m*.
sinus ('sainəs) *n* (Neben)Höhle *f*. Sinus *m*.
sip (sip) *n* Schlückchen *neu*. *vt* nippen.
siphon ('saifən) *n* **1** Siphon *m*. **2** Siphonflasche *f*. *vt* absaugen.
sir (sə:) *n* **1** Herr *m*. **2** *cap* Sir *m*.
siren ('sairən) *n* Sirene *f*.
sirloin ('sə:lɔin) *n cul* Lendenstück *neu*.
sister ('sistə) *n* **1** Schwester *f*. **2** *med* Oberschwester *f*. **sisterhood** *n rel* Schwesternschaft *f*. **sister-in-law** *n* Schwägerin *f*.
sit* (sit) *vi* **1** sitzen. **2** tagen. **sit down** sich (hin)setzen. **sit-in** *n* Sitzstreik *m*. **sitting** *n* Sitzung *f*. **sitting room** *n* Wohnzimmer *neu*.
site (sait) *n* **1** Lage *f*. **2** Bauplatz *m*. **3** Gelände *neu*.
situation (sitju'eiʃən) *n* **1** Lage *f*. **2** Stellung *f*. **be situated** liegen, sich befinden.
six (siks) *adj* sechs. *n* Sechs *f*. **sixth** *adj* sechste.
sixteen (siks'ti:n) *adj* sechzehn. *n* Sechzehn *f*. **sixteenth** *adj* sechzehnte.
sixty ('siksti) *adj* sechzig. *n* Sechzig *f*. **sixtieth** *adj* sechzigste.
size (saiz) *n* **1** Größe *f*. **2** Maß *neu*. *v* **size up** *inf* einschätzen.
sizzle ('sizəl) *vi* zischen. *n* Zischen *neu*.
skate[1] (skeit) *n* Schlittschuh *m*. *vi* Schlittschuh laufen.
skate[2] (skeit) *n* Rochen *m*.
skeleton ('skelətn̩) *n* **1** Skelett *neu*. **2** Gerippe *neu*.
sketch (sketʃ) *n* **1** Skizze *f*. **2** Entwurf *m*. *vt* **1** skizzieren. **2** entwerfen.
skewer ('skjuə) *n* Fleischspieß *m*. *vt* spießen.
ski (ski:) *n* Schi *or* Ski *m*. *vi* Schi *or* Ski laufen. **ski-lift** *n* Schilift *m*.
skid (skid) *n* **1** Rutschen *neu*. **2** *mot* Schleudern *neu*. *vi* **1** ausrutschen. **2** schleudern.
skill (skil) *n* Geschicklichkeit *f*. **skilful** *adj* geschickt. **skilled** *adj* gelernt, Fach—.
skim (skim) *vt* entrahmen. **skim over** dahingleiten über. **skim through** durchblättern.
skimp (skimp) *vi* knapp halten. **skimpy** *adj* knapp.
skin (skin) *n* **1** Haut *f*. **2** Fell *m*. **3** Schale *f*. *vt* **1** enthäuten. **2** schälen. **skin-diving** *n* Sporttauchen *neu*. **skin-tight** *adj* hauteng. **skinny** *adj* mager.
skip (skip) *vi* **1** hüpfen. **2** seilhüpfen. *n* Sprung *m*. **skipping-rope** *n* Springseil *neu*.
skipper ('skipə) *n* Schiffsherr, Kapitän *m*.
skirmish ('skə:miʃ) *n* Scharmützel *neu*. *vi* plänkeln.
skirt (skə:t) *n* Rock *m*. *vt* en-

tlangfahren. **skirting board** *n* Scheuerleiste *f*.
skittle ('skitḷ) *n* Kegel *m*.
skull (skʌl) *n* Schädel *m*. **skull and crossbones** *n* Totenkopf *m*.
skunk (skʌŋk) *n* Stinktier *neu*. Skunk *m*.
sky (skai) *n* Himmel *m*. **sky-high** *adj* himmelhoch. **skylark** *n* Feldlerche *f*. **skyline** *n* Horizont *m*. **skyscraper** *n* Wolkenkratzer *m*.
slab (slæb) *n* **1** Platte, Tafel *f*. **2** Holzschwarte *f*.
slack (slæk) *adj* **1** schlaff. **2** lose. **3** nachlässig. **slacken** *vi* **1** schlaff werden. **2** nachlassen. *vt* **1** schlaff machen. **2** nachlassen.
slacks (slæks) *n pl* Damenhose *f*.
slalom ('slɑːləm) *n* Slalom *m*.
slam (slæm) *vt* **1** zuschlagen. **2** knallen. *vi* zuschlagen. *n* **1** Zuschlagen *neu*. **2** Knall *m*.
slander ('slændə) *n* Verleumdung *f*. *vt* verleumden.
slang (slæŋ) *n* Slang, Jargon *m*.
slant (slɑːnt) *n* Schräge, Neigung *f*. *vi* schräg liegen. **slanting** *adj* schräg, schief.
slap (slæp) *n* Klaps, Schlag *m*. *vt* klapsen, schlagen. **slapdash** *adj* **1** hastig, übereilt. **2** unbekümmert. **slapstick** *n* Schwank *m*.
slash (slæʃ) *vt* **1** (auf)schlitzen. **2** *inf* drastisch kürzen. *n* Schnitt *m*.
slat (slæt) *n* Lamelle *f*. Streifen *m*.
slate (sleit) *n* **1** Schiefer *m*. **2** Schiefertafel *f*.
slaughter ('slɔːtə) *n* **1** Schlachten *neu*. **2** Blutbad *neu*. *vt* **1** schlachten. **2** niedermetzeln. **slaughterhouse** *n* Schlachthaus *neu*.
slave (sleiv) *n* Sklave *m*. *vi inf* schuften. **slavery** *n* Sklaverei *f*.
sledge (sledʒ) *n* Schlitten *m*. *vi* Schlitten fahren.
sledgehammer ('sledʒhæmə) *n* Schmiedehammer *m*.
sleek (sliːk) *adj* geschmeidig, glatt.
sleep* (sliːp) *vi* schlafen. *n* Schlaf *m*. **go to sleep** einschlafen. **sleeper** *n* **1** Schläfer *m*. **2** (railway) Schwelle *f*. **sleeping-bag** *n* Schlafsack *m*. **sleeping-car** *n* Schlafwagen *m*. **sleeping-pill** *n* Schlafmittel *neu*. **sleepwalk** *vi* nachtwandeln. **sleepy** *adj* schläfrig.
sleet (sliːt) *n* Graupelregen *m*. *vi* graupeln.
sleeve (sliːv) *n* Ärmel *m*. **have something up one's sleeve** etwas im Schilde führen.
sleigh (slei) *n* Schlitten *m*.
slender ('slendə) *adj* **1** schlank. **2** gering.
slept (slept) *v* see **sleep**.
slice (slais) *n* **1** Scheibe *f*. Schnitte *f*. **2** Kelle *f*. *vt* in Scheiben schneiden.
slick (slik) *adj* **1** glatt. **2** raffiniert.
slide* (slaid) *vi,(vt)* gleiten (lassen). *n* **1** Gleiten *neu*. **2** *phot* Dia(positiv) *neu*. **3** Schlittenbahn *f*. **slide-rule** *n* Rechenschieber *m*.
slight (slait) *adj* **1** schmächtig. **2** gering. *n* Geringschätzung *f*.

vt geringschätzig behandeln. **slightly** *adv* etwas.

slim (slim) *adj* **1** schlank. **2** dürftig. *vi* Schlankheitskur machen, abnehmen.

slime (slaim) *n* Schlamm *m*. **slimy** *adj* schlammig.

sling* (sliŋ) *n* **1** Schleuder *f*. **2** *med* Schlinge *f*. *vt* **1** schleudern. **2** umhängen.

slink* (sliŋk) *vi* schleichen. **slink off** sich wegschleichen.

slip[1] (slip) *vi* rutschen, schlüpfen. *vt* schlüpfen lassen. **slip on/off** überstreifen/abstreifen. **1** (Aus)Rutschen *neu*. **2** Fehltritt *m*. **3** Fehler *m*. **slippery** *adj* schlüpfrig, glitschig.

slip[2] (slip) *n* Zettel *m*.

slipper ('slipə) *n* Pantoffel, Hausschuh *m*.

slippery ('slipri) *adj* schlüpfrig, glitschig.

slit* (slit) *n* Schlitz *m*. Spalte *f*. *vt,vi* (zer-, auf-)splittern.

slobber ('slɔbə) *vi* sabbern. *n* Sabber *m*.

sloe (slou) *n* **1** Schlehe *f*. **2** Schlehdorn *m*.

slog (slɔg) *vt* (heftig) schlagen. *vi inf* schuften. *n* **1** Hieb *m*. **2** Plackerei *f*.

slogan ('slougən) *n* **1** Schlagwort *neu*. **2** Werbeslogan *m*.

slop (slɔp) *vt* verschütten. **sloppy** *adj* **1** labberig. **2** schlampig. **slops** *n pl* Spülicht *neu*.

slope (sloup) *n* **1** Abhang *m*. **2** Neigung *f*. *vi* **1** abfallen. **2** sich neigen. *vt* abschrägen. **sloping** *adj* schräg.

slot (slɔt) *n* Schlitz *m*. **slot-machine** *n* **1** Warenautomat *m*. **2** Spielautomat *m*.

slouch (slautʃ) *vi* latschig gehen *or* sitzen.

slovenly ('slʌvənli) *adj* schlampig.

slow (slou) *adj* **1** langsam. **2** schwerfällig. **3** langweilig. *vt* verlangsamen. *vi* langsamer werden *or* gehen.

slug[1] (slʌg) *n* **1** Schnecke *f*. **2** Kugel *f*. **sluggish** *adj* **1** träge. **2** faul.

slug[2] (slʌg) *vt* (mit dem Faust) heftig schlagen. *n* heftiger Schlag *m*.

sluice (sluːs) *n* Schleuse *f*. *vt* (aus)spülen.

slumber ('slʌmbə) *n* Schlummer *m*. *vi* schlummern.

slump (slʌmp) *n* **1** (Preis)Sturz *m*. **2** Tiefstand, Rückgang *m*. *vi* **1** stürzen. **2** hinplumpsen.

slums (slʌmz) *n pl* Elendsviertel *neu*.

slung (slʌŋ) *v* see **sling.**

slur (sləː) *vt* verschlucken. **2** *mus* binden. *n* **1** Fleck, Tadel *m*. **2** *mus* Bindebogen *neu*.

slush (slʌʃ) *n* **1** Matsch *m*. **2** *inf* Kitsch *m*.

sly (slai) *adj* schlau. **on the sly** heimlich.

smack[1] (smæk) *n* (Bei)-Geschmack *m*. *v* **smack of** schmecken nach.

smack[2] (smæk) *n* **1** Klatsch, Klaps *m*. **2** Schmatz *m*. *vt* klatschen, jemandem einen Klaps geben. **smack the lips** mit den Lippen schmatzen.

small (smɔːl) *adj* **1** klein. **2** gering. **in a small way** bescheiden. **make someone feel small** einen beschämen.

smallholding *n* Kleinbauernbesitz *m.* **small-minded** *adj* kleinlich, engstirnig. **smallpox** *n* Pocken *f pl.*
smart (smaːt) *adj* **1** heftig. **2** adrett. **3** fein. **4** gescheit. *n* Schmerz *m.* *vi* schmerzen. **smarten up** *vt* herausputzen. *vi* sich schön machen.
smash (smæʃ) *vt* **1** zerbrechen. **2** vernichtend schlagen. *vi* **1** zerbrechen. **2** zusammenstoßen. **3** krachen. *n* **1** Krach *m.* **2** Zusammenbruch *m.* **3** Zusammenstoß *m.*
smear (smiə) *vt* **1** beschmieren. **2** verleumden. *n* **1** Schmiere *f.* **2** Fleck *m.*
smell* (smel) *n* Geruch *m.* *vt* riechen. **smelly** *adj* übelriechend.
smile (smail) *vi* lächeln. *n* Lächeln *neu.*
smirk (sməːk) *vi* grinsen. *n* Grinsen *neu.*
smog (smɔg) *n* Smog, rauchiger Nebel *neu.*
smoke (smouk) *n* Rauch *m.* *vt* **1** rauchen. **2** *cul* räuchern. *vi* rauchen.
smooth (smuːð) *adj* **1** glatt. **2** fließend. **3** sanft. **4** gewandt. **smoothen** *vt also* **smooth 1** glätten. **2** ebnen. **smoothly** *adv* reibungslos, glatt.
smother ('smʌðə) *vt,vi* ersticken.
smoulder ('smouldə) *vi* **1** glimmen, schwelen. **2** glühen.
smudge (smʌdʒ) *vt* beschmieren. *n* Klecks *m.*
smug (smʌg) *adj* selbstgefällig, überheblich.
smuggle ('smʌgəl) *vt* schmuggeln. **smuggler** *n* Schmuggler *m.* **smuggling** *n* Schmuggel *m.*
snack (snæk) *n* Imbiß *m.* **snack-bar** *n* Imbißstube *f.*
snag (snæg) *n* **1** Aststumpf *m.* **2** Schwierigkeit *f.* Haken *m.* **3** Nachteil *m.*
snail (sneil) *n* Schnecke *f.*
snake (sneik) *n* Schlange *f.* *vi* sich schlängeln.
snap (snæp) *vt* **1** schnappen. **2** *phot* knipsen. **3** knicken. *vi* **1** (zu)schnappen. **2** knacken. **snap at** anschnauzen. ~*n* **1** Schnappen *neu.* **2** Knacks *m.* **snapshot** *n* Schnappschuß *m.*
snarl (snaːl) *vi,vt* knurren. *n* Knurren *neu.*
snatch (snætʃ) *vt* **1** haschen, packen. **2** ergreifen. *n* **1** Haschen *neu.* Griff *m.* **2** Stückchen *neu.*
sneak (sniːk) *vi* **1** schleichen. **2** *sl* petzen. *n* **1** Schleicher, Kriecher *m.* **2** *sl* Petzer *m.*
sneer (sniə) *vi* **1** hohnlächeln. **2** spotten. *n* **1** Hohnlächeln *neu.* **2** Spott *m.*
sneeze (sniːz) *vi* niesen. *n* Niesen *neu.*
sniff (snif) *vt* riechen. *vi* schnüffeln. **sniff at** die Nase rümpfen über. ~*n* **1** Schnüffeln *neu.* **2** Naserümpfen *neu.*
snip (snip) *vt* schnipseln. *n* Schnipsel *m.*
snipe (snaip) *n zool* Schnepfe *f.* *vt,vi* aus dem Hinterhalt schießen. **sniper** *n* Heckenschütze *m.*
snivel ('snivəl) *vi* **1** aus der Nase triefen. **2** wimmern, schnüffeln, heulen.
snob (snɔb) *n* Snob, Vornehmtuer *m.*

snooker ('snuːkə) *n* eine Art Billardspiel *neu*.
snoop (snuːp) *vi* (herum)-schnüffeln.
snooty ('snuːti) *adj* hochnäsig, arrogant.
snooze (snuːz) *vi* ein Schläfchen machen. *n* Schläfchen *neu*.
snore (snɔː) *vi* schnarchen. *n* Schnarchen *neu*.
snort (snɔːt) *vi* schnauben. *n* Schnauben *neu*.
snout (snaut) *n* **1** Schnauze *f*. **2** (of a pig) Rüssel *m*.
snow (snou) *n* Schnee *m*. *vi* schneien. **snowball** *n* Schneeball *m*. *vt* mit Schneebällen bewerfen. **snow-drift** *n* Schneewehe *f*. **snow-drop** *n* Schneeglöckchen *neu*. **snowflake** *n* Schneeflocke *f*. **snowman** *n* Schneemann *m*. **snowplough** *n* Schneepflug *m*.
snub (snʌb) *vt* (kurz) abweisen, zurückweisen. *n* Zurückweisung, Abfertigung *f*.
snuff (snʌf) *n* Schnupftabak *m*. **take snuff** schnupfen.
snug (snʌg) *adj* **1** behaglich. **2** eng.
snuggle ('snʌgəl) *vi* **snuggle up to** sich schmiegen an.
so (sou) *adv* so. *conj* deshalb, so. **so that** damit ~*interj* so, also. **and so on** und so weiter. **so-and-so** *n* so und so. **so-called** *adj* sogenannt. **so-so** *adj,adv* so so.
soak (souk) *vt* **1** durchnässen. **2** durchtränken. *vi* **1** einweichen. **2** durchsickern. **soak up** aufsaugen.
soap (soup) *n* Seife *f*. *vt* einseifen. **soap-powder** *n* Seifenpulver *neu*. **soapy** *adj* seifig.
soar (sɔː) *vi* **1** sich erheben. **2** sich aufschwingen. **3** schweben. **4** (auf)steigen. **5** *comm* in die Höhe schießen.
sob (sɔb) *vi* schluchzen. *n* Schluchzen *neu*.
sober ('soubə) *adj* nüchtern. *vt* ernüchtern. **sober up** nüchtern werden.
social ('souʃəl) *adj* **1** gesellschaftlich. **2** sozial, Sozial—. **Social Services** *n pl* soziale Einrichtungen *f pl*. **sociable** *adj* gesellig, gemütlich. **socialism** *n* Sozialismus *m*. **socialist** *n* Sozialist *m*. *adj* sozialistisch.
society (sə'saiəti) *n* **1** Gesellschaft *f*. **2** Verein, Verband *m*.
sociology (sousi'ɔlədʒi) *n* Sozialwissenschaft, Soziologie *f*. **sociological** *adj* soziologisch. **sociologist** *n* Soziologe *m*.
sock[1] (sɔk) *n* Socke *f*.
sock[2] (sɔk) *sl vt* (ver)hauen. *n* Schlag *m*.
socket ('sɔkit) *n* **1** *anat* Höhle, Pfanne *f*. **2** *tech* Muffe *f*. **3** (electrical) Steckdose *f*.
soda ('soudə) *n* Soda *f,neu*. **soda-water** *n* Sodawasser, Mineralwasser *neu*.
sofa ('soufə) *n* Sofa *neu*.
soft (sɔft) *adj* **1** weich. **2** leise. **3** weichlich. **soft drink** *n* alkoholfreies Getränk *neu*. **soft-hearted** *adj* weichherzig. **soften** *vt* weich machen. *vi* **1** (sich) erweichen. **2** mildern.
soggy ('sɔgi) *adj* durchnäßt, feucht.
soil[1] (sɔil) *n* Boden *m*. Erde *f*.

soil[2] (sɔil) *vt* **1** beschmutzen. **2** beflecken.
solar ('soulə) *adj* Sonnen—.
sold (sould) *v* see **sell.**
solder ('sɔldə) *vt* löten. *n* Lötmetall *neu.*
soldier ('souldʒə) *n* Soldat *m.*
sole[1] (soul) *adj* einzig, Allein—. **solely** *adv* allein, ausschließlich.
sole[2] (soul) *n* Sohle *f.* *vt* besohlen.
sole[3] (soul) *n* Seezunge *f.*
solemn ('sɔləm) *adj* **1** feierlich. **2** ernst. **solemnity** *n* Feierlichkeit *f.*
solicitor (sə'lisitə) *n* Anwalt *m.*
solid ('sɔlid) *adj* **1** fest. **2** dauerhaft. **3** kräftig. *n* Körper *m.* **solidarity** *n* Solidarität *f.* **solidify** *(vi),vt* (sich) verfestigen.
solitary ('sɔlitri) *adj* **1** einsam. **2** einzeln, allein. **solitary confinement** *n* Einzelhaft *f.*
solitude ('sɔlitju:d) *n* Einsamkeit *f.*
solo ('soulou) *n mus* Solo *neu.* *adj* Allein—, Einzel—.
solstice ('sɔlstis) *n* Sonnenwende *f.*
soluble ('sɔljubəl) *adj* löslich, (auf)lösbar.
solution (sə'lu:ʃən) *n* **1** Lösung *f.* **2** *sci* (Auf)Lösung *f.*
solve (sɔlv) *vt* (auf)lösen. **solvent** *adj* **1** (auf)lösend. **2** *comm* zahlungsfähig. *n* Lösungsmittel *neu.*
sombre ('sɔmbə) *adj* düster, trübe.
some (sʌm) *adj* **1** irgendein, irgendwelche. **2** einige. **3** etwas. **4** gewisse. **5** manche. **6** etwa, ungefähr. **somebody** *pron also* **someone** jemand. **somehow** *adv* irgendwie. **something** *pron* **1** etwas. **2** irgendetwas. **sometime** *adv* irgendwann, eines Tages. **sometimes** *adv* manchmal. **somewhat** *adv* etwas, ziemlich. **somewhere** *adv* irgendwo(hin).
somersault ('sʌməsɔ:lt) *n* Purzelbaum *m.* **turn a somersault** einen Purzelbaum schlagen.
son (sʌn) *n* Sohn *m.* **son-in-law** *n* Schwiegersohn *m.*
sonata (sə'nɑ:tə) *n* Sonate *f.*
song (sɔŋ) *n* **1** Lied *neu.* **2** Gesang *m.*
sonic ('sɔnik) *adj* Schall—.
sonnet ('sɔnit) *n* Sonett *neu.*
soon (su:n) *adv* **1** bald. **2** gern. **as soon as** sobald wie. **sooner** *adv* **1** eher. **2** lieber. **no sooner than** kaum...als. **no sooner said than done** gesagt, getan.
soot (sut) *n* Ruß *m.* *vt* verrußen.
soothe (su:ð) *vt* **1** beruhigen. **2** lindern.
sophisticated (sə'fistikeitid) *adj* **1** verfeinert. **2** hochentwickelt. **3** kultiviert.
soprano (sə'prɑ:nou) *n* Sopran *m.*
sordid ('sɔ:did) *adj* schmutzig, gemein.
sore (sɔ:) *adj* **1** wund, weh. **2** schlimm. **3** verletzt. *n* wunde Stelle *f.*
sorrow ('sɔrou) *n* **1** Trauer *f.* **2** Kummer *m.* Leid *neu.* *vi* trauern. **sorrowful** *adj* **1** traurig, betrübt. **2** elend.
sorry ('sɔri) *adj* **1** bekümmert.

2 erbärmlich. *interj* Verzeihung! **I am sorry** es tut mir leid.
sort (sɔːt) *n* Sorte, Art *f.* **what sort of** was für. *vt* sortieren. **sort out 1** aussortieren. **2** *inf* erledigen.
soufflé ('suːflei) *n* Soufflé *neu.* Auflauf *m.*
sought (sɔːt) *v* see **seek.**
sought-after *adj* gesucht, begehrt.
soul (soul) *n* Seele *f.* **soul-destroying** *adj* seelentötend, bedrückend. **soulful** *adj* seelenvoll. **soulless** *adj* seelenlos.
sound[1] (saund) *n* **1** Ton, Laut *m.* **2** Klang *m.* **3** Geräusch *neu.* *vi* **1** klingen. **2** tönen, lauten. *vt* ertönen *or* erklingen lassen.
sound[2] (saund) *adj* **1** gesund. **2** ganz. **3** fest. **4** vernünftig. **5** kräftig.
sound[3] (saund) *vt* **1** *naut* loten. **2** sondieren.
soup (suːp) *n* Suppe *f.*
sour (sauə) *adj* **1** sauer, scharf. **2** bitter, mürrisch. *vi* sauer *or* bitter werden. *vt* **1** säuern. **2** erbittern.
source (sɔːs) *n* **1** Quelle *f.* **2** Ursprung *m.*
south (sauθ) *n* Süd(en) *m.* *adj* Süd—, südlich. *adv* sudwärts, nach Süden. **south-east** *n* Südosten *m.* **south-eastern** *adj* südöstlich. **southerly** *adj* südlich. **southern** *adj* Süd—, südlich. **southwards** *adv* südwärts, nach Süden. **south-west** *n* Südwesten *m.* **south-western** *adj* südwestlich.
South Africa *n* Südafrika *neu.*
South America *n* Südamerika *neu.*
South Pole *n* Südpol *m.*
souvenir (suːvə'niə) *n* Andenken *neu.*
sovereign ('sɔvrin) *adj* **1** souverän. **2** höchst. *n* Souverän, Monarch *m.*
Soviet Union ('souviət) *n* Sowjetunion *f.*
sow*[1] (sou) *vt* **1** (aus)säen. **2** besäen.
sow[2] (sau) *n zool* Sau *f.*
soya bean ('sɔiə) *n* Sojabohne *f.*
spa (spɑː) *n* Kurort *m.* Bad *neu.*
space (speis) *n* **1** Weltraum *m.* **2** Platz *m.* **3** Zwischenraum *m.* **4** Zeitraum *m.* *vt* **1** einteilen. **2** sperren. **spaceship** *n* Raumschiff *m.* **spacious** *adj* **1** geräumig. **2** weit.
spade[1] (speid) *n* Spaten *m.* *vt* graben.
spade[2] (speid) *n game* Pik *neu.*
Spain (spein) *n* Spanien *neu.* **Spaniard** *n* Spanier *m.* **Spanish** *adj* spanisch. *n* (language) Spanisch *neu.*
span (spæn) *n* **1** (Zeit)Spanne *f.* **2** Spannweite *f.* *vt* **1** (um-, über-)spannen. **2** (aus)messen.
spank (spæŋk) *vt* schlagen. *n* Schlag *m.*
spanner ('spænə) *n* Schraubenschlüssel *m.*
spare (spɛə) *adj* **1** spärlich. **2** mager. **3** übrig. **4** Ersatz—. *n* Ersatzteil *neu.* *vt* **1** (ver)schonen. **2** übrig haben für. **sparing** *adj* sparsam.
spark (spɑːk) *n* Funken *m.*
spark plug *n* Zündkerze *f.* ~

vi Funken sprühen. **spark off** auslösen.

sparkle ('spɑːkəl) *vi* **1** funkeln. **2** sprühen. **3** schäumen. *n* Funkeln *neu.*

sparrow ('spærou) *n* Sperling, Spatz *m.*

sparse (spɑːs) *adj* spärlich, dünn.

spasm ('spæzəm) *n* Krampf *m.* **spasmodic** *adj* **1** kramphaft. **2** unregelmäßig. **spastic** *adj* spastisch, Krampf—.

spat (spæt) *v* see **spit.**

spatial ('speiʃəl) *adj* räumlich, Raum—.

spatula ('spætjulə) *n* Spatel *m.* Spachtel *f.*

spawn (spɔːn) *n* Laich *m. vi* laichen. *vt* hervorbringen.

speak* (spiːk) *vi* sprechen, reden. *vt* (aus)sprechen, äußern. **speaking!** am Apparat!

spear (spiə) *n* Speer, Spieß *m. vt* (auf)spießen.

special ('speʃəl) *adj* **1** besonder. **2** Sonder—, speziell, Spezial—, extra. **specialist** *n* **1** Spezialist, Fachmann *m.* **2** *med* Facharzt *m.* **speciality** *n* **1** Besonderheit *f.* **2** Spezialfach *neu.* **3** Spezialität *f.* **specialize** *vi* sich spezialisieren.

species ('spiːʃiːz) *n, pl* **species** Art, Spezies *f.*

specify ('spesifai) *vt* spezifizieren. **specific** *adj* **1** spezifisch. **2** bestimmt. **specification** *n* Spezifizierung *f.*

specimen ('spesimən) *n* Muster, Exemplar *neu.*

speck (spek) *n* Fleck *m. vt* flecken.

spectacle ('spektəkəl) *n* **1** Schauspiel *neu.* **2** Schau *f.* **3** *pl* Brille *f.* **spectacular** *adj* **1** auffallend, spektakulär. **2** eindrücksvoll.

spectator (spek'teitə) *n* Zuschauer *m.*

spectrum ('spektrəm) *n* Spektrum *neu.*

speculate ('spekjuleit) *vi* **1** nachsinnen. **2** *comm* spekulieren. **speculation** *n* **1** (theoretische) Betrachtung *f.* **2** *comm* Spekulation *f.*

speech (spiːtʃ) *n* **1** Sprache *f.* **2** Rede *f.* **speechless** *adj* sprachlos.

speed* (spiːd) *n* **1** Geschwindigkeit *f.* **2** Eile *f.* **3** *phot* Lichtempfindlichkeit *f.*

speed-boat *n* Rennboot *neu.*

speedometer *n* Geschwindigkeitsmesser *neu.* ~*vi* schnell fahren. **speed up** beschleunigen. **speedy** *adj* geschwind.

spell*[1] (spel) *vt* **1** buchstabieren. **2** *inf* bedeuten. *vi* richtig schreiben. **spelling** *n* Rechtschreibung *f.*

spell[2] (spel) *n* Zauber(spruch), Bann *m.* **spellbound** *adj* gebannt.

spell[3] (spel) *n* **1** Schicht *f.* **2** Weilchen *neu.*

spend* (spend) *vt* **1** (money) ausgeben. **2** (time) verbringen. **3** (energy) verwenden. **spendthrift** *n* Verschwender *m. adj* verschwenderisch.

spent (spent) *v* see **spend.** *adj* erschöpft, matt.

sperm (spəːm) *n* Same *m.* Sperma *neu.*

sphere (sfiə) *n* **1** Kugel *f.* **2**

Sphäre *f.* Bereich *m.* **spherical** *adj* kugelförmig.
spice (spais) *n* Gewürz *neu.* Würze *f. vt* würzen. **spicy** *adj* pikant, würzig.
spider ('spaidə) *n* Spinne *f.*
spike (spaik) *n* Spitze *f. vt* **1** festnageln. **2** aufspießen. **spiky** *adj* spitzig.
spill* (spil) *vt* **1** verschütten. **2** vergießen. *vi* **1** verschüttet werden. **2** überlaufen.
spin* (spin) *vi,vt* **1** spinnen. **2** wirbeln. **3** (a coin) hochwerfen. **4** (a tale) ausdenken. *n* Wirbeln *neu.* **spin-dry** *vt* schleudern. **spin-dryer** *n* Wäscheschleuder *f.*
spinach ('spinidʒ) *n* Spinat *m.*
spindle ('spindḷ) *n* Spindel *f.* **spindly** *adj* spindeldürr.
spine (spain) *n* **1** Rückgrat *neu.* Wirbelsäule *f.* **2** Stachel *m.*
spinster ('spinstə) *n* **1** unverheiratete Frau, Junggesellin *f.* **2** alte Jungfer *f.*
spiral ('spairəl) *n* **1** Spirale *f.* **2** Wirbel *m. adj* **1** spiralig. **2** schraubenförmig. *vi* sich schrauben.
spire (spaiə) *n* Turmspitze *f.* Kirchturm *m.*
spirit ('spirit) *n* **1** Geist *m.* **2** Temperament *neu.* **3** Mut *m.* **4** Spiritus *m.* **5** *pl* Stimmung *f.* **6** *pl* Spirituosen *pl. v* **spirit away** wegzaubern. **spirited** *adj* lebhaft. **spiritual** *adj* **1** geistig. **2** geistlich.
spit* [1] (spit) *vi* **1** spucken. **2** (of rain) sprühen. **spit out** ausspucken. *n* Spucke *f.*
spit [2] (spit) *n* **1** Bratspieß *m.* **2** Landzunge *f.*
spite (spait) *n* Bosheit, Gehässigkeit *f.* **in spite of** trotz. ~ *vt* ärgern. **spiteful** *adj* boshaft, gehässig.
splash (splæʃ) *n* **1** Spritzfleck *m.* **2** Patschen *neu. vt* (be)spritzen. *vi* patschen.
splendid ('splendid) *adj* **1** herrlich. **2** großartig. **splendour** *n* Herrlichkeit, Pracht *f.*
splint (splint) *n med* Schiene *f. vt* schienen. **splinter** *n* Splitter *m. vi,vt* (zer)splittern.
split* (split) vt **1** (zer)spalten. **2** teilen. *vi* **1** sich spalten. **2** sich entzweien. **split hairs** Haarspalterei treiben. ~*n* **1** Spalt, Riß *m.* **2** Spaltung *f.*
splutter ('splʌtə) *vi* **1** spritzen. **2** stottern, plappern. *n* **1** Spritzen *neu.* **2** Geplapper *neu.*
spoil* (spɔil) *vt* **1** verderben. **2** (a child) verwöhnen. **3** plündern. *vi* schlecht werden. **spoils** *n pl* Beute *f.* Gewinn *neu.* **spoil-sport** *n* Spielverderber *m.*
spoke [1] (spouk) *v* see **speak.**
spoke [2] (spouk) *n* Speiche *f.*
spoken ('spoukən) *v* see **speak.**
spokesman ('spouksmən) *n* Wortführer *m.*
sponge (spʌndʒ) *n* Schwamm *m. vt* mit einem Schwamm (ab)wischen. *vi* schmarotzen.
sponsor ('spɔnsə) *n* **1** Pate *m.* **2** Bürge *m.* **3** Förderer *m. vt* **1** fördern. **2** finanzieren.
spontaneous (spɔn'teiniəs) *adj* **1** spontan. **2** freiwillig. **3** *tech* Selbst—. **spontaneity** *n* **1** Spontaneität *f.* **2** Freiwilligkeit *f.*
spool (spuːl) *n* Spule *f.*
spoon (spuːn) *n* Löffel *m. vt*

löffeln. **spoonfed** *adj* verhätschelt.

sport (spɔːt) *n* **1** Sport *m.* **2** Scherz *m.* **a good sport** *n* feiner Kerl *m.* **do** *or* **play sport** Sport treiben. **sportsman** *n* Sportler *m.* ~*vi* scherzen. *vt* zur Schau tragen.

spot (spɔt) *n* **1** Fleck *m.* **2** Stelle *f.* **3** Pickel *m.* **be on the spot** zur Stelle sein. **spotlight** *n* Scheinwerfer *m. vt* **1** beflecken. **2** bemerken. **spotless** *adj* fleckenlos.

spouse (spaus) *n* Gatte *m.* Gattin *f.*

spout (spaut) *n* **1** Schnauze *f.* **2** Ausgußröhre *f.* **3** Wasserstrahl *m. vi* (heraus)spritzen.

sprain (sprein) *vt* verrenken. *n* Verrenkung *f.*

sprang (spræŋ) *v* see **spring.**

sprawl (sprɔːl) *vi* **1** sick rekeln. **2** *bot* wuchern.

spray[1] (sprei) *n* **1** Gischt *m.* **2** Spray *m. vt* besprühen, spritzen.

spray[2] (sprei) *n* **1** Zweig *m.* **2** Blütenzweig *m.*

spread* (spred) *vt* **1** (aus-, ver-)breiten. **2 aufstreichen** *vi* sich verbreiten. *n* **1** Verbreitung *f.* **2** Spanne *f.* **3** Brotaufstrich *m.*

spree (spriː) *n* **1** Jux *m.* **2** Orgie *f.*

sprig (sprig) *n* **1** Sproß *m.* **2** Sprößling *m.*

sprightly ('spraitli) *adj* lebhaft, munter.

spring* (spriŋ) *vi* **1** springen. **2** entstehen. *vt* sprengen. **spring a leak** leck werden. ~ *n* **1** Sprung *m.* **2** Sprungkraft *f.* **3** Triebfeder *f.* **4** Quelle *f.* Brunnen *m.* **5** Frühling *m.* **springboard** *n* Sprungbrett *neu.* **spring-cleaning** *n* Frühjahrsputz *m.*

sprinkle ('spriŋkəl) *vt* (be)streuen. *vi* sprühen.

sprint (sprint) *vi* sprinten. *n* Sprint *m.*

sprout (spraut) *vi* sprießen. *n* Sproß *m.*

sprung (sprʌŋ) *v* see **spring.**

spun (spʌn) *v* see **spin.**

spur (spəː) *n* **1** Reitsporn *m.* **2** Ansporn *m. vt* (an)spornen.

spurt (spəːt) *vi* **1** *sport* spurten. **2** herausspritzen. *n* **1** Spurt *m.* **2** Wasserstrahl *m.*

spy (spai) *n* Spion *m. vt* (er)spähen. *vi* spionieren. **spy on someone** jemandem nachspionieren.

squabble ('skwɔbəl) *vi* sich zanken. *n* Zank *m.*

squad (skwɔd) *n* Gruppe *f.* Trupp *m.* Kommando *neu.*

squadron ('skwɔdrən) *n* **1** *mil* Schwadron *f.* **2** *aviat* Staffel *f.* **3** *naut* Geschwader *neu.*

squalid ('skwɔlid) *adj* armselig, verwahrlost. **squalor** *n* Schmutz *m.* Verwahrlosung *f.*

squander ('skwɔndə) *vt* verschwenden.

square (skwɛə) *adj* **1** viereckig. **2** quadratisch. **3** ehrlich. **4** quitt. *n* **1** Viereck *neu.* **2** Quadrat *neu.* **3** (in a town) Platz *m. vt* **1** viereckig machen. **2** quadrieren. **3** (an account) ausgleichen. *vi* passen.

squash (skwɔʃ) *n* **1** Gedränge *neu.* **2** Fruchtgetränk *neu.* **3** *sport* Squash *neu. vt* **1**

(zer)quetschen. **2** (er)drücken, zerdrücken.
squat (skwɔt) *vi* **1** kauern, hocken. **2** unbefugt besetzen. *adj* **1** kauernd. **2** untersetzt. **squatter** *n* Siedler ohne Rechtstitel, Squatter *m*.
squawk (skwɔːk) *vi* kreischen. *n* Kreischen *neu*.
squeak (skwiːk) *vi* **1** quietschen. **2** knarren. *n* **1** Gequieke, Quietschen *neu*. **2** Knarren *neu*.
squeal (skwiːl) *vi* **1** quieken, quietschen. **2** *inf* verpfeifen. *n* Quieken, Quietschen *neu*.
squeamish ('skwiːmiʃ) *adj* **1** überempfindlich. **2** heikel.
squeeze (skwiːz) *vt* **1** drücken, pressen. **2** bedrängen. *vi* dringen, drängen. *n* **1** Druck *m*. **2** *inf* Gedränge. **squeezer** *n* Presse *f*.
squid (skwid) *n* Tintenfisch *m*.
squiggle ('skwigəl) *n* Kritzelei *f*. Schnörkel *m*. *vi* kritzeln.
squint (skwint) *vi* schielen. *n* Schielen *neu*.
squire ('skwaiə) *n* Landjunker, Gutsherr *m*.
squirm (skwəːm) *vi* sich winden, sich krümmen.
squirrel ('skwirəl) *n* Eichhörnchen *neu*.
squirt (skwəːt) *vt* spritzen. *n* Spritze *f*.
Sri Lanka (sriː'læŋkə) *n* Sri Lanka *neu*.
stab (stæb) *n* Stich *m*. **stab in the back** hinterlistiger Angriff *m*. ~*vt* erstechen. *vi* stechen.
stabilize ('steibəlaiz) *vt* stabilisieren. **stability** *n* **1** Stabilität *f*. **2** Festigkeit *f*.
stable[1] ('steibəl) *n* Stall *m*. *vt* einstallen.
stable[2] ('steibəl) *adj* **1** stabil. **2** beständig.
stack (stæk) *n* **1** Schober *m*. **2** Schornstein *m*. **3** Stapel *m*. *vt* (auf)stapeln.
stadium ('steidiəm) *n* Stadion *neu*.
staff (stɑːf) *n* **1** Stab *m*. **2** Personal *neu*. Belegschaft *f*. *vt* (mit Personal) besetzen.
stag (stæg) *n* Hirsch *m*.
stage (steidʒ) *n* **1** Bühne *f*. **2** Schauplatz *m*. **3** Stufe *f*. **4** Teilstrecke *f*. **stage manager** *n* Regisseur *m*. ~*vt* inszenieren, vorführen.
stagger ('stægə) *vi* taumeln, schwanken. *vt* **1** verblüffen. **2** staffeln. *n* Schwanken *neu*.
stagnant ('stægnənt) *adj* **1** stagnierend **2** träge. **stagnate** *vi* stocken, stagnieren.
stain (stein) *n* **1** Flecken *m*. **2** Makel *m*. **3** Beize *f*. *vt* **1** beflecken. **2** beizen. **stained glass** *n* buntes Glas *neu*. **stainless** *adj* **1** fleckenlos. **2** (of steel) rostfrei.
stair (stɛə) *n* **1** Stufe *f*. **2** *pl* Treppe *f*. **staircase** *n* Treppenhaus *neu*.
stake[1] (steik) *n* Pfahl *m*.
stake[2] (steik) *n game,sport* Einsatz *m*. **be at stake** auf dem Spiele stehen.
stale (steil) *adj* **1** alt, schal. **2** fad.
stalemate ('steilmeit) *n* **1** *game* Patt *neu*. **2** Stillstand *m*.
stalk[1] (stɔːk) *n* **1** Stiel *m*. **2** (of corn) Halm *m*.
stalk[2] (stɔːk) *vt* beschleichen. *vi* stolzieren.

stall[1] (stɔːl) *n* **1** Pferdebox *f*. **2** (Markt)Bude *f*. **3** *pl Th* Parkett *neu*. **4** Chorstuhl *m*. *vt* einstallen. *vi mot* aussetzen, stehenbleiben.
stall[2] (stɔːl) *n inf* Verwand *m*. Ausflucht *f*. *vt* ausweichen. *vi* Ausflüchte machen.
stallion ('stæliən) *n* Hengst *m*.
stamina ('stæminə) *n* Ausdauer, Vitalität *f*.
stammer ('stæmə) *vi* stammeln. *n* Stammeln *neu*.
stamp (stæmp) *n* **1** Stempel *m*. **2** (Brief)Marke *f*. **3** Gepräge *neu*. *vt* **1** stempeln. **2** frankieren. **3** prägen. *vi* stampfen.
stampede (stæm'piːd) *n* Panik, wilde Flucht *f*. *vi* flüchten, durchgehen.
stand* (stænd) *vi* stehen. **stand by 1** treu bleiben. **2** in Bereitschaft halten. **stand-by** *n* Beistand *m*. **stand for 1** bedeuten. **2** ertragen. **3** kandidieren für. **stand up** aufstehen. ~*n* **1** Stand *m*. **2** Standpunkt *m*. **3** Bude *f*. **standing** *adj* **1** stehend. **2** (be)ständig. *n* **1** Stellung *f*. **2** Ruf *m*. **standstill** *n* Stillstand *m*. **come to a standstill** zum Stehen kommen.
standard ('stændəd) *n* **1** Standarte *f*. **2** Standard *m*. Norm *f*. **3** Stufe *f*. *adj* maßgebend, Normal—, Standard—.
stank (stæŋk) *v* see **stink.**
stanza ('stænzə) *n* Strophe, Stanze *f*.
staple[1] ('steipəl) *n* **1** Krampe *f*. **2** Heftklammer *f*. **stapler** *n* Heftmaschine *f*.
staple[2] ('steipəl) *adj* Haupt—, Stapel—. *n* **1** Haupterzeugnis *neu*. **2** Hauptgegenstand *m*.
star (stɑː) *n* **1** Stern *m*. **2** Star *m*. *vi* die Hauptrolle spielen. **starfish** *n* Seestern *m*.
starboard ('stɑːbəd) *n* Steuerbord *neu*.
starch (stɑːtʃ) *n* (Wäsche) Stärke *f*. *vt* stärken. **starchy** *adj inf* steif.
stare (stɛə) *vi* große Augen machen, starren. **stare at** anstarren. ~*n* **1** Starren *neu*. **2** starrer Blick *m*.
stark (stɑːk) *adj* **1** steif, starr. **2** völlig. **stark naked** *adj* splitternackt.
starling ('stɑːliŋ) *n* Star *m*.
start (stɑːt) *vi* **1** anfangen. **2** starten. **3** abgehen, abfahren. **4** auffahren. *vt* **1** in Gang bringen. **2** starten lassen. **3** anfangen. *n* **1** Auffahren *neu*. **2** Anfang, Beginn *m*. **3** *sport* Start *m*.
startle ('stɑːtl̩) *vt* erschrecken.
starve (stɑːv) *vi,(vt)* verhungern (lassen). **starvation** *n* (Ver)Hungern *neu*. *adj* Hunger—.
state (steit) *n* **1** *pol* Staat *m*. **2** Zustand *m*. **get into a state** *inf* sich aufregen. ~vt **1** angeben. **2** darlegen. **3** feststellen. **4** aufstellen. *adj* Staats—. **stately** *adj* **1** stattlich. **2** prächtig. **3** erhaben. **statement** *n* **1** Angabe *f*. **2** Darlegung *f*. **3** Kontoauszug *m*. **5** Behauptung *f*. **statesman** *n* Staatsmann *m*.
static ('stætik) *adj* statisch.
station ('steiʃən) *n* **1** (railway) Bahnhof *m*. **2** (Polizei)Wache *f*. **3** Platz *m*. **4** Station *f*. *vt mil*

stationieren. **station-master** *n* Stationsvorsteher *m*.
stationary ('steiʃənri) *adj* **1** stillstehend. **2** stationär.
stationer ('steiʃənə) *n* Schreibwarenhändler *m*. **stationery** *n* Schreibwaren *f pl*.
statistics (stə'tistiks) *n pl* Statistik *f*.
statue ('stætju:) *n* Statue *f*. Standbild *neu*.
stature ('stætʃə) *n* **1** Statur *f*. Gestalt *f*. **2** Größe *f*.
status ('steitəs) *n* **1** Rang *m*. **2** Status *m*.
statute ('stætju:t) *n* **1** Statut, (Landes)Gesetz *neu*. **2** Satzung *f*. **statutory** *adj* gesetzlich.
stay[1] (stei) *vi* **1** (sich) aufhalten. **2** bleiben. **3** wohnen. *n* Aufenthalt *m*.
stay[2] (stei) *n* Stütze *f*.
steadfast ('stedfa:st) *adj* **1** fest. **2** (of a look) unverwandt. **3** standhaft.
steady ('stedi) *adj* **1** (be)ständig. **2** sicher. **3** fest. **4** ruhig. *vt* **1** sicher machen. **2** (sich) festigen. **3** (sich) beruhigen.
steak (steik) *n* **1** Steak *neu*. **2** (Fisch)Filet *neu*.
steal* (sti:l) *vi,vt* stehlen.
steam (sti:m) *n* **1** Dampf *m*. **2** Dunst *m*. *vi* dampfen. *vt cul* dünsten. **steam-engine** *n* Dampfmaschine *f*. **steam-roller** *n* Dampfwalze *f*. **steamer** *n* **1** Dampfer *m*. Dampfschiff *neu*. **2** Dampfkochtopf *m*.
steel (sti:l) *n* Stahl *m*. *adj* stählern, Stahl—. *vt* stählen.
steep[1] (sti:p) *adj* **1** steil, jäh. **2** *inf* stark.
steep[2] (sti:p) *vt* **1** einweichen. **2** versenken.
steeple ('sti:pəl) *n* Kirchturm *m*. **steeplechase** *n* Hindernisrennen *neu*.
steer (stiə) *vt* steuern. **steer clear of** vermeiden. **steering-wheel** *n* Steuerrad *neu*.
stem[1] (stem) *n* **1** Stamm *m*. **2** Stengel *m*. *v* **stem from** stammen von.
stem[2] (stem) *vt* eindämmen.
stencil ('stensəl) *n* **1** Schablone *f*. **2** Matrize *f*. *vt* schablonieren.
step (step) *n* **1** Schritt *m*. **2** (Fuß)Tritt *m*. **3** Stufe *f*. **4** Maßnahme *f*. *vi* **1** schreiten. **2** treten, gehen. **stepladder** *n* Trittleiter *f*.
stepbrother ('stepbrʌðə) *n* Stiefbruder *m*.
stepdaughter ('stepdɔ:tə) *n* Stieftochter *f*.
stepfather ('stepfa:ðə) *n* Stiefvater *m*.
stepmother ('stepmʌðə) *n* Stiefmutter *f*.
stepsister ('stepsistə) *n* Stiefschwester *f*.
stepson ('stepsʌn) *n* Stiefsohn *m*.
stereo ('steriou) *adj* Stereo—. *n* Stereoanlage *f*. **stereophonic** *adj* stereophonisch.
stereotype ('steriətaip) *n* Stereotype *f*. *vt* stereotypieren. **stereotyped** *adj* stereotyp.
sterile ('sterail) *adj* **1** steril. **2** unfruchtbar. **sterilize** *vt* **1** sterilisieren. **2** unfruchtbar machen. **sterilization** *n* Sterilisierung *f*.
sterling ('stə:liŋ) *adj* **1**

gediegen. **2** Sterling—. *n* Sterling *m*.

stern[1] (stəːn) *adj* streng, hart.

stern[2] (stəːn) *n naut* Heck *neu*. Spiegel *m*.

stethoscope ('steθəskoup) *n* Stethoskop *neu*.

stew (stjuː) *n* Schmorgericht *neu*. *vt* schmoren.

steward ('stjuːəd) *n* **1** Steward *m*. **2** Verwalter *m*. **3** Ordner *m*. **stewardess** *n* Stewardeß *f*.

stick[1] (stik) *n* Stock *m*. **get hold of the wrong end of the stick** die Geschichte in den falschen Hals kriegen.

stick*[2] (stik) *vt* **1** ankleben. **2** stecken. *vi* **1** kleben. **2** steckenbleiben. **sticker** *n* Klebzettel *m*. **sticky** *adj* klebrig. **come to a sticky end** ein schlimmes Ende nehmen.

stiff (stif) *adj* **1** steif. **2** starr. **3** (of a drink) stark. **stiffen** *vt* steifen. *vi* **1** sich versteifen. **2** erstarren.

stifle ('staifəl) *vt* ersticken.

stigma ('stigmə) *n* Stigma *neu*.

stile (stail) *n* Zauntritt *m*. Steige *f*.

still[1] (stil) *adj* still. *adv* **1** immer noch. **2** noch, immer. *conj* doch, dennoch. *vt* **1** stillen. **2** beruhigen. *n* Photographie *f*. **stillborn** *adj* totgeboren. **still life** *n* Stilleben *neu*.

still[2] (stil) *n* Destillierapparat *m*.

stilt (stilt) *n* Stelze *f*. **stilted** *adj* gespreizt, geschraubt.

stimulus ('stimjuləs) *n* **1** Antrieb *m*. **2** Reizmittel *neu*. **stimulate** *vt* anreizen, stimulieren.

sting* (stiŋ) *vi,vt* **1** stechen. **2** schmerzen. *n* **1** (of an insect) Stachel *m*. **2** Stich *m*.

stink* (stiŋk) *vi* stinken. *n* Gestank *m*.

stint (stint) *vt* einschränken. *n* **1** Einschränkung *f*. **2** Schicht *f*.

stipulate ('stipjuleit) *vt* festsetzen, vereinbaren. **stipulation** *n* **1** Festsetzung *f*. **2** Bedingung *f*.

stir (stəː) *vt* **1** rühren. **2** aufregen. *vi* sich rühren. *n* **1** Rühren *neu*. **2** (Auf)Regung *f*.

stirrup ('stirəp) *n* Steigbügel *m*.

stitch (stitʃ) *n* **1** Stich *m*. **2** Masche *f*. *vt* nähen, heften.

stoat (stout) *n* Hermelin *neu*.

stock (stɔk) *n* **1** Vorrat *m*. **2** Stamm *m*. **3** Stock *m*. **4** *pl* Aktien *f pl*. **5** *cul* Brühe *f*. **take stock of** abschätzen. ~*adj* **1** Standard—. **2** stereotyp. *vt* **1** versehen. **2** vorrätig haben. **stockbreeding** *n* Viehzucht *f*. **stockbroker** *n* Börsenmakler *m*. **stock exchange** *n* Börse *f*. **stockpile** *n* Vorrat *m*. *vt* aufstapeln. **stocktaking** *n* Inventur *f*.

stocking ('stɔkiŋ) *n* Strumpf *m*.

stocky ('stɔki) *adj* untersetzt.

stodge (stɔdʒ) *n* schwerverdauliches Essen *neu*. **stodgy** *adj* **1** schwer. **2** schwerfällig.

stoical ('stouikl̩) *adj* stoisch.

stoke (stouk) *vt* (an)schüren.

stole[1] (stoul) *v* see **steal.**

stole[2] (stoul) *n* Pelzkragen *m*. Stola *f*.

stolen ('stoulən) *v* see **steal.**

stomach ('stʌmək) *n* Magen *m*. *vt* **1** verdauen. **2** ertragen.

stomach-ache *n* Magenschmerzen *m pl*.

stone (stoun) *n* **1** Stein *m*. **2** Kern *m*. *vt* **1** steinigen. **2** (fruit) entsteinen. **stony** *adj* **1** steinig. **2** steinern.

stood (stud) *v* see **stand.**

stool (stu:l) *n* Hocker *m*.

stoop (stu:p) *vi* **1** sich bücken. **2** sich erniedrigen. **3** krumm gehen.

stop (stɔp) *vt* **1** (an)halten. **2** hindern. **3** aufhören. **4** verstopfen. *vi* **1** anhalten. **2** aufhören. **3** stehenbleiben. *n* **1** Halt *m*. **2** Pause *f*. **3** Hemmung *f*. **4** (Bus)Haltestelle *f*. **5** Punkt *m*. **stopgap** *n* Notbehelf *m*. **stopwatch** *n* Stoppuhr *f*. **stoppage** *n* **1** Stockung *f*. **2** Einstellung *f*. **3** Sperrung *f*. **stopper** *n* Stöpsel *m*. *vt* zustöpseln.

store (stɔ:) *n* **1** Vorrat *m*. **2** Lagerhaus *neu*. **3** Fülle *f*. **4** *pl* Kaufhaus *neu*. **5** Schiffsbedarf *m*. *vt* lagern, aufbewahren. **set store by** Wert legen auf. **storage** *n* **1** Aufbewahrung, Lagerung *f*. **2** (of electricity) Speicherung *f*.

storey ('stɔ:ri) *n* Stock *m*. Stockwerk, Geschoß *neu*.

stork (stɔ:k) *n* Storch *m*.

storm (stɔ:m) *n* Sturm *m*. *vt* stürmen. *vi* toben. **stormy** *adj* stürmisch.

story ('stɔ:ri) *n* **1** Geschichte *f*. **2** Erzählung *f*. **3** Handlung *f*.

stout (staut) *adj* **1** stark. **2** dick. **3** tapfer. *n* Starkbier *neu*.

stove (stouv) *n* **1** Ofen *m*. **2** (for cooking) Herd *m*.

stow (stou) *vt* verstauen.

stowaway *n* blinder Passagier *m*.

straddle (strædl̩) *vi* breitbeinig gehen *or* stehen. *vt* spreizen.

straggle ('strægəl) *vi* **1** verstreut liegen. **2** umherschweifen. **3** wuchern. **straggling** *adj* weitläufig, lose.

straight (streit) *adj* **1** gerade. **2** aufrichtig. **3** glatt. **get straight** klarmachen. **put straight** in Ordnung bringen. **straight ahead** *adv* geradeaus. **straight away** *adv* sofort, unmittelbar. **straighten** *vt* geradeachen. *vi* gerade werden. **straightforward** *adj* **1** gerade. **2** redlich.

strain[1] (strein) *n* **1** Anstrengung *f*. **2** Druck *m*. **3** *med* Zerrung *f*. *vt* **1** anstrengen. **2** zerren. **3** (durch)seihen. *vi* sich anstrengen. **strainer** *n* Seiher *m*. Sieb *neu*.

strain[2] (strein) *n* Abstammung, Rasse *f*.

strand[1] (strænd) *vi,(vt)* stranden (lassen).

strand[2] (strænd) *n* Strähne *f*.

strange (streindʒ) *adj* **1** fremd. **2** seltsam. **stranger** *n* **1** Fremde(r) *m*. **2** Neuling *m*.

strangle ('stræŋgəl) *vt* **1** erwürgen. **2** unterdrücken.

strap (stræp) *n* **1** Riemen *m*. **2** Träger *m*. *vt* festschnallen.

strategy ('strætidʒi) *n* Strategie *f*. **strategic** *adj* strategisch.

straw (strɔ:) *n* **1** Stroh *neu*. **2** Strohhalm *m*. *adj* Stroh—.

strawberry *n* Erdbeere *f*.

stray (strei) *vi* **1** sich verirren. **2** abirren. *adj* verirrt. *n* verirrtes Tier *neu*.

streak (stri:k) *n* **1** Streifen *m*. **2**

Spur *f.* *vt* streifen. **streaky** *adj* **1** streifig. **2** (of bacon) durchwachsen.

stream (striːm) *n* **1** Bach *m.* **2** Strom *m.* *vi* **1** strömen. **2** flattern. **streamer** *n* Papierschlange *f.* **streamline** *n* Stromlinie *f.* *vt* modernisieren.

street (striːt) *n* Straße *f.*

strength (streŋθ) *n* Kraft, Stärke *f.* **on the strength of** kraft. **strengthen** *vt* (be)kräftigen, (be)stärken. *vi* erstärken.

strenuous ('strenjuəs) *adj* **1** emsig. **2** eifrig. **3** anstrengend.

stress (stres) *n* **1** Ton *m.* Betonung *f.* **2** Nachdruck *m.* Gewicht *neu.* **3** *med* Streß *m.* *vt* **1** betonen. **2** unterstreichen.

stretch (stretʃ) *vt* **1** strecken. **2** (aus)dehnen. **3** anspannen. *vi* **1** sich erstrecken. **2** sich dehnen. *n* **1** Strecke *f.* **2** Dehnung *f.* **at a stretch** in einem Zug. **stretcher** *n* Tragbahre *f.*

strict (strikt) *adj* **1** streng. **2** genau. **strictly speaking** streng genommen.

stride* (straid) *vi* schreiten. *n* (langer) Schritt *m.*

strike* (straik) *vt* **1** schlagen. **2** treffen. **3** auffallen. **4** anzünden. *vi* **1** schlagen. **2** streiken. *n* Streik *m.*

string* (striŋ) *n* **1** Schnur *f.* **2** *mus* Saite *f.* **3** Reihe *f.* *vt* **1** aufreihen. **2** *mus* besaiten. **stringed instruments** *n pl* Saiteninstrumente *neu pl.*

stringent ('strindʒənt) *adj* **1** streng. **2** fest. **3** knapp. **stringency** *n* **1** Strenge *f.* **2** Härte *f.* **3** Knappheit *f.*

strip[1] (strip) *vi* sich ausziehen. *vt* **1** entkleiden. **2** entblößen. **3** abreißen. **striptease** *n* Striptease *neu.*

strip[2] (strip) *n* (schmaler) Streifen *m.*

stripe (straip) *n* Streifen *m.* **striped** *adj* gestreift.

strive* (straiv) *vi* **1** streben. **2** ringen.

stroke[1] (strouk) *n* **1** Schlag, Hieb *m.* **2** Streich *m.* **3** Strich *m.* **stroke of luck** *n* glücklicher Zufall *m.*

stroke[2] (strouk) *vt* streicheln.

stroll (stroul) *vi* **1** bummeln, schlendern. **2** spazierengehen. *n* **1** Bummel *m.* **2** Spaziergang *m.*

strong (strɔŋ) *adj* **1** stark. **2** kräftig. **3** fest. **stronghold** *n* Festung *f.* **strong-minded** *adj* willenstark.

struck (strʌk) *v* see **strike.**

structure ('strʌktʃə) *n* **1** Bau *m.* **2** Struktur *f.* **structural** *adj* **1** Bau—. **2** strukturell.

struggle ('strʌgəl) *vi* **1** sich (ab)mühen. **2** kämpfen, ringen. **3** zappeln. *n* **1** Kampf *m.* **2** Ringen *neu.*

strum (strʌm) *vi,(vt)* klimpern (auf).

strung (strʌŋ) *v* see **string.**

strut[1] (strʌt) *vi* stolzieren. *n* Stolzieren *neu.*

strut[2] (strʌt) *n* Strebe, Stütze *f.*

stub (stʌb) *n* **1** Stumpf *m.* **2** Stummel *m.* *vt* stoßen. **stub out** ausdrücken.

stubborn ('stʌbən) *adj* **1** hartnäckig. **2** halsstarrig. **stubbornness** *n* Hartnäckigkeit *f.*

stud[1] (stʌd) *n* **1** Beschlagnagel

m. **2** Kragenknopf *m.* *vt* **1** beschlagen. **2** bestreuen.
stud[2] (stʌd) *n* Gestüt *neu.*
student ('stju:dnt) *n* Student *m.* Studentin *f.*
studio ('stju:diou) *n* **1** Atelier *neu.* **2** Senderaum *m.* **3** Studio *neu.*
study ('stʌdi) *n* **1** Studium *neu.* **2** Studierzimmer *neu.* **3** *Art* Studie *f.* *vt* **1** studieren. **2** genau beobachten. *vi* studieren. **studious** *adj* **1** fleißig. **2** beflissen.
stuff (stʌf) *n* **1** Stoff *m.* **2** Zeug *neu.* *vt* **1** (voll-, aus-)stopfen. **2** *cul* füllen. **stuffing** *n* **1** *cul* Füllung *f.* **2** Polsterung *f.* **stuffy** *adj* **1** muffig. **2** *inf* spießig.
stumble ('stʌmbəl) *vi* stolpern. **stumble upon** stoßen auf. *~n* Stolpern *neu.* **stumbling block** *n* Stein des Anstoßes *m.*
stump (stʌmp) *n* **1** Stumpf *m.* **2** *sport* Stab *m.* *vt* *inf* verblüffen. *vi* stapfen.
stun (stʌn) *vt* betäuben. **stunning** *adj* **1** betäubend. **2** *inf* sagenhaft, toll.
stung (stʌŋ) *v* see **sting.**
stunk (stʌŋk) *v* see **stink.**
stunt[1] (stʌnt) *vt* im Wachstum hindern.
stunt[2] (stʌnt) *n* **1** Kunststück *neu.* **2** Trick *m.*
stupid ('stju:pid) *adj* **1** dumm. **2** blöd. **stupidity** *n* Dummheit *f.*
sturdy ('stə:di) *adj* **1** derb. **2** stämmig.
stutter ('stʌtə) *vi* stottern. *n* Stottern *neu.*
sty (stai) *n* **1** Schweinestall *m.* **2** *med* Gerstenkorn *neu.*
style (stail) *n* Stil *m.* **in style** *adv* vornehm. **stylish** *adj* **1** stilvoll. **2** elegant.
stylus ('stailəs) *n* **1** Griffel *m.* **2** Grammophonnadel *f.*
subconscious (sʌb'kɔnʃəs) *adj* unterbewußt. *n* Unterbewußte *neu.*
subcontract (sʌbkən'trækt) *n* Nebenvertrag *m.*
subdue (səb'dju:) *vt* **1** unterwerfen. **2** dämpfen.
subject (*n,adj* 'sʌbdʒikt; *v* səb 'dʒekt) *n* **1** *pol* Untertan, Staatsangehörige(r) *m.* **2** Thema *neu.* **3** Fach *neu.* **4** Subjekt *neu.* *adj* **1** unterworfen. **2** abhängig. **subject to** vorbehaltlich. *~vt* **1** unterwerfen. **2** unterziehen. **3** aussetzen. **subjective** *adj* subjektiv.
subjunctive (səb'dʒʌŋktiv) *n* Konjunktiv *m.* *adj* konjunktivisch.
sublime (sə'blaim) *adj* **1** erhaben. **2** *inf* großartig.
submachine-gun (səbmə 'ʃi:ngʌn) *n* Maschinenpistole *f.*
submarine (sʌbmə'ri:n) *n* Unterseeboot *neu.* *adj* Untersee—.
submerge (səb'mə:dʒ) *vt* **1** untertauchen. **2** überschwemmen. *vi* untertauchen.
submit (səb'mit) *vt* vorlegen. *vi* **1** sich unterwerfen. **2** sich ergeben. **submission** *n* **1** Vorlage *f.* **2** Unterwerfung *f.* **submissive** *adj* unterwürfig.
subnormal (sʌb'nɔ:məl) *adj* unternormal, subnormal.
subordinate (sə'bɔ:dinət) *adj* **1** untergeordnet. **2** Neben—. *n* Untergebene(r) *m.* *vt* **1** unter-

ordnen. **2** unterwerfen. **subordination** *n* Unterordnung *f.*
subscribe (səb'skraib) *vt* **1** unterschreiben (mit). **2** (money) zeichnen. *vi* **subscribe to 1** abonnieren. **2** zustimmen. **subscriber** *n* Abonnent *m.* **subscription** *n* **1** Unterzeichnung *f.* **2** Abonnement *neu.* **3** Mitgliedsbeitrag *m.*
subsequent ('sʌbsikwint) *adj* folgend. **subsequently** *adv* **1** hinterher. **2** anschließend.
subservient (səb'səːviənt) *adj* **1** unterwürfig. **2** dienlich.
subside (səb'said) *vi* **1** sich senken. **2** sich legen. **subside into** verfallen in. **subsidence** *n* Senkung *f.*
subsidiary (səb'sidiəri) *adj* Hilfs—, Neben—.
subsidize ('sʌbsidaiz) *vt* (mit Geld) unterstützen, subventionieren. **subsidy** *n* **1** Beihilfe *f.* **2** Subvention *f.*
subsist (səb'sist) *vi* **1** leben. **2** bestehen. *vt* unterhalten. **subsistence** *n* **1** Lebensunterhalt *m.* **2** Dasein *neu.*
substance ('sʌbstəns) *n* **1** Substanz *f.* **2** Wesen *neu.* **3** Inhalt *m.* **4** Wirklichkeit *f.* **substantial** *adj* **1** wesentlich. **2** wirklich. **3** solid. **substantive** *adj* **1** *gram* substantivisch. **2** selbständig. **3** fest. *n* Substantiv *neu.*
substitute ('sʌbstitjuːt) *vt* ersetzen. *vi* vertreten. *n* **1** Ersatz *m.* **2** Stellvertreter *m. adj* Ersatz—.
subtitle ('sʌbtait) *n* Untertitel *m.*
subtle ('sʌtl̩) *adj* **1** fein(sinning). **2** spitzfindig.
subtlety *n* **1** Feinheit *f.* **2** Spitzfindigkeit *f.*
subtract (səb'trækt) *vt* subtrahieren, abziehen. **subtraction** *n* Subtraktion *f.* Abzug *m.*
suburb ('sʌbəːb) *n* Vorstadt *f.* Vorort *m.* **suburban** *adj* vorstädtisch, Vorstadt—.
subvert (sʌb'vəːt) *vt* umstürzen. **subversive** *adj* umstürzlerisch, subversiv.
subway ('sʌbwei) *n* Fußgängerunterführung *f.*
succeed (sək'siːd) *vi* **1** Erfolg haben. **2** gelingen. **3** (nach)folgen. *vt* (nach)folgen.
success *n* Erfolg *m.* **successful** *adj* erfolgreich. **be successful** Erfolg haben. **succession** **1** Nachfolge, Reihenfolge *f.* **2** Erbfolge *f.* **3** Thronfolge *f.* **in succession** *adv* nacheinander. **successive** *adj* aufeinanderfolgend.
succulent ('sʌkjulənt) *adj* **1** saftig. **2** fleischig.
succumb (sə'kʌm) *vi* **1** unterliegen. **2** sich ergeben.
such (sʌtʃ) *adj* **1** solch. **2** derartig. **3** so. *pron* solch. **suchlike** *adj* dergleichen.
suck (sʌk) *vt* **1** saugen. **2** ansaugen. **3** (sweets, etc.) lutschen. **suck up to** *sl* sich einschmeicheln bei.
sucker ('sʌkə) *n* **1** Sauger *m.* **2** *bot* Sprößling *m.* **suckle** *vt* säugen, nähren.
suction ('sʌkʃən) *n* **1** Saugen *neu.* **2** Ansaugung *f. adj* Saug—.
Sudan (suː'dæn) *n* Sudan *m.* **Sudanese** *adj* sudanesisch. *n* Sudanese *m.*
sudden ('sʌdn̩) *adj* plötzlich.

suds (sʌdz) *n pl* (Seifen)Lauge *f*.

sue (suː) *vt* verklagen. *vi* klagen.

suede (sweid) *n* Wildleder *neu*. *adj* Wildleder—.

suet ('suːit) *n* **1** Nierenfett *neu*. **2** Talg *m*.

suffer ('sʌfə) *vi* leiden. *vt* erdulden, erleiden. **suffering** *n* Leiden *neu*.

sufficient (sə'fiʃənt) *adj* genug, genügend. **be sufficient** genügen.

suffix ('sʌfiks) *n* Nachsilbe *f*. Suffix *neu*.

suffocate ('sʌfəkeit) *vi,vt* ersticken. **suffocation** *n* Erstickung *f*.

sugar ('ʃugə) *n* Zucker *m*. *vt* **1** zuckern. **2** versüßen. **sugar beet** *n* Zuckerrübe *f*. **sugar cane** *n* Zuckerrohr *neu*. **sugary** *adj* **1** zuckerig. **2** zuckersüß.

suggest (sə'dʒest) *vt* **1** vorschlagen. **2** andeuten. **3** eingeben. **suggestion** *n* **1** Vorschlag *m*. **2** Andeutung *f*. **3** Eingebung *f*. **suggestive** *adj* **1** andeutend. **2** zweideutig.

suicide ('suːisaid) *n* **1** Selbstmord *m*. **2** Selbstmörder *m*. **suicidal** *adj* selbstmörderisch.

suit (sjuːt) *n* **1** (Herren)Anzug *m*. **2** (Damen)Kostüm *neu*. **3** Bitte *f*. **4** *game* Farbe *f*. *vi,vt* passen. **suit oneself** tun, was einem beliebt. **suitcase** *n* (Hand)Koffer *m*. **suitable** *adj* passend, geeignet.

suite (swiːt) *n* **1** Gefolge *neu*. **2** Garnitur *f*. **3** *mus* Suite *f*. **suite of rooms** Zimmerflucht *f*.

sulk (sʌlk) *vi* schmollen. **sulky** *adj* **1** schmollend. **2** mürrisch, launisch.

sullen ('sʌlən) *adj* verdrossen.

sulphur ('sʌlfə) *n* Schwefel *m*. **sulphuric** *adj* Schwefel—.

sultana (sʌl'tɑːnə) *n cul* Sultanine *f*.

sultry ('sʌltri) *adj* **1** schwül. **2** stechend heiß.

sum (sʌm) *n* **1** Summe *f*. **2** Rechenaufgabe *f*. **do sums** rechnen. *v* **sum up** zusammenfassen.

summarize ('sʌməraiz) *vt* zusammenfassen. **summary** *n* Zusammenfassung *f*.

summer ('sʌmə) *n* Sommer *m*. **summertime** *n* Sommerzeit *f*.

summit ('sʌmit) *n* Gipfel *m*. **summit conference** *n* Gipfelkonferenz *f*.

summon ('sʌmən) *vt* **1** auffordern. **2** rufen. **3** vorladen. **summon up** aufbieten. **summons** *n* **1** Aufforderung *f*. **2** gerichtliche Vorladung *f*.

sun (sʌn) *n* Sonne *f*. **sunny** *adj* sonnig. *v* **sun oneself** sich sonnen.

sunbathe ('sʌnbeið) *vi* ein Sonnenbad nehmen.

sunburn ('sʌnbəːn) *n* Sonnenbrand *m*.

Sunday ('sʌndi) *n* Sonntag *m*.

sundial ('sʌndaiəl) *n* Sonnenuhr *f*.

sundry ('sʌndri) *adj* verschieden. *n pl* Verschiedenes *neu*.

sunflower ('sʌnflauə) *n* Sonnenblume *f*.

sung (sʌŋ) *v* see **sing**.

sunglasses ('sʌnglɑːsiz) *n pl* Sonnenbrille *f.*
sunk (sʌŋk) *v* see **sink.**
sunlight ('sʌnlait) *n* Sonnenlicht *neu.*
sunrise ('sʌnraiz) *n* Sonnenaufgang *m.*
sunset ('sʌnset) *n* Sonnenuntergang *m.*
sunshine ('sʌnʃain) *n* Sonnenschein *m.*
sunstroke ('sʌnstrouk) *n* Sonnenstich *m.*
suntan ('sʌntæn) *n* Sonnenbräune *f.*
super ('suːpə) *adj inf* prima, erstklassig.
superannuation (suːpərænju'eiʃən) *n* **1** Pensionierung *f.* **2** Ruhegehalt *neu.* Pension *f.*
superb (suː'pəːb) *adj* **1** prächtig. **2** herrlich.
superficial (suːpə'fiʃəl) *adj* oberflächlich.
superfluous (suː'pəːfluəs) *adj* überflüssig.
superhuman (suːpə'hjuːmən) *adj* übermenschlich.
superimpose (suːpərim'pouz) *vt* auflegen.
superintendent (suːpərin'tendənt) *n* **1** Aufseher *m.* **2** Inspektor *m. adj* aufsichtführend.
superior (su'piəriə) *adj* **1** ober. **2** höher. **3** besser, überlegen. *n* **1** höherer Offizier *m.* **2** Vorgesetzte(r) *m.* **3** *rel* Superior *m.* **superiority** *n* Überlegenheit *f.*
superlative (su'pəːlətiv) *adj* **1** höchst. **2** *gram* superlativisch. *n* Superlativ *m.*
supermarket ('suːpəmɑːkit) *n* Supermarkt *m.*
supernatural (suːpə'nætʃrəl) *adj* übernatürlich.
supersede (suːpə'siːd) *vt* **1** ersetzen. **2** verdrängen. **3** überholen.
supersonic (suːpə'sɔnik) *adj* Überschall—.
superstition (suːpə'stiʃən) *n* Aberglaube *m.* **supersititious** *adj* abergläubisch.
supervise ('suːpəvaiz) *vt* beaufsichtigen. **supervision** *n* **1** Beaufsichtigung *f.* **2** Aufsicht *f.* **supervisor** *n* Aufseher *m.*
supper ('sʌpə) *n* Abendessen, Abendbrot *neu.*
supple ('sʌpəl) *adj* biegsam, geschmeidig.
supplement ('sʌplimənt) *n* **1** Ergänzung *f.* **2** Nachtrag *m.* **3** Beilage *f. vt* ergänzen. **supplementary** *adj* **1** Ergänzungs—. **2** Nachtrags—.
supply (sə'plai) *vt* **1** (be)liefern, versorgen, besorgen. **2** decken. *n* **1** Versorgung *f.* **2** Vorrat *m.* **3** Angebot *neu.* **4** *pl* Vorräte *m pl.* **supply and demand** Angebot und Nachfrage. **supplier** *n* Lieferant *m.*
support (sə'pɔːt) *vt* **1** (unter)stützen. **2** tragen. *n* **1** Unterstützung *f.* **2** Stütze *f.* Träger *m.*
suppose (sə'pouz) *vt* **1** annehmen. **2** voraussetzen. *vi* vermuten, glauben.
suppress (sə'pres) *vt* **1** unterdrücken. **2** hemmen. **suppression** *n* Unterdrückung *f.*
supreme (sə'priːm) *adj* höchst, oberst.
surcharge ('səːtʃɑːdʒ) *n* Zus-

chlag *m*. *vt* mit Zuschlag belegen.

sure (ʃuə) *adj* **1** sicher, gewiß. **2** zuverlässig. **surely** *adv* **1** gewiß, sicherlich. **2** vermutlich. **surety** *n* **1** Bürge *f*. **2** Sicherheit *f*.

surf (səːf) *n* Brandung *f*.

surface ('səːfis) *n* **1** Oberfläche *f*. **2** Äußere *neu*. *vi* auftauchen. *adj* oberflächlich.

surfeit ('səːfit) *n* Übermaß *neu*. *vt* übersättigen.

surge (səːdʒ) *vi* **1** branden. **2** aufwallen. **3** vorwärtsdrängen. *n* **1** Brandung *f*. **2** Flut *f*.

surgeon ('səːdʒən) *n* Chirurg *m*. **surgery** *n* **1** Chirurgie *f*. **2** Sprechzimmer *neu*. **3** Sprechstunde *f*.

surly ('səːli) *adj* mürrisch.

surmount (sə'maunt) *vt* **1** übersteigen. **2** überwinden.

surname ('səːneim) *n* Zuname, Familienname *m*.

surpass (sə'pɑːs) *vt* übertreffen.

surplus ('səːplis) *n* Überschuß *m*. *adj* überschüssig.

surprise (sə'praiz) *vt* **1** überraschen. **2** ertappen. *n* Überraschung *f*. **surprised** *adj* überrascht, verblüfft.

surrealism (sə'riəlizəm) *n* Surrealismus *m*.

surrender (sə'rendə) *vt* **1** übergeben. **2** aufgeben. *vi* sich ergeben. *n* Übergabe *f*.

surreptitious (sʌrəp'tiʃəs) *adj* heimlich, verstohlen.

surround (sə'raund) *vt* **1** umgeben. **2** umzingeln, einschließen. **surrounding** *adj* umgebend. **surroundings** *n pl* Umgebung *f*.

survey (sə'vei) *n* **1** Überprüfung *f*. **2** Überblick *m*. **3** Landvermessung *f*. *vt* **1** (über)prüfen. **2** überblicken. **3** vermessen.

surveyor (sə'veiə) *n* **1** Feldmesser, Geometer *m*. **2** Aufseher *m*.

survive (sə'vaiv) *vt,vi* überleben. **survivor** *n* Überlebende(r) *m*.

susceptible (sə'septəbəl) *adj* empfänglich, anfällig.

suspect (*v* sə'spekt; *n,adj* 'sʌspekt) *vt* **1** verdächtigen. **2** vermuten. **3** mißtrauen. *n* Verdächtigte(r) *m*. *adj* verdächtig.

suspend (sə'spend) *vt* **1** aufhängen. **2** verschieben. **3** einstellen. **4** unterbrechen. **suspense** *n* **1** Spannung *f*. **2** Ungewißheit *f*. **suspension** *n* **1** Aufhängung *f*. **2** *mot* Federung *f*. **3** Verschiebung *f*. **4** Einstellung *f*.

suspicion (sə'spiʃən) *n* **1** Verdacht *m*. **2** Vermutung *f*. **3** Spur *f*. **suspicious** *adj* **1** verdächtig. **2** mißtrauisch.

sustain (sə'stein) *vt* **1** aushalten. **2** unterstützen.

swab (swɔb) *n* **1** Tupfer *m*. **2** Scheuerlappen *m*. *vt* **1** aufwischen, scheuern. **2** betupfen.

Swabia ('sweibiə) *n* Schwaben *neu*. **Swabian** *adj* schwäbisch. *n* Schwabe *m*.

swagger ('swægə) *vi* **1** stolzieren. **2** prahlen. *n* **1** stolzierender Gang *m*. **2** Prahlerei *f*.

swallow[1] ('swɔlou) *vt* (ver)schlucken, verschlingen. *vi* schlucken. *n* Schluck *m*.

swallow[2] ('swɔlou) *n zool* Schwalbe *f*.

swam (swæm) *v* see **swim.**
swamp (swɔmp) *n* Sumpf *m.* *vt* überschwemmen.
swan (swɔn) *n* Schwan *m.*
swank (swæŋk) *n inf* Prahlerei, Angeberei *f.* *vi inf* aufschneiden, prahlen.
swap (swɔp) *vt also* **swop** (aus)tauschen. *n* Tausch *m.*
swarm (swɔːm) *n* Schwarm *m.* *vi* **1** schwärmen. **2** wimmeln.
swastika ('swɔstikə) *n* Hakenkreuz *neu.*
swat (swɔt) *vt* zerquetschen, schlagen.
sway (swei) *vi* schwanken, schaukeln. *vt* **1** beeinflussen. **2** mitreißen. *n* **1** Herrschaft *f.* **2** Einfluß *m.*
swear* (swɛə) *vi* **1** fluchen. **2** schwören. *vt* (be)schwören. **swearword** *n* Fluchwort *neu.*
sweat (swet) *vi,vt* schwitzen. *n* **1** Schweiß *m.* **2** *inf* Plackerei *f.* **sweater** *n* Pullover *m.*
swede (swiːd) *n* Steckrübe *f.*
Sweden ('swiːdn̩) *n* Schweden *neu.* **Swede** *n* Schwede *m.* **Swedish** ('swiːdiʃ) *adj* schwedisch. *n* (language) Schwedisch *neu.*
sweep* (swiːp) *vt* **1** fegen, kehren. **2** durchstreifen. *vi* vorbeirauschen. *n* **1** Schornsteinfeger *m.* **2** Fegen *neu.*
sweet (swiːt) *adj* süß. *n* **1** Bonbon *m.* Süßigkeit *f.* **2** Nachtisch *m.* **sweetbread** *n* Bries *m.* **sweet corn** *n* Zuckermais *m.* **sweetheart** *n* Liebchen *neu.* Liebste(r) *m.* **sweet pea** *n* Wicke *f.* **sweeten** *vt* **1** süßen. **2** versüßen.
swell* (swel) *vi* (an)schwellen. *adj sl* **1** prima. **2** vornehm.
swelter ('sweltə) *vi* vor Hitze umkommen.
swept (swept) *v* see **sweep.**
swerve (swəːv) *vi* **1** (plötzlich) abbiegen. **2** ausweichen.
swift (swift) *adj* schnell, rasch.
swig (swig) *inf n* Schluck, Zug *m.* *vt* saufen, hinunterschlucken.
swill (swil) *n* **1** Schweinefutter *neu.* **2** Spülwasser *neu.* *vt* spülen.
swim* (swim) *vi* schwimmen. *vt* durchschwimmen. *n* Schwimmen *neu.* **swimming** *n* Schwimmen *neu.* **swimming costume** *n* Badeanzug *m.* **swimming pool** *n* Schwimmbad *neu.* **indoor swimming pool** *n* Hallenbad *neu.*
swindle ('swindl̩) *vt* betrügen, beschwindeln. *n* Schwindel, Betrug *m.*
swine (swain) *n* Schwein *neu.*
swing* (swiŋ) *vi,vt* schwingen, schaukeln. *n* **1** Schwung *m.* **2** Schaukel *f.*
swipe (swaip) *vt,vi* hauen. *n* wilder Schlag *m.*
swirl (swəːl) *vi,vt* (herum)-wirbeln. *n* Wirbel *m.*
swish (swiʃ) *vi* **1** schwirren. **2** rascheln. *vt* schwirren lassen. *adj* schick, elegant.
Swiss (swis) *adj* schweizerisch. *n* Schweizer *m.*
switch (switʃ) *n* **1** Schalter *m.* **2** Umstellung *f.* Wechsel *m.* **3** Rute *f.* *vt* **1** wechseln, tauschen. **2** umstellen. *vi* umstellen, übergehen. **switch off** ausschalten. **switch on** anschalten. **switchboard** *n* Schalttafel *f.*

Switzerland ('switsələnd) *n* Schweiz *f.*
swivel ('swivəl) *(vi),vt* (sich) drehen.
swollen ('swoulən) *adj* geschwollen.
swoop (swu:p) *vi* sich stürzen, herabschießen. *n* plötzlicher Angriff, Sturz *m.*
swop (swɔp) *v* see **swap.**
sword (sɔ:d) *n* Schwert *neu.* **swordfish** *n* Schwertfisch *m.* **swordsman** *n* Fechter *m.*
swore (swɔ:) *v* see **swear.**
sworn (swɔ:n) *adj* **1** eidlich. **2** geschworen.
swot (swɔt) *vi inf* pauken. *n* Streber *m.*
swum (swʌm) *v* see **swim.**
swung (swʌŋ) *v* see **swing.**
sycamore ('sikəmɔ:) *n bot* Bergahorn *m.*
syllable ('siləbəl) *n* Silbe *f.*
syllabus ('siləbəs) *n* **1** Lehrplan *m.* **2** Verzeichnis *neu.*
symbol ('simbəl) *n* Symbol, Sinnbild *neu.* **symbolism** *n* **1** Symbolismus *m.* **2** Symbolik *f.* **symbolize** *vt* symbolisieren.
symmetry ('simitri) *n* Symmetrie *f.* Ebenmaß *neu.* **symmetrical** *adj* symmetrisch.
sympathy ('simpəθi) *n* **1** Mitgefühl, Mitleid *neu.* **2** Sympathie *f.* **sympathetic** *adj* **1** mitfühlend. **2** verständnisvoll. **3** wohlwollend. **sympathize** *vi* **1** mitfühlen, Mitleid haben. **2** übereinstimmen. **3** wohlwollen.
symphony ('simfəni) *n* Sinfonie, Symphonie *f.*
symposium (sim'pouziəm) *n* **1** Konferenz *f.* Symposion *neu.* **2** Tagungsbericht *m.*
symptom ('simptəm) *n* Symptom, Anzeichen *neu.* **symptomatic** *adj* symptomatisch.
synagogue ('sinəgɔg) *n* Synagoge *f.*
synchronize ('siŋkrənaiz) *vt* synchronisieren.
syndicate (*n* 'sindikət; *v* 'sindikeit) *n* Syndikat, Kartell *neu. vt* zu einem Syndikat vereinigen.
syndrome ('sindroum) *n* Syndrom *neu.*
synonym ('sinənim) *n* Synonym *neu.*
synopsis (si'nɔpsis) *n* Übersicht *f.* Abriß *m.*
syntax ('sintæks) *n* Syntax *f.* Satzbau *m.*
synthesis ('sinθəsis) *n* Synthese, Zusammensetzung *f.* **synthetic** *adj* synthetisch.
syphilis ('sifəlis) *n* Syphilis *f.*
Syria ('siriə) *n* Syrien *neu.* **Syrian** *adj* syrisch. *n* Syrier *m.*
syringe (si'rindʒ) *n* Spritze *f.*
syrup ('sirəp) *n* Sirup *m.*
system ('sistəm) *n* **1** System *neu.* **2** Verfahren *neu.* Methode *f.* **systematic** *adj* systematisch, methodisch.

T

tab (tæb) *n* Aufhänger *m.* Etikett *neu.* **keep tabs on** kontrollieren.
tabby ('tæbi) *n* getigerte Katze *f.*
table ('teibəl) *n* **1** Tisch *m.* **2** Tafel *f.* **3** Liste *f.* **tablecloth** *n* Tischtuch *neu.* **tablemat** *n* Untersatz *m.* **tablespoon** *n* Eßlöffel *m.* **table tennis** *n* Tischtennis *neu.*

tablet ('tæblət) *n* **1** *med* Tablette *f.* **2** Tafel *f.*

taboo (tə'buː) *n* Tabu *neu.* *adj* tabu, verboten.

tachograph ('tækougraːf) *n* Fahrtenschreiber *m.*

tack (tæk) *n* **1** Zwecke *f.* **2** Heftstich *m.* **3** *naut* Lavieren *neu.* *vi naut* lavieren. *vt* (an)heften, befestigen.

tackle ('tækəl) *n* **1** Gerät *neu.* Ausrüstung *f.* **2** *naut* Takelwerk. **3** *sport* Angreifen *neu.* *vt* **1** angreifen. **2** angehen.

tact (tækt) *n* **1** Takt *m.* **2** Feingefühl *neu.* **tactful** *adj* taktvoll.

tactics ('tæktiks) *n pl* Taktik *f.* **tactical** *adj* taktisch.

tadpole ('tædpoul) *n* Kaulquappe *f.*

taffeta ('tæfitə) *n* Taft, Taffet *m.*

tag (tæg) *n* **1** Etikett *neu.* Anhängezettel *m.* **2** Stift *m.* *vt* anheften. **tag along** hinterherlaufen.

tail (teil) *n* **1** Schwanz *m.* **2** Ende *neu.* *vt* beschatten, verfolgen.

tailor ('teilə) *n* Schneider *m.* *vt* schneidern.

taint (teint) *vt* **1** beflecken. **2** verderben. *n* Makel, Fleck *m.*

take* (teik) *vt* **1** nehmen. **2** bringen. **3** ergreifen. **4** gewinnen. **5** fangen. **6** halten. **take in 1** aufnehmen. **2** einschließen. **take off** *vi* abfliegen. *vt* ausziehen, abnehmen. **take-off** *n aviat* Abflug *m.* **take-over** *n* Übernahme *f.* **take place** stattfinden.

talcum powder ('tælkəm) *n* Talkpuder *m.*

tale (teil) *n* **1** Erzählung *f.* **2** Lüge *f.*

talent ('tælənt) *n* Begabung, Talent *neu.*

talk (tɔːk) *vi* reden, sprechen. *n* **1** Rede *f.* **2** Gespräch *neu.* **3** Gerede, Geschwätz *neu.* **talkative** *adj* geschwätzig, gesprächig.

tall (tɔːl) *adj* **1** groß. **2** hoch. **3** lang. **tall story** *n* Spinnerei, unglaubliche Geschichte *f.*

tally ('tæli) *n* Rechnung *f.* *vi* übereinstimmen.

talon ('tælən) *n* Kralle, Klaue *f.*

tambourine (tæmbə'riːn) *n* Tambourin *neu.*

tame (teim) *adj* zahm, gezähmt. *vt* zähmen.

tamper ('tæmpə) *vi* **tamper with 1** sich einmischen in. **2** herumbasteln an.

tampon ('tæmpɔn) *n* Wattebausch, Tampon *m.*

tan (tæn) *n* **1** Lohe *f.* **2** Bräune *f.* *adj* gelbbraun. *vt* **1** gerben. **2** bräunen. *vi* braun werden.

tangent ('tændʒənt) *n* Tangente *f.*

tangerine (tændʒə'riːn) *n* Mandarine *f.*

tangible ('tændʒəbəl) *adj* **1** greifbar. **2** fühlbar.

Tangier (tæn'dʒiə) *n* Tanger *neu.*

tangle ('tæŋgəl) *n* Wirrwarr *m.* Verwirrung *f.* *vt* **1** verwirren, verwickeln. **2** verknoten.

tank (tæŋk) *n* **1** Zisterne *f.* **2** Tank *m.* **3** *mil* Panzer *m.* *v* **tank up** tanken. **tanker** *n* Tanker *m.*

tankard ('tæŋkəd) *n* Kanne *f.* Bierkrug *m.*
tantalize ('tæntəlaiz) *vt* quälen.
tantrum ('tæntrəm) *n* Wutanfall *m.*
tap[1] (tæp) *vt,vi* klopfen. *n* Klopfen *neu.*
tap[2] (tæp) *n* Hahn, Zapfen *m.* *vt* **1** anzapfen. **2** (a telephone) anzapfen.
tape (teip) *n* **1** Band *neu.* **2** Tonband *m.* *vt* **1** auf Band aufnehmen. **2** mit einem Band befestigen. **tape measure** *n* Maßband *neu.* **tape-recorder** *n* Tonbandgerät *neu.*
taper ('teipə) *vi,(vt)* spitz zulaufen (lassen). *n* dünne Kerze *f.*
tapestry ('tæpistri) *n* Wandteppich *m.*
tapioca (tæpi'oukə) *n* Tapioka *f.*
tar (tɑː) *n* Teer *m.* *vt* teeren.
tarantula (tə'ræntjulə) *n* Tarantel *f.*
target ('tɑːgit) *n* **1** Zielscheibe *f.* **2** Ziel *neu.*
tariff ('tærif) *n* **1** Zolltarif *m.* **2** Preisliste *f.*
Tarmac ('tɑːmæk) *n* *Tdmk* Asphalt *m.*
tarnish ('tɑːniʃ) *vt* **1** trüben. **2** beflecken. *vi* sich trüben.
tarragon ('tærəgən) *n* Estragon *m.*
tart[1] (tɑːt) *adj* **1** sauer, herb. **2** beißend.
tart[2] (tæːt) *n* **1** (Obst)Torte *f.* **2** *sl* Dirne *f.*
tartan ('tɑːtn̩) *n* **1** karierter Wollstoff *m.* **2** kariertes Schottenmuster *neu.*
task (tɑːsk) *n* Aufgabe *f.* **take someone to task** jemanden zur Rede stellen.
Tasmania (tæz'meiniə) *n* Tasmanien *neu.*
tassel ('tæsəl) *n* Quaste *f.*
taste (teist) *vt* **1** schmecken. **2** kosten. *vi* schmecken. *n* **1** Geschmack *m.* **2** Kostprobe *f.*
tasty *adj* schmackhaft.
tattoo[1] (tə'tuː) *n* *mil* Zapfenstreich *m.*
tattoo[2] (tə'tuː) *vt* tätowieren. *n* Tätowierung *f.*
taught (tɔːt) *v* see **teach.**
taunt (tɔːnt) *vt* sticheln. *n* Stichelei *f.*
Taurus ('tɔːrəs) *n* Stier *m.*
taut (tɔːt) *adj* **1** gespannt, straff. **2** steif.
tautology (tɔː'tɔlədʒi) *n* Tautologie *f.*
tavern ('tævən) *n* Schenke, Kneipe *f.*
tax (tæks) *n* Steuer *f.* *vt* **1** besteuern. **2** anstrengen. **income tax** Einkommensteuer *f.* **tax evasion** *n* Steuerhinterziehung *f.*
taxi (tæksi) *n* Taxi *neu.* *vi aviat* rollen.
tea (tiː) *n* **1** Tee *m.* **2** Teemahlzeit *f.* **high tea** *n* Abendbrot *neu.* **tea-bag** *n* Teebeutel *m.* **tea-break** *n* Teepause *f.* **tea-cloth** *n* Geschirrtuch *neu.* **teacup** *n* Teetasse *f.* **tealeaves** *n pl* Teesatz *m.* **teapot** *n* Teekanne *f.* **teaspoon** *n* Teelöffel *m.*
teach* (tiːtʃ) *vt* lehren, unterrichten. *vi* unterrichten. **teacher** *n* Lehrer *m.* Lehrerin *f.* **teacher training college** *n* pädagogische Hochschule *f.*

teak (ti:k) *n* **1** Tiekbaum *m.* **2** Tiekholz *neu.*
team (ti:m) *n* **1** *sport* Mannschaft *f.* **2** (of horses) Gespann *neu.* **3** Team *neu.* *v* **team up** sich zusammentun.
tear[1] (tiə) *n* Träne *f.* **tear-gas** *n* Tränengas *neu.*
tear*[2] (tɛə) *vt* (zer)reißen. *vi* **1** (zer)reißen. **2** zerren. **3** *inf* rasen. *n* Riß *m.*
tease (ti:z) *vt* **1** necken, ärgern, quälen. **2** *tech* (aus)zupfen, kämmen.
teat (ti:t) *n* **1** Brustwarze, Zitze *f.* **2** Lutscher *m.*
technical ('teknikəl) *adj* **1** technisch. **2** fachlich. **technician** *n* Techniker *m.* **technique** *n* Technik *f.* Verfahren *neu.* **technology** *n* **1** Technologie. **2** Gewerbekunde *f.*
tedious ('ti:diəs) *adj* langweilig, ermüdend.
tee[1] (ti:) *n* *tech* T-Stück *neu.*
tee[2] (ti:) *n* *sport* Abschlagestelle *f.* *v* **tee off** den Ball abschlagen.
teenage ('ti:neidʒ) *adj* jugendlich, Teenager—. **teenager** *n* Teenager *m.*
teetotal (ti:'toutl̩) *adj* antialkoholisch, abstinent. **teetotaller** *n* Abstinenzler *m.*
telecommunications (telikəmju:ni'keiʃənz) *npl* Telekommunikation *f.*
telegram ('teligræm) *n* Telegramm *neu.*
telegraph ('teligrɑ:f) *vt* telegraphieren. *n* Telegraph *m.* **telegraph pole** *n* Telegraphenstange *f.*
telepathy (ti'lepəθi) *n* Telepathie *f.*
telephone ('telifoun) *n* Telephon *neu.* Fernsprecher *m.* *vt,vi* telephonieren, anrufen. **telephone box** Telephonzelle *f.* **telephone call** Anruf *m.*
telescope ('teliskoup) *n* Fernrohr, Teleskop *neu.*
televise ('telivaiz) *vt* im Fernsehen übertragen. **television** *n* Fernsehen *neu.* **television (set)** *n* Fernsehapparat *m.*
telex ('teleks) *n* Fernschreibnetz *neu.*
tell* (tel) *vt* **1** sagen, erzählen. **2** mitteilen. **3** erkennen. **4** unterscheiden. *vi* **1** erzählen. **2** Wirkung haben. **telltale** *adj* verräterisch. *n* Zuträger *m.*
temper ('tempə) *n* **1** Laune *f.* **2** Wut *f.* **3** *tech* Härtegrad *m.* *vt* **1** mildern. **2** *tech* härten. **temperament** *n* Temperament *neu.* **temperamental** *adj* temperamentvoll. **temperate** *adj* **1** mäßig. **2** mild. **temperature** *n* Temperatur *f.* **have a temperature** Fieber haben.
tempestuous (tem'pestjuəs) *adj* stürmisch.
temple[1] ('tempəl) *n* *rel* Tempel *m.*
temple[2] ('tempəl) *n* *anat* Schläfe *f.*
tempo ('tempou) *n* Tempo *neu.*
temporal ('tempərəl) *adj* **1** weltlich. **2** zeitlich. **temporary** *adj* vorübergehend, vorläufig.
tempt (tempt) *vt* **1** versuchen. **2** verlocken. **temptation** *n* **1** Versuchung *f.* **2** Anreiz *m.*
ten (ten) *adj* zehn. *n* Zehn *f.* **tenth** *adj* zehnte.
tenacious (tə'neiʃəs) *adj* beharrlich, zäh.

tenant ('tenənt) *n* Mieter, Pächter *m.* **tenancy** *n* Mietverhältnis *neu.*
tend[1] (tend) *vi* **1** neigen. **2** führen, gehen.
tend[2] (tend) *vt* **1** pflegen, hüten. **2** bedienen.
tendency ('tendənsi) *n* Neigung, Tendenz *f.*
tender[1] ('tendə) *adj* **1** weich, zart. **2** empfindlich. **tenderness** *n* Zartheit *f.*
tender[2] ('tendə) *vt* anbieten. *n* Angebot *neu.*
tendon ('tendən) *n* Sehne *f.*
tendril ('tendril) *n* Ranke *f.*
tenement ('tenəmənt) *n* **1** Mietwohnung *f.* **2** Miethaus *neu.*
tennis ('tenis) *n* Tennis *neu.* **tennis court** *n* Tennisplatz *m.*
tenor ('tenə) *n* **1** *mus* Tenor *m.* **2** Sinn *m.*
tense[1] (tens) *adj* gespannt, straff. *(vi),vt* (sich) anspannen. **tension** *n* Spannung *f.*
tense[2] (tens) *n gram* Zeit(form) *f.*
tent (tent) *n* Zelt *neu.*
tentacle ('tentəkəl) *n* Fühler *m.*
tentative ('tentətiv) *adj* **1** Versuchs—. **2** zögernd. **tentatively** *adv* versuchsweise.
tenuous ('tenjuəs) *adj* **1** dürftig. **2** dünn.
tepid ('tepid) *adj* (lau)warm.
term (tə:m) *n* **1** Termin *m.* **2** *educ* Trimester, Semester *neu.* **3** Ausdruck *m.* **4** *pl* Bedingungen *f pl.* **5** *pl* (persönliche) Beziehungen *f pl.* **6** *pl* Zahlungsforderungen *f pl.* *vt* (be)nennen.
terminal ('tə:minḷ) *adj* letzt, End—. *n* **1** Endstation *f.* **2** (electricity) Pol *m.* **3** Flughafengebäude *neu.*
terminate ('tə:mineit) *vt* **1** (be)endigen. **2** kündigen. *vi* aufhören, zu Ende kommen.
terminology (tə:mi'nɔlədʒi) *n* Terminologie *f.*
terminus ('tə:minəs) *n* **1** Endpunkt *m.* **2** Endstation *f.*
terrace ('terəs) *n* **1** Terrasse *f.* **2** Häuserreihe *f.*
terrestrial (tə'restriəl) *adj* irdisch, Erd—.
terrible ('teribəl) *adj* schrecklich, furchtbar.
terrier ('teriə) *n* Terrier *m.*
terrify ('terifai) *vt* erschrecken. **terrific** *adj* **1** fürchterlich. **2** *inf* großartig.
territory ('teritri) *n* Gebiet *neu.*
terror ('terə) *n* **1** Entsetzen *neu.* Schrecken *m.* **2** *pol* Terror *m.* **terrorist** *n* Terrorist *m.* **terrorize** *vt* terrorisieren.
Terylene ('terili:n) *n Tdmk* Terylene *neu.*
test (test) *vt* **1** prüfen, testen. **2** untersuchen. *n* **1** Prüfung, Probe *f.* **2** Test *m.* **test-tube** *n* Reagenzglas *neu.*
testament ('testəmənt) *n* Testament *neu.*
testicle ('testikəl) *n* Hoden *m.*
testify ('testifai) *vt* bezeugen. *vi* Zeugnis ablegen.
testimony ('testiməni) *n* **1** Zeugenaussage *f.* **2** Beweis *m.* **testimonial** *n* **1** Empfehlungsschreiben *neu.* **2** Gedenkzeichen *neu.*
tether ('teðə) *n* Haltestrick *m.* **be at the end of one's tether** nicht mehr weiter wissen. ~ *vt* anbinden.

Teutonic (tjuː'tɔnik) *adj* teutonisch.
text (tekst) *n* Text, Wortlaut *m.* **textbook** *n* Lehrbuch *neu.*
textile ('tekstail) *n* **1** Webstoff *m.* **2** *pl* Textilien *pl. adj* gewebt, Textil—. Web—.
texture ('tekstʃə) *n* **1** Gewebe *neu.* **2** Struktur *f.*
Thames (temz) *n* Themse *f.*
than (ðən; *stressed* ðæn) *conj,prep* als.
thank (θæŋk) *vt* danken. **thanks** *n* Dank *m. interj also* **thank you** danke (schön), vielen Dank. **thankful** *adj* dankbar.
that (ðæt) *adj,pron* jener, jene, jenes, der, die, das. *pron* der, die, das, welch. *conj* **1** daß. **2** daß, damit. **in that** insofern als. **so that** so daß.
thatch (θætʃ) *n* Dachstroh *neu. vi* mit Stroh decken.
thaw (θɔː) *vt,vi* (auf)tauen. *n* Tauwetter *neu.*
the (ðə; *stressed* ðiː) *def art* **1** der, die, das. **2** *pl* die. **the...the** je...desto.
theatre ('θiətə) *n* **1** Theater, Schauspielhaus *neu.* **2** *med* Operationssaal *m.* **theatrical** *adj* **1** bühnenmäßig. **2** theatralisch.
theft (θeft) *n* Diebstahl *m.*
their (ðεə) *poss adj 3rd pers pl* ihr.
theirs (ðεəz) *poss pron 3rd pers pl* ihrer, der ihre *or* ihrige.
them (ðəm; *stressed* ðem) *pron 3rd pers pl* **1** sie. **2** ihnen. **themselves** *pron 3rd pers pl* **1** sich. **2** sich selbst. **3** sie selbst.
theme (θiːm) *n* Thema *neu.* **thematic** *adj* thematisch.
then (ðən; *stressed* ðen) *adv* **1** dann, da, darauf, damals. **2** dann, demnach, weiter. *conj* also, dann. **until then** bis dahin.
theology (θi'ɔlədʒi) *n* Theologie *f.* **theologian** *n* Theologe *m.* **theological** *adj* theologisch.
theorem ('θiərəm) *n* Lehrsatz *m.* Theorem *neu.*
theory ('θiəri) *n* Theorie *f.* **theoretical** *adj* theoretisch. **theorize** *vi* Theorien aufstellen.
therapy ('θerəpi) *n* Therapie *f.* Heilverfahren *neu.* **therapeutic** *adj* therapeutisch.
there (ðεə) *adv* dort(hin), da(rin). *interj* na nu! na also! **over there** dort drüben. **there is** es gibt, es ist. **there are** es gibt, es sind. **thereabouts** *adv* **1** da herum, in der Gegend. **2** so etwa, ungefähr. **thereafter** *adv* danach. **thereby** *adv* dadurch. **therefore** *adv* deshalb, deswegen, infolgedessen. **thereupon** *adv* darauf, danach. **therewith** *adv* damit.
thermal ('θəːməl) *adj also* **thermic** **1** thermisch. **2** warm.
thermodynamics (θəːmoudai'næmiks) *n* Thermodynamik *f.*
thermometer (θə'mɔmitə) *n* Thermometer *neu.* Temperaturmesser *m.*
thermonuclear (θəːmou'njuːkliə) *adj* thermonuklear.
Thermos ('θəːməs) *n Tdmk also* **thermos flask** Thermosflasche *f.*
thermostat ('θəːməstæt) *n* Thermostat *m.*

these (ðiːz) *adj,pron pl* diese, die.
thesis ('θiːsis) *n, pl* **-ses 1** These, Behauptung *f.* **2** Dissertation *f.*
they (ðei) *pron 3rd pers pl* sie. **they say** man sagt.
thick (θik) *adj* **1** dick, dicht. **2** *sl* dumm. **thick-skinned** *adj* dickfellig. **thicken** *vt* **1** dick machen. **2** eindicken. *vi* **1** dick werden. **2** sich verdichten. **thickness** *n* **1** Dicke *f.* **2** Dichtheit *f.*
thief (θiːf) *n, pl* **thieves** Dieb *m.* **stop thief!** haltet den Dieb!
thigh (θai) *n* (Ober)Schenkel *m.* **thigh-bone** *n* Oberschenkelknochen *m.*
thimble ('θimbəl) *n* Fingerhut *m.*
thin (θin) *adj* **1** dünn, mager. **2** spärlich. *vt* **1** dünn machen. **2** verdünnen. **thin-skinned** *adj* empfindlich. **thinness** *n* **1** Dünnheit *f.* **2** Dürftigkeit *f.*
thing (θiŋ) *n* **1** Ding *neu.* Sache *f.* **2** Geschöpf *neu.* **among other things** unter anderem. **no such thing** nichts dergleichen. **the very thing** genau das.
think* (θiŋk) *vt,vi* **1** denken. **2** sich vorstellen. **3** überlegen. **think of/about** denken an/ über, halten von. **I think so** ich denke schon.
third (θəːd) *adj* dritte. *n* Drittel *neu.* **third party** *n* Dritte(r) *m.* **third-party insurance** *n* Haftpflichtversicherung *f.* **third person** *n* dritte Person *f.* **third-rate** *adj* drittrangig.
thirst (θəːst) *n* **1** Durst *m.* **2** Sehnsucht *f.* *vi also* **be thirsty** dürsten, Durst haben. **thirsty** *adj* **1** durstig. **2** begierig.
thirteen (θəː'tiːn) *adj* dreizehn. *n* Dreizehn *f.* **thirteenth** *adj* dreizehnte.
thirty ('θəːti) *adj* dreißig. *n* Dreißig *f.* **thirtieth** *adj* dreißigste.
this (ðis) *adj,pron* dieser, diese, dies(es). **this minute** augenblicklich. **this morning** heute morgen.
thistle ('θisəl) *n* Distel *f.*
thorn (θɔːn) *n* Dorn *m.* **thorny** *adj* dornig.
thorough ('θʌrə) *adj* **1** vollständig. **2** gründlich. **thoroughbred** *n* Vollblüter *m.* *adj* Vollblut—. **throughfare** *n* **1** Verkehrsader *f.* **2** Durchfahrt *f.* **thoroughly** *adv* **1** gründlich. **2** höchst.
those (ðouz) *adj,pron pl* jene, diejenigen.
though (ðou) *conj* **1** obgleich, obschon. **2** zwar. **as though** als ob.
thought[1] (θɔːt) *n* **1** Denken *neu.* **2** Gedanke *m.* **3** Überlegung *f.* **4** Rücksicht *f.* **thoughtful** *adj* **1** rücksichtsvoll. **2** gedankenvoll. **thoughtless** *adj* **1** rücksichtslos. **2** gedankenlos. **3** unbesonnen.
thought[2] (θɔːt) *v* see **think.**
thousand ('θauzənd) *adj* tausend. *n* Tausend *neu.* **thousandth** *adj* tausendste.
thrash (θræʃ) *vt* **1** prügeln. **2** besiegen.
thread (θred) *n* **1** Faden *m.* **2** *tech* Gewinde *neu.* *vt* einfädeln. *vi* sich durchziehen. **thread-**

bare *adj* fadenscheinig, abgedroschen.

threat (θret) *n* Drohung *f*. **threaten** *(vt),vi* (be)drohen.

three (θriː) *adj* drei. *n* Drei *f*. **three-cornered** *adj* dreieckig. **three-dimensional** *adj* dreidimensional. **threequarters** *adj* dreiviertel. **threesome** *n* Dreier *neu*. Dreiergruppe *f*.

thresh (θreʃ) *vt* (aus)dreschen.

threshold ('θreʃhould) *n* Schwelle *f*.

threw (θruː) *v* see **throw.**

thrift (θrift) *n* Sparsamkeit *f*. **thrifty** *adj* sparsam.

thrill (θril) *n* **1** Schauer *m*. **2** Sensation *f*. *vt* **1** erregen. **2** durchschauern. *vi* beben. **thriller** *n* **1** Sensationsfilm *m*. **2** Sensationsroman *m*.

thrive (θraiv) *vi* gedeihen.

throat (θrout) *n* Kehle *f*. Schlund *m*.

throb (θrɔb) *vi* pochen, klopfen. *n* **1** Klopfen, Pochen *neu*. **2** Erregung *f*.

throne (θroun) *n* Thron *m*.

throng (θrɔŋ) *n* **1** Gedränge *neu*. Andrang *m*. **2** Menge *f*. *vi* (sich) drängen. *vt* bedrängen.

throttle ('θrɔtl̩) *n* Drosselventil *neu*. *vt* **1** erdrosseln. **2** ersticken.

through (θruː) *prep* **1** durch. **2** mit Hilfe (von). *adv* durch. **throughout** *prep* **1** überall in. **2** während. *adv* **1** überall. **2** durchaus.

throw* (θrou) *vt* werfen, schleudern. *n* Wurf *m*. **throw away** wegwerfen. **throw off** abwerfen. **throw out** hinauswerfen. **throw up** *inf* kotzen.

thrush (θrʌʃ) *n zool* Drossel *f*.

thrust* (θrʌst) *vt* **1** stoßen. **2** stecken. *vi* stoßen. *n* Stoß *m*.

thud (θʌd) *n* dumpfer Schlag *m*. *vi* dumpf aufschlagen.

thumb (θʌm) *n* Daumen *m*. *vt* durchblättern. **well-thumbed** *adj* (of a book) abgegriffen.

thump (θʌmp) *n* (dumpfer) Schlag, Puff *m*. *vt* schlagen. *vi* klopfen.

thunder ('θʌndə) *n* Donner *m*. *vi* donnern. **thunderstorm** *n* Gewitter *neu*.

Thuringia (θju'rindʒiə) *n* Thüringen *neu*.

Thursday ('θəːzdi) *n* Donnerstag *m*.

thus (ðʌs) *adv* so, also, auf diese Weise.

thwart (θwɔːt) *vt* durchkreuzen, vereiteln.

thyme (taim) *n* Thymian *m*.

thyroid ('θairɔid) *adj* **1** Schilddrüsen—. **2** Schildknorpel—. *n* **1** Schilddrüse *f*. **2** Schildknorpel *m*.

tiara (ti'ɑːrə) *n* Tiara *f*. Stirnreif *m*.

tick[1] (tik) *vi* **1** ticken. **2** *inf* funktionieren. *vt* abhaken. *n* **1** Ticken *neu*. **2** Häckchen *neu*.

tick[2] (tik) *n zool* Zecke *f*.

ticket ('tikit) *n* **1** Karte *f*. **2** Fahrschein *m*. Fahrkarte *f*. **3** Zettel *m*. **return ticket** Rückfahrkarte *f*. **season ticket** Zeitkarte *f*. **single ticket** einfache Fahrkarte *f*. **ticket collector** *n* Bahnsteigschaffner *m*. **ticket-office** *n* Fahrkartenschalter *m*.

tickle ('tikəl) *vt,vi* kitzeln. **ticklish** *adj* **1** kitz(e)lig. **2** heikel.

tide (taid) *n* **1** Ebbe und Flut *f.* **2** Strom *m.* **high tide** Flut *f.* **low tide** Ebbe *f.* **tidemark** *n* Gezeitenmarke *f.*

tidy ('taidi) *adj* ordentlich, sauber. *vt also* **tidy up** aufräumen.

tie (tai) *vt* (ver)binden, schnüren. *n* **1** Schlips *m.* **2** Band *neu.* **3** *sport* Unentschieden *neu.*

tier (tiə) *n* Reihe *f.* Rang *m.*

tiger ('taigə) *n* Tiger *m.*

tight (tait) *adj* **1** fest. **2** dicht. **3** eng, knapp. **4** straff, gespannt. **5** *sl* beschwipst. **tight-fisted** *adj* knauserig. **tightrope** *n* Drahtseil *neu.* **tights** *n pl* Strumpfhose *f.* **tighten** *vt* **1** straff spannen. **2** enger machen. **3** zusammenziehen.

tile (tail) *n* **1** Dachziegel *m.* **2** Fliese *f.* *vt* mit Ziegeln *or* Fliesen decken.

till[1] (til) *prep,conj* bis.

till[2] (til) *vt* bebauen, bearbeiten.

till[3] (til) *n* Kasse, Geldschublade *f.*

tiller ('tilə) *n* Ruderpinne, Steuerstange *f.*

tilt (tilt) *(vi),vt* (sich) kippen, (sich) neigen. *n* Neigung *f.* Hang *m.*

timber ('timbə) *n* **1** Bauholz, Nutzholz *neu.* **2** Balken *m.* *adj* hölzern.

time (taim) *n* **1** Zeit *f.* **2** Mal *neu.* **3** *mus* Takt *m.* **4** *pl* Zeitalter *neu.* *vi* **1** die Zeit bestimmen. **2** die Zeit messen von. **time bomb** *n* Zeitbombe *f.* **timetable** *n* **1** Stundenplan *m.* **2** Fahrplan *m.*

timid ('timid) *adj* **1** furchtsam. **2** scheu.

tin (tin) *n* **1** Zinn, (Weiß)Blech *neu.* **2** Dose, Büchse *f.* *adj* zinnern. *vt* **1** konservieren. **2** verzinnen. **tin-opener** *n* Büchsenöffner *m.*

tinge (tindʒ) *n* **1** Färbung *f.* **2** Anhauch *m.* *vt* **1** färben. **2** einen Anhauch geben.

tingle ('tiŋgəl) *vi* **1** prickeln. **2** klingen. *n* **1** Klingen *neu.* **2** Prickeln *neu.*

tinker ('tiŋkə) *n* Kesselflicker *m.* *vi* basteln.

tinkle ('tiŋkəl) *vi* klingeln. *n* Geklingel *neu.*

tinsel ('tinsəl) *n* **1** Flitter *m.* **2** Lametta *neu.*

tint (tint) *n* Tönung *f.* *vt* leicht tönen.

tiny ('taini) *adj* winzig.

tip[1] (tip) *n* Spitze *f.* *vt* mit einer Spitze versehen. **tiptoe** *vi* auf Zehenspitzen gehen.

tip[2] (tip) *vt,vi* umkippen. *n* Abladeplatz *m.*

tip[3] (tip) *n* **1** Trinkgeld *neu.* **2** Wink, Tip *m.* *vt* **1** ein Trinkgeld geben. **2** einen Wink geben.

tipsy ('tipsi) *adj* beschwipst.

tire ('taiə) *vt* **1** müde machen. **2** erschöpfen. *vi* müde werden. **tired** *adj* **1** müde. **2** erschöpft. **be tired of something** etwas satt haben.

tissue ('tiʃuː) *n* **1** (feines) Gewebe *neu.* **2** Papiertaschentuch *neu.*

title ('taitl̩) *n* Titel *m.* *vt* betiteln.

to (tə; *stressed* tuː) *prep* **1** zu. **2** vor. **3** nach. **4** an. **5** gegen. **6** auf. *conj* um zu. **to and fro**

adv hin und her. **to-do** *n* Getue *neu.*
toad (toud) *n* Kröte *f.* **toadstool** *n* Giftpilz *m.*
toast[1] (toust) *n* Toast *m.* *vt* **1** toasten, rösten. **2** wärmen.
toast[2] (toust) *n* Trinkspruch *m.* *vt* trinken auf.
tobacco (tə'bækou) *n* Tabak *m.* **tobacconist** *n* Tabakhändler *m.*
toboggan (tə'bɔgən) *n* Rodelschlitten *m.* *vi* rodeln.
today (tə'dei) *adv* heute, heutzutage.
toddler ('tɔdlə) *n* kleines Kind *neu.*
toe (tou) *n* Zehe *f.* **toenail** *n* Zehennagel *m.*
toffee ('tɔfi) *n* Karamelle *f.* Toffee *neu.*
together (tə'geðə) *adv* **1** zusammen, miteinander. **2** zugleich.
toil (tɔil) *vi* arbeiten, sich mühen. *n* Mühe, Plackerei *f.*
toilet ('tɔilət) *n* **1** Toilette *f.* **2** Klo(sett) *neu.* **toilet paper** *n* Klosettpapier *neu.*
token ('toukən) *n* **1** Zeichen *neu.* **2** Andenken *neu.* **3** Gutschein *m.*
told (tould) *v* see **tell.**
tolerate ('tɔləreit) *vt* **1** dulden. **2** aushalten. **3** tolerieren. **tolerance** *n* Duldsamkeit, Toleranz *f.* **tolerant** *adj* tolerant.
toll[1] (toul) *vt,vi* läuten, schlagen.
toll[2] (toul) *n* **1** Wegegeld *neu.* Zoll *m.* **2** Tribut *m.* **tollgate** *n* Schlagbaum *m.*
tomato (tə'mɑːtou) *n, pl* **-oes** Tomate *f.*
tomb (tuːm) *n* Grab(mal) *neu.*
tomorrow (tə'mɔrou) *adv* morgen. **the day after tomorrow** übermorgen. **tomorrow morning** morgen früh. **tomorrow week** morgen in acht Tagen.
ton (tʌn) *n* Tonne *f.*
tone (toun) *n* **1** Ton *m.* **2** Tönung *f.* *vt* abtönen.
tongs (tɔŋz) *n pl* Zange *f.*
tongue (tʌŋ) *n* **1** *anat* Zunge *f.* **2** Sprache *f.* **hold one's tongue** den Mund halten. **tongue in cheek** ironisch. **tongue-tied** *adj* stumm. **tongue-twister** *n* Zungenbrecher *m.*
tonic ('tɔnik) *adj* **1** tonisch, stärkend. **2** *mus* Grundton—. *n* **1** Stärkungsmittel *neu.* **2** *mus* Grundton *m.* **tonic water** *n* Sprudel(wasser) *m,neu.*
tonight (tə'nait) *adv* heute abend *or* nacht.
tonsil ('tɔnsəl) *n* Mandel *f.* **tonsilitis** *n* Mandelentzündung *f.*
too (tuː) *adv* **1** (all)zu. **2** sehr. **3** auch, dazu. **all too** viel zu, allzu.
took (tuk) *v* see **take.**
tool (tuːl) *n* Werkzeug, Gerät *neu.*
tooth (tuːθ) *n, pl* **teeth** Zahn *m.* **toothache** *n* Zahnweh *neu.* Zahnschmerzen *m pl.* **toothbrush** *n* Zahnbürste *f.* **toothpaste** *n* Zahnpasta *f.* **toothpick** *n* Zahnstocher *m.*
top[1] (tɔp) *n* **1** Spitze *f.* Wipfel, Gipfel *m.* **2** Oberfläche *f.* Oberteil *m.* **3** Deckel *m.* *adj* **1** oberst, höchst. **2** best. *vt* **1** übertreffen. **2** köpfen. **3**

anführen. **top hat** *n* Zylinder *m.* **top-heavy** *adj* kopflastig.
top² (tɔp) *n* Kreisel *m.*
topaz ('toupæz) *n* Topaz *m.*
topic ('tɔpik) *n* Gegenstand *m.* Thema *neu.* **topical** *adj* **1** aktuell. **2** *med* örtlich.
topography (tə'pɔgrəfi) *n* Topographie *f.*
topple ('tɔpəl) *vi* kippen, stürzen. **topple down** *or* **over** umkippen, niederstürzen.
topsoil ('tɔpsɔil) *n* Ackerkrume *f.*
topsy-turvy (tɔpsi'tə:vi) *adj,adv inf* das Oberste zuunterst, drunter und drüber.
torch (tɔ:tʃ) *n* **1** Taschenlampe *f.* **2** Fackel *f.*
tore (tɔ:) *v* see **tear.**
torment ('tɔ:mənt) *n* Qual *f. vt* quälen.
torn (tɔ:n) *v* see **tear.**
tornado (tɔ:'neidou) *n* Tornado, Wirbelsturm *m.*
torpedo (tɔ:'pi:dou) *n* Torpedo *m. vt* torpedieren.
torrent ('tɔrənt) *n* **1** Sturzbach *m.* **2** Wolkenbruch *m.* **3** Strom *m.* **4** Wortschwall *m.*
torso ('tɔ:sou) *n* Torso *m.*
tortoise ('tɔ:təs) *n* Schildkröte *f.*
tortuous ('tɔ:tʃuəs) *adj* gewunden, krumm.
torture ('tɔ:tʃə) *n* Folter, Marter, Qual *f. vt* foltern, martern, quälen.
Tory ('tɔ:ri) *n* britische(r) Konservative(r) *m.*
toss (tɔs) *vt* **1** (hoch)werfen. **2** schütteln. *vi* **1** sich unruhig bewegen. **2** schlingern. *n* Wurf *m.*
tot¹ (tɔt) *n* Schluck *m.*
tot² (tɔt) *vt* **tot up** zusammenrechnen.
total ('toutl̩) *adj* **1** gesamt. **2** ganz, völlig, total. *n* **1** Ganze *neu.* **2** Summe *f.* Gesamtbetrag *m. vi* sich belaufen auf. **totalitarian** *adj* totalitär.
totem ('toutəm) *n* Totem *neu.* **totem pole** *n* Totempfahl *m.*
totter ('tɔtə) *vi* schwanken, wanken.
touch (tʌtʃ) *vt* (an-, be-) rühren. *vi* in Berührung kommen, berühren. **touch down** *aviat* landen. **touch up** auffrischen. ~*n* **1** Berührung *f.* **2** Tastsinn *m.* **3** Spur *f.* Hauch *m.* **4** Hand *f.* **touchy** *adj* reizbar, überempfindlich.
tough (tʌf) *adj* **1** zäh. **2** hart. **toughen** *vt* zäh(er) machen, abhärten.
toupee ('tu:pei) *n* Toupet *neu.*
tour (tuə) *n* Tour, Reise, Rundfahrt *f.* Rundgang *m. vt* bereisen, besuchen. *vi* reisen. **tourism** *n* Fremdenverkehr, Tourismus *m.* **tourist** *n* Tourist *m.*
tournament ('tuənəmənt) *n* Tournier *neu.*
tow (tou) *vt* **1** (ab)schleppen. **2** bugsieren. **towrope** *n* Schlepptau *neu.*
towards (tə'wɔ:dz) *prep also* **toward** **1** gegen. **2** nach (...zu), auf...zu *or* hin. **3** entgegen.
towel ('tauəl) *n* Handtuch, Badetuch *neu.*
tower ('tauə) *n* Turm *m. vi* sich erheben, emporragen. **towerblock** *n* Hochhaus *neu.*
town (taun) *n* Stadt *f.* **town**

clerk *n* Stadtsyndikus *m*. **town hall** *n* Rathaus *neu*. **town-planning** *n* Städteplanung *f*.

toxic ('tɔksik) *adj* giftig, toxisch.

toy (tɔi) *n* Spielzeug *neu*. *v* **toy with** spielen mit.

trace (treis) *n* Spur *f*. *vt* **1** folgen, nachgehen. **2** zurückverfolgen. **3** durchzeichnen.

track (træk) *n* **1** Weg, Pfad *m*. **2** (of a railway) Gleis *neu*. **3** Spur *f*. **4** *sport* Bahn *f*. *vt* (ver)folgen, nachspüren. **tracksuit** *n* Trainingsanzug *m*.

tract[1] (trækt) *n* **1** Strecke *f*. **2** *anat* System *neu*. **3** Zeitraum *m*.

tract[2] (trækt) *n* *rel* Traktat *m,neu*.

tractor ('træktə) *n* Schlepper, Traktor *m*.

trade (treid) *n* **1** Handel *m*. **2** Gewerbe *f*. Geschäft *neu*. *vi* handeln. *vt* austauschen. **trademark** *n* Schutzmarke *f*. **tradesman** *n* Ladenbesitzer, Händler *m*. **trade union** *n* Gewerkschaft *f*.

tradition (trə'diʃən) *n* **1** Tradition, Überlieferung *f*. **2** Brauch *m*. **traditional** *adj* traditionell.

traffic ('træfik) *n* **1** Verkehr *m*. **2** *comm* Handel *m*. **traffic jam** *n* Verkehrsstockung *f*. **traffic lights** *n pl* Verkehrsampel *f*. **traffic warden** *n* Verkehrsaufseher *m*.

tragedy ('trædʒədi) *n* Trauerspiel *neu*. Tragödie *f*. **tragic** *adj* tragisch.

trail (treil) *n* **1** Spur *f*. **2** Schweif *m*. *vt* **1** nachschleppen. **2** verfolgen. *vi* schleifen.

trailer *n* **1** *mot* Anhänger *m*. **2** (of a film) Vorschau *m*.

train (trein) *n* **1** Zug *m*. **2** Reihe *f*. **3** Gefolge *neu*. *vt* **1** schulen, ausbilden. **2** *sport* trainieren. *vi* *sport* trainieren. **trainee** *n* Lehrling, Praktikant *m*.

traitor ('treitə) *n* Verräter *m*.

tram (træm) *n* Straßenbahn *f*.

tramp (træmp) *vi* **1** wandern. **2** trampeln, treten. *n* **1** Landstreicher *m*. **2** Wanderung *f*.

trample ('træmpəl) *vt* zertrampeln. *vi* herumtreten.

trampoline ('træmpəli:n) *n* Trampoline *f*.

trance (trɑ:ns) *n* **1** Verzückung *f*. **2** Trance *f*.

tranquil ('træŋkwil) *adj* still, ruhig, gelassen. **tranquillity** *n* **1** Ruhe *f*. **2** Gelassenheit *f*. **tranquillizer** *n* Beruhigungsmittel *neu*.

transact (træn'zækt) *vt* durchführen. **transaction** *n* Geschäft *neu*. Verhandlung *f*.

transatlantic (trænzət'læntik) *adj* transatlantisch.

transcend (træn'send) *vt* übersteigen, überschreiten.

transcribe (træn'skraib) *vt* **1** umschreiben. **2** *mus* umsetzen.

transfer (*v* træns'fə:; *n* 'trænsfə:) *vt* **1** übertragen. **2** versetzen. **3** (money) überweisen. *n* **1** Übertragung *f*. **2** Versetzung *f*. **3** Überweisung *f*. **4** Versand *m*. **5** Abziehbild *neu*.

transform (træns'fɔ:m) *vt* verwandeln, umformen. **transformation** *n* Verwandlung *f*. **transformer** *n* *tech* Transformator *m*.

transfuse (træns'fju:z) *vt* **1** *med* übertragen. **2** durchtränken. **transfusion** *n* **1** *med* Blutübertragung *f*. **2** Durchtränkung *f*.

transistor (træn'zistə) *n* Transistor *m*. **transistor (radio)** Transistorradio *neu*.

transit ('trænsit) *n* **1** Durchgang *m*. **2** Durchgangsverkehr *m*. **in transit** unterwegs.

transition (træn'ziʃən) *n* Übergang *m*.

transitive ('trænsitiv) *adj* transitiv.

translate (trænz'leit) *vt* übersetzen, übertragen.

translucent (trænz'lu:sənt) *adj* **1** nicht ganz durchsichtig. **2** lichtdurchlässig.

transmit (trænz'mit) *vt* **1** (by radio, etc.) (über)senden, übertragen. **2** überliefern. **transmitter** *n* Sender *m*. **transmission** *n* **1** (by radio, etc.) Sendung *f*. **2** *tech* Getriebe *neu*. **3** Übersendung *f*.

transparent (træns'pærənt) *adj* durchsichtig.

transplant (*v* træns'pla:nt; *n* 'trænspla:nt) *vt* **1** umpflanzen. **2** *med* transplantieren. *n* **1** Umpflanzung *f*. **2** Transplantation *f*.

transport (*v* træns'pɔ:t; *n,adj* 'trænspɔ:t) *vt* befördern, transportieren. *n* **1** Beförderung, Spedition *f*. Transport *m*. Versand *m*. **2** Begeisterung *f*. *adj* Transport—.

transpose (træns'pouz) *vt* **1** umsetzen. **2** *mus* transponieren.

trap (træp) *n* Falle *f*. *vt* (ein)fangen, erwischen. **trapdoor** *n* Falltür *f*.

trapeze (trə'pi:z) *n* Trapez *neu*.

trash (træʃ) *n* **1** wertloses Zeug *neu*. Kitsch *m*. **2** Unsinn *m*. **3** Abfall *m*.

trauma ('trɔ:mə) *n* Trauma *neu*.

travel ('trævəl) *vi* reisen. *vt* bereisen. *n* **1** Reise *f*. Reisen *neu*. **2** *pl* Reisen *f pl*. **travel agency** *n* Reisebüro *neu*. **traveller** *n* Reisende(r) *m*. **traveller's cheque** *n* Reisescheck *m*.

trawl (trɔ:l) *n* Schleppnetz *neu*. *vi* mit dem Schleppnetz fischen. **trawler** *n* Schleppnetzfischerboot *neu*. Trawler *m*.

tray (trei) *n* Tablett, Servierbrett *neu*.

treachery ('tretʃəri) *n* Verrat *m*. Untreue *f*. **treacherous** *adj* **1** verräterisch. **2** gefährlich.

treacle ('tri:kəl) *n* Sirup *m*. Melasse *f*.

tread* (tred) *vi* treten. *vt* betreten. *n* **1** Schritt, Tritt *m*. **2** *mot* Reifenprofil *neu*.

treason ('tri:zən) *n* Verrat *m*. **high treason** Hochverrat *m*.

treasure ('treʒə) *n* Schatz *m*. *vt* **1** (hoch)schätzen. **2** anhäufen. **treasurer** *n* Schatzmeister, Kassenwart *m*. **treasury** *n* **1** Schatzkammer *f*. **2** Finanzministerium *neu*.

treat (tri:t) *vt* **1** behandeln. **2** freihalten. *n* Genuß *m*. Vergnügen *neu*. **treatment** *n* Behandlung *f*.

treatise ('tri:tiz) *n* Abhandlung *f*.

treaty ('tri:ti) *n* Vertrag *m*. Abkommen *neu*.

treble ('trebəl) *adj* **1** dreifach. **2** *mus* Sopran—. *n mus* Sopran, Diskant *m*.

tree (tri:) *n* Baum *m*.

trek (trek) *vi* trecken. *n* lange Reise *f*. Treck *m*.

trellis ('trelis) *n* **1** Gitter *neu*. **2** Spalier *neu*.

tremble ('trembəl) *vi* zittern, beben.

tremendous (tri'mendəs) *adj* **1** furchtbar. **2** *inf* riesig, gewaltig.

tremor ('tremə) *n* Zittern, Beben *neu*.

trench (trentʃ) *n* Graben *m*. *vt* mit Gräben durchziehen.

trend (trend) *n* **1** Neigung, Tendenz *f*. Trend *m*. **2** Mode *f*.

trespass ('trespəs) *n* **1** unerlaubtes Betreten *neu*. **2** Vergehen *neu*. *vi* **1** widerrechtlich betreten. **2** verstoßen.

trestle ('tresəl) *n* Bock *m*. Gestell *neu*.

trial ('traiəl) *n* **1** Gerichtsverfahren *neu*. Prozeß *m*. **2** Versuch *m*. Probe *f*. **3** Prüfung *f*.

triangle 'traiæŋgəl) *n* **1** Dreieck *neu*. **2** *mus* Triangel *m*. **triangular** *adj* dreieckig.

tribe (traib) *n* (Volks)Stamm *m*. **tribesman** *n* Stammesangehörige(r).

tribunal (trai'bju:nl̩) *n* **1** Gericht, Tribunal *neu*. **2** Gerichtshof *m*.

tributary ('tribjutəri) *adj* **1** zinspflichtig. **2** zufließend. *n* Nebenfluß *m*.

tribute ('tribju:t) *n* **1** Tribut *m*. **2** Lob *neu*.

trick (trik) *n* **1** Streich *m*. **2** Trick, Kniff *m*. **3** *game* Stich *m*. *vt* überlisten, betrügen. **tricky** *adj* **1** schlau. **2** verwickelt, heikel.

trickle ('trikəl) *vi* tröpfeln. *n* Tröpfeln *neu*.

tricycle ('traisikəl) *n* Dreirad *neu*.

tried (traid) *adj* erprobt.

trifle ('traifəl) *n* **1** Kleinigkeit *f*. **2** *cul* (süßer) Auflauf *m*. *v* **trifle with** tändeln, spielen.

trigger ('trigə) *n* Abzug, Drücker *m*. *vt* auslösen.

trill (tril) *vi* trillern. *n* Triller *m*.

trim (trim) *adj* **1** nett, hübsch. **2** ordentlich, in Ordnung. *vt* **1** beschneiden. **2** garnieren. **3** *naut* trimmen. *n* **1** Schmuck *m*. **2** Ordnung *f*.

trio ('triou) *n* Trio *neu*.

trip (trip) *n* **1** Reise *f*. **2** Ausflug *m*. *vi* stolpern. *vt* ein Bein stellen.

tripe (traip) *n* **1** *cul* Kaldaunen *f pl*. **2** *inf* Quatsch *m*.

triple ('tripəl) *adj* dreifach. *(vi),vt* (sich) verdreifachen. **triplet** *n* **1** *lit* Dreireim *m*. **2** Dreiergruppe *f*. **3** Drilling *m*.

tripod ('traipɔd) *n* Dreifuß *m*.

trite (trait) *adj* abgedroschen, platt.

triumph ('traiʌmf) *n* Triumph *m*. *vi* triumphieren, siegen. **triumphant** *adj* triumphierend, jubelnd.

trivial ('triviəl) *adj* trivial, unbedeutend.

trod (trɔd) *v* see **tread.**

trodden ('trɔdn̩) *v* see **tread.**

trolley ('trɔli) *n* **1** (Hand)Karren *m.* **2** Kontaktrolle *f.* **trolley bus** *n* Obus *m.*

trombone (trɔm'boun) *n* Posaune *f.*

troop (truːp) *n* **1** Truppe *f.* **2** Trupp *m.* Schar *f. vi* sich sammeln, sich scharen.

trophy ('troufi) *n* Trophäe *f.* Siegeszeichen *neu.* Preis *m.*

tropic ('trɔpik) *n* **1** Wendekreis *m.* **2** *pl* Tropen *pl.*

trot (trɔt) *vi* traben, trotten. *n* Trab *m.* **trotter** *n* **1** Traber *m.* **2** *pl cul* Hammelfüße, Schweinsfüße *m pl.*

trouble ('trʌbəl) *n* **1** Unruhe, Schwierigkeit *f.* **2** Kummer *m.* Unglück *neu.* **3** *tech* Störung *f.* **in trouble** in Verlegenheit *or* Not. ~*vt* **1** beunruhigen, stören. **2** belästigen. *vi* sich bemühen. **troublemaker** *n* Unruhestifter, Störenfried *m.* **troublesome** *adj* lästig, störend.

trough (trɔf) *n* Mulde *f.* Trog *m.*

troupe (truːp) *n* (Theater)Truppe *f.*

trousers ('trauzəz) *n pl* Hose *f.* Hosen *f pl.*

trout (traut) *n* Forelle *f.*

trowel ('trauəl) *n* **1** Maurerkelle *f.* **2** Ausheber *m.*

truant ('truənt) *n* **1** Schulschwänzer *m.* **2** Müßiggänger *m. adj* **1** schulschwänzend. **2** müßig. **play truant** (die Schule) schwänzen.

truce (truːs) *n* Waffenstillstand *m.*

truck (trʌk) *n* **1** Güterwagen *m.* **2** Lastkraftwagen *m.*

trudge (trʌdʒ) *vi* sich (mühsam) schleppen.

true (truː) *adj* **1** wahr, richtig. **2** echt, wirklich. **3** treu. **truly** *adv* **1** wirklich, tatsächlich. **2** aufrichtig. **yours truly** Hochachtungsvoll.

truffle ('trʌfəl) *n* Trüffel *f.*

trump (trʌmp) *n* Trumpf *m. vt* stechen.

trumpet ('trʌmpit) *n* Trompete *f.*

truncheon ('trʌntʃən) *n* Knüttel, Knüppel *m.*

trunk (trʌŋk) *n* **1** *bot* Stamm *m.* **2** *anat* Rumpf *m.* **3** *zool* Rüssel *m.* **4** (Schrank)Koffer *m.* **5** *pl* Badehose *f.*

trust (trʌst) *vt* (ver)trauen, sich verlassen auf. *vi* **1** vertrauen, sich verlassen. **2** (zuversichtlich) hoffen. *n* **1** Vertrauen *neu.* **2** *comm* Kartell *neu.* **3** *law* Pflegschaft *f.* **trustworthy** *adj* zuverlässig, vertrauenswürdig. **trustee** *n* Treuhänder, Vermögensverwalter *m.*

truth (truːθ) *n* Wahrheit *f.* **truthful** *adj* **1** ehrlich, wahrhaftig. **2** wahrheitsgemäß.

try (trai) *vt* **1** versuchen. **2** probieren. **3** *law* verhören. **4** proben. *n* Versuch *m.* **trying** *adj* **1** unangenehm, lästig. **2** anstrengend.

tsar (tsɑː) *n* Zar *m.*

T-shirt *n* Trikot, Sporthemd *neu.*

tub (tʌb) *n* **1** Faß *neu.* **2** (Bade)Wanne *f.* **tubby** *adj inf* rundlich, dickbauchig.

tuba ('tjuːbə) *n* Tuba *f.*

tube (tjuːb) *n* **1** Rohr *neu.* Röhre *f.* **2** Schlauch *m.* **3** Tube *f.* **4** Untergrundbahn, U-Bahn *f.*

tuber ('tjuːbə) *n bot* Knolle *f*.
tuberculosis (tjuːbəːkju'lousis) *n* Tuberkulose *f*.
tuck (tʌk) *n* **1** Falte *f*. Umschlag *m*. **2** *sl* Süßigkeiten *f pl*. *vt* **1** falten. **2** einschlagen. **tuck away** wegstecken. **tuck in** *inf* zugreifen, einhauen.
Tuesday ('tjuːzdi) *n* Dienstag *m*.
tuft (tʌft) *n* Büschel *neu*.
tug (tʌg) *vt* **1** zerren, ziehen. **2** *naut* schleppen. *vi* ziehen. *n* **1** Ruck *m*. **2** *naut* Schlepper *m*. **tug of war** *n* Tauziehen *neu*.
tuition (tjuː'iʃən) *n* Unterricht *m*.
tulip ('tuːlip) *n* Tulpe *f*.
tumble ('tʌmbəl) *vi* **1** (hin)fallen. **2** purzeln. *vt* (um)stürzen. *n* Sturz, Fall *m*. **tumble drier** *n* Wäschetrockner *m*. **tumbler** *n* Becher *m*. Trinkglas *neu*.
tummy ('tʌmi) *n inf* Magen, Bauch *m*.
tumour ('tjuːmə) *n* Geschwulst *f*. Tumor *m*.
tumult ('tumʌlt) *n* Tumult *m*. Getümmel *neu*. Aufruhr *m*.
tuna ('tjuːnə) *n* Thunfisch *m*.
tune (tjuːn) *n* **1** Melodie *f*. **2** Stimmung *f*. *vt* stimmen. **in tune** (gut) gestimmt. **out of tune** verstimmt. **tuneful** *adj* melodisch.
tunic ('tjuːnik) *n* **1** Bluse *f*. Überkleid *neu*. **2** Soldatenrock *m*.
Tunisia (tjuː'niziə) *n* Tunesien *neu*.
tunnel ('tʌnl̩) *n* Tunnel *m*.
tunny ('tʌni) *n see* **tuna.**
turbine ('təːbain) *n* Turbine *f*.
turbot ('təːbət) *n* Steinbutt *m*.
turbulent ('təːbjulənt) *adj* **1** unruhig. **2** aufgeregt, stürmisch, turbulent.
turf (təːf) *n* **1** Rasen *m*. **2** Torf *m*. **3** Pferderennen *neu*. *vt* mit Rasen belegen. **turf accountant** *n sport* Buchmacher *m*.
Turk (təːk) *n* Türke *m*.
turkey ('təːki) *n* Truthahn *m*. Pute *f*.
Turkey ('təːki) *n* Türkei *f*. **Turkish** *adj* türkisch. *n* (language) Türkisch *neu*. **Turkish bath** *n* Schwitzbad *neu*.
turmeric ('təːmərik) *n* Gelbwurz *f*.
turmoil ('təːmɔil) *n* Aufruhr, Tumult *m*.
turn (təːn) *vt* **1** drehen. **2** machen, verwandeln. **3** (um)wenden. **4** lenken, abbringen. **5** werden. *vi* **1** sich drehen. **2** werden. **3** sich umwenden. **4** gehen. **turn down** ablehnen. **turn off 1** abbiegen. **2** abstellen, abdrehen. **turn on** anstellen, einschalten. **turn up** auftauchen. ~*n* **1** Drehung *f*. **2** Wendung *f*. **3** Runde *f*. **4** Versuch *m*. **5** Veränderung *f*. **turning** *n* **1** Drehen *neu*. **2** Kurve *f*. **3** Ecke *f*. **4** Querstraße *f*. **turnover** *n* **1** Umschwung *f*. **2** *comm* Umsatz *m*. **3** *cul* (Apfel)Tasche *f*. **turnstile** *n* Drehkreuz *neu*. **turntable** *n* Plattenteller *m*.
turnip ('təːnip) *n* (weiße) Rübe *f*.
turpentine ('təːpəntain) *n* Terpentin *m*.
turquoise ('təːkwɔiz) *n* Türkis *m*.

turret ('tʌrət) *n* Türmchen *neu.* Turm *m.*
turtle ('tə:tḷ) *n* Schildkröte *f.*
tusk (tʌsk) *n* Stoßzahn *m.*
tussle ('tʌsəl) *n* Kampf *m.* Balgerei *f. vi* kämpfen, sich balgen.
tutor ('tju:tə) *n* **1** *law* Vormund *m.* **2** (at a university) Tutor *m.* **3** Privatlehrer *m. vt* Unterricht geben.
tweed (twi:d) *n* Tweed *m.*
tweezers ('twi:zəz) *n pl* Pinzette *f.*
twelve (twelv) *adj* zwölf. *n* Zwölf *f.* **twelfth** *adj* zwölfte.
twenty ('twenti) *adj* zwanzig. *n* Zwanzig *f.* **twentieth** *adj* zwanzigste.
twice (twais) *adv* zweimal.
twiddle ('twidḷ) *vt* müßig herumdrehen, spielen mit.
twig (twig) *n* Zweig *m.*
twilight ('twailait) *n* Zwielicht *neu.* Dämmerung *f.*
twin (twin) *n* Zwilling *m. adj* doppelt, Zwillings—.
twine (twain) *n* Bindfaden *m.* Zwirn *m. vt* (ineinander) verflechten, winden. *vi* sich winden, sich verflechten.
twinge (twindʒ) *n* **1** (stechender) Schmerz *m.* **2** Gewissensbiß *m.*
twinkle ('twiŋkəl) *vi* blinken, funkeln. *n* Blinzeln, Funkeln *neu.*
twirl (twə:l) *vi,vt* zwirbeln, herumwirbeln. *n* Wirbel *m.*
twist (twist) *vt* **1** (zusammen)drehen, winden. **2** verdrehen. **3** biegen. *vi* sich drehen, sich winden. *n* **1** Drehung, Windung *f.* **2** Biegung *f.* **3** Verdrehung *f.*
twitch (twitʃ) *vi* zucken. *vt* zwicken. *n* Ruck *m.* Zucken *neu.*
twitter ('twitə) *vi* zwitschern. *n* Gezwitscher *neu.*
two (tu:) *adj* **1** zwei. **2** beide. *n* Zwei *f.* **in twos** zu zweit. **in two** entzwei. **two-faced** *adj* **1** doppelgesichtig. **2** heuchlerisch. **twosome** *n* Paar, Pärchen *neu.* **two-way** *adj* **1** Doppel—. **2** Gegen—.
tycoon (tai'ku:n) *n inf* Industriekapitän *m.*
type (taip) *n* **1** Typ *m.* Art, Sorte *f.* **2** Klasse, Kategorie *f.* **3** Muster *neu.* **4** Type *f. vi,vt* tippen, mit der Maschine schreiben. **typewriter** *n* Schreibmaschine *f.* **typical** *adj* typisch, kennzeichnend. **typify** *vt* verkörpern, typisch sein für. **typist** *n* Maschinenschreiberin *f.*
typhoid ('taifɔid) *n* Typhus *m.*
typhoon (tai'fu:n) *n* Taifun *m.*
tyrant ('tairənt) *n* Tyrann *m.*
tyranny *n* Tyrannei *f.*
tyre ('taiə) *n* Reifen *m.*
Tyrol (ti'roul) *n* Tirol *neu.*

U

ubiquitous (ju:'bikwitəs) *adj* allgegenwärtig.
udder ('ʌdə) *n* Euter *neu.*
ugly ('ʌgli) *adj* häßlich. **ugliness** *n* Häßlichkeit *f.*
ukulele (ju:kə'leili) *n* Ukulele *neu.*
ulcer ('ʌlsə) *n* Geschwür *neu.*
ulterior (ʌl'tiəriə) *adj* **1** jenseitig. **2** verborgen.
ultimate ('ʌltimət) *adj* **1** äußerst. **2** letzt. **ultimatum** *n* Ultimatum *neu.*

ultraviolet (ʌltrə'vaiələt) *adj* ultraviolett.
umbrella (ʌm'brelə) *n* Regenschirm *m*.
umlaut ('umlaut) *n* Umlaut *m*.
umpire ('ʌmpaiə) *n* Schiedsrichter *m*.
umpteen (ʌmp'ti:n) *adj inf* zahllos. **umpteen times** x-mal.
unable (ʌn'eibəl) *adj* unfähig.
unacceptable (ʌnək'septəbəl) *adj* unannehmbar, nicht akzeptabel.
unaccompanied (ʌnə'kʌmpnid) *adj* unbegleitet.
unanimous (ju:'næniməs) *adj* einstimmig.
unarmed (ʌn'ɑ:md) *adj* unbewaffnet.
unattractive (ʌnə'træktiv) *adj* reizlos.
unavoidable (ʌnə'vɔidəbəl) *adj* unvermeidlich.
unaware (ʌnə'wɛə) *adj* **1** nicht bewußt. **2** ahnungslos. **unawares** *adv* unversehens, unerwartet. **catch unawares** überraschen.
unbalanced (ʌn'bælənst) *adj* **1** unausgeglichen, unstet. **2** (of mind) gestört.
unbearable (ʌn'bɛərəbəl) *adj* unerträglich.
unbelievable (ʌnbi'li:vəbəl) *adj* unglaublich, unglaubhaft.
unbend* (ʌn'bend) *vi* **1** sich entspannen. **2** gerade werden. *vt* entspannen, losmachen. **unbending** *adj* unnachgiebig.
unbreakable (ʌn'breikəbəl) *adj* unzerbrechlich.
unbridled (ʌn'braidḷd) *adj* zügellos.
uncalled-for *adj* unnötig, unangebracht.
uncanny (ʌn'kæni) *adj* unheimlich.
uncertain (ʌn'sə:tṇ) *adj* **1** unbestimmt, **2** ungewiß. **3** unzuverlässig.
uncle ('ʌŋkəl) *n* Onkel *m*.
uncomfortable (ʌn'kʌmftəbəl) *adj* **1** unbequem. **2** unbehaglich.
unconscious (ʌn'kɔnʃəs) *adj* **1** bewußtlos, ohnmächtig. **2** unbewußt. *n* Unbewußte *neu*.
unconventional (ʌnkən'venʃənəl) *adj* unkonventionell, ungezwungen.
uncooked (ʌn'kukt) *adj* ungekocht, roh.
uncouth (ʌn'ku:θ) *adj* grob, roh, ungebildet.
uncover (ʌn'kʌvə) *vt* **1** aufdecken. **2** bloßlegen.
uncut (ʌn'kʌt) *adj* **1** ungeschnitten. **2** (of a gem) ungeschliffen.
undecided (ʌndi'saidid) *adj* unentschlossen.
undeniable (ʌndi'naiəbəl) *adj* unleugbar.
under ('ʌndə) *prep* unter. *adv* (nach) unten.
under age *adj,adv* minderjährig.
undercharge (ʌndə'tʃɑ:dʒ) *vt,vi* zu wenig berechnen.
undercoat ('ʌndəkout) *n* (of paint) Untergrund, Grundanstrich *m*.
undercover ('ʌndəkʌvə) *adj* Geheim—.
undercut (ʌndə'kʌt) *vt comm* unterbieten.
underdeveloped (ʌndədi'veləpt) *adj* unterentwickelt.
underdone (ʌndə'dʌn) *adj* nicht gargekocht.

underestimate (ʌndər'estimeit) *vt* unterschätzen.
underfoot (ʌndə'fut) *adv* unter den Füßen.
undergo* (ʌndə'gou) *vt* **1** erleben. **2** erdulden. **3** sich unterziehen.
undergraduate (ʌndə'grædjuət) *n* Student *m*. Studentin *f*. Nichtgraduierter *m*.
underground (*adv* ʌndə 'graund; *adj,n* 'ʌndəgraund) *adv,adj* **1** unterirdisch. **2** geheim. *n* Untergrund *m*. **underground (railway)** *n* Untergrundbahn, U-Bahn *f*.
undergrowth ('ʌndəgrouθ) *n* Unterholz *neu*.
underhand (ʌndə'hænd) *adj* hinterlistig.
underline (ʌndə'lain) *vt* unterstreichen.
undermine (ʌndə'main) *vt* untergraben.
underneath (ʌndə'ni:θ) *adv* unten, darunter. *prep* unter(halb).
underpants ('ʌndəpænts) *n pl* Unterhose *f*.
underpass ('ʌndəpɑ:s) *n* Unterführung *f*.
underprivileged (ʌndə'privilidʒd) *adj* benachteiligt, unterprivilegiert.
understand* (ʌndə'stænd) *vt* verstehen, begreifen. **understanding** *n* Verständnis *neu*. Verstand *m*. *adj* verständnisvoll.
understate (ʌndə'steit) *vt* untertreiben.
understudy ('ʌndəstʌdi) *n* **1** Ersatzschauspieler *m*. **2** Ersatzmann *m*.
undertake* (ʌndə'teik) *vt* **1** unternehmen. **2** zusagen. **undertaker** *n* Leichenbestatter *m*. **undertaking** *n* **1** Unternehmen *neu*. **2** Versprechen *neu*.
undertone ('ʌndətoun) *n* **1** gedämpfte Stimme *f*. **2** Unterton *m*.
underwear ('ʌndəwɛə) *n* Unterwäsche *f*.
underworld ('ʌndəwə:ld) *n* Unterwelt *f*.
underwrite* ('ʌndərait) *vt* **1** unterschreiben. **2** *comm* versichern, übernehmen.
undesirable (ʌndi'zaiərəbəl) *adj* unerwünscht.
undo* (ʌn'du:) *vt* **1** aufmachen. **2** aufknöpfen, losbinden. **3** rückgängig machen. **4** ruinieren.
undoubted (ʌn'dautid) *adj* unbezweifelt.
undress (ʌn'dres) *(vi),vt* (sich) ausziehen.
undue ('ʌndju:) *adj* **1** unangemessen, ungebührlich. **2** unnötig. **3** unzulässig.
undulate ('ʌndʒəleit) *vi* wogen, wellen.
unearth (ʌn'ə:θ) *vt* **1** ausgraben. **2** ans Licht bringen.
unearthly *adj* **1** unirdisch. **2** unheimlich.
uneasy (ʌn'i:zi) *adj* unruhig, ängstlich.
uneducated (ʌn'edjukeitid) *adj* ungebildet.
unemployed (ʌnim'plɔid) *adj* **1** arbeitslos. **2** unbeschäftigt. **the unemployed** *n* die Arbeitslosen *pl*. **unemployment** *n* Arbeitslosigkeit *f*.
unequal (ʌn'i:kwəl) *adj* ungleich.

uneven (ʌn'iːvən) *adj* **1** uneben. **2** unausgeglichen.
unfair (ʌn'fɛə) *adj* unfair, ungerecht.
unfaithful (ʌn'feiθfəl) *adj* treulos, untreu.
unfamiliar (ʌnfə'miliə) *adj* nicht vertraut.
unfit (ʌn'fit) *adj* **1** untauglich. **2** unfähig.
unfold (ʌn'fould) *(vi),vt* (sich) entfalten.
unfortunate (ʌn'fɔːtʃunət) *adj* unglücklich.
unfurnished (ʌn'fəːniʃt) *adj* **1** nicht ausgerüstet. **2** unmöbliert.
ungrateful (ʌn'greitfəl) *adj* undankbar.
unhappy (ʌn'hæpi) *adj* unglücklich.
unhealthy (ʌn'helθi) *adj* ungesund.
unicorn ('juːnikɔːn) *n* Einhorn *neu.*
uniform ('juːnifɔːm) *adj* gleich(förmig), einförmig. *n* Uniform *f.*
unify ('juːnifai) *vt* vereinheitlichen, vereinigen.
unilateral (juːni'lætərəl) *adj* einseitig.
uninhabited (ʌnin'hæbitid) *adj* unbewohnt.
uninterested (ʌn'intrəstid) *adj* uninteressiert.
union ('juːniən) *n* **1** Vereinigung, Verbindung *f.* **2** Union *f.* **3** Verein *m.* **4** Einheit *f.*
Union Jack *n* britische Nationalflagge *f.*
unique (juː'niːk) *adj* **1** einzigartig, einmalig. **2** einzig.
unison ('juːnizən) *n* **1** Einklang *m.* **2** *mus* Unisono *neu.*
unit ('juːnit) *n* Einheit *f.*
unite (juː'nait) *(vi),vt* (sich) vereinigen *or* vereinen. **unity** *n* **1** Einheit *f.* **2** Einigkeit *f.*
United Kingdom *n* das Vereinigte Königreich *neu.*
United States of America *n* die Vereinigten Staaten *m pl.*
universe ('juːnivəːs) *n* Weltall, Universum *neu.* **universal** *adj* **1** allgemein, universal. **2** allumfassend.
university (juːni'vəːsiti) *n* Universität, Hochschule *f.*
unjust (ʌn'dʒʌst) *adj* ungerecht.
unkempt (ʌn'kempt) *adj* zerzaust, ungepflegt.
unkind (ʌn'kaind) *adj* unfreundlich, herzlos.
unknown (ʌn'noun) *adj* unbekannt.
unlawful (ʌn'lɔːfəl) *adj* ungesetzlich.
unless (ən'les) *conj* **1** es sei denn, daß. **2** wenn...nicht.
unlike (ʌn'laik) *adj* unähnlich, ungleich. *prep* im Gegensatz zu. **unlikely** *adj,adv* unwahrscheinlich.
unload (ʌn'loud) *vt* ausladen, entladen.
unlock (ʌn'lɔk) *vt* aufschließen.
unlucky (ʌn'lʌki) *adj* unglücklich.
unmanned (ʌn'mænd) *adj* unbemannt.
unnatural (ʌn'nætʃərəl) *adj* unnatürlich.
unnecessary (ʌn'nesəsri) *adj* unnötig.
unofficial (ʌnə'fiʃəl) *adj* nicht amtlich, inoffiziell.

unorthodox (ʌn'ɔːθədɔks) *adj* unorthodox.
unpack (ʌn'pæk) *vt,vi* auspacken.
unpleasant (ʌn'plezənt) *adj* **1** unangenehm. **2** unfreundlich.
unpopular (ʌn'pɔpjulə) *adj* unbeliebt.
unprecedented (ʌn'presidentid) *adj* einmalig, unerhört, beispiellos.
unravel (ʌnrævəl) *vt* entwirren.
unreasonable (ʌn'riːzənəbəl) *adj* unvernünftig, unsinnig.
unrelenting (ʌnri'lentiŋ) *adj* unerbittlich.
unreliable (ʌnri'laiəbəl) *adj* unzuverlässig.
unrest (ʌn'rest) *n* Unruhe *f*.
unruly (ʌn'ruːli) *adj* unbändig, ungestüm.
unscrew (ʌn'skruː) *vt* abschrauben, losschrauben.
unsettle (ʌn'setl̩) *vt* verwirren, durcheinanderbringen, ins Wanken bringen.
unsightly (ʌn'saitli) *adj* unansehnlich.
unsound (ʌn'saund) *adj* **1** ungesund. **2** unsicher. **3** unsolid(e). **4** falsch.
unsteady (ʌn'stedi) *adj* **1** wackelig. **2** unstet, unbeständig.
unsuccessful (ʌnsək'sesfəl) *adj* erfolglos.
untangle (ʌn'tæŋgəl) *vt* entwirren.
untidy (ʌn'taidi) *adj* unordentlich.
untie (ʌn'tai) *vt* aufbinden, auflösen.
until (ʌn'til) *prep,conj* bis. **not until** nicht vor, erst.
untrue (ʌn'truː) *adj* falsch, unwahr.
unusual (ʌn'juːʒuəl) *adj* ungewöhnlich, seltsam.
unwell (ʌn'wel) *adj* unwohl.
unwind (ʌn'waind) *vt* abwinden. *vi* **1** sich abwickeln. **2** *inf* sich entspannen.
unwrap (ʌn'ræp) *vt* auswickeln.
up (ʌp) *adv* **1** auf(wärts). **2** hinauf. **3** empor. **4** nach oben. **5** oben, hoch. *prep* auf. **be up against** gegenüberstehen. **what's up?** *inf* was ist los?
upbringing ('ʌpbriŋiŋ) *n* Erziehung *f*.
update (ʌp'deit) *vt* auf den neuesten Stand bringen.
upheaval (ʌp'hiːvəl) *n* Erhebung *f*. Umsturz *m*.
uphill (ʌp'hil) *adv* bergauf. *adj* **1** ansteigend. **2** anstrengend.
uphold (ʌp'hould) *vt* aufrecht(er)halten.
upholster (ʌp'houlstər) *vt* polstern. **upholstery** *n* Polsterung *f*.
upkeep ('ʌpkiːp) *n* Instandhaltung *f*.
uplift (*v* ʌp'lift; *n* 'ʌplift) *vt* emporheben. *n* Hebung *f*.
upon (ə'pɔn) *prep* auf.
upper ('ʌpə) *adj* ober, höher. **upper class** *n* Oberklasse *f*. **upper house** *n* Oberhaus *neu*. **uppermost** *adj* oberst, höchst. *adv* am höchsten.
upright ('ʌprait) *adj* **1** aufrecht. **2** aufrichtig.
uprising ('ʌpraiziŋ) *n* Aufstand *m*. Erhebung *f*.
uproar ('ʌprɔː) *n* Aufruhr, Lärm *m*.
uproot (ʌp'ruːt) *vt* entwurzeln.

upset* (*v*, *adj* ʌp'set; *n* 'ʌpset) *vt* **1** umkippen. **2** (um)stürzen. **3** bestürzen. *adj* **1** umgekippt. **2** außer Fassung. *n* **1** Umsturz *m*. **2** Verstimmung *f*.
upshot ('ʌpʃɔt) *n* (End) Ergebnis *neu*. **in the upshot** am Ende.
upside down (ʌpsaid 'daun) *adv* **1** mit dem Kopf nach unten. **2** drunter und drüber.
upstairs (ʌp'stɛəz) *adv* **1** (nach) oben. **2** die Treppe hinauf. *adj* ober.
upstream (ʌp'striːm) *adv* stromaufwärts.
uptight (ʌp'tait) *adj* angespannt.
upward ('ʌpwəd) *adj* ansteigend. *adv* aufwärts. **upwards** *adv* aufwärts.
uranium (ju'reiniəm) *n* Uran *neu*.
Uranus (ju'reinəs) *n* Uranus *m*.
urban ('əːbən) *adj* städtisch.
urge (əːdʒ) *vt* **1** (auf)drängen. **2** dringend bitten. *n* Drang *m*.
urgent ('əːdʒənt) *adj* dringend.
urine ('juərin) *n* Urin, Harn *m*. **urinate** *vi* urinieren.
urn (əːn) *n* Urne *f*.
us (ʌs) *pron 1st pers pl* uns.
usage ('juːsidʒ) *n* **1** Brauch *m*. **2** Gebrauch *m*.
use (*vt* juːz; *vi,n* juːs) *vt* **1** benutzen, gebrauchen. **2** anwenden. **3** ausnutzen. *vi* pflegen. *n* **1** Gebrauch *m*. **2** Anwendung *f*. **3** Nutzen *neu*. **useful** *adj* nützlich, brauchbar. **useless** *adj* **1** nutzlos. **2** unbrauchbar.
usher ('ʌʃə) *n* Platzanweiser *m*. *vt* (her-, hin-)einführen. **usherette** *n* Platzanweiserin *f*.
usual ('juːʒuəl) *adj* gewöhnlich, üblich.
usurp (ju'zəːp) *vt* an sich reißen. *vi* sich widerrechtlich bemächtigen. **usurper** *n* **1** Usurpator, Thronräuber *m*. **2** Eindringling *m*.
utensil (juː'tensəl) *n* Gerät *neu*.
uterus ('juːtərəs) *n* Gebärmutter *f*.
utility (juː'tiliti) *n* Nützlichkeit *f*.
utmost ('ʌtmoust) *adj also* **uttermost** äußerst, höchst. *n* Äußerste *neu*.
utter[1] ('ʌtə) *vt* äußern, sagen.
utter[2] ('ʌtə) *adj* **1** äußerst. **2** endgültig. **3** vollkommen.

V

vacant ('veikənt) *adj* **1** leer. **2** frei. **3** unbewohnt. **4** ausdruckslos. **vacancy** *n* **1** freie *or* offene Stelle *f*. **2** Leere *f*.
vacate *vt* **1** räumen. **2** niederlegen. **vacation** *n* Ferien *pl*.
vaccine ('væksiːn) *n* Impfstoff *neu*. **vaccinate** *vt* impfen.
vacillate ('væsəleit) *vi* **1** schwanken. **2** zaudern.
vacuum ('vækjuəm) *n* Vakuum *neu*. **vacuum cleaner** *n* Staubsauger *m*. **vacuum flask** *n* Thermosflasche *f*.
vagina (və'dʒainə) *n anat* Scheide *f*.
vagrant ('veigrənt) *n* Landstreicher *m*. *adj* wandernd.
vague (veig) *adj* vage, ungenau, undeutlich.
vain (vein) *adj* **1** eitel. **2** leer. **in vain** umsonst.
valiant ('væliənt) *adj* tapfer, mutig.

valid ('vælid) *adj* gültig. **validity** *n* Gültigkeit *f*.
valley ('væli) *n* Tal *neu*.
value ('vælju:) *n* Wert *m*. *vt* **1** bewerten. **2** (hoch)schätzen. **valuable** *adj* wertvoll. **valuables** *n pl* Wertsachen *f pl*.
valve ('vælv) *n* **1** Ventil *neu*. **2** Klappe *f*.
vampire ('væmpaiə) *n* Vampir, Blutsauger *m*.
van (væn) *n* Lieferwagen, Lastwagen *m*.
vandal ('vændl) *n* Vandale *m*. **vandalism** *n* Vandalismus *m*.
vanilla (və'nilə) *n* Vanille *f*.
vanish ('væniʃ) *vi* verschwinden.
vanity ('væniti) *n* Eitelkeit *f*.
vapour ('veipə) *n* Dunst, Dampf *m*.
variety (və'raiəti) *n* **1** Vielfalt, Auswahl *f*. **2** Art *f*. **variety show** *n* Varietévorstellung *f*.
various ('vɛəriəs) *adj* verschieden(artig).
varnish ('vɑ:niʃ) *n* **1** Firnis *m*. **2** Politur *f*. **3** Lack *m*. *vt* **1** firnissen. **2** polieren. **3** lackieren.
vary ('vɛəri) *vt* **1** (ab-, ver-)ändern. **2** wechseln. *vi* variieren. **variable** *adj* **1** veränderlich, wechselnd. **2** *tech* regelbar, variabel. **variant adj** abweichend. **variation** *n* **1** Veränderung *f*. Wechsel *m*. **2** Variation *f*.
vase (vɑ:z) *n* Vase *f*.
vasectomy (væ'sektəmi) *n* Vasektomie *f*.
vast (vɑ:st) *adj* **1** riesig. **2** ausgedehnt.
vat (væt) *n* Faß *neu*. Bottich *m*.
Vatican ('vætikən) *n* Vatikan *m*.
vault[1] (vɔ:lt) *n* **1** Gewölbe *neu*. **2** Stahlkammer *f*. **3** Grabgewölbe *neu*. Gruft *f*.
vault[2] (vɔ:lt) *vi* springen. *vt* überspringen.
veal (vi:l) *n* Kalbfleisch *neu*.
veer (viə) *(vi),vt* (sich) drehen, (sich) wenden. *vi* umschwenken.
vegetable ('vedʒtəbəl) *n* **1** Gemüse *neu*. **2** Pflanze *f*. **vegetarian** *n* Vegetarier *m*. *adj* vegetarisch. **vegetation** *n* Vegetation *f*.
vehement ('vi:imənt) *adj* heftig, vehement.
vehicle ('vi:ikəl) *n* **1** Fahrzeug *neu*. **2** Vehikel *neu*.
veil (veil) *n* Schleier *m*. *vt* verschleiern.
vein (vein) *n* **1** *anat* Vene *f*. **2** Ader *f*.
velocity (və'lɔsiti) *n* Geschwindigkeit *f*.
velvet ('velvit) *n* Samt *m*. *adj* **1** samtartig. **2** sanft.
vendetta (ven'detə) *n* Blutrache *f*.
veneer (vi'niə) *n* Furnier *neu*. *vt* furnieren.
venerate ('venəreit) *vt* (ver)ehren, hochachten.
venereal disease (vi'niəriəl) *n* Geschlechtskrankheit *f*.
Venetian (vi'ni:ʃən) *adj* venezianisch. **Venetian blind** *n* Jalousie *f*.
vengeance ('vendʒəns) *n* Rache *f*.
Venice ('venis) *n* Venedig *neu*.
venison ('venisən) *n* Wildbret, Rehfleisch *neu*.
venom ('venəm) *n* Gift *neu*.

vent[1] (vent) *n* **1** Luftloch *neu.* **2** Öffnung *f.*
vent[2] (vent) *vt* freien Lauf lassen, auslassen.
ventilate ('ventileit) *vt* (durch)lüften.
venture ('ventʃə) *n* **1** Wagnis *neu.* **2** Unternehmen *neu.* *vt* wagen.
Venus ('vi:nəs) *n* Venus *f.*
verb (və:b) *n* Zeitwort, Verb(um) *neu.*
verdict ('və:dikt) *n* **1** *law* Urteilsspruch, Wahrspruch *m.* **2** Urteil *neu.*
verge (və:dʒ) *n* Rand *m.* *vi* grenzen.
verify ('verifai) *vt* **1** prüfen. **2** bestätigen. **3** beglaubigen.
vermin ('və:min) *n* Ungeziefer *neu.*
vermouth ('və:məθ) *n* Wermut *m.*
vernacular (və'nækjulə) *n* **1** Landessprache *f.* **2** Umgangssprache *f.* **3** Jargon *m.*
versatile ('və:sətail) *adj* **1** vielseitig, wendig. **2** wandelbar.
verse (və:s) *n* **1** Vers *m.* Strophe *f.* **2** Poesie *f.*
version ('və:ʃən) *n* **1** Gestaltung *f.* **2** Auffassung, Version *f.*
vertebrate ('və:tibreit) *n* Wirbeltier *neu.*
vertical ('və:tikəl) *adj* senkrecht, vertikal.
verve (və:v) *n* Begeisterung *f.* Feuer *neu.*
very ('veri) *adv* sehr. *adj* **1** genau. **2** bloß. **3** derselbe.
vessel ('vesəl) *n* **1** *naut* Schiff *neu.* **2** Gefäß *neu.*
vest (vest) *n* Unterhemd *neu.*
vestment ('vestmənt) *n* Gewand *neu.*
vestry ('vestri) *n* Sakristei *f.*
vet (vet) *inf n* Tierarzt *m.* *vt* untersuchen.
veteran ('vetərən) *n* Veteran *m.*
veterinary surgeon ('vetərənəri) *n* Tierarzt *m.*
veto ('vi:tou) *n* **1** Veto *neu.* Einspruch *m.* **2** Einspruchsrecht *neu.* *vt* verbieten.
vex (veks) *vt* ärgern, plagen. **vexation** *n* **1** Ärger *m.* **2** Belästigung *f.*
via ('vaiə) *prep* über, via.
viable ('vaiəbəl) *adj* **1** lebensfähig. **2** praktisch, ausführbar.
viaduct ('vaiədʌkt) *n* Viadukt *m.* Brücke *f.*
vibrate (vai'breit) *vi* schwingen, vibrieren. **vibration** *n* Schwingung, Vibration *f.*
vicar ('vikə) *n* Vikar, Pfarrer *m.*
vicarious (vi'kɛəriəs) *adj* **1** aus zweiter Hand. **2** stellvertretend.
vice[1] (vais) *n* **1** Laster *neu.* **2** Fehler *m.*
vice[2] (vais) *n* Schraubstock *m.*
vice-chancellor *n* Vizekanzler *m.*
vice-president *n* Vizepräsident *m.*
vice versa ('və:sə) *adj* umgekehrt.
vicinity (vi'sinəti) *n* Nähe, Nachbarschaft *f.*
vicious ('viʃəs) *adj* **1** bösartig. **2** lasterhaft.
victim ('viktim) *n* Opfer *neu.* **victimize** *vt* **1** (auf)opfern. **2** quälen, belästigen.
Victorian (vik'tɔ:riən) *adj* **1**

viktorianisch. **2** prüde. *n* Viktorianer *m*.
victory ('viktri) *n* Sieg *m*. **victorious** *adj* siegreich.
video-tape ('vidiouteip) *n* Magnetbildband *neu*.
Vienna (vi'enə) *n* Wien *neu*. **Viennese** *adj* wienerisch. *n* Wiener *m*.
Vietnam (viet'næm) *n* Vietnam *neu*. **Vietnamese** *adj* vietnamesisch. *n* Vietnamese *m*.
view (vjuː) *n* **1** Aussicht *f*. **2** Ansicht *f*. **3** Einstellung *f*. **with a view to** zu dem Zweck. **view-finder** *n* Sucher *m*. *~vt* **1** anschauen. **2** besichtigen.
vigil ('vidʒil) *n* Nachtwache *f*. **vigilant** *adj* wachsam.
vigour ('vigə) *n* **1** Kraft, Lebenskraft *f*. **2** Intensität *f*. **vigorous** *adj* **1** kräftig. **2** lebhaft.
vile (vail) *adj* **1** widerlich. **2** gemein.
villa ('vilə) *n* **1** Landhaus *neu*. **2** Villa *f*.
village ('vilidʒ) *n* Dorf *neu*. **villager** *n* Dorfbewohner *m*.
villain ('vilən) *n* Schurke *m*.
vindictive (vin'diktiv) *adj* rachsüchtig.
vine (vain) *n* **1** Rebe *f*. **2** Weinstock *m*. **vineyard** *n* Weinberg *m*.
vinegar ('vinigə) *n* Essig *m*.
vintage ('vintidʒ) *n* Lese *f*. *adj* hervorragend.
vinyl ('vainil) *n* Vinyl *neu*.
viola (vi'oulə) *n* Viola *f*.
violate ('vaiəleit) *vt* **1** verletzen, brechen. **2** schänden.
violence ('vaiələns) *n* **1** Gewalt(tätigkeit) *f*. **2** Heftigkeit *f*. **violent** *adj* **1** gewalttätig, gewaltsam. **2** heftig.
violet ('vaiələt) *adj* violett. *n* **1** *bot* Veilchen *neu*. **2** Violett *neu*.
violin (vaiə'lin) *n* Violine, Geige *f*. **violinist** *n* Violinist *m*.
viper ('vaipə) *n* Viper, Natter *f*.
virgin ('vəːdʒin) *n* Jungfrau *f*. *adj also* **virginal** jungfräulich.
Virgo ('vəːgou) *n* Jungfrau *f*.
virile ('virail) *adj* männlich.
virtue ('vəːtjuː) *n* **1** Tugend *f*. **2** Vorzug *m*. **by virtue of** kraft. **virtual** *adj* eigentlich, tatsächlich. **virtuous** *adj* tugendhaft.
virus ('vairəs) *n* Virus *m,neu*.
visa ('viːzə) *n* Visum *neu*. Einreisebewilligung *f*.
viscount ('vaikaunt) *n* Vicomte *m*.
vision ('viʒən) *n* **1** Sehvermögen *neu*. **2** Erscheinung *f*. **3** Anblick *m*. **visible** *adj* **1** sichtbar. **2** offensichtlich.
visit ('vizit) *vt* besuchen. *n* Besuch *m*.
visual ('vizjuəl) *adj* visuell, Seh—. **visualize** *vt* sich (klar) vorstellen.
vital ('vaitl̩) *adj* **1** lebenswichtig. **2** Lebens—. **3** vital. **vitality** *n* Lebenskraft, *f*.
vitamin ('vitəmin) *n* Vitamin *neu*.
vivacious (vi'veiʃəs) *adj* lebhaft, munter.
vivid ('vivid) *adj* lebhaft, deutlich.
vixen ('viksən) *n* *zool* Füchsin *f*.

vocabulary (və'kæbjuləri) *n* **1** Wortschatz *m*. Vokabular *neu*. **2** Wörterverzeichnis *neu*.
vocal ('voukəl) *adj* **1** mündlich, stimmlich. **2** stimmhaft. **vocal chords** *n pl* Stimmbänder *neu pl*.
vocation (vou'keiʃən) *n* **1** Berufung *f*. **2** Beruf *m*.
vodka ('vɔdkə) *n* Wodka *m*.
voice (vɔis) *n* Stimme *f*. *vt* äußern.
void (vɔid) *adj* **1** leer. **2** unwirksam. **3** ungültig. *n* **1** Leere *f*. **2** Lücke *f*.
volatile ('vɔlətail) *adj* **1** flüchtig. **2** vorübergehend. **3** unbeständig. **4** lebhaft.
volcano (vɔl'keinou) *n, pl* **-oes** Vulkan *m*.
volley ('vɔli) *n* **1** *mil* Salve *f*. Hagel *m*. **2** *sport* Flugball *m*.
volt (voult) *n* Volt *neu*.
volume ('vɔljuːm) *n* **1** Umfang *m*. **2** Inhalt *m*. Volumen *neu*. **3** Lautstärke *f*. **4** Band *m*.
volunteer (vɔlən'tiə) *n* Freiwillige(r) *m*. *vi* sich freiwillig melden. *vt* freiwillig anbieten. **voluntary** *adj* freiwillig.
voluptuous (və'lʌptʃuəs) *adj* **1** wollüstig. **2** sinnlich.
vomit ('vɔmit) *vi* sich erbrechen *or* übergeben. *vt* auswerfen, ausspeien. *n* Erbrochene *neu*.
voodoo ('vuːduː) *n* Wodu, Wudu *m*.
vote (vout) *n* **1** Stimme *f*. **2** Stimmrecht *neu*. **3** Wahl *f*. *vi* abstimmen, wählen.
vouch (vautʃ) *vi* **vouch for** bürgen für.
voucher ('vautʃə) *n* **1** Gutschein *m*. **2** Unterlage *f*.
vow (vau) *n* Gelübde *neu*. *vt* geloben.
vowel ('vauəl) *n* Vokal *m*.
voyage ('vɔiidʒ) *n* (See)Reise *f*. *vi* reisen.
vulgar ('vʌlgə) *adj* **1** gemein, vulgär. **2** unanständig. **3** gewöhnlich.
vulnerable ('vʌlnrəbl̩) *adj* **1** verwundbar. **2** anfällig.
vulture ('vʌltʃə) *n* Geier *m*.

W

wad (wɔd) *n* **1** Bündel *neu*. Stoß *m*. **2** Bausch *m*. **wadding** *n* Watte, Wattierung *f*.
waddle ('wɔd) *vi* watscheln. *n* Watscheln *neu*.
wade (weid) *vi* waten. **wade through** sich durcharbeiten durch.
wafer ('weifə) *n* **1** Waffel *f*. **2** *rel* Oblate *f*.
waft (wɔft) *vt,vi* wehen. *n* Wehen *neu*.
wag (wæg) *vt* **1** schütteln. **2** (a tail) wedeln.
wage (weidʒ) *n* Lohn *m*.
waggle ('wægəl) *vt* wackeln.
wagon ('wægən) *n* **1** Lastwagen *m*. **2** Güterwaggon *neu*.
waif (weif) *n* verwahrlostes Kind *neu*.
wail (weil) *vi* wehklagen. *n* Klagen. *neu*.
waist (weist) *n* Taille *f*. **waistband** *n* Bund *m*. **waistcoat** *n* Weste *f*.
wait (weit) *vi* **1** warten. **2** bedienen. **wait for** erwarten, warten auf. **waiting list** *n* Warteliste *f*. **waiting room** *n* **1** Wartezimmer *neu*. **2** (of a station) Wartesaal *m*. **waiter**

n Kellner *m*. **waitress** *n* Kellnerin *f*.
waive (weiv) *vt* verzichten auf.
wake* (weik) *also* **wake up** *vt* (auf-, er-)wecken. *vi* erwachen, aufwachen. **waken** *vi* erwachen, aufwachen. *vt* (auf-, er-)wecken.
Wales ('weilz) *n* Wales *neu*.
walk (wɔːk) *vi* **1** laufen, (zu Fuß) gehen. **2** wandern. *n* **1** Spaziergang *m*. **2** Gang *m*. **go for a walk** spazierengehen. **walking stick** *n* Spazierstock *m*. **walkout** *n* Streik *m*. **walk-over** ('wɔːkouvə) *n* leichter Sieg *m*.
wall (wɔːl) *n* **1** Mauer *f*. **2** Wand *f*. **wallflower** *n* **1** *bot* Goldlack *m*. **2** *inf* Mauerblümchen *neu*. **wallpaper** *n* Tapete *f*.
wallet ('wɔlit) *n* Brieftasche *f*.
wallop ('wɔləp) *inf vt* prügeln, (heftig) schlagen. *n* (heftiger) Schlag *m*.
wallow ('wɔlou) *vi* sich wälzen.
walnut ('wɔːlnʌt) *n* Walnuß *f*.
walrus ('wɔːlrəs) *n* Walroß *neu*.
waltz (wɔːls) *n* Walzer *m*. *vi* Walzer tanzen.
wand (wɔnd) *n* **1** (Zauber)Stab *m*. **2** *mus* Taktstock *m*.
wander ('wɔndə) *vi* **1** wandern. **2** irregehen. **3** abbiegen.
wane (wein) *vi* **1** (of the moon) abnehmen. **2** nachlassen, schwächer werden.
wangle ('wæŋgəl) *vt sl* **1** hinkriegen, organisieren. **2** abluchsen.
want (wɔnt) *vt* **1** wollen. **2** benötigen. *vi* mangeln. *n* **1** Bedürfnis *neu*. **2** Not *f*. **3** Begierde *f*.
wanton ('wɔntən) *adj* **1** mutwillig. **2** geil.
war (wɔː) *n* Krieg *m*. **wage war** Krieg führen. **warfare** *n* Kriegsführung *f*. Krieg *m*.
warble ('wɔːbəl) *vi,vt* trillern, singen.
ward (wɔːd) *n* **1** Abteilung *f*. **2** *med* Station *f*. **3** *law* Mündel *neu*. *v* **ward off** abwehren.
warden *n* **1** Vorsteher. *m*. **2** Jugendherbergsvater *m*.
warder *n* (Gefängnis)Wärter *m*.
wardrobe ('wɔːdroub) *n* **1** Kleiderschrank *m*. **2** Garderobe *f*.
warehouse ('wɛəhaus) *n* Lagerhaus *neu*.
warm (wɔːm) *adj* warm. *vt* (er)wärmen. *vi* sich erwärmen. **warm-blooded** *adj* warmblütig. **warm-hearted** *adj* warmherzig.
warn (wɔːn) *vt* warnen. **warning** *n* Warnung *f*. *adj* warnend.
warp (wɔːp) *(vi),vt* (sich) werfen, (sich) verziehen. *n* Verwerfung, Verkrümmung *f*.
warrant ('wɔrənt) *n* **1** Vollmacht *f*. **2** Rechtfertigung *f*. **3** Haftbefehl, *m*. *vt* **1** rechtfertigen. **2** haften für. **warrant officer** *n* **1** Stabsfeldwebel *m*. **2** Stabsbootsmann *m*.
warren ('wɔrən) *n* Gehege *neu*.
warrior ('wɔriə) *n* Krieger *m*.
wart (wɔːt) *n* Warze *f*.
wary ('wɛəri) *adj* vorsichtig, behutsam.
was (wəz; *stressed* wɔz) *v* see **be.**
wash (wɔʃ) *vt* **1** waschen. **2**

spülen. *vi* (sich) waschen. **wash up** spülen. ~*n* **1** Waschen *neu.* **2** Wäsche *f.* **3** *naut* Kielwasser *neu.* **washbasin** *n* Waschbecken *neu.* **washer** *n* *tech* Dichtungsring *m.* **washing** *n* **1** Wäsche *f.* **2** Waschen *neu.* **washing machine** *n* Waschmaschine *f.* **wash-out** *n sl* Fiasko *neu.* **washroom** *n* Toilette *f.*

wasp (wɔsp) *n* Wespe *f.*

waste (weist) *vt* **1** verschwenden. **2** verwüsten. *vi also* **waste away** abnehmen, schwinden. ~*adj* **1** wüst. **2** unnütz. **3** Ab—. *n* **1** Müll, Abfall *m.* **2** Öde *f.* **3** Verschwendung *f.* **wastepaper basket** Papierkorb *m.*

watch (wɔtʃ) *vt* **1** bewachen. **2** beobachten. **3** zusehen. *vi* **1** aufpassen. **2** zuschauen. **3** wachen. **watch television** fernsehen. ~*n* **1** Armbanduhr *f.* **2** Taschenuhr *f.* **3** Wache *f.* **watchdog** *n* Wachhund *m.* **watchful** *adj* aufmerksam, wachsam.

water ('wɔːtə) *n* Wasser *neu.* **drinking water** Trinkwasser *neu.* ~*vt* (be)wässern, (be)gießen. **water down** verwässern. **watering-can** *n* Gießkanne *f.*

water-closet *n* Klosett *neu.*

watercolour ('wɔːtəkʌlə) *n* **1** Aquarell *neu.* **2** Wasserfarbe *f.*

watercress ('wɔːtəkres) *n* Brunnenkresse *f.*

waterfall ('wɔːtəfɔːl) *n* Wasserfall *m.*

waterlily ('wɔːtəlili) *n* Seerose *f.*

waterlogged ('wɔːtəlɔgd) *adj* vollgesogen.

watermill ('wɔːtəmil) *n* Wassermühle *f.*

waterproof ('wɔːtəpruːf) *adj* wasserdicht. *n* Regenmantel *m.* *vt* imprägnieren.

water-ski *n* Wasserschi *m.* *vi* Wasserschi fahren.

watertight ('wɔːtətait) *adj* wasserdicht.

waterway ('wɔːtəwei) *n* Wasserweg *m.*

waterworks ('wɔːtəwəːks) *n pl* Wasserwerk *neu.*

watery ('wɔːtəri) *adj* wässerig.

watt (wɔt) *n* Watt *neu.*

wave (weiv) *n* Welle *f.* *vi* **1** winken. **2** wehen. *vt* **1** winken. **2** schwingen. **3** wellen. **waveband** *n* Frequenzband *neu.* **wavelength** *n* Wellenlänge *f.* **wavy** *adj* wellig, gewellt.

waver ('weivə) *vi* schwanken, zittern.

wax[1] (wæks) *n* Wachs *neu.* *vt* bohnern, wachsen. *adj also* **waxen** *or* **waxy** wächsern.

wax[2] (wæks) *vi* **1** wachsen, zunehmen. **2** werden.

way (wei) *n* **1** Weg *m.* **2** Mittel *neu.* **3** Richtung *f.* **4** Weise *f.* **by the way** übrigens, nebenbei. **under way** **1** unterwegs. **2** im Gange. **way in** Eingang *m.* **way out** Ausgang *m.*

waylay (wei'lei) *vt* auflauern.

wayward ('weiwəd) *adj* **1** widerspenstig. **2** launisch.

we (wiː) *pron 1st pers pl* wir.

weak (wiːk) *adj* schwach. **weak-minded** *adj* **1** schwachsinnig. **2** charakterschwach.

weak-willed *adj* willensschwach. **weaken** *vt* **1** schwächen. **2** verdünnen. *vi* schwächer werden. **weakling** *n* Schwächling *m*.
wealth (welθ) *n* Reichtum *m*. **wealthy** *adj* wohlhabend, reich.
weapon ('wepən) *n* Waffe *f*.
wear* (wɛə) *vt* tragen. *vi* haltbar sein. **wear out 1** abtragen, abnutzen. **2** ermüden.
weary ('wiəri) *adj* erschöpft, müde. *vt* **1** ermüden. **2** langweilen.
weasel ('wi:zəl) *n* Wiesel *neu*.
weather ('weðə) *n* Wetter *neu*. *vt* überstehen.
weave* (wi:v) *vt* **1** weben, wirken. **2** (ver)flechten. *vi* **1** weben. **2** sich verflechten.
web (web) *n* **1** Gewebe *neu*. **2** Netz *neu*.
wedding ('wediŋ) *n* Hochzeit *f*. **wedding anniversary** *n* Hochzeitstag *m*. **wedding ring** *n* Trauring *m*.
wedge (wedʒ) *n* Keil *m*. *vt* verkeilen.
Wednesday ('wenzdi) *n* Mittwoch *m*.
weed (wi:d) *n* Unkraut *neu*. *vt* jäten. **weed out** aussondern.
week (wi:k) *n* Woche *f*. **weekday** *n* Wochentag *m*. **weekend** *n* Wochenende *neu*. **weekly** *adj,adv* wöchentlich. *n* Wochenzeitung *f*.
weep* (wi:p) *vt,vi* weinen.
weigh (wei) *vt* (ab)wiegen, abwägen. *vi* wiegen. **weighbridge** *n* Brückenwaage *f*. **weight** *n* **1** Gewicht *neu*. **2** Last *f*. **weight-lifting** *n* Gewichtheben *neu*.
weird ('wiəd) *adj* **1** unheimlich. **2** *inf* ulkig.
welcome ('welkəm) *adj,interj* willkommen. *vt* willkommen heißen, begrüßen. *n* Willkommen *neu*.
weld (weld) *vt* schweißen.
welfare ('welfɛə) *n* Wohlfahrt *f*.
well[1] (wel) *n* Brunnen *m*. *vi* quellen. **well up** hervorquellen.
well[2] (wel) *adv* **1** gut. **2** wohl. *adj* gesund. *interj* also, na. **as well** auch. **do well 1** gut tun. **2** wohlauf sein. **3** Erfolg haben. **feel good** wohlauf sein. **just as well** ebenso gut.
well-bred *adj* wohlerzogen.
well-built *adj* gut gebaut.
well-known *adj* (wohl)bekannt.
well-off *adj* wohlhabend.
well-paid *adj* wohlbezahlt.
well-spoken *adj* redegewandt.
well-worn *adj* abgenutzt.
Welsh (welʃ) *adj* walisisch. *n* (language) Walisisch *neu*. **Welshman** *n* Waliser *m*.
went (went) *v* see **go.**
wept (wept) *v* see **weep.**
were (wə:) *v* see **be.**
west (west) *n* **1** West(en) *m*. **2** *cap* Westen *m*. Abendland *neu*. *adj* westlich. *adv* westwärts, nach Westen. **westerly** *adj* westlich. *n* Westwind *m*. **western** *adj* westlich. *n* Wildwestfilm *m*. **westward** *adj* nach Westen. **westwards** *adv* westwärts.
West Indies ('indiz) *n pl* Westindien *neu*. **West Indian** *adj* westindisch. *n* Westindier *m*.
Westphalia (west'feiliə) *n* Westfalen *neu*.

wet (wet) *adj* naß, feucht. *n* Nässe *f.* *vt* naßmachen, nässen. **wet suit** *n* Taucheranzug *m.*
whack (wæk) *inf vt* schlagen. *n* **1** heftiger Schlag *m.* **2** Anteil *m.*
whale (weil) *n* Wal(fisch) *m.*
wharf (wɔːf) *n* Kai *m.* Landungsbrücke *f.*
what (wɔt) *pron,interj* was, wie. *adj* welch, was für ein. **what for?** wozu? **what sort of?** was für? **whatever** *pron* was auch immer, alles was. *adj* **1** welch auch immer. **2** überhaupt.
wheat (wiːt) *n* Weizen *m.*
wheedle ('wiːdl̩) *vt* beschwatzen, überreden. *vi* schmeicheln.
wheel (wiːl) *n* Rad *neu.* *vt* **1** rollen. **2** drehen. *vi* rollen. **wheelbarrow** *n* Schubkarren *m.* **wheelchair** *n* Rollstuhl *m.*
wheeze (wiːz) *vi* keuchen. *n* Keuchen *neu.*
whelk (welk) *n* Wellhornschnecke *f.*
when (wen) *adv* wann, zu welcher Zeit. *conj* als, wenn. **whenever** *adv* wann auch immer. *conj* wenn (immer), so oft als.
where (wɛə) *adv,conj* wo, wohin, woher. **whereabouts** *n pl* **1** Aufenthalt(sort) *m.* **2** Verbleib *m.* *adv* wo herum. **whereas** *conj* während. **whereby** *adv,conj* wodurch, wie. **whereupon** *adv,conj* worauf. **wherever** *adv* wo(hin) auch immer.
whether ('weðə) *conj* ob.
which (witʃ) *pron* **1** welch. **2** der. **3** was. *adj* welch. **whichever** *pron* welcher auch immer.
whiff (wif) *n* Hauch *m.* *vt,vi* paffen.
while (wail) *conj also* **whilst** während, solange. *n* Weile *f.*
whim (wim) *n* Laune, Grille *f.*
whimper ('wimpə) *vi,vt* wimmern.
whimsical ('wimzikəl) *adj* wunderlich.
whine (wain) *vi* wimmern, winseln.
whip (wip) *n* Peitsche *f.* *vt* **1** peitschen, schlagen. **2** reißen.
whippet ('wipit) *n* Whippet *m.*
whirl (wəːl) *vi,vt* wirbeln. *n* **1** Wirbeln *neu.* **2** Wirbel *m.* **whirlwind** *n* Wirbel(wind) *m.*
whirr (wəː) *vi,(vt)* schwirren (lassen). *n* Schwirren *neu.*
whisk[1] (wisk) *vt* **1** fegen. **2** rasch wegnehmen.
whisk[2] (wisk) *cul vt* schlagen. *n* Schneebesen *m.*
whiskers ('wiskəz) *n pl* **1** Backenbart *m.* **2** *zool* Schnurrhaare *neu pl.*
whisky ('wiski) *n* Whisky *m.*
whisper ('wispə) *vi* flüstern. *n* Geflüster *neu.*
whistle ('wisəl) *vi,vt* pfeifen. *n* **1** Pfeife *f.* **2** Pfiff *m.*
white (wait) *adj* weiß. *n* **1** Weiß *neu.* **2** Weiße(r) *m.* **whitewash** *n* (weiße) Tünche *f.* *vt* **1** tünchen, weißen. **2** reinwaschen. **whiting** *n* Weißfisch *m.*
Whitsun ('witsən) *n* Pfingsten *neu.*
whiz (wiz) *vi* sausen. *n* Sausen *neu.*
who (huː) *pron* **1** wer. **2** der,

welch. **whoever** *pron* **1** wer auch immer. **2** jeder der.
whole (houl) *adj* ganz, vollständig. *n* Ganze *neu.* Gesamtheit *f.* **wholehearted** *adj* rückhaltslos. **wholemeal** *adj* Vollkorn—. **wholesale** *n* Großhandel *m. adj* **1** Großhandels—. **2** vollständig. *adv* **1** im großen. **2** en gros. **wholesome** *adj* gesund, heilvoll. **wholly** *adv* ganz, völlig.
whom (huːm) *pron* **1** wen, wem. **2** den, welchen.
whooping cough ('huːpiŋ) *n* Keuchhusten *m.*
whore (hɔː) *n* Hure *f. vi* huren.
whose (huːz) *pron* **1** wessen. **2** dessen.
why (wai) *adv, conj* warum, weshalb, wozu. *interj* nun, doch.
wick (wik) *n* Docht *m.*
wicked ('wikid) *adj* böse, boshaft.
wicket ('wikit) *n sport* Tor *neu.* Dreistab *m.*
wide (waid) *adj* breit, weit. **widely** *adv* **1** weit, breit. **2** in hohem Maße. **widen** *vt* erweitern. **widespread** *adj* weit verbreitet.
widow ('widou) *n* Witwe *f.* **widower** *n* Witwer *m.*
width (widθ) *n* Breite, Weite *f.*
wield (wiːld) *vt* **1** handhaben. **2** ausüben.
wife (waif) *n, pl* **wives** (Ehe)Frau *f.*
wig (wig) *n* Perücke *f.*
wiggle ('wigəl) *vi,(vt)* wackeln (mit).
wigwam ('wigwæm) *n* Wigwam *m.*
wild (waild) *adj* wild. **run wild 1** sich austoben. **2** wild wachsen. **wildlife** *n* Wild *neu.*
wilderness ('wildənəs) *n* Wildnis, Wüste *f.*
wilful ('wilfəl) *adj* **1** eigensinnig. **2** absichtlich.
will* [1] (wil) *v mod aux* **1** werden. **2** wollen. **3** sollen.
will [2] (wil) *n* **1** Wille *f.* **2** Testament *neu.* **willpower** *n* Willenskraft *f.*
willing ('wiliŋ) *adj* (bereit)willig.
willow ('wilou) *n* Weide *f.*
wilt (wilt) *vi* (ver)welken.
win* (win) *vt* **1** gewinnen. **2** erlangen. *vi* gewinnen, siegen. *n* Sieg *m.*
wince (wins) *vi* zusammenzucken.
winch (wintʃ) *n* Winde, Kurbel *f.*
wind [1] (wind) *n* Wind *m.* **windbag** *n* Windbeutel *m.* **windfall** *n* **1** Glücksfall *m.* **2** Fallobst *m.* **wind instrument** *n* Blasinstrument *neu.* **windmill** *n* Windmühle *f.* **windpipe** *n* Luftröhre *f.* **windscreen** *n* Windschutzscheibe *f.* **windscreen wipers** *n pl* Scheibenwischer *m.* **windswept** *adj* sturmgepeitscht. **windy** *adj* windig.
wind* [2] (waind) *vt* **1** winden, wickeln. **2** drehen. *vi* sich winden.
windlass ('windləs) *n* Winde, Haspel *f.*
window ('windou) *n* Fenster *neu.* **window box** *n* Blumenkasten *m.* **window-shop** *vi* einen Schaufensterbummel machen.

wine (wain) *n* Wein *m*.
wing (wiŋ) *n* **1** Flügel *m*. **2** *aviat* Tragfläche *f*. **3** Gruppe *f*. *vi* fliegen. **wing commander** *n* Oberstleutnant der britischen Luftwaffe *m*.
wink (wiŋk) *vi,vt* blinzeln. *n* Blinzeln *neu*.
winkle ('wiŋkəl) *n* Strandschnecke *f*.
winter ('wintə) *n* Winter *m*. *vi,vt* überwintern.
wipe (waip) *vt* (ab)wischen. *n* Wischen *neu*.
wire ('waiə) *n* **1** Draht *m*. **2** Telegramm *neu*. *vt* **1** telegraphieren. **2** mit Draht versehen.
wise (waiz) *adj* weise, klug.
wish (wiʃ) *vt,vi* wünschen. *n* Wunsch *m*.
wisp (wisp) *n* **1** Wisch *m*. **2** Streifen *m*.
wisteria (wis'tiəriə) *n* Glyzine *f*.
wistful ('wistfəl) *adj* sehnsüchtig.
wit (wit) *n* **1** Witz, Esprit *m*. **2** Verstand *m*.
witch (witʃ) *n* Hexe *f*. **witchcraft** *n* Hexerei *f*.
with (wið) *prep* mit, bei.
withdraw (wið'drɔː) *vi* sich zurückziehen, ausscheiden. *vt* zurückziehen.
wither ('wiðə) *vi* (ver)welken, vertrocknen.
withhold (wið'hould) *vt* **1** zurückhalten. **2** vorenthalten.
within (wið'in) *prep* in, innerhalb, binnen. *adv* drinnen.
without (wið'aut) *prep* ohne. *adv* (dr)außen.
withstand* (wið'stænd) *vt* widerstehen.
witness ('witnəs) *n* Zeuge *m*. *vt* **1** bezeugen. **2** Zeuge sein von.
witty ('witi) *adj* geistreich, witzig.
wizard ('wizəd) *n* Zauberer, Hexenmeister *m*.
wobble ('wɔbəl) *vi* wackeln.
woke (wouk) *v* see **wake.**
woken ('woukən) *v* see **wake.**
wolf (wulf) *n* Wolf *m*.
woman ('wumən) *n* **1** Frau *f*. **2** Weib *neu*.
womb (wuːm) *n* Gebärmutter *f*.
wonder ('wʌndə) *n* **1** Wunder *neu*. **2** Verwunderung *f*. *vi* **1** sich fragen. **2** sich wundern. **wonderful** *adj* wunderbar.
wonky ('wɔŋki) *adj inf* schwankend, wackelig.
wood (wud) *n* **1** Holz *neu*. **2** Wald *m*. **woodcock** *n* Waldschnepfe *f*. **wooden** *adj* **1** hölzern. **2** ausdruckslos, steif. **woodland** *n* Wald *m*. Waldland *neu*. **woodpecker** *n* Specht *m*. **woodpigeon** *n* Ringeltaube *f*. **woodwind** *n* Holzblasinstrument *neu*. **woodwork** *n* Holzwerk *neu*. **woodworm** *n* Holzwurm *m*.
wool (wul) *n* Wolle *f*. **woollen** *adj* wollen, Woll—. **woolly** *adj* **1** wollen. **2** wollig. **3** verschwommen.
word (wəːd) *n* Wort *neu*. *vt* ausdrücken.
wore (wɔː) *v* see **wear.**
work (wɔːk) *n* **1** Arbeit *f*. **2** Werk *neu*. **3** *pl* Werk *neu*. Betrieb *m*. *vi* **1** arbeiten. **2** funktionieren. *vt* **1** bearbeiten. **2** betätigen, bedienen. **3** *min* ausbeuten. **worker** *n* **1** Arbeiter *m*. **2** *pl* Arbeiterschaft *f*. **working class** *n* Arbeiter-

klasse *f.* **workman** *n* Arbeiter, Handwerker *m.* **workmanship** *n* **1** Kunstfertigkeit *f.* **2** Arbeit *f.*

world (wə:ld) *n* Welt *f.* *adj* Welt—. **not for the world** um keinen Preis. **man/woman of the world** *n* Weltmann, Weltdame *m,f.* **worldly** *adj* weltlich. **worldwide** *adj* weltweit.

worm (wə:m) *n* Wurm *m.*

wormwood ('wə:mwud) *n* Wermut *m.*

worn (wɔ:n) *adj* abgenutzt.

worry ('wʌri) *vi* sich sorgen *or* beunruhigen. *vt* **1** beunruhigen. **2** plagen. *n* **1** Sorge *f.* Kummer *m.* **2** Ärger *m.*

worse (wə:s) *adj,adv* schlechter, schlimmer. **worsen** *(vi),vt* (sich) verschlechtern, (sich) verschlimmern.

worship ('wə:ʃip) *vt* anbeten, verehren. *vi* beten. *n* Anbetung, Verehrung *f.*

worst (wə:st) *adj* schlechtest, schlimmst. *adv* am schlimmsten. *vt* überwältigen.

worth (wə:θ) *n* Wert *m.* *adj* wert. **it is worth doing** es lohnt sich, es zu tun. **worthwhile** *adj* der Mühe wert. **worthy** *adj* würdig, wert.

would (wəd; *stressed* wud) *vi* see **will**[1].

wound[1] (wu:nd) *n* Wunde, Verletzung *f.* *vt* verwunden, verletzen.

wound[2] (waund) *v* see **wind**[2].

wove (wouv) *v* see **weave.**

wrangle ('ræŋgəl) *vi* zanken. *n* Zank *m.*

wrap (ræp) *vt* (um-, ein-)wickeln. *n* **1** Hülle *f.* **2** Schal *m.* **wrapper** *n* Hülle *f.* Umschlag *m.* **wrapping** *n* Hülle, Verpackung *f.* **wrapping paper** *n* Packpapier *neu.*

wreath (ri:θ) *n* **1** Kranz *m.* **2** Gewinde *f.*

wreathe (ri:ð) *vt* **1** winden. **2** bekränzen. *vi* sich winden *or* kräuseln.

wreck (rek) *n* **1** Wrack *m.* **2** Schiffbruch *m.* *vt* **1** zertrümmern. **2** zerstören. **wreckage** *n* Trümmer *pl.*

wren (ren) *n* Zaunkönig *m.*

wrench (rentʃ) *vt* verrenken, verdrehen. *n* **1** (heftiger) Ruck *m.* **2** *tech* Schraubenschlüssel *m.*

wrestle ('resəl) *vi* ringen, kämpfen mit. *vt* ringen *n* Ringkampf *m.*

wretch (retʃ) *n* Elende(r) *m.* **wretched** *adj* elend, unglücklich.

wriggle ('rigəl) *vi* sich winden. *n* Winden *neu.*

wring* (riŋ) *vt* **1** (aus)wringen. **2** (an animal's neck) abdrehen. **3** (one's hands) ringen.

wrinkle ('riŋkəl) *n* Runzel, Falte. *f.* *(vi),vt* (sich) falten, (sich) runzeln.

wrist (rist) *n* Handgelenk *neu.* **wristwatch** *n* Armbanduhr *f.*

writ (rit) *n* **1** Erlaß *m.* **2** *law* Vorladung *f.*

write* (rait) *vt,vi* schreiben. **write down** aufschreiben, niederschreiben. **write off** abschreiben. **write up** (ausführlich) beschreiben. **writer 1** Verfasser *m.* **2** Schriftsteller *m.* **writing paper** *n* Schreibpapier *neu.*

writhe (raið) *vi* sich krümmen, sich winden.
wrong (rɔŋ) *adj* **1** verkehrt, falsch. **2** unrecht. **3** irrtümlich. *adv* falsch, verkehrt. **be wrong** unrecht haben. **go wrong** schiefgehen. **something is wrong** etwas stimmt nicht. **what is wrong?** was ist los?
wrote (rout) *v* see **write.**
wrought iron (rɔːt) *n* Schmiedeeisen *neu.*
wrung (rʌŋ) *v* see **wring.**
wry (rai) *adj* schief, verzogen.

X

xenophobia (zenə'foubiə) *n* Fremdenhaß *m.*
Xerox ('ziərɔks) *Tdmk n* Photokopiergerät *neu. vt* photokopieren.
X-ray *n* Röntgenstrahl *m. vt* röntgen.
xylophone ('zailəfoun) *n* Xylophon *neu.*

Y

yacht (jɔt) *n* Jacht *f. vi* segeln. **yachtsman** *n* **1** Jachtsegler. **2** Jachtbesitzer *m.*
yank (jæŋk) *vi,vt inf* heftig ziehen.
yap (jæp) *vi* kläffen.
yard[1] (jɑːd) *n* Yard *neu.* **yardstick** *n* Maßstab *m.*
yard[2] (jɑːd) *n* Hof *m.*
yarn (jɑːn) *n* **1** Garn *neu.* Faden *m.* **2** Erzählung *f.* **spin a yarn** ein Seemannsgarn spinnen.
yawn (jɔːn) *vi* gähnen. *n* Gähnen *neu.*
year (jiə) *n* Jahr *neu.* **yearly** *adj,adv* jährlich.
yearn (jəːn) *vi* sich sehnen. **yearning** *n* Sehnsucht *f.* Sehnen *neu.*
yeast (jiːst) *n* Hefe *f.*
yell (jel) *vi,vt* (gellend) schreien. *n* gellende(r) Schrei *m.*
yellow ('jelou) *adj* gelb. *n* Gelb *neu.*
yelp (jelp) *vi* kläffen.
yes (jes) *adv* ja, jawohl. *n* Ja *neu.*
yesterday ('jestədi) *adv* gestern. *n* der gestrige Tag *m.* **the day before yesterday** vorgestern. **yesterday's** *adj* gestrig.
yet (jet) *adv* **1** (schon) noch. **2** sogar. **3** schon. **4** bis jetzt. *conj* jedoch. **not yet** noch nicht.
yew (juː) *n* Eibe *f.*
Yiddish ('jidiʃ) *n* Jiddisch *neu.*
yield (jiːld) *vt* **1** hervorbringen, einbringen. **2** hergeben. **3** tragen. *vi* **1** nachgeben. **2** sich ergeben. **3** tragen. *n* Ertrag *m.*
yodel ('joudl̩) *vi* jodeln.
yoga ('jougə) *n* Joga *m.*
yoghurt ('jɔgət) *n* Joghurt *m.*
yoke (jouk) *n* Joch *neu. vt* anjochen.
yolk (jouk) *n* Dotter *m.* Eigelb *neu.*
yonder ('jɔndə) *adv* dort drüben. *adj* jener.
you (juː) *pron 2nd pers* **1** *fam* du, dich, dir. **2** *fml* Sie, Ihnen. **3** *pl fam* ihr, euch. **4** *pl fml* Sie, Ihnen. **5** *imp* man, einen, einem.
young (jʌŋ) *adj* jung. **youngster** *n* Junge *m.*
your (jɔː, juə) *poss adj 2nd pers* **1** *fam* dein. **2** *fml* Ihr. **3** *pl fam* euer. **4** *pl fml* Ihr. **yours** *poss*

pron 2nd pers **1** *fam* deiner, der deine *or* deinige. **2** *fml* Ihrer, der Ihre *or* Ihrige. **3** *pl fam* eurer, der eure *or* eurige. **4** *pl fml* Ihrer, der Ihre *or* Ihrige.
yourself *pron 2nd pers s* **1** *fam* dich, dich selbst, du selbst. **2** *fml* sich, sich selbst, Sie selbst.
yourselves *pron 2nd pers pl* 1 *fam* euch, euch selbst, ihr selbst. **2** *fml* sich, sich selbst, Sie selbst.
youth (ju:θ) *n* **1** Jugend *f.* **2** Jüngling *m.* **youth hostel** *n* Jugendherberge *f.*
Yugoslavia (ju:gou'slɑ:viə) *n* Jugoslawien *neu.* **Yugoslav** *n* Jugoslawe *m. adj* jugoslawisch.

Z

Zambia ('zæmbiə) *n* Sambia *neu.*
zeal (zi:l) *n* Eifer *m.*
zebra ('zebrə) *n* Zebra *neu.*
zebra crossing *n* Zebrastreifen *m pl.*
zero ('ziərou) *n* **1** Null *f.* **2** Gefrierpunkt *m.*
zest (zest) *n* Begeisterung *f.* Reiz *m.*
zigzag ('zigzæg) *n* Zickzack *m. adj, adv* im Zickzack.
zinc (ziŋk) *n* Zink *neu.*
Zionism ('zaiənizəm) *n* Zionismus *m.*
zip (zip) *n* Zischen *neu. vi* sausen. *vt* mit einem Reißverschluß schließen. **zip (fastener)** *n* Reißverschluß *m.*
zodiac ('zoudiæk) *n* Tierkreis *m.*
zone (zoun) *n* **1** Zone *f.* **2** Erdgürtel *m.*
zoo (zu:) *n* Zoo m. **zoology** *n* Zoologie *f.* **zoological** *adj* zoologisch. **zoologist** *n* Zoologe *m.*
zoom (zu:m) *vi* **1** summen. **2** *aviat* hochschnellen.
Zurich ('zjuərik) *n* Zürich *neu.*